W9-AFF-522

Contemporary Literary Criticism

Volume 4

# Contemporary Literary Criticism

Excerpts from Criticism
of the Works of Today's
Novelists, Poets, Playwrights,
and Other Creative Writers

**Carolyn Riley, Editor**

Gale Research Company
Book Tower
Detroit, Michigan 48226

## STAFF

Carolyn Riley, *Editor*
Phyllis Carmel Mendelson, *Associate Editor*
Bernadette Meier, *Research Assistant*
Karen M. Hilker, *Editorial Assistant*

Elizabeth Cheslock, *Permissions Manager*


Library of Congress Catalog Card Number 76-38938
ISBN 0-8103-0106-7

## ABRAHAMS, Peter 1919-

**Abrahams, a "Cape Coloured" South African, has lived in Jamaica since 1957. He is an English-speaking novelist, short story writer, poet, and staff writer for *Holiday Magazine*.**

[The] position of Abrahams in the [modern African literary] movement is not clear: perhaps it is best described as 'transitional.'. . . [A] summary of typical subject-matter in modern African novels, 'the rise of nationalism, the process of de-colonization, developments in new governments, the tensions before and after independence between the tribal and the national, between the traditional and the modern, throughout the whole of Africa,' is adequate as a summary of *A Wreath for Udomo* but has little bearing [on] works such as *Wild Conquest* or *Mine Boy*. . . .

Part of the problem of interpretation lies in uncertainty about the use of literary tradition. . . . His literary tradition is closely related to the society which he describes. His novels arise from the novels of the nineteenth and twentieth centuries, from prose works by Hardy, Lawrence and Steinbeck, and from writers upon South African subjects. . . .But we can find a strength in his work which comes from a profoundly felt personal experience at work upon a well understood tradition.

In his first five novels Abrahams gives his rendering of the people and history of South Africa. An artist hero in one of his early sketches gives a partial insight into his method of writing: 'And with my pen and my burning heart I built canvas after canvas. The words became pictures. The pictures became stories. The stories became people'. *Dark Testament* [gave] pictures of South African life in a manner caught in part at least from the sketches of William Saroyan. . . .[This] was a new departure in writing about South Africa. . . .

Abrahams has a freedom of movement among the social and racial groups which is without parallel in any other novelist from South Africa. Though strained, his picture is authentic, and gives a view of a tragic society, though the artists' [sic] eye is cool rather than mocking or clinical. . . .But Abrahams is not coldly dispassionate. . . .

Abrahams attempted increasingly ambitious themes in his next four novels. *Wild Conquest* (1951) is a South African's view of the Great Trek without the conventional northwards slant. Abrahams looks southwards as well and shows the process of expansion and invasion from both sides. *A Night of Their Own* (1965) is a fragment, again showing both sides, from the modern politics of subversion and mass imprisonment in South Africa. *A Wreath for Udomo* (1956) shows the rise to power and betrayal of his aides and a South African confederate by a modern African political leader. *This Island Now* (1966) sketches the rise to power and the enfeebled tyranny of a black nationalist party in a Caribbean island. Despite their flaws these are works which provided a new impetus in writing about African subjects. They have a new objectivity in historical or political writing about modern relationships between the racial groups. . . .

This impartiality of Abrahams's writing is frequently noted by reviewers. . . .Nevertheless [they] are not impartial studies. . . .[His] portrayals reveal his bias. . . .Abrahams urges that understanding comes first but does not conceal the current of his feelings, as in *Return to Goli* where the 'lump in my throat and the burning anger in my heart and mind' are never far from the surface. . . .

In his three political novels, . . . *A Wreath for Udomo* (1956), *A Night of Their Own* (1965) and *This Island Now* (1966), the mannered aestheticism of the early work is replaced by a greater stringency and economy of expression. The characteristic inclusiveness of Abrahams, his portrayal of men from both sides of a variety of colour lines, persists. In many ways these works catch the mood of the times. *A Wreath for Udomo* suggests, like Golding's *Lord of the Flies,* that there is a depravity in the mind of men which requires a ritual sacrifice: but Abrahams directs this into the formula of melodrama and causes death to be a punishment for a political misjudgement and not a mere fact as in the witch-hunt scene of *Wild Conquest. A Night of Their Own* is a thriller with a purpose in the Graham Greene manner. . . .

In *Return to Goli,* Abrahams notes that the problems of South Africa are his for life: he is 'a child of Goli—forever rooted in its problems'. His critical attitude to Coloured men who show 'the same mentality as most of the whites' . . .[re-appears] in the later novels. . . .

The early novels offer no cures and the later ones portray dying hopes rather than solutions. Abrahams's purpose appears to be moral and artistic rather than public. . . .

[Criticism] of Abrahams's language can be sustained. Abrahams can be factual and exact, especially in scenes based on childhood memory and recent close observation; but [there is] a . . . weakness. . . .The cause of failure [sometimes]. . .lies. . .in Abrahams's lapse from ordinary speech rather than in the failure of professed beliefs. In his description of the lovers on the beach in *This Island Now,* 'the tall handsome black boy and the statuesquely beautiful black girl', he. . .fails in precision: words such as 'handsome' and 'statuesquely beautiful' say little about the appearance of the objects being described. . . .

Perhaps the strongest restriction in Abrahams's work is to be found in the language itself. As a member of an African people whose distinguishing mark is that 'they speak no African language'. . ., Abrahams had a choice between two Germanic languages: Afrikaans or English. . . .In [choosing English] he left behind what was for him the language of warmth, feeling and humour. . . .

But the choice of English as a literary language, with all the pitfalls both in the language and in the act of choice, was inevitable for Abrahams. English is the language of Countee Cullen, Langston Hughes, W. E. B. DuBois and others who brought Abrahams to a new vision. On reading their works he saw his country afresh, with 'the objective eyes of a stranger', he records in *Tell Freedom.* His novels explore what DuBois calls 'the problem of the twentieth century . . . the problem of the colour line' with great fullness and detail. In this area his writing is most assured, and the language rid of vagueness. . . .Abrahams observes colour conflicts and the various shades of men with humour and detachment. Although a reviewer suggested that humour was lacking in *Dark Testament,* Abrahams's later work, and especially *Jamaica,* has flashes of humour: racial, or perhaps 'African' humour, crossing the numerous colour lines available only in modern societies with an African experience at their roots.

*Christopher Heywood, "The Novels of Peter Abrahams," in* Perspectives on African Literature, *edited by Christopher Heywood (copyright © 1971 by University of Ife; published in the United States in 1971 by Africana Publishing Company, a Division of Holmes & Meier Publishers, Inc. and reprinted by permission), Africana, 1971, pp. 157-72.*

A novel written by a black South African is often remarkably different from a West African or an East African one. The ties that South Africa has had with Europe go back considerably further than do those of most areas of tropical Africa, and in this century at least it has been possible for the black or Coloured South African to grow up in an urban milieu where English is his first language. . . .South African writing tends to be almost totally devoid of anthropological background, and the influence from oral literary materials is usually quite negligible.

The fact that South Africa is multi-racial, as well as that it has been a white-dominated society for so many years, has also had a major influence on its writers. . . .

As a result of these and other conditions, characterization in South African fiction is more closely aligned with characterization in Western fiction than with that in writing from tropical Africa, and the novel itself is in many ways an extension of the traditional English novel because there are few African innovations. . . .

The most prolific novelist from South Africa is Peter Abrahams; and his early novel, *Mine Boy,* which was published in 1940. . .is representative of the South African novel as a whole. The story itself is relatively uncomplicated—an account of a young man's exposure to life in Johannesburg and his work as leader of one of the work crews in a gold mine. The concentration, however, is on life in Johannesburg itself; thus *Mine Boy* is a novel with urbanization as its theme. . . .

There is little plot in *Mine Boy.* Rather, Abrahams' story is one of character and atmosphere, for, like Cyprian Ekwensi's Lagos, Abrahams' picture of Johannesburg's Malay Camp is in many ways the prime concern of his novel. Blacks, Coloureds, and whites are all in the novel, but it is only the sections of the story that are set in the Malay Camp among the African characters that are truly alive. The brief sojourns that Xuma makes in the segregated white areas of the city are flat and considerably less realistically drawn; Abrahams' white characters are often given to mouthing ideas of racial equality—rather than living these ideas as the African characters do. . . .

*Mine Boy* differs. . .greatly from other African fiction where the family still plays a significant part. In *Mine Boy* the family has been completely destroyed, there is no sense of the communal consciousness. People band together out of a common need. There is no sense of the basic filial unit which plays such an important function in tropical African fiction. Nor are there any children to give the novel warmth and humor and the happiness we have seen in other African novels. Abrahams has created an adult world instead—in a city which eventually destroys its inhabitants. The strong characters, other than Xuma, are all women, and in spite of the optimistic and overly didactic ending, one cannot foresee much of a future for Xuma. He is still young; the city will eventually count him in its toll.

*Charles R. Larson, in his* The Emergence of African Fiction, *Indiana University Press, 1971, pp. 160-66.*

Peter Abrahams is a novelist of ideas. He writes about the machinery of politics and power, but he uses his considerable grasp of this area of activity to serve his central interest, which is the problem of individual freedom in contemporary human affairs. . . .[Most of] his novels . . . are set . . . in South Africa. . . .It is possible, and I would say likely, that without the influence of the American Negro writers of the 'twenties and 'thirties as mediated through Abrahams' work, as well as the influence of that work itself, the initial development of literature in English in Nigeria and Kenya would have taken rather a different course.

It should be stated at the outset that Abrahams' ability as a writer of fiction is in the middle range, and the grandiose claims made for his work from time to time by propagandists of African literary culture have been misguided. He is a skilful, if flawed, writer, and there is evidence that he finds the writing of fiction arduous. What is most apparent about his fiction is the complete sincerity and honesty of the author. He has not chosen an easy path; he feels every word he writes and seems incapable of writing conscious pot-boilers. The subjects he returns to again and again in his fiction are the problems which have most exercised—and come near to paralysing in the process—the liberal mind in the West since the end of the second world war. They are the problems of how to reconcile the liberal conscience to the unpleasant consequences of necessary action; how to resist inroads made into the integrity of the individual, especially where these inroads are the results of justified attempts to set others free, to put them on the road to the liberal goal of individual fulfilment. Abrahams invokes and even to some extent typifies the liberal dilemma of the twentieth century. (pp. 4-5)

Abrahams' first novel, *Song of the City,* was published in 1944. It is an immature work, clumsy in dialogue and almost completely lacking conviction in characterization; the language is cliché-infected and the structure disorganized. But it also initiates certain themes which develop in complexity throughout Abrahams' later work, and it is informed by a quality of youthful ardency and sincerity which augurs well for the integrity of Abrahams' later achievement. Novelists of ideas need to be sincere, even when conviction has long given way to a helpless awareness of complexity and confusion. *Song of the City* confronts issues head-on with the certainty of innocence, but at the same time one of Abrahams' most clear-cut convictions is that the world is not made up of black and white. This is also a good augury; this conviction, with increased maturity, becomes a genuine awareness. (p. 14)

Abrahams' decision to take up the theme of urbanization was both courageous and obvious. Though it had been extensively used by white South African authors, the only honest and sympathetic treatment of any literary merit had been William Plomer's *Ula Masondo,* published in 1927. But Abrahams' purpose exceeded that of Plomer: writing from a different kind of commitment to the South African scence, fresh from recent and intense political activity within the non-racial left-wing movement, he was determined to explicate the human realities of the phenomenon in political terms. And, in this, he was right, since to ignore this level would constitute a falsification, and to treat it with Plomer's subtlety would have been beyond the range of Abrahams' powers and would also have necessitated writing from a point of view—that of the articulate and urbane white liberal—that lay outside his experience. Point of view is everything in Abrahams' novels, and it is a level on which his natural and somewhat transparent honesty seldom, if ever, fails him. (p. 15)

*Mine Boy* must be considered Peter Abrahams' first substantial novel. (p. 26)

After the woodenness of characterization, the improbability of diction, the failure to create a convincing matrix of work experience (a serious drawback in a novel of this kind) and unevenness of plot have all been duly noted and condemned, *Mine Boy* remains an important novel, even in some ways a powerful one. Its power is derived from the imaginativeness of the undertaking and the originality and scope of the underlying idea, which turns the literary stereotype of the inevitable corruption of the innocent black man by the white city on its head. (p. 48)

*The Path of Thunder* was Abrahams' third novel. . . .It relies heavily on early materials and memories of the author's South African experiences, and at the same time betrays a distance growing increasingly difficult to bridge between the remembered perception of the real situation and the fictive interpretation of it. There is thus little that is fresh or vital about the book: it is impassioned and highly subjective, a fierce cry for elementary justice in a crude fictive framework. It constitutes the uneasy climax to Abrahams' first phase of development. Between it and *Wild Conquest* there is a world of difference, of careful thought and studied detachment.

In a way these remarks tend to undermine the novel's main virtues which are precisely those of passion, of energy, of commitment, of a direct belief in humanity and civilized values. (p. 52)

*Wild Conquest* marks an important development in Abrahams' work. It. . .represents an attempt to summarize, as it were, objectively, his South African experience. He achieves the distance necessary for impersonality by making it a historical novel, hinging on the central event in modern South African history, the great northward expansion of white power known as the Great Trek. (p. 74)

Abrahams wrote before the great stock-taking began which led to the current interpretation of South African history. . . .He is a victim of the authorized version, and his contribution consists in his attempt to break away from this, to be impartial, to see the African side of this stirring epic. In this it should be said without delay, . . . he fails: but it is an interesting, even peculiar failure which had the effect of transforming his stature as an author.

As we have seen, up to this time Abrahams' fiction has been influenced more by his relationship to political attitudes and even ideologies than by interest in human beings. Problems of personality and character have been treated with facile optimism, and his books have not abounded in living characters. He has been too involved in the need to communicate his own youthful experiences in South Africa, and in *The Path of Thunder* it is clear that this vein had reached exhaustion without any new inspiration presenting itself.

The artistic necessity of breaking free from this source of material must have been clear to Abrahams, and *Wild Canquest* is an attempt to dig beneath the exhausted vein, to examine its origins, and to interpret them. Needless to say, absolute historic accuracy has been sacrificed without qualms. (p. 75)

[He] has a further end in view which, however trite it may sound, may also be seen as his governing obsession in writing about South Africa. This is to demonstrate that underneath their skins, whatever their differences of race or colour, human beings are fundamentally alike in their makeup. This characteristic—and very basic—humanist idea caused Abrahams, more than anything else, to deviate from his early specifically Marxist convictions and general ideological orientation, and to settle for a much more vulnerable liberal outlook—which finds its first clear manifestation in *Wild Conquest,* and dominates the second and third phases of his literary output. It is therefore natural that in *Wild Conquest* he should emphasize by contrast superficial differences, in order to stress basic similarities. Unfortunately, his imaginative range was too narrow to sustain two convincing illusions side by side, which had to bear very little superficial resemblance to each other while interpenetrating completely at a deeper level of significance. (p. 78)

The novel also marks the beginning of Abrahams' alienation from those forms of African nationalism or Pan-Africanism orientated towards the traditional past in Africa. His rejection of tribal life is not as fully explicit as it becomes in *A Wreath for Udomo*: the conscious commitment to Western liberal humanism is also rather exclusive—a not unknown phenomenon among other Western authors who lose faith in their youthful Marxism. In Abrahams the rejection of the tribal group leads to (or is accompanied by) a total involvement with the typical liberal humanist preoccupations with the fate of the individual and his need for and prospects of personal fulfilment, in relation to himself rather than society. This has its clear beginnings in *Udomo,* but its foundation is in the rejection of the group, of man in the mass, implicit in *Wild Conquest*: and it develops in Abrahams' later work into the peculiarly aristocratic position (which includes a strong feeling of mixed fear and contempt for ordinary people) of his last two novels, *A Night of Their Own* and *This Island Now*. (p. 97)

[The] novelistic element in *Tell Freedom* is quite organic to the work. It is in no sense 'pure' autobiography, but a highly dramatized, one is even tempted to say experimental, version. (p. 109)

Indeed, certain qualities which inform the writing in *Tell Freedom*—qualities such as humour and liveliness—are precisely those most lacking in his works of fiction. (p. 117)

One may as well remark in passing that nowhere in his novels does Abrahams manage dialogue as skilfully or as naturally as in *Tell Freedom*. (p. 117)

*A Wreath for Udomo* (1956) marks the culmination of the second phase of Abrahams' creative development, and shows substantial progress towards artistic maturity. In a sense it is the result of crucial events in the author's life: a return for a visit to his family in South Africa, the self-examination produced by this, as well as the uneasy process of writing a work of autobiography. *Return to Goli* and *Tell Freedom* are Abrahams' best books: in them he achieves the fresh and honest realism he consistently falls short of in his novels. Writing them he was in a rich creative vein, something of which carries over to make *Udomo* his best achievement to date in the novel.

The second stage of Abrahams' development began with *Wild Conquest,* which was sharply distinguished from the preceding novels simply because it dealt with a major historical event, lengthily and in a fairly complex manner. Despite its other distinguishing features, which have already been discussed, it must be judged a failure, subject to many of the faults found in the early works. *Udomo* is similar in scope and deals with many of the same themes, but is much more advanced in technique, character presentation and the handling of moral issues.

*A Wreath for Udomo* is the story of a group of Africans involved in the struggle to free their continent from colonial rule. The book was highly topical when it was written, but few of its original readers who approached it sympathetically would have suspected it to be as full of prophetic insight as time has shown it to have been. (p. 132)

The characteristic themes of the second phase of Abrahams' writing are present in highly developed forms. They arise out of his political transition from naive historical materialist to committed Western Liberal, aware of individual shortcomings but retaining a superficial optimism in ultimate terms about the human condition in general. . . .The clearest manifestation of Abrahams' liberalism is a deeply felt commitment to the idea of the human being as an individual.

The most obvious and perhaps startling result, in thematic terms, of Abrahams' conversion to liberalism, is the passionate identification with certain mythical beliefs of Western industrialized society, which are grouped around polarities such as 'past-future!', 'primitive-civilized', 'corrupt-efficient', 'tribal-modern'. Indeed, the conflict between traditional and modern is one of the main themes of the book. The personal and political levels of action are inter-related by the operation of this theme in the lives of the major characters. Thus adherence to traditional social attitudes in politics is seen as a negation of individuality in personal life. (pp. 133-34)

Stylistically the book is occasionally subject to clichés and picture-postcard descriptive writing, as most of his work, but the really awkward moments are few, which places it in the same prose period as *Wild Conquest*: a glossy woman's magazine patina has been achieved, though the subject matter is rather more serious. Of course, this has unfortunate consequences for the total effect and is always one of the crucial factors which prevents Abrahams from being as important a writer as his potential might have allowed. (pp. 150-51)

*Udomo,* published in 1956 when the only independent states in sub-Saharan Africa were Ethiopia, Liberia and South Africa, not only sketches a chillingly accurate paradigm of events to come: it also assigns causes for these events, suggests their origins with some subtlety, and is understanding of human weaknesses that had not yet come into play in a situation that was not even half created. This kind of insight amounts to prophecy. Politically *Udomo* is the best thing Abrahams has ever done, and as a novel the same judgment may be made with some confidence. (p. 152)

*A Night of Their Own* constitutes something of a special case in Abrahams' development, the direction of which follows the classical post-World War II Western pattern. This is a movement from decisive involvement with mass political deprivation and action to equally decisive withdrawal from and rejection of almost all kinds of action, and emphasis on a mystique of individuality which is a sort of decadent romantic (and essentially élitist) loneliness. . . .Abrahams participates fully in the historic confusion of bourgeois Western artists of our day. (p. 173)

*This Island Now* may be regarded as a culminative step in the latest stage of Abrahams' development. In it the author seems preoccupied with the need to define as clearly as possible the outlines of the social and political philosophy which he has been in the process of adopting since the early 'fifties. The book is, perhaps, better constructed and less hastily written than its immediate predecessor, and is not so closely tied to a specific real situation, which partly explains why its conclusions contradict those of *A Night of Their Own,* published only a year earlier. There is not much doubt that *This Island Now* constitutes the more genuine expression of Abrahams' world view. (p. 174)

Of all the writers in English in the field defined as 'African literature' none is as 'European' as Peter Abrahams, in regard to intellectual as well as artistic development. (p. 197)

*Michael Wade, in his* Peter Abrahams, *Evans Brothers, 1972.*

* * *

## ADAMOV, Arthur 1908-1970

**A Russian-born French playwright and translator, Adamov wrote absurdist, surrealistic dramas until 1957 and epic, realistic dramas from 1957 to 1970. He is best known for *Ping-pong,* the finest example of his earlier plays. (See also *Contemporary Authors*, Vols. 17-18; obituary, Vols. 25-28.)**

Arthur Adamov's early plays illustrate in their purest form the principles of the avant-garde drama. In all the dramas of the current avant-garde the purpose is protest against the hopelessness of the human condition and against the strictures imposed on the individual by society. The method by which this protest is conveyed is the method of paradox, in which a truth is presented by an exaggerated emphasis on its opposite.

Like most modern dramatists, Adamov has a thoroughly pessimistic outlook on life. His themes are the tyranny of parental love; the innate cruelty of the society in which we are forced to live; and the meaninglessness, futility, and confusion of everyday life. . . .

He protests against the merciless cruelty of the world—a cruelty that is at once inhuman and superhuman, omnipresent in the external and immanent in the individual's inner world, an almost tangible entity in itself and at the same time an emanation of a greater, instinctively malicious entity. . . .

The sense of cosmic cruelty that appears in Adamov's work is accompanied and balanced in most cases by a narrower, specifically human type of cruelty. The sense of helplessness that man experiences when confronted by the metaphysical world is intensified by his confrontation with the same helplessness and thwarted desire when he turns to his fellow men. Man becomes a dumb animal frustratedly bellowing back and forth across a crowded space that seems to him a void. . . .

The theme of cruelty within the social system shows up in *Tous contre Tous* (All Against All, 1953) and *Paolo Paoli* (1957). In the earlier play the theme is treated in general symbolic terms; in the later one in specific, individual terms. *Tous contre Tous* is undoubtedly Adamov's best play. It is about the instinctive mutual enmity human beings display toward each other. The play is not so much an indictment of a social system which forces human beings to act in their habitual dog-eat-dog manner as an implication that the social system is a result of human nature. A social system, Adamov is saying, is no more than a conglomeration of individuals and their traits.

*George Wellwarth, "Arthur Adamov: The Way Out of the Void," in his* The Theater of Protest and Paradox: Developments in the Avant-Garde Drama *(reprinted by permission of New York University Press; copyright © 1964 by New York University), New York University Press, 1964, pp. 27-36.*

Adamov's post-absurd plays have disappointed many of his earlier admirers. Throughout his work there has generally been a lack of human feeling, partly because the author is always the victim of ideas and doctrines: he sometimes seems like Pierre in *The Invasion,* trying to decipher meaning from heaps of manuscripts. If the plays of Adamov do not hold together in dramatic cohesion with the interrelationship of people and ideas implemented, he has nevertheless provided some fine theatrical moments, as in the terror conveyed in parts of his dramas about dictators.

*Harry T. Moore, in his* Twentieth-Century French Literature Since World War II *(© 1966 by Southern Illinois University Press; reprinted by permission of Southern Illinois University Press), Carbondale: Southern Illinois University Press, 1966, pp. 163-64.*

*Le Ping-Pong,* like Adamov's first play, *La Parodie,* is concerned with the futility of human endeavour. But while *La Parodie* merely asserted that whatever you do, in the end you die, *Le Ping-Pong* provides a powerful and closely integrated argument to back that proposition—it also shows *how* so much of human endeavour becomes futile, and *why.* It is in losing themselves to a *thing,* a machine that promises them power, money, influence over the woman they desire, that Victor and Arthur waste their lives in the futile pursuit of shadows. By making a machine, a means to an end, an end in itself, they pervert all those values of their lives that are genuine ends in themselves—their creative instinct, their capacity to love, their sense of being part of a community. *Le Ping-Pong* is a powerful image of the alienation of man through the worship of a false objective, the deification of a machine, an ambition, or an ideology.

The pinball machine in *Le Ping-Pong* is more than just a machine; it is the centre-piece of an organization and of a body of thought. The moment the objective—the improvement of pinball machines—becomes an ideal, it embodies itself in an organization with its own struggles for power, its own intrigues and politics, its own tactics and strategies. As such it becomes a matter of life and death for all who serve the ideal. . . .Adamov achieves the difficult feat of elevating the pinball machine to a convincing image of the objectives of *all* human endeavour. He does so by the poetic intensity with which he invests his characters when they talk about the most absurd aspects of that absurd apparatus with a conviction and obsessive concentration that sound utterly true. . . .

What is perhaps the most original feature of *Le Ping-Pong* is the way in which an inner contradiction, a dialectical relationship, is established between the action and the dialogue. This is a play that may well appear completely meaningless if it is merely read. The speeches about improvements in the construction of pinball machines may seem trivial nonsense; the meaning of the play emerges precisely at the moment when the actor delivers these nonsensical lines with a depth of conviction worthy of the loftiest flights of poetry. It is a play that has to be acted *against* the text rather than with it. . . .

*Le Ping-Pong* belongs in the category of the Theatre of the Absurd; it shows man engaged in purposeless exertions, in a futile frenzy of activity that is bound to end in senility and death. The pinball machine has all the fascinating ambiguity of a symbol. It may stand for capitalism and big business, but it may equally well stand for any religious or political ideology that secretes its own organization and apparatus of power, that demands devotion and loyalty from its adherents. . . .

The role played by pinball machines in *Le Ping-Pong* is in *Paolo Paoli* taken by commodities no less absurd—butterflies and ostrich feathers. Yet these objects of trade and manufacture have far greater reality. As one of the newspaper projections before the first scene points out, ostrich feathers and products manufactured from them formed France's fourth largest export in 1900. Adamov brilliantly shows the far-reaching social and political ramifications and implications of the trade in these absurd articles. . . .[In] a few strokes, Adamov has shown the connexion between the seemingly absurd object of trade and the penal system of French society, foreign politics, and the workings of the Church. The same is true of Hulot-Vasseur's ostrich feathers in relation to the Boer War, and, as the plot develops, the labour and trade-union troubles of his factory and his fight against German competition are very convincingly made explicit within the narrow circle of the play.

As in *Le Ping-Pong,* the characters are obsessed with their pursuit of money and power, represented by the absurd commodities they deal in. . . .

It is precisely because it does succeed in maintaining the extremely delicate balance between the incurable and the curable aspects of the human condition that *Le Ping-Pong* must be regarded as Adamov's finest achievement to date. The pinball machine stands for all illusory objectives, material and ideological, the pursuit of which secretes ambition, self-seeking, and the urge to dominate other human beings. There is no necessity to fall victim to such illusory aims, so there *is* a social lesson in the play. And yet the absurdity of all human endeavour in the face of death is never quite forgotten, and is finally put before our eyes by a telling and compelling image. *Paolo Paoli,* on the other hand, is marred not only by the intrusion of oversimplified economic and social theories, but, above all, by the introduction of a wholly positive and therefore less than human character, Marpeaux, and by the even less credible conversion of a hitherto negative character, Paolo, to provide a climax and a solution. This noble character and this noble action are clearly the consequence of the author's special pleading for the curable aspect of things, which leads to an underplaying of the incurable side of the human situation.

*Martin Esslin, "Arthur Adamov: The Curable and the Incurable" (copyright © 1961, 1968, 1969 by Martin Esslin; reprinted by permission of Doubleday & Co., Inc.), in his* The Theatre of the Absurd, *Doubleday-Anchor, revised edition, 1969, pp. 66-99.*

Arthur Adamov's play, *Ping-Pong,* uses the image of a pinball machine to embody the hazards and caprices of fortune. The players are motivated by the desire to achieve success and gain power, though the game ends inevitably in death. The erratic behavior of the ball, the numbers that light up, the use of the left flipper, the possibility of achieving control, the jamming of the machine—all this makes for ingenious metaphoric implications. The epitome of amusement, the pinball machine offers "Action! Conflict! Participation!" That is how Adamov represents the mysterious element of contingency. How can one learn to master the machine? Why does it regularly fall out of order? . . .

The last scene, which drops the image of the pinball machine, also drives home the meaninglessness of the game of life. The two close friends in the play, Victor and Arthur, now old and white-haired, engage in playing ping-pong on a table divided into eight black and white squares. The game goes on, though they still have not decided what they are playing for. Victor decides to get rid of the squares. Then they remove the net, after which they throw their paddles away and play with their bare hands. The volleys grow wilder and wilder; the players make spectacular but clumsy leaps in returning the ball. Victor's movements are becoming progressively weaker. When Arthur hits the ball high, Victor leaps for it but falls to the floor, dead. The game is over.

*Ping-Pong,* like Samuel Beckett's *Endgame,* reveals the futility of the struggle; the game is ended, though the machine keeps on running. Adamov later abandoned the theater of the absurd and took to writing plays with a markedly social content. He decided to play the game according to rules that were close to the redemptive ideology expressed in Bertold Brecht's epic dramas. By shifting his perspective he arrived at a different version of reality.

*Charles I. Glicksberg, in his* Modern Literary Perspectivism, *Southern Methodist University Press, 1970, pp. 59-61.*

* * *

## ADAMS, Richard 1920-

**Adams, an Englishman, is the author of the successful novel *Watership Down.* (See also *Contemporary Authors*, Vols. 49-52.)**

*Watership Down* is a very grand book, but a simple outline of what happens in it makes it sound strictly for kids and/or idiotic. (Why is it, by the way, that idiot entertainment is thought okay for children?) . . .

There are a lot of things that make this book work, including the traditional and here expertly employed device of cliff-hanging chapter endings. But mainly it is Richard Adams's wonderfully rich imagination, together with an extraordinary and totally disarming respect for his material. Tone is all-important in a tale like this, and Adams's is straight, confidently controlled, never maudlin, never cute. Occasionally the author steps aside to tell us something about rabbits (he seems to know everything), but for all the necessary anthropomorphism, including just enough of a fine invented language—*hrududu,* for example, means motorcar or tractor—and separate character delineation, he keeps the rabbits convincingly rabbity, true to themselves and to their nature. One is drawn into their world, and once in, everything—from their constant fears and skittishness to the great rabbit folk-tales they tell each other—is perfectly believable. There is, of course, a considerable allegorical element (rabbit politics plus a stern defense of nature, with man seen as its destroyer—the one sentimental note in the book), but it is not pressed or made too heavy. In sum, a marvel, a wise and sunny book, a suspenseful epic that readers twelve and up are going to enjoy for a long time to come.

*Eliot Fremont-Smith, in* New York Magazine *(© 1974 by NYM Corp.; reprinted by permission of* New York Magazine *and Eliot Fremont-Smith), March 4, 1974, p. 60.*

All the praises and prizes that *Watership Down* has received have gone to it as the kind of nature-loving and highly literate juvenile that British children can read much younger than their American counterparts. . . .

As for mystical profundities, there are references to a death symbol known as the Black Rabbit and stories-within-the-story concerning a rabbit folk hero called *El-ahrairah.* There is a brief glossary of rabbit terms. The quotations at the head of each chapter derive from Aeschylus, Xenophon, *Pilgrim's Progress, Morte d'Arthur.* But otherwise *Watership Down* offers little to build a literary cult upon. On the American-whimsy exchange, one Tolkien hobbit should still be worth a dozen talking rabbits.

*Melvin Maddocks, "Rabbit Redux," in* Time *(reprinted by permission from* Time, The Weekly Newsmagazine; *copyright Time Inc.), March 18, 1974, pp. 92-3.*

Because indiscriminate hostility toward modern animal fiction is generally sound critical practice, we must marvel that so fresh a twig can sprout from such a battered branch of literature. "Watership Down" is an adventure story of an epic scope that takes place within a few months and a few square miles of English soil. It is a story of exile and survival, of heroism and political responsibility, of the making of a leader and of a community. And it is more: through a remarkably sustained thrust of the imagination, Richard Adams has constructed a complete civilization, with its own governments, language and mythology. . . .

Adams handles his suspenseful narrative more dexterously than most authors who claim to write adventure novels, but his true achievement lies in the consistent, comprehensible and altogether enchanting civilization that he has created. His fantasy is firmly rooted in the world we know. . . .

*Peter S. Prescott, "Rabbit, Read," in* Newsweek *(copyright Newsweek, Inc., 1974; reprinted by permission), March 18, 1974, p. 114.*

The relations of rabbit to man and warren to warren are sometimes invested with horror and have chillingly suggestive political overtones, but [*Watership Down*] is not parable because its naturalism is too technically detailed. They transcend rabbitdom by talking and can make alliances with other animals. . . .

They have many of the values and anxieties of public school England. A well-meaning, weak-minded mouse speaks broken English with an Italian flavor. The book leaves out the only really heroic physical accomplishment of the rabbit, sex. So perhaps it isn't strange that they don't feel at home in nature, need the drama of action to confirm their identities, and, curiously stranded between life and make-believe, often feel little and lost. While I appreciated the degree of imaginative validity of this small world, something within me balks when an author tries to teach me how to turn into a British rabbit.

*Martin Washburn, in* The Village Voice *(reprinted by permission of* The Village Voice; *© 1974 by The Village Voice, Inc.), March 21, 1974, p. 25.*

Modern literature is notoriously lacking in [heroes and adventure], which is perhaps why serious readers sometimes indulge themselves in spy stories, detective novels, science fiction—the literary equivalent of lollipops. Since *Watership Down,* which makes no claim to deal with human life and hence doesn't belie it, is arguably less puerile than such debased survivals of epic tradition, one can perhaps understand what impels Macmillan to market the book in America not as a children's story but simply as "a novel."

But how to explain the dimensions of the campaign in behalf of this clever little saga? The initial 75,000-copy printing, $13,000 ad budget and endorsements of pundits like Bruno Bettleheim and Buckminster Fuller suggest more than confidence in a sturdy tale. Do the publishers think they have another *Jonathan Livingston Seagull* on their hands: an animal story susceptible to reading as a self-help book? Certain elements in the text bear out this suspicion.

To begin with there are the epigraphs, culled from important adult literature, which remind us that similar events have been recounted about humans. Moreover the rabbits are given a stock of legends—about a heroic likeness named El-ahrairah, a sun god named Frith, and the Black Rabbit of Inlé—that invites speculation on the role of tradition in any pattern of behavior. Such devices constitute a gentle appeal to analogical reasoning, and although Adams, who is an environmentalist by profession, emphasizes specifically animal behavior and makes his rabbits too individual for allegory, he does occasionally seem to be sending us a message. . . .

Among the pleasures offered by Adams' book is the implication that some of man's victims are clever enough to keep us from getting away with it, and that we might even learn from them something about escaping the beastliness ourselves. But it scarcely needs pointing out that rabbits, unlike men, live in a world where harsh threats are also simple ones and hence amenable to simple physical solutions. So it is discomfiting to read Fuller's praise for the book ("one of those great ones that every once in a while lets us know that the universe has something really mysteriously great 'going' for humanity"). Or to learn that the same firm that broke records for the privilege of reprinting *Jonathan Livingston Seagull* and *I'm OK–You're OK* has already offered a recordbreaking sum—pre-publication—to get *Watership Down* into paperback. It would be a pity if Adams' *tour de force* were taken as a wish-fulfilling fable for ecologists.

*Charles Thomas Samuels, "Call of the Wild," in* The New Republic *(reprinted by permission of* The New Republic; *© 1974 by The New Republic, Inc.), March 23, 1974, pp. 28-9.*

"Watership Down" is in some ways a delightful book, at times an affecting one. But faced with the extraordinary praise given the book in England, one has to draw back some distance. Lacking the high wit and imaginative force of "Alice in Wonderland" or the triumphant (if occasionally purple) lyricism of "The Wind in the Willows," the book seems to me a good deal less than the "classic"—with the implication in the word of settled universal appeal—that British commentators have so reflexively proclaimed it. . . .

Structurally, [the tale] is composed of a number of set-pieces, the longest and most dramatic of which is a dangerous and ultimately successful excursion by the rabbits to another warren, one run along totalitarian lines, in search of females through whom the race or species can be perpetuated.

The group is led throughout by a rabbit called Hazel, a figure of natural authority, whose chief assistants include Fiver, the clairvoyant, Bigwig, a tough, courageous fellow, and Blackberry, known for his cleverness. At times this division of qualities comes to resemble that of a Hollywood war movie, the kind with the brave guy, the prankster, the brooder, etc. But for the most part the characterizations work surprisingly well, and this is because Adams is able to get past the usual sentimentalities about bunnies and afford his creatures a rough plausibility as representatives of embattled life.

As in all such fiction, the plausibility issues from the detail and consistency with which the animal life is rendered, and above all from the resemblances we can discern to aspects of our own lives. (We can identify, for example, with the phenomenon of worker bees serving a queen, but not with the physiological process of making honey.) To this end Adams offers a remarkable wealth of information on rabbit existence—much of it gained, as he tells us, from R. M. Lockley's study, "The Private Life of the Rabbit"—and wisely concentrates on matters of sustenance, living arrangement, behavior toward other animals, and the like.

But as anthropomorphic fantasy replaces observation (the book is set in an actual area of Berkshire, England, and Adams is particularly fine on landscapes and flora, weathers and seasons) he sees fit to give his rabbits a folklore and folk-heroes, a mythology complete with creation-myth and, finally, a language. . . .

If I remember correctly, the great writers of animal fiction let their characters unselfconsciously speak the authors' own languages, and this is proper because the imaginative act is complete once the literary decision has been made to allow animals to speak in words; to let them use their own words, their own verbal language, is to tempt the pathetic fallacy beyond its acceptable limits. This may seem a small point, especially since the Lapine is a very minor element of the rhetoric, but I think it symptomatic of what is wrong with "Watership Down," or rather what keeps it from being wholly right.

There is a subtle indecisiveness or doubt on Adams's part as to just how convincing his fiction is. . . .

The point is that if you are going to anthropomorphize you had better do it all the way, relying on the pure inventedness of your tale, the same outrageous conceit which is at the back of the March Hare, Mowgli and Pooh, however differing their literary realities.

Now I know there are going to be readers for whom such questions of literary strategy and imaginative rightness couldn't matter less. For some, particularly the younger ones, the narrative will be enough and, as I've said, that works perfectly well, as adventure and melodrama. For the other kind of readers . . ., the ones I think will give "Watership Down" its cachet, the narrative will have more complex uses, being in the service of the book's "meanings," the lessons it teaches, its allegorical élan; such readers are just as unlikely to be troubled by inconsistencies or excesses.

For what is chiefly wanted from a book like this is *utilitarian* fantasy, qualities of reassurance and inspiration, a consoling legend. The morale it seems likely to instill, whatever its intentions, is that peculiar sort which consists in a strength gained through having been first made to feel ashamed, in this case ashamed of our oblique, acquisitive, "insincere" lives in the face of candid and undevious nature. It isn't that Adams (who I ought to have said before was until recently an air-pollution expert with the British Department of the Environment) has sentimentalized his rabbits—the book is no "Jonathan Livingston Seagull"—but that the shadowy presence of man is almost always characterized by hint and threat of evil, a theme on occasion made wholly explicit.

*Richard Gilman, in* The New York Times Book Review *(© 1974 by The New York Times Company; reprinted by permission), March 24, 1974, pp. 3-4.*

[*Watership Down*] is a real place, and the book has a map based on the Ordnance Survey to show its precise location, south of Newbury, west of Kingsclere, north of the railway line to Salisbury down which roared the force like a thousand thunderstorms. It is this down-to-earth reality that has enabled Mr. Adams to succeed in his desperate venture. For to endow the story of rabbits migrating from one warren to another with a sense of epic grandeur (hence the high-flown style of my first paragraphs) does strike me as something of a tall order. I think he has pulled it off. . . .

Mr. Adams knows what he's talking about, and thus [makes] one readier to credit him when he is describing desperate chases and hairbreadth escapes. He is a master of menace and suspense. I have no special feeling for rabbits, indeed mildly dislike them, but I read the last hundred pages at a gulp, heart thumping at the crisis when Bigwig goes alone to the grim warren of Efrafa, or when those powerful bullies mount a surprise attack on Watership Down. . . .

Now and then Mr. Adams points to a likeness in the way men and rabbits behave in a certain situation (after working to overcome an obstacle, success will be followed by a pause) but in no way is this a fable of human behavior like *Animal Farm.* For all their way of talking, Holly, Hazel, Bigwig, and the rest are not stand-ins for any humans; within the conventions of the story, they remain true to the nature and ways of rabbits. George Orwell wrote his tale to make us think about men and politics; Richard Adams wants us to think about rabbits and nature. *Watership Down,* which started as a tale to keep Mr. Adams's daughters entertained during car drives to Stratford, was published in Britain last year as a straightforward children's book. Like any good children's book, it pleased a lot of adults too (*Treasure Island* had no keener reader than Mr. Gladstone). But the American publishers present it simply as "A Novel," and by so doing may well encourage readers to go looking for the wrong things. For who would write a novel for adults about rabbits—unless the tale were a fable or a myth? I foresee an outbreak of symbol hunting in the burrows; mythic explications will drop like *hraka* on the grass. I think the publishers sniff a campus cult on the wind, and this underlies their proclaimed expectation that the book will be "one of the major literary and commercial successes of 1974."

Certainly, it appears at a time when we are becoming increasingly skeptical of our species' ability to live its life decently; there is an inclination to look, if only in fancy, for alternative models in other species, other worlds. I don't think *Watership Down* has much to tell us of how to set about transforming ourselves and our institutions, or how to find a short cut to the promised land. In as much as Mr. Adams has a message for his readers, I'd say it is to make them more sensitive to the complex balance of nature, more aware of the needs and ways of other species (and the effect of human actions on them), more mindful that we are creatures too, and must live in harmony with the others who share our world. . . .

Several times—in reading, for instance, of the old warren's destruction so that men might have homes—I thought of Thomas Hardy's "The Field of Waterloo":

> *Yea, the coneys are scared by the thud of hoofs,*
> *And their white scuts flash at their vanishing heels,*
> *And swallows abandon the hamlet-roofs.*
>
> *The mole's tunnelled chambers are crushed by wheels,*
> *The lark's eggs scattered, their owners fled;*
> *And the hedgehog's household the sapper unseals. . . .*

Hazel and Bigwig are to succeed Gandalf and Frodo as heroes of a cult, then a good book will have been demeaned and misunderstood.

*Janet Adam Smith, "Exodus," in* The New York Review of Books *(reprinted with permission from* The New York Review of Books; *© 1974 by NYREV, Inc.), April 18, 1974, pp. 8-9.*

I'm writing my seventh novel: it's called *Herbert Cunningham Gnu.* I know a bandwagon when it runs me over: 1971, dolphins; 1972, seagulls; 1973-74, rabbits. From the land of Beatrix Potter and nationalized strikes, has come *Watership Down,* Richard Adams' lapine odyssey. Believe me, nothing depresses the spirit more surely than a sententious rabbit. Yet *Watership Down* has had "unanimous praise from England."

"An exceptional book, a true original." "It doesn't fit any known formula, thank goodness." Nonsense: it fits five or six. This bunny squad could be a John Wayne platoon of GIs. The foresighted, tactful rabbit leader. The fast rabbit. The clever rabbit. The blustery, hard-fighting noncom rabbit. Athos, Porthos, and D'Artagnan on a diet of grass. *Watership Down* is pleasant enough, but it has about the same intellectual firepower as *Dumbo.* "Refreshes a reader's feeling for the world of man." Apparently more than one reviewer has been rabbited out of his critical faculties. After all, if your dog started speaking French you'd be loath to criticize his pronunciation. Yet if Hazel and Bigwig and Dandelion were men, they'd make very commonplace characters. What seems a moral, an insight, is just a novelty.

"A true classic." Right. *Watership Down* goes blue in the face being classic. Adams has tagged a scholarly quotation onto each of 50 chapters. These indicate an Oxford education; also a lust for the irrelevant. "The centurion commanded that they which could swim should cast themselves first into the sea . . . (Acts of the Apostles, chapter 27)." That means the rabbits are about to cross a stream. Scripture and three dozen masterpieces of Western literature have their go at goosing this children's tale into sham relevance. . . .

I can sniff an allegory when I'm downwind of one, and this book leaves no such spoor—as the reviewer lamely goes on to concede, ". . . although there is no actual political parallel." The rabbits encounter two warren societies: one totalitarian and one effete. You get that kind of "political suggestiveness" in old *Star Trek* reruns. The spaceship from a good, democratic civilization lands among Nazis, hedonists . . . whatever. There aren't the one-to-one correspondences, the particular images that you encounter, say, in *Gulliver's Travels* or in the aforementioned *Animal Farm. Watership Down* is an adventure story, no more than that: rather a swashbuckling, crude one to boot. There are virtuous rabbits and bad rabbits: if that's allegory, *Bonanza* is an allegory. . . .

I suspect that the "unanimous praise from England" tells us more about England than it does about *Watership Down.* This is an okay book; well enough written. But it is grossly overrated. The extravagant notices come from a people sick to death of men things, of the political process. "Human" fiction, which promises to teach about real life, will suffer from the national despondency. British readers seem to have lost their nerve. Trapped between the badger Wilson and the weasel Heath, they have crept, on quick all fours, back into a second childishness. I'm curious—and somewhat afraid—to see the American reviews of *Watership Down.*

*D. Keith Mano, "Banal Bunnies," in* National Review *(150 East 35th St., New York, N.Y. 10016), April 26, 1974, pp. 484-85.*

Adams has no qualms about anthropomorphizing his male rabbits—depicting them as capable of the most extraordinary displays of loyalty, courage and affection. Yet their humane camaraderie does not extend to females. . . .

Overall, Adams's work is a glorious paean to man's (or rabbit's) resilience, to the instinct for survival against all odds. Though the novel spans little more than eight weeks in time and a mere six miles of English countryside in space, Adams has created within these modest confines, a rich new world full of beauty and truth. Yet, one must note with passing regret that so remarkable a maiden flight of the literary imagination is marred by an attitude toward females that finds more confirmation in Hugh Heffner's Playboy than R. M. Lockley's "The Private Life of the Rabbit."

*Selma G. Lanes, in* The New York Times Book Review *(© 1974 by The New York Times Company; reprinted by permission), June 30, 1974, p. 39.*

[*Watership Down,* the] rabbit tale of adventure and awakening, told with disarming élan and happily devoid of rabid anthropomorphism, owes a great deal more to Tolkien than to Jack London, as animal stories go. It chronicles a small group of rabbits as they leave their old warren and migrate over the Berkshire countryside, through thick and thin, to find a new home. One can argue the merits of fantasy, animal stories, picaresque novels of escape, Edgar Rice Burroughs, fables, or going through the looking-glass until the bunnies come home, but this is pleasant reading well told.

Virginia Quarterly Review, *Vol. 50, No. 3 (Summer, 1974), p. lxxxii.*

* * *

## AGNON, S(hmuel) Y(osef) 1888-1970

**Born in Galicia, Austria-Hungary (present-day Poland), Agnon lived in Palestine (Israel) from 1924 until his death. He spoke no English and was the first Israeli author, and the first author writing in Hebrew, to receive the Nobel Prize for Literature. Drawing upon ancient Jewish folk materials, Agnon fashioned his lyrical, humorous, and ironic stories around the themes of Jewish myth, legend, and tradition. (See also *Contemporary Authors*, Vols. 17-18; obituary, Vols. 25-28.)**

Agnon first became known in Hebrew literature because he eschewed the innovations that had been introduced by some of his older contemporaries and chose to base his style on a pattern which had been used for a thousand years or more in the writing of children's stories and "popular" narrative. Moreover, the heroes of his tales were not those who were trying to escape from and change the course of Jewish tradition, but rather those who lived within it. As a result his work first attracted notice in the circles of Germany and Central Europe where a reaction against nineteenth-century rationalism, particularly in the Hebraic form known as the *Haskala,* was setting in. By the middle 'twenties, Agnon had won himself a place entirely his own in Hebrew literature, as a classic of a new kind, and he is now universally acknowledged as one of the leading figures of contemporary Hebrew literature.

The tales by which he is best known deal with Galician Jewish life, first in the post-Napoleonic period, then in and about the early days of the Zionist movement, and finally in the period between the two world wars. In addition he has written a large number of timeless and universal Jewish legends, often based on folk stories, but equally frequently of his own private vintage. . . .

Agnon's stories of life a hundred years and more ago are shrouded in a mellow nostalgia, a family-chronicle warmness similar to that of a grandmother telling the tales of her clan. The closer he comes to the contemporary scene, however, the less pleased with his subject matter he appears to be. His tales of life fifty years ago are marked by an almost photographic realism, while when he comes to the present day a certain undercurrent of asperity can be detected in the apparent serenity that characterizes all he writes.

*I. M. Lask, headnote to "Tehilla," by Samuel Joseph Agnon, in* Tehilla and Other Israeli Tales *(copyright © 1956 by Abelard-Schuman Limited), Abelard-Schuman, 1956, pp. 9-10.*

Utilizing vast sources of midrashic, hasidic and folk literature, [Agnon] created a unique Hebrew prose style. His work links historic Jewish piety and martyrdom with the longing for Palestine. He is the portrayer *par excellence* of the saintliness and simplicity of Eastern European traditional Jewish life before the advent of the modern temper. In [later] years he [became] preöccupied with the epic of Jewish rebirth in the land of Israel. . . .

When Samuel Joseph Agnon began to write, the new chapter of modern Hebrew literature was dominated by the general European spirit. . . . The young passionate poets were anxious to forget the Jewish village together with the traditions of their fathers and to become part of European civilization. They extolled man, the human being, and not the Jew within him. . . . They used the national tongue, Hebrew, but the song they sang was a universal one. They were all possessed by a common desire—to capture outposts in a newly opened world, to become equal partners in universal human attainments, to create values that would command respect in world literature—but to do so in the language of the Jewish renaissance, in Hebrew. Their Jewishness they would assert by the language in which they wrote, their universalism through its content. . . .

Agnon appeared on the scene and began a counter-revolution. He reversed the trend from Europe homeward again, from alien ways back to the native road. He did not burst upon the scene in stormy fashion. He brought no theories or arguments with him. He said not a single word *pro* or *contra.* He simply began to write in a different manner, different from all other Hebrew writers of that time. His novelty lay in his old-fashionedness. His uniqueness consisted in his return to the old sources, to the folk-character and its traits of simplicity and sincerity, purity and piety. . . .

With Agnon the Hebrew short story reaches artistic heights. He has the secret of the perfect blend of content and form, style and rhythm, inner beauty and outer grace. He has tapped new sources of Jewish ethical and esthetic values, revealing the spiritual grandeur in Jewish life. He has done what others have sought in vain to do: to convert simplicity and folk-naiveté into a thing of consummate art and beauty. . . .

In the serenity of Agnon's world, "the weariness, the fever and the fret" of living are forgotten. The piety and simplicity of his hasidic style had led many to believe mistakenly that his is merely an imitative technique. But one entering Agnon's world is caught by the spell of his narrative and touched by something more pervasive and more deep-rooted than mere stylistic novelty. While it is true that his literary style is graceful, his real power lies in his vision. This is manifested in his character portrayals. His style is not a question of "literature" but of "life." It mirrors the very soul of his characters. It radiates the mild and kindly humor of brotherly understanding and forgiveness, the humor of an artist who is at one with his characters, their suffering, their faith and hope, their silent study and their fervent prayers.

Only one who denies the basic truth underlying all creative art could suspect Agnon of creating a "style for style's sake." If naiveté were not a genuine and integral part of his characters, he would not have been able to portray with such consistent infallibility the inner state of their minds, their inevitable reactions and their particular speech. But even were one to insist that Agnon consciously stylizes his narratives, playing only the part of a weaver of tales, projecting himself with conscious effort into the role of his heroes, one would still have to admit that Agnon is an unusually brilliant artist.

However, careful observation of Agnon's creative technique shows that his true greatness lies in his knowledge of Jewish folk-life. . . .

In the travels and adventures of Menasseh Haim as well as in the wanderings of Reb Yudel in *The Bridal Canopy,* we see the life of the people vividly depicted. It is marked by two dominant characteristics—poverty and the study of the Torah. In the despair and hope of the motley assortment of characters who cross Menasseh Haim's path, there is something sublime and majestic. One is moved by the sight of so much suffering and yet one cannot help admiring the people's simple faith. At times one gets the impression that these are not beggars and paupers but princes in disguise who at any moment may throw off their tattered rags and appear before us in shining splendor. Though they wear no splendid garments they are possessed of an inner spiritual beauty. Midas-like, the hand of a great artist has transmuted the grime of poverty into a golden dust. Agnon endows his characters with divine qualities without making an effort to emphasize the mystical. One senses this most strongly in his cycle of legends, *Poland,* in his short stories and in some parts of his *Stories of Love*. . . .

In his works, just as the boundaries disappear between reality and dream, this world and the next, so too do the boundaries between diaspora [Jewish life apart from Israel] and the Land of Israel almost vanish. . . . The Holy Land, in Agnon's works, is a land of mystical purity. It is for him more than just a geographical term, more than a politico-social entity. It is a place where the old become young again, the weak strong again. When an old man merits the privilege of going to Palestine, then all the years he has lived in the diaspora are erased from his allotted number and he begins the days of his life anew. For living in Palestine is like getting a foretaste of the next world—and in that next world life begins again. That is why Agnon scarcely needs any young characters in his stories in order to portray youth. The old are his youth.

*Menachem Ribalow, "Samuel Joseph Agnon: Major Novelist of Yesterday and Today," in his* The Flowering of Modern Hebrew Literature, *edited and translated by Judah Nadich (copyright 1959 by Mrs. Menachem Ribalow; reprinted with the permission of Twayne Publishers, a Division of G. K. Hall & Co.), Twayne, 1959, pp. 273-305.*

Agnon, the distinctive artist, is, it need hardly be said, much more than a Hebrew Kafka. Even his "Kafkaesque" stories bear the unmistakable marks of Agnon's own special vision; in any case, they constitute only one segment of his varied literary production over more than half a century. But beyond all similarities, there is one radical difference between the two writers: while Kafka exemplifies the distress of rootlessness that has characterized so many Jews in modern times, Agnon's uniqueness derives from the fact that he is so deeply rooted in a tradition. Agnon is in many ways the most profoundly Jewish writer to have appeared in modern Hebrew literature, and it is in his role as heir to a Jewish religious and cultural heritage that much of his artistic distinctiveness is to be sought. . . .

While . . . [his] Jewish erudition has served as an inexhaustible mine of materials—both verbal and conceptual—from which Agnon has fashioned his creative vision, the relation between Agnon the author and Agnon the learned and pious Jew is to some extent ambivalent. There are times when he looks ironically on his own role as writer (or *sofer,* which in traditional Hebrew meant Torah scribe, and in modern usage generally means author); a Jew, he implies, ought to be an inscriber of holy scrolls, not someone who simply tries to write pretty things. In at least two of his stories he attempts to resolve this conflict by imagining himself as a *sofer* in both senses of the word—a writer whose stories and novels form one long Torah scroll. . . .

[There] is really no analogue among the Western languages to the body of Hebrew upon which Agnon draws. One tends to think, for example, of older literary English, at least since the later Middle Ages, as more ornate, more rhetorically elaborate and consciously artificial, than its modern counterpart, while Old English has for most of us the roughhewn look of a less developed language. The Hebrew of the Midrash, on the other hand, does not suffer from either old-fashioned ornateness or from even the appearance of crudeness. The style of this great medieval collection of homiletic and legendary variations on biblical themes is simple, even-toned, quietly modulated (and consequently Agnon's own style can be deceptively "easy and simple"), but it possesses a peculiar lyric grace, and its flexibility of syntax and breadth of vocabulary make it capable of representing minute details of action and fine nuances of feeling.

Midrashic Hebrew is, moreover, much closer to the modern Hebrew reader than its history of nearly two thousand years would suggest. The source books in which it is used have been traditionally studied from childhood on with the sort of application that would make them as familiar to the cultivated reader of Hebrew as, say, *Pilgrim's Progress* once was to English schoolchildren. Agnon's Hebrew stands with the readers for whom it is intended on a footing of old and intimate acquaintance, in all its archaic accouterment. It has a distinctive poetic charm that necessarily disappears in translation, and because of the deliberate simplicity of the style, Agnon in a Western language is likely to look rather wan and anemic. . . .

Together with the words of tradition, Agnon has adopted for his own uses a wide variety of motifs and symbols from this religious—and often highly poetic—literature. In effect he has found in it one solution to a problem that has typically concerned modern writers beginning with Yeats, Eliot, and Joyce: the need for a living body of mythology from which the artist can draw symbols meaningful to his audience to use in his own work. Agnon discovered a virtually untapped reservoir of symbolic richness in Jewish tradition, and, most particularly, in the Midrash. His development of traditional motifs endows his vision with an unusual poetic coherence, even over the apparently ambling stretches of some of his longer novels. A novel by Agnon is likely to prove to be, among other things, an extended variation on several symbolic themes, frequently themes he has taken from the Midrash. . . .

Of all his achievements in adapting the materials of Jewish tradition to his own fictional modes of expression, the most important has been his remarkable success in weaving the legendary tapestry of the medieval Midrash into the texture of the twentieth-century world lived in and experienced by Shmuel Yosef Agnon. One significant instance of this process is his treatment of the theme of the house. Perhaps the greatest single concern in Agnon's writings is the problem of modern man who, spiritually, finds himself with no place to live. Though this theme is almost everywhere in Agnon's fiction, it receives its most extensive and resonant expression in *A Guest for the Night:* the very title of that novel suggests the uneasy fate of transience to which most of his central characters are condemned, and the main action is the futile, finally self-deceiving attempt of the protagonist, who has returned from Jerusalem to his native Szybuscz, to revive there the old studyhouse, the key educational and religious institution that in fact had been the sheltering spiritual "home" for East-European Jewry in recent centuries. . . .

Jewish tradition always opposes to the hut of exile the image of the house that was, which is also the image of the house that will be; the dark reality of exile is confronted in the unswerving belief in a redemption to follow the exile. There are many moments in Agnon's stories when his dispossessed protagonists seem on the point of being wholly submerged by the forces that threaten them, but what ultimately distinguishes Agnon from an uprooted Jew like Kafka is the fact that at times he can honestly envisage a restoration of the shattered order, a rebuilding of the ruined house. To be sure, it is often difficult to know quite how to take Agnon: even his occasional images of hope flicker ambiguously, are gravely threatened by the world of shadows around them, but they possess an imaginative reality that cannot be entirely discounted.

Agnon has in his varied literary enterprise confronted some of the most disturbing aspects of the contemporary world, and he is too shrewd, too tough-minded an observer to be capable of deceiving himself about the way things are. Yet by remaining constantly in touch—both in his art and in his private life—with the spiritual wholeness of the past, he has preserved the conviction that such wholeness of spirit is both indispensable and still possible to achieve, however unreachable it may now seem.

*Robert Alter, "S. Y. Agnon: The Alphabet of Holiness" (originally published in a slightly different version as "The Genius of S. Y. Agnon," in* Commentary, *August, 1961), in his* After the Tradition *(copyright © 1962 by Robert Alter; reprinted by permission of the publishers, E. P. Dutton & Co., Inc.), Dutton, 1969, pp. 131-50.*

[*The*] *Bridal Canopy* [is] one of Agnon's major novels and a highpoint in modern Hebrew literature. . . .

An element [in this work] is the search for a past, a probing into a once-upon-a-time way of life. In *The Bridal Canopy,* Agnon is the literary archivist of Galician Jewry, the comprehensive preserver of a now destroyed civilization. As Reb Yudel and his driver Nuta wander through early 19th-century Galicia trying to collect enough alms to dower Reb Yudel's three daughters, they listen to and exchange countless stories with the people they meet. There is an enchanting inner rhythm to the work where the adventures blend with the "told" stories. The tales the characters tell are often an extension of their personality and relate artistically to the main plot. . . .

Realism and fantasy mingle in this enchanting storybook world. Horses converse, men speak in formal rhyme—reminiscent of the rhymed prose picaresques written by Spanish Jews 800 years ago. Yet the total fabric of Galician Jewry—its beliefs, traits, humor and folklore—is described in epic grandeur with absolute fidelity of detail. Yiddishkeit suffuses this book, as it does most of Agnon's works. . . .

Like *The Bridal Canopy,* the novella *In the Heart of the Seas* is a retrospective glance at early 19th-century Jewish life; but whereas *The Bridal Canopy* is a huge canvas, the novella is a fine miniature. Here Agnon focuses only upon a small group of Hasidim who decide to make the *aliya* to the Land of Israel. Since this is a story about Hasidim, the spirit of Hasidism pervades the work. . . .

As usual, Agnon makes use of the entirety of Hebraic lore. . . . In the tale he assumes the same role he has carved out for himself during the past sixty years—a teller of stories who sweetens the passing time for the company of travelers. On the one hand this displacement of self may seem like a charming literary gesture. However, on the other hand, given the problem of spiritual tension that pervades Agnon's fiction—man perpetually seeking tranquility and faith—the removal of self may be a form of wish-fulfillment, an escape from the problem-laden 20th century into the security of the past.

*Curt Leviant, "Mirror of The Jewish Past," in* Congress Bi-Weekly, *September 25, 1967, pp. 20-21.*

[Agnon's] fiction spans five to six generations of Jewish life in East Central Europe and Palestine, from the Hasidic revival at the end of the eighteenth century through the Zionist revival at the end of the nineteenth, and beyond that into the present worlds of European and Israeli Jewry. (p. 1)

Agnon's powers are not primarily the powers of a novelist; he has no gusto, no thirst for experience, no substantial gift of empathy. He has never been concerned with the plastic creation of character, and he has, on the whole, shunned the task of fleshing out human responses within the finely meshed web of social relationships. His gift is essentially a lyric one, though his lyricism is coupled with a nearly misanthropic thrust of satiric imagination. The grand felicities of his prose, like those of Mann and Proust, of Kafka and Joyce, come to serve as a vehicle for meditation upon the life of the soul, for a meditation that appropriates the actualities of the outer world in order to evoke the sense of an elusive subjectivity. (pp. 1-2)

Agnon in his fiction plays continually with the redemptive, messianic associations of Jerusalem, the Holy City, which signifies security and integrity, as opposed to the Diaspora (the Exile), where rootlessness and insecurity prevail. Yet the city of Jerusalem is also of this world, is a modern environment of alienation, disruption, and fragmentation. (p. 7)

[In] parables like "Ido and Enam" and in a still later story, "Forevermore," he attempts to formulate an attitude toward the entire experience. The final perspective is neither so clear nor so definitive as Agnon's best work promises it could or would be. But it is a wide perspective, and one that, like these parables themselves, includes the greatest dilemmas of modern Jews and, in some respects, of all modern men. (p. 9)

*The Bridal Canopy* represents Agnon's emergence from the twilight of the early tales. I find it at times tedious, labored, and too sustainedly coy. It displays his remarkable architectonic gifts, however, and it seems to have confronted him with the crucial problem of history, of the relation between the past and the present, which forms the central concern of the late parables and of his major fiction. Even as he was summoning up a vision of the old world of the "fathers," he seems to have begun to come to grips with his own problematical relation to it. Agnon's later novels deal with the impact of that world's decline upon people like himself who must bear the body of its death. His own historical situation becomes the focus of his work—a situation in which the individual remains sentimentally bound to a decaying social and cultural order which magnetizes his sensibility and prevents him from shaping a satisfactory life in a changing universe. . . . [The] ancestral past continues to serve Agnon as the foundation of his consciousness and even of his judgment, as a source of stability and the basis of his alienation from modernity. His *judgment* of that foundation remains achingly obscure, but his novelistic manipulation of it is almost uniformly impressive. (p. 17)

Much of Agnon's short fiction since the early 1930's has been concerned with representing either the radically equivocal states of being that arise when one is unwillingly possessed by the past or when one willfully tries to recapture it. These stories fall roughly into three groups. There is the usually brief nightmarish tale, rather Kafkaesque in technique, that renders the experience of an individual whose life is disrupted by an onrush of incomprehensible events obscurely related to his wishes and fears. Then there is the expressionist tale, directly related to the last volume of Hermann Broch's novel *The Sleepwalkers,* but with affinities to the art of Frank Wedekind, Robert Musil, and even the early Bertold Brecht. These present an utterly fragmented and demented outer world which often reflects a disrupted inner world but which has independent validity as an image of chaos and upheaval. And finally there is the self-conscious parable of a quest, like "Ido and Enam," in which characters consciously and unconsciously seek out ways of resuscitating the old, sanctified modes of existence, trying to order their experience and find goodness, beauty, and truth in a wayward, desperate present.

One notes the persistence, in all three types of story, of certain motifs, involving what we might call an Agnon figure—that is, involving a writer or scholar . . . who deliberately tries to contact, record, or preserve a lost or elusive reality. All these characters share an alienation from ordinary experience; all of them pursue their interest in relative or complete isolation, often with a Magian intensity. . . . Curiously, however, these special characters are not essentially different from the more commonplace figures who move through Agnon's work. Agnon's ordinary protagonist is a little man who tends toward a bewildered incomprehension of the things that happen to him. He is—one might say—an archetype of bewilderment.

This figure represents the peculiar strength as well as the peculiar limitation of Agnon's achievement. He has been compared to Kafka's heroes, just as the modernist tales about him have been compared in style and form to Kafka's work. If one seeks analogies in modern literature, however, one would do better to look to Faulkner, whose characters remain caught up in the traditions of the old South and continue to live within its mythos without being able to evolve viable relationships in the world which has supplanted it. The difference is that Faulkner's people respond to this situation with glorified self-dramatization in postures of defeat, while Agnon's people respond to their circumstances with Chaplinesque incomprehension and a reflexive shrug of the shoulders, in which wit and imbecility coincide. (pp. 23-4)

In view of Agnon's own "Zionist" choice to write in Hebrew, and in view of his massive contribution to the development of modern Hebrew as a literary medium, it is supremely ironic that his language should often seem a transmogrified, quintessential rendering in Hebrew of something native to Yiddish at its most reflexive. His prose is a language never heard on land or sea, impeccably Hebraic and yet molded in the cadence of another mode—a Yiddish one—another language, another form of consciousness. Indeed, the pleasures which Agnon's prose style affords are themselves a symptom of the underlying difficulty. So much is invested by Agnon in the language that, instead of serving as a pane of clear glass through which we might envision a world, it often seems one of those finely wrought products of vitreous art in which figures are etched into the glass itself. His language ultimately points back to itself, rather than outward into an objectified fictional universe. There is an objective attunement to the outer world and its problems. But there is also always the self-regarding, aestheticizing intrusion of Agnon's sensibility. I insist, in contrast to some of Agnon's more sensitive readers, that he is not a mere aesthete; his work is too rich and too deeply engaged with some aspects of reality for him to be seen as one. But I hold that he does not achieve a vigorous substantive engagement with the ultimate implications of his experience.

In a sense, his range is too narrow, and the historical scope of his fiction fails to make up for the limited span of experience it encompasses. Agnon lacks gusto, and so do his characters. Their inherent passivity—their incapacity to engage in passionate struggle—oppresses the reader and, in the end, makes for a lack of conviction as to the integrity of the total vision. One always feels that something is left out—that some range of energies and impulses remains unconfronted.

The common comparison to Kafka suggests one source of the weakness. Within the psychic smog of Kafka's world there is a tensed, even compulsive will to be, to achieve, to escape. . . . Such tension is largely absent in Agnon. (pp. 25-6)

More damaging, ultimately, is the underlying irresolution in Agnon's attitude toward his material. The late parables bespeak the hopelessness of attempting to embody the high aims and ravening dreams of the Rechnitzes, Ginats, and Gamzus. Yet they may also be said to constitute a kind of elegiac celebration of that fond, foolish effort—the only effort worth making in this shattered world. It is surely no accident that Agnon's first novel had *Don Quixote* in its background; *The Bridal Canopy* and all the work that follows are riddled with a Cervantesque ambivalence toward the figure of the hero—treating him as saint and fool, martyr and "fall guy". . . . It is the sort of ambivalence that mocks the objects of its heroes' desire, and it accounts in part for the quality of unpleasantness in Agnon's work. The price of the remarkable lyricism of the pathetic comedy of his own and his people's journey through the anterooms of modernity into the center of its hell is a faint nastiness, an uneasy afterstench of self-indulgence which precludes wisdom, passion, and even the larger energy of a truly hellish ordeal. (p. 27)

Agnon's finest noncomic work in the traditionalist mode has a kind of luminous loveliness and musicality, reminiscent of the medieval tale at its best. In it there is a fine orchestration of feelings that spring from pain and loss, but never a direct representation of the rawness and anguish they involve. . . . It is as though Agnon turns to the ancestral past partly because he finds within it a set of attitudes that permit a deeply desiderated transcendence of the harshness of inner conflict and a deeply felt need to circumvent the horror of death itself. (p. 50)

*The Bridal Canopy* is an extraordinary book, in its handling of both [its] world and Agnon's ambivalence toward that world. . . . [It] renders, as no other work does so extensively, the unique *shtetl* sense of nature and history. Much admired for this, it has been hailed as *the* "epic" of the old village culture, and as *the* representation of the *shtetl* before its decline. . . . One can say that the tales of the ancestral world "diminutivize" the denizens of that world and substitute quaintness for vigor and active striving. (pp. 72, 75)

Agnon's gift is such that it provokes the highest expectations and impels us to make the most aggressive demands. The pleasures the work affords compensate for many limitations: the terrible muting of his peoples' passions, whether they be of love or of rage; the chilling lack of sympathy with ordinary human aspiration; the tamping of dramatic urgencies; and the cloying indulgence of sheer verbal effect. These limitations often yield in the face of the sheer beauty of Agnon's evocations and of his astonishing architectonic virtuosity in the projection of themes and of worlds. More than anything, they yield, for those who have the patience to follow the development of the entire body of his work, in terms of the larger architecture of the revelation that is apparent in the context of the whole: an architecture that indeed has "epic" dimensions, and that embraces so much that is vital to the history of his culture over hundreds of years. The awareness of Agnon's strengths, however, is somehow again subordinated to the intuition that something essential is missing: the agony of final confrontation, which will bring muscle and bone and blood and guts into the wrestling with the angel of nullity—not so much sweet singing and exquisite purling of song. (pp. 189-90)

*Baruch Hochman, in his* The Fiction of S. Y. Agnon *(copyright © 1970 by Cornell University; used by permission of Cornell University Press), Cornell University Press, 1970.*

For generations, the Jewish way of life . . . was a religion and a culture at the same time. It enveloped the life of the individual and the community from the cradle to the grave. You could make your own list of parallel characteristics: the Sabbath candles, the black mantle, gefilte fish, pickled herring, dumplings; playing with a spinning top on *Hanukah* and with nuts on Passover; tearing the hem of the coat as a sign of mourning, kissing a holy book when it dropped to the floor, never kissing your beloved in front of strangers; singing traditional songs for every occasion; your grandmother, her spectacles perched on her nose, reading old tales of the pious from a book on her lap at Saturday twilight . . . thousands of customs and habits that everyone observed and followed and was imbued with. A paradise for writers, as it were. S. Y. Agnon . . . who was conceived in the womb of this all-embracing "religion-cum-culture" and grew up in its bosom, demonstrates in every story of his the pleasure of this writer's paradise. . . .

[The] Hebrew style, typically Agnonian as it is—economical, legend-like, with ironic undertones alluding to the naivety of popular beliefs—is at the same time traditional, derived from Hassidic tales and holy Scriptures. The distinction of it lies in this very combination of individuality and convention, when the single voice ripples with the echoes of past generations. Thus, reading a story of Agnon is like looking into a deep well, where your own image is reflected through mysterious half-darkness encircled by ancient stones.

*Aharon Megged, "How Did The Bible Put It?," in* Encounter, *January, 1971, pp. 39-43.*

Now that *Shira* has been published . . . the novel has perplexed many of Agnon's devoted readers. Agnon is known as a master of synoptic perception. His work is read and interpreted on literal, allegorical, symbolic, and mystical levels, but in *Shira* he has shifted from connotative to denotative meaning. What is perplexing is that the scholar of the cabala and its intricacies, the teller of Hassidic tales and Kafkaesque fables should leave as his last work an explicit, open story dealing with a sexual affair, a story about real people, set against the background of Jerusalem in the 1930s and early 1940s. The Agnonite labryinth has given way to a vivid picture of mundane life.

Perhaps the explanation is that his shift from the religious to the secular in this novel—from the symbolic to the realistic, from the connotative to the denotative meaning—is itself part of the "symbolic" content of his work as a whole. Seen in this light, the "matter" of the novel reflects the general transition from a symbolic to a realistic Weltanschauung in Jewish culture as a whole; and the "manner" of the novel is entirely consistent with this process. Thus, Agnon has written a secularized novel, after having witnessed the long process of secularization in Jewish culture.

In the face of this process Agnon's novels nevertheless kept their connotative richness, and his readers came to expect symbolic material which they could interpret in a variety of ways. And now, as well, commentators have continued this many-sided interpretation of Agnon; they have hurried to point out that the name of the heroine, Shira, means "poetry" in Hebrew, while the name of the hero, Herbst, means "autumn" in German. There is also a Weltfremd, German for "alien to the world," as well as a Wechsler, German for "money-changer" or "one who produces changes." Yet the fact that commentators must latch onto such obvious symbols points to the breakdown of a deeper symbolic orientation in general culture. It is exactly this breakdown which Agnon seems to have made one of his main themes in a novel which departs entirely from his symbol-filled writing. . . .

[In] all his novels before *Shira,* the surface story provided a key to a wider perception of a totality of life, a symbolic perception greater than that carried by the narrative. In *Shira* the motifs are confined in their meaning to the particular event or anecdote, and they do not permeate the book as a whole. This is exactly what one would expect, since the world he describes is a world lacking any transcendent or pervasive meaning. His Jerusalem (like his protagonist) is a secular city in a secular world, a world having to search for a meaning within itself. But this search can proceed only if this world believes that its past is truly dead and that it therefore must look within itself in its present. . . .

[In *Shira*, the] religious theme involves a change in character; but in the secular theme, the character is merely thrown against himself, he never comes out of himself and therefore remains unchanged. The theme of love, so rich with symbolic meaning in Agnon—in *Agunoth* God is the male figure weaving a relationship with the female Israel—is here reduced to a physical level which is meaningless not only to the characters but also to the reader. The love of Herbst and Shira only accentuates their loneliness.

The novel is much more significant as the last work of a great writer than it is as a work on its own terms. Considered on its own, it loses its breath and momentum as well as the causal connectedness expected in a novel. Viewed, however, as Agnon's last statement, it expresses his realization that the Westernization of Judaism represents its decline as a living, generative, and ever-meaningful spiritual power.

*Gila Ramras-Rauch, "'Shira': S. Y. Agnon's Posthumous Novel," in* Books Abroad, *Vol. 45, No. 4, Autumn, 1971, pp. 636-38.*

*Sippur Pashut* (A Simple Story) is . . . set in Galicia in the declining world of Eastern European Jewish life [of about 1910].

The broad outlines of the story are indeed quite simple, although the novel is far more complex in its symbolic structure, character development, and potential "levels of meaning." A seventeen-year-old boy, Hirshel Horowitz, is trapped between the values of his bourgeois parents, Baruch Meir and Tsirel Klinger Horowitz, and his own spiritual needs in the changing world. The novel treats the conflicts and resolutions which grow out of his situation. Galician society of 1910 decreed that Hirshel would marry the respectable Minah Tsiemlich (meaning "so so") instead of the night blooming Blumah Nacht, whom he truly loves and who represents eros and freedom as well as personal fulfillment. The forced marriage and its implications for Hirshel's freedom contribute to what really amounts to a nervous breakdown which Agnon perceives in metaphysical terms. Hirshel's cure is coupled with his return to society, acceptance of his "so so" wife, and the regeneration of a new family. Hirshel strives throughout the novel to "correct his attributes" by breaking away from his family and establishing an independent ground of operation, and thus the conclusion of the novel is a surprise and, indeed, a disappointment. He rejects his idealistic gropings and settles down into the family business, inheriting his grandfather's store in the same way that he inherited a family curse, another cause of his mental disturbance.

For Agnon, no less than for Shakespeare, human events have metaphysical implications, and an incorrect marriage reflects a state of the universe, just as fixing what is wrong in the world has possible messianic implications. The time is definitely "out of joint" in Shibbush, Hirshel's town; something is rotten there, though the narrator hides the rottenness under layers of irony. The name "Shibbush" in Hebrew means something like "malfunction" and seems to be a distortion of the name of Agnon's own hometown, Bucacz.

A debate has been conducted around this novel with regard to the narrator's feelings about Hirshel's resolution. Scholars have suggested the levels of irony within the story; on the one hand, Hirshel's capitulation to bourgeois norms is disgusting, but on the other, it seems to be the only resolution. Is Hirshel to be scorned for having given up his ideals? Or is the world unfixable, in which case his capitulation is not only tolerable but appropriate? A line which appears throughout the novel is the narrator's assurance that "the bourgeoisie are the essence of the world"; and while the line strikes a biting tone each time it is said, one cannot help but feel that Agnon meant it in the most literal sense. . . .

Setting enriches the problems of *Sippur Pashut* by adding layer upon layer of paradox to an already paradoxical and ambiguous world. Agnon is always implying that things are not what they seem. He means this, also, quite literally. . . .

*Sippur Pashut* is in part a novel of manners and morals, . . . and Hirshel's emotional disorder and subsequent "adjustment" is directly related to his ability or inability to "belong" to that setting in which those manners and morals find expression. The settings are rarely metaphoric in nature, rather they operate as extensions of the protagonist. The social environment yields synecdochic details which contribute to the recurring motifs that take the story beyond its social levels. As a novel in which social environment plays such a great part, *Sippur Pashut* is replete with rich descriptions of setting. . . . A consideration of varying aspects of setting will demonstrate that setting is used not to clarify the status of the protagonist, but to complicate it. . . .

Agnon uses his setting to maximum advantage, without forcing the reader to be aware of the importance of the role of setting within the novel. He creates metaphor, metonymic settings, and synecdochic details; often the detail becomes symbolic of Hirshel's changing personality at a given time. Setting in the novel is central to the descriptions of Hirshel's efforts to draw near to and away from his social surrounding. . . . The vacillating hostility and friendliness of a variety of settings suggests that Hirshel really belongs nowhere. His residence in Shibbush may be uncertain in the same ambiguous and paradoxical way in which setting (and indeed the entire universe) is treated throughout the novel.

*William Cutter, "Setting as a Feature of Ambiguity in S. Y. Agnon's 'Sippur Pashut'," in* Critique: Studies in Modern Fiction, *Vol. XV, No. 3, 1974, pp. 66-79.*

* * *

## Ai (pseudonym of Florence Anthony) 1947-

**A Black American poet, Ai chose as her true—as opposed to given—name the sound of a cry.**

Ai's "Cruelty" will be taken for kinky, black-leather stuff; it is not. The poet has been called (by Anne Sexton) "All woman—all human"; she is hardly that. She is more like a bad dream of Woody Allen's, or the inside story of some Swinburnean Dolorosa, or the *vagina dentata* itself starting to talk. Woman, in Ai's embodiment, wants sex. She knows about death and can kill animals and people. She is hard as dirt. Her realities—very small ones—are so intolerable that we fashion female myths to express our fear of her. She, however, lives the hard life far below our myths. And her man lives it with her. . . . Murder, suicide, sexual violence, simple lust, whoredom, child-beating occur with utmost flatness. . . . The speakers of these poems—most of whom are not the poet, and almost a third of whom are in fact men—are playing out the dramas of their lives in isolated small-town and small-farm settings, where their lives count for nothing more than that of a slaughtered goat, where desire is like the smell of fresh meat. Each is savage, each is victim. None blames another, none complains. Their voices form a chorus. The cruelty is theirs because it is nature's. Though she is just beginning, Ai has set herself in a league with Faulkner's novels, or with Ted Hughes's "Crow"; with those who will not take yes for an answer.

*Alicia Ostricker, in* The New York Times Book Review *(© 1974 by The New York Times Company; reprinted by permission), February 17, 1974, p. 7.*

Not only has Ai approached new ground in exploring the human consciousness in poetry, but she is covering it in lucid style. . . . [She] is herself lost (transformed) among the people and events she witnesses and records. So totally does she identify with what she sees that all her poems become, successfully, the voices of men, 40-year-old whores, mad hitchhiker killers, starving tenant farmers, child-beaters, even corpse-haulers. . . .

Ai has not spared herself or mistrusted the reality of her own perception of experience; she has chosen honesty over politics. Expressions of personal knowledge are always arguable; if you want nice poems to "like" [*Cruelty*] is not your book.

To read *Cruelty* is to wonder peculiar wonders: How is it, for example, that Woman—who is in her own life constantly and intimately conscious of blood—has written so little poetry with blood, bloodiness, as a recurring image? And how is it that women—the only people capable of knowing the truth of childbirth—have written so little that is graphic about that bloody truth? And how is it that women—who spend so much of their lives knowing that love and passion are a sometime thing—write so many poems in which those feelings alone exist? The answers to these questions have been so prolific in the past few years that the questions themselves must be posed almost rhetorically; yet Ai's poems raise them again. . . .

*Alice Walker, "'Like the Eye of a Horse'," in* Ms., *June, 1974, p. 41.*

* * *

## ALGREN, Nelson 1909-

**Algren is an American novelist and short story writer best known for *The Man With the Golden Arm*. "Poet of the Chicago slums," Algren is the chronicler of America's bars and brothels, drunks and pimps. (See also *Contemporary Authors*, Vols. 13-14.)**

As early as 1935, in *Somebody in Boots,* his first novel, Algren had confronted the standard interpretation of American life—prosperity and success—with his own chronicles of poverty and failure. His first hero, a "poor-white" Texas boy, growing up during the depression years, takes to the road and becomes a vagabond and petty criminal. The book is dedicated to "those innumerable thousands: the homeless boys of America." It may remind you of Jack London's earlier study of American tramps and vagabonds called *The Road,* or of certain parts of John Dos Passos' *The 42nd Parallel.* There is indeed a whole body of literature dealing with this area of the national scene, as far back as the 1890's.

The emphasis of Algren's first novel is on the scenes of brutality which mark the life of the "lumpen-proletariat," the social scum, the passively rotting mass of people who lie at the bottom of the social scale. . . . [The] novel is also in the straight documentary style of the 1930's: a thesis novel of social protest in which the characters are social types—if they are lucky. The prose is "poetic" in a bad sense; the tone of the novel is sentimental and melodramatic. *Never Come Morning,* seven years later, in 1942, was a very different story. . . .

Perhaps the best comparisons are with the Chicago Irish of James T. Farrell's novels and the tormented black souls of [Richard] Wright's . . . work; but you get in Algren's book even more clearly the sense of stunted (and potentially vicious) children. . . .

Algren's powerful effects are usually in his big scenes rather than in the portrayal or development of character. He is almost at his best in this volume of short stories [*The Neon Wilderness*] where he can suggest the whole contour of a human life in a few terse pages. There is more warmth and humor here, too, than in the earlier books. It is, all in all, an excellent collection of short stories, perhaps one of the best we had in the 1940's. And, opening the new decade of the 1950's, *The Man With the Golden Arm* brought together the various strains in Algren's work. . . .

The structure of the book is panoramic; there are a host of minor characters. The language is rich, if not ornate with the idiom of punks, cranks, and petty gangsters. This is a *Winesburg, Ohio* of the slum dwellers; and one remembers that Sherwood Anderson wrote his nostalgic country tales while living in these miserable Chicago buildings, at the ragged end of life, where the streets run on and on, "out of nowhere into nothing.". . .

Algren's typical figures are failures even at vice. They are the underdogs of sin, the small souls of corruption, the fools of poverty, not of wealth and power. Even the murders they commit, out of blind rage or through sheer accident—or through another ironic twist of their impoverished destiny—are not important. . . .

Algren's work represents an extreme phase of the native American realism which opened, in the 1900's, with Stephen Crane's *Maggie,* Frank Norris' *McTeague,* and Dreiser's *Sister Carrie.* All these authors were concerned with the dispossessed, but still retained the notion of hope and chance in a blind and very often hostile but not absolutely fatal universe. These writers believed that human character was both a social and a biological (or hereditary) product. Or rather, they did not see character as a "product" at all, but as that "mystery of personality" which continued to fascinate the older generation of American artists up to Sherwood Anderson and Ellen Glasgow. (Nor should I exclude, in the "aristocratic" branch of our letters, Edith Wharton and Henry James himself.) Algren moves on a much narrower base than this—the range from the documentary novel of social misery in the 1930's to the later depiction of human beings who are caught in the trap of social circumstance. The scale is always weighted, in his view, the odds are too heavy, the universe *is* fatal.

He is the poet of this underworld, a high verbal talent, and one is not sure that he is even interested in character, or his characters, except in so far as they contribute another offbeat dissonance. (The true comparison of Algren's work may be with jazz, or bebop, or rock 'n roll.) At least *A Walk on the Wild Side* (1956), Algren's sequel to *The Man With the Golden Arm,* contributes to this impression. . . .

The narrative is filled with brilliant little profiles of very dubious characters indeed. There are passages of inimitable dialogue. There are comic interludes of a Rabelaisian hilarity, marked by a deliberate sensationalism which is also a take-off on our conventional notions of romantic love.

Algren has moved closer here to the San Francisco school of "Zen hipsters," as Herbert Gold has described them. ("Zen Strikes Back.") This is the group centered around jazz music—progressive or rocky—those sick sounds and weird reverberations whose . . . spokesman is Jack Kerouac, whose philosopher-poet is Kenneth Rexroth, whose aging prophet is Henry Miller. But both Miller and Algren are mature artists, deriving from other periods and other roots. For Algren himself, *A Walk on the Wild Side* is also a kind of hit-and-run book. The trouble is that very often the poetic inspiration—exuberant, gay, outrageous as it is—runs away with the narrative; sometimes the narrative seems to be only inspiration. Here the earlier limitations in the writer's work also become dominant; and in a sense he seems indifferent to them.

Is this also the end of the whole tradition of social protest which, as we have seen, Algren has embodied in his previous work and career? That tradition is unfashionable today (though half the world is in the throes of social revolution). A writer like Algren must at times regard himself as an isolated figure. It is easier to give up; it is easier to become the popularizer of the lower depths, rather than the poet—or to move in the direction of Steinbeck and make theatrical "primitives" out of these native American paisanos. To a certain degree Henry Miller has also done this in his later "sex" books, which are diluted summaries of his earlier ones. The humor of *A Walk on the Wild Side* is a little too facile; the people are abstracted; their tragedy is muted. The writer is relying on his verbal talent to cover the loss of human material. (A book much in the same vein, Erich Remarque's *The Black Obelisk* [1957], a satiric and poetic chronicle of post-World-War-I Germany, has much more humanity and warmth.). . .

Nelson Algren should remind himself that he represents a solid and enduring part of the American literary heritage; that he derives from this past, and writes not for the contemporary stage alone. That Iron Sanctuary, the source and center of his earlier work, still haunts our civilization. And Algren, like John Hersey, is a writer who carries with him our hope and concern for something more than entertainment.

*Maxwell Geismar, "Nelson Algren: The Iron Sanctuary" (originally published in a slightly different version in* College English, *March, 1953), in his* American Moderns: From Rebellion to Conformity *(reprinted by permission of Hill and Wang, a division of Farrar, Straus & Giroux, Inc.; copyright © 1958 by Maxwell Geismar), Hill & Wang, 1958, pp. 187-94.*

What we have . . . in this big fat volume ["The Last Carousel"] is a cockeyed chrestomathy of 37 Algren pieces from 1947 to 1972. . . . Short fiction, travel sketches, reminiscences, character assassinations, pop history material deleted from "A Walk on the Wild Side," odes to Chicago springs. Even occasional lapses into poetry. . . .

Mr. Algren hates waste, finds nothing dispensable. When he latches on to a snappy line or anecdote, he really milks it, even throws it into his nonfiction to hype the action or distract attention from his greased deal. "I've always thought," he confesses, "I could make it as a standup comic." I guess he figures that the guys he breaks up in the Carefree Corner Bar aren't likely to catch his act the next month at Caesar's Palace. But I suspect he just doesn't give a damn, or else he'd have edited out the repeats and overlappings in this catch-all volume. . . .

[What] about all the familiar complaints about Algren's work—his pretending to be a tough-minded naturalist when he's really a closet transcendentalist, his sentimentalizing of the world's losers as if only the fringe-people retained freedom and purity, his shameless exploitation of the dispossessed for easy laughs from the coupon-clippers? Well, all of these charges can be documented from "The Last Carousel." Admitted. Lots of chocolate-covered cherries ooze through these pages: "a thousand heartbroken dawns," "dimly fell the shadows, one by one, of bars," "memory ties rainbows of forgetfulness about old lost years," "the fly-a-kite spring," "the broken-handled cups of hopes that had never come true."

The eschatological imagery wears thin: merry-go-rounds going around for the last time, the golden arm failing at last, the ferris-wheel sinking forever downward into dust, tote-board lights going blind with dusk. . . .

[But anyone] daring to review Nelson Algren today stands in grave danger of being a "past-poster"—a party who puts down a heavy bet on a horse that has already won.

*James R. Frakes, in* The New York Times

*Book Review (© 1973 by The New York Times Company; reprinted by permission), November 11, 1973, pp. 20, 22.*

No writer has been more relentlessly faithful to his scene and cast of characters than Nelson Algren. His scene is the "wild side," the "neon wilderness," the seamier sprawls of Chicago and its spiritual extensions across this broad land —America as Chicago. And his characters are the drifters and grifters, clowns and carnies, pimps and pushers, hustlers and hookers, gamblers and touts, junkies and lushes, marks and victims, conmen and shills, freaks and grotesques—the born losers who constitute a half-world, an anti-society to the society that never appears, not even as a sensed or felt presence, in Algren's work. Over the four decades of his life as a writer, scene and characters have never changed. Atmosphere, obsessions, talk, ways of putting in the time—all are fixed, held in suspension, dreamed and long after hazily recalled, caught not as they once were but as they are remembered, just as they are about to dissolve and become ballads. The mythical time, whatever the calendar reads, is always the '30s, somewhere around the longest year of 1935.

Except when it's time for settling old scores. Since *The Last Carousel* is for the most part an ingathering of magazine pieces, many of them from the pages of *Playboy*, anything goes. . . .

[The] book takes its echoing tone from Algren's chronic weakness for "fine" writing, the kind of overblown elegaic lyricism—tremulous, quivering, cadenced, or wistful, celebratory, nostalgic, poignant—that used to be called prose-poetry. It was widely practiced by sensitive young writers in conscious quest of an American demotic voice, some suitable song for the open road—the endless, receding plains, prairies, rivers of the imagined West. Of that chorus, Algren's voice was the most prominent and is the longest lasting, the others have long since faded. Decidedly a literary manner, it came on aggressively anti-literary: tough-tender and bittersweet, sentimental and swaggering, robust, keen-eyed, sprung from the soil, epic, open to the full spectrum of American experience, defiantly outside the mainstream of literary modernism and contemptuous of it, a strong dose of salts for the university wits and nancies—in short a species of literary populism and native romanticism, a nervously American preoccupation of the '30s.

The trouble with "style," with any strongly marked literary manner, is that it can become its own object of contemplation. Algren has always been a gifted yarn-spinner, a teller of tall tales and manner as to be finally strangled by them. Helplessly our sorely strained attention shifts from story and character. Typically the story outgrows its limits, expands, without warrant, toward legend. Characters degenerate into "colorful characters"; and our attention, having been thus wrenched from its ostensible objects, centers on the evocative voice of the poet singing of summer with full-throated ease. Not a page is free ofit. . . .

Algren is a maverick of American letters: a solitary, impervious writer in possession of a true though narrow talent. . . .

Algren, our only poet of the lumpen proletariat, is the rambling minstrel of times that never were and are now long gone. He alone has remembered their voices and restored their lives. In order to make them memorable, the stuff of lore, figures in the American landscape, he provides the amplification, with reedy winds, often one lonesome oboe, off-key, and augmented strings, some of them snapped.

*Saul Maloff, "Maverick in American Letters," in* The New Republic *(reprinted by permission of* The New Republic; *© 1974 by Harrison-Blaine of New Jersey, Inc.), January 19, 1974.*

* * *

## AMBLER, Eric 1909-

**Ambler, according to Graham Greene, is England's best thriller writer. Although best known for his realistic espionage tales, particularly *Epitaph for a Spy* and *The Mask of Dimitrios,* Ambler has also written many successful screen plays. (See also *Contemporary Authors*, Vols. 9-12, rev. ed.)**

Not until Eric Ambler began writing in the late thirties did any degree of sophistication about the powers of darkness enter the thriller. And even then his perspective is, from our point of view, rhetorical and simplistic. . . .[It] is in *Background to Danger* that torture makes its delayed entrance into the spy story. Ambler's books reflect the stages of contemporary conflict, from the early days of Fascism and Nazism to the cold war.

In *Background to Danger* also Ambler displays for the first time in thriller literature a critical attitude toward capitalism. . . .[Earlier thriller writers] would have castigated Ambler's insistence that "at some point in the business structure there is always dirty work to be done" [*Background to Danger*]. "International business may conduct its operations with scraps of paper, but the ink it uses is human blood" [*The Mask of Dimitrios*]. Ambler himself was a little ashamed of such emotionalism. . . .Nevertheless, Ambler's antipathy toward Big Business was consistently expressed in novel after novel, and he shared the view of young English intellectuals in the late thirties that "political ideologies had very little to do with the ebb and flow of international relations. It was the power of business" [*Background to Danger*].

*Ralph Harper, in his* The World of the Thriller, *The Press of Case Western Reserve University, 1969, pp. 32-4.*

Ambler is a superb technician. Anything but avant-garde, he is descended from Maugham and certain Edwardian stylists. . . .Slowly, smoothly, he involves the reader with his characters, and in a short time everything becomes real.

*Newgate Callendar, in* The New York Times Book Review *(© 1972 by The New York Times Company; reprinted by permission), July 16, 1972, p. 32.*

In the six novels he wrote before the outbreak of World War II, Eric Ambler . . . infused warmth and political color into the spy story by using it to express a Left Wing point of view. . . .The central character is an innocent figure mixed up in violent events who slowly comes to realize that the agents and spies working on both sides are for the most part unpleasant but not important men. They murder casually and without passion on behalf of some immense corporation or firm of armaments manufacturers whose interests are threatened. These, rather than any national group, are the enemy. *The Dark Frontier* (1936) is the least important of his books, but it contains one prophetic note in the detonation of the first atomic bomb. . . .

The political side of the books lies under the surface. Almost all the best thrillers are concerned, in one form or another, with the theme of the hunted man. Ambler was fascinated by European cities, and his hunts take place against a convincing background of places like Istanbul, Sofia, Belgrade, and Milan. He was interested also in the problems of frontiers and passports, so that the difficulty of moving from place to place plays a large part in the stories. And he showed from the beginning a high skill, which became mastery, in the construction of plot. His finest book of this period, a masterpiece of its kind, is *The Mask of Dimitrios* [in America, *A Coffin for Dimitrios*], in which flashback follows flashback in the attempt of the crime novelist Latimer to trace the career of the dead Dimitrios, and there is little direct action until three-quarters of the way through the book. To develop interest through a book composed in such a way is a mark of the highest technical skill. The story sparkles with incidents, like the interview with the retired spy, or the account of the white-slave traffic, that could be extracted as separate stories and yet continue to advance the plot. . . .

Ambler's later books are more like plain thrillers than spy stories. The best of them, *The Night Comers* (1956) [in America, *A State of Siege*], *The Light of Day* (1962), and *Dirty Story* (1967) are less sensational than some of the prewar novels, and they show the same mastery of construction. Something has been lost, however; a certain world-weariness has replaced enthusiasm and hope. They are detached from events rather than involved in them. There is much to admire and enjoy, but nothing to equal *The Mask of Dimitrios*.

*Julian Symons, in his* Mortal Consequences: A History—From the Detective Story to the Crime Novel *(copyright © 1972 by Julian Symons; reprinted by permission of Harper & Row, Publishers, Inc.), Harper, 1972, pp. 238-39.*

* * *

## AMIS, Martin 1950?-

**An English novelist and critic, Amis is the son of the novelist Kingsley Amis.**

Martin Amis . . . shows great promise in his first novel, and this is all the more hopeful since in *The Rachel Papers* he is labouring under the disadvantage of having to build his story of romantic mishaps and youthful self-discovery around a peculiarly obnoxious hero. Charles Highway is that drearily familiar specimen of post-adolescent English youth, the Early Bloomer, the Sixth Form Sneerer, that combination of middle-class privilege and A-level meritocracy who is such a delight for the dons and such a damn trial to everybody else until a few years pass and, mercifully, he either fizzles out or, more rarely, manages the breakthrough into rejoining the rest of the human race. . . .

I can't help thinking that Mr Amis may have been slightly premature in tackling this particular subject. I hope that doesn't sound patronising; indeed, Mr Amis in his early twenties shows confidence and talent enough to take on anything—except perhaps Charles Highway at 19 years of age. I just feel that a couple of years further away from that age-group might have usefully distanced the author from his subject-matter; at the moment he sometimes gives the impression of still being rather intimately bound up in its concerns, and I think it makes him at once both too indulgent and too harsh in his judgments. Too indulgent, because every now and then one senses from the author a furtive, rather wistful desire to believe that there *is* after all something of value in Charles Highway's messy chatter, in all those dingy little *aperçus* and corny paradoxes and fifth-hand aphorisms. Too harsh, because Mr Amis, perhaps through fear of being thought sentimental, refuses to give us any indication that there may be—as in life there almost always is—something much finer in the human being lurking behind the smokescreen of Charles's defensive old chat.

What is truly depressing in the average university-bound bright young English thing is that the characteristic verbosity so often masks a deeper inarticulateness, in which the spirit struggles and fails to find outlet in true communication. This is a vision that Mr Amis declines to offer, though in Charles Highway he looks to have the perfect medium for it.

*Peter Prince, in* New Statesman, *November 16, 1973, p. 744.*

Well, you old fogies, you were right after all. Martin Amis has exposed the younger generation for the evil and wretched creatures you always supposed them to be, and his only consolation for them is that, once over the hill of adolescence, they may perhaps improve. *The Rachel Papers* is to its crypto-hero, Charles Highway, what the *Confessions* were to St Augustine, both of them enlarging on the motif of "but not yet." In Highway's strange case, the menace is not so much chastity (although that will come in time, no doubt) but maturity. His is a personal record of the pains and pleasures that loom before the age of twenty, and it is one apparently written during the five long hours before that particular number comes up for him. . . .

Highway has the young man's gift for dissecting appearances: accents and social mannerisms are relentlessly exposed, while his own become self-conscious in the extreme. The narrative is often very funny indeed, but I suspect that Martin Amis is getting the last laugh. Charles Highway is so much the archetypal youth, of a certain time and a certain class, that he is necessarily a comic creation. . . . Martin Amis has fashioned a substantial character out of the rag-ends of our frantic contemporaries, and he has done so without any facile commitment to their means and ends.

*Peter Ackroyd, "Highway of Good Intentions," in* The Spectator *(© 1973 by* The Spectator; *reprinted by permission of* The Spectator*), November 24, 1973, p. 674.*

The demands of a comic novel, such as *The Rachel Papers* by Martin Amis, . . . often [depend] on maintaining a distance between the reader and the butt of the joke: too much sympathy means no laughter. But so does too little: we laugh, surely, because we identify with the character in a comic situation, without for a moment believing or caring what the consequences may be. . . .

Most of the sympathy in Martin Amis's very funny first novel *The Rachel Papers* is reserved for his randy, scheming narrator, a privileged middle-class youth loose in London, just coming up to his 20th birthday, and almost getting trapped on the way by true love and a possibly pregnant girl-friend. Certainly the novel is obsessive: the only aim of young Charles Highway—*there's* a name for a Time Traveller—is to get the nubile if faceless Rachel into bed as quickly and often as possible. The obsession, however, seems merely indicative of ribald good health; sickness is limited to adolescent pimples, hangovers and a mild sexual disease. Martin Amis directs a determined, deadpan stare at his chosen patch of the lush teenage jungle, teeming with characters who are about as appealing as bacilli on a face flannel, described with the detached, excessively detailed physicality common to satirists down the ages. What holds the attention are not these limited characters, but the author's verbally inventive scrutiny of them; any time-travelling in this narrow environment can only be in the language itself.

*Clive Jordan, in* Encounter, *February, 1974, pp. 61, 64.*

*The Rachel Papers* impressed me hugely, though more with promise and felicities en route than with achievement. Amis is a moralist, equipped with some of the talents and Anglo-Saxon attitudes of Angus Wilson, a satirist dismayed, like Swift, by the body's incongruities and treacheries, a literary craftsman concerned with the difficulties facing the self-critical novelist in the 1970s who has 'seen it all before' in other writers from Aeschylus to Henry Miller. . . .

The main defect in *The Rachel Papers* is that narrator and milieu lack the weight and texture needed to hold the author's themes and theses. Nevertheless, Martin Amis has made a brilliant start. Mutatis mutandis, as one of Highway's derided dons might have said, this book is Amis's *Crome Yellow,* and he is going to have to beware the same pitfalls that hampered and finally prevented the full development of Aldous Huxley's early brilliance.

*John Mellors, in* London Magazine, *February/March, 1974, pp. 133-34.*

In this lively first novel [*The Rachel Papers*], whatever you may think of the subject matter, it is the language itself that is most striking. Never faltering, Martin Amis moves the narrative with speed, sureness and wit through a complicated tale of a pre-scholarian autumn spent cramming for Oxford Entrance and in bed, at one time with a girl he fancies and for the rest, with a girl he loves. . . .

Charles Highway, let it be said, could be one of the most annoying characters in contemporary fiction; his self love and personal admiration society, plus an overgrown larynx that leads to endless intellectual musings, mean that our view of the supporting characters is heavily coloured by his pontificating eyes. Our sympathy is brought out though, for Charles, because he does suffer from acne, asthma and alienation. In fact, it is only through his callow approach to life that the novel gains its vitality; and Martin Amis is able to display an extraordinarily wide range of knowledge and verbal-play-skills.

Although *The Rachel Papers* is tight, bright and full of talent, if I have one criticism, it is that the novel is not really placed in its time. . . . [The] novel could just as well be criticising the social banalities of the Twenties or Thirties, given a change of vocabulary.

*Carol Dix, in* Books and Bookmen, *April, 1974, pp. 92-3.*

[*The Rachel Papers* is] a moving book, winsome without being cloying, and a delight—perhaps the best teenage sex novel I've read since Philip Roth's *Goodbye, Columbus,* and that was fifteen years ago. *The Rachel Papers* is one of those books that make you feel good: oh, it's very graphic (but how hard it is to do this well) and unabashedly sexist, but it shows once again what a greatly saving grace humor is, what a necessary complement to decency—and that Mother Nature works. Which, every once in a while, is nice to hear.

*Eliot Fremont-Smith, in* New York Magazine *(© 1974 by NYM Corp.; reprinted by permission of* New York Magazine *and Eliot Fremont-Smith), April 29, 1974, p. 76.*

Genes matter; they really do. For years Kingsley (Amis *père*) has been writing sour, witty novels combining manic energy with crapulous fastidiousness, and now Martin (Amis *fils*), 24, comes on peddling hard, seemingly determined in his first novel to outrace Daddy's excesses. . . .

Readers like me, . . . who respond to fiction through a layer of scar tissue, should have an entertaining time, for after a shaky start ["The Rachel Papers"] works very well, propelled by its author's absolute self-confidence over many a failed aphorism and clangorous conjunction of words. "The Rachel Papers" may not be as spectacular a debut as was "Lucky Jim," but it is forceful enough—funny, coarse and extremely energetic.

*Peter S. Prescott, "Love's Highway," in* Newsweek *(copyright Newsweek, Inc., 1974; reprinted by permission), May 6, 1974, pp. 78-9.*

*The Rachel Papers* offers a candid, groin-level view of teenage sex, circa 1970, in Swinging Britain. Amis' hero, Charles Highway, is no slouch at telling us exactly what-he-did-and-then-she-did. But since he is also a precocious and totally self-absorbed intellectual, this indefatigable swordsman is more interested in what he thought, pretended, felt, and above all what he *wrote* in his journal about his sexual happenings, than he is in the act itself. No experience is real for him until he's written it down. (Like Gwendolen Fairfax in Oscar Wilde's *The Importance of Being Earnest,* Charles never travels without his diary, to make sure he always has something sensational to read.). . .

Unfortunately, *The Rachel Papers,* though it has some wildly funny lines, is less a work of fiction than a collage of brightly malicious cinematic takes about that hoary first-novel chestnut, young love and early sorrows. Amis' very with-it bites and snarls occasionally capture his generation's uninhibited idiom, but too many of the book's jokes are labored and unfunny. *The Rachel Papers* is quite short. Nonetheless, it soon seems long-[winded], a one-note tirade of teenage *angst* and absurdity that is basically more narcissistic than mocking. In the novel no less than in life, an unvaried diet of sexual activity is like the toil of Sisyphus, a futile, interminable expense of energy that never reaches the top.

*Pearl K. Bell, "A Surfeit of Sex," in* The New Leader, *May 13, 1974, pp. 19-20.*

[Martin Amis] has performed the rare and hazardous feat of extending his family's mastery of the comic novel to a second generation. While the younger Amis admittedly owes much to his father in terms of style, he is quite his own man in the subject he has chosen. "The Rachel Papers" is a chronicle of the end of adolescence. On the eve of his twentieth birthday, the protagonist, Charles Highway, reviews his latter teens with a wry nostalgia for a time that can never be recaptured—and one; he implies, that he has no wish whatever to recapture.

Amis's vision of adolescence is an unvarnished, terrifying, and hilarious one. It is casually crude, scatological, and obscene. Charles Highway applies the clever brain of an almost-man to the solution of all kinds of problems of gratification, sexual and intellectual alike. He is both a gilded and a repulsive creature; his charms and talents are thickly overlaid with a variety of impostures, on the one hand, and physical preoccupations—spots, dress, hair styles, toilet habits, sexual protocol—on the other. . . . He is the complete adolescent, and in that capacity a memorable figure.

But this is not a novel of stasis, though it might have been a most respectable one; Amis is more ambitious than that. He wants to show us *process*—the advent of Charles Highway's manhood in the form of a series of comeuppances and realizations—and he does just that. The first hundred and fifty pages of the novel are bright, lively, witty, clever, and rapid, but sometimes a little flat and labored, as if the author were just warming up his undoubted skills. In setting out the terms of Highway's teen-age existence, his irony and satire, his comically intense malignity (an Amis family specialty) seem a little too casual, too offhand to be really persuasive. But when Highway meets his match—first in his own mind, during the long-awaited (and very funny) seduction of poor Rachel, and then at the hands of a hip Oxford don who sees right through his phony-erudite examination papers—the novel springs blazing to life, and Amis, like Highway, comes of age. The book is well worth reading for these last seventy-five pages and their promise for the author's future. It is significant that Highway begins his adult life—at the stroke of midnight on his twentieth birthday—by wondering "what sort of person I can be" and by taking up pen and paper and writing the first amateurish paragraph of an intended work of fiction. I await Martin Amis's next novel with impatient interest.

*L. E. Sissman, in* The New Yorker, *June 24, 1974, p. 102.*

What is surprising about Mr. Amis is that at 24 he already possesses the authority and sophistication that most reviewers take years to acquire. . . .

*Ronald De Feo, "The Joy of Sex?," in* National Review *(150 East 35th St., New York, N.Y. 10016), July 5, 1974, pp. 770-71.*

*The Rachel Papers* has caused a stir in Britain—and, it may be, a dreadful thrill of excitement at what may by some be regarded as the spectacle of a crusadingly nasty adolescent unburdening himself in print. In fact, Mr. Amis is witty, clever, and concise, and has devoted himself to writing about, more than to being, a young person out to shock. But it's quite true, too, that there's an interest in its being a book by someone recently an adolescent: in Britain, adolescents don't often drop their cool long enough to write a novel, and don't usually divulge at any length what it's like to be cool. . . .

Mr. Amis's novel is nasty, British, and short. This is nastiness aforethought: the scabrousness and scornfulness are highly calculated. Mr. Amis believes that the nastier things are, the funnier. . . .

It may be that the novel, which is marshaled as a satire on the writer's age group, does not altogether take the measure of its hero's charm and success. He is a winner, and I would bet that this has helped to make the novel a winner. Equally, I would bet that many of those attracted to the novel are older, by a bit, than its author. The British have gone in fear of their exotic young, from whom they expect a nasty princeliness, by whom they expect to be thrilled and despised. I wonder if Mr. Amis knows the pleasure he has given.

*Karl Miller, in* The New York Review of Books *(reprinted with permission from* The New York Review of Books; *© 1974 by NYREV, Inc.), July 18, 1974, p. 26.*

* * *

## ASHBERY, John 1927-

**Ashbery is an American experimental poet whose work is characterized by obscure syntax and elusive imagery. *The Double Dream of Spring* is considered his finest work. Ashbery has also written plays and, with James Schuyler, a novel, *A Nest of Ninnies*. (See also *Contemporary Authors*, Vols. 5-8, rev. ed.)**

Ashbery is *avant-garde,* obscure, abstract, and one of our two or three best. Each of his first three books was a striking new departure. At last [in *The Double Dream of Spring*] we have something that looks like a consolidation—but not a retreat, certainly not a retreat. The poetry is philosophical without being pretentious: rather, a fantastic control of tone balances these poems on a witty edge between comedy and tears. "Some Words," for example, written in consciously terrible couplets, stops being funny after a page or so; the reader becomes uneasy, as he realizes that on another level Ashbery means it. . . .

Paradox and ambiguity have always been central to Ashbery's sensibility. He sees the world as a series of random events, events which are open to a variety of interpretations—with no way to choose between. Each interpretation will have a certain validity; likewise each will be false to the total picture. "For these are moments only, moments of insight,/And there are reaches to be attained,/A last level of anxiety that melts/In becoming, like miles under the pilgrim's feet." No one interested in contemporary directions in poetry can afford to ignore John Ashbery.

Virginia Quarterly Review, *Vol. 46, No. 4 (Autumn, 1970), p. cxxxii.*

Few will disagree with at least two propositions about Ashbery's poetry: 1) it is stylistically unique, and 2) it is enigmatic. *The Double Dream of Spring* retains the unique Ashbery signature, but adds a new dimension of clarity and cohesiveness to his work. What I find in this volume are the *best* qualities of Ashbery's three previous volumes. It has the infatuation with the pursuit of beauty that we find in *Some Trees,* the startling newness of syntax ("words in unexpectedly brilliant new combinations") notable in *The Tennis Court Oath,* and what I can only call the "objectified feeling" of *Rivers and Mountains* (after W. C. Williams' famous dictum, "Say it not in words, but in things"). What is added in this volume is a sense of Ashbery himself *in* the work rather than icily apart from it. There is less the *artiste* here and more the poet, although that poet would not be John Ashbery without the inclusion of a sestina or two and a smattering of other French forms. What I like best about these poems is the feeling that this sophisticated, urbane, eminently "civilized" poet has experienced something of a breakthrough—that he is able to convey a sense of wonder *beyond* the literary sophistication which often tries to mask it.

*Fred Moramarco, in* Western Humanities Review, *Winter, 1971, p. 96.*

When John Ashbery took over the title of de Chirico's painting ["The Double Dream of Spring"] as the title for his fifth book of verse, he was confronting [the] problems of knowledge [that is, "what can be known and how can we know it?"] which had grown directly out of his earlier work. In his earlier books, Ashbery had demonstrated his ability to speak in several voices, to strike different poses regarding certain aspects of human experience, but his work seemed too gamey, too playful, his several poetic personalities spread so thin that the verse and the emotions it expressed seemed glib, untenable. He seemed to be more a tourist in the world of human experience than a resident. Such poetry has some value. It delights, but it doesn't entirely satisfy. It seemed, however, that the poetic intelligence behind the early work was itself restless and dissatisfied, as if it knew that a game was being played which would soon turn dead serious. Ashbery's early virtuosity sometimes seemed to be a nervous habit, a distraction from the crucial questions which he sensed as being imminent.

Ashbery's first important book, *Rivers and Mountains,* was his fourth published, and in it he began to address directly, and painfully, the issues which he had skirted in his earlier work. . . . Ashbery wonders at the processes of change he sees in people, in the seasons, in language, but his perception of the things about him also persuades him that nothing has ever really changed. . . . What we believe to be the deepest sources of our own humanity and our claim to a unique and changing present may then merely be footnotes to the "Fables that time invents/To explain its passing." If all things, all thought and feeling, are subject to time's revisions, then what can we ever know? What events, what feelings, can we ever trust?

In exploring questions such as these, Ashbery has experimented with forms of dislocated language as one way of jarring things into order; his notorious twisting of syntax is really an attempt to straighten things out, to clarify the problem at hand. Critical response to Ashbery's stylistic eccentricities have been almost amusing. On the one hand are those who berate him for lacking the Audenesque "censor" (that little editing machine in a poet's head which deletes all superfluous materials) or who accuse him simply of being willfully and unreasonably perverse. On the other hand are those reviewers who, queerly enough, praise the difficulty of Ashbery's verse as if difficulty were a positive literary value in itself, while ignoring what the poet is saying. I think that Ashbery's "difficulty" (grammatical ellipses, misapplied substantives, fragmented verb phrases, etc.) is a function of his meaning, which is a simple and unoriginal way of saying that sometimes the poet's methods work to support his meaning and sometimes they don't. . . .

Unlike Yeats, Ashbery avoids generalized declarations of his vision of our fragmented, unpredictable world. Instead, he gives us a feel for the elusive processes of change which he is in the very act of describing; we experience the nervousness, the sudden insane calm, the cageyness and rawness of it all, because those very qualities comprise the greater part of Ashbery's method. We are not so much asked to believe, as we are compelled to feel. The sadness which suffuses Ashbery's work is never rhetorical, never programmatic or literary; the sorrow is compressed, genuine, and somehow baffingly complete. At the center of it all beats a kind of urban anguish over what we have made of ourselves and what our furious past continues to make of us. . . .

Ashbery has always been possessed by a desire to posit a person or relationship at a particular point in time then slip that unit of time into the larger sequence of past and future. It's an attempt at redemption which strives to account for both visible and invisible aspects of life. Beginning with the poems in *Rivers and Mountains,* Ashbery becomes a kind of dream-interloper, looking to snatch from the fierce runaround of physical and spiritual events a sudden though elusive clarity. He strives to compute the distance between nightmare and vision, between fire and flame. . . .

Ashbery's arguments with himself sometimes sound like a civilization talking to itself, recollecting and seeking to clarify the reasons for all the past pain, the sometimes enforced deprivations of the human imagination, the uncountable slaughters, the ghouls and glamour girls who have strutted through history's nightmares. . . .

Ashbery's verse has always seemed more or less "prosy" insofar as it has been characterized by the unpinned rhythms and relaxed diction common to prose. When lesser talents try to write "prose poems", they do so in order to create merely gratuitous effects. The results are usually tedious and flimsy. Ashbery, however, resorts to a prose format in order to achieve a heightened concentration of sensibility, a firmer unity of feeling and thought which would otherwise be impossible to achieve in stanzaic verse. The prose sections in [*Three Poems*] cannot be broken down into lines of free verse. They can exist as poems only when rendered in prose. . . .

The poet [of *Three Poems*] is in search of a perfect medium, an imagination warp so to speak, wherein the pure light of revelation condenses, filling past, present and future simultaneously with the constant illumination of truth. Truth, to Ashbery, is clarity, even when truth gives the lie to nature's appearances. Clarity means the perfect coincidence of dreamt knowledge and waking knowledge, of projection and articulation, of futureness and whatever is not futureness. Arguing against the possibility of such coincidence here on earth, Ashbery would instead pursue and embrace such imperfections as are available to him. . . .

The constant analogue which links the poet to his poetic environment, to the poem and its making, is the engagement which exists (or should or could exist) between two persons. The random flux of joy and pain, inspiration and desperation, which drives people toward and away from one another, duplicates the tension lines drawn between the poet and his poetry. It's sometimes difficult to know whether Ashbery is addressing a real second person, his poetic past, or his present self. Though this at first appears to be a rather gratuitous ambiguity, it turns out to be the major unifying grammatical device in the book, since each of these secondary personae is derived from and symbolic of one essential source: Change.

*W. S. Di Piero, "John Ashbery: The Romantic As Problem Solver," in* The American Poetry Review, *August/September, 1973, pp. 39-42.*

I remember purchasing *Some Trees,* Ashbery's first commercially published volume (Yale Press, 1956, Introduction by Auden) in December, 1956, after reading the first poem ("Two Scenes") in a bookstore. The poem begins: "We see us as we truly behave" and concludes with "In the evening/Everything has a schedule, if you can find out what it is." A skeptical honesty, self-reflexive, and an odd faith in a near-inscrutable order remain characteristic of Ashbery's work after sixteen years. Also still characteristic is the abiding influence of Stevens. . . .

Where the middle Ashbery, the poet of the outrageously disjunctive volume, *The Tennis Court Oath,* attempted too massive a swerve away from the ruminative continuities of Stevens and Whitman, recent Ashbery goes to the dialectical extreme of what seems at first like a barrage of bland commonplaces. . . .

He is, in temperament, more like Whitman than like Emerson or Stevens. Even the French poet he truly resembles is the curiously Whitmanian Apollinaire, rather than Reverdy. . . .

Let us, swerving away from Apollinaire, call these Ashbery's two contradictory spiritual temptations, to believe that one's own self, like the poem, can be found in "all the things everywhere," or to believe that "there is still only I who can be in me." The first temptation will be productive of a rhetoric that puts it all in, and so must try to re-vitalize every relevant cliché. The second temptation rhetorically is gratified by ellipsis, thus leaving it all out. I suppose that Ashbery's masterpiece in this mode is the long spiel called "Europe" in *The Tennis Court Oath,* which seems to me a fearful disaster. In Stevens, this first way is the path of Whitmanian expansiveness, which partly failed the not always exuberant burgher of Hartford, while the second is the way of reductiveness, too great a temptation for him, as Stevens came to realize. The road through to poetry for Stevens was a middle path of invention that he called "discovery", the finding rather than the imposition of an order. Though there are at least three rhetorics in Stevens, matching these three modes of self-apprehension, none of the three risks Ashbery's disasters, whether of apparently joining together bland truisms or of almost total disjunctiveness. But I think that is close to the sorrow of influence in Ashbery, which is the necessary anxiety induced in him by the siren song of Stevens' rhetorics. Ashbery (who is not likely to be pleased by this observation) is at his best when he is neither re-vitalizing proverbial wisdom nor barely evading an ellipsis, but when he dares to write most directly in the idiom of Stevens. This point, and Ashbery's dazzling deflection of it, will be my concern when I arrive at *The Double Dream of Spring*. . . .

In *Some Trees,* Ashbery was a relatively joyous ephebe of Stevens, who evidently proved to be too good a father. . . . The Ashbery of *The Tennis Court Oath* may have been moved by DeKooning and Kline, Webern and Cage, but he was not moved to the writing of poems. Nor can I accept the notion that this was a necessary phase in the poet's development, for who can hope to find any necessity in this calculated incoherence?. . .

*Rivers and Mountains* (1966) is a partial recovery from *The Tennis Court Oath,* though only one poem in it, "The Skaters", seems to me major Ashbery when compared to what comes after. . . .

Though the leap in manner between *Rivers and Mountains* and *The Double Dream of Spring* is less prodigious than the gap between *The Tennis Court Oath* and *Rivers and Mountains,* there is a more crucial change in the later transition. Ashbery at last says farewell to ellipsis, a farewell confirmed by *Three Poems,* which relies upon "putting it all in," indeed upon the discursiveness of a still-demanding prose. The abandonment of Ashbery's rhetorical evasiveness is a self-curtailment on his part, a purgation that imparts simplicity through intensity, but at the price of returning him to the rhetorical world of Stevens and of the American tradition that led to Stevens. . . .

What the elliptical mode truly seeks to omit is the overt continuity with ancestors, and the mysterious compulsion operative here is a displacement of what Freud charmingly called "the family romance".

Ashbery's own family romance hovers uneasily in all-but-repressed memories of childhood; his family-romance-as-poet attains a momentarily happy resolution in *The Double Dream of Spring,* but returns darkly in *Three Poems.* Ashbery is a splendid instance of the redemptive aspect of influence-anxiety, for his best work shows how the relation to the precursor is humanized into the greater themes of all human influence-relations, which after all include lust, envy, sexual jealousy, the horror of families, friendship, and the poet's reciprocal relation to his contemporaries, ultimately to all of his readers. . . .

Nothing is more difficult for me, as a reader of poetry, than to describe *why* I am moved when a poem attains a certain intensity of quietness, when it seems to wait. Keats, very early in his work, described this as power half-slumbering on its own right arm. I find this quality in only a few contemporary poets—Ashbery, Ammons, Strand, Merwin, James Wright, among others. Recent Ashbery has more of this deep potential, this quietness that is neither quietism nor repression, than any American poet since the last poems of Stevens. Webern is the nearest musical analogue I know, but analogues are hard to find for a poem like "Evening in the Country". For, though the poem is so chastened, it remains an Orphic celebration, as much so as Hart Crane at his most ecstatic. . . .

"Fragment" [is] the crown of *The Double Dream of Spring* and, for me, Ashbery's finest work. Enigmatically autobiographical, even if it were entirely fantasy, the poem's fifty stately ten-line stanzas, orotundly Stevensian in their rhetoric, comment obliquely upon a story never told, a relationship never quite a courtship, and now a nostalgia. Studying this nostalgia, in his most formal and traditional poem, more so than anything even in *Some Trees,* Ashbery presents his readers, however faithful, with his most difficult rumination. But this is a wholly Stevensian difficulty, neither elliptical nor obscure, but a ravishing simplicity that seems largely lacking in any referential quality. . . .

What the all-but-perfect solipsist *means* cannot be right, not until he becomes perfect in his solipsism, and so stands forth as a phantasmagoric realist (one could cite Mark Strand, a superb poet, as a recent example). "Fragment", I take it, is the elegy for the self of the imperfect solipsist, who wavered before the reality of another self, and then withdrew back into an interior world. The poem being beautifully rounded, the title evidently refers not to an aesthetic incompleteness, but to this work's design, that tells us only part of a story, and to its resigned conclusion, for the protagonist remains alone, an "anomaly" as he calls himself in the penultimate line. . . .

Much of the difficulty, and the poignance, of "Fragment" is generated by Ashbery's quasi-metaphysical dilemma. Committed, like the later Stevens, to the belief that poetry and *materia poetica* are the same thing, and struggling always against the aesthetic of the epiphany or privileged moment, with its consequent devaluation of other experience, Ashbery nevertheless makes his poem to memorialize an intense experience, brief in deviation. This accounts probably for the vacillation and evasiveness of "Fragment", which tries to render an experience that belongs to the dialectic of gain and loss, yet insists the experience was neither. There are passages of regret, and of joy, scattered through the poem, but they do little to alter the calm, almost marmoreal beauty of the general tone of rapt meditation.

*Harold Bloom, "John Ashbery: The Charity of the Hard Moments," in* American Poetry Since 1960: Some Critical Perspectives, *edited by Robert B. Shaw (reprinted by permission of Dufour Editions, Inc.), Carcanet, 1973, pp. 83-108.*

* * *

## ATWOOD, Margaret 1939-

**Ms Atwood is an accomplished Canadian poet and novelist whose richly complex work has been awarded several important Canadian prizes. (See also *Contemporary Authors*, Vols. 49-52.)**

Much of what Margaret Atwood says in [*Procedures For Underground*] she has said in her previous books. She presents a world of peripheries, under-surfaces, divisions and isolation similar to the one in *The Circle Game,* but it would be a mistake to think that *Procedures For Underground* is simply a repetition of her earlier work. Certainly the surface of these poems remains the same; many of the images of drowning, buried life, still life, dreams, journeys and returns recur and the book is locked into a very repressive and inhibited atmosphere, even though the time-scope of the book is large, covering the chronological stretch from pre-history to the present. As in *The Circle Game,* personal relationships offer only minimal hope, yet most of the second half of this book expresses a promise of breaking-out that did not occur in the earlier work.

Even the title suggests that people need not be trapped or buried in stasis but that they can take action: there are motions that will push life and the individual forward. This volume moves in its second half more and more to the notion that words can break the authorities and inhibitions that fetter us and even a cry of agony is worth shouting, for it expresses that deep underside with its "mouth filled with darkness". This howl may be an automatic response to fear or pain, simply "uttering itself", but it is a statement, and, as such, is preferable to the blankness of "a white comic-strip balloon/with a question mark; or a blank button."

People still live on the edge in these poems, surrounded by flux, impermanence and repression, haunted by bad dreams, menaced by objects but

in fear everything
lives, impermanence
makes the edges of things burn

brighter.

In our present pre-historic state of human relationships we are at least evolving; "we are learning to make fire." Flux and disintegration continue but the poet has the means of preserving experience—"Over all I place/a glass bell". . . . Things may frighten man but he is a creator; he may in fact create his own fears, his own divisions, his own dreams and nightmares but the act of creation, in particular the act of poetry, becomes an important procedure. . . .

The progression in the book is towards a fundamental belief in the prerogatives of poetry in a threatening, tense world. Even the lining of the poems, still the usual broken, tentative expression she has used before, somehow sounds firmer, playing some kind of strength against the details of violence, repression, doubt and fear, finally emphasizing the courage of coming to terms with that lower layer where "you can learn/wisdom and great power,/if you can descend and return safely."

Margaret Atwood has returned safely, broken the circle, shaken off the persona of Susanna Moodie [the nineteenth-century Canadian poet and novelist] which to my mind was a restriction on her own personality as a poet. Her own clear voice rings out from this book to give us her best collection to date.

*Peter Stevens, "Dark Mouth," in* Canadian Literature, *Autumn, 1971, pp. 91-2.*

Margaret Atwood's "Surfacing" invites comparison with Sylvia Plath's "The Bell Jar": both novels by poets, both about a young woman who has been made desperate by a stifling social milieu and who can find relief only by abandoning what those around her have defined as sanity. Yet Plath's novel, written 10 years ago, expresses only a pure and private suffering; her heroine, Esther, can make no more impression on the conditions of her life . . . than a fly on the walls of the jar enclosing it. . . .

Miss Atwood's nameless heroine expresses a more sweeping revolt than Esther, but she is able at the novel's end to come up for air, to move confidently out of the destructive element and into freedom. The more recent novel, then, avoids the tone of flat, sealed-off resignation on which "The Bell Jar" ends; rather, it invigorates by its heroine's resolve to trust herself to the world while refusing, at the same time, to be a victim of it.

Victimization, and how to avoid it, is also the theme of Miss Atwood's companion volume to "Surfacing"—"Survival" (1972), a thematic guide to Canadian literature. In the latter book she indicts the literary tradition of her country for perennially reducing its heroes to victims, whether of confining social institutions, Canada's harsh geography, American power, or just their own inanition. Together, "Surfacing" and "Survival" have brought into sharp focus for Canadian literary intellectuals the problem of their country's cultural identity in the seventies.

Miss Atwood . . . has thereby outsoared her previous status as a widely-respected younger poet, author of five volumes of verse; she has become the literary standard-bearer of a resurgence of nativism and nationalism in Canada, eclipsing established Canadian writers of more cosmopolitan outlook. . . . Her work is also distinguished from theirs by its acute responsiveness to the Canadian landscape; we are constantly reminded that her formative years were passed largely in the sparsely settled "bush" of Northern Ontario and Quebec, rather than in the cities adjacent to the United States border. . . .

Within the novel, anti-Americanism serves to construct a new version of the 19th-century contrast between the English novel, concerned with man as he is shaped by social institutions, and the American romance, concerned with man in relation to moral absolutes and to nature. Then, the typical American hero was represented as an innocent being, untainted by Europe's moral obliquities. But now, when America's claim to innocence has been discredited by the brutalities of power politics, Atwood can assert the Canadian's claim to have virtue in his very powerlessness and uncertainty about his mission, if not in any more positive quality. Like her mute and destructive heroine, he must "clear a space" before he can know who, or where, he is. . . .

At a time when many novelists restrict themselves to a single mode of expression, such as documentary realism or unrestrained fantasy, Miss Atwood has undertaken a more serious and complex task. Denying Emerson's maxim that the true art of life is to skate well on surfaces, she shows the depths that must be explored if one attempts to live an examined life today.

*Paul Delany, in* The New York Times Book Review *(© 1973 by The New York Times Company; reprinted by permission), March 4, 1973, p. 5.*

Margaret Atwood is a Canadian poet, one of the best, and [*Surfacing*] is a poet's novel. The story takes place on an island two miles long in the wilderness of northern Quebec, on the last rim of marginal civilization. Miss Atwood's sense of the place, of the lake in its various moods, of the animal life retreating before the intruder, is beautifully conveyed. In the most intense passages of the book her writing reminds me of Iris Murdoch. . . .

There are . . . passages of fine writing in this book, and scenes of considerable power [as well as] identification of sensibilities in this North country which I believe to be true. I think it a pity that at the end . . . the heroine's behavior and her future . . . are so hard to believe.

*Edward Weeks, in* The Atlantic Monthly *(copyright © 1973 by The Atlantic Monthly Company, Boston, Mass.; reprinted with permission), April, 1973, p. 127.*

If the "argument" of Sidney's *Astrophel and Stella* is "Cruel Chastity," the argument of Atwood's *Power Politics* is cruel sexuality. . . . In *Power Politics,* as in Atwood's two novels, the unrequited love of courtly myth gives way to its equally frustrating modern form, a hedonistic, yet somehow mechanical union. The woman in *Power Politics* feels that her being is lacerated and her capacity for vision destroyed by subjection to a sadomasochistic sexual love. . . .

Atwood's ironic inversion of courtly love connects her art with the revelations of MacLuhan, Millett, Roszak, and Chesler about the social mythology of Western culture. Romantic obsession with lover or husband is presumed to provide the woman with her most satisfying form of existence. . . .

To Atwood, the love-aggression complex is an historical-personal fact. The cover of *Power Politics* expresses the predicament of women in the sexist society. . . .

The theme of *Power Politics* is role-engulfment: "You refuse to own/yourself, you permit/others to do it for you. . . ." The self is lost to the social role of romantic lover, warrior, wife, superman: fulfilment means incarnation within the archetype. . . . Beyond the mask of social role lies the paradox of Western culture: a postulated uniqueness of self that may not exist, or perhaps cannot be known, if it does exist. . . . The antithesis of the mask is the "face corroded by truth,/crippled, persistent," asking "like the wind, again and again and wordlessly,/for the one forbidden thing:/love without mirrors and not for/my reasons but your own." . . . [The] implicit quest is always for some alternative to the sadistic penetration and destruction of the [sadomasochistic sexual] relationship, for some "reality" behind the engulfing political role, and for some communion with that "reality". *Power Politics* confronts us with an entropic modern world in which a formerly solar masculinity now operates as a suction pump to exhaust and destroy the environment. . . .

The imagery in Atwood's novels also expresses mechanization and destruction, but there the woman's helpless suffering or retaliation changes into an urgent desire for liberation. [Onley notes, though, that "the movement from bondage to liberation is not a chronological development of theme.] . . .

A persistent strain in Atwood's imagery, appearing in the poetry as well as in *Surfacing,* is the head as disconnected from, or floating above, the body. . . . Often the imagery describes the body as a mechanism remotely controlled by the head; sometimes the neck is sealed over; always the intellectual part of the psyche is felt to be a fragment, dissociated from the whole. The "head" of Atwood schizoid persona is the "Head" described in Michael McClure's

"Revolt" (reprinted in Roszak's *Sources*), the Head that "quickly . . . fills with preconception and becomes locked in a vision of the outer world and itself. . . . The Head [that] finally may act by self-image of itself, by a set and unchanging vision that ignores the demands of its Body.". . .

Through the perceptions of her narrator [Anna in *Surfacing*], Atwood records again the pathology of a sexual relationship in which the male asserts his masculinity by inflicting physical or psychological pain. . . .

Throughout *Surfacing,* as in Sadian fantasy, sex is linked with mechanization, coercion, and death. . . .

To Atwood's intuitively psychoanalytical consciousness of human nature, engulfment in the sexual role, as she satirically exposes it in *Surfacing,* means that the ego of the cultural personality tends to become fixated at the stage of anal-sadism, condemned to the hellish circle of self-definition through violence, in which each man kills the thing he loves, in one way or another. . . .

The basic metaphor of descent and surfacing is a transformation of Atwood's inherited romantic image of death by drowning. The last part of the novel is thus a paradigm of descent into and ascent from the fluid ego boundary state of schizophrenia. But it is a carefully controlled, artistically simulated descent, of therapeutic purpose and value within the psychoanalytic dimension of the novel. The ego core (or inner self) of the narrator always retains its integrity, except for a fleeting moment during the peak experience of hallucinatory oneness with nature where Atwood seems to be synthesizing a primitive state of mind analogous to Lévy-Brühl's "participation mystique". Like [R. D.] Laing, Atwood seems to believe that schizophrenia is a form of psychic anarchy: a usually involuntary attempt by the self to free itself from a repressive social reality structure. . . .

In *Surfacing* and *The Edible Woman,* it is as if Atwood had inferred from the glittering surfaces of our social images the Freudian theory of personality as narcissistic, accomplishing self-definition through various forms of aggression, ranging from overt coercion to the subtle forms of unconscious "induction" revealed by Laing. . . .

A fusion of many literary forms, Menippean satire, diary, wilderness venture, even the Canadian animal story, *Surfacing* is the classic human animal story: the wilderness guide as social deviant becomes a scapegoat, driven out of the technological society for her sexist peers so that they may define themselves by their rejection of her.

By the end of the psychological quest, it is clear why, as Atwood stated earlier in *The Circle Game,* "Talking is difficult" and why in *Surfacing* "language is everything you do". The difficulty in human relations, metaphored in *Surfacing* as exile from the biosphere, is metaphysically related to the exploitative use of language to impose psychological power structures. The need for communion in *Power Politics* is paralleled by the realization that language tends to warp in the hand from tool to weapon. . . .

In Atwood's poetry, the psychological basis and the value in human relationships of the individualism of Western man is very much in question: partly by reference to her sense of self-definition by violence explored in the transactional social worlds of the two novels, where individualism becomes a potent carrier of death; and partly by reference to a presumed primitive, non-linear, and pluralistic state of being which functions as a mythic reference in most of her poetry from the earliest work on, emerging in *Surfacing* as a utopian alternative to alienation. In the love poems the tension between individuality and isolation, on the one hand, and loss of identity and sexual fulfilment on the other, is extreme and cannot be resolved. Imagistically it is an anguished oscillation within the *either/or* psycholinguistic structures of Western man, the existentialist trap the wilderness guide describes as the "walls" of "logic". An oscillation between the polarities of civilized/primitive, individual/generic, male/female (in terms of Atwood's camera imagery, focussed/unfocussed), in which reciprocity of being, psychosomatic, wholeness, and a sense of genuine communion, as *integrated qualities of experience,* remain mythic states forever beyond reach. The channels of communication and action are patriarchal almost beyond redemption: ". . . you rise above me/smooth, chill, stone-/white . . . you descend on me like age/you descend on me like earth". . . .

The anguished lack of communion between the lovers in *Power Politics* is, for Atwood, the inability of the alienated self to break through the thought structures of Western culture. . . .

To read Atwood's description of insanity by social definition and of psychic iconoclasm in "Polarities" [a short story published in *The Tamarack Review,* 58 (1971)] and *Surfacing* in conjunction with contemporary works which analyze the social construction of reality is to realize that what Atwood calls "mythologizing" is usually a conscious or unconscious enforcement of the sexual "polarities" inherent in the myths of romantic love, nuclear marriage, the machismo male, and the "feminine" woman. As an intelligent woman and a poet, Atwood indicates that we must somehow escape from this alienating cultural definition of personality and human relations. . . .

The narrator of *Surfacing* returns to sanity with the realization that she can refuse to participate in the destructive "mythologizing" of her society: "This above all, to refuse to be a victim. . . . The word games, the winning and losing games are finished; at the moment there are no others but they will have to be invented, withdrawing is no longer possible and the alternative is death." Arising renewed from the non-evaluative plurality of nature, the wilderness guide comprehends that reality is, as William James said, a "multi-dimensional continuum." For the first time she understands and has compassion for the subjective dimensions of others. She realizes "the effort it must have taken [her father] to sustain his illusions of reason and benevolent order," and how her mother's "meticulous records" of the weather "allowed her to omit . . . the pain and isolation." Her perception of her lover is altered. "He isn't an American, I can see that now . . . he is only half-formed, and for that reason I can trust him." She has escaped her former sense of total closure, thus achieving a liberated self and a basis for action within the world.

*Gloria Onley, "Power Politics in Bluebeard's Castle," in* Canadian Literature, *Spring, 1974, pp. 21-41.*

We sense right from the opening poem of *The Circle Game*—"This is a Photograph of Me"—in which the poet is unable to place herself in any sort of harmony with the landscape, that the haunting mood of isolation in the book is associated, in some undefined way, with geographical wilderness. No human form is visible in the photo; we get the feeling that wilderness somehow precludes human existence. . . .

Owing in part to the repeated conjunction of wilderness setting with moods of fear and alienation, physical landscape very soon comes to imply a good deal more than neutral, external reality. . . . [The] unspecified conflict between poet and landscape is internalized within the poet herself to the extent that the wilderness world comes to stand for the outside correspondent of some internal state. The element of schizophrenia evident in several poems is, in this light, not only explicable, but indeed quite justified.

Atwood's treatment of civilization—what we might be tempted to regard as the opposite of wilderness—affords evidence, if any be needed, that her use of landscape is predominantly and consistently figurative. Modern writers have, of course, long made use of the ironical truism that as more people crowd into an area, the more superficial becomes the contact among them. In other words, the city (and all it implies) has long supplied writers with contexts and symbols of human alienation. But Atwood provides her own twist: she portrays the city as nothing more than a variation on the wilderness theme. Civilization is a glass and steel and asphalt veneer, not a change so much as a disguise ("the landscape behind or under/the future cracks in the plaster"), and a temporary one at that. . . .

Like the wilderness, the city exists in an emotional vacuum. Civilization obliterates humanity as surely as a flood or the plague. . . . In whatever setting, people are trapped, impotent. The poet can say "outside there is a lake/or this time is it a street" ("Playing Cards"), because it really makes no difference. The outer world, in whatever form, is wilderness.

But the wilderness, we have said, symbolizes something within the poet. That something, the barren side, the gravitation toward chaos, the isolation, prevents any type of valuable human relationship. An assimilation is never achieved, never even a happy alignment; instead there is always actual or potential repulsion, the reaction against, a jerky attraction reversed, like magnets. . . .The need for love is real and strong, but it finds little sustenance and no parallel outside itself. Wilderness is dominant. . . .

The problem, however, refuses such a simple solution. Love itself turns out to be a dubious blessing. As the need for an involved human relationship approaches satisfaction, a counter-reaction grows proportionally stronger. Hence the poet, struggling to escape isolation, suddenly finds herself saying "How could you invade/me when/I ordered you not/to." Whenever the existence of a love relationship is assumed, this repellent force is very powerful. New variables are brought into the equation of self, and these are as difficult to understand and solve as the old. . . .

An important question thus arises: how does one reconcile the need for individual identity, for separate wholeness, with the simultaneous and equally urgent need for others, an escape from total isolation? In other words, we have come full circle and arrived at the question that has been implicit from the outset: how to reconcile the inner and outer worlds?

It would be a gross oversimplification to say that physical wilderness is neutral, incapable of love, and that the inner, private world of self resembles external nature only when the capacity for love goes unused; but surely the poetry is drawing us in the direction of such an understanding. At the least we could say that nature, generally, is benign when the perception of it is shared. Even a landscape of threat is less terrifying through a common lens. We could say also that those poems dealing directly with the two-person relationship ("Eventual Proteus", "A Meal", "The Circle Game", "Letter, Towards and Away") tend to contain very little wilderness imagery.

"The Islands" is irrefutable evidence that physical landscape reflects quite clearly the inner state of the perceiver. . . . We have [in this poem] for the first time, an acceptance of aloneness, of personal isolation, and the very acceptance robs the fact of its terrifying connotation. Again, a kind of freedom is attained. The most significant point, though, is that she can accommodate herself to the condition of solitude only in the presence of someone else. What enables her to accept with such equanimity is the realization that her state is shared; everyone is cut off. Ironically, when things are shared—even things like despair and alienation—bonds are made, invisible bridges formed between islands, and insularity overcome.

The effect of landscape is altered by an alteration in attitude towards it. The change has come about through the poet's recognition of her affinities with others, and, by extension, with the outside world. It is not the conflicts between self and nature that she dwells on now, but the likenesses; and once you start seeking overlappings, affinities, you find them. . . .

A tentative balance has been struck, a reconciliation achieved. The poles of isolation and community are not mutually exclusive. The poet is on her way toward creating a viable inner order; it remains now only to extend the integration by applying its implications back out to the real, physical wilderness. The connection is made through the direct juxtaposition of the outer landscape with the personal one, its human correspondent. . . . Inner and outer worlds do not differ in kind; the two selves need not conflict. Each is an integral part of something more. . . . In the recognition of this identity, the terror of landscape disintegrates.

*Gary Ross, "'The Circle Game'," in* Canadian Literature, *Spring, 1974, pp. 51-63.*

When the dart is an icicle aimed right between your eyes it is difficult to separate the magic from the magician. Reading the novels and poetry of Margaret Atwood is an intensely personal experience which culminates in a confrontation with the ubiquitous image of the poet on the back cover of the book. . . .

The used words subside like snowflakes as Atwood, the magician, hypnotizes with the brilliant image which dazzles without illuminating. The hypnotic subject participates involuntarily in a grotesque, dances without knowing the steps. There is nothing shared in the experience of manipulation. The puppet learns nothing of itself or of the puppeteer.

The refusal to be known, except as female god or witch doctor is articulated in the motif of invisibility as the Atwood persona struggles to extricate herself from personal relationships. Like the extraterrestrial cliché of popular science fiction, she cannot feel, exists only to comment. In *Surfacing,* the protagonist "prayed to be made invisible, and when in the morning everyone could still see me I knew they had the wrong god." She is always the outsider, existing only to shatter the illusions of her fellow beings. . . .

The world stripped of emotions and words is left visual and tactile and this is where Margaret Atwood finds her real strength. Her poems are petroglyphs indelibly printed on the brain. It is the image which persists when the words, often cruel and bitter, subside. Words are a substitute for and distortion of her world, which is silent and concerned only with survival and the passing seasons. One of the reasons *The Edible Woman* fails as a novel is the awkwardness of the dialogue. Atwood is self conscious in the urban environment which requires language. There is little dialogue in *Surfacing* to disturb the sounds of the country and this is one of the strengths of the more mature novel.

There is no warmth in the natural world where she takes refuge, only a lack of hypocrisy. Atwood, the observer, knows she has no control over the northern landscape she describes as no one else does and she admires its proud refusal to submit, except to death. In spite of her identification with animals, the fur coats, the leather jackets and startled grace, the Atwood persona is left to salvage what she can of the human condition. She knows a language and is burdened with a personal and social history. She cannot be animal. In *Surfacing,* she proves her dependance upon society. She cannot live alone in the wilderness. . . .

There is a pervasive chill in her imagery. Death is cold. Love is cold. Snow is cold. The lack of a warming counterpoint in her work is the failure of compassion in the characters who dance in an involuntary circle around her ice-woman. No one is strong enough to challenge her supremacy at the centre of the universe and this is a weakness, as her voice becomes too strident, losing conviction. There is no dialogue on any level.

There is no life-giving warmth in her metaphorical water either. The ascent from drowning is no resurrection, just a return to conventional reality. In or out of the water, the drowned soul persists. Even life in the womb is surreal, grotesque. There is no state of innocence and there is no state of grace. The nightmare overcomes the dream. There is no escape. The fiction is a glassy mirror to cold realities.

The poet is the agent of beauty and the sharp instrument of death. She is a knife cutting through onion. Each layer falls away in beautiful symmetry. But there is no relationship between the layers and the centre is hollow.

*Linda Rogers, "Margaret the Magician," in* Canadian Literature, *Spring, 1974, pp. 83-5.*

* * *

## AUCHINCLOSS, Louis 1917-

**American novelist, short story writer, playwright, and critic, Auchincloss is also a practicing attorney. He is a member of a large, wealthy, and important New York family. Considered one of America's only true novelists of manners, Auchincloss writes skillful and authoritative fictional chronicles of New York aristocracy. (See also *Contemporary Authors*, Vols. 1-4, rev. ed.)**

*Venus in Sparta* is, as it turns out, only incidentally a novel about business, but Auchincloss's knowledge proves useful as he introduces us to his leading character, Michael Farish, at forty-five vice president and senior trust officer of the Hudson River Trust Company, with good reason to expect to occupy the presidency, as his grandfather had done in his time. Most businessmen in fiction are annoyingly nebulous or else their functions are described in massive and confusing detail. Auchincloss does not tell us much about Michael's duties, but what he does tell defines exactly the nature of his success and the reasons for it. . . .

Auchincloss is a deft prober, and he shows us how a sense of inadequacy and guilt can be created and how it can shape a life. To me the psychological problem to which he addresses himself in *Venus in Sparta* is less interesting than the ethical problem with which he was concerned in his preceding novel, *The Great World and Timothy Colt.* In its portrayal of a particular milieu, however, of a world in which there not only is money but has been money for several generations, the novel demonstrates that Auchincloss knows his stuff and knows how to use it to literary advantage.

*Granville Hicks, with Jack Alan Robbins, "'Venus in Sparta'" (originally published in* Saturday Review, *September 20, 1958), in their* Literary Horizons: A Quarter Century of American Fiction *(reprinted by permission of New York University Press; copyright © 1970 by New York University), New York University Press, 1970, pp. 187-88.*

After the violence of James Baldwin's *Another Country,* the turgidity of Philip Roth's *Letting Go,* and the complexity and intensity of Doris Lessing's *The Golden Notebook,* Louis Auchincloss's *Portrait in Brownstone* is a pleasant change. Auchincloss knows so well what he can do and goes about his job with such quiet competence that his novels are always satisfying, and *Portrait in Brownstone* is Auchincloss at his best.

Auchincloss, as has often been said, is a novelist of manners, one of the few extant. Like Edith Wharton, for whom he has strong but not uncritical admiration, he writes about people of wealth and position, about what is sometimes called "good society." No part of American society is or ever has been stable, but in good society there is at least an air of stability. Certain assumptions are shared, for a time at any rate, and there is some agreement as to what constitutes proper behavior. Against such a background the subtler human relationships can be studied with a precision that is quite impossible in more turbulent situations, and this is the great virtue of the novel of manners as written by Jane Austen and Henry James and all the rest of Auchincloss's predecessors.

*Granville Hicks, with Jack Alan Robbins, "'Portrait in Brownstone'" (originally published in* Saturday Review, *July 14, 1962), in their* Literary Horizons: A Quarter Century of American Fiction *(reprinted by permis-*

*sion of New York University Press; copyright © 1970 by New York University), New York University Press, 1970, pp. 188-89.*

Were there a literary prize for the anti-anti-novel, how could it be withheld from Louis Auchincloss? But since craftsmanship, good storytelling, tepid and unpornographic sex, social criticism that is subtle rather than screaming no longer attract the critics, [*A World of Profit*] (like his others —*The Rector of Justin, The Embezzler, Tales of Manhattan*) will have to suffer in the best-seller lists and at the hands of book clubs. However, for all its style and its fascinating treatment of unfamiliar undercurrents of New York life, *A World of Profit* is not quite in the brittle sophisticated class of the earlier works. Its controlled and understated yet savage criticism of contemporary business activity is finally vitiated by a pervasive sense of placidity.

The Antioch Review *(© 1969 by The Antioch Review, Inc.; reprinted by permission of the editors), Vol. XXIX, No. 2, 1969, p. 261.*

Louis Auchincloss most nearly resembles Henry James in the emphasis he gives to the moral issues that grow out of the social lives of the very rich in New York City. And because he has described himself as a "Jacobite," many reviewers have concluded that it is therefore enough to describe him as merely an imitator of the Master. Auchincloss most differs from James, though, in the informed analysis he is able to give to the nice problems of ethics in the legal profession—a command of the world of Wall Street brokers and bankers which James himself sorely regretted not having. Auchincloss calls himself a Jacobite because so much of his lifetime's reading has been "over the shoulder of Henry James". . . . But Auchincloss has always, once started, gone his own way—often qualifying and contesting, as well as enlarging, the social insights of the nineteenth-century novelist of manners.

The world brought to life in his novels is the nineteenth- and twentieth-century life of the metropolitan rich in New York City—particularly the lives of the lawyers, bankers, trust officers, corporation executives, and their wives and daughters. As a lawyer, Auchincloss knows them in their Park Avenue apartments and in their Wall Street offices. He sees the glitter and glamour of their world, its arrogant materialism and its unexpected generosities. He knows the rigidity of its conventions—just how far they can be bent, at what point they break, just when convention may break a character. He understands what happens to the idealistic men and the unfulfilled women of this world. And he is able to tell their stories with unusual sympathy. Rarely has Auchincloss ventured from this small but exclusive world, because it is the world he knows best. For this "narrowness," I suppose, it is possible to criticize him. . . . The New York *haut monde* is Louis Auchincloss's backyard. His ten novels are his Austenean two inches of carefully carved ivory.

Not all of his novels are novels of manners—he is fascinated by the unexhausted possibilities of the novel of character—but most of them hinge upon the imperatives of private morality in a world where social morality no longer, apparently, exists. In many of these books Auchincloss explores the ambiguities of selfhood, affirming, finally, the freedom and autonomy of the human personality. . . .

*The House of Five Talents* (1960) and *Portrait in Brownstone* (1962), Auchincloss's best novels of manners, are set in New York City. Both deal with rich and "aristocratic" families during a period of several generations. Both portray the emergence of a woman as matriarch of the tribe (although one is an old maid). And both offer a bittersweet portrait of "the image of lost elegance and virtue." . . .

In semipolitical literary criticism there are sometimes objections to the kind of people Auchincloss writes about. It is sometimes said, for example, that the world of New York society people is somehow not as interesting as that of share-croppers, boxers, or big-game hunters. . . . But there is no necessary reason why this claim should be true. *The Assistant* and *Herzog* may be better novels than *The Embezzler* and *The Rector of Justin*. But their superiority has nothing to do with the subject matter or the "relevance" of these books—it has only to do with the greater artistry by which the novels of Malamud and Bellow are brought to life. . . .

I submit that Auchincloss . . . sees that the differences between classes are superficial and that there is therefore no adequate reason why one should not deal with headmasters and lawyers, bankers and brokers, if they permit the kind of social analysis that illuminates our essential human predicament. The problem implicit in his choice is that of making us believe that this universe is—if not *the* universe —at least a *believable* universe, and describing his characters so fully and convincingly that we do not care about the class they belong to. It is Auchincloss's difficulty that, as good as some of his novels are, he does not always so convince us. But the limitation is one of his talent, not of his material.

*James W. Tuttleton, "Louis Auchincloss: The Image of Lost Elegance and Virtue," in* American Literature *(reprinted by permission of the Publisher; copyright 1972 by Duke University Press, Durham, North Carolina), January, 1972, pp. 616-32.*

This staggeringly silly novel [*I Come as a Thief*] is Louis Auchincloss's twenty-first published book and ought to put a stop, once and for all, to those rumors that surface periodically about his being hearth keeper of the manners-and-morals tradition. He has merely appropriated its drawing rooms. . . .

Does it matter . . . that the book is relentlessly superficial or that the characters have no more life than a connect-the-dots puzzle or that the language has the elegance of an over-reaching governess? . . . Probably not, for Mr. Auchincloss is no longer even writing the fantasies of the upper-middle class—he has taken on their soap operas, and such stuff works on a level beyond argument. At least he makes no demands, his story is sprinkled with interior-decorating touches, and his publisher doesn't embarrass his readers with a lurid jacket. But it is a sobering thought that our melodrama has come to this. By comparison, old Joan Crawford movies are epics. Epics.

*Joseph Kanon, in* Saturday Review of the Society *(copyright © 1972 by Saturday Review/World, Inc.; reprinted with permission), August 26, 1972, pp. 60-1.*

Louis Auchincloss is the only writer of our time who has done something interesting with something like the novel of manners. An admirer of Henry James and a discriminating critic of James's principal American disciple, Edith Wharton, Auchincloss has deliberately limited his scope. He has set aside as his particular province—his Yokapatawpha County, so to speak—a small part of the population of New York City, made up of people of some means but not rich in the Hollywood sense of the term and usually but not always belonging to old families. They constitute, in short, what is still called in some quarters "good society."

Here Auchincloss has found what James might have described as a "sufficient field" for the exercise of his particular talents. His is a small world and perhaps not an important one; indeed, it isn't a world at all when compared with the compact, well-ordered and self-sufficient world of the great novelist of manners, Jane Austen; but it does present moral problems of a sort Miss Austen would have understood. In a society in which there is little agreement as to what is valuable and what isn't, moral problems of the subtler and therefore more interesting kind tend to vanish, but they may persist in certain segments of that society, what Arnold Toynbee called "fossils in fastnesses."

In his many novels and stories Auchincloss has circumnavigated his little world, gone back and forth across it, explored above and below it. Sometimes he has concentrated on people who belong to good society and are for the most part satisfied with their lives, but more often he has been concerned with rebellion, usually unsuccessful. The rebels are sometimes thrown off the track by sexual passion, their own or their wives', or they may be derailed by external forces. . . .

My recurrent quarrel with Auchincloss is that the little world in his novels usually seems to me to be detached from the real world, the world to which this newspaper devotes thousands and thousands of words every morning. Even ["The Rector of Justin"], his best novel in my opinion, presents a model of the little world, an exclusive school for boys. ["I Come As a Thief"] has a different quality because it portrays a man who escapes from *his* little world not by changing his social class but by moving into a realm of absolutes. In literature, one does not have to believe in the validity of a vision but merely that the visionary believes in it. The quality of a religious experience cannot be communicated; one of its distinguishing marks, the authorities agree, is its ineffability. But its effect may be great, not only on the man who has it but on those whose lives are touched by his.

*Granville Hicks, in* The New York Times Book Review *(© 1972 by The New York Times Company; reprinted by permission), September 3, 1972, p. 6.*

*The Embezzler* and other novels by Auchincloss, such as *Venus in Sparta, Portrait in Brownstone,* and *A World of Profit,* reflect a concern for the breakdown of the old values of genteel New York. The author's criticism of old values held together by a kind of outmoded innocence, as well as of the new principles and methods used to exalt a new class into place, is reminiscent of Edith Wharton, who was so averse to the barbarians and Invaders who began infiltrating New York in the 1880's and severe with the decadent aristocracy which hid behind closed blinds hoping that the newcomers would soon go away. As the Invaders settled on Fifth Avenue, speculated with their newly-made fortunes on the Stock Exchange and hunted for titles on the Washington Square reservation in Wharton's fiction, so do the outsiders in Auchincloss' novels poach on the preserves of old New York society and rise in social significance by their exploits on Wall Street. Both novelists portray the slow and natural process of extinction of the aristocratic species.

*Wayne W. Westbrook, "Louis Auchincloss' Vision of Wall Street," in* Critique: Studies in Modern fiction, *Vol. XV, No. 2, 1973, pp. 57-66.*

Auchincloss . . . writes mainly about the declines and cushioned falls of good-family New Yorkers. He is a lucid, confident and tidy observer of this small community; yet many critics (expecting, maybe, Henry James) refuse to accept Auchincloss as the teller of well-tailored stories that he is.

In *The Partners,* Louis Auchincloss could not be plainer about how he operates within his chosen limits. His 20th work of fiction, the book is not truly a novel but a set of stories loosely linked by principal characters who happen to be members of the same Wall Street law firm. Each incidental anecdote and character sketch is arranged to show how time and change have affected the values and manners of Auchincloss's narrowing circle.

This casual form fits the author like an old sports coat. Indeed, he used it ten years ago in *Powers of Attorney. . . .*

Despite his rather reserved, fiduciary tone, Auchincloss generates some psychological subtlety and emotional range.

*R. Z. Sheppard, "Fiduciary Matters," in* Time *(reprinted by permission from* Time, The Weekly Newsmagazine; *copyright Time Inc.), February 4, 1974, p. 76.*

[Although] it is called a novel, *The Partners* is actually an assemblage of autonomous sketches or episodes, tenuously related and sometimes not related at all save by the fact that there's a lawyer lurking about somewhere, most often the lawyer who may be called the principal character by virtue of the persistence of his lurking. In several instances the episodes have been included, one feels, as an afterthought, so inconsequential are they. They contain a lawyer or lawyers, who appear once, and never again. The overall effect is that of a maze of offices, occupying the premises of a firm, each enclosing its little tale. Nothing in the narrative gathers up its energies toward a destined end; instead the scale of the book seems determined by something so arbitrary as the cubic feet of office space, the number of inhabited cubicles and offices.

Such unity as the book possesses is conferred by a tone of voice—and therein lies the problem. For what are we to make of a tone uneasily situated somewhere between solemnity and irony, respect and ridicule, as its objects seem ready to collapse beneath satire into slapstick? How can we possibly take seriously, much less regard sympathetically, men who are at best pompous bores or sanctimonious buffoons? The problem is an interesting one of perspective: instead of fixing our attention on the characters, we are compelled to watch the author constantly shifting and adjusting to find the appropriate angle from which to regard them. Better: to listen to the voice as it seeks the right pitch. That voice: orotund, grave, stately, scoffing; faintly archaic, Augustan, ambassadorial, more royalist than the king. Call it Tory.

Now, making much of a name is a dirty business; but in a fiction where a word, a nuance, the arch of an eyebrow can decisively tip the balance of our attitudes, the difference between Beekman Ehninger and "Beeky," as any farceur knows, is the difference between Old New York and snickering. . . .

Auchincloss' intention is obviously satiric, indeed heavy-handedly satiric, and there's an end of it. One either finds this sort of thing amusing or one does not. How can anyone respond save with distaste to a world in which Beeky is not only not the least of persons but by far the least appalling; one need only glimpse the others to recoil. Yet it is by no means certain that the intention is, as bottom, satiric. However absurd at times, these are honorable men, good at their vocation, the best of them formidable; they are bulwarks of the societal order. God help us. . . . [For] all their foibles, the value of their enterprise is never in question nor, in essence, are the men who staff it. Where, after all, would we be without them? A satirist might have suggested, if ever so lightly, the nature of that far better place.

Playfully scoffing, yes; satiric, no: the authorial voice (which is not necessarily the author's) resembles too closely those it mocks. There is no distancing; indeed there is no distance.

*Saul Maloff, in* The New Republic *(reprinted by permission of* The New Republic; *© 1974 by Harrison-Blaine of New Jersey, Inc.), February 23, 1974, pp. 29-30.*

[Auchincloss] writes about realities you can verify, an orderly society with values your dad understands, and he believes in telling stories. If Auchincloss himself is to be found in his fiction, it's through his perceptions rather than his visions. Far more important to a reading of Auchincloss is his profession as a Wall Street lawyer than any possible artistic rearrangement he has in mind concerning the non-art of living. Auchincloss is a poured-in-concrete realist, although the concrete is always the best that money can buy. He stands for class and tough-mindedness, as the reader may remember from such previous works as "The Injustice Collectors," "Portrait in Brownstone" and "The Rector of Justin." . . .

Auchincloss observes like a cat. He makes judgments with subtlety and sophistication, usually about human character under the strain of slowly compressing environment. In Auchincloss's fiction there is no escape from the self because the enveloping environment also consists of the personality operating within it. Outsidedness is a cop-out. . . .

Auchincloss defines his people by what they want. He examines and reveals them in what they do and say. And all are caught up in struggles with a world they cannot alter. They must change themselves since they can control little else. Conflict stretches them. They are in struggles with forces so deep in the structure of society that they cannot win except at the expense of the ego they would preserve. . . .

He is the gentlest of moralists. He takes us inside human beings. He makes us believe they are worthy of our interest and concern. For a while we are caught up in the narrowness of other lives and are reminded that we may expand our own.

*Webster Schott, in* The New York Times Book Review *(© 1974 by The New York Times Company; reprinted by permission), February 24, 1974, p. 2.*

Throughout his long writing career . . ., Auchincloss has been thought of, correctly, as a novelist of manners, a chronicler of life among the well-born Waspy wealthy, the professional upper class. His fiction is "old-fashioned" in the sense that it brings, conveys, "the news." It is not personal or soul-searching or chest-beating—no instant catharsis of the *writer* visible—but is, rather, made up of reports on how rich Eastern Establishment types (mostly New Yorkers, mostly Episcopalian) try to live their lives and do their jobs *appropriately*. They think of themselves not as prime movers of society but as guardians of society, the people who, just below or discreetly behind the top levels of power, are responsible for keeping things going. Their occupations reflect this: many of Auchincloss's characters are in—or, rather, they *serve* in—the legal profession. . . .

Auchincloss deals not with classes, plural, but essentially with one class—a class that is assumed (its money is assumed, too) and that is defined not by its relationship to other classes but primarily by its sense of duty, its self-assumed role of guardianship, its commitment to what it sees as a proper way of doing things. The "way" is what is all-important. Unlike his made-up novelist [in *The Partners*], who is really a fading fashion-monger, Auchincloss is a novelist of manners in the most literal sense. . . .

As the profile of a type, *The Partners* is vintage Auchincloss—sensitive, ironic, sympathetic, affecting. Auchincloss is particularly good with the interior reality of seemingly minor conflicts; he also shows, over and over again, that seemingly large and dramatic conflicts are often not the important ones. He is marvelous about money—the attitudes of old-monied very rich about their wealth. . . . He is observant, too, of the behavior, cooperative and abrasive, of the women and wives though the world of *The Partners* is very much a man's world. He is less acute with peripheral characters—the overbearing lawyer of the first episode, the novelist, the forger-for-art—who border on caricature. . . .

Auchincloss is a deliberately distanced writer—he keeps himself at arm's length, and then some, from the reader—and is therefore, I suppose, vulnerable to the charge of being clunkishly traditional. (Clunkish because he is an able writer, not an elegant one.)

*Eliot Fremont-Smith, in* New York Magazine *(© 1974 by NYM Corp.; reprinted by permission of* New York Magazine *and Eliot Fremont-Smith), February 25, 1974, pp. 62-3.*

[In *Literary Horizons*, Granville Hicks states that Auchincloss] "has written for the most part about 'good' society, the well-to-do and the well-bred. And he has written about them with authority. What bothers me is not that he writes about this little world but that he seems to be aware of no other. Although he is conscious of its faults, he never questions its values in any serious way." This is fascinating. I have read all of Auchincloss's novels and I cannot recall one that did not in a most serious way question the values of his "little world." Little world!

It is a fascinating tribute to the cunning of our rulers and to the density of our intellectuals (bookchat division, anyway) that the world Auchincloss writes about, the domain of Wall Street bankers and lawyers and stockbrokers, is thought to be irrelevant, a faded and fading genteel-gentile enclave when, in actual fact, this little world comprises the altogether too vigorous and self-renewing ruling class of the United States—an oligarchy that is in firm control of the Chase Manhattan Bank, American foreign policy, and the decision-making processes of both divisions of the Property Party; also, most "relevantly," Auchincloss's characters set up and administer these various foundations that subsidize those universities where academics may serenely and dully dwell like so many frogs who think their pond the ocean. . . .

Of all our novelists, Auchincloss is the only one who tells us how our rulers behave in their banks and their boardrooms, their law offices and their clubs. Yet such is the vastness of our society and the remoteness of academics and bookchatterers from actual power that those who should be most in this writer's debt have no idea what a useful service he renders us by revealing and, in some ways, by betraying his class. But then how can the doings of a banker who is white and gentile and rich be *relevant* when everyone knows that the only meaningful American experience is to be Jewish, lower-middle-class, and academic? Or (in Mr. Hicks's words), "As I said a while ago and was scolded for saying, the characteristic hero of our time is a misfit." Call me Granville. . . .

In a society where matters of importance are invariably euphemized (how can an antipersonnel weapon actually kill?) a writer like Louis Auchincloss who writes about the way money is made and spent is going to have a very hard time being taken seriously. For one thing, it is now generally believed in bookchat land that the old rich families haven't existed since the time of Edith Wharton while the new-rich are better suited for journalistic exposés than for a treatment in the serious . . . novel. It is true that an indiscriminate reading public enjoys reading Auchincloss because, unlike the well-educated, they suspect that the rich are always with us and probably up to no good. But since the much-heralded death of the Wasp establishment, the matter of Auchincloss's fiction simply cannot be considered important.

This is too bad. After all, he is a good novelist, and a superb short-story writer. More important, he has made a brave effort to create his own literary tradition—a private oasis in the cactus land of American letters. He has written about Shakespeare's penchant for motiveless malignity (a peculiarly American theme), about Henry James, about our women writers as the custodians and caretakers of the values of that dour European tribe which originally killed the Indians and settled the continent.

Mr. Hicks with his eerie gift for misunderstanding what a writer is writing about thinks that Auchincloss is proudly showing off his class while bemoaning its eclipse by later arrivals. Actually, the eye that Auchincloss casts on his own class is a cold one and he is more tortured than complacent when he records in book after book the collapse of the Puritan ethical system and its replacement by—as far as those of us now living can tell—nothing. As for the ruling class being replaced by later arrivals, he knows (though they, apparently, do not) that regardless of the considerable stir the newcomers have made in the peripheral worlds of the universities, showbiz, and bookchat, they have made almost no impact at all on the actual power structure of the country.

Auchincloss deals with the movers and shakers of the American empire partly because they are the people he knows best and partly, I suspect, because he cannot figure them out to his own satisfaction. . . .

Finally, most unfashionably, Auchincloss writes best in the third person; his kind of revelation demands a certain obliqueness, a moral complexity which cannot be rendered in the confessional tone that marks so much of current American fiction good and bad. He plays God with his characters, and despite the old-fashionedness of his literary method he is an unusually compelling narrator, telling us things that we don't know about people we don't often meet in novels—what other novelist went to school with Bill and McGenghis Bundy? . . .

Not since Dreiser has an American writer had so much to tell us about the role of money in our lives. In fascinating detail, he shows how generations of lawyers have kept intact the great fortunes of the last century. With Pharaonic single-mindedness they have filled the American social landscape with pyramids of tax-exempt money, for the eternal glory of Rockefeller, Ford, et al. As a result, every American's life has been affected by the people Auchincloss writes so well about. . . .

[In *The Partners,* the] author's virtues are well displayed: almost alone among our writers he is able to show in a convincing way men at work—men at work discreetly managing the nation's money, selecting its governors, creating the American empire. Present, too, are his vices. Narrative is sometimes forced too rapidly, causing characters to etiolate while the profound literariness of the author keeps leaking into the oddest characters. I am sure that not even the most civilized of these Wall Street types is given to quoting *King Lear* and Saint-Simon quite as often as their author has him do. Also, there are the stagy bits of writing that recurrom book to book—hands are always "flung up" by Auchincloss characters; something I have never seen done in real life west of Naples.

One small advance: in each of Auchincloss's previous books sooner or later the author's Jacobite fascination with the theater intrudes and, when it does, I know with terrible foreboding that I shall presently see upon the page that somber ugly word "scrim." I am happy to report that in *The Partners* there is no scrim, only the author's elegant proscenium arch framing our proud, savage rulers as they go singlemindedly about their principal task: the preserving of fortunes that ought to be broken up.

*Gore Vidal, "Real Class," in* The New York Review of Books *(reprinted with permission from* The New York Review of

Books; © *1974 by NYREV, Inc.), July 18, 1974, pp. 10-12, 14-15.*

* * *

## AUDEN, W(ystan) H(ugh) 1907-1973

**Auden was an Anglo-American poet, critic, translator, librettist, anthologist, and, with Christopher Isherwood, dramatist. Auden has been called "our most catholic virtuoso, without whom our conception of who the poet is and what he does would be greatly impoverished." (See also *Contemporary Authors*, Vols. 9-12, rev. ed.; obituary, Vols. 45-48.)**

The recent work [note, though, the date of Wilson's essay] of W. H. Auden has . . . taken the direction of returning to the older tradition of serviceable and vigorous English verse. His *New Year Letter* must be the best specimen of purely didactic verse since the end of the eighteenth century, and the alliterative Anglo-Saxon meter exploited in *The Age of Anxiety* has nothing in common with prose. It may, however, be pointed out, . . . that in the speech of the girl over the sleeping boy in the fifth section of the latter poem, the poet has found it easy to slip into the rhythms and accents of Mrs. Earwicker's half-prose soliloquy at the end of *Finnegans Wake*.

*Edmund Wilson, "Is Verse a Dying Technique?," in* The Triple Thinkers: Twelve Essays on Literary Subjects *(copyright © 1938, 1948 by Edmund Wilson; reprinted with the permission of Farrar, Straus & Giroux, Inc.), Oxford University Press, revised edition, 1948, pp. 15-30 (in the Galaxy paperbound edition).*

Leavis apart, the majority of critics would seem to grant Auden his just place as the most accomplished and versatile of living poets, and one who has been, and who remains, exceptionally influential. Clearly, he dominated the generation of the 1930s with a power and range that few could approach. Master of an impressive number of forms, from the Ballad to the Blues, he was all the more able to contain the see-sawing beliefs and passions of the time. Committed, yet distanced, his poetry was remarkable for its surface calm, the pincers moving obliquely but firmly over their subject. . . .

The influence of music on Auden's verse. . .throughout the longer works, has always been salient: even his worst lines often "sound" impressive. Indeed the poems on which his reputation will finally come to rest may well be the magnificent early lyrics—far away from the world of Spain and Fascism against which he cried out so forcefully in much-quoted poems he no longer favours.

With his move to America in 1938, Auden's area of interest and commitment changed visibly. By 1940 the Auden conception of love had moved away from an ideal union of man and woman, or of a brotherhood of man ("we must love one another or die") to a Christian ideal, making one aware of what Spender has called "the odd impersonality" of Auden. Coated more with the philosopher's semantics, the four long poems of this later period *(New Year Letter, For the Time Being, The Sea and the Mirror, The Age of Anxiety)* are in the main colder, more distant, more cerebral than any of Auden's previous work. . . .

[Questions] of How, Why, and What, indeed the whole gamut of Existentialist Choice which *New Year Letter* raises, are as relevant to Western society now as they were to Auden then. Whether or not they are organic to the poetry as a whole is another matter. For all the range and muscle of the verse, the refined hypnotic couplets falling just so, the ideas appear to be somehow removed from the poetry in a way they rarely are in either the earlier or later short poems. There are marvellous sections, to be sure, whole passages (short poems almost) where the verse opens out suddenly from close arguing into poetry of great dignity; but these are often linked to memories, or are lyrical asides touching the "real" world, and as such are only incidentally related to the poem's high theme and dialectics.

*Jeremy Robson, "Auden's Longer Poems," in* Encounter, *January, 1970, pp. 73-4.*

I could never hang onto Auden poems—that high-pressure "watch me be impossibly cultivated" and "let me ENTERTAIN you," those low phrases, as irritating as Eliot's "get the good of it hot," ho ho. I'm too young to be awed by his reputation; what threw me was how his prose could be so crisp and true compared to his impossibly self-conscious poems. Those that didn't bore impressed but did not engage; the poet was difficult to love. How could a man of his taste, learning, and good sense write like that? Why didn't he grow up and come across?

[*City Without Walls*] knocked me down—pages of wonderful, effortless verse. It's as if he gave up all hope of writing for effect—or no longer needs to write for fame. The book's navel is an excellent poem called "The Horatians," which is that thing. The songs are real songs this time. "Insignificant Elephants" is a theological poem St. Teresa would love to read. For the first time he makes *no* stylistic apology for his sense of play. The title poem is Auden knifing the Auden Poem to death, and the rest of the book he's daring someone to catch him. No more pitching you wisdom for the price of your attention, which is all backwards. An aunt should have told him never to be arch. He *would* apply the standard dilettante-varnish the British finish their work in, if they're experts, so it won't look as if they're in trade. Not this time. "Elegy," "Since," even the Moore mosaic in its new dress are tired kinds of poems which aren't tired any more. It's like opening an old cupboard and smelling pizza instead of lavender.

*Gerald Burns, in* Southwest Review, *Spring, 1970, pp. 213-14.*

For Auden myth has served as a major and continuous mode of expression and always as a deeply personal one. His use of myth, moreover, indicates a consistency and continuity within all the diversity of his thought and poetic form. From his early work to the present day, in the persona of classical healer and in that of Christian poet-preacher, Auden has employed myth and ritual to suggest through the body of his work a definition of his poetry as public, ceremonial, and efficacious in alleviating emotional and spiritual disorder.

In his poetry of the late thirties, myth reveals man's lonely struggle with the unconscious forces of his own nature unaided by faith in any supernatural power; in the poetry written after his conversion to Christianity, "dogmas become myths" as he attempts to understand and control the unconscious drives revealed in myth through Christian faith and devotion. When Christian dogma becomes his ultimate psychological reality, he adapts and converts it to mythical expression.

Auden's approach to myth and ritual was influenced by his knowledge of the works of Freud and, to a much lesser extent, those of Jung. In employing myth as an expression of the unconscious, Auden, like Freud, exploits its possibilities as an analytic tool; it is an instrument of fantasy, most effective in exposing the irrational; even as it creates illusion, it shatters it. Unlike Yeats, Auden did not begin by contesting the insight that myth provided. For him there was no initial "flight into fairyland." Yeats created a mythical structure as both a defense against and a unique means of releasing unconscious insight and knowledge; Auden, relying on a scientific structure provided by the new psychology, approached myth as a guide to unconscious drives in man and society. . . .

Though Auden's use of myth to reveal unconscious feelings and conflict is varied and extensive, it manifests itself in four main modes: he employs large mythical concepts or "entities"; he mythicizes the scene and atmosphere of contemporary life; he alludes to well known mythical figures or legends, which provide a background of feelings and associations to which he relates a contemporary experience; he relies for contrast or irony on the reader's memory of specific mythical references in the works of ancient poets. . . .

Spear's discussion of Eros in Auden's poetry oversimplifies both his conception and its expression in the poems. . . .

The key to Eros in Auden, as in Freud, lies in the fact that it is a mythical term and concept. Though in depth and significance the Freudian Eros goes far beyond the ancient mythical figure of the god of love, it includes his ambivalent nature, his capacity to bring suffering and pleasure, to cause destruction and death, and to inspire creation. In ancient literature Eros is at once a child god and a childish one, and also a powerful productive force. . . .

For Freud, Eros exists side by side with death, with which it is continually engaged in warfare, but which is by no means its only enemy. The capacity of Eros to cause suffering results in part from its own nature: pain, dependence, and loss are intrinsic to it, the variety and extent of its power threaten organized life, and possibly "not only the presence of civilization but something in the nature of the function itself . . . denies us full satisfaction and urges us along other paths." . . .

In adopting as his own the Freudian Eros, Auden slowly came to apprehend it as the complex and ambiguous force Freud explored and described. Auden's early poems emphasize the inherent strength of Eros in its opposition to death, but it is only in his mature work that he recognizes love as an instinctual drive which can most accurately be delineated through a mythical or legendary image. Furthermore, the struggle of Eros against social and political as well as personal adversaries suggested to Auden its intrinsic relationship to other basic needs denied by a repressive society. . . . [See Auden's 1935 essay, "Psychology and Art"]

In Auden's poetry Eros does not achieve its full Freudian instinctual and mythical implications until the beginning of his conversion to Christianity. Then he can no longer maintain his earlier belief in the power of Eros, since its association with suffering and conflict and its tie with Thanatos seem to preclude optimism or even acceptance. For reassurance Auden gropes toward a new ideal—Agape. The new struggle in his poetry is indeed between Eros and Agape, but while the mythical concept Eros deepens in scope and depth with each new question and challenge, the religious ideal Agape seldom seems to provide the final answers Auden sometimes patiently, and at other times desperately, seems to hope it will offer. . . .

Auden's most recent extensive use of myth as a vehicle for exploring the unconscious mind is in *The Bassarids, Opera Seria with Intermezzo in One Act,* written in collaboration with Chester Kallman. Employing the myth of Dionysus as it appears in Euripides' *The Bacchae,* Auden and Kallman create an original poetic drama which revitalizes the myth and its associations accumulated for centuries. Their range in exploring and interpreting the myth of Dionysus is enormous. As their tone shifts from tragic to comic, from ironic to burlesque, they seem to uncover layer by layer the traces of instinct and memory in the unconscious mind.

*Lillian Feder, "W. H. Auden: Myth as Analytic Instrument," in her* Ancient Myth in Modern Poetry *(copyright © 1971 by Princeton University Press; reprinted by permission of Princeton University Press), Princeton University Press, 1971, pp. 136-80.*

Auden uses ritual allusions and effects in a variety of ways, but always as a means of invoking and releasing hidden elements in man and nature: the suffering, power, or knowledge of his persona or his protagonist, the inner drive or the inner faith. In his early poems he uses ritual mainly to disclose desires and conflicts and to call upon the healing powers of nature; in the later ones it reveals and celebrates the infinite in the finite, the spiritual essence of ordinary reality. . . . [In his 1956 lecture "Making, Knowing, and Judging," included in *The Dyer's Hand,* Auden writes:] "In poetry the rite is verbal; it pays homage by naming." . . . [Elsewhere in that lecture he states:] "A poem is a rite; hence its formal and ritualistic character." . . .

Auden's poetry has always been ritualistic; even in his earliest poems, in which he hardly uses traditional myth, when he writes of love, war, sickness, and death, he is the communicant of a "sacred encounter" with such phenomena and with the persons, seasons, and landscapes which enact or reflect the conflict and drama inherent in them. Through this encounter he has become aware of the secret meaning of such experience, and his persona is often that of an initiate who would draw the reader into a hidden society of symbolic revolutionaries, spies, and informants. . . .

This sense of deep and secret communication with experience, awesome because of the intensity of fear or pain or the recognition of danger, is present throughout the poems of [*Poems* (1930)]. Though there are few explicit references to ritual objects or acts, Auden's prophetic and admonitory tone in these poems imbues daily experience with the anticipatory tension of ritual, in which the participant, despite all the evidence to the contrary, strives to control reality by symbolic action. . . .

As love, or the mythical entity Eros, becomes a major theme of Auden's poetry, he employs allusions to ritual and ritual effects to convey the ambiguity of its nature and to trace the devious courses it takes when denied or misused. . . .

In Auden's poetry, ritual not only discloses a general unconscious struggle with the ambiguous powers of Eros; it is also a vehicle of self-revelation through which the poet publicly tests the drive of his own talent against the destructive forces within himself and external nature. . . .

Though Auden has employed ritual effects throughout his career to depict the poet's "sacred encounter" with experience—his power to elicit the secrets of nature and man and to exert control by exposure and invocation—it is mainly in his latest phase as a conscious composer of rites that he "pays homage by naming."

*Lillian Feder, "W. H. Auden: '. . . homage by naming,'" in her* Ancient Myth in Modern Poetry *(copyright © 1971 by Princeton University Press; reprinted by permission of Princeton University Press), Princeton University Press, 1971, pp. 243-69.*

In his prose and poetry of the thirties Auden reveals his commitment to an analysis of man's history through a fusion of psychoanalytic, economic, anthropological, and philosophical concepts in unifying myths, which are essentially scientific instruments. . . .

One of the most striking features of Auden's intellectual development is his capacity to assimilate diverse and even contradictory ideas which he synthesizes in a myth that symbolizes their "common and fundamental truth." In ["Jacob and the Angel," ostensibly a review of Walter de la Mare's *Behold This Dreamer*], Auden denies the validity of a deterministic and mystical conception of Destiny, such as Spengler's, through his interpretation of the contest between Jacob and the Angel as symbolic of the struggle between society's "daemon" and its rational will. Only when such a contest is accepted as inevitable can "the day . . . be reconciled with the night, Freedom with Destiny.". . .

Auden's concern with the unconscious forces that influence the nature of human society and are always an essential factor in its history is undiminished by his conversion to Christianity; nor is his approach to the problem of controlling and directing these forces essentially changed by religious conviction. Characteristically, he adapts his basic position regarding such unconscious elements to his new acceptance of a spiritual presence in the universe. . . .

Auden's scientific attitude toward man's role in history is constant throughout his career; he may waver and change in his interpretation of Eros, and certainly the addition of a Christian deity to his world view is significant, but more so is his consistent emphasis on man as at once "a social political individual" and as "a unique person who can say *I* in response to the *thou's* of other persons," who "transcends his time and his place, can choose to think and act for himself, accept personal responsibility for the consequences, and is capable alike of heroism or baseness, sanctity or corruption" [*The New York Review of Books,* August 18, 1966, p. 17]. . . .

"September 1, 1939," in which Auden speaks in the first person, reveals his deeply personal involvement with history. "Uncertain and afraid," he sees the "anger and fear" of the decade "Obsessing our private lives. . . ." He interprets the violence of past and present history in psychoanalytic terms—as resulting from sickness, obsession, and delusion. The struggle against the psychopathology of the age is also personal. The poet's hope is fragmented by his experience of the limitations of Eros, the sole productive element in history, which too often operates in both individual and social life as a narcissistic and deceptive influence.

In his poetry of the early forties, Auden's growing conviction that individual knowledge and will cannot control the unconscious aggression responsible for "the crimes of history" is expressed in his depiction of Eros as a primarily destructive social and political force. Though in "New Year Letter" he continues to probe for potential regenerative functions of Eros, the evidence of history can only convince him that "Love's vigour shrinks to less and less". . . .

To Auden, man's history since the Renaissance indicates that freedom and will can exist as agents in history only if they operate in relation to a principle or law more dependable than the protean instinctual drives and the "Self-known, self-praising, self-attached" ego of man.

The religious position Auden takes in the poetry he has written since the forties is consistently related to his view of the Incarnation as a climactic historical event. . . .

Auden seeks to replace the "collective and political myth of Eros" with the Christian myth of Incarnation and redemption as historical "Law," guiding man "so that his Eros may have the courage to take decisions." What he calls "self-actualization" [in "Eros and Agape"] can occur in human society only when love, its essential productive element, functions as a spiritual power of more stability, unity, and selflessness than the human Eros can achieve, and as one to which instinctual drives are continually directed.

*Lillian Feder, "W. H. Auden: Unconscious Forces in History," in her* Ancient Myth in Modern Poetry *(copyright © 1971 by Princeton University Press; reprinted by permission of Princeton University Press), Princeton University Press, 1971, pp. 317-43.*

Auden's early work, Mr. Buell suggests [in *W. H. Auden as a Social Poet*], was both colored and limited by the narrowness of his audience, work limited to a certain generation, class and sexual coloration among English intellectuals. Hence the quality of in-joke so often noted in his early poems. Knowing the language of his circle and its fashions of mind and loyalty, Auden became the entertainer and in some part the enlightener of a special group. His problem, if he was to continue in poetry, was one of how to expand the "we," the audience that might respond to so particular a talent, without at the same time flattening out the profile of his own poetic sense of things.

*Bernard Duffey, in* American Literature *(reprinted by permission of the Publisher; copyright 1974 by Duke University Press, Durham, North Carolina), March, 1974, p. 121.*

## AVISON, Margaret 1918-

**Ms Avison, a masterful Canadian poet, has forged a unique and complex diction for her poems. Closepacked, allusive, artful, her language strains toward perfect expression of her peculiarly visual sensibility. Her recent work, Christian mystical poetry, has reminded critics of Donne, Herbert, Hopkins, and Eliot. (See also *Contemporary Authors*, Vols. 17-18.)**

[Some] of [Avison's] finest poems . . . are cryptic, but what she experiences is 'mysterious', and easy writing is not possible.

Under the scrutiny of her intellect the world sometimes becomes austere, but the poems are never unfeeling. 'Thought' *becomes* 'feeling', and Romanticism is thus inverted—not to find its values valueless, or to praise the social world as the best of all possible, but to find another expression for a metaphysical sensibility by which 'that' world of understanding and 'this' one of perception can be brought together. The brief moment for which this may be possible is still stable, and by being, it becomes part of the future experience, or field of vision, of the poet-perceiver. Sensitivity to word and sound is not irrelevant to this pursuit, but rather the key. The very momentariness of perceptions, and the continuous shifting in point of view, are communicated to our understanding when they are rendered in sound; the multiple meanings inherent in puns immediately suggest this flux, which is the medium in which Margaret Avison looks for a self, and for both release and illumination. . . .

[Poems] during the 1940's and 1950's, were to explore the ambiguities raised by the question of perceiving, ambiguities of existence and response, inexactnesses which linguistic ambiguities could be employed to convey. So rhyme is largely cast aside, her verse becomes intentionally cryptic, and the pun becomes one of her main techniques for exploring not only the multiple meanings in the self and the world but also the ironies to which they in turn give rise. The pun inherent in the word *sense* illustrates what is going on. Images, sounds, surfaces: these are all understood both by *sense perceptions* and by the intellect by *sense*. The linguistic ambiguity (often 'offstage' in her poems, like many of her allusions) allows the two to become one; the mind 'possesses' the body then, analysing one of its perceptions and still 'perceiving' more, postulating a series of permutations that immediately clouds the issue, making the initial perception at once justifiable and suspect. The complexity and confusion of her earlier poetry—a confusion of response, consciously understood, not of poetic organization—stems from the exploration of the mind's relationship with the world. (To see her poetry strictly as "poetry of ideas," then, . . . is a little too narrow a view.) . . .

Margaret Avison's best poems . . . play with words to reveal what words can convey, working with them carefully to reveal their brilliance: their glitter and their meaning.

*W. H. New, "The Mind's Eyes (I's) (Ice)" (originally published in* Twentieth Century Literature, *1970), in his* Articulating West: Essays on Purpose and Form in Modern Canadian Literature, *New Press, 1972, pp. 234-58.*

Miss Avison's . . . poetical achievement in *Winter Sun* (1960) and *The Dumbfounding* (1966) merits consideration as spiritual quest and discovery. The first of her books is marked by a continual seeking, while the second speaks of fulfilment in lyrics which have been hailed [by A. J. M. Smith] as "among the finest religious poems of our time" [*Canadian Forum,* 46 (1966)]. Aside from sheer literary excellence, what makes the two collections remarkable is that, far from being tacked on as a "Christian" afterthought to her previous verse, Miss Avison's later poems seem to grow out of her earlier searching ones in a sequence which if not that of simple cause and effect, is yet that of authentic experience. Search and discovery are thus like two sides of one coin, or like two main parts of that one thing Claudel declares every poet is born to say in the totality of his works. . . .

If to be secular means to be fully engaged in the world of the "here and now", then all of Miss Avison's poetry is secular. If to be religious means to care about meaning, to have (in Tillich's language) an "ultimate concern", little of her poetry is not religious. The search for the ultimately significant in life stands out as a main feature of *Winter Sun,* but it is not always obtrusive. . . .

Just as the piled-up consonants in [some of the *Winter Sun* poems] help convey the sense of obstruction, the prevailing complexity of surface and structure throughout Miss Avison's first book reflects the difficulties of an as yet unrewarded search. . . .

Facing man's situation is an indispensable necessity, but, as the poet of *Winter Sun* realizes, what matters beyond that is how one responds to it. In these poems of search, Miss Avison explores various alternatives, but does not advocate any particular response—she is not ready yet, and the search itself, together with her hopes or fears, is all that she can share. In "Unfinished After-Portrait", a poem of mourning, the poet expresses her own dissatisfaction with the repeated frustrations of her quest. . . .

Gradually in this first volume of Miss Avison's there begins to emerge a realization that some radical renewal, some transforming rebirth might be possible, and might, if attained, turn out to be the true goal of the search. . . . In "Voluptuaries and Others", a very Auden-like poem in its long lines and blend of clinical precision with casual tone, Miss Avison speaks of two kinds of discovery, one being like that which occasioned Archimedes' "Eureka":

> The kind of lighting up of the terrain
> That leaves aside the whole terrain, really,
> But signalizes, and compels, an advance in it.

The accumulation of human experience "makes the spontaneous jubilation at such moments" of scientific discovery "less and less likely though", since genuine significance is only to be found in that "other kind of lighting up/That shows the terrain comprehended, as also its containing space." This latter illumination, then, is the object of the poet's search. . . .

*The Dumbfounding* contains further poems of inner search and debate, but they may be retrospective, and in any case they give the impression that the period of spiritual gestation has come to a close. "The Two Selves" pictures two opposing aspects of the poet discussing the "birds in the sky," which somehow stand for spiritual realities. . . . The response to the sceptical self reveals a maturing confidence. The "Two Mayday Selves" . . . are more mutually in harmony, yet the more hesitating one is urged to respond wholly to the new experience. . . . It is the voice of a true finder speaking, one who can call for an end to talk and self-centred questioning, and in the simplest, most forthright language invite to participation in a new joy, a release. In "Many As Two," reminiscent of Christina Rossetti's "Uphill" or of Marvell's dialogue poems, the objections are now external to the new Christian, serving both to challenge and to define his life of discovery. . . .

Having become fully taken up in the new life, Miss Avison can look back at the first moment of discovery, and attempt to picture the miracle of transformation. One such portrayal is given in "Ps. 19", a personal interpretation of the statement, "The fear of the Lord is clean, enduring for ever.". . .

Authenticity is the keynote of [the] specifically Christian poems [in *The Dumbfounding*]. They have the ring of truth that comes, in part, from the genuine search experience that preceded them, which in Amos Wilder's terms might be called the poet's "baptism in the secular", her coming "face to face with the reality of the first Adam". . . .

Miss Avison's poems, whether of search or of discovery, cannot be dismissed as "propaganda". Their rich sensitivity to all aspects of life, amounting to a wholesome "secularity", their deep and incisive engagement in the world of thought and meaning, their full exploitation of all the modern resources of language and technique—all these mark them with the vitality which is the essence of true poetry. The poems of Christian discovery are fully contemporary and dynamic, deeply rooted in the experiential. By a union in the truly human, they manage to avoid the seeming dichotomy of Christianity and art that perturbed Auden. In and through their value as poetry they have another value, a religious one which might well be appreciated by believers and others alike: they "body forth" an answer to man's searchings that one may accept or reject, but not dismiss.

*Daniel W. Doerksen, "Search and Discovery: Margaret Avison's Poetry," in* Canadian Literature, *Spring, 1974, pp. 7-20.*

# B

## BAINBRIDGE, Beryl 1933-

**Ms Bainbridge is a British novelist. (See also *Contemporary Authors*, Vols. 21-22.)**

This spare and lethal piece [*The Dressmaker*] must be one of the best novels of 1973. Within the most astringent limits Miss Bainbridge has created a sense of powerful emotions, has given a most tremendous sense of time and place. The writing is lithe, economical and muscular. . . .

At no time does one get a sense that the writer has 're-searched' and 'placed' her period and local colour. Pop songs, references, details of fashion, attitudes to the war and the Americans are natural and unforced. Miss Bainbridge, incidentally, uses a simple device that forces the reader to start again at the beginning immediately the last page is finished . . . and this is, if a touch artful, the most chilling touch of all.

*Roger Baker, "'The Dressmaker,'" in* Books and Bookmen, *January, 1974, p. 71.*

Perhaps because she writes of mean people in drab places, perhaps because her plot devices are at times so deceptively sensational that her fiction is confused with crime stories—whatever the reason, Beryl Bainbridge has been scandalously neglected. On the evidence of *The Secret Glass,* she is an author of extraordinary power whose touch is at once steel-hard and delicate. Indeed, she is a more remarkable, far more original writer than Lessing or Murdoch or Spark. . . .

[The] plot of this domestic tragedy is less important than Miss Bainbridge's precision, the quiet perfection with which she renders the quality of life in this suppressed, anguished household, and her wit, which has Nellie sitting down to her Singer "like the great organ at the Palladium cinema before the war." When Rita brings the American to tea with her aunts, Margo knows instantly what sort of man he is, and Miss Bainbridge defines the menace of his heartless, animal greed by means of a bleak spareness that only a superbly gifted writer can manipulate with such awesome resonance.

So intense, pure and unsentimental is the feeling Miss Bainbridge draws from these lives of proud desperation, of pleasureless obedience to unquestioned imperatives of convention, that a great stillness comes over the reader. As we follow Nellie and Margo and Rita and Ira to their catastrophic climax, our involvement in their experience—through the novelist's brilliant shaping—becomes an act of uncluttered concentration and total assent. Judgment is there—it must be there—yet it is tempered at every point by Miss Bainbridge's knowledge and humor, her affection and pity, her unique and wholly arresting talent.

*Pearl K. Bell, "The Overblown and the Overlooked," in* The New Leader, *September 2, 1974, pp. 17-18.*

Not a confirmed thriller reader, I am not a very reliable judge of the genre, but I suspect that neither [*Harriet Said* nor *The Secret Glass*] is successful in that vein. They do not manage to keep the serious novel and the entertainment both going at once. To me they are psychological novels trapped in another genre, emotional evocations forced toward violent endings that are not implicit in the situations. The "abnormality" of Bainbridge's characters is released not by the final act of horror but by the characters' becoming briefly the center of attention.

The best of Bainbridge lies in the interior of her characters, the most important of which is the same girl who keeps recurring in different disguises. The bookish middle-class little girl of *Harriet Said* is the naive Rita in the working-class setting of *The Secret Glass,* and either or both might have grown up to be the Maggie of *A Weekend with Claud,* a physically and emotionally untidy young woman vibrating constantly on the edge of possibility. . . .

[The] sense of inevitable loss—the "isolation" that . . . pervades the books . . . is far more disquieting than the conventional violent endings. More important—artistically, at least—is Bainbridge's sure sense of the conflict in her characters between self-knowledge and self-deception, between the person and the role, between the situation and its idealization. Neither of these novels is finally satisfying, but if both of them testify to a strong talent at work—and I think they do—it is because their central figures are uncertain creatures, part fact and part fancy, into whose shoes any of us could step.

*Gerald Weales, "Acts of Horror," in* The New Republic *(reprinted by permission of*

The New Republic; © *1974 by The New Republic, Inc.), September 28, 1974, p. 27.*

* * *

## BALDWIN, James 1924-

**A Black American novelist, essayist, short story writer, and playwright, Baldwin is one of America's most eloquent spokesmen, insistently pursuing personal and racial freedom in our morally and intellectually impoverished society. (See also *Contemporary Authors*, Vols. 1-4, rev. ed.)**

*Blues for Mr. Charlie* . . . is the embodiment of everything [Baldwin] once professed to deplore, being "notoriously bloodthirsty" propaganda of the crudest sort, with little existence either as truth, literature, or life. Uncontrolled, hysterical, self-indulgent, employing a clumsy flashback technique and proceeding by means of a surprisingly flabby rhetoric, it is a play of thumbs—fashioned, I would guess, to gouge the eyes of the audience.

It is well known that Baldwin has radically changed his conception of himself over the past few years [note that Brustein was writing in 1964], suppressing the private side of his character to become an Official Spokesman for a Cause. I have not been among those who admired him in this new role, but I never assumed the decision was easy—or even wholly avoidable, for it may be, as Irving Howe suggests, that the Negro writer cannot find "freedom and fulfillment" until he achieves his Cause. On the other hand, Baldwin's race, formerly authentic and precise, has begun to seem increasingly mechanical, trumped-up and free-floating, while his self-righteousness has been expressed at the cost of complexity and scruples. In this play, for example, he is—despite a usually delicate awareness of the deadening effect of racial abstractions—dedicated to perpetuating stereotypes, and doing so in a manner which can only create confusion or dissension. The characters have no life apart from narrow racial categories, and the categories themselves are based on prejudice. . . .

The most disappointing thing about the play, however, is not its aesthetic flatness but rather its moral and intellectual deficiency. . . .

The ultimate difficulty . . . is not a racial difficulty at all; it is the difficulty of the modern intellectual, torn between the way of influence and the way of truth. This conflict has driven more than one gifted individual of our time to a sorry abuse of his talents, as well as to that almost pathological frustration that usually accompanies it; and I suspect that much of the exasperation in this play stems from Baldwin's inability to reconcile the private and public aspects of his character. Until he does, however, he has ceased to illuminate our consciousness. Early in his career, James Baldwin declared it his ambition to be "an honest man and a good writer." In *Blues for Mr. Charlie* he is neither. There, the complex man of sensibility has been totally absorbed by the simplistic man of power—and that constitutes what Baldwin himself once called "his corruption and our loss."

*Robert Brustein, "Everybody's Protest Play" (1964), in his* Seasons of Discontent: Dramatic Opinions 1959-1965 *(© 1959, 1960, 1961, 1962, 1963, 1964, 1965 by Robert Brustein; reprinted by permission of Simon and Schuster, Inc.), Simon & Schuster, 1965, pp. 161-65.*

The truth is that *Blues for Mister Charlie* isn't really about what it claims to be about. It is supposed to be about racial strife. But it is really about the anguish of tabooed sexual longings, about the crisis of identity which comes from confronting these longings, and about the rage and destructiveness (often, self-destructiveness) by which one tries to surmount this crisis. It has, in short, a psychological subject. The surface may be Odets, but the interior is pure Tennessee Williams. What Baldwin has done is to take the leading theme of the serious theater of the fifties—sexual anguish—and work it up as a political play.

*Susan Sontag, "Going to Theater, etc." (1964), in her* Against Interpretation and Other Essays *(reprinted with the permission of Farrar, Straus & Giroux, Inc.; copyright © 1961, 1962, 1963, 1964, 1965, 1966 by Susan Sontag), Farrar, Straus, 1966, pp. 140-62.*

The implication of Baldwin's first two novels [*Go Tell It on the Mountain* and *Giovanni's Room*] is that the primitive Negro who could accept suffering and deny guilt could save white America and white Europe from the burden of guilt imposed by the inhibitions of civilization. But his romantic primitivism is so extreme that it necessarily contradicts this framework of social salvation. He can posit no reality beyond the particular individual. For him, the abstract is artificial, the artificial is civilization, civilization is inhibition, inhibition is guilt, and the whole purpose of spiritual salvation for the individual is the transcendence of guilt. He must end with Norman Mailer in a theology of personal salvation which separates the particular saint from the sinful brotherhood of mankind. And if the Baldwin saint is not physically impotent, he is yet as sterile as [Mailer's] Rojack. . . . This is the tragic impasse of . . . *Another Country.*

*David W. Noble, in his* The Eternal Adam and the New World Garden: The Central Myth in the American Novel Since 1830 *(George Braziller, Inc.; reprinted with permission of the publisher; copyright © 1968 by David W. Noble), Braziller, 1968, pp. 214-15.*

In early 1949, early in his career, James Baldwin published a now legendary essay, "Everybody's Protest Novel," in which he took a stand that at the time was astonishing to encounter in a Negro novelist. Writers with a Cause such as Harriet Beecher Stowe and Richard Wright, Baldwin argued, are not novelists but pamphleteers, and though their moral sincerity is unexceptionable, they reduce their characters to pawns on a chessboard of social injustice, members "of a Society or a Group or a deplorable conundrum to be explained by Science." . . .

The true business of the novelist, Baldwin insisted, was not the inflammatory manipulation of social responsibility and reform, but the far more difficult and courageous revelation of man's complexity. "Only within this web of ambiguity, paradox, this hunger, danger, darkness, can we find at once ourselves and the power that will free us from ourselves."

The essay was an extraordinarily self-assured performance for so young and so *Harlem* a writer. Yet shortly before it was published, Baldwin had in fact left Manhattan and America altogether, hoping through exile in Europe to escape from a suffocating society that not only seemed to lock every black writer into the crude simplicities of propaganda and protest, but was also peculiarly inimical to a homosexual like himself. Europe did not of course prove to be the unconstrained color-blind paradise of Baldwin's naïve expectations. It did, however, make possible a personal change of perspective that enabled him to complete his first and best novel, *Go Tell It on the Mountain,* an autobiographical chronicle of his evangelical-preacher father: "In America, the color of my skin had stood between myself and me; in Europe, that barrier was down. . . . The question of who I was had at last become a personal question, and the answer was to be found in me."

Until the early 1960s, that answer, for Baldwin, consisted largely of a literary and intellectual cosmopolitanism that freed him, for a time, from the racial shibboleths and platitudes of "Negro" fiction. Thus in his second novel, *Giovanni's Room,* he told the troubled story of some white homosexuals in Paris in the first person—out of a defiantly cocky need to prove that a Negro novelist could successfully obliterate the facts of race from his work, if not from his life.

Oddly, while he was programmatically right about the objectives of fiction for the artist, Baldwin's own novels have been on the whole uninteresting and fatally strained. If *Giovanni's Room* was a startling experiment in audacity, it was nonetheless a feeble novel; and *Another Country* and *Tell Me How Long the Train's Been Gone* are lazy and sentimental, full of hackneyed violence and tin-ear dialogue, thin and unrealized characters, speciously "shocking" melodrama.

Indeed, Baldwin has never been altogether at home in the novel. His real power as a writer is to be found in his autobiographical essays, particularly in that small and lacerating masterpiece, "Notes of a Native Son." . . .

In the early 1960s, in his now characteristic pattern, Baldwin published a pedestrian novel, *Another Country,* and a magnificently eloquent memoir and lamentation, *The Fire Next Time,* a reflective inquiry, dark with foreboding, into the lessons his own private chaos could derive from black history. . . .

Passionate and lucid in its melancholy recognitions, in its beautifully sustained tension of rage and intelligence, *The Fire Next Time* was a black jeremiad spoken with incredible dignity. Baldwin did not bludgeon the guilty white reader into reaching for his consoling and stuffed hair shirt. One did not have to consent to Baldwin's prophecy of doom and conflagration in order to be moved by his vision of black suffering. . . .

Yet less than a decade later, in *No Name in the Street,* Baldwin repudiated temperateness and insight to take up the torch of apocalypse. This violently bitter requiem for the civil rights movement, published in 1972, degenerated almost immediately into indiscriminate sniping, mindless contumely ("White Americans are probably the wickedest and most dangerous people . . . in the world today"), myopic nonsense ("White America remains unable to believe that black America's grievances are real"), and paranoid malediction (America is "the Fourth Reich"). Where the tone of *The Fire Next Time* had been at once intensely personal and free of egoism, *No Name in the Street* revealed a Baldwin indecently self-important about his own celebrity. The elegiac compassion and unflinching self-scrutiny that had given his earlier essays such grace and authority were smothered by a nervous pomposity about the trivia of fame, and an ungovernable indulgence in the irresponsibilities of bigotry and hate.

The gifted young maverick who wrote "Everybody's Protest Novel" a quarter of a century ago will be 50 this year and he has just published his fifth novel, *If Beale Street Could Talk*. . . . It is not only Baldwin's shallowest work of fiction, but ironically it commits those very atrocities of distortion and stereotyping that he long ago deplored in *Native Son*: Richard Wright's acquiescence in the pervasive American fantasy that the Negro "is a social and not a personal or a human problem."

*Pearl K. Bell, in* New Leader, *May 27, 1974, pp. 3-4.*

As a novel [*If Beale Street Could Talk*] is not a success, being too sentimental and predictable by half. But it has the makings of a splendid opera. . . .

*Beale Street* is . . . a form of social realism. It is hard to speculate how a writer of Baldwin's quality succumbed to such timeless bathos. It is even more difficult to accept that a man capable of writing the dense, seductive prose of *Giovanni's Room* could turn out a slack bromide like "Trouble means you're alone."

Possibly Baldwin, who now lives in France, took to long fiction for the first time in six years out of disgust with the slag heaps of sociology about blacks.

*Martha Duffy, "All in the Family," in* Time *(reprinted by permission from* Time, The Weekly Newsmagazine; *copyright Time Inc.), June 10, 1974, pp. 94, 96.*

"I'd rather be here, than any place I know," sings the *boulevardier* of Handy's great blues song, unintimidated by having seen the seven wonders of the white world for he is sure that Beale Street had more than enough life and love for anyone until they closed down the saloons. As an account of black experience in America this has obvious limitations, and the irony in the title of James Baldwin's bitter new novel of black lovers in the repressive hands of white justice tells us clearly enough the point he wants to make. But the novel itself does not succeed in telling a story that convinces us of that point. . . .

Simplicity and directness will do very well for any story with the polemical intentions of *If Beale Street Could Talk*; but even simplicity requires that a writer take the trouble to get things right, imagine his world in ways that aren't contradictory, not be careless about the occasions created for emotional invitations.

It is these occasions that go wrong in this novel whose governing situation seems at least improbable. . . .

Baldwin's incontrovertible thesis, that being black makes it much harder to get justice in America, leads him into incredibility. . . .

To read *If Beale Street Could Talk* as accurate social drama seems to me virtually impossible. I can't care as much as I want to about Fonny and Tish unless the system that victimizes them is described in a way that I can recognize. No one can doubt that terrible things are done to good and innocent black people. But Baldwin writes so flatly and schematically that he drives one to imagining ways in which his story might be more "believable." . . .

So one must try to read this novel allegorically, taking Tish and Fonny as Romeo and Juliet (as they're in fact teasingly called by some of their friends), cop-crossed lovers victimized by a repressive order whose exact workings don't really matter. They are credible and often affecting as lovers, but the fantasy on which Baldwin's allegory relies may disturb some of Baldwin's readers, particularly black ones: blackness in a white system becomes here a condition of helpless passivity, of getting screwed by the man; persecution and violation are emphasized so insistently and despairingly that enduring them becomes a kind of acceptance. . . .

[If] Baldwin's political meanings carry an essentially sexual message, the frustrated rage in this novel needs a clearer relation to its inner subject. As it is, I unhappily suggest that an important and honorable writer has failed to make us believe in his vision of horrors that surely do exist, but outside his book.

*Thomas R. Edwards, in* The New York Review of Books *(reprinted with permission from* The New York Review of Books; © *1974 by NYREV, Inc.), June 13, 1974, pp. 37-8.*

Over the past twenty years Baldwin has become the most influential prophet and polemicist and perhaps the most distinguished writer of his race, and he has earned a position in the moral community of our time comparable only to that of Norman Mailer as a monitor of conscience and a remaker of consciousness. His fame now secure, we have accorded him the highest honor we can bestow upon a public intellectual: We have disarmed him with celebrity, fallen in love with his eccentricities, and institutionalized his outrage (along with Mailer's obscenity and Capote's bitchiness) into prime-time entertainment.

Yet his role as America's favorite token black is not without its advantages for Baldwin the writer, however responsible it may have been for converting the realities of his cause into the clichés of rhetoric. His strategy has always been to keep constantly before us the reminder that he is a *black* writer and that black is his subject. The absolute rightness of his cause coupled with his self-righteousness in proselytizing for it have very effectively kept at bay many commentators who might otherwise have approached him with the critical skepticism they habitually bring to the work of his white contemporaries. Baldwin has, to be sure, been the object of negative criticism, but all too often its force has been blunted or misdirected to peripheral issues seemingly in deference to the idea that the act of critical discrimination just might possibly be considered discriminatory. Where other writers may be judged on the strength of their artistry, Baldwin's artistry has frequently been placed beyond judgment because of the sacredness of his subject. One can only wonder whether his other and, in some respects, more central subject, interracial sexuality and homosexuality, would be quite so effective as a silencer of opposition. . . .

Baldwin's blackness has caused him to perceive and conceive experience almost exclusively within the charged polarities of black and white, and in spite of his intelligence and remarkable powers of narration—qualities displayed more impressively in his essays than in his novels—he has repeatedly produced fictional characterizations that represent the most simplistic vision of the racial conflict. There is considerable irony in this because Baldwin, very early in his career [in the essay "Everybody's Protest Novel"], brilliantly stated the case against the very kind of fiction he later came to write. . . . However sensitive Baldwin may be to the unique quality of the individual human being, he has been generally unsuccessful in creating characters who exist independently of their categorization. . . .

[Baldwin's failure] would appear to be the result of an inability to extricate his powerful feelings for individuals from his far more powerful feelings for them as victims of racial oppression.

Perhaps in an effort to break out of the confines and to generalize the implications of his own form of the protest novel, Baldwin has repeatedly tried to convince his readers that there is finally no difference between the dilemma of his black characters and that of just about everybody else in our corrupt society. . . .

Baldwin's preoccupation with sexual love between blacks and whites may be yet another symptom of his effort to extend the thematic range of his fiction beyond the boundaries of race. Sexual love emerges in his novels as a kind of universal anodyne for the disease of racial separatism, as a means not only of achieving personal identity but also of transcending false categories of color and gender. . . . As the forces of discrimination grow stronger in the outside world, the characters grow more undiscriminating in their sexuality, achieving through countless combinations and recombinations of relationships some brief sense that they are still alive. . . . The remarkable thing about these people, apart from their indefatigability, is that they are really not interested in one another at all. In fact, they are no more real to one another than they are as characters. . . . One might have assumed on the evidence of his essays and early fiction that Baldwin would be consumed in the fires of hate and that his future as a novelist could well depend on his achievement of compassion and objectivity. But it seemed probable after the appearance of *Another Country* and the later novel, *Tell Me How Long the Train's Been Gone,* that he might instead be destined to drown in the throbbing seas of sentimental love, and, regrettably, his new novel, *If Beale Street Could Talk,* only makes that probability seem a certainty. . . .

It is extremely sad to see a writer of Baldwin's large gifts producing, in all seriousness, such junk. Yet it has been evident for some time that he is deteriorating as a novelist and becoming increasingly a victim of the vice of sentimentality. This seems a particular pity because Baldwin may have one great novel left within him which it would take the most radical courage to write, the story of a talented black writer who achieves worldwide success on the strength of his anger and, in succeeding, gradually loses his anger and comes to be loved by everybody. Clearly, such acceptance can be considered a triumph for a black man in America, but it can be death for a black writer in whom anger and talent are indivisible.

*John W. Aldridge, "The Fire Next Time?," in* Saturday Review/World *(copyright © 1974 by Saturday Review/World, Inc.; reprinted with permission), June 15, 1974, pp. 20, 24-5.*

[*If Beale Street Could Talk*] is Baldwin's fifth novel, and his first in six years. It's also a major work of black American fiction. It's the story of Tish, a 19-year-old Harlem girl, and her lover, Fonny, a young black sculptor. . . .

[It] is Tish herself who holds us. . . . In what is arguably Baldwin's most painful novel, she spites pain and bewilderment, and goes on loving not only Fonny but also the tribute to his struggle for his manhood that she is carrying inside her. . . .

The narrative is a remarkable blend of lyricism and speed, and beneath the whisper and hurry of the story you can feel Baldwin and Tish in a kind of subtextual dialogue. Tish engages, even astonishes Baldwin as no other character he has ever written about. It's the hoariest of critical clichés to say so, but he's exactly the right distance from her. I've never encountered anyone quite like Tish in American fiction. But America's streets are full of her. We all know Tish. She works for some of us, rides the bus beside others of us, is sister to still others. But, as she says of the depth of her rage: "People don't know." And who can say she's wrong? At the very least, Baldwin makes it clear how little Tish has to count on, how incalculably dangerous her life would become—all but unlivable, really—if she didn't have Fonny to love. And love is hard. It brings Tish agonizingly close to despair. It keeps her from falling into it.

Tish is uniquely 19, black, scared and born up by a tremendous natural dignity—and all of this is what keeps her going. She's at a time in her life that will never come again, and part of the sweet ache the book makes us feel is that we can see this more clearly than she can.

*Ivan Webster, in* The New Republic *(reprinted by permission of* The New Republic; *© 1974 by The New Republic, Inc.), June 15, 1974, pp. 25-6.*

Baldwin was gifted with one of the most elegant, precise and conscious prose styles ever bestowed on any modern writer—it made all his early work coldly shine. Perhaps he ceased to value this wonderful and delicate instrument; perhaps it could not contain his rage; but whatever the reason, [*If Beale Street Could Talk*] has a central problem with its voice. A story of young black lovers crossed by a vicious white judicial system—Fonny, a sculptor, is jailed for a rape he could not have committed, while Tish, the narrator, carries his child—[the novel] contains much affecting writing, but often wanders among the tallest corn, while giving Tish a wide-eyed governessy style which is the very emblem of the unengaged, lazing imagination.

Fonny is just too good, Tish is too innocent, the law is too wicked. Baldwin's hate collapses everything into a rigid scheme. Yet the book, astonishingly, isn't dead; a disturbing sexual allegory, working far below the stylistic lapses and the schema, keeps it going. The most vivid scenes are violently, explicitly sexual—Tish's defloration, Fonny masturbating in jail. Fonny's sexuality, which will give him a child, is what motivates his lover's family to work to save him; in jail, he fears rape, for his friend Daniel has been warped by it; he is raped by the legal system, which charges him with a false rape. Anger is the conscious response to this cycle, but the actual way out seems to be passivity. Fonny, Baldwin hints, is more than a man when he abandons hope. The ending suggests that the only release is in art or childbearing, a profoundly despairing, profoundly shocking implication.

*Peter Straub, "Happy Ends," in* New Statesman, *June 28, 1974, p. 930.*

* * *

## BARNES, Djuna 1892-

**An American novelist, dramatist, and short story writer, Djuna Barnes is best known for her novel *Nightwood.* (See also *Contemporary Authors*, Vols. 9-12, rev. ed.)**

In *Nightwood* the nostalgia of transient details becomes transmuted to an anguish in whose crepuscular heaving objects lose their literal, narrative base of reference to become pure metaphors, at once freer and less fictional than in other novels. . . . It is no disparagement to the vision of this novel to say, with T. S. Eliot, that it exists at the margin of its genre and of another, poetry. Literal or not, the metaphors still extend the characters who handle them or name them. . . . The splintered narrative, the striking exfoliation of unliteral detail, exist here in a hypertrophy reminiscent of *Ulysses*; and its characters, like those of *Ulysses,* tend to petrify into types, to twist, through the style, into grotesques more distorted than those of *Winesburg, Ohio.*

*Albert Cook, in his* The Meaning of Fiction *(reprinted by permission of the Wayne State University Press; copyright © 1960 by Albert Cook), Wayne State University Press, 1960, p. 126.*

Djuna Barnes, who belonged to what Gertrude Stein called "the lost generation," wrote very different plays at the beginning and end of her writing career. . . . As melodramatic as O'Neill's early shockers . . . , Barnes' plays did not eventually lead her toward her own experience, as did those of O'Neill. . . .

It is impossible to consider [her early] plays seriously, in their modish poses and pseudo-poetic dialogue. The sure touch of Barnes' novels seems to come from some other mind. But nearly four decades after these dubious plays, Djuna Barnes again turned to drama. Still melodrama in that the emotion seems to exceed the vehicle, the dialogue of that vehicle is distinctive—different from anything else written by Djuna Barnes, and different from any other play of the twentieth century.

The title *Antiphon* (1958) suggests an archaic and static form, for an antiphon is a verse reply, as in an antiphonic hymn. Elizabethan in phrasing, the drama is antiphonal in several scenes; that is to say, a verse speech calls forth its immediate reply, rather than fitting into an overall action. Though the verse of *The Antiphon* is archaic, setting and plot are relatively modern—the one recalling Eliot and the other Yeats. Like Eliot's *Family Reunion, The Antiphon* is set in an English country house; curiously, the date of production of *Family Reunion* is the date within *The Antiphon* —1939, the beginning of World War II. The war is the play's present, but the characters are mired in the past, as in Yeats' *Purgatory*. In both plays, a woman has betrayed her aristocratic heritage by lust for a commoner. . . .

The heavily imaged verse embraces all three acts of [*The Antiphon*] but the theatrical mood of each act is different. . . .

[Matter] extracted from manner betrays *The Antiphon* more than most plays. The seventeenth-century speech reflects the theme, carrying conviction of the Burley past. Djuna Barnes' lines tease with echoes of Webster and Tourneur, and yet the idiom is original. In Yeats' *Purgatory* we have the Old Man's word that "Great people lived and died in this house." But in Barnes' *Antiphon* the language imposes those people upon us.

As in her novel *Nightwood,* Djuna Barnes makes some effort to differentiate the speech of the several characters. . . . In spite of differences, all six characters utter free pentameters, freer images, and the two women use a syntax that is perhaps too convoluted to be understood in the theater.

Unlike T. S. Eliot, who forced his verse into the mold of modern conversational prose, Djuna Barnes resolutely resurrects techniques of Elizabethan drama—soliloquy, aside, catalogue, pun, and above all metaphor. At its worst, the imagery swallows denotative sense. . . . More often, though, the imagery concentrates paragraphs of dialogue. . . .

There are few sustained threads of imagery, but these few are significant. Miranda is often a voyager or traveler; Augusta is both hunted and hunter. . . .

The dialogue of *The Antiphon* is astonishing. As drama, *The Antiphon* has many flaws: Jack Blow's opening exposition is obscure; descriptions are gratuitous of Augusta's sister Elvira and of Titus' mother Victoria. Even the coupling of Miranda's ruin with a Paris ruined by war is skillful in its horror rather than organic in its link. Too often, connotations muffle denotations; sound buries sense. In spite of these serious faults, however, *The Antiphon* contains extraordinarily rich diction and varied rhythms. For literary accomplishment, the play begs comparison with Eliot or Yeats. But unlike their plays, *The Antiphon* has not yet—1970—tempted theatermen. Which implies its own critique of the play, or of the theater.

*Ruby Cohn, "Djuna Barnes," in her* Dialogue in American Drama, *Indiana University Press, 1971, pp. 207-11.*

[*Nightwood*] as a whole is deeply concerned with the perception, memory, and association of its characters and their consequent behavior. It draws heavily on images from nature, childhood, and religion, both in portraying the present and past of the characters. In the passage [concerning] . . . the doctor and his room, and the question, "tell me everything you know about the night" all suggest not only psychological but also religious significance. Specifically, there is the suggestion of a rite of initiation at a sacred time and in a sacred space.

Traditionally, religions require the initiate to undergo symbolic torment, suffering, and death. His death, in turn, signifies his return to the womb, to his creator, and thence to rebirth and a higher plane of awareness. Nora, indeed, fulfills these requirements of the initiate, albeit on a psychological plane. . . .

Thus far we have considered *Nightwood* as a novel concerned with pyschology—that is, portraying the memory, perception, symbols, dreams, myths, fantasies, and behavior of its characters—saturated with religious allusions. The novel draws the structure of its conflict from a conception of the mind in tension; historically and individually created in unknown, unknowable circumstances akin to concepts of Dionysian darkness, chaos, and formlessness, yet shaped unconsciously by a fusion of actual memory and given religious-cultural myths. By these the characters perceive and act in the Apollonian world of form. The central myth is the religious myth of rebirth, a myth which, however consciously lost in a character, still resides, a dark force of the unconscious but dimly perceived. In short, *Nightwood* draws a parallel between certain historically recognized myths and certain personal myths in much the same fashion as certain contemporary psychologists. This is not to say, however, that Barnes and Jung share the same point of view towards this phenomenon nor that their objectives are parallel.

The characters are repeatedly defined by religious allusions. . . .

The religious references are themselves linked to the basic religious longing to be other than what one is; the individual is lost, unfulfilled. In religion this longing is played out by creation of sacred space, time, and rituals which are recreations of the divine acts of creation and so promise to unite the human with the divine from which he came. In both psychology and religion, the natural earthly counterpart to Edenic existence and identification with God is the child's experience of the mother. She represents security, power, and unity experienced by the child when he is consciously undifferentiated from the mother. In the womb is the sacred time and space and the most sacred rite of personal experience. Both religion and psychology share the symbol of the mother, the archetype of a greater identity the offspring cannot know, yet longs to know again. But, in religion and psychology, the mother and God both have a dual nature, great and terrible, because they define our mortality. The wish to return, the longing to transcend, demands an undifferentiated consciousness which can only be experienced in death. Thus the longing for the ideal becomes the longing for death. *Nightwood* uses these concepts.

The novel presents characters who act out their unconscious personal myth in terms of given cultural and religious myths. Essentially, they believe, as religious man does, that the practice of certain rituals or exercises will give them knowledge and power to unite with the forces of control, defying death and transcending their situation, the human predicament. The novel sets out the abundance and appeal of symbols that represent this belief, while ironically undermining it. In the circus, wild beasts are controlled and made to conform to human wishes. Further, humans not only have power to control nature, but to defy its laws. Frau Mann, the trapeze artist, presents the illusion that the human being can achieve a surreal existence, united with form that defies gravity and death. . . . Likewise, the "man of magic'' moves through ''a series of 'honesties' '' (p. 35) to give the illusion of impossibility achieved, the illusion of form created out of nothing. The opera and theater present actors who seem to function on their own, but in fact are directed by unseen instructions. Their music is the wedding of the Dionysian and Apollonian, giving form to the formless, fusing meaning with sound. The church presents the most central symbol. The impersonality of the Roman Catholic rituals suggests that one is in contact not merely with men but with God. Behind its form and ritual it promises a true, ultimate form by which we were created and which we may obtain. God may be witnessed in human form, Christ, and he, our salvation, was delivered to earth through a virgin, divinely exempt from the human condition. O'Connor says of the Catholic church, it ''is the girl that you love so much that she can lie to you'' (p. 20). The novel sets this myth as complement to childhood remembrance so that the characters confuse or infuse their own birth with the myth of sacred creation and hopes of salvation. . . .

At first, Robin does not seem to connect the sex act with pregnancy. As a representation of unconsciousness, she connects conception with divine creation, turning to the Catholic church and the image of Virgin Mary, losing herself in wandering. The church, then, represents the divine wish, but the wandering is the profane, degraded, and bestial. Robin, who has the ''iris of wild beasts who have not tamed the focus down to meet the human eye'' (p. 37), desires the divine, but in the form of a beast. In this the novel suggests the universal unconscious wish of human procreation if the beast may be taken to serve as an image of human form. Instead, Robin experiences only pain, a sense of loss, a ''lost land,'' the coming of consciousness, all represented by Guido, the child, neither beast nor divine, but an image of suffering and arrested physical and mental development.

Thus, Robin has tricked Felix, but has herself been tricked, to which she responds by attempting to lose herself, in ''love and anonymity'' (p. 55). . . .

To the end that he may not be deceived or tricked by existence, as he feels he has been in being born in male form, [O'Connor] practices a religion of withdrawal from the world. Yet his very attempts to imitate Christ as healer and divine draw him into involvement and action which his prophetic powers see as inevitably leading to evil. Knowledge becomes then not power to overcome a condition, but only heightened awareness of it. . . . Hence, the doctor's bedtime transvestitism becomes an emblematic gesture of the novel's theme: that love is an act of the self reaching toward an unconscious myth of one's past in an effort to create one's self anew, to be born again. O'Connor represents man's sincere attempts to raise his self-love to a higher level only to face the unconquerable limitations of his human existence. O'Connor's chief symbol of this is the body itself. . . .

A vast range of imagery is bound together and drives the principle theme. The range and depth of Barnes's style, its imagery and motifs, have hardly been pricked here, nor have all the existential implications been dealt with. Yet it is enough to enable a return to the initially presented, psychological moment, Nora's ''sensation of a thought.'' One can now review the complex concentration of images and theme suggested by the childhood remembrance of a fairytale in the mind of Nora.

The story of Little Red Riding Hood, of course, involves the young girl of that name who goes to deliver cookies to her grandmother and meets, instead, a wolf masquerading as her grandmother, with an appetite for Red Riding Hood herself. That children ''like'' this scene suggests the child's affinity for the power and amoral, unconscious mind of the beast. But this affinity exists in adulthood also, where it is disciplined consciously in moral terms. . . .

The beast in grandmother's clothes represents both the unconscious unity of the child's mind and its degradation, the profanity that Nora is succumbing to in an attempt to achieve her own myth of nobility, even as in her dream Robin moves further away the more passionately Nora summons her. Yet, the wolf is there to devour Nora, in so far as she is identified with Riding Hood, and this suggests the process of being ''eaten away.'' Behind the profanity of this desire ultimately lies death, and the loss of self sought after in life.

To continue probing these associations, Nora and Robin are transferring predicaments. Nora, by trying to unite with Robin, is abandoning the cultural myths and going into chaos. Robin is developing a myth of Nora as creator, awakening consciousness endowed with divinity. This Robin acts out in her confusion: Nora becomes the Virgin Mary, the divine exemption from the human predicament, yet fated to take on suffering. Nora's dog is then taken by Robin for herself, that which is unconscious and without myth and with which Robin attempts to unite, to devour, as it were. Robin's final act, that concludes the book, completes the imagery of the sort of atavism that lies behind the myth of rebirth as acted out in the cultural and love aspirations of the characters. Finally, what does the fairytale indicate O'Connor's fate to be? He himself, as the wolf, is longing to taste of innocence. But when confronted with Nora, he is ''extremely put out, having expected someone else'' (p. 80). For O'Connor, innocence will never come, but only the human predicament, Nora. And so long as only the human predicament presents itself, his appetite for salvation is chained to the evil of that situation. . . .

The novel expresses the old phrase that life is a comedy to the intellect but a tragedy for the emotions. It is a universal theme, but one which few but the invert [experience], deprived of even the illusive reflection of himself, of the potential future of the child, and confronted with his profound alienation even from himself.

*Edward Gunn, ''Myth and Style in Djuna Barnes's 'Nightwood',''* in Modern Fiction Studies *(© 1974, by Purdue Research Foundation, Lafayette, Indiana), Winter, 1973-74, pp. 545-55.*

* * *

## BEAUVOIR, Simone de 1908-

**Simone de Beauvoir is a French existentialist philosopher, novelist, essayist, and autobiographer. Although her fiction is usually considered artistically masterful, it is most often studied as the exegesis of her philosophical thought. (See also *Contemporary Authors*, Vols. 9-12, rev. ed.)**

The main reason why Simone de Beauvoir's feminism deserves very careful attention is because *Le Deuxième Sexe* may frequently be misunderstood by opponents and supporters. . . . [One] misunderstanding is to consider her feminism as an isolated aspect, rather than to see her views in *Le Deuxième Sexe* as a central feature of her fiction and thought; in this way, the immediate problems, both social and political, which are posed in *Le Deuxième Sexe,* can be conveniently overlooked. . . .

A brief examination of *Le Deuxième Sexe* is, however, bound to be a dangerous undertaking, for there are immediately two risks: that of obscuring the essential unity of her work, visible in the close resemblances between novels, essays and autobiography; and that of over-simplification. . . . It will be seen that, for Simone de Beauvoir, woman has currently two unsatisfactory functions: she is both object and image. Once man has branded her with the stigma of otherness ("altérité"), she has been throughout history a mere object in a male society; thereafter, when the object is obliged to incarnate man's dream, she becomes an image. This representational function accounts for the inauthentic attitude which Simone de Beauvoir calls woman's "être-pour-les-hommes," which will, at least in part, explain . . . the frequent references to mirrors and looking-glasses in her novels and autobiography as well as in *Le Deuxième Sexe*.

[In] *Le Deuxième Sexe,* and in her further remarks on womankind in U.S.A. and China, Simone de Beauvoir decides to take upon herself the function of looking-glass and thus reveal to the less privileged members of her sex the imperfections of Woman the Object and of Woman the Image. . . . To avoid any accusation of hypersensitivity, let us agree that Simone de Beauvoir is probably right about the male; but let us also suggest that the converse weighting of the argument in favour of women raises a reasonable doubt about the just or unjust methods of argumentation elsewhere in the book. It may be that Simone de Beauvoir's mirror gives only a distorted image to suit her own theories, outlook and aims. [An] examination of her feminism will reveal flaws which arise from the intrusion into the feminism of her three other preoccupations . . . the existential, the autobiographical and the political. . . .

In every novel which Simone de Beauvoir has written, man is shown as the controller of society in every sphere. . . . The clearest and, in many ways, fairest demonstration which she gives of this state and of the difficulties facing Woman the Object and Woman the Image is to be found in *Les Belles Images*. . . .

Simone de Beauvoir's frequent references to mirrors in novels, essays and autobiography are far from being mere imitations of a literary device which can be traced from the legend of Narcissus to the works of Cocteau and Sartre. In her work mirrors are mentioned for a variety of reasons, which range from the creation of an interesting visual effect to the symbolical illustration of her philosophy; and an examination of these will not only [describe] the unfair image which she believes man to have created, but will, at the same time, illustrate how her personal preoccupations are apparent even in the relatively minor stylistic devices which she uses. . . .

It is . . . possible to relate this frequent use of mirrors not only to her philosophical but also to her feminist views, for the heroines who observe themselves are trying to find some meaning in their own lives, trying to achieve a proper identity: and the usual conclusion is that they have been duped, reduced to an empty image. . . .

For Simone de Beauvoir, woman is denied a true individuality, she is torn between the traditional cultural heritage of a man-made society and the desire of every human being to transcend the immanence. Woman is constantly seeking her true identity and it is this fruitless search which explains the frequent use of mirrors in Simone de Beauvoir's novels. . . . She claims that the mirror or mirror substitute is woman's normal solution in a society which has refused her adequate education and economic opportunity. . . . Thus the mirror in which Woman the Image gazes to find or to lose herself gives little comfort; reflections show up the inevitable emptiness of life, the inevitable emptiness of death. Woman the slave and the idol, woman the Object and the Image is denied a true existence. . . . *Les Belles Images* is also a commentary upon the illusory nature and emptiness of which these characters are the product. . . .

[*Les Belles Images*] presents many of the feminine problems and responses mentioned in *Le Deuxième Sexe* and, at the same time, it reveals the existentialist, autobiographical and political preoccupations which mark all Simone de Beauvoir's works.

*C. B. Radford, "Simone de Beauvoir: Feminism's Friend or Foe?," in* Nottingham French Studies, *October, 1967, pp. 87-102.*

Only a confirmed and utterly prejudiced misogynist would condemn every one of [the] proposals [in *Le Deuxième Sexe*]: only Simone de Beauvoir would advocate all of them in the particular way which she has chosen. The vehement and aggressive style and the extreme nature of many of her views show a personal flair and an outspokenness which are rare in any other feminist writer. In fact, far more than the theories, it is the personal flavour which is the distinctive element of her feminism. . . . More important at present, is the need to consider the way in which Simone de Beauvoir's views are, like man's, a distortion of woman. . . .

It is significant that in every novel the women are freed from many of the major problems which face women in real life. . . . In the lives of these heroines there are few social responsibilities; they escape from the difficulties of mediocrity; and most of Simone de Beauvoir's wives contrive to have a lover without marital disapproval or discovery. In this way her novels can only be seen as reflecting a reduced part of the feminist problem.

There is a danger that *Le Deuxième Sexe* has been influenced by the same narrowness of personal experience and outlook. A footnote which is frequently overlooked emphasizes the reality of this danger and suggests that, however far Simone de Beauvoir may delve into history and myth, however wide the range of countries from which she chooses examples to fan her anger, her primary concern is with Western Woman. . . . *Le Deuxième Sexe,* in spite of its length and the comprehensive nature suggested by the title, may have a narrower scope than appears at first sight. If then it can be shown that Simone de Beauvoir's own interpretations of the feminine situation have been attributed in some cases to an excessively large proportion of her sex, it will be clear that *Le Deuxième Sexe* is at times of limited value to the broad movement of feminism. . . .

It would, of course, be extravagant to suppose that Simone de Beauvoir has consciously tried to shape the whole of the female sex to some preconceived pattern closely resembling her own choice: such a suggestion would immediately be contradicted by the spirit of existentialism and her aim to bring women to a state of authentic liberty. It would be harder to refute the suggestion that, just as novels and *Le Deuxième Sexe* at times reveal a narrowness of personal experience even in someone as inquisitive and energetic as Simone de Beauvoir, so the individual problems of the writer herself may assume an exaggerated importance in her discussions of femininity. Suspicions that *Le Deuxième Sexe* presents an image which is distorted by autobiographical influences may be strengthened by a brief glance at three facets of the essay: the bourgeois element, the interpretation of myths, and lastly, a comparison between what she says is generally true and what she shows is personally true, the distinction being particularly noticeable when she discusses such subjects as death, maternity, family, shame and guilt.

The likelihood that *Le Deuxième Sexe,* beneath the comprehensive title, is primarily a middle-class document has already been mentioned. Some justification for this could be made, as it is within the range of middle-class women that a number of difficulties of purely social origin are most acutely experienced. On the other hand, some of Simone de Beauvoir's remarks about working-class women suggest, by traces of fantasy and sentimentality, that the author may be far happier when dealing with the class to which she has always belonged. Her description of adolescence is evidently made from a middle class viewpoint. An illustration of this can be seen in her account of the young girl's attitude towards nature. . . . Regrettably, not every girl has the opportunity to immerse herself in the beauty of natural surroundings; nor is the opportunity always enjoyed in quite the way which Simone de Beauvoir suggests. The description which is presented as common to all girls has instead the familiar ring of Simone de Beauvoir's own exuberant delight when she escaped to Meyrignac as a girl, when she went on a bicycling holiday with Sartre, when she wanders through French or Algerian countryside. . . .

Simone de Beauvoir is hardly original in seeing the link between feminism and socialism, nor in advocating educational reform and economic independence. . . . The originality of her contribution would therefore be limited to providing a link, whose importance would depend upon the breadth of her concerns and upon the modernizing of certain themes. . . . There can be no doubt that criticisms of her methods of argumentation, style, factual accuracy and the absence of a clearly defined route may, however valid, encourage the positive features of her work to be ignored.

*C. B. Radford, "Simone de Beauvoir: Feminism's Friend or Foe?," in* Nottingham French Studies, *May, 1968, pp. 39-53.*

Since the appearance of *Le Deuxième Sexe,* in such works as *Les Mandarins, La Force des Choses,* and *Une Mort très Douce,* her readers have seen Mme. de Beauvoir increasingly concerned with another "destiny". [In] *La Vieillesse* [in America, *The Coming of Age*], she has kept a promise made in *La Force des Choses* and given us a work on a topic that some of her readers have considered to be her particular obsession. Even more than in her book on women [*The Second Sex*], Simone de Beauvoir is concerned in *La Vieillesse* with the political economy of her problem. Perhaps this book will also come to be seen as the tocsin of some new liberation movement, this time of the old. But *La Vieillesse* bears the stamp of the deepened interest in limitations that has characterized French Existentialism since the early 1950s. . . . The givens and limitations of old age are much more compelling and depressing than those of femininity, and in *La Vieillesse* Mme. de Beauvoir is given a tougher run for her money: wrinkles, senility, physical decay and—most important of all—the gradual disappearance for the aged of the future that had made sense of the existentialist "projet", all serve to mock the freedom of the aged "pour-soi". In this respect *La Vieillesse* reveals a new dimension of that concern of Phenomenology and Existentialism with the human body. It treats a feature of the body not found in the work of Sartre and Merleau-Ponty: the body in decline.

Simone de Beauvoir does not wish to be accused of having slighted the facts of old age, and much of her book bears witness to a wide reading in the literature of science, medicine, anthropology, and history on the topic of aging. . . . [The] anti-scientific tone that some readers have detected in Existentialism is nowhere in evidence. If such a "new" respect for science does exist in *La Vieillesse* it may well represent the fifteen-years debate in France between adherents of Sartrean Existentialism and those of the Structuralism associated with Claude Lévi-Strauss. . . .

[Much] of this book . . . reveals, at the level of one "vécu", that of Simone de Beauvoir, how the difficulty of growing old can come to haunt one of the privileged. For *La Vieillesse* allows us to glimpse how she has lived her own growing old—the sense of "déja vu", the deaths of friends. . . .

They were wrong, those who saw in Existentialism only a modern form of despair. They had ignored the incredible optimism that found in the project a means for attaining real values in a world bounded by "non-sens". Although it is written in the glum style characteristic of Simone de Beauvoir, *La Vieillesse* maintains much of the spirit of that optimism. But in old age one Existentialist, at least, has found a tougher opponent than in other forms of determinism, and the horns of optimism have been drawn in ever so slightly. . . .

*T. H. Adamowski, "Death, Old Age, and Femininity," in* The Dalhousie Review, *Autumn, 1970, pp. 394-401.*

Like the children who clap for Tinkerbell, you have to believe in Simone de Beauvoir if you are going to take on [*All Said and Done*]. She is a very serious person and she expects to be taken very seriously. You have to remember exactly what she said about feminism in 1949 and be interested in how her views have altered; you have to know who were the friends of her youth and care what has happened to them since; you must recall what other people said about her and Sartre in the past, and mind if they were wrong. This is the fourth volume of her autobiography. . . . But it is really more like the last volume in a set of collected works, the one with notes, addenda, errata and so on, which no one would think of reading from cover to cover.

Simone de Beauvoir refuses 'to have the notion of "a work of art" attached to [her] autobiography. . . . [That] is a consumer term and to me it is shocking that it should be applied to the works of a creative writer.' This puritanically anti-capitalist attitude may be one of the reasons why her book has such an unlovely shape: after a couple of introductory chapters, the contents of her life are grouped under headings such as friends; books; travel; films; music; dreams; progressive causes—lists follow. Sometimes what she says is marvellous (for instance—unexpectedly, in view of her austerity—about Oscar Wilde); but sometimes it is so perfunctory and pedestrian that only a PhD student of her work could be expected to read on.

She has always been interested in time, in how people experience it and what it does to them: but, instead of a *Temps Retrouvé,* her account of what has happened to her friends reads like a Christmas news letter from across the Atlantic. . . .

When she published the preceding volume the critics accused her of pessimism because she told the truth; and the truth, especially about old age, was horrible. She argues that, on the contrary, she is an optimist: 'It is because I reject lies and running away that I am accused of pessimism; but this rejection implies hope—the hope that truth may be of use.' . . .

In her third volume she grumbled that middle-class women liked her first, *Memoirs of a dutiful daughter,* for the wrong reason. 'They enjoyed the accuracy with which I had depicted a milieu they recognised, but without being at all interested in the effort I had made to escape from it.' Well, middle-class or not, I wish there were a few more milieux in this volume. And, anyway, it was not just the milieux: the book was a wonderful account of what it is like to be young and thoughtful. Simone de Beauvoir can write so well, but she seems to think it frivolous to do so.

She can be petty and mildly paranoid about literary squabbles and political disagreements. She has little sense of humour, though some of her tales of the progressive conferences and marches that she and Sartre attended with tireless assiduity are full of involuntary comedy. . . .

It is a comedy of insensitivity, but the book is full of reflections and analyses which are quite the opposite.

*Gabriele Annan, "Serious Lady," in* The Listener, *June 6, 1974, pp. 740-41.*

Simone de Beauvoir's fourth (one can not with her predict any finality) autobiographical volume, *All Said And Done,* . . . offers us ten years (1962-72) not so much of experience realised (although this is exceptionally packed with incident) as an imaginative and intellectual transmutation of such experience. It is a deeply serious, wholly absorbing, and marvellously stimulating testimony which gives a complete feeling of maturity and confidence in the autobiographer who comes through with tremendous honesty and admirable lucidity and precision. Whatever reservations one may previously have had for one jocularly known as *La Grande Sartreuse,* are here thrown out. This is a splendid person, who had looked at herself, her friends and the world they share with an instinctive respect for truth, having, herself, in her own right, as Simone de Beauvoir, brought her best to a peak of creative achievement in this most contemporary *document de nos temps.* . . . One is full of admiration and respect for the wholeness of Simone de Beauvoir's world, meaning her total capacity to take it all in, to accept it, to learn it yet again, and assimilate its new findings as being part of any one person's natural capacity and experience.

*Kay Dick, "La Bonne Bouche," in* The Spectator *(© 1974 by The Spectator; reprinted by permission of* The Spectator*), June 8, 1974, p. 708.*

A portrait one might call "The French Intellectual in Majesty" belongs in every reader's imaginary museum. Your intellectual sits enthroned; a few of the saved cluster like cherubim overhead, while the naughty ones who would not listen to Reason writhe beneath his left foot. He wears a decipherable political label, though nothing else may be clear. He has left an account of a doomed world in which he apparently intended to be the sole survivor; he has also provided us with sublimely inaccurate and humorless descriptions of places and societies he was unable to fathom, for the simple reason that he was indifferent to them in the first place. In ["All Said and Done"] the [fourth] volume of her autobiography Simone de Beauvoir lives up to the set criteria. . . .

Her books have never been warm; this one is bloodless. . . . Her reports read like prim diaries, or, unforgivably, like tacked-together newspaper cuttings. There is an absence of vitality, of generosity, even of intellectual coherence. . . . The book abounds in misconceptions, in outright mistakes, in pointless exposition. . . . [We] are given one trifling fact after the other, in a style that has the dazed, ruminative rhythm of a French schoolgirl chewing gum at a concert in time to Bach. . . .

Gradually we wonder if the book was not after all written as a conscientious account of 10 years of the late 20th century for a civilization still to come, or for a civilization cut off from the world we take for granted; if it was not planned, in fact, for people who do not know how to read. If so, then it should not be judged as an ordinary autobiography. [In 1973] Simone de Beauvoir wrote to Le Monde protesting the refusal of Syria to give out information about Israeli prisoners. Because the plea ran counter to her known political views, the letter was treated as a news item and boxed on page two. . . . I mention it only because her letter had more grace, point, purpose and feeling than the entire 463 pages of "All Said and Done."

*Mavis Gallant, in* The New York Times Book Review *(© 1974 by The New York Times Company; reprinted by permission), July 21, 1974, p. 4.*

[Simone de Beauvoir] is sometimes a long-winded and humorless writer, and tutorial in a ponderous way. The first volume of her autobiography or a novel like *Les Mandarins* (1954) had more vivacity and direction than [*All Said and Done*], and one has to say that artists become diffuse when they become commentators. They generalize where they were once sharp and actual. But her confidence, her sanguine and energetic concern for the human condition are still bold. She is firm in her feminism and keeps her head about it. She fights back against the merely conventional notion that the minds of atheists are bleak and despairing because they do not believe in the afterlife; she is warm in her belief in the value of happiness and truth-telling; she has always been the enemy of stagnant "serenity": the incurious are, for her, the self-starved. She . . . willingly examines with detachment the differences she sees between the self of today and the self of twenty years ago. The energy, the genetic tonnage of vitality remains, but there *is*, she says, a loss of the sense of the future. . . .

The book does lack intimacy; but intimacy is impossible when one is writing about one's immediate past, except to occasional artists. The author has hardened too much into seeing people "in the light."

There are some interesting comments on reading—but these seem rather like republished reviews. . . . I prefer those pages in this long book when we get some sight of the woman inside the views. I cannot believe that she is all social conscience, all teacher, all self-management.

*V. S. Pritchett, "Simone Says," in* The New York Review of Books *(reprinted with permission from* The New York Review of Books; *© 1974 by NYREV, Inc.), August 8, 1974, p. 24.*

[*All Said and Done*] is the fourth volume of Simone de Beauvoir's autobiography; it is presented as being the last, but who knows? . . .

[It] has to be admitted . . . that *All Said and Done* is a much duller book than the previous volumes, perhaps because it does not really take us much beyond the stage reached in volume three. Simone de Beauvoir abandons the chronological sequence of narrative she had followed up till then to concentrate more on themes, and this she sees as an advantage. But she may have made the change unconsciously, because for the time being experience is not impinging upon her in any new way. Like most famous people, she is no doubt cushioned off from reality by her own celebrity and the part she has played; the role or the persona gets in the way of freshness of impression, without her being aware of this. . . . It is true that most people become more general and predictable as they grow older, because collective forces erode the gem of originality they started with. But this should happen less to existentialists than to others, since existentialism preaches the novelty of every fresh moment. Strangely enough, De Beauvoir frequently sounds quite bourgeois in her complacency, although anti-bourgeoisism is her staple attitude. Is this an effect of age or of an intellectual flaw?

She certainly remains a true Absurdist, because the book opens with a meditation on the basic bewilderment of the conscious mind faced with the mysterious fact that it belongs to *this* particular individual with *this* particular identity. So far so good. But the crucial problem for De Beauvoir, as for Sartre, remains the relationship between the Absurd and commitment, since their Absurdism is so much more subtle than the fluctuating dogmatism of their commitment. If the Absurd runs through everything, why does De Beauvoir remain so boringly leftist, when leftism has so often proved inadequate and its validity is far from self-evident? Once could accuse both Sartre and herself of being guilty of antibourgeois bad faith. Perhaps they have formed too close a mutual admiration society; perhaps their marriage of true minds was, in a sense, its own impediment. At any rate, there is something wrong, because volume four fails to show any deepening of perception or widening of perspective. But we can always look forward with existentialist hope to volume five.

*John Weightman, "Don't Be Absurd," in* Book World—The Washington Post *(©* The Washington Post*), August 18, 1974, p. 1.*

My disappointment with Simone de Beauvoir's . . . *All Said and Done* is very great. She is, of course, a serious writer who has usually written important and serious things (*The Coming of Age, The Second Sex,* etc.) but who now has very little new left to say. . . . She has always been a writer who writes too much and in this respect the new book does not disappoint us. Her interminable description of the geriatrical story of Sartre's mother's life illustrates both her indiscriminate inclusion of detail and her curious sense that everything of interest to her will be of interest to us, including all the stops on every journey, every opinion of films and plays she has seen, every book she wishes to discuss.

The interesting part of this book comes in the final seven . . . pages. Here she reexamines her important feminist views with an eye to changing some of her opinions in *The Second Sex.* The last paragraphs on her atheism are cogent and convincing. When she writes this way no one speaks more forcefully than does Beauvoir. But for the rest, it is long-winded, self-congratulatory, repetitious and pompous.

*Doris Grumbach, in* The New Republic *(reprinted by permission of* The New Republic; *© 1974 by The New Republic, Inc.), September 7, 1974, pp. 28, 30.*

* * *

## BECKETT, Samuel 1906-

**Beckett, born in Ireland, has lived in Paris, writing almost exclusively in French, since 1937. He is a novelist, short story writer, poet, translator, and essayist. But as a playwright, he is one of the major and most controversial literary figures of our time. His first play, *Waiting for Godot,* which has been called "not a play at all but an abstruse metaphysical disquisition," continues to perplex and infuriate, amuse and profoundly move its audiences. (See also *Contemporary Authors*, Vols. 5-8, rev. ed.)**

The only puzzling thing about *Godot* now is not the play, but the way we take it: why on earth has it ever accumulated such a reputation for determinism?

Part of the trouble is perhaps the way Beckett has been bracketed with Ionesco. Ionesco's characters often do talk like ticker tapes, and they are indeed pushed around helplessly by the circumstances of the world, by goods and chattels and uninspected banalities; but Beckett's characters are freely eloquent, with a speech that flies up out of the mundane and tugs in the air like a kite, and they live in a void which they alone have any power over or any obligation to change.

Whereas Ionesco's plays are crammed with disagreeably dynamic objects, cupboards that assume the initiative and chairs as fertile as rabbits, Beckett's plays habitually happen in an unfurnished void where the only significant object is the human figure, more or less ugly or infirm but all the same often wonderfully oblivious to it. Beckett's characters are anything but pure-dyed pessimists: like most people in real life, they are capable of feeling at one and the same time that existence is both insupportable and indispensable, and that they are both dying and also amazingly well. . . .

The urns and mounds that encumber the people in the later plays are not imposed; they are annexes of the characters' temperaments, traps created by their own past. Their physical equipment may be grotesquely inadequate for their tasks, but it is all they have, and they are constantly and comically pulling themselves together to mount another feeble attack on the objective, which is "to represent worthily for once the foul brood to which a cruel fate confined us." Beckett's characters are perpetually trying to carve out of the boundless gray flux a piece of time that will have some form and gaiety. They are devoted, in fact, to trying to make art out of the unpromising material of life, and to bringing off at least one achieved stylistic feat as a way of beating the dark. This isn't determinism.

In *Godot* the two tramps behave as though they had a sacred obligation to turn the day into a piece of music hall. It is impossible for them to sustain the effort for long, but they keep nerving themselves to have another go, standing back after a burst of backchat to have a look at the result as though they had to be their own audience in the void. "That wasn't a bad little canter," says Estragon encouragingly to them both after one spurt. *Godot* is a very affectionate play. . . .

In the first act the idiot . . . has a twitching tirade that employs a breakdown of language with more grief and horror than any other speech I can think of in our half century of experiments with incoherence. . . .

When a man writes with this noble comic stoicism he can break any rules he likes.

*Penelope Gilliatt, "Beckett" (1965), in her* Unholy Fools: Wits, Comics, Disturbers of the Peace: Film & Theater *(copyright © 1973 by Penelope Gilliatt; all rights reserved; reprinted by permission of The Viking Press, Inc.), Viking, 1973, pp. 21-3.*

[Beckett's] writing shows how artists are more sensitive to the burning theme that is hidden or repressed in any given period than the sociologists or reformers are. And indeed see it sooner.

Beckett is not moved by meliorist ideas but presents his old men and women as creatures who have entered a culture of frenzy, complete in itself, with its own rage of inquiry, its feverish speed of acute and changing sensation. They are at war not with death but with their own vitality. His old people are agonized by the life force that prevents them from dying. "What tedium!" cries his Molloy, continuously, contemptuously. Beckett joins those writers who reject the idea of serenity with the frightful hilarity of people forced to survive. His fever is different from the fever of Chateaubriand's eloquent self-loathing, but both contain their truth and an illumination: when we recognize the inevitable, we are strengthened to bear it or (more important in a selfish society that values long life) to endure it in others.

*V. S. Pritchett, "Growing Old," in* The New York Review of Books *(reprinted with permission from* The New York Review of Books; *© 1972 by NYREV, Inc.), July 20, 1972, pp. 3-4.*

The English in this review [of *The Lost Ones*] has been translated from the original French by the present writer and the French has been translated from the original English by the present writer. Le cheval trottait au bord de la mer. Enter Murphy, Watt, Molloy, Krapp, Malone (before he dies) displaying more pricks than kicks. Eh Joe, are you listening now, you who are as old as yonder elm standing erect among the hitherandthithering waters of where-you-will? Une jolie place, avec un square, des vélums crème ou orange, à toutes les maisons. Beckett keeps playing the old tune, is it in Dublin now at Trinity College and saying yes yes yes I will yes or is it in Paris where he says no no no I won't no and has has had at least three conversations with Georges Duthuit? Jacques Joyce avait son imperméable sur lui pendant sa neuvaine. Samuel Beckett was born in Ireland, God help him, but has lived most of his life out of it, mainly in France. The best day's work he ever did was to clear the hell out of Dublin where literary men live on peanuts and Guinness and hate each other's guts and become drunks or failures with as much chance of getting the old Nobel as a castrated donkey. Yeats got it but he never drank with the boys. Beckett alone has dared to name the Unnamable and tell us frankly How It Is. How Is It, Sam? C'était le crépescule. Elles portaient des paquets? Oui, oui, there's wee Willie Wee. But who was I talking about? Ah, yes I remember him well. Beckett, so rumour has it, was a great friend of Maurice Chevalier who influenced Jacques Joyce himself who laid hands on young Sam (well, in the literary sense). Did I tell you *The Lost Ones* (I am reviewing it in case you have forgotten you illiterate twerp) was translated by S Beckett from S Beckett's *Le Dépeupleur* and that those two intellectual rubbishers Calder and Boyars say it is S Beckett's most sustained text to appear for many years. Well now, doesn't that news warm the cockles of yer poor ole 'eart. It was written in 1966, according to C and B, except for the last paragraph which was added in 1970. Last paragraphs are the very devil. That's why it's better not to write in paragraphs at all. Quand ils avaient bu, ils voyaient le monde autrement. I'd write the whole effing review in Voltaire's tongue but for one thing. No, it doesn't worry me that you stupid buggers wouldn't catch on. A purely practical reason—no accents on my Remington Home Portable. There are 63 pages in this book including what the rubbishers call prelims and the type is so big it reminds me of those cards opticians show you with real big print. I'm no accountant but I've worked out the cost at roughly 20p per 1,000 words. Not bad, as any ICA culture vulture would tell you. Est-ce qu'il y avait encore besoin d'explications? Excuse me now, I've a date with Murphy, Watt, Molloy, Krapp and Malone. Then we will all wait for Godot.

*Robert Greacen, "'The Lost Ones'," in* Books and Bookmen, *October, 1972, p. 78.*

In practice, . . . though Beckett's are anti-novels, anti-plays, and anti-short-stories—that is, anti-constructive—they cannot quite achieve nothingness, the formal perfection of formlessness, or we should have no evidence that zero is what they are moving towards: a deathly negation. It is significant, however, that his volume of collected non-short-stories is entitled *No's Knife,* his latest non-play *Not I*. The nihilism of which this urge to negation is an expression can, of course, be hilarious—by debunking, for instance. . . . In *Waiting for Godot* the philosophic generality —one place, in leaf and leafless, to stand minimally for Space and Time, two pairs of characters all with different national names, to stand for Mankind—allows us to laugh at sufferings we need not pity (as these are notions rather than persons). The devices of non-sequitur, non-listening and non-action—typical of most theatre of the absurd—amusingly undermine common assumptions, allow an audience the pleasure of relaxing the daily effort of politeness, attention, and purposiveness. A similar claim can be made for *Endgame* and, a little more dubiously, for *Happy Days*. But these plays all retain some links with the theatre of *vital* form in which, as in life, the disintegrative temptation of the death-wish is held at bay. Such form controls, without killing the human energies of the content. Beckett's plays simply by getting shorter—down to half a minute—have less and less working form: a fact, of course, inseparable from their having less and less to say about less and less (till *Breath,* logically, says nothing about nothingness and is itself formally next to nothing). The characters keep pace: at first doddery and down-and-out, but mobile, next almost immobilised in dustbins, then quite immobilised in earth, and finally annihilated. It is sometimes said that their broken utterances mysteriously "add up to a life." No, they subtract down to a death, and the play's formal progress towards symbolic burial and annihilation, towards absence, perfectly parallels the contentual progress towards silence.

This inevitably follows from Beckett's basic premises. . . . A nihilist is one for whom everything has no value and no price, so that living is seen as a matter of finding ways to pass the time (which would pass anyway) till death relieves us of the unwelcome burden of life. A view that can produce much amusement by mocking the pursuits and beliefs we normally take seriously, some of them, perhaps, genuinely more seriously than they deserve. But such an idea necessarily implies that there is no point in positive effort. The only point therefore is to point out the pointlessness of everything—and why not, then, the pointlessness of pointing? That is why the only logical end is silence and a form that disappears up its own analogical end. Equally clearly the only bearable attitude in face of such a belief—especially when decrepitude is taken as the human norm—is stoicism.

Traditionally, "stoicism" rings of nobility, whether real, as with Boethius and Socrates, or religious (putting the clock fast) as with Seneca. Beckett is different. His is an ignoble stoicism. His non-character in "The End" refers to ". . . the story I might have told, a story in the likeness of my life, I mean, without the courage to end or the strength to go on." . . . This *is* the story Beckett tells, over and over, edging to a literary death as his impersonages edge to a literal one—sans action, sans character, sans plot, sans words, sans everything. Like Buddha, Beckett desiderates Nirvana, but it is for him not a spiritual progress to an abstract state; it is a physical regress to a material one. While waiting, passing the time, his derelicts are not so much *going* to ground as stoically letting the ground get them back. Being down to earth is certainly an anti-romantic virtue; carried to logical but absurd lengths it becomes a form of decadent romanticism, for it indulges a despair in excess of that warranted by the full facts, necessarily dangerous to life and art, and destructive of both form and content: "All I say cancels out, I'll have said nothing" ("The Calmative," *No's Knife*, p. 26).

Actually, Beckett is exaggerating, making the worst of things as usual. Even in his late works he says—or, anyway, implies—just a little more than nothing; and they can still be gruesomely funny, though less consistently so than *Waiting for Godot* and *Endgame*. Minimal as they are, they still exist, at the common vanishing-point of tragedy, farce, and nihilistic comedy. It is even true that they have some value apart from that of being debunking, pessimistic correctives to over-optimistic attitudes. For Beckett's is the bitter grin of displaced pity; and this affects both content and form, neither being quite so negative as it seems. . . . This results at its best in mithridatic tragi-comedy, enabling us to endure, if not to enjoy life. It forces us to face the plight of the badly stricken, and allows us to bear the sight, by defensive laughter. To put it in more specific, practical terms, Beckett indicates a way of death-in-life for the aged, the imprisoned or the bedridden; shows the spirit of non-resistance needed to pass the time with fewer and fewer resources, to make do with less and less, make the best of bad businesses, be thankful for ever-smaller mercies, "keep faith with death." His works are, as it were, Get Worse cards for those in hospital, in the end bed. And that is something. The question is whether it is enough—let alone the feast that would ratify his current reputation. The answer, surely, is surely not; and the reason for that answer lies precisely in the admired logic of his development, since it is a logical progression, as we have seen, from fallacious premises.

The basic flaw, the hole in your Beckett, seems to be this: for all their façade of modernism his plays are medieval in their assumption that the end of life is the whole of life, that if there is no purpose or reason beyond life there cannot be any purposes or reasons within it—false conclusions, both of them. He is, then, philosophical but not reasonable. In the long view, it may be just to see life as essentially a painful progress to the grave, disguised by self-deception and play-acting. But on nihilistic premises themselves the long view should be no more valid than short views, the essential than the contingent; and this particular long view happens not only to be false, but also to be psychologically and artistically stultifying. In fact, as we read or watch, we know that for the better part of their lives most people are not ill, poor, impotent, crippled and bored, nor even bedevilled by spiritual despair; that along with the loneliness of the human situation goes the sociability of people, along with some misery some happiness—at any rate until we become too badly stricken. This secret knowledge is what makes the gruesomeness funny and the toughmindedness sentimental.

Beckett, in short, springs a typically symbolist trap: making a part stand for the whole, but choosing an unrepresentative part. We fall for it, if we do, because the apparently unsentimental toughness of attitude and the formally seamless, "uncluttered" world created, con us into taking his truthfulness about the part as the Whole Truth about the whole.

Paradoxical to the end, he exaggerates by *minifying* reality. The more negative he is, the more exaggerated his claim. The more unflinching his gaze the less he sees—and reveals. And, it would seem, the less he creates, the more we admire. Perhaps they were right, those admen who took for their selling-point to a gullible public not the solid mint but that perfect form of negation, the hole in the middle.

*Allan Rodway, "There's a Hole in Your Beckett," in* Encounter, *February, 1974, pp. 49-53.*

In the beginning was the Word, the Word was made Flesh, but Word forsook the Flesh, Flesh cried aloud but no one could hear it and Word rattled and shook and grew bigger.

And then, quite by accident, Samuel Beckett became fashionable. He murdered silence with a bauble of truth, and grew and grew until he became a cautionary tale. He was fashionable for the right reasons, and nothing would go right any more.

True, he is the last of his kind. He is the last romantic, threshing about in the darkness of a more and more constricted space, and his prose is as lyrical on his own behalf as anything in the *Prelude* or *Les Fleurs Du Mal*. The scene has changed from the gleaming hills and allies of the pathetic fallacy, but the pigmy 'I' still frets across the stage and makes its own kind of peace: "I am down in the hole the centuries have dug, centuries of filthy war, flat on my face on the dark earth sodden with the creeping saffron water it slowly drinks." Ah, how pleasant it is to be whole again, to be capable of hurt and with the breath to sing of it. Even if it is your last breath. Beckett is something of a humanist, and humanists prefer unhappy endings.

*Texts for Nothing* has thirteen steps. The 'texts' were written during the period of *Godot* and *Molloy*, and they are codicils to that creative self-destruction which seemed then to be the lovely, hopeless riposte to death and megadeath. The 'voice' or 'tone', that machine which grinds on when all else fails, is constant and uniform. This is the portrait of the artist as old and woe-begone, but using harmonies like nobody else.

Of course it has become common knowledge that Beckett, as the blurb says in its indefinably vulgar way, "has destroyed the continuing possibilities of the competent narrative novel and the well-made play seen in terms of art." The common knowledge is wrong. Beckett's little me is perfectly aesthetic, a harmoniser, a teller of truths, a "character." The whole work is as stylised and as constructive as a sonnet by Sir Philip Sidney.

Only a rhetorician could be so melancholy, and Mr Beckett has chosen his devices with an academic's care. *Anacolouthon,* grammatic incoherence, *aposiopesis,* the abrupt pause, and *litotes,* deliberate understatement, are only the most obvious in a pantheon of special effects. *Antonomasia* is, naturally, the goddess and it is through her that a tramp can lie in the gutter and not only see the stars but be them, too. Mr Beckett, as I said, is a humanist and will reify 'man' precisely because it is at its worst.

Only a humanist could employ rhetoric so that it became popular again, but only a romantic would need to. The omnipresent 'I', the collage for all ages, is defended by the strict conventions of Mr Beckett's prose and at the same time it is lost among them. Little Me is continually looking for an origin, a point of entry, a time when Word and Flesh were conjoined for better or worse. In the present tense, it dips and floats on the surface of a continuing monologue: "But there is not silence. No, there is utterance, somewhere someone is uttering." It has not escaped Beckett that Beckett is responsible. Anxiety is a precious bloom; it must be handled carefully and not allowed to disappear. Beckett may be a writer by default, but he knows exactly what he must do: "Nothing ever but nothing and never, nothing ever but lifeless works."

*Peter Ackroyd, in "Baubles, Bangles, Pearl Beads," in* The Spectator *(© 1974 by* The Spectator; *reprinted by permission of* The Spectator*), March 30, 1974, pp. 393-94.*

[*Texts for Nothing*] represents the culmination of Beckett's prose tetralogy, which starts with *Molloy, Malone Dies* and *The Unnamable*. More concise, more concentrated and filled with deeper and more pregnant silences than the books which precede them, these *Texts for Nothing* are perhaps more difficult of access to the unprepared reader than the *Three Novels,* but they are certainly no less rewarding. None of Beckett's *novels* really [belongs in] the category of narrative prose usually defined by that term: they are internal monologues, profound and rigorous descriptions of introspective experiences and as such both more *documentary* and, at the same time, far more *lyrical* than the conventional novel. The *Texts for Nothing,* being shorter and even more devoid of any 'narrative content' than the three 'novels', are purer and more lyrical—they are far nearer to 'poems in prose', a transition towards the even more rigidly formal late Beckett of *The Lost Ones* and *Lessness.*

Here then is Beckett in his essence, in his most concentrated form: a writer to be savoured slowly and with full attention, read and reread, pondered and digested, not a superficial read but an existential experience which, when it is truly assimilated, enters into the very fabric and fibre of the reader's being and effects a lasting change in the manner of his perception of the world.

What concerns Beckett in all his writings, and in these *Texts for Nothing* more clearly than most of his other works, is an exploration into the nature of the Self, of human identity. The stream of consciousness, which inevitably is also an endless stream of language, of words, that passes through our brain and which comprises all our awareness, awake or dreaming, is perceived by Beckett as a succession of voices telling stories. But—whose voices are they? If we could track down the source of these voices, if we could penetrate to the ultimate speaker we would have found our own identity. But there is a snag: if we listen to the voices of our own consciousness: who *is* it who *listens* and *who* speaks? And is the *speaker* the true self? or the *listener*? The moment we become aware of this dichotomy, of this schizophrenic split in our minds between the observer and the observed, we have created a further split: for now a third entity observes the observer—and so forth ad infinitum: '. . . who's this speaking in me, and who's this disowning me, as though I had taken his place . . .' (Text No XII).

The ultimate observer, the last listener who listens to all the voices of consciousness, is ever elusive; to find the Self would mean to transcend the Self, to throw off the shackles of its endless compulsion to listen. Ultimately therefore Beckett's quest is the mystic's quest for the loss of the Self, or rather, the illusion that there is such an entitiy as the Self; and through losing the Self to enter into Union with the ultimate essence of the universe which has no voice and no shape and is free from the frustrations and limitations of *being in the world,* of existence. Non-being, however, is 'being nothing'. The mystic's striving is a striving for non-being, a striving to become Nothing. Hence the title *Texts for Nothing*. But to be free from consciousness, to be nothing, also means that the suffering being who aches and writhes under the torments of being, will never, never in all eternity be able to enjoy the pleasure of knowing that he no longer *is*. The mystic's striving is therefore paradoxical: it is this irony which produces the laugh, 'the long silent guffaw of the knowing non-exister . . .' (Text No XII).

And if, alas, Man can never enjoy that irony and the pleasure of that long laugh, he can, having had the courage to face the inevitable pain of existence, at least revel in the sense of that irony. That is why Beckett, having plunged into the deepest reaches of human despair emerges from it, triumphantly, with a laugh. Beckett is a humorist, a comic writer, simply because having confronted the worst and having come to terms with it, there is nothing left but to laugh at the ridiculousness of the human condition and its hopelessness. It is a kind of divine gallows-humour, the serenity of one who has come to terms with the full inevitability of his condition. What is inevitable and cannot be helped causes no pain; only the disappointment of frustrated expectations and shattered illusions makes us suffer. Having realised the illusoriness of the Self, how can we take *ourselves* seriously?

And why should the artist, Beckett himself, take the trouble of creating his work, which, seen against the ultimate futility of endless time and inevitable death, also is, literally *for nothing?* . . . Why write it down? The answer lies plainly before us as we read: it lies in the beauty of the language, the power of the images and their intrinsic truth, which is born from the courage of a noble mind, bold enough to face the truth. The serenity of a mind able to laugh about the realities of the human condition is the ultimate positive element in the gloom. For this is what the Greeks called *catharsis,* the feeling of exaltation and peace which arises at the end of the most horrifying tragedy, namely that the human spirit is able to face up to harsh realities and transform horror into beauty.

*Texts for Nothing* is undoubtedly a masterpiece—not easily accessible, but endlessly rewarding for those who have the good fortune of possessing the power of concentration and the humility to approach it. They will return to it over and over again.

*Martin Esslin, "Worth the 'Wait'," in* Books and Bookmen, *June, 1974, pp. 91-2.*

* * *

## BENCHLEY, Peter 1940-

**Benchley is an American novelist and writer for children. (See also *Contemporary Authors*, Vols. 17-18.)**

The jaws are a white killer shark's; their maulings keep a Long Island resort in terror. Like that shark, this first novel by Peter Benchley—third in the line of writing Benchleys—survives by steady motion: to still it for close scrutiny is to sink it. But "Jaws" keeps its pace; it is a fluid entertainment.

The shark's shreddings provide the novel's supports; the story is strung between them. . . .

Even for a fish story, "Jaws" may be a mite malodorous. The shark is as disconcertingly omnipresent as the town is defenselessly flaccid before its peril. "No mortal man is going to catch that fish," intones Minnie the postmistress, and the way *these* mortals hand it she doesn't have to hedge her bets. Briney connections, occasional florid or sentimental lapses, stark manipulations impair the narrative. Passages of hollow portentousness creep in, as do clattering allusions—perhaps inevitable—to the Great American fish felon, Moby Dick. But the shark is so menacingly adequate an [embodiment] of imagined malignity that, even though its attacks are telegraphed, they fix one's attention. In these scenes the novel's faults are forgotten. Other times, they circle restlessly like fins.

*Andrew C. J. Bergman, in* The New York Times Book Review *(© 1974 by The New York Times Company; reprinted by permission), February 3, 1974, p. 14.*

"Jaws" is awful.

"Jaws" has rubber teeth for a plot.

"Jaws" is stunningly bad, a . . . fish-opera featuring cardboard people and an overblown shark. "Jaws" is a failure in almost every way possible for a novel to fail. It's boring, pointless, listless, bewitched by banality; if there's a trite turn to make, "Jaws" will make that turn. It seeks new reaches of tedium. It packs more padding than a pound box of surgical cotton. It is weary; vacant; tasteless. . . .

Remember Huston's rubber whale in "Moby Dick"? Or Disney's 100-foot rubber squid in "20,000 Leagues Under the Sea"? Perhaps a 20-foot man-eating shark doesn't sound like much rubber beside a rubber whale or a rubber squid, but Peter Benchley's moviebound "Jaws" tries hard to stretch its dummy fish to the same big evil—the Devil in fish flesh.

The first 230 pages are a shuddering yawn, a mind-sapping yawn, a yawn that topples the stone-heavy reader into a poisoned coma, canyons of bottomless falling, falling, down into the belts of sleep below 300 fathoms where the nerves flake into fish fluff. . . .

The climax does have a scenery-chewing, ballbreaker harpooner, Quint, a storm, more blood, and a Melville parody ending. And it's phony, Quint's phony, . . . Benchley's phony, even the shark's phony. There's not a single detail that convinces me that Benchley ever grabbed anything more dangerous than the stem of a martini, and certainly not the tail of a shark.

I think what hurts most is the shark. It lacks sharkness, a marvelous, strange sharkness to imperil my dreams. I could forgive everything, maybe, if at least I got some sense of poetry from the shark. All I get is the smell of research. Never do I feel the shiver of reading a sentence by a man who has looked a shark straight in the eye and grabbed me by the shirt to tell me about it.

*Donald Newlove, in* The Village Voice *(reprinted by permission of* The Village Voice; *© 1974 by The Village Voice, Inc.), February 7, 1974, pp. 23-4.*

In Peter Benchley's first novel, *Jaws,* the animal is the bad guy: a huge white shark that appears off the coast of a small Long Island resort town and proceeds to lunch on hapless bathers, much to the chagrin of the local tourist industry. . . . Much tension here, or so one would think: Should they close the beaches? Who's going to get eaten next? How are they going to catch the creature? Who (in a distinctly contrived subplot) is screwing the police chief's wife?

One dutifully finishes the book to find out the answers, which probably qualifies this as a page-turner, but somehow the suspense and snap just really aren't here. Benchley claims he wanted to keep this a serious novel, as well as a best seller, and that was probably his mistake. None of the humans are particularly likable or interesting; the shark was easily my favorite character—and, one suspects, Benchley's also. But then sharks don't buy books. Maybe if the sex subplot had paired the police chief's wife with the shark . . . but that, most certainly, would have been a whole different kettle of fish.

*Michael Rogers, in* Rolling Stone *(© 1974 by Straight Arrow Publishers Inc.; all rights reserved; reprinted by permission), April 11, 1974, p. 75.*

Peter Benchley's best-selling first novel *Jaws* is haunted intermittently by the shades of *Moby Dick* and *The Old Man and the Sea.* At its centre is the duel between a man and a monster fish—a killer shark which terrorises the beaches of a small Long Island holiday resort. The metaphysical overtones are played down but the faint resonance they leave is enough to make the book more than a good thriller. The characterisation of the humans is fairly rudimentary and better so, for when Benchley attempts more detail he achieves only the ready-made. The shark, however, is done with exhilarating and alarming skill and every scene in which it appears is imagined at a special pitch of intensity.

*John Spurling, in* New Statesman, *May 17, 1974, p. 703.*

* * *

## BENEDIKT, Michael 1935-

**Benedikt is an American poet, critic of art, film, and music, and translator. (See also *Contemporary Authors*, Vols. 15-16.)**

Benedikt's poetry strikes me as being New and Improved, like soap. This is too bad, because his first book, *The Body,* was so good. In *Sky* he is slicker, more clever, more polished in his own Ogden Nashian unpolished way, but he has lost the sense of discovery that he had in *The Body.* There's no doubt that many of the poems in *Sky* are funny, but beyond that they don't do much for me. . . . I do like it when Benedikt's humor fastens on mundane or arbitrary things. He gives you a sense of the completely arbitrary structure of many aspects of life. . . . Benedikt's strategy is to take things literally, as they manifest themselves; this gives his poetry a point of view slanted enough and yet familiar enough so that ordinary things become strange and humorous and random. But the trouble is, this is pretty one-sided. When *everything* is random and arbitrary, poetry is finished; there's no sense in writing anymore. Ideas for poems become more or less expendable. You have to start writing list poems, as Benedikt does. List all the names for the baby, all the ways people undress, the various things an arm can do, the things that don't work, etc. Or simply list the things you see walking down the street. . . . This is that same kind of languid eagerness to record, without any selectivity, that one associates with a lot of New York art, especially with Andy Warhol's movies. Selectivity implies that some things are more important than others, for any number of reasons; poetry, in fact, is the act of discovery of those things and those reasons. What was good about Benedikt's first book, *The Body,* was the sense you got of wading through lots of junk and clutter in order to find important things and to find weird and new connections between them. In *Sky,* there is the junk and clutter, and a slightly more polished style, as well as a little more wit, but nothing else, no discovery, no important things, no weird connections. Everything is flattened out and exists side by side, the interesting and the dull. It's all a rather mildly entertaining background with no figure or figures set against it. Benedikt wants you to like it, although he doesn't want to appear to try too hard; and so he describes it, makes a few funny observations, artlessly disparages himself and his artlessness, and moves on, never engaging anything that he's described, and consequently never engaging the reader.

*John Vernon, in* Western Humanities Review, *Spring, 1971, pp. 193-94.*

Modern poetry has accomplished the significant task of extending the range of poetic humor. Lightness, parody, and sheer giggle have been combined to elbow out a little more dimension. Michael Benedikt's newest book, *Mole Notes,* is a collection of digs toward another fantastic nether-netherland.

Mole is Benedikt's protagonist. He burrows and squints his way into terrestial activities, makes a few down-to-earth comments, concludes with an appropriate understatement, and wriggles back into the ground. Mole is seen only on occasion, though he is usually felt to be somewhere underfoot. He likes to read and "if Mole seems to be a sort of bookworm it's probably because of all the literature he finds in the garbage can." His discourses are erudite enough to include a lecture on (who else?) Molière. Mole is an innocent whose simplicity cuts through muddy platitudes, whose blindness is only physical. . . .

*Mole Notes* is composed of a series of prose poems, and all too often it exhibits the pitfalls of the genre. It has a frequent tendency to get carried away, leaving the reader baffled and irritated. The humor sometimes becomes shrill; the free-form associations sometimes seem interminable and dull. The fun often seems silly, and whatever profundity may creep beneath the whimsy is probably lost forever. At his best, Benedikt's prose poems are quick and amusing. At his worst, they are only paragraphs in shambles.

Contriving a method for presenting humor through poetry has always been a difficult task. And for this, *Mole Notes* may be more admirable for what it attempted than for what it achieved.

*W. G. Regier, "Demolition," in* Prairie Schooner *(©1973 by University of Nebraska Press; reprinted by permission from* Prairie Schooner*), Spring, 1973, pp. 86-7.*

* * *

## BERGSTEIN, Eleanor 1938-

**Ms Bergstein is an American novelist and short story writer. (See also *Contemporary Authors*, Vols. 53-56.)**

*Advancing Paul Newman* is two stories, with the same characters, told contrapuntally. . . .

For a novel, especially a first novel, to remain compulsively readable for almost 400 pages in which short sequences intercut two levels of time is a feat; here the conception works completely. Instead of rendering a sense of displacement, each fragment blends into the text with an urgency that increases as the book goes on. Bergstein's ear is very fine; the prose rhythms are superbly controlled, and the slightly elegiac tone of the retrospective segments brings a satisfying throb to the infighting and couplings of the campaign. The two narratives play on each other, just as Ila's and Kitsy's sexual involvements and political activities merge in a way that makes it impossible to separate cause and effect. Bergstein combines her materials to create an extraordinarily rich mixture. . . .

In *Advancing Paul Newman,* memories of Manhattan and the Beatles and sex and assassinations and movies come together to form the texture of a decade that has been lived through; and, despite the speed of the prose, the novel has the leisurely feel of a reverie. In getting to the essence of how we look back on a just-vanished era, Bergstein does what the makers of *American Graffiti* were said to have done, and without the aid of a soundtrack for instant nostalgia.

Ila and Kitsy are swallowed up into the fecundity of this texture; during the reading I was caught up in their ambitions and griefs and rivalries, but in thinking of them afterward they don't exist for me outside of the novel's locales and events. They are clearly set, and I don't forget them; but I don't connect them with people I meet in life, as I do the characters in some other novels that are close to me. Although Bergstein probably intended for Ila and Kitsy to be more vivid than they are, their evanescence isn't a flaw. If they were stronger the novel's carefully achieved balance between contrasting moods might be thrown off, and the book might lose its air of constant surprise. The men are easily identifiable while you're reading about them, but when you've finished it's hard to remember which was which. In a novel that gave us nothing but characters reacting to each other, this kind of blurring would be fatal; but the forgettableness of these possibly tiresome males who do keep things going without any bother makes it easier to enjoy everything else. . . .

Better than any other novel I can think of, *Advancing Paul Newman* tells us the way part of the American experience of the '60s was; but it doesn't tell us why. If it did, it would be a complete vision; but to engross us and even to transform our view of the past as it does, its vision doesn't need to be complete. Effortlessly assured, it has none of the tentativeness of a "first novel." Eleanor Bergstein knows how to bring emotion to the surface without leaving her readers to wallow in it. She knows how to begin a long novel on a high and sustain it, even while including elements of tragedy. Her debut is exhilarating from start to finish and is a major work.

*John Alfred Avant, in* The New Republic *(reprinted by permission of* The New Republic; *© 1974 by Harrison-Blaine of New Jersey, Inc.), February 23, 1974, pp. 26-7.*

The characters [in *Advancing Paul Newman*] live brilliantly in stroboscopic flashes, but try to see them whole and they vanish before your eyes. Well, that's "the point," perhaps; but I wish the novel were able to transcend the problem it sets for itself, for I fear it too will evanesce sooner than it should. To read *Advancing Paul Newman* with perfect sympathy and understanding you ought to remember the look of the lipstick marks on the cover of *Goodbye, Columbus,* still feel frissons at the mention of the Janice Wylie murder—after all, didn't you live just a couple of blocks away?—and be at least able to identify Sam and Curtis and Jessica in the McCarthy campaign. Read now, with the decade just slipping from one's own imaginative grasp, it stirs continual feelings of recognition, of rightness. A reader twenty years hence may find it just as baffling as *Finnegans Wake.*

*Richard Todd, in* The Atlantic Monthly *(copyright © 1974 by The Atlantic Monthly Company, Boston, Mass.; reprinted with permission), May, 1974, pp. 130-32.*

* * *

## BERRIGAN, Daniel J. 1938-

**Berrigan, an American, was formerly a Jesuit priest. He is a**

**poet, essayist, and social activist. (See also *Contemporary Authors*, Vols. 33-36.)**

[*Love, Love at the End*] is a thing of great potency. While it contains very few "poems" as one gets into the habit of defining poems, nearly all of these "parables, prayers and meditations" take structure from imagery. . . .

[While] it is true that both Berrigan and his brother have certainly gone as fervently to the streets as anybody, it seems to me the poet and priest have survived without being corrupted—that the priest has prospered greatly, and the poet has found new spine for his work. . . .

In all, this is a strong book, both religious and worldly—a scarifying vision, even when oblique, of the kind of adventure we have pursued in Southeast Asia.

*Robley Wilson, Jr., "Five Poets at Hand," in* The Carleton Miscellany, *Fall, 1968, pp. 117-20.*

Daniel Berrigan, priest and poet, flew to Hanoi to bring three captured American fliers home. [*Night Flight to Hanoi*] is his journal and, as well, a set of eleven poems based on the experience. It is certainly a promising subject, and Father Berrigan has proven himself in the past to be a poet of some skill. What the book is, however, is a manifestation of the moral hysteria which has swept the minds of so many good men over the past few years. Father Berrigan, motivated by love and moral anguish, condemns the United States for its behavior in an "immoral" war, but then he goes on to exalt Lenin and Ho Chi Minh to the status of modern saints. He condemns the fliers he rescued because they still believed in America after their confinement, because they did not succumb to the Communist teachings of their captors. What began as a book of love ends as a book of hate. Father Berrigan becomes the merciless accuser of a God of revenge and violence. The book is a frightening document, for in it poet becomes mouthpiece for propaganda and priest becomes prosecutor. It is a flight into a night of moral rage; there is no dawn of new love and understanding at the end of that flight.

Virginia Quarterly Review, *Vol. 45, No. 1, Winter, 1969, p. xx.*

A considerable part of my purpose in this review [is] to suggest that contemporary poetry in America finds it difficult to make simple, unadulterated statements. . . . Of all the poets I have been reading, I should have supposed Daniel Berrigan would have been most direct: here, after all, is a man involved in action as very few of us have allowed ourselves to become involved. But action must have another idiom than the one I would have assigned to it; the man acting is something other than what I thought he was, or is reflected in different mirrors. Berrigan's work, which I would have supposed revolutionary and absolute, is instead involute: the mind that can consider the possibility of action is extraordinarily intricate before it starts. . . .

I do not think that this poetry [*Encounters*] is very public . . . , rather, it seems the poetry of a public position, what is said by someone who has confused the private and the public roles. I think that such a confusion is easier than it ought to be in our time, and I can hardly fault Berrigan for having allowed it. But I still feel that the nimbus of his language is instructing me without having the direct right to instruct me. The elevation of the language is like and unlike the elevation of the Host; the first elevation assumes that I share a ritual in which, as it happens, I am not a participant.

*William Dickey, "Public and Private Poetry," in* The Hudson Review *(copyright © 1972 by The Hudson Review, Inc.; reprinted by permission), Vol. XXV, No. 2, Summer, 1972, pp. 295-308.*

Father Berrigan's major purpose [in *America is Hard to Find*] is to defend his anti-government actions and those of his associates. This purpose is inseparable from another purpose, the attack upon America, the decent, healthy heart of which is, for the author, hard to find. It's difficult to find out from the book what it is which makes up this hard-to-find America but the tone suggests that it is that magnificent potential for greatness to which Nick Carraway referred in another expression of disillusion with American life, "The Great Gatsby." But if the elements of this America are hard to find in the book, the elements which have crushed it are not: the military mind, police power, the F.B.I., and the collapse of American morality under the weight of American technology. "Who owns this land anyway?" Berrigan asks and though he answers that we, the people, do he implies that it is being taken from us by the powers just mentioned.

Father Berrigan's anger and bitterness are great and of contemporary commentators on the American civilization few whites have spoken so harshly. Strangely enough, this passionate Jesuit sounds like the wild-eyed Henry Miller who could digest neither American food nor American manners. But where Miller took refuge in rancor and concentration on human aberrations which, unfortunately, he could not transcend himself, Father Berrigan concentrates his actions and ideas into a revolutionary role which at times, alas, takes on the appearance of a sought-for martyrdom. There is, however, no single picture of Father Berrigan to be taken from the book. In those sections which read like prose poems he appears as a sort of visionary, Whitman-like in his symbolic vision of American life. In his letters home he is the attentive son and brother, attached to his family with restraint, dignity, yet with passion. In the essays, which seem to be the backbone of his expression from the underground (hiding from the authorities) he is both an expositor of the conditions of American life and an exhorter to overt action against the government, the military, and police mentality.

As exhorter Berrigan fluctuates between exhortations to overt actions and admiration for the quiet yet deep and significant moral life. Unfortunately, the tone of the former dominated that of the latter. Though moved by his call to overt action, I was also troubled by it for it rendered hollow his professions of belief in a quiet life—for example, one dedicated to the moral and physical stability of family. When he recommended such overt action as that of individuals and their families camping on the White House grounds until specific decisions are made I said yes, yes, yes, but almost simultaneously wondered at the potential horror and even absurdity of its impracticality. Could I bring eight small children to the White House grounds without the whole of my personal venture crumbling into an absurd exhibition of the waywardness, frailty, and innocence of these children? I don't wish to overemphasize this particular recommendation of Father Berrigan, yet I do wish to stress that possibly the quiet life (his mother's for example) is not devoid of revolutionary tactics, that after the captains and kings depart and after the shouting and the tumult has died "the humble and the contrite heart" remains.

On the other hand I wish to praise Father Berrigan for helping me to understand him better; for his choice of hero for our time, Dietrich Bonhoeffer, who returned to wartime Germany and persecution so that he could earn his right to an eventual peace; for his clarification of and gentle dismissal to the "near" hero; for his insight into and condemnation of such half truths as that which stolidly dictates that "one who acts against the law, if he is to act virtuously and responsibly, must always take the consequences."

*Frank L. Ryan, in* Best Sellers, *October 1, 1972, p. 301.*

Berrigan's most mature poetry [*Prison Poems*] was probably written during his nearly fatal 30 months in Danbury Federal Penitentiary, to which he was sentenced in October, 1968, as one of the so-called Catonsville Nine. . . . In style, tone, imagery, idiom and insight, these three-score poems convey a toughened singleness of vision that is no less religious, even mystical, for all its resort to a blunt, sardonic vernacular. . . . Berrigan moves in close to "whiff the cup" of prison life; his glimpses of brother prisoners are moving, his message is *hang on.*

Publisher's Weekly *(reprinted from July 23, 1973, issue of* Publisher's Weekly, *published by R. R. Bowker Company, a Xerox company; copyright © 1973 by Xerox Corporation), July 23, 1973, p. 68.*

[As demonstrated by "Prison Poems,"] Berrigan's faith and humor never seem to flag, even under the worst circumstances. . . . The effect [of the poems] is to deflate the innate tragedy of the circumstances. Often the effect is also to escape the real issue at hand.

Berrigan insists on [a] stream-of-consciousness method and defiant sense of irony throughout the book, both I think to a poetic disadvantage. . . . Berrigan's wit and "craziness" too often preclude a serious atmosphere in which the poetic facts can breathe. . . .

[But he] is capable of a fine short lyric now and then. . . .

Berrigan's debt to Hopkins is noticeable.

*Paul Kameen, in* Best Sellers, *October 1, 1973, p. 298.*

It is Dan's talent for publicity that accounts for the swiftness of his elevation to the ranks of the exalted. Unlike [Thomas] More, Dan has written a play about his own martyrdom—probably the first to do so—in which he is likened to Jesus Christ and Socrates. Thus he serves as his own chronicler, being unwilling, the times being what they are, to wait for an apostle or a Plato or Xenophon, or to trust them with the nuances of the material. *The Trial of the Catonsville Nine* has been a smash hit in theaters in Europe and Canada, as well as in the United States; and now, thanks to Gregory Peck and the actor who plays Dan, and managed to catch his "essential soul," there is the film, capable of bringing the message to millions. The third act is the important act; here the nine defendants speak to the court and, through the agency of Dan's poetry, to Gregory Peck and the rest of mankind. Dan sees to it that his brother Philip speaks first and that he himself speaks last, sort of wrapping it up for the defense, and not only last, but longest, getting 14 and a half pages to John Hogan's one and a half, for example, or Mary Moylan's three and a half. Anyone can burn a draft card, but only a poet can be trusted to immortalize the event, because only the poet, or someone like him, can see its full significance. Only the poet will know what to say in the dramatic presentation of the trial, because only the poet can see the significance of The Trial. . . .

It is surely not the profundity of his political thought that accounts for his fame and the esteem in which he is held. . . . The fact is, it does not make sense; there was no relation between his analysis of the political situation and the action he proposed by way of remedy or solution. . . .

*The Trial of the Catonsville Nine* may be a dramatic and propagandistic triumph, but its poetry, and the license enjoyed by poets (in general and by this one in particular), conceals the absurd or, alternatively, the pernicious character of the doctrine it espouses. . . .

*The Dark Night of Resistance,* won the Thomas More Medal as the "most distinguished contribution to Catholic Literature in 1971," and it will not do for an Episcopalian political scientist to question this award or to suggest that 1971 must have been a particularly poor year for Catholic literature. Dan recounts in this book how in Hanoi, where he had gone to assist in the repatriation of the first American fliers released by the North Vietnamese, he experienced one of his rather frequent spiritual awakenings, this one brought on when he encountered Buddha, the "many faces of Buddha," at a time when "the United States of America was taking an Infant Jesus to its religious heart, changing His underpants on major feast days. A culture of infancy savored and prolonged; a religion for infants."

One might have thought that the Thomas More awards committee would be put off by such talk—I mean, it certainly does not *seem* very Catholic, or even very Christian, not, at least, to someone brought up on the Book of Common Prayer; but in the day of *Godspell* and *Jesus Christ Superstar* and *Hair* and *Oh! Calcutta!* one must be prepared to acknowledge the possibility that there is some truth in the old saying that all roads lead to Rome. Still, Christianity a "religion for infants"? Nowadays you get Christian prizes for that?

*Walter Berns, "The 'Essential Soul' of Dan Berrigan," in* National Review *(150 East 35th St., New York, N.Y. 10016), November 9, 1973, pp. 1231-43.*

Although Daniel Berrigan insists in his introduction to the published version of *The Trial of the Catonsville Nine* that he has "worked directly with the data of the trial record, somewhat in the manner of the new 'factual theatre,'" his play differs not only from most plays produced by that theatre of fact, but from most other courtroom dramas. It is more document than documentary, more personal testimony than play. It does not argue with the audience; it makes no revelations; it partakes of no "reconstructions" or dramatizations of the events that lead the nine defendants to where they are. . . . It offers no hypertensive confrontations between court and defendants or defendants and prosecution. Yet it is surprisingly, even intensely, dramatic, more so than many more deliberately theatrical works. . . . Although it is a mediocre "play" by traditional standards, it is provocative politics and exceptional theatre. . . .

Berrigan's play is tendentious and at times simplistic. . . .

Daniel Berrigan has one great advantage over most other writers of political drama: he is a poet. . . . His lines have a resonance where others' frequently are earthbound; he can evoke, where they usually can only expound.

*Catharine Hughes, "'The Trial of the Catonsville Nine'," in her* Plays, Politics and Polemics, *Drama Book Specialists, 1973, pp. 83-90.*

Daniel Berrigan is not a poet. He hasn't the equipment. His imagery, his language are humdrum as check stubs. . . . We endured his trivial crimes; now we endure his trivial punishment [*Prison Poems*]. Verses on: a tooth extraction, a visiting skunk, an anal search. Your average pickpocket has as much to say. . . . Jesus and Vietnam and Watergate are overwhelmed by peevish complaint. He seems to say merely "I—I—was imprisoned. I was made uncomfortable. I.". . .

The man who, in *Catonsville,* spoke for his superior moral passion has been outpassioned. Diminished. Daniel Berrigan's time has come. And, as suddenly, it has gone.

*D. Keith Mano, "Berrigan Agonistes," in* National Review *(150 East 35th St., New York, N.Y. 10016), March 1, 1974, pp. 263-64.*

Berrigan has searched for some years for the proper literary medium to tell his life story. He has produced 14 books of prose, including an effective and successful experiment in "factual theater," *The Trial of the Catonsville Nine,* and eight books of poetry, including *Time Without Number,* which received the Lamont Poetry Prize in 1957. His characteristic writing style is highly metaphysical, and not always appropriate to the basic lessons in morality and politics that he offers to teach. It makes use of extravagant metaphor and wit, hyperbole that often achieves confusion rather than clear thought. His skill as a writer showed itself best in older, short prose pieces, like his invitation to Catonsville during the time of the trial; his letter to the Weathermen while he was underground, or, in the present prose volume [*Lights On In the House of the Dead*], "Acknowledgements and Dedication, Sort Of"; letters to his brother Jesuits, and other occasional pieces where he seems to have a particular audience well in mind.

Frequently the prose is hard to read—rhetorical displays that serve no useful purpose. . . .

[Sympathetic] as I am to Daniel Berrigan, teacher of a generation of passive resistors, and to his book as one kind of record of the Danbury experience, I wish it were better as a literary work. As a reader I need some help, some way of participating in the experience, rather than this account in which he rarely reveals any concrete detail about himself or others. . . . In many of the diary commentaries on conversations with prisoners, the reader waits for important facts, the size, shape, distinctive characteristic of the people one hears about, but seldom sees. Berrigan seems too impatient, too concerned with message and thus careless about his listener, too hurried, so he fails to respond with so much as a nod to the reader before moving on.

The problem is one of distance in the prose, distance from people, from time, as if the speaker in his diary lived in a world beyond. Perhaps it is the voice of the prophet of one who sees what no one else sees, hears what no one else hears. But how can I be sure? Maybe it's only that detached, unworldly voice of the Sunday sermon, the newspaper editorial, the government document, the college catalog—the "we" of the papal bull. Why should I, as reader, trust the voice when it shows so fragile a link with my world, my time, when it speaks in such a stilted way about the ordinary person's wish for common things, when it shows so little sense of other people involved, either in the American past or the antiwar present, in common struggle?

It is the *voice,* after all, in prose that the reader must trust before he can take on the heavy message of the writer as prophet. In this, one cannot help but compare Daniel's account with his brother's, since both deal with roughly the same time span. In Philip Berrigan's *Widen the Prison Gates,* one finds all the details that one misses in *Lights On In the House of the Dead*—people named, conditions described, the hard, patient facts of day-to-day existence in prison: the struggle to survive the harassment of the screws, the betrayal of the media, the gossipy and empty concern of the public.

Daniel Berrigan is not patient enough in prose to let the dogged and simple facts, the natural shape of things, speak for themselves. He intrudes on them, wearying us with the snap, crackle, pop of verbal display. As a prose writer he needs a good dose of Orwell.

The poems [in *Prison Poems*] are another matter. They are the best poems of his career, frequently brief lyrics, where the telling metaphor brings the event to life, tuned to the music of natural speech. . . .

"My Father," an elegy of 500 lines, written during Holy Week 1971, . . . is, quite simply, one of the most beautiful extended lyrics in contemporary poetry.

Taken together these two books remind us of what Daniel Berrigan's war resistance cost him in physical illness and mental anguish. For this reason alone they are useful records, written for the same purpose that he "confessed or read or kept silent": to guard his sanity. In the poems, particularly, one gets a strong sense of the courage and talent he had for giving new life to plain moral truths, in word and in action, at Catonsville and from prison.

*Michael True, "Verbal Display," in* The New Republic *(reprinted by permission of* The New Republic; *© 1974 by The New Republic, Inc.), April 13, 1974, pp. 27-8.*

## BERRY, Wendell 1934-

**Berry is an American poet, novelist, and essayist.**

Wendell Berry is a spokesman for the rural and natural. His subjects and images come almost exclusively from the outdoors, yet *Openings* is an introspective volume in which the speaker seeks to understand himself and his world of rural Kentucky, a world to which he has made strong allegiance.

At times *Openings* reveals a good sense of movement, but while there are triumphs, there are failures in Berry's manner that are capable of producing an image like "eats/ at my heart," which is consistent with the feeling in the poem but which is, no matter where it is found, bad writing. And I question why he includes some poems, such as "The Winter Rain," "March Snow," and "April Woods: Morning," three in succession in which the speaker states or suggests meanings occasioned by observation or experience; the poems lack the special quality of implied force a calm, colloquial poetry needs in order to be remembered. . . .

Berry can be wordy and rather endless when he hooks on to a subject. I much prefer his shorter poems, such as "The Change," "The Quiet," "The Snake," and "Before Dark," each of which is distinctly good, bearing the firm control yet loose manner of Berry at his best.

*Ronald Moran, in* The Southern Review, *Vol. VIII, No. 1, Winter, 1972, pp. 249-50.*

[*The Memory of Old Jack*] is a simple, quiet story, told in elegant but restrained prose; it has the pace and mood of an elegy. What makes it far more than a sentimental celebration of a flawed but good man is the variety of distinct but interrelated themes it explores. One can, if one wishes, read it as merely the story of the life of a small town's revered elder statesman, the first fellow in a fellowship of friends. But *The Memory of Old Jack* is also about such matters as laboring for one's own fulfillment rather than that of others; attempting to use others for private, selfish purposes; and the "immemorial kinship" between man and the land he loves.

*Jonathan Yardley, in* Book World—The Washington Post (© The Washington Post), *March 3, 1974, p. 3.*

Distressingly few novelists treat both their characters and their readers with the kind of respect that Wendell Berry displays in [*The Memory of Old Jack,* a] deeply moving account of the final day in the long life of a remarkable human being. . . .

Mr. Berry largely avoids cornball sentimentality by letting us see the warts on his hero—his stubborn pride, his sick marriage, his adultery with Rose ("She was a woman without devices, who possessed her body in her eyes"), his sometimes suffocating narrowness. And the occasional highflown over-insistence on rural virtuousness in this agrarian elegy is redeemed by the solid ballast of chapters like "Hunger"—a root-touching evocation of the cooking and eating of a noontime meal during tobacco harvest. . . .

In the driving, near-Biblical rhythms of his prose, Berry does at times get a little preachy about modern ignorance, laziness, frivolity and the curses of technology. And I'm still not quite sold on the sublimity of "the yeoman's tradition of sufficiency to himself, of faithfulness to his place," especially since this tradition seems to suggest that a man who submits himself to the demands of the land ("that complexity of returns between labor and hunger") is by definition a superior being. Yet all this is more than salvaged by the handling of Old Jack's dignified death, ceremonial viewing and funeral, which may well rival even James Agee's subtler and more complex treatment in "A Death in the Family."

*James R. Frakes, in* The New York Times Book Review *(© 1974 by The New York Times Company; reprinted by permission), March 31, 1974, p. 38.*

*The Memory of Old Jack,* Wendell Berry's compassionate and profound third novel, celebrates a pastoral life which our nation in this century has abandoned. Our loss of the pastoral ideal is built into [its] structure and texture. . . .

The pastoral life celebrated here is stunningly rich. Jack is "faithful to his land, through all its yearly changes from maiden to mother, the bride and wife and widow of men like himself since the world began." This marriage brings him peace through toil, through the cycles of work and season: depletion, repetition, bounty. Often the work is its own reward. The most telling sign that a man does not easily accept the sweat of his brow is the constant teasing into work. "Settle for the half-assed, and then, by God, *admire* it!" "If you're going to talk to me, you'll have to walk." Laggards are coaxed into the fields with taunting praise. Work must be faced with comedy.

The book makes us grieve that these rhythms of work and speech are lost to us, as they are lost to Jack's daughter Clara, married to city banker Glad Pettit, who can buy anything, but who passes from car to porch steps without touching earth. . . .

Jack's world is lost to us. The second loss is more profound: Eden must contain loss; not the serpent but the condition of occupancy. And only here this magnificent novel fails us, for Berry does not permit Jack to work out the consequences of his painful dilemma. Rose is killed off and Jack remains: pained, bereft, yet essentially unchanged, in many ways a moral innocent. He and Berry both get off easily.

But this is the only misstep in a novel filled with a sense of humor in the face of pain and a sense of loss as the price of completion. At its center we behold Jack: "When he stepped into the first opening furrow of a new season he was not merely fulfilling an economic necessity; he was answering the summons of an immemorial kinship; he was shaping a passage by which an ancient vision might pass once again into the ground." Berry's prophetic language gives that vision voice; Old Jack's life and death gives it flesh.

*Joan Joffe Hall, in* The New Republic *(reprinted by permission of* The New Republic; *© 1974 by The New Republic, Inc.), April 6, 1974, pp. 26-7.*

Faulknerian in tone and intent, [*The Memory of Old Jack*]

manages to be only soporific in effect. For, uniformly, the characters lack passion. And therefore they lack depth. They spend the better part of each day coping grimly with grim realities. They seldom speak and even less often enjoy themselves.

In fact, the big orgasm in Port William, Ohio, is paying off the mortgage. And this state of affairs simply does not make for either an engaging or pertinent sort of fiction.

*Jack Friedman, in* The Village Voice *(reprinted by permission of* The Village Voice; *© 1974 by The Village Voice, Inc.), April 18, 1974, p. 31.*

* * *

## BERRYMAN, John 1914-1972

**Berryman, one of the best-known American poets of his generation, won both the Pulitzer Prize and National Book Award for *The Dream Songs,* his complex and idiosyncratic masterpiece about love and death. (See also *Contemporary Authors*, Vols. 15-16; obituary, Vols. 33-36.)**

*The Dream Songs* is a poem about falling and the Fall. From the first song where "nothing fell out as it ought" to the last in which the poet acknowledges that "fall is grievy, brisk. Tears behind the eyes/almost fall. Fall comes to us as a prize/to rouse us toward our fate," Berryman explores the significance of the fallen. "All we fall down & die" (190) and "Ashes, ashes. All fall down" (253) provide the sense of loss and mortality with which Henry struggles to find something or someone that stays, and what he [finds] in his love of work, his children, his friends is a ripeness of spirit, a compassion, a love for which, in the season that announces a death, the poets have found an appropriate metaphor.

Being a poem about the fallen, *The Dream Songs* is also a book of lamentations. This is important because it deepens the texture of religious significance. Henry's condition resembles that of Jeremiah, the poet of the Old Testament book of *Lamentations*. In that book misery and desolation have fallen about the holy city, as if God had departed, and Jeremiah is haunted by the utter solitude in which he finds himself. He suffers imprisonment, a type of death-in-life, from which he is rescued by his friendship with a black man, the Ethiopian eunuch, Ebed-Melech. The *Lamentations* of Jeremiah are very carefully structured. There are five elegies, each divided into twenty-two stanzas, with each beginning with a letter of the Hebrew alphabet. *The Dream Songs* are also carefully structured. Each song is eighteen lines long and the total number of lines as well as the total number of songs is divisible by seventy-seven, the number of songs Berryman first published in 1964. Such structuring may have some significance, but the real importance of Berryman's poem is that it is a complex and meaningful investigation of love and death that is both terrifying and comforting.

By any criteria *The Dream Songs* is a major poem. It speaks to fundamental problems of man, and, for the most part, it speaks brilliantly and honestly. It is not, of course, a perfect poem. Most readers will find it difficult, filled with allusions to historical and contemporary events that are sometimes little known or too private. Sometimes the syntax is bewildering, and sometimes Henry seems to be just a little too coy and sentimental. But, finally, it is a poem that rightly demands much of the reader, and I think it rewards him amply.

*Larry P. Vonalt, "Berryman's* The Dream Songs," *in* Sewanee Review *(reprinted by permission of the editor; © 1971 by The University of the South), Summer, 1971, pp. 464-69.*

*Love & Fame* is [an] uneven book; published so soon after *The Dream Songs,* it is the kind of book to put fear into any critic for what he might, and might not, find. Knowing all this, I found the book to be a distinctive part of Berryman's development as a man and as a poet, and to contain a number of very powerful poems. If the poems in the first half of the book often are too close to gossip and something less than a full art, those in the second half recover much of the force that Berryman, at his best, is able to muster.

As a book, *Love & Fame* poses major questions about the relationship between love and fame, and between art and life. . . .

*Love & Fame* raises the same major difficulty that *The Dream Songs* did—of an art which comes increasingly to rely upon a life for its weight and source.

*Arthur Oberg, "Deer, Doors, Dark," in* The Southern Review, *Vol. IX, No. 1, Winter, 1973, pp. 243-56.*

It will take years for readers to understand as well as like these quirky, topical, exorcistic poems [*The Dream Songs*] about Henry Pussycat (Celtic Henry, Rabbi Henry, Forgestic Henry, Anarchic Henry). Hater, lover, straightman Charlie Brown, gamester, martyr, savior, from Japan in the East to Ireland in the West, Henry ducks in and out of places and times past and present, but mostly it is America ruled over by Ike, whose subjects include Mark Twain, Bessie Smith, Charles Whitman, Shirley Jones, Walter Lippman, and George C. Scott (Hé would be prepared to líve in a world of Fáll"). Specified events merge and split, meanings coalesce and disintegrate, and Buoyant Henry alternately reveals and conceals.

Like *The Bridge* and *The Waste Land, The Dream Songs* is an anatomy of modern life, its narrative disjunctive, its language a melange of the arcane, the prissily elevated, and the demotic, and its purpose to invest the poor poet with a mystical health-giving role for ordering a disordered age. The craftsmanship in the poem is brilliantly executed. Berryman writes 385 songs, each one (with only occasional variation) an eighteen-line poem comprised of three six-line stanzas with irregular line lengths and casual, but sometimes intricate, rhymes. With his given form, it would take a genius to sustain his or our interest in the limited manipulations, and Berryman isn't quite that genius. There are simply too many dream songs. . . . I do not doubt for a moment that this is one of our century's most impressive Big Poems, and, appropriately, *The Dream Songs* will take much longer to explicate than its author took to write it. Like its distinguished predecessors, it will eventually require extensive annotation—if for no other reason to make sense of our floating, eminently topical times.

Countering the form, which is coherent in an almost mathematical way, are the vocal continuities, which are richly derived from many sources, including the tradition of American minstrelsy and its parodic highjinks . . . , and the extensive thematic patterns supplied by history, psychology, and myth. . . .

Inventive, even innovative, in a way that puts to shame his louder, younger contemporaries, Berryman glides, rocks, bounces, skips, and Perishable Henry croons, babbles, moans.

Reading these poems is a little like watching those old newsreels of space experiments in which speeding rockets are really controlled by tracks and drogue parachutes. The form oddly combines release and control in inevitable balance: the aggressively energetic diction and syntax push against the confines of disciplined stanzaics. And in this appropriate form for our age, Berryman stuffs it all. . . .

There's a lot of malarkey in Berryman's dream songs, and sometimes the odor of burnt cork is too overpowering to be able to make nicer discriminations. But there is no doubt that, in Auden's category, he's a poet who takes his making seriously. *The Dream Songs* may be the most important single work of the middle generation poets.

*James H. Justus, "Some Middle Generation Poetry," in* The Southern Review, *Vol. IX, No. 1, Winter, 1973, pp. 261-68.*

Anyone who writes about *The Dream Songs* puts himself in a dangerous position. The poem's landscape resembles in some places a minefield where an explanatory footstep triggers explosions of warning and invective, bursting in the face not only of critics but of all readers. Berryman's mildest warning to his expositors is both a simple renunciation and a complex, tragic claim:

> These Songs are not meant to be understood, you understand.
> They are only meant to terrify & comfort.

Henry (Henry Pussycat, Henry House, Mr Bones, Berryman's verbal standin, the poem's agonist) maintains that the "ultimate structure" of the Songs is inaccessible to critical analysis, that the Songs lack the regular articulated structure that informs "cliff hangers and old serials," that his "large work . . . will appear, / and baffle everybody." . . .

Berryman's ludditisms (there are dozens of them) against the critical act amount to an elliptical statement about the poem's organization, its way of being. Unlike most of the recent verse that gets filed away in one's memory under the heading "confessional," Berryman's poem invents a form and language assertively its own, an achievement possible only because Berryman wrestled successfully the master voices of Hopkins, Auden, Cummings and Pound. He also has a strategy of his own, one which looks at first like the familiar confessional self-justification ("Miserable wicked me,/How interesting I am," Auden parodied in another context) but is in fact far more complicated. The title *The Dream Songs* asserts the subjectivity of the poem's occasions: dreams are events absolutely inaccessible to shared or common experience. But neither are they events subject to the organizing power of the dreamer himself. The poem claims to derive from mental activity at a place so deep in the poet's self that the self is no longer in control. Berryman makes an explicit disclaimer of responsibility in a forenote to the completed work. . . . [The] Songs are not what they appear to be, a transparently autobiographical series of dramatic monologues (trespassed by other voices now and then), but a verbal corporation whose members are uncontrolled responses to—and translations from—the world of experience, and whose rules are flexible and mostly hidden.

Yet the poems are not only dreams but "Songs", and they are always patterned and often musical. Berryman suggested the solution to the paradox of the title *The Dream Songs* in an interview: "Henry? He is a very good friend of mine. I feel entirely sympathetic to him. He doesn't enjoy my advantages of supervision; he just has vision." *Entirely sympathetic*: Berryman is too shrewd not to mean this in its fullest sense, that Berryman's feelings and Henry's are precisely the same. *My advantages of supervision*: though the statements in the poem are in Henry's voice, the Apollonian will to pattern and outline is the poet's own. The portion of the Songs which is the most regular in form and meter, most grave in language, is the Opus Posthumous series, written after Henry's "death" (in the center of the poem) when he is most subject to supervision by the living. . . .

The Songs have a formal frame, and, despite dozens of variations, each Song is built upon a regular pattern. . . . Berryman said that the Songs are not individual poems but "parts" of a single poem. . . . Berryman wrote that one problem involved in a long poem is "the construction of a world, rather than the reliance upon one existent which is available to a small poem"—and this is an invitation to a phenomenological rather than structural reading of the Songs.

This issue deserves further definition. Everything in a poem that makes its world different from that of life is derived ultimately from the *closure* of art, its beginning and middle and end. In life no one has any clear sense of one's beginning, nor, after the fact, can one have any sense at all of one's end. (In a late Canto Pound put it simply: "No man can see his own end.") One can close one's life, as Berryman did, but one cannot look up at the clock afterwards and begin something new. . . . Though Henry "moves on in the world," and, at the end of the first volume of the Songs, is explicitly "making ready to move on," the whole poem is finished and sealed. . . . The world of *The Dream Songs,* the world that is "according to [Henry's] nature," depends *from* the kind of events that happen there, the verbal events that translate the dream. . . .

Berryman's special kind of transformation of extended personal experience into finished forms is probably his most important achievement, a model of method, if not a model of what to do with a method. At a time when most "confessional" verse tends to the dreary anecdote told in formless chat, Berryman's enterprise towards an idiosyncratically appropriate language, in an appropriate form, is courageous and rare. . . .

With *Homage to Mistress Bradstreet* (1956) Berryman first successfully fused his by now perfected syntax into a thoroughly personal form and subject. This remarkable poem, probably the most consistently successful that Berryman ever wrote, has a narrative "plot" which may be described briefly. The poet imagines the body of Anne Bradstreet, and "summons" her from the centuries; she speaks her history, which, through one of Berryman's best imaginative leaps, turns out to be a grimly witty narrative of modern, almost suburban isolation and detachment, set in Puritan New England; Berryman and Anne, each to the other a ghostly presence, speak a dialogue, and each *almost* takes the other for a lover. But Anne escapes the (to her) temptation offered by the twentieth-century voice, and asserts her seventeenth-century independence. Berryman's voice returns to the poem only after Anne's death. The structural device through which Berryman first creates Anne Bradstreet, then is thrown off by his own creation, might appear to be a conventionally modernist sleight-of-hand, a familiar form of play with the status of appearances, but Berryman summons a vast emotional universe of personal loss and assertion to the device, and succeeds in rendering it as deeply moving as it is artificial. . . . *Homage to Mistress Bradstreet* is among other things an historical narrative, yet its central statements are "about" isolation and love. Anne Bradstreet seems at times an historical convenience. She is not a Yeatsian "mask" but a *projection*. In *The Dream Songs* the poem's universe is that of a man at the extremes of noisy passion and unhappiness, but also, alas, when considered outside his world of private eros and thanatos, *l'homme moyen social*. Berryman and Lowell admire each other enthusiastically in print, but their phenomenal worlds are vastly different: where Lowell takes everything in the *polis* for his subject, Berryman's social commentary . . . is nearly as crazy as the later Yeats, and much less sonorous. . . .

Berryman is no naif. His power-plays are not simply subject matter for his poem, but are enacted in the poem itself. Berryman is smart enough to realize that he presents himself in the least prepossessing manner he can imagine: his personal offensiveness is not accidental but entirely deliberate, for what he wants from his readers is their critical approval despite their personal disapproval, their assent despite their awareness of what they are assenting *to*. What Berryman hopes to enjoy is not the power to delight or enchant, but the power to control those who are both conscious and unwilling. . . .

*Love and Fame* (1970) . . . continues Berryman's development of a personal voice. He drops the Henry-doppelgänger and speaks autobiographically and directly in his own name. The title of one poem, "Regents' Professor Berryman's Crack on Race", would have been impossibly direct only a few years earlier, but with directness came a dangerous facility and self-importance. The book makes pleasant reading, but the struggles of *The Dream Songs* have diminished to chat. Berryman's last book, *Delusions, etc.*, indicates that the mad-lyric mode was Berryman's mainstay to the end, intensely personal, slightly desperate, persistent in its survivals, its paradoxes, and its celebrations.

Finally the survivals gave out.

*Edward Mendelson, "How to Read Berryman's 'Dream Songs'," in* American Poetry Since 1960: Some Critical Perspectives, *edited by Robert B. Shaw (reprinted by permission of Dufour Editions, Inc.), Carcanet, 1973, pp. 29-43.*

Most of those who have written on John Berryman's poems have found it reasonable to assume that his work poses—even postures—as "difficult." It has been considered a poetry for which certain clues must be known beforehand in order to gain access, let alone understanding. . . .

The problem is partly Berryman's fault. He complained in prefaces and in interviews that his work was discussed in wrong ways, that critics missed the point. As well as that, readers, and critics, especially British ones, have been put off by Berryman's syntax and orthography. Even worse, his scholarly affectations, his cultural reach, not only manifest themselves in poems as allusive details, but are held by some to be the stiffening in a larger theological argument. Few British readers can take *that* seriously. These indifferent reactions are the grumbling of an Age without vision. They can be held to one side. What must be asserted about Berryman's work is its humanity. Berryman himself may have thought that beside the point too; but it is what, in my opinion, is strongest in his poems. . . .

Berryman's life-in-his-poems has been probed, about as far as is decent. The poems ask for this. Autobiography was an adjunct of his understanding of Fame. But Henry is so unanimously accepted as Berryman himself that the imaginative function of the person-who-behaves-like-the-self in a poem has been neglected.

The self-as-subject is one of the problems raised, not only by Berryman's work, but by many contemporary poetries, those of Plath and Lowell in particular. . . . Berryman is not Henry; but Henry *is* Berryman. . . .

Whether this process results in a creation that can be called a "literary device" is questionable. It appears to be more personal, more to do with the nature of the poet's mind, and the consolations it needs to compensate for solitude and the nature of what he knows about himself. It could also be said to be fundamental in a poetry in which the self is exploited through imaginative recreations—as in Jarrell's monologues. . . .

Consider the despair, the predicament, of a man whose disciplined and large intellect allowed him to create an imaginary friend out of himself, whose fears, guilts, doubts and escapades he could describe and condemn. And is not that despair, that predicament, the substance of Berryman's writing? . . . Is it not also . . . an extreme instance of the dilemma of the contemporary poet, brought partially into the open, as it is here, by poetic form, by a technique which can be tentatively explained in psychological terms? . . . For Berryman never allowed his personal difficulties to intrude on an enduring fascination with metrics and all the stylistic problems of poems. . . .

As a search for an individual and spiritual haven in which he could wait for the inevitable with an honest resignation, Berryman's poetry is a fair sample of a continuing phenomenon, albeit in his case magnified by genius. He writes about what it is like to possess formidable intelligence in a society where all aspirations appear negative, or frustrated from the start. His intelligence appears to have had no objective beyond that of writing poems. He recoils from public worsening, but not publicity. Personal disasters repeat themselves or return in shuddering, nerve-racking memories. His past is full of grief—his father's suicide, the deaths of his friends, his affairs and marriages. His drinking continues. His lapses of sanity come and go and recur. Yet all the time it is a poetry of waiting, a poetry of impending solutions, which were to come in the religious poems that close *Love & Fame,* and constitute much of *Delusions etc.* . . .

*Recovery,* Berryman's posthumous and incomplete novel, [is] in its own right a remarkable dramatisation of the agonies of alcoholism. His poems are so close to a sense of life, an imparting of truth complete with the bias of technique and personality, that they have the true flavour of fiction. An enormously comprehensive and unsentimental pathos slips out of his work, complicated and perplexing. We realise that although it may all be about ordinary Berryman, it generalises itself, it has compass.

His generous humanity is neglected by those who shy away from the oddness of his voice, or the grotesque inventions of his imagination. . . . But Berryman has much to say, wisely and with pleasure, of the human condition. . . .

The seriousness with which Berryman engaged with the problems of writing, of achieving a contemporary idiom as a matter of priority, is what marks him off from most British talents. At times, his erudition on the subject of styles, practical though it was, is inhibiting. In his *Sonnets* especially, though elsewhere too, he courts the traditions of writing as self-consciously as he seeks the truths of experience. . . .

His religious poems in *Love & Fame* are intended to "criticise backward" the earlier, scandalous sections; and, presumably, the carnality, comedy and religious doubts of *Dream Songs* as well. . . . Berryman may have discovered faith, and its attendant certainties; but a nervous edge, an incompletion, was to remain. Nor was his language to be greatly altered in these later poems.

*Douglas Dunn, "Gaiety & Lamentation: The Defeat of John Berryman," in* Encounter, *August, 1974, pp. 72-7.*

* * *

## BIOY CASARES, Adolfo 1914-

**Bioy Casares is an Argentinian short story writer, novelist, and essayist. With his friend Jorge Luis Borges, he has written several volumes of short stories and one of film scripts. (See also *Contemporary Authors*, Vols. 29-32.)**

We hear sad murmurs that our century lacks the ability to devise interesting plots. But no one attempts to prove that if this century has any ascendancy over the preceding ones it lies in the quality of its plots. . . . I believe I am free from every superstition of modernity, of any illusion that yesterday differs intimately from today or will differ from tomorrow; but I maintain that during no other era have there been novels with such admirable plots as *The Turn of the Screw, Der Prozess, Le Voyageur sur la terre,* and [*The Invention of Morel*], which was written in Buenos Aires by Adolfo Bioy Casares.

[One] popular genre in this so-called plotless century is the detective story, which tells of mysterious events that are later explained and justified by a reasonable occurrence. In this book Adolfo Bioy Casares easily solves a problem that is perhaps more difficult. The odyssey of marvels he unfolds seems to have no possible explanation other than hallucination or symbolism, and he uses a single fantastic but not supernatural postulate to decipher it. My fear of making premature or partial revelations restrains me from examining the plot and the wealth of delicate wisdom in its execution. Let me say only that Bioy renews in literature a concept that was refuted by St. Augustine and Origen, studied by Louis Auguste Blanqui, and expressed in memorable cadences by Dante Gabriel Rossetti:

> I have been here before,
> But when or how I cannot tell:
> I know the grass beyond the door,
> The sweet keen smell,
> The sighing sound, the lights around the shore.

In Spanish, works of reasoned imagination are infrequent and even very rare. . . . *The Invention of Morel* (the title alludes filially to another island inventor, Moreau) brings a new genre to our land and our language.

I have discussed with the author the details of his plot. I have reread it. To classify it as perfect is neither an imprecision nor a hyperbole.

*Jorge Luis Borges, "Prologue" to* The Invention of Morel and Other Stories, *by Adolfo Bioy Casares, translated by Ruth L. C. Simms (copyright © 1964 by Adolfo Bioy Casares; reprinted by permission of University of Texas Press), University of Texas Press, 1964, pp. 5-7.*

Bioy Casares is a close friend and collaborator of Borges, and Borges's influence is very clear in his work (if we knew more about him, we might also say that his influence is very clear in Borges's work). He is in one sense more inventive than Borges, better able to create a plot and sustain a narrative. But he appears to lack Borges's eeriest and most important gift: the ability to suggest the uncanny lurking in the quietest, most unlikely corner of a house or a phrase. *Diary of the War of the Pig* has the logic of dream, or seems to invite such a logic, but it doesn't have the intensity of a dream, although it seems to be seeking it. . . .

A young man shoots an old man, and explains to the court that he was so irritated by the sight of a bald head, and by the old man's slow reflexes, that he just couldn't resist the temptation to kill him. The jury understands, and he is acquitted.

What is interesting about the book is less its premise and the competent but uninspired execution of its consequences, than the psychology of the old men, who are busy either trivializing the whole thing, arguing about whether the war of the pig ought not to be called the war of the hog, or caving in wholesale to the arguments of the young, secretly agreeing to despise themselves, to feel ashamed at the course of nature. Bioy is plainly thinking here of that damaging impulse so common in persecuted groups, and memorably dramatized in Kafka: the impulse to believe that your persecutors are in some sense right about you.

*Michael Wood, in* The New York Review of Books *(reprinted with permission from* The New York Review of Books; *© 1973 by NYREV, Inc.), April 19, 1973, p. 37.*

Casares' *Diary of the War of the Pigs* [might be called] "magic realism".... Its theme—to over-simplify—is the pain and problem of growing old. This is expressed through a group of aging men, with one, Vidal, at the centre, who live in a city in which, as we gradually become aware, groups of young men are waging a campaign of terrorism against the old. This terrorism Casares keeps very effectively in the background: no *Clockwork Orange* exhibitionism of blood and horror, only the thud of bombs in the distance and Vidal's awareness, now and then, that one of his friends has disappeared. The true drama, of which the terrorists' acts are a sort of symbol (though one which, like all effective symbols, is only reality pushed one stage further, the reality of our generation-obsessed age-fearing society)—the true drama lies in Vidal's ever-increasing sensitiveness, his awareness of the isolation of old age, his striving to accept the humiliations it entails. All this we found convincing and moving. Where the story seems to falter is in its delineation of a belated love-affair which, one gathers, was to save Vidal from utter despair—and in its dubious ending, which seems to leave everything ambiguous: did Vidal stay with his love? did the young men call off their "war of the pigs"? And if they did, why? But even if the ending is unsatisfying, the work as a whole has real imagination, intense but controlled.

*Patrick Cruttwell and Faith Westburg, "Fiction Chronicle," in* The Hudson Review *(copyright © 1973 by The Hudson Review, Inc.; reprinted by permission), Vol. XXVI, No. 2, Summer, 1973, pp. 417-18.*

* * *

## BIRNEY, (Alfred) Earle 1904-

**Birney is one of Canada's foremost writers. A poet, short story writer, novelist, and critic, Birney is most frequently concerned with contemporary Canadian life. (See also *Contemporary Authors*, Vols. 1-4, rev. ed.)**

Mr. Birney has a nose for the picaresque situation, and his poems frequently partake of the nature of travellers' observations. He also has the nicest of ears for national accent (his Australian and New Zealand pieces are a hoot).

Behind the satirical equipment, there lies the basic lyrical impulse which he is careful not to overwork but whose existence presents his credentials as that more recognised species of poet. Sometimes this is found in verse like the snatches of some melody:

I met a lady
  on a lazy street
hazel eyes
  and little plush feet

or in his imagistic love-poem *There are delicacies.* At other times, it reveals itself in a descriptive line: 'the sky's blue is hard as bakelite.' But whether addressed to the senses or the intelligence, these poems—for all their chosen limitations—are seldom other than bang on centre. Such marksmanship is a joy to witness.

*Derek Stanford, in* Books and Bookmen, *November, 1973, pp. 108-09.*

In the making of *What's so Big About Green?*, Birney must once again have driven Jack McClelland and his printers batty. This new collection continues in the anti-book tradition of *Rag and Bone Shop,* featuring such vagaries as a see-through poem, boxes of print, differing type sizes, unusual spacings, and especially noteworthy here, two-tone print, in this case black and green.

Looking back at earlier books, one notices that Birney has always been interested in visual effects on the page, and in the carrying over into the poem of found objects such as tourist brochures, wall-signs, *etc.* But in the last decade he has moved bodily into the area called the interface, between poem and visual art.

One wants to remark that his moves through the interface are often academic, somehow at the spectator's vantage point; but then there are his "Alphabeings", the creatures, animals and others, crudely drawn with the letters that make up their names. Now that is something that every ten-year-old kid has done, and there Birney plunges, into the risk, the dare. Aw, my kid could do that. So why is that a criticism? Indeed.

But I still feel that all this is not really the avantgarde. Birney is usually, in these japes, doing something exciting and playful for his own amusement, and that is okay. But the reader is not similarly energized. The reader is having a story without a storyteller, and he and Birney might wave at one another, as the boy in the swimming hole and the driver of the passing locomotive might wave at one another. If you remember that, you'll know it's a nice experience.

So one looks through the book, enjoying some parts more than other, the way you did with your Christmas stocking. Personally, I don't like a certain mixing of visual and sound, the making a poem about a mountain appear mountain-shaped. Is one supposed to contemplate it? I think that once that has been done, with for instance Herbert's altar, it's done. What more can further shaped poems offer but more shapes? And we already have those shapes anyway.

More interesting is a concrete poem that makes one pay attention to the design of the print, or the design the print makes anew. Rather than copying a design already more interestingly made by a skyline or a mountain or a falling airplane. Even with concrete poetry one does better to imitate than to copy nature.

That is why Birney does magically (?) with his black and green. A curious thing happens—sometimes when you tilt the page the black type seems to turn green, especially if you've been looking at green, the alternative. I mean this is right now happening even with the black ink (I think) I am using to make these notes. Often in a poem that is nearly all black, the line you are presently reading seems to turn green before your eyes, while the others in the periphery remain black.

There's the thematic contention of the book taking place. The book takes place. The green of life and nature versus the black of industrial (industrious) greed and death. The dialectic or rather struggle is of green vs. greed, both energetic but not to be confused. But in the shifting light they are....

[Birney] has very clear line notation, not for a syncopated or moment-oriented rhythm, but the sure sense that comes when clause and line find their junctures equal....

But finally Birney's great concern is the dying earth. He does not offer any hope or method of salvation. He has been here long enough to see the changes wrought on the earth, sea and sky of Vancouver. He is Canadian enough to take the geology as theme and its aeons as scope (as did Pratt and Scott), but he is far enough into the century Laurier promised us to see how "puny" men could not only subdue but obliterate the wild. It is as if the Group of Seven paintings could include an oil slick or some sawed-off hillsides.

*George Bowering, "Suitcase Poets," in* Canadian Literature, *Summer, 1974, pp. 97-100.*

* * *

## BISHOP, Elizabeth 1911-

**Elizabeth Bishop, a Pulitzer Prize-winning American poet, has lived in Brazil since 1952. She writes witty, fanciful, and imaginative poems. (See also *Contemporary Authors*, Vols. 5-8, rev. ed.)**

Elizabeth Bishop's *Poems* seems to me one of the best books an American poet has written, one that the future will read almost as it will read Stevens and Moore and Ransom. Her poems are quiet, truthful, sad, funny, most marvelously individual poems; they have a sound, a feel, a whole moral and physical atmosphere, different from anything else I know. They are honest, modest, minutely observant, masterly; even their most complicated or troubled or imaginative effects seem, always, personal and natural, and as unmistakable as the first few notes of a Mahler song, the first few patches of a Vuillard interior. . . .

The poet and the poems have their limitations; all exist on a small scale, and some of the later poems, especially, are too detailedly and objectively descriptive. But the more you read her poems, the better and fresher, the more nearly perfect they seem; at least half of them are completely realized works of art.

*Randall Jarrell, "Fifty Years of American Poetry" (1962), in his* The Third Book of Criticism *(reprinted with the permission of Farrar, Straus & Giroux, Inc.; copyright © 1941, 1945, 1955, 1956, 1962, 1963, 1965 by Mrs. Randall Jarrell; copyright © 1963, 1965 by Randall Jarrell), Farrar, Straus, 1969, p. 325.*

Elizabeth Bishop is not a poet who finds inspiration in public events, political issues, or socioeconomic ideology; reading her, one is unaware of Hitler and World War II, just as one is unaware of Napoleon and his wars when reading the works of Jane Austen. Unlike many of her Auden-influenced contemporaries, she distrusts history, with its melodramatic blacks and whites, and prefers geography, with its subtle gradations of color. . . . And, like a geographer, she delights in the landscapes, animals, customs, climates, and changing lights of the world, which are very real to her: she is no solipsist. Her sense of the existence of objects relates her to William Carlos Williams and, especially, to Marianne Moore, who has a similar passion for precise rendering of the scenes and inhabitants of the world. Restless as an explorer or a tourist, Miss Bishop moves along many roads in search of objects and insights. . . .

As a peripatetic poet and geographer, Miss Bishop avoids that concentration on the self which often leads to emotion that "too far exceeds its cause," like that which a map maker perhaps feels as he runs the names of cities across neighboring mountains. Perhaps it is an extraordinary vulnerability that makes her look outward rather than inward. At any rate, she registers those increments of awareness that experience of many latitudes brings. Her verse does not lack feeling—it is merely directed to the objects that elicit feeling. These objects point to the ambiguities, beauty, and suffering of a world subject to time and death. . . .

The poet's characteristics are fully evident in her first book, *North and South,* which appeared in 1946 and contained poems written mostly before 1942. It reveals her wonder and excitement as she looks at the world and describes what she sees. Some of this excitement derives from her discovery that language can perform miracles of exactness in description. . . .

Much of the effectiveness of these descriptions derives, of course, from the figures of speech, from the correspondences that the poet discovers between the objects she is describing and other objects, not present, that her imagination entertains. For example, who besides Miss Bishop has ever seen a relationship between the grating sound of a wet match and the croak of a cock at dawn? One often finds such a delighted yoking together of disparate elements. . . .

Most of the poems in *North and South* are strikingly imagined and ordered, but, now and then, as in the case of the poem "Florida," the poet's exuberance provides a scattering of images whose relevance to the total structure is open to question. It is as though Miss Bishop stopped along the road home to examine every buttercup and asphodel she saw. The images are dazzling; they call attention to themselves like ambitious actors in minor roles; but they contribute very little to the total effect. Some of the descriptive poems are saved from disintegration by a metaphor, an apt unifying image, in the concluding lines. . . .

[The poems in the] group entitled "A Cold Spring" . . . are rich in reports of the colors, shapes, and temperatures of the world; they contain vivid contrasts, sometimes held in paradoxical suspension as unities. . . .

Again, as in *North and South,* it is the beauty, pain, wealth, poverty, and sorrow of a world caught in the processes of time that stir Miss Bishop; she is indifferent to politics. When she writes about Washington, D.C., it is not to make a comment on the political scene or to describe congressmen in debate, but, rather, to suggest the power of the sun and the trees. . . .

Clearly, then, Elizabeth Bishop is a poet who, early in her career, chose to avoid politics and public issues without, at the same time, abandoning the objective realities that constitute the otherness of the world. She believes in that world, especially when it shocks or baffles her, and she renders it with precision and clarity.

*Stephen Stepanchev, "Elizabeth Bishop," in his* American Poetry Since 1945: A Critical Survey *(copyright 1965 by Stephen Ste-*

*panchev; reprinted by permission of Harper & Row, Publishers, Inc.), Harper, 1965, pp. 69-79.*

Despite her high reputation among poets and critics, Elizabeth Bishop has never had the recognition she deserves. . . . Though the body of her work is small, very few poets have a record of such consistent, stunning excellence. Miss Bishop has chosen not to repeat herself; she has the imaginative resourcefulness to surprise us over and over again. Like Marianne Moore, she has perfected a form, a tone, a style that is unmistakably her own; like Miss Moore, she is humble and honest, profound without rhetoric and subtle without obscurity; and she might vie with Miss Moore for the title of the World's Greatest Observer. But she never imitates Miss Moore; she imitates no one. Her poems have the effortless, natural grace that can only belong to poets who hear their own voice with utter clarity. Her best poems—such as "Roosters," "The Fish," "The Prodigal Son"—will surely be among the enduring poems of this century. "The Complete Poems," so full of insight and wisdom, and of language of astonishing beauty, is one of those books that makes us marvel, gratefully, at the gift of speech.

Virginia Quarterly Review, *Vol. 45, No. 4 (Autumn, 1969), p. cxxxii.*

All the way through [*The Collected Poems* of Elizabeth Bishop] the purpose appears to be one of rendering what she sees (occasionally, what she imagines) as accurately as possible. The view, put more plainly though in more complex a manner in the later poems, is of men and all other creatures suspended, incomplete and without complete comprehension, among the beauties and perils of this particular world. . . .

Miss Bishop is perhaps willing to circumscribe the limits of our comprehension more straitly than many would like; beyond the immediately visible circumstances, of which she is very sure, the mystery closes in. She has made it her business, though, to make poems out of what does come clear, out of . . . isolated patches of understanding and vision.

*H. T. Kirby-Smith, Jr., in* Sewanee Review *(reprinted by permission of the editor; © 1972 by the University of the South), Summer, 1972, p. 484.*

Elizabeth Bishop seems never to approach the questionable, whether in matters of good taste or topic or intention. She corresponds to none of the feminine stereotypes [Ms. Rizza refers specifically to three—Formlessness, Feminine Hysteria, and Female Confinement—defined by Mary Ellmann in *Thinking About Women*]: she is "confined" in neither her subject matter nor in her ways of seeing; hysterical emotion is hardly a consideration, since her poems seldom reveal her own emotions; her verse forms are at least as rigorous and consistent as those of Robert Lowell or Richard Wilbur. There is little autobiography in her poems that indicates that the writer is a woman. Yet, there is a delicacy of description, a certain mildness or innocence that might first be considered "girlish," though a deeper reading reveals a maturity and worldliness that has somehow failed to corrupt the writer's immaculate freshness. The pages of *The Complete Poems* offer constant alternations of type and form, on one page a song, and on the next, blank verse. And so it is with subject matter, a selection of garden flowers in a vase, none of them offensive or horrifying, all of them presented with considerate formality.

Great balance and integrity distinguish Miss Bishop's poetry. Neither subjective nor sterile, it possesses the qualities that we look for in writing: sensitivity, intelligence, artistry and compassion. We read poetry with the expectation that the poet will do a certain amount of fishing for us, so that, casting in unseen places, she will eventually serve us some undreamed of catch. We enjoy being surprised, but we also want to understand the poetry, we want to be touched exactly by the mention of something we might ourselves have experienced. Miss Bishop satisfies this wish by never writing about experiences limited to herself. She lets one feel that, in the special circumstance, one might have perceived the same thing.

Discipline is the key to Miss Bishop's achievement. And for her, discipline means not only writing in a specific form: it means avoiding the flamboyant statements of "apocalyptic" poets for whom reality warps to fit the metaphor or the imagination. Her discipline includes an almost objectivist restriction to the data perceived by the senses, described without recourse to abstraction. Always looking outward, she treats the visual world compassionately, but not sentimentally. The style is conversational, never flat or argumentative; it sometimes has the language but never the verbosity of prose. . . . Miss Bishop's descriptions demand careful deliberation, as though they were beautifully formed, internal dialogues. . . .

Without qualifying as "apocalyptic," Miss Bishop treats objects, natural things, people, as though she loves them for themselves, and not for how she can use them to reflect herself or her metaphors. She possesses what might be called an "objective imagination."

*Peggy Rizza, in* American Poetry Since 1960: Some Critical Perspectives, *edited by Robert B. Shaw (reprinted by permission of Dufour Editions, Inc.), Carcanet, 1973, pp. 169-70.*

* * *

## BLAIS, Marie-Claire 1939-

**Mlle Blais is a French Canadian novelist, born in Quebec. Although her fiction is not localized in Canada, Mlle Blais employs the "painful vision of her imagination" to explore familiar Canadian themes. (See also *Contemporary Authors*, Vols. 21-22.)**

In approaching the novels of Marie-Claire Blais, there is one widely current assumption that it is important to dismiss from one's mind: the supposition, that is, that her work has anything in common with that of Françoise Sagan. . . . Mlle Sagan is a highly sophisticated Parisian, who goes in for fast cars and destructive drugs and complicated love affairs. . . . Mlle Blais, on the other hand, comes out of a bleak bigoted Quebec and is not at home on the boulevards. Her fictions, up to [*Une Saison dans la vie d'Emmanuel*], have been usually obsessed and tormented dreams that took place—like a number of Canadian novels —in a never identified country. *La Belle Bête,* the first of her novels, published in 1959 (translated as *Mad Shadows*), is a kind of tragic fairy tale; *Tête Blanche* (translated with its French title) of 1960 is somewhat closer to a recognizable social world but it does not quite make connections with the probable behavior of such a world; *Le Jour Est Noir* of 1962 scarcely makes such connections at all: it is an agonizing phantasmagoria, full of ever-shifting nightmarish relationships that involve the desertion of children, the compulsive abandonment by a wife of her husband and the suicide, obscurely motivated, of another unhappy husband; *Les Voyageurs Sacrés,* which appeared in 1963 in the collection *Écrits du Canada Français,* though a narrative, is labelled "Poème," and rather resembles certain productions of Virginia Woolf's. This last has been, up to *Emmanuel,* the only one of Mlle Blais's books which was given a definite locale: it is supposed to take place in France.

But, now, in *Une Saison dans la Vie d'Emmanuel,* the writer has made a definite new departure. The clairvoyant's crystal ball that revealed the diminished, remote and somewhat mysterious visions englobed in the early novels has been suddenly darkened and filled with the turbid and swirling sediment of the actual French Canadian world—with the squalor and the squirming life that swarms in the steep-roofed cement-covered houses of the little Canadian towns. . . . Though the material of *Emmanuel* is that of an actual milieu in all its prosaic and sordid detail, it is not presented prosaically nor even, in spite of its horrors, sordidly, but infused—and sometimes a little blurred—by the fantasies of adolescence, saturated with the terrors and appetites, the starving and stifled aspirations of these young people in their prisoned overpopulated world. . . . Certainly, to the non-Canadian, the appearance of such a book as this—so far, it seems to me, much the best of Mlle Blais's novels and the best I have read from French Canada except some of those by André Langevin—would seem to show that French Canadian literature, after producing a good deal of creditable work of merely local interest, is now able to send out to the larger world original books of high quality.

*Edmund Wilson, "Foreword" (reprinted with the permission of Farrar, Straus & Giroux, Inc.; copyright © 1966 by Edmund Wilson) to* A Season in the Life of Emmanuel, *by Marie-Claire Blais, translated by Derek Coltman, Farrar, Straus, 1966, pp. v-ix.*

Marie-Claire Blais is a young French Canadian with some half dozen novels and a book of poems behind her. Her previous novel, *A Season in the Life of Emanuel,* has at its center an autobiographical sketch by a consumptive child whose writing is a cry of defiance against the misery of his life and the approach of his death. The manuscripts of a suffering child, a structural detail of that novel, are the sum and substance of its successor. *The Manuscripts of Pauline Archange* take us through memories of almost unmitigated horror rendered bearable, redeemed even, for us as for the novel's heroine, by the fluid, re-creative medium of her prose. . . .

What Pauline remembers does not fall into a conventional plot or lend itself easily to summary. Her life is lived out in the mental and physical squalor of a French Canadian slum, under the tyranny of repressed, frustrated adults who visit their failures in blows upon their consumptive, lamed offspring. To survive is to escape, to rebel, above all, to avoid pity. Pity "stinks of death," and only leads to torture and rape of the victims it cannot help. Pauline writes her manuscripts because, as her family tells her, she "has no heart." Only at such a cost does she live and speak to us.

The novel has its faults. Some of the people we meet in Part 2 (published separately in French as *Vivre! Vivre!*) seem arbitrarily bizarre. And yet the novel's total effect, its strange world of suffering children preternaturally old, is so convincing that I am not sure that I would not reverse these judgments on another reading.

*Daniel M. Murtaugh, in* Commonweal *(reprinted by permission of Commonweal Publishing Co., Inc.), November 13, 1970, p. 180.*

Marie-Claire Blais' *David Sterne* first appeared in French in 1967, following *A Season in the Life of Emmanuel,* the most naturalistic and most successful of her books. In the earlier novel she placed her characters in the recognizable social world of rural, church-dominated Quebec though their behaviour and reactions remained as extreme and obsessed as in her previous books, *Mad Shadows* and *Tête-Blanche.* But, in *David Sterne* Mlle. Blais has again left naturalism far behind and created a passionate prose-poem in which her highly sensitive and tormented characters struggle, in an urban landscape full of shadows and nightmares, to break free from their own moral and existential dilemmas. . . .

With *David Sterne,* Mlle. Blais has placed herself firmly and uncompromisingly in the literary tradition of the French moralists leading back through Camus, Genet and Gide to Baudelaire. The book deals in one way or another with many of the themes explored by these writers, and this makes it somewhat derivative. It owes most, perhaps, to the more abstract and less sensational works of Jean Genet, in which the passionate existential wranglings, the rebellion, the life of crime and sensation are so prominent. The confessional and didactic style of the book will also strike echoes in the reader's mind. Some of the poetic passages have the same broad expansiveness and rhythms, and indeed sentiments, of Walt Whitman. But *David Sterne* survives and transcends these comparisons. What allows it to do so is the immense compassion and tenderness Mlle. Blais displays for her characters in their whirlwind of struggle and suffering. The hard cold eye she cast on the cruel world of *Mad Shadows* has grown into one full of pity and profound sadness for the fate of men condemned to do battle with themselves.

With its exploration of abstract existential problems, *David Sterne* lacks the strong imaginative power of some of Mlle. Blais' other work. It is not her best book, but it is a provocative and moving one. . . .

*Brian Vintcent, "In a Landscape of Nightmares," in* Saturday Night, *November, 1973, pp. 53-4.*

* * *

## BOGAN, Louise 1897-1970

**An American poet and critic, Louise Bogan served as poetry**

**critic for *The New Yorker* for thirty years. She was a fine lyric poet whose "spiritual ancestors," according to Theodore Roethke, were Campion, Jonson, and the anonymous Elizabethan writers. Her work won many important prizes. (See also *Contemporary Authors*, obituary, Vols. 25-28.)**

Miss Bogan's themes are the reasons of the heart that reason does not know, the eternal strangeness of time in its periods and its passage, the curious power of art. Her mood is oftenest a sombre one, relieved not by gaiety but by a sardonic wit. She is primarily a lyricist. Not for nothing does the word "song" recur repeatedly in her titles, as, among others, "Juan's Song", "Chanson Un Peu Naïve", "Song for a Slight Voice", "Song for a Lyre", "Spirit's Song". It is the spirit's song that Louise Bogan sings, even when her subject is the body. The texture of her verse is strong and fine, her images, though few, are fit, her cadences well managed. Her lyrics display her gifts more happily than do her excursions into free verse, yet even an imperfect example of this shows of what durable stuff her poetry is made.

*Babette Deutsch, in her* Poetry in Our Time *(copyright by Babette Deutsch), revised edition, Doubleday, 1963, p. 266.*

This fine gathering of poems [*The Blue Estuaries: Poems 1923-1968*] gives us Louise Bogan's selections from the five books of poetry she has produced since 1923, and to these selections is added a collection of new poems. Evident up and down the line is Miss Bogan's dedication to the strictest demands of poetry. Never is there a sign of frantic casting about for catchy modes; the voice has been her own throughout a half-century of work. And yet, as the new poems will bear witness, she has refused to allow her voice to become static. . . . Here, too, can be seen the economy and cleanness which have been consistent qualities of Miss Bogan's lines. These same technical qualities are faithful to the emotions which subsume the poems. As the late Theodore Roethke pointed out, Miss Bogan is a woman "who scorns the open unabashed caterwaul so usual with love poets," a woman "who shapes emotion into an inevitable-seeming, an endurable, form." None of the emotions called on are exempt from her requirements. In a new poem, "Night," she finds among "the cold remote islands/And the blue estuaries" a metaphor for life's inescapable progression, but the emotions evoked by night's coming are held in check by her insistence on an ever-renewing nature: "—O remember/In your narrowing dark hours/That more things move/Than blood in the heart." Tight lines on emotions which threaten clarity. It is this kind of power under control that has marked her as one of our most accomplished poets.

Virginia Quarterly Review, *Vol. 45, No. 1, Winter, 1969, p. xviii.*

I think that one of the things poetry ought to do is prepare us for what is ahead. This is one of the senses in which poetry is prophecy. I have to have the feeling that a poet is living in the same world I'm in, that he walks on the ground, that he knows the scenes of his own crimes and the images of his own hope, that he has been where I'm headed. Louise Bogan's poems tell me what I only half want to know. I mean this, of course, as a compliment. . . .

In Bogan life is neither all one thing or another. The life force giveth and the life force taketh away. Hers is a poetry of meditation. Where to stand in a changing world, a world in which both our desires and the objects of our desires change?—this is the question. . . .

The great strength of Louise Bogan's poetry is its compression. No poet has been more adamant than she in demanding the uncluttered line and the precise image. Some of her early poems, I believe, blur in the mind. There is too much abstraction, too many big, bumbling nouns in "Fifteenth Farewell," "Winter Swan," and "The Alchemist," for example. . . . But in *The Blue Estuaries* this kind of poem is certainly in the minority. At her best Miss Bogan achieves what she has described as "effects truly fitted for the condensation of language and the production of 'memorable speech.'". . .

*Blue Estuaries* is a cold, comforting book.

*William Heyen, "The Distance From Our Eyes," in* Prairie Schooner *(© 1969 by University of Nebraska Press; reprinted by permission from* Prairie Schooner*), Fall, 1969, pp. 323-26.*

Louise Bogan is a poet who generates affectionate approval. . . . [The] feeling pervades that Miss Bogan never received the recognition due her work; and those who write about her verse go extra weight to correct the imbalance. . . .

*A Poet's Alphabet* is a delight to read. The arrangement takes us from Auden to Yeats, from American Literature to the Yale Series of Younger Poets. The dates of composition take us from 1923 to 1969, the year before Miss Bogan's death in February, 1970. The chief experience one undergoes in *A Poet's Alphabet* is admiration for Miss Bogan's generosity, which however is bestowed never at the expense of truth. Miss Bogan finds the strengths of her writers and emphasizes these in deft, bright, compact, and perceptive analyses. It is instructive to any critic or reviewer that Miss Bogan, in assessing the work of over 120 authors, approves (my count was casual) a round 100. . . . Miss Bogan almost never is negative completely. Some of these censured are admired elsewhere in her reviews. . . .

Evidence of a certain conservatism is found frequently in the early materials. . . . In her reviews of the 'fifties and 'sixties, Miss Bogan appears to have come to some terms with the experimentalists and vers librists, whom for a long time she held off. . . . Yet her need of form dies hard. One of the longer essays in her book is a defense of formal poetry under the guise of espousing its delights. . . .

Perhaps the service that Miss Bogan has done for letters during her life is discernible best in her constant approval of the significant literary movements on the continent and her vigorous support of translation as a means of making available, no matter how imperfectly, the thought of the influential cultures of France, Germany, Spain, and to a lesser extent of modern Greece and the Orient.

*Harry Morris, "Poets and Critics, Critics and Poets," in* Sewanee Review *(reprinted by permission of the editor; © 1972 by The University of the South), Autumn, 1972, pp. 627-29.*

[When] I was writing poetry myself and was young enough to be looking for signals that women wrote and wrote well [,] I had no notion then of whether or not they wrote as women—or even of what that might mean. If the question had been put to me, I would have dismissed it, for I would not have understood it as a desirable quality. To write as a woman of things that concern woman would have meant to me then soft prose, fine writing and poetical musings by three-named lady writers. I intended to avoid all of it. But Louise Bogan suggested something deeper: a lack of options as part of the condition of being a woman, a narrow life chosen by women because they were unwilling, if not unable to take risk. And yet wasn't there something of a risk in the act of being the person who wrote the poem? . . .

I thought . . . her anthologized poems seemed too careful; they lacked bite. I do not mean to imply that she was no academic poet—for she believed deeply in the lyric as a cry —only that too often she weakened her poems by tidying them up in the final lines, thereby undercutting their full strength.

Because she wrote well and because she had a critical honesty as unmistakable and durable as granite she knew this perfectly well. . . .

I would have given a great deal in those days of forming myself as a writer . . . to have found "Little Lobeila's Song," "Masked Woman's Song," "The Sorcerer's Daughter" and "After the Persian."

For these are the cries of a woman—cries against the turning of luck or of bad timing, and they speak of the ability to face the mirror or the bottle, of the courage to go to the "mad-house" (as she called it in a letter to Theodore Roethke) when life went down on her and she could not pull herself up alone any more. There is a loss implied in these poems for all women who are alone and aging. . . .

*Nancy Milford, in* The New York Times Book Review *(© 1973 by The New York Times Company; reprinted by permission), December 16, 1973, pp. 1-2.*

An elegant lyric poet and the *New Yorker's* highly influential poetry reviewer through most of four decades, Louise Bogan poured out a tireless flow of letters, keeping her friends informed of everything that went on in her complicated mind and life. That mosaic of dailiness has now been put together by her close friend Ruth Limmer, and ranks with the letters of Keats, Henry James and Rilke. For *What the Woman Lived* is not simply the informal accounting of events one expects from such a collection. Ardent, opinionated, eloquent, self-mocking, often wonderfully funny, the letters should be read, as Miss Bogan herself remarked of Rilke's correspondence, as "part of the body of [the poet's] imaginative work." William Maxwell observed in his *New Yorker* obituary of Louise Bogan: "In whatever she wrote, the line of truth was directly superimposed on the line of feeling." No book of hers more perfectly accomplished this than *What the Woman Lived*. . . .

In the poems of her old age, Louise Bogan took a dry, unsentimental look at women who face the dwindling hoard of years vulnerably on their own. If she allowed herself a rare stifled cry ("She is possessed by time, who once/Was loved by men"), her poems remained as passionately reticent and spare as ever. And her letters continued, for the most part, to tap a vein of careless panache, of hyperbolic and reckless abandon which was never permitted into her poetry and criticism (this may be the reason she wrote so many letters—that side of her had to come through somewhere). Nonetheless, during her 60s she sometimes sounded rather strained in her correspondence, indeed a trifle cautious—particularly in comments to her friend, the poet and novelist May Sarton. To Ruth Limmer, she complained, "If [May] would only stop writing sentimental poems!" Yet she was kinder and more circumspect when corresponding with Miss Sarton, less exuberantly outspoken and therefore less interesting. One misses the swift unself-conscious chop that in her youth she delivered straight to the jaw without a second thought. Of course, it had always been men, not women, who brought her to the top of her form as a letter-writer: She was a beguiling, if ironic, flirt.

*Pearl K. Bell, "A Woman of Letters," in* New Leader, *February 4, 1974, pp. 23-4.*

* * *

## BOND, Edward 1934-

**Bond is a controversial English playwright whose brilliant but violent and cruel plays were twice banned by Lord Chamberlain. He is best known for *Saved,* one of the formerly censured plays. (See also *Contemporary Authors*, Vols. 25-28.)**

In retrospect one might guess that *Saved* represents a transitional phase in Bond's work, one in which he is, more or less consciously, striving to free himself from the naturalistic style of *The Pope's Wedding,* with its meticulous notation of local country speech and recreation of a recognizably real world for its characters to live in, and reaching out towards the overtly non-realistic manner of *Early Morning*. . . . *Saved* could have made a thoroughly effective play in Bond's entirely naturalistic manner, or, seen in a different light, if he had managed to divorce it entirely from naturalism. But the text as it stands seems to me an interesting but finally unsatisfactory compromise. No question of compromise with *Early Morning,* though. Here naturalism is thrown right out of the window, and Bond is able to get straight down to what he has to say, without the necessary periphrases of superficially naturalistic drama.

Which is just as well, seeing that what he has to say is quite complex enough without the superimposition of purely technical subterfuges as well. If *The Pope's Wedding* and *Saved* can be seen as about—among other things—the corruption of man's natural innocence by 'upbringing and environment', which is to say by the forces exerted on him by abstractions like society, Christian mortality, the repressive rule of order, *Early Morning* moves a stage further, or if you like starts at the other end. The two earlier plays are about the suffering classes; *Early Morning* is about those who impose the suffering, exert the pressures. The play is a nightmare comic fantasy. . . .

The themes are completely consistent from *The Pope's Wedding* to *Saved* and from *Saved* to *Early Morning*. Each has an innocent (or relatively innocent) martyr-figure who with saintly or perhaps merely masochistic devotion opens himself to the worst that life has to offer. Each assumes some pervasive Oedipal situation in which humanity is seen as divided into put-upon, ill-used children and cruel, arbitrary, inscrutable parents who mete out punishments and occasional rewards with the savagery and unassailable authority of Old Testament gods. And each allows us to suppose that something may remain uncorrupted, some shred of natural goodness may survive; there is always a straw, if no more than a straw, to clutch at. . . .

It is easy to accuse [*Early Morning*] of naïvety. And of course on the level of ideas it is naïve; so are all Bond's plays. Life is not quite as simple as all that: society is not just Us and Them, the tyrants and the tyrannized, parents and children. Nor is it quite so easy for most of us to assume the position of lofty dissociation from it all that Bond seems to assume in *Early Morning,* remote from human sympathy, tolerant, if at all, because the human beings shown are as small and insignificant as the flies Queen Victoria is constantly swatting. But happily in the theatre such considerations have little to do with the case. It is not so much the abstract validity of the image presented, its power to change our own ideas on the subject, as the effectiveness of the image in itself—something which comes from the strength of the author's conviction in what he is saying, his complete commitment to his own position, however remote it may be from yours or mine. And here *Early Morning* really scores. It is not, heaven knows, a likeable play (none of Bond's, I think, is), but it packs a formidable punch in performance, and even in reading, because the strength of Bond's own obsession bludgeons us into suspending disbelief. . . .

*Early Morning,* of course, had even more trouble with censors and the censorious than *Saved.* And yet somehow, as has so often happened in the new drama in Britain, things were subterraneously working in Bond's favour, so that what started as incomprehensible, shocking, inducive of immediate, unthinking fury gradually came, without anyone's knowing quite how, to be accepted as, at the very least, an inescapable fact of theatrical life, so that even those who did not like Bond's plays very much found themselves agreeing to his importance. . . .

[*Narrow Road to the Deep*] marks a new stage in Bond's mastery of his material and his ability to display it to best advantage. The dialogue is pared to the bone, and placed with a poetic wit and economy which shows the hand of a master stage craftsman—something which before one would hardly have put in the forefront of Bond's qualifications as a dramatist. And above all, the play bears the mark on every page of Bond's maturing as a dramatic thinker, his increasing awareness of the complexities of life and moral decision.

*John Russell Taylor, "Edward Bond," in his* The Second Wave: British Drama for the Seventies *(reprinted by permission of Hill and Wang, a division of Farrar, Straus & Giroux, Inc.; copyright © 1971 by John Russell Taylor), Hill & Wang, 1971, pp. 77-93.*

[Bond is] a dramatist whose talent has never been in question, though the uses he has put it to have satisfied only sensationalists. But in *The Sea* Edward Bond displays a range of human sympathy brutally overlaid in most of his earlier work. True, he has not yet got back to writing about the three-dimensional people he presented in *The Pope's Wedding* and indeed in *Saved*; but the characters in *The Sea* have a faceted complexity, a comic ambiguity, which is quite new in Bond's work, and very welcome. No less so the almost total absence of that slavering cruelty which has marred, even ruined, much that has gone before. . . .

I should not care to describe *The Sea* as a well-made play, but it has about its many fine moments, both comic and pitiful, a stature which Bond has never touched before.

*J. W. Lambert, in* Drama, *Autumn, 1973, pp. 14-16.*

It goes without saying that this Shakespeare [in Bond's *Bingo*] won't be very easily reconciled with the one who rounded off *The Winter's Tale* so serenely, or, for that matter, the one who appears to rejoice at the prospect of Iago being exquisitely and endlessly tortured to death. A despairing, disgusted suicide seems scarcely less historically credible than a lesbian love-affair between Queen Victoria and Florence Nightingale. And yet, whether he's writing of the treatment of vagrants in 17th-century England or the details of Shakespeare's own dealings in Stratford, Bond consistently aims at an authenticity he never contemplates in that mad fantasy, *Early Morning.* Even the saloon-bar binge with Jonson has a basis in tradition, though Shakespeare's fatal acquisition is supposed to have been a fever, not a phial. Indeed, his account of the enclosure controversy seems rather more accurate than that of the redoubtable Rowse, who misreads a vital document in order to be able to claim that Shakespeare was opposed to the landgrabbers. Bond isn't interested in offering us a fictional archetype of suffering mankind, like his own (or Shakespeare's) Lear: he wants our attention for a specific period, an actual person. How is it (we're to ask) that a man whom we worship for his humanity could bear to live in a society we know to have been so cruel? How can we, his descendants, bear to live in a society directly derived from it?

This is the sort of question that Bond asks again and again, in play after play. All, from *Saved* to *The Sea,* may be seen as the dramatic equivalents of those insistent Oxfam ads which thrust children with sparrow-legs and pigeon-bellies under our well-nourished noses. Each insists that we face the kind of realities that make us instinctively drop our eyes and change the conversation; each consciously, perhaps presumptuously, attempts to make us more sensitive and responsible to the world's suffering.

*Benedict Nightingale, "The Bourgeois Bard," in* New Statesman, *November 23, 1973, p. 783.*

* * *

## BORGES, Jorge Luis 1899-

**Borges, an Argentinian, is a master of the short story, a poet, essayist, and man of letters. His inimitable fictions, or "parables," are not merely anti-realistic; they define, according to one critic, "new orders of reality." (See also *Contemporary Authors*, Vols. 21-22.)**

Somewhere, at a point coincident to their two orbits, Joyce and Borges meet. . . . Both have worked on their respective cities, Dublin and Buenos Aires, like mythographers resurrecting from sounds, local sights, houses, and streets, a timeless vision of their inhabitants. And, although at home in several languages and literatures, a shocking parochialism locates the center of their cosmopolis. Both are Daedalian architects of word structures, of labyrinths. Both are exorcists of the shadowy feelings and meanings, the mystery and power of words: literary exorcists of consciousness. Both betray that predilection for compounding the erudite and trivial, the esoteric and the oecumenical, implicating, at its most sensitive, our twentieth-century sensibility. And of course both have pressed an obsession with form, with style and technique, to bounds that dazzle even where they seem familiar. Some of their most brilliant moments are strictly parasitic and parodistic, and even self-parodistic. There is, moreover, an influence of one on the other, for Borges, in the twenties, was one writer of that vanguardist generation feeling the full impact, the contemporary impact, of *Ulysses*. His essay on Joyce ["El *Ulises* de Joyce"] and a translation of a fragment of the closing monologue ["Traducción de James Joyce, La última hoja del *Ulises,*" in *Proa,* January, 1925] comprise a singular event in literary history. Borges' experiments with style, in his poetry of the twenties, [reflect] a Joycean awareness of a new sensibility in search of expression. Several of the structural ideas of *Finnegans Wake* acquire a dialectical form in some of Borges' stories, essays, and poems. His poem *"La noche cíclica"* owes at least the adjective of its title to Joyce. Perhaps the decisive point of comparison is that their interpretative vision of the intellectual, social, and moral world of man is esthetic, and that their attitudes, tastes, literary ends and means are apolitical, frequently hermetical, and heretical. It is this affinity of nonconformists that attracts attention to their use of irony for fusing style to subject. Also, we owe to a similar use of the cyclical view of time, history and personalities, some of their most inimitable and intimate revelations about themselves as writers. And a final point: Borges, like Joyce in his later years, suffers from blindness. . . .

While we proceed in the two essays [Murillo studies Joyce and Borges, in this book, in two separate essays] by different means of analysis, the unity of the essays rests on the analogy between the reflective act that both authors accomplish through irony. The reflective act, that is, rendered an esthetic act. Here are two writers who intensify our awareness of the intellectual and esthetic phases by which irony communicates an unstated "impersonal" and "objective" meaning. Here irony, as a mode, is inseparable from the significance of works in prose and from the means of our access to that significance. We find here the *how* of ironical expression increasingly provoking and drawing attention to itself. Increasingly the effect becomes that of provoking the reaction that this *how* is attempting to simulate both the thing represented and our intellective and esthetic notions arrested by (Joyce) or converging upon (Borges) our apprehension of the thing represented. The more immediately it provokes our awareness of the mechanics of its operation, the more intensified and effective this *how.* Its aim is both to produce a counter-reflection through the impulses of the reader and to redirect them in a conspiratorial action between him and [the] author back upon the facets of reality or life represented. In Borges' stories we . . . find that our perceptions of the multiple relations between things and persons, and the causal connections between events, constitute the "meaning" of events, of lives and things, their *whatness* established by the *howness* of Borgian irony and its quality. The residue of mockery and ridicule in this mode is directed as humor or play at our impulse to attempt and to possess an omniscient view of human events and an infallible understanding of the universal laws of causality. The result of the conspiratorial action, as part of an impersonal and objective resolution of meanings, is to betray "reality," "fact," "life," into exposing themselves in our perceptions as image, or symbol, or, to use Borges' term, a *simulacrum.*

At the center of the analogy between Joyce and Borges are the effects each produces by redirecting the representation of certain states of consciousness onto the perceptions of their readers. Yet here precisely lies the cause for proceeding on two separate essays. The analogy results from their techniques for attaining a simultaneity of expression and multiple equivalences of form to subject. The underlying contrasts are harder to trace to their source. A basic one is the central position held by metaphysical speculation in Borges' dialectical designs. Or we could compare the dreaming consciousness of *Finnegans Wake* with the hallucinatory ordeals of some of Borges' heroes. Both, as dream structures, are labyrinthine and cyclical. But the verbal obscurities of Joyce's dreamer-narrator are controlled to work their way from the irrational inconclusiveness of a sleeping mind toward coherent resolutions of rational statement; whereas in Borges style and idea impel his rational disquisitions out to fantasy, non-reason, and hallucination. In more conventional terms, we may say that in Joyce's verbal patterns we have a "stream," in Borges' compact, conceptual ones, a "structure" of consciousness.

The states of consciousness in *Finnegans Wake,* however verbally obscure, appear transparently evident in their linear and sequential movement because they are conceived in the dream as states of nonviolence. They are inner reflections of the human *mea culpa* taking place or projected upon a glass of innocency. The Borgian states of consciousness, nearly always scared by acts of violence, are radical conflicts between the subjectivity of will and illusion and their objectivization in time, conflicts between dimensions of being and the process of their impersonalization that gives rise to archetypes and symbols. Thus Borges furnishes what I call "total" conflicts because the progression and movement of their warring tensions build up and impart to us through reiteration and recapitulation (a horizontal and vertical compression of themes) a total opposition between all of their components as that dichotomy of symbolical realities that is human consciousness, both personal and collective. The effect is to heighten the reader's perceptive awareness of his own consciousness, so to speak, as a counterpart to that antagony of irresolvable forces and symbolical dissonances. The Joycean effect is then quite unlike the Borgian because, although both authors impel the inductions of ironical readings to a highly logical and, stylistically, logistical point of resolution, the tensions of the Joycean ironies which I call dis-tensions neutralize their opposition at this point to provide entry into the myth that *Finnegans Wake* enacts; whereas in Borges' stories the conflict of tensions remains irresolvable in order to produce, in their mutual annihilation or effacement, the effect of a predicament of consciousness compounded, localized, and centered in the reader's intellective and emotive response.

*L. A. Murillo, "Introduction" to his* The

Cyclical Night: Irony in James Joyce and Jorge Luis Borges *(copyright © 1968 by the President and Fellows of Harvard College; excerpted by permission of the publishers), Cambridge, Mass.: Harvard University Press, 1968, pp. ix-xix.*

Jorge Luis Borges makes strange and compelling word-music. He plays only one instrument—the intellectual, the epistemological—but the strumming of his cerebral guitar sets into vibration all the strings of emotion, intuition, and esthetic longing that are common to sentient humanity. In his short stories alone he has written a symphony of the human consciousness—unfinished, not because he has left it incomplete, but because he sees human thought as unconsummated. Men may possibly have truth, his fictions tell us, and they can believe they have it, but they cannot know they have it. Tantalized by truth, they juggle their thoughts and words and haply achieve the dazzling suggestion of the imminence of a revelation. On this Borges has based his "esthetic of the intelligence." (pp. 3-4)

What Borges gives us is uncanny in the Freudian sense: untrue, but somehow true—or, as Plato said of his myths, they are not true but there is something like them that is true. It is in this sense that Adolfo Bioy Casares and Ana María Barrenechea have said that Borges' fantasies are more real than reality. His stories suggest other ways of interrelating the parts of the universe, other ontologies that we have forgotten or have not yet made.

This is only to say that Borges is mythic. In the ancient mythmaker and the radical philosophical idealist the wheel comes full circle. Because both are lacking an overriding perspective or mental commitment, their worlds are in flux, and each momentary contour of thought is as valid as another. An idea's value to the consciousness is the criterion of its truth. (p. 5)

Borges does not pretend, and we do not expect, that some ultimate, objective revelation will really spring from his dissolution and reformation of reality; the symphony can never be finished. But it can be played infinitely. Meaning, beauty, and satisfaction lie in the crescendo that culminates in climactic moments of near-fulfilment, when a Name seems about to be called, a summary note struck, and the face of Truth revealed. (p. 6)

[Borges] does not suppose, apparently, that in reading his tales we are going to lose ourselves in the mood or the action; instead, he gives us, with deceptive and very deliberate casualness, the symbols of an idea. Through his symbols and images he repetitiously and systematically *alludes*, and his allusions comprise much, if not most, of the real substance of his narratives. The semantic payload is given largely by suggestion. (p. 7)

Having to do with creation as such, many of his fictions comprise a literature about literature—art about art. . . . Borges' stories in the aggregate comprehend, almost omnisciently, the abstract forms of literature and of its creation and its manner of being. It is almost as if Borges had uttered the hundredth word, calling the summational Name of literature; but, courteously, he speaks it obliquely, as if to spare literature the humiliation of fulmination.

It is for this reason that Borges is rightly called a Baroque writer. The Baroque is, essentially, a time or a circumstance in which the creative intellect ceases to find value in the results of thought and turns to contemplating the form of its own activity. (p. 8)

The esthetic experience is essentially intellectual, but it is not usually self-conscious; it does not analyze itself in the moment of its occurrence. But when, in literature, this happening consists precisely in its looking at itself through symbolic or allegorical forms, the reader is given a degree of control over the event. Because he has some awareness of what is happening, as it happens, he can surrender to the esthetic enjoyment, or he can concentrate on the manner of production of the esthetic occurrence with intellectual appreciation, or he can do both at once with the effect of unifying and heightening his experience. A person can read and reread Borges with the enjoyment he feels in replaying his favorite music.

The Symbolists made their poetry self-symbolizing, but perhaps took the matter too seriously. . . . They looked for God through poetry; they tried to be mythic in order to restructure the universe. But Borges, both as poet and as fiction-maker, knows that modern man cannot be mythic, not really, and that imagination only confirms idealism as the nearest substitute for a mythic view; for in order to be mythic, the mind must lack a structured rationality. Only man's reason can call into question the hierarchy of reality it has created. The conceptual fluidity of the mythmaker can exist only as a mentality that radically doubts the validity of its own constructs, or as one which consciously forays into fancy without expecting to transcend or fulminate the vast system of practical fictions that men live by. Borges will not ride with Valéry on the seesaw of momentary subjective renewal followed by reentry into mundane reality; this smacks of psychedelic self-hypnosis, of religion, of escape. Borges will not lose psychic control over the game; he will remain the chess player as well as the pawn. (pp. 16-17)

If I seem to treat Borges' short stories as if they were primarily the artistic reflection of a few ancient ideas about the functions of the mind, it is because I must be simplistic for the sake of putting this one aspect of his work into clear relief. It is one of the most important aspects of his fictional creation. (p. 18)

Borges' intellectual esthetic, his "imminence of a revelation," his "mental process," and his penchant for the depiction of ambiguity, are facets of the self-expression of a mind inverted upon itself. . . . What, then, is the essential nature, the identity, of the mountains and horses and persons with whom Borges peoples his literature, if in the end they trace the image of Borges, who knows them for what they are? They are ideal beings, the constructions of a self-conscious mind, and we can expect them to behave as such, not as the mountains and horses and persons that we know in the outer world. . . . The world in which Borges' fictive creations move about is a primeval world and has all the earmarks of the archaic cosmology.

This is owing precisely to the fundamental fluidity of Borges' thought. Borges is an idealist, a skeptic, a freethinker, and above all, an artist. The human mind imagines and conjectures in the same degree that it does not know, or in the degree to which it does not choose to know or does not believe it knows. Radical speculation—

imagination—is the special property of archaic man, who has little fixed knowledge to guide him; of children for the same reason; and of the artist, the poet, and the skeptic. Where facts have not yet been chosen or have been rejected for scientific or esthetic reasons, fantasies compete for honor. Every truth begins as metaphor, useful fiction, or esthetic dream. (p. 19-20)

Isaiah Berlin, the British historian, has noted . . . a psychic difference in the mentalities of many great writers. He makes his point by quoting Archilochus: "The fox knows many things, but the hedgehog knows one big thing" (*The Hedgehog and the Fox,* p. 7). Shakespeare, Goethe, and Aristotle are foxes in this scheme; Dante, Plato, and Dostoevsky are hedgehogs. Perhaps the distinction is merely that of Nominalism versus Realism, Aristotle against Plato. (p. 24)

I would say that Borges is philosophically a fox who longs for the simplicity and certainty of the hedgehog but cannot bring himself to be one. He searches, without hope of finding, something which transcends fox and hedgehog. He finds only substitutes and metaphors for that transcending something. Intellectually, he finds idealism; esthetically, myth. Borges is both an Anglophile and an Argentine. He is steeped in the mood of Schopenhauer and Nietzsche and in English literature, but emotionally he is a product of Spanish American *criollismo.* He has made the conflict between perspectivism and universal vision (Zahir and Aleph) one of his central artistic concerns (I would maintain that it is *the* central concern), and he depicts the transcendence of this contradiction as myth, the near-abstraction or esthetic fact. Because of this central concern, Borges is literarily a hedgehog.

This is the most important point to be made in this study of Borges' fiction. The system that is apparent in Borges' imagery and symbol hinges upon the simple idea of pyramidal thought, of thing and attribute, with all of its vast implications. I shall try to show that when Borges speaks of twilight and noon, swamps and towers, blood and sand, tigers and walls, and dozens of other things that recur in his fiction, he is talking about being and non-being, the created and the uncreated; and always he is talking about them with the implication that the contradiction between them is transcended—or as I see it, underlain—by myth. [Wheelock's careful explication of the word "myth," central to his argument, is found on pages 20-25.] . . . [Only] the poets and the mystics seem able to prolong [the "moment of myth"]; they stretch it out by declaring that the world and all of its details are somehow provisional and illusory. The idealist prolongs or converts the "moment" into an intellectual attitude. We call it pantheism, nihilism, skepticism, or intellectual mysticism, but Borges is nearest to right in calling it an esthetic of the intelligence. (pp. 24-5)

Since man's ideas cannot be validated by outside criteria, one idea is as good as another. A man can demolish and reconstruct the world, making it less banal and more beautiful, and he can do this with the complete freedom of the self-sufficient mind. With regard to this idealist solipsism, Anderson Imbert says that what interests Borges is the beauty of the theories, myths, and beliefs that he cannot believe in; he feels free to choose "a multiplicity of simultaneous paths" (*Literatura hispanoamericana,* II, 268). As this critic goes on to say, Borges sees man as lost in a labyrinth, capable of producing mental labyrinths of his own as explanations of the chaotic Great Labyrinth. But while men in general engage in serious hypostatization as the only form of "explanation," Borges stands above this attempt to account for the universe; his truth does not depend on the things that can be called true, but upon the assumption that nothing can be so called. For him the goal of thought is not knowledge, but distraction.

Borges' most lucid symbol of this mental isolation from objective reality is the Minotaur of "The House of Asterion." This story can be read coherently and meaningfully if one keeps in mind that the narrator, Asterion, is the idealist consciousness and that the labyrinth he lives in is the conceptual universe. (p. 27)

What does Borges mean by "dream"? This is a critical question for anyone who approaches Borges' fiction as symbolic expression. . . . In the first place, Borges' idea is the same as Descartes': existence and thought are the same thing. (pp. 44-5)

Borges' "dream," then, is imagination, the creation of the esthetic fiction. But here I do not intend to imply only *literature,* but what C. S. Lewis has called "fantasy that hovers between the allegorical and the mythopoeic." Such fantasy is not limited to writers, as Borges would quickly agree. It is precisely because Borges' stories and prose pieces (his *thoughts*) have thought as their real subject that they are detached from mundane reality and hence are finally independent of language. Says Lewis [in his preface to *George Macdonald: An Anthology*]: "The critical problem . . . is whether this art—the art of mythmaking—is a species of the literary art. . . . [The] Myth does not essentially exist in *words* at all."

Borges' esthetic is an esthetic of the intelligence, and he usually makes dreaming equivalent to thinking—the kind of thinking, or imagination, that brings the elements of the world together into a pregnancy through extreme, almost hypnotic concentration: separation from immediate sense-perceptions and the deliberate inversion of the mind upon its contents, as if, by the heat of attention, to melt them into oneness, or to cause them to yield up something palpable, something real. In other words, dreaming or thinking is an effort to escape from language, from the idea of the world which language imposes upon us. By "dreaming" the consciousness hopes to escape its own solidified thought-history, its fixed categories, the dead words that represent memory badly and petrify the world. What the mind finally seeks is a new arrangement of reality, and to achieve this it must go back to the mythical condition prior to the gods, before language; for out of that pregnancy some more adequate God, some better language may come, though it be faceless and wordless. (pp. 45-6)

Borges longs for the Alephic vision that is given only to mystics; or rather, he longs for that cerebral mysticism which is able to hypostatize all attributes simultaneously instead of successively; to do this would be to destroy linear time. But he cannot have this, and he lives by making hypostatizations, each having its distinct moment.

The tension or interplay between longed-for universality and necessary perspectivization is a recurring preoccupation in Borges, best exemplified in "The Aleph" and "The Zahir." But this interplay is not as prevalent as a more fundamental tension that we may call hypostatic rivalry: competition among the hypostatizations of the mind, or between a hypostat and its attributes. Most of the stories in *El Aleph* and *Ficciones* are (from the standpoint of motif) only variants of this form. Two ideas, two aspects of reality, two attributes or "beings" vie for the attention of the consciousness; one must be victorious over the other; so Scharlach kills Lönnrot, the Negro kills Martín Fierro, Bandeira kills Otálora, and so on. The fate of the subordinate idea is a cause for lament, in Borges' view, and although the victory of one is necessary, it is nevertheless deplorable because the victor is only a perspective, a partial image of reality. When a dominant hypostatization becomes a fixation, a dogma, it is not a rival who kills him, but the consciousness itself (the "universe"). Fire is an entity that finally tests the contents of the mind, and only the expedient and provisional beings survive. Dogmas perish because they are too fixed, too objectively real.

The symbols of the Zahir, its modifications, its opposites, and its alternatives are repeated with monotonous persistence throughout all of the stories in the two collections. (pp. 64-5)

To dispense with the accepted verities and create fictions out of other fictions is to think freely in the most radical sense. It is to start from, and return to, the primordial home ground of myth in forming and re-forming one's ideas of the world. This makes it possible to see reality in many perspectives, all of them fresh and free of blinding dogmatism. If a man cannot have an Aleph, he must at least have a panorama of views, none of which claims to be ultimate and thus blots out the rest. Borges says it all beautifully in "Pierre Menard, Author of the *Quijote*". . . . (pp. 68-9)

*Carter Wheelock, in his* The Mythmaker: A Study of Motif and Symbol in the Short Stories of Jorge Luis Borges *(copyright © 1969 by Carter Wheelock), University of Texas Press, 1969.*

Borges writes of sceptics overwhelmed by mystical event and of gangsters with the logic of Auguste Dupin. [His] remarkable stories which mix cabbalism with science fiction and the detective story deride, in their ironic reversals, the fictions of communication with others and make the communication of one with oneself the greater puzzle. In his stories, narratives, and prose pieces, Borges is among the leading writers of our time who are extending the boundaries of fiction into autobiography and essay.

Virginia Quarterly Review, *Vol. 47, No. 2 (Spring, 1971), pp. lvi-lvii.*

In his own work, Jorge Luis Borges has practiced, among other offices, that of chronicler of insomnia and of its equally unsleeping counterpart, nightmare. The states of the insomnia that he notes have included poignant and lucid memory. His degrees of dreaming or waking nightmare have been characterized by prescient insight, by epiphany. (His epiphanies we understand in the sense in which Joyce employed the term, the larger sense of passages of revelation and vision. . . .) Borges' own obsession with a dream state—in the individual, in the created (or dreamt) world, in the gods or God—has forced his hand when writing, so that he writes of dreams which must be dreamt in the future, of man's fates which were dreamt in the past. And so we find that "the memory of the future" is of exactly the same potential as "the hope in the past". . . .

From the time of his first, particular, sense of the infinite, Borges has apparently suspected that everything has been dreamt before. He offers constant proof of this suspicion. . . .

Borges, the subtlest of historians, understands that history is not *merely* a nightmare (not just a nightmare from which we are struggling to awake, as in Joyce's cosmology, but perhaps also a nightmare we are preparing to dream?); it is also a sequence of vividly insomniac epiphanies to be repeatedly relived. In these states of pre-nightmare the personae of the action step to the music of others as well as their own, inhabit the dreams of others as well as their own, are duplicated as brothers, antagonists (second actors), chance counters of a dream lottery. Borges suspects a cyclical nihilism in it all, an annihilating repetition, a repetitious similitude, a simulacrum. . . .

Borges is a crypto-classic. And the secret *(kruptos)* of his classicism is in [his] texts, and they in themselves are cryptic, which, as well as secret, means concise, laconic, succinct. His shorthand serves in making *précis* of numberless mythologies, personal as well as popular. In expounding his own unique vision, he establishes a valid syncretism of his own for uniting synopses of antique plots which have classically repeated each other. Previous tellers of antique tales, "synopsizers" of antique plots, seem less excruciatingly aware that they are retelling the eternal tales, re-synopsizing the plots. . . . Borges is so aware that he is summing-up that he finds it natural to reproduce some of the previous synopses for us so that we may marvel in comparing the "Extraordinary."

In [his] "brief and extraordinary tales," most of the pieces are not tales so much as suggestive passages of para-Kabbalistic meaning: not the Kabbalistic theory of language, but a theory of key passages: not Word/World, but Sentence/Judgment. As it is for the Kabbalist, history here is a symbolic *repetition* in every man's soul. . . .

We change each day. In his own work, Borges has shown us that we change each moment in regard to a mirror, the moon, a door, a book.

*Anthony Kerrigan, "Foreword," to* Extraordinary Tales *by Jorge Luis Borges and Adolfo Bioy Casares, edited and translated by Anthony Kerrigan (© 1971 by Herder and Herder, Inc.; reprinted with permission), Herder & Herder, 1971, pp. 7-15.*

The laying on of heavy strokes of local colour has always been one of [Borges's] predominant traits and the more one reads of him—outside of his twenty or so 'metaphysical' tales and fables—the more limited seem his means and aims. His predictable reliance on the basic elements of gothic stories gets to be ennervating. (In this he has, I think, been rather poorly served by his recent English publishers who [in *A Universal History of Infamy*], greedily and carelessly include pieces which have appeared up to four times previously in other volumes. . . .)

In the introduction to the first edition Borges makes an acknowledgement the implications of which he seems, uncharacteristically, to ignore. He says that the early films of

Von Sternberg were a great influence on these tales—in fact all they have in common with movies like *Morocco* and *Shangai Express* is an emphasis on decor and setting and props.

Now it must be patently evident to everyone that the camera, and so the spectator, can take in a great deal in the way of 'atmosphere' whilst concentrating on the action of the narrative being played out before it; in print we have to depart from the drama to gather data of this (secondary) nature—in a novel such diversions need not bother us, indeed such diversions may well form the novel, but in a story of a couple of thousand words an author's concern for ambience can often come to be mistaken for his over indulgence of a facility for listing the graphic and incongruous elements of the backdrop.

*Jonathan Meades, "Borges's Documentary Tales," in* Books and Bookmen, *January, 1974, p. 47.*

Like the frugal stars he mentions in "Rubaiyat," [Borges'] poems [in *In Praise of Darkness*] hold their treasures back. Like those stars, his poems are distant, they are cool, they are tiny, they are remotely bright. Most of all, though, they are only and lastingly themselves.

I don't mean that Borges' poems display the extravagant stinginess of much modern poetry, the pharisaic abuse of the commandment "less is more." Not at all. Nor that he pays out in fashionably flat diction. (Although phrases like "that white thing, the moon" are the kind of achieved failure, the signal frustration this sort of diction aims at, or should.) Nor even that the real voice of Borges is in his short stories and that his poetry is metrical ventriloquism. (That, after all, is the vulgar temptation and so the easiest to avoid.) No, I mean that reading his poems is like listening to someone pacing in a carpeted study next door: we strain, we hear, we imagine, but we never do see. . . .

Borges has only been able to give by taking away and he imagines the taking away has been a giving back—his sight for his vision, for instance. What's at stake is not the truth of his statements, their autobiographical or even "poetic" truth; rather, it is the hazard of an imagination acting on the less, on the *least* in order to see the *most*. As always, Borges' imagination is precisely superlative. Or, as Norman Thomas di Giovanni beautifully renders the poet's *"admirablemente mezquinos,"* "wondrously paltry."

Here, then, is the latest collection of poems by one of the three greatest writers alive today. It is the slimmest of slim volumes. Unpretentious in its diction, in its imagery, in its praise of "plain things" and even in its invocation of famous figures like the near-blind James Joyce, it in fact pretends to offering the "center," the "algebra" and the "key" to Borges. But the book will no doubt be passed over in favor of more obviously assuming works by a man who says here that he wants "to be remembered less as a poet than as a friend" anyway. This book does much to create that sense of Borges as a friend, an old friend, whose richness lies not in splendid moments but in our extended relationship. So let us not forget that it is the poet who creates the friend. Let us remember that darkness lets us see the stars. Let us, too, praise darkness.

*Ronald Christ, in* Commonweal *(reprinted by permission of Commonweal Publishing Co., Inc.), March 8, 1974, pp. 18-9.*

Borges is the modern poet who best expresses not the power of the imagination but the seductiveness of the imaginative intellect, not one who evokes emotion raw or lyrical on the page but one who offers a highly idiosyncratic consciousness just prior to the awakening of an emotion or just after the emotion has passed. Immediacy has always been lacking in his works. And yet the world of Borges has its own majesty, its own penetrating cadences and charm, full of spheres within spheres, thought about thought, a parabolic shadow play continually unfolding, doubling back, and then returning (to use one of Borges's persistent motifs) like a river to its unimaginable source. . . .

If [the poems in *In Praise of Darkness*] have a certain twilit convalescent air, recording Borges's familiar fascination with mirrors and mazes, to which have been added two new themes, "old age and ethics," they nevertheless have the beauty of faded cameos, of museums of shifting forms, as well as Borges's poignant, stoical apprehension of his approaching death: "I reach my center, / my algebra and my key. . . . Soon I shall know who I am."

The New York Review of Books *(reprinted with permission from* The New York Review of Books; *© 1974 by NYREV, Inc.), April 4, 1974, p. 44.*

Borges frequently questions his own existence, and characteristic fictive strategies include reviewing non-existent books, inventing obscure texts to quote from, and writing biographical sketches of imaginary writers.

In *Doctor Brodie's Report,* his first collection of new tales for some years, Borges claims he is trying to escape from the elaborate literary games and fantastic contrivances with which he is associated and write 'straightforward stories' in the style of the early Kipling. . . . Only three or four of these 11 stories are Borges at anywhere near his peak. I think especially of *End of the Duel,* in which a pair of gauchos continue their rivalry up to and just after the moment of death, and *Guayaquil,* which involves a mystical conflict between two scholars who briefly take on the identities of the historical figures they are discussing. Others, for all the skill and economy of their narration, lack the intellectual excitement and resonance of his best work. They are plain tales from the foothills of a genius. But while he may have set aside the puzzles, the old epiphanies remain, and the stories reflect again and again the familiar obsessions—with time, labyrinths, doubles, chance and destiny. . . . There is much about history in *Doctor Brodie's Report,* but as usual there is virtually no interest shown in political questions or social problems. Nor is there much concern for character, though he creates people with vivid presences and convincing minds. There are however no stories here that eschew human protagonists and rely upon the excitement of ideas, as several of his most memorable fictions do. . . .

Borges appeals to academics in part because his small, coherent, but infinitely suggestive body of work lends itself to endless exegesis. More than that though, he comforts the campus author by refuting the cult of experience, by showing so triumphantly that to be a writer you don't have to hunt big game, go to the wars or walk the corridors of power. Further, he combines in an unusual degree the cultivation of the mind and an admiration for the primitive, lucid ratiocination and freewheeling mysticism, while showing that you do not have to be either alienated from society or too closely involved in its problems. As the writer's writer, he embodies and articulates a powerful concern for craft, for vocation, for tradition. . ., for the invincibility of the book.

*Philip French, "Labyrinthine," in* New Statesman, *May 3, 1974, pp. 628-30.*

* * *

## BRESLIN, Jimmy 1930-

**Breslin, an American writer, is well known in New York for his syndicated newspaper columns and his political activities.**

Breslin is a local colorist of this city [New York], particularly of Queens; he has the place, the time and the speech. . . . Breslin writes prose in a New York idiom with a shrewdness all his own, but for things beyond our borders his style has limitations. He employed it to good comic effect in "The Gang That Couldn't Shoot Straight" and he has adopted it sagely in the New York chapters of this chilling book [*World Without End, Amen*]. Among the horrors of Belfast and Derry, however, it often seems inappropriate. That is something one does not like to say of a writer so much to be valued for his rightness about things on his own turf.

*Harvey Gardner, in* The New York Times Book Review *(© 1973 by The New York Times Company; reprinted by permission), August 26, 1973, pp. 6, 18.*

In *World Without End, Amen,* Breslin weighs in as a serious novelist, then takes himself too seriously. The narrative's bog-slogging pace is a shame, because Breslin clearly cares, and can teach much about people who seldom turn up in current fiction: frustrated cops, tiresome racists, lower-middle-class wives with horizons defined by mortgage payments and broken washing machines. Breslin knows this turf, but he seems to have taken his title too literally. Under his ministrations, an instructive tour is slowly transformed into an endless vigil.

*Paul Gray, "Emerald Blues," in* Time *(reprinted by permission from* Time, The Weekly Newsmagazine; *copyright Time Inc.), September 17, 1973, p. 100.*

[Breslin] . . . writes as he speaks (on television and in his periodical journalism), not in the Queen's English, but in an "ethnic" Irish Queens (NY) accent. He knows that world as only a native son can, and that knowledge is the source of his strength as a writer. He is racetrack wise and street-corner funny, and he can smell a con through three feet of concrete. He is the only honest Irish cop on the force.

When he is on home ground in the first third of his new novel [*World Without End, Amen*], writing about Irish cops in Queens, his ear and eye pick up everything within range. If his portrait of life at home and on the beat is accurate—and there can be no doubt of its authenticity—then that is where hell is located, in the bars, courtrooms and those endless rows of two-family houses of "neighborhood" New York. This is not the black ghetto or the central city; no one goes hungry and at the end of the line there is a pension. This is the white, ethnic, lower middleclass, embattled "suburb" of the most depressing drabness, meanness, sloth, squalor—the spiritual equivalent of hopeless dead-end poverty; it would make drunkards of Carrie Nation and Billy Sunday and an atheist of Billy Graham.

But Breslin is not content to be our chronicler of this desiccated corner of the city. He is aflame with a mission. . . .

[But *World Without End, Amen*] collapses; it collapses into some good on-scene reportage of the unholy war in Belfast and Derry and elsewhere—but as a novel it nonetheless collapses utterly. . . . Breslin at his worst has always been a beery sentimentalist who does not scruple at bathos and has a marked weakness for soggy movie finishes.

The New Republic *(reprinted by permission of* The New Republic; *© 1973 by Harrison-Blaine of New Jersey, Inc.), September 29, 1973, p. 31.*

In "World Without End, Amen," Breslin, to my surprise and delight, outruns his writ as a New Journalist and becomes, in the best sense, an Old Novelist. . . .

His savage depiction of life in the Davey family and life on the Force is meant to instruct, not to amuse, and it carries much of the authority of Robert Coles' recent studies of Middle American rage and frustration. . . .

The scenes in Ulster belong to the people of Ulster, and the principal figure of these scenes is actually the Protestant-Catholic struggle. Breslin's reportorial skill tells here: I have not read a more persuasive account of the modern Troubles. Though the author seems to side with the Catholic faction, and though he adduces many instances of their oppression, there is no feeling of polemic in his pages. One is reminded of Morley Safer's television reports from Vietnam, telling us, between the lines, that this is really how it is.

*L. E. Sissman, in* The New Yorker, *October 8, 1973, p. 166.*

I understand that in the United States *World Without End, Amen* is rather widely taken to be a revelation of the nature and origin of the troubles in Northern Ireland. There are reasons for being skeptical about this revelation. Certainly anyone who tries to understand the situation in Northern Ireland today with the aid of Mr. Breslin's book will find himself or herself far out at sea. . . .

As a political guide to the Northern Ireland situation, either in 1970, 1974, or at any other time, *World Without End, Amen* is worse than useless, since it is plausibly and persistently misleading. Considering it as a work of fiction, I do not find it any more satisfactory. . . .

The pity of it is that Mr. Breslin could have written quite a good book about Northern Ireland; vestiges of it are embedded in *World Without End, Amen.* He is a reporter who describes very well what he actually sees: his descriptions of riots, of the outward appearance of people and their clothes, of houses, rooms, bars, and streets are accurate and telling. (His *ear* is much less good, most of his Irish dialogue is unspeakable, in every sense of the word.) If he had put his meager ideological equipment on the shelf, had put cotton wool in his ears, and had described what he actually saw in Northern Ireland that summer, day by day, the result would have had to be much nearer to the truth, and also more interesting, than *World Without End, Amen*.

*Conor Cruise O'Brien, "An Ulster Fable," in* The New York Review of Books *(reprinted with permission from* The New York Review of Books; *© 1974 by NYREV, Inc.), February 21, 1974, pp. 13-14.*

* * *

## BRODSKY, Joseph 1940-

**Brodsky, a Russian poet, was exiled by the Soviet government in 1972 and has since served the University of Michigan as poet-in-residence. (See also *Contemporary Authors*, Vols. 41-44.)**

[It] is clear from the translations that Mr. Brodsky commands many tones of voice, from the lyric ("A Christmas Ballad") to the elegiac ("Verses on the Death of T. S. Eliot") to the comic-grotesque ("Two Hours in an Empty Tank"), and can handle with equal ease a wide variety of rhymes and meters, short lines, long lines, iambics, anapaestics, masculine rhymes and feminine. . . .

Mr. Brodsky is not an easy poet, but even a cursory reading will reveal that, like Van Gogh and Virginia Woolf, he has an extraordinary capacity to envision material objects as sacramental signs, messengers from the unseen. . . .

Unlike the work of some of his contemporaries, Mr. Brodsky's seems to stand outside what might be called the Mayakovsky tradition of "public" poetry. It never uses a fortissimo. Indeed, original as he is, I would be inclined to classify Mr. Brodsky as a traditionalist. To begin with, he shows a deep respect and love for the past of his native land. . . .

He is also a traditionalist in the sense that he is interested in what most lyric poets in all ages have been interested in, that is, in personal encounters with nature, human artifacts, persons loved or revered, and in reflections upon the human condition, death, and the meaning of existence.

His poems are apolitical, perhaps defiantly so, which may explain why he has, so far, failed to win official approval, for I can find nothing in them which the sternest censor could call "subversive" or "immoral." . . .

For Brodsky, as for Rilke and Eliot, poetic language has the same degree of "reality" as the world; words regularly interact with things. In "Isaac and Abraham" (1963) the transformation, in Isaac's dream, of the word *kust* ("bush") into the word *krest* ("cross"), which takes place painfully, letter by letter, symbolizes the transformation of a part of nature into the altar on which Isaac is to be sacrificed. Even Isaac's name becomes an anagram of his fate: the Cyrillic letter *s* (which is shaped like the Latin *c*) mirrors the form of the victim—a sacrificial lamb with forelegs and hindlegs bound together. . . .

Brodsky assumes, with the Pasternak of "The Poems of Yuri Zhivago," an essential "unity of poetry and life." And he continues, with extraordinary energy, to hurl his poetic speech against the silence that surrounds us all.

*W. H. Auden, "The Poems of Joseph Brodsky," in* The New York Review of Books *(reprinted with permission from* The New York Review of Books; *© 1973 by NYREV, Inc.), April 5, 1973, pp. 10-11.*

Among us, by the accident of history and the connivance of a more subtle tyranny—the knowledge that the West celebrates and consumes its celebrities—is the greatest poet of his generation, the Soviet Jewish exile, Joseph Brodsky, whose "Selected Poems" is a revelation of the power of the word living in the cracks of silence. . . .

These—silence and death, creation, birth and beginnings—are the outer limits of Joseph Brodsky's universe. Spinning at the center is the poet: young man, lover, father, exile, Mr. Out-of-step, madman, traveler, celestial wanderer, Jew, Christ-bearer, legatee of a language . . ., creator of a new language, master of traditional forms and inventor of new ones.

How does one know that Joseph Brodsky is, at 33, a major poet, not simply a major poet to whom majority is accorded as a complementary addendum to the details of heroic biography? Nothing needs to be known about Brodsky other than the poems. Anything else that is known—and already there is too much of that—is irrelevant. I confess that for me the mark of the gift is not alone the congeniality of the vision, that Brodsky is moved by many of the same sources that move me, the Bible, Dante, Goethe, Lev Shestov, Nicholas Berdyaev, Vladimir Soloviev, the progenitive myths and their slightly deranged Russian interpreters, but more than these that he never lets himself off easily. . . .

The poet thinks beyond the poem and writes again. The reader is abandoned to his own reflections. The poet and the audience are abjured by the poem to rethink their existence. If poetry can compel such renewal what it may display as harshness, angularity, sheer complexity and difficulty is justified by the magnitude of the reality incanted.

It is quite true that Joseph Brodsky is a private voice. He has nothing to do with the spectacles and spectaculars which have become the hallmark of the vagabond poets of the Soviet Union, to whom the United States has been so hospitable in recent years. But to apostrophize Brodsky's privacy, to underscore his apparent indifference to ideology is to make a familiar mistake about poems, however accurate an opinion it may be about poets. . . .

Brodsky does not assist his audience to feel righteously martial sentiments, to purge their rage in the face of historical brutality; but his poetry, these poems, are covered with a sense of evil, the diabolic irrationality of human history, contempt for the cynicism and venality of those who claim possession of operational truth.

Against the vectors of antihumanism Brodsky sets a tensed and tough version of justice, justice within nature and creation which *must* be believed and sustained. And to him, sustaining his sense of strangeness in this world (not alienation), aloneness and isolation (undepressed and without despair), anguish (but not anxiety) is a vision, not yet classically Jewish nor yet dogmatically Christian, which might be described as Christ-bearing or Messianic. Brodsky's liturgical poem "Nunc Dimittis" or his pictorial "Nature Morte" are poems that depict faith, rather than pointing toward it. . . .

"Gorbunov and Gorchakov" . . . is the equal of any major poem written within reasonable memory. This poem . . . persuades me that the high argument of our times can be conducted in a poem. This interlocution between two inmates in a madhouse, written throughout in implicit dialogue, is the argument between matter and spirit, social particularity and transcendent claim, aggression and passion, torture and love, manipulation, control, order and the free play of the moral imagination. It is quite simply a poem that evokes all that lives and calls itself man.

*Arthur A. Cohen, in* The New York Times Book Review *(© 1973 by The New York Times Company; reprinted by permission), December 30, 1973, pp. 1-2.*

Brodsky's not stirringly quotable in translation, he has to be taken by the loaf—all 168 pages [of *Selected Poems*]. And read twice, at least.

Time after time his poems begin like set-pieces or exercises. Long middles treading water. Then, surprisingly, the poem *lifts*. A sudden release of spirit swims up, a satisfying light shines back through the poem. *Ahh!*

Without fail? Let's say there's a high record of success. The suprise is that poems which often begin conventionally wind up cloudborne and warbling, with the poet insisting on outdoing himself. At least I suspect he's warbling in Russian, since I see that he's cloudborne even in English.

These poems were written between 1962 and 1972. Since Brodsky was born in 1940, he was 22 to 32 years old. Naturally, the later dated poems become more intense, searching, rewarding. But even at 23, his quite long "Elegy for John Donns" shows the same enviable mastery (and surprising *lift* that shakes us when reading young Stephen Crane's "The Red Badge of Courage." In both cases, the poets observe graphically from afar a scene they never witnessed. . . .

His best poems, for me, are Yes-poems to God. Success after success shows a terrific variety of forms. A few poems explore the tone of Beckett-Burroughs, the sound of a mind scratching on silence, but hope returns as if with a grave blasted open. A marvelous strength hardens the poet's eye.

*Donald Newlove, in* The Village Voice *(reprinted by permission of* The Village Voice; *© 1974 by The Village Voice, Inc.), March 14, 1974, pp. 26-7.*

* * *

## BROOKS, Gwendolyn 1917-

**Ms Brooks is a Pulitzer Prize-winning Black American poet. She has been called one of America's most "objective" poets and her imaginative and powerful poems have reminded some critics of the work of Wallace Stevens. (See also *Contemporary Authors*, Vols. 1-4, rev. ed.)**

In [*In the Mecca*], Gwendolyn Brooks is more self-consciously a Negro than ever before. The long title poem is both an impressionistic and naturalistic journey through a huge ghetto apartment house, through the black precincts of despair. It is a strong poem, displaying the same raw power and roughness that marked and marred Richard Wright's fiction. Miss Brooks preaches a sermon of life in the face of her despair; she invokes the examples of Medgar Evers and Malcolm X to counter the chaos of poor life in the Mecca. It is a new manner and a new voice for Miss Brooks, better than her earlier work in its honesty, poorer in its loss of music and control. Perhaps the exchange was necessary; it proves that Gwendolyn Brooks, the poet, is still alive in the fullest sense.

Virginia Quarterly Review, *Vol. 45, No. 1, Winter, 1969, p. xx.*

Miss Brooks is a poet of the contemporary world, and her works reflect the semi-heavens and hells of the black people of this world. Although she displays insight and wisdom, her treatment is objective, and her characters speak for themselves. The idiom is often local, but the language is universal. Her work sometimes resembles a poignant social document, but her poems are works of art. . . .

From the city-folk poetry of Gwendolyn Brooks, one can reconstruct a vivid picture of Bronzeville, U.S.A. Her characters are usually the unheroic black people who fled the land for the city—only to discover that there is little difference between the world of the North and the world of the South. One learns from them their dismal joys and their human grief and pain. Miss Brooks, whose material is often incendiary, remains detached as she writes about the bodies and souls of Bronzeville, U.S.A.

*Jeanne-Marie A. Miller, "Bronzeville, U.S.A.," in* The Journal of Negro Education, *Winter, 1970, pp. 88-90.*

In *Riot,* as in all her later poetry, many lines are cryptic and compressed. The impact of her words is powerful. She does not preach; her work is not polemical. As a vital poet Miss Brooks merely responds to the climate in America, the varied moods and the changing times.

*Jeanne-Marie A. Miller, "Riot," in* The Journal of Negro Education, *Fall, 1970, pp. 368-69.*

*Report From Part I* affirms the riot in the world of Gwendolyn Brooks as it uses family pictures and selected poems to make clear the new woman and the new poet found in today's Gwendolyn Brooks. . . .

As an autobiographer, Gwen Brooks deals with facts in a straightforward manner while remaining true to her times and true to herself. She presents facts to show the development of her career. Then she interprets them and evaluates her career. . . .

"Collage" defines her Black womanhood first in relation to her personhood, selfhood, or humanness and then in relation to her femininity. For Gwen Brooks, peoplehood or race is not limited to continental boundaries. When she crosses from continent to continent, she realizes that racial unity becomes a necessity for survival; however, she further realizes that the achievement of unity becomes more difficult when it reaches beyond continental boundaries. This section offers a spontaneity with its brief and varied discussions. Moreover, it draws a relationship between each of these topics and Miss Brooks' individuality.

*Report From Part I* offers a blend of inner thoughts with outer actions as it makes private and public aspects of Gwen's life interesting and inspirational. *Report From Part I,* like Gwendolyn Brooks, is rich enough to expand minds and to grow people. Both the woman and the book have separate dignities that each communicate "an appropriate glory."

*Annette Oliver Shands, "'Report from Part One'," in* Black World *(copyright © March, 1973, by* Black World; *reprinted by permission of* Black World *and Annette Oliver Shands), March, 1973, pp. 70-1.*

Gwendolyn Brooks, the Pulitzer Prize-winning poet and Poet Laureate of Illinois, is known as one of the world's great living poets. But she also is a novelist. . . .

*Maud Martha* is included in *The World of Gwendolyn Brooks* among various collections of poems. Within the novel, Miss Brooks explores the theme of humanness. She gives value to places, things and localities as they are identified with people and their feelings. Human feelings growing from one's innermost thoughts, the interactions between a man and a woman, the interracial relations between Black and whites, the impressions seeded in the Black community, and the most perplexing questions relating to mankind are posed and examined. They are examined with the possibility of change. Throughout the novel Miss Brooks presents ideas and techniques that are evident in her poems. A striking difference is that the novel has less subtlety than her poems. . . .

As a novelist, Gwendolyn Brooks presents an impressionable analysis of the life of a young Black woman. Her novel antedates the 1954 desegregation court decision, laying bare a part of the impetus behind today's surge toward "the Black and the beautiful." Unlike many of the earliest Black writers, Miss Brooks does not specify traits, niceties or assets for members of the Black community to acquire in order to attain their just rights. For as Maud Martha listens to Howie Joe Jones, she feels there is something special about nameless, but "private identities." So, this is not a novel to inspire social advancement on the part of fellow Blacks. Nor does it say *be poor, Black and happy*. The message is to accept the challenge of being human and to assert humanness with urgency.

*Annette Oliver Shands, "Gwendolyn Brooks as Novelist," in* Black World *(© June, 1973, by* Black World; *reprinted by permission of* Black World *and Annette Oliver Shands), June, 1973, pp. 22-30.*

* * *

## BUECHNER, Frederick 1926-

**Buechner, an American, is a Christian novelist. (See also *Contemporary Authors*, Vols. 13-14.)**

It is a common presumption that Frederick Buechner is the delight of the more precious academic critics. His novels, it is said, honor their stately edicts on the art of fiction, and his exquisite sensibility—hushed comparisons are made with Henry James, Elizabeth Bowen, Truman Capote—offends no canons of taste. True, Buechner is sometimes the willing victim of his most elegant vices, but he is also the victim of a larger controversy in which the word acádemic has become a shibboleth. Buechner has taught in preparatory schools; he is also an ordained Presbyterian minister, and a novelist who has tried, with uneven success, to harmonize a world of subtle human feelings and complex religious ideas. Steeped, by his own admission, in the great prose writers of the seventeenth century—Jeremy Taylor, Sir Thomas Browne—he has also schooled himself in the theology of Buber and Tillich, and he has lately shown unexpected interest in the broils of American politics. After *A Long Day's Dying,* 1949, a novel written when the author was 23 years old—its aura still hangs about his name—Buechner produced two others. *The Season's Difference,* 1952, is an over-refined account of a mystical experience, the way it infiltrates the consciousness of children and adults in a narrow circle of people. In *The Return of Ansel Gibbs,* 1958, Buechner makes a more decisive departure from his earlier manner. The book is reasonably forthright; its material, though rich in moral ambiguities, is topical rather than mythic, dramatic more than allusive. But though it calls for the resolution of complexities in action, it fails to unify the political, moral, and ideological questions which distend the framework of its story. All in all, and hackneyed as it may seem to say so, Buechner remains a writer of distinct promise rather than incontrovertible achievement. His failures are not the product of a trivial imagination. They happen, in fact, to reflect some chronic difficulties of fiction in our time. . . .

*Ihab Hassan, in his* Radical Innocence: Studies in the Contemporary American Novel *(copyright (© 1961 by Princeton University Press; Princeton Paperback, 1971; reprinted by permission of Princeton University Press), Princeton University Press, 1961, pp. 153-54.*

Buechner is a fine writer, and he is one who delights in the common things of life. His novel [*The Entrance to Porlock*] will appeal particularly to those "academic" readers who joy in asking: Does this mean that? Is Strasser the demon lover? Is the rain storm at the end of the journey the "mighty fountain momentarily . . . forced"? Is the land on Tinmouth mountain the equivalent of Xanadu? If such questions apply, then Mr. Buechner has given us a literary companion piece to those elaborate paintings of the Renaissance whose symbolism was so complex that only the painter knew for sure what it all meant—and even he was probably doubtful at times. Such works usually endure either as curiosities or as beautiful pieces of workmanship so stunning that the observer can find pleasure in them even if he ignores the symbolism entirely. I think the latter case will be true of this work. Buechner has written a much better book than he intended.

*Richard Marius, "Prisoners of Dreams," in* The Christian Century *(copyright 1970 Christian Century Foundation; reprinted by permission from the April 1, 1970 issue of* The Christian Century), *April 1, 1970, pp. 393-94.*

A lot of recent fiction—most of it? all of it?—is about people who are unable to believe in anything and how they go about accommodating the emptiness of their souls or transcending, sometimes, their own cruel gracelessness. *Open Heart* . . . is about people who individually believe, or try to believe, in something and about what this belief does to them. The novel suggests, with at times a too-cozy certainty, that everyone really believes in something. . . .

Buechner lays down his narrative as effortlessly as a fly-caster drops fifteen yards of line on the surface of a still pond, and expresses his most profound doubts with fluid decisiveness. The author has also listened carefully to the way people really talk to each other, and his accurate report of their words, in the mouths of his characters, lends considerable humor to the novel. Still, I am left with the feeling that *Open Heart* hasn't taken me anywhere. I've spent several hours inside a few extraordinary people, and they manage to become "ordinary" in the best sense of the word; I feel hope for them because they show me the remarkable resilience that most people possess. But if *Open Heart* is about something more than staying alive as best we can and doing it with a simple readiness to receive epiphanies along the way, then I missed it.

*George Malko, in* Saturday Review of the Society *(copyright © 1972 by Saturday Review/World, Inc.; reprinted with permission), July 29, 1972, p. 64.*

*Open Heart* is the second novel in a trilogy about an American evangelist, which Frederick Buechner began last year in *Lion Country*. The characters, interests and style remain the same—and so does the leisurely pace. The narrator, Antonio Parr, relates the story in a folksy, introspective manner which allows him room to ramble through psychology, philosophy and theosophy as sidelights on the character and deeds of Leo Bebb, his father-in-law. . . .

Mr Buechner is more accomplished with the minor than the major incidents. He has a fine eye for the quirks and oddities of situations and people, and the small moments that alter large issues. . . .

[As] in earlier novels Mr Buechner insinuates his Christian affirmatives and an acceptance of mystic revelations. He is quite content to suggest that one character might be a government inspector, an angel, or a man from outer space, and leave the question unresolved. This approach creates not merely ambiguities, but a lack of resolution in the novel as a whole.

*"Rogue Preacher," in* The Times Literary Supplement, *December 29, 1972, p. 1588.*

"There are *poetry* books and *poetic* books—the first a book with poems in it, the second a book which may or may not have poems in it but which is in some sense a poem itself."

So speaks Frederick Buechner, developing a distinction by which we identify his newest book [*Wishful Thinking*] outside the sequence of his seven novels which have placed him in the first ranks of American writers. He goes on: "In much the same way there are *religion* books and *religious* books." The latter are transparencies through which we can "experience firsthand what a *religion* book can only tell about." Such, he says, rightly, are "The Brothers Karamazov" and "King Lear." His present volume, small but powerfully concentrated, is "a *religion* book," explicitly about "religious ideas, symbols, attitudes."

The same stylistic power, subtlety and originality that have distinguished his novels, from "A Long Day's Dying" (1950) to "Open Heart" (1972), lift "Wishful Thinking" far above commonplace religion books nearly to the level of C. S. Lewis's "Screwtape Letters." An artist is at work here in the vineyard of theology, an able aphorist with a natural gift for gnomics, a wit with wisdom.

*Edmund Fuller, in* The New York Times Book Review *(© 1973 by The New York Times Company; reprinted by permission), May 13, 1973, p. 20.*

* * *

## BURGESS, Anthony 1917-

**An English novelist, critic, essayist, and composer, Burgess writes brilliant and fiendishly witty novels. His best known work is *A Clockwork Orange*. (See also *Contemporary Authors*, Vols. 1-4, rev. ed.)**

*Nothing like the Sun* is a clever, tightly constructed book, reminiscent in its much smaller and more sensational way of Mann's *Doctor Faustus,* full of the author's old verbal ingenuity (with something of Shakespeare's to boot), and likely to be one of the most remarkable (if most ambiguous) celebrations of the Bard's quatercentenary—although what it celebrates is pretty clearly something other than the Bard. It is a *tour de force*: a little too much force has been applied, in the wrong places. Mr Burgess has set himself so awesome a task that it seems hardly proper to complain at all. Only a gifted word-boy could have managed an Elizabethan-style idiom which most of the time strikes one as simply good lively English, if rather gamy. Of minor false notes there are few. . . .

The false note, it seems to me, is not a minor one, and it peals out full-bodiedly. In the case of a book subtitled 'A Story of Shakespeare's Love-life' it would be perverse to complain of the amount of sex present. But the point here is not the amount but the nature of it. Mr Burgess's narrative might help to account for the rougher bits in the Sonnets, for Lear's remarks on the gentler sex, for Othello, Troilus, Leontes—but not for Hermione, Miranda, Imogen, Cordelia, nor exactly for that other dark lady, the serpent of old Nile. WS's sexual history—love-life seems hardly the word—is not so much grim or terrible as horrific and grotesque.

*D. J. Enright, "A Modern Disease: Anthony Burgess's Shakespeare" (1964), in his* Man Is An Onion: Reviews and Essays *(© 1972 by D. J. Enright; reprinted by permission of Open Court Publishing Co. and Chatto & Windus), Open Court, 1972, pp. 39-43.*

If language is the house of being, Anthony Burgess has always gone with a pair and three of a kind and, in *MF,* his thirteenth novel, he has dealt the house of Atreus into play as well. A winner? A house of cards? Well, if you liked *A Clockwork Orange* and *Enderby* (revised) better than his others, you may feel that in *MF* Burgess has brought his special talent to a post-citric fruition. . . .

Unless you like stories whose underpinnings are the myths of Greek tragedy, you are not going to like *MF*. Unless moral generalizations elevated on the antipodes of incest and miscegenation interest you, you are not going to be interested in *MF*. One would feel a good deal happier about this novel if it did not seem so open an invitation to be made the subject of interpretative papers in *PMLA*.

With *MF*, Burgess invites, even demands, comparison with writers of the ilk of Nabokov and Joyce. And yet, despite his exuberance and creativity and clear delight in all he does, he seems here to have chosen a roadway of fiction on which there is no mirror. Most novels provide forms for experience by insinuating themselves into the kinds of emotion out of which ordinary experience is constructed. A novel like *MF* assumes language as its subject, language as it has been used in art of the more direct sort but as no longer functioning directly. We are tugged, not toward the concrete or a simulacrum of it, but rather in the direction of abstraction, of bloodless cogitation, and it is on that level, if at all, that this artifact to the second power connects with life, by connecting with abstractions formulated against backgrounds other than art. Could this be said of Nabokov and Joyce? I think not. Burgess suffers from the comparison he invites. The second-order, "literary" delight *MF* occasions leaves one curiously dissatisfied, or maybe the dissatisfaction is not curious after all. A reader who, like myself, prefers the trilogy *The Long Day Wanes* and novels like *Devil of a State, A Vision of Battlements, The Right to an Answer*—indeed *Enderby* in its original form (*Inside Mr. Enderby*)—has a way, within the Burgess canon, of explaining his dissatisfaction with *MF*. Those novels came out of Burgess' entrails; *MF*, like *A Clockwork Orange,* issued from his extraordinary mind and no amount of symbolic sex and violence gives them flesh, tactility, artistic substance.

Anthony Burgess is among the half dozen most important English novelists writing today. He is surely one of the most intelligent. No writer can know too much but a writer's knowledge has to be assimilated and rendered almost visceral in order to count in a novel. In most of his novels, Burgess harnesses his learning to his imagination and the results are exceptional eliciters of aesthetic effect. . . . *MF*, seen within his *oeuvre,* appears to be a finger exercise, a display, an unrealized piece of pyrotechnic for which, as for second class relics, we should be grateful.

*Ralph McInerny, in* Commonweal *(reprinted by permission of Commonweal Publishing Co., Inc.), May 28, 1971, pp. 290-91.*

That superlative writing machine called Anthony Burgess doesn't hit a false note in this deadpan divertissement [*One Hand Clapping*], which he probably scribbled down over a long weekend.

*Audrey Foote, in* Book World (© The Washington Post)*, March 5, 1972, p. 7.*

Burgess's love of language is becoming proverbial, and [*MF*] is a philologist's delight. Many of the words he uses as English are to be found in neither first, second, nor third edition of the unabridged. Browsing through dictionaries, including Classical Greek dictionaries, is part of the fun of reading this book, and was presumably part of the fun of writing it. . . .

*MF* also manages to be a book about poetry; it is, in short, a Protean work which all lovers of language will have to read. The only flaw is that a single, offhand sentence in the epilogue changes the complexion of the entire book. Are such clues as may exist a fair preparation for the reader, or did Burgess cheat and decide as an afterthought to bomb the reader with a cheap surprise? The book should be read carefully, no matter what the answer to the question.

*Thomas Winter, "A Protean Work," in* Prairie Schooner *(© 1972 by University of Nebraska Press; reprinted by permission from* Prairie Schooner*), Spring, 1972, pp. 82-3.*

One of the most contemporary pictures of Britain's nagging *Götterdammerung* is the Malayan trilogy of Anthony Burgess, called in the American edition *The Long Day Wanes*. In theme and action these three novels—running together to a little over five hundred pages—set about to show the twilight of British rule in Malaya and the dawn of freedom for the Malayan states. Burgess's fidelity in treating the problems of a nation that has often seemed about as fathomable as a gibber of apes at a conference table opens new doors of perception on unpublicized reaches of empire and on the failed British mission. Less interested in exploring the hypersensitivity of Forster's "good" Indians and "bad" Englishmen (or vice versa), the metaphysics of evil of Conrad's, or the grotesque parodies of institutions and people of Waugh's darker continents, Burgess, a writer of wit and incredible verbal control, digs in to the nitty-gritty of the political, religious, and cultural mess in the Far East.

What he comes up with is a tragi-comic view of imperialism and an anatomy of the heart of Malaya. In technique Burgess is close to Waugh, but in sensibility he is closer to Orwell. Both understand the tempers of peoples pitted against the Western brand of progress, self-consciously and nationalistically dedicated to their emergence. But unlike Orwell, who views Burma as a force of homogeneous wills (and consequently *one* will) bent upon undermining and overturning the white man's power, Burgess sees Malaya in all its heterogeneity; sees its timeless conflicts arising as much from indigenous human nature as from abstractions like "brutality and jingoism" (to quote Orwell on Kipling) of imperialism; sees its people given to the same vices, vanities, frustrations, desires, and excesses, be they black, white, or yellow, English, Chinese, Eurasian, Malaysian, or Indian, Christian, Moslem, Buddhist, or Hindu.

Tough-minded, at bottom an ironist and comedian rather than a satirist, Burgess keeps the proper artistic distance from problems that obviously speak for themselves. Yet he is anything but cautious and tentative. . . .

Throughout the trilogy, history and hero interpenetrate. Both are extremely viable, history being for Burgess not memory but the living pattern that Crabbe (agent, reflector, commentator, pawn) experiences. . . .

Via James Joyce—Burgess is a Joycean scholar as well as a practicing disciple—has come, undoubtedly, a concern with Vico and cyclical theories of history. Burgess is less attracted by Vico's general laws of growth, decay, and regrowth through which all civilizations must pass, than by his analogy of civilizations evolving parallel to children developing—acquiring knowledge, that is, through growing experience. Thus with Crabbe and thus with Malaya. As freedom dawns for the new nation, in the jungle is written the ironic coda to his own education. . . .

Hegelian thought, too, sifts through *The Long Day Wanes*. The interpreter of Vico for the post-Renaissance world, the intellectual antecedent of Spengler and Toynbee, Hegel placed the keystone, if not the foundation, of the arch through which all modern students of history must pass. Cold, precise, deterministic in its metaphysics, the Hegelian dialectic is both logical and phenomenological, but ultimately antihumanistic and ethically deplorable to anyone who sees the historical process continually renewing itself at the expense of human beings, to anyone who views as hopeless and nihilistic a process by which ends not only justify means, but are sacrificed to them. Thesis, antithesis, synthesis; the unholy trinity of materialism! And the synthesis that becomes a new thesis in this eternal genesis of organization and reorganization may be stronger, though not necessarily better, as Burgess suggests at the opening of the trilogy's final volume, *Beds in the East*. . . .

[The] *Malayan Trilogy* is not just a composite of rhetorical fripperies, wit, puns, flirtations with language, and love affairs with technique. It is not merely a comedy of misplaced idealism, alienation, despair, impotence, or transparent ideologies—though it is, of course, all these as well. It is foremost a continuing drama of change: how one man encounters and experiences it, founders upon and succumbs to it. It is a novel of one man borne by one current while beating against another, of one hard-shelled but vulnerable, of one aloof but involved, of one not deep, but sensitive and sincere. It is a novel of one better than so many, yet, in the end, not quite sufficient.

*Robert K. Morris, "Anthony Burgess—'The Malayan Trilogy': The Futility of History," in his* Continuance and Change: The Contemporary British Novel Sequence *(copyright © 1972 by Southern Illinois University Press; reprinted by permission of Southern Illinois University Press), Carbondale: Southern Illinois University Press, 1972, pp. 71-91.*

Anthony Burgess, novelist, composer, prolific book reviewer, and current smash on the college lecture circuit, seems able to be defined only in terms of sharply conflicting opposites of much the same type as those which very wittingly characterized the structure of his novels. A thoroughgoing traditionalist in his moral values and philosophy, Burgess has strong and self-pronounced anarchical tendencies. Seemingly an abrasively satiric critic of the Rock Culture, he is becoming, increasingly, a best-seller in college bookstores. A vigorous advocate of moral commitment, he is a firm antagonist of the simplistic moral viewpoint that so frequently obtains for the zealously committed. An amazingly productive novelist who writes, avowedly, to make money, and who thoroughly understands Pop Art, he is in many ways unmistakeably a Modernist, an embittered disciple of the Old High Art whose death seems likely to be witnessed in our own day.

The Burgess phenomenon is instructive, I think, in that his novels are a marriage—perhaps a violent and almost profane union—of popular and elitist literature. Burgess, a perceptive (even hip) critic of the novel, knows, it would seem, exactly what he is doing: the violent and sudden oscillations of mood and event in his novels are certainly purposeful and could even be termed, with some fair accuracy, metaphysical. He is assuredly one of the most vibrant and intriguing examples of a novelist of the "new sensibility" on either side of the Atlantic, and he is clearly, by far, the most major British novelist of the present day to turn so pronouncedly from high art to popular art. Burgess himself seems to know exactly where he should be placed: in his urbane but tuned-in handbook of the contemporary novel, *The Novel Now,* he places his own fiction in the chapter titled "On the Margin," the margin that is, between "serious fiction" and "entertainment." . . .

One might argue that Burgess is, although with some exception, still Modernistically elitist at core, and basically satiric in his intent. Examination will not bear this out. His principal theme, and structural technique, involves always a demonstration of the remarkable interpenetration of seemingly irreconcilable opposites in the world (which, in the case of good and evil, is denoted by Burgess's frequent references to Manicheanism); thus no individual, party, or group has any monopoly on wisdom, morality, culture or goodness. One might possibly suppose that Burgess would advocate, as a remedy to the vulgar debasement and tawdriness of life in our times, a return to the great and ennobling art of the past. Burgess, however, (like William Golding whose grotesques are used to much the same point) sees evil as endemic to man's nature; simplistic solutions such as an advocacy of a return to cultural values he sees as hopelessly and dangerously naive. Characteristically, he exposes the truth about man's moral (largely immoral) nature by means of vigorous paradox. . . .

Burgess does, of course, sometimes satirize what he considers to be tawdry and debased elements in contemporary society, but unlike traditional satire in which certain individuals, groups, or types are exposed to judgment as knaves or fools, Burgess's satire is thoughtful and even ultimately compassionate; it stimulates new ontological and metaphysical perceptions rather than adverse judgments on our fellow men. . . .

It might be said in short that Burgess satirizes nearly everyone and everything—if we are willing, that is, to accept a definition of satire that is broader and more relaxed than the traditional one. But at the same time we must not presume that Burgess is a nihilist or that his intention is to draw a manic image of absurdity, disorder, or evil. Burgess actually comes closer to being a romantic at heart; he shows us the myriad wonders of the earth and the fascinating behavior of its divergent peoples, the pleasures and pains of being human, the good and evil mingled everywhere together in the world. Basically, Burgess is happy to accept the world as it is, although his is an acceptance that is tinged with some satire and with much humor. The art that Burgess gives us is, in fact, very much akin to that of the Pop Artists of the graphic arts, chiefly in the fact that the countless mundane objects he gives us come very near themselves to being the subject matter, although also as in the graphic arts, they are superinflated (in Burgess by a bursting sort of neo-Jacobean language) so as to bring us to new perceptual and ontological levels of awareness. . . .

Burgess is a novelist who is on the margin in many ways.

By virtue of real craft and talent he incorporates in an imaginative and integral way the considerable influence of writers so diverse (besides those already indicated) as Shakespeare and Sterne, Nabokov and Graham Greene, James Joyce and Wyndham Lewis. He absolutely defies pigeonholing and would himself obviously resent the attempt. Like other writers of the "new consciousness" he is acutely aware of a pluralistic universe and an ever-changing world; with such a recognition, literary genres, categories, and modes must almost of necessity dissolve. This is altogether congruent with his prime thematic technique—the dark and forceful coming together of opposites. It is likely, too, that Burgess would reject the distinction between elite and popular literature. Not infrequently Burgess uses the standard devices of the modernist elitists—allusion, irony, paradox, ambiguity—but uses them to strikingly original purposes, bouncing them incongruously off more "popular" elements, or even more incongruously, merging them. Brilliant invention and obvious convention (blatant artifice, in fact) tumble strangely over each other in his fiction and finally become indiscernible one from the other. He warns us (only slightly ironically) against trying to extrapolate a paraphrasable meaning from his fiction: "Don't try distilling a message from it, not even an espresso cupful of meaningful epitome or a Sambusca glass of abridgment, *con la mosca*. Communication has been the whatness of the communication. For separable meaning go to the professors" [*MF*]. . . .

Neither a zealot of Art, a champion of popular culture, nor an exponent of a programmatic *via media*, Burgess is simply one novelist who is trying hard to find life-giving forms to impart to his work. He obviously feels, though, that present-day art can be viable only if it honestly and imaginatively attempts to reflect a distinctly contemporary consciousness. For Burgess, a totally switched-on center of energy, this necessarily involves an attempt, from his position on the margin, to forcibly bring together all opposites. Some successful fusions can only help toward restoring the novel form to a state of health and vitality not experienced for a long time.

*John J. Stinson, "Anthony Burgess: Novelist on the Margin," in* Journal of Popular Culture, *Summer, 1973, pp. 136-51.*

There are linguistic studies of Joyce which give statistics about the frequency of 'the' in a given work—a calculation more efficiently performed by a computer programmer than a literary critic—but *Joysprick* is not such a book. Mr Burgess sets out to explore two basic questions: how does Joyce use language, and why does he use it in that way? The answers involve not only linguistics, but practical criticism, literary theory, and biography: language is not isolated from life, words on the page are continually being referred back to their common usage as Mr Burgess picks his way through what he calls 'the wiry heathpacks' of Joyce's prose.

A useful distinction is made at the beginning of this book between the novelist in whose work 'language is a zero quantity, transparent, unseductive, the overtones of connotation and ambiguity totally damped' (Class I), and the novelist who makes his books out of words as well as out of character and incident (Class II). It is to the second category that Joyce belongs—within which, indeed, he is preeminent, and his exploitation of 'opaque language' unparalleled.

Mr Burgess, a composer as well as a novelist, is very good on the melodies of Joyce's prose. A sentence from *Ulysses* is shown to play a tune independent of the sense and reveals just how extensively Joyce uses the full keyboard of vowel phonemes: 'By Brady's cottages a boy for the skins lolled, his buckets of offal linked, smoking a chewed fagbutt.' In the style, as Mr Burgess characterises it, of 'one of the American Irvings, say: Stone or Wallace', this might read, 'A boy sent to collect pelts waited languidly outside Brady's cottages with his arm through the handle of a bucket of animal offal; he was smoking a cigarette end.' The differences between Class I and Class II are immediately apparent; the value of this study is that the qualities of each are sensitively analysed in several series of practical criticism, and the fundamentals of Joyce's aesthetic approach to language are explained.

*Robert Chapman, "Jabberwocky and Joyce," in* Books and Bookmen, *September, 1973, p. 60.*

In an age of dull prose, jargon of sociology, and psychology, incessant buzz of gossip, journal, the endless dribble of weepy-eyed ghetto hysterics, tin clatter of avant-garde mobiles, hollow academic puling: a reader who delights in succulent phrase, unctuous pap, the zest of word play and a saucy paragraph, must fall on each new work of Anthony Burgess with ravenous appetite. If some of his dishes have been mere dessert tarts, hasty puddings, gooseberry trifles like *M/F*, I can now rave that a full, groaning, gourmand's table has been set in his present opus, *Napoleon Symphony*.

Sweeping though the panorama of the French emperor's life, rolling with a beat that makes us feel a Corsican teenager bounding in the general's creamy pants, half hoodlum, half genius, an adolescent whose energy animates an empire; it is of course Burgess, line by line, vibrating in Napoleon's boots. But who is to say that this is not the truest form of biography, for the music, its dashing erratic, brilliant voice, compels us to believe we are in the presence of a Napoleon. . . .

How does Bonaparte/Burgess handle such a vast calendar of battle, civil reform, amour, intrigue? By jumping from critical moment to moment with a dazzling generalship of the raw materials of biography, showing that mastery which bends the rule of the fallacy of imitative form, just enough chaos, confusion, event tumbling upon event in the text for us to feel Napoleon's genius for the exact moment to push, shove, win through, echoed in the chronicler's talent for the precise cut, collage, surprise arrangement in ordering what seems like an endless roster. . . .

[As] myth, fiction, it has that uncanny ring of psalmody whereby we believe that the songs and dreams of the scribe are truly the king's, the emperor's. Despite a far-ranging third person, Burgess's voice and Napoleon's are so well harmonized that Burgess can violate a hundred laws of fictional narrative leaping from Josephine, Louis Antoine, General MacDonald, an anonymous army engineer, without ever losing the shadow of Bonaparte's cloak *uber alles*. . . .

At the end the author stretches prose credulity to the breaking point in a set of parodies almost as elaborate as his real hero, First Consul James Joyce. Here in a final burst of fireworks, Burgess at his most characteristic, craziest, surpasses the high fun of the invented language in *Clockwork Orange*. The emperor finishes as a chuckle in the divine symphony. A rococo performance of Prometheus, lovemaking in Poland, past battles, return to haunt Napoleon on Saint Helena, as the author floats into a deft, rapid splicing of the hero's last fevered days, his life now all reflection and therefore all Burgess's, all dreams, all poetry.

*Mark Mirsky, "A Musical Offering With Heroic Overtones," in* Book World—The Washington Post (© The Washington Post), *May 26, 1974, p. 1.*

Essentially [*Napoleon Symphony*] is not so much about Napoleon as about Anthony Burgess writing a novel. As such it has many pleasures. All of the Burgess embellishments are here, and they sing alluringly each to each, even if they don't swell into a larger harmony. (You get it: love-heartburn; water-*l'eau*.) Burgess's most impressive successes, "Nothing Like the Sun" and "A Clockwork Orange," have been novels in which the play with language and literature has been part of the larger intent, essential to a concerted whole. The flourishes often seem gratuitous here—except of course for the fun of it. And that is saying a good deal. Even when we don't know what all the pyrotechnics are celebrating, we can still enjoy a good display.

*Sara Sanborn, in* The New York Times Book Review *(© 1974 by The New York Times Company; reprinted by permission), June 9, 1974, p. 5.*

Twelve years ago Burgess published *A Clockwork Orange* and *The Wanting Seed,* books which made serious play with notions of human freedom and responsibility and with religious definitions of man. A year later, under the name of Joseph Kell, appeared *Inside Mr Enderby,* in which our embattled hero was first introduced. These three novels are the richest and most verbally dazzling comedies Burgess has written, and there is, not surprisingly, an air of contrivance about the present attempt [*The Clockwork Testament, or Enderby's End*] (dedicated, for some pleasant reason, to Burt Lancaster) to wind things up. . . .

Burgess is faced both with recalling the distinctive glories of his poet's life-style and showing how that style gets him in trouble when he moves beyond the kitchen or toilet. There are respectable amounts of satisfyingly dyspeptic activity as well as less engaging chunks of poems-in-progress (though an imagined filmscript starring Pelagius and Augustine has its moments). Enderby's students at Manhattan U. are vicious, stupid and lazy; there is no suggestion that the novelist holds any more complicated views of them. And in fact a case could be mounted against Burgess, as sharing enthusiastically his hero's self-pity and misanthropically slobbish grunts toward life—could be mounted, though, only by remaining resolutely impervious to moments of high entertainment and to the stylistic energies infusing them. It is the liveliness of the routines that counts. . . .

*William Pritchard, "Exile's Return," in* The Listener, *June 13, 1974, pp. 776-77.*

[Buried] at the foot of the gaudy lettering of the main title [*The Clockwork Testament*], and set in infinitely smaller type, is a sub-title: *Enderby's End.* At first glance this seems a somewhat shuffling way to introduce the final volume in the hitherto triumphant trilogy devoted to that dedicated poet and flatulent glutton. By the end of *The Clockwork Testament,* however, one has to conclude that the subdued introduction strikes just about the right note. This is not, in fact, a very glorious exit. Poor Enderby doesn't so much 'end' here as get mislaid somewhere along the way by a creator who clearly has too many other things on his mind to pay proper attention to his charge.

Briefly, what is preoccupying Mr Burgess in this book is his contempt for American culture and particularly for its academic environment. . . . Mr Burgess has chosen to let Enderby stand in for him on this issue. . . . The one thing American educators cannot be said to suffer from is a shortage of advice. It is not ignorance of the alternatives that determines the character of big-city universities in the United States. Rather their development is a result of mainly conscious decisions about what role they should play in their society—and what would have to be sacrificed to attain it. Enderby is entitled to disagree with these decisions, of course. But not to come on like an Old Testament prophet bringing Light to a totally benighted people.

Moreover, Enderby makes a very unimpressive, as well as a redundant, prophet. It is sad to watch his stature shrink in this alien setting. The egotism, the slovenliness, the indifferent poetry, which were all such fun in earlier volumes, seem rather dispiriting now that their possessor is actually proposing himself as an arbiter, even a model, of cultural excellence. And more seriously, Enderby's insularity and his racism—at various times, though prudently only to himself, he refers to his students under such headings as 'cannibal kike', 'black bitch', 'redskin sod'—seem merely contemptible now that he has been translated from the easy-going bigotries of his native turf to this tense, angry city, one of the world's great black and Puerto Rican (and Jewish) capitals. It is all meant to be a jolly joke, of course, just part of Enderby's lovable British rumbunctiousness. Except it looks here like a case of incorrigible immaturity and loutishness, much more grave indeed than the mild juvenile iconoclasm that Enderby diagnoses and deplores among his American students. And unhappily, as with his heart condition, it's clear that Enderby's at least is a terminal case.

*Peter Prince, "Intramural," in* New Statesman, *June 21, 1974, p. 894.*

How refreshing it is when a writer these days sets out on a monumentally impossible adventure—in this case to create a musical novel—and admits he's just doing it because he wants to. If "Napoleon Symphony," to take its conceit a step further, were translated into a painting, it would be filled with the breathless plenty of one of those incomparably sunny, baroque Italian ceilings wafting its massive machinery around on rose petals. But it's not all roses: somehow Burgess can sing too of dirty deaths and diarrhea, the gory trails of defeated armies, the insane effects of military errors. . . .

In boudoir and battle Burgess's narrative powers, putting you half in the character's mind and half behind his back, are magnificent. The sweep assimilates literary as well as military and musical history. . . .

Burgess isn't writing just about Napoleon, but about everything that happened in and around the tyrant—including Beethoven's torn-up dedication to the Eroica. The moral imagination which keeps the monster's tyranny in perspective is Beethoven's, so that you don't get the misleading effects of being shown a world in which there is no mature power to judge the way you do in that other book about a conqueror, "The Clockwork Orange," with its Alexander the Great.

Someday someone will explain Burgess's preoccupation with heroes whose utter lack of second thoughts—never mind moral restraint—unleashes on the rest of mankind instinctual forces of historical dimensions. Impossible to resist speculation in the case of a novelist of Burgess's powers: is it an expression of his own literary restraint and the fact that, with all his gifts, he himself forgoes literary heroism and chooses not to write an *entirely* unconventional novel?

Not to cavil, "Napoleon Symphony" has splendor.

*Martin Washburn, in* The Village Voice *(reprinted by permission of* The Village Voice; *© 1974 by The Village Voice, Inc.), July 4, 1974, p. 19.*

In the fertility of his enterprise, his louche congenial knockabout confidence, Mr. Burgess may remind us of one of those Elizabethan professionals, like Nashe or Deloney, who tried their hands at practically every species of literary composition, always coming up with something readable and rewarding, but curiously unsettling too, as if their freewheeling methods cast a kind of doubt on the more accepted kinds of literary achievement. . . . Burgess, no less than Nashe, is an artificer in his own line, but he does not seem to take us so far from presentness and actuality as do in their various ways James Joyce or Scott Fitzgerald or Saul Bellow or Anthony Powell. . . .

Mr. Burgess, whenever we remeet him in a literary setting, seems to be standing knee-deep in the shavings of new methods, grimed with the metallic filings of bright ideas. *A Clockwork Orange,* for example, was a book which no one could take seriously for what was supposed to happen in it—its plot and "meaning" were the merest pretenses—but which contained a number of lively notions, as when his delinquents use Russian slang and become murderous on Mozart and Beethoven. In a work by Burgess nothing is connected necessarily or organically with anything else but is strung together with wires and pulleys as we go.

Thus we can discount at once the claim, hopefully supplied by the blurb, that what we have here [*Napoleon Symphony*] is "a grand and loving tragicomic symphony to Napoleon Bonaparte." The symphonic stuff—a novel in four movements and so on—is no more than bits of string, and it is one of the many endearing things about this author that he does not really bother us (and possibly irritate us) by pretending it is anything else. He is as enterprising as Nabokov, but his flair does not need pretension to keep it going: he is not an aesthete but a man of letters. Why should he have wanted to write about Napoleon? Probably because of the interesting technical challenge involved—an almost impossible challenge, but writers like Burgess and his predecessors are not worried about finicky matters of possibility provided they can keep a workshop going and amuse themselves and their public. . . .

[Burgess's] Napoleon is reminiscent, it must be admitted, of his portrait of Shakespeare in an earlier historical fantasy, and both have a good deal in common with the durable figure of Enderby, the protofigure of many of Burgess's fictions. They are, that is to say, observant, civilized, distracted, victimized, and endowed with a rich stream of consciousness. . . .

Mr. Burgess's problem, which he cannot be said to have solved, is that his more informed readers cannot really need this kind of thing to imagine themselves into the Napoleonic era, while all the sound knowledge—of corps commanders, horse batteries, Continental System—which he strews so prodigally but inconspicuously around cannot do much to edify his more popular readership. . . .

After the retreat from Moscow Napoleon said that from the sublime to the ridiculous is but a step: he did not, however, add that they are both the same thing. Mr. Burgess is far too intelligent and thoughtful a writer not to have reflected on the curious fact that we can no longer render the past in terms of its pomp and circumstance, the sublime as well as the ridiculous. We can only do it—perhaps we can only do ourselves too?—as creatures of fantasy and farce.

*John Bayley, "From the Ridiculous to the Ridiculous," in* The New York Review of Books *(reprinted with permission from* The New York Review of Books; *© 1974 by NYREV, Inc.), September 19, 1974, pp. 32-3.*

# C

## CALISHER, Hortense 1911-

**Ms Calisher is an American novelist, short story writer, and autobiographer. It has been said that, in her poetic fiction, she limns characters who are "boundless states of mind." (See also *Contemporary Authors*, Vols. 1-4, rev. ed.)**

All of Miss Calisher's manifold characteristics as an author, both positive and negative, are magnified and distorted in [*The New Yorkers*], patently designed to be her magnum opus, for here in all their glittering opulence are to be found her predilection for ambiguity, opacity, ellipses, and prolixity—all so much a part of her charm, deftness, fluency, and sureness of touch. Adherence to story lines is not one of her fetishes, and in consequence her book often dawdles from page to page in desultory fashion, introducing meanwhile a cast of characters bewildering in their variety, actors all, in a drama centered on a New York City Jewish family. The leading figure in particular, a "lace-curtain Jew and a lapsed one," now a retired judge of the appellate court, is clearly intended to be a strong and warmly human being. Unhappily for the author her considerable talents fail to confer upon him the breath of life just when vigor and animation are required rather desperately to offset the pedestrian qualities of the narrative.

Virginia Quarterly Review, *Vol. 45, No. 3 (Summer, 1969), p. lxxxviii.*

This generation's subject has been selfhood, and, despite all the evidence, it is after all possible to write well of it. That is, if one writes well. Miss Calisher, who does not want her readers to be aware of her prose style, has one—at its best a blend of letting go and containment that reaches the heart. . . . There are parts of [*Herself*], in the middle, that no one should have been required to read. Miss Calisher shares with the reader her journal. . . . [It] is a variety of gush perfected by the British (and that only for talking); its inclusion here in such volume—it was meant to take the place of daily letters—causes a serious drop at the center of the book. Confronted with this, with the inclusion of whole texts of her letters on Viet Nam to the *Times,* letters to critics, one asks whether it is necessary to take it all. The answer is yes, with some impatience, for so good a writer is involved here, one so rich in temper, so capable in the use of words for spirit, that one takes the whole display.

*Dorothy Rabinowitz, in* World *(copyright © 1972 by Saturday Review/World, Inc.; reprinted with permission), October 10, 1972, p. 55.*

In her complex, surrealistic style Miss Calisher in [*Standard Dreaming*] creates a dream world in which her characters move as automatons in the course of their search for themselves, for the children who have forsaken them, and for a world having some recognizable attributes of reality. Her book is not actually a novel in any conventional sense, nor are her characters more than shadowy figures at best, but she does write out of a sense of pain and anguish in a most beguiling style about lost souls doomed to failure. If her theme be basically the classic one of search, she pursues it with unwavering diligence.

Virginia Quarterly Review, *Vol. 49, No. 1 (Winter, 1973), p. xii.*

Hortense Calisher is a shrewd observer of our social ills—displacements of youth, futilities of the rich—but she is more than a naturalist noting easy details, cataloguing crimes or sins. She is a maker of fictions; she insists upon private consciousness—even when this consciousness is extreme, obsessive and "poetic". . . .

Calisher begins [*Eagle Eye*] with a convenient plot, but she refuses to structure her fiction in a straightforward manner. She knows that linear plots are lies that rarely get at the heart of perception. Thus there is for her no one Vietnam, no single youth cult, no simple family. Social "realities" are as "real" as *one mind perceiving them.* Radical truth is inevitably more alarming and convincing than editorial prescriptions. . . .

Calisher stuns us with the "magic, forbidden leaps" of her imagination. She forces us to enter—and withdraw from—her narrator's mind; she offers few clues to his ultimate condition. But by testing us with her sharp vision she emerges here as a true creator—an eagle of fiction-makers.

*Irving Malin, "Supremacy of Consciousness," in* The New Republic *(reprinted by permission of* The New Republic; *© 1973 by Harrison-Blaine of New Jersey, Inc.), November 3, 1973, pp. 26-7.*

*Eagle Eye* is a spare, skillful book I loved on second reading, but fought with all through the first. It is tightly controlled, often as difficult as a poem—but as rewarding.

Experiencing this work of Calisher's imagination is a matter of learning the economics of her highly individual language (all the characters speak an allusive shorthand, understanding one another with maddening ease even when we miss what they are talking about), and of adjusting to a complex world composed of voices, moods, and textures, more than of keeping track of the linear plot. . . .

Finding yourself, this novel suggests, means finding that your visions and actions touch and are touched by the lives of others. . . .

Calisher has elsewhere treated . . . the problems of relationship between parent and child, male and female, humanist and scientist. If her work is seen as a continuing discussion of these conflicts, *Eagle Eye* is an optimistic part of her vision, an affirmation of our capability for such daring and offbeat combinations as may save us.

*Joan Larkin, "Twice Over Heavily," in* Ms., *January, 1974, pp. 39-40.*

Hortense Calisher's latest exploration of man's heart and head is as perilous and fascinating a voyage as any reader could hope to make this year. Few American writers deserve such praise. But Calisher is uniquely gifted and in *Eagle Eye* she has created a durable masterpiece, intriguing as a spider's web, a novel so absorbing that the idea of abandoning the fictional Bronstein family became impossible; two readings were required before I could say goodby. I could say I stayed on quite willingly. But the truth is that the Bronsteins refused to let me go.

The ties that bind the Bronsteins together are those dull, deadly twins, circumstance and habit. But in *Eagle Eye,* a family that less gifted writers would surely have wronged with all the old clichés has been made real, blessed with cowardice and frailty. Here, the Bronsteins represent the family of the universal rising executive, so very like my upward-bound yet needy relatives and friends that I felt sure I'd met them somewhere before and more than once. The same uncanny ability to evoke submerged traces of experience, the same disturbing sense of *déjà vu* that so distinguishes *False Entry,* is delightfully in evidence here.

But more than sorcery and polished technical skills are at work in *Eagle Eye*. . . .

Call *Eagle Eye* a novel, then. Some people will. But others will say it is a work of art. Count me among the latter, the faithful who are glad to wait and see what Hortense Calisher will think up next, the grateful ones who cherish the company of living beings she has molded with her wise hands.

*Bonnie Stowers, "'The Same World-Dwarfing Stories'," in* The Nation, *June 29, 1974, pp. 829-30.*

* * *

## CAMUS, Albert 1913-1960

**Camus was an Algerian-born French novelist, dramatist, and existentialist essayist. His "philosophy of the absurd," developed in *The Stranger,* a novel, and *The Myth of Sisyphus,* essays, became a point of reference for an entire generation during the forties and fifties.**

Modern literature is oversupplied with madmen of genius. No wonder, then, that when an immensely gifted writer, whose talents certainly fall short of genius, arises who boldly assumes the responsibilities of sanity, he should be acclaimed beyond his purely literary merits.

I mean, of course, Albert Camus. . . . Being a contemporary, he had to traffic in the madmen's themes: suicide, affectlessness, guilt, absolute terror. But he does so with such an air of reasonableness, *mesure,* effortlessness, gracious impersonality, as to place him apart from the others. Starting from the premises of a popular nihilism, he moves the reader—solely by the power of his own tranquil voice and tone—to humanist and humanitarian conclusions in no way entailed by his premises. This illogical leaping of the abyss of nihilism is the gift for which readers are grateful to Camus. This is why he evoked feelings of real affection on the part of his readers. Kafka arouses pity and terror, Joyce admiration, Proust and Gide respect, but no modern writer that I can think of, except Camus, has aroused love. His death in 1960 was felt as a personal loss by the whole literate world.

Whenever Camus is spoken of there is a mingling of personal, moral, and literary judgment. No discussion of Camus fails to include, or at least suggest, a tribute to his goodness and attractiveness as a man. To write about Camus is thus to consider what occurs between the image of a writer and his work, which is tantamount to the relation between morality and literature. For it is not only that Camus himself is always thrusting the moral problem upon his readers. (All his stories, plays, and novels relate the career of a responsible sentiment, or the absence of it.) It is because his work, solely as a literary accomplishment, is not major enough to bear the weight of admiration that readers want to give it. One *wants* Camus to be a truly great writer, not just a very good one. But he is not. It might be useful here to compare Camus with George Orwell and James Baldwin, two other husbandly writers who essay to combine the role of artist with civic conscience. Both Orwell and Baldwin are better writers in their essays than they are in their fiction. This disparity is not to be found in Camus, a far more important writer. But what is true is that Camus' art is always in the service of certain intellectual conceptions which are more fully stated in the essays. Camus' fiction is illustrative, philosophical. It is not so much about its characters—Meursault, Caligula, Jan, Clamence, Dr. Rieux—as it is about the problems of innocence and guilt, responsibility and nihilistic indifference. The three novels, the stories, and the plays have a thin, somewhat skeletal quality which makes them a good deal less than absolutely first-rate, judged by the standards of art. Unlike Kafka, whose most illustrative and symbolic fictions are at the same time autonomous acts of the imagination, Camus' fiction continually betrays its source in an intellectual concern.

What of Camus' essays, political articles, addresses, literary criticism, journalism? It is extremely distinguished work. But was Camus a thinker of importance? The answer is no. Sartre, however distasteful certain of his political sympathies are to his English-speaking andience, brings a powerful and original mind to philosophical, psychological, and literary analysis. Camus, however attractive his political sympathies, does not. The celebrated philosophical essays *(The Myth of Sisyphus, The Rebel)* are the work of an extraordinarily talented and literate epigone. The same is true of Camus as a historian of ideas and as a literary critic. Camus is at his best when he disburdens himself of the baggage of existentialist culture (Nietzsche, Kierkegaard, Dostoevsky, Heidegger, Kafka) and speaks in his own person. This happens in the great essay against capital punishment, "Reflections on the Guillotine," and in the casual writings, like the essay-portraits of Algiers, Oran, and other Mediterranean places.

Neither art nor thought of the highest quality is to be found in Camus. What accounts for the extraordinary appeal of his work is beauty of another order, moral beauty, a quality unsought by most 20th century writers. Other writers have been more engaged, more moralistic. But none have appeared more beautiful, more convincing in their profession of moral interest. Unfortunately, moral beauty in art—like physical beauty in a person—is extremely perishable. It is nowhere so durable as artistic or intellectual beauty. Moral beauty has a tendency to decay very rapidly into sententiousness or untimeliness. This happens with special frequency to the writer, like Camus, who appeals directly to a generation's image of what is exemplary in a man in a given historical situation. Unless he possesses extraordinary reserves of artistic originality, his work is likely to seem suddenly denuded after his death. . . .

Camus is the writer who for a whole literate generation was the heroic figure of a man living in a state of permanent spiritual revolution. But he is also the man who advocated that paradox: a civilized nihilism, an absolute revolt that acknowledges limits—and converted the paradox into a recipe for good citizenship. What intricate goodness, after all!

*Susan Sontag, "Camus' Notebooks" (1963), in her* Against Interpretation and Other Essays *(reprinted with the permission of Farrar, Straus & Giroux, Inc.; copyright © 1961, 1962, 1963, 1964, 1965, 1966 by Susan Sontag), Farrar, Straus, 1966, pp. 52-60.*

Throughout [Camus'] career he remained an artist who was also an intellectual, rather than an intellectual, like Sartre, who used the arts for polemical and theoretical ends. Although he did his university work in philosophy—his thesis was on Plotinus—he was never a professional, or even a particularly natural philosopher; he was a moralist who managed to make a persuasive system out of his novelist's preoccupation with conduct. *The Rebel* may be a remarkably probing and sustained intellectual performance for a man of letters, but it is also, for such a difficult, abstruse work, curiously beautiful. The man of letters triumphed over the philosopher, not only in the lucid rhetoric of the close, but in the texture itself of the book. What gives it that sombre, unexpected beauty is something beyond mere style as artifice; it is the quality that forms and controls style: an unwavering sense of justice, a tense humility. . . .

One of his greatest strengths as a thinker was that he demonstrated from the inside just how hopeless the liberal humanist position has become. It is not simply that modern industrial states are too vast and highly organized for the creed to be effective, or even meaningful. It is rather that they are organized in such a way that they exert on all beliefs an intolerable pressure which forces them into totalitarianism. Both the nineteenth century's nihilism and its revolutionary utopianism produced their separate brands of totalitarianism—of the right and the left, Hitler's and Stalin's. Against them, liberal humanism was too vaguely loving, hopelessly enlightened and full of optimistic intentions to be a viable alternative.

What Camus set in its place was not a philosophy but a personal stance that assumed nothing, expected nothing and was critical of everything. His early concept of the Absurd was, I suppose, a secularized sense of tragedy, an analysis of the way a meaningless death gratuitously calls in question a life without meaning, or a life amounting, at best, to no more than that death. 'Nothing, nothing had the least importance, and I know quite well why. . . . From the dark horizon of my future', says Meursault the Outsider, 'a sort of slow, persistent breeze had been blowing towards me, all my life long, from the years that were to come.'. . .

[By] cutting the roots to his childhood [as Camus did], a writer not only cuts off much confusion and mess and darkness, he also runs the risk of cutting himself off from the sources of real feeling. Camus avoided this by giving himself with extraordinary generosity to the present. He did so without drama or self-pity, without preconceptions, regrets or illusions, with great intelligence and modesty, and by creating a style which was lucid, unfailingly objective, yet humane, tentative and lonely. He was courageous without making claims; he had, above all, no conceit. Simply by recognizing the present impossibility of systematized morality he emerged as the one genuine imaginative moralist of our time.

*A. Alvarez, "Albert Camus" (originally published in* The Spectator, *1965), in his* Beyond All This Fiddle: Essays 1955-1967 *(copyright © 1968 by A. Alvarez; reprinted by permission Random House, Inc.), Random House, 1968, pp. 123-27.*

For Camus, the greatness of man, that which releases him from absurdity, lies in his 'consciousness' and his power of rebellion—a rebellion which Camus calls 'metaphysical'. It is a rebellion, not so much against the terms in which existence is given, as against the submissiveness, the unthinking acceptance, which allows those terms to determine human reality. This Sisyphean theme is the basis of Camus' novel, *The Plague,* which could be said to be an extended working out, in a modern setting, of the old myth. . . .

'To leave all justice to God', says Camus in *The Rebel,* 'is to sanctify injustice', and that is why 'it is better to die on one's feet than live on one's knees'.

In the work of Camus, then, we see the human rebellion hurling itself against a meaningless universe and claiming for itself the power to justify happiness. The rebellion is not an individual act of Promethean defiance, but a work of human compassion, and it neither seeks nor requires any absolute to vindicate it. In the words of Colin Smith, 'Rebellion has its own meaning as the final action of which man is capable when everything else dissolves into irrationality and death.' The meaning is in the rebellion itself: it is not in the *results* of rebellion, which may be nothing but failure and which in any case can never create permanent values. . . .

The obvious difference between Camus and Sartre is that the former gives an important place to human relatedness and avoids the latter's loveless individualism. For both writers there can be only one kind of meaning, and that is the meaning created by man himself; but for Camus this meaning is found not so much in individual as in corporate action, and the metaphysical rebellion which he demands issues in a sense of human solidarity. . . .

[In *The Stranger,*] Camus cannot subscribe to any 'objective' theory of the atonement: the cross is meaningful because it typifies the human rebellion against the senselessness of existence, but we make a serious mistake if we think that it has created new conditions in which meaning has somehow become 'given' and permanent. This is precisely the mistake which the Church *has* made. If there is resurrection, if a supernatural order has now imposed its solutions upon absurdity, then Christ's death is no longer the desperate throw of man against futility; it is surrender, not rebellion, and it is therefore 'inhuman' in the sense that it ends by denying the need for rebellion and proclaims acceptance as the way of salvation. So man loses one of his essential dimensions, and turns into an ideology the values which have no existence except in unceasing, ever-renewed struggle.

Camus distinguishes sharply between 'the only two possible worlds that can exist for the human mind': they are 'the world of grace' and 'the rebel world'. The former is Christian, the latter is not. Either we deny all power to justify ourselves and wait submissively for supernatural blessings; or we decide that meaning can come only from our own efforts, and act accordingly. . . .

*The Plague* is one of those rare novels which release the tragic protest and deepen our awareness of what is 'genuinely human'. We recognize ourselves in it, and yet we did not know that we could be as admirable as this. Given the conditions of the plague, we might all hope to act like a Rieux or a Tarrou or an Othon.

Camus is surely right in thinking that to understand oneself as 'genuinely human' is to understand oneself as a rebel. It is important, however, to remove political overtones from the word 'rebel'. While it is true that the human rebellion may and often will find political forms of expression, the 'metaphysical' rebellion of which Camus speaks refers to something which preexists specific forms of rebellion and stands for a characteristic of our existential awareness as such. The word is not used to mean an attempt to overthrow some constituted authority: it points rather to the vision, the questioning, the *protest* which man finds in himself. The starting-point of rebellion is the recognition that the world provides no objective correlate which is coincident with man's interior vision, and it lays upon him the necessity of acting in the light of that vision while refusing to be an instrument of the forces which threaten it. . . .

Of course there are limits to human understanding beyond which God *is* inscrutable and his ways past tracing out; if this were not so, God would be nothing more than an idol—a projection of human fantasies and ambitions claiming authoritative status. But the prophets of Israel will have none of this. The divine word is not an echo of human ambitions: it is a word of judgment as well as promise; it summons men to depart from iniquity and to ally themselves with the divine compassion.

There are thus two kinds of rebellion open to man: the false, self-destroying kind which is rebellion *against* God; and the true, liberating and life-giving kind which is rebellion *with* God. To obey God is to become a rebel against sin and evil, against all that separates man from the source of life and virtue, against all the destructive forces inside and outside man which masquerade as God. To obey God is also to align oneself with meanings and values which have their source in God but which man himself is called to actualize in human history—in politics, economics, social organization, as well as in the individual himself. The fact that these meanings and values always transcend the power of man to grasp or achieve is the reason why the human rebellion always has a Sisyphean character and never attains finality; at the same time, it also forces upon man the realization that he is not God. Only a transcendent God can give the lie to the absolutist claims of man; only a transcendent God is our safeguard against attributing divine authority to human programmes. Camus is right when he points to the terrible consequences which follow when man introduces 'absolutes' into his affairs and claims to be acting in their name. But this is precisely the primal sin of man in the biblical doctrine: 'ye shall be as gods' are the words which lead to the Fall; it is man at the height of his aspiration who forgets the limits of rebellion and plunges into disorder and misery. But without the transcendent God to remind him of his imperfect insights and the hidden 'cellarage' of his self-regard, there is no reason why he should ever do otherwise or understand the cause of his collapse.

The transcendence of God is therefore both the source of the human rebellion and its limitation. . . .

I think we must say that Camus is mistaken when he places in opposition to each other the world of grace and the rebel world. To live by grace is to live as a 'rebel' and to find one's power of rebellion increased. This may seem a startling statement to those who see in the Church nothing but submission and inaction, but I agree with Harvey Cox in his belief that it is one of the great biblical correctives to the distortions of 'tradition'. Catholic and Protestant alike have too often understood 'grace' or 'justification' in essentially *static* terms having little to do with the ongoing challenge of the secular conditions of man's existence. This is not to deny the Church's historic role in the relief of need and suffering, but generally speaking this role has been performed without much radical questioning by the Church of the political, social, and economic orders themselves.

*David Anderson, in his* The Tragic Protest *(© SCM Press Ltd., 1969; used by permission of John Knox Press), John Knox, 1969, pp. 82-103.*

Camus's Don Juan is not 'innocent'. He has decided to live as if he were innocent, which is a very different thing. Such a choice is already reflective, already rational, and the life thus chosen must at least sometimes be beset by the alternatives which the choice has excluded. No doubt it is true that man is 'penetrated by the absurd', as Camus says, but it is no less true that he is penetrated by a sense of moral realities—which may, indeed, be ignored, but which cannot simply be excluded from consciousness by an initial choice. The philosophy of the absurd makes all purposive action—including the choice of absurdity itself—impossible. If, as Camus suggests, consciousness of the absurd makes all actions equal, then there can be no basis for choosing anything at all and life becomes a mere succession of random impulses. . . .

Camus moved away from this position in *The Plague* and *The Rebel.* He did so by trying to fit a philosophy of revolt into his philosophy of the absurd. I have suggested that the two philosophies are inconsistent with each other: there is no reason for being a healer in an absurd world, and Camus was right when he said in *Le Mythe de Sisyphe* that in such a world we can be virtuous only by accident. But *The Plague* shows that there *are* moral values: the whole novel can be read as a passionate protest against totalitarian political systems which are founded on murder and outrage. The philosophy of the absurd cannot account for the existence of the categorical imperative which summons men to revolt against human suffering; on the contrary, the fact that the world contains this imperative must be counted as evidence against absurdity. It must also make untenable the view that man can choose 'innocence'. . . .

Throughout the novel one feels the intensity of Camus's sympathy for ordinary people, who may indeed have lost the innocence of childhood but whose guilt can never merit the monstrous tyranny of a hideous death. It is hard to disagree with this verdict, and the fact that the problem is a very old one which has called forth many attempts to justify God is hardly a sufficient answer to Camus's agonized question. One cannot help feeling that Camus has shown that all theodicies are in the end nothing but callous sophistry.

If *The Plague* were merely about external evil for which man is not responsible, we should have to concede that Camus had made his point. But we have noticed that this is not so. The disease is also meant to be a symbol of the evil in man, and it is a weakness of the novel that microbes are very inadequate symbols of human motives. The plague bacillus creates no moral conflict: it must simply be opposed and eliminated. The matter is clear-cut and the appropriate human action is obvious to any reasonable man. But if the plague represents the evil element *in* man—the desire to dominate, for example—then moral conflict must arise and the problem of appropriate action will become incomparably more complex. The weakness of *The Plague* is that it tries to treat the latter kind of case as though it were the former kind, with the result that the moral ambiguity of human motives is hard to fit into the framework of the parable. . . .

It is impossible to achieve personal sanctity, with or without God, in a world which does not offer unambiguous moral choices. Our very existence is a kind of 'fall' into unfulfilled potential in which there are no hard outlines and no escape from the anxiety which conditions all our becoming. Christ himself was not exempt from the tragic destiny which marks all genuinely human existence. To seek to abstract oneself from a sinful world in order to cultivate a detached rectitude is to be guilty of what Berdyaev called a transcendent egoism. It turns out that the pursuit of individual moral integrity is itself morally blameworthy, and may even be a subtle way of achieving that very sense of domination which, in its overt political forms for example, we righteously condemn. It is to this problem that Camus turns his attention in *The Fall*. . . .

It is certainly a mistake to suppose, as some have been all too ready to do, that in *The Fall* Camus shows himself to be a convert to the orthodox Christian doctrine of original sin. Camus has not abandoned his theory of limits: excessive claims to virtue and excessive accusations of guilt are both disastrous, leading inevitably to tyranny and servitude. Man is not wholly innocent, and Clamence's recognition of the presence of self-regarding motives in his life of virtue is an advance on Rieux's simplistic morality of 'doing his job'. But to swing as Clamence does to the opposite extreme of unremitting self-denunciation is to forget that there are also limits to guilt. Camus is suggesting that denial of man's *relative* innocence is as catastrophic as denial of his relative wickedness. . . .

I think Camus is implying that, although we are guilty, our only hope lies in our being treated *as if we were innocent*. He is hinting at something that is surprisingly like the doctrine of grace. . . . Camus sees that this is the only exit from the crushing morality of merit and desert, but he has failed to notice the emphasis of the New Testament on the cost and sacrifice which made it possible. The conclusion which Clamence seems to draw from the Gospel is the optimistic one that human guilt is not, after all, a very serious matter—a view which is very much in line with Camus's idea of the secret 'innocence' of man which we have noticed in his earlier books. . . .

[For] all the shrewdness of its insights and the clarity of its language, *The Fall* is finally a disappointing book: it offers only an ironical commentary on a serious human question. We are left with a false prophet, and the solution to the problem of human guilt seems to vanish into the rain and fog of Amsterdam where the judge-penitent carries on his profession. Perhaps Camus is simply saying that there *is* no solution and that we must be content to live ambiguously in the strange half-light between guilt and innocence without claiming virtue and without losing heart. This is an attractive, almost Epicurean view, and probably most of us are able to live by it for most of the time. But it does not help us 'in the sombre season or the sudden fury', and it is hard to see how it can include the kind of challenge and sacrifice which made Camus's earlier imperative of revolt so exhilarating. There are limits to the living of life within limits.

*David Anderson, in his* The Tragic Protest *(© SCM Press Ltd., 1969; used by permission of John Knox Press), John Knox, 1969, pp. 144-55.*

It is true that, compared to the Arthur Koestler of *Darkness at Noon,* to the Malraux of *La Condition humaine,* to the Orwell of *1984* or of the essays on Mahatma Gandhi and Burnham, or to the Sartre of *Les Mains sales* or *Les Séquestrés d'Altona,* Camus does tend, because of [his] obsession [with the death penalty], to look at politics from a very narrow angle. He sees little but the problem of violence, and always in the highly generalized terms of a philosophy which, in his view, justifies killing in the name of historical inevitability. He offers nothing of Sartre's or Koestler's feeling for the complexity and unpredictability of history, little of Orwell's detailed analysis of how doctrines and attitudes change in response to different situations, none of Malraux's ability to dramatize the wide general sweep of the historical process and thus make it emotionally as well as intellectually comprehensible. But if he sees things narrowly, Camus also sees them sharply. The concern for the living individual already implicit in his early work, and essential to his view of the artist's calling, recurs in its most intense and moving form in those books and articles in which he is striving to protect men against the two worst things on ideology can do to them: kill them outright or deprive them of their individuality. It is this concern to protect the individual against both these dangers which inspires what is, from a political standpoint, his most complex and probably his most satisfying work: *The Plague*.

From the moment of its publication, in 1947, this novel was interpreted in political terms: as an allegory of the German occupation and French Resistance movement and as an interpretation of this movement presented by a man once involved in it, as a more general description of totalitarianism in action, and as a novel that recommended, though without leaving the plane of allegory, a certain form of political behavior. While it is on the first level that its transposition of the definite ambitions of the Nazi movement into the more impersonal activity of the plague is most open to criticism, it is nevertheless here that its immediate appeal to the 1947 reader was to be found. . . .

[Paneloux] is, in fact, forced to confront the dilemma which Camus himself presents, in *The Rebel* and elsewhere, as the major objection to Christianity: that if God is all-powerful and all-good, it is impossible to understand why he should allow the innocent to suffer through natural causes. Such considerations are, of course, only tangentially relevant to the political content of the novel. No philosopher of history, however providential his vision, has maintained that absolutely everything is for the best, and that the progress of the dialectic knoweth even the fall of the sparrow. What the introduction of these wider issues does illustrate, however, is the extent to which the Camus of *The Plague* avoids the major pitfalls of the political novel: relevance to only one period and to only one problem.

*The Plague* treats the problem of totalitarianism from a number of different angles, and it also recommends an attitude of tolerant agnosticism in political matters. But it is also a novel of the human condition, an attempt to show the problem of suffering in a metaphysical as well as in a political context. It may well be that, with the passage of time, its immediate applicability to the problems confronting France or Europe in the 1940's will become less immediately visible. It is already difficult for young readers to grasp the references to the German occupation and to the Resistance movement, and the gradual liberalization of even the French Communist party will make Camus's attack on totalitarianism increasingly difficult to understand. Nevertheless, three aspects of *The Plague* will more than outweigh these possible disadvantages: the excellence of Camus's prose, especially in the imagery which serves to emphasize both the naturalness of the plague and the delights of the natural life; the criticism of all forms of abstract thought; and the plea for tolerance, which has a far wider applicability than the immediate circumstances for which Camus was writing. . . .

[The] political meaning [of *The Fall*] is linked to a particular interpretation of why bourgeois intellectuals are attracted by the absolute discipline of the Communist party which seems to have occurred to Camus during the controversies over *The Rebel*. They feel guilty at the privileges and freedom which they enjoy in a society where so many others are neither rich nor free, and they lack the strength of character to adopt a reasonable attitude toward their guilt. Acceptance of communism enables them to see this guilt as a necessary phenomenon and also offers them a way of escaping from it through the highly disciplined revolutionary struggle for a classless society. This meaning is not, however, something that leaps immediately to the eye, and it has never been as widely discussed as the relevance of *The Plague* to the German occupation. Indeed, it could even be argued that it is so well disguised by the other aspects of the novel, and especially by the light which *The Fall* casts upon Camus's attitude to Christianity, that a political interpretation is almost a classic example of the intentionalist fallacy. . . .

[The] political meaning of *The Fall* is clear only to the reader who has been told that it is there, and the book is much less obviously a political novel than *The Plague*. There is no point in being committed unless people can see what you are being committed about, and the same criticism of relative obscurity can also be leveled at the short story "The Renegade," whose political implications are apparent only to someone with a fair understanding of *The Rebel*. . . . *The Fall* and "The Renegade" are thus concerned, like *The Plague,* with totalitarianism, and both recommend, as did Camus's earlier novel, the same attitude of moderation: We must guard against exaggerating either our sinfulness or our initial revolt, lest we become infected with the intolerance and lust for power which characterize the bacillus of the plague.

All three works express the same agnostic humanism, but the second two are particularly open to the criticism that the diagnosis which they offer involves a considerable oversimplification of the issues involved. . . .

Almost everything which Camus says about politics in the two volumes of his *Carnets* that have so far been published indicates that he took part in politics only reluctantly and always tried to give priority to artistic considerations. Had he been born in a different age, when political questions presented themselves with less urgency, there is little doubt that he would have remained a more detached artist, and that his work would have reflected more of his declared ambition to write prose as Mozart composed music. In a way, this would have been a pity. The great appeal which Camus made in the 1940's was as a moralist, and his intense concern for ethical questions fitted in remarkably well with the political mood of the time. The excellence of *The Plague* lies precisely in the way that this encounter between his conscience and the political atmosphere of postwar France gives rise to considerations that are applicable to the permanent problems of political action and not solely to one period. Without the impact that politics made on Camus in the 1940's, we should be poorer by a masterpiece; and without the political concerns that continued to inspire part of his work in the 1950's, we should lack the opportunity of seeing how some very good books can be written under the inspiration of some rather limited ideas.

*Philip Thody, in* The Politics of Twentieth-Century Novelists, *edited by George A. Panichas (reprinted by permission of Haw-*

*thorn Books, Inc.; copyright © 1971 by The University of Maryland; all rights reserved), Hawthorne, 1971, pp. 189-206.*

*The Plague* will endure partly because it achieves something rare in fiction: its theme and plot resemble each other closely, each in itself demonstrating the same concept. Considering the horse and rider or chest and treasure relationship of plot and theme in most fiction, Camus' is a remarkable accomplishment. Much of the power of this powerful work is found in the natural interweaving of plot and theme which here, because of their similarity, peculiarly reinforce and electrify each other. . . .

The plot of the story is revealed in five parts. Of these the middle one is smallest and the second and fourth largest, so there is in the structure some symmetry which is not, however, worked out down through the level of the individual chapters. Why then bother with dividing the novel into parts? Obviously Camus feels that each is doing a distinct job. . . .

I believe the best one-word summary of the five parts of the book, in order, would be: unawareness, awareness, death, commitment, and life. First the people of Oran, and they are not extraordinary in this way, are characterized as making no effort to reach the true nature of each other, and, unaware of the reality of their world and its other inhabitants, they are unfit to become easily aware of the coming plague. Then the brutal statistics awaken them, and they psychologically gird for battle. In the third part, they are crushed both physically and psychologically; their bodies die, and so do their minds and hearts; they are ready to surrender, and their hearts are emptied of love. But in part four they learn how to fight; they learn that their resistance must be organized; they learn that only by fighting beside and for one another do they have any hope of surviving themselves. When in part five the plague leaves, the survivors, despite their tendency to isolate themselves once again, are keenly alive; and they have learned how to live better. Unawareness, awareness, death, commitment, life: that is the shape of the plot. . . .

The theme of the plague is this: in life we choose either to live or to die. To die we first cease truly to communicate; to live we first communicate truly and then we commit ourselves to our fellow man. So this is the shape of the theme of *The Plague:* death—noncommunication—communication—commitment—life. Notice how very similar this is to the shape of the plot: unawareness, awareness, death, commitment, life. (Unawareness and awareness are so like non-communication and communication in this book that they are virtually the same.) Therefore, between the plot and the theme the only difference is that the concepts are in a slightly different order: compared to the order of the plot, the theme's parts are ordered 2, 3, 1, 4, 5; compared to the order of the theme, the plot's parts are ordered 3, 1, 2, 4, 5. The obvious reason for this juxtaposition is that death, which is thematically at the opposite pole from life, must dominate the fulcrum of the book for dramatic reasons. Either way, . . . both plot and theme demonstrate the same concept, a concept which, when applied in an analysis of all the works of its remarkable author, should shed new light on his landmark thinking.

*Francis J. Henninger, "Plot-Theme Fusion in "The Plague'," in* Modern Fiction Studies *(© 1973, by Purdue Research Foundation, West Lafayette, Indiana), Summer, 1973, pp. 216-21.*

* * *

## CARRUTH, Hayden 1921-

**An American poet, novelist, and critic, Carruth has won several important prizes for his lyrical and controlled poems. He is most often praised for his sustained meditations, of which *Journey to a Known Place* is a notable example. (See also *Contemporary Authors*, Vols. 9-12, rev. ed.)**

As I think of *The Crow and the Heart,* I find myself believing not in its sustained power or concentration of language, but in a carefulness which bursts, once or twice or three times, into a kind of frenzied eloquence, a near-hysteria, and in these frightening places sloughing off a set of mannerisms which in the rest of the book seems determined to reduce Carruth to the level of a thousand other poets who can do, just as easily as he, most of the things he does in about three-fourths of these poems. Often, Carruth appears not to have learned the Gresham's Law of poetry, which states that the more sounds and images you crowd into a line, the less effect they have. He seldom lets you forget that you are reading something which has been written, and written again, and then written some more. These poems strike me as being completely mechanical and lifeless, with more than a hint of academic dilettantism about them. They are Suspect, and I for one cannot take them seriously. . . .

What kind of thing, here where my mother's
  flowers
Bark colors only, like a tranced bazaar,
Is my late lingering love for you, which
  flows
Beyond all those events, past the Azores?

I guess (and I am only guessing) that "bark colors" is intended to indicate that the colors are raucous and irritating, and call attention to themselves mindlessly and unnecessarily. Actually, though, this is not what happens in the beholder's mind. He thinks momentarily only of a preposterous image of flowers like dogs, or like sideshow barkers, and then dismisses it, his attention having been retained by neither flowers nor dogs. Because the objects which are called to our attention are vertiginously disembodied in language, considerable doubt is cast on the veracity and imagination of the mind that brought them up and presented them in this way. As Auden says, the poet's job is to find out the images "that hurt and connect," and a great many of Carruth's don't, at least not for me. They are like musical exercises that one wants to hear dissolve into the real playing. . . .

"On a Certain Engagement South of Seoul" is as fine a poem as an American has ever written about the ex-soldier's feelings, and that takes in a lot of territory. It is only after the Inevitable has clamped us by the back of the neck that we go back and look carefully at the poem, and see that it is written in *terza rima.* And so, hushed and awed, we learn something about the power of poetic form, and the way in which it can both concentrate and release meaning, when meaning is present. This poem suggests, too, that Carruth is one of the poets (perhaps all poets are some of these poets) who write their best, pushing past limit after limit, only in the grip of recalling some overpowering experience. When he does not have such a subject at hand, Carruth amuses himself by being playfully skillful with internal rhyme, inventing bizarre Sitwellian images, being witty and professionally sharp. . . .

Hayden Carruth is a writer with strange and terrifying shifts in quality. His last year's *The Crow and the Heart* contained the finest sonnet sequence that I have read by a contemporary poet, "The Asylum," and a great deal of ordinary, jargoning stuff which Mr. Carruth should have been ashamed to print in the same volume. "The Asylum" showed, however, that Mr. Carruth might be one of the few modern poets capable of writing a good long poem. *Journey to a Known Place* is it. . . .

Like his man-bird, Mr. Carruth is "skilled now in the / profound and lovely / necessities," and his wonderful new poem, very possibly a great poem, which begins with a huddle of refugees and ends in the City of the Sun, is bound to be discussed and reread for many years. *Journey to a Known Place* is a painful and magnificent poem; it really hurts and it really sings, and I can only urge readers to buy it and live with it.

*James Dickey, "Hayden Carruth" (1961), in his* Babel to Byzantium *(reprinted with the permission of Farrar, Straus & Giroux, Inc.; copyright © 1956, 1957, 1958, 1959, 1960, 1961, 1962, 1963, 1964, 1965, 1966, 1967, 1968 by James Dickey), Farrar, Straus, 1968, pp. 127-31.*

[*For You*] is a collection of five long poems by Hayden Carruth that have appeared previously only in magazines or limited editions, one of them being the 1963 Balch prize winning poem, "North Winter." They are, perhaps, Carruth's finest work, although his book-length sequence, "The Norfolk Poems," may hold that honor. In any case, these are major poems by a poet who has never received the wide acclaim his work deserves and who is certainly one of the most important poets working in this country today. And these five long poems show him at his best, technically skilled, lively, never less than completely honest, and as profound and deeply moving as one could ask. The speaker of the poems is a man who has been sorely wounded by life, but has found in that wounding the necessary strength to continue to live and more, to take deep joy in living, in the movement of seasons, the names and natures of birds and flowers, the hurting and loving of human beings. "Come," he says at the end of "Contra Mortem," the fourth of these poems, "let us sing against death." And sing that song he does, whether in the sharp descriptions of winter's coming and going in "North Winter," or in the moving farewell to his father in "My Father's Face"; he sings against death and for life always, life with all its hurt and sting, the nothing that is everything. Let us celebrate this book's appearance and hope that it will at last give to these fine poems the wide audience they so truly deserve.

Virginia Quarterly Review, *Vol. 47, No. 3 (Summer, 1971), p. cv.*

As a poet, a friend of poets, an editor, a critic, Hayden Carruth is one of the preservers of the life of poetry in his time. . . .

When the worlds of so many poets are made of words, as though poetry were accessible to no more than talent and ambition, it is a moving reaffirmation of the power of poetry that [*From Snow and Rock, From Chaos*] does not make a world of its own. It does not attempt or desire to do so. Instead, it accepts the obligations of the world outside itself that it did not make. Its principal subjects are love, work, poverty, mortality, and the difficult, beautiful land and weather of Vermont. The poems have been fretted and abraded in their bearing of this world's knowledge and mystery. Like weathered carvings, they have been both made and worn the way they are.

And when so many poets record their obsession with their own sufferings and their own deaths, it seems an estimable strength and grace in this book that it fulfills itself in the realization of other lives and other deaths, and keeps the heavy accounts of that devotion. . . .

Out of their burden of knowledge and mystery, "from snow and rock, from chaos," these poems render their gifts of orderly speech. . . . They delineate and accept the terms of human love. . . . And their stern fidelity to those terms verifies their profound gentleness. . . . The poet speaks of, and out of, what he has known again and again, touching lightly in passing the sources of his endurance. . . .

*Wendell Berry, "On Carruth's Poetry," in* American Poetry Review, *January/February, 1974, p. 39.*

* * *

## CASSILL, R(onald) V(erlin) 1919-

**Cassill, an American novelist, short story writer, and essayist, is best known for his fictional studies of the American Midwest. (See also *Contemporary Authors*, Vols. 9-12, rev. ed.)**

Cassill's most insightful and esthetically complete accomplishments to date have been in his short stories; his novels, despite their considerable merit and consistently similar thematic concerns, do not manage to present that essence of embodied vision necessary to the finest artistic performance. Paradoxically, the novels may be seen to attach themselves as tangential illuminations in the over-all expression which finds its artistic keystone in the faceted, mosaic structure of a whole conglomeration of autonomous and independent shorter works. . . .

"This Hand, These Talons" is not an early story in the sense that it confronts us with an immature theme or imperfect mastery of techniques; it is early only in the sense that it states a major concern of Cassill's fiction with as much clarity as its ironic and understated conventions will allow. The story falls short of that ultimate clarity of vision which relinquishes the felicities of ambiguity in favor of that more willful explicitness which must be termed prophetic, however; and in view of his further attempts, that is the gambit which Cassill has accepted. It is a sign of his insight and tenacity and his rockbound humanistic bias that in his subsequent fiction he has forged beyond such grim realities and found an affirmation of the heart's plight—at the end of its tether, the mind must turn back and recreate its willful illusions, and those illusions may be annealed once again into functional ideals.

"And in My Heart," a story of very different substance from the earlier "This Hand, These Talons," similarly confronts us with the individual's dilemma within the voiding forces of circumstance and the inadequate alternatives open to action, but ultimately affirms the struggle because that struggle itself can seek its completion in the form of art. . . .

In the stories as a whole, one finds several signal threads by which the thematic development here polarized might be traced; in addition, of course, these threads may very well be viewed from nonthematic perspectives. One finds, for instance, a repeated portrayal of abnormal mental states in Cassill's characters, salient enough that one might well construct a thesis to the effect that in his works the psychic disorders which are ordinarily judged as failures of the individual to come to terms with the milieu in which he lives, are in fact the tragic *means* of evaluation and insight into a world which has lost its traditional moorings. Such stories as "The Outer Island," "The Puzzle Factory," and "The Father," in addition to "This Hand, These Talons," might profitably be examined from such a normative psychoanalytic point of view. . . .

In a different vein, a number of Cassill's stories may be seen as comprising one of the most dexterous efforts among contemporary writers at creating new forms for fiction. The scholarly narrator of *Clem Anderson,* Cassill's most satisfying novel, says of a group of writers of whom Clem was one: "Some years ago [they] had shared with Clem an enthusiasm for 'the new short story.' The story was to be a consolidation of the gains made by Joyce, Crane, Porter, Hemingway and Faulkner. As I recollect the eager theorizing, the new story was to be as compact as poetry. . . . It was to keep the suppleness and repertorial virtues of traditional fiction while it added a range of subtleties unknown before the twentieth century." I submit that the production of such a story has been an effort and aim of a not inconsiderable number of writers since 1940, and that a portion of Cassill's work fits this category exemplarily. . . .

One has, finally, the possibility of considering the whole body of Cassill's stories in the light of their consciously-wrought function of describing individual experience as a measure for the archetypal experience of man as it is re-enacted in our time.

> *David Roberts, "The Short Fiction of R. V. Cassill," in* Critique: Studies in Modern Fiction, *Vol. IX, No. 1, 1966, pp. 56-70.*

Second—but still troubled—thoughts have persuaded us to give mention to [*Doctor Cobb's Game,* an] outrageous but nonetheless unforgettable novel. Can R. V. Cassill be right, can the 1963 Profumo scandal in the higher echelons of the British power-structure somehow be fictively if not otherwise believably "explained"? Can such a novel work? The answer has to be "yes" to both questions. For the real source of power is the sexual drive, and if by Svengali-like string-pulling and brainwashing a cynical and sinister mesmerizer like Dr. Michael Cobb gains dominance, the ruinous "game" can be destructively won. Cassill's game is won as well. He has control and in many passages of bravura writing is most exciting; there is talent here that is superbly sure of itself. A repugnant reading experience—so be it. Evil is evil and must be nothing less than frightening.

> The Antioch Review *(© 1970 by The Antioch Review, Inc.; reprinted by permission of the editors), Vol. XXX, Nos. 3 & 4, 1970, pp. 459-60.*

Perfectly at home in the New York art world in which it's set, R. V. Cassill's new novel ["The Goss Women"] is also heavy with device and bloated with a portentous, idealized sexuality that is its undoing. Dean Goss, nearing 70, is America's acknowledged old master of modern painting, a giant of continuing accomplishment, "protean." Goss's life and work is being recorded and celebrated in a book by Susan, a novelist whose teenaged daughter is having an ecstatic, mystical affair with Goss's youngest son, Jason. . . .

Cassill has novelistic gifts that place him well above the usual constructers of plots like this, and it's sad to see him in the company of such stuff. In addition, I'm constantly surprised at how many of the no-longer-young attribute gargantuan sexual appetites—and activities—to young people, and how often hippie-hating and hippie-revering seem to share this common source. For Cassill, sex and sensuality are the property of the very young and of the Creative Artist, and the novel, dangling its secondhand mystical-occult apparatus, pumps toward the eventual coupling of these featured characters with a vengeance that's faintly unpleasant.

Plot devices included (the only up-to-the-minute one that's missing here is an exorcism), this is a remarkably old-fashioned novel that creaks with its stale assumptions about youth, art, sensuality. It would be unfair not to mention that Fay Weldon's thoroughly original and neglected 1972 novel, "Down Among the Women," is, almost line-by-line, a witty antidote to all the myths of this book—especially the one about the artist's appetite.

> *Sara Blackburn, in* The New York Times Book Reivew *(© 1974 by The New York Times Company; reprinted by permission), April 21, 1974, pp. 36-7.*

* * *

## CELA, Camilo José 1916-

**Cela is a Galician with Italian and English ancestors. He has written many short stories and travel books about Spain in addition to the novels for which he is well known. *The Family of Pascual Duarte,* according to one critic, "brought new preoccupations and language to the Spanish novel." (See also *Contemporary Authors*, Vols. 21-22.)**

Camilo José Cela, like the other members of his generation in Spain, . . . reacted violently against the "dehumanizing" tendencies so pronounced in the post-World War I novelists such as Ramón Pérez de Ayala, Jarnés, Unamuno and Miró. Seeking a foothold in traditional Spanish realism, [the more recent] novelists eschew intellectualized figures and abstractions, preferring to focus their attention on flesh-and-blood characters and the realities of the world which surrounds them. In spirit their works are probably closest to the late nineteenth-century realistic masters such as Galdós, Pereda, Blasco Ibáñez.

The history of the Spanish novel records few cases of such stern and merciless realism as Cela's. [This] Galician has little to say in favor of mankind. Few if any rays of sunshine penetrate his pages, in which ugliness, brutality, selfishness and the principle of "homo homini lupus" predominate. Cogent reasons exist for classifying him as a full-fledged naturalistic writer. From the very beginning of his career, Don Camilo has exhibited a predilection and a genius for portraying life, man and society at their worst.

In his first novel, *La familia de Pascual Duarte* (1942), Cela adopted the form and even the archaic style of the Golden Age picaresque novel to present the autobiography of a criminal awaiting execution. Born into the most squalid and loveless of environments, Pascual is incapable of rising above his milieu. Despite a basically kind disposition, his life is a series of brutalities and killings. He kills in turn a dog which always appeared to regard him reproachfully, a horse which had thrown his wife and caused her to abort, his wife's lover and finally his hateful, nagging mother. The novel, to a large extent a *succès de scandale*, abounds in shocking incidents. Pascual Duarte merits comparison with some of Dostoevsky's psychopathic protagonists. It is difficult to find in Spanish literature a novel which approaches *La familia de Pascual Duarte* in its sustained atmosphere of impending catastrophe, its powerful portrayal of human malevolence, and in nightmarish effects.

Cela's second novel, *Pabellón de reposo* (1943), consists of a series of letters by supposed tuberculosis patients in a sanatorium. The young writer dips his pen in blood to portray the anguished and tortured soul-states of his protagonists, in the last stages of consumption. So realistically convincing were the letters, which first appeared in serial form in *El Español*, that Cela received a letter from a physician imploring him to discontinue the series, since his patients were identifying themselves with the hapless characters in *Pabellón de reposo* and this was retarding their progress!

In *Nuevas andanzas y desventuras de Lazarillo de Tormes* (1946), the novelist presents a modern *Pícaro*. The new Lazarillo, of no more illustrious parentage than his sixteenth-century forerunner, successively serves a trio of wandering musician-sharpers, a hermit, a group of French acrobats and finally a witch-healer. The twentieth-century Spanish rogue is less a caricature, more a flesh-and-blood character than the Golden Age prototype.

A careful and conscientious workman, Don Camilo devoted five years to the writing of his fourth and most recent novel, *La colmena*, published in 1952 in Argentina. As if manipulating a powerful camera, Cela focusses upon one after another of the *habitués* who frequent Doña Rosa's bar, located in a shabby section of Madrid. *La colmena* is the collective tragedy of pathetic individuals existing in a material and spiritual vacuum and devoid of any altruism of idealism. Spanish criticism has been almost unanimous in acclaiming this novel as Cela's masterpiece, both for its vigorous simplicity and for the author's artistry in evoking the atmosphere of Madrid during the final days of World War II and the years immediately following. . . .

Don Camilo has himself supplied a number of statements which afford insight into his aims and methods. Among foreign writers he renders special tribute to Dostoevsky, while among Spaniards it is Baroja who influences him most strongly. To certain critics Cela is largely a cultivator of the *novela barojiana*. It is indeed true that there is much that is reminiscent of the venerable Basque novelist in his works: their episodic and rambling structure, the rich galaxies of types presented, the kaleidoscopic views of society, the strong attraction for outcasts and marginal personalities, the pessimistic view of life. . . .

Much like Pío Baroja, he conceives of the novel as a malleable and flexible instrument for the mirroring of life's realities. The novelist is to him "the keeper of the conscience of his times and his world" whose duty it is to lash out against deceit, dishonesty and sham.

His pessimism is stubborn and unrelieved. He has not hesitated either in his novels or in his critical statements to make this clear. [He has] commented: "Life is not good; neither is man. . . . Upon occasion it appears that man is kind and intelligent. But let us not be deceived. He is only hiding behind hs mask."

*Jacob Ornstein and James Y. Causey, "Camilo José Cela: Spain's New Novelist," in* Books Abroad, *Vol. 27, No. 2, Spring, 1953, pp. 136-37.*

[Not] only has Cela been responsible for revitalizing the Spanish novel by giving it impetus with a series of artistically excellent works, but he has chosen as well to make his career one of a complete re-examination and reconsideration of the novel as an art form. Cela's consistent refusal to adhere to any a priori assumptions concerning the novel and his insistence on being the most unpredictable writer since the tempestuous Unamuno have not endeared him to all literary critics. . . .

Cela's novels have often attracted more attention to their form than to their themes, and the author has stated his interest in trying out various modes of the novel. It is unnecessary to discuss why Cela is interested in experimenting with different modes of fiction. Why does any author experiment with form and technique if it is not in order to find the most convenient form of self-expression? . . . In trying several different theoretical orientations, Cela has sought directly to improve his skill as a novelist and indirectly to serve as bellwether for the postwar Spanish novelists. It remains to be seen how much impression Cela's work will have on novelists in general and whether his importance will be felt sufficiently outside of Spain to influence non-Spanish novelists.

From a theoretical point of view, the principal concern of Cela's novels has been the mode of the novel as a reflection of human experience. Cela's various attempts with narrative prose fiction may be seen as seeking to establish an optimum balance between the novel and the living reality it pretends to reflect. In this respect, Cela's novels may be grouped into four broad categories: (1) traditional in form (*La familia de Pascual Duarte*); (2) novel of psychological introspection (*Pabellón de reposo*); (3) novel of the social complex (*Nuevas andanzas y desventuras de Lazarillo de Tormes, La colmena, La catira*, and *Tobogán de hambrientos*); and (4) new novel in form (*Mrs. Caldwell habla con su hijo, Garito de hospicianos*, and *La familia del héroe*. *Tobogán* also shares characteristics of this group.). . .

*Tobogán de hambrientos* demonstrates to an abundant degree all of the tendencies and characteristics of Cela's novels as a whole. Cela continues to advance the idea that mankind can be seen only as a totality of individuals who share common desires, problems, and emotions. *Tobogán de hambrientos* views individuals essentially as objects to be used as raw material in a commentary upon mankind. With this novel, Cela reaches a plateau of technical achievement where successive novels threaten to become repetitions of what has already been said. Although Cela has firmly established the right of the novel to explore mankind communally from a superior point of view, it remains to be seen to what extent such a procedure can make the necessary transition from caricature to profound statements of synthesis. *Tobogán de hambrientos*, which has its obvious merits as a novel, unfortunately tends to be more caricature than profound synthesis in spite of the structural design employed in order to simulate narrative unity. . . .

Although the illusion of objectivity is sought after in Cela's previous works, *Mrs. Caldwell habla con su hijo* is the first novel to work out a series of structural devices for this purpose. Cela's satisfaction with them is evident in their incorporation into the structures of both *La catira* and *Tobogán de hambrientos*.

*Tobogán de hambrientos*, in particular, employs many of the devices of the new novel, especially in its use of pattern and in the rejection of chronology, definable plot, and unified points of view. Cela's *Garito de hospicianos* is an extreme example of the rejection of the more conventional narrative or fictional aspects of the novel. . . .

Cela's role as a novelist and his role as a man constitute a fundamental paradox that accounts for many of the technical and structural pecularities of his novels. Cela has come to believe that the function of the novel is to give the illusion of reflecting life as it is being lived, although, of course, the final result is but one novelist's personal vision. Cela's novels stand back to record the scurrying and the scuffle, both tragic and comic, of everyday life. In so doing he has expressed his belief that man is essentially unaware of the role he plays in the vast complex of human existence. Cela has stated both in his prologues and in his novelistic asides that the majority of men and women are unconscious of life above the level of their basest needs and desires. . . . These beliefs have been brought out particularly in *La colmena* and *Tobogán de hambrientos*, but they are valid also with reference to others of Cela's novels, for example, in the central irony of *La familia de Pascual Duarte*. . . .

In believing that men are basically the same and in writing novels that utilize typical and archetypal human personalities, Cela is basically neoclassic as a philosopher and as a theoretician on the content of art. That the novel must portray what is typical about man and mankind rather than what is singular and particular has hopefully been established as a working premise for Cela as a novelist.

Yet, the structure of Cela's novels is as far removed from traditional or classic forms as is possible. Structurally and formally speaking, Cela's novels are free forms. In a sense they are singular in their very rejection of any a priori assumptions concerning the novel in the same way that Cela's characters refuse to behave in accordance with any preconceived moral or ethical notions. This is not to say that Cela's novels lack form any more than free forms lack form. They merely adjust themselves conveniently to the stresses of the situation at hand.

Basically, however, the principal condemnation of Cela as a novelist results not from his radical designs for the novel, but from his departure from the romantic-realist pattern in which the novelist is responsible for the creation of individuals who, although they may reflect the broader outlines of their society, must also exist as well-defined and unique individuals. It is the latter that Cela refuses to have his characters do. The characters of Cela's novels gather any importance they may possess as individuals solely from their identity with the larger human society to which they belong. Since Cela seems to feel that it is unnecessary to create individuals—perhaps even impossible—he can with little trouble reject the form, devices, and ends of the realist novel. A significant step toward understanding Cela's work as a novelist is made by the reader who is able to allow himself to accept for the moment the possibility and the desirability of the novelist's speaking purely on the level of human universals. The fact that those universals may be the basest—as opposed to the lofty virtues usually associated with the classic perspective in literature—is certainly of a secondary consideration.

*David W. Foster, in his* Forms of the Novel in the Work of Camilo José Cela *(reprinted by permission of the University of Missouri Press; copyright © 1967 by the Curators of the University of Missouri), University of Missouri Press, 1967, pp. 13-160.*

With *The Family of Pascual Duarte* (1942), the first of two major novels on which his reputation rests, Camilo José Cela catapulted himself into the first rank of Spanish writers. This thin, first novel shattered the literary vacuum left by the Civil War. In form, it purports to be the autobiography of a criminal awaiting execution in a rural prison during the war years. Pascual Duarte is termed a "sweet lamb harassed and frightened by life." But, like Lenny in John Steinbeck's *Of Mice and Men,* he had hands that seem to be meant to kill. A deceptive objectivity masks the presentation of cruel and monstrous scenes, including murder and matricide. In a taut style, with emotion carefully reined, Cela evokes an atmosphere of extreme brutality, one which a nation suffering from the after-effects of a brutal civil war could readily understand and believe. It was this brutality that ushered in a neo-realist style of writing, "Tremendismo," which has been widely imitated in Spain.

Since this novel appeared the same year as Albert Camus' *The Stranger,* critics were quick to point out similarities between the two works. While there are some existentialist overtones in Cela's novel, his major inspiration lies closer to home—in the picaresque tradition of Spanish writing rooted in the sixteenth century, and in a peculiarly Spanish fascination for grotesque deformation of reality. . . .

In his second major novel, *The Hive* (1951), Cela abandons the traditional narrative structure to follow the lead of John Dos Passos's *Manhattan Transfer.* Here, the Spanish novelist pries the lid off the human beehive of Madrid during the 1942-3 period, to lay bare a panoramic view of decadence, sex, and hunger, seen mainly in the cafe, the brothel, and the bar. This anti-epic of Madrid has no story-line for its 160 characters, only sketches and endless dialogue. . . .

In these and other novels in the neo-realist tradition, Cela has gradually forged one of the most expressive Spanish prose styles since Cervantes. It is the rich vernacular of oral speech, so fresh off the tongues of the common people that one can almost detect the scent of garlic behind the words. It is a style redolent of popular slang, savory vocabulary, and a peculiarly masculine charm.

But the neo-realist is but one of three faces Cela turns to the literary world. . . .

He also excels in the "quasi-novel," really books of travel and local-color sketches. Like many Spanish writers before him, Cela has taken to the dusty back roads of his country, on foot, toting a rucksack, in an effort to experience at first hand the scruffy reality of life in the towns, hamlets, and the open countryside. He is regularly taken for a shabby traveler, not a writer. . . .

Cela's engaging local-color sketches have deep roots in national history. Spanish writers have long delighted in capturing the quivering vitality of real life on the wing, not recreating it in the study. In this field, known as "articulos de costumbres" Cela stands with the finest Spanish writers of all time. It is very possible that his lasting fame will rest more on these sketches than on his novels. . . .

But Cela has still another literary face—that of the conscious artist concerned with universal problems, which he presents with little or no reference to his normal Spanish habitat. In this vein, he has produced two novels noted for their lyrical recreation of somewhat depressing themes. In *Rest Pavillion* (1943), the Spanish novelist, drawing partly on personal experience, evokes the atmosphere of a sanitarium for tubercular patients. Once again he abandons the story-line and substitutes a series of vignettes to give the reader a vicarious taste of the misery, suffering, nostalgia, and sense of abandonment felt by his characters in their cruel vigil, watching the hall clock in its steady rush toward a future they will never know. In this work, Cela probes deeply into man's true purpose in life and questions the materialistic values by which many live today.

His second literary novel is *Mrs. Caldwell Speaks to Her Son* (1953), which has recently found its way into English translation. This is a poetic diary of an incestuous mother, directed to her dead son. Turning his back again on the traditional mold for a novel, Cela employs short letters (chapters)—215 of them in less than that number of pages—to recreate the thoughts and hallucinations of his one major character. From the outset, the author indicates that Mrs. Caldwell had died in London's Royal Insane Asylum. With this as a background, the poetic and often surrealist imagery in which Mrs. Caldwell clothes her fanciful memories becomes understandable. . . .

Although there is much fine writing in Cela's two literary novels, both are disappointing. They lack pace and offer no true development of character. Both stand as evidence that a fine prose style cannot of itself insure a rewarding novel. . . .

Over the years, Cela's powers of novelistic invention have declined somewhat, but this has been offset by his growing mastery in the field of travel and local-color sketches. It is that faculty for transferring the still-breathing Spanish reality to the pages of his works, and his two early neo-realist novels, which assure him an honored place in Spanish literature.

*Francis Donahue, "The Three Faces of Camilo José Cela," in* Michigan Quarterly Review, *Summer, 1969, pp. 201-03.*

Camilo José Cela appeared dramatically on the literary scene in 1942 with *La familia de Pascual Duarte (The Family of Pascual Duarte)*, which not only caused a sensation, but, more important, secured a wide foreign acceptance. It has the virtues and defects of a first novel. Even greater acclaim for *La colmena (The Hive)*, 1951—a work of maturity and originality without the earlier shortcomings—assured his place at mid-century as one of Europe's outstanding novelists. In view of Spain's internal and international situation, his accomplishment is all the more remarkable, indicating that these books were sufficiently timely to receive immediate attention. (Preface)

*La colmena* [*The Hive*], still considered Cela's masterpiece by many, evolved in the years from 1945 to 1950. . . . It is important to bear in mind his developing technique of this period because critics have seriously proposed Dos Passos' *Manhattan Transfer* as his model for the presentation of urban life in a series of loosely connected sketches. This American novel had been translated in Spain before the war, but . . . Cela has been steadily elaborating his own method. The action of *La colmena* is concentrated, whereas that of Dos Passos' rambling novel covers twenty years and the sections are much longer. Evidently, *Manhattan Transfer* is cited in an effort to explain the great evolution in Cela's writing after *Pascual Duarte*. In *La colmena* Cela for the first time deals at length and effectively with everyday urban life, thereby assuring his status as Spain's foremost novelist. (p. 83)

*D. W. McPheeters, in his* Camilo José Cela *(copyright 1969 by Twayne Publishers, Inc.; reprinted with the permission of Twayne Publishers, a Division of G.K. Hall & Co.), Twayne, 1969.*

* * *

## CÉLINE, Louis-Ferdinand (pseudonym of Louis-Ferdinand Destouches) 1894-1961

**Céline was a French novelist and physician. His nihilistic, misanthropic novels employ a unique idiom originally based on Parisian argot. (See also *Contemporary Authors*, Vols. 1-4, rev. ed.)**

Céline's greatest books . . . are: *Voyage au bout de la nuit* and *Mort à crédit,* written at the start of his literary career; *D'un château l'autre* and *Nord,* produced during the last decade of Céline's life. Everything characteristic of the writer is contained in these four works: all the main themes and stylistic innovations, every stage of the evolution his writing underwent. In themselves, they constitute a whole, a statement as complete as anything designed to define an author's vision of man's position in the universe. At the same time, they can also be seen as a cycle, for it has been noted that Céline's last great work, *Nord,* meets and in many respects parallels his first, *Voyage au bout de la nuit.* (p. 15)

Céline, the arch-individualist among modern French novelists, refuses to be labeled or categorized. . . . If we wish to do so at all, we must provide only the largest and broadest sort of lineage for Céline. We might then point to his relatedness with the ancient tradition of irrationalist, mystical, obscurantist literature which, in French writing, would link him most closely to the Middle Ages and the sixteenth century and to a tradition which preceded that of the Classical Age with its emphasis on reason, formal beauty, elimination of excess. We might also ally him to this current as it comes to the surface again in the nineteenth century and manifests itself in the rejection of the dictates of classicism.

Linking Céline to particular writers, such as Aristophanes or Rabelais, Rousseau, Voltaire, Swift, and Cervantes, has its attractions. However, while such comparisons emphasize his capacity to produce laughter of a robust or satirical sort, it seems even more important to dwell on Céline's adherence to another, blacker current in literature. It is one filled with militant pessimism and violent derision, denoting a vision that spares nothing of man's existence, and a humor that is no less somber than its poetic strength. This stream flows from Villon to Beckett. . . . One of its tributaries . . . is that of existentialism. . . .

Céline's link with existentialist thought is much more crucial than the obvious influence he has exercised on the best known exponent of the doctrine, Jean-Paul Sartre. It is based not only on his ability to figure in the ranks of those who are its precursors—for, like them, he has seen and voiced all the pain, hideousness, meaninglessness, and despair of the human condition—but also on the fact, and this is one of his major contributions, that he has translated his vision into a particularly modern idiom. His work can thus be considered as a juncture of existentialist thought and contemporary style, that is, the eruption of the spoken word into literature. (pp. 17-18)

Céline's contribution is vital not only because it is a journey to the end of past statements on the nature of human existence, but also because it points the way to an expression of these ideas through stylistic means that force the reader into direct contact with basic emotions and spoken language. Thus, the stripping away of protective layers of consolation, illusion, contingency which may serve as palliatives, occurs on two planes at once: the sweeping demand for a *tabula rasa* is met both by thought and expression. In this resides Céline's unusual power as a writer, as well as the anger or terror of the reader, who is subject to such ruthless and exacting action.

There can be no doubt that Céline belongs in the ranks of the great destroyers. Uprooting secure concepts of existence and literature at the same time, he commits what for many is an unpardonable sin—that of leaving us no refuge of any kind, no exit from the trap he has shown our world to be. The first attack is leveled at beliefs we generally cling to in order to maintain a safe view of our universe: thus, religion is dismissed or rejected; moral codes are proven a sham, an empty shell; human brotherhood reveals itself as a hollow dream. The second uprooting is no less thorough, for traditional literary style is scrupulously dismembered, exploded, destroyed. Céline's entire work—both in theme and style—is an illustration of the view that existence is an endgame played out on a cannibal isle or in a cosmic jungle, in an irrational and vicious setting with a multiple décor of slaughterhouse, asylum, and dunghill. Moreover, this vision is hammered into us in a language as brutal, direct and visceral as raw human emotion—the apparent directness being due to Céline's consummate skill as a writer which allows him to produce this effect of style, while hiding the meticulous craftsmanship that lurks behind it. (pp. 18-19)

Although the impact of Céline is not specific, it runs in a deeper—if often hidden—current. Essentially, it consists of the creation of a new tone, a literary ambiance which pervades an entire sector of modern letters and exceeds the limits of national boundaries or personal orientation and background. It has made possible the indebtedness to Céline felt by French authors of such diverse persuasion as Aymé, Queneau, and Bernanos, as well as the kinship expressed by foreign writers like the Slovakian Céjra Vanos, the Americans Henry Miller, William Burroughs, Allen Ginsberg, and Jack Kerouac, among others. (p. 20)

The greatness of Céline resides not only in his stylistic revolt, but also in his having ventured to the very end of an already desperate line of thought and feeling. (p. 25)

Céline's interest . . . in the falling apart, the liquefication, the melting away of the individual . . . is a part of that firsthand exploration of all man's lower depths, physical or mental. Madness, . . . whether confined to the asylum or rampant in that open-air madhouse, . . . must be illuminated.

The novels are filled with explorations of this nature. From *Semmelweiss* to *Nord,* there stretches an almost endless line of "madmen," "nuts," "imbeciles," and other creatures who are suffering from dementia, from alienation of one sort or another. It is, however, more than the description or analysis of madness that interests Céline. . . . It becomes quite apparent that for Céline there are two kinds of madness: that of victim and that of torturer. For the first, he has compassion; for the second, he reserves a good deal of his anger. Thus, it is only half true that the author feels that "man in his illness is essentially malevolent," since he castigates solely those sick individuals who are also vicious, and spares the harmless or innocent, even if they are mad. (pp. 104-06)

Diametrically opposed to the humanistic ideal which places man on an ever-ascending stairway leading to the perfection of all his attributes, Céline's view emphasizes the downward path, the escalator going to a basement of impotence, futility, absurdity, decomposition. . . . According to the former, man is lucid, creative, meaningful, capable of joy, dignity, perfectibility. According to Céline, he flees lucidity, is destructive, meaningless, absurd, capable of endless misery, cowardice, prone to continual decay and corruptibility. (pp. 106-07)

It is as if the author demanded true heroism from his audience rather than from his characters. . . . While the protagonists of the novels are allowed to choose detachment, *évasion,* apathy, paralysis—the reader is not. He is trapped, snared by the work of art, fastened to his terrible reflection in the mirror, with eyes pried open. Actually, his is the most horrible fate. Céline's attack is directed primarily against him. (p. 113)

Céline *does* sometimes speak of what is delicate, or filled with emotion; when this happens, the incident or single phrase has the startling brilliance of a luminous stone against black cloth, a piercing point of light in otherwise total darkness. Their very rarity, their intensely lyrical quality, make these passages both striking and deeply moving.

In general, they seem like a momentary pause in the violent storm of invectives, a brief respite in the description of the vicious battle of existence. It is as though Céline, while unleashing the black *déluge* of his writing, set afloat a small ark of human beings and animals whom he will spare. (p. 115)

[Reality], which in Céline has only the vilest connotations, continually intrudes or forces its way into the realms of the imagination, of fantasy, of art.

In the last works, however, we find a development of a trend already visible in the early novels: reality takes on such a hallucinatory aspect that it is hard to separate it from the realm of fantasy. . . . The implacable exploration of this delirious reality, as well as the attempts to overcome it by a kind of exorcism, create an important part of the dynamism of these works of Céline. At the same time, one may also note a quest for delirium, as an escape from time, failure, horror. This has already been true for such works as *Voyage* and *Mort à crédit*. . . . In the last novels it is no longer even a momentary truce of this kind, but the briefest of respites, a sudden—if brutal—removal from reality. In the first writing of Céline as in the last, it is clear that one must take the leap if one wishes to turn one's back on existence: "In order to truly flee, one has to pass through the mirror, into the domain of dream or madness." (p. 185)

*Erika Ostrovsky, in her* Céline and His Vision *(reprinted by permission of New York University Press; copyright © 1967 by Erika Ostrovsky), New York University Press, 1967.*

There can be no doubt about the historical importance of Louis-Ferdinand Céline in the literature of anarchistic revolt. He was the first great foul-mouthed rhapsodist of the 20th century to proclaim a satanic vision of a godless world, rolling helplessly through space and infested with crawling millions of suffering, diseased, sex-obsessed, maniacal human beings. *Voyage au bout de la nuit,* which appeared in 1932, was not simply a continuation of the pessimistic literature of the 19th-century "realists". It was Zola-esque in its blackness, but it had a frenzy, a speed, and a virulence which made the average Zola novel suddenly seem almost as old-fashioned as a horse-drawn bus. Zola had toyed with the idea of using the working-class vernacular as a medium for the expression of social reality, as had Jean Richepin and a number of minor satirical poets, but no one before Céline had exploited the figurative obscenities and racy syntax of the spoken language in such a thorough-going and masterly fashion. It was as if the underdog had suddenly found a voice. . . .

Since nothing is ever absolutely new, Céline would probably not have been what he was without the French tradition of revolt, which one can trace back almost as far as one likes. . . . God-defiance or God-rejection, wild satirical exaggeration, scatological and pornographic hyperbole are not novel elements in French literature. . . . Céline may not have absorbed much of this tradition consciously, but it was in the air he breathed. . . .

It would be interesting to know whether or not Henry Miller had actually begun writing his "Tropics" before he read *Voyage au bout de la nuit*. The . . . similarities between his books and Céline's two major novels, the *Voyage* and *Mort à crédit* (1936) seem too striking to be explained merely as a coincidence, or as two separate manifestations of the *Zeitgeist*. One gets the impression that Céline pulled out some kind of stopper and released a flood of vituperative literature, which since his time has flowed as strongly in the English language as in French. The vengeful, apocalyptic note . . . sounds first in Miller, then in Mailer, Kerouac, Baldwin, Ginsberg, *et al*. . . . Céline had a lot to do with the development of the poetics of paranoia. . . [and he] is a novelist only in autobiography. . . . The writing is demential in that Céline does not tell a story nor explain anything, but instead produces a vast, swirling monologue in which glimpses of real-life episodes, worked up to Céline's usual feverish pitch, alternate with repetitive diatribes against all those people against whom he has a grudge. . . . After producing *Voyage au bout de la nuit* and *Mort à crédit,* which were widely and justifiably assumed to be expressing a predominantly left-wing sensibility, he suddenly turned into the most scurrilous kind of anti-Semitic pamphleteer and, when the Germans occupied France, allowed himself to be associated with one of their most revolting enterprises, the anti-Semitic exhibition in Paris. . . .

I think one has to assume either that Céline was not quite right in the head, or that his metaphysical despair was so great that he thought it didn't much matter whom he attacked or what he said, provided the theme he was dealing with could be translated into his particular brand of rhapsodic prose. The most one can say on his behalf is that he didn't play safe. His literary reputation stood high in the late '30s and, since anti-Semitism was not a popular theme in France, he had no personal axe to grind in suddenly switching to it, apart, perhaps, from the technical need to find a new source of invective, after using up the material of his early life in the two major works. Nor are the later volumes in any sense an apologia. He doesn't try to explain or justify his behaviour; he just carries on in his usual tone, hitting out in all directions. . . . The style [of *Castle to Castle*] is characteristic of his later manner, *i.e.* it bears as little resemblance to traditional narrative writing as Turner's last pictures do to representational painting. The reader has to surrender himself to an impressionistic, paranoiac monologue, in which more often than not the sentences are left unfinished, the transitions from one idea to the next are not explained and many of Céline's contemporaries are referred to elliptically and derisively under transparent nicknames. . . .

The technique is always the same: detail is piled upon detail in a mad rush, as if the intolerable nature of creation were being suggested by a proliferation of instances. The phenomenon is very close to the hysteria of the Absurd in Ionesco. . . .

The basic feeling in paranoia may be that the individual consciousness is being stifled by the infinite number of other existences and by the pressure of the unassimilable weight of material things. . . .

Independently of its moral obtuseness, [its] all-or-nothing rhythm is, in the long run, very monotonous, and *Castle to Castle,* apart from one or two good, nightmarish passages, is quite a tedious book. . . . I would suggest, rather, that after 1936 he went so peculiar that he involved himself in experiences which did not correspond to the whole of his personality as it had existed in the earlier phase. The increasing stridency of his later works shows that there is something wrong with the experiences themselves and that he is not digesting them properly into literature.

*John Weightman, "Céline's Paranoid Poetics," in* The, New York Review of Books *(reprinted with permission from* The New York Review of Books; *© 1969 by NYREV, Inc.), June 5, 1969, pp. 25-9.*

Céline's work stands as a monument to . . . dissonance, rage, and madness. . . . When Céline died in 1961, he was still at work on one more novel [*Rigadoon*], in which he continued to pour forth his vituperation against the lie, against all lies that blind men to their misery.

Yet Céline never really offered any belief in the truth, that is, in any truth beyond the recognition of man's horrible necessity to grow sick and die and of the anguish that accompanies that recognition. Perhaps it is inappropriate to speak of truth and falsehood in Céline's case, for his novels propose a form of discourse that lies beyond the realm of normal verification and beyond the paradox that springs from the antithesis of lie and truth. His novels are, in essence, discourses in the delirium that springs from his intolerable awareness of human misery; and as discourses in delirium, Céline's novels are an inexhaustible source of truths and countertruths.

From his first to his last novel Céline's work can be compared to a journey, or, more precisely, to a flight that leads into the night of existential, metaphysical, and, finally, historical darkness. There are momentary flickers of light in this night, such as Céline's lyricism in *Guignol's Band* or the joy he finds in the dance. There is also his anti-Semitic polemic, the outrageous pamphlets that constituted an insane effort to bring illumination to the night. *Voyage au bout de la nuit* first sets forth the theme of flight into darkness and thus serves as a kind of preface to the entire body of Céline's work. It is a preface complete in itself, yet it points beyond itself to the journey that ends in the disaster of Céline's last novels in which he narrates pseudohistorical "chronicles" of his flight across Nazi Germany.

Céline's flight into darkness is more than a physical or even literary journey, for his works trace a descent into a night of another sort, one in which the light of reason has been extinguished. This snuffing out of the light of reason means quite simply that Céline's journey leads to the darkest reaches of madness. Céline's novels present extended travels into the delirium of men, things, history, of existence itself. Madness is his favorite metaphor to explain the nature of being. Hallucination is his favored mode of perception. (pp. 3-5)

[When] *Voyage au bout de la nuit (Journey to the End of the Night)* appeared on the literary scene in 1932, . . . Céline's cynicism and denunciations seemed to speak for everyone. . . . [His] popular, obscene language was like a violent gust of fresh air breaking into the literary climate. The Right and the Left, both Daudet and Trotsky, were ready to applaud *Voyage*'s scandalized portrayal of a society in dissolution as well as its bewildered outrage at man's innate viciousness. Neither group was entirely wrong in its interpretation, for in *Voyage* Céline had succeeded in writing a work in which a social sense of human exploitation coexisted with a sense of man's incapacity to rise above his dreary propensity for self-destruction. In short, he had composed a radical novel based on reactionary premises. (p. 7)

In terms of the narrative structure *Mort à crédit* is undoubtedly Céline's best novel. The work is virtually seamless. Céline is in complete control of his narrative material, never losing sight of its development nor yielding to the urge to incorporate extraneous horrors. *Mort à crédit* is longer than *Voyage*, but the reader follows its organic unfolding with no sense of formless wandering. The mad rush of events often possesses a forceful if demented logic that carries the reader along at a rapid pace. To a large degree Céline's control of his temporal perspectives in the key to his structural success. He first posits a narrator in an undefined present and then changes the narrative point of view to an earlier point in time. The illusion of two temporal perspectives adds another dimension to the work as it moves chronologically from the earlier time toward the narrator's present. Time lost is recovered—or at least purged—by the structural movement.

The structure of *Mort à crédit* gives the impression of an author not only firmly in control of his artistic vision but, in one sense, even disengaged from it. This disengagement is a corollary of Céline's choice to present his fictional world in an essentially comic manner; for to see a world as comic is, necessarily, to see it from a vantage point of emotional and intellectual distance. . . . For both the reader and the author the aesthetics of comedy are founded on disengagement.

To say that *Mort à crédit* is a comic novel is to say that all elements in the novel are subordinate to its comic vision. Thus one of the main differences between *Mort à crédit* and *Voyage* is the difference between the satirical and the comic, though this is not to say that elements of mordant satire are not found in *Mort à crédit* and that comic devices are not used in *Voyage*. . . . *Voyage* shows that satire can blend into the formless scream of revolt at another extreme. . . . *Mort à crédit* presents a vision of a world in which delirious, comic automatons blindly act out their obsessions with predictably cataclysmic results. (pp. 74-6)

From *Voyage au bout de la nuit* to *Mort à crédit* Céline considerably changed his approach to the novel. . . . [However] it is obvious that the deliriously hostile world of *Mort à crédit* is akin to *Voyage*'s disintegrating world. Common to both novels is Céline's view of life's destructiveness as a projection of the insanity that lies at the core of existence. Understanding Céline's approach to the novel is thus fundamental to understanding the differences between the two works. Rather than trying to combat this madness through a total revolt doomed to failure by its very contradictions, he has chosen to exorcize it through comic reduction. Céline's refusal of his world through comic negation is still a form of protest, but the mechanisms of comedy he so brilliantly uses also show that Céline has accepted madness insofar as it can be transformed into laughter. In this sense, the violence of total rejection has become the hyperbole of extravagant comedy. (p. 77)

Cosmic buffoonery, coming from Céline's pen, is still an accomplishment that many lesser writers would envy. His frantic slapstick and burlesque *délire* endow the novel with a curious force. As a gratuitous verbal performance, *Féerie pour une autre fois* probably has no equal in modern literature. Céline is visibly present in his efforts to bend his obsessions and paranoia to fit a mythical mold that will dramatize and explain his very real misery. The reader is inevitably struck with admiration for the very frenzy of Céline's struggle. He sees that Céline is grappling with a problem whose solution can never be found through mere verbal energy, that Céline is wrestling with a personal demon that he tries to shout down—and Céline's volume has never been greater. The greater the incomprehensibility of his disaster, the more Céline seems to believe that his verbal magic can work a counter-spell against the evil that has caused it. Yet the reader also sees that Céline's revolt has turned into a parody of itself. His refusal has become a series of comic obsessions that generate an incredible amount of noise, but represent ultimately no more than a cosmic belch of disgust. Taken together, then, *Féerie I* and *Normance* are Céline's last expression of a visceral refusal of the undigested and indigestible past that the earlier novels tried to purge. They are also the first expression of his revolt against history and its collective manifestations of *délire* that the last novels will present on the scale of nations, if not the cosmos. (p. 168)

Céline's outcry against the incomprehensible unfolding of events that has led to his downfall is, ultimately, grounded in a paranoid clown's view of history as a personal apocalypse. . . . Yet Céline's refusal to go beyond his own misfortunes reduces his revolt against *délire* and its eviscerating agent, History, to a sterile caricature. Moreover, in spite of Céline's often brilliant pyrotechnics, in spite of the comic angle of vision his pariah complex gives him, one must regret that Céline's paranoia, seemingly founded on an obstinate will to perceive only what pleased him, appears to be a defense mechanism by which he shields himself from knowledge that could destroy him. Céline could never have been called an intellectual; he always wrote from beneath the solar plexus. But it is more than regrettable that his obsessive revolt could not have been tempered, if not by understanding, at least by compassion. In the trilogy of chronicles Céline has lost that sense of compassion that was one of the most admirable sides to the negation he expressed in his earlier works. It is this narrowness that makes these works oppressive, though at the same time it intensifies their comedy. Céline's work ends, then, with a paradox much like the one that began it in *Voyage*: the very source of the strength of his vision makes it intolerable. (pp. 198-200)

Finally, Céline's legacy is his use of language. Language, *délire,* comedy, and revolt are inseparable in Céline. It is through his blend of argot, neologisms, popular expressions, and obscenities, through his blend of fractured syntax and popular speech patterns, and through his furious, rhythmic punctuation that Céline emulates chaos, emotional distress, and madness. It should be stressed again that neither his originality nor his stylistic force resides in his use of argot and slang. (p. 210)

The Célinian novel is then, if only through the immediate force of language, one of the most naked revelations of the tormented self in modern literature. . . . Language mimics madness and destruction in Céline. It also mimics a riotous joy, the joy of shouting down all the misery and injustice with which life can crush a man. It is this exuberance that will not allow us to abandon Céline. (pp. 211-12)

*Allen Thiher, in his* Celine: The Novel as Delirium, *Rutgers University Press (New Brunswick, N.J.), 1972.*

*Rigadoon* completes the trilogy begun with *Castle to Castle* (1957) and *North* (1960). . . . The book is a sort of *Paradisio* to the *Inferno* and *Purgatorio* of its two predecessors, and it triumphantly concludes Céline's career. . . .

In *Castle to Castle,* Céline is patiently making a final try for the brass ring, straining to recapture the buoyant energy, the creative self-esteem of *Journey to the End of the Night* (1932) and *Death on the Installment Plan* (1936), in the face of private wretchedness and public indifference or obloquy. But poignant as is his sense of banishment from the republic of letters, there is a major problem to the book: as he sardonically doctors the hungry, rumor-ridden, backbiting colony of French fascists and collaborators at Sigmaringen, he is inescapably trapped in his own public role as an alleged collaborator, the author of the notorious anti-Semitic polemics of the late '30s and early '40s. He had not in fact been a collaborator, despite his prewar enthusiasm for Hitler's racial policies, and after the war he amply paid for his pestilential anti-Semitism. But in the absence of any hint of remorse for it in the book or any acknowledgment of the scale of the Nazi infamies, there is something edgily disingenuous about his repeated insistence on his postwar sufferings, his scathing counterattacks against his literary accusers, his mordant challenges to the official cliché version of a nobly resisting France. They suggest rather too much a brilliant defense attorney with a shaky brief.

*North* is considerably more relaxed, partly no doubt because of the favorable reception of *Castle*. . . . The book sags a bit toward the end as Céline tries to manufacture some novelistic action, and it is still politically unendearing in places. But there are indications, too, of a certain amount of authorial role-playing, of Céline's presenting himself knowingly as "the foremost living stinker," giving his public their thrills, aware of the duplicity of their attitudes toward suffering and disasters in a disastrous world. And the kind of reader whose imagined complaints about his ramblings and abrasiveness he takes note of at various points is obviously not perceived as hostile. . . .

Céline himself, as he writes [*Rigadoon*], is consciously nearing sanctuary at last, an anachronistic survivor, the old enmities almost done with, though he goes through the motions for form's sake.

With death near, with the promise of rest and the certainty of his own literary immortality, there is a new and deserved self-acceptance, an acknowledgment of his youthful skills and idealism, his abiding sense of duty, his stubborn endurance. . . .

His works are the most eloquent testimony that we have to the madness of Europe that resulted in the two holocausts. But the eyes through which he regarded that madness, as the present book reminds us, were not only those of the prodigious genius-victim of *Death on the Installment Plan* and *Journey to the End of the Night* and the brutal polemicist of the swollen so-called pamphlets. They were also those of the deeply compassionate doctor who wrote that poignant brief study of medical genius and folly, *The Life and Work of Semmelweiss* (1924). *Rigadoon* deserves its bugle call, it takes its place alongside *Semmelweiss,* and the two of them, while not of the stature of his two masterpieces, are the works that most satisfyingly complement them.

*John Fraser, "Bulls-Eye," in* The New Republic *(reprinted by permission of* The New Republic; © *The New Republic, Inc.), May 18, 1974, pp. 22-3.*

Our short focus may explain why most war novels are so unsatisfactory: they show us a melodramatic theater—tanks, planes, bombs, guns, whole battlefronts—but they don't convey the day-by-day domesticity of a war, they make it exciting, interesting, meaningful, life-enhancing . . . pornographic! Céline is different. No great battles for him; no omissions either. "I'll tell you as I go along . . . all the more or less amusing vicissitudes. . . . [Takes] all kinds of crap to make a world . . . not to mention a book!" He knows that we don't much like his kind of book, that we'd prefer evasions, rhetoric, the old style: "I guess you think I'm an awful sap. . . . I could easily have stayed home taking a lofty view of events, and written about the stirring adventures of our intrepid armies of the Great Shit Parade, the way they managed to come home in triumph, [welcomed] by marshals under the Arch . . .". Well, we did like all kinds of crap, but on the other hand we don't much trust lofty views of events. Pedestals put us off. Women complain that literature falsifies them because writers have so limited a sense of what women are like inside. Wars might validly make the same complaint—but not, one suspects, about the war novels of Céline.

A stylistic innovator and chronicler of grasping, foundering, lower-middle-class Parisian life, Céline was as narrow, suspicious, cynical and elaborately bigoted as the people he described. His anti-Semitism led to his being suspected of pro-German sympathies during the Second World War (actually he had *no* sympathies), and toward the end of that war he fled—with his wife "Lili" and his cat Bébert—into Germany, where they underwent a complicated odyssey back and forth from Baden-Baden to Berlin, from Sigmaringen to eventual escape into Denmark . . . where he was jailed for over a year. After the war he was condemned and then cleared by French courts, practiced medicine outside Paris and wrote several novels about his war years.

*North* focuses on the destruction of Berlin and Céline's first internment; *Castle to Castle* evokes the black-comic opera world of the Vichy government in exile; and *Rigadoon* is a travel book, in which we shuttle with Lili, Bébert, and Céline, on trains under bombardment, from one bombed-out city to another, until we reach the illusory haven of the Hotel d'Angleterre in Copenhagen. . . .

[For] the evocation of a world at war, all this is reported by a participant whose mental quirks evoke the mental and emotional reality of life in such a world. Suspicious, ignorant of what's going on and reticent about what he knows, hypocritical, sleepless, insistently factual and yet self-contradictory, self-justifying, cynical and yet living for the moment optimistically, shrewd, shepherding idiot children but abandoning their tubercular leader, looking forward enthusiastically to the death of Europe but willing to risk his life for Bébert—Céline quite deliberately makes us feel the inescapable, mind-rotting horror of endless chaos, the fact of war as Americans have never known it . . . although we have been inflicting it on others from the air, in Asia now as we did 30 years ago from our Flying Fortresses.

*J. D. O'Hara, "War on the Installment Plan," in* Book World—The Washington Post (© The Washington Post), *June 2, 1974, p. 3.*

"Rigadoon" does not succeed for me. As early as page 44, with the appearance of the lepers, I began to find the voice of the narrator too wayward, and his inappropriate and unexpected reactions to calamities, which in his earlier works made me laugh, became artistically ineffective. Since the background is the real destruction of much of Europe, Céline's smart-aleck tone seems not simply unattractive but inadequate. . . .

Violence is a staple of Céline, and I now think (dismayed because I felt so remote from "Rigadoon," I went back and reread him) that he chooses approaches to the subject which are incompatible. His narrator-protagonist is occasionally on the wrong side of the law, but, verbally aggressive though not physically violent, he frequently insists that he is a physical coward. Yet the narrative voice just as frequently speaks as a connoisseur of destruction, the way an impotent man might become a connoisseur of obscene shows. So, in "Rigadoon," Céline describes with relish how Restif kills the general in command of the soon-to-be-destroyed train, and he establishes his superiority over his audience by knowing more than it does about killing. Sometimes, speaking as the doctor, he assumes professional detachment, but on these occasions he is almost invariably being Dickens' Fat Boy: he wants to make our flesh creep by talking about loathsome diseases and painful deaths, though now and then he just wants to get in a few words about the inferiority of women. The other superiority Céline seeks is in suffering. The Céline protagonist has done nothing to deserve the dreadful things that happen to him; he always hurts more than anybody else, and his pain justifies his hatred. . . . The Céline narrator is forever alone. . . . And the concept of the narrator as the lonely coward among millions of heroes, which seemed comical the first time I read "Journey," became less plausible, especially now that specialists, from anthropologists to zoologists, have been fretting that combat creates a unique solidarity among men, a staunchness and fraternity that no other human enterprise evokes. . . .

An artistic difficulty about Céline's racism in "Rigadoon" is that it calls attention to his knockabout, night-club-comedian cast of mind. . . .

There is a coherence in Céline's works, but it represents not so much a consistent comic point of view as it does an enduringly hostile personality who will use any trick to dominate the audience. . . . Since he regards his reader as his enemy, Céline is alert to outwit him. . . .

And, of course, there is his writing—the style that seems to me as stunning as ever. His use of language—his inventions or discoveries of rhythms, echoes, verbal and tonal surprises—reflects an innocent enjoyment, a playfulness that astonishes, entertains, dazzles. I am troubled now not only because of the use he made of these gifts but because I have so far accepted it. Ought he to have mocked the poor, narrow people from whom he sprang? Ought he to have made fun of their ignorance and ineffectuality? Ought I to have laughed with him? On my first reading of "Castle to Castle," I felt like an accomplice when I joined Céline in deriding men who, whatever evil they had done, were at the end of their rope. Now I do not wish to share his guilt. I find myself saying to Céline what Mrs. Weston says to Emma: "You divert me against my conscience." That is a moral rather than an artistic judgment, but is there not a point at which a moral failure becomes an aesthetic flaw?

*Naomi Bliven, "Connoisseur of Destruction," in* The New Yorker, *June 10, 1974, pp. 129-32.*

Nobody knows quite what to do with Louis-Ferdinand Céline . . .: this multi-personality, split Gemini driven by the passions of Scorpio (with the scorpion's desire to sting himself to death), healer and reveler in destruction, history's clairvoyant and mud-spattered participant, verbal-visionary genius and hack pamphleteer. It is difficult for most of us, living in the either-or world of morality, engaged in the endless, futile struggle to separate good from evil, to cope with the lightning-like ambivalence of genius. We want our heroes to be good. (And yet, Blake: "Energy is eternal delight.") . . .

If . . . the reader [of "Rigadoon"] survives [the] opening barrage—which by the time of "Rigadoon" has become almost an obligatory song-and-dance for Céline, a self-parody—he will find a very different Céline, one whose relationship to the reader is conspiratorial, confiding, engaging, variously that of bum to fellow bum, showman to spectator, cold sober crystalline philosopher to suddenly awestruck, silent student. . . .

The trilogy is essentially a firsthand account of the collapse of European civilization, though "collapse" is too polite a word, orgiastic death-throes would be more like it, and "firsthand" is too tame a phrase for a man who planted his own life right in the midst of the sickness and death of Europe and let it rage—reprehensible and Lear-like—through his soul. . . .

[What] is being finally and utterly pulverized in "Rigadoon" is not just a landscape, but the very essence of a civilization—the agreed-upon structure of perception. . . .

As in his other books . . ., Céline's scalding and secretly moral contempt for human nature, its inveterate selfishness, sensationalism and inertia (which *is* his vision, and which perhaps lies—as in the eye—right next to his blind spot), exists side by side with his physician's unflinching, unforgiving gaze at suffering and his fundamental care for life.

*Annie Gottlieb, in* The New York Times Book Review *(© 1974 by The New York Times Company; reprinted by permission), June 30, 1974, pp. 6-7.*

* * *

## CLARKE, Arthur C(harles) 1917-

**An English astronomer, science fiction novelist, and short story writer, Clarke is best known for his novel *Childhood's End* and for his screenplay for Stanley Kubrick's "2001: A Space Odyssey." (See also *Contemporary Authors*, Vols. 1-4, rev. ed.)**

It is interesting that one of the best-known science fiction writers, long a prophet of space travel and its implications, should espouse a fundamentally negative conception of nature, insofar as nature can be identified with matter. But such seems to be the case with Arthur C. Clarke, author of *2001: A Space Odyssey, Childhood's End,* and a spate of other fascinating inquiries into the world of science and the future. In *Childhood's End,* alien space creatures establish a benevolent dictatorship on earth, just as man is about to penetrate outer space. Poverty, war, ignorance, and disease are eliminated; there is even an attempt to erase the resulting boredom by the development of universal education and participation in the arts. Only one basic restriction is placed on man: He is barred from research in the field of parapsychology.

The golden age is disrupted when a young child begins having dreams during which his mind leaves his body and travels to distant planets. Other children begin to have similar experiences. The wandering child-minds develop the capacity to manipulate matter. Then, as more children are affected, the minds begin to merge beyond the bodies. After a period of playing with their/its newfound power, the common mind leaves the earth, destroying it in the process. It ascends into the heavens to merge with an "overmind" which has infinite capacities to travel and manipulate matter. Man has ceased to exist. The creatures who arrived to rule the earth turn out to be the midwives of the "overmind," sent to earth to save man from self-destruction before the "birth" of the new form, and to keep him from aborting the birth of the children's common mind by stemming his advances in parapsychology. Salvation is attained in Clarke's novel by an elaborate process by which man is delivered from the tyranny of matter.

In the novel *2001: A Space Odyssey*—which Clarke published after his collaboration with Stanley Kubrick on the screenplay of the film—Clarke again introduces a free-floating mind. It is the power which intervenes at various points of human history and which lies behind the release of the astronaut at the book's end. In *2001,* the released mind seems to retain units of individual consciousness, but otherwise there is no change in Clarke's attitude toward matter. . . .

[Clarke's] objectification of evil in matter can lead to a disregard of the natural environment, the consequent increase of sickness, and the encouragement of escapism and a distortion of truth in our perception of reality. . . .

Another problem with *Childhood's End* and *2001,* if taken as possible sources of metaphysical speculation, is that individual freedom and self-consciousness are components which are devalued, and man is made subject to forces which he can neither comprehend nor control. Mind is all; it functions in a predetermined manner; it is finally a mere atom in the vague mass of "overmind."

*Lois and Stephen Rose, in their* The Shattered Ring: Science Fiction and the Quest for Meaning *(© 1970 by M. E. Bratcher; used by permission of John Knox Press), John Knox, 1970, pp. 48-53.*

Mr. Clarke's fantasy [in *2001*] shows us that science fictionists cannot escape a compulsion toward metaphysics even while they have to express it in a style conducive to their own habit of thinking in terms of gadgets. . . .

Clarke, an inveterate and hardheaded despiser of philosophers, seems to stammer in amazement as he finds himself caught up—one suspects greatly to his surprise—in the ancient dreams some philosophers have harbored about "Spirit . . . and even beyond." "If there was anything beyond *that,* its name could only be God.". . .

There is something gratifying in seeing a fanatic of technology like Clarke become converted to the mysticism of Father Teilhard de Chardin. His conversion would be more satisfying, however, if this advance toward the spiritual were understood as something more and other than an increased skill with computers and information machines. And we notice too that obsessive habit of technological utopians, to which E. M. Forster has called our attention in "The Machine Stops," to debase the poor archaic vessel of the body until here, in this most advanced technological phase, it is simply shed like an inefficient and worthless husk.

*William Barrett, in his* Time of Need: Forms of Imagination in the Twentieth Century *(copyright © 1972 by William Barrett; reprinted by permission of Harper & Row, Publishers, Inc.), Harper, 1972, pp. 357-58.*

Clarke particularly likes to set forth apparently complex, threatening situations and then resolve them with simple common sense. . . .

The Hermian attempt to destroy Rama [in *Rendezvous with Rama*] is the most dramatic illustration of Clarke's belief that man is his own greatest enemy. Rama is "an element of total uncertainty" in the universe. Man cannot tolerate uncertainty, and in his desire for knowledge, his destructive impulses rear their heads. . . .

Perhaps Clarke's disinterest in characterization results from [his] view that the universe is indifferent to man. All the characters are one-dimensional—either defined by their scientific theories and specialties or stereotyped to fit a particular role in space exploration.

*Melody Hardy, in* Best Sellers, *October 1, 1973, p. 291.*

Although it lacks some of the metaphysical fireworks and haunting visionary poetry of "Childhood's End" or "The City and the Stars," this thoughtful scientific romance [*Rendezvous with Rama*] is happily representative of the man who is both our most distinguished writer of speculative fiction and one of the important literary figures of our time. Clarke handles his generic stocks-in-trade—the strange creatures and hallucinatory landscapes—with splendid imagination, but "Rendezvous with Rama," like all of his work, is essentially an expression of wonder in the presence of Mystery, for this excellent scientist and entertainer has remained above all a moralist, preoccupied with the transformations of man, the infinite possibilities of time, the reverence for life, and the transcendental destiny of the human spirit. One customarily praises a science-fiction by remarking that it is original or ingenious, but Clarke's books inspire a search for more ambitious adjectives. Try "lofty" or "noble"—or even "saintly."

Virginia Quarterly Review, *Vol. 50, No. 1 (Winter, 1974), pp. viii, x.*

*   *   *

## CONDON, Richard 1915-

**Condon, an American novelist and playwright, is best known for *The Manchurian Candidate.* (See also *Contemporary Authors*, Vols. 1-4, rev. ed.)**

Richard Condon's first two novels—"The Oldest Confession" . . . and "The Manchurian Candidate" . . . are brilliant, highly individualistic, and hopelessly unfashionable demonstrations of how to write stylishly, tell fascinating stories, assemble plots that suggest the peerless mazes of Wilkie Collins, be very funny, make acute social observations, and ram home digestible morals. They demonstrate, in short, a good many of the things that were expected of the novel before the creative-writing courses got its practitioners brooding in their mirrors. Indeed, Mr. Condon knows his business so well that in his first novel he goes one step further. "The Oldest Confession," which puts the reader in that rare and agreeably painful situation of knowing that each irresistible page is shortening his pleasure, is at once a galloping novel in the grand manner and a parody of a galloping novel in the grand manner. . . . Yet, like all expert parody, which tints a perfect imitation of its model in just the right places, much of this is subtly and outrageously exaggerated. Although persuasive, the book's hair-raising ending, which involves a dizzy roundelay of murder and deception, is preposterous. . . . The same double standard appears in Mr. Condon's prose. Basically smooth, meticulous, and spare, it is always breaking into perfectly timed sweats of tough, outlandish, wise-guy imagery that are memorable takeoffs of all the self-indulgent writing in contemporary novels. . . . But parodists are bilious entertainers. Thus, with an unexpected-bonus feeling, one suddenly realizes at the close of "The Oldest Confession" that most of Mr. Condon's high-wire stunting has been compelled by an intense, barely reined-in disgust for the irreparable damage that human beings, out of passion and stupidity, do to each other almost every day of their lives.

This disgust turns to bugling derision in "The Manchurian Candidate," a furious pummelling of some of the cheaper aspects of present-day America that recalls, in its wrathfulness, the pyrotechnic loathings of the Philip Wylie of "Finnley Wren" and "A Generation of Vipers." The result is a wild and exhilarating satire, which keeps succumbing to the heartburn of heavy sarcasm. . . .

Very likely, many of "The Manchurian Candidate"'s liberal readers will clap their hands over its savage parade of bourgeois decadence and the wicked political deception it outlines, while an equal number of conservatives will disbelievingly humph and bridle at such soiled, un-American images. Both groups, of course, will have missed its heartening and robust intent, and for a simple reason. The book is about them.

*Whitney Balliett, in* The New Yorker, *May 30, 1959, pp. 101-03.*

The cultural handicappers who tick off lists of the Ten Best Books To Be Stranded in Toledo With have missed a bet. Far more interesting might be a compilation of the Ten Best Bad Novels—books whose artistic flaws are mountainous but whose merits, like Loreleis on the rocks above, keep on luring readers. A place on such a list would go to Author Condon's second novel [*The Manchurian Candidate*], an almost complete catalogue of humanity's disorders, including incest, dope addiction, war, politics, brainwashing and multiple murder. The book carries a superstructure of plot that would capsize Hawaii, and badly insufficient philosophical ballast. Yet Condon distributes his sour, malicious humor with such vigor and impartiality that the novel is certain to be read and enjoyed. . . .

Man's fate, as Condon sees it, is to work hard, sacrifice much, lead an intelligent, just and fruitful life, and then show up at the Last Judgment minus his pants. Sooner or later, like the blind beggars toppling after their blind leader in Bruegel's chillingly ironic painting, all the author's characters stumble into the ditch of mortality. Satirist Condon is not afraid to set up outrageously improbable situations to achieve his effects. In his first novel, *The Oldest Confession* (1958), an Achilles among criminals was brought to heel while trying to hijack Goya's *The Second of May,* from the Prado. In the current fable [*The Manchurian Candidate*], a brilliant Chinese disciple of Pavlov—a sort of Marxist Dr. Fu Manchu—directs the capture, brainwashing and reflex-conditioning of an entire American patrol during the Korean war. Before grinning Russian brasshats, he shows off his success. The Americans pull contentedly on yak dung cigarettes and delicately avoid G.I. profanity—they imagine they are attending a meeting of the garden club in Spring Valley, N.J. They are so thorougly Pavloved, in fact, that they are ready to commit murder on signal. . . .

In the end, the effort at global satire proves too strenuous. In spite of a climax as apocalyptic as any since King Kong was shot off the top of the Empire State Building, Author Condon falters as he battles both cold-war antagonists simultaneously. But in his comic set pieces, he is wickedly skillful.

*"Pantless at Armageddon," in* Time *(reprinted by permission from* Time, The Weekly Newsmagazine; *copyright Time, Inc.), July 6, 1959, pp. 78-9.*

If Condon's Manchurian candidate was a thinly veiled Joe McCarthy, Mulligan [in *The Vertical Smile*] leaves even less to the imagination. He is described as an "Amish lawyer from California." He has a persistent "blue, black underbeard." He speaks stiffly about making one thing perfectly clear. His nickname is "Funky Dunc." Get it?

Candidate Mulligan *does* have one interesting after-dark fetish (tight black rubber evening gowns) the average reader would hardly credit to the Nixon imagination. But Condon's dirty-joke allegory is not the type of novel to quibble over details. At all costs, it is determined to prove that the grotesqueries of our politics and government are engendered by the sexual repressions and perversities built into our character.

If this book hadn't been so heavily loaded with Redeeming Social Value, it might have made amusing lightweight pornography. . . .

In the past, I've found that the faster I read Condon's novels the better I like them—and that at top speed some are excellent thrillers. In this one, even though the pace and tone are ostensibly "madcap," the usual fast surface is pitted with authorial asides—all of which are designed to explain the psycho-social significance of just about everything.

*Ron Rosenbaum, in* The New York Times Book Review *(© 1971 by The New York Times Company; reprinted by permission), October 10, 1971, p. 44.*

The main problem with [*The Vertical Smile*] by Richard Condon is that the author is potentially a much better writer than he seems willing to allow himself to be. . . .

Whenever he can bring himself to stop sandbagging the reader with quips and lectures, Condon reveals himself as an ingenious and original writer with a genuine gift for dialogue and characterization.

*L. J. Davis, in* Book World (© The Washington Post), *October 31, 1971, p. 15.*

Mr Condon's prose style [in *The Vertical Smile*] is hard-boiled, cynical and often very funny. Who but Mr Condon could describe the eyes of an avid filmgoer as being so bloodshot from watching so many movies that it looked as though someone had thrown ketchup in them? Well, Peter de Vries or S. J. Perelman, perhaps. But all Mr Condon's own are the loving descriptions of conspicuous consumption, of feats of prodigious skill, and of the preparation and consumption of food (though there may be too much about hamburgers for the taste of gourmets on this side of the Atlantic).

Unfortunately, however, though the parts of the book are entertaining enough they do not add up to a satisfactory whole. As the book progresses one gets the uneasy feeling that Mr Condon is losing his cool on the subject of the corruption and violence of American society and politics. The characters show an increasing tendency to lecture one another about the American constitution, the American way of life and the real meaning of democracy. For Mr Condon's style to work it needs to be totally cynical, hard-hearted as well as hard-headed. At times in this book the mask seems to slip. It is as though Swift had given equal time in his "Modest Proposal" to a spokesman of the NSPCC. Though humanly entirely understandable, the result is sometimes artistically unfortunate.

*"Rot Around the Clock," in* The Times Literary Supplement *(reprinted by permission), April 28, 1972, p. 500.*

Anyone who has read much of the current output of America's giants of fiction could not be surprised to be told once again that all is not well with the US in the matter of social conditions. Yankee materialism has been condemned many times, the breakdown of US society through crime, drug taking, booze—you name it, we've had plenty of evidence.

Mr Condon seems to think it time that he climbed aboard the bandwagon—but no, how could he? Mr Condon *is* the bandwagon. This book is described as 'an entertainment' but it's nearer to being a self-indulgence. The USA is bad:

very well. We accept that not everything there is perfect. But in *The Vertical Smile* all, *all,* is rotten. The author throws in everything, but everything, with the abandon and lack of discrimination of a delinquent 10-year-old doing his best to be naughty in every possible manner. . . .

If there is anyone or anything in the book that could be recognised as 'normal' I failed to find it. Did the author intend the work to be funny? Comic? *Mole ruit suâ.*

*The Vertical Smile* has all the attraction of a mud pudding, all the wit of the six-hundred and fortieth throwing of custard pie. Every oddity and quirk is placed not under a magnifying glass but under an electron-microscope that enlarges to such an extent that nothing under its scrutiny is recognisable as bearing any relation to the known.

*John Boland, in* Books and Bookmen, *May, 1972, pp. 71-2.*

The most original novelistic style of the 1960's was the style of paranoid surrealism. As created by such novelists as Joseph Heller, William Burroughs, Norman Mailer, Thomas Berger, Ken Kesey and Thomas Pynchon, the paranoid novel drew equally on the facts of national life and the cliches of popular fiction to create a world where technology, politics and history had run wild and the only possible humanism was gallows humor. The dream of community that had inspired the Popular Front (and the literary methods of Dos Passos, Farrell, Bellow and the Mailer of "The Naked and the Dead") had been replaced. . . .

Richard Condon was one of the most distinguished members of this group and through the controlled corrosiveness of his two great early novels—"The Manchurian Candidate" (1959) and "Some Angry Angel" (1960)—has some claim to being a founder. But something seemed to fall apart in the five novels that followed "An Infinity of Mirrors" (1964). Condon became a cult novelist, a little paranoid epicycle of his own, cutting easy slices from the same chunk of multicolored, hyperdense imagination, producing novels without any real qualities of invective and intelligence, stuffed with in-jokes and obvious parodies, a kind of virtuoso shoddiness.

"Winter Kills," Condon's 11th novel, seems to come on in much the same way. . . . But "Winter Kills" is not another Condon novel like the last few, filled with the forgettable frenzy of a mechanical satirist. "Winter Kills" is instead a triumph of satire and knowledge, with a delicacy of style and a command of tone that puts Condon once again into the first rank of American novelists. . . .

How can the paranoid intensities possible in art compete with the normal paranoias of everyday life? . . . The form of the novel has always implied paranoia: the reader and writer alone with each other and themselves, the plot that organizes the world for your benefit. Joyce reestablished what Laurence Sterne already knew: the added paranoia of the writer trapped with his words, the closed moment of history and language he believes it is his mission to recreate.

Joyce finally withdrew into his words totally. But novelists like Condon and Thomas Berger have completely moved away from the modernist obsession with literary language and are experimenting instead with the ability of the rhythms of daily speech and popular culture to embody the plain-speaking clarity of their satire. By destroying the gap between "serious" and "popular" culture, they make us realize that the myths and images we may consciously disdain affect us more deeply for our ignorance of them.

"Winter Kills," then, is "some kind of bummer through American mythology," in which almost all of Condon's characters, from highest to lowest, are driven by the American dream of being someone, making a difference, having power and control. "Winter Kills" isn't the world; it's the way we think about the world. . . . Condon has created a paranoid novel that does not leave us trapped inside its world, but functions instead as a liberation, exposing through the gentler orders of fiction the way we have been programmed to believe anything in print. By mingling historical reality with his own fabulous invention, Condon savagely satirizes a world in which fiction and reality are mingled to manipulate, exploit and kill.

*Leo Braudy, in* The New York Times Book Review *(© 1974 by The New York Times Company; reprinted by permission), May 26, 1974, p. 5.*

[Condon's] early books, *The Oldest Confession, The Manchurian Candidate* and *A Talent for Loving,* are among the maddest funny novels of the last couple of decades. They seemed to have been written by Mephistopheles, raucous with glee at the insane excesses of the human creature. But Condon's last several books have been querulous and scolding.

It should be enough to say that *Winter Kills* is a gothic farce about the assassination in the early 1960s of U.S. President Tim Keegan. . . .

[It] is in grossly bad taste, although cynicism prompts the additional observation that taste might not matter if the book were funny. It is not. It is paranoid. Condon clearly wrote the novel to take his suspicions for a stroll, and what he suspects is that the very rich are in conspiratorial control of the country. . . .

Condon has unraveled. The world's villainy simply does not work so simply. To pretend that it does is mindless mischief.

*John Skow, "Obscurity Now," in* Time *(reprinted by permission from* Time, The Weekly Newsmagazine; *copyright Time, Inc.), June 24, 1974, pp. 91-2.*

Of that group of novelists who re-create fiction from news stories Richard Condon has proved himself one of the most adept. He has constructed a series of sly intricate thrillers out of the pop fantasies on which the weeklies thrive. At the same time he has tried to distend his stories with his own stubborn, eccentric, almost malevolent sensibility into something beyond mere suspense and parody.

His clipped style, cartoon plots, and magazine metaphors are, of course, not the stuff of literature in the grand tradition. In . . . "Winter Kills," his hero Nick Thirkfield wonders openly if he's living in a John Wayne movie or in a "bummer through American mythology.". . .

Condon's is a curious genre, parasitic on the Nightly News and the weeklies yet trying to transcend in fiction some of the comic strip banalities of the other media. And "Winter Kills" is one of his more successful efforts, a witty, readable, neatly plotted pop allegory, but it suffers nevertheless from a confusion of purpose.

For at times it seems Condon entirely believes that the mass media, particularly television, generate by themselves both the substance and the nonsense of our lives. He seems to regard the so-called American dream, whatever that is, as a creation of tv journalists and media executives. All the other institutions of our lives serve merely as illusory backdrops on a picture tube.

According to Condon, literature as we have known it, with its intimacies and niceties and internal convolutions, cannot survive except as a gloss on the television news. Outmoded language and metaphor must be replaced by a pop vocabulary . . . , and 1000 brand names the honors of allusion which were once reserved for gods and heroes only. . . .

In "Winter Kills" he exaggerates the pop fantasies about wealthy men, power, and glamor until they appear grotesque and completely unlivable. . . .

But "Winter Kills" is a competent novel, neat and quick and clever, and that alone elevates it above the usual fare. Those seeking great literature or a first-class intelligence had best look elsewhere, but those who want light and mildly provocative entertainment will find Richard Condon a congenial companion.

*Leonard Orr, in* The Village Voice *(reprinted by permission of* The Village Voice; *©1974 by The Village Voice, Inc.), June 27, 1974, p. 29.*

* * *

## CONNELL, Evan S(helby), Jr. 1924-

**Connell is an American novelist and epic poet. (See also *Contemporary Authors*, Vols. 1-4, rev. ed.)**

[Evan S. Connell, Jr.'s "Points For a Compass Rose" contains no] plot, no consistent retinue of characters, no delimited venue, but [is] actually a semidramatized commonplace book in which mind-boggling saliences from every field of knowledge swirl around as if in some epistemological spiral galaxy, and all the rest—rumors, guesses, ruminations, asides, riddles, cries, jokes, recipes, prayers, chess moves and map coordinates—is gas clouds, the shapelessness of things to come. . . .

I think Connell intended a ventriloquial roll call during a drum roll, or some such effect: an American Express Tiresias who's both magus and Ancient Mariner, both mouthpiece and voices off, a Mister Everybody forever striking out in front of a mirror. As it is, his protagonist's patently a man of conscience, a disciple too of Paracelsus, Sir Thomas Browne, and Borges, an admirer of the cosmos who'd rather be a liker of humans (as distinct from their artifacts). But, as we go, we have to reconcile successive informations. The narrator is Pope Gregory VII, but also Dom Helder Camara (Archbishop of Recife), Lully, Kepler, Newton, a plowman of Bohemia, and many others. Formerly in the army, he has his portrait in the Louvre, has had two sons, has never had any children or been married, is married to Margaret, has an awkward hippo of a daughter, is neither Goya nor Henry the Navigator, though he resembles both. It's like waiting for the human race to jell back into Adam, the Many into the One. And the absurd thing is: he fails to add up only a little bit more than he doesn't.

On the one hand, I welcome this summary, synoptic, anachronistic mode of fiction, which more ambitiously resumes the method of Connell's novel of 10 years ago, "Notes From a Bottle Found on the Beach at Carmel." The anthropological novel (what Cortázar calls the anthropophanic) is overdue, and it's good to find someone promenading *homo sapiens,* with grade C branded on that creature's brow, through the House of Knowledge. On the other hand, I think Connell has missed exploiting some opportunities of his own making: over the book's length the data mode might have shrunk while the synthesized hero swelled (a matter of proportional plasticity); and, instead of being delivered undifferentiated, the verse paragraphs might have reached crescendo or whimper (a matter of transforming thematic materials, of not leaving them intact).

The book works, and I'd rather read it than "straight" fiction, but I'd like to have seen it moving a good deal farther from the diffident-personalized scrapbook, or the cloth sampler allowed to ripple in the *Zeitgeist's* draught.

*Paul West, in* The New York Times Book Review *(© 1973 by The New York Times Company; reprinted by permission), April 29, 1973, pp. 7-8.*

Evan S. Connell, Jr., is the author of *Mrs. Bridge* and *Mr. Bridge,* both of which explored the claustrophobia of modern domestic life. *Points for a Compass Rose* is a more ambitious book, a meditation on the horrors of public experience in the twentieth century, a record of how present shock drives the mind back into history, only to find little solace there. For Connell mere prose is scarcely up to such a task, and he resorts to what is at least typographically verse, in which high and low styles consort together, sometimes nervously. . . .

The book sounds pretty much like that throughout, as if some crazed, tone-deaf antiquarian—with Sir Thomas Browne, Theophrastus, Sir John Mandeville, and Albertus Magnus much in his mind, perhaps because he is drawing on them—were lecturing to us interminably on the curious beliefs of past and present, worrying all the while lest we miss the "relevance" of (for example) the odd dietary customs in Teber and elsewhere. . . .

But the pedantry is deliberate, not to say insistent. Connell's *persona,* "sick of old devices," can only try to convey his disgust about Vietnam and the Nazi death camps through a kind of imitative form, in which some 8,000 lines of flat, repetitious verse create in the conscientious reader something like the numbed stupefaction that human history merits. Probably few readers will be sufficiently conscientious; but, having had no other choice than to read on, I found myself sometimes, grudgingly, moved by the very anger that must have made Connell write such a book. . . .

But *Points for a Compass Rose,* however admirable and moving its motives, finally seems wasteful itself in its treatment of the waste of history. "After such knowledge, what forgiveness?" was a good question when Eliot asked it fifty years ago, and it still is; but I'm afraid that, like other urgent questions, it loses its force when asked too insistently and for too long. Connell's version of cultural nightmare will perhaps impress those who have grown up not knowing *Gerontion* and the *Pisan Cantos,* but those who do know them will find themselves thinking, however unfairly, that they have been here before.

*Thomas R. Edwards, "Surprise, Surprise," in* The New York Review of Books *(reprinted with permission from* The New York Review of Books; *© 1973 by NYREV, Inc.), May 17, 1973, pp. 35-7.*

[*Points for a Compass Rose*] isn't a novel. [Connell] has carefully disconnected section from section and item from item so that there is no logical or even chronological progression from one to the next; and of course there is nothing even remotely like a story. Still, there are characters of a sort, and events, and the author himself speaks in many voices—identifying himself alternately as Geoffrey Chaucer, a medieval knight named John Mandeville, most often as a Jewish historian named Simon Dubnow who was a prisoner of the Nazis—and so on. In fact, this little game of shifting identities becomes almost an obsession with Connell as the book goes on. He keeps riddling us with his "who am I?"—dropping hints, then skipping cutely away. . . .

It is a book—plainly and simply that, gracefully written in fine ironic style expressing very well the moral tensions of the inner man who is the author. The work most like it, of course, is Connell's earlier *Notes from a Bottle Found on the Beach at Carmel,* for both of these must have found their origin in his journals. But *Points for a Compass Rose* also calls to mind J. G. Ballard's collection of grotesqueries, *The Atrocity Exhibition,* and William S. Burroughs's *Naked Lunch.*

His purpose is didactic—and now beware, for we are into the meaning of it all. Connell seems constantly to be adjuring us to "look" or "listen," or challenging us, "Do you understand?" Clearly, he wants us to understand, for this work which he calls "a gnomic book about America" has been written to show us what we have become. "Of what value is life," he asks, "if it's not woven on history's loom into other lives?" Well, in *Points for a Compass Rose,* Evan S. Connell Jr. attempts to do just that. Our civilization, our culture, our lives are on his loom here. We may not like the pattern of moral disaster that emerges, but there is no denying a certain cruel accuracy in the lineaments of his design.

*Bruce Cook, "Prose by Any Other Name . . .," in* Book World—The Washington Post (© The Washington Post), *May 27, 1973, p. 10.*

Evan S. Connell Jr. . . . finds any and all points relevant for inspection in his excursion through the galaxies of knowledge. Man's consciousness/historicity is the subject of [*Points for a Compass Rose*]. The verse, however, is pure prose and this is not a failing. I am sure the author intended the simple prose style while setting the page in versets as a smooth vehicle. He succeeded; for the visual aspect is rather atmospheric, e.g., like skimming through old Merlin's scrapbook, and the cut line also offers the best method of scanning the short cosmic blurbs. This mural is painted with sketches of ancient ritual, little known quotes, special (I suppose) latitudes & longitudes, fairy-tale-like gossip, recipes, jokes, riddles, and obviously anything else Connell's mind can conjure. But, does it work?

If the author plans to weave some sort of tapestry, unifying sense or spiral direction into a portrait of man by use of confused past, then it fails. The movement of the book is repetitious and the end result is a massive picture so tacked by endless footnotes that the face becomes indistinguishable. But, if the work, contrary to the cover jacket's presumptions, weaves no mystical web, no plot, no saucy message, then I recommend it for the absurd fun of it all. The only criticism is that the work should funnel into some concrete focus so that the cosmological catalogues might gain more credence. The author's many voices are only a hindrance to the movement and give the reader [neither] insight nor centralized position.

*James Fahey, in* Best Sellers, *June 15, 1973, pp. 136-37.*

When I first heard that Evan S. Connell, Jr. had brought out another epic-length poem, I was exhilarated for days. We have here on the planet with us a man of such courage and strength of spirit that he has not lost what Alfred Adler calls "the nerve for excellence." He has kept it despite the burden of an awareness not only of the enormity of his project and of the limitations of his own human understanding, but also of the abject ignorance and indifference of his audience.

Viking published a long poem, *Notes from a Bottle Found on the Beach at Carmel,* in 1963. The world shrugged. Later, with the publication of *The Diary of a Rapist* and *Mister Bridge* (the latter a companion to the best-selling *Mrs. Bridge*), critics paid some attention to Connell's fiction; they mentioned the poem only as a curiosity, or ignored it altogether. Now, with the Knopf publication of a second long poem, *Points for a Compass Rose,* it is time—past time—to approach Connell's poetry seriously, with meek heart and due reverence.

*Notes from a Bottle Found on the Beach at Carmel* is a poem 243 pages—or 40 yards—long. It takes the form of a spiritual journey "towards penance and redemption," a journey through all the fabulous and fiery cruelties of history that purge the spirit's basest dross and purify it to gold. On the page it is a dazzling series of disparate chunks. These are the "notes from a bottle" written in increasingly apocalyptic haste by the poem's speaker, or "note-taker," who is, among other things, a man at sea.

The note-taker, like the Wandering Jew, ranges over centuries of Western civilization, witnessing marvels and abominations. "I gather, preserve, collate, and set down." His notes, presumably shaken together in their bottle by Providence, the roiling sea against which he is constantly "hammering" and to which he finally yields, are "a juxtaposition of all things." Any bit of the lore is fascinating. . . . The notes cover all history with a careful emphasis on those rapacious centuries that followed—or precipitated—the shattering of medieval faith. The annihilation of South American cultures at the hands of the Conquistadores is here, as well as, pointedly, the flight of the *Enola Gay*. Cruelty is Connell's theme, especially cruelty in the name of Christ, and ignorance, courage, dissimulation, miracle, murder, credulity, and the decay of vital cultures. The tone is merciless and meticulous; the alien landscapes are spare. Between the snippets of church Latin, between the confounding parables, latitude and longitude coordinates, *cris de coeur,* and fragments of fantastic narration, the blank spaces of mystery, mute, weave the intricate weft of the poem. . . .

The note-taker's very submission to this journey into the soul's dark night is itself a kind of penance for the sins of the whole world. He is in this way both the Wandering Jew, who harried Christ, and Christ himself. In a final note he also drops an allusion to himself as Job's servant, that anguished witness who alone has escaped to detail for us disaster after disaster, the reduction of everything to nothing. But Job's fortunes are restored; earth's may be also, if not to this civilization, then to the next: "Thus the mighty cycle of the ages shall begin again."

I cannot begin to suggest the intricate tensions of the poem's complexity. After you have read it once, you can get lost on any page. . . .

Somehow, Connell makes you care. Many modern poets demand a good deal of work; Connell *excites* it. Sometimes the note-taker's tone is hectoring, even belligerent; if you have any competitive spirit at all, you seize a thread—any thread—follow it, and, lo, it traces a pattern. He did it. "I am Magus. Trust in me." And you understand at last that these notes are not tentative explorations, and far less are they "expressions": they are instead the magnificent artifices of a giant intellect. . . .

[The poetry] is powerful stuff. It is not the done thing; neither is this choleric spluttering the language of poetry to which we have become accustomed. But Connell always knows what he is doing. The speaker of *Points for a Compass Rose* has of himself made a living sacrifice: he risks our disgust, and all but destroys his own spirit, in order to sustain his hatred, lest we forget. It is astonishing what he cares about. He drags out the ecclesiastical repression of scientific advances, the folly of the Crusades, the rapaciousness of the Conquistadores, the insanity of witch trials, and so forth, with an innocent and fresh rage. It all happened yesterday, and nobody gives a tinker's damn; and so it is all happening today.

Any despot, ecclesiastic or secular, requires not only the meekness but especially the gullibility of the society he would rule. And we are not one whit less gullible, credulous, or superstitious than any people of the past. The genius of this poem, and its play, lies in Connell's treatment of this matter of fact and fraud, of credulity and belief. . . .

These poems [*Notes from a Bottle Found on the Beach at Carmel* and *Points for a Compass Rose*] are masterpieces. You could bend a lifetime of energy to their study, and have lived well. The fabric of their meaning is seamless, inexhaustible. I have not even mentioned, for instance, the staggering possibilities for a poetry of fact that Connell unfurls by using, without apology or explanation, the language of technical prose. It is almost as though, had his note-taker and speaker no recourse to these dry and cadenced prose measures, they would both lapse into glossolalia, into ecstatic tongues and fatidic howls.

Instead, their language is steely and bladelike; from both of its surfaces flickering lights gleam. Each page sheds insight on every other page; understanding snaps back and forth, tacking like a sloop up the long fjord of mystery. Thinking about these poems, one at a time or both together, is a sweet and lasting pleasure to the mind.

*Annie Dillard, "Winter Melons," in* Harper's *(copyright © 1974, by Harper's Magazine, Inc.; reprinted from the January, 1974 issue of* Harper's Magazine *by permission of Annie Dillard), January, 1974, pp. 87, 88-9.*

In Evan S. Connell's novels the characters, prudent and cautious folk with healthy talents for survival, walk into traps so interesting of prospect and so cleverly disguised that they seemed before they snapped shut to be the very plan of a successful life. . . .

In "The Connoisseur" a well-to-do New York insurance man knows that he is moving toward a trap. He has the native wit to elude 40 traps; naturally by the last page of this novel he is inextricably inside the trap he assiduously avoided. The plot is as delicious as that of a folktale or a detective story.

The trap is pre-Columbian Art [collected by] Muhlbach, our hero. . . .

Mr. Connell, himself a connoisseur of the inner contradictions of Western capitalist civilization ("Notes From a Bottle Found on the Beach at Carmel" and "Points for a Compass Rose," two scrapbooks of learned indictment which for all their diligence are not nearly as powerful in meaning as his novels), is fascinated by (and fascinates us with) the encounter of an intelligent man, his imaginary nobody Muhlbach, with the shards of a civilization which European man once obliterated with fanatic thoroughness and is now interested in as so many knicknacks to squirrel away in a museum or private collection. . . .

This is a deceptively short novel. Evan Connell has perfected a style that is all onwardness, losing no richness of detail to the fastness of his pace. Everything contributes to the total effect. The real hero of the novel is an idea. We watch it enter a man's mind and after much discomfort and hesitation root itself like a stubborn weed. . . .

There is much more to this novel than I've been able to suggest. The wonderful problem of the relation of fake to original is a theme (and clue to the meaning of the book). . . . In Mayan art there are probably more forgeries to admire with awe than real objects. Will it occur to Muhlbach in his trap that nothing, nothing at all, is what it seems?

*Guy Davenport, "The Connoisseur," in* The New York Times Book Review *(© 1974 by The New York Times Company; reprinted by permission), September 1, 1974, p. 4.*

* * *

## COZZENS, James Gould 1903-

**Cozzens, an American Pulitzer Prize-winning novelist, writes fiction characterized by careful craftsmanship about the rela-**

**tionship between men and society. (See also *Contemporary Authors*, Vols. 9-12, rev. ed.)**

Cozzens began his career with several pieces of juvenilia and then wrote two short works, *S.S. San Pedro* and *Castaway,* both of which are livelier in technique and less stagnant in moral assumption than his later books. . . .

After these experiments Cozzens turns to what might as well be called his dominant manner. He now becomes a quite conventional novelist, either uninterested in or unable to use the twentieth century advances in techniques; he strives for and often achieves a strong, efficient but rather flavorless style. It is a decent, workmanlike style, neither exalted nor corrupt, and generally most useful when approaching the tone of anonymous objectivity. It serves far better for locating objects in the external world than for projecting a vision of life through accumulation of metaphor or nuances of inflation. Ithis a style, in short, that is likely to reassure people who find modern literature bewildering.

Structurally, Cozzens worked out a scheme that does represent a certain deviation from—though hardly an improvement upon—the conventional novel. What seems particularly to interest him as a writer is the weight of social and moral pressures that a community brings to bear upon one of its significant members, generally a professional man who both leads and serves it. It is this idea of friction that is central to Cozzens' work, far more so than the patterns of drama or the risks of tragedy. As a result he does not generally use plot in his novels, at least in the traditional sense of a coherent action moving through time and guided toward climax and resolution. Instead, he concentrates on the moment before climax. We are brought very quickly to this moment and then are stopped for a series of dogged investigations of group after group, representative figure after figure, as each of these impinges on the protagonist and multiplies the pressures to which he is subject. Meanwhile the action, to the extent that there is one, hangs suspended, waiting for Cozzens to amass the necessary data that might have come more dramatically and organically through a use of plot. . . .

The leading characters . . . are frequently sentimentalized, not through the usual identification with suffering and sensitiveness, but through a perverse admiration for their ordinariness of spirit, their rudeness of manner, and their contempt for tenderness of feeling. When Hemingway struts about to show how tough he is, he usually irritates us with his need for wearing a silly mask; when Cozzens tries to show how hard-bitten and illiberal his attitudes are, he can be very convincing.

*Irving Howe,* "By Love Possessed" *(copyright © 1958 by Harrison-Blaine, Inc.; reprinted by permission), in* The Critic As Artist: Essays on Books 1920-1970, *edited by Gilbert A. Harrison, Liveright, 1972, pp. 167-80.*

The most alarming literary news in years is the enormous success of James Gould Cozzens' *By Love Possessed.* It sold 170,000 copies in the first six weeks of publication—more than all eleven of the author's previous novels put together. . . .

There's nothing new in all this—after all, *something* has to be the No. 1 Best-Seller at any given moment. What is new appears if one considers Grace Metalious' *Peyton Place*, which was at the top for a full year, before *By Love Possessed* displaced it. *Peyton Place* is a familiar kind of best-seller, a pedestrian job, an artifact rather than a work of art (putting it mildly) that owes its popularity to nothing more subtle than a remarkably heavy charge of Sex. . . . But Cozzens is not of the company of Kathleen Winsor, Edna Ferber, Daphne Du Maurier, Lloyd C. Douglas, and other such humble, though well-paid, artisans. Nor can he be "placed" at the middle level of best-sellerdom, that of writers like Herman Wouk, John Hersey, and Irwin Shaw, nor even (perhaps) on the empyrean heights occupied by Marquand and Steinbeck. He is a "serious" writer, and never more serious than in this book. That so uncompromising a work, written in prose of an artificiality and complexity that approaches the impenetrable—indeed often achieves it—that this should have become what the publishers gloatingly call "a run-away best-seller" is something new. . . .

The requirements of the mass market explain a good deal of bad writing today. But Cozzens here isn't writing down, he is obviously giving it the works: *By Love Possessed* is his bid for immortality. It is Literature or it is nothing. Unfortunately, none of the reviewers have seriously considered the second alternative. . . . This sincere enthusiasm for a mediocre work is more damaging to literary standards than any amount of cynical ballyhoo. One can guard against the Philistines outside the gates. It is when they get into the Ivory Tower that they are dangerous. . . .

Perhaps we should now take a look at what Cozzens has to say in *By Love Possessed*, and how he says it. The normative hero is Arthur Winner, a reputable, middle-aged lawyer and family man who is exposed, during the two days and nights covered by the action, to a variety of unsettling experiences, which stimulate in him some even more unnerving memories. Winner is presented as a good man—kind, reasonable, sensitive, decent—and so he is taken by the reviewers: "The grandest moral vision in all Cozzens' work—a passionately good, passionately religious, yet wholly secular man, whose very failures are only bad dreams," as one wrote. . . . Passion seems to me just what is most obviously missing in Arthur Winner; he's about as passionate as a bowl of oatmeal.

He is, in fact, a prig. His responses to the many appeals made to him in the course of the story—he's always on top, handing down advice and help, a great temptation to priggishness—while decent enough in form ("genteel") are in reality ungenerous and self-protective. . . . That he is right in each case . . . is beside the point. A prig is one who delights in demonstrating his superiority on small occasions, and it is precisely when he has a good case that he rises to the depths of prigocity.

Although Winner behaves like a prig, he is not meant to be one, if only because the main theme of the novel, the moral testing and education of a good man, would then collapse, and the philosophical tragedy that Cozzens has tried to write would have to be recast in a satiric if not a downright farcical mode. Here as elsewhere, the author is guilty of the unforgivable novelistic sin: he is unaware of the real nature of his characters, that is, the words and actions he gives them lead the reader to other conclusions than those intended by the author.

His characters often speak brutally, for example, not because they are supposed to be brutes, but because their creator apparently thinks this is the way men talk. An elderly lawyer, civilly asked by a client to make some changes in the investment of her trust funds, replies, "You're getting senile, Maud. Try not to be more of a fool than you can help." A doctor, presented as a gentleman, meets the wife of a friend at a party and, no dialogue or motivation given before, opens up: "What's your trouble, baby? Or can I guess? . . . Tell Pappy how many periods you've missed. . . . You know as well as I do you're one of those girls who only has to look at him to get herself knocked up." She leaves the room "indignantly" (the adverb implies she's a mite touchy). No reason is given for any of these onslaughts, aside from the fact that all [the] recipients are women; this seems to be Cozzens' idea of manly straight-from-the-shoulder talk. Curious. Curious, too, Winner's pooh-poohing attitude when he is appealed to by the feminine victims. For Winner, too, is something of a brute, without his creator suspecting it. . . .

This leads us, in a way, to sex. The crucial episode, the one that more than any other shakes Winner's faith in himself and in the uprightness of his life, is something that happened years before the action begins and that keeps coming back into his mind: his affair with Marjorie, the wife of his close friend and law partner, Julius Penrose. . . . At no time is love or even lust involved: "Far from coveting his neighbor's wife, he rather disliked her, found her more unattractive than not." The only reason given for Winner's reaction to Marjorie is that she was there. Like that mountain climber. . . .

The formula for a best-seller now includes a minimum of "outspoken" descriptions of sexual activities, and *By Love Possessed* doesn't skimp here. Its inventory includes rape, seduction, marital and extra-marital intercourse, with touches of sadism, lesbianism, onanism, and homosexuality. *By Sex Possessed* would be a more accurate title. There is very little love, which the author presents as at best a confusing and chancey business, to be patiently endured, like the weather. . . . The Chattanooga *Times* wonderfully summed up the theme as "the situation of rational man beset by passion," adding: "Cozzens regards each form of love as a threat to Arthur Winner's power to reason, to his ability to live life with meaning." . . . [But] love, even passion, is not an extraneous monkey wrench thrown into the machinery of life, but rather a prime mover which may burst everything apart but which must function if there is to be any motion at all. This is, at any rate, how the makers of our literature, from Homer to Tolstoy, Proust, and James, have treated the theme; Cozzens' efficiency-expert approach (Gumming Up the Works) is echt-American but creatively impoverishing. . . .

[Perhaps] the real title should be *By Reason Possessed.* I have the impression that Cozzens is as suspicious of sex as of love. Most of the sexual encounters he conscientiously describes are either fatuous (Winner and his first bride), sordid (Ralph and Veronica), or disgusting (Winner and Marjorie). Far worse—from a sales viewpoint—they are written in his customary turgid and inexpressive style. Take, for example, the two pages (264-5) on Winner's love-making with his second wife, the most concrete description of the sexual act in the book and also the only place sex is presented, as one might say, positively. This passage sounds partly like a tongue-tied Dr. Johnson: "the disposings of accustomed practice, the preparations of purpose and consent, the familiar mute motions of furtherance." But mostly like a *Fortune* description of an industrial process: "thrilling thuds of his heart. . . . moist manipulative reception. . . . the mutual heat of pumped bloods. . . . the thoroughgoing, deepening, widening work of their connection. . . . the deep muscle groups, come to their vertex, were in a flash convulsed."

The reviewers think of Cozzens, as he does himself, as a cool, logical, unsentimental, and implacably deep thinker. . . . In reality, Cozzens is not so much cool as inhibited, not so much unsentimental as frightened by feeling; he is not logical at all, and his mind is shallow and muddy rather than clear and deep. I think Julius Penrose may fairly be taken as Cozzens' beau ideal of an intellectual, as Winner is his notion of a good man. If Penrose is meant to be taken ironically, if his pompous philosophizings are supposed to be burlesques, then the novel collapses at its center—leaving aside the fact they would be tedious as parodies—since it is Penrose who throughout the book guides Winner toward the solution of his problems. There's a Penrose in Homer, but he's not confused with Ulysses. His name is Nestor. . . .

The three earlier Cozzens novels I've read, *The Last Adam, The Just and the Unjust,* and *Guard of Honor,* were written in a straightforward if commonplace style. But here Cozzens has tried to write Literature, to develop a complicated individual style, to convey deeper meanings than he has up to now attempted. Slimly endowed as either thinker or stylist, he has succeeded only in fuzzing it up, inverting the syntax, dragging in Latin-root polysyllables. Stylistically, *By Love Possessed* is a neo-Victorian cakewalk. [Footnote: "'Cakewalk': a form of entertainment among American Negroes in which a prize of a cake was given for the most accomplished steps and figures."] A cakewalk by a singularly awkward contestant. Confusing laboriousness with profundity, the reviewers have for the most part not detected the imposture. . . .

Cozzens' style is a throwback to the palmiest days of 19th-century rhetoric, when a big Latin-root word was considered more elegant than a small Anglo-Saxon word. The long, patient uphill struggle of the last fifty years to bring the diction and rhythms of prose closer to those of the spoken language might never have existed so far as Cozzens is concerned. He doesn't even revert to the *central* tradition (Scott, Cooper, Bulwer-Lytton) but rather to the eccentric mode of the half-rebels against it (Carlyle, Meredith), who broke up the orderly platoons of gold-laced Latinisms into whimsically arranged squads, uniformed with equal artificiality but marching every which way as the author's wayward spirit moved them. Carlyle and Meredith are even less readable today than Scott and Cooper, whose prose at least inherited from the 18th century some structural backbone.

That a contemporary writer should spend eight years fabricating a pastiche in the manner of George Meredith could only happen in America, where isolation produces oddity. . . .

How did it happen? Why did such a book impress the reviewers? We know whodunit, but what was the motive? Like other crimes, this one was a product of Conditions.

The failure of literary judgment and of simple common sense shown in *l'affaire Cozzens* indicates a general lowering of standards. If this were all, if our reviewers just didn't know any better, then one would have to conclude we had quite lost our bearings. Luckily, there were other factors. . . .

The . . . most important, I think, [was that it] is difficult for American reviewers to resist a long, ambitious novel; they are betrayed by the American admiration of size and scope, also by the American sense of good fellowship; they find it hard to say to the author, after all his work: "Sorry, but it's terrible." In Cozzens' case, it . . . would have meant that a lifetime of hard work in a good cause had ended in failure, which would have been un-American. . . .

The other factor in the book's success is historical. It is [an] episode in The Middlebrow Counter-Revolution. In the 20's and 30's, the avantgarde intellectuals had it pretty much their way. In 1940, the counter-revolution was launched with Archibald MacLeish's essay, "The Irresponsibles," and Van Wyck Brooks's Hunter College talk, "On Literature Today," followed a year later by his "Primary Literature and Coterie Literature." The Brooks-MacLeish thesis was that the avantgarde had lost contact with the normal life of humanity and had become frozen in an attitude of destructive superiority; the moral consequences were perversity and snobbishness, the cultural consequences were negativism, eccentricity, and solipsism. [Footnote: "Brooks and MacLeish assumed it was good for writers to identify themselves with society because they assumed that society was healthy. But if society had been showing increasing symptoms of disease, then it was sensible of the avantgarde to isolate itself from the infection. Sensible or not, the gross empirical fact is that practically all the major art in every medium since 1850 has been produced by that avantgarde whose contemptuous rejection of bourgeois culture so infuriates the middlebrow."] The thesis was launched at the right moment. By 1940 the avantgarde had run out of gas—unfortunately no rear-guard filling stations have been opened up, either—while the country had become engaged in a world struggle for survival that made any radically dissident, skeptical attitude a luxury. . . .

[There] is, in fact, a . . . pigeonhole for Cozzens: the Novel of Resignation. *By Love Possessed* is, philosophically, an inversion, almost a parody of a kind of story Tolstoy and other 19th-century Russian novelists used to tell: of a successful, self-satisfied hero who is led by experiences in "extreme situations" to see how artificial his life has been and who then rejects the conventional world and either dies or begins a new, more meaningful life. In the Novel of Resignation, the highest reach of enlightenment is to realize how awful the System is and yet to accept it *on its own terms*. Because otherwise there wouldn't be any System. Marquand invented the genre, Sloan Wilson carried it on in *The Man in the Grey Flannel Suit,* and Herman Wouk formulated it most unmistakably in *The Caine Mutiny*. Wouk's moral is that it is better to obey a lunatic, cowardly Captain Queeg, even if the result is disaster, than to follow the sensible advice of an officer of lower grade (who is pictured as a smooth-talking, destructive, cynical, irresponsible conniver—in short, an intellectual) and save the ship. Because otherwise there wouldn't be any U.S. navy. (If there were many Captain Queegs, there wouldn't be a navy either, a difficulty Mr. Wouk seems not to have considered.) In short, the conventional world, the System, is confused with Life. And since Life is Like That, it is childish if not worse to insist on something better. This is typically American: either juvenile revolt or the immature acceptance of everything; there is no modulation, no development, merely the blank confrontation of untenable extremes; "maturity" means simply to replace wholesale revolt with wholesale acceptance. . . .

From Winner's climactic six-page interior monologue that ends the book we can take three formulations that sum it up: (1) "Freedom is the knowledge of necessity." (2) "We are not children. In this life we cannot have everything for ourselves we might like to have." (3) "Victory is not in reaching certainties or solving mysteries; victory is in making do with uncertainties, in supporting mysteries."

But what is the reality behind these unexceptionable bits of philosophy? It is that Winner, for complicated pragmatic-sentimental reasons, decides to cover up an embezzlement he has just discovered, an embezzlement of trust funds by his venerable law partner, Noah Tuttle, and that he has been eased of his guilt toward his other partner, Julius Penrose, about his old affair with Marjorie, Penrose's wife. . . .

In short, Ivan Ilyich feels free because he is compelled to reject his past as "not the right thing." Arthur Winner feels free because he is allowed to accept his past. (He is even thanked by his best friend for having concealed from him the fact that he had cuckolded him!) The last words of the book are Winner's, as he returns home: "I'm here." It's all right, nothing has to be changed: "I have the strength, the strength to, to—to endure more miseries," thinks Winner, gratefully. . . .

It is as if Tolstoy's *The Death of Ivan Ilyich* ended with the hero, after his atrocious sufferings, concluding that, as a high official of the Court of Justice, it was in the nature of things that he should die horribly of cancer, and that he must therefore bear his torment like a man (or rather like a cold, correct, respectable dignitary) as an example for the good of the service. In the actual story, however, he is driven by his "extreme situation" to reject his whole past way of life. Only when he is at last able to give up "the claim that his life had been good" can he experience, for the only time in his existence, anything significant: love (the young servant's gentle care) and then death.

But, as William Dean Howells memorably observed, "What the American reading public wants is a tragedy with a happy ending." And this Mr. Cozzens has dutifully supplied.

*Dwight Macdonald, "By Cozzens Possessed" (abridged from* Commentary, *January, 1958, pp. 36-47; slightly revised for this reprinting by Dwight Macdonald and included here with his permission), in his* Against the Grain: Essays on the Effects of Mass Culture *(copyright by Dwight Macdonald), Random House, 1962, pp. 187-212.*

[*Men and Brethren, The Just and the Unjust,* and *By Love Possessed* are all] novels . . . set in relatively small communities situated well off the beaten track, where progress is slow and change hardly distinguishable from decay. And because he sees such places for what they are, Cozzens explores a kind of American life which the ordinary run of novelists do not touch. The characters in [the first two of these three novels] and even more in *By Love Possessed* live in the unhappy assurance that almost any change that overtakes them will be for the worse, because their own status is entirely dependent upon, and identifiable with, the status quo. . . .

Many of his critics have been distressed that Cozzens should feel, and reveal, sympathy for characters like Arthur Winner. I have to agree that there are times when I share their feeling. But just because of the relationship between Winner and his community, a good share of the critical disapproval is misplaced: the critic, who is a product of one kind of American culture, looks upon a character who is the product of another kind—and scorns the character when, if he could only see it, what really repels him is the other culture. Or, to return to an old refrain, things are not always seen clearest when seen from New York.

Such a fault in perspective seems to underlie the famous hatchet job by Dwight Macdonald called "By Cozzens Possessed". . . . He is less a critic than a polygraph operating on the periphery of intellectual journalism. . . .

Amid the din of applause raised by the reviewers of the dailies and weeklies, who gave *By Love Possessed* something more than its full meed, Macdonald raised the always relevant question about the emperor's clothes. The book was, he declared, a dismal swamp of clumsy and pretentious writing. He was not the only one to say so, of course, but he was easily the most vociferous, and he quoted samples until his point was made beyond cavil—as well as beyond endurance. He was right. When writing is bad there should always be someone ready to say—perhaps to shout —that it is nothing short of terrible. There should also be someone, of course, to ask whether, in a long novel, bad writing makes a really momentous difference. . . .

[It] is clear in his article that Macdonald's violence was also stirred by the feeling that this novel had been written for "middlebrows," and that its commercial success was a middlebrow phenomenon. . . .

What Macdonald forgot is that by right of birth the novel is blatantly middlebrow anyhow. It became respectable only when the Industrial Revolution brought forward a new class with money to buy books, leisure to read them, and too little old-fashioned classical education to support prejudices in taste. . . .

What Macdonald was getting at was that the whole system of values in *By Love Possessed*, those a man like Arthur Winner, Jr. would live by, are also such as the middlebrow would hold and as would appeal to middlebrow readers. No doubt he is right again. But again he is somewhat beside the point. The charge brought against any novel of embodying the wrong values makes sense only so long as the tone of the book remains immediately contemporary; as soon as history moves forward enough so that there is no longer a conflict between the code which the novelist treats as valid and some other code which is held by a considerable number of the novelist's fellow-citizens, the whole criticism evaporates. . . .

A good part of the code by which men like Arthur Winner live would seem laudable by any standard: there is nothing wrong that I can see with, for instance, responsibility and loyalty—both of which mean a great deal to Winner, and never more than when events make it difficult for him to know where his responsibilities and loyalties really lie. But I want to grant Macdonald his due, and recognize in Cozzens' characters a certain stuffiness. The rest of the point is that this stuffiness—make it even a Philistine stuffiness, though I doubt that the qualifier is fully justified—is not the whole story, and that a critical perspective which sees it loom so large is one which lets it mask such qualities as Cozzens, as novelist, really possesses. . . .

Cozzens' principal distinction, which has made him an increasingly better novelist from year to year and in *Guard of Honor* makes him excellent, lies in his having the imagination to place in the very center of a novel a mature man capable of accepting the responsibilities of his age and experience. Taken by and large, the world of the serious American novel is rarely a country for old men. . . .

Cozzens' evident ability to understand characters as being molded by profession, and to see the world as such characters see it, is just about unique in American writing. . . .

There would seem to be a very visible connection between the presence in Cozzens' novels of such professional characters, these older and more experienced men, and his deep interest in the kind of community he so often writes about. Such communities are where such men are to be found most easily, and where they stand out the best. . . .

Just to see the world through the eyes of an older man opens a fresh set of perspectives, and these perspectives function in *By Love Possessed*—whatever the book's other defects—as much as they do in *Guard of Honor*.

*W. M. Frohock, "Cozzens and His Critics: A Problem in Perspective," in his* Strangers to This Ground, *Southern Methodist University Press, 1961, pp. 63-83.*

One of the most distinguished of contemporary American social novelists is James Gould Cozzens, more impressive and more politically engaged than Marquand, but, like him, seized with the passion to record. Cozzens did his best work of that kind in his days of comparative obscurity before the publication of *By Love Possessed* (1957). . . . By any reasonable standards, Cozzens is an important novelist, even if he is unlikely ever to write a great book. . . .

Certainly *Guard of Honor* is characterized by an attempt, akin to that made in many other American novels, to create a social world through profusion and precision of detailed notation. The attempt succeeds to a remarkable degree, and *Guard of Honor* remains not only Cozzens's outstanding achievement but one of the finest novels to appear in America since the end of the Second World War.

*Michael Millgate, "James Gould Cozzens" (© 1964 by Michael Millgate), in his* American Social Fiction: James to Cozzens, *Oliver & Boyd, 1964, pp. 181-94.*

The work of Cozzens suggests certain generalizations on the relation of characterization to such elements as description, interior monologue, and auctorial commentary. . . .

Where the plot is, as Aristotle said, "of a certain magnitude," . . . [the] speculations of the characters, being tied to the plot, bring richness and fullness to the situations in which they make their crucial decisions. The reason for this fact is that everything depends upon what the character's thoughts are *about*. If he thinks in circles about everything—about the plight of the world and his disbelief, for example—he comes out a shadow; the ideas are there, but they are not meaningfully *his*. He could talk forever in this vein without taking on personal form and meaning. But if what the character thinks about is always related to the decisions he will face, if it fills out the body of ideas and intentions that he will bring to the decision, then it will continually enrich the characterization.

This latter is what happens through *By Love Possessed* and the other fine novels by Cozzens. Arthur Winner has a very elaborate mind; it is full of ideas, opinions, information, poems, passages of Shakespeare. As he moves through his eventful weekend he is turning these ideas over and over, and they are comments on the situations, on his part in them, and on the values and the goals that he will bring to his decisions. Thus they constitute a rich body of *self*; they make a rounded, integrated man who is known in far greater detail than one might know his own illustrious uncle. The rhythms of his thought reflect the rhythms of his town, the flow of the life all around him, the give and take of his intercourse with a score of people. The whole complex of what he thinks, how he thinks, and how he acts makes for an extraordinarily rich characterization. The "rhythms of his thought," which come out in a style that has been strenuously condemned as needlessly involuted and difficult, embody the intercourse between the hero and the whole life of the town; they make his relation a felt, an almost physical sensation to the receptive reader.

Rhythm of thought, action, speculation, and final decision, then, conspire to bring out the idea that bursts at the end of this remarkable novel. The action is tremendously exciting, the style is compelling, the theme is profoundly rooted in the study of man in society. Woven into this rich and beautiful texture, characterization is as full and satisfying as one might think possible.

*Charles Child Walcutt, in his* Man's Changing Mask: Modes and Methods of Characterization in Fiction *(© 1966, University of Minnesota), University of Minnesota Press, Minneapolis, 1966, pp. 285-86.*

Cozzens has never participated in the literary politics and public-relations activities to which most writers devote a good deal of their energy; in any event, his views would, as it amuses him to recognize, make him ineligible. . . . He thinks the whole bag of tricks about the alienation of the artist and intellectual in America is absurd and that, if anything, such people get more attention than they deserve. . . .

But unlike most writers of his period, Cozzens feels a strong obligation to see the world for what it is: not to be content with it, but to recognize its nature and its strength. . . .

Cozzens has paid a price for his independence. For years he was the most unpublicized writer of anything like his talent in America, and when, with the publication of *By Love Possessed,* it looked for a moment as if he might get the recognition he deserved, Dwight Macdonald, the ablest critic of his kind in New York, made a carefully planned attack on Cozzens that undoubtedly damaged his reputation. From Mr. Macdonald's point of view, it was a wise move; Cozzens' novels represent a conception of experience that is a danger to what Mr. Macdonald cares about. . . .

Cozzens' respect for life as it is gives him an exceptional interest in the actual world. This interest ranges all the way from his pleasure in the ingenious organization of things like department stores and air force bases to his almost anthropological curiosity about the customary life of social institutions like the small town or of professions like the law and medicine. He has a deep respect for men who can function effectively in the world, whether they are skilled mechanics or talented pilots, able generals or smart judges, and this respect, because it is not dictated by a theory, is without condescension. Both *The Just and the Unjust* (1942) and *By Love Possessed* (1957) are legally impeccable novels about the law; the hero of *The Last Adam* (1933) is a doctor, and the hero of *Men and Brethren* (1936) is a priest. Three of these four novels show a fascinated intimacy with the social life of the American small town. *Guard of Honor* (1948) is a novel about life on an Army Air Force Base during the war; no one has ever been able to find a flaw in its minutely detailed account of that life.

Because of this respect for the actual world, Cozzens represents it with a fullness and a lack of distortion by self-interest very unusual in American literature. He is himself a man of very considerable intelligence; the actions of his novels are bathed in a glow of brilliant good sense that is a continuous pleasure, and the intellectual powers of his clever characters are actually demonstrated in his novels, not, as is so often the case in novels, merely asserted to exist. At the same time his respect for the actual world will not let him distort what it is in order to convince us that it can—or at least ought to—be what he would like it to be, though the temptation to do so must attack him as often as it does any intelligent man. He can see as quickly as anyone how raw the deal most people get from life is, but he never allows himself to forget that "life is what life is." Cozzens confronts squarely the rawness of the deal that drives the subjective novelists to a defiance of life itself. He knows as well as Melville and Faulkner how strong the passions of the heart are. But since he never loses sight of the simple, obvious fact that life is what life is, he is always conscious that it is not what these passions so often convince men it is, or may be. To him their effect on men is a kind of possession—in the sense of being influenced to the point of madness. . . .

Faced by [the] absence of the familiar, fashionable devices for giving novels a range and depth of subjective reality, critics are inclined to jump to the conclusion that Cozzens' novels have no subtlety. Unprepared for the different kind of subtlety the novelist of objective reality is concerned with, they simply miss the beautiful, intricate pattern that makes every one of the minutely observed realistic events in Cozzens' novels contribute to his meaning, to his vision of what life is, without the help of any distortion of objective reality or any special rhetorical appeal.

For a writer like this, one of the most attractive qualities in men is their ability to take pleasure in what life offers them, their natural responsiveness to the drama that is always a part of the ordinary business of life. His novels are full of attractively unintellectual—though often quite impressively talented—men of action (a very rare kind of character in modern fiction) who take an amusingly unliterary delight in such things. . . .

For anyone not blinded by the spectacular achievements of the great, impassioned idealists who have written many of the twentieth century's best novels, Cozzens' achievement must have a special interest, precisely because he does realize with astonishing insight and intelligence an aspect of our experience that has almost disappeared from serious fiction and that confronts us in his novels like a new discovery. In order to do so he has recreated the full-scale realistic novel—the kind that deals with the manners, not of a limited class and kind of people, but a whole society—for a culture that has scarcely ever seen itself before in that undistorting mirror.

*Arthur Mizener, "James Gould Cozzens: 'Guard of Honor'," in his* Twelve Great American Novels *(copyright © 1967 by Arthur Mizener; reprinted by arrangement with The New American Library, Inc., New York, New York), New American Library, 1967, pp. 160-76.*

[*Morning, Noon and Night* (Cozzens' thirteenth novel] although he no longer acknowledges the first four) represents no shift from his central thematic concern: man must live in uncertainty and pretend to the world that he does not. The prose style here represents a partial retreat from some of the pseudobaroque extravagances of "By Love Possessed," and can in part be explained by the narrator and central figure, an aging and successful management consultant. Like the heroes of Cozzens' last half-dozen novels, Henry Worthington is a successful professional man, skeptical in temper, resentful of human appetites, and determined to be free of illusion. But, like the others, he is victimized by an anti-romantic sentimentality, a self-indulgence in Psalmist pithiness or classical wisdom updated. Worthington's heavy allusions come mostly from the seventeenth century—the King James Bible, Bacon, Shakespeare—and reflect, of course, Cozzens' own tastes. But the allusions only underline the odd and smug consolation that Cozzens and his heroes feel they deserve for lives of seeming self-abnegation.

Virginia Quarterly Review, *Vol. 45, No. 1, Winter, 1969, p. xiv.*

Far from being a "researched" novel, *Guard of Honor* owes its distinction from other novels of *America*'s war to Cozzens's espousal of the virtue in old-fashioned virtue—principles, ability, self-control, measure. The moral law—not handed down from on high but won by stoic upperclass Protestants through long practice in the values necessary to survival (and by putting down darker, more hysterical races)—was more urgent than any inflamed insistence on equality. . . . [His] belief in "society," the country, the air force, is the reason for Cozzens's almost provocative illiberalism, and still reflects the dominating ethical point of view that novels of social rivalry used to take in America. . . .

No Cozzens protagonist will stand up any longer to the New Disorder. The center will not hold. But possibly a minutely organized, well-made novel may? *Guard of Honor* offers in structure and style the vision of a moral intactness that the chosen few have lost in everything but memory. An old-fashioned solidly worked up novel set up against a bad time and getting worse! But in *By Love Possessed* (1957) the neutral, self-satisfied irony of Cozzens's usual style has been replaced by the effort to contain Cozzens's own disarray. . . .

Cozzens had always made a cult of "the man of reason" and obviously felt himself to be one, perhaps the last one, in American writing, for most of which his contempt is notorious. But it is the fate of a "man of reason" to be utterly surprised, like Arthur Winner Sr., in the face of death. Trying to remain in urbane perfect control, the style of *By Love Possessed* strains itself into a complicatedness that reflects Cozzens's loss of respect for his own class. Cozzens had always been a dry, close, methodical and unpretentious writer. The law was his great love and each novel competently closed in on itself as evidence. Now the style broke down, tried to conceal Cozzens's conflict by unnatural fussiness. A world is supposed to have died. After discovering Noah's peculations, Arthur Winner Jr. says out loud—"I am a man alone." But perhaps that was only Cozzens himself. The "well-made" novel has not survived the shapely class distinctions on which it modeled itself.

*Alfred Kazin, in his* Bright Book of Life: American Novelists & Storytellers from Hemingway to Mailer *(copyright © 1971, 1973 by Alfred Kazin; reprinted by permission of Little, Brown and Co. in association with the Atlantic Monthly Press), Atlantic-Little, Brown, 1973, pp. 99-104.*

* * *

## CREELEY, Robert 1926-

**Creeley, one of the founders of the "Black Mountain movement," is an American poet, novelist, and short story writer. Hayden Carruth calls Creeley a "superb technician" whose poems are "self-completing gestures of tone, syntax, logic, image, measure and connotative feeling." (See also *Contemporary Authors*, Vols. 1-4, rev. ed.)**

Superficially [Robert Creeley's] poems look like the cameos of Mallarmé—such still lifes as *"Autre Éventail"* or *"Petit Air"*—or the intense little epigrams of William Carlos Williams—the plums in the icebox, the wheelbarrow glazed by the rain or the cat stepping over the window sill. On close inspection Creeley's poems turn out to be anything but Imagism. They are erotic poems, but what gives them their terrific impact is neither love nor lust. Each is an excruciating spasm of guilt. It is obvious that so limited a subject matter hardly provides the scope for major poetry. But there is no question of Creeley's effectiveness within his self-imposed or perhaps inescapable limitations. In the last couple of years he seems to have become more at ease in the world and less haunted by his relations with others, and his poetry is, however slowly, gaining in humanity and breadth. What distinguishes it is the same thing that keeps Mallarmé important—remarkable skill and special sensitivity to the inflections of speech—however special a speech either Creeley's or Mallarmé's may be.

*Kenneth Rexroth, "The New Poetry," in* The New York Times Book Review *(© 1961 by The New York Times Company; reprinted by permission), February 12, 1961.*

In *St Martin's*, a small collection of poems occasioned by a visit to the West Indies, Mr Creeley maintains his normal austerity of manner. Clipped and quiet, his speech combines a mild surface with sharp signs of turbulence below. His strenuous allegiance is to reality, to the truth of his unyielding nature and the bleak limitations of all human existence. The colourless imprecision of his language directs the reader to those burdens and pleasures of friendship and love that supply Mr Creeley with his special themes.

*"Dubious Seer," in* The Times Literary Supplement *(reproduced by permission), July 23, 1971, p. 855.*

Even when the surface of the poem is almost opaque, as dulled in its reflections as a black marsh pool, it is difficult not to respond to Creeley's poetry. There is always some movement, some breaking of the surface to the emotion below it. The surface is hard, but it isn't unyielding, and in the poems which are less opaque his voice has a presence and a distinctness that gives his poetry a sense of bitten, hard clarity. In long reaches of his poems the hardness gives a sense of difficulty—of difficulty with the words, the expression, with the poem, with the emotion—and in first encounters with Creeley's poetry there is a problem of deciding if the difficulty comes from a complexity in his poetic conception or if there is something in the poet that comes between the poem and its language. . . .

Nothing draws him out—even a deeply felt emotion is terse and hard. Creeley is a poet who is driven to speak—but is almost unable to listen to the sound of his own voice. Not unable, since he does listen and write, but certainly guarded. And the tension of his poetic diction seems to be involved with this discomfort, not with any confusion in the poem itself. It's difficult, in many ways, to confront something as muted and withdrawn as the emotion in Creeley's poetry—it's even more difficult to realise that the poetry has in some ways become more withdrawn and more elusive as his concept of the poem has extended and deepened. . . .

He has widened the limits of his poetry—the book *Pieces*, published in 1969, is a brilliant extended work, with a range of place and concern, of scene and accent, that gives his work an entirely new dimension—but the language is even more tightly drawn. He has thinned it down to the point where he has eliminated continuities, and the perception is left almost as word clusters—just as they must have been when they forced themselves on him. His honesty—and he is as honest as a poet as he is as a human being—can sometimes be a harrowing experience.

I don't feel at any point that Creeley is trying to make a poetic form out of emotions that are obscure or misunderstood—build a frame out of poles that are warped and splintered—or that he is trying to force poetry out of a kind of barren intellectualization that leaves the poem too heavily weighted down to have movement or direction—but that he's trying to bare himself, as a poet has to leave himself bare, as the poem at some point has to become the act of baring, and at the same time keep his bareness covered. The gestures have to be small, not move far from his body, his hands can't grasp or hold, but have to outline, suggest. The emotional power of the poems is in their half-glimpsed expression of the deeper emotion that forced him to the sudden act of baring that is the poem. . . .

The effectiveness of the small movements is their interrelationship with the form of the poem. One of Creeley's greatest strengths as a poet is his nearly flawless sense of the word, its dissonances, its assonances, and its full and implied point of meaning. The strokes are short, the tonality muted, but each one is subtly placed and there is no touch that alters the tonal balance of the design. . . .

In his refusal to use much of the clutter of contemporary poetic diction as a kind of impersonal concealment he has given his work its immediate identity. . . .

If his language is difficult, if he has limited the range of the poetry, he has still—with oblique strokes—sketched in a self that we can respond to—even be drawn to. In his hesitancies, in his insistence on his inadequacies, the bareness of his hopes, he has become fierce in his honesty and soft in his gentleness. And the poem does exist on this other level as an expression of the poet's self, and in our response to this self, this person, then the poem becomes an incident in the expression of this self, and we can reach through it to the poet.

*Samuel Charters, "Robert Creeley," in his* Some Poems/Poets: Studies in American Underground Poetry Since 1945, *Oyez, 1971, pp. 85-96.*

These poems [*St. Martin's*] . . . are suffused with that same kind of uneasy idyllic atmosphere we find in "The Tempest." And, like Prospero, the poet confronts the contraries of life and nature, and, finally, brings them into a delicate balance of light and dark, identity and love, confidence and joy. The opening poem, "Do You Think . . ." is surely one of Creeley's finest. We can see now, more clearly than ever, that his poems are destined to be regarded as among the very best of his generation.

Virginia Quarterly Review, *Vol. 48, No. 1 (Winter, 1972), p. xxiii.*

[My] admiration for [Creeley's] earlier work is enthusiastic—and for reasons not unlike those held by Creeley's large audience: the right words and rhythms, the clear complexities, and the stories consistently told. I know that if *Pieces* came unsolicited by an unknown author to Scribner's, Creeley's publisher, or for that matter to any reputable publishing house, it would have been sent back by return mail or, failing that, it would not have made it past the first reader. What, then, is so bad about *Pieces?* It reads as if it were scattered entries in a personal journal. In this respect, the title is honest. There is little cohesion, drama, flair, or purpose to this book, which is comprised of brief poems, prose passages, and incidental statements.

*Ronald Moran, in* The Southern Review, *Vol. 8, No. 1, Winter, 1972, p. 252.*

If one could only harness the energy that must be in Creeley's mind. He has a knack for making the world recklessly sensual and vibrant. His poetry is deeply self-analytic and emotional. This latest effort [*A Day Book*] merits any awards it may win.

Virginia Quarterly Review, *Vol. 49, No. 2 (Spring, 1973), p. lxii.*

*The Gold Diggers and Other Stories* . . . is fiction that demands too much effort from the reader, for the little it offers in return. Most of the stories are difficult, with grammatical ambiguities such as doubtfully identifiable pronouns and "squinting modifiers." . . . Many modern writers are accused of obscurity, and some with justice; for deliberately to confuse a reader can succeed only if there are strong lures to make him decipher the puzzles. Creeley's stories in this volume lack these enticements. . . . The best of the collection are "The Grace," "Mr Blue," and "The Unsuccessful Husband," in that they suffer less from obscurity and mannerism. The plot of each of these three is satisfying; one is persuaded that the characters are real and complex; and one can draw a thematic inference from each. Too many of the others, departing from the forms and techniques many readers expect from fiction, yield too few hints to permit a reader to adjust his expectations to fit these stories.

*Jeanette Gilsdorf, in* Prairie Schooner (*© 1973 by University of Nebraska Press; reprinted by permission from* Prairie Schooner), *Spring, 1973, pp. 91-2.*

The particular value of Creeley's book [*A Sense of Measure*] is that it is not a statement of theory, but a personal testament. In a number of pieces, written from 1951 onwards, he muses over the way he himself writes, and over what the writing of his contemporaries means to him. Though his terms are all concrete, the effect of his syntax is to give them a curiously abstract value—it's rather like talking with a pillar of cloud. Nevertheless, he makes certain beliefs clear: that within the space/time continuum we now recognize, older concepts of category, a contained plot, for instance, or a completed thought, in fact any man-centred universe of art, become impossible. Art must not manipulate time and place, but express its belonging within them—since space/time is a continuum, the relations it expresses will always make sense. Similarly, the particular work of art is itself a time and place, which must not be infringed by considerations imported from outside.

*Roger Garfitt, in* London Magazine, *June/July, 1973, Vol. 13, No. 2, p. 119.*

# D

## DEIGHTON, Len 1929-

**An English novelist, Deighton is best known for his spy thriller *The Ipcress File*. (See also *Contemporary Authors*, Vols. 9-12, rev. ed.)**

[Deighton's] sure handling of technicalities is reminiscent of Kipling, who could absorb unfamiliar detail and then write about it so convincingly that, for instance, men who had spent a lifetime at sea were convinced that he, too, must have been a sailor. Deighton's picture of men going through well-learned movements while their senses were being assaulted by great fear on the one hand and stimulated by the primitive exhilaration of killing and destroying on the other, reminded me of Stephen Crane who, though without experience of battle himself, wrote more truthfully about it than many who had actually fought.

In the 13 stories which make up *Declarations of War* the research, as meticulous as ever, no longer obtrudes [as it did, one critic charged, in *Bomber*] and we are at least as interested in the characters as in their machines and their technique. Some of the characters—an ex-colonel, now a car enthusiast, a battered First World War ace, a young GI in Vietnam, a regular Army sergeant in India—have been touched with the rare magic which makes them live on in the memory long after their story is forgotten. Two or three of the stories are only a little short of masterpieces.

The exciting thing about Len Deighton is that he develops with each new book. He could have gone on repeating the formula of *The Ipcress File* with undoubted success, but instead he tried for more subtlety, for more convincing, more substantial characters. . . . I do not think it is too far-fetched to suggest that one day Len Deighton will write a novel which will warrant the most careful critical attention and will rank him among the best.

*Peter Elstob, in* Books and Bookmen, *December, 1971, p. 60.*

[In] *The Ipcress File* (1963) and his subsequent books, Len Deighton . . . gave a new twist to the [spy story]. His anonymous central character (called Harry Palmer in the films) is a working-class boy from Burnley, opposed to all authority, who dislikes or distrusts anybody outside his own class. He is set down in a world of terrifying complexity, in which nobody is ever what he seems. The Deighton stories are elliptically—sometimes too elliptically—told, but their sudden shifts of tone and scene are extremely effective, and the technological expertise is impressive because it is not just there for show. Deighton's fascination with what in another writer would be gimmicks comes through . . ., and there is something almost lyrical about his re-creation of the dangerous and transitory lives of agents, as well as something sharp and knowing. From his most brilliant performance, *Billion-Dollar Brain* (1966), one carries away admiration for a plot as intricate as the lock of a good safe and for the characterization of the clownish double agent Harvey Newbigin, but even more for the evocation of General Midwinter's dotty neo-Fascist organization in Texas and the wonderfully vivid picture of the shooting of Harvey in the snow outside the Russian train. Writing of this quality, combined or contrasted with the constant crackle of the dialogue, makes Deighton a kind of poet of the spy novel.

*Julian Symons, in his* Mortal Consequences: A History—From the Detective Story to the Crime Novel *(copyright © 1972 by Julian Symons; reprinted by permission of Harper & Row, Publishers, Inc.), Harper, 1972, pp. 245-46.*

Len Deighton's plots are made like certain kinds of cheese: the holes they have in them are intended. His art of the spy story, deftly exemplified once again by *Spy Story,* contrives to strand you guessing even after everything's blown over. The snags in the web, the sundered connectors, the absences of information that leave you puzzling and straining to join up the middles whose ends are flamboyantly tied, evince an authorial omniscience more tauntingly grudging than Milton's God on a bad day with Satan.

*Valentine Cunningham, in* The Listener, *May 9, 1974, p. 606.*

[In *Spy Story,*] Mr. Deighton returns to international espionage by leading us into the computerized insanity of the Joint Anglo-American Strategic (Naval) War Game Studies Centre, in London, and showing us what the staff is really up to. The action, hobbled by much technical information, tends to move by fits and starts, and our mystification by what we seem to be seeing is almost total, but the information is grimly instructive and the mystification is irresistibly beguiling. It might be added that Mr. Deighton has never written more cleanly, and that he has also pretty much curbed his tendency to long-windedness.

The New Yorker, *September 23, 1974, p. 147.*

*  *  *

## DICKEY, James 1923-

**Dickey is an American poet, critic, and novelist. Although his novel *Deliverance* was enormously successful, he considers himself primarily a poet. (See also *Contemporary Authors*, Vols. 9-12, rev. ed.)**

Mr. Dickey's materials have a noble simplicity, a constancy extending through many poems. Merely to catalogue them is no use; to project in a single relation their somewhat delicate developments is perhaps impossible, but I shall have to make some more or less compromised try at it.

My impression of the process of his poetry is that it runs something like this: water—stone—the life of animals—of children—of the hunter, who is also the poet. It is rarely or never so simple as this, yet the intention seems often enough this, a feeling one's way down the chain of being, a becoming the voice which shall make dumb things respond, sometimes to their hurt or deaths, a sensing of alien modes of experience, mostly in darkness or in an unfamiliar light; reason accepting its animality; a poetry whose transcendences come of its reconciliations. Salvation is this: apprehending the continuousness of forms, the flowing of one energy through everything. There is one other persistently dramatized relation, that of the child to his father, and one that is more autobiographical, that of the poet to a brother who died before he was born. And now to particularize this matter.

These are poems of darkness, darkness and a specialized light. Practically everything in them happens at night, by moonlight, starlight, firelight; or else in other conditions that will make ordinary daytime perception impossible: underwater, in thick fog, in a dream—I note especially a dream of being in a suit of armor—, inside a tent, in a salt marsh where because of the height of the grass you "no longer know where you are."...

The power of poetry, which is to perceive all the facts of the world as relation, belongs in these poems equally to both parties: to the hunter and his victim; to the child and the father he is trying to become; to the father and the child he was, whom he has lost and is trying to find again. The paradoxical continuousness of all disparate forms one with another, in this generated world, is what Mr. Dickey's poems concentrate on representing, often by the traditional lore of the four elements. . . .

There is this major virtue in Mr. Dickey's poetry, that it responds to attention; the trying to understand does actually produce harmonious resonances from the poems; it seems as though his voyage of exploration is actually going somewhere not yet filled with tourists: may he prosper on the way.

*Howard Nemerov, "James Dickey," in* Sewanee Review *(© 1963 by The University of the South), Winter, 1963; reprinted in his* Reflexions on Poetry and Poetics, *Rutgers University Press (New Brunswick, N.J.), 1972, pp. 71-6.*

The giants—Eliot and Williams, Frost and Stevens—are so recently dead that we have not yet accustomed ourselves to a world of lesser poets. Somehow the self-denigrating whiners who ask us to buy their books or listen to their readings as if we were their analysts serve only to remind us of the passing of confident, commanding greatness. Perhaps this accounts for the cordial welcome critics and reviewers have given James Dickey, a poet who is larger-than-life, raucous, Brobdingnagian. Here we have a book [*Poems, 1957-1967*] by which we can take his measurements: three hundred large pages of the poetry he wants to preserve from his first decade of writing. There is no question about the dimensions: he is a *big* poet; but his work is also massively blemished, sprawlingly disordered; and its disorder stems from haste, not from art. Dickey deserves praise for his energy, his independence, and his election of subjects from real life, but one hopes that during the next decade he will give us more finished poetry and perhaps a little less of it.

Virginia Quarterly Review, *Vol. 43, No. 4 (Autumn, 1967), pp. clxviii-clxix.*

Dickey's power as a poet has depended upon a fairly repetitive technique: a human psyche is situated in some natural setting and proceeds surrealistically toward a metaphorical merger with any of various forms of plant, animal or human life. The process is always accompanied by an accumulative verbal intensity and excitement. As Dickey himself has said of his own work, "I meant to try to get a fusion of inner and outer states, of dream, fantasy and illusion where everything partakes of the protagonist's mental processes and creates a single impression." . . .

I would suggest, however, two reasons why Dickey's newer poems do not reach the mark of some of his earlier work. The energizing power of Dickey's language has always depended upon the free flow of successive participal and gerund phrases, long, loose lines, frequently run-on: the effect must be accumulative. . . . [In *The Eye-Beaters,*] verbal power has succumbed to artificial gimmickry.

Secondly, and perhaps more pervasive, the focus of a number of these poems [in *The Eye-Beaters*] is blurred by a tendency toward verbosity and overstatement. "Turning Away" and "Pine" are examples of poems too discursive to sustain interest. Part of this is the result of the almost total prose-like effect of many of these poems: Dickey has moved far away indeed from the anapestic cadences of his earlier poems. . . .

Finally, no one expects Dickey to be able to sustain through every poem the authentic lyric force of poems like "The Lifeguard" and "Hunting Civil War Relics at Nimblewill Creek." The nature of his poetry is such that it demands strong emotive risks, but it should be undertaken with acute consciousness of the dangers along the way.

*George Lensing, in* Carolina Quarterly, *Spring, 1970, pp. 90-1.*

Resurrection, regeneration, death in life and life in death, the struggle to keep alive those ancient intuitive powers of the mind that link man to his biological past—these are Dickey's abiding concerns. . . . [One] is conscious of this poet's passion for life and his desperate insistence that every human experience, however painful or ugly, be viewed as a possible occasion for the renewal of life. With Dickey any renewal inevitably requires struggle; sometimes it is intense physical strife, other times a battle of the inner life. . . .

In many of [his] poems Dickey . . . is striving toward something in the past, some primitive source, . . . which perhaps will provide the illumination needed to "re-invent the vision of the race." Some of [his poems] . . . are among the finest his generation has produced.

Virginia Quarterly Review, *Vol. 47, No. 1 (Winter, 1971), p. xviii.*

In *The Eye-Beaters,* Mr. Dickey displays a style that seems daring or difficult while lacking invention. It is founded on the exclamatory sentence, treated with an expansiveness that makes one long for Whitman and a violence that makes one wince for Hopkins. To suggest intensity of feeling, he repeats words often and erratically, as if in a stammer of ecstasy. This does not mean that the words are carefully chosen. To distract one from his lack of grace, Mr. Dickey makes a showy distribution of words on the page, to look like elaborate stanza forms with touches of concrete poetry. Since these shapes have little foundation in rhythm, they are largely arbitrary. . . .

In effect, Mr. Dickey tramples on the slogan of "fit audience though few" and reveals a degree of ambition that would raise a claque for him in an underground station. The loudest, most visible effects, clearly designed to gather the biggest, most miscellaneous audience, are the standard elements of his work.

*"In Search of an Audience," in* The Times Literary Supplement *(reproduced by permission), May 21, 1971, p. 580.*

Owl imagery is quite prominent in James Dickey's *Deliverance* and may be understood as a symbol for an antiromantic view of primitive man in nature. . . .

Three well-known qualities of owls pertain to their function in the novel. First, owls are naturally birds of prey. The one that perches on the tent spends the night hunting. The four characters on the canoe trip are in the process of becoming animals of prey. Lewis Medlock, the organizer of the trip, insisted from the beginning that it was an exercise in survival, and the men intend to kill what they eat. After they meet the two mountaineers, their lives depend on their ability to kill for a different reason. Killing a man to protect oneself has a different moral meaning from killing an animal to eat. Killing a man is killing on the same level with oneself, as opposed to killing a lower animal; but since lower animals usually kill on the same level with themselves, Gentry becomes like them when he undertakes to kill a man. Thus he has to undergo a transformation, to become an animal, in order to accomplish his purpose: "I'll make a circle inland, very quiet, and look for him like I'm some kind of animal. What kind? It doesn't matter, as long as I'm quiet and deadly. I could be a snake" (149). Second, in literature an owl is a bird of ill omen. Its function in the novel in this respect hardly needs comment. The artificial owl at the beginning prefigures the real owl on the tent, which forebodes the horrible experiences of the next day. Third, in folklore the owl is a bird of wisdom. Numerous nursery rhymes and folk proverbs testify to this point. *Deliverance* is obviously an initiation story, a story in which the major character or characters come to a deep understanding of something fundamental to human nature. Lewis and Ed certainly come to a realization of the natural savagery of man in nature, though the shallowness of Bobby's character prevents him from plumbing the situation beyond its surface horror. Though Drew's death may prevent us from concluding how meaningful the experience was to him, the fact that he was the only one to argue that the situation should be resolved through civilized procedures of justice indicates that he had to be killed in the wilderness because he was unable to adjust to its laws (cf. 105-13). But at least half the characters acquire the knowledge that the owl symbolizes.

The owl has a fourth symbolic quality, different in kind from the previous three. The story begins in civilization, represented by the artificial owl, in which man's instinctive savage nature has to be repressed. . . . When the characters move into the woods, savagery becomes an actuality and violence a necessity; therefore, the artificial owl is replaced with a real one. After the three survivors have returned to civilization, Ed again thinks of the innocuous artificial owl. His calling it a "wind-toy" emphasizes the contrast between the artificial and the real. Their problem now is not to be violent but to cover up all traces of their past savagery and violence. That they finally become civilized again is evidenced at the end of the novel by the submerging of the horror in the casual activities and quiet tone of the conclusion. In three days they have retraced the course of human development and have found in the natural state not the romantic ideal of beauty in nature coupled with brotherhood among men but beauty in nature coupled with the necessity to kill men, coolly and in the course of things.

*C. Hines Edwards, Jr., "Dickey's 'Deliverance': The Owl and the Eye," in* Critique: Studies in Modern Fiction, *Vol. XV, No. 2, 1973, pp. 95-101.*

James Dickey has been attempting to write, during the last decade, what none of his contemporaries seems capable of or interested in attempting—a poetry of the common man: about his obsessions, failures, uninspiring everyday life and attempts to escape it, and above all, his successes, which would not perhaps have been considered as such in another age or country. . . .

What seems to me most striking, . . . reading over all of Dickey's poems, is the great change, not entirely in style, but obviously in format of the work in such a short period of time. When I mentioned . . . that Dickey attempted to write a poetry of the common man, it was because the attempt seems particularly to have engaged his subconscious. Though in his first book he did not entirely succeed in the attempt, in each successive volume, culminating in the latest—the title of which, *The Eye-Beaters, Blood, Victory, Madness, Buckhead and Mercy,* seems designed to attract the divergent desires of as many readers as possible—he has moved farther and farther towards the common man and away from poetry, as if admitting that the two are just not compatible, but trying, nonetheless, to stretch the definition of the latter because the former is not, unfortunately, as malleable. The result of this movement away from the focus of poetry has been to center Dickey's ellipse about the common man and his preferences, and the poet has given up even the pretense of indentation and line break and told again the story of one of his poems, dressed up and dressed out, in prose, with an almost too appropriate title, *Deliverance,* and deliverance it surely is, from any responsibility—no matter how little there was to begin with —for the placement of his words in a stricter order than their sense. . . .

It is possible that James Dickey will concentrate, in future, on writing more outdoor adventure stories like *Deliverance,* and will write less and less of [the] sort of "poetry" [presented in *Buckdancer's Choice* and subsequent volumes]. When he started writing poems in the late 'fifties there was no one quite like him, and therefore his sort of poetry, better then than it is now, was interesting, as novel. Some of the earlier poems may last as examples of his style—some are good enough even as poems, compared to so much of what has been passed off in the past decade. But, as is true of almost any unusual, personal style, imitations abound as soon as it succeeds in attracting much attention, and those styles which are personal to begin with—if they are not also based on personal perception, and a thorough knowledge of poetic practice, which assures that few would-be mimics will be competent enough for the forgery —are taken over quickly by a crowd. Dickey's style has been imitated excessively already, so that if he does not again write the massive number of poems he once did, our loss will be compensated by the many poems of others written after his fashion. As fashions go (and this one will like so many others) this is not the most attractive that America produced in the 1960's.

James Dickey's poetry appeared like a tidal wave to flood the poetic landscape of the 'sixties, washing inland as far as it could, but then settled into one of the lowest depressions in that landscape, producing one of our newest imaginative swamps, where the imitative bull-frogs have taken up residence and taken up the cry, exchanging their stories in indistinguishable croaks.

*Michael Mesic, "A Note on James Dickey," in* American Poetry Since 1960: Some Critical Perspectives, *edited by Robert B. Shaw (reprinted by permission of Dufour Editions, Inc.), Carcanet, 1973, pp. 145-53.*

I am trying to uncover what [*Deliverance*] says rather than what Dickey wants it to. I think Dickey was the victim of his own trap, which ultimately is his secret belief that men are free when they are straying and breaking away, not when they are in a living homeland. Dickey has it that Ed, despite his apathetic attitude, contains within him the spark of life which simply needs liberating. Lewis is just the man to liberate it, and the story concerns transference of life energies from master to apprentice. This theme of ritual initiation into manhood Dickey no doubt recognized as being at the center of much American literature. Ed grows up, meets the challenge, gets in touch with himself, with nature, and with "life," and eventually the two self-made heroes are properly humanized and forced to accept their limitations. Bobby of course remains an obvious foil; he never learns and appropriately slips off at the end to the easy life in Hawaii. We feel no pain for his humiliation. We might even accept it as cosmic justice appropriate to such a mental and physical coward. But what about Drew? In order for the grand pattern to become emotionally significant, a tragic waste has to be built in somewhere along the line. Bobby obviously isn't good enough to be the scapegoat victim. Drew is at once the innocent bystander drawn into the tragic conflict and at the same time the Orphic poet, dismembered by a society that cannot tolerate the artist's inner freedom and power of expression. Someone has to die to illustrate the gravity of the theme, and Dickey is careful to delineate the guilt for the scapegoat's death. First Drew is wounded by a member of the country culture (ironically, since Drew is their one link with the city culture, as seen by the interchange between Lonnie and Drew and also by the fraternal touch on the shoulder given Drew by Lonnie's father). But the gunshot wound is apparently superficial; it is the river that finishes him off. Drew is too good to be done in by man alone—or is it that he senses the futility of it all and gives it up?

So the river kills him, but Drew has the last word. When the others finally find him he is seated somewhat comfortably in the middle of the river (not, as in the movie, with one arm grotesquely twisted around his head). He appears strangely serene in the midst of chaotic turbulence; he faces upstream and is jammed into what appears to be a natural throne or altar, eyelids "propped open by the current, seeming to see out of the open water back up into the mountains, around all the curves of the river, infinitely." Even in death Drew's firm center shines forth. The river might have temporarily conquered him, yet he seems to be prophesying in his "all-seeing and clear" way its own impending demise—as well, perhaps, as the demise of the Lewises of the world. This is what the novel tells us, and this is the Drew we are going to remember, as well as the Drew who is no doubt going to haunt Ed and Lewis later in life. Drew the musician, Drew the tamer of the wild, Drew the magician. We'd like to know more about him. He is our link with the future.

But of course Dickey can't tell us more. I think one part of him knows that Drew is the real hero, but the other part has to stereotype him, has to simplify and categorize him as a "straight-forward quiet fellow . . . devoted to his family" who believes in the things his soft drink company stands for to the point of keeping a copy of the company history on his living room coffee table. Something in Dickey has to sacrifice Drew to Lewis: immediately after describing Drew he has Ed say, "But Lewis and I were different" and explains what sets them (especially Lewis at this point) apart in their praiseworthy attempt to "rise above time . . . take a chance, as though the burden of . . . laborious immortality were too heavy to bear." Come on, Dickey. We'd like to believe you know better.

What is it then that kills Drew? Dickey wants to tell us it's his adaptiveness, his willingness to compromise, his middle-of-the-roadness. But we know enough about Drew to recognize that he is just as adamant in his beliefs as Lewis is—in fact more so, since Lewis knows he has Ed and Bobby on his side. It can't be Drew's character flaw that kills him, then, but his *strength.* For as soon as Drew objects, he becomes the voice of civilization reprimanding the outlaw duo. It is Lewis and Ed that kill Drew—the brotherhood of good outlaws, the song of the open road, the song of freedom and individuality. Society be damned, the individual must take a stand against the group if he is to achieve his personal salvation. Drew is merely a superego sacrificed to the id's greater demands. In face of Ahab's dark quest, Drew looks a lot like tame Starbuck. The die is cast. But where is Ishmael?

Dickey should be Ishmael (since in this novel Ed can't be), but Dickey has cast his lot with Lewis and Ed. In order to test this out we might examine the various characters' responses to music and art. Bobby, of course, is totally insensitive. Lewis seems to *know* about the music Drew and the country people make but never seems to *hear* it, whereas Ed learns by listening to it. Moreover, Ed, not Lewis, is the potential artist who has a rudimentary "ability to get the elements of a layout into some kind of harmonious relationship." It is Ed who makes the connection between the real owl and its artistic representation (the wind-chime owl which rings from his patio), as it is Ed who appreciates Holley's transformation of a "dead" work of art into a "live" work (one of Braque's birds into a Pegasus). The question revolves around the artist's role in society. Lewis, the antinomian hero, has no room in his life style for art. Drew, the artist, has no room in his life for antinomianism. Ed has room for both.

We wonder, then, what Dickey is going to make of Ed. Unfortunately Dickey chooses to tell us it is Lewis' influence that saves Ed, whereas the novel tells us it is Drew's. For this reason *Deliverance* has the potential of becoming a classic. . . .

The point is that Drew's music ultimately becomes the prophet's music, the artist's music which, as Frost says, is at best a "momentary stay against confusion." The artist's music works for the artist, and if we believe Shelley, works in the long run for society as well. But the artist in our Western culture usually suffers Orpheus' fate. So Drew, the man who knows too much and sees too clearly, must be sacrificed. Perhaps he sees that the brotherhood of man can be built, but not on Lewis' individualistic premises—the old antinomian urge of Natty Bumppo to escape man's limitations for once and for all and build a new society in the wilderness. Instead, Drew, and perhaps even Dickey, might possess more conservative notions of what it is that keeps men together. Music and law, not reckless freedom and salvation through violence.

*William Stephenson, "*Deliverance *from What?" in* The Georgia Review, *Spring, 1974, pp. 114-120.*

* * *

## DONLEAVY, J(ames) P(atrick) 1926-

**An American-born novelist, playwright, and short story writer who became an Irish citizen, Donleavy is best known for *The Ginger Man,* an experimental novel in a post-Joycean mode. (See also *Contemporary Authors*, Vols. 9-12, rev. ed.)**

Compared to *The Ginger Man, A Singular Man* is an extremely neat presentation of the hero consenting to the trap of his society. For all of its incidental invention, however, it is a repetitive and finally rather dull book. *The Ginger Man* shows some of the same tendencies, but, in it, the style has not yet become mannered. The rhetoric, hovering between bathos and mockery, is suitable to Sebastian. The stylistic device—and a very clever one—which allows sudden shifts from first to third person within a paragraph suggests that Sebastian speaks as himself and then steps back to see himself, that he is always both sufferer and observer. The interplay between Sebastian's reality and his fantasies give a richness to the novel which is diluted only by the recognition that, in fact or in fancy, he is a somewhat tiresome man to spend much time with. *A Singular Man* tries to go a step beyond *The Ginger Man*. George Smith's only reality is mythic. Like the hero of the Donleavy play *Fairy Tales in New York,* he is a fantasy figure in a fantasy setting, suggesting some satirical truths about our society. Yet, like Sebastian, he wears disguises, invents situations, plays many parts; unlike Sebastian, he never touches ground. The implications are fascinating—the relationship between the fantasies society imposes and the ones we invent to escape from it—but the book is not. Its style defeats it. It is not simply that some devices (the shift in person, the verse-like tags) seem merely hangovers from the earlier book. The second novel's chief stylistic innovation is self-defeating. Except for the dialogue, the book is written almost entirely in sentence fragments, as though it had been dictated by Mr. Jingle. Although Donleavy may intend these fragments to tell us something about George Smith or about his society, the fragmentation becomes a surface annoyance and serves finally to reinforce the impression that we are being given the same thing over and over.

*Gerald Weales, "No Face and No Exit: The Fiction of James Purdy and J. P. Donleavy," in* Contemporary American Novelists, *edited by Harry T. Moore (© 1964 by Southern Illinois University Press; reprinted by permission of Southern Illinois University Press), Carbondale: Southern Illinois University Press, 1964, pp. 143-54.*

[Reviewers have called *The Beastly Beatitudes of Balthazar B*] Donleavy's best book since *The Ginger Man.* Which is saying a lot, since *The Ginger Man* is a first-rate novel. But it is also not to say all one would wish about *The Beastly Beatitudes of Balthazar B.* For this is not so much Donleavy's best book since *The Ginger Man,* as it is *The Ginger Man*—in its flashiest parts most especially.

And that's the rub. Donleavy is dangerously close to writing his old book all over again. Oh, the characters and the story are different, but oftentimes only accidentally so. Move from surface to substance and one encounters the familiarities of mode and technique that made *The Ginger Man* a triumph. The exotic chef has returned to the book of recipes, tried and true. . . .

Curiously, this does not seem to be what Donleavy intended. A mature Donleavy, far more sophisticated than the Donleavy of *The Ginger Man,* opens his book in Paris, and sets about some serious mood and character delineation. This is vintage Donleavy: serious and characteristically humorous; perceptive and feeling, and always within identifiable contexts, even when he is introducing 12-year-old Balthazar to the wonders of sex (and fatherhood) through his 24-year-old nannie. The situation is heavy with the components of farce, and one would expect Donleavy to pull all the stops. But he plays it straight—or reasonably straight—handling Balthazar as delicately and gracefully as a Mike Nichols directing a Dustin Hoffman. . . .

But Donleavy doesn't maintain his directions. At a given point his story gets away from him, and precisely when he brings Balthazar across the Irish Sea and enrolls him at Trinity. Whether it is Trinity or Dublin, or, as I suspect, a bit of each, the two have a wildly exhilarating effect on Donleavy; he reminds one, for all the world, of the old grad who never gets college or the college town out of his system and who makes an ass of himself at every reunion. . . .

This is a hard thing to say about a writer so talented as J. P. Donleavy; it is said only because Donleavy, being talented, should be above stunting, just as he should be above warmed-over *Ginger Man.* In point of fact, he gives the reader more, much more, in the first hundred pages of *Beatitudes,* but then the serving goes stale, except for the later time when Donleavy is busy with the romance of Balthazar and classmate Elizabeth Fitzdare. Again Donleavy puts aside highjinks and settles down to some sober storytelling. But soon he is bored and impatient, so Fitzdare is thrown from a horse, dies and is buried. Balthazar and the reader are back in the hands of the impulsive stunt man.

*John Deedy, in* Commonweal *(reprinted by permission of Commonweal Publishing Co., Inc.), March 7, 1969, pp. 710-12.*

Though eager to succeed, the Donleavy hero has an aristocratic disdain for Success. He insists on playing the game his way, even though the prospect of failure makes him giddy. In his aggressive phase, he is willing to employ violence, cunning, and a ruthless energy in the pursuit of his goals; in his passive guise he offers his vulnerability as proof of his goodhearted innocence. He may be wise in the ways of the world, but he is never worldly wise. . . .

In the twenties Scott Fitzgerald offered the innocent but sophisticated young an image of flaming youth. To live in the high style meant using money while spurning the money-getting process. The fun, while it lasted, depended on the camaraderie of a set of people sharing values that clearly distinguished them from the lesser breeds unable to afford either material or spiritual luxury. In the sixties Donleavy has attracted a considerable "underground" following, especially on campuses in the East. He, too, offers an image of rebellious youth, but the company of the elite is sadly diminished. More single-minded and more embattled in their quest for erotic pleasure, apparently born with the taste of defeat in their mouths, they invent (or their creator does) a style of life for themselves, nervous and lyrical, compounded of tough-minded vulgarity and tender-minded elegance. The glamor of fine clothes, good food, and handsome bodies is still very much in evidence, but the hero is more and more isolated. To dream of the good life in any substantial sense would be a hypocrisy beyond his spiritual means; the best he can manage is a defiant protest on behalf of the single man against the world that would unman him.

*John Rees Moore, "Afterword" (1969) to his essay, "Hard Times and the Noble Savage: J. P. Donleavy's 'A Singular Man'," (1964), in* The Sounder Few: Essays from the "Hollins Critic," *edited by R. H. W. Dillard, George Garrett, and John Rees Moore, University of Georgia Press, 1971, pp. 14-15.*

Mr Donleavy has imagination, unfortunately of a rather obsessive and repetitive order. Where it is apparently freed entirely, as in *The Onion Eaters,* the obsessive and repetitive elements are inclined to take over, somewhat to the reader's discomfort. Both the scenes of violence and the sexual encounters suggest an attitude to the human body and its functions, weaknesses and pleasures, which is anything but tender, compassionate, or celebratory. The book is written in the present tense, a device over-used to suggest narrative energy, in staccato, frequently verbless sentences which do not make for easy reading and which seem to occlude rather than reveal the occasional flash of real humour or feeling.

*"Three's Company," in* The Times Literary Supplement *(reproduced by permission), July 23, 1971, p. 849.*

J. P. Donleavy is a master of some of the most glorious nonsense to have been written since Sterne fell dead.

When Donleavy first came on with *The Ginger Man,* there was some hint that he too was an angry young man, and was rich in meaning, which, to be sure, he was keeping up his sleeve.

Not so, at all. There is a kind of comedy that may well begin in the traditional comic solicitude for a liquid articulateness to life on this planet but which soon forgets such noble guff and goes for the horselaugh. Donleavy has simply chosen to be as funny as he can, and does not sit down to the typewriter until he has several pages' worth of high-class insanity to record.

*The Onion Eaters* is therefore an outrageous performance from first page to last, with no mercy shown in any quarter. There is a plot, but it is in shambles before very long. There are characters whose achievements in idiocy reach heights undreamed of by Jerome K. Jerome, Wodehouse or Stella Gibbons. The only parallel fit to put beside Donleavy is his master Beckett. . . .

Donleavy is uninterruptedly bawdy, yet his obscenity is so grand and so open, that it rises above giving offense into a realm of its own, unchallenged and wild. Even the most prudish reader, however, might profitability stomach Mr. Donleavy's Gaelic randiness for the sake of his wit, which is as keen as can be found in comic writing in this dreary century, and for the sake of his invention, which belongs in Ben Turpin's league, and Chaplin's and Keaton's. A man as funny as J. P. Donleavy may write what he will. The clown's privileges are utterly free, for it is his art that keeps us sane.

*Guy Davenport, in* National Review *(150 East 35th St., New York, N.Y. 10016), October 8, 1971, p. 1124.*

How does a man weakened by an awareness of death survive in a world experienced as magical with malevolence? This is the question the heroes of J. P. Donleavy's novels answer in their own, progressively inefficacious ways. To evade his consciousness of mortality, Sebastian Dangerfield of *The Ginger Man* lives a hedonistic life in the present and dreams of relaxed ease for the future. George Smith of *A Singular Man* separates himself from the world in a parody of Howard Hughes' and John Paul Getty's attempts to avoid the disease of life. In *The Saddest Summer of Samuel S* and *The Beastly Beatitudes of Balthazar B,* the heroes find heterosexual love the combatant of mutability's sadness. Donleavy's most recent hero, Clayton Claw Cleaver Clementine of *The Onion Eaters,* tries an uneasy synthesis of his fictional cousins' survival strategies, but his attempt to live the life he wants fails more miserably than the similar attempts of his predecessors. The degree of misery in Clementine's role of powerless victim seems to signal Donleavy's reaching the dead end of a theme—victimization—developing in his work since *The Ginger Man. The Onion Eaters* also introduces a fiction different in kind from that which precedes it, for although familiar features are here, often in exaggerated form, the psychological exploration which helped unify and made serious the earlier rambling plots is much diminished in *The Onion Eaters*. Whether dead end or new beginning, *The Onion Eaters* furnishes a useful perspective on the rhetorical strategies of Donleavy's always comic novels, for the rhetoric of this latest novel both parallels and significantly differs from the rhetoric of his early work. . . .

The jagged syntax of Donleavy's early work does not, as one might expect, become progressively fragmented with his development of victimization as a central theme. In fact, the syntax of *Beastly Beatitudes* and *The Onion Eaters* is less wrenched than the syntax of *The Ginger Man* and *A Singular Man.* The fractured syntax of those two novels was a good correlative of the active desperation of their protagonists, for the interrupted sentences gave the impression of consciousness anxious in threatening time. Sentences do not reach their natural end because their speakers fear they themselves may end first. Working away from the comedy of dynamic desperation to a comedy of sadness and resignation, Donleavy finds conventional syntax adequate for the more conventional perceptions of a Balthazar or Clementine. Living a life after the death of others, they are not threatened by time, feel no need to hurry up their speech and thoughts to the extent that earlier heroes did. As passive victims who are less able to honor the aristocratic code of style than their predecessors and as men not anxious for conversation, Balthazar and Clementine tend toward silence. . . .

*The Onion Eaters* is ultimately the nightmare of a small boy whose faithful dog (Elmer) provides no protection against the castrating females and mysterious wizards who haunt his lonely room (Charnel Castle). In *The Ginger Man, A Singular Man,* and *Beastly Beatitudes,* the male alliance against the world lies just below the surface sexuality, but this adolescent response has become increasingly retrograde until, in *The Onion Eaters,* it dissolves into the sentimental situation of boy and dog in a cold world, a kernel difficult to make into adult fiction. In *The Ginger Man* the hero's fantasies were nearly equal to his fears; victim and victimizer were one. With *A Singular Man* began the hero's acquiescence to his victimization until, in *The Onion Eaters,* the reader rebels at the helplessness of a man both too much and too little like Sebastian Dangerfield to be entombed in Charnel Castle.

*Thomas LeClair, "'The Onion Eaters' and the Rhetoric of Donleavy's Comedy," in* Twentieth Century Literature, *July, 1972, pp. 167-74.*

Sad to say, J. P. Donleavy remains the author of *The Ginger Man.* His first novel read like Henry Miller on the loose in James Joyce's Dublin and made Britain's so-called Angry Young Men sound rather docile and good-natured. But the *Ginger Man* style has become a prison: even the prefaces in [*The Plays of J. P. Donleavy*] are partly written in Donleavy's patented, whimsical version of stream of consciousness. As for the plays—*The Ginger Man, Fairy Tales of New York, A Singular Man, The Saddest Summer of Samuel S,* all based on his published or unpublished fiction—they prove repeatedly that a series of duologues and monologues need not add up to a real play. The first three have been produced in London, but they contain hardly a scene that goes, or even seems to be going, anywhere. Oddly, Donleavy's trump card—the daft things people say to themselves and partners while making love—is never played. Even so, the Roman Catholic Archbishop of Dublin was displeased, as the preface "What They Did in Dublin with *The Ginger Man*" relates. It may be Donleavy's most lasting contribution to theater history.

*Vivian Mercier, in* World *(copyright © 1972 by Saturday Review/World, Inc.; reprinted with permission), July 18, 1972, p. 66.*

J. P. Donleavy's *The Onion Eaters* . . . proves suspicions many critics voiced after the publication of *The Saddest Summer of Samuel S.*: Donleavy has stagnated in the brilliant formal and thematic gimcrackery which made his first novel, *The Ginger Man,* such an unusual and exciting book. Donleavy has gone nowhere since then. There is still the picaresque hero with unusual genital endowments, beset by sex-hungry, voracious females, finally finding refuge with a sweet, innocent, but sexy country-girl; there is still the lonely, underdog protagonist, thrown into a grotesquely hostile world, desperately wanting to be rich and happy beyond any possible measure, intruded upon by weird characters who seem to have escaped from the paintings of Hieronymus Bosch. . . . Donleavy emerges as the author whom one likes to remember for having created Sebastian Dangerfield, that most pathetic, yet moving antihero of *The Ginger Man,* and, maybe, for *The Beastly Beatitudes of Balthazar B.* His latest novel, regrettably, is just another layer of the same onion, without getting us any closer to the core.

*Franz G. Blaha, in* Prairie Schooner *(© 1972 by University of Nebraska Press; reprinted by permission from* Prairie Schooner*), Fall, 1972, p. 276.*

"A Fairy Tale of New York" . . . is provisioned with the malign Niebelungen of our urban land: power jobbers, sexual self-destructs, kamikaze eccentrics. It's about social impotence and despair. Valleys of humiliation, sloughs of despond: all the grim topography of that other Christian's progress. [Donleavy's hero is Cornelius Christian.] Salvation for Cornelius is pessimistic: emigration. He returns to Europe. Yet Donleavy's thunderous, superb humor has the efficacy of grace. It heals and conquers and ratifies.

The style is adaptable as Plastic Man. A stream of consciousness with wild cataracts in it. The whole should be italicized: it has the unsyntactical terseness of stage directions. Donleavy's style is cantilevered to support strong feeling. "When I was a little boy. Left in a brand new foster home. I went out playing the afternoon around the block. Got lost, so busy telling all the other kids a fairy tale of New York. That my real father was a tycoon and my mother a princess." And it has the resilience, the necessary amplitude, for boisterous laughter. "Stand here in the vestibule. When I first heard that word. Thought that's what women had. And they asked you in." A modern style: streamlined as some compact, collapsible appliance. And Donleavy is master of it.

Yet the novel has a stellar fault: one that might just as easily be admired. It's too funny. Even if you accept a fairy tale ambience, the big dialogue set pieces with their uproarious verbal confusions, their crazy reversals and accurate characterization, distract from the narrative's structural line. . . . Donleavy, I think, has disfigured "A Fairy Tale of New York" for the sake of entertainment. There is a musical comedy unevenness: disquieting pauses for chorus and duet and long, glad applause.

Yet I mean to be grateful. J. P. Donleavy is a writer of explosive, winning imagination. I loved "A Fairy Tale of New York." For its faults; for its several successes.

*D. Keith Mano, in* The New York Times Book Review *(© 1973 by The New York Times Company; reprinted by permission), September 23, 1973, p. 6.*

In Donleavy's fiction gravity and absurdity go hand in hand. . . .

The composition by phrases and full stops, and the substitution of present participles—putting up, smoking, getting out—for more active and transitive verb forms are essential Donleavy and impart a dance-like movement. . . .

In picaresque narrative characters other than the hero tend to be used up and discarded as the *picaro* makes his progress through the shams and facades of the represented society. In *A Fairy Tale* two characters—Fanny Sourpuss, an ex-prostitute turned millionaire widow, and an ancient Jewish physician expounding the spiritual efficacy of regular bowel movements—stay present and compelling. These are mentor figures teaching a wisdom, in bed and consulting room, that is obscene and true.

Donleavy's investigation and fantastication of the New York he grew up in and regularly, secretively, visits are thorough. No borough except Richmond is left unturned. Affection, loathing, nostalgia and fear are main components of the attitude he brings to bear upon his native place. The language, especially in certain set scenes taking place in mortuaries, courtrooms, taverns, penthouse apartments and in the streets and subway stations, is electrically alive. Hidden away in the book for those who can find it is a good deal of personal revelation, a good deal of alembicated and metamorphosed autobiography. . . .

Since *A Fairy Tale of New York* is Donleavy's best book to date and ample evidence of his staying power, I predict that his Boswell will appear in time. Candidates for the job should be quick on their feet, handy with the mitts (for sparring, shadow boxing and bobbing and feinting sessions only), and infinitely tolerant of the put-on and the leg-pull.

*Julian Moynahan, "The Rake's Progress," in* Book World—The Washington Post (© The Washington Post), *September 30, 1973, p. 5.*

"A Fairy Tale" is not among Donleavy's better books. At his best, this man is rather a magician, stitching idiosyncratic fantasies together into almost the texture of myth. At his least, he is simply a sleight-of-hand artist, a master of languidly easy effects. "A Fairy Tale of New York" finds him in perigee. . . .

There are some felicities in the writing, most of it in a spare, disjunctive, Joycean stream-of-consciousness style, but without Joyce's puns or allusions. . . .

*L. E. Sissman, in* The New Yorker, *October 8, 1973, pp. 168-69.*

From *The Ginger Man* on, J. P. Donleavy's novels have been simultaneously cruel, sentimental, repetitive and sporadically funny. Donleavy heroes are ridiculous figures who wallow in self-pity behind their mannered fronts and anesthetize deep personal hurts with sex and alcohol.

Time *(reprinted by permission from* Time, The Weekly Newsmagazine; *copyright Time, Inc.), October 29, 1973, p. E3.*

Four hundred and ten pages of fairy tale is a bit much, isn't it? . . . But Donleavy, I'm told, has a cult following, and as we know—already knew, in fact, but know especially well in the pop age—cult fans can't get too much of a bad thing. And here's our Irish American dutifully churning out 410 pages of it for them. . . . All minced into bits and pieces of sentences, which is at least something to be thankful for.

Margaret Drabble, in a broadcast, found [the] hamburger-style prose [of *A Fairy Tale in New York*] tiresome. But one burps to think how soggily indigestible it would have been, served up in long, sinuous sentences. Like 410 platefuls of congealed spaghetti. Give me a stale, early 1960s-style hamburger, or a Ginger Man, any day. Or, on second thoughts, no, please don't.

*James Brockway, in* Books and Bookmen, *November, 1973, pp. 96-7.*

* * *

## DONOSO, José 1925-

**Donoso is a Chilean novelist and short story writer, now living in Spain, whose novel *The Obscene Bird of Night* is considered a major contribution to Latin American literature.**

How do you review a dream? *Pájaro* [*The Obscene Bird of Night*] is a nightmare. It changes while you do so that trying to describe it is hopeless. If ever a work contained all the characteristics Umberto Eco has found for the *opera aperta* it surely is this one. True, we meet again the preoccupations Donoso has expressed in his earlier novels—*Coronación. . . , Lugar sin límites, Este domingo*—namely: youth versus old age, the poor versus the rich, servants versus masters (if in Sábato's *Sobre héroes y tumbas* the blind rule the world, in *Pájaro* it is the old, retired, decrepit servants that govern it), freaks versus "normal" people, illness versus health, impotence, transmutations (here even grotesque transplants), charity and its hidden motives, family histories, et cetera, but this time they are virtually all reflected in each other. It is as though reality mirrored dreams, history showed us legend or myth, as if each were a form of all others. People change into each other, into animals, and back. The whole novel strikes one as the delirium of a physical and metaphysical hypochondriac, almost a schizophrenic.

The narrator's viewpoint shifts continually; identities are conjugated in time and space; at the end, the only consciousness left, sewn up tight in a series of sacks from which it is unable to free itself, gets thrown into the fire and apparently burns: the creative imagination has eliminated itself. This literal and literary reductio ad absurdum is in fact the most intimate movement of the novel: a consciousness that, dreading chaotic and unclean reality, shrinks from it, and shrinks and shrinks into self-extinction. At what I take to be the center of the novel there is a straight, conventionally told folk-myth about erotic witchcraft, something like a musical theme. Slowly the book turns into a series of variations on the myth, and the variations themselves, too, enter into strange combinations: everything becomes everything else—as in a dream.

Donoso worked eight years on this novel. The result is superb and unique; a complicated book, true, one that requires much effort from the reader, but a novel that causes what is called an "intense experience." I consider *Pájaro* a masterwork.

*Wolfgang A. Luchting, in* Books Abroad, *Vol. 46, No. 1, Winter, 1972, pp. 82-3.*

[Donoso] writes in Spanish like an Englishman, like one of the no-nonsense reviewers in the *TLS,* say, who has decided to chuck criticism for fiction. Donoso is intelligible even in his most "poetic" moments, a quality to be appreciated, surely, when compared to all that "intense" prose and *écriture* that has lately been coming out of Latin America. This holds true even for such complex books (and their *asuntos*) as his latest novel, *El obsceno pájaro de la noche*. . . . In comparison to it, *Cuentos* is as digestible as skimmed milk, when compared to sour cream. . . .

I am partial to Donoso: I like practically anything he writes (with one minor reservation, his first novel *Coronación* . . .) and consider him one of the most fascinating Latin American writers. Not all the stories in *Cuentos* are impressive, but most are. In certain ones there is that sometimes irritating disproportion between the preparation for a plot and the execution of it ("Charlestón," "El güero," for instance), or, also, the impression one occasionally gets of what might be termed a "desganada" attitude in the author toward what he tells ("La puerta cerrada"). As for the narrative techniques, I detect a certain minor abuse of the story-within-the-story approach. But none of these (unimportant) objections is serious. Reading *Cuentos* is ninety percent sheer pleasure, not only for the ad hoc effects they may achieve, but also for the insights they permit into his "workshop." They are all there, his obsessions, his hang-ups, and it is revealing to see how even years ago they were decisive in forming what were to be Donoso's later writings: *El lugar sin límites* . . . and *Este domingo*. . . . In short, no serious student of Latin American literature can afford not to read this book, for Donoso's is unquestionably one of the most skillful works that continent and a half has produced.

*Wolfgang A. Luchting, in* Books Abroad, *Vol. 46, No. 2, Spring, 1972, pp. 275-76.*

[The] forest of this long novel [*The Obscene Bird of Night*] is unsubdued (it could advantageously have been thinned out) and the feral cacophony within it is unstinting. Yet there is, embedded as a figure in the luxuriant ground of the whole, like a witches' Sabbath in a greenhouse, an outrageously brilliant novella about a Chilean grandee who secretes a deformed son on the remote family estate and combs the world for other human sports of nature to keep him company. I know of no more compelling stretch of prose in modern Latin American fiction. I just wonder why Donoso added so much to it, muffling and weakening it. If he felt it gained through contrast, he was surely mistaken: we supply our own contrasts to anything gruesome, freakish, willful—indeed, self-styled "normality" needs no boost in its smugness. Not that any part of this book is badly written (or badly translated); it just has so exceptional a core that what I suppose is the shielding seems a bit humdrum and sometimes superfluous. . . .

Far from prolific, José Donoso, born in Chile in 1925, has published two volumes of stories and a previous novel *Coronation* (Englished in 1966), but little in those essentially societal servant-master studies prepares one for this phantasmagorical impasto of magic, madness and misery. He has learned to multiply by myth and this gives his work a resonance and amplitude that puts him alongside Carpentier, Cortázar and García Márquez.

*Paul West, "Into a Fiery Green Furnace," in* Book World—The Washington Post (© The Washington Post), *May 27, 1973, p. 6.*

"The Obscene Bird of Night" is a dense and energetic book, full of terrible risk-taking, populated with legendary saints and witches, mad old crones and a whole estate-full of freaks and monsters, and narrated by a disturbed deaf-mute, many times disguised. The story line is like a great puzzle with everything in it from burlesque to romance, magic to murder, often bizarre, yet always—for Donoso is himself possessed by an astonishingly agile imagination—invested with a vibrant, almost tangible reality. Even the very setting is a kind of maze-within-a-maze, yet as vivid in its details as the hairs on an old crone's chin. . . .

[In] spite of all its surface disorder, "The Obscene Bird of Night" has been carefully, intelligently—even cabalistically—designed. There are three parts to the book, the first two containing nine chapters each, the third a magical twelve. The three parts are dominated, respectively, by Mudito, Boy (Don Jerónimo's monstrous heir), and the Blesséd Inés—the author-Father, freakish Son and somewhat perverse Holy Spirit, who blows through the book like some kind of ironical Original Sin, like "the obscene bird of night" itself, an image borrowed, appropriately, from a letter written by Henry James Sr. to his sons Henry and William. . . .

I have no idea what fate awaits [this book], but it certainly deserves to take its place alongside the major works of Asturias and Fuentes, Cortázar, Borges and Rulfo, Vargas Llosa and García Márquez, and never mind that "the old woman plotted everything." She and "The Obscene Bird of Night" are part of our mainstream, after all, Anglo- and Hispano-American alike. The horrible bat-winged head of the beautiful Blesséd Inés pursues us all.

*Robert Coover, in* The New York Times Book Review *(© 1973 by The New York Times Company; reprinted by permission), June 17, 1973, pp. 1-2.*

In his excellent novella, "Hell Has No Limits" . . . , the Chilean writer, José Donoso, dealt with themes of identity—the dissatisfaction with self and existence, and the adoption of roles to alleviate that dissatisfaction. In his new book, a huge, striking and at times very puzzling novel [*The Obscene Bird of Night*], Donoso explores a strange, decaying world, given to ritual and madness, and populated by discontent, isolated souls often longing for a change of skin. . . .

As Donoso describes this absurd world of ritual and deception, he also traces the deterioration of various characters and settings—the decline and eventual demise of the de Azcoitía family, the fall of the convent home, and Humberto's passage from vague being to non-being. Throughout the novel, the author is in complete control of his material, handling complex monologues and time transitions with ease and, except for a few lapses, subtly dramatizing his ideas. I would be dishonest to pretend that a book as long, dense and claustrophobic as this is not a challenge and a chore for the reader. At times it does seem tedious, too repetitious. And after reading parts of it a second time, I still couldn't decide whether certain scenes were "real" or simply products of Humberto's imagination. But for all its difficulty, *The Obscene Bird of Night* is a stunning and original book by an unusually gifted and serious writer. Though the world Donoso has created seems quite closed and distant, the odd, desperate inhabitants, with their games and crises of identity, are simply representative of the confused and tortured players who perform on the vast stage we know so well.

*Ronald DeFeo, in* Commonweal *(reprinted by permission of Commonweal Publishing Co., Inc.), September 21, 1973, pp. 509-10.*

Among . . . recent Latin American narratives, . . . three novels in particular—*From Cuba with a Song* by Severo Sarduy, *Three Trapped Tigers* by Guillermo Cabrera Infante, and *The Obscene Bird of Night* by José Donoso—have reaffirmed the destruction of conventional reality by installing the grotesque in order to depict most effectively a shapeless world that cannot find its center. In these novels, a new language is created in the space of the text itself: fragmentation is used as an expressive unit of the irrational, implying an ever-changing structure.

Within this new literary reality, *The Obscene Bird of Night* is a singular work, for it portrays the universe in a continuous metamorphosis where ambiguity is an all-encompassing principle that reflects a world in constant contradiction. Although this novel marks the culmination of Donoso's work, his previous novels, especially *This Sunday* and *Hell Has No Limits,* contain the germ of that delirious world presented in *The Bird*. . . .

The characters in *The Bird* . . . are transformed by constant mutation into metaphoric figures. In Donoso's novel, transformation is a mirror of the world, and in that sense it approaches the great myths of metamorphosis: Ovid's *Metamorphosis,* Apuleius' *The Golden Ass,* and especially Hieronymus Bosch's *The Garden of Delights,* to which Donoso's cosmos is clearly related. . . .

Bosch's universe, in consonance with the perspective of the fifteenth and sixteenth centuries reflects the terror of God's absence in a world where Satan is triumphant, pointing to a destructive reality rather than to religious hope of salvation. In Donoso's world, man is a recluse who is never the Self but always the Other. Therein lies his rejection of religion, institutions, and reality. But Donoso's cosmos rests totally on earth, the only place without limits, where we are "given" heaven and hell. . . .

In both Bosch's and Donoso's world, woman, acting as the intermediary between man and the universe, is the reason for the fall from paradise into earthly chaos. Woman is thus united to the magical ritual and is the possessor of both the angelic and satanical powers that have been irrationally conceived, but rationally exercised. . . .

There is an exuberant nature in both Bosch's painting and Donoso's novel, a supernature that exalts the telluric. It is a savage desire that goes from the idealization of the sensuous (the idyllic fishbowls of *The Garden*) to the most repugnant and monstrous. . . .

What is unique in Donoso's work is that metamorphosis as a literary reality is both a myth and a poetic metaphor. All myth is born from contradiction and is at the same time a transformation of reality. Myths are expressed in algebraic form and are found at the boundaries of a logical supernature where the balance of the world undergoes a never-ending mutation. Every transformation is ruled, however, by a recurring and ordered process: 1) opposition (vertical axis); 2) mediation (transit and passage, horizontal axis), and 3) transformation (new paradigmatic structure, vertical axis). The intermediary resolves the ambiguity and conditions all changes. It is significant that the figure established in the third moment does not remain static, since it has a potential for a new transformation. Thus, an unstable and constant rhythm is created. In Donoso, the metamorphosis is a language that is made within the *literalness* of the text. The narrative mode is a surprising mixture of I-thou-he interwoven in a context in which the reader must imagine the mutations of identity. The reader, as a privileged intermediary, becomes part of the magical act of reading to fathom the "weave" of the text. When the chaotic world demands it, there is a corresponding chaotic language. When the motive is idealized, the language is also endowed with traces of "Darío's *modernismo,*" such as in the idyllic walks of Jerónimo and Inés through the parks of La Rinconada. The Language is also baroque, like a cornucopia of colors in the luxurious and Pantagruelian banquets of La Rinconada, with similar sensual connotations conveyed by the feathers, flowers, and fruits of *The Garden*.

However, if *The Bird* is myth as language, it is also a metalanguage. That is a critique of unyielding reality, of institutions, of the alienation of man who is never the Self and will never know who he is: a world without escape, without a beginning or an end—the ultimate trap.

*Zunilda Gertel, "Metamorphosis as a Met-*

*aphor of the World," in* Review, *Fall, 1973, pp. 20-3.*

It would be useless to try to find a vantage point within the gigantic verbal construction of *The Obscene Bird of Night* from which to contemplate the totality of its magnificent disorder. And to search for a supreme point (as Breton would say) from which the real and the imaginary—the *logos* and the *mythos* mixed up within the interminable convolutions of the novel—would cease to be perceived contradictorily, would also be an enterprise doomed to failure from the very start. Like a murmuring void, a body mutilated a hundred times and healed a hundred times, a muted tongue which nevertheless is obliged to talk for pages and pages, the nameless (or many-named) narrator envelopes the world with his scandalous prattle and wisely warns us that his fiction can only lead us into chaos. . . .

At times, the reader despairs of ever knowing which theme to believe. But he realizes very soon that the novel is precisely the product of conflicting themes. . . .

The constant reflection of one theme in another produces not only a repetitious world, but also a world of disguises and inversions, or what Severo Sarduy has called, referring to the other great Donoso novella (*Hell Has No Limits*), the phenomenon of writing as a *travestismo* (transvestism). But if the narration and the story are out of phase in *Hell Has No Limits,* in *The Bird* they come together in an astonishing way. *Hell Has No Limits* is constructed in a classical way, while *The Bird* is a baroque building, a labyrinth of terraces in which everything is held together with sticking plaster. Or, to use Jean Rousset's expression, we are dealing with a renaissance building reflected in a shimmering pool.

*Francisco Rivera, "A Conflict of Themes," translated by Deborah Davis, in* Review, *Fall, 1973, pp. 24-6.*

Practically all the commentary on Donoso's fiction has centered upon his preoccupation with Chilean reality and his skill in portraying the decadent upper classes. Readers and commentators continue to seek in his fiction features that constituted essential ingredients of the nineteenth-century novel. With very few exceptions, they have been inclined to define the Chilean writer's fiction from the outside rather than from within. . . .

For these commentators the artistry of Donoso is to be seen in his plot development, the depth of the psychological and sociological preoccupations of his characters and the author's ability to reproduce in written prose the speech patterns of a particular social class. Ironically, however, since the appearance of his first novel in 1957, Donoso's narrative has undergone an acute process of internalization, and his identification with a specific external reality has given way to a hermetic world whose bizarre creatures and events render the traditional principles of verisimilitude virtually meaningless. Donoso's latest novel, *The Obscene Bird of Night* is the culmination of this process and poses an unending source of difficulty and frustration for the reader accustomed to traditional fiction.

Any attempt to understand and appreciate this novel must take into consideration two of its principal features: the peculiar nature of its fictional characters and the use of a highly complex narrative structure. Living in a hostile universe, Donoso's characters seek refuge in an inner self, only to discover that the disharmony of their inner world is no less painful than that of its external counterpart. Faced with the task of identifying themselves, they become highly introspective but find self-knowledge to be as elusive as a comprehension of the world around them. Donoso immerses us in a world of darkness, symbolic of the obscurity engulfing the identity of his characters, where a clear delineation between persons and things is blurred and the law of opposites is never valid. By artistically weaving the external reality with the characters' internal agony he succeeds in presenting a terrifying and grotesque account of human existence. . . .

Throughout the novel Donoso rejects the notion of psychological unity and seems to suggest the dissolution of the self into a plurality of masks, with each mask developing its own possibility within the self that has been transformed. By denying the unequivocal identity of his characters, he makes all of them undergo a metamorphosis whereby things can become their opposites while at the same time preserving the ability to assume their original identity. The stability, therefore, between signifier and signified begins to lose its customary integrity, so that a *mundo al revés* emerges in which objects tend to be signs to their opposites. What ensues is a world in which master-servant, virgin-prostitute, priestess-witch, beauty-monster, God-Satan, male-female are no longer mutually exclusive categories but interrelated aspects of one another. . . .

The second and no less innovative aspect of *The Bird* which adds to the difficulty of its reading is the writer's use of a unique narrative structure. Donoso presents his novel through a narrator-agent—not in itself a very revolutionary procedure—but given the nature of his fictional character, he achieves a literary expression never before experienced in the Latin American novel. Circular in structure, the novel opens in the Casa de la Encarnación with the death of Brígida, one of the forty retired servants in residence there, and closes with the evacuation and the imminent destruction of the building. What occurs between these two poles of the novel defies any attempt at a logical explanation. The narrator as character undergoes a series of transformations, adopts a number of fluctuating yet autonomous identities as he tells the story. . . .

Central to Mudito's narration is the use of an interior monologue which from one moment to the next suddenly externalizes itself by representing the conversations of all of the other characters. As a kind of roving eye limited by neither time nor space, Mudito has the power not only to record the conversations of those around him, but to reproduce conversations that may or may not have taken place. . . . Because there is no distinction made between what a person thinks and what he actually verbalizes, dialogues become embedded within Mudito's continuous monologue. Such a blending of the presentational forms of narration into the body of the text results from Donoso's refusal to differentiate between a character and the idea of that character in his narrator's mind. . . .

All of the action in the novel transpires in an atmosphere that exists outside the confines of physical time. . . . Donoso does not destroy time in his novel—for certainly all of his characters are very much aware of its passage and their inevitable extinction. He does destroy, however, chronology. Through the use of discontinuity he obtains a destruction of linear progression similar to that which occurs in filmmaking. Like many contemporary writers, he replaces the sequential nature of storytelling with the principle of juxtaposition which allows him to undermine the logical development of the plot. The outcome is a novel in which time is suspended and events become spatialized in the sense that our point of reference to a particular occurrence is never *when* but *where* it takes place.

This fusion of the temporal and spatial realms, together with the previously discussed multiplicity of character and the complexity of the narrative voice, makes unrelenting demands upon the reader. Donoso does not offer us in *The Obscene Bird of Night* a novel to simply read, but one to experience in which we are continuously called upon to give the text some order by discovering its unities and repetitions.

*John J. Hassett, "The Obscure Bird of Night," in* Review, *Fall, 1973, pp. 27-30.*

José Donoso has produced one of those difficult, chaotic novels so marked by talent and invention that critics tend to overpraise them, vivid imagery and originality prompting many to see as genius what is merely disarray. Thus, although *The Obscene Bird of Night* is not a masterpiece, it is already being called that in several quarters.

Donoso, a Chilean who writes with undeniable vigor and imagination, eschews literary realism, like so many of the Latin Americans whose works have been published here in the last few years. Combining elements of legend and witchcraft with astute sociological observation, he creates his own intense, intricate world. But along with an almost tactile sense of mood and character and some superb vignettes, he also attempts to convey a wobbly metaphysical vision. Fortunately his symbols, if not his philosophy, are arresting. . . .

[Often] in a style that blurs traditional distinctions between objectivity and subjectivity, so that it is difficult to separate what is truly perceived from what is only imagined . . . [the] narrative jumps from past to present and back again, piling symbols on top of legends. As in a dream, identities shift, time and events are distorted. Myths and suggestions of witchcraft color and alter the most ordinary affairs. . . .

While this interweaving and repetition of symbols is interesting, what it leads to is seldom clear. The criticism of Humberto's writing made by a character in Donoso's book is equally true of the work at hand: "Humberto had no talent for simplicity. . . . [He] complicated and deformed his original project so much that it's as if he'd lost himself forever in the labyrinth he invented. . . ." *The Obscene Bird of Night* becomes, similarly, not an account of chaos, but chaos itself. All the conventional rules are discarded yet no new ones are introduced to replace them. The result is less a novel than an antinovel, a work from which all prevailing notions of order have disappeared.

In this context, ambiguous passages seem more the product of carelessness than of any reasoned deliberation. . . . The pointlessness of these ambiguities casts doubt on the validity of others. In the end, the reader is left wondering how much of the book's obscurity stems from an attempt to express the unfathomable, and how much from a refusal to organize material.

*Eugenie Bolger, "Lost in the Labyrinth," in* New Leader, *October 1, 1973, pp. 20-1.*

Many Latin American novels simply exist as states of the imagination rooted in the landscape, history and legend of the region. They are mood pieces. Speaking about his celebrated *One Hundred Years of Solitude,* García Márquez said:

> I merely wanted to tell the story of a family who for a hundred years did everything they could to prevent having a son with a pig's tail.

The tangled skein linking the successive tiers of fantasy in Donoso's [*The Obscene Bird of Night*] is witchcraft. . . .

This novel, which took eight years to write, comes armed with a recommendation by Luis Buñuel. Still, at the risk of *lèse majesté* one must ask what it is all about. 'An indictment of a corrupt, doomed society,' the blurb trumpets. Without so much as a pig's tail to clutch at, there is, I suppose, always that interpretation to fall back on. . . .

Nearly all Latin American writing has the quality of being a virtuoso performance. The reader is trapped inside the writer's head. Occasionally, this may be diverting and even clever. [*The Obscene Bird of Night* illustrates] this tendency to literary acrobatics. But the fact is that surreal divagations and electronic adumbrations are not enough.

*Shiva Naipaul, in* New Statesman, *March 1, 1974, p. 300.*

* * *

## DOS PASSOS, John 1896-1970

**Dos Passos, an American novelist, is best known for the gigantic, innovative, *U.S.A.* trilogy, novels based on American social and economic conditions during the 1920's. (See also *Contemporary Authors*, Vols. 1-4, rev. ed.; obituary, Vols. 29-32.)**

The Communist critical movement in America . . . tended to identify their ideal with the work of John Dos Passos. In order to make this possible, it was necessary to invent an imaginary Dos Passos. This ideal Dos Passos was a Communist, who wrote stories about the proletariat, at a time when the real Dos Passos was engaged in bringing out a long novel about the effects of the capitalist system on the American middle class and had announced himself—in the *New Republic* in 1930—politically a 'middle-class liberal.' The ideal Dos Passos was something like Gorky without the mustache—Gorky, in the meantime, having himself undergone some transmogrification at the hands of Soviet publicity—and this myth was maintained until the Communist critics were finally compelled to repudiate it, not because they had acquired new light on Dos Passos, the novelist and dramatist, but because of his attitude toward events in Russia.

*Edmund Wilson, "Marxism and Literature," in* The Triple Thinkers: Twelve Essays on Literary Subjects *(reprinted with the permission of Farrar, Straus & Giroux, Inc.; copyright © 1938, 1948 by Edmund Wilson), Oxford University Press, revised edition, 1948, pp. 197-212 (in the Galaxy paperbound edition).*

[The] shadowy image of a brilliant purpose shows through in *Manhattan Transfer.* It can be seen in the complex panorama of many-sided life which gives the novel the look of having been photographed rather than written; it can be sensed in the quick, raw-nerved violence of the prose which, although it is not yet a "style," seems to have been compounded out of the same dirty concrete as that of the city it describes. It is present, particularly, in the truly remarkable energy and daring of Dos Passos' conception. But it is, as yet, blurred and undirected. The energy and the violence lead to nothing because they have no object. There is no frame in which they can be concentrated and no purpose which they can be used to serve.

For Dos Passos, at the time he wrote *Manhattan Transfer,* there seems to have been no cause great enough to impel him toward a supreme integration of his powers. He had all the vitality and insight he needed to produce a major work of art; and he certainly had all the idiosyncrasy and passion he needed. But he had to believe once more in the necessity of taking a stand, of affirming a principle, before he could display his powers in a way that would be more meaningful than a mere cataloguing of disgust.

It is generally believed that the bitterness engendered in Dos Passos by the injustice done to Sacco and Vanzetti provided him with the focus and purpose he needed to write his immense trilogy *U.S.A.* However true this may be, one can just as easily explain his achievement in that work in terms of natural creative evolution. . . .

[As] the result of the experiments he made in *Manhattan Transfer,* Dos Passos was able to return to the material he had begun to explore in that book and see in it implications which had previously escaped him. He sensed now that the real victims of the system were the working classes and that the real evils of the system stemmed from wealth and power. He was thus able to focus his sympathies upon a specific social group and set them against his hatred of another social group, just as in his earlier work he had focused his sympathies upon the individual aesthete and set them against his hatred of war. He was able to write now within the frame of two distinct and separate worlds, two nations, and to bring to his writing the full power of his protest (for he believed in the cause of the working classes as he had formerly believed in the cause of the aesthete) as well as the full power of his futility (for he knew, in spite of his belief in their cause, that the working classes under capitalism must always be defeated).

The dramatic intensity of *U.S.A.* derives from the perfect balance of these conflicting forces within Dos Passos. There is, on one side, the gradual corruption and defeat of the characters whose lives are depicted in the straight narrative sections. There is, on the other, the implicit indignation of the harsh, cutting style, which runs persistently counter to the drift of the narrative and comments upon it. Then, in the "Camera Eye" and "Biography" sections the style picks up additional counterforce. . . .

This hypothesis of universal ruin, introduced lyrically through the "Camera Eye" and historically through the "Biographies," is given dramatic proof in the narrative proper. Here all the social classes of *U.S.A.* are represented. There are J. Ward Moorehouse, Charley Anderson, Richard Ellsworth Savage, Eveline Hutchins, Eleanor Stoddard, the prototypes of privilege; and Joe Williams, Ben Compton, Mary French, the prototypes of unprivilege. Each has a different story, but all come to the same end. . . .

The U.S.A. which Dos Passos describes is thus more than simply a country or a way of life. It is a condition of death, a wasteland of futility and emptiness. In it, the best and the worst must be defeated; for defeat can be the only answer for the inhabitants of a world in which all goals are unattainable and the most powerful gods are corrupt. Yet, although the thing he describes is death, Dos Passos brings to his description a savage kind of power which saves it from becoming dead too. Through it all, he has consistently hated and condemned; and he has expressed his hatred with great strength and purpose. This has given meaning to the meaninglessness of his characters, value to their valuelessness. His style has been the perfect instrument of that meaning, protesting at every step in its development against the horror of the thing it was disclosing.

*John W. Aldridge, "Dos Passos: The Energy of Despair," in his* After the Lost Generation, *McGraw, 1951, pp. 70-6.*

The relation of the individual to society has consistently been the key problem for Dos Passos, both as writer and citizen; and his conviction that individual freedom was being lost within a steadily congealing social organism attracted him from the very beginning of his career to any expression of revolt. The revolt could be aesthetic or social, but preferably both simultaneously. . . . Dos Passos was not himself split between aesthetic and rebel [and] he did not see art and politics as antitheses, but as facets of a unified whole. . . .

[In *U.S.A.*] the historian, the artist, and the social rebel are fused. The trilogy is an acid analysis of thirty years of American capitalism, an analysis that envisages the country as split between the exploited and the exploiters; yet none of the fourteen characters important enough to carry the interwoven stories in their own names comes from other than the working class or the lower or middle layers of the middle class. What Dos Passos is concerned with is the efforts of ordinary people to survive in a business civilization and the disintegrative effect that such a civilization has upon them through their experience of economic injustice, war, and financial boom. The class analysis undoubtedly owes something to Marx, but the spirits of other men preside more powerfully here. As the trilogy develops, one sees that it is the history of the rise and incipient decline of yet another empire, chronicled with the ironic detachment of a twentieth-century Gibbon who happens also to be a novelist. More importantly, when one reaches *The Big Money,* the basis of Dos Passos's economic criticism becomes at last almost explicit, for it is in this third, climactic volume that he places the key "biography," that of Thorstein Veblen, whom he had read so much. . . . If one accepts the fact of Dos Passos's reliance on Veblen more than on Marx, it likewise becomes clear why there are no major characters from the owning class; they would simply be in the way of the author's intent. . . .

Because of its dependence for ideological basis on Veblen's

bitter drink, *U.S.A.* seems a somber and negative book; yet it contains a tentative affirmation. The positive hope of *U.S.A.* comes from Walt Whitman, of whose revolutionary quality Dos Passos [once] wrote. . . . Even more than in *Manhattan Transfer* one sees that Whitman's love of the American spoken word lies behind Dos Passos's own colloquial style in the stories, and like the poet, the novelist has tried to include, not just New York, but all America in his work. Equally important, Dos Passos looks for the cure of his sick country, not to a dictatorship of the proletariat, but to a restoration—the word is significant—of the democratic vista.

*Walter B. Rideout,* The Radical Novel in the United States 1900-1954, *Harvard University Press, 1956, pp. 157-62.*

A writer seldom retrieves a long-lost reputation at a single stroke, but John Dos Passos has probably done just that with *Midcentury,* by far his best novel since he completed the *U.S.A.* trilogy with *The Big Money* in 1936. It is written with a control of narrative styles, a grasp of character, and a sense of the American scene. In its fictional passages this panoramic novel recaptures the Dos Passos verve and intensity of a quarter-century ago, while the background sections, made up of sociological tidbits and pertinent biographical sketches, show much of the old Dos Passos skill at manipulating the devices which helped to give *U.S.A.* originality and force. . . .

In repeated, vigorous, and one-sided attacks on labor unions, Dos Passos hammers away at racketeering of the kind we all know exists. But he hardly suggests that there are good as well as evil unions. About three-fifths of the way through the volume, however, when the antiunion poundings threaten to become tiresome, he introduces two new and interesting characters, Jasper Milliron and his son-in-law, Willoughby Jenks, who take part in exciting battles at management levels where the villainy of unions is only incidental. In adding this dimension, Dos Passos proves again that he can write about business—which doesn't have to be a dull subject—better than anyone since Theodore Dreiser. The sequences concerned with it in *Midcentury* are worth a dozen grey-flannel-suit and executive-suite novels. Here the author gives fictional life to some of the phases of American civilization recently noted by popularizing sociologists, but he does so with pronounced individuality and the stamp of authority. If the sociologists look, with a scientific eye, at outwardly directed and herd-motivated men, Dos Passos regards them with deep pessimism and gloom—here projected fictionally in the downfall of Jasper Milliron and in the ensnaring of Will Jenks in an unhappy compromise.

Not that Dos Passos has ever been a cheerful writer. He began his career in the early 1920s with two despairing war books, long before such novels became fashionable. In 1925 his *Manhattan Transfer* displayed a gallery of unhappy city dwellers, but readers hardly noticed the mood of the book as they admired its cinematically shuttling episodes. This technique was elaborated in the "collective" novels comprising *U.S.A.,* which perhaps didn't really champion the masses so much as this author's enthusiasts of the time thought they did, but rather celebrated individualism.

With his next trilogy, *District of Columbia,* completed in 1949, Dos Passos suffered a loss in critical reputation and, presumably, in readers. It wasn't merely a matter of disagreement with the opinions he set forth, but rather, in most cases, with the excessively dogmatic and story-spoiling way in which he expressed them. *District of Columbia* and the novels following it lacked the concentrated power of *U.S.A.* and gave their readers almost no hint that the author had left in him the kind of imaginative energy that manifests itself in *Midcentury*. . . .

The prose of *Midcentury* has fewer color shadings than the earlier volumes. But it is recognizably Dos Passos' in its sparing use of the commas that hook a reader's eye and in its Joycean ramming together of words ("a shortnecked grayhaired man"). The writer's distinctive cadences are also noticeably present, in the choral chants of the biographies and, more emphatically, in the hard-surfaced narrative passages and in the crackling realism of the dialogue, all of it good American-built writing.

*Harry T. Moore, in* The New York Times Book Review *(© 1961 by The New York Times Company; reprinted by permission), February 26, 1961, p. 1.*

Of all the recorders of what happened last summer—or last decade—John Dos Passos is the most dogged. Not since the brothers Goncourt has there been such a dedication to getting down exactly what happened, and were it not for his political passions he might indeed have been a true camera to our time. He invents little; he fancies less. He is often good when he tells you something through which he himself has lived, and noted. He is well equipped to be a good social critic, which is the role he has cast for himself: conscience to the Republic, stern reminder of good ways lost, of useful ways not taken.

With what seems defiance, the first two pages of John Dos Passos's . . . novel *Midcentury* are taken up with the titles of his published work, proudly spaced, seventeen titles to the first page, sixteen to the second: thirty-three books, the work of some forty years. The list is testament to Dos Passos' gallantry, to his stubbornness, and to his worldly and artistic failure. . . . Admired extravagantly in the '20's and '30's, Dos Passos was largely ignored in the '40's and '50's, his new works passed over either in silence or else noted with that ritual sadness we reserve for those whose promise to art was not kept. He himself is aware of his own dilemma, and in a . . . novel called *The Great Days* he recorded with brave if bewildered objectivity a decline similar to his own. I shall not try to ring the more obvious changes suggested by his career. Yet I should note that there is something about Dos Passos which makes a fellow writer unexpectedly protective, partly out of compassion for the man himself, and partly because the fate of Dos Passos is a chilling reminder of those condemned to write for life that this is the way it almost always is in a society which, to put it tactfully, has no great interest in the development of writers, a process too slow for the American temperament. As a result our literature is rich with sprinters but significantly short of milers.

*Gore Vidal, "John Dos Passos at Midcentury" (originally published in* Esquire, *May, 1961), in his* Homage to Daniel Shays: Collected Essays 1952-1972 *(copyright © 1960,*

*1961, 1971 by Gore Vidal; reprinted by permission of Random House, Inc.), Random House, 1972, pp. 96-102.*

No American writer has attempted more, and few writers anywhere have brought to successful completion novels of the size and scope of *U.S.A.* Dos Passos' ambition was impossibly grandiose, and as an attempt to present in fictional terms the development of American society from 1900 to 1929, *U.S.A.* was doomed to at least partial failure. Yet it remains, for all its faults, the fullest and most impressive fictional treatment of that period, and it firmly establishes Dos Passos's claim to be considered the most important social novelist since Dreiser.

Dos Passos is a more subtle writer than Steinbeck, but we can recognise something of the same attitude—individualistic, agrarian, fundamentally conservative—throughout his work. In almost all his novels there is an underlying emotional commitment, closely akin to Veblen's and not unlike that in such novels as Howells's *A Hazard of New Fortunes* and Anderson's *Poor White,* which finds its most nearly explicit statement in one of the later books, *The Grand Design* (1949), the final section of the *District of Columbia* trilogy.

*Michael Millgate, "John Dos Passos (© 1964 by Michael Millgate), in his* American Social Fiction: James to Cozzens, *Oliver & Boyd, 1964, pp. 128-41.*

Dos Passos' most significant image of the man on the road as representative of America is the anonymous youth of the prose-poem entitled "Vag" which caps *The Big Money.* For this somewhat improbably seedy hitchhiker, the road reveals only defeat and Dos Passos' repulsion. . . .

The punch, the slam, the grab, the twist, the snarl—"the big knee brought up sharp into the crotch"—come not just from the cop who roughed up the poor vag but from all of American "history [as] the billion-dollar speedup." This violent motion without catharsis is the intellectual theme of Dos Passos, and one which leaves no individual freedom of experience, on the road or in the sky. The broad social perception and compassionate anger presented in the image of the vagrant frenziedly turns apotheosis to stink and abstraction. The narrowing of responsiveness—in Dos Passos and more generally in literary naturalism—reveals a revulsive obsession with failure which may also be the inversion of the pathological American insistence on success. Curiously, the hobo as more victim than rebel, which recurs in so much moralistic American fiction—as a case of social fatality and stinking pathos without sensibility or elan—denigrates the impetus to rebel and wander outside.

*Kingsley Widmer, in his* The Literary Rebel *(copyright © 1965 by Southern Illinois University Press; reprinted by permission of Southern Illinois University Press), Carbondale: Southern Illinois University Press, 1965, p. 117.*

Dos Passos' novels are out of fashion at the moment, partly because his later work is inferior to the work he did in the thirties, but largely because the sense of private reality is momentarily the fashion in the intellectual marketplace, where an astonishing number of one-time intellectual Leftists are busy burning their old political draft cards for newspaper reporters and making a public career out of the happy conviction that their private experience—especially of political events—is not as that of other men. But this violent shift of attitude among the couturiers of the intellectual world ought not to conceal from us the importance for the American novel of Dos Passos' work or of the sense of reality it expresses. . . .

Despite Dos Passos' commitment [in *The Big Money*] to the kind of outer reality represented by social history, despite his sympathy with the radical political tradition that has persisted throughout American history, he writes neither social history nor political propaganda. Behind his image of American society in the 1920's is an image of human experience as a whole; behind his political dislike of the Big Money is a despair of the human situation itself that justifies Malcolm Cowley's description of *The Big Money* as "a furious and sombre poem." If his wonderfully particularized, brilliantly organized portrait of America in the boom years of the twenties shows us what the Big Money does to simple, hopeful Americans, it also suggests what organized society does to all such men in all times.

Dos Passos is the only major American novelist of the twentieth century who has had the desire and the power to surround the lives of his characters with what Lionel Trilling once called "the buzz of history"—the actual, homely, everyday sounds of current events and politics, of social ambitions and the struggle for money, of small pleasures and trivial corruptions, amidst which we all live. He has given us an image of a major aspect of our experience that has hardly been touched by any other novelist of our time.

*Arthur Mizener, "John Dos Passos: 'The Big Money'," in his* Twelve Great American Novels *(copyright © 1967 by Arthur Mizener; reprinted by arrangement with The New American Library, Inc., New York, New York), New American Library, 1967, pp. 87-103.*

Dos Passos . . . is a tireless social commentator, whatever the genre. The introduction to his collected plays is a diatribe against the commercial theater, which is disparagingly compared to a socially meaningful theater. . . .

His first play, *The Garbage Man,* was written in 1923, before Dos Passos had found his fictional voice. Like O'Neill, Wolfe, and Elmer Rice, Dos Passos at this period saw Expressionism as a more viable form than Realism in which to register social protest. German Expressionist plays tend to be stridently social (e.g. Toller) or, stemming more directly from Strindberg, to focus on the poetic quest of the protagonist (e.g. Kaiser's *From Morn to Midnight*). Dos Passos mixes the two streams, and writes a confusing play. . . .

Dos Passos' Production Note indicates that he feels the play rests upon popular forms such as musical comedy, but, far from popular, the dialogue of the protagonists is painfully literary. A poetic quest play demands a poet—Brecht's *Baal,* Strindberg's *Road to Damascus,* even Williams' *Camino Real*—but Dos Passos is a journalist. What we best remember in Dos Passos' novels are the journalistic inserts that build a society—the Camera Eye, headlines, biographies. But the maudlin love story of *The Garbage Man* barely reflects the society in the background, while the dialogue is inflated by pseudo-poetry and Expressionist sighs.

Dos Passos clings to realism in his next two plays, the one focused on a family and the other on a place. *Airways, Inc.* (1928), as its title suggests, deals with a big business corporation, but it deals even more with the disintegration of a family under capitalism. . . .

The play is agit-prop melodrama: capitalist sympathizers are stupid and vicious, whereas the few radicals are humane and selfless. Unlike old-fashioned theatrical melodrama, however, violence is banished off stage, while the dialogue rambles on stage. . . . Neither image nor rhythm is distinctive. . . .

Though Dos Passos avoids direct didacticism in his Depression play, *Fortune Heights* (1933), the diction is again dull, because Dos Passos has no ability to make us care about his characters. Or perhaps we find their diction dull because we do not care about his characters. There is, of course, no more facile criticism than to say that a play has or has not convincing or credible characters. And yet, this is a particular problem of realistic drama with a social orientation, if it is not to be a tract in dialogue form. We may debate about whether or not *Death of a Salesman* is a tragedy, but we do so only because we care about Willy. We may or may not respond to a play with Aristotelian pity and terror, but if we do not respond with *any* emotion, mere dialogue cannot create a drama. . . . [In *Fortune Heights* the] hesitant speech of Dos Passos' mid-westerners recalls that of O'Neill's New Englanders, but Dos Passos is never able to focus on the large, dramatic character; his eyes are busily darting all over the worn canvas. . . .

At about the time he wrote *Fortune Heights,* Dos Passos was working on *USA,* where he found the journalistic voice for which he is celebrated; he conveys a cross section of a big city in the grip of depression, through Camera Eye, Newsreel, biographies, legends, headlines. And he had the wisdom not to attempt drama again.

*Ruby Cohn, "John Dos Passos," in her* Dialogue in American Drama, *Indiana University Press, 1971, pp. 179-83.*

Never forgetting his initial indoctrination in aesthetics at Harvard—in the midst of that Eliot-Cummings-Hillyer coterie—Dos Passos has striven to advance his theses with artfulness as well as indignation. As a consequence, his works demonstrate technical inventiveness and a freshness of style which, along with their "message," give them life —indeed, enable them to contribute to the maturing of twentieth-century American fiction. . . .

It is in *U.S.A.* that Dos Passos is seen to greatest advantage, both as an "architect of history" and as a skillful novelist. The trilogy, covering the years from 1899 to 1929, develops the theme of power throughout, illustrating how the corporation (for example, the United Fruit Company) thwarts the individual and produces economic injustice, how war is a moral cheat and a waste, how "socialism" fails to benefit the common man. The woes of the country are summed up for Dos Passos in the Sacco-Vanzetti case, the clearest violation, he felt, of America's fundamental principle of individual liberty. . . .

The trilogy, growing stronger and more fierce as it progresses, steadily develops the author's thesis that the world is a gray horror, filled with oppression, inequity, and false values. War and war profiteering, the bludgeoning of strikers, the abrupt dispatching of undesirable aliens, are the norm. At the center lies the Ward Moorehouse success story, the Fords and Samuel Insulls in the forefront, the Randolph Bournes and Joe Hills in the rear, the working people disregarded. Benjamin Disraeli's "two nations" have come to roost in America.

Though Dos Passos does not register his opinion about all this directly in *U.S.A.,* preferring to preserve the documentary approach and the objective narrative pattern, still, the reader can detect his tone and must define it as disillusioned, and decidedly so. . . .

We are reminded that the work falls within the tradition of polemical writing, demonstrating both the virtues and the vices of the genre, a clarity, gusto, and force on the one hand, an excessive degree of denunciation and one-sidedness on the other. If impressed by the moving account of the Sacco-Vanzetti trial, one is at the same time distressed by the unfair portrait of Wilson as a hypocritical politician. If appreciative of the brilliant vigor of the Body of an American profile, one is at the same time bothered by the occasional didactic statement ("And you ask why the prestige of our nation has sunk so low in the world") or oversimplification (for example, Franklin Roosevelt as a power-hungry Caesar). Happily, Dos Passos avoids, for the most part, the shortcomings of "exposure literature," refusing to employ its rhetoric, character manipulation, and too simple structure and relying instead upon an original and lively technique. . . .

His concern for technique is repeatedly demonstrated in *U.S.A.,* reflected, for one thing, in his utilization of a carefully thought out form. He sets up an elaborate structural pattern for the work, a scheme of enormous scope and containing multiple elements, most notably his four pioneering devices, the newsreels, Camera Eyes, profiles, and intertwined "life histories." All these function as separate entities yet at the same time fuse to enforce the leading ideas, lift and enliven the narrative, and produce a strong sense of mood. Above all, they bring into focus what is finally the book's protagonist—or antagonist—twentieth-century American civilization.

The newsreel sections, consisting of headlines, songs, slogans, and advertisements, serve to establish chronology and to create mood. Mixing the trite with the crucial, showing the inconsistencies in the American public image ("Army casualties soar," "peace dove in jewels given Mrs. Wilson"), they generally convey a sense of the shoddy, restless wartime and postwar boom period.

Perhaps more interesting because less mechanically ironic and more specific are the Camera Eye passages. Written in a semi-stream-of-consciousness style, they are primarily devoted to an impressionistic rendering of the author's autobiography, yet they, too, establish time and atmosphere, giving some sense of how the private life is of a piece with the culture complex. The satirical mood often predominates, with reflections on the horrors of war as felt by a participant and on the absolute futility of his postwar military activity of piling scrap. Most charged with emotion, indeed a prose poem, is the Sacco-Vanzetti section in *The Big Money,* expressing intense unhappiness about the injustices cropping up in the American "way of life." As a rule, however, the Camera Eye confines itself to reflecting the character of the author, partly the sensitive artist but partly, too, the "protestant," questioning the assumptions of the genteel bourgeois class to which he belonged. . . .

The substance of the novels stems, of course, from the fourth device, the series of fictional biographies, twelve in all, which crisscross through the trilogy. Almost invariably recording a drifting, meaningless existence, the sketches attach to the individual destiny a strong sense of futility. . . .

The panoramic format of *U.S.A.,* with the special devices for the most part deftly inserted and with a swift and flexible narrative sustained throughout, works well for Dos Passos. The structure has the fragmented chaotic quality needed to accentuate the fractured lives and fractured values. The tumbled-together headlines of the newsreels, sensory ramblings of the Camera Eyes, rushed phrasing of the profiles—all accentuate a headlong pace, one which crystallizes the concept of going nowhere, of lives involved in a weary treadmill.

In keeping with the mood of the work, the style and language employed by the author are almost uniformly flat. Perhaps the method might be called documentary-graphic or the deadpan voice. Enlivening this, however, is a staccatolike rhythm, achieved through the Dos Passos reliance on short paragraphs, sentence fragments, and a general lack of formal syntax and punctuation, and producing an impressively harsh, spasmodic effect. The controlling principle of the style appears to be directness, the nuances and shadings eschewed. Whether setting forth a character description, an action sequence, or a propaganda speech, Dos Passos uses simple language, often resorting to colloquialisms and profanity and rather seldom introducing an image or a figure of speech. . . . Conceivably, the flatness causes a certain sense of monotony over the long span of the trilogy, but it usually succeeds in accentuating the vapidity and aimlessness and in heightening the irony (for example, the final lines of the Unknown Soldier profile—"Woodrow Wilson brought a bouquet of poppies"). The flatness is relieved, too, by the strong epithet ("toadfaced young man"), the chantlike repetitions, and the usually suitable talk of the characters (the vaporous phrasing of the "laborfaker" Barrow, the polished drawl of Judge Cassidy). The jargon and popular rhythms of the newsreel, the brisk fragments of the profiles, and the more image-strewn Camera Eye passages, filled with sounds and colors, contribute to the variety as well. Dos Passos's survey of the restless, simmering urban American environment is effected in wiry, terse, appropriately restless prose.

*W. Gordon Milne, "John Dos Passos (1896-1970)," in* The Politics of Twentieth-Century Novelists, *edited by George A. Panichas (reprinted by permission of Hawthorn Books, Inc.; © 1971 by The University of Maryland; all rights reserved), Hawthorn, 1971, pp. 263-77.*

The trilogy of novels recording what he learned from his travels is an impressive work that embodies a paradox. Dos Passos was primarily interested in presenting his *material*—that is, in offering a panorama of American life at all levels over a period of thirty years. But no previous novelist had found a method of painting such a panorama. Tolstoy? one asks. His *War and Peace* had achieved a breadth beyond the dreams of other novelists, but even Tolstoy had devoted most of his attention to four great families of the Russian nobility. Dos Passos wanted to present typical persons from many levels of society, giving sharp attention to each—even using their special idioms—while suggesting the movement of society as a whole. To do so he was forced to invent devices of his own. . . . There were to be hundreds of characters, but the substance of the novel would be the life stories of twelve more or less typical men and women. . . . At this point . . . [he] was setting out to make himself a master technician.

The paradox is that the technique, much more than the observed material it was designed to present, has had an effect on literary history in more than one country. Dos Passos' picture of America succumbing to decay as competitive capitalism gave way to monopoly capitalism is powerful, but in the end subjective; one is not obliged to accept his notion of a catastrophic decline and fall. One has to acknowledge, however, that his technical inventions soon reappeared in the mainstream of fiction. *The Grapes of Wrath, The Naked and the Dead,* and scores of other American novels . . . have owed a debt to Dos Passos for solving some of their problems in advance. So have novels by famous Europeans, as Jean-Paul Sartre explained in the *Atlantic Monthly*:

> . . . it was after reading a book by Dos Passos that I thought for the first time of weaving a novel out of various, simultaneous lives. . . .

[Nothing] he wrote after *U.S.A.* had the same widespread and lasting effect. . . .

His loss of literary stature might tempt one into making a false generalization about fiction and politics. Dos Passos was a radical and wrote works of great inventiveness and power; then he became conservative and produced such bald, embittered tracts as *Most Likely to Succeed* and *The Great Days*; so therefore—but that is entirely too simple. The history of fiction seems to show that great novelists can hold almost any sort of position, radical or conservative, aristocratic or egalitarian; they can be monarchists like Balzac or angry reformers like Dickens, or they can shift positions like Dostoyevsky without necessarily harming their work—but on one absolute condition, that they should believe in their characters more firmly than they hold to their opinions. Dos Passos in his later work often failed to meet that condition, and there too he broke another rule that seems to have been followed by great novelists. They can regard their characters with love or hate or anything between, but cannot regard them with tired aversion. They can treat events as tragic, comic, farcical, pathetic, or almost anything but consistently repulsive. . . .

In . . . books he published during the later years there are admirable passages, though it must be added that almost all of them are retrospective. . . . It is as if [he] were saying that the best times were all in the past, or as if, in the various prospect of desolation, he could not bear to contemplate his literary decline and fall.

*Malcolm Cowley, "Dos Passos: The Learned Poggius" (originally published in* The Southern Review, *Vol. IX, No. 1, Winter, 1973), in his* A Second Flowering *(copyright © 1973 by Malcolm Cowley; reprinted by permission of The Viking Press, Inc.), Viking, 1973, pp. 88-9.*

[We] have yet to account for the contradictory qualities of [Dos Passos'] best work, *U.S.A.*, for example, which presents a fictive world dominated by failure and frustration that nevertheless dazzles us with its energy and vitality. No one yet has come to grips with the significance of the fact that an apparently political novelist presents us with instance after instance of the futility of political action. . . . Dos Passos' ideas about political action and the exercise of power have an important source, not in an historian or political theorist or even in another novelist, but in a poet, Walt Whitman. . . .

In Camera Eye (46) of *U.S.A.*, Dos Passos identifies with Whitman in a context which throws . . . light on this question of the incongruity of such a political vision. . . . Dos Passos' shame at the futility of what he is asking men less well off than he is to do is mixed both with self-contempt and a somewhat mocking though essentially serious rededication to a task he is not at all sure can be accomplished. He sharply differentiates the world where men fight for power and get their heads broken from the sheltered room where the power is reached for theoretically, and democracy is fiction, not history. . . .

The worthlessness of the highflying America, the America which overtook and replaced imperial Britain in the American century, and of all who spiritually live in her, is one great theme of Dos Passos' work. The other is the articulation of the true, obscured America, in the double sense of giving it a voice and a definition, thereby bringing it into existence. All the true American possesses in Dos Passos' vision is his voice and his hunger. It is, in a sense, astonishing that the very great vitality, abundance, and excitement of the book should emerge from so many stories of disappointment and defeat. . . .

Dos Passos' sense of history ill-disguises the notion of a legendary golden age analogous to Whitman's primal innocence . . . and his goal, like that of Whitman's voyage, is a return to that original purity and unity, to "storybook democracy." . . . Clearly such a belief in a golden age is necessary for the fervid characterization of the world of power that he gives us as well as for the fidelity to the voice of the submerged groups which is one of the triumphs of *U.S.A.* But it is myth, not history; it generates expressive and rhetorical power, not political. For . . . equally fundamental in Dos Passos is the belief in the ultimate impassibility from history to myth, diversity to unity.

*Lois Hughson, "In Search of the True America: Dos Passos' Debt to Whitman in 'U.S.A.'," in* Modern Fiction Studies *(© 1973, by Purdue Research Foundation, West Lafayette, Indiana), Summer, 1973, pp. 179-92.*

Generations of bright high school kids learned their attitudes toward manliness, love, and style from Hemingway, Fitzgerald, and Steinbeck; and toward America from James T. Farrell and John Dos Passos. As the America they defined has frayed, Farrell and Dos Passos have joined the general neglect. Some may recall that Dos Passos followed an orbit of youthful estheticism toward a burning socialism to a final distaste for the ugliness of the time that was more than a reversion to preciosity. Ultimately, he became something of a right-winger and wrote novels that have been dismissed as the maundering complaints and naggings of an aging mandarin. As he wrote of his own father, he knew "the loneliness of one who has outlived his generation." . . .

*USA* and other books of Dos Passos's prime are not read very much any more, but those familiar Modern Library editions helped to form the generation of writers now garnering the fame and esteem for which Dos Passos longed and which, briefly, like them, he tasted. Despite his political drift and a curious self-indulgent privacy of style, a personal isolation unpenetrated by this book [*The Fourteenth Chronicle*], his concern with individual liberty was constant. . . .

Decline is probably a merely conventional way to characterize the shift in Dos Passos's approach to interpreting American life. He was more consistent than we realized. His first radical work is animated by boyish bitterness and anger—combined with the youthful ambition to make a literary mark. The later conservative or right-wing work is animated by aging bitterness and anger—combined with the older man's desire to take a few revenges on a time that has passed him by. What remains constant, and of constant value in a writer who never quite achieved his ambitions, is a passion that might be derived from both the paltriest and the deepest of sources: the sense of his unique self. His libertarian views, his lyrical privacy, his belief in the primacy of will—never fully dramatized in his novels—are most touching. They come clear in these letters and notes [*The Fourteenth Chronicle*] as they never did in his more ponderous constructions. Mauriac said that the poet can be defined as the soul of a boy carried in the body of a man. Dos Passos hid his poet's soul in the practice of stylish politics, make-work journalism, and one striking effort at an all-encompassing vision of America. He left behind him neither a perfectly exemplary work nor an exemplary life, but how many writers leave either?

*Herbert Gold, "The Literary Lives of John Dos Passos," in* Saturday Review/World *(copyright © 1973 by Saturday Review/World, Inc.; reprinted with permission), September 11, 1973, pp. 32, 34-5.*

*"America our nation has been beaten by strangers who have turned our language inside out who have taken the clean words our fathers spoke and made them slimy and foul . . . we stand defeated America."*

One of time's ironies is that these passages from Camera Eye (50) in *The Big Money* are probably John Dos Passos' most remembered words; and yet, given to students today, they would likely be identified as belonging to Allen Ginsberg's "America" poem. Triggered by the Sacco-Vanzetti execution, they represent the furthest left position in Dos Passos' political thinking; his arrival at that point and his consequent turn to the right are movingly documented in *The Fourteenth Chronicle,* a large (643 pages) collection of Dos Passos' letters and diary entries covering 60 years, 1910-1970.

The comparison with Ginsberg is not gratuitous, though the elder Dos Passos would have disliked it. Dos Passos was in many ways a poet manqué (his diary is filled with poems) and his early letters, which compose the bulk of *The Fourteenth Chronicle,* often read remarkably like the travel poems in Ginsberg's *The Fall of America*: sharp descriptions of the sounds, sights, smells and tastes encountered on Dos Passos' endless wanderings through Europe, Asia, Africa and, finally, America. This book shows him to be in that main American tradition beginning with Whitman that seeks to grasp the American experience by accumulation of detail, by great width and scope, by swallowing America whole, as it were, rather than carving out deep chunks from certain sections as his friends Hemingway, Fitzgerald, Faulkner and Cummings did.

Two reasons for Dos Passos' lack of popular success (compared to, say, Hemingway and Fitzgerald) are the negative thrust of his work—he always insisted his writing was satirical—and his failure to create characters with whom readers could identify either themselves or the author. He never became a personality like his friends, and in the endless stream of anecdotes about the "lost generation" writers, Dos Passos was always the one who was listening while Cummings regaled the company with his wit and musical improvisations or who watched while Hemingway battled the huge marlin and the sharks that were made famous in *The Old Man and the Sea.* My favorite picture of Dos Passos is in Carlos Baker's *Ernest Hemingway,* where Dos Passos looks like the poor squire to the resplendently ski-clad Hemingway and Gerald Murphy.

*The Fourteenth Chronicle* should help in fleshing out Dos Passos for his readers. And while the book is ultimately sad, with the elderly out-of-step writer exclaiming that "the rank idiocy of the younger generation is more than I can swallow" (echoing a letter of his father's 56 years earlier), the main impression one gets from reading it is that of a decent and generous man of boundless enthusiasm and energy; if a satirist is a romantic with 20/20 vision, Dos Passos fits the description.

His writing reflects a natural blend of theory with personality; personally modest and shy, he replaced Whitman's cosmic and Ginsberg's orgasmic "I" with his "Camera Eye," the main stylistic influences being Flaubert, Joyce, Eisenstein and Hemingway. Dos Passos' multiple-protagonist novels in turn became very influential, leading to Norman Mailer's *The Naked and the Dead* and the wave of New Journalists. But where the latter tend to be marked by self-indulgence or self-display, Dos Passos' style retains its basic objectivity and intelligence, even in his later works. . . .

Dos Passos was congenitally allergic to abstract formulae—he had the poet's distrust of words—and the letters [in *The Fourteenth Chronicle*] deal with events, adventures, battles with censors, his long fight against rheumatic fever, impressions of cities, reports of friends, etc. Whenever he lectures or makes some general statement about life, literature or politics, he invariably tacks on some disclaimer, notably "This is all bullshit!" The letters show over and over that he was attached to people, not dogma or schools or slogans; he constantly refused to join the Communist Party even while he saw it as the hope for the future. Just as his left turn, and much of his early writing, was focused by Sacco-Vanzetti, his turn to the right was incurred in large part by the Communist assassination of Dos Passos' Spanish friend José Robles in 1936. (This event, fictionalized in *Adventures of a Young Man,* 1939, also ended his close friendship with Hemingway; Dos Passos could remain friends despite ideological differences, but Hemingway couldn't.) . . .

All along Dos Passos insists that he has *not* changed his stance, that he has always fought for the "individual's rights," for the worker, against Big Business *(USA),* Big Government *(District of Columbia),* Big Labor *(Midcentury).* His strong stand against Russia reflects his belief not that capitalism is good, but that it's better than communism. One of his letters about the oppressiveness of Russia, which he visited in 1928, reads remarkably like a recently published letter by Alexander Solzhenitsyn. In fact many of Dos Passos' letters (the artist as prophet) have a distinctly contemporary sound. . . . The few letters that actually *are* contemporary, written shortly before his death in 1970, sound like a more generous, lower-keyed William Buckley (in fact the last letter in the book is a recommendation that Buckley be admitted to the Century Association). . . .

One feels growing in Dos Passos a clear intellect, a sympathy with the downtrodden that is not sentimental, an integrity that is not dogmatic, a belief in hard work without self-pity. . . .

I think that Dos Passos succeeded in writing several "permanent" books *(Three Soldiers,* the USA trilogy, *Manhattan Transfer)* and that much of his other writing is greatly underestimated. I hope that this important book will send readers back to Dos Passos.

*Peter Meinke, "Swallowing America Whole," in* The New Republic *(reprinted by permission of* The New Republic; *© 1973 by Harrison-Blaine of New Jersey, Inc.), September 22, 1973, pp. 28-31.*

The best letters have always been written for a purpose of some importance to the author: letters edged with desperation, like Scott Fitzgerald's, or set out as if they were essays, like Shaw's. The best of these collections do more than add to our knowledge of the author's life; they are an extension, however informal or involuntary, of his work. As much cannot be claimed for [*The Fourteenth Chronicle*]. John Dos Passos's letters are of excellent value to students of his life and of the remarkable generation of which he was a part, and they show him to be both a good and an energetic man, but they are rarely of literary interest in themselves. "Letters are largely written to get things out of your system," Dos Passos wrote, but little of what he wanted to purge himself of seems particularly striking, or even original, now.

Dos Passos—who will be remembered for such novels as "Three Soldiers," "Manhattan Transfer" and the trilogy "U.S.A."—wanted even in 1917 to create a new form in fiction: "I'm dying to write—but all my methods of doing things in the past merely disgust me now. . . . The stream of sensation flows by—I suck it up like a sponge—my reactions are a constant weather vane." It is an accurate appraisal of himself, but like so much of what he wrote in these letters, it is expressed in mangled clichés, such as "See all you can, do all you can, eat all you can," and so on. . . .

[In] the '30s, after he had recovered from his leftist despair of the country's future, he wrote remarkably sensible statements about Communism, which, in its Stalinist guise, he correctly saw to be the obverse of the Fascist coin. "I'm now at last convinced," he wrote early in 1935, "that means cant be disassociated from ends." He was right, of course, but the writers whom he knew at the time tended to disagree. . . .

And when he reached the end of his life, and wrote in defense of the invasion of Cambodia, he was long past his best days of defending the little man against the juggernaut.

*Peter S. Prescott, "Long Trip With a Good Man," in* Newsweek *(copyright Newsweek, Inc., 1973; reprinted by permission), October 15, 1973, pp. 107, 110, 112.*

In 1938 Jean Paul Sartre concluded his extraordinary essay on "John Dos Passos and '1919'" with the statement, "Dos Passos' world—like those of Faulkner, Kafka and Stendhal—is impossible because it is contradictory. But therein lies its beauty. Beauty is a veiled contradiction. I regard Dos Passos as the greatest writer of our time." The judgment startles, no matter how often one reads it. Who in the United States has ever thought of Dos Passos in such terms? Even in 1938, when the novels in the *U.S.A.* trilogy were just being put under one cover and *Manhattan Transfer* and *Three Soldiers* still seemed new and exciting, Dos Passos was seen essentially as the writer who (in Alfred Kazin's words) "rounds out the story of (the lost) generation and carries its values into the social novel of the thirties." And now, more than 30 years later, the question to be asked is not whether anyone but Sartre ever thought of Dos Passos as our greatest writer, but whether anyone still thinks of him at all. . . .

The publication of *The Fourteenth Chronicle* is not likely to alter the situation. . . . [It] is more tedious, and less informative, than any of Dos Passos's later (and least interesting) books. Of course Dos Passos knew most of the literary figures of his time: Anderson, Fitzgerald, Dreiser, Hemingway, Cummings, Wilson, Cowley, Dwight MacDonald, John Howard Lawson and so on, and letters to all of them are included. And, indeed, Dos Passos seems to have been witness to many important political and social events of the time. . . . But none of this can compensate for the fact that he was neither a very interesting nor a particularly revelatory writer of letters.

What is most distressing about *The Fourteenth Chronicle* is that there is little . . . which explains why Dos Passos, like most American novelists, was unable to sustain the level of his craft as he grew older. . . . [What] we get in this collection of letters and diaries is the chronicle—"a kind of autobiography," as the editor sees it—of a gentle man of letters who enjoys traveling but who, for all the good will in the world, seldom rises above the banal. Whether he is writing to a Walter Rumsey Marvin, Dudley Poore, or Edmund Wilson, Dos Passos more often than not sounds as if he is a character in a Dreiser novel. . . .

Perhaps *Century's Ebb,* completed just before Dos Passos's death and due for publication next year, will help us understand why Sartre wrote that he knew of no writer whose art "is more precious, more touching or closer to us" than that of Dos Passos.

*Jack Salzman, "Portrait of the Artist as a Dog," in* Book World—The Washington Post *(©* The Washington Post*), October 28, 1973, p. 4.*

*   *   *

## DÜRRENMATT, Friedrich 1921-

**Dürrenmatt is a Swiss dramatist, novelist, and painter. His powerful, sometimes shocking, plays examine the plight of men forced to contend with a hostile society. (See also *Contemporary Authors*, Vols. 17-18.)**

When *The Visit* opened on Broadway on May 5, 1958, it was an instant success, and the name of Friedrich Dürrenmatt, known throughout Europe for some years, was suddenly brought to the attention of the American theater world. So profound an impression did this one play make that Dürrenmatt has shot up in the estimation of American theater people to a place on a level with Jean Anouilh as one of Europe's foremost current dramatic authors.

Dürrenmatt's plays can be characterized as fantasies from which lessons may be learned. . . . Philosophy, Dürrenmatt insists, cannot be transmitted through drama. He feels that the theater exists solely as a medium for the creation of a special world—that the audience, in other words, comes to peep in at a new, wonderful, and strange world, a contrived set of circumstances in which fantastic things can happen quite as matter-of-factly as the spectators wistfully wish they might in real life. Beyond this Dürrenmatt refuses to go. He maintains that he does not care what lesson may be drawn from his plays, if any. Like T. S. Eliot, he is often enlightened as to the inner meaning of his works by reading the critics. His own attitude is simply that each person will choose from these created worlds whatever appears desirable or useful to him.

All of Dürrenmatt's created worlds seem to fasten upon and revolve (in a manner sometimes savage and bitter, sometimes impersonal and amused, sometimes ferociously jocular—but always detached and bitingly sardonic) around death. In Dürrenmatt's works death seems to be almost personified—a vague, grey shape leaning mockingly over the shoulders of his leading characters and edging them slyly on. . . . Death is the culmination of life, but it is an anticlimactic and basically insignificant culmination. A process that culminates in an anticlimax can only be treated as a ridiculous joke. Hence the mordantly sardonic, lacerating note in Dürrenmatt's plays—"Man is ridiculous because he must die." Dürrenmatt's world is like a Punch and Judy show in which audience and puppeteer are part of the ridiculous antics. . . .

Throughout his works Dürrenmatt has a viewpoint that can best be described as sardonic. Dürrenmatt is a disillusioned analyst of the human character. Even the plays with political themes are ultimately about the human beings rather than the issues. Like Ionesco, like Beckett, like all the writers of the dramatic avant-garde in fact, Dürrenmatt feels deep down in himself that the problems of humanity are insoluble. And so he takes refuge from this knowledge in a mordantly sardonic portrayal of life. He himself remains detached. . . .

Although Dürrenmatt derives his technique more from Thornton Wilder than from Antonin Artaud and the surrealists, he does resemble the authors of the current dramatic avant-garde in that his plays are dominated by the two qualities of protest and paradox. Dürrenmatt's two main themes are based on (i) the paradox that the power to do good corrupts the doer so that the goodness is negated and the power becomes purely evil; and (ii) the paradox that the omnipresence of death renders human acts trivial. What distinguishes Dürrenmatt from Beckett, who also feels that the events of life are basically meaningless, is that Beckett feels this to the point where he asserts that all events are flattened out and equally insignificant, whereas Dürrenmatt does recognize that events may have an immediate significance to those affected. . . . Nothing is inevitable and determined in Dürrenmatt. The fact that things are insignificant from a cosmic viewpoint does not alter the fact that they are significant in the immediate present: it merely argues that they are finally insoluble and will always repeat themselves.

*George Wellwarth, "Friedrich Dürrenmatt: The Sardonic View," in his* The Theater of Protest and Paradox: Developments in the Avant-Garde Drama *(reprinted by permission of New York University Press; copyright © 1964 by New York University), New York University Press, 1964, pp. 134-61.*

Dürrenmatt's writing owes much to the German tradition of grotesque fantasy: Kafka, E. T. A. Hoffmann, Büchner, and Wedekind are among his literary forebears. But there is an Anglo-Saxon streak in Dürrenmatt as well; he owes much to the English detective novel which also takes murder for granted in the most well-ordered of middle-class societies; and his vein of anachronistically ironic treatments of historical or mythological subjects is clearly based on Shaw.

An affluent, highly mechanized society, teeming as it may be with violence, cannot, in Dürrenmatt's view, give rise to tragedy because it is so mechanized that violence happens by remote control. There is no responsibility in an ant heap, and there can be no tragedy without responsibility: "In the muddle of our century," Dürrenmatt has said, "there are no longer guilty or responsible human beings. Everybody claims that *he* is not to blame, that *he* did not want it to happen. And indeed, things would have happened without anyone in particular doing anything about making them happen. We are far too collectively guilty, far too collectively embedded in the sins of our fathers and of their fathers. We are merely the children of their children. That's our bad luck, not our guilt. Guilt presupposes personal action, a religious act. Only comedy can deal with *us*. Our world has led us into the realm of the grotesque, as it has led us to the atom bomb; just as the apocalyptic paintings of Hieronymus Bosch are also merely grotesque." . . .

And so Dürrenmatt confronts his audiences with a world that may be horrifying and grotesque but that, he hopes, they will face with courage and a sense of humor.

*Martin Esslin, "The Neurosis of the Neutrals: II. Friedrich Dürrenmatt," in his* Reflections: Essays on Modern Theatre *(copyright © 1961, 1962, 1963, 1966, 1967, 1968, 1969 by Martin Esslin; reprinted by permission of Doubleday & Co., Inc.), Doubleday, 1969, pp. 107-14.*

Friedrich Dürrenmatt has been celebrated for the ingenuity of his plots. . . . Equally ingenious is the catalogue of names, principally for the dramatis personae, which he has devised for his plays. Dürrenmatt's names run the gamut in inventiveness. . . . The variety manifest in "Dürrenmatt's delight in evocative names" points, it would seem, to his basic concept of the function of the theater and the characters in a play. Although he has protested that he means to put living beings on the stage . . ., he concerns himself in his plays primarily with ideas. . . . Basically, the label Dürrenmatt has chosen for his plays—tragicomedy—makes clear his intent to paint the complexity of the individual only in broad, satiric strokes (as the artist Dürrenmatt's pictures indicate, too).

That some of his dramatis personae are only types Dürrenmatt makes clear by identifying them no further than as to their function or relationship. . . . The tendency to abstract and to limit characterization so as to regard only relationships germane to the situation in the play predominates in the work of the expressionists, Dürrenmatt's immediate predecessors in creative writing for the stage and his models, among others. . . .

While unnamed characters occur in many plays, they never preponderate. As a salient feature, there are the fanciful names, based on word-play, intended as a pun or an elaborate joke. . . .

The names which allude to historical personages, although not intended to evoke the characters themselves, indicate yet another direction in which Dürrenmatt's fascination with names has led. Occasionally the characters have been christened by their author with a view to the literary associations they may call up. . . .

Occurring somewhat more frequently but also involving subtlety (at least generally) is Dürrenmatt's practice of choosing names with symbolic values which underscore the thematic content of the play. . . .

Dürrenmatt, whose concern it has been to make the drama a vehicle for ideas—sometimes bizarre, but always challenging—has exploited the entire range of types of names for his characters, from the colorless to the clever, from the allusive to the metaphoric. By his ingenuity he has integrated the names of his dramatis personae and the play, making them a part of the wide-ranging humor which animates his "tragicomedy."

*Kurt J. Fickert, "Wit and Wisdom in Dürrenmatt's Names," in* Contemporary Literature *(© 1970 by the Regents of the University of Wisconsin), Vol. II, No. 3, Summer, 1970, pp. 382-88.*

After the premiere of a new play by Dürrenmatt the reviews almost always contend that the work lacks formal and internal unity. Even when Dürrenmatt constantly uses the general term *comedy* as a designation for works of a highly different nature, he cannot conceal the fact that it applies only to one basic element in his plays, often just a surprise effect. The critics argue that Dürrenmatt's productions are in need of central themes and ideas to hold them together. Thus far, his works have shown themselves to be rather spotty attempts to dramatize a comical idea. Sometimes they stretch a mere paradoxical statement into a play and sometimes into a prose narrative, as in the novel *Grieche sucht Griechin (Once a Greek)* and in *Die Panne,* the short-story version of the radio play *Traps.*

In actuality all Dürrenmatt's works can be clearly arranged and classified. The transition from one literary genre to another does not have to be forced but develops from a new intellectual situation and from structural necessity. Even the detective novels of his earlier period are anything but the embarrassing products of a writer who had to scrape money together to support his family, and hence, it would be best not to talk about them. In fact, they are authentic Dürrenmatt and belong to the volume of his early prose works which he himself edited under the title *Die Stadt (The City)*. . . .

Dürrenmatt is far from sacrificing the actual structure of his work to ingenious ideas. It is the other way around: Dürrenmatt is a master at transforming all structure into a new formation of themes and investigations. This is a skill that he has had ever since his debut in the literary limelight, and he has stubbornly held onto this skill and has constantly modified it. . . .

Basically, Dürrenmatt works with a theology without God in his plays. The original situation of man is paradoxical; yet God does not take on a meaning or explain things—even if he may have meant something in the past. . . .

The strands in the dramatic works of Friedrich Dürrenmatt are held together by this outlook. God is there, but he is useless in human relations. Man must learn to master these relations himself, even the dramatist, who works with fictional figures created in man's image. For Dürrenmatt, the son of a pastor, transcendence is always present but mainly as the opposite position and a threat. When Dürrenmatt calls for the preservation of the "human point of view," he does not do so because he is considering a move toward "existentialism" and the "integral atheism" of Sartre. . . .

Dürrenmatt himself has no desire to be a star slugger along Sartre's lines. In his work, death dies. Meaningless death. Corpses pile up on the stage. Farcical death is experienced, and one is disconcerted about not being able to understand and explain the deaths. . . . Religion is inhumane. It is only capable of disturbing because it makes a farce out of serious humane things. . . .

His main concern is to portray the condition of a world that must manage itself without God. This is why it is anything but a joyous exultation when Dürrenmatt replies to his critics in the note to one of his recent plays, *Die Wiedertäufer,* that he who sees only nihilism in the comedy merely reflects his own.

It is from this theme that Dürrenmatt has derived all his dramaturgical theory and practice. . . .

[The] dramatist Dürrenmatt has moved closer and closer to the playwright Brecht. After *The Marriage of Mr. Mississippi,* which had been a great success and simultaneously had led up a dead end, it was apparent that Dürrenmatt began more and more to employ Brechtian motifs. . . . For Brecht, even gangsters are good citizens. For Dürrenmatt, the good citizens are actually gangsters. . . .

Dürrenmatt does not seem to acknowledge the dialectical relationship between theory and practice in the Brechtian sense. Evidently he would never think of founding a new art of writing plays in the manner of Brecht, nor of initiating a new "art of participation" for the audience. . . .

*Es steht geschrieben* was typical of his entire early work, which constantly propounded the primacy of sacrifice over any type of action. The sufferer stood morally and metaphysically higher than the man of action. Here the young Dürrenmatt proved himself to be a conscious disciple of Frank Wedekind and the expressionist dramatists. The ideal situation for all of Dürrenmatt's early plays was set by Wedekind's comedy *Der Marquis von Keith*. . . .

At the end of *Die Wiedertäufer* there is a real-life torture and murder. However, the actor Bockelson returns to the stage after his monumental flight onto the world stage. This is a new Dürrenmatt. He has gone beyond Wedekind and beyond Brecht. Just as in the beginning of his literary career, the life substance seems to be penetrating his work more and more strongly—the relation between the man and his work. Along with this, we can see that a new qualitative change has become possible: from the worst possible turn of events to comedy, there is now a turn to a realm which allows for tragic situations. A new form of tragedy as the highest form of comedy thought to its finish. One will have to wait to see how it turns out.

*Hans Mayer, "Friedrich Dürrenmatt: The Worst Possible Turn of Events," in his* Steppenwolf and Everyman, *translated and with an introduction by Jack D. Zipes (copyright © 1971 by Hans Mayer; reprinted with permission of Thomas Y. Crowell Co., Inc.), Crowell, 1971, pp. 163-80.*

Friedrich Dürrenmatt is well-known for his legerdemain. In *The Pledge,* not only the parody of the "thriller" format, but the language play, the toying with points of view, the hints that lead nowhere, the comic *deus ex machina,* the fairy-tale in the environment of realistic detail—these elements are all characteristic of Dürrenmatt's other detective stories of this period. *The Judge and his Hangman, Suspicion, The Pledge,* and *The Quarry* are all murder mysteries with a waggish surface. . . .

[*The Pledge*] is a mystery story—not in the tradition of the *Kriminalroman,* for that is attacked in the story and mocked by it, but in the sense of real mystery, the ultimate lack of knowledge. Faith in mystery is not parodied; the commitment to puzzle-solving is. And since *The Pledge* remains full of mystery, the novella itself is the meaning.

*Roger Ramsey, "Parody and Mystery in Dürrenmatt's 'The Pledge'," in* Modern Fiction Studies *(© 1971, by Purdue Research Foundation, West Lafayette, Indiana), Winter, 1971-72, pp. 525-32.*

Dürrenmatt writes in German, and has obviously been much influenced by Expressionism. His work is relentlessly moralistic, and every social point is driven home with the insistent irony of an Emil Jannings film. The most important of his short novels is *Der Richter und Sein Henker* (1952), translated as *The Judge and his Hangman* (1954), a book masterly in its control of the crime-story medium for the author's symbolic and moral purposes. . . . In this book, Dürrenmatt uses much of the apparatus of the detective story. Why did young Lieutenant Schmied wear evening dress on days which he marked with a "G" in his diary? What happened to the body of the dog killed by Barlach's assistant Chanz when the dog attacked the Inspector? The apparatus is used as part of a fantastic game which Barlach is playing with the other characters, and which Dürrenmatt is playing with the reader. The revelation of the murderer comes as a surprise, but it is subservient to the points the author is making about the nature of justice and the need to extirpate evil by violence.

Dürrenmatt's other crime stories do not fuse the investigatory and symbolic elements quite so successfully, but they are all remarkable for their originality. *Der Verdacht* (1953), translated as *The Quarry* (1962), finds Barlach in hospital, slowly recovering from what had been thought a fatal illness. The doctor treating him thinks he identifies in an old picture from *Life* a German concentration-camp doctor who took pleasure in operating on inmates without anesthetics. Has this man committed suicide, or is he in fact still alive and the head of a clinic which takes in only wealthy patients? There follows a struggle of wits and wills between Barlach and this man, which is also a struggle between freedom and nihilism. . . .

*Das Versprechen,* translated as *The Pledge* (1958), is about the transformation of Inspector Matthäi from an emotionless machine into a man with a passion for justice, intent to discover the murderer of three young girls. In pursuit of the man, Matthäi becomes for years a petrol station attendant, and with the utmost ruthlessness uses another young girl as bait for the killer. The bait is not accepted; the girl becomes a sluttish prostitute; the defeated Matthäi sinks into a sodden wreck. At the end of the story, it is revealed that he was "a genius, more so than any of your fictional detectives," and that all of his deductions were correct. Again, what might have been a mere clatter of ironies is kept finely under control.

*Julian Symons, in his* Mortal Consequences: A History—From the Detective Story to the Crime Novel *(copyright © 1972 by Julian Symons; reprinted by permission of Harper & Row, Publishers, Inc.), Harper, 1972, pp. 195-96.*

Like Bertolt Brecht and Max Frisch, Switzerland's Friedrich Duerrenmatt is one of those didactic dramatists who regard the theater as a classroom, the stage as a blackboard, the pen as a pointer and the playgoers as barely educable dolts. These playwrights take a dim view of man, dividing the species into two arbitrary categories: predators and prey, the fleecers and the fleeced. No one would deny that such characters are abundantly present in life, but to see the entire pattern of human behavior in these terms is one-eyed vision.

*T. E. Kalem, "Salome's Revenge," in* Time *(reprinted by permission from* Time, The Weekly Newsmagazine; *copyright Time, Inc.), December 10, 1973, pp. 86, 88.*

* * *

## DUNCAN, Robert 1919-

**Duncan, an American poet of the Black Mountain school, writes dense and experimental poems in the Christian visionary tradition. (See also *Contemporary Authors*, Vols. 9-12, rev. ed.)**

*Roots and Branches* is characteristic in its title, as in all other respects, of a continuing work which no brief note can report with much accuracy. For one thing, Robert Duncan is of that most rare order of poets for whom the work is not an occasional exercise, nor a demonstration of metrical abilities, nor any other term of partial commitment, however interesting. This book is the eleventh of a sequence, of a life, in fact, which can only be admitted or experienced in that totality. . . .

[Of] the major insistences of his work as one meets with them in this book as well as in every other which he has written,[most] primary is the assertion that what one *can* say, in any circumstance of poetry, is informed by a "voice" not ours to intend or to decide.

*Robert Creeley, "'To disclose that vision particular to dreams'," in* Humanist, *January-February, 1966.*

Complete with footnotes and an allusive richness breathing life into dust, Robert Duncan is truly an academic poet. His lines are the hard-earned result of an intensive classical education of the traditional mode. [*Bending the Bow*] continues his open series of poems, "Structures of Rime," and begins a new one, "Passages." And there are as well a fine set of disconnected poems. Attacks on President Johnson comparing him to Hitler and Stalin rub shoulders with quotations from Victor Hugo and Jacob John Sessler; the contrast says a great deal about this modern time. Duncan uses the insane rantings against Johnson to show the hollowness of such modern academic "protest" poetry. And they are insane, screaming, pointless, absurd. How rich and true then does his woven texture of the past appear, cool, intelligent, with the curves of marble in every line. How brilliantly he has shown the lie of his angry contemporaries in the classic calm of his inquiring poetic mind.

Virginia Quarterly Review, *Vol. 44, No. 3 (Summer, 1968), p. civ.*

*Bending the Bow* and *Tribunals* carry on Robert Duncan's tradition of instant poetry. Coherence and clarity one has learnt to forgo in his work. As for rational syntax, good grammar, and correct idiom, these evidently give way to a higher value, fidelity to impulse, which Mr Duncan mistakes for fidelity to oneself. If such a principle deserved attention, it would still not compensate readers for the tedium produced by Mr Duncan's writing. But not even a façade of integrity appears in the style of these poems. Pastiche, collage, syncretistic pseudo-thought are the deliberate methods he employs.

In a man who finds Boehme as authoritative as Dante, who receives his philosophical principles from both Plutarch and Ezra Pound, one is hardly surprised to discover some degree of moral confusion. But that he should then pose as an *illuminatus,* through whom the true order of the universe seeks expression, is still remarkable. Probably those admirers who feel puzzled by Mr Duncan's opacity console themselves with a delight in his high-mindedness. . . .

Those who are at a loss for literary reasons to praise Mr Duncan can rejoice in his radical orthodoxy. The tone of anguish, the claim that righteous fury must overwhelm the author's expressive power, the eruptive use of asyndeton and ellipsis, are standard tokens of virtuous character, and Mr Duncan displays them like stigmata.

*"Dubious Seer," in* The Times Literary Supplement *(reproduced by permission), July 23, 1971, p. 855.*

Duncan, in so many ways, does battle for us all. His battle for poetry and for the experience of the poem is so determined and so persistent that anyone involved with poetry in the United States today is in his debt. . . .

Perhaps because of this deep responsiveness Duncan has the widest range of concerns and fascinations of all his contemporaries. In some of the Passages there is the Poundian heaviness of encyclopedic reading summaries, but when he became immersed in the Cantos Pound virtually gave up writing anything else. Duncan began the Passages when he was already fully formed as a poet, and they have continued to express his fullest range of subject. The Passages have even opened out into bitter denunciation of America's war in Vietnam. . . .

[But] despite the concern for the present, the searching for theme in the present, it would still be difficult to call him a modern poet. The things that most characterize modern poetry aren't present in his work. He isn't deeply concerned with the image. He is concerned with imagery, but not with imagism. He describes, but he doesn't have the kind of visual realizations that Williams or Creeley or even Olson have. The rhythm of the poetry also has no sense of the breath's measure or limitation. Often the poems have been assembled from groups of notes and their different cadences make it impossible to find a breath rhythm that lies through all of them. It is poetry without a place. Lacking the sentimentality of the 19th Century, the order and precision of the 18th, the religious passion or courtly posturing of the 17th, it has to go back to this point where the medieval and the renaissance mingle, where everything is suddenly being picked up and looked at anew, and for the first time in so many centuries there is no boundary to what can be considered. This is the sense of the ornateness as he fills his poems with objects and attitudes; the reach of the work as he leans out to gather what he can into the image and the idea. He has been displaced, and he has to struggle again and again to find his place anew.

*Samuel Charters, "Robert Duncan," in his* Some Poems/Poets: Studies in American Underground Poetry Since 1945, *Oyez Press, 1971, pp. 47-56.*

In [*The Truth & Life of Myth,* Duncan] tries to make a harmony of all knowledge as he delves into his theme, the mythopoeic nature of poetry. He is a very shaman of the craft, a poet-priest, who sounds unfortunately like a savant among the dullards of his professional tribe. An explicator rather than an illuminator of ideas, he interlards his sentences with fragmented, if choice, examples of his erudition. Nothing in ancient or modern philosophy, eastern or western theology, anthropology or psychoanalysis fazes him. He stands on slippery ground, since his essay abounds in cluttered prose, each sentence loaded with parenthetic quotation. Of his writing he admits, ". . . my sentences knot themselves to bear the import of associations." He has read widely and deeply; his erudition is so vast, his citations so profuse, the varied strands of his theme become entangled, as he combines them to make a synthesis of his ideas.

*I. L. Salomon, "Duncan on Myth," in* Michigan Quarterly Review, *Fall, 1973, p. 389.*

Robert Duncan is sometimes spoken of as not only the most talented but also the most intelligent of modern poets. Though both claims may be close to the truth, part of the credit for intelligence surely grows out of the unintelligibility of much of his poetry. . . . [Jim Harrison, in *The New York Times Book Review,* September 29, 1968, suggests that in] reading Duncan "it simply helps to be familiar with Dante, Blake, mythography, medieval history, H. D., William Carlos Williams, Pound, Stein, Zukofsky, Olson, Creeley, and Levertov." To this list we might add Cabalistic literature, Hermetic writings, Indian lore, *The Golden Bough,* the pre-Socratic philosophers, Christian mysticism, and the *Oxford English Dictionary.* Lacking these familiarities the reader can penetrate some distance into the complex syncretism of Duncan only by a dogged persistence. . . .

It is not only that Duncan's mythic foragings are incredibly wide-ranging: gods and goddesses, songs and rituals may with patience be traced down. But more difficult is the aura of the mythic that invades the language at all levels. . . .

From Duncan's redundant mythologies, then, we are not apt to distill any private mystic vision, but perhaps we may discover a private *mythos,* shaped by the circumstances of the poet's life and time. If it is to be distilled, it will be, one expects, in the alembic of Duncan's poetic—for . . . it has become evident that the poet's world-view is intimately bound up with his poetic, and that that poetic is inextricably tied to the poet's reaction to the Vietnam War. . . .

Duncan's homosexuality brought him to poetry as an area of freedom, a private order that demanded no revolt—society and its systems could be disregarded. Moloch need not be bearded, he could be ignored. But not easily ignored—for the early poems are haunted with images of disease, self-doubt, loneliness, and isolation. But they are a beginning toward the mature poetic of Duncan, exploring the possibilities of love and growth, and finding in eros and the beloved a step on the ladder toward the Primal Eros and the Beloved.

Love is the first interest of Duncan: he sees his own life as a struggle to learn to love, and the life of the universe as an unfolding toward the Perfect Form of Love. Love is the one Law (Gospel, "God-Spell") written in all things, but a law that is brought to flower only with great travail. . . .

Duncan is painfully aware that the love he is able to give is not worthy of the word (or Word), not equal to his idea of what Love participating in Primal Love should be. . . .

Duncan's is, of course, an organic theory of poetry—few poets today do not claim that sobriquet for their poetic, though it often means only that they do not impose strict traditional forms upon their work. . . . But Duncan's organicism goes beyond Emerson's "ask the fact for the form" or Creeley's "form is the extension of content." It not only claims that the poem unfolds according to its own law, but envisions a compatible cosmology in which it may do so. It is not the poem alone that must grow as freely as the plant: the life of the person, the state, the species, and indeed the cosmos itself follows a parallel law. All must follow their own imperatives and volition; all activity must be free of external coercion. But first the poem. . . .

In his ideas of cosmic order, Duncan appears to be a Platonist by natural inclination, an Aristotelian by choice, and an evolutionist (Darwin/Chardin) by desire and necessity of circumstance. . . . [Concerning] the *bodilessness* of his poetry, he tends to deal with the material world as though it were but a copy of the divine *eidos* and interesting chiefly as the metaphor or signature of the spiritual. He does so in spite of his intentions and assertions to the contrary. With Aristotle he insists, however, that this world is the real world, and that its Form is innate rather than remote. . . . The real world, he adds, is the source of all our knowledge and devotion; we take our revelation from it, and it is not to be despised as it was by the Gnostics. The actual, the literal, is the primary ground out of which we create the linguistic, the universal. . . .

Duncan is not unaware that the Greek *kosmos* meant "order," and his own poetry takes its dramatic center in the tension between order and disorder, *kosmos* and *kaos*. The manner in which these seeming polarities are related is perhaps the knottiest critical problem his poetry poses. In ordering chaos one creates cosmos and participates in the original work of the Grand Designer. Yet Cosmos is for Duncan not an eradication of Chaos, but an awakening of and an awakening to the harmony with which Chaos is already suffused. His poetry intends not an ordering of experience, but an experiencing of its order. The divine harmonies with which Chaos is pregnant are of an order different from our human order, and it is precisely for this reason that the poet must, so to speak, keep his hands off his poem. . . .

The order that men would impose upon chaos would resemble a gridwork of regular lines—a graph-paper sky (or a rectangular and "level" breadboard). But nature supplies the body's needs by an altogether erratic (seemingly) branching of arteries; and the tree spreads its branches through the chaos of monotonous air with an order that is excitingly disorderly. For Duncan, such is the difference between life and death. The dead matter of the universe science dissects into tidy stackables; the living significance of creation, the angel with which the poet wrestles, is a volatile whirlwind of sharp knees and elbows threshing with a grace beyond our knowledge of grace. . . .

The poem, one's life, the life of the cosmos, the dance of things in time, have no plan or end or pattern or goal, other than the imperatives of the unfolding law of their own activity in space and time. The only law the dance has is love of the Dance itself, which in practice means love of all persons and objects that are a part of it. Evil is that which is antagonistic to the dance, the resistant medium through which the dance honeycombs its erratic patterns. Life, Poetry, Godhead is the light coming out of darkness, cosmos radiating through chaos, the God's eye opening in the murky ambience. . . .

There is in Duncan's work none of the intense visceral experience of the war's suffering that we find in Levertov, but instead a remoteness and grandeur like that in Milton's battle on the plains of heaven. Duncan does not *experience* the war but repeatedly attempts to place it in its large spiritual perspective. His protest and the war fall into the patterns of the classic struggle between good and evil, light and darkness. Perhaps it is already clear that it is not war itself that Duncan considers evil, but rather its coercive implications in modern times. . . .

All hatred and all evil, Duncan believes, grow out of *a failure of the imagination to put together a condition in which love can function*. . . .

Duncan's virtues as poet are also his shortcomings—the mythic and cosmic perspective allows him to transcend narrowness and hatred, but fails to communicate vividly to any sizable audience. . . .

In summary: Duncan believes that paradise is a matter of the here and now in the community and free volition of man; that the City of God is hidden in the cities of man; that love is evolving naturally out of hatred like a God's eye opening in darkness, but needs a total freedom in which it may grow; and that not death but coercion and loss of community are the real evils of war. Duncan's outrage, then, is not merely against [the Vietnam] war in particular, and yet not indiscriminately against all war in general. But it is unlikely that any modern war can ever again meet the conditions of community and free volition that would justify it—and so Duncan's reservations are in a way academic. Nevertheless, they are exactly the reservations we should have expected him to make. A poet of Duncan's mythological mind could hardly be expected to relinquish from his cosmology all possibilities of heroic combat against the monsters of evil. It is only that in an increasingly sophisticated world both St. George and the dragon must inevitably play out their drama under new forms. The "irreal"—that level of spiritual reality one step beyond our commonplace awareness—has new weapons: the actual hallucinogens that expand consciousness, the new music, and the new morality, the new spirit of poverty and anti-materialism, and the new adventures in nonviolence. Duncan's own protest against coercion and lovelessness grows directly and spontaneously from his poetics and biography and is but one manifestation of a truly different kind of consciousness, either a very old or a very new spirituality.

*James F. Mersmann, "Robert Duncan: Irregular Fire–Eros Against Ahreman," in his* Out of the Vietnam Vortex: A Study of Poets and Poetry Against the War, *University Press of Kansas, 1974, pp. 159-204.*

## DURRELL, Lawrence 1912-

**Durrell, an Indian-born English novelist, poet, and travel book writer, has lived in France since 1957. His sensuous and poetic fiction, particularly *The Alexandria Quartet,* has reminded critics of work by De Quincey, Conrad, and Nabokov. (See also *Contemporary Authors*, Vols. 9-12, rev. ed.)**

[Durrell's] style is a mosaic. Each word is set in its precise and luminous place. Touch by touch, Durrell builds his array of sensuous, rare expressions into patterns of imagery and tactile suggestion so subtle and convoluted that the experience of reading becomes one of total sensual apprehension. . . . No one else writing in English today has quite the same commitment to the light and music of language.

But this does not mean that this jeweled and coruscated style springs full-armed from Durrell's personal gift. He stands in a firm tradition of baroque prose. . . . Durrell, with his Shakespearean and Joycean delight in the sheer abundance and sensuous variety of speech, may strike one as mannered and precious. But the objection arises in part from our impoverished sensibility. . . .

Durrell's style is more than a formal instrument; it carries the heart of his meaning. *Justine, Balthazar, Mountolive,* and *Clea* are founded on the axiom that the ultimate truths of conduct and the world cannot be penetrated by force of reason. Where truth can be apprehended at all, in brief spells of total illumination, the process of insight is one of total sensuous absorption. In a conceit which is the very crux of his argument, Durrell instructs us that the soul enters truth as man enters woman, in a possession at once sexual and spiritual. Again, this is a view which has existed before Durrell. It plays a vital role in oriental and medieval mysticism; it is at work in Dante and in the erotic metaphors of the seventeenth-century metaphysical poets. Moreover, it is crucial in the theories of Gnosticism and the citadel of Gnosticism was Alexandria. And it is here that the example of D. H. Lawrence is relevant. The presence of Lawrence is felt through the four novels and one of the main characters is in personal touch with him. Like Lawrence, Durrell believes in a wisdom of the senses truer and subtler than that of the predatory mind. Both men see in the act of love the crucial affirmation of human identity and the only true bridge for the soul. Durrell's personages pursue each other in an elaborate cross-weaving of sexual encounter, for only thus can the ghostliness of the human spirit be given the substance of life. . . .

The long, glittering arabesques of adjectives with which Durrell surrounds objects are not only exercises in verbal acrobatics. They are successive assaults on the inner mystery of things, attempts, often exasperated and histrionic, to trap reality inside a mesh of precise words. Being equipped with a superb apparatus of sensual receptivity, Durrell is aware of the myriad movements of light, scent, and sound. . . . Durrell's Alexandria . . . is one of the true monuments in the architecture of imagination. It compares in manifold coherence with the Paris of Proust and the Dublin of Joyce.

The technique of accumulated nuance, the painter returning constantly to the same scene in the changes of the light, applies not only to the portrayal of the city but also the entire plot. . . .

Durrell must explore the ambiguities and covertness of sensual lust precisely because he believes that it is only in the lambent or desperate contact of the flesh that we can gain access to the truth of life. In his treatment, moreover, there is little of prurience or the snigger of the eroticist. Love in Durrell has an ashen taste. . . . As in so many dandies able to experience the fullness of sensuous life, there is in Durrell a touch of the Puritan.

But although its range of material and emotion is great, the Alexandria Quartet leaves one, at the last, with a suspicion of triviality. There lies the real problem for the critic. Why should there be at the center of this superbly contrived fable of life an undeniable hollowness? There are, I think, two reasons.

Durrell dramatizes a wide spectrum of sensibility; but his cast of characters is of an exceedingly special kind. All these fascinating and exotic beings share a high degree of nervous intelligence; they articulate their emotions with lyric power and unfailing subtlety; they live life at a constant pitch of awareness, more searching and vulnerable than that of ordinary men. They are cut from the same fragile and luminous stone and so they reflect each other like mirrors disposed in cunning perspectives. . . .

The angle of vision, moreover, is rigorously private. The gusts of social and political life blow across the scene, but they are not accorded much importance. . . . Now no one would be so absurd as to demand from him a novel of "social consciousness." But by severing his imagined world from the intrusions of political and social fact he makes it even narrower and more fragile than it need be. . . . The legend of Lady Chatterley is as narrow and private as that of Darley and Melissa; but *Lady Chatterley's Lover* is a profoundly intelligent study of class relations.

Because of its enclosedness and utter privacy, the Alexandria Quartet is more convincing in its details than in its broad design. . . . It is not so much the main plot which sticks in one's memory, as it is the digressions and minor episodes. . . . As in medieval illuminations, the fringe is often brighter than the center.

But there is also a particular failure. *Clea* marks a drastic falling-off. It is a brittle, self-conscious gloss on the three preceding volumes. . . .

Yet even when we make such reservations, there can be little question of the fascination of Durrell's novel. Anyone caring about the energies of English prose and the forms of prose fiction will have to come to grips with this strange, irritating work. We are too near the fact to say what place the Alexandria Quartet will hold in future estimates of twentieth-century English literature. I would guess that it will stand somewhere above the range of *Green Mansions,* with the less complete but more central performance of Malcolm Lowry. That Durrell will have his place is almost certain.

*George Steiner, "Lawrence Durrell and the Baroque Novel" (1960), in his* Language and Silence: Essays on Language, Literature and the Inhuman *(copyright © 1967 by George Steiner; reprinted by permission of Atheneum Publishers, U.S.A.), Atheneum, 1967, pp. 280-87.*

Critics who have ventured to revisit and review Lawrence

Durrell's *Alexandria Quartet* in the five years since its completion have been remarkably hesitant, however strongly (or reservedly) they profess their admiration, to make any claims for its longevity or future acceptance. The best of them did go so far once as to risk putting it somewhere between *Green Mansions* and *Wuthering Heights,* which seems to me hedging one's bet so safely as not to be betting at all; there is a tolerably vast region between. The oddity is that most of them *have* liked it, have found great wonders to sing of in this four-storied monument to the imagination. They have also found, again almost universally, defects and deficiencies—a certain lack of seriousness, a thinness of "content"—but very few seemed to doom it altogether for these. The French, in fact, who consider Durrell more theirs than ours, were delighted at the escape it offered from their own increasingly, distressingly overcerebral fiction. . . .

The Durrellian Imagination is a creative organ of awesome fertility: its equal for power and inventiveness has rarely been seen since Dickens. It can charge a single word or phrase or image into stunning surreality; it can capture all Alexandria with a play of random notes. . . . Like the heroes of Dickens novels, the title-characters of the *Quartet* —even that Zionist sphinx, the near-mythical Justine—tend to pale somewhat, to elude one on rereading. But again like Dickens, the minor characters—Scobie of course, De Capo, Melissa, Memlik Pasha, Pombal, Leila, the Virtuous Samira—Narouz!—are the surest signs of their author's imaginative powers, and destined to at least some kind of immortality. . . .

Dickens, like Durrell, had a multitude of "selves" he felt forced to push forward, a multitude of voices: high-comic, low-comic, ironic, sentimental, suspenseful, reformist. The sentimental-serious self was forever being tripped up by the ironic-intrusive, and he finally gave in in *Bleak House* and divided himself in two. With a century of narrative experimentation behind him, Durrell can more comfortably split his intentions among a dozen *personae*—though essentially, perhaps, only three: Darley, the romanticist; Scobie, the comic; and Purswarden, the serious, cynical critic. Behind them, as with Dickens, there is a confusion of intention that keeps the *Quartet* from ever cohering into a single, memorable experience; a confusion that allows each reading to be a sequence of varying *kinds* of experience of undiminished imaginative intensity—but that leaves us with nothing solid to hold onto in between.

*David Littlejohn, "The Permanence of Durrell" (1965), in his* Interruptions *(copyright © 1970 by David Littlejohn; reprinted by permission of Grossman Publishers), Grossman, 1970, pp. 82-90.*

[*The Ikons*] shows no great advance in Durrell's poetic manner or matter, but it is, like his earlier poems, controlled and classically cool, perceptive and alive with imaginative vision. The poems are like ikons, small and exquisite, worthy of meditation for they are numinous and meaningful. Durrell's "The Alexandria Quartet" remains the towering work of the fifties. These poems, like his verse plays "An Irish Faustus" and "Acte," are small but worthy additions to the varied body of work of which that great novel is the center.

Virginia Quarterly Review, *Vol. 43, No. 3 (Summer, 1967), p. cxi.*

Durrell is not an inventor of new poetic concepts. . . . He is content, like an Elizabethan poet, like Shakespeare in his sonnets, with perennial topics, the beauty of the world, its transience, its danger, the triumph of time, the battle of love and art against time. For him, as for the Elizabethans whom he loves, the originality of the poet lies not in the discovery of new topics, new moods, but in ingenuity, in invention, in what the Elizabethans called 'device', in handling the old ones. (p. 55)

[For] all its patches of the cruel, the horrible, the macabre, for all its maimings and deaths, its transformations and reductions, *The Alexandria Quartet* is not a tragic novel like *Anna Karenina,* nor an epical one, like *War and Peace*; it is lyrical romantic comedy in which the working-through of the life-force, the It, is celebrated in its very absurdity. Durrell has a gross, schoolboyish, but very hearty appetite for life. Life can be very humiliating, it tends to put one in one's place, but only the mortally sick, the broken, or incurable egoists (like Rochefoucauld, in Durrell's poem about him) reject it. Love, like art, like death, like power-games, is a means by which the It or the Life-Force (Shaw's phrase) works itself out; nothing is a final consummation, nothing is an end-stop. But the working out leaves in our mouths not only the taste of grapes or of wine but the taste of iron, a tingling and dangerous sadness. And the wild laughter that echoes through *The Alexandria Quartet,* Pursewarden's laughter, *is,* as Darley says, a reversed glove: tenderness turned inside out. (pp. 147-48)

Durrell's gifts as a writer are those of a lyrical and sympathetic comedian, with an occasional taste, but not a dominating one, for the frightening and the grotesque. His gifts as a master of language are for bravura, for rich excess, though he can write when he wants to with a plain elegance, as in many pages of *Mountolive*. In his deep self, he is a quietist and almost a mystic. Bubbling over though he is with ideas, one does not have to accept the ideas behind *The Alexandria Quartet* to enjoy the book—to accept them, that is, other than as elements in a composition. His personality is in a sense everything in his books and yet it is a remarkably elusive one, what he himself calls an 'ingenuous mask'. He is a great conjurer. . . . Durrell is a near-mystic, or a near-mage, who has to 'rejoice that all things are'. He has to see evil as a dark and puzzling aspect of a cosmic unity which ultimately has to be accepted as good, or as beyond good and evil. Nevertheless, in the realm of charity, as of the spirit, for all his dallyings with darkness, he strikes me as a more compassionate man than some of the critics who dismiss him as immoral, amoral, a mere belated aesthetic fantasist. Alas, the terror of life, which he sometimes represents so frighteningly, is no more a fantasy than life's promise, its delight, its painful power of growth and of rebirth. He is a serious, though never a solemn writer. (pp. 162-63)

*G. S. Fraser, in his* Lawrence Durrell: A Critical Study *(copyright © 1968 by G. S. Fraser; reprinted by permission of the publishers, E. P. Dutton & Co., Inc.), Dutton, 1968.*

The "Einsteinian" concept that every moment contains in

itself all time seems to be at the foundation of Durrell's application to literature of the space-time continuum in what he calls his "relativity poem": so Pursewarden [in the *Alexandria Quartet*] sees the "n-dimensional novel" as "a marriage of past and present with the flying multiplicity of the future racing towards one."... The first three volumes of the *Quartet* are meant to represent the dimensions of space, while only the fourth is to be associated with time, in "a continuum, forsooth, embodying not a *temps retrouvé* but a *temps délivré*" . . .—a remark assuming differences between Durrell's and Proust's methods and goals much more sweeping than those that really exist. Some of Durrell's other analogical adaptations of the concept of "relativity" qualify even further our acceptance of his stress on the contradictions between his work and Proust's. "Our view of reality," says Pursewarden, "is conditioned by our position in space and time"...; from a notion of truth, then, kindred to that of *Remembrance of Things Past*—or *Absalom, Absalom!*—Durrell makes use of kindred narrative forms. Especially in *Justine* and *Balthazar,* Darley reconstructs a number of scenes out of his imagination, asking us, in effect, to suspend disbelief; and we do, proceeding with him under the assumption that, as Balthazar puts it, "to imagine is not necessarily to invent." . . . "At every moment in Time the possibilities are endless in their multiplicity": out of this attitude toward reality arises "the intercalation of fact and fancy" . . . that is the *Alexandria Quartet.*

*Morris Beja, in his* Epiphany in the Modern Novel, *University of Washington Press, 1971, pp. 217-18.*

The *Alexandria Quartet* is easily one of the best works of the past decade. The city it evokes is exotic, vibrant, sensual, and fluid. Its characters are diverse, many quite actually "round," most symbolically relevant. Its imagery is directed toward some splendid effects; its multiple and multileveled narrative toward creating memorable (in places notorious) scenes; its sweep is broad; and, above all, it is most ambitious in its attempt to get at one of the great archetypal literary and philosophical problems: namely, the nature of love and art and the erosion of both by time and change. In every way Lawrence Durrell has written the modern, rather than merely contemporary, novel.

The temptation, however, to read it in a certain way—as a technical and pyrotechnical tour de force—is still around even after ten years, and suggests something of its limitations. For the *Quartet* is not, despite a plethora of characters, a novel of character; it is not, despite a show of polymathic learning, a novel of ideas; it is not, for all the shadow play of narrative devices, a novel of complex plot or action. . . . Actually, the *Quartet* offers scant illumination on anything not part of its insulated hermetic world. Somewhere within the peripheries of its diffuse narratives and its lush atmosphere is, one suspects, a hub of meaning from which all else radiates. Yet again and again the center eludes us, and the sequence seems too specifically, too purely one of form, of art: a law unto itself, and a law still uncodified. . . .

The game of the realist is that of turning "selected fictions" into realities, and of a writer like Durrell, of heightening such selected fictions as already exist. It is this last that the *Quartet* sets out to do. Life, never art but eventually transformed into art, operates in a continuum of change. The question is really how (and if) both can be kept fluid, moving, kinetic during the process of transformation, without distorting either. For life, though it may be viewed from differing perspectives, cannot be reordered except through art. Retrospectively, the *events* of life are sequential, static, historic (Pursewarden's "causality") the *interpretations* of events (the motives involved with them, if one prefers) are alone open to reconstruction ("indeterminacy"). On such terms it seems as justifiable to write the same novel four different ways as to write four novels one way, i.e., to persist in "drowsily cutting along a dotted line." Art, therefore, not life, becomes the principal focus of the artist's changing vision.

To put it another way, Durrell is writing his own "pure novel," and in form (not necessarily spirit) the *Quartet* is closer to Gide's *Counterfeiters,* say, or Nabokov's *Ada,* than to either *Remembrance of Things Past* or *Ulysses,* both of which are rigidly structured. . . .

The collective desires and the collective wishes of those who live in Alexandria and those who move through it are fused by Durrell in a symphonic-scientific metastasis of memory. Each section of the *Quartet* provides additional insight and material for turning disparate memories into a coherent pattern, for making the city "real." . . .

Alexandria is, at one extreme, the solid base of the novel, and, at the other, the most palpable symbol of change. Like Proust's Paris or Combray or Balbec, Alexandria is dormant, amorphous until quickened and shaped by imagination and memory, both differing functions of a single process that for Durrell is pretty much reserved for the artist. The reality of the city—what one might think of as its "life"—remains constant; the changes it undergoes are related to a widening artistic perception and the growth of the artist who is not only changing from day to day, but is part of a changing history and changing ethos. Alexandria mirrors the changes of those who live within its unravelling mystery, but with that reversal peculiar to all mirrors. . . .

What Durrell is about here is at once the fusion and disintegration of space-time: rendering the continuing quality of life (its routine, regularity, boredom) just as one might imprison an image in a mirror, and at the same time projecting the subtle or wild fluctuations of events beyond those narrative and historic methods—the conventional modes of fiction—that demand a finite ending or cyclical return. Hence, concern with "relativity" (what has drawn much too much hullabaloo over the sequence) is more nominal than actual. Actually, the *Quartet* defines change by moving off fixed points on a space-time continuum to become (substantiating for the moment the distinction of Darley's) "a work of memory rather than imagination." Durrell does not (like Joyce or Proust) mythicize an event, but the memory of it in the mind of one artist or another. Change (interpreted by memory as well as mythicized and refined by it) can no longer be thought of as the only permanent thing, but as a shifting thing in itself. And these along with time and space, normally treated as novelistic motifs, supportive props for capturing life and art, are directed to capturing the *movement* of life and art. . . .

[The] *Quartet* is not an artist's novel so much as the artists' novel. Those who have a hand in creating it—namely, Arnauti, Pursewarden, Darley, and Durrell himself—are to a greater or lesser degree concerned with this very interplay of memory and imagination as it relates to time. . . . The *Quartet* does not establish any hierarchy of artists; more precisely, one understands an ordering by way of continuity, for the act of creation is continuously and differently renewing itself. Thus of the many continuums in the sequence the principal one is this continuum of writers—a continuum that transforms a novel of passion, love, sadism, espionage, and good old grand guignol into a formal, logical, classically ordered work of wholeness. The square within the circle is the image for the *Quartet*. . . .

To a large extent the *Quartet* is Darley: composed, collated, reshuffled, and woven by him. It is his "intercalating of realities," as he moves from Arnauti's subjective vision to Pursewarden's objective one, rejecting both but spinning out strands and threads along the way. But even the weaver may find himself woven. In *Mountolive* Darley is shuttled through the warp and woof of action over which he has little effect and no control. *Mountolive* is more or less a piece of straight nineteenth-century naturalism, but it is a tour de force in so far as the sequence is concerned. Durrell, now the "omniscient narrator" is calling the shot. He gains his own purchase on reality by showing how subject (Darley) can turn object; how the gothic patina, the baroque sensibilities, the esoterica, perversion, decadence, the permeating mythicness and mirrorness of Alexandria become (through a simple and relative shift of the artist's vision) mere bas reliefs on the greater frieze of history. . . .

Moving in space freed from time must always appear to the critical and analytical intelligence more exciting than moving in time without space. For the artist, art cannot but appear more intimate and meaningful than life itself, even when art supposedly *is* life itself. For Darley, the artist who comes of age in the *Quartet,* and for Durrell, who implies that this is the way such genesis comes about, the supreme artistic vision is that fine recreation and balancing of all three things comprising time—history, imagination, memory; the supreme artist is one who can turn the common stuff of realities into triumphs of art; and the supreme art is that which all the while seeks to gain the "purchase on reality," to become ever stable while it is ever changing.

*Robert K. Morris, "Lawrence Durrell–The 'Alexandria Quartet': Art and the Changing Vision," in his* Continuance and Change: The Contemporary British Novel Sequence *(copyright © 1972 by Southern Illinois University Press; reprinted by permission of Southern Illinois University Press), Carbondale: Southern Illinois University Press, 1972, pp. 51-70.*

Durrell's 'savage charcoal sketch of spiritual and sexual etiolation', as he calls [*The Black Book*] bears all the scars of having been written under great pressure. Everything in the writing has been geared up to such stylistic pitch that talent runs away with itself in the search to restore a lost quality of life. *The Black Book* seeks to infect the world with its despair, to insult with verbal blows 'The old Babylonian whore that is England, burnt out, gutted, with the disease melting her eyes in their sockets.' For all its mannerisms, black-plush decadence and aureate vocabulary, the book has power, a vivid oddness and extremity of perception, tilting at times towards the gross Gothic, or a social realism of despair. . . .

*The Black Book* courts Modernism with the fidelity of a young writer of the 'thirties anxious not only to be in the swim, but from a pressure to slough off native restraints and reach his real writing self. In this last respect, the book is an *exemplum.*

Henry Miller praised Durrell's treatment of the theme in this way: *The Black Book,* he said, 'expanded the womb feeling until it includes the whole universe'. In the contemporary climate of accuracy and plainspeaking, Durrell's theme is likely to be thought hysterical. My own view is unsteady. Durrell's psychology might be as much part of his dandified despair as his style. Both the theme and the brilliantly inventive phrase-making have been taken too far, and seem a colossal, dithyrambic exaggeration, an over-compensation for the English Death, just as the way out—a ticket to the Med—is a personal solution, hardly a general truth. But whatever flaws it has, *The Black Book* is enthralling testimony, violently galvanized by fierce talent. Linguistically, it may be the most 'poetic' novel in the language, an ornate addition to the long line of works by melancholy, aggressive malcontents whose disease was England. It is certainly an important book, a missing link from the literature of the 'thirties—most of which Lawrence Lucifer despises—now belatedly restored to the canon.

*Douglas Dunn, in* London Magazine, *June/July, 1973, p. 152.*

The pleasure I derive from Lawrence Durrell's verse comes, I think, from my regarding it as a well-stocked arsenal of memorable phrases rather than as so many faultless poems. One can always rely on Mr Durrell for a phrase, but the perfectly rounded-out and cut-away poem is a rather different matter. Having said which, I should like to add that there are at least half a dozen pieces by him which I would count among the most accomplished poetry of the century. The present volume *Vega and Other Poems* does not add to this number; but is nevertheless not without its surprising and original compositions.

It is one of the charms of Mr Durrell that he can come up with a virtuoso piece which, at the same time, wears the air of improvisation. . . .

Mr Durrell's damnable facility is no doubt his chief enemy. He can give to . . . slick impermanent thought so comely or modish a dress that to restrain him might seem to be the work of a literary spoilsport.

*Derek Stanford, "Virtuoso Verse," in* Books and Bookmen, *July, 1973, p. 96.*

During the 'sixties [Durrell's] poems grew plummier. Rich syllables oozed (an oystershell was a 'valve of nacre'). Sumptuous decay thickened the Mediterranean air. In *Vega* things have dried out. Death's print is on the sky—'a white-washed moon with/Frost in the bulb'. Corpses are respected, envied almost, for their 'corpsely wise' look and their 'marvellous/Property of withoutness'. . . . The quivers of memory or regret that still disturb his quiet are finely subdued into images of submersion or burial. . . . Among the pleasures of the collection, and emblematic of it, are the lines on a dead cicada's husk, fleshless as mica.

*John Carey, in* London Magazine, *August/September, 1973, p. 126.*

* * *

## DYLAN, Bob 1941-

**Dylan, an American folksinger and songwriter, pioneered the "complex and unsentimental love song in the modern idiom." (See also *Contemporary Authors*, Vols. 41-44.)**

[The] stylistic presentation [of *Tarantula*] is diffuse and unusual, though the book cannot be categorized as a novel. There are no chapter divisions nor a story line; it is a conglomeration of poems, letters and other writings, full of imagery, symbolism, allusion, satire, cant, argot, and jargon. The line of demarcation between reality and fancy is very inexact, leaving the reader halfway informed about people and places of our time, halfway entertained, and short on inspiration to change the world around us. Dylan's fusion of panorama and organic form could be better understood (if not enjoyed), if a catalog were provided. "Tarantula" loses something through the passage of time which it perhaps would not if it were a work of greater literary merit. . . .

Where was Bob Dylan's head when he put together Tarantula?

*Denise R. Majkut, "'Tarantula,'" in* Best Sellers, *October 1, 1971, p. 299.*

*Tarantula* didn't work. Dylan was doing songs and albums, going on the road a lot and taking his typewriter with him to write the book, and very upset that he had a deadline. It became a drag for him. It grew less lucid as he went along, more stream of consciousness that both defied meaning and lacked the emotion of poetry. Much of it was absurdist word-play. Dylan was unhappy with it, but still he plunged ahead, forcing himself to write. There was a feeling among some friends that he was seeking some sort of approval from the literary establishment which had ignored him.

*Anthony Scaduto, in his* Bob Dylan *(copyright © 1971 by Anthony Scaduto), Grosset & Dunlap, 1971, p. 185.*

Bob Dylan certainly deserves considerable credit for having, almost single-handed, made both symbolism and verbal complexity acceptable in pop music. But that he should be considered a part of a wider *avant-garde* is merely a measure of how far popular song has lagged behind the development of literature, for his achievement consisted of introducing into the former art techniques which had been commonplace in the latter for forty years or more. If some poets find Dylan or John Lennon genuinely important influences on their own art, they are testifying only to the extent to which they have lost touch with the poetic tradition. An indication of serious defects in our society and its culture, certainly; but scarcely a fact that should lead us in itself to expect anything very new in their writing.

*Grevel Lindop, in* British Poetry Since 1960: A Critical Survey, *edited by Michael Schmidt and Grevel Lindop (reprinted by permission of Dufour Editions, Inc.), Carcanet, 1972, pp. 92-3.*

[There] are three strands to Dylan's work I'd like to [say] something about.

One is its Jewishness. No one can come from a Jewish background without being profoundly influenced by it, whether the process is one of acceptance, compromise or rejection. Dylan is no exception, and one doesn't need to know much about his change of name or his contradictory, carefully disguised relationship with his parents to realize it. . . .

Recently Dylan seems to have been rediscovering his Jewishness all over again, coming to terms with it. But the important thing is what it means for his music. It explains, I think, a certain self-pity which slops over into sentimentality in some of his songs (*pace* Albert Grossman); except for his very early work, and one or two songs on [his album] *John Wesley Harding,* Dylan has always reserved most of his compassion for himself. Its most obvious effect, however, has been to make religion one of the major themes—perhaps *the* major theme—in Dylan's music. Not only does he make use of Biblical symbolism and allusions throughout his work; the central problem of what one is to believe, of Man's relationship to God, recurs in song after song. . . .

A second strand to Dylan's music which has been largely undiscussed is its "gay" component. It's almost as though the critics have maintained a conspiracy of silence about this. . . .

Dylan is a master of masks. If any proof were needed, his skillful manipulation of the mass media and his deliberate choosing among images to present to the public are sufficient. More importantly, Dylan uses masks in his songs as well. In many of them he seems to be writing about himself in the second or third person, as though distancing himself from and then addressing himself; so that the "you" in the song is really "I." It's a common enough device in literature and everyday speech, but Dylan has taken it further by seeming to create an alternative persona; and often the persona he chooses is a woman. . . . Of course, Dylan's songs characteristically work at different levels of meaning; like any great work of art, the best of them set up reverberations which defy reduction to a single, unalterable explanation. And often it is impossible to separate the man from the mask. Dylan's involvement in, or response to, the gay scene has probably enriched and deepened his music, though it may also have introduced an unnecessary obscurity. And it may also explain why, like Jagger's, some of its sexuality rings a little false.

Finally, it's worth emphasizing again the personal nature of Dylan's music. Those who try to force him into one ideological straightjacket or another don't realize that Dylan has never been a political thinker, that if anything he is both anti-political and anti-intellectual; he seems to work more by instinct than anything else, and what we value about him are his insights and his poetry, his artist's ability to distill and shape, not to order. Some critics accept this, but foist a substitute title upon him: that of Culture Hero, or Spokesman For His Generation. Fans search his latest songs for messages to the world, commentators with stethoscopes search for the heartbeat of the counter-culture. But Dylan has always insisted he writes only for himself. Throughout his career he has shrugged off old roles and adopted new ones like sport jackets; those who hunger after his old declamatory songs of dissent, or the apocalyptic visions of the mid-sixties, are demanding from him a consistency which he has never claimed.

*Craig McGregor, "Introduction," to* Bob Dylan: A Retrospective, *edited by Craig McGregor (abridged by permission of William Morrow & Co., Inc.; copyright © 1972 by Craig McGregor), William Morrow, 1972, pp. 11-15.*

It seems to me that Dylan first revealed the individual directions of his creative career in his second album, *The Freewheelin' Bob Dylan*; his first album, as we know, was more a record of Dylan as performer (of the songs of others) than of Dylan as a "song poet." But in *Freewheelin',* Dylan presented his own songs largely, and it was here that he sang love lyrics, such as "Girl from the North Country," that he sang "Blowin' in the Wind," which became so useful to freedom movements; and it was also on this record that Dylan sang "Hard Rain." And the substance of these three songs, but significantly not the style, suggested the contents of all subsequent Dylan albums. The love songs were not to dominate any album—until *Blonde on Blonde,* perhaps—but the protest songs and the songs which can be called apocalyptic songs, in keeping with the temper of the times—songs which prophesied and described violent destruction and some sort of eschatological revelation—were to take turns at dominating individual albums, the particular emphasis in each case depending entirely on the evolution of Dylan's mind, emotions, and concerns. The upshot is that *Freewheelin'* can be seen as an announcement of balanced possibilities and as a presentation of thematic concerns. But the album which followed it, *The Times They Are A-Changin',* was his most striking protest album, while Dylan's sixth album, *Highway 61 Revisited,* was the most apocalyptic. Overall, the perceptible shift from protest to apocalyptic—and later to the personal—was a shift from public to private, from the temporal to the universal to the more narrowly personal. . . .

In the time between "Hard Rain" and *Highway 61,* Dylan himself seems to have undergone more than a sea change. He moved through his period of public protest to a discovery that for himself the devastation he had been trying to sing about and the wasteland he had seen were really internal and personal. He discovered that apocalyptic imagery said more about an individual's soul than about what happens to the physical world. It was a Romantic discovery in the same way that many other poets, from William Blake and Coleridge to Eliot, Hart Crane, and Richard Wilbur, have discovered the significance of apocalypse for the human imagination. It is no accident that songs listed on this album—for example, "Tombstone Blues," "Desolation Row," and "Just Like Tom Thumb's Blues"—are greatly indebted to the wasteland imagery of the early poems of T. S. Eliot: "Gerontion," "The Hollow Men," and, of course, . . . *The Waste Land.*

It is *The Waste Land* which provides source and background for much of "Just Like Tom [Thumb's] Blues" with its Easter rain and aura of spiritual malaise. And it is *The Waste Land,* crossed with Tennessee Williams' apocalpytic play *Camino Real* which provides principles of structure and considerable substance for the brilliant song "Desolation Row," with its death dance of characters and circus vignettes. . . . Circus, and dance of death, and ship of fools.

But there is still another twist. For Dylan's apocalyptic songs are something that Eliot's apocalyptic lines are not—they are comic, discordant, and ultimately absurd. It is true that there is imagery and incident in *The Waste Land* that border on the comic, but they are always directed in some way to the purpose of satirizing social types and society at large. The apocalyptic imagery in the latter portions of Eliot's poem is another matter, for it is traditional and singularly uncomic. Still, Dylan's admixture of the apocalyptic and the comically absurd, if *not* anticipated by Eliot, is nevertheless *not* unprecedented. "Desolation Row," for example, as I have noted, owes as much, in imagery, character, and structure, to Tennessee Williams' *Camino Real* as it does to Eliot. This song, and others, moreover, owe more, one might even venture, to the theater of Jean Genet, than they do to any of Dylan's generously acknowledged debts to folk and popular performers.

Even more significantly, however, I should like to propose that these apocalyptic songs constitute the most recent contribution to and manifestation of that American literary tradition defined by R. W. B. Lewis as stemming from Herman Melville's novel of disguises and metamorphoses, *The Confidence Man* (1857), and a tradition given new impetus through the absurd visions of Nathanael West's *The Day of the Locust* (with its title borrowed from Revelation), and renewed quite possibly by such novels as Joseph Heller's *Catch-22,* Thomas Pynchon's *V,* and Flannery O'Connor's *Wise Blood*. . . .

[It] is apparent to me that no *poet* has worked the *comic* apocalypse with as much success as the "song poet" Dylan has. His success in this vein makes *Highway 61 Revisited,* in my opinion, his most valuable single album to date, his most original contribution. And a genuine understanding of the "literary" content of these songs and of their place in a discernible literary tradition helps to explain still another phenomenon.

In their evocation of the comically but absurdly apocalyptic vision, these songs, despite the gaiety and the jauntiness of much of the music—but perhaps in part because of these very qualities—are disturbing, disconcerting, even frightening. . . .

[It] was in his apocalyptic songs that Dylan expressed, and undoubtedly faced, the terrifying truths of his own imagination and psyche. But the rub is that it could not end with his own confrontation with the reaches of the self. In rejecting songs of protest against munitions manufacturers, and in attacking those righteous people who wage war, confident that God is with them; in rejecting all songs which project *society* into an externalized villain, standing somewhere out there to be overcome, Dylan unleashed for the multitudes what in the past, historically, was available only to a handful of readers. For in the "electric age" of instant communication through oral and visual image, these ideas are no longer the province of literature exclusively; they are no longer by necessity limited, in their most artistic forms (and propagandistic forms, too), to the initiates of a *literate* culture.

*George Monteiro, "Dylan in the Sixties," in* South Atlantic Quarterly *(reprinted by permission of the Publisher; copyright 1974 by Duke University Press, Durham, North Carolina), Spring, 1974, pp. 160-72.*

*Nashville Skyline, New Morning* and *Self-Portrait* did have some moments of invention and purity, but what passed for mellowness did so only by pathetic comparison, and was mostly bland and monotonic.

Now Dylan has come alive again. In *Planet Waves* (Asylum Records) he incorporates the density of his nightmare vision of America with a new sweet richness, a *credible* romanticism, a hope. The reality of this time is not contained in his lyrics, which are more subtle than the "moon/June" period of *New Morning*—though still a little too close for comfort—but in the revived brilliance of his music. . . .

[If] the lyrics are still not consistently up to his earlier visionary lyrics, this is only to say that Dylan, thank God, is not complete. His longings, his hopes, mostly about love, are evident; a separate peace also contains its own warfare, and clarity is purchased not by running away from reality but by finding within it the strength to go on, to go *through,* with energy and style, and not to quit by abdicating one's humanity. He is not, like so many ashram seekers these days, "blissed out"; he is, we might say, "blissed *in*"—alive not at the price of mind and emotions, but within them. "It's never been my duty to remake the world at large/Nor is it my intention to sound the battle charge," he sings. Does he protest a tiny bit too much? His energy speaks for itself, and where there is intelligent energy these days there is a battle charge of sorts, like it or not. His love-visions, especially in the two versions of "Forever Young," in "You Angel You," "Something There Is About You," and "Wedding Song," have the stuff of lived life in them. Where so much of contemporary mass culture, especially Hollywood, tries to short-circuit the traumas of love with utter cynicism, Dylan embraces the *effort* of love. So his declarations of love have weight precisely because we know they have not come easily. The sweet wistfulness of "Forever Young"—a '70s version of Kipling's "If," and more to the contemporary point—is all the more poignant when set against the luminous mournfulness of "Dirge" ("I Hate Myself for Loving You"). With several dimensions rippling through *Planet Waves,* each becomes more than what it, by itself, would amount to. Even "Dirge" is multidimensional, moving from "You were just a painted face on a trip down suicide row" through "In this age of fiberglass I'm searching for a gem" to "I paid the price of solitude but at least I'm out of debt," and then "No use to apologize, what difference would it make?" Even the most tender "Wedding Song" admits: "What's lost is lost, we can't regain what went down in the flood." Like Paul Simon, whose *Here Comes Rhymin' Simon* is one of the loveliest albums of the '70s, Dylan has survived with his clarity and imagination intact.

In the '60s Dylan helped make anxiety, desperation, vision, the will to transcend and combativeness credible in the culture. Now he helps make faith credible: not blind faith, but faith that sees. As Auden said of Yeats, in the prison of his days he teaches the free man how to praise.

*Todd Gitlin, in* The New Republic *(reprinted by permission of* The New Republic; *© 1974 by Harrison-Blaine of New Jersey, Inc.), April 20, 1974, p. 25.*

# E

## EKWENSI, Cyprian 1921-

**A Nigerian-born Ibo novelist, short story writer, and pharmacist, Ekwensi is considered a masterful stylist, most skillful in his depiction of rural Africans forced into developing urban centers. (See also *Contemporary Authors*, Vols. 29-32.)**

If [Ekwensi] were an American we would not have much difficulty in assessing his position. He would be a best-selling book-of-the-month-club author. But it needs little knowledge of the contemporary African scene to appreciate the significant difference between a writer such as Chinua Achebe, intellectual, classic, and a novelist who can declare, "I am a writer who regards himself as a writer for masses." With such a determination, it is easy to see where the obvious strengths and weaknesses of Ekwensi's writing will lie. He often dangerously approaches the sentimental, the vulgar and melodramatic. Behind his work stands a reading of American popular fiction and paperback crime stories. Yet Ekwensi's writing cannot be dismissed with such assertions. The very practice of writing, the developing professionalism of his work, makes us find in Ekwensi a new and perhaps important phenomenon in African writing. By constant productivity, his style is becoming purged of its derivative excess and his plots begin to take on a less picaresque structure. Ekwensi is interesting because he is concerned with the present, with the violence of the new Lagos slums, the dishonesty of the new native politicians. Other Nigerian novelists have sought their material from the past, the history of missionaries and British administration as in Chinua Achebe's books, the schoolboy memoirs of Onuora Nzekwu. Ekwensi faces the difficult task of catching the present tone of Africa, changing at a speed that frighteningly destroys the old certainties. In describing this world, Ekwensi has gradually become a significant writer. His development can be traced through the three novels that have been published in this country. If there are disconcerting intrusions into his later work of bad writing and scenes of sheer silliness, there is also a growing understanding of what he can achieve, the description of the face of the new Nigeria which has become the new Africa. Only Ekwensi has dared to approach the contemporary scene with critical satire. For others the fact of independence seems too triumphant for the more recent changes to be recorded.

It is in his latest novel *Beautiful Feathers* that Ekwensi best exhibits those characteristics that will make him important in the African literature. His earlier books had their commendable moments, but the melodrama and the falseness of their situations make them remarkable largely for their energy and enthusiasm. In his first novel, *People of the City* (. . . 1954), we have a surfeit of incidents, enough for three normal books. . . .

By the time Ekwensi's second novel *Jagua Nana* was published in 1961 there were already promising changes. The major character is a whore with the heart of gold who only wants to find true love. This is an obvious stereotype from western fiction. But Jagua Nana has a stagey life of her own, and if not subtle, she has an urgent liveliness. Perhaps we regret what a popular film script some elements of this book will make and we learn that this is to be the first film produced with a Nigerian story. But there is a more significant element in this book than the adventures of Jagua's generous promiscuity. Jagua meets Uncle Taiwo, the secretary of the major political party. He becomes Ekwensi's most successful character. He has a tremendous power. He is grossly amorous, shamelessly venial, crass and vicious. His huge laugh roars without humor at the follies of his challengers. Perhaps he has some part of his origin in the Huey Long type of American politician but Uncle Taiwo remains African; an African who has taken from the west all its evil, its greed and corruption, its tricks of shabby political manipulation. This figure is the most sure and powerful creation of modern African fiction in spite of all the praise of Achebe's noble priests.

Ekwensi's third novel called *Burning Grass* is a tale of the Fulani tribe and outside the normal themes of his work, but with the publication of *Beautiful Feathers* in 1963, he begins to show achievement as well as potential. There are lapses in the style and the old sentimentality pushes itself in occasionally, but the moments are rarer and only emphasize the many superior sections of the book.

The story of *Beautiful Feathers* concerns Wilson Iyari who, like Ekwensi, is a druggist and is also ambitiously forming his own political party to foster the cause of pan-African solidarity. Ekwensi structures his book to balance Iyari's increasing prominence and success as a politician against his failure as a husband and a father. The literary sophistication of this construction is in total contrast to the, at best, picaresque organization of *People of the City*. . . .

The writing in . . . scenes [in *Beautiful Feathers*] is a measure of Ekwensi's growing confidence. When it is employed in the political scenes, his characterization is even more effective. It suggests that one day Ekwensi will write a full scale political satire of present day Nigeria; vicious, sardonic, and pointed. In this novel there is no single character with the grand solidity, the Falstaffian grossness of Uncle Taiwo [in *Jagua Nana*], but there are others of a similar caliber. . . .

The satiric portraits are more effective than the idealistic description of politics. The portrait of the president of the republic is too nobly wise, improbably benign, with virtues that read like the praises of Joseph Stalin some years ago. Less successful too, are the scenes where Wilson represents his country at the Pan-African Conference. Perhaps Ekwensi has little conviction about the probable efficacy of the Pan-African movement. Certainly pious platitudes take the place of sharp perception. This might determine Ekwensi on the best direction for his future writing, but one must admit that Ekwensi does not even seem very certain of what are the relative qualities of his writing. The latter part of the book has much less to recommend it and shows the ever threatening influences of bad movies and cheap magazine stories on Ekwensi. . . .

It may seem after these comments that the total of Ekwensi's achievement is not very extensive. Some bits of *People of the City,* a character in *Jagua Nana,* several scenes from *Beautiful Feathers.* But Ekwensi is a prolific writer and each novel has shown a development in his control and creativity. Until that sloppy ending, *Beautiful Feathers* can be measured against any novel we have yet had from Africa. It may be that Ekwensi's very weaknesses will prove to be the source of his future promise. If his attempt to be popular and modern leads him into the trivial and shallow, it also saves him from the contrary threat that makes pedagogic competence and mediocrity the common flaws of some African writing. His energy and liveliness may be controlled by a more serious subject and indeed there is already evidence of this. I shall expect Ekwensi's next novel to show this increasing depth and sophistication. Some critics apparently feel that his attempt at the merely popular makes his writing unworthy of serious critical consideration. I believe that they may be missing not only a new phenomenon in African writing, but a novelist who will have the potential to create books far more profound and complex than those he has so far achieved.

*John F. Povey, "Cyprian Ekwensi and 'Beautiful Feathers,'" in* Critique: Studies in Modern Fiction, *Vol. VIII, No. 1, 1965, pp. 63-9.*

Cyprian Ekwensi is the earliest and most prolific of the socially realistic Nigerian novelists. His first writings were mythological fragments and folk tales. From these African materials he turned to the city and its urban problems, which he now feels are the major issues confronting his people. . . .

Certainly his realism is his predominant characteristic; his reliance on sociological material often mars his fiction with the superficial patina of a journalistic exposé, but at his best moments his vision of the animal vitality of human struggle is powerful and evocative. Even at his weakest, when he indulges in what his critics call a "true detective" or "modern romance" level, he still exhibits narrative agility and inventiveness. . . .

[The] journey motif—that of the young man's initiation into an awareness of adult responsibilities and burdens, into a choice between the magical past (his father's mysterious "wandering") and a present time shorn of the gift and charm of potent superstition—is what impels all of Ekwensi's fiction, even his most urban book, *Jagua Nana,* in which Jagua goes back to the Eastern section to find a potency she has squandered in the modern city. *Burning Grass,* though entirely devoted in setting to the rural North, refers at many points to what has become the central thesis of Ekwensi's work: the ambivalent, destructive-invigorating city life of Lagos. . . .

Ekwensi's thematic symbols [may be found in *Beautiful Feathers*]. The beautiful but errant woman sacrifices herself for the virtuous man; the life of the city is represented as another kind of hell: "Lagos was rapidly becoming Nigeria's divorce centre. It was the mark of its outward sophistication that nowhere did a happy marriage really exist" . . .; the inhabitants of the city are beautiful people turned bestial and captive.

*Beautiful Feathers* is a familiar story, and very familiar territory for Ekwensi. It is, however, Ekwensi's most economically written work; the journalistic and sociological conglomeration of details which marred his earlier urban novels have been carefully avoided. In its portrayal of urban realities and the secrets of men behind locked apartment doors, the novel is powerful, but it is also a quasi-fairy tale, with its solution to political problems lying in the hands of beautiful wives and mistresses sacrificing their lives for the cause of a virtuous man.

*Martin Tucker, in his* Africa in Modern Literature: A Survey of Contemporary Writing in English, *Ungar, 1967, pp. 74-5, 82.*

* * *

## ELKIN, Stanley 1930-

**Elkin is an American novelist and short story writer whose technically brilliant fiction is episodic in nature, often constructed around vignettes or anecdotes. (See also *Contemporary Authors*, Vols. 9-12, rev. ed.)**

The first story in [*Criers and Kibitzers, Kibitzers and Criers*] sounds a note of unrelieved despair, but the final one echoes with a moving shout for the human spirit—drowning both criers and *kibitzers* with its improbable splendor, and even if the misfits who crown Union Square fail to recognize its significance, the reader of these nine remarkable stories can hardly fail to do so, for their blend of farce and pathos, their sheer mastery of style and martinet-like understanding of the human condition surely make *Criers and Kibitzers, Kibitzers and Criers* one of the most important collections of short stories published in recent years.

*David Galloway, in* The Southern Review, *Vol. IV, No. 3, Summer, 1968, p. 860.*

That literature, like all our institutions and rationalizations, is counterfeit is no matter for despair. On the contrary,

[the] recognition of absurdity helps the humanist to remain merely human since he is aware of the lies of life and of his own pretense. He refuses to jump over the times that test his humanity. . . .

The humanist transvaluates within a world of lies. The absurdist, tortured by this world, cannot get beyond the shock that it is not true; he devises perspectives of pasts and futures, histories and fantasies, the fields of the galloping imagination, in order to keep the imagination untested by this life. . . .

Parody in the contemporary absurdist novel [in this instance, Elkin's *A Bad Man*] is a serious matter. It clears the way for the heroism of language. The old character, morality, and metaphysics are mere shadows with which substantially fleshed words can box. The maker of metaphors is, like Barth's Burlingame, master of infinite disguises, and this lying, like Kierkegaard's, is meant to deceive us into the one truth—that fiction is a holy compensation for the loss of consoling gods. The novelist as hero uses his words to parody social relationships or spiritual yearnings, not as much in scorn of moral or metaphysical seriousness as in protest against aesthetic limitations. . . . Stanley Elkin's bad man [is] conceived as a cluster of rhetorical attributes and [is] actually a parody of a bad man (the moral competition between good and bad is simply the deck of cards). . . .

The fantasy of identity through victimization, the search for use, becomes a structural metaphor that displays itself lavishly and has nothing to do with moral value or metaphysical possibility. It is no wonder then that the final trial in Elkin's novel deliberately pretends to offer a qualitative judgment but merely teases us with it; the verdict nullifies any potential moral or metaphysical contest between crowd and hero and leaves the novelist in solitary liberation, "free to plunder and profane" . . ., victorious over morality, philosophy, and his clutter of characters.

*Naomi Lebowitz, "The Twentieth-Century Novel: Old Wine in New Bottles," in* Humanism and the Absurd in the Modern Novel, *Northwestern University Press, 1971, pp. 125-26, 128.*

Elkin does not theorize about laughter, but it is everywhere in [*A Bad Man*]. It is used, as the bulk of the writers in the sixties use it—in black humor, mixing it with pain, stirring our consciences without moralizing, and gaining some control over the despair that threatens to hand the plaguey mess over to everyone's Warden Fisher. In one parenthetical comment, Feldman mentions laughter: "It is in the long sad tradition of my people to pluck laughter from despair." Even as Feldman says it, Elkin means it, demonstrates it, and mocks it; this is, in small, an example of how he uses laughter.

Because *A Bad Man* removes . . . the last toehold on reality—the formal distinctions between good and evil—it is a good example of the kind of fable that was written in the sixties. It is not really a creation of fantastical characters moving in a fantastical world for the sake of escape or to illustrate abstract moral principle. It is a demonstration of what is fabulous about the actual world we live in. Filled with moments that shock us with their seeming fidelity to the known . . ., the book drives us back and forth from saying it is no world we know to saying it is exactly the world we know. *A Bad Man* removes all doubt that abstractions about Meaning could have any value. It is simply a world incredibly fabulous, filled with some force called Warden Fisher that overwhelms us, but against which we can still say with Feldman that life is worth affirming. Faced with so vast a confusion between fact and fiction, good and evil, life and death, and faced with a choice between Fisher's sterility and Feldman's madness, all that can be said is what Feldman's secretary tells him: "The world is getting to be a terrible place, and I don't know if it's your kind or their kind who makes it more awful, but if we must have terror, let it be gay and exciting, I say." . . .

*Raymond M. Olderman, "The Fisher King Turns Warden," in his* Beyond the Waste Land: A Study of the American Novel in the Nineteen-Sixties, *Yale University Press, 1972, pp. 52-71.*

Plots are only secondary . . . in Elkin's work, mere frameworks from which to deluge the reader with a Niagara of words—all controlled by a virtuoso. His narrator-heroes talk, dream, fantasize, backflash, surprising us in every paragraph, showing ennui at times, but never becoming inarticulate.

Publisher's Weekly *(reprinted from August 13, 1973, issue of* Publisher's Weekly, *published by R. R. Bowker Company, a Xerox company; copyright © 1973 by Xerox Corporation), August 13, 1973, pp. 47-8.*

Certainly [Elkin's] is a remarkably various talent, and the stories in "Searches and Seizures" nicely illustrate its range. . . .

This is an art that takes time—his scenes are comic turns that build cunningly toward climax in deflative bathos, and in the novels there's an inclination toward the episodic, the compulsive storyteller's looseness about connections and logic. . . .

In Elkin's fiction, violence may bring at least the illusion of renewal . . .; or it may bring a recognition, however appalling, of how one's own fate fits into the general fate of humankind. . . . In any case, the seizure that follows the search is an act of possessing, or being possessed by, something worth knowing, and Stanley Elkin is finally a good deal more than just another comic novelist.

*Thomas R. Edwards, in* The New York Times Book Review *(©1973 by The New York Times Company; reprinted by permission), October 21, 1973, p. 3.*

Stanley Elkin is one of those talented but quirky writers who seem always to stand on the brink of both popularity and critical acclaim without, somehow, achieving either. Critics tend to carp at him—and I am afraid I am about to do so, too—giving with the one hand and taking with the other, while the public has simply refused to respond to him in any manner commensurate with his considerable gifts. In his previous novels and collection of stories . . ., he has demonstrated himself to be both an extraordinarily funny writer and an unusually complex and serious one. His language is unfailingly superb; he is, without question, one of the finest prose stylists that we have. Unfortunately, these qualities have not been an unmixed blessing, as we shall see.

In the three novellas that make up [*Searches and Seizures*] . . . Elkin's virtues are on prominent display. His language has never been more brilliant, his metaphors never more apposite and finely tuned, his erudition never more dazzling. . . . All of [the central characters] are rootless wanderers; all of them in their various fashions are seekers not only after truth but logic, structure, rationality. Like most human beings, they ask only to be given something to live for. Like most human beings, they fail to find it. At the heart of each of these stories lies the death of God and the failure of philosophy. It is at once our bitterest dilemma and the source of our greatest fiction, a nettle to be grasped and grasped again: the heartbreaking quandary of the human condition.

Yet for all Elkin's acuity, formidable skill and astonishing inventiveness, two of these tales do not succeed and the third—*The Condominium*—seems both overlong and occasionally overwrought. Elkin's characters are artifacts, superbly sculptured statuary adorned with rich garlands of prose. Sedentary, separate from us, their gestures frozen, they are meant to be observed but not experienced, admired but not touched. The strength of the writing imbues them with a kind of static life, but it does not bestow upon them either an autonomous vitality or a poignant humanity. They exist to prove a point. The way in which they are written about is more important than the way they react to their surroundings, and they are trundled from place to place like demonstration models, more for the purpose of description than for faltering and imperfect reasons of their own. In a way, the prose itself becomes the hero.

Only in *The Condominium* is the protagonist acted upon by his environment, his dilemma shaped by circumstance and not by language. . . . Despite a certain ornate feverishness, it shows us what Elkin is capable of when he is able to liberate himself from the chains of his own artistry and contemplate his plot as closely as he contemplates his faultless metaphors. One fervently wishes that he would do it more often; once he grants himself such freedom, it seems as though there is nothing he cannot do.

*L. J. Davis, in* Book World—The Washington Post (© The Washington Post), *October 28, 1973, pp. 10-11.*

In *Boswell, A Bad Man* and *The Dick Gibson Show,* Stanley Elkin demonstrated lavish verbal and comic gifts, a generosity of spirit and a talent for staging extravaganzas of the absurd. If his plots lurched and his ideas went off like random flares, Elkin's characters commanded attention because of the manic way they acted out their necessities.

In *Searches & Seizures,* a collection of three novellas, each Elkin hero obeys his needs with results that vary from the bitterly funny to the preposterous and pathetic. . . .

Elkin, one of America's most inventive comic writers, is also adept at old-fashioned realism.

Time *(reprinted by permission from* Time, The Weekly Newsmagazine*; copyright Time Inc.), October 29, 1973, pp. E3, 122.*

Character, like language, is a defense against disorder, and the real subject of the three short novels contained in *Searches and Seizures* is a complicated invention of character by means of snowballing language. The writer invents characters who invent themselves as they talk and thereby invent him, the writer. . . .

What guides and gives structure to these fictions is Elkin's fidelity to the oddness of his own imagination, which in turn simulates a fidelity to the jerky, arbitrary movements of the real world. This means that the pieces of the fictions—patches, paragraphs, sentences, gags—tend to be better than the wholes they hardly turn out to be parts of, and William H. Gass's allusion (on the dustjacket of the book) to Henry James's notion of the "beautiful and blessed nouvelle" is so inapt as almost to constitute a definition in reverse of what Elkin is doing. Of the three stories here, only the third comes together to make the comic, desperate sense the other two hint at rather darkly.

*Michael Wood, in* The New York Review of Books *(reprinted with permission from* The New York Review of Books; © *1974 by NYREV, Inc.), March 21, 1974, pp. 20-1.*

I must have been mad or blind or ignorant to have missed, when it first appeared in 1965, *Criers & Kibitzers, Kibitzers & Criers* by Stanley Elkin. But no matter. I've now caught up with him . . ., and I've spent days reading (and rereading some) these superb stories. One I've read three or four times, "A Poetics for Bullies," which comes as close to running, colloquial, irresistible poetry as anything I've ever read. To be able to sustain a teenaged first-person narrative like this which convinces completely and yet pleases by the beauty of its prose is a major achievement. In that much-maligned and often-neglected genre the short story, there are indeed still some giants in the English language, and I now count Elkin among them.

*Doris Grumbach, "Fine Print," in* The New Republic *(reprinted by permission of* The New York Republic; © *1974 by The New Republic, Inc.), March 23, 1974, pp. 32-3.*

* * *

## ENRIGHT, D(ennis) J(oseph) 1920-

**An English novelist, poet, and essayist of great range and learning, Enright is highly regarded for his intelligent, witty, and compassionate fiction. (See also *Contemporary Authors,* Vols. 1-4, rev. ed.)**

Enright's sympathies, humor and talent are best suited to writing little vignettes, such as his "University Examinations in Egypt" and "The Tourist and the Geisha." But too frequently his impulse to write poems appears to have been vitiated by his fear of pretentiousness, and his unwillingness to recognize that the poet who respects poetry as an art has sufficient reasons for creating it.

*William Van O'Connor, in his* The New University Wits and the End of Modernism *(© 1963 by Southern Illinois University Press; reprinted by permission of Southern Illinois University Press), Carbondale: Southern Illinois University Press, 1963, p. 113.*

A series of books by D. J. Enright shows one kind of partial solution to the characteristic problem of mere articulateness. Enright's form is usually very flat and conversational, approaching in a way the 'minimal' style of Robert Creeley, and though actually the poetry is intellectually oriented the statement is kept as simple as possible. He sometimes sounds a more rational Lawrence, or a plainer Empson. A tremendous identification with the betrayed innocents of the earth marks his writing and, together with his tart self-knowledge, accounts for the basically sympathetic speaking character he presents. Enright's subject matter gives him a great advantage, for he has lived and taught literature in various foreign parts, particularly in Asia, and the hard-bitten realism of what he reports is intrinsically of the greatest interest. In his most telling collection, *Addictions* (1962), the bitterness of his encounters with official repression in a 'new' nation explicitly enters a number of the poems. His disillusionment—that of the Western radical with the developing, altered world which he himself has helped create—is all the more convincing because Enright, despite his own unfortunate experience, does not allow himself to condemn humanitarianism or social progress. It is, rather, the impersonality, the inevitable philistine indifference of political process to the ordinary person, and at the same time certain doubts about his own motives, that disturb him. An unusual sequence of poems (for Enright) in this same volume concerns a love-affair that has gone wrong in very much the same sense as modern history has gone wrong. Somehow, things went awry; the dreamt-of came to pass and yet was not what it should have been. In his highly candid and precise speech and his amateurish free-verse, he involves us, wearies us, stamps his personality on our sympathies.

*M. L. Rosenthal, in his* The New Poets: American and British Poetry Since World War II *(copyright © 1967 by M. L. Rosenthal; reprinted by permission of Oxford University Press, Inc.), Oxford University Press, 1967, pp. 222-23.*

One can see that the humanist poet, with his particularly strong sense of the real, objective existence of human problems—and his feeling that, while as a poet he may be called upon only to describe them, as a man he is partially responsible for helping in their solution—would begin to have misgivings about his art *qua* art. Certainly Enright's Japan poems show that his occasional hankerings for poetic purity are outweighed by his doubts about poetry itself: for him, literature is subordinate to life. . . .

Despite, however, Enright's scruples about the possible pitfalls of humanist poetry, one's final judgment is decidedly not that he falls into them. Rather one admires the unending effort to balance the respective claims of life and art, realizing that the emphasis placed on the former demands of the poet considerable artistic self-denial without bringing the man the compensating sense of having solved the problems of the world in which he lives.

*Philip Gardner, "D. J. Enright Under the Cherry Tree," in* Contemporary Literature *(© 1968 by the Regents of the University of Wisconsin), Vol. 9, No. 1, Winter, 1968, pp. 100-11.*

[Enright's] poems themselves disclose the little faith that [he] seems to have in them. When he attempts a technical device, he makes it obvious, as though the skillful use of his craft were an embarrassment. He is a verse-writer treating subjects that call for serious poetry. He is unwilling to abide in his poems. It is this unwillingness, I think, that makes it impossible for him to condense and sharpen his poems to the point of conviction and which prevents him, except occasionally, from surprising us with the vitality of language. . . .

Behind these poems [in *The Typewriter Revolution & Other Poems*] selected from an entire career, there is a refusal—an unwillingness to engage language at any but a most obvious or trivial level; perhaps from a fear of failure, perhaps from a belief that poetry no longer can bear the excitement of a real commotion. Whatever the case, Mr. Enright resembles altogether too much those people he so acutely described as thinking "of a piece of poetry as if it were some kind of pussy cat which will sit and purr on their knees while they stroke it lazily." . . .

*John R. Reed, "Magicians and Others," in* Poetry *(© 1973 by The Modern Poetry Association; reprinted by permission of the Editor of* Poetry*), April, 1973, pp. 48-9.*

D. J. Enright writes of his childhood with beguiling ease. The poems [in *The Terrible Shears*] seem cut-up prose, until you pick at them. Then you find they're sharp as glass. As undistorting, too. . . .

He seems to me the wittiest poet writing, and the wit constantly suggests well-springs of pity and anger beneath it.

*John Carey, in* London Magazine, *August-September, 1973, pp. 125-26.*

For many years D. J. Enright's verse has drawn its subject-matter chiefly from his experiences as 'a mendicant professor' in places as distant from one another, and from England, as Berlin, Cairo, and Singapore. In this . . . collection [*The Terrible Shears*] the poet comes home: not, however, to the England of today, but to that of his childhood in Leamington during the Twenties. . . .

Technically many of the poems have the appearance of being as casual as they can be without lapsing into prose; they are given to unrhymed, conjunctional line-endings, broken rhythms, and a deliberate avoidance of sonority. Yet one does not feel for a moment that they have been easy to write. Candour is never easily come by. Nor is the capacity steadfastly to deny that the pains inflicted upon us by the world have in some way been good for us, or have become emblematic of a truth larger and more important to us than life itself. For all its humour, delicacy, and gentleness of tone, perhaps the highest praise one can give to *The Terrible Shears* is to say that the book is unforgiving. It isn't a sense of present injury on the part of the author that the poems express: far from it. If time and subsequent experience have not allayed these griefs, it is because there was no experience subsequent to them, then, and no time existed other than that in which they occurred. That is precisely the condition which the poems evoke.

*Dan Jacobson, "Life and Hard Times," in* New Statesman, *September 28, 1973, p. 432.*

D. J. Enright's reviews and essays [*Man is an Onion*] are generally first-rate pieces of literary journalism. Having accomplished their original purposes, however, they do not deserve to be enshrined in the pages of a book. Witty, urbane and knowledgeable, his comments on subjects ranging from British, American and European fiction and poetry to oriental literature and philosophy undoubtedly entertained and instructed readers of [various] journals. . . . As a collection, though, his judgments of a biography of Samuel Richardson, Doris Lessing's series of novels in *Children of Violence,* Mann's letters, and books of minor poems and critical essays simply do not add up to any meaningful particular perspective on literature or any profound esthetic statement.

To be sure, Enright can be devastatingly clever (although grammatically careless), as when he says, "It only took God six days to create the whole world. It really shouldn't require six hundred pages for Miss Lessing to destroy a part of it." He can be most sensible, as in his response to the tone of Anthony Burgess's book on Shakespeare: "It is unwise for an author to tyrannise—and rashest of all, perhaps, to tyrannise over our more than national poet." In dealing with devotees of Nabokov, he can be tellingly shrewd: "The Nabokovites find nothing so shockingly immoral as morality."

His assessments of Hermann Hesse's artistic limitations, Chairman Mao's appeal to the Chinese past and national character, and Yukio Mishima's tragic death reveal a sensitive, cosmopolitan critic. In its parts, then, the volume is unobjectionable; unfortunately, in this instance, the whole is considerably less than the sum of its parts.

*Robert D. Spector, in* Books Abroad, *Vol. 48, No. 2, Spring, 1974, p. 423.*

Although reviewers and critics have been kind to D. J. Enright and his poems, he has, for the most part, been the butt of ossified opinion, treated to the same review, sometimes by the same reviewer. Minds have been made up. Enright is to be thought of as a poet of manner. Descriptions like 'mordant', 'sardonic', 'laconic', and 'mischievous' crop up with embittering regularity as the sum of what he has been about for the 20 years or more of his publishing life, as if he has been, and is, little more than a tone of voice. Unsurprising then that he was once forced to say how he wished a little attention might be paid to what he said. . . .

One of the difficulties with Enright is assessing his affiliation with The Movement. Reading his poems, I find myself thinking he was a non-member, a subversive associate from the very beginning. And bother his inclusion in *New Lines.* On the other hand, in a few poems he writes as if he had been the *only* poet to take what The Movement allegedly stood for with any seriousness. . . .

But Enright's poetic antagonisms do appear to have arisen more from urgent social necessity than concern for the health or otherwise of poetry-writing. Lucidity is humane, obscurantist symbol-making and verbosity little more than dandified avoidance of important realities. While Enright believed something on these lines, The Movement as a whole approved of 'purity of diction', an altogether more literary concern, urgent enough in their eyes, but an animating impulse which, if not drastically opposed to Enright's more thematic concerns, was at least strikingly different.

Enright claims to be unpolitical, or anti-political. . . .

Many of his Eastern poems conjure situations of the underdog beset by politicians. He sees the goodness of life riddled with doctrinaire racketeering after power and sway. Again and again, despite the liberalism of his stance, he shows his toughest poetic allegiance to be with Brecht, the Brecht of *Buckow Elegies,* suspicious of authority, of governments, fearful for people, unsure of where he is going, of whether there can be any worthwhile direction. His human tactic is imitated from the Chinese whom he admires. Survival at all costs is his maxim. Cunning, connivance, resistance, patience, silence, and anything else which helps the skin grow thick, are all permissible.

In his . . . book of poems, *The Terrible Shears,* about his working-class childhood and adolescence in Leamington Spa in the 1920s and 1930s, Enright's un- or anti-political gestures collapse. Some, if not all, of his attitudes approach closely on the positions of Amis, Conquest and Larkin. This opens up an enormously interesting area for speculation on the political implications that might always have been inherent in The Movement. In Enright's case, the interest is redoubled. His origins are markedly different. His literary life bears the scars of struggle. Yet, and with what ease, his humanity, his detestation of the 'vituperative humming' of politics, converts in the context of Britain's class-ridden society to what seems suspiciously like complacency. In Britain, there is no such approach as the 'unpolitical', while the 'anti-political' is, as it must be, in the context of practising institutions and vituperatively humming politicians, the most political approach of all, negative only in the sense of being inactive. . . . Enright's poems offer, and with admirable fullness, many of the problems which concern contemporary poetry.

*Douglas Dunn, "Underwriter," in* New Statesman, *June 28, 1974, p. 927.*

# F

## FARRELL, James T(homas) 1904-

**Farrell is an American novelist, short story writer, and essayist. Considered a leading practitioner of contemporary American realistic fiction, Farrell is best known for his trilogy, *Studs Lonigan*. (See also *Contemporary Authors*, Vols. 5-8, rev. ed.)**

Self-education comes high in America, and Farrell has paid for it—as in differing respects did Faulkner and Hemingway—with his whole career. Its cost to him consists in the fact that the attitudes it has given him are largely provincial; the morals are parochial; and the modes are pedantic, for it appears to be the case with the self-educated literary man in America that he tends always to confuse learning and pedantry and that in pursuing the one he will caricature the other. . . .

It becomes clear in reading over the prose in [*Reflections at Fifty*] that Farrell went to school, but it is just as clear that he went to school to the wrong teachers. His prose is a savage compound of jargon and rhetoric derived from French naturalist novels, the writings of William James, John Dewey, the Marxists, and the German philosophers, political manifestoes, and behaviorist psychology, and it appears to have got into the book by way of the dump truck and shovel. It has no rhythm, grace, warmth, or subtlety of style, and it is overlaid with a heavy-footed earnestness and zeal like that of a frightened schoolboy, pompous and pop-eyed, reciting a speech cribbed largely from the *Encyclopaedia Britannica*. In content it is approximately vintage 1910. I do not mean that the questions it raises are necessarily no longer in force. It is rather that one no longer expects to see them discussed in quite this fashion and at this level.

*John W. Aldridge, "The Education of James T. Farrell," in his* In Search of Heresy, *McGraw-Hill, 1956, pp. 186-91.*

[In] the Chicago of Studs Lonigan, Danny O'Neill, and Gas House McGinty, there was not only no attempt to find the sophistication and subtletly of an earlier decorum; there was absolutely no experience of it. *Young Lonigan* (1932), *The Young Manhood of Studs Lonigan* (1934), and *Judgment Day* (1935)—the novels of the Studs Lonigan trilogy were written in the self-effacing and reductive idiom of Studs himself. Herein are the demands of a point of view reduced to their lowest level; the style had not only to be equal to the subject, it had literally to *be* the subject. The consciousness was that of the spiritually impoverished lower middle class of a section of Chicago which is slowly deteriorating under social and economic pressures. It is true that Farrell, especially in the second of these novels, echoed and imitated the experiments of his more daring contemporaries, noticeably Joyce and Dos Passos; and in *Gas House McGinty* (1933) he very deliberately and with a measure of success, tried to transport the mind of Leopold Bloom from Dublin to Chicago. Aside from these experimental excursions, Farrell relied upon a literal rendering of his subject, at once subjective in its following of point of view and objective in its freedom from sentimentality of record. . . .

[The] Irish-Catholic world of a section of Chicago . . . was not a slum neighborhood; nor were the stages in Studs's decline designed to illustrate an economic thesis. "The social milieu in which he lived and was educated was one of spiritual poverty," in short, the effect of a failure of moral sanctions rather than of economic dislocation. . . .

No one has so thoroughly and so doggedly described a single area of American society as we find in the seven novels of Studs Lonigan and Danny O'Neill. The constant reiteration of the trivial and the vulgar, the thoroughly naturalistic view of the ugly and terrifying lives of these people, have a cumulative effect which is chiefly the result of Farrell's conscientious fidelity to the subject's idiom. The style, therefore, is consistently a documentary record of this world from the point of view of those who live in it and share its limitations—who in a real sense, *make* its limitations. An important part of the effect, therefore, lies in the conscientious vulgarity, profanity, and obscenity of the language—as well as the earnest inelegance of the narrative's loose and repetitive structure. There is a quality of tone, however, which enables us to see Farrell's characters more clearly (that is, to understand the tone of their feeling) than we can ever do in the case of Dos Passos' novels.

*Frederick J. Hoffman, in his* The Modern Novel in America, *Regnery, revised edition, 1963, pp. 155-58.*

[In *Judith and Other Stories,* Farrell] continues to write

about ordinary people and ordinary lives in a manner that's familiar, a bit on the old-fashioned "naturalistic" side, but still interesting and absorbing. . . . The theme of exile, from country, from the past, from self, runs quietly throughout these simple tales of people we recognize whether Farrell speaks of marriage, or love affairs, or families, or just the solitary being. The writing is mellow, not stylish, and is refreshing for its openness and genuine simplicity.

Publisher's Weekly *(reprinted from August 13, 1973, issue of* Publisher's Weekly, *published by R. R. Bowker Company, a Xerox company; copyright © 1973 by Xerox Corporation), August 13, 1973, p. 48.*

"Judith and Other Stories" is James T. Farrell's forty-fourth book, and it is a sizable one. In an introduction, the author speaks of his stories as stories "of time." The book is a continuation of his lifework: the attempt to "create out of the life I have seen, known, experienced, heard about, and imagined, a panoramic story of our days and years, a story which would continue through as many books as I would be able to write."

The time-span of "Judith" is enormous, especially since it is contained within a single individual's memory: some stories are set in 1973, the earliest in 1918. They are evidently forms of reverie, some of them sheer stream-of-association reminiscence, like "Sister" (which takes us back to a Catholic school similar to the one in the first volume of "Studs Lonigan"); some are journal-like accounts of the experiences of one Eddie Ryan, a writer originally from Chicago who now lives in New York, at the Hotel Chelsea. The most interesting stories in the book are those dealing with Eddie, who, despite his having evidently achieved recognition of sorts as writer, is an incurably lonely man. He both wants and does not want permanence; he is fairly romantic at times—he falls in love easily—and at other times so reasonable about the failures of his various love affairs that he seems almost inhuman. . . .

The difficulty with fiction that originates so firmly and authentically in "real life" is that artistic arrangement, compression with necessary distortion and the introduction of non-naturalistic elements like the symbolic (which is really a kind of shorthand, not a violation of the real), might seem a betrayal of what really happened. If a man has loved and been loved by a multitude of women, it might seem a distortion of the truth to compress them all into two or three women, in order to dramatize their personalities more vividly. How tyrannical the ostensible freedoms of literary naturalism turned out to be, after all—once the censorship battles were won, and what was shocking could not carry its own inherent dramatic value. . . .

It may be, however, that there is an inherent and perhaps extra-literary virtue in "naturalism"—that is, the scientific and objective setting-forth of the truth, at least as the writer sees it—that bypasses any critical assessment of it. Since James T. Farrell has written American classics, and since his naturalistic technique is obviously a deliberate and conscious expression of his philosophy, it would be audacious for any reviewer to suggest that he change. Perhaps simply the introduction of newer themes, as in "Judith," will be refreshing, and lead to a reorganizing of thought.

*Joyce Carol Oates, in* The New York Times Book Review *(© 1973 by The New York Times Company; reprinted by permission), November 25, 1973, pp. 14, 18.*

The works of James T. Farrell cannot be discussed singly. His 22 novels, 14 collections of short stories, essays, literary criticism and poetry all center on his pessimistic determinism, conditioned by personal experiences and confirmed through intense observation of the human scene. He is indeed considered by some to be the literary heir of Upton Sinclair and Theodore Dreiser through his consistent depiction of urban decay, social corruption and individual despair.

In *Studs Lonigan* (1935) Farrell created an epochal document detailing as no one has surpassed, the environment of prejudice, inferiority, foamy sentiment and violence of lower working class Chicago. This was succeeded by the Danny O'Neill pentalogy, the Bernard Carr trilogy (major but unevenly written novels) and over 200 short stories—often peopled with recurring characters, like faces in changing crowds, contorted always by the same hopeless grimace.

*Judith and Other Stories* presents few surprises. It possesses both the major deficiencies and cumulative persuasion of many of Farrell's preceding works. The themes of the 11 stories are familiar, the style is flat and the characters one-dimensional. These are dwarfish people even when the author, as in the title story, stresses monotonously his protagonists' highly applauded musicianship and literary productiveness. The banality of their relationship and the drone of their self-expression belie the credibility of Farrell's insistence upon their artistry.

Of the 11 stories, reflective of the author's organic thesis that "the conditions of American life create alienated and truncated personalities," only three succeed in arousing interest or empathy. "Tomorrow and Tomorrow" is a moving account of the tedious hardship experienced by the common laborer. One is pierced by the meaningless work, futile resentment and unnoticed hysteria in Bill Eliot's daily life. In "Mr. Austin," Eddie Ryan, a Farrell spokesman, effectively relates the struggle of a petty stockbroker to maintain respectability against inevitable, faceless defeat. "Tom Carroll," a lengthy and perhaps partly autobiographical story, concerns the faded days of a former radical, "hero" and esteemed historian. He is betrayed by his wife, denounced as a fascist by his son and viewed with estranged puzzlement by drifting friends. But Carroll is too tired to express his political insight which far excels that of his detractors. Fatigue overcomes him—as it does most of the characters in the other stories.

Nevertheless the complete collection succeeds in presenting a compassionate kaleidoscope of man's limitations and hapless yearning for a meaningful existence.

*Regina Barnes, "Old Master," in* The New Republic *(reprinted by permission of* The New Republic; *© 1973 by Harrison-Blaine of New Jersey, Inc.), December 22, 1973, p. 30.*

[While] Farrell's stories often present many of the same themes and characters from his novels, there are examples when the shorter form is the more successful. He has a way of perceiving the hidden occasions of success or failure (more often of failure, in Farrell) which are the kernel of good short stories, and transmuting them through his own unmistakable vision and voice.

As a theorist of the short story form, however, Farrell seems to sell himself short. "You've written books with warmth," the wife of Tom Carroll, a Farrell alter-ego says in one of these new tales [*Judith and Other Stories*]. "But people can get only so much out of a book, Tom. They can't get the warmth of a man out of his books. They must get it out of him."

Wrong. In the best short stories, as Sean O'Faolain has shown, one encounters a combination of both plausibility and personality. Without the charge of personal voltage, we get the yarn and not the man. Fortunately, there is plenty of Farrellian warmth in *Judith and Other Stories,* and it is as much for this distinctive, communicated personality so many of us continue to read him, as it is for his objective recording of an historical time and place.

Yet the voice sounds more autumnal here—as it well might: Farrell will be 70 this month. As before, the elementary forces of the universe still provide the drama and the tension. But that pertains to plot only. The personality informing the plots seems mellower. The themes of the volume are the death of love and feeling in the world (a death Farrell sees as far worse than physical death), and the humiliation of pain to man. . . .

Thus, *Judith and Other Stories* is a gallery of characters for whom the peak of life is passed, if it were ever attained at all—people reviewing their pasts in what Farrell here calls "the memory of lost ecstasies.". . .

The settings range from New York to Paris to Rome and even on to Jerusalem—some distance from the Chicago Farrell is often accused of writing about exclusively. But the Farrellian vision of a struggle between the will and the passions, with the passions always winning, remains much the same as in his first book, *Young Lonigan,* published in 1932.

*Robert Phillips, in* Commonweal *(reprinted by permission of Commonweal Publishing, Co., Inc.), February 15, 1974, pp. 493-94.*

* * *

## FIEDLER, Leslie A(aron) 1917-

**Fiedler, an American critic, novelist, and man of letters, is best known for his major critical work, *Love and Death in the American Novel.* (See also *Contemporary Authors*, Vols. 9-12, rev. ed.)**

[*Love and Death in the American Novel*], indeed, [is] a pantograph, a treatise that sets out to explain not only, as avowed, the American novel and its relation to American life, but also American social, moral, sexual, cultural, anthropological and psychological history, in fact the whole of American life, in fact America, in fact everything, or at least everything American—a qualification of, to him, fluctuating importance. Everything and everybody, accordingly, may turn out to be relevant: Conan Doyle, *Beowulf,* the Marquis de Sade (but of course), Gary Cooper, Rabelais, *Frankenstein,* Dylan Thomas. And any source, any method may supply the right answer, a possible answer, significant information, something: *The Allegory of Love,* Marxism either neat or with a *Partisan Review* admixture, Freud and Jung and their commentators, Lawrence's *Studies in Classic American Literature.* My point about this last lot is not so much that it indicates a welcome sense of being at home in the analytical armoury, an eclecticism of the kind that informs some of the best criticism now being written in English, though there is that. Rather I want to direct attention to the fact that Dr Fiedler, so far from attempting to conceal his use of these sources, makes a neat catalogue of them in his preface. Thus casually to lay one's critical kit out for inspection seems very American, or anyway non-British; our own instinct is to assume, even to pretend, that writer and reader have long ago got hold of and absorbed everything that counts, and we all know what counts. Similarly, it takes an American to feel that illumination may come from the least expected quarter, that the relative importances of things are never settled; in England, as Mr Malcolm Bradbury wrote . . . in a more general context, 'everything has happened before'. . . .

He is concerned not to shock or titillate but to explain, to demonstrate in concrete terms, the gap between American fiction and American fact. If he often, as he must by now be weary of being told, 'goes too far', he as often goes in a new and illuminating direction. He is at his most convincing when he finds and traces a division in the American novel between the sentimental strain and the Gothic. . . .

A guarded summing-up—guarded because, for all its length, this is a book of fearful compression, requiring several re-readings and re-thinkings—can lead off with the query whether some of the hard questions may not have been left unanswered. Granted that the American novelist has moved away from the centre of sex (marital, physical) to its periphery (perverted, rarefied), what in him or his environment is responsible? Granted that the bestseller in the United States preceded the serious novel instead of following in its wake, why are the two levels so often inextricably confused to this day, so that, just as in jazz, that essentially American art-form, one is shifted from this moment to that between the authentic and the banal? There are some, especially on this side of the Atlantic, who will feel that, even if fully answered, such questions lie partly, perhaps wholly, outside the brief of the literary critic, as do some of the questions the book has fully answered. To use the American novel as a couch-monologue wherewith to analyse the American psyche is a valid enterprise (and Dr Fiedler's achievement is nowhere near exhausted by being so described), but, again, there is the objection that criticism, rather than tearing aside the surface of a literary work in order to unearth one kind of truth, should concern itself with illuminating that surface ever more truthfully. . . .

[But it] does sometimes look as if the novel in English, rather than the American or the Anglo-American novel, is tomorrow's proper study; and for that purpose, as for the one he sets himself, Dr Fiedler's witty, exasperating, energetic, penetrating book will prove indispensable.

*Kingsley Amis, "Men Without Women" (1961), in his* What Became of Jane Austen? and Other Questions *(copyright © 1970 by Kingsley Amis; reprinted by permission of A. D. Peters and Company and Harcourt Brace Jovanovich), Jonathan Cape Ltd., 1970, and Harcourt, 1971, pp. 98-102.*

*Pull Down Vanity and Other Stories,* predictably enough, suffers from numerous improprieties of language; the frenzied twistings of style in these eight tales published in various periodicals between 1948 and [1963] seem to represent now Fiedler's juvenilia, now his insincere concessions to colloquial idiom, now his tendon-pulling reach for the profound. . . . Fiedler's self-doubts and uncertainties come out in his fiction. Even on the rare occasion when Fiedler's language is commensurate with his theme, there is still a spectacle of an ignoble non-hero coming to judgment.

Once he leaves the dim ancestral past for the upbeat struggles of the eastern metropolis or the midwestern university town, Fiedler's language changes from artfully direct to stridently unnatural. . . .

The stories in *Pull Down Vanity* are only in part frontier yarns of territory disputes in which the bad bourgeois society confronts the good artist or some other pair of classes strike sparks against each other. . . . A more likely common theme seems to be the removing of a counterfeit face, a shield which represents some harmful kind of innocence. Unmasked, the individual experiences reality and admits what he's been covering up all along. Following this view, the title phrase, "Pull down vanity," seems to refer to the idea of removing vain shows, taking away masks. . . .

Despite Fiedler's apparent reductive attitude—we are all dirty, we all wear the "minister's black mask"—it is his protagonists who are left holding the bag, who fight the border war; theirs alone is the mask that drops away. . . .

In summary, the [Communist] Party and the Shoestore seem to be two of Fiedler's major frontier areas. The others: the academy, the old-world Jewish *shtettl,* the Negro's societal fringe, the provincial hinterland into which the Jewish writer strays, a bachelor girls' apartment seen as love's tender trap. It is of course impossible to know the real Leslie Fiedler, for all his voluble confessions, apologias, and self-unmaskings. But in the final analysis there is a charming sincerity and inexpungable innocence in a man who can write eight diversified frontier tales of Promethean (or would-be Promethean) heroes who get humiliated and come to grief, a man who can state openly, as he did in a review of Shapiro's *Poems of a Jew*, "We are all spiritual Stalinists engaged in a continual falsification of our own histories, and we must pray for critics capable of pointing this out."

*Samuel I. Bellman, "The Frontiers of Leslie Fiedler," in* Southwest Review, *Winter, 1963, pp. 86-9.*

[There] are reasons for not reading *Back to China* in the abstract, for not writing it off as a fizzle. For one thing, Fiedler often does better on short runs; he has trouble sustaining himself in a distance effort, despite the fact that he is capable of formidable spurts. Moreover, he is still one of the most imaginative and provocative critics around, and a fictionist of real power: a number of the tales in his story collection, *Pull Down Vanity* (1962), are excellent. . . .

He seems not to have intended *Back to China* as a major work, or even as serious in effort as his first novel, *The Second Stone* (1963), echoes from which appear in the new book. More importantly, *Back to China* contains a number of themes and ideas that are of genuine importance, whatever the quality of the narrative itself.

*Back to China* is a harrowing picture of academic futility and aridity; the barren Montana terrain ("steep rock and sparse trees") seems an objective correlative of rootless, enervating pedagogy. In a nightmare vision we see a projection of the Montana Fiedler as a sterile, academic clown who realizes that all his father-figures and son-figures have failed him just as he has failed them, who can't get along with anybody, and who continues to eke out an absurd and unbearable existence. Although he will father a son, he tells himself at the end, "yet I am sterile." Always, we are told, Baro feels "caught between an impulse to play the clown, and a resolve to act the professor." . . .

[The] novel marks a decided shift in mood on Feidler's part. *The Second Stone* featured a "No!"-thunderer of relentless persistence who then sold out to the philistines (another secret fear and self-suspicion of Fiedler's?), while crowing a self-exultant "cock-a-doodle-doo." *Back to China* has a weak, fatuous agonist who is always ready to cry or say or do the wrong thing. What does this betoken for one of the few really challenging gadfly writers of our time?

*Samuel I. Bellman, "Baro Led a Barren Life," in* Saturday Review *(copyright © 1965 by Saturday Review/World, Inc.; reprinted with permission), May 1, 1965, p. 40.*

Leslie A. Fiedler, a well-known belligerent American writer, occasionally turns out verse and fiction of not very substantial merit, but most effectively functions as a polemical "literary critic." More exactly, he is a literary critic of non-literature. Using the left-handed strategy that the modern methods of literary criticism provide revelatory techniques in themselves, he writes about criminals, politics, social fads, religion, popular entertainment, bohemian ideologies, sex, and cultural power politics—his real interests—as if he were dealing with particularly obscure literary texts. Perhaps Fiedler displays his inverse best on a subject like "comic books." Playing an Aristotle of sub-literary popular culture, he uses mock-erudition to categorize comic book forms and types as significant allegories of good and evil and mythic expressions of urban folk consciousness. The argument claims more than it should, often gaining suggestiveness at the price of tangential forcing. (As in the analogy of comic books with jazz music, which ignores that jazz is not only of much different quality but, unlike comic-books, has always had a life separate from its mass-technical reproduction on records.) Fiedler does not take his burlesque scholar-criticism of comic books altogether seriously. For he makes much of the more pertinent point that the artifact of mass entertainment acquires most of its meaning as a reduction of expression to a "commodity" rather than as individual art or collective symbolism. His inversion of comic books into richer significance serves as a defiance of those who righteously attack them. Fiedler's main purpose in "The Middle Against Both Ends" comes out in the assault on the banality of standardized middleclass taste and morals because the "middle-brow" who denies the vulgar also denies the intellectual. From his opening assertion of reading comic books "with some pleasure," through his defense of all arts—elitist and popular—which concern the "instinctual and dark" (death, sex and guilt), to his final insistence on a hierarchy of intellectual values, he strikes at the "drive for conformity on the level of the timid, sentimental, mindless-bodiless genteel."

Some of the strength of Fiedler's polemic derives from his awareness that some past literary rebels' intellectual egalitarianism and cultural democracy results in both comic books and the righteousness of those that attack them. The weaknesses of the argument reveal not only the forced posture of defending comic books but a self-indulgent eagerness to win against fools—the minds inspired by the more mawkish best-selling novels and the charms of resentfully easy virtue. Why so vehemently fight cripples about toy dragons?

*Kingsley Widmer, in his* The Literary Rebel *(copyright © 1965 by Southern Illinois University Press; reprinted by permission of Southern Illinois University Press), Carbondale: Southern Illinois University Press, 1965, pp. 160-62.*

Two-thirds of [Fiedler's *The Last Jew in America*] represent a fantastic degree of ineptness and literary falsity. His stereotypes of white gentile, Indian, and Negro, for example, are utterly unreal and hence meaningless. The hysteria and frenzy that in true Fiedler-fashion underlie these stories indicate clearly not that his message is urgent or that the time is sadly out of joint, but simply that he is one of the outstanding Spasmodic prose-poets of our time. As with the Victorian Spasmodic poets or the nineteenth-century American Spasmodic fictionist John Neal, Fiedler's imaginative writing represents a series of emotional fits. And as with early American film comedies, *The Last Jew in America* and much of Fiedler's other fiction also depend heavily on the wild melee, the uninhibited free-for-all that releases a lot of pent-up tension but otherwise doesn't make much sense. . . .

The one thing needful for Fiedler: less matter and more art. Mere stereotypes and anti-stereotypes don't make good stories. The "class war" approach, so basic in Fiedler's narrow outlook (capitalism vs. socialism, artist vs. society, male vs. female, Jew vs. gentile, white vs. Negro, West vs. East), is another fond fixation of adolescence that should long ago have been given the "No! in Thunder" treatment.

*Samuel I. Bellman, "In Groups Within Groups," in* Saturday Review *(copyright © 1966 by Saturday Review/World, Inc.; reprinted with permission), July 30, 1966, pp. 31-2.*

Leslie Fiedler's new book [*The Return of the Vanishing American*] completes the "venture in literary anthropology" begun with *Love and Death in the American Novel* and continued in *Waiting for the End.* Having dealt with "*eros* and *thanatos*" and with "the hope of apocalypse and its failure," he now turns to "the Indian," which sounds odd and anticlimactic and I'm afraid finally is so, taking *The Return of the Vanishing American* as an individual critical performance. The significance of the whole venture I leave to the American Studies people to worry out—part of the fun of reading Fiedler (and of *being* him, I dare say) is imagining their solemn outrage. I am more interested in figuring out why so lively and intelligent a book leaves me feeling disappointed and annoyed.

By now the objections to Fiedler's procedures are virtually standardized. He can be careless about little accuracies . . . and silly with his analogies . . ., and his habit of melodramatizing history will not be to everyone's taste. . . . Fiedler is an incorrigible rascal, and to forbid him his tricks would deprive us of the often brilliant insights he has up his sleeve.

The insights in *The Return of the Vanishing American* are, however, achieved at a pretty high price. . . .

I don't think that Fiedler's way of treating myth is as easily transferable into prescriptive program as he wants it to be. His methods do damage not just to literature, by breaking up whole works to salvage the "authentic" fragment, but to life, making it only a kind of *materia mythica* to be arranged and manipulated without entering very deeply into the particular experiences that compose it. He doesn't mean to do this, and his career is a deserved and salutary rebuke to those who would insulate art from its human motives and consequences; but *The Return of the Vanishing American,* for all its admirable intentions and its achieved pleasures and illuminations, is finally bad medicine.

*Thomas R. Edwards, in* Partisan Review *(copyright © 1968 by Partisan Review, Inc.), Fall, 1968, pp. 606-10.*

Together, [Fiedler's *Collected Essays*] reveal [his] weaknesses—most particularly his fondness for repetition and his inability to develop a theme—but they also reveal his strengths, and, among contemporary critics, Fiedler's strengths are unique. . . .

He writes with vigor and style. He is arrogant, contemptuous of those who cannot see what he sees, but he has an uncommon wit and a talent both for satire and for pithy axioms. If he does not develop his themes, he develops the position from which they are observed: "I have been *thrice* born," he says, "first into radical dissent, then into radical disillusion and the fear of innocence, finally into whatever it is that lies beyond both commitment and disaffection." He delights in generalizations, condemning "the fact-snufflers, the truffle-hounds of science" who bring in harvests of data, all of which, he says, are "a democratic substitute for something so aristocratic as ideas, some bureaucratic ersatz for the insight of the individual thinker." Unlike most critics, Fiedler has sunk roots into American popular culture—into films and comic books—although he is often surprised that he likes it and is always more convincing when pop culture is the background, not the subject of his argument.

Fiedler is rarely boring. To be dull, a man must be either modest or incompetent, and Fiedler is neither. His writing, he is the first to say, is "the basis for a new understanding of our classic books and of our culture in general." It nearly is. . . . He tries a few close readings of texts but seems to sense that these are aberrations, gestures toward conformity. Fiedler's true lust (there is no other word for it) is for connections, for the patterns of culture he finds behind the surface forms of art. . . .

Fiedler enjoys reducing art and life to a kind of dramatic nicety. How neat for Fiedler that the unlikable Whittaker Chambers should be the just man and Hiss, the Harvard man, a traitor. Even Chambers's whispered accusations become proof of his virtue, whereas another dramatist

(Shakespeare, perhaps) would have made them proof of villainy. Theatrical jargon pops up everywhere: the uproar over Joe McCarthy was no more than "our modern East Lynn, a melodrama" and the Rosenbergs' pleas of innocence a "comedy"—a particularly irritating comedy because the actors never confessed, which would, of course, have made the play come out as it should have. Fiedler, in his first attempts to show America its political innocence, pipes the cold-war tunes; he did not know then how dishonest our own government could be.

Most of Fiedler's major themes touch upon innocence, either in our literature or in our politics, and the tenacity with which we hold to it. . . . Fiedler extends his theme of innocence—I think accurately—to cover a certain ignorance and regressiveness in American culture, an "implacable nostalgia for the infantile, at once wrong-headed and somehow admirable. The mythic America is boyhood."

Fiedler's essays with a narrow focus are generally acute; his broader essays may be in part mistaken but they are always exciting. . . . We have less need of critics who are right than we have of critics like Fiedler who set up a perspective that forces us to look again on art, on culture we once thought familiar. Fiedler is part mystic, part romantic, part Hebraic truth teller. He insists that the artist's role is to say a "Hard No": "to fulfill its essential moral obligation, [serious] fiction must be negative." By this he means the artist must show the gap between what man dreams of and is able to accomplish, and in this he is correct.

But Fiedler, in his desperate flight from sentimentality, from the treacherous optimism of commercial fiction, forgets that many of the world's great writers—Chaucer, Congreve, Fielding and Jane Austen among them—have made an honorable accommodation that a critic of Fiedler's romantic and apocalyptic temperament would find it hard to accept. It is difficult to imagine Fiedler talking to Laurence Sterne or to any of the writers who admit the absurdity of man's customary performance while insisting still on the joy of the human condition. It is not enough to write truly of the gap between man's dream and his accomplishment—one must come to love frailty as well.

*Peter S. Prescott, "Americans as Innocents," in* Newsweek *(copyright Newsweek, Inc., 1971; reprinted by permission), August 2, 1971, pp. 76-9.*

Fiedler has always been delighted to hurl himself into the immediate moment, not just to live that moment but to rewrite history or politics or mythology from the perspective of that moment. He obsessively defines the characteristics of recent historical periods, not just content with setting off the fifties from the sixties or having one lead to the other but making minor demarcations everywhere: the *early* thirties, the *middle* sixties, etc. Fiedler never tires of setting out a current problem or issue, comparing it to something else a decade or a generation ago, redefining the problem given the context of the past, then projecting a large-scale present and future from that redefinition.

When you do things this way, and also write a lot, you inevitably change your mind a good deal, and Fiedler has never been one to try to hide his many shifts in opinion and emphasis over the years. Though the "Collected Essays" look monumental and imply settledness, in fact they describe the history of a sensibility as it leaped and darted through the last twenty years. For Fiedler the important task has always been to be abrasive, to say "No! in Thunder," and in as many different ways as he can.

The shift from the *chutzpah* of being a truth-telling and sometimes naughty *enfant terrible* to the *chutzpah* of one who wants his essays collected and enshrined can be explained by Fiedler's apparently recently acquired sense that he has found an audience that does not revile him, as he used to hope would happen, but that listens gratefully, as he now delights in thinking. . . . Fiedler [implies that he] is now our guru, and [does sound] rather like Leavis at that. No wonder, then, that he collected his essays. . . .

It is perhaps unjust to complain about such collections that there is a great deal of repetition in them, but in this case it is more marked and more revealing than in most. Fiedler has certain subjects—being a Jew in America, American Jewish writers, liberal politics and taste, the mythology of chaste homosexual relations at the center of classic American literature—to which he returns over and over, and about which he has had, essentially, one idea. . . .

It begins to seem that Fiedler is constantly plunging himself into the present, into some apparently new context, in order to avoid his or our seeing that he has a rather small stock of ideas. . . . He has never pretended to be rich in ideas, but he has meant to be profuse in contexts and challenges. . . .

The real point about Fiedler, which we can make praise or blame as we choose, is that he is always a political writer, always putting himself into situations where he is speaking against this fashion or that obsolescence, deriding some official line, jockeying for some new position. He always acts as though we might be deceived by some other hawker of myths and contexts if he did not set us straight, and he loves doing this so much that he will take any opportunity that presents itself to keep us informed, protected, reminded. But he also just plain loves to hear himself talk, too, and as long as he is excited by an idea he will go on saying it.

This means not only that he repeats himself but that his relation to literature remains essentially impure, and that, in turn, means that much of what he writes dates rather quickly. Because he is most interested in his own ideas, he doesn't quote enough, or find enough other ways to treat books on their own rather than on his terms. He tends to make contexts control works rather than the other way around, which leads not so much to distortion, because Fiedler is a good and therefore honest man, but to overrating whatever will fit his context. . . .

It is hard, finally, to admire Leslie Fiedler as much as he deserves, as much as his best work needs. That best may consist of no more than a dozen essays or chapters, but it is work of a high order. . . . Perhaps the penchant for battle and for immersion in the present tense need not always be at odds with the penchant to tell truths, to be wise and impersonal. They are not always at odds in Fiedler's work. But the *habit* of battle is a punishing one, as is clear to anyone who finds himself becoming a little weary of Fiedler's otherwise splendid and necessary *chutzpah.*

*Roger Sale, in* The New York Times Book

Review (*© 1971 by The New York Times Company; reprinted by permission*), *October 10, 1971, pp. 6, 10, 12.*

Fiedler has become what he set out to be: a living myth, a part of his criticism itself. For he—of all our contemporary critics—has been the one most concerned with creating an "image" of himself. . . .

In the "Introduction to Volume I" [of *The Collected Essays of Leslie Fiedler*], [he] bemoans the fact that he has been so frequently misunderstood. Three of the essays in *An End to Innocence,* he informs us, have been "badly read." As a group they represent, I believe, the three major concerns of all of Fiedler's "occasional" writings: the political, the social, and the literary. Brought together, of course, they constitute a record of Fiedler's lifelong love affair with American culture: from his Populist, man-in-the-street approach, to the much more academic-*cum*-liberal vantage point of the professor become guru. The first of these "badly read" essays, "Afterthoughts on the Rosenbergs," is a fascinating piece of writing, although a lesser piece than "McCarthy and the Intellectuals," the essay that follows it. Read together, however, as he intends they should be, they show him at his best: Fiedler has always had a startling ability to analyze real people as if they were characters in books. These political essays lead directly into Fiedler's later writings on innocence and evil in American fiction. . . .

It is the last of these three essays, however, that is the most notorious—Fiedler's much discussed essay on homosexuality in American fiction, "Come Back to the Raft Ag'in, Huck Honey!" While its insights may seem pretty tame now that we have Fiedler's treatment of this theme in his later books on American literature, it is easy to see why critics were in a constant flap in those days when Fiedler was just beginning to publish his literary criticism. He says, for example, "the dressing of Jim in a woman's gown in *Huck Finn* . . . can mean anything or nothing at all. . . ." Just enough to upset his critics. Fiedler has always known how to play cat and mouse.

This desire to taunt, goad, and generally annoy the critical establishment has, I believe, formed a major portion of Fiedler's intent in all of his writings. And with the publication of each succeeding volume expounding his critical theory he has admirably succeeded in so doing. The result is that Fiedler's essays—at their most extreme—provide a counterbalance for some of the opposing theories of a number of his contemporaries, and, in this respect, Fiedler is a kind of necessary angel. As Fiedler has said of literary criticism, "I long for the raised voice, the howl of rage or love." This is exactly what his own criticism accomplishes. If nothing else, it never bores the reader. (It should be pointed out, too, that his critical essays range far beyond the merely American cultural scene: to Sophocles, Dante, Shakespeare, Kafka, Pavese, etc.) I still think that "In the Beginning Was the Word" and "Archetype and Signature," the two essays on theory that conclude *No! in Thunder* (and Volume I of these *Collected Essays*), are among the finest things he has written. Conceptually, both began as an attack on the New Critics, on the "a poem should not mean, but be" school, as Fiedler calls it. And, within them, he brilliantly illustrated the limitations we place on any piece of writing if we ignore the conditions under which it was written—*i.e.,* the writer's own given "signature," as Fiedler puts it. . . .

What holds true for the poet holds equally true for the critic. In an essay called "My Credo"—which should be included in *The Collected Essays,* but isn't—Fiedler insists: "The voice of the critic must be his own voice, idiosyncratic, personal, for without real style (and true style is never safe, choosing to court extravagance) he carries no conviction except what charts and tables accidentally provide." Willing to dissent, Fiedler is always telling us: "No, there is another way to look at things." Thus, his criticism works by a process of cancellation. He opposes what others have said; then, after he's won the debate (at least to his own satisfaction), he knocks his own theories.

*Charles R. Larson, "The Good Bad Boy and Guru of American Letters," in* Saturday Review *(copyright © 1971 by Saturday Review/World, Inc.; reprinted with permission), December 25, 1971, pp. 27-8, 35.*

* * *

## FORREST, Leon 1937-

**Forrest, a Black American novelist, poet, and playwright, has been called a "fastidious" writer, producing a small amount of high quality work.**

Leon Forrest, author of "There Is a Tree More Ancient Than Eden," is one of those black writers who appear to suffer from the unhappy delusion that they are really William Faulkner. That is to say, his book is written in what seems to be stream-of-consciousness and is pervaded by a sense of what might very well be doom. What it's all about is anybody's guess, although the jacket copy makes a game try. Stream-of-consciousness is just fine, but only if we know from whom it is streaming and why it is streaming that way and not another. And a pervading sense of doom is certainly a nasty thing to have, but it is helpful to the reader to have some notion about what is being doomed, why it is being doomed and who is doing the dooming.

No doubt the author's somewhat involved symbolism—trains, angels, cantaloupes—means something to him, but what it is supposed to mean to the reader remains a moot and unanswered question to the very last page. Characters flit in and out. Sometimes they speak loud, but not in voices that were ever heard on this earth. They appear to be up to something. It's impossible to discover what. One might as well be holding a board up to one's face.

*L. J. Davis, in* The New York Times Book Review *(© 1973 by The New York Times Company; reprinted by permission), October 21, 1973, pp. 48-9.*

In many ways [*There Is a Tree More Ancient Than Eden*] represents simply one act in a Black drama. It falls on that side of the bifurcation labelled complexity, wit, ambiguity, mythopoeia—the Black writer's attempt to come to terms with a multifaceted experience in a rich, poetical style. Intelligence is the norm here, an acuity laden with college bells and polysyllable cadences dense in signification. Ishmael Reed, George Cain, and N. J. Loftis all fall into this camp and look backward to Ralph Ellison, James Baldwin, and the later Melvin Tolson, their spiritual ancestors. This is what some have glibly called the assimilationist side of our culture. Against it they have juxtaposed no-nonsense, quick punching, monosyllabic literary nationalism. Of course, the dichotomy—like all broad divisions—is much too neat. . . . Suffice it to say, Forrest is not an existential artist crying in a barren wilderness. The ground has been covered before, and there are echoes of his forerunners. . . .

The criterion of stainless originality, however, goes along with inspirational aesthetics: the afflatus descends or the windy muse whispers dawn-fresh words into the creator's ear. *There Is a Tree More Ancient Than Eden* is first of all a studied book that shows the careful labor of the file and more than a modicum of self-consciousness. Only the naïve reader will assume the author trudged home from work each evening and allowed the words to flow in random order. There are five major divisions of the work that carry us back and forth in time with great deftness. We never get beyond one chronological sequence—the movement of the funeral procession of young Nathan Witherspoon's mother. Psychologically, or in terms of what Melville called horological time, however, we move through the childhood of the narrator, his New Orleans' ancestry, one of his fractious relative's escape from bondage, his junior high school days at Robert E. Lee, and ceaselessly through "a landscape of the tossed and driven mind and the bruised blood erupting brain." . . .

The book finally represents an awe-inspiring fusion of American cultural myth, Black American history, Black fundamentalist religion, the doctrine and dogma of Catholicism (stations of the Cross and the Precious Blood Cathedral), and an autobiographical recall of days of anxiety and confusion in the city. . . .

If it is not the ideal volume to take to a political rally, or to lay on the nightstand for pre-bed comfort, it is certainly an effort that contains insight, streaks of brilliance, and a finely-informed intelligence that promises further revelations.

*Houston A. Baker, Jr., in* Black World *(copyright © January, 1974 by* Black World; *reprinted by permission of* Black World *and Houston A. Baker, Jr.), January, 1974, pp. 66-9.*

[In *There Is a Tree More Ancient Than Eden,*] Forrest has woven an hypnotic fabric with words that are part jazz, part blues, part gospel. It is a music that moves with a mystic reality that, at times, accurately records the multi-faceted Black experience in America.

There is little of the usual story line or dialogue here, but Forrest does wonders in acquainting you with this mulatto family through the stream-of-consciousness approach to his youthful protagonist, Nathaniel (Turner) Witherspoon. Not since Ellison's *Invisible Man* has this reviewer read anything as moving and forceful in its poetic flow. However, in spite of this magnificent ambivalence with words I was left with an uneasy feeling. . . .

[One] may conclude that, in spite of the need of a Black awareness direction, this author has chosen to go the route of the "art for art's sake" advocates.

This last statement, perhaps, is a little too harsh because if one lends an attentive ear, deciphers the sounds and counter-sounds and searches deeply into the symphony of his music, one may emerge with a tune that is not only healthy and Black, but also understood.

After reading and re-reading *There Is a Tree More Ancient Than Eden,* to me, it all boils down to this rather pertinent question: Is Forrest only a verbal manipulator doing excessive gymnastics with words, or is he a deep and serious writer probing and exploring new areas in the human psyche?

*Zack Gilbert, in* Black World *(copyright © January, 1974, by* Black World; *reprinted by permission of* Black World *and Zack Gilbert), January, 1974, p. 70.*

For those of us who struggle to grow as individuals—tied to history yet constantly peering into the future, self-impressed but ashamed, self-centered though socially committed, finished with church-going and yet always seeking faith, *There Is a Tree More Ancient Than Eden* is a welcome companion. To read it is to travel with the author on his spiritual, historical and personal odyssey—moving through a series of intense descriptions and responses, drawn from life in the streets, in the home and in black history. Using dialogue, testimony (the personal and religious kind), stream of consciousness and brief narratives, Forrest has produced a powerful work of literature. The book is written like a jazz composition: it begins with a core theme and then moves on to elaborations and explorations of the theme's possible variations. All the tensions of personal growth, race and religion which Forrest later treats are presented in a six-page self-portrait at the beginning of the book. The resolution, the book's conclusion, is one of themes rather than plot. . . .

Forrest's descriptions of people and places present a wealth of details from the black and the American experiences. The "lives" which follow the first self-portrait are brief but amazingly comprehensive portraits of people who have influenced Forrest's life. Each portrait has a completeness which is characteristic of other parts of the book; they can be read and appreciated separately. The book is held together, however, by Forrest's spirit which searched on all the levels of his experience and imagination for a place, a coherence, on this "faithstripping, long journey road that life is. . . ." The artistic achievement of this book lies in Forrest's mastery of a wide variety of forms which accompany his many changes of subject and mood. The language and rhythm of each section are beautifully suited to its subject.

Forrest's expression of spiritual searchings is particularly fine. The sense of a black man's spiritual odyssey—an odyssey with historical causes and deeply personal effects—is communicated in several moving passages. . . .

The mixture of contemporary and historical vision, the transcending symbols and images all combine to produce a new form of expressing the black, and indeed the human, experience. Faulkner mastered a writing style which used long, expansive sentences to convey the weight of history on his characters. Forrest borrows heavily from Faulkner, but he builds on Faulkner's mode. By infusing it with new rhythms and subjects he expands that writing style into a new medium for conveying the black, and particularly the urban-black, experience.

*Joel Motley, in* The Harvard Advocate *(© 1974 by* The Harvard Advocate; *reprinted by permission), Vol. CVII, No. 4, special issue, 1974, pp. 59-60.*

* * *

## FORSTER, E(dward) M(organ) 1879-1970

**Forster, an English novelist, short story writer, and essayist, was one of the major writers of our time. In many ways, as one critic noted, Forster was "the outstanding literary spokesman for humanist values." (See also *Contemporary Authors*, Vols. 13-14; obituary, Vols. 25-28.)**

From many points of view [Forster] was a superb literary critic. He felt this himself, and had a pert way of exclaiming how acute he was, and what an easy business criticism turned out to be. His letters of literary advice to friends are admirable. No one was better, as they acknowledged, at sensing their intentions or putting his finger on the spot where things went wrong. As a critic he *looked,* he scrutinised the object as if nothing else like it had ever existed, and he emerged with a brand new, freshly-minted formula, fitting not only the work in question but, potentially, a whole new class of works. His published criticism has the same virtues; many of his judgments in *Aspects of the Novel* seem dated now, but his formulae are as lively as ever.

However, there was a price to pay for this *ad hoc* approach to criticism. He was so distrustful of system in all matters of art, as in matters of the heart and conduct, that he could not enter into the frame of mind of artists to whom system mattered. He could never get his mind round Henry James, for instance, though he thought about him, off and on, all his life. He would write James off as a futile cobweb-spinner; then he would pick up a new novel of his and be astonished at its marvellous power and solidity. The thing seemed a great mystery to him; it never occurred to him that James might have wanted to do one thing in one novel and another in another—that there was a system and larger artistic plan in his literary career. . . .

I mention his limitations as a critic because they help to define his virtues, which were also his virtues as a thinker and writer in general. His mind was a vast breeding-ground for discriminations. He endlessly picked and chose and could distinguish between two blades of grass. No one ever made such restrictive remarks. I can hear them so vividly: "So-and-so, with an intelligent face, fairly"; or, "I am devoted to so-and-so's son, slightly." . . . Again, both as a critic and a creator, he was a master of *angle.* As all his friends remarked, nobody came at things from queerer angles. It was not whimsicality; it arose from his seeing things more concretely than other people. (It shows his respect for the concreteness of the world that he always realised his metaphors. Describing himself as having, like a rat, deserted the ship of fiction, he continues "and *swam* towards biography.") He planted himself firmly in the world and took sighting from where he stood; there was this that one could see and that which was concealed by the lie of the land. Of course, one could change one's viewpoint. . . . His great strength as a novelist was his sense for the angles at which people stood to one another and to the universe surrounding them and the constant dance of changing angles from which he makes us view them. For him, the art of fiction, like the art of life, lay in finding one's bearings. "One must face facts," a friend once said to him. "How can I," he replied, "when they're all around me?"

This leads me to what you might call his "secret" and his deepest originality; I mean his feeling for life. His knowledge of society was not particularly remarkable; what was superior to him was his knowledge of the possibilities of life. It seemed he could see through to life; it was not a vague generality to him but a palpable presence, and he could hear its wingbeat.

*P. N. Furbank, "The Personality of E. M. Forster," in* Encounter, *November, 1970, pp. 61-8.*

[One] of the effects of reading E. M. Forster is to feel a bit ashamed . . . at one's own obtuseness at not being able to see things—important things about relationships, about society, about the condition of being human—as he saw them: with lucidity, sympathy and absolutely in the round. . . .

Technically, . . . Forster's novels form a connection between the ethical-culture and traditional forms of the 19th-century novelists and the main preoccupations of the novelists of the 20th—Forster takes up, that is, where George Eliot leaves off and leaves off where D. H. Lawrence takes up. But to place Forster in the immense stretch of literary landscape between George Eliot and D. H. Lawrence is really not to place him at all.

To find a writer of comparable position in the hearts and minds of his readers one has to go outside English literature—one has to go all the way to Russia and to the figure of Chekhov. How alike the two writers seem in their virtues: in possessing temperaments of exquisite balance, in being firmly anchored in their respective national cultures, in holding at all times to an essential decency. "People must never be humiliated—that is the main thing." Chekhov wrote that, but it could as easily have been Forster. . . .

While "A Passage to India" is certainly Forster's most ambitious novel—it is also, incidentally, his most "teachable," which may account for its being far and away the best known of his books—Lionel Trilling among others has judged (rightly, I think) "Howards End" to be his masterpiece. . . .

Thick with life, consummate in pace and plot, written in a tone of offhand elegance that is perfect to its subject, ["Howards End"] also displays a knowledge of human nature, with its quirks, range and complexities, that attains to nothing less than wisdom. . . .

Forster's novels are fraught with the most surprising twists and turns of plot, including quite violent ones. He could kill off a character almost as fast as Evelyn Waugh, who, when he was working well, could do it faster than God. . . .

The writing of "Maurice" must have been part of an act of deep personal liberation on Forster's part—a novel that, for complex reasons, he needed to write, just as he may have needed to imagine a happy ending for a homosexual life. One likes to think that his own coming to terms with homosexuality ended happily, which it may well have, for he had an enormous talent for living an ordered life. Nor does having written one deeply flawed novel in any way invalidate all that is so very fine in the body of his work. The obvious nature of the flaws in "Maurice" somehow serves to make Forster seem even more human than before. "Maurice" after all, illustrates a very odd and very common point in the history of literary creation: in literature, psyche's gain is often art's loss.

*Joseph Epstein, in* The New York Times Book Review *(© 1971 by The New York Times Company; reprinted by permission), October 10, 1971, pp. 1-2, 28-9.*

Since comparison [of *Maurice*] with *Lady Chatterley's Lover* is inevitable, perhaps all that needs to be said is that, as always, Lawrence had the greater imaginative force and intensity and depth of perception. The inner life of his protagonists seems to break out of the fissures which he points to in English society, and he knew how the poor thought and talked, and what working-class culture was, in a way that was denied to Forster.

Both novels, when set against the masterpieces each man wrote, are failures. All the more tragically, for both felt themselves possessed when they wrote and were convinced of the supreme importance of what they had to say about sexual relations. Perhaps for that reason the novels also have to perform the work of tracts, and creation gets elbowed aside by argumentation. If Lawrence's ambition, range, and achievement were greater, so too was his failure, and there is nothing in Forster so overwritten as some of the passages of sexual achievement in *Lady Chatterley's Lover*. . . .

Forster knew he was writing a tract. . . . Tracts are rarely funny and we get hardly a glimpse of his humor. Those fierce contoured plots have disappeared. . . . [The] book feels thin in the way that Forster's other novels never do.

Nevertheless, *Maurice* is not negligible. We never doubt, as we so often do in the novels of our time, that Forster believes in the supreme importance of human beings, and hence of their actions, and hence of the moral meaning of those actions. His characters are never diminished by their environment. They are not allowed to shuffle off their responsibilities upon the inevitable processes of history or excuse themselves by identifying with the case histories in psychoanalysis. . . .

He knew perfectly well that other homosexual worlds existed, such as the international set, and that numbers of homosexuals camped about as pansies and transvestites or felt impelled to solicit rough trade in public lavatories or to comb the pubs, or were in his time especially susceptible to guardsmen and sailors.

But he was not interested in them any more than he was interested in womanizers. He liked the comedy of sex but he disliked sexual boasting. . . . The great myth of potency which has so affected post-First World War American literature from Hemingway's heroes to Updike's couples never enthralled Forster. Forster thought sex was an attribute of love and, though ultimately indispensable, by no means the most important attribute. Loyalty was as indispensable and so was truthfulness. Love meant, as it did to others born Victorians, a lifelong involvement, changing its shape no doubt, but not something that in the nature of things would turn out to be a transitory affair. . . .

Forster as a living artist had a long inning. The poets and writers of the Thirties admired and accepted him. In the Forties when it became clear that his main work was completed, Lionel Trilling acclaimed him, and he passed into the universities as a classic. The young in England continued to read him until he was over eighty. Then they stopped, and he became a monument. [*Maurice* and *Albergo Empedocle and Other Writings*] will be invaluable to those who want to pull it down and say that it is made of scrap iron and not bronze.

It does not matter. What they say will be virtually irrelevant. Forster the man has yet to appear and he will be found to have as many echoes and mysteries as his novels. The oddity of his mind expressed itself in the originality of his judgments (not, of course, always right) and of his perceptions about the nature of things (nearly always fertile, fruitful, and still sprouting). He was one of the greatest moralists of his time. He wrote one of the greatest novels of the twentieth century. Nothing else need be put in the scales.

*Noel Annan, "Love Story," in* The New York Review of Books *(reprinted with permission of* The New York Review of Books; *©1971 by NYREV, Inc.), October 21, 1971, pp. 12-19.*

Flaubert's imagined orgy in which the slumbering spirit of man wakens to an apocalyptic anarchy of sight and sound is a hope never dreamed of in Forster's philosophy. No one knows better than Forster the dictionaries of commonplace that define much of life and the fictions by which we attempt to transcend the prosaic. . . . But because Forster accepts the day that is and views the past as "a series of disorders," he seeks no escape into history, no grounds for an aesthetic martyrdom. That his novel is being written is neither an existential heroic cry against the conspiracy of silence nor a magical act of exorcism. Whatever superiority there is in the order of art consists in its recognition that knowledge is *not* power. Because art is not a history "pressed into shape from outside," it makes the unique claim of being the "only material object in the universe which may possess internal harmony" ["Art for Art's Sake," p. 92]. It is one order of life whose fiction, through its humor, may console us for our inability to remain silent and unjustified.

The novelist is not god, saint, or tortured artist; he is defined like his characters on the wirework of experience and expression, and all the alternatives of perspective and attitude that he cares about and can envisage are contained within the novel. His novel uses occasion; it cannot preserve experience from the attrition of time. By tolerating imperfections of cultures and personalities, the author refuses the nobility of tragedy for the self. Forster's conviction is that the days we live through provide the material to explore spirit. The word cannot release time into space; it is the superhistorical temper that insists on this conversion. . . . Forster's history is forever encased in a human mind and contradicts the spatial histories of Flaubert's Fontainebleau and George Eliot's Zionism. He does not lead us, however, to a frustrating nihilism, unless that is where we want to go. . . .

Forster's humanism never allows an invulnerable history or nature to destroy or expand his subject permanently. . . .

The humanist novelist challenges abstraction wherever he finds it, especially in varieties of humanism. If nature cannot annihilate men, neither can men control nature. The lordly imperialism of the superhistorical mind, which allegorizes culture and nature to possess them, is overcome by, as often as it re-forms, the exuberant independence of the universe. And the significant contribution of humanist fiction is that it does not choose sides but knows it must live with both. Chapter 10 of *A Passage to India* is a good illustration of Forster's endurance of both nature's indifference and man's compulsion for order. Here he typically undermines the props of his own novel: story and density of character. Following one of the several inconclusive talks between the characters, Forster takes us perilously near to utter unraveling: "The inarticulate world is closer at hand and readier to resume control as soon as men are tired" (p. 114). Both the wise and the ignorant suffer the fatigues of ordering. The habit of personification, a temporary strategy of human superiority, is regularly exposed by a tireless humor. . . .

As he steps down from the sky, Forster shows us how he manages to control the risky pitch that sounds throughout the novel, a bold blending of derision and compassion. At first we are led to think that Forster's description will follow the deterministic line to its reductive finale. By using allegory familiarly, he implies that he has shared the habit of mankind in general to reach the unfamiliar by myths, to control it by such fictions as writing novels. . . .

Forster does little to elevate the modest gesture of humanism, the attempt to be sensible, honest, subtle. But there is a tiny charity that helps it to persist. When Forster, however provisionally, rises above his characters' habitual perspective to criticize it, he compensates them by relinquishing his own superiority. . . . [We are led] to ask how far dignity can be enhanced by *not* being absorbed into the comedy. Is the evident poise of Mrs. Moore and Professor Godbole a permanent superiority? When Fielding is involved up to his neck, do we think less of his wisdom? For Forster, as for his most sensitive characters, there is no stopping point at nobility. The will is humbled by the spirit, the moral by the mystic, but these terms are explored by the stuttering word and felt by the faltering handshake. . . .

Aziz's attraction to poetry . . . is that it dissolves distinctions by raising individual tragedy to universal pathos. This is the function of its romance—to overrate, for better and for worse, the possibilities of communion between man and man, man and his universe, culture and culture, history and apocalypse, the body and the spirit. . . .

Romance unchecked by evidence caused Aziz's difficulties; now his dream of love fosters suspicion of the foreigner and his friend. It is the oldest of tensions, that between brother and brotherhood, between the difficulties of loving one's neighbor and dreams of love. But Forster goes beyond a simple dialectic. Even in dreams, Aziz's love distinguishes between national and universal. What Forster is ultimately telling us is that poetry or religion, where love may dwell without tension, cannot further the kind of personal relationship that is the center of the humanist novel, the relationship that barely holds on with dwarfed hands. Explicitly and in allegories of nature mocking man, Forster indicates that Western poetry, religion, and myth help us to order the universe and to relieve us from absurdity by yoking together man and man, man and nature, with imperative fictitious commands. . . .

In contrast, Indian poetry deals with the absurd by dissolving distinctions between man and flower. It relieves anxieties brought on by the compulsion to moral order with the perspective of pathos, that view which sees all victory as fate. Aziz's divorce of poetry from friendship, with the separation of grace from justice, is an agonizing human pattern. . . . The humanist's recognition of the absurd is essentially the recognition of this separation.

*Naomi Lebowitz, "'A Passage to India': History as Humanist Humor," in* Humanism and the Absurd in the Modern Novel, *Northwestern University Press, 1971, pp. 67-85.*

Forster's work *is* built on a traditional intellectual and literary inheritance. . . . What the tradition is he himself has brought alive for us by showing, in many essays and in books like *Marianne Thornton,* his own intellectual origins and lineage, which go back to the world of the Victorian upper-middle-class, dissenting intelligentsia from which he descended, and beyond that to Romanticism. To the cultural historian the fascination of this intelligentsia lies in its responsible and unconditioned spirit, its capacity to act beyond interest and to embody without a sense of radical alienation the critical intelligence in society, the demand for culture and wholeness. This in turn goes back to the beginning of the nineteenth century, and especially to that engaging synthesis, in Wordsworth and Coleridge, of the romantic imperative of the imagination and the social imperative to right reason and moral duty. There could be, then, a romantic critique of society, a critique which took it as solid, real, and worthy, which is precisely what Forster's kind of novel assumes. His novels also assume the compelling power of the imagination in human dealings; he demands a personal connection between inner and outer worlds, demands that both man and society be whole, which is why his novels are about individual redemptions and personal relationships and at the same time very social novels, in which the passion to see life steadily and see it whole provides the moral thrust, in which the object of criticism is those 'vast armies of the benighted' who fail not only the heart but also the brain. . . .

Forster is an historical ironist; he knows the problems of his lineage very well. His last two novels, and his finest works, *Howards End* and *A Passage to India,* are both about that—which is why they are, differently, complex modern works. *Howards End* (1910) is a romantic novel about emotional and social wholeness, the reconciling of the prose and the passion, the commercial bourgeoisie and the intellectual, the material activity of society and the ideal of felt, living personal relationships. A classic kind of comedy which is also a deep inquiry into the state of the nation and the state of the culture, it is a very central and exemplary kind of English novel. *A Passage to India,* which comes fourteen years and a World War later, is about human and cosmic wholeness, the reconciling of man to man in a global sense, and then of man to the infinite. A book of decidedly symbolist aspirations, its world is one in which social existence is dwarfed and made a feeble invasion on the surface of a harsh, implacable, yet also spiritually demanding earth. But the difficulties are patent and turn ironically back on both books, so that the thrust of their values is unfulfilled. In *Howards End* Forster touches in with the greatest power those processes in history which will destroy the favoured world and cannot be gainsaid; the proliferating energy of urbanization and industrialism attacks his own metaphors and symbols, and the spirit of a pastoral England which seems the one offered base for wholeness. *A Passage to India* contains one of the most powerful evocations of modern nullity we have in our literature: the worlds within us and without, at the extreme of romantic dejection, echo together the sound of *boum* from the caves; visionary hope faces an alien, unspeaking, self-reflecting nature. In both books the will to vision, the liberal drive to right reason, the urgent claims of the holiness of the heart's affections, are confronted with unyielding forces in history; it is the irony resulting from that confrontation that makes Forster's works so very modern, a modernity that intensifies as we read his novels in sequence. . . .

Forster's first three novels were social comedies with romantic moral implications, works set in a relatively stabilized world in which the bearers of the Forsterian virtues—the virtues of the developed heart, spontaneous passion, trust in the imagination—battled with the armies of the benighted and won their illuminating moral victories. So is *Maurice,* mostly written in 1913-14. But *Howards End,* though still very much concerned with a mode of social comedy open towards the world of the unseen and the visionary, turns on a new historical acceleration, an instability in the world order; the relationship between the formal world of art and the historical world of time is central. Hence the book has been seen as divided inside itself; the social metaphor Forster distils in connecting two of his central characters, Margaret Schlegel and Henry Wilcox, and the spiritual metaphor Margaret inherits from Wilcox's previous wife, seem imposed on the worked and felt life of the novel. . . .

*Howards End* I take to be a novel, treated in the comic mode, about the circumstances in which the moral life, which is also the full life of the imagination, can be led in society, about the compromises it must effect with itself in order to do so, about the moral and imaginative value of making certain compromises, and about the historical pressures underlying them. The concerns here are deeply associated with Forster's 'liberalism'—his devotion to what is decent, human, and enlarging in daily conduct, to personal relationships and responsiveness to life, to finding that truth and goodness coincide—but the book also considers questions of whether this moral life can become transcendent, and by what means reality may be known. There is in the novel a push, on these lines, towards wholeness, and contact with the infinite; and Forster's liberalism apparently proposes to justify itself when it mirrors infinity—intimations of which can reside in personal relationships, harmonious living, and contact with the earth. . . . It is thus possible to read the novel as a dialectical work moving towards synthesis, which is spiritual completeness. But to see *Howards End* like that is to underplay what is also in it: a real devotion to society, an ironic spirit, an ambiguous ending. For the book is also concerned with the necessary conditions of life in a particular community, and indeed with those 'great impersonal forces' that Mr. Wilcox complacently appeals to when he wants to purge the personal from conversation. This makes Forster very quizzical, and one of the main functions of the comic tone here is surely to enforce this, indeed to let Forster be sceptical about his spiritualizing thrust. This makes *Howards End* more ironic than the very positive interpretations the novel has earned suggest; and that irony is of the essence, for it is a mediating presence between the parts of the book that are pre-eminently social comedy and those concerned with the poetic, which is also the infinite. . . .

In the end, Forster seems to say both, to indicate both total unity, the oneness of the world and what lies behind it, and total multiplicity. He does so because comedy and poetry share [*A Passage to India*] between them in perpetual interplay, proliferating muddle, yet manifesting formal order. The human world may be unredeemable, but Forster venerates those who try to redeem it; it may be plurally incomprehensible, existence without value, but [he] values those who seek to comprehend it. Yet the world of wholeness and vision is, in a sense, too easy, and not enough; the material and human world must subsist first before it may have credit. The task of the full novel must therefore be undertaken not alone by the social novelist, and not alone by the symbolist one, as Virginia Woolf undertakes it. The result is, finally, a dualistic world, a world founded on contradictions at once potentially mystery and muddle. As Virginia Woolf—who shared Bloomsbury with him, but maintained her novel as a rather purer species—complained, Forster is a materialist novelist, very much aware of the powers of time, refusing to live life at the level of perpetual vision: for to him vision is rare and not always redemptive. So the human plot tells of life in time, and Forster awards enough meaning and tone and style to that to make it matter fully; the verbal plot tells of transcendence, of epiphany, through art, through suggestion, pattern, and leitmotif, the opening out of meanings, and Forster gives wholeness to that too, the wholeness which is the unity of art.

*Malcolm Bradbury, "E. M. Forster as Victorian and Modern: 'Howards End' and 'A Passage to India'," in his* Possibilities: Essays on the State of the Novel *(© 1973 by Malcolm Bradbury; reprinted by permission of Oxford University Press, Inc.), Oxford University Press, 1973, pp. 91-120.*

Altogether, [Forster] stood in an odd relation to time. He remained current, a writer speaking to men here and now, unusually long; and yet, at the same time, he was peculiarly Edwardian. He seems to have received his vision of life and art more or less complete at a very early age; and insofar as this vision was a social one, the figures peopling it were and remained Edwardian. His Anglo-Indians in *A Passage to India* are pre-First World War Anglo-Indians. And when, in old age, he wrote that very fine story 'The Other Boat', it was Edwardians his imagination dwelt on still. This trait would not have been significant in a poet, but for a novelist, depicting society, it created difficulties.

More and more, *Howards End* strikes one as *the* Edwardian novel, taking up the common preoccupations of its age and interpreting them originally. The age was concerned about physical degeneracy, and Forster commended athleticism—but an athleticism of love: it was love, he said, which must develop 'thews'. Edwardian England—this was part of the same preoccupation—was obsessed with Germany, and Forster's novel subtly probes this obsession, so that, for instance, Mr. Wilcox stammers when the word 'Germany' rises to his lips: 'England will never keep her trade overseas unless she is prepared to make sacrifices. Unless we get firm in West Africa, Ger . . . untold complications may follow.' Forster carpeted the common notion that Prussian strength spelled 'manhood' and let it discredit itself. He even gave weight, a limited weight, to the idea of war as a purifier: thus, it is a German sword, sheathed after Sedan, which finally cuts through the tragic muddle in *Howards End*.

*Howards End* is the novel of Forster's which most worries present-day critics. Some, partly as a result, take the line that *A Passage to India* is his only acceptable work. This seems to me too much of a manoeuvre; though to my mind *Howards End,* magnificent as it is, has one glaring fault, the treatment of Leonard's wife Jacky. Here I do think one runs up against grave limitations in Forster. He truly couldn't imagine a Jacky, and here charity failed him as well as imagination; one feels offended with him over it.

*P. N. Furbank, in* The Listener, *January 31, 1974, p. 155.*

The tone of Forster's essay, 'Not Looking at Pictures,' is similar to his ironic and satiric use of art in his two Italian novels [*Where Angels Fear to Tread* and *A Room With a View*]. In these books the English characters learn to see life through the medium of art, which revives both their visual and their sensual feelings, and awakens their 'fantasies' about painting as well as their capacity to love. . . .

Though the effect of Forster's wit and playfulness is frequently humorous, the themes of both novels are serious and even sombre; and Forster uses the paintings of Ghirlandaio and Giotto in a subtle way to suggest the symbols, reveal the characters and emphasize the themes of his books. The subject and content of the paintings provide numerous allusions and analogies to the substance of the novels, and the characters are often defined by their response to the paintings. And Ghirlandaio [called Giovanni da Empoli in *Where Angels Fear to Tread*] and Giotto are also used as aesthetic models for significant scenes so that the visual element matches and heightens the psychological significance of the action. . . .

Ghirlandaio's fresco, like Donizetti's opera that the English visitors see in Monteriano, provides an aesthetic model for *Where Angels Fear To Tread,* for the novel is composed of a series of operatic and dramatic scenes ('The vista of the landing and the two open doors made [Gino] both remote and significant, like an actor on the stage'), and the English regard Italy as a 'pageant' and a 'spectacle'. When Philip sees Gino and Caroline just after they have bathed the baby and at the crucial moment when she realizes that she loves Gino they form a composition like the Ghirlandaio fresco—with a similar view and a similar copper pot—that is at once theatrical, aesthetic and religious. . . .

The 'sweetness and barbarity' of the saint's life, portrayed in the fresco, is not only an aesthetic model for certain scenes in Forster's novel, but also a thematic source that relates the characters to a single image. For like Fina, Lilia dies an exemplary and expiatory death, liberating Caroline and Philip, as she had freed herself, from 'the idleness, the stupidity, the respectability, and the petty unselfishness' of Sawston. Caroline's rescue of Philip, the fictional equivalent of Fina's miraculous cure of Beldia's paralyzed arm, is also presented in a dramatic, aesthetic and religious composition similar to the 'Virgin and Child, with Donor'. . . .

Ghirlandaio's fresco records the life of a saint who struggled against the devil, and the novel's theme is an ambiguous and ironic reversal of the painting. Gino is twice called the 'devil', but he is also the agent of self-discovery for the principal characters. Like Fina, first Lilia, then Caroline *Abbott* and finally *Fra* Filippo are tempted by the attractive but unfaithful Gino, who is associated with the powers of evil. . . .

The legend of Santa Fina also provides a major symbol in the novel, for when the saint died the rotten wood of the bed was covered with violets and masses of violets were seen flowering suddenly on all the towers of the town. When Philip first arrives in Monteriano his caustic interrogation of Caroline is suddenly interrupted by a long and lyrical description in water imagery of the violets that seem to symbolize Italy. . . .

The characters and themes of *Where Angels Fear To Tread* are repeated three years later in *A Room With A View,* where Gino becomes George, Philip is Cecil, Caroline is Lucy, and Harriet is Charlotte. In the later novel, however, George and Lucy achieve a fulfilment of love, analogous to the divine love portrayed in Giotto's painting, that is denied to Philip and to Caroline.

The second chapter of *A Room With A View* (1908), 'In Santa Croce with no Baedeker,' focuses on Giotto's fresco *The Ascension of St John,* and the significance of the painting reverberates throughout the novel. For just as Giotto presents, in the characters grouped around St John, two distinct ways of viewing experience, so Forster reveals his characters' approach to life through their approach to art. One character complains of the Italians, 'From the cab-driver down to—to Giotto, they turn us inside out': images lead to ethics. In the course of the novel the heroine, Lucy Honeychurch, moves from a separation to an integration of art and life, and her development is measured by her change from a purely aesthetic object to a mature woman awakened through art to self-knowledge. . . .

Like Baedeker and the violets, the 'compositional' scenes of *Where Angels Fear To Tread* reappear in *A Room With A View*. George's kisses, prompted by the example of the driver Phaeton, take place in the context of an aesthetic landscape: the view over the Sussex weald is compared to pictures in a gallery and the Italian view is similar to the one that Alessio Baldovinetti was fond of introducing into his paintings. . . .

In *A Room With A View* Forster first uses Giotto's *The Ascension of St John* to reveal his themes through the characters' approach to the painting. But as the novel develops these purely aesthetic responses become identified with moral issues. Forster constructs a witty analogy between Lucy and St John, for whenever Lucy follows Mr Emerson's advice and moves toward illumination (portrayed in the painting by the golden rays that emanate from Christ), she is described in the imagery of ascension. . . . The theme of *A Room With A View* is Lucy's reticent yet triumphant response to the call of life, and the victory of the intuitive and impulsive over the rational and repressive modes of experience. Italy and its art work some marvel in Lucy: they make her aware of her craving for sympathy and love, and manifest their power to evoke passion and bring it to fulfilment.

*Jeffrey Meyers, "The Paintings in Forster's Italian Novels," in* London Magazine, *February/March, 1974, pp. 46-62.*

* * *

## FOWLES, John 1926-

**Fowles is an English novelist whose outstanding fiction displays keen psychological, historical, and sociological insight. (See also *Contemporary Authors*, Vols. 5-8, rev. ed.)**

Following the blaze of approval initially greeting [*The French Lieutenant's Woman*], a few flickers of dubiety, of critical reserve, and of modest apprehension may now be discerned; for the indisputably talented Mr. Fowles while writing a romance in Victorian style has not hesitated to adopt a wholly modern viewpoint and quite contemporary techniques. His book is indeed placed in the London of one hundred years ago with manners and morals accurately represented. He departs from convention by allowing the author to intrude from time to time in his own person and with a present-day commentary, thus breaking the spell; then, too, he outrages narrative proprieties characteristic of the genre by advancing not one dénouement but a series of them, all equivocal and each suspect, none of them conclusive or persuasive. His tale of two women and a man, though based on an ancient formula, simply does not conform to the pattern, leading directly to a suspicion that the author, well aware of his virtuosity, has succumbed to the temptation of dazzling his readers with a display of his skills, or else with Freudian games out of key with his material. Artificial profundity has been in any case conferred upon a story unable to sustain the burden. Refuge must be sought in frank admiration for the dexterity and agility thus to be seen, whatever the ultimate success or failure of a brave effort to afford novelty. Mr. Fowles' thoughtful, always entertaining book is patently of more than transitory importance, for all his idiosyncratic obtrusions and affectations.

Virginia Quarterly Review, *Vol. 46, No. 2 (Spring, 1970), p. xl.*

Fowles is, without question, a brilliant storyteller, in the simple and fundamental sense that he keeps one reading out of sheer curiosity to know what he's going to produce next, and he can put on an impressive parade of learning, though it can't be said that he wears it "lightly, like a flower." . . .

Fowles' second book, *The Aristos,* is subtitled a "self-portrait in ideas." An attempt to present the author's views on the role of man, in terms of belief and action, in the contemporary world, it is written as a collection of aphorisms. As Fowles notes himself, in a recent interview, "The pensée form is very antipathetic to the English palate." Fowles' book is full of interesting notions, but I'm afraid it has to be called pretentious. In other words, it falls far short of what it promises. This was probably inevitable, the masters of the form, or rather the masters of the aphorism as a means of philosophical discourse, being at once so few and so great. Whether a writer is wise to present himself as in competition with Pascal and Nietzsche is a matter of opinion; but at least it can be taken as an indication of the writer's ambition.

And ambition is probably the first thing that strikes one about Fowles' second novel, *The Magus* (1966). It runs to more than 600 pages and is a very elaborate structure indeed. Again I find it difficult to avoid the word pretentious. It is certainly grossly self-indulgent, though it is only fair to add that Fowles himself now seems to consider it a failure. . . .

Fowles himself, challenged to state the meaning of the novel by one interviewer, says: "I was trying to tell a fable about the relationship between man and his conception of God." Well yes; good enough as far as it goes. But if this is so, and I don't doubt that it is, all one can say is that Fowles invented the wrong fable. *The Magus* is a difficult novel; but then I think of another difficult novel, which could also be said to tell a fable about the relationship between man and his conception of God, Kafka's *The Trial* and there is a world of difference between the two and the nature of the difficulties implicit in them. In Kafka the difficulties are inherent in the problem as dramatised in the fable, and indeed the problem *is* the fable. We are faced with the ultimate questions, the ultimate riddle, and the fable is stated in what may be called naturalistic terms. We are all the time in a city of the Austro-Hungarian Empire; the setting is palpable and tangible. It is there, like external reality.

I don't find anything like this in *The Magus*. . . .

There is a credit side to the novel. Fowles' renderings of the Edwardian age, his descriptions of fighting in the first World War and of the German occupation of Greece in the second, are splendid feats of the historical imagination, and they indicate, in my view, the true nature of Fowles' talent.

Which brings me to *The French Lieutenant's Woman.* It is a most interesting novel, a genuine achievement, though not, I think, quite in the way some American reviews have seen. It is, first and foremost, an historical novel, and for all its up-to-date asides, an historical novel of an old-fashioned kind. Among scholars and some writers, the Victorian age has been "in" for almost thirty years. But I suspect that the educated layman, in the United States particularly, was jerked into full awareness of the Victorian age and its manifold and curious differences from our own only by the appearance, four years ago, of Steven Marcus' *The Other Victorians. The French Lieutenant's Woman* gives us a post-Marcus view, as it were, of the Victorian age. This is not to say that Fowles' theme is Victorian sex; it is much wider than that; but he does give his Victorian hero a sexual life of a kind that, though modest and unspectacular enough, would scarcely even have been hinted at in a Victorian novel. . . .

What fascinates me, though, is that the sudden authorial intrusion, the dropping of the novelist's *persona* as narrator, is itself thoroughly Victorian. Fowles' Chapter 13 is, as it were, the mirror-image of George Eliot's Chapter "In Which the Story Pauses a Little" in *Adam Bede.* Fowles is a very clever man.

The significance of *The French Lieutenant's Woman* doesn't lie in its "experimental" features. These are much more apparent than real and, in my view, are a boring red herring. *The French Lieutenant's Woman* stands up in its own right as a remarkably solid historical novel in which Fowles recreates a large part of the ferment in English life a century ago, the intellectual ferment, the class ferment, the shifting of classes, the shifting of power, and the effects of these on the assumptions by which men and women live. It is a quite considerable achievement.

*Walter Allen, "The Achievement of John Fowles," in* Encounter, *August, 1970, pp. 64-7.*

I want to examine the unity of Fowles's fiction, taking note of the existential continuity which the author himself has frequently drawn attention to, and emphasising their generic similarities as romances. Both the gothic romance, beginning with Walpole's *Castle of Otranto* (1764), and the historical romance, beginning with Scott's *Waverley* (1814), evolved popular traditions which Fowles's three novels—despite their author's posture as a realist—can be seen as inheriting and revitalising in order to re-create multi-levelled romance fictions of considerable complexity and depth.

The gothic novel and the historical romance have traditionally been regarded as sub-literature, fringe reading unsuited to the mature and educated sensibility. . . . Though the objections to romance can be intellectual, the scorn of the professional writer for the often uneven and shamelessly derivative style of the romance novelist (evidenced for example in Coleridge's angry dismissal of Scott's work as 'Wretched trash'), the usual objection . . . is moral. . . . The romance found an unexpected defender in Henry James, who regarded it as an 'attribute' that the genre dealt in experiences remote from a normative social ethos . . ., a point of view significantly amplified by the meaningful way in which each of Fowles's three novels begins with the precise location of time and place, moves into dimensions of myth, and then gravitates back to the secure identity of an English social landscape. . . .

Fowles inverts the traditionally assumed dichotomy between the romancer and the realist writer, manipulating the romance form to effect both a sceptical examination of the romance experience and, more radically, a critique of contemporary realist fiction for its absence of moral responsibility. . . . While maintaining the element of exotic distance which inheres in the romance form, Fowles permits his works to function as parables of human character which he regards as of immediate relevance to contemporary English social realities. English society becomes a mythic battleground for Fowles, in which solitary individuals engage in a conflict for moral and imaginative survival against 'the great universal stodge' . . . of social conformity. . . .

Fowles is very far from being unaware of the strains involved in being a didactic writer, and the security of his narratives is frequently questioned by elements of ambiguity and self-parody. . . . The parody does not however ultimately detract from the seriousness of Fowles's exploration or the relationship which figures in the 'godgame' involved in any novel, an exploration which is dramatically assimilated to his existential philosophy of freedom by the radical device of offering the reader three alternative conclusions to the plot action. Whether or not the choices manifest in this gesture are meaningful at anything more than a conceptual level and do not instead have their posited equality eroded by the linear nature of the novel form remains debatable. Either way these highly self-conscious manipulations of romance situations testify to the originality and awareness underlying Fowles's exploitation of the genre, conferring a discernible structural continuity on to his novels and showing them to be something more than the simple entertainments which many reviewers and critics originally perceived them to be. . . .

*The Collector* is entirely credible at a 'realistic' level. . . . At the same time a variety of literary allusions and echoes convert the action of the story towards a mythic resonance, while the novel itself cannot be said to possess the 'unique plot' attributed to it by Fowles's interviewer. On the contrary, the theme of the persecuted maiden has a long literary heritage and became a stock property of the gothic romance. . . . Fowles takes this romance situation and updates it, infusing it with psychological, metaphysical and moral dimensions. . . . Miranda ultimately dies because there is simply no moral level on which she can communicate with Clegg; his moral atrophy has reached a stage where any potential for change has become ineluctably frozen. Fowles emphasises the fine balance that exists in the individual between a potential for good or evil, but in Clegg's case the descent into the pathological is the ingrown result of years of environmental repression, and it is the incurability of his delusions which makes *The Collector* such a tragic and bleakly pessimistic novel. . . .

*The Collector* contains in embryo the psychological and philosophical ideas which in the later two works appear as the mature expression of a personal and anglicized brand of existentialism, bridged by the appearance of *The Aristos* (1965), a pensée-like collection of pithy definitions of man's social and metaphysical condition. . . . *The Aristos* is a brave statement of his personal views and testifies to the seriousness and scope of the ideas underlying his sensational novels, but the originality of Fowles's existentialist philosophy locates itself more in the eclectic unity it makes when moulded into a dramatic fictional situation, rather than in the ideas themselves, which largely seem to derive from Kierkegaard, Heidegger and Sartre. The emphasis on personal choice is central to Fowles's philosophy. . . . [It] is in Fowles's conception of character that we come more centrally to the dramatic persuasiveness of his existentialist philosophy, realized in the way moral growth springs dialectically out of the tissue of contradictions which his major protagonists embody. . . .

[His] affirmative and optimistic attitude towards life distinguishes Fowles's novels from the existential fictions of Sartre and Camus, as well as from the chic pessimism of the Waste Land mentality. Instead of nausea and disgust Fowles's existentialist characters experience moments of epiphany when they capture a sense both of the continuity of time alive in every moment (in Fowles's terminology 'the horizontality of existence') and of the richness and density of the contingent world; instead of dramatising despair or gratuitous acts of rebellion his novels propose a stoic endurance and a sharp recognition of the possibilities open to every individual at each moment when choices demand to be made. . . .

The two main criticisms levelled against *The Magus,* that it is both unrealistic in its fabulously contorted plot and hollow in its meaning, are criteria of judgement which have been used against romances from the earliest days of the novel. . . . The assumption that *The Magus* is an entertaining but ultimately frustrating and vacuous thriller is quite mistaken. . . . [The] novel as a parable is open to the same structural ambiguity as that . . . in *A Portrait of the Artist as a Young Man*: are Nicholas Urfe and Joyce's Stephen finally transfigured, or is the last upward movement merely a gesture, another turn in an endless cycle? . . . Just as *Tristram Shandy* arrives at the sardonic conclusion that the whole novel has simply been a cock and bull story, so at the centre of *The Magus* is the joke that this is a mystery novel which contains no mystery at all. . . . *The Magus* is a novel turned in on itself, crammed with Chinese boxes which ironically mirror the broader meaning of the narratives. . . .

*The French Lieutenant's Woman* is clearly not, like the previous two novels, in the mainstream of the gothic romance tradition, but is rather in the genre which developed out of the gothic, that of the historical romance. . . . To see the novel as an historical romance allows us to understand the generic continuity of Fowles's fiction in a way that other definitions such as 'anti-novel' or 'reconstructed Victorian novel' tend to blur. Fowles's third novel contains all the characteristic properties of the historical romance, including a Persecuted Maiden, the motif of flight, and dramatization of 'history—*real* history, as distinguished from legend and myth,' backed up by an impressive array of documentation. The naive use of mobility which the historical romancer makes is turned to comic effect by Fowles in a novel which proceeds with a quirky, Chaplinesque narrative rhythm, luxuriating in ironically redundant social-historical data and self-conscious authorial wit. *The French Lieutenant's Woman* is not substantially any more of an 'anti-novel' than *The Magus,* though its fictive self-consciousness is made very much more overt, and it is structurally very different [from] 'anti-novels' such as Flann O'Brien's *At Swim-Two-Birds* or Malcolm Lowry's *Through the Panama,* where the narratives explode in exuberant confusion and never quite come back together. A perceptive reviewer recently characterised Iris Murdoch's *The Black Prince* as an 'anti anti-novel' and despite the ponderousness of the term it's a definition which could also be usefully applied to Fowles's novel for the way in which the reductive ironies, the structural critiques and the sardonic digressions do not irrevocably violate narrative progression but are instead absorbed into it. . . .

Though romance plots, existential ideas and psychological dramas provide a coherent continuity to Fowles's fiction his final meaning remains moral. Seeing him as a romancer enables us to recognise both the structural unity of his fiction and the radical way in which he enforces a reappraisal of customary responses to romance, challenging the traditional cognition of the genre as escapist entertainment and pointing towards a new and morally-ambitious direction in post-war British fiction which satisfies the usually conflicting demands of both an academic and popular readership.

*Ronald Binns, "John Fowles: Radical Romancer," in* Critical Quarterly, *Winter, 1973, pp. 317-34.*

Fowles puts right at the centre of his work a superb generative energy, a history-making gift, a power of what, until the word 'story' weakened in critical credit, was called story-telling, of such an order that the philosophical and aesthetic articulation of his works seems modified by its presence. The aesthetic problem, the problem of fictions, is in fact created very deep inside *The Magus,* made less an aspect of its construction and management than of its theme. It remains, of course, a book about art; it is the sort of book a novelist might write in order to assert, for himself and others, a sense of the possibilities open to fiction in a time when our ideas and notions of freedom, of selfhood, and of significant order are in ferment, and complex problems of modern history, modern psychic life or consciousness, modern notions of selfhood and of reality, and modern aesthetics of form have to be synthesized. These, we may propose, though the reviewers did not, are the inner themes of *The Magus*; and the hypothesis has a fair confirmation in *The French Lieutenant's Woman,* where a number of these themes rise explicitly to the presentational surface, implicating the novelist himself and becoming part of his technical self-questioning and self-development. In both books the hero is led towards a state of exposure or self-discovery, led out of one state of consciousness into another, in a world in which the historical determinants of consciousness are extremely significant and in which the capacity to learn through fictions is central. . . .

Fowles does not dissolve the tradition of realism completely, and . . . in many respects his aim, like Iris Murdoch's, seems to be to preserve as much humanism for the novel as can be got. If the traditional novel may, by the linearity and rigour of its plot and by authorial omniscience, seem to control and limit, the modernist one may, by the placing of character in long formal perspectives, tend to dehumanize, to ironize. Fowles has reason to claim his contemporaneity, but also some to question it; and both these things I think he does. He knows his modernity, systematically, as a deep structure in consciousness; and his essential theme, the encounter of his heroes with the dreadful freedom pushed upon us out of history, supports his more flamboyant aesthetic pretensions. But his work has something of the air of forcing itself towards a formal self-consciousness of surface, rather than inherently needing it. So in *The French Lieutenant's Woman* one feels left, as I have said, with a sense of mystification. The realistic Victorian mode of the novel, in which Fowles seems capable of working at high intensity, is also represented as authoritarian and containing; the modern mode, which comports with Sarah's modernizing consciousness and also opens the door of formal opportunity, allows for unpredictability and contingency. Yet Fowles's real intensity of achievement lies above all in what he does in the former mode, and what he does there is only to be explained in terms of a realistic aesthetic that responds to the intensities created by living with the object or person the writer invents and develops. The larger framing apparatus has the air of being functional and enabling, and in some ways doesn't so much free the material as reify and distance it. The book actually succeeds, I suspect, on the level of its sheer impurity. Fowles is, in the end, an ethical novelist with a predilection for disguise; and he requires, clearly, many 'liberal' constituents in his novel which are not present in the formal wholeness of a novel by, say, Robbe-Grillet. His typical novel is perhaps a bridging enterprise, an aesthetic marriage of phrases of style. This may explain something of the oddity of *The Magus,* a rather more mysterious and I think commanding novel than *The French Lieutenant's Woman*. . . .

*The Magus* is concerned with the familiar obsessions of modernism—with the hope that beyond the ordinary, contingent, and disillusioned world of real life there lies a meaning of fullness, balance, and regard for mystery, and the suspicion that this transcendent hope is one beyond life and time and therefore can only be a translucent, literary image. But it is also very much aware of the unsatisfactoriness of asserting simply a formal salvation, hope of redemption through an aesthetic unity. And Fowles does indeed manage to create the sense that his structures and obsessions are not borrowed properties but fulfil a logical need to consider how the imagination now may design, shape, and give meaning to the world. . . .

*The Magus* is generically a mythic novel or perhaps rather a romance, and this kind of fiction of the mysterious web has a long and honourable ancestry. Indeed, Fowles himself draws on a number of significant literary allusions. Conchis is Prospero, magician, psychopomp—the mysterious creator of mysteries, the symbolist of the world of the unseen, the agent of the supernatural, the psychic force that can lead us through to a new version of reality. He is a splendid impresario, rather like the figure of the author who appears, in his lavishly embroidered summer waistcoat, to spy on the agents of *The French Lieutenant's Woman*. But Fowles deals with him in an ambiguous way, though in a way not unfamiliar in much modern fiction. An obvious comparison can be made to Iris Murdoch, some of whose novels—*A Severed Head, The Unicorn,* and others—involve a mythic universe in which mystery suggests the problems of a lost order or structure not available in liberal-conventional notions of reality. Like Iris Murdoch, Fowles is clearly concerned not simply with mystery for its own sake, or the vague evocation of powers undreamt of in our philosophy, but with forces and structures that underlie our rational being, sociopsychic forces that are not readily registered in the fiction of documentary modes. In Iris Murdoch it is, I think, fairly evident that we are invited 'out' of society in order to see the powers which underpin it, powers which presume new relationships and new risks with selfhood that must by necessity be explored. The problem of the mode is that it characteristically involves a high degree of fictional faking, and there is a strong temptation for the novelist to create a sense of mystery and special insight which is no more than a numinously dramatic satisfaction, a building up of myth for its own splendid sake. Fowles obviously piles on the suspense by making Urfe at times less aware of what has to be going on than he should be, and the elaborate forgeries and ruses employed by Conchis require a kind of good luck to sustain the illusion which Fowles as novelist always grants.

*Malcolm Bradbury, "The Novelist as Impresario: John Fowles and His Magus," in his* Possibilities: Essays on the State of the Novel *(© 1973 by Malcolm Bradbury; reprinted by permission of Oxford University Press, Inc.), Oxford University Press, 1973, pp. 256-71.*

* * *

## FROST, Robert 1875-1963

**Frost, an American, was one of our most honest and masterful poets. His personal and deceptively simple lyrics, usually in a pastoral mode, chronicle his unceasing pursuit of the nature and meaning of life.**

We have seen the growth or revival in this country of a narrow nationalism that has spread from politics into literature (although its literary adherents are usually not political isolationists). They demand, however, that American writing should be affirmative, optimistic, not too critical, and "truly of this nation." They have been looking round for a poet to exalt; and Frost, through no effort of his own —but more through the weakness than the strength of his work—has been adopted as their symbol. Some of the honors heaped upon him are less poetic than political. He is being praised too often and with too great vehemence by people who don't like poetry, especially modern poetry. He is being presented as a sort of Sunday-school paragon, a saint among miserable sinners. And the result is that his honors shed little of their luster on other poets, who in turn feel none of the pride in his achievements that a battalion feels, for example, when one of its officers is cited for outstanding services. Frost's common sense and his "native quality" are used as an excuse for belittling and berating all his contemporaries, who have supposedly fallen into the sins of pessimism, obscurity, obscenity, and yielding to foreign influences; we even hear of their treachery to the American dream. Frost, on the other hand, is depicted as a loyal, autochthonous, and almost aboriginal Yankee. We are told not only that he is "the purest classical poet of America today"—and there is truth in Gorham B. Munson's early judgment—but also that he is "the one great American poet of our time" and "the only living New Englander in the great tradition, fit to be placed beside Emerson, Hawthorne and Thoreau."

But when he is so placed and measured against them, his stature seems diminished; it is almost as if a Morgan horse from Vermont, best of its breed, had been judged by the standards that apply to Clydesdales and Percherons. Height and breadth and strength: he falls short in all these qualities of the great New Englanders. And the other quality for which he is often praised, his utter faithfulness to the New England spirit, is hardly a virtue that they tried to cultivate. They realized that the New England spirit, when it stands alone, is inclined to be narrow and rigid and arithmetical. It has reached its finest growth only when cross-fertilized with alien philosophies. Hinduism, Sufism, Fourierism, and German Romanticism: each of these contributed its share to the New England renaissance of the 1850's. . . .

[Frost] is a poet neither of the mountains nor of the woods, although he lives among both, but rather of the hill pastures, the intervales, the dooryard in autumn with the leaves swirling, the closed house shaking in the winter gales (and who else has described these scenes more accurately, in more lasting colors?). In the same way, he is not the poet of New England in its great days, or in its catastrophic late-nineteenth-century decline (except in some of his earlier poems); he is rather a poet who celebrates the diminished but prosperous and self-respecting New England of the tourist home and the antique shop in the old stone mill. And the praise heaped on Frost in recent years is somehow connected in one's mind with the search for authentic ancestors and the collecting of old New England furniture. One imagines a saltbox cottage restored to its original lines; outside it a wellsweep preserved for its picturesque quality, even though there is also an electric pump; at the doorway a coach lamp wired and polished; inside the house, a set of authentic Shaker benches, a Salem rocker, willow-ware plates and Sandwich glass; and, on the tip-top table, carefully dusted, a first edition of Robert Frost.

*Malcolm Cowley, "Robert Frost: A Dissenting Opinion" (originally published, in two parts, in* The New Republic, *September 11, 1944 and September 18, 1944), in his* A Many-Windowed House *(copyright 1970 by Southern Illinois University Press; reprinted by permission of Southern Illinois University Press), Carbondale: Southern Illinois University Press, 1970, pp. 201-12.*

Time has made it evident that "The Oven Bird" stands at the center of Robert Frost's early poetry. Indeed, this sonnet struck a note which was to become central to the themes of many of the major poets of the first quarter of the twentieth century. Anticipating by several years that sorrowful observation of his younger contemporary, T. S. Eliot, that in our time the ancient song of the nightingale had degenerated into the "Jug Jug" of dirty ears, Frost focused on the transformation and diminution of Whitman's central symbol for the poet. In the mid-summer, mid-wood song of the ovenbird Frost hears a parable of the modern poet who, unlike those poets who can burst into song only in the spring, has learned the ovenbird's paradoxical trick. He has learned how to sing an unlyrical song in those times that are not at all conducive to joyous song. . . .

Like his ovenbird of mid-summer song, the poet that Frost continued to recognize in himself was one who faced the hardest of facts: seasonally, but above all historically, the world has diminished, and "dust is over all." Still, the difficulty of the situation cannot reduce the durable poet to compliance: he resists the fact and his resistance becomes the impulse—bone and sinew—for his poem.

*George Monteiro, "Robert Frost's Solitary Singer," in* The New England Quarterly, *March, 1971, pp. 134-40.*

[It] is . . . possible that [Frost's] success in playing the role of the Great Poet prevented him from developing as a great poet as he became less of a farmer and more of a performer, cutting himself off from the life which had given a hard core of factuality to the fiction in the early narratives. Talking to his audience directly he lost his own voice in his public voice. He had always thought of the making of a poem as a performance, but latterly he was distracted by the performance he knew he was going to give on the platform, allowing his talent for pleasing his public to draw him away from the talent that really mattered.

But there is also something perverse about his refusal to commit himself more deeply. A poem called "At Woodward's Gardens" in the 1936 volume *A Further Range* describes how two monkeys in a cage get the better of a boy who has been burning them with a magnifying glass. Incapable of understanding how the glass focuses the sun's rays, they nevertheless succeed in gaining possession of it. "It's knowing what to do with things that counts" concludes the poem, and in some editions it is sub-titled *Resourcefulness Is More than Understanding.* Frost's poetry is a monument to this doubtful precept.

*Ronald Hayman, "A Talent for Pleasing," in* Encounter, *September, 1971, pp. 76-7.*

[The] feeling of being drawn down into the depths, the sensation of being lured on by elusive perspectives arises in us when we enter Robert Frost's poetry for the first time, a feeling which keeps growing as we keep reading and absorbing it. . . . Frost reproduces reality in such a manner that the very scene presented to our view entices us bit by bit, then involves us completely.

His images . . . are stereoscopic. They surround the viewer like trees in a wood from behind which now and then other trees—and clearings—gaze at us, creating the illusion that there beyond the next turn the goal will be reached, the goal which we involuntarily keep pursuing until we realize that there is no end to the woods. But by then the original purpose of our walk, strictly speaking, is already behind us.

This analogy of a walk in the woods confronts us strikingly on reading Frost. His lyric poems are not only rich in motifs of this kind (a natural phenomenon for the man living close to nature), but one could also say that they are based on a corresponding "entrance" of the poet (and, along with him, of the reader too) into the world he himself depicts, a world presented three-dimensionally and charged with mysterious, alluring depths and significant happenings. We are fascinated by the close attention paid by the poet to the most ordinary things, by his clear focus upon the actual, the concrete. We are even intrigued by the scrupulousness with which he reports about everything surrounding him. It is a kind of scrupulousness rich in suggestion. And we come to suspect that life's occurrences are not as simple and commonplace as they may have seemed at first glance. . . .

For Frost it is extraordinarily essential to bring different levels together: life and death, past and present, external and internal, spring and autumn, lake and wood. This kind of conjunction may take place in Frost by an exchange of views: "Two had seen two, whichever side you spoke from"—but by such a momentary contact the sought-for fullness and an all-embracing universal integrity are achieved—the internal concatenation of phenomena that may be remote from one another but still appear in the poetic image as a unity. According to Frost, there is "something" in the very nature of things "that doesn't love a wall, that wants it down." For this reason, for example, racial discrimination, social and spiritual segregation, everybody's living for himself alone according to the principle "good fences make good neighbors" found in Frost a definite enemy. . . .

In his insistence upon the unity of the world, which in our consciousness frequently appears to be divided and atomized into countless cells, nuclei, poles, lies the ethical and the actual aesthetic program of Frost. He wished he could embrace both heaven and earth ("Birches"). His work, the work of artists in general, consists of building a short bridge from one man to another, of establishing connections between man and nature, body and soul, of demonstrating reality in the wonderful interaction of its individual parts.

Frost's landscapes and genre scenes—with all their realistic delicacy and liveliness of portrayal—contain something that is more than just a mere imitation of life, a copying of nature. At the same time the metaphysical essence of nature and existence which he abstracts from everyday life surrounding him are always in Frost rooted deep in the soil of reality. Poetry and prose, abstract philosophy and sober everyday occurrences are so closely interwoven in his poetry that the one becomes now the source, now the shell of the other. Like his characters, Frost himself, to use his own expression, "mingled reckless talk of heavenly stars with hugger-mugger farming." Physical work he coupled with poetic inspiration and gave himself to philosophy, meditation, contemplation, whether he was chopping wood or gathering hay. . . .

Undoubtedly Frost, the poet-philosopher who preferred to "walk" through the world in order to observe life closely and contemplate its origins, goes contrary to modern rhythm. He looks into the depth of things, not merely at their spectacular, sparkling surfaces; and consequently his slow and easy, pensive step outruns the field time and again. His whole art sounds in fact like an invitation to a walk along an old familiar country road where behind every apparent trifle a new miracle is waiting to be revealed.

*Andrei Sinyavsky, "Come Walk With Us," in his* For Freedom of Imagination, *translated and with an introduction by Laszlo Tikos and Murray Peppard (copyright © 1971 by Holt, Rinehart and Winston, Inc.; reprinted by permission of Holt, Rinehart and Winston, Publishers), Holt, 1971, pp. 64-70.*

Few poets have elaborated images and metaphors more insistently than Robert Frost or mixed them so judiciously at times with controlling axioms and guiding philosophic commentary. . . . Ultimately, the context of any single image in Frost is not merely the poem in which it occurs but the special language that develops throughout the collected poems. Taken as a related set of symbols, these elements of Frost's habitual landscape form a particularly comprehensive view of many . . . pastoral themes . . . and allow us to realize their modern potential in perhaps the only way it can be fully realized—in the densely compacted medium of the lyric. Frost's insights into the nature of pastoral can thus be of valuable help to us in understanding those aspects of pastoral that have managed to survive and get translated into modern terms. They have an additional value in that, like Stevens, Frost is very conscious of the nature of the poem in its fusion of the imagination and reality and its creation of an order pleasing to the mind in the midst of potential confusion and chaos. . . .

To define its engagement and disengagement, to winnow the grain of rationality from the chaff of meaningless objects in the landscape, is in effect the mind's special "georgic" labor. For Frost, pastoral is an easier set of correspondences that come about in scenes where wonder and beauty thrust themselves forward, like the tuft of flowers, without need of arduous probing. One simply crosses a fence and discovers an abundance he has not expected. In contrast, georgic requires a muscular effort against a resistant terrain, and Frost's poetry frequently works hard at creating its rational, axiom-filled order in a universe at odds with it. "The Most of It" is an impressive balance of these two impulses because the laboring poet has not forced himself to encapsulate the grain in axioms: he merely brings the central revelation far enough forward for us to wonder at it with him as the poem remains arrested between plunging in and withholding. . . .

In each of these images—the road, the unharvested area, the swamp and the woodpile, the witness tree, and spring pools—Frost explores the basic metaphysical reasons that nature cannot be idyllic and that, by implication, the poet cannot compose himself in final acts or pure poems as he might like. Another way of putting it is to say that neither the design nor the language of poetry can derive from a realm of Ideas abstractable from nature's forms but must try to be reflections of real things in passage in a local geography obviously quite unlike the permanent landscape of an Eden or Arcadia. Even the kind of songs that nature offers (like the ovenbird's) are a guide to the poet's songs and symbols for them; they are clearly not those of the romantic cuckoo, skylark, or nightingale, who bear little resemblance to the real songsters that pass under those names. . . .

Frost's poetry . . . survives between the flux of the wilderness and the order that people choose to enact, in the difficulty of living on the "edge." For the place the poet most seeks to establish form is the boundary between himself and the Alien, where form is negotiation rather than an artifice of eternity.

Typical of these places of discovery, and perhaps an appropriate one to cite as a summing up of the pastoral aspects of Frost's clearing operations, is "Far-away Meadow" in "The Last Mowing." . . .Though echoes of romanticism are strong plangencies here, Frost's meadow compromises between them and the world of necessary mowing and plowing. Unlike mythological scenes, Far-away Meadow is a real place (or could be), and unlike the infinitude that lies beyond boundaries for the romantic, the distance beyond it is unknowable and inhospitable: one does not want to go farther, and the trees will soon erase all human marks even there. . . . [Especially in *Far-away Meadow*], Frost places the age-old concerns of pastoral in a new context. Like the main poets of the tradition, he seeks for ways to transform into the harbored order of poetry the momentary perfection that he glimpses in the landscape of New England. But these moments exist for him only perilously between social disturbances of one kind or another and the shadowy claims of an impenetrable nature. At times they exist only in the poet's verbal enclosures, which like woodpiles are not permanent but are more long-lived than most things. Thus poems are momentary havens from the confusion that presses insistently into the life of the real Frost, the struggling farmer and poet. Not only his success as a poet but his peace of mind depended upon his reconstituting of pastoral and discovery of forms to withstand those dark powers that "blot out and drink up and sweep away."

*Harold E. Toliver, "Frost's Enclosures and Clearings," in his* Pastoral Forms and Attitudes *(originally published by the University of California Press; reprinted by permission of The Regents of the University of California), University of California Press, 1971, pp. 334-60.*

[The] Robert Frost whom I knew in his old age as a friend (closer than casual but not close enough for intimacy) contained in various proportions humanity and genius, jealousy and spitefulness, generosity, careerism, ease of access and an ultimately obsessive secrecy. He was a man who on the one hand spoke to every acquaintance with the unaffectedness of a lifelong friend; but who on the other hand succeeded in concealing some of the important elements of his life even from his authorized biographer.

The fulfillment of Robert Frost's character, his maturing, took something like 20 years to gather momentum and then washed him up very suddenly on the shore of himself. Most poets find their voices in their 20s. Frost had to wait, in irritable obscurity until, at the age of 37, through an act of conscious will, his character finally changed, deepened and arrived. . . .

In discussing Robert Frost's character I have chosen to concentrate on the few months before his English adventure, centering on January 1912, when I believe he lost himself and found himself at once. He never spoke much in his later life about this period, except in parables. The character he chose to embody in his middle and old age was one he had created as a form out of the deepest uncertainties. . . .

The Robert Frost who took up residence in Derry in 1900 was arrogant, touchy, neurasthenic, sickly and shy. Contemporary photographs show us a smooth, stubborn, cold-eyed, sensitive face with sensuous lips. His handwriting was indecisive, scattered and slanting. He was preternaturally sensitive to slights and indignities and had long lived in resentment of his mother's struggle against genteel poverty. In the poems he had already written, and in the poems he would soon write, he often speaks of running away, of losing himself in the woods. In fact this theme would repeat itself again and again from the first poem of *A Boy's Will* until the very last poem of *In the Clearing*. He was perhaps more troubled by the fear of weakness than by weakness itself. . . .

By 1906 the worst of his depression was over, and Frost little by little emerged from his isolation, began teaching school again, became inventive as a teacher and revered by many of his students. He was writing and sometimes publishing poems. In 1909 the Frosts left the Derry farm to share a house in Derry Village. Two years later Frost was invited to teach psychology at the Normal School in Plymouth, New Hampshire. He seemed to be displaying a new confidence in himself, for reasons not immediately clear, reasons he himself never made explicit in later years. . . . For the inward record we will have to turn to the poetry, for the biographers and Frost himself tell us all but nothing. . . .

"Directive" tells us much about rage and division, about moving back from the present into the past, from the valleys to the mountains, into the psychically deserted New England culture. Can Robert Frost be suggesting, in the lines that conclude the poem, that he had found "wholeness" by returning to his own New England sources after a long resistance? That, "possessing what he still was unpossessed by," he had finally "found salvation in surrender"? . . . The external signs were all there in 1911: Frost's breakaway from Derry, his newly mannered speech, his evident confidence, his new cheerfulness and wit—all these must be taken as signs of self-definition, most particularly his new-found humor. . . . Frost's new style, like his new personality, was calculated to be both charming and bearable. Once the new style had been achieved and Frost knew he had mastered it, he minced no words: "To be perfectly frank with you I am one of the most notable craftsmen of my time . . . I alone of English writers have consciously set myself to make music out of what I may call the sound of sense."

I believe that before the end of the year 1911, in Plymouth, Robert Frost had begun "taking himself" differently enough to make this new style, this craftsman's revolution, possible. . . .

Like many American writers Frost had been drawn from the West to the East. Henry James and Mark Twain, to name but two, had relished the eastward movement; Frost, until this time in his life, had begrudged that motion eastward because to him it meant disgrace and failure. But now he had recognized the validity of Bergson's retrograde movement, "obliged, though it goes forward, to look behind," and was willing to pay what he would later call "the tribute of the current to the source." Now he inwardly accepted the retrograde movement, the existence of his past, and he found himself whole at last. Wholeness so freed him, in fact, that he was able not only to liberate himself from Derry, that haunted place, but, a year later, to launch out on another great leap.

In the summer of 1912 the Frosts are said to have flipped a coin to decide whether to move to Vancouver or England. "The coin chose England," Frost reported. It pointed them toward the East, recapitulating the movement of 1885 from California; but this move eastward brought with it a tremendous access of new energy. Not a month after arriving in England, Frost was at last able to dust off the poems in *A Boy's Will*—almost all of them except "one or two things to round out the idea" long since completed during the Derry years—and take them to a publisher.

Throughout the fall of 1912 he went on writing poems in his adopted Yankee voice, in the *North of Boston* style, giving himself over to his sense of New Hampshire language and landscape and people. . . . By the late summer of 1913, a year after leaving the United States, not only was *A Boy's Will* already published, but *North of Boston* seems also to have been complete, and it was published in England the next year. Frost marveled a little at what had happened to him. The change was evident in a dozen ways. His very handwriting altered significantly during the year 1912, showing new traits that a graphologist might identify as increases in both boldness and secretiveness. Not only had Frost arrived at a new poetic style, but at a new personality that the style reflected. The style was indeed "the way the man took himself," with "outer humor but with inner seriousness."

*Peter Davison, "The Self-Realization of Robert Frost, 1911-1912," in* The New Republic *(reprinted by permission of* The New Republic; *© 1974 by Harrison-Blaine of New Jersey, Inc.), March 30, 1974, pp. 17-20.*

[In] trying to place Frost in our cultural history, it is important not to lose sight of the most evident peculiarity of his career: unlike many of his great contemporaries in poetry—Yeats, Lawrence, Stevens, and Eliot—Frost was from the start a truly popular poet. Before he belonged to the profession of criticism, he belonged to the general public. He still does. It would be presumptuous, if it were even possible, to say that the Frost who enthralled readers and listeners across the nation was mostly a kind of front, that there is a "real" Frost underneath who can be reached only by those able to stand the pressures of supposedly uncharted depths. . . .

The attention [Frost asks for] is quite alien to the kind of reading we have been habituated to by most twentieth-century poetry and by most twentieth-century criticism of it. Usually, by close inspection of metaphors or of tones of voice, by recognition of philosophically or psychologically structured images, the reading moves gradually outward, the poem is expanded, techniques are translated into meanings. The line between the poem and mythology gradually becomes blurred; drama and voice become at last little more than a pretext—in a literal sense of that word.

Frost is a poet who obstinately resists that process. It's not too much to say that he writes *against* the disposition—poetic, critical, human—just described. This reluctance to reward the kinds of attention to which readers of Yeats and Eliot had become accustomed—quite aside from whether it ever gave a good picture of either Eliot or Yeats—would by itself be enough to make him both popular and unfashionable. But to compound the difficulty, the rewards Frost does offer require, I think, an even more strenuous kind of attention. Once you have decided, that is, to look for the remarkable power hidden behind the benign-ironic masks of his personality, you discover that Frost is quite without gratitude for small favors. He makes you work very hard indeed, simply to find out how much he's denying you by way of large significances. He will not let you have him as a poet in the style of Eliot or of Yeats; he will not let you even discuss him in the same terms. So that while, in the care you lavish upon him, you find yourself resolutely treating him like a very great poet, he is just as resolutely disqualifying the terms normally used to describe one. . . .

Frost, more than Eliot, is pleased enough with momentariness, with his quite extraordinary satisfaction in the poem as a human performance, in the poem as an exemplification of how to perform in the face of the confusions of life or the impositions of authority, including literary authority.

It is this that makes Frost so unique and his genius so hard to account for. It can only be accounted for by the most precise notation of *how* he performs, of how he momentarily achieves a stay in particular poems and particular lines, even particular feet. It is as if the world of other people and of things, including again other poets and poems, existed in a sound which is not his and to which he will succumb if he does not fashion a sound of his own. Each poem is an act of such confrontation starting from scratch and with a chance of his losing. In poem after poem, all that is other than himself is identified by sound, either seductive or threatening, either meaningful or brute. There is the sound of the wind and the rain, of trees in their rustling, of the scythe in the field, the cry in the night, the beating on a box by a lonely old man, the movement of a beast, the song of birds, the voice of a lover or her silence.

It is a commonplace of romantic poetry, this obsession with sound and its possible clues, with silence and its promise of visionary afflatus. But nowhere is the person who is vulnerable to these sounds and silences so often characterized not as a common man but as the common man who is a poet, a "maker" of poetry. . . .

Reuben Brower offers a good comment on "Mowing" when he says: "In feeling reverence and love in the common thing and act Frost renews the Wordsworthian sympathy between man and his world, but he does so in a decidedly American accent. The higher value for Frost is pragmatic, the fruit of action is *in* the moment." The action *in* the moment is not only the acting dramatized by the poem but the poem itself as an enactment, an act of "earnest love." Many of the early poems, wherein I think one finds some of the psychological and structural source of all Frost's poetry, are about the relation of love to poetic vision and poetic making, of "making" it in all those senses. And they are also poems about sound and the danger of being silenced by failure in love. . . .

[The] biographical material doesn't tell us as much about the man as the poetry does. By that I mean that the poetry doesn't necessarily come from the experiences of his life; rather the poetry and the life experiences emerge from the same configuration in him prior to his poems or to his experience. Sex and an obsession with sound, sexual love and poetic imagination partake of one another, are in some sense the same. As he observes in "The Figure a Poem Makes" (again note that sense of the poem as an action, as not merely a "made" but a "making thing"), "The figure is the same as for love." And as he continues, the metaphors, without his even having to intend it, so central is the identification of making love and making poems, assume a peculiarly sexual suggestiveness. . . .

*Richard Poirier, in* The Atlantic Monthly *(copyright © 1974 by The Atlantic Monthly Company, Boston, Mass.; reprinted with permission), April, 1974, pp. 50-5.*

* * *

## FULLER, Roy 1912-

**Fuller is an English poet, novelist, and writer for children. Although better known as a poet, Fuller has committed himself more seriously to fiction, in which genre his best achievement, according to George Woodcock, is the "restraint and sureness with which he establishes [a] network of relationships." (See also *Contemporary Authors*, Vols. 5-8, rev. ed.)**

[Roy Fuller's *Collected Poems, 1936-1960*] ought to be a more impressive collection than it is—Fuller is a capable and serious writer; of the two hundred or so poems collected from about twenty-five years' writing, there is no real dross, a large number of good poems, and a few better than that. It's not easy to see why as a volume it doesn't make a more distinct impression. Fuller is not, for instance, the product of any movement or "school". (The two strong influences on his work—Auden in the early poems, plus Yeats in the later—are dominant in other poets today (e.g. Larkin and Gunn) but not in the 1944-55 period when nearly half of the poems in this volume first appeared.) Repetitiveness within a narrow range of feeling has something to do with it, but not enough: you read on, nonetheless, on the lookout for the fully-achieved memorable poems the general level leads you to expect. Nor is it any overt lack of "experience", or a flight from what the last decades have offered. Though he despairs of the public world, he has nothing but scorn for contemporaries who have given up trying to cope. . . .

One main trouble is, I think, that Fuller has never found a wholly personal voice. Instead, he has a style. This emerged in the 1944 volume [*A Lost Season*] and from then on the poems are assured and fluent, the poet fully, it seems, in command. But, if there is such a thing, it's an approximate style. There is always a constant (and even a chosen?) distance between the meanings it achieves and the meanings which, after a while, you begin to feel are missing. And this remains true, despite a steady development and growth still going on. . . .

Somewhere near the centre of all of his writing . . . there is this final emphasis on life as grotesque and terrible. Reason (or neurosis) barely control its menace, so barely that even though all specifically human life depends on it, the control seems to him not far short of pointless. It is this vision that shuts the artist out of directly satisfying life, that drives him to art; but since art is one of the questionable activities on which human life depends, the meaning of the vision saps continuously at the value of his activity as artist.

*Graham Martin, "More Wound Than Bow," in* Review, *August/September, 1962, pp. 3-11.*

Throughout Fuller's [*New Poems*] we find the singular voice, the syntactic skill, and the probing intellect that, along with his poetry's emotive force, brought critical attention to his work and recently won for him the poetry chair at Oxford. Fuller can move without difficulty from a gently self-derisive poetry (as in "Chinoiserie": "How much happier I'd have been/Had I . . . been less timid and considerate,/And voted Tory, and stuck to prose.") to a poetry which penetrates deeper into universal experience, as in "Disasters": "Didn't in fact/Primaeval fluids hold terrors for newly/Created proteins about to find out how/To perpetuate themselves?" The pervading tone of the book is created by a relaxed yet incisive wit. In "Mind to Body" Mind concludes, "Likely to be a sad affair,/Lean flesh, our final reconciliation." This low-keyed quality is often deceptive, however, for beneath the surface of many of the poems one senses a complexity of emotions. For example, in "On the Railway Platform" after touching the head of an infant the poet muses, "This Mad Hatter figure scarcely knows/Whether he longs for your innocence/Or the youth of your nearby mother/Or a generalised human love," and, failing to engage the infant's attention, he sees the rightness of its response and offers the following admonition: "Beware, child, of your hand in crazy/Crashing doors and of ostensibly/Benevolent, unknown gentlemen." In short, the collection is rife with masterful poems—quietly passionate, joyous, pensive, sometimes mysterious, but always alive with the interplay of human experience.

Virginia Quarterly Review, *Vol. 45, No. 3 (Summer, 1969), p. xciii.*

[Roy Fuller] has written three crime stories, interspersed between orthodox novels and poems. . . . All are marked by the exactness and elegance of his poetry, but perhaps the most successful of them is *With My Little Eye* (1948). The subtitle calls the book "a mystery story for teenagers," but this is deceptive, for it means only that the murder and other crimes are seen through the eyes of an intelligent adolescent narrator, conscious of the pain and loneliness of growing up. . . .

*With My Little Eye* is a little-known book, yet it is in its small way a perfect example of a modern crime story, finely constructed and balanced, with the solution to the various problems that baffle Frederick French (what could make a man move from one bookmaker to another on a racecourse, putting five pounds on every one of the nine horses in a race?) dropping perfectly into place. *The Second Curtain* (1953) finds George Garner, a timid publisher's reader, nursing the hope that through the box files in which he keeps carefully the whole of his correspondence he will one day be acknowledged as "a sort of Horace Walpole." Garner becomes immersed in the problem posed by the disappearance of his constant correspondent and old friend Widgery, and his quest for the truth about Widgery (for that is what it proves to be) leads him up to an abyss of violence into which he looks for a moment before flinching away. The book, again beautifully composed, might serve as a model of how little rather than how much violence is needed to make a successful crime story. *Fantasy and Fugue* (1954) looks back to Godwin in its central character who is both hunter and hunted. It is less successful than the other books chiefly because the theme is treated with a too insistent Freudianism. Since then Fuller has given up crime as a theme in his novels, and one can only hope, without great expectation, that he will return to it.

*Julian Symons, in his* Mortal Consequences: A History—From the Detective Story to the Crime Novel *(copyright © 1972 by Julian Symons; reprinted by permission of Harper & Row, Publishers, Inc.), Harper, 1972, pp. 193-94.*

[Why is *Professors and Gods: Last Oxford Lectures on Poetry*] not very much better? One reason is the very tolerance, the amiability, that contribute to the initial appeal. He begins by aligning himself with Leavis's essential values: 'On re-reading him I start assenting again and again out of my deepest convictions.' But the very next sentence makes the nullifying proviso: 'Certainly it is not possible, without condemning oneself to Leavis's harshness, to judge the literature created by one's contemporaries by the standards of the literature that has survived from the past. The natural, built-in indulgence one must show to those creators who are grappling with the problems and phenomena of our time is enough to enable one to admit as valid and good sufficient of present-day art.' . . . Amiability is not enough. It is the outstandingly good who need the 'harshness' of the highest standard: the fifth-rate will always be cared for by their own innumerable kind.

A second source of weakness—partly, but not entirely, due to the nature of lecturing—is Mr Fuller's reliance on the expressed opinion, without sufficient demonstration by detailed reference to texts. We may agree with his assessment of Mailer and Sylvia Plath, but there is nothing to enforce it if we don't, nor enough to enforce his appreciative opinions. His loyal tenderness for the political poets of the Thirties, with Auden as his touchstone of merit, fails to persuade me of their literary interest. . . . One's sense of having so often to agree or disagree merely with his opinion is relevant to his discussion of Leavis and the 'two cultures' of Snow. . . .

Strong, and provisional, conviction is enough for private enjoyment of what we read. But literary discussion demands the 'evidence'—the discriminated aspects of the work and what we find they do for us—in order to make conviction at the same time intelligible and open to intelligible demur. Only here and there does Mr Fuller quote enough, and point enough to the facets of what he quotes, to show the basis of his opinions and make discussion profitable. Lacking this, the critical tradition of which his book is an engaging example must fail to meet the obligation he says we owe to scientists—'to make our discipline not less great nor less arduous than theirs'. The scientist reading such a book enters the other culture and finds himself at sea, with waves of opinion colliding or combining, and no good reason for choosing between them unless he goes for the biggest wave in sight and helps to swell the fashion of the moment.

*D. W. Harding, "Tolerance," in* The Listener, *February 7, 1974, pp. 182-83.*

[Fuller is] tightly packed into his regular metres, end-rhymes and stanzas, cautious, prudent, reserved, distant and assured. . . .

He subscribes to the tired provincial myth that sees the right tradition as proceeding from Hardy, somehow through Auden, to Larkin and the weak neat poets of the 'fifties: poets surely as ideologically crippled as Rupert Brooke in their different circumstances and ways. He demonstrates the necessity for a proper historical perspective, and therefore the possible necessity for an epic, but doesn't see the significance of *The Cantos*.

*Herbert Lomas, in* London Magazine, *February-March, 1974, pp. 125, 130.*

# G

## GINSBERG, Allen 1926-

**Ginsberg, an American poet, is a gentle, generous man, and the "leading apostle" of the Beat Generation. As much a public as a literary figure, Ginsberg writes "mystical-rhetorical" poetry which is inseparable from his performance of it. (See also *Contemporary Authors*, Vols. 1-4, rev. ed.)**

The same themes, the same attitudes, and the assumptions that all of the poets around Ginsberg share—the intense idealism, the social naivete, the centering on the lyric of the self, the use of familiar linguistic materials—all of this is expressive of Ginsberg's concerns. His own definiteness as poet is a verbal fluidity, a line's length and form growing around his involvement with the spoken, rather than the read, poem; and an even more intense idealism. He has, also, a brilliant intensity of image, the poem shaped by his conception of material as image. His insistence on the unity of his work is an expression of the emphasis on the conception. . . .

In Ginsberg . . . language and . . . attitudes are entirely personal, and . . . excitement is direct, unabashed. And in the smallest objects he finds an image source that clarifies most of his deepest concerns. . . .

Only someone who was sure of his attitudes toward his society could find an imagery as coherent, as consistent, as Ginsberg finds in his responses to something as casual as loose money ["American Change"]. In another poet this kind of consistency comes from a kind of intellectual insistence, but with Ginsberg it comes from his deep moralism. It is this, perhaps, of all the concerns in his poetry that gives it its strongest thrust. He insists on the moral necessity of idealism, even when he seems to laugh at his own extravagant imagery, even when he's writing the loose sections of the work for reading performance. He has written, is writing, a long poetic expression of this morality, all of it implicit in the lines of the long segments, "Howl" and "Kaddish," and as clearly stated, as intensely, in the shortest poem and fragment. The poem, from this view of it, has become Ginsberg, and he, in an involved, complex reflection of the realities of his life, has become his dark, tense, tangled poem.

*Samuel Charters, "Allen Ginsberg," in his* Some Poems/Poets: Studies in American Underground Poetry Since 1945, *Oyez, 1971, pp. 71-6.*

The best-known poem of the Beat movement is Allen Ginsberg's "Howl" (1956). . . . Written in long-line parallel verse-clauses that pile up into huge sentences, "Howl" invites comparison with the "Song of Myself" of Whitman, whom Ginsberg claims as a father. But unlike Whitman's poem of praise, "Howl" is a frenzied protest against the indignities of life in Ginsberg's America. . . . Also unlike Whitman's poem, which is addressed to all men and proclaims the universality of human experience. . . . [It is, in] its appeal to the special attitudes and experiences of an alienated group, rather than to mankind at large, . . . an in-group poem. . . .

Written at great speed, according to his own testimony, Ginsberg's lines give the impression of an excited outpouring of language rather than a "combing out" or selection from common speech. Because of its sensationalism and frequent obscenity, Ginsberg's verse often makes a considerable initial impact upon readers or listeners. Despite his frequent protestations of cosmic piety and disinterested benevolence, "Howl" is largely a tirade revealing an animus directed outward against those who do not share the poet's social and sexual orientation.

*Walter Sutton, in his* American Free Verse: The Modern Revolution in Poetry *(© 1973 by Walter Sutton; reprinted by permission of New Directions Publishing Corporation), New Directions, 1973, pp. 182-84.*

In [*The Fall of America: Poems of These States 1965-1971*] Ginsberg has further brought to perfection certain poetic techniques introduced in the memorable poem "Wichita Vortex Sutra," published in his previous book, "Planet News." Ginsberg has pointed out a wonderful new direction for poetry to take—that is, for poetry to become once again, as in ancient days when history was sung and chanted, the vehicle for the description of history.

The poetry is difficult. Every image, every line, has its "data," i.e. its references which engender satellite data-clusters hanging together in the best poems like an exquisite painted Buddhist world-wheel. But you have to be willing to jump into the Ginsbergian brain-stream, where the ride is gentle, comradely, and brilliant. He has become a master at the description of nature, and he has tied up and captured the horror and gore of the world within the frame of anarcho-buddhist-SkyArt, if you can dig where I'm coming from, muh fuh, so that one can cry, sneer, laugh, or sigh in the safety of a friendly bard's Words.

It is a seething poetry, restless with energetic data-fragments and data-clusters, a technique used with stunning possibility by Ezra Pound in the "Cantos," and later by Charles Olson when he opened his wonderful case file on Gloucester, Massachusetts, in the "Maximus Poems." The poetry emerges, as it were, from a plexus of memories, historical references, quotes, newspaper headlines, radio broadcast shrieks, auld lang blowjobs—whereupon, on a sudden, flash! an exquisite line begins and a cadence of purest verse thrills the eye-brain. Maybe it's time for the poets to bump the Schlesingers from the set.

*Ed Sanders, in* The Village Voice *(reprinted by permission of* The Village Voice; *© 1974 by The Village Voice, Inc.), April 18, 1974, p. 27.*

One hesitates to say it, but Allen Ginsberg's . . . *The Fall of America: poems of these states 1965-71* is not a very good book. The title—an uneasy blend of Whitmanian majesty with Cummings-like whimsy—pretty well sums up the author's intentions: to continue "*Planet News* chronicle tape-recorded, scribed by hand or sung condensed, the flux of car bus airplane dream consciousness Person during Automatic Electronic War years . . ." Huh? Despite evocative traces of Flash Gordon and Fu Manchu, this last is sheer Newspeak, no more distinguished or less chilling than the flood of Bureaucratalk issuing from Washington these days. The text of *The Fall of America* is similarly disappointing. Ginsberg the Constant Enemy of the oppressors continues to write poetry that is baldly oppressive. . . . In Ginsberg's favor it can be said that his new book contains passages of true poetry, moments of touching whimsy . . . or flashes of delicate urban lyricism. . . . Unfortunately, passages like this seem only to be the accidentally poetic by-products of some more cosmic, more pretentious design. . . .

Engaging and likable a culture hero as Ginsberg may be, those same qualities that have gone to earn him his superstardom in life turn sour on the page, emerging in *The Fall of America* as mindless ticker-tape rhythms, hackneyed political sentiments, and a pseudo-Futurist vocabulary that would, I think, make a Martian blush. Why then do I hesitate to dismiss Ginsberg's work? Maybe it's because he's such a very good culture hero, one whose heart is wholeheartedly in the right place—which is to say, always on his sleeve. There's no doubt that Ginsberg takes an enormous risk in gathering the effects of that slapdash, patchwork sort of journalism-of-the-soul that he goes in for and calling it poetry, laying himself bare to all sorts of criticism and, indeed, mockery. Again, though, the impulse here would seem to be more melodramatic than poetic, or, more precisely, more messianic than aesthetic—an impulse which no critic of poetry is really empowered to judge. In the midst of this confusion I come back, with qualification, to my original statement: the poems in *The Fall of America* aren't much as poems, but there's one whale of a *mensch* behind them.

*Gerrit Henry, "Starting from Scratch," in* Poetry *(© 1974 by The Modern Poetry Association; reprinted by permission of the Editor of* Poetry*), August, 1974, pp. 292-93.*

Ginsberg is not the best, and surely not the most typical, poet of the [sixties] but the impulses that find exaggerated statement in his life and poetry are found in more muted tones in the writings of nearly every poet at work in this period; and though his poetry and poetic creed may still be at the periphery of general poetic practice, he seems to express the *Zeitgeist,* or that portion of the larger poetic spirit that is peculiar to this moment in history, unique to this time. . . .

If the reader is to appreciate the integrity of Ginsberg's outcry against all forms of spiritual and psychological oppression, he needs first to appreciate how cruel Ginsberg's experience of those forces has been. If Ginsberg's poetic rantings are generally successful and convincing where others fail, it may be largely because he speaks from experience and has earned his right to shout. . . .

Though it is not overtly political, anti-war, or social protest, the little *Empty Mirror* volume demands treatment here because (1) it establishes the autobiographical nature of Ginsberg's poetry and demands from us a different critical approach, (2) it records the origin and source of Ginsberg's rebellion, (3) it demonstrates that his poetry is essentially all "anti-war" poetry, and (4) it points to an important relation between the content and form of his writing. . . .

We must, if we care about humanity and are not entirely caught up in art, objects, abstractions, and arguments, find something interesting in the passions and doubts displayed in such poems. It is true that Ginsberg's poems are not so polished and permanent as to be interesting as finished figurines and sculpture; but they are interesting as flowing amoebas engulfing or fleeing the random particulate experience they encounter, or as naked, shaggy, fibrillating paramecia, shuddering with excitement or revulsion. They offer the soul, brain, guts, and jissum of the man with unique honesty—fully and boisterously in the later work, tentatively and sadly in these early poems. . . .

Apparently written before Ginsberg had his Blakean visions, this poem encapsulates many of the issues with which his entire life and poetic career have been concerned. There is here the painful gap between known spiritual facts and vitally experienced truth; the alienation and separateness; the inadequate and guilt-ridden self-image; the feeling of sordidness; the sensation that all things lack any ultimate significance; and the societally conditioned response. . . .

In many of the poems Ginsberg is simply talking to himself, sorting through things, implicitly or explicitly formulating precepts by which to endure. Occasionally [as in "The Terms in Which I Think of Reality," p. 29] he achieves an objectivity free of guilty self-laceration and captures his own and modern man's predicament, the predicament against which he later devotes all his energies. . . .

*The Empty Mirror* is the one volume of Ginsberg's poems that is not "anti-war." It is the volume in which he is busy discovering the enemy. Subsequent poetry is a war against the Moloch not named but experienced in *The Empty Mirror.* In *Empty Mirror* he is not on the outside describing and criticizing but on the inside agonizing. . . .

["Sakyamuni Coming Out from the Mountain" represents]

a new vista opening for Ginsberg, a new avenue of adjustment, a new stance to take with regard to the "separation" he experiences. The poem . . . shows that he understands and identifies with a "beatness" that need not be guilty, but which is common to spiritual men. It is the opening of a new and alternative reality, the beginning of his *experiences* of the "spiritual facts" he had known were true but didn't feel in *The Empty Mirror*. . . . This poem . . . marks a beginning and is an important milestone along the road toward "Howl" and beyond. . . .

The one poem of *The Empty Mirror* ["Paterson," p. 39] where the verse form points toward the later cataloguing and bardic breath of "Howl" is also the one poem that threatens open rebellion against the system; and it is here that Ginsberg first speaks of this contention as war. . . . Implicit here is the assumption that the same dispositional complex or "wrath" that brings physical mutilation on the battlefield is also the source of the psychic scars and existential wounds of competitive American society. . . .

Surprisingly, Ginsberg's special way of juxtaposing war and sex was anticipated at the time of World War I by none other than the surprising Amy Lowell. . . . Like Ginsberg, Amy Lowell senses that war is a "pattern" closely related to other patterns that constrict, stiffen, and stifle life. . . .

"Howl" is the moment of breakthrough, the violent externalization of the ulcerous guilt of Ginsberg's discontent. Poetry is act, not object; but the more genuine the act, the more fully shaped is the object that is left behind. . . .

More so than most readers have realized, "Howl" is a vehement anti-war poem. It is anti-war in its specific statements and in its stance towards "control." The poem describes, blames, purges, and transcends the world of relative consciousness, the It-World as described by Martin Buber in his *I and Thou* classic, the world of things, of walls, and doors, and inhibitions, and discriminations. . . .

As Ginsberg draws it, the twentieth century is the dotage of the once vigorous enlightenment of the seventeenth and eighteenth centuries, the prurient and senile old man suffering from the hardened arteries of the intellect. Now that there is little further room for beneficial exploration, the values that were so necessary to man as he pushed back the frontiers of science and the New World have turned to rend their master and suck his soulblood. . . .

It would be wrong to think that Ginsberg is describing only a particular American culture; he is attacking the radix or soul of which our culture is but the body. In that sense Ginsberg is indeed a *radical* poet and thinker. His particular radicalism is not by any means original (it is essentially Christ's battle with the Pharisees, Siddhartha's struggle with Vedic Brahmanas, Tolstoy's struggle with Russian orthodoxy, Lear's struggle with Goneril and Regan), but it is unique in its passion and in its grounding in Ginsberg's own personal suffering. . . .

[Surely] with Ginsberg one ought to avoid what Northrop Frye has called the "debauchery of judiciousness." A poet and a poetry that draw inspiration from the battle against Moloch, the heavy judger, may perhaps be granted the boon of our nonjudgment. They deserve attention and description, but are not illuminated by qualitative tags. This poetry purposely seeks to throw away, violate, and make such standards inoperative. It is perhaps formless, but it may be formless as a living amoeba compared to an inanimate clam shell; it is perhaps mixed, but it may be mixed as a rich stew compared to purer but plainer broth. It may be without art, but it is also without artificiality and carries its own natural inscape. . . .

As a poet Ginsberg associates language with the deepest spiritual impulses of man. Language that has been made to serve the judgmental rational faculty rather than the imagination and the deeper self will necessarily become as superficial and dangerous as the master it serves. The proliferation and prostitution of language through the mass media has transmogrified the natural magic power of language, words to express the ineffable and the transcendent, into evil black-magic language that denies the ineffable and transcendent and elevates the spiritless untruths of modern politics and culture.

A chief virtue of "Wichita Vortex Sutra" is that it makes the reader *experience* the proliferation and abuse of language. Its technique is to notice and reproduce the language that inundates the senses everyday, and in doing so it makes one painfully aware that in every case language is used not to communicate truth but to manipulate the hearer. . . .

Ginsberg is not a great poet, but he is a great figure in the history of poetry. We do not win from him many new insights or subtle understandings, but we do take from his poetry a simple intensity and a certain freedom. His poetry has made it easier for others to speak honestly. His unabashed admission of his own insufficiency and anguish have helped make others aware of their own deprivations and insensitivity. Certainly we might have wished for a more tidy apostle of compassion, one who would spare us the unhappy details of his sex life, one who might combine reticence and discrimination with his genuine openness and honesty. . . . But prophets do not come made to order. Ginsberg is a flawed but necessary prophet, a man desperately crying in the wilderness for love, searching the world's religions for a sustaining vision, witnessing nakedly to man's timeless spiritual and physical desires. . . .

*James F. Mersmann, "Allen Ginsberg: Breaking Out," in his* Out of the Vietnam Vortex: A Study of Poets and Poetry Against the War, *University Press of Kansas, 1974, pp. 31-76.*

* * *

## GIONO, Jean 1895-1970

**Giono was a French novelist, the author of one play, and translator of *Moby Dick*. His early novels, the "novels of the soil," grandly depict Mediterranean peasant culture; the post-war novels tend toward "classical tragedy and . . . the sweep of history." (See also *Contemporary Authors*, Vols. 45-48; obituary, Vols. 29-32.)**

Jean Giono, a determinedly pagan writer, . . . will not let the reader be. He must continually point out how right his characters are, how beautifully attuned they are to the universe—that is to say, Giono's universe, so basically different from ours. (p. 100)

Giono's universe is animated to the point of agitation. Everything in his novels is in motion, and everyone is engaged in some precise action. . . . No tree in Giono—and they are there by the hundred—no stream of water, no small seed, no large glacier, fails to vibrate with human feeling. The transfer is solemnly made. Everyone in Giono's novels must approach every phenomenon of nature as if it were humanly animated; so persistent is this trait that the grandeur of Giono's natural world often gives way to a sort of crowded fussiness. We lack air, so concretely busy is the wind, so intent on its affairs. A strong sense of the great cosmic flow of life presides over the genesis of Giono's tales, but all too often he is content to express it by way of a monotonous, pervasive and all too simple animism. (pp. 107-08)

*Germaine Brée and Margaret Guiton, in their* An Age of Fiction: The French Novel from Gide to Camus, *Rutgers University Press (New Brunswick, N.J.), 1957.*

The reader familiar with Giono's early work will already have glimpsed flashes of epic power in the three short novels comprising the *Trilogie de Pan,* in the opening pages of *Le Grand Troupeau,* and in the festival of shepherds . . . in *Le Serpent d'étoiles*. Though surpassed perhaps in grandeur and poetic beauty by individual passages in its two successors, *Le Chant du monde* (1934) is universally regarded today as the masterpiece of Giono's epic period. The reason for this esteem is the perfect balance which Giono only here has achieved among pictorial richness, interest and credibility of intrigue, and development of characters which blend into and are explained by their background. With its three divisions representing autumn, winter, and the glorious rebirth of the world in the spring, *Le Chant du monde* possesses at the same time the coherence and unity of great drama and the musical harmonies of a symphony. (p. 77)

*Le Chant du monde* deserves to be called an epic novel not only because of its grandiose background of natural forces but also because of its characters and narrative. (p. 79)

At first glance *Que ma joie demeure* seems much less epic and more realistic than either the preceding or following novel. The narrative, which relates the efforts of Bobi, the wandering acrobat, to bring a sense of joy and beauty to the monotonous and lonesome life of these isolated peasants, is discursive and rambling, filled with the details of husbandry and descriptions of the seasons. The style in the main is simple and free from the exuberant prolixity of imagery of the earlier volumes. Yet, on the whole, in spite of the brooding melancholy which has only temporarily given way to Bobi's poetic magic, the general atmosphere of the book is replete with quiet charm and appreciation of humble things which here are tinged with spiritual beauty. (p. 81)

In his epic lyricism Giono is especially effective in his sense of the movement of natural forces, such as the wind rolling clouds into fantastic and monstrous images, or the melting of mountain glaciers and snowfields in the spring. (p. 82)

*Batailles dans la montagne* (1937) is the most ambitious, the most truly epic of the novels in this cycle. (p. 84)

*Batailles* marks the extreme limit of Giono's epic inspiration. He realized that he had exhausted this poetic vein, for this is the last novel of what has been called his first manner. This novel is followed by the very different style of the *Chroniques,* in which the lyric rhapsodies of nature are subordinated to a sobriety of expression almost metallic in its hardness, even though his fondness for strange, mysterious adventures still persists. (p. 87)

The lush richness of Giono's fertile creativity reminds one indeed of a tropical jungle in which the explorer must first thrust aside the underbrush in order to feast his eyes on the exotic splendor of the foliage and fauna.

In this very profusion, however, lies one of Giono's greatest failings. . . . Of his enormous production, it is certain that much will prove merely ephemeral; it is unlikely that his dramas, motion picture scenarios, travelogues, propaganda pamphlets, even most of his short stories and sketches, will be long remembered.

What will remain will in all likelihood be only a handful of his novels—but enough to assure him a permanent and distinguished rank among the great novelists of France. Literary prophecy is perhaps the most dangerous and futile of all human temptations, and full of temerity is he who dares to foretell the taste of future generations. . . . I will suppress my own personal fondness for *Pour saluer Melville* and *Voyage en Italie,* and venture my nominations for survival among Giono's works. Of Giono's first period this list would include *Jean le bleu,* the short volumes of the *Trilogy of Pan* now available in inexpensive editions for the masses, and especially that beautiful and poetic *Chant du Monde*; of the post-war period the strangely haunting *Un Roi sans divertissement* and *Les Ames fortes,* and certainly *Le Hussard sur le toit.* (pp. 173-74)

Giono's numerous weaknesses as a novelist stem primarily from the characteristics already mentioned: prolixity and proliferation. In most of them there is great unevenness, resulting in majestic mountain peaks worthy of an anthology that alternate with dreary wasteland and monotonous marshes in which the reader is bogged down. In the earlier period Giono's verbosity keeps him from resting until he has almost smothered the reader with adjectival synonyms and breathless metaphors. On other occasions his quest for naturalness led him into the artifice of elementary dialogue, replete with irregular syntax and repetition. His absorption with natural forces sometimes tended to diminish his human figures until they were scarcely distinguishable from plant or animal creation. (pp 174-75)

But, if Giono has several faults, they are more than redeemed by virtues which in many cases are merely the obverse of the medal and spring from the same source. Thus his prolixity is only the price he pays for verve and intensity—a richness of the creative imagination which few writers have exceeded. (p. 175)

Giono is first of all a great poet in prose. It is now generally recognized that, like Chateaubriand in the preceding century, he has brought a new freshness, warmth, and color to the French language. . . . Uniquely open to the physical universe, he has given man a new vision of the reality about him, and expressed it with a wealth of imagery and symbol. Closely akin to this quality in Giono is his ability to transport us into a world of fantasy and mystery which yet seems entirely credible and real.

If Giono has succeeded in readapting to our blasé, sophisticated society the long-forgotten tradition of the primitive epic, he has also shown himself a precursor and initiator in the technique of the modern novel. Better than any other contemporary French novelist, perhaps, he has practiced the method of Faulkner and the American novel in allowing the reader to participate more fully in the explanation of events and characters overlapping in time as they are related in the first person by one or more humble narrators.

In one respect, however, Giono is far removed from contemporary practice. Recent tendencies in the novel seem to subordinate the story itself to the "stream of consciousness" technique until one critic has complained that "the history of fiction is simply the history of the decay of the plot." Other than his poetic spontaneity, the most persistent quality in Giono as a novelist has been his marvelous capacity for telling a story that holds the reader breathless until the end. (p. 176)

And finally, the last paradox we shall mention in regard to this paradoxical writer, Giono the regionalist is at the same time a universal writer. . . . [Giono's novels are mostly] concentrated in the comparatively wild and primitive valleys and plateaux of upper Provence and Dauphiné. But, though we recognize the scenery and even the faces of his characters, Giono is far more than a regional novelist. His themes are universal and timeless—the struggle of man for survival against the great forces of nature; the elemental and eternal instincts of love and friendship, ambition and revenge. (p. 177)

*Maxwell A. Smith, in his* Jean Giono *(copyright 1966 by Twayne Publishers, Inc.; reprinted with the permission of Twayne Publishers, a Division of G. K. Hall & Co.), Twayne, 1966.*

Giono is little concerned with verisimilitude and the situations he describes are often scarcely credible. He could even be accused of falling into melodrama. What he is really aiming at is tragedy, classical tragedy with its choruses and recitatives. The old Giono, who tried to raise ordinary events of village life to the grandeur of epic, has not entirely been effaced. But this grandeur is now provided more by history than by folklore and the old poet of the earth and the stars turns more and more to historical reconstruction. This escape into the past saves Giono from having to take sides in the controversies of our time and allows him even more than before to turn away from a world that has disappointed him and which he totally rejects.

*Maurice Nadeau, in his* The French Novel Since the War, *translated by A. M. Sheridan-Smith (reprinted by permission of Grove Press, Inc.; copyright © 1967 by Methuen and Co. Ltd.), Methuen, 1967, p. 47 (in the Grove-Evergreen paperbound edition, 1969).*

At the very moment when her political and economic leaders seemed powerless to avert an impending catastrophe, France produced a number of writers whose robust audacity and faith were scarcely equaled elsewhere in Europe. Jean Giono is probably the most original among these men; his appearance in the French literary firmament was truly meteoric. . . . The novels of that newcomer to literature were not skillfully built; they ignored academic subleties and the fashions of the day. Their heroes were not poisoned by complexes, nor did they blend desire and hatred in 'that mutual torture,' which was, for Proust, synonymous with love. In them the tone of a psychological dissector had given way to that of a poetical master of suggestive language and an epic storyteller.

Giono was also a prophet, and his message was soon acclaimed by eager disciples. He rejected much of our urban and analytical civilization; but he held out hope for despairing moderns. He aimed at rebuilding a new unity in man and endeavored to instil in him the sweet, or bitter, 'lore that nature brings.' . . .

The chief actors in Giono's stories are the great elemental forces: the wind, the torrents of spring unleashed over field and marsh, the parched earth in summer, the Dionysian dance of reeling odors, which intoxicate his men and his women, and above all, the stars that guide their works and their humble meditations. The novelist's purpose is to create living beings not unworthy of such a simple and yet grandiose setting, and the best of Giono's books are those in which he has conjured up the people who enchanted his childhood and taught him the meaning of life and the acceptance of fate. . . .

[The] early novels of Giono reflected the radiant search for joy of a young man exulting in his rediscovered bonds with the mythical forces of nature and eager to rebuild a new communion through love. Soon, however, the author became obsessed with the memories of war . . . [and in *Batailles dans la Montague* (1937)] the dramatic and even the plain human quality of Giono's earlier works seems gone. Words are rich in sap and juicy as sunny grapes, but their impetuous torrent appears no longer controlled by the author. Giono's epic qualities have swollen dangerously. . . .

More and more, as he became sensitive to the evils of the world, the prophet in him triumphed over the teller of tales.

His gift of style has not left him. His message, earnestly felt, is often expressed with great force. An anthology of Giono's thoughts, detached from a certain verbose repetitiousness, which weakens them in their context, would include some of the most convincing denunciations of the social and moral wrongs of modern life, couched in sumptuous language. But Giono's books [became] loose in structure, occasionally declamatory, and wearying in their revolt against the inevitable. The distinction the Stoics make between evils that we may hope to cure and evils that are not under our control is not observed by this old pagan wisdom. . . .

Giono is significant in French letters because he is, primarily, a great artist. . . . His first astonishing gift is sensation. Giono plunges into the world with a freshness of perception denied to most adults. But that freshness is not the delicate sensitiveness of children, which blends the concrete and the magical. His sensations are as robust and earthy as they are intense. They do not diffuse objects in a halo of evanescent glimmering light; they accept them whole and capture their essence, concrete and spiritual. The novelist's world is a world of smells, tastes, palpable masses and shapes, caressed by the body; visual sensations account for little, and the intellectual content of perceptions is sacrificed to their sensuous revelation.

What he has perceived is almost instantaneously rendered through images. Giono is one of the most prolific creators of images in modern literature. He has occasionally abused his gift, but he has seldom indulged in the tricky metaphorical phrases for which [some of his older contemporary compatriots] became famous. Giono's images do not aim at surprising the reader, even less at debasing the person or the object, as was the fashion when a 'gentleman' would compare his lady's pale complexion to 'that yellow paper in which butchers wrap up meat.' Giono's rarest gift is his inexhaustibility to create precise, yet expanding and soaring, images. He fixes the essence of reality through them and ennobles it at the same time; he simplifies, and yet transfigures. . . .

Giono is no master of the art of fiction in the traditional sense of the word; and his wealth of digression and lavish use of description deprive his books of the purity of outline associated with many French novels. . . . [His novels] are often loosely built. Even in character creation, where Giono is far stronger, he can lay no claim to having molded individuals overflowing with life, as are the heroes of Balzac or Proust. His women in particular remain indistinct. We know much of what takes place in their sensations and, as it were, along and under their skin, but much less about their feelings and less still about the intellectual side of their nature, their moral or social reactions. They are nevertheless real human beings and as true peasants as exist in fiction. . . .

Giono is also an artist with words. His vocabulary is extraordinarily varied—one of the richest in French since Balzac and Hugo. He seems to have the right word always ready at his disposal to express any part of a flower, of a tree, of an animal, or of a house, for the precise sensation received from the wind or the rain. His language is as robust as it is rich. The reader actually smells Giono's verbs, breathes the fragrance of his adjectives, feels the caress of his adverbs on his skin. . . .

[Giono] realizes that no regression is possible for men; machines will not be scrapped and probably should not be; but 'the true riches' should be shared by many of those who are at present absorbed in machines. If we cannot deny or undo mechanical civilization, we can go beyond it. To the suffering man of today, oppressed by a load of monstrous drudgery and living in terror of fierce cataclysms, Giono extends words of solace and hope. . . . A passionate protest against man's fate—this is the significance of Giono's work. Some will smile at these outbursts against modern civilization and affix the familiar labels: romanticism, primitivism, anti-intellectualism. There will doubtless be a measure of truth in their scoffing. But Giono's art laughs in turn at such philosophers who treat man as a purely logical and reasoning animal, or rather as hardly an animal or plant at all, while he differs only in degree from trees and horses. His creed is not likely to be long discussed by professional thinkers or to be weighed carefully by experts on economic science. But it is the living faith of a poet, the passionate and anguished cry of a sensitive man protesting against 'what man has made of man.'

*Henri Peyre, "Jean Giono," in his* French Novelists of Today *(copyright © 1955, 1967 by Oxford University Press, Inc.; reprinted by permission), Oxford University Press—Galaxy, 1967, pp. 123-53.*

At some point in each of Giono's works there is a climax—an explosion and a release. In *Colline,* the basic world of earth, water and fire is freed from the malignant hostility, or revenge, of nature when the spring restarts to flow, as if the putrid swelling on the hill had been pricked. In *Regain,* spring brings an outburst of new life after years of congested desires. In *Un de Baumugnes* and *Le Chant du Monde,* lovers escape from prison. Peace at the end of *Le Grand Troupeau* comes as a high-point, an end to slaughter, a start to living. Bobi looses longings; Saint-Jean dynamites the blocked waters. Langlois blows himself to bits; Angelo liberates himself from both plague and rebellion; the narrator of *Les Grands Chemins* can only wander at random again by killing his too magnetic companion. It is a literature of uncorseting, as un-Voltairian as possible. But, though it explodes outwards, it is from a fixed centre: Ulysses sloughs off fears by inventing a dream-world, but he must one day return to less tractable matter—his fellow-beings. So, Giono's world opens outwards, in the most expansive kind of egocentricity imaginable. In the country of notoriously *indoors* fiction and mainly psychological landscapes, Giono's private world includes the great outdoors. (p. 191)

Giono's peculiar genius has been to describe joy, freedom and achieved love more sensuously than most other, non-mystical, writers. Yet such intense sensory awareness does transcend ordinary experience, and is almost mystical. . . . Giono replaces reality with his own fabrication. . . . He has always advocated imaginary building, to fill the gaps in reality, and having, like Zola, a taste for the gigantic, he fills to overflowing. Indeed, like Zola, after knowing material poverty in his youth, ever after he seems to compensate by a sustained exaggeration, an orgy of rich imaginative experience. The result, for both, is a basic grossness, a disproportion, but undeniable force, despite the impression that the process of *démesure* in both writers becomes *automatic,* and enslaves the would-be omnipotent creator. It is less impressive than it might have been if it had paid more homage to dialectics. (p. 192)

It seems unlikely that he handles genuine moral problems so much as titillating enigmas. His people tend to have one instinctive and exclusive code of action, and rarely know the succession of disappointments lit up by only occasional triumphs and interspersed with much blankness which probably makes up an average human condition. He never shows us an individual truly wrestling with a recalcitrant inner self. . . . Giono stressed harmony before he added discord, so that the first seems willed and ingenuous, and the second contrived, an afterthought. The wheels on which Giono's world careers along are too well oiled. In omitting such a large area of human experience, Giono, apparently working for a unified picture, in fact produces a highly relative view, characterized by his quixotic treatment of external reality. Convinced that this century's civilization has been commercialized and atomized, he has tried to construct in opposition a fictional world, self-contained and internally coherent. Yet this is to foster hermeticism. He cannot share this with readers who do live in their times, at least not the whole of it. . . . So that, despite all the escapism, it is hard to avoid a feeling of inadequacy in the organization of contemporary life when reading Giono. Garden cities, national parks, week-end rambles, are only substitutes. It is not even Provence that Giono exalts in antithesis to urban civilization, but an ideal country of the mind: he has invented even what he hankers after. (pp. 192-93)

His books can enthrall, flood the reader with sense-impressions, shock, captivate, but they never move. . . . Strange how a literature which stresses the continuous transformation of all matter gives the appearance of being static. Perhaps, despite the cult of roots, Giono's world, being one essentially of words, is really of surfaces. Nevertheless, the spectacle of his imagination operating in full flight provokes an exhilaration rare to-day. (pp. 195-96)

*W. D. Redfern, in his* The Private World of Jean Giono *(reprinted by permission of the Publisher; copyright 1967 by W. D. Redfern), Duke University Press, 1967.*

I not only liked [*The Horseman on the Roof*] when I first read [it] and continue to like [it] on rereading; I think [it is a minor masterpiece] in the range with such esteemed works as Fitzgerald's *The Great Gatsby,* Gide's *Strait Is the Gate,* Mann's *Felix Krull,* or Greene's *The Labyrinthine Ways*. . . .

I have a theory. In [his book], Giono did not do homage to the great god Zeitgeist. Not only did [he] neglect honoring him; [he] did not even set out to flout him—flouting, after all, is an admission of importance. [He] simply behaved as though he were of no great consequence, no more than he had been before Hegel puffed him up. . . .

To artists in general Zeitgeist says, not *Make it beautiful,* but *Make it new* (think of fashionable Shakespeare productions, and Jan Kott's *Shakespeare Our Contemporary*). . . .

To novelists in particular, Zeitgeist says *Reveal Thou Me,* and of course they do. In fact, they were doing it before he told them to. They can't help doing it, at least a little. A *novel* brings *news* of the subtlest ways people are connected, and not even sociology and psychology between them can beat fiction at that game. . . . So, one of the best ways to find out what Zeitgeist is like in any given locale is to read good novels; but that does not mean that novelists necessarily adore him, write in order to reveal him or even to understand him. . . .

I suspect, though I am not quite sure of this, that a novel written in obedience to Zeitgeist's command to reveal him, make it new, be modernist, revolt, will not amount to much; the best form for that enterprise, it seems to me, is journalism (think of Orwell's fiction and then of his superb journalistic essays). . . .

[*The Horseman on the Roof*] is a story of wandering, and in the course of it Giono invents plenty of adventures to show us how people of every stripe behave; moreover, Angelo is a great theorizer, and Giono lets us eavesdrop on his thoughts as well as on the occasional speculative discussions he becomes involved in with people he meets. We have every opportunity to find in the pattern of these adventures the book's message, for we are guided not only by Angelo's theories but also by comments which Giono makes in his own person. (An instance of his old-fashioned, tale-telling, pre-Jamesian, authorial ease with the reader: "For a heart like his, smitten with liberty, these inhuman solitudes had a certain charm." But for a novelist to manifest himself instead of Z is a mortal sin against the Art of Modern Fiction, one of Z's lesser avatars.) What we find by delving into this novel is that there isn't any message, at least not of a variety favored by holy Z. Giono instructs us on the spirit of neither that age nor ours. The plague does not symbolize anything, it is neither a punishment from God nor a product of social injustice nor a disaster in whose glare the wickedness of society may be exposed; it is just there in the world, a given, like hot weather. . . . [The] reader is on everybody's side, even on the side of the despicable characters. Worse, he is with Angelo less because Angelo has right opinions than because he is charming and full of vitality. The novel provides victims aplenty; in fact, all the characters are victims either of the plague or of fear of it. But our delight in the fortitude with which Angelo and a few others face the horror commingles with our contempt for the abject baseness with which most face it, to impurify our victim-pitying till it does not lead to indignation or other easy sentiments but to contemplation and thence to a kind of acceptance. . . . For the offenses of permitting shameless thoughts . . . to enter his liberals' heads and of telling a victim-story that deplores not at all and delights a great deal, that is not Relevant to any of the Problems of Our Age, Giono will not be lightly forgiven.

*George P. Elliott, "Ramon Sender's 'A Man's Place' and Jean Giono's 'The Horseman on the Roof'," in* Rediscoveries, *edited by David Madden (© 1971 by Crown Publishers, Inc.; used by permission of Crown Publishers, Inc.), Crown, 1971, pp. 104-14.*

Because of his scholarship, obvious intellectual independence, and study of such artists as Melville, Proust, Gide, Breton, Sartre, and Faulkner, [Giono] became a craftsman and technician par excellence of the novel, the tale, and story collection or cycle.

Self-educated, a lone visionary residing mainly in his native Manosque, thus isolating himself from Parisian notables by distance, climate, and way of life, Giono established himself for a wide, international reading public as an unrepentant social critic, as champion of the poor, as theologian, mythographer, scholar, revolutionary, and humanist. (p. 4)

Jean Giono widened our understanding of the uses and the possibilities of prose fiction. He elevated the novel particularly, the very form thought by many to be moribund, to new artistic preeminence. Working experimentally in book after book . . . Giono demonstrated over forty odd years of daily practice how brilliantly the novel fulfills the conditions, and therefore meets the needs customarily satisfied by several hallowed literary modes.

A learned man, very well read, with a personal library of over 7,000 volumes, Giono often experimented by placing certain of his novels carefully within literary traditions. In such cases he proceeded by first arousing and then meeting in his readers a thirst for literary decorum, where components fit properly into what are recognizable modes. Various of his novels thus clearly recreate long-established sets, or literary structures. Such books read as if the author, having first categorized human experience, set forth its mysteries upon which he imposed order and form. Behind his approach, in other words, underlie not only the super-narrator's watchful decision made *a priori,* as Giono explained in the Preface to his *Chroniques romanesques*

(1962), concerning the basis for each conception but, even more important, his awareness of those certain issues—political, moral, religious, historical, aesthetic—best treated traditionally by each mode. Thus, adapting in some cases old formats to present use, Giono handled with striking originality various reconstitutions of a frightening, mysterious world. He hoped meanwhile, he added, that his *modus operandi* passed unperceived.

Adopting several different attitudes towards reality, then, and studying mankind from several different perspectives, Giono began by writing fiction according to the pastoral mode, which to the great comfort of his pre-war reader he initially preferred as an explanation of the world. Then he branched out into what we shall suggest is an apocalyptic mode, when in a spirit of prophecy he chose to treat history and theology. Much later he chose a surrealistic mode, when he undertook unearthly, fictional voyages through time and space; a symbolic mode, when he felt constrained to convey, or to suggest, by patterns, knowledge not made explicit in the text, and/or not comprehended fully by him either; an epic mode, when he proposed the ways of saints and barbaric heroes, lest their stories were thought irrelevant to modern life; a tragic mode, either according to Sophocles or to Shakespeare, when he realized that sacrificial offerings were still being made, even in the twentieth century; and twice an autobiographical and Proustian mode, when he resumed his puzzling about motherhood, creativity, and childhood, relying here, of course, upon the *Bildungsroman,* or portrait of the artist. (pp. 5-6)

No depth of mature consciousness, no great awareness of craft, and no accession to bitter adulthood occur in Giono much before his first near-masterpiece, *Batailles dans la montagne* of 1937. (p. 7)

Like William Faulkner, Giono not only rejected the city and foresaw grass growing at the Paris subway exits, but he constructed from bits and geographical particulars what he acknowledged to be a mythical "High Country" peopled by hypothetical beings like those in Jefferson, at the hub of equally mythical Yoknapatawpha County in northwest Mississippi. As early as his novel *Nassance de l'Odyssée* of 1930—the novel so titled because it humorously offers a theory and practice for the creation of Homer's *Odyssey*—Giono had selected two of his chief themes: the happiness of man released from society into the wide world as a free adventurer like Ulysses, and the privileged position of the artist, also like Ulysses, creating tales for the delight and knowledge of himself and anyone else. As an apocalypticist, Giono grappled later on at least two major occasions, 1931 and c. 1960, with the catastrophic end of modern civilization, and each man's personal abyss and absorption into the cosmos. As a surrealist rejecting reason and logic and summoning other ways of knowing, Giono imagined trips back into time in *Noé* and forward into space in *Fragments d'un paradis*. When he chose a symbolic mode, he summoned reader collaboration for *Les Grands chemins* as for *Le Hussard sur le toit,* soliciting theories and conclusions from the mazes of oblique referential patterns relating to twinships and brotherhoods, blacks and whites, warfare between nations and sexes. The epic novels call upon modern humanists to review the behavior of men and women, to decide upon what now in our days can be salvaged from what once were worshipful stances and actions, and to view the heroic women leaders of the future, after our present revolution. Always in the most noble mode, the tragic novels of Giono very movingly treat crimes and justice, triumphs, revenge, and ghastly sacrifices to olden gods, perhaps upon a frozen planet. (pp. 18-19)

The great ironic novels of Jean Giono appeal, . . . not only because he succeeded in clothing his vision in aesthetically admirable and identifiable forms, which allow the reader the pleasure of placing the works severally into familiar and rich literary traditions; they also afford shelter and comfort by reminding the modern reader, with whom the world is much too much, that beyond his routine and narrow horizons lies a vast, adventuresome universe of freedom and pure delight. They thrill some readers with their portraits of brave men and magnificent women, who trust the earth and their own bodies. Last of all, they delight eye and ear and bring joy to many hearts because, more than most authors, Giono possessed what Aristotle considered the surest mark of a born genius: the gift of abundant metaphor. There lies his waspish humor, and there also the reader's enjoyment. (p. 23)

When, passing suddenly to the mature novelist, we open a discussion of Giono's chronicle *Noé,* we see spread before us a most brilliant innovation in fictional form. . . . The ideas of Noah, ark, flood, and voyage produced three Giono works, all published closely together, in 1947 and 1948: *Noé, Fragments d'un déluge,* and *Fragments d'un paradis. . . . Noé* remains . . . not only one of Giono's richest and most intricate books, but also a novel closely related to a collection of short stories—a splendid innovation in fictional form. In addition, due to its sheer originality, *Noé* is in my opinion the most readable, even after many readings, of "modern" or "new" novels. (pp. 55, 74)

In 1951, twenty years into his career as a novelist, Giono came to the attention of literary critics at home and abroad with a major novel. His *Hussard sur le toit* deals with a celebrated novelistic subject, the bubonic plague, set by Giono as a background to the adventures of a central character, the aristocratic Angélo Pardi. . . . [As] probably Giono's greatest work, it presents problems common to the most distinguished of our modern novels. (pp. 111-12)

While establishing the fact that [Camus'] *La Peste* and *Le Hussard sur le toit* are, despite their mutual subject matter, largely dissimilar, the critics wavered in their assessments of the more troublesome, because much more complex, Giono work. The major problem shared by the critics of this novel was precisely whether the book could be best treated in terms of another familiar literary genre, the epic perhaps, or the medieval allegory. It would seem now that the romance, the *roman courtois* from the Middle Ages, better interprets this Giono novel, which is further complicated by the presence of symbolic patterns. (p. 112)

*Norma L. Goodrich, in her* Giono: Master of Fictional Modes *(copyright © 1973 by Princeton University Press; reprinted by permission of Princeton University Press), Princeton University Press, 1973.*

* * *

## GIOVANNI, Nikki 1943-

**Ms Giovanni is a Black American poet and author of the autobiographical work *Gemini*. Angry, joyful, sensuous, melan-**

**choly, energetic, Ms Giovanni's work is more and more frequently placed at the center of contemporary Black literary culture. (See also *Contemporary Authors*, Vols. 29-32.)**

Nikki writes about the familiar: what she knows, sees, experiences. It is clear why she conveys such urgency in expressing the need for Black awareness, unity, solidarity. She knows how it was. She knows how it is. She knows also that a change can be affected. . . .

[When] the Black poet chooses to serve as political seer, he must display a keen sophistication. Sometimes Nikki oversimplifies and therefore sounds rather naive politically. . . .

Nikki is at her best in the short, personal poem. She is definitely growing as a poet. Her effectiveness is in the area of the "fast rap." She says the right things at the right time. Orally this is cool, but it doesn't come across as printed poetry.

*Don L. Lee, "Nikki Giovanni," in his* Dynamite Voices I: Black Poets of the 1960's, *Broadside Press, 1971, pp. 68-74.*

The poet Nikki Giovanni looks upon her world with a wide open penetrating gaze. She sees her world as an extension of herself, she sees problems in the world as an extension of her problems, she sees herself existing amidst tensions, heartache, and marvelous expressions of love. But the tensions, heartaches, and expressions of love do not overwhelm the poet. She controls her environment—sometimes with her mind, often with her heart.

*My House* is the poetic expression of a vibrant black woman with a special way of looking at things. A strong narrative line runs through many of the poems: a familiar scene is presented, and the poet comments upon the people or the events. The poems are short, the language is simple; each poem contains a single poignant image. The people in Nikki Giovanni's poems are insulated from one another by carefully constructed walls of personal superiority: the old lady in "Conversation" is proud of the knowledge she assumes she has because of her advanced age; the woman in "And Another Thing" maintains an uncertain status by constantly talking. When a reader enters *My House,* he is invited to savor the poet's ideas about a meaningful existence in today's world.

*John W. Conner, in* English Journal, *April, 1973, p. 650.*

A lot of us moved into Blackness aided by Nikki's poems. And now, many of us are trying to stretch out and make it real and find ourselves. And we find ourselves in turns, at different times, confused, angered, mystified, saddened, delighted, disgusted and various other "-eds" by Nikki's new work. Which is because, somehow, Nikki has turned out to be a kind of person many of us never saw or expected her to be: *Wow, not Nikki Giovanni?!*

But wow, the relevance of Nikki Giovanni is that she is really not too quite different from how many of us see ourselves in our lonesome lanky watchtower hours. . . .

*My House* is not just poems. *My House* is how it is, what it is to be a young, single, intelligent Black woman with a son and no man. Is what it is to be a woman who has failed and is now sentimental about some things, bitter about some things, and generally always frustrated, always feeling frustrated on one of various levels or another. And lost in life.

But—and we had better begin recognizing our oppression for what it is, for how it is—it is not enough to simply sing the blues. Lost love lyrics will not change our oppression, which is real and is planned every step, every tear, every pain/pleasure. Our poets do us a disservice when all they present is reactions to, rather than analyzations of, our *collective* oppression. . . .

"The Inside Rooms" besides "Rituals" and a few other dreams and wishes is mostly romanticism come riding straight out the west/ern civilization literature. . . . And somehow the feeling is presented that if simple love can be achieved, well then, everything would be alright. . . .

The philosophy of *My House* is strictly European literature regurgitated.

*Kalumu Ya Salaam, in* Black World *(copyright © July, 1974, by* Black World; *reprinted by permission of* Black World *and Kalumu Ya Salaam), July, 1974, pp. 64-70.*

* * *

## GOLD, Herbert 1924-

**Gold is an American novelist and short story writer concerned in his fiction with power, competition, sex, and love in America. (See also *Contemporary Authors*, Vols. 9-12, rev. ed.)**

If we need to be reminded of the injustices and humiliations to which Negroes are subjected in our society, *The Prospect Before Us* does the job, and does it all the more effectively for its gentle air of objectivity. . . .

And Gold makes us feel them as few novelists, white or black, have succeeded in doing. But they are not what the book is about.

The book is about the triumph-in-failure of Harry Bowers, and in order to make us feel that, in all its truly tragic implications, Gold must arouse in us a sense of Harry's greatness. . . .

He is a man who knows on what terms he wants to live his life and is willing to pay the price for doing so. That his principles are tested by way of the Negro problem is an accident, though perhaps no other test could so well define his elements of greatness. What matters is the way he stands the test. . . .

One of the important elements in Gold's success is his mastery of a colloquial style. The dialogue is so perfect that it seems artless, and, when it serves his purpose, he uses the same style in his narrative. The effect is to immerse the reader in the garish world of Harry Bowers.

. . . . .

Carnival jargon fills [*The Man Who Was Not With It*]. In the *Prospect Before Us,* Gold displayed his mastery of a vernacular style, but he has gone much farther in the new novel. Sometimes, perhaps, too far. There are passages in the beginning that leave an uninitiated reader baffled. "Marko" and "pitch" and "mainline" and "hay-rube" are familiar or explain themselves, but "countstore" and "skillo" and "patch" and "geek," for me at any rate, took some guessing. Basically, however, Gold places no great reliance on this exotic vocabulary. What he does depend on is the rhythms, the imagery, and the quick twists of everyday speech. Miraculously, in spite of tired journalese, the glib announcements on radio and TV, the hard-worked phrases of the advertising agencies, there persists, below the literary level, a creativeness in the use of words. This kind of talk Gold has attentively listened to, and he has made it the foundation of his style. He has adapted it so successfully that, when one comes to the last sentence of the novel, one knows what it means and knows that its meaning could not have been otherwise communicated. The last sentence reads: "There's a good and with it way to be not with it, too."

. . . . .

[*The Optimist*] is Burr Fuller's book, and everything hinges on whether or not the reader can really lay hold of this character. I find Burr elusive, and that is the basis of my dissatisfaction. In scene after scene he is perfectly real, but then he slips away from me, and, in the end, I cannot put my hands on him. In a way, I can see, this is all to Gold's credit, for he has refused to content himself and gratify us with a superficial view of Burr's character. Burr is no more elusive than I am to you or you are to me. We never really know anyone, either in life or in fiction. But in a successful novel one feels, not that the mystery of personality has been solved once and for all, but that a precious secret has been revealed. For me the moment of revelation never comes in *The Optimist*.

I have another ground for complaint. In its latter half this is the story of the disintegration of a marriage, and a powerful account it is that Gold gives. But the failure of the marriage tells us little about Burr. I think it was Gold's intention to show that Burr and Laura are both responsible for the collapse of the marriage and that behind their short-comings lie faults of the society in which they have grown up. What the reader is made to feel, however, is that, Laura being what she is, the marriage could not possibly have succeeded. . . .

After these negative remarks, it seems almost offensive to mention again the many fine scenes or to point out that Gold's mastery of the vernacular is now complete, but something must be said to make it clear that Gold is just as much as ever a first-rate novelist. If this novel is in some sense a failure, it is the kind of failure only a first-rate man could produce.

. . . . .

*Therefore Be Bold* continues the study of love, and this time Gold is scrutinizing the love of adolescents. It is a theme that often has been treated humorously though sometimes with morbid seriousness. Gold is serious enough but a long way from being morbid. There are comic episodes in the book, and the narrator, who is looking back over twenty years, knows as well as anyone that he and his boyhood friends were making fools of themselves in a variety of ways. But at the same time he feels both tenderness and respect, and he has a sense that anything is possible for these boys and girls. . . .

[Gold] has been working steadily towards greater freedom and freshness in the use of words, not for the sake of shocking the reader but in order to rouse him out of lethargy, in order to compel him to see more clearly and feel more strongly. One may feel that he is not always successful and yet respond sharply to the total effect. The book vibrates with energy. It is full of the hopefulness and courage of the young, full of belief in love, full of the sense of human possibility.

*Granville Hicks, with Jack Alan Robbins, selections from four essays (originally published in 1954, 1956, 1959, and 1960, respectively), in their* Literary Horizons: A Quarter Century of American Fiction *(reprinted by permission of New York University Press; copyright © 1970 by New York University Press), New York University Press, 1970, pp. 153-54, 160, 162-64, 165-67.*

Witty, vital, and prolific—he can be slick too—Herbert Gold has published five novels to date [1961], and written a large number of stories and essays. The latter, crowded as they are with insight and prejudice, jubilantly express his views on fiction. . . . The need to bounce with life, to take risks with its incompleteness, to celebrate the "tin and hope" of human existence, knowing all the while that reality may be its own end (the mode of comedy) or, less frequently, that ambition contains its own death (the manner of tragedy)—these are the primary concerns of Herbert Gold when craft and vision meet in the felicity of a fictional moment. When craft and vision fall asunder, the style of Gold crackles with forced gaiety, and his wisdom degenerates into a knowing wink, a mere knack for poetic sapience. The writing, it then seems, gets ahead of itself; the author strives to attain his goal too easily or too fast. . . .

*The Optimist* is a parable of man refusing to accept less than his full share of life. The limit is death, and death, as everyone knows, throbs in the heart and courses in the blood. For the time being, however, why not ask for more of everything? This is the question which Burr Fuller must constantly answer—and learn to ask.

*Ihab Hassan, in his* Radical Innocence: Studies in the Contemporary American Novel *(copyright © 1961 by Princeton University Press; Princeton Paperback, 1971; reprinted by permission of Princeton University Press), Princeton University Press, 1961, pp. 180-81.*

Herbert Gold is a neat stylist, sometimes too neat. He can upon occasion master words, use them to bring out exactly what he needs to say about people and incidents; but he often slips too easily into rhetoric. He has a sensitivity for the nuances of speech and can frequently catch the precise accent, rhythm, and tone of dialogue and dialect. But here too he can slip, simply by making the characters themselves speak a little too brightly, as for example in *Salt.* On the other hand, in *The Man Who Was Not With It,* Gold's use of carnival idiom is exactly in key. He shows its tricks of insincerity, an important part of the story, but also displays its force in expressing the deepest feelings of the people who speak it. . . .

Burr Fuller, the center of attention in *The Optimist* (1959), is one of today's schizoid Americans who at mid-life find themselves split between an urge to make slow but steady progress and a compulsion to keep speeding frantically ahead. This kind of American futility has so often been presented that it can now be taken as a basis for serious literature only when the treatment of it sounds new depths. *The Optimist* doesn't do that; it is mostly a skillful reflection of surfaces. . . .

In describing Burr's army years, Gold's gift of realistic observation is given full play. In his use of dialogue here he shows that he has an eager and expert ear for regional varieties of speech, and among his characters in that first part of the book he includes some out-of-the-way personalities of the kind that appeared so zestfully in his first three novels. . . .

[The] last part of the book, with its suburban agonizings and all too sketchily presented picture of politics, fails to fulfill the promise of the first part. These later sections fail to bring to the hackneyed themes the freshness they need.

Little can be said about Gold's next novel, *Therefore Be Bold* (1960), except that it is charming. It is also unambitious and indeed hardly seems to be a novel at all, but rather a memoir of what it was like to be adolescent in Cleveland in the 1930s. . . . This book, which took its author more than ten years to write its less than two hundred and fifty pages, is an attempt to see life through the hot-eyed innocence of youth. The vision may not be deep, but the picture of adolescent, depression-era morals is vital and attractive.

*Salt* (1963) is highly ambitious and, except for a surprisingly strong conclusion, seems to me somewhat of a failure, at least in not realizing all the ambitions it implicitly announces. . . .

Unfortunately, . . . the author, in attempting to show the falsity of New York existence, is too often too slick. The people he introduces are mostly fringe types of journalism, television, and show business, and far too epigrammatically clever. Some of their behavior reflects the results of the author's shrewd observation, but their speech is always sprinkled with verbal gold dust; the people talk like characters put forth by Scott Fitzgerald before he matured. That this level of New York social existence is glittering and brittle, the reader would hardly dispute, but the total effect of its representation here is one of a high artificiality, in which the dialogue makes the purposeful artificiality of the characters into something not always believable. That is, if one may use the expression, they are often just too artificially artificial. In these passages the author is of course trying for satire, and while he occasionally succeeds—once again, through the actions rather than the speech of his people—the satire is not sharply enough fanged to bite very deep.

*Salt* nevertheless shows Herbert Gold as still a writer of more than promise. . . . *The Man Who Was Not With It* [is] evidence of what Gold can accomplish when he brings together his varied gifts—observation, comedy, and ear for dialogue. And the moral implications usually found in Gold's fiction are all emphatically present in this book. . . .

In having Bud tell the story in carnie slang, Gold makes full use of his own ability to handle colorful idiom. It crackles. But the language isn't flashed just for its own sake; it is organic. Through it, the author is able to present nuances of character and investigate the depths of his particular kind of people in a way which would have been less intimate with straight language. Herbert Gold's tendency toward the bizarre in style exactly matches the subject matter in this book.

Let me say once again that the whole novel needs to be read for its story to be appreciated. And it is a good story, one of a redemption or partial redemption, and of a failing attempt at redemption. To use this last word is to oversimplify, something which Herbert Gold avoids doing in this story. But the word is a kind of semaphore to indicate partially what happens in the novel. And such matters, involving important changes in character, are never simple, as Bud carefully suggests at the end of the book.

*Harry T. Moore, "The Fiction of Herbert Gold," in* Contemporary American Novelists, *edited by Harry T. Moore (copyright © 1964 by Southern Illinois University Press; reprinted by permission of Southern Illinois University Press), Carbondale: Southern Illinois University Press, 1964, pp. 170-81.*

The attempt to poeticize the wandering naturalistic American Joe and give him moralistic resolution takes [various] forms. In the quite over-written but best novel of Herbert Gold, *The Man Who Was Not With It,* Bud Williams, a young carnival barker and part-orphan, gains his education into moral identity on the road and in the lovingly elaborated underside of life. The wandering, father-defying, drug addiction, sexual voyeurism, crime and varied gross experiences elucidate such aphorisms as "You drink from the cup of wisdom? I fell into it." . . . The wisdom, however, is that the ordinary American Joe learns the hard way back to being the urban worker and family man that he originally rebelled against being. Degradation and the road, not convention and culture, provide the truest way to adaption and acceptance. "Down is the long way up." Slanged-over Heraclitean wisdom summarizes the traditional violations and final affirmations of monogamy, loyalty, honesty, filial acceptance, forgiveness and going back home again. The road through extremity provides the leap of faith into ordinary moral life by which the con-man can, once again, become an authentic "mark." "There's a good and with it way to be not with it, too"—which means that you can be a rebel without being rebellious.

*Kingsley Widmer, in his* The Literary Rebel *(copyright © 1965 by Southern Illinois University Press; reprinted by permission of Southern Illinois University Press), Carbondale: Southern Illinois University Press, 1965, p. 126.*

Herbert Gold's open feeling and generous sympathy in

*Fathers* are initially appealing . . .; and I admired the self-criticism apparent in Mr. Gold's new quieter style: the strenuous lyricism, the boastful emotionality of the earlier work have been subdued. But to my taste they have not been transmuted into the genuinely imaginative love and insight that *Fathers* needs. I wish I could feel more enthusiastic about a novel so humane in intention and so courageously direct in its approach to large simple feelings. But sympathy and piety can be willful too; quiet acceptance can be only an assertion, though it may be the right assertion. Mr. Gold wants to honor his father in honest terms, to bridge by faith the "abyss" of incommunicability between paternal and filial love, to express filial love by imagining what can never be experienced—the sufficiency of paternal love. And he fashions a highly attractive image of his father's energy and freedom, above all of his father's charm. But in so doing he makes himself too small—or so it seems to me, and Mr. Gold's frank autobiographical novel seems to ask for a similarly frank response from his reader. The father is a man of fact and commercial action, of will and property, the son's values are opposed, and this opposition is meant to be important. But Mr. Gold underplays his own values to protect his father. This seems to me false piety to begin with, and it badly upsets the balance of the book: it makes the son's imagination of his father's virtues too fluent.

*Robert Garis, in* The Hudson Review *(copyright © 1967 by The Hudson Review, Inc.; reprinted by permission), Vol. XX, No. 2, Summer, 1967, pp. 329-30.*

The . . . flexibility of tone [in *Fathers*] is astonishing. A prevailing buoyancy—sustained by the fact that the action, even when painful, is always safely recollected—can modulate rapidly into poignance, satire, or sententiousness. This provides a good deal of reading pleasure but it also raises a problem. The writing is often too obviously a performance, a striving for effect. Gold juggles his feelings. The breathless speed of his style at first lulls, then irritates our critical faculties, and we find ourselves asking if this or that really happened, a question which ought not to arise. The writer's virtues slide into vices: exuberance into overheartiness, wit into flippancy, shrewdness into smugness, poignance into corniness. The problem is one of sincerity.

Gold's sincerity seems most questionable in three aspects of his novel. Least disturbingly, because most openly, in the broadness of the satire, at times a sort of verbal slapstick: "'Your father earned his own living when he was twelve,' Mother remarked contentedly in explanation, 'and he is proud of it. *Proud* of it.' 'Thirteen he said,' I said. 'Proud he said,' she said." (His handling of the Jewish Mother is often scarcely above the level of stand-up comedy routines. Women in general come off rather badly in *Fathers,* partly because of the thematic emphasis on masculine love of risk in defiance of feminine craving for security: "When the banks closed in '33, my mother said 'We've lost everything'; my father said 'We'll start again.'") The problem of sincerity also arises in connection with Gold's awkward reticence about the failure of Herbert's marriage; one suspects that Herbert understood manhood more surely than he achieved it. Finally I distrust the frequently facile idealizations of the father. In fact what is presented as the father's style, his living "in a fury of using himself," seemed really the writer's need. (One or two passages actually suggest such a connection, but it is not clearly worked out.)

Yet Gold's virtues are more solidly present here than in his earlier novels. One reason may be that the constantly colorful idiom he seems to require is, in part, justified dramatically by the Yiddish-English speech of the parents. Another reason may be that his subject touches a deeper layer of feeling—feeling that is most sincere, most authentic, when he links the hurtling energy of father and son to an underlying sense of loss, when he both defies and admits his dread of the irreversibility of time.

*David J. Gordon, in* The Yale Review *(© 1967 by Yale University; reprinted by permission of the editors), Autumn, 1967, pp. 106-07.*

In writing about the by now tattered fringes of hippy-yippy life in San Francisco in [*The Great American Jackpot*] Mr. Gold by his very choice of locale and subject matter gives his new book a faintly old-fashioned air. Few observers deny the fact that Haight-Ashbury, Berkeley, and related areas are dying phenomena, barely surviving that time in the early sixties when the "beat" movement largely flourished, out of which all the rest followed. Thus when the author might have aroused susceptible readers with a parade of eccentric characters intent on doing their "thing" he is apt today to encounter only boredom; where his curiously plotted novel with its emphasis on improbabilities might once have brought approving smiles and some words of commendation there can today be nothing more than polite toleration. In the past Mr. Gold has given us good journeyman performances. All hope must not be abandoned for so fluent and facile a writer.

Virginia Quarterly Review, *Vol. 46, No. 3 (Summer, 1970), p. lxxxix.*

Herbert Gold, through his theoretical essays and fictional practice, . . . [has] shown [his] intention of writing metaphysical novels in the activist mode; and if the metaphysical activist novel indeed has a uniqueness—a spiritual emphasis suggested by K.'s quest in *The Castle*—which defines its particular excellences, then Gold . . . [produces] inferior work in that mode.

The world is, perhaps, too much with [him], and [he], like [his] heroes, [seems] to cherish experience for its own sake. . . .

We can tell from the surface of Gold's novels, by the philosophical interjections and dialogues which he supplies, that Gold intends to give us in *The Optimist* and in *Salt* the presentation of a metaphysical quest beyond the limits of the worldly environment which his hero—usually a well-brushed lawyer, like Burr Fuller in *The Optimist,* or a well-brushed advertising man, like Dan Berman in *Salt*—inhabits; but we cannot tell this from a level other than the surface. *The Optimist,* Gold's first novel in the activist mode, and *Salt,* a more recent novel, also in this mode, are not informed by [an] . . . urgent sense of self or separation (not necessarily alienation) of self from the masses.

Gold's Burr Fuller wants more of worldly experience; he loves life; he does not separate himself from this experience or from its worldly patterns. Although Gold satirizes ordinary middle-class life and ordinary sophisticated life, the comforts and the evils of the corrupt world from which the hero would disengage himself, nevertheless there is always the nagging suspicion that Gold is forced to satirize the world to keep himself, and his hero, from embracing it. Ordinary life is not nearly unpleasant enough. . . . [It] is pleasant; it is seductive. . . .

It is enough, and yet not enough. It is enough for life, perhaps, but not enough for the novel. Each novel needs to define itself structurally, whether the structure be traditional or antitraditional and activist; and part of structural definition lies in theme. The theme of becoming in the successful activist novel demands a basically open structure to reveal the hero-in-process, but there must be something besides this openness to make the structure complex and to give it its narrative significance: some conflict, opposition, or tension is necessary. The process of becoming posed against a personal concept of ideal being, the existential fact against the awareness of possibilities, especially the transcendent possibility of the self—must be dramatized if the narrative of the activist hero's adventures is to be considered as more than picaresque, as a new pattern for modern man's metaphysical and spiritual investigation. K. is always a surveyor of the castle's land, never the Land-Surveyor. A continuing frustration of the will to ideality is coupled with an ironic realization of his ideal self in the process of his existence: this duality is at the root of the art of the activist novel. It is this duality which Gold does not achieve.

*Helen Weinberg, in her* The New Novel in America: The Kafkan Mode in Contemporary Fiction *(copyright © 1970 by Cornell University; used by permission of Cornell University Press), Cornell University Press, 1970, pp. 179-82.*

Perhaps the nicest thing about Herbert Gold's informal autobiography [*My Last Two Thousand Years*] is that it reminds one of Henry Miller without the sexual posturings. The two are similarly self-referential, bedeviled by the need to be more than America seems to allow, exhilarated by the hope of remaking the self through acts of exuberant storytelling. But where Miller's is an art of improvisational variety, Gold elects to pursue a Meaning, committing himself from his opening words to a kind of thematic overkill. . . .

It would be stupid to blame a man because his life, in outline, sounds like someone's first novel—whose life wouldn't? But Gold's treatment, by insistently dwelling upon incidents that carry the theme of tribal discovery, doesn't sufficiently complicate and enliven the scenario. Time and again the necessary and interesting irrelevancies of a life seem to have been sacrificed for the sake of a "significant" experience. . . .

Even so, his account of his youth and early manhood is often quite wonderfully funny and poignant. It's later, when his theme seems to demand heavy thinking and large conclusions, that the life goes most troublingly out of focus and the writing gets soft and woolly. . . .

Gold makes sense of his life . . . by bringing to it a kind of tunnel vision. Where Henry Miller, for all his self-concern, remains fascinated by other existences and their own stories, the conditions, real or fictive, that have made them what he takes them to be, Gold has only one story to tell, his own, and the other people who figure in it seldom have much individuality apart from what that story requires of them.

*Thomas R. Edwards, in* The New York Times Book Review *(© 1972 by The New York Times Company; reprinted by permission), October 15, 1972, pp. 4, 18.*

*My Last Two Thousand Years* [is] an autobiography-with-a-theme by Herbert Gold that is intelligent, lively, and provocative, and yet, in the end, a disappointment. I fear that Gold is too nice a man ever to write an autobiography in which heart and soul are laid bare, which is what the theme—a Jew's discovery of himself as a Jew—deserves at this point in history if it is to engage us at a level deeper than curiosity. However, in a novel, freed from the obligation to be factual on the one hand and discreet on the other and drawing upon his considerable gifts as a writer, he might have created out of the raw material of his experience a character who would endow the theme with a blazing, life-enhancing urgency it never quite achieves here. . . .

[Many] of the episodes and their settings are by now traditional elements in any literary success story and would be just as likely to turn up if the tale were told by Herbert Gould, Unitarian.

*William Abrahams, "Backgrounds," in* Saturday Review of Education *(copyright © 1972 by Saturday Review/World, Inc.; reprinted with permission), November 11, 1972, pp. 69, 72.*

* * *

## GOMBROWICZ, Witold 1904-1969

**Gombrowicz, a Polish novelist, was a masterful prose stylist. He is best known for *Ferdydurke* and *Pornografia*. (See also *Contemporary Authors*, Vols. 19-20; obituary, Vols. 25-28.)**

[Is] *Ferdydurke* real? Is it a picture of the Polish realities in 1938? Contrary to what you might at first believe, it most certainly is. Admittedly everything seems completely dreamlike and fantastic. . . . Everything depicted as the consequence of associations. The language (actually, the words) are arranged musically like leitmotifs not according to their meaning—as in the case of Thomas Mann—but according to their tonal and emotional power of expression. One is reminded of E. T. A. Hoffmann, of the etchings by Alfred Kubin, of the eery dream scenes in Kafka's novel that take place in courtrooms located somewhere in an attic.

All the literary, musical, and visual associations which the reader of *Ferdydurke* feels welling within himself convey a dream world. And this is what Gombrowicz would have wanted. As a writer he entered the realm of dreams, created dream pictures. He abandoned himself to the flow, creation, fables, and associations in order to bring about new dream worlds for the reader—not merely to bring about the reproductions of his own visions, but to allow for the free associations of the reader and those to whom the work is addressed. . . .

The word "Ferdydurke" functions immediately as the formula "step into the realm of dreams." We still have a Polish reality of 1938. (When one writes about Gombrowicz, one is drawn almost naturally into the mire of a narrative style that moves along with the aid of leitmotifs and tonal pictures and even orgiastically enjoys the principle of the repetition of words and ideas at times. The compulsion to repeat is a basic element in the thinking of children. Repetition is an element of propaganda and also infantilism.) In the realm of dreams there is no absolute. The dreamer, dreaming, still lives in the real world. His visions and emotions may be spaceless and timeless. They may dispense with all causality. However, they can only produce something that has not been experienced from the reproduced bits and pieces of past experience. The old dreambooks distinguish themselves from the new Freudian ones by their relation to this phenomenon. In the former it is dream as anticipation, as preexperience of the future. In the latter it is dream as a strange and unsuitable reproduction of past experience. The epic dreamworld of Witold Gombrowicz would like to be both: the interpretation of dreams in a double sense—according to the biblical Joseph and Professor Sigmund Freud. Planted between past and future. In the hollow of the present. . . .

The theme of immaturity as the basic motif is modified in *Ferdydurke,* Gombrowicz's first novel. . . . Yet, as the decisive force behind it all, there is the *immaturity of a country,* the Polish state in 1938. . . . Social immaturity and social maturity rubbing elbows with one another. This is true of the unresolved relationships between the city and the country, the feudal world and the bourgeois world in Poland of that time. This is also true, however, as the novel demonstrates, of the corresponding ideologies and "superstructures."

Viewed superficially the schoolyard duel of making faces which leads to the defeat of the idealist seems merely to be a grotesque dream that is superbly narrated. However, what Gombrowicz intended to represent was the two extreme doctrines that were set against each other at that time in Poland: official messianic and ecstatic idealism ostensibly derived from the Polish romantic writers Mickiewicz and Słowacki versus the exaggerated popular trend of the urban intellectuals and ideologists who, like the nineteenth-century Russian Narodniki, wanted to become brothers with the common people, above all the peasants. . . .

His last novel *Pornografia* not only brings new elements that are reminiscent of Sartre and that parallel certain Ionesco themes, but it also contains considerable chunks of narrative, and the raw material seems to have been supplied by Jean Genet.

In spite of this fact, the reader who is familiar with Gombrowicz's earlier works will immediately recognize the author's peculiar thematic structure in *Pornografia,* which is unmistakably a counterpart to *Ferdydurke*. The real and the imagined Poland. . . .

In *Ferdydurke,* dreamlike tales of absurd duels, the processes of infantilism, and grotesque spiritual antitheses were related. However, behind it all stood the real Poland of 1938. Visions of immaturity both general and specific as representative of the real environment in Poland. On the other hand the novel *Pornografia* describes scenes that are, to be sure, gruesome, agonizing, and repulsive (all these adjectives are actually meaningless, for there are no corresponding values), but all these scenes are possible, conceivable, even probable. Apparently a "realistic story," artfully constructed besides. Composed like a play. Unity of place determined essentially by the landowner's house and its environs. Unity of time that is maintained by the passage of only a few days. Unity of action in which five men "in their best years" are confronted with three young people about seventeen, two boys and a girl. A novel in two parts which both end like the final act of a play. The first part ends with the murder of the landowner's wife Amelia. The novel ends with three murders, and only the murder of Simian has a rational basis to it.

Everything depicted with precision, blood, horror, and agony. Presented in conformity with the classical unities, which can be fixed and repeated. Nevertheless, as Gombrowicz correctly explains, an imaginary Poland. The complete opposite of *Ferdydurke*. This time an apparently realistic story that can say nothing about the real Poland during the period of occupation. . . .

Moreover, to dispel immediately any ideas to the contrary, it has nothing to do with "pornography" in its traditional sense. Anyone who is somewhat familiar with Gombrowicz's clowning would already suspect as much from the first glance at the title *Pornografia*. Nowhere is there even a realistic sexual situation depicted. If one can speak of intellectual obscenity (which is entirely possible here), then it lies precisely in the fact that there is not one *natural* sex act described among the young people, nor is there one between the young and the old. No sexual *reality*. Everything remains in a condition of sexual potential. It is exactly this that Gombrowicz calls pornography. . . .

Someone like Gombrowicz, who is in love with immaturity and at the same time strives to reach maturity and form, finds the ideal medium for expression in the literary genre of the diary. This form does not allow for the completion of anything, for anything to reach maturity. Everything remains in progress, everything is provisional, noted down always with the possibility of being retracted later by another note. In extreme cases the diary form recommends itself as an escape from really giving shape to ideas. What is once committed to a diary will in all likelihood not be resurrected in another artistic form. . . .

Gombrowicz is an unusual figure in contemporary literature, and the ingeniousness of this artist cannot be understood by going back to the man Gombrowicz nor by a detailed dissection of his theses and thoughts. The literary phenomenon of Witold Gombrowicz lies beyond all assertions and biographical facts. . . .

With Gombrowicz, nothing gets finished because he simultaneously desires and fears the connection between the "I" and its present world. He would be a loner who nevertheless achieves harmony with others. . . .

[There] can only be unresolved questions in the relationship between Gombrowicz and others, including his critics. He will never admit that a critical analysis interprets him correctly. On the other hand, literary critics must avoid equating their final judgment of Gombrowicz with Gombrowicz's judgment of Gombrowicz. . . . The uniqueness of Witold Gombrowicz in literary history lies in the fact that this warped relationship between artist and critic, between the "I" and its surroundings, was made into the peculiar theme of his literary work. Into the peculiar theme of Witold Gombrowicz. Into his only theme.

*Hans Mayer, "The Views of Witold Gombrowicz" (originally published in* Ansichten zur Literatur der Zeit; *© 1962 by Rowohlt Verlag GMBH), in his* Steppenwolf and Everyman, *translated and with an introduction by Jack D. Zipes (copyright © 1971 by Hans Mayer; reprinted with permission of Thomas Y. Crowell Co., Inc.), Crowell, 1971, pp. 240-55.*

*Pornografia* is a skilful composition of gossamer threads, and altogether different from the pronounced (if poeticised) physicality of *Lolita*. Noticing the superficial kinship with Nabokov, a British reviewer has remarked that Gombrowicz festers less. True, gossamer doesn't fester. But this seems a doubtful point of superiority in the present case, for if a story of this sort doesn't fester, it is hard to see what it can do. The oldsters are not sex maniacs, they are simply incomprehensible, simply weirdies. It would seem a perverse complaint to make at a time like the present, but one is tempted to reproach the book with failing to live up to its title.

Gombrowicz's earlier novel, *Ferdydurke* (first published in English in 1961, though first published in Warsaw as far back as 1937), prompts the reflection that what is amiss with *Pornografia* is that it isn't fantastic enough and so is merely odd. *Ferdydurke* is very nearly fantastic enough. The apparent preoccupations and theories of the later novel are already present here, indeed are more overt from the start. . . .

Without knowing of the book's strange and sad publishing history and its suppression in Poland, I doubt whether one would have spotted its supposed (and premonitory) political relevance, though one perceives and appreciates its timeless and unlocalised mockery. . . .

The book's superiority to *Pornografia* consists in its density of anecdote and even (however 'unrealistic') of character—among other items there is a very funny bedroom scene involving an unusually large cast—and its greater willingness to be comic, grotesque, wild, fantastic. Frothier on the surface, it none the less impresses as a more substantial piece of work. Perhaps it doesn't make much more sense than *Pornografia,* but it certainly provides more amusement. . . .

And yet there are passages in *Ferdydurke* so shrill and insistent (and passages so repetitious and tedious) that they will scarcely be denied 'interpretation': what else could they be crying out like that for? Even so, you can dance with the book quite merrily for much of the time, whereas with *Pornografia* you won't stagger more than a few steps before tripping over your partner.

*D. J. Enright, "Dancing the Polka" (1966), in* Man Is An Onion: Reviews and Essays *(© 1972 by D. J. Enright; reprinted by permission of Open Court Publishing Co. and Chatto & Windus), Open Court, 1972, pp. 92-5.*

Gombrowicz understood his national identity because he was partly in love with *La Gloire* of his own ego. Perhaps the Pole is an *enfant terrible* among the Slavs, asking awkward questions, always on the run from the parental myth. A squire or a peasant, he has enough aristocratic defiance to accept disillusionment.

Writers do not, on the whole, acknowledge those literary debts which have affected their style: these are probably too intimate to reveal, even if one keeps a diary for public confessions, as Gombrowicz did. His manner of writing stemmed from his Polish predecessors, both 19th century and more recent. Parody and mimicry need models to work on: a style cannot pull faces at nothing. The past was more useful to Gombrowicz than the present. And there were iconoclasts of genius before him. Irzykowski was one of them. His *Paluba,* a very early psycho-analytical novel (1903), owed nothing to Freud, but it probed deeply into patterns of self-deception, into bashful moments hiding behind big words and poses, it exposed both social and patriotic cant. [Irzykowski] saw his experiment as the triumphant comedy of character. Ferdydurke's comedy is in essence triumphant. . . .

*Operetta* comes towards the end of Gombrowicz's development, a stylistic résumé, full of conscious echoes and obvious borrowings. . . . As an artistic instrument the operetta is a sort of pianola, with Gombrowicz banging it until the whole pretence breaks to pieces. . . .

Undoubtedly, much of the 1930s is reflected in Gombrowicz's mimicry: the grand gestures of the silent films, the teasing eroticism of popular entertainment, the impoverished families that could still afford servants. And the intellectual mania for paradox. . . .

He cared about language. . . . The idiosyncratic style of Gombrowicz has structural patterns which can be reproduced in another language, and on the whole he translates better than most Slavonic novelists. He is essentially the writers' writer. Will he ever become popular?

The next thirty years should determine Gombrowicz's place in European literature. How his books will read in the future is difficult to predict. They are light, not ponderous, and the charm is in their lightness. The public unfortunately confounds weight with seriousness, length with permanence. Brevity may be the soul of wit, but the immortality of that soul is another question.

*Jerzy Peterkiewicz, "The Fork & the Fear," in* Encounter, *March, 1971, pp. 57-60.*

* * *

## GOODMAN, Paul 1911-1972

**Goodman, an American poet, novelist, short story writer, playwright, urban planner, psychotherapist, social, political, literary, and educational critic, was an intellectual of tremendous energy and range. During the 1960's, his suggestions for educational and social reform were widely disputed. (See also *Contemporary Authors*, Vols. 19-20; obituary, Vols. 37-40.)**

If you compare Goodman's deliberately utopian thesis [in *Growing Up Absurd*] with the two kinds of social criticism that are now in vogue—the merely descriptive sociology of a Vance Packard that exploits the present uneasiness of the American middle class, and the obstinate "position" taking that one sees in C. Wright Mills's self-consciously defiant "line" in favor of Castro and other unpopular causes—a book like *Growing Up Absurd* seems better than it is, since it is full of the intellectual dignity of the old-fashioned radical independent thinking things out for himself. Goodman is not only an extremely intelligent and acute social observer of troubled young men, delinquents, beatniks, Village apaches; he is also the last person in the world to take existing society as necessary and he is incapable of flattering it. He is free of the superficiality that seems to possess so many social commentators in America just now—writers who are no longer able to see their society from outside, and who, like Max Lerner and how many others, just now talk as if they were osteopaths and America were their patient. It is ridiculous to talk about the waste makers and the Mom complex, the lonely crowd and status symbols, without addressing oneself directly to the historic nature of the profit system, our middle-class culture, and the obvious imbalance between our wealth and the deprivations suffered by most other human beings. Too many Americans now want to remain fully attached to our social system and at the same time to draw the rewards of a little sophisticated (and wholly external) criticism of it.

Goodman, by contrast, is a thoroughgoing philosophic and intellectual radical. Not only is he able to see American society in perspective; he frees the reader, page after page, of the intellectual vagueness that comes from so much identification with our present scheme of things; the current alternative—identification with historical "destiny" in the shape of a Gomulka or a Castro—is equally impossible for him. Goodman thinks for himself; and in upholding the sanctions and demands of a human nature freed from contemporary American fears and shibboleths, he brings home the constant stimulus to independence of thought that lies in psychoanalysis (Goodman is a lay practitioner). . . .

Goodman's tradition is that of the literary Romantics—the belief in a suppressed capacity in human nature that unites the Romantic poets to the psychology of Freud. His essay is often exhilarating in its independence and is full of penetrating insights into the intense quarrel with society that rumbles under the prosperous surface of our society. But I don't believe in his book as a diagnosis of youth in general. When Goodman talks about youth, he seems to be talking not about the suburban youth whose games he has never seen but about a whole class of consciously alienated young men in the city. . . .

Although Goodman ends his book with a list of the many modern revolutions whose frustration, he thinks, explains the impasse of youth today, it is noteworthy that he speaks always of "fellows," "lads," "boys," "kids," and never of the actual social, economic, and racial categories among youth who are in rivalry with the established order and who are now making their way up. His analysis virtually overlooks the disaffections of young girls, who he thinks always have a vocation anyway as mothers and housekeepers. . . . Goodman's analysis is most valuable, I think, as an articulation of what those who are actively independent of society really want for themselves. The acuteness of many of his observations articulates the radical energy and spiritual freedom of the kind of intellectual who is fast disappearing in favor of the organization-manager-turned-critic-of-himself and the nostalgic radical who has become desperate for a "position."

*Alfred Kazin, "Youth Is a Pressure Group" (copyright © 1960 by Alfred Kazin; reprinted by permission of Little, Brown & Co. in association with The Atlantic Monthly Press), in his* Contemporaries, *Little, Brown, 1962, pp. 438-42.*

Goodman's poetry, as one might expect from his career as a critic of American mores and institutions, is filled with forthright political statement, following the model of Wordsworth and Shelley in such matters. . . . For many years he has advanced a half-mystical conception of the relation between our civilization and its neglect of the resources that should be made available to the citizenry. . . .

One might view Goodman's work as in some degree a throwback to the romantic and polemical style of the best popular poets of the last century. To some extent his refusal to internalize the ills of the age as thoroughly as many other modern poets do, obliterating their character as social issues and offering up their own psyches as more interesting symbolic substitutes, points toward such a throwback. But there is a thoroughly contemporary side to his poetic style and thought as well. . . .

Goodman has written [some] inward poems that bring his work into rapport with the confessional tendency of the age—particularly his poems about love, both homosexual and normal, and poems like 'Long Lines' that recall the sonnets of Wordsworth (or the tone of his and Coleridge's odes) but are thoroughly modern in their dislocations of syntax and of the hexameter pattern, their shifts of focus, their specific diction, and, most important, their essential attitude. . . .

*M. L. Rosenthal, in his* The New Poets: American and British Poetry Since World War II *(copyright © 1967 by M. L. Rosenthal; reprinted by permission of Oxford University Press, Inc.), Oxford University Press, 1967, pp. 313-16.*

I've reservations about [Goodman's] poems, which are very unequal and often sloppy, not the work of a man who's put poetry first, but still very interesting reading. (Some quite accomplished technicians seem to have forgotten it's all a waste of time unless the poems are interesting.) The stories are undoubtedly [his] best [work], and some of them—'Our Visit to Niagara' for instance—seem to me of a very high order indeed. *Five years* gave me the sort of satisfactions Gide's *Journals* were supposed to give but didn't—because, I think, Goodman's a great deal more intelligent than Gide and without the awful encumbrance of Gide's pretensions and concept of himself. Neglect accounts for a lot of Goodman's gay strengths as well as his sloppy weaknesses. But mostly what wins admiration—or, for some, I expect, repels—is the person: the unbeatable aboriginal artist, turning his wounds into sources of power and affirmation, essentially living out of his passions, yet distinguished by his shining level-eyed observation and polished intellect, his sense of humour, plain speech and courage, learned in the human sciences, with a vigorous analytical power and an ability to synthesize his findings into fiction with 'vision': that is, it's all his own, wherever he got it from, and it makes you see the world differently. And it's *relevant*—it's *about* the world, about where we are as a race; not private, not humped-off out. . . .

Goodman's not adventurous enough in form for me, and he's often too easily satisfied with getting out the basis for a poem; but he writes very cleanly and simply in his own voice, and he gets the essential information down.

*Herbert Lomas, "Coming Across," in* London Magazine, *April-May, 1973, pp. 152-57.*

By his own count Paul wrote forty books. The apparent diversity of his work is actually the unfolding of one large underlying theme: the search for harmony of the life made by man, and the life not made, but given.

It was a theme that entailed many duties. We find him, for example—especially in the poems, and the autobiographical *Five Years*—speaking of the task of creating a self. ("Long have I labored to make me Goodman.") It was such a self, however, as stands in contrast to the familiar *persona* of art (as a poet imagines a bardic figure and tries to live it), for it was the minimal, or transparent self implicit in Aristotle's definition of the highest good: the unimpeded functioning of the powers that are distinctly human. . . .

Paul's . . . public and the private self became one. The therapist and the poet were the same man. Paul's writings on psychotherapy are intrinsically political. His political writing is philosophic. In short, wherever one touches his work, one finds his major theme, which was a task of living as well as of writing.

There are other ways of saying this. He lived "the examined life." His tools were art, psychotherapy, and philosophy. Or one can say simply that thought was real to him, and that the truth as he saw it was never a mere intellectual proposition, but a commandment. Or one can say—as Paul does, in many poems—that he "staggered from need to need," was an exile among men, had come "from another planet." The fact remains that most of his thought is devoted to the nature that is prior to ego, its progress through the self, and the requisites of the human home (political, social, ethical, etc.) necessary to fulfillment. (His name for the whole, at times, is Adam.) These are the subjects not only of his social criticism but also of *Gestalt Therapy,* and in more imaginative forms, of his short fiction and his major work *The Empire City*. . . .

Paul's poetry is much distinguished by its immediacy of feeling and meaning, its daylight actuality, over a wide range of experience. His learning appears unabashedly as the way he looks at things (not as a map of culture), and he suffers no convention of "the poetic," but every significant turn of thought, emotion, and event seems to have shaped a poem. The classic themes of love and death recur often, and recur in their classic form, that is, not as themes but as persons and emotions. There are somber prayers, and poems of an elevated nature, and poems of humor, sometimes of hilarity. At all periods there are simple lyrics beautifully realized: the early "A Cyclist," and "The flashing pigeons as they wheel"; and the late haiku, of which he wrote many. . . .

He wrote ballades, and ballads, sonnets, narrative poems like the stern and strong "The Well of Bethlehem"; and analytic odes like "The Character of Washington," and the early "The Death of Leon Trotsky."

Like D. H. Lawrence, Paul is a poet "without a mask." The voice of the poetry is persuasively the man himself . . . and he is in his real city of New York. In our present extravagantly metaphoric conventions, with their elaborate *personae,* and multiple (finally rather dim) refractions of experience, I find the brilliant actuality of his poems infinitely refreshing.

Paul's is "occasional poetry" (and he was fond of quoting Goethe: "the highest kind"). Technically, he is often brilliant. The prevailing effect, however, is of spare accuracy capturing experience already deeply felt and thought. Poem by poem his aim is modest. The poems accumulate to an *oeuvre* of striking presence and magnitude; the more so in that the life embodied here was itself a rare venture in our time. . . .

Paul's powers as an artist are not merely striking, or praiseworthy. As powers, they are powers of greatness. They were the endowment and the triumphs of a man who, like Coleridge, was also beset by ills and was injured by his own age. Both powers and failings are broadly visible in his art. Some of Paul's stories and poems, and the late novel *Making Do,* are very seriously flawed. The best of his short work, however, has already been compared—justly, I believe—with that of Melville and Hawthorne. And in the span from Chaucer until now, *The Empire City* must be counted one of our grand eccentric books.

*George Dennison, "In Memory of Paul Goodman," in* The New York Review of Books *(reprinted with permission from* The New York Review of Books; *copyright © 1973 by the Estate of Paul Goodman), December 13, 1973, pp. 50-3.*

[Goodman's *Collected Poems*] will, I think, last a long while, longer perhaps than his social criticism. . . .

The writing of poetry was essential to Goodman, because it was an immediate way for him to examine, if not always to understand, what was happening in his life. . . . [He] never stopped turning over the consequences of the "plain facts" that obsessed him, and he could not permanently down his wit. . . .

Some of his poetry—sometimes bulky stretches of it—is only poetry because he said it was. . . .

But, as F. O. Mathiessen, his fire turned blue, would tell his classes, "Clarity does not necessarily make poetry." . . .

There is much suffering, only rarely and transiently purged, in these poems because Goodman, as he put it, was "an orphan who had had a home." But there is also much about music, and pleasures of being and seeing in the New Hampshire countryside he loved. There is also much about sex, largely unrequited lust, and no little love. . . .

Paul Goodman was a various man. "A man of letters in the old sense," he described himself, Goodman was also a man of the streets and of the academy (which he loved, though not most of its tenured priests). The voice of Paul Goodman's poetry, George Dennison writes in his characteristically honest and complexly compassionate memoir, "is persuasively the man himself—and he is in [his] real city of New York."

*Nat Hentoff, in* The Village Voice *(reprinted by permission of* The Village Voice; *© 1974 by The Village Voice, Inc.), January 24, 1974, p. 31.*

Like many writers who feel an obligation to promote social change, and so devote their energies to criticism (James Agee was one, Harold Rosenberg is another), Goodman was more interested in the production of literature than in anything else. He himself was "that mystery of mysteries, the reformist radical," or so he describes a character from his immense novel, *The Empire City.* And nowhere is this desire to reform entire institutions more evident than in his poetry, where the "institution" is nothing less than life itself. . . .

Goodman emphasized the importance of colloquial speech in his writing. He was a master of idiom, a brilliant stylist who knew how to turn language into a subtle instrument responsive to what he saw. One of his most original poems, "Epode. The New Bus Terminal," celebrates in ironic high style the completion of the Port Authority, alternating between the grandiose ("this new/ this marvel where the buses overhead/ roar to the provinces") and the demotic ("so I came inside/ out of the lousy season"). In this he was like Delmore Schwartz, whose comic, exaggerated poetry took advantage of the tradition in order to satirize or elevate his subject.

More than Schwartz, though, I would say that Goodman's poems resemble Berryman's late religious phase. Less metered, less intense than Berryman's "Address to the Lord," much of Goodman's poetry is in the form of prayer, the wish to speak directly with God. His theology was uncomplicated, wanting only explanations about why things were as they were, and was expressed, like all his poetry, in the most economical speech possible. . . .

Because he wrote so copiously, these poems vacillate between Utopian hope and a sort of Nietzschean stubbornness; one can learn from them nearly all the details of Goodman's own life, the trials encountered, the successes and loss.

I don't mean to make too large a claim for these poems. They depend on what he called elsewhere "the glorification of simple overt acts," and often require patience to read through simply because their intentions are so limited. Goodman wrote poetry with a deliberate awkwardness. Perhaps he thought it would be more democratic to practice a style so plain and rude.

*James Atlas, "First Person," in* The New Republic *(reprinted by permission of* The New Republic; *© 1974 by Harrison-Blaine of New Jersey, Inc.), March 2, 1974, pp. 30-1.*

As a writer, Goodman was a naturalist who analyzed human behavior and thought, often using his own as a model on which to center investigation. He was a Gestaltist, and his insistence was to see an object in its field, particularly where field and object touch. He became widely known in 1960 for *Growing Up Absurd,* an analysis of youth gangs, junior executives and Beats, written at the time *Life* magazine was running inspirational pieces on "Our National Purpose," and the nations were fighting the cold war. In this book Goodman argued that people had hardly any world to live in, even less to devote themselves to except, perhaps, the little life in the stances their egos had managed to eke out for them.

He, too, had etched, as a poet and writer, a self from the blocks of his intelligence and passion:

*Fatherless I was, nobody offered*
*me to the muses. I imposed on them.*

And done it in a world that he felt hindered not only his but most people's fundamental needs. He did not take seriously such a notion as a nation's providing a purpose. Psychologist and anarchist, Goodman knew that the realities of nations take one too far from actual experience and satisfaction (or disappointment) and, therefore, become dangerous. His poetry often records an encounter, in himself, where words and experience become each other, where experience is named into being and the boundaries of the self are discovered. . . . Or it is poetry that is written as a response to some occasion in the world: a government's resumption of nuclear testing, his finishing a book, his seeing a sunflower, a lover departed. . . .

Just as students beginning to read Wordsworth read the preface to the *Lyrical Ballads* for his poetics and philosophy of language, so readers of Goodman might read the seventh chapter of the second volume of his *Gestalt Therapy* and the concluding chapters of his *Speaking and Language: Defense of Poetry.* Homespun as his poetry may sometimes appear, Goodman has wrought it with an intelligence well rooted in Western and non-Western literatures.

And, I will say it, there is sublimity in his poetry.

*Neil Heims, "Who Sang the Lordly Hudson," in* The Nation, *June 29, 1974, pp. 824-26.*

* * *

## GORDONE, Charles 1925-

**Gordone is a Pulitzer Prize-winning Black American playwright.**

Charles Gordone's Pulitzer Prize-winning drama [*No Place to Be Somebody*] depicts the black experience, but it is also concerned with people, black and white, who are filled with despair but who continue to hold on to their dreams, dreams shaped by their surroundings. . . .

The action in Gordone's play is harsh and raw. The confrontations between the characters are many and striking as they engage in their love-hate relationships. . . .

The action of *No Place to Be Somebody* is episodic; the construction, complex. But with a few exceptions Gordone weaves all of these elements into an integrated whole. The action, which sometimes seems overburdening on stage, becomes less so when the play is read. Then the architecture of the play reveals itself more clearly. The character Machine Dog, the symbol of black militancy in the mind of Johnny, is one of the elements that remain separate from the whole. Though I understand the playwright's intention, to deepen the meaning of the character of Johnny, Machine Dog remains a flaw. I am struck by the richness of Gordone's language—witty, lyrical, convincing. The dialogue, though sometimes humorous, is filled with pathos and insults.

By the standards of the black revolutionary dramatists, Gordone is a conservative. His play does not fulfill LeRoi Jones's challenge to black playwrights: "Everything we do must commit us collectively to revolution, i.e., National Liberation." Gordone, on the other hand, believes that the idea of the black theatre is dead. . . .

*No Place to Be Somebody,* which recalls Eugene O'Neill's *The Iceman Cometh,* began as a workshop production in Joseph Papp's Public Theater and went on to win the Pulitzer Prize for Drama in 1970. Its creator, Charles Gordone, has been described as "the most astonishing new American playwright to come along since Edward Albee."

*Jeanne-Marie A. Miller, "A Drama of the Black Experience," in* The Journal of Negro Education, *Spring, 1971, pp. 185-86.*

The central interest of *No Place [to be Somebody]* . . . obtains, as does its form, from what is in essence a dialectic between Gabe and his alter ego, Johnny. Theirs is a dialectic about the nature of life and possibility, dispossession and affirmation; about, in short, the blackness of Blackness. Informing it is the most deadly seriousness, for its outcome determines nothing less than the working out of Gabe's fate. Very shortly on in the play, it becomes a confrontation between art and anarchy, style and substance, subversion and accommodation. . . .

*No Place* is a tragicomedy, a "Black-black" comedy true to both the letter and the spirit of the blues in its near-comic, near-tragic duality. Herein lies the most stylized element of the drama, this ordering of experience faithful to the complexity of life and testament to the inviolable diversity of experience, which is a matter both for the tears of the clown and the tragedian. That Gabe is able to resist the utter bleakness of self-pitying despair for a vision which accommodates the rude, vigorous humor of even his own scarred experience is a triumph of no small dimensions.

*Ronald Walcott, "Ellison, Gordone and Tolson: Some Notes on the Blues, Style and Space," in* Black World *(copyright © December, 1972, by* Black World; *reprinted by permission of* Black World *and Ronald Walcott), December, 1972, pp. 4-29.*

Johnny's Bar. It is in Greenwich Village, and it is in Gabe Gabriel's head—perhaps more in Gabe's head. . . . It is real, as real as his pain, as real as the torment, the pain, and the anguish of nearly all the characters in Charles Gordone's powerful and lacerating "Black-black comedy" *No Place to Be Somebody. . . . No Place to Be Somebody* is a play of dying dreams. . . .

The tone [of the epilogue] is somehow wrong, false even. It fails to jibe with the harsh and bitter reality and the ironic humor that have gone before. For what has gone before, for all its melodrama and its sometime lack of discipline, has a pungency, an immediacy, and a cohesiveness that that last gesture somehow violates. But it is one of the very few wrong steps. *No Place to Be Somebody* vibrates with a kind of vitality all too seldom found on contemporary stages. It may sprawl; it may on occasion become self-indulgent or sentimental; it never bores. It is alive.

*Catharine Hughes, "'No Place to Be Somebody'," in her* Plays, Politics and Polemics, *Drama Book Specialists, 1973, pp. 53-8.*

* * *

## GOULD, Lois

**Ms Gould, an American novelist and nonfiction writer, formerly served as executive editor of *Ladies' Home Journal.***

[*Such Good Friends*] borders on soap opera: suffering wife stunned by sensational revelations! Can her love overcome her hurt and cure the dying daddy? But Lois Gould's tone is too bitchy to be soft, her observations too acerbic to allow for sentimentality and her details of a "middle-class-but-with-it" New York milieu too keenly observed and solid for the pasteboard backing of "As the World Turns." . . .

Miss Gould has larded her first novel with as many four-letter words as can be gratuitously jammed into her gratuitous sex passages. Unhappily, dirty words do not a female Portnoy make. But despite what appears to be either innate vulgarity or a cynical bid for sales, she has written a very funny, keenly observed chronicle of middle-class manners.

*Paul D. Zimmerman, in* Time *(reprinted by permission from* Time, The Weekly Newsmagazine; *copyright Time Inc.), June 1, 1970, p. 88.*

*Such Good Friends* is more personal and honest and graphic than *Portnoy's Complaint.* But Philip Roth's crazy, hilarious irony is one thing: Lois Gould's depressive, desperately unhappy bitterness, another. Like Roth's, her novel may induce tears—but not from laughing. . . .

Lois Gould's frantic, cruel rectital of modern middle-class woman's lot is an imaginative chapter in the feminist struggle. It is also another of the many recent signposts of social and psychological and political change going on. . . .

It does no good to call Julie Messinger insensitive and tactless. Her life is loveless and barren, the friends around her loveless and insensitive and tactless. She doesn't know how she got into her uptight, jammed-up mess, nor how to break out of it: the whole depressing chaos started so long ago for her, as it has for others. How many Julie Messingers are out there now, trying to find some point for the absurd catastrophe of their lives?

Even though this is her first novel, Lois Gould writes as idiomatically and naturally and truthfully as an old pro. And, notwithstanding the curious unconscious insensitivity of its acutely sensitive author, *Such Good Friends* is an important, awful, believable book. Many men will resent it, but the novel will change the lives of many women. Certainly, I don't see how the marriage of any couple can be the same after they have read it.

*Joel Lieber, in* Saturday Review *(copyright © 1970 by Saturday Review, Inc.; reprinted with permission), June 13, 1970, p. 43.*

Here is that paradox of paradoxes—a novel clearly destined for best-sellerdom that actually deserves to be widely read.

*Such Good Friends* is a brilliant, compulsively readable first novel recalling Alison Lurie at her bitchy best. It is both tough-minded and moving; a passionate cri de coeur about such knee-slappers as death, betrayal, and Women's Liberation that is sustainedly funny.

The good friends of the title are a band of hip, affluent New Yorkers who flock to the bedside of Richard Messinger, a magazine art director, when the news spreads that he is in a coma induced by a fluky reaction to anesthesia he was given for minor surgery. When it becomes advisable to replace all of Richard's blood, hordes of donors jam the hospital corridors until "it was like Friday night outside the Cinema Rendezvous. What could possibly be playing? *Coma!* Starring Somebody You Really Know!" . . .

The finest scenes are at the hospital. A former reporter and magazine editor, Mrs. Gould has an extraordinarily sensitive eye for the telling detail. . . . The whole psychology of the death-watch is explored brilliantly here. . . .

This eye for detail is Mrs. Gould's major gift as a novelist, and goes far to compensate for makeshift plotting and relatively shallow characterization (none of the friends is really memorable on his own). The novel is obviously deeply autobiographical, and I wonder whether Mrs. Gould will be able to write a second one in which she is less personally involved, because her traumatic experience here has not been fully objectified into the serenely universal condition of art.

As it stands, though, *Such Good Friends* is a tour de force of journalistic narrative—fast-paced, and written in a no-nonsense style. Above all, a rueful, malign wit cuts through any potential self-pity in it like a shot of lemon juice in a bowl of borscht.

*Richard Freedman, in* Book World (© The Washington Post), *June 21, 1970, p. 5.*

With commendable candor, Lois Gould has chosen Erica Jong's poem "Autobiography" as the epigraph of [*Final Analysis*]. ("The lover in these poems/is me . . . All this is true.") At its best, it is the slight but cleverly written and curiously moving story of a thirtyish woman journalist as she wars with herself and her masculine-dominated world in search of . . . well, a little dignity. . . .

In [some] passages we see Gould's protagonist whole and entire, a very real and affecting figure in a landscape of ghastly familiarity, as she comes to grips with the invidious sexual programming that is every woman's lot and burden: to lie about her age and worry compulsively about her looks, to clean up frantically after men, to be humble before them, and—above all—not to compete with them, especially on their own terms. The yoke she bears is not of her own devising and yet, like some rebellious serf, she must carry it throughout her days and feel its weight upon her shoulders every hour she lives. And the loneliness of that burden is a terrible one.

All too soon, however, the book veers almost frantically in another less profitable direction, and before we know it, we are back in picture-puzzle land again. Try as we will to avert our eyes and suspend our curiousity, pull though we do for the author (wing it, girl! wing it!), there is no way to avoid the inevitable: all those real people keep trotting out, and to our dismay we find ourselves hotly engaged in the same old guessing game: Who is the magazine editor, *really?* Is the abominable novelist supposed to be Norman Mailer or Irving Wallace? And what names can we put to those faces in the crowd at the Hamptons? It is like some hideous bout of charades during a long weekend in the provinces, boring, inescapable, distracting, and enraging. We would give much to tear ourselves away from it, but some mysterious force holds us; and anyway, there is nothing else to do. Saddest of all, through it all there still flickers—at times faintly and at times with a tantalizing, warm, but impossibly distant glow—the light of a much finer and far more important book that simply is not getting written. There was so much to be said.

*L. J. Davis, in* Book World—The Washington Post (© The Washington Post), *April 14, 1974, p. 3.*

Now I could bite the bullet and read ["Final Analysis"] as an infatuated account of an obsessed woman's unrelieved self-loathing, an explicit study of masochism, with a rare candor that both excites and repels. Lois Gould is no novice at the examination of masochism. In "Such Good Friends," the author's first and fiercely interesting novel, there was another female victim, this one a betrayed wife who sits in the hospital waiting room, receiving merciless reports on her dying husband's concealed, complex erotic life. Here too, the woman had wept, neglected—and shoved to her side of the kingsized bed. One felt the wife's rage, her terror, all the unmanageable feelings stirring out of her numbed narcissism.

Yet Lois Gould has somehow refused these valuable feelings, and even suggests that, oh, well, he wasn't really so bad, and the wife laments after his death, "I miss something that must have been us. Because we were something, in spite of each other, weren't we?" What they were was married, and the women in Lois Gould's novels seem to share the conviction that with husbands they are something, without them they are nothing, orphans of the storm.

*Iris Owens, in* The New York Times Book Review (*© 1974 by The New York Times Company; reprinted by permission), April 14, 1974, p. 7.*

While creating the fluff of women's glamor magazines, Gould's freelance femme lives in a generally sustained manic giggle, which, when seasoned by drink, dexies, or the threat of personal happiness, turns into floods of tears. "Final Analysis," like a wet Kleenex, is a by-product of women's dependency problems. . . .

One virtue of Gould's book is that it creates a feminine universe, in which the doctor's stick-figure existence is at least partial reply to centuries of male-oriented fiction. There are no direct exchanges about the content of their relationship because Dr. Foxx is such a foil, and the reality comes across simply through the totality with which the heroine is consumed by her problem.

Both characters lack curiosity about who and why they are, just as Gould lacks awareness that her consciousness as a writer is made possible by the struggles of women writers in the past. . . .

There is, finally, little sense of [the heroine's] having

learned from her struggle or problems; Lois Gould has penetrated the universe of women and come back with a box of chocolate-covered teardrops.

*Martin Washburn, in* The Village Voice *(reprinted by permission of* The Village Voice; *© 1974 by The Village Voice, Inc.), April 18, 1974, pp. 30-1.*

[*Final Analysis* is] a slick romance about a lonely, disaffected psychiatrist and his guilt-ridden, weepy ex-patient which is occasionally quite funny but pushes feminism and enlightenment-through-psychiatry in the same way that old-fashioned romances used to push love and moral rectitude. The characters here—the woman's friends in a consciousness-raising group, the piggy publishing men who treat her so badly, and even the sloppy, absentminded psychiatrist—never really jell, because they are more like peripheral exhibits in the woman's case history than believable people. The woman herself is sharp and clear. Like most Gould heroines, she's a rather endearing schlemiel who *knows* she deserves a better life than the one she is living, but even she is subjected to too much labeling and packaging (expressions like "I'm functioning" and "needing someone emotionally" appear with depressing frequency), and, throughout, the author's tart, irreverent sense of humor is undercut by the heavy-handed politicking.

The New Yorker, *April 22, 1974, p. 154.*

Miss Gould has assayed a satiric novel [*Final Analysis*] about an analyst, an analysand, and that portion of the literary world which is presided over by male magazine editors. It would be one of those novels that might be passed over without a word were it not for its inordinately irritating qualities, notable among them the archness and the sentimentality that lie at the core of it. It is a peculiarly unpleasant—one might be tempted to say unhealthy—form of sentimentality, coming as it does at the heels of Miss Gould's version of satire. Satire, one is given to understand from the execution of this novel, is that vision which proceeds from hatred and wretchedness; love is what proceeds from health and openness. Miss Gould perpetrates this simple, if unconscious, belief on a novel about which it ought to be said only that it has, at heart, the point of view of a daytime TV serial, with none of the saving brevity of that form, and that it can be counted on, page after page, to serve up with singular self-confidence most of the clichés of our time about analysis and male chauvinism and the politics of personal relationships.

*Dorothy Rabinowitz, in* Saturday Review/World *(copyright © 1974 by Saturday Review/World Inc.; reprinted with permission), May 18, 1974, p. 28.*

* * *

## GRASS, Günter 1927-

**Grass is a West German novelist, playwright, poet, painter, and sculptor. His novelistic sensibility is primarily a comic one, and his exuberant, fantastical, fugal fictions are completely unique. (See also *Contemporary Authors*, Vols. 13-14.)**

[Grass's] plays . . . are essentially images seen with the eyes of a painter who is so obsessed with his images that they also seek expression as poetic metaphors; a lyrical poet so eager to see his metaphors come to life that he is compelled to write for the stage. Or, to put it differently, so vivid were the images in the painter's, the poet's mind that they had to start to talk in dialogue. . . .

Grass's subject matter, the degradation of Germany in the time of Hitler and in the aftermath of war, is sordid in the extreme. And in his writings—poems, plays, and novels—he never tries to evade the most direct confrontation with these nauseating facts. But because he deals with them so directly, with the total lack of self-consciousness, the innocence of a child, the disgusting facts can be accepted without the physical reactions of disgust that would make them intolerable as the subject matter of an artist's vision. Brecht spoke of naïveté as one of the most precious of aesthetic categories; Grass possesses that innocence of vision to a degree unparalleled by any other writer of our time.

It is the vision of a Douanier Rousseau, a Paul Klee. And Grass's plays can best be seen as images from that sphere brought to life on a three-dimensional canvas. . . .

It has been said that Grass's dramatic works lack the documentary quality, the descriptive, autobiographical detail that he incorporates in his novels. But this, to me, seems to overlook the essential difference between the narrative and the dramatic form. If Grass wrote plays filled with details about his early years in Danzig he would be producing naturalistic drama wholly at variance with his own artistic personality. In the novels it was possible to combine the most abundant autobiographical detail with the wildest flights of grotesque fantasy. There is no time in drama to preserve both of these elements. Yet, precisely because the dramatic form demands more conciseness, more concentration, because it makes Grass confine himself to a limited number of images in each of his plays, it brings out his lyrical quality, the quality of his vision as a carrier of images. Nor is it a coincidence that each of his long novels contains passages written in dialogue and, indeed, that these dialogue passages could be performed in the theatre: the episode of the nuns on the Atlantic Wall from *The Tin Drum* was staged in Düsseldorf, the discussion chapter from *Dog Years* at Munich.

Indeed, for a writer of Grass's chaotic and anarchic exuberance as a storyteller, the dramatic form provides a most salutary discipline; on the other hand, the dramatist is to a much greater degree in the hands of his directors and performers. His plays' relative lack of success in the theatre may well be due to the difficulty of finding the right style for their performance. Grass himself has criticized the timidity of German producers in tackling unusual works like his plays, and there certainly is some substance in these strictures. His play *The Plebians Rehearse the Uprising* did indeed cause a stir, but here the more topical—and more sensational—subject matter played its part. For in this play Grass managed simultaneously to attack the sacred cows of Eastern and Western Germany, which is no mean feat. . . .

Günter Grass is a committed writer; it is one of the most hopeful signs for the future of Germany that her leading literary figures have broken with a long-standing tradition that artists of all kinds should keep aloof from politics. However fantastic and unrealistic Grass's plays may appear at first sight, the social comment is present and very much to the fore: in *Flood* there is a powerful warning against any nostalgia for the times of calamity and *camaraderie*; the murderer in *Mister, Mister* and the murderous teen-agers have obvious implications for members of both generations in present-day Germany; in *The Wicked Cooks* there are clear reflections of power struggles and intrigues; even the slight, parodistic curtain-raiser *Only Ten Minutes to Buffalo* can, ultimately, be seen as an attack against illusions, a plea for realism in looking at the contemporary scene. There is thus no split between Grass the author of seemingly abstruse, absurdist plays, and Grass the indefatigable campaigner for the Social Democratic party in the German elections of 1965 and 1966.

*Martin Esslin, "Günter Grass the Dramatist" (originally published in a slightly different version as an introduction to* Four Plays, *by Günter Grass, published by Harcourt, Brace & World), in his* Reflections: Essays on Modern Theatre *(copyright © 1961, 1962, 1963, 1966, 1967, 1968, 1969 by Martin Esslin; reprinted by permission of Doubleday & Co., Inc.), Doubleday, 1969, pp. 143-50.*

*Local Anaesthetic* . . . is worth reading by anyone who still thinks there is a dividing-line between "the novel" and "poetry." It adds up to a very powerful and remarkable picture of one man's mental landscape, and not just any man chosen at random but the characteristic sensitive and intellectual inhabitant of West Germany. All the social realities and the uncomfortable historical legacies are *there*; on the other hand, the continual switching into and out of fantasy, and the pivoting of the story on enormous symbols, take it right out of the domain of that kind of documentary or social-realist novel that would have been, twenty years ago, the natural way of dealing with this kind of subject. Towards the end of the book, there is a passage in which the hero seems to be recollecting the experience of helping his student to set fire to the dog, and being attacked by the crowd, dragged away by the police, thrown into a cell, etc., etc., but there is no indication of any kind whether these things have actually happened or whether he is day-dreaming. This, like the T.V. commercials presented by his ex-fiancée, is simply an example of the kind of thing that, whether it takes place or not, fits naturally into the mental, moral and emotional atmosphere the hero is living in, and which is the real subject of the book.

The dachshund blazing to death in front of the cake-eating ladies, the unattainable girl lying wrapped in cellophane in the deep freeze—these are metaphors, and the ability to communicate primarily in metaphor has generally been thought of as a mark of the poetic mind. Aristotle thought it the special distinguishing mark of the poet that he could create original metaphors, which presumably means that Aristotle would have classed *Local Anaesthetic* as a poem.

*John Wain, "A Salute to the Makers," in* Encounter, *November, 1970, p. 59.*

The density of Grass's writing derives in part from his documentation—for instance, the naval expertise in *Cat and Mouse* and the faustball and ballet material in *Dog Years*—though at times this documentation appears to be posing as a sort of autonomous allegory. In the new novel, *Local Anaesthetic,* there is a fair amount of technical information about dental methods through the ages, and about geology, and more than a fair amount (for its relevance is more dubious) about the manufacture of cement. . . .

Generally in Dickens, documentation—what a person does for a living, where he lives, his favourite food and drink—is properly indistinguishable from characterisation—what a person is. And there is less room for inoperative material in this relatively short novel than in the mammoth *Dog Years. Dog Years* was a notably energetic work: as in *The Tin Drum,* a lot was going on even if some of the activity remained enigmatic. By comparison—by comparison with other novels by Grass, for when all is said, he is one of the very few authors whose next novel one has no intention of missing—*Local Anaesthetic* is a little on the tired side. Admittedly, that is inherent in its theme: a wearied, worried bafflement, the apparent homelessness in the affluent state of passion and ideals, even their possible dangerousness. After all, an Economic Miracle isn't as hateful as a Master Race in arms. . . . If the citizens have their eyes glued to the idiot-box, then just remember the commandants of concentration camps who read Hölderlin or played Schubert sonatas. The plump ladies stuffing themselves with *Torte* in the *Konditoreien* along the Kurfürstendamm are not a pretty sight, but are they moral monsters? 'Freedom of choice and second helpings. That's what they mean by democracy,' says a thin-skinner student. . . .

Grass has been most courageous. He has turned from the meaty material of Nazism and post-war moral chaos to the stolidly triumphant bourgeoisie of today's Bonn and West Berlin, from 'de-demonizing' the Third Reich (if that was what he was up to, and personally I never found him that cosy) to Chancellor Kiesinger and the aforementioned undemonic Ku'damm cafés. . . . My God, it almost seems that, but for the Americans misbehaving in Vietnam, we could all live at ease with our consciences for the first time since. . . . Grass's subject here is essentially this: what does St. George do when the local dragon is 'relatively' not such a bad beast and the villagers are not especially terrorised by it? Yet dragons are dragons—and do we want St. George to lay aside his sword and let it rust? . . .

We don't need these concluding words to persuade us that Grass has not sold out to the comforts of comfort, the complacency of middle age, the ethos of 'I'm all right, Johann,' the convenient silence of the mouth-stopped cake-eaters. And, *pace Time Magazine,* I see no evidence [in *Local Anaesthetic*] that he believes in 'the apparently helpless and surely tragic bankruptcy of liberalism'. He has simply noticed that clean sweeps leave a lot of room for more dirt, that revolution exacts a very high price for its problematical benefits.

*D. J. Enright, "Always New Pains" (1970), in his* Man is an Onion: Reviews and Essays *(© 1972 by D. J. Enright; reprinted by permission of Open Court Publishing Co. and Chatto & Windus), Open Court, 1972, pp. 96-102.*

A Bildungsroman requires that outer events transform themselves into casual factors in the development of a character. This is not at all the case with Oskar [of *The Tin*

*Drum*]. He does not change. The stopping of his growth and the gratuitous toleration of a small increase in growth do not derive from experiences with society or reactions against it. Oskar imbibes parts of the social but owes nothing to society. He relates to it like a free-loader and pirate not like a *zoön politikon*. . . .

Oskar Matzerath as a "monad without windows." As the self-reliant individualist who views society merely as an object. Oskar Matzerath without "faith, hope, and love"—to quote the horrendous title of the last chapter in Book One. It is all quite clear: the narrative account completely resists the attempt of a critic to take seriously the ideas of the literary theorist Matzerath and his role as hero of a conventional novel. Oskar is neither a hero nor a character of a novel as he himself understands the norms of the traditional novel. The essential meaning of the book will be missed if one wants to understand it—and in this way to be taken in by Oskar's ideas—as an epic account.

This is not what *The Tin Drum* is. And Oskar is not an individual in the sense of Tom Jones or Madame Bovary, Leopold Bloom or Baron de Charlus. Oskar is an artifice in a completely new and momentous sense. His existence in the novel is an artistic process that keeps itself as far away as possible from simulating any kind of "nature." The ingredients of this artifice gradually become visible. Above all, Oskar is pure awareness that can manage with a minimum of corporeality. To compensate for this awareness, he had already demonstrated a high capacity for reflection to protect himself while yet in his mother's womb, and most definitely from birth up to the present. The awareness intends to reveal as little as possible and to resist pressures of society. . . .

Since Oskar does not have any emotions and, aside from small crises of the nerves and attacks of sensuality, would like to remain pure consciousness without communication with things social, it must be assumed that Grass is attempting to portray a special social pattern with the help of a supposed hero who is fit for neither the Bildungsroman nor the picaresque novel.

Oskar as an artifice is important chiefly as a location and standpoint, and this is at the far end of normal human dimensions. Oskar sees only the bottom of everything. He is the gnome, the perpetrator, who is neither seen nor heard. In this way he avoids (along with his author) the difficulties that the realistic narrator of the old school encounters, who can portray the actions of his characters only the way the general public is able to see. . . .

[In] writing the novel *The Tin Drum,* Grass wrote the satirical novel of a modern version of a man of the Enlightenment with the help of his grotesque artifice. . . . [If] one wants to speak about tradition in the first great novel by Grass, one is most compelled (as far as form is concerned) to think about Laurence Sterne, Jean Paul, and E. T. A. Hoffmann. . . .

It is most typical of the comic-satirical novel that the narrator, or rather the author, sets up a secret agreement with the reader by occasionally shoving aside the persona who is supposedly reporting the events as though he were a hindrance. This is done—behind the back of the chronicler—in order that the author may address the public himself. . . .

[But the] forms of the grotesque and satire, of irony and humor, demand distance. They never allow the narrator to lose himself completely in the narration. Only a novelist who prefers not to use a narrator as function, and yet cannot do without one (as in the case of Flaubert), will strive to present the story by itself and nothing but the story, a narration without a narrator. But a novel such as *The Tin Drum,* which is concerned with functions, needs the interplay between narrator and reader—mostly with the help of a persona, often in contrast to the persona.

*Hans Mayer, in his* Steppenwolf and Everyman, *translated and with an introduction by Jack D. Zipes (copyright © 1971 by Hans Mayer; reprinted with permission of Thomas Y. Crowell Co. Inc.), Crowell, 1971, pp. 184-88.*

Satire . . ., especially in the grotesque mode, prevails in Grass's treatment of the more blatantly political subject matter in [*The Tin Drum*]. But Grass is protean in his use of other materials and devices. Closely related to the author's views on Hitlerism is his emphasis on history: Through historical summary, anecdote, place legends, superstitious lore, allegory, myth, and symbolism, Grass tries to convey the reality of living through a certain continuity of events in historical space and time—"great" events which in their totality are no more but no less real than the mishaps and the fortunes of the individuals in the historical continuum. . . .

Making the characters a part of history forces Grass to raise, at least indirectly, the question of whether they have free will or are moved by social and political currents beyond their control and in consequence bear no moral responsibility for their actions. In *The Tin Drum,* unlike his stance in *Dog Years* and in *The Plebeians Rehearse the Uprising,* Grass evades giving a clear-cut answer to the question by presenting the entire narrative as the artistic re-creation of a possibly disordered and certainly immature mind. In a novel which, regardless of the elaborate pose of objectivity, is one long *j'accuse,* this evasion is a moral inconsistency and possibly an artistic flaw. However, two arguments may be advanced in defense of this evasion. First, Oskar has been called a moral monster; he is not one, but he may be schizoid, as is implied by the frequent shifts in viewpoint between the first and third person, and throughout most of the book he is definitely a child who, when he reaches thirty, is still far from being full-grown, physically and mentally. . . .

Second, despite his concern with history, Grass presents history as meaningful only in its effect on individuals. In one of his essays he criticizes Hegel's theory of history as a "fatal guide," and in his fiction he is indifferent to any alleged laws or principles of historical development that might lighten the individual's load of responsibility. This indifference is consistent with his general distrust of systematic ideologies.

This distrust is part of his artistic as well as his political credo. He felt no obligation to present positive alternatives to the situation of Oskar and his society. In suggesting that involvement is better than withdrawal, Grass scarcely goes beyond Camus's *The Stranger*. . . .

The theme of involvement and withdrawal likewise dominates *Cat and Mouse,* a novella in which, as in *The Tin*

*Drum,* the problem involves religious belief as well as psychological growing up. But the political element is always present, though often submerged. Again Grass has constructed his tale in the form of a reminiscence written long afterward by a major character, a framework that allows the author to present all judgments as provisional. . . .

[The] overtly political content of *Dog Years* is greater than in his two previous novels. As a whole, the work still lies within the tradition of the realistic, panoramic novel, but the political and religious allegory tends to dehumanize the characters; their voices tend to merge into the single voice of the author. Moreover, much of the social and political satire is aimed at language and ideas rather than at actions —for example, the many parodies of Martin Heidegger. In an author less brilliant at re-creating scenes with vivid, sensuous detail, the increase in allegory and parody might be a gain; in Grass it is a net loss.

This tendency to talk and allegorize more and to re-create less may have developed because Grass's increasingly political orientation drew him into a task beyond even his powers, nothing less than awakening the consciousness and conscience of the entire German people by offering a cross-sectional history of the German middle class before, during, and after the war. . . .

Grass seems to imply that one ingredient of the new Germany is art perverted by technology and industry, which, thus perverted, helps to create a grotesque, materialistic caricature of what a society should be. The social and political satire of the postwar leaders who base their policies on the predictions of the mealworms is specific and relatively good-natured; the satirical allegory of the scarecrow mine is far-reaching, savage, and much more radical than anything Grass has said in his nonliterary speeches and writings.

Since the 1965 campaign, Grass's art has come progressively closer to undiluted political discussion—with results not altogether pleasing. *The Plebeians Rehearse the Uprising* (1966) had a promising theme: a theatrical producer and playwright (inspired by, but not a portrait of, Bertold Brecht) who refuses to support the East German workers' uprising in 1953 partly because it is badly planned and partly because it is not good theater. However, like Brecht's weaker plays, *The Plebeians* bogs down in long-winded discussion, and it was coolly received by reviewers and audiences. *Davor* (*Therefore*), which opened in West Berlin early in 1969, is reportedly little more than a series of interconnected dialogues, largely on political and philosophical themes. . . .

Though the juxtapositions of episodes and dental conversations [in *Local Anesthetic*] are often comic in their incongruity, the speech and narrative lack the baroque richness and excitement of Grass's prose in *The Tin Drum* or even in parts of *Dog Years*. Moreover, *Local Anesthetic* lacks the multidimensionality of his earlier fiction: *The Tin Drum* was a religious and a picaresque novel as well as a political novel and a *Bildungsroman*. Finally, as reviewers of *Local Anesthetic* have noted, Grass is here too often content to state his views in discussion rather than to embody them in description, action, or characterization. . . .

The content, or substance, of Grass's work has always included ideas consonant with his belief in practical reform rather than in doctrinaire programs of either the left or the right. One commits a logical fallacy in saying that Grass's increasing preoccupation with the role of the artist as militant citizen has led him to overstress political themes in his work with the enthusiasm of the doctrinaire liberal and to impose the form of political discussion on his raw material quite arbitrarily rather than making a genuine attempt to overcome its "resistance"—that is, doing full justice to the complexities, nuances, and grotesque elements latent in that material and which he actualized so effectively in *The Tin Drum*. But whatever the causes of this doctrinaire imposition, the effect has been a debilitation of his art.

*Norris W. Yates, in* The Politics of Twentieth-Century Novelists, *edited by George Panichas (reprinted by permission of Hawthorn Books, Inc.; copyright © 1971 by The University of Maryland; all rights reserved), Hawthorn, 1971, pp. 215-28.*

With the rise of Nazism, the German artist became dramatically implicated in his historical milieu. This implication is one of the chief concerns of the works of Günter Grass; the artist-heroes of his novels find themselves in difficult and finally contradictory positions, *vis-à-vis* their contemporary society, so that they typically have to engage in a series of disguises or changes of identity in order to survive. From one standpoint this is simply a variation on the familiar theme of the modern artist without an identity; at the same time, the cliché was made more pointed and even grotesque by the impact of Nazi history. More important, however, is that Grass is writing in the tradition of the *Künstler-* and *Bildungsroman* and, more specifically, in the wake of Thomas Mann; as such, he is very aware of how the artist has been used symbolically, particularly in *Doktor Faustus,* as a means of voicing and representing the essential forces at work in German history and culture. As in the traditional *Künstler-* and *Bildungsroman,* the artistic careers of Oskar in *Die Blechtrommel* [*The Tin Drum*] and Amsel in *Hundejahre* [*Dog Years*] interact with and symbolically epitomize the circumstances and the structure of German history and culture; at the same time, however, Grass has given new dimensions to this interaction and symbolic relationship.

Oskar's relationship to his historical milieu is exceedingly difficult to define. At one extreme, he is the kind of person whom the Nazis persecuted ruthlessly because of his physical deformity and counterfeited mental retardation; indeed, he is threatened once explicitly with such persecution, and the possibility of his extermination is always in the background. At the other extreme, he becomes at one point in his career an active collaborator with the Nazis, for he works in a propaganda troupe on the Atlantic front, and, just after the uprising at the Polish post office has been brutally quelled, he allows himself to be "rescued" by the assailants, while remarking that he, Oskar, "zählte sich zu den Heimwehrleuten" [that he, in other words, was counting on the "folks back home"]. . . .

Bebra [his *Meister*] tells Oskar that, given his dwarfed body, he cannot afford to remain passive during the coming times; if he does so, he will doubtlessly be destroyed by the Nazis. Instead, Oskar must compensate by assuming somehow a more active role in society than he has yet done. In this way, he becomes a highly comic realization of the unconventional artist's dilemma during the Hitler years, for, if an artist did not fit the Nazi idea of what he should be, he had to assume some kind of false identity in order to escape persecution. Oskar's comically literal response to this advice from Bebra comes shortly thereafter; he drums waltz time under the rostrum of a Nazi gathering in what is, as he argues it at least, an aesthetic rather than a political protest against the Nazis. . . .

[As] Oskar plays the role of both persecuted and collaborating artist, he reveals in the kind of art he practices traits which smack both of fascism and what fascism rejected. On the one hand, his narrative style may be seen as often marked by a cruel aesthetic elitism. . . . The maintaining of such elitist aesthetic distance, one of the most essential forms of Oskar's language, and the attempt to see poetic beauty in death and destruction are familiar forms of fascist rhetoric. . . .

At the same time that Oskar is using this rhetoric, however, he is also criticizing it; by calling attention to what he has done and by being so callous as to suggest that he could footnote the number of the Polish dead, he screws his statement up to such a point of brutality that we cannot help being aware of the grotesque image it makes. In making use of a form of fascist rhetoric, then, Oskar similtaneously becomes a type of artist which the Nazis loathed: a satirist, a parodist, a negator.

Behind this dualism in Oskar's voice lies a deeper paradox; Oskar embodies and simultaneously deflates the myth which the Nazis built up about the nature of the artist. This myth was itself self-contradictory, as the career of Oskar shows us; at the same time the Nazis habitually venerated artists and poetic vision in their propaganda, they persecuted and censured them in actual fact. More important though is the fact that, under Hitler, art and politics were identified in an appalling way; the fascist dictator was seen as the counterpart to the poet, in that they both possessed a vision which elevated them above their fellow men and the unpoetic restrictions of rational thought. . . .

[On] a deeper level, we can see Oskar as an inclusive symbol for Nazi Germany; he is an exemplification and a parody of the chief elements that lie behind the Nazi mythology of art and society. The Nazi attempt to achieve a creative unity of members of the Aryan race in which social unity was also artistic wholeness involved . . . a willful rejection of rationality in favor of some deeper mythic, emotional, and somehow poetic bond. Viewing the Nazi era in retrospect, we see how such an attempt would have two chief tendencies, both of which we find in Oskar's parodic rendering of them; it would represent, on the one hand, a willed regression, reflected in Oskar's choice to remain a child and in his consciously grotesque infantilism, and, on the other hand, the willed assumption of a state close to madness, reflected in Oskar's present status, as the inmate of a "Heil- und Pflegeanstalt." Here the irony of Oskar's position comes full circle: by embodying the essential aspects of Nazism, he becomes a creature which the Nazis, with their persecution of the insane and deformed, would have sought to exterminate. Moreover, through his paradoxical character he provides us with a broader portrayal of history than either a patently fascist or antifascist artist could: he is both what the Nazis were and what they rejected, and he simultaneously presents to us in his narrative the Nazi dream and the Nazi reality.

*Ann L. Mason, "Günter Grass and the Artist in History," in* Contemporary Literature *(© 1973 by the Regents of the University of Wisconsin), Vol. 14, No. 3, Summer, 1973, pp. 347-62.*

In this century of analysis, when the obsessions of interior fantasy become the objects of medical, scientific and literary research, is it any wonder that those old practitioners of dream witchcraft, storytellers, should turn to autobiography and begin to debate fiction and fact? The publication within the last few years of two stunning books in Germany, diaries of Günter Grass and Max Frisch . . . which defy conventional boundaries between the novel and personal narrative, convince me that we are witnessing the creation of a new genre, a literature inhabited by creatures with the mouth of human confession and the loins of beasts, fabulous wing or haunch. Of course, it has its antecedents, Kafka's diary, Dostoyevsky's, but these were not conscious attempts to set autobiography and fantasy before the reader in deliberate collage. Certainly among the poets we have seen this introspective charting.

Whatever its predecessors, Günter Grass's *From the Diary of a Snail* is an astounding new book. In the next breath I must say that this yoke of fiction and biography does not entirely work but the attempt is masterful and through long passages it sounds the humanistic clarion of the melancholy angels, Camus, Orwell. The form is bold as if in one structure, the diary, to house the three mansions of these predecessors, story, autobiography, political essay. . . .

Throughout the book creeps the snail, as image, metaphor, magical talisman, presiding beneficent deity; the emblem of Grass's faith in the patient invisible inching forward of mankind to a better world, justifying his efforts in the election campaign, mocking our pretensions of "Superman," reminiscent of Kafka's cockroach in *The Metamorphosis,* but with a certain sly low-to-the-ground humor that laughs away the latter's despair and sets us back on the road, moving by infinitesimal degrees forward with wry and "earthy" satisfaction. . . .

It is more than just another book—an event in the fall of 1973, a diary which we must all inhabit, make part of our own biography. Not only are the events of 1939 and 1969 set in parallel, but again and again Grass reminds us how the sirens tempt us to leap into intolerant, righteous charge on the horse of the Apocalypse. So the storyteller with his bitter, ironic parable sings the fall of the old animal heroism, blood lust, and would make us adopt a new heraldry, self-depreciating and humble to the point of comedy, snail.

*Mark Jay Mirsky, in* Book World—The Washington Post (© The Washington Post), *September 23, 1973, pp. 1, 8-9.*

Writers nearly always imagine it is easy to be a reporter, not to speak of a moral philosopher. The latter is simpler. One of the hardest things in the world is to describe what happened next.

Perhaps because of this, because his great gift is for fiction, Grass's Germany, the Germany he bravely stumps for Brandt, bringing the good word about old-age pensions, comes out gray and flat [in "From the Diary of a Snail"]. He is doing this for the young, for their own good: the writing takes on a nervous finger-shaking quality, as though he knew perfectly well, under the gloom and goodwill, that it is no use telling children what they are to remember.

*Mavis Gallant, in* The New York Times Book Review *(© 1973 by The New York Times Company; reprinted by permission), September 30, 1973, pp. 4-5.*

Günter Grass addresses his newest book, "From the Diary of a Snail" . . ., to his four children. The eldest of *my* four children once, under the illusion that she could turn pebbles into jewels, acquired a bright little machine that, loaded with gray sludge and plugged into a socket, revolved and tumbled to a hypothetical lustre whatever bits of the material universe were put inside. That curious device (now defunct) offers the best analogy I can think of to Grass's present authorial method. The gray sludge is "fug" or "melancholy"—the leaden aura of staleness and inertia possessed by compromised, relative, muddled, hashed-over, snail's-pace reality. The electricity is Grass's phenomenal energy, not only intellectual but personal, soulful, human; however farfetched his fancies, Grass (like the not dissimilarly mustachioed Kurt Vonnegut) convinces us that his heart remains in the right place. The bits of rough matter are whatever obsessions he finds simultaneous within him: in this book, snails, children, hermaphroditism, Dürer's print entitled "Melencolia I," the fate of the Danzig Jews, the suicide of Manfred Augst (real), the adventures of Hermann Ott (fictional), and the 1969 West German elections, wherein Grass contributed nearly a hundred speeches to Willy Brandt's successful campaign. While functioning, Grass's narrative engine, like the polishing machine, seems inexhaustible and distinctly unmusical, at least in translation. Though my daughter's polisher ran for days and weeks without stopping, the rocks and shards inside never shed, along with their incidental roughnesses, the core of obduracy that makes sea-smoothed stones so dryly disappointing when arranged on the summer-cottage mantelpiece. And when "From the Diary of a Snail" stops shuddering and churning, what tumbles out, though of a certain sheen, is not a work of art.

Not that art is overtly aspired to. "From the Diary of a Snail" began as a *Sudelbuch,* a scribble book, a book of jottings Grass carried with him on the campaign trail: "My entries come to me on the road. . . . I mean to speak to you by roundabout bypaths: sometimes offended and enraged, often withdrawn and hard to pin down, occasionally brimful of lies, until everything becomes plausible." . . .

Upon this campaign diary Grass permits to intrude—or has imposed in two years of revision—a number of other concerns, tales, devices, and designs. . . .

What we want from our great imaginers is not fuel but fire, not patterns but an action, not fragmented and interlaced accounts but a story. . . .

In fairness, and with no aspersion on the efforts of Mr. Manheim [Grass's translator], who for all I know has done the best of all possible jobs, one feels that exceptionally much has been lost in translation. The poems flung into this diary must be better than they seem. For every piece of wordplay that is explained in a footnote, there must be several too delicate to unravel. Grass's curious trick of unpunctuated word-triplets ("bitter tired finished," "went stood lay") must appear less gratuitous in German. Throughout, the skin of words feels a little raw in English, as if it lacked the epiderm of intelligent verbal nervousness, of voiced sensitivity. And of course the many references to contemporary political figures strike chords muffled here. We do not so much read this book as overhear it: a German is speaking to Germans, intimately and urgently. For Grass, in addition to the universal duties of a writer, has the local duty, with all the German writers of his generation, of guarding and barring the path back into Hell.

*John Updike, "Snail on the Stump," in* The New Yorker, *October 15, 1973, pp. 182-85.*

Reading "Diary of a Snail" made me think of Grass as a hairy Thomas Mann, with smelly feet. He has a similar sense of meaningful congestion. His interrupted literary style makes you feel like your mind has a bad cold, but it is a cold which could be the occasion for an important re-ordering of the psychic life. But caution: it's like whole-grained bread—you chew it reflectively and put it down often. Too hasty ingestion and its rough richness may interfere with your stomach.

*Martin Washburn, in* The Village Voice *(reprinted by permission of* The Village Voice; *© 1973 by The Village Voice, Inc.), October 25, 1973, p. 33.*

At no point of Günter Grass' heady career as contemporary Germany's most powerful and widely read novelist has it been possible to fit this clowning but desperately earnest maverick into any conventional literary slot. Not for him the Olympian detachment, high seriousness and smooth narration that was once the earmark of German novelists. Instead, Grass has recaptured the cruelty and remose of 20th-century German history through a tumultuous, unsparing manipulation of fantasy, fairy-tale nightmare and the appalling reality of the grotesque: in *The Tin Drum,* the dwarf Oskar Matzareth's magic drum beats out the dread Nazi years in his own disruptive rhythms; in *Dog Years,* the subterranean army of mechanical scarecrows waits to unleash its Grimm vengeance on the postwar world; the teenager Mahlke, in *Cat and Mouse,* with his monstrous Adam's apple, desecrates the Iron Cross—to the horror of piously nationalistic German readers. Nothing has delighted Grass more than to turn his countrymen's passion for *Ordnung* upside down and let the past tumble guiltily out of the nation's pockets.

Most recently, in *Local Anaesthetic,* a novel deliberately meant to set the reader's teeth and soul on edge, Grass turned to the smug present-day prosperity of the "economic miracle" to dramatize the generation gap between jaded, enervated liberalism and chaotic, revolutionary youth. There, more than ever, he refused to make any conventional concessions to his readers. . . .

A chatty, helter-skelter potpourri, *From the Diary of a Snail* contains an embarrassment of truncated, unassimilated riches that do not always prove their worth. In part, the work is a manual on the anatomy and mating habits of the snail—the novelist has always had a passion for facts—submitted both as Grass' self-image ("I am the civilian snail, the snail made man . . . with my tendency to dwell, hesitate, and cling") and as a symbol of true progress ("It seldom wins and then by the skin of its teeth. It crawls, it goes into hiding but keeps on, putting down its quickly drying track on the historical landscape . . . far from well-situated theories, skirting retreats and silted revolutions").

The book is, moreover, a short history of German Socialism. . . .

There is, however, an excess of tedium involved in plowing through everything that Grass has thrown indiscriminately into *From the Diary of a Snail*. If a subtle order to his selection and arrangement of details exists, it is impossible to tell. Furthermore, Grass indulges in breathlessly incomplete sentences, to no discernible purpose. . . . There is too much . . . mannered coyness, too much about snails and electioneering and food, too many cute children's questions with heavily ironic answers.

Yet it is not the whirl of miscellaneous dailiness that eventually defeats the reader, and certainly not Grass' moderate, antiapocalyptic, antiextremist position on social change, which is altogether admirable in its robust sanity and responsible intelligence. What ultimately drags him down is the book's lazy anything-goes organization, a formlessness that resembles a random-entry notebook. One's attention is forced to shift gears so frequently, and without warning, that the work becomes blurred, difficult to read, and not worth the effort—except, that is, for the too-brief novelist's story of Doubt.

*Pearl K. Bell, "Of Mollusks and Men," in* New Leader, *October 29, 1973, pp. 15-16.*

The eponymous hero of [*From the Diary of a Snail*] engages in a melancholy symbiosis by collecting rare and lovely gastropods, just as Grass collects odd stories, recollections and conversations which strike his moonish fancy during his campaign progress through the Federal Republic. The structure of the piece is that of self-reflectiveness, a vain and necessarily incomplete process which does less than justice to the tokens and ideas which swim to the surface of the ordinarily unembarrassed and unselfconscious mind. But for Grass it is the staple of his 'fiction' (it takes little effort to dramatise ourselves right off the teeming surface of the world) and he has taken yet one more step backward by creating an alter and ulterior ego, a factoid, an untruth expressly designed to behave like the truth and resurrect the prone and melancholy self. . . .

[The] voice drones on, endlessly analysing, dissecting the facts of its own inadequacy. It is as if the will were seeking some kind of identity with history, an aspiration at once weighty and futile. The book is Germanic in just that sense, and it can be terribly dull.

Grass invents himself everywhere, but none of his pieces will fit into anything but the meretricious mood which would only last a moment were it not cosily ensconced within the generalisations of the scholars. His political persona is no more plausible—and it is to his credit that he seems to realise this—than any of the more imaginative personae who are dreamt and then forgotten. Even that image of the snail as unconsidered but remorseless destiny bears precious little meaning any more, just as the snail of dialectic can only make its way by wreaking violence and twisting the world all out of recognition. Everything becomes the figment of system, and it is only when Grass's backroom weariness emerges and the heat of Utopia has cooled that the whole business is seen for the transparent fraud it is. It is ironic to note, of course, the publication of this swan-song in the week that Willy Brandt goes down at the hand of secret services, managers and technocrats. This must seem another weight on Melancholy's shoulders, as Grass sits bent double over the typewriter, the ladders and globes and scales refusing to come together even for that one line which offers the promise of his wholeness, and the forgiveness for whatever private nightmare is consuming him within this book.

*Peter Ackroyd, in* The Spectator *(© 1974 by* The Spectator; *reprinted by permission of* The Spectator*), May 18, 1974, p. 614.*

* * *

## GRAU, Shirley Ann 1929-

**Ms Grau is a Southern American regional novelist and short story writer. (See also *Contemporary Authors*, Vols. 1-4, rev. ed.)**

As was demonstrated by several of the stories in her first book, *The Black Prince,* published when she was in her early twenties, Shirley Ann Grau has a gift for dealing with nature and the kind of people who live close to nature. Her second book and first novel, *The Hard Blue Sky* . . . made good use of this talent, telling a story of a community of fishermen living on an island in the Gulf of Mexico. In *The House on Coliseum Street* . . . she showed that she is by no means limited to this sort of material, but in *The Keepers of the House* . . . she has returned to it and I think she is happy to do so, as I am happy to have her. . . .

It is a novel of considerable dramatic force. Miss Grau makes her point—the absurdities as well as the cruelties to which prejudice leads—sharply enough, but this is a story, not a tract. The characters are striking, Margaret as well as William, and vigorously portrayed. The manner of telling the story, partly in the first person and partly in the third, permits Miss Grau to achieve both perspective and immediacy. And always there is the sense of the land and the seasons. . . .

All the virtues of Miss Grau's earlier books are here, together with a new power. I think it is her best novel, and I shall be surprised if it is not her most popular one.

*Granville Hicks, "Only the Countryside Was Serene," in* Saturday Review *(copyright © 1964 by Saturday Review, Inc.; reprinted with permission), March 21, 1964, pp. 33, 51.*

The violent history of a Southern family from the early 19th century to the present; miscegenation and its effects on the children it produces; the politics of racial hatred in the modern Deep South; an eruption of vengeance and counter vengeance between victims and victimizers, all bound together in the consequences of slaveholding days—these are the themes of ["The Keepers of the House"]. . . . They are, of course, the same old Southern Gothic themes, and the reader of this review will be forgiven if he groans at seeing them dredged up after so many neo-Yoknapatawphans have sunk them into cliché. For most of us one Faulkner is quite enough, and if we are morally engaged by what is happening in the South today, we still reserve the right to be bored by seeing it reworked once again in fiction.

I say this, however, only to preface a defense of "The Keepers of the House" as an excellent novel. It is not Miss Grau's fault that her world overlaps with Faulkner's. She is obviously writing about the South she knows at first hand. Readers who have followed her career through "The Black Prince and Other Stories" (1955), "The Hard Blue Sky" (1958) and "The House on Coliseum Street" (1961) will not need to be told that she is a gifted storyteller. Her [work is characterized by] lucidity, . . . narrative directness, [and] . . . reliance on the bare details of her plot instead of on ponderous philosophizing. . . .

Ultimately "The Keepers of the House" succeeds, not as a political novel or a tale of violence, but as an exercise in imaginative sympathy.

*Frederick C. Crews, "Unto the Third Generation," in* The New York Times Book Review *(© 1964 by The New York Times Company; reprinted by permission), March 22, 1964, pp. 4-5.*

If a good many Southern novels lean rather more heavily on incident than on character, show more concern for parochial details than for general truth, and have a greater respect for dialect than for dialogue, it is partly because the Southern ethos is so firmly established as a literary convention that only the boldest imagination dares challenge it. The novelist's task of expressing his own conception of life through the representation of an environment so familiar becomes formidable.

It is a task that Miss Grau, in her third novel, does not quite accomplish, although she comes as near to it as any living Southern novelist. While the psychological realities of "The Keepers of the House" are undeniable, toward the end the story itself threatens to render them meaningless and even fraudulent. This is not because the events of the story lack credibility. It is because the events are not amenable to the symbolic interpretation that the epigraph from the Book of Ecclesiastes suggests. And obviously Miss Grau intended them to be. Obviously she meant her novel to have a moral center of gravity.

From the moment Abigail Tolliver appears, bringing into the inhospitable present the pride of blood, the independence of mind and the eccentricities of character, as well as the legends of her family's history, we come face to face with the operation of psychic forces, commonly described as Southern, in a series of incidents of the kind that generations of novelists and the gossips of history have persuaded us can occur only in the South. Here are the dateless legends of white men back from the wars, of murderous Indians, of loyal, inscrutable blacks. Here are blood and bitterness, lust and glut, love and the absence of love. . . .

[The ending] is the unexpected climax to a story that might have ended sooner and to more purpose. It is before this point is reached that Miss Grau begins to slight literary artistry and resorts to a kind of literary mechanics, which she employs with great skill, but at the expense of truth.

*Saunders Redding, "Enough of a Drawl to be Distracting," in* Chicago Tribune Book Week, *March 22, 1964, p. 4.*

Plot aside, [*The Keepers of the House*] is a Southern novel alright, and one often beautifully written. . . .

Shirley Ann Grau has been demonstrating her gifts as a sensitive observer of human development and growth for some time now. With a few words she can establish a mood, mixing man's emotions with appropriate reflections of them in landscape. She knows her heavy, low Southern moon, her Southern turtles and snakes and herb gardens. She knows the old houses with their long windows and the nodding breezes which come upon thankful, clammy skin. She knows the people, knows the ambiguities of race relations, the devices, pretenses, ironies, absurdities, and incredible frustrations, all of them constant reminders of the mind's capacity for illusion, rationalization and even delusion under an irrational but powerfully coercive social and economic system. . . .

Most significantly, she writes at a time when she can know some answers, too. For this is a novel which in its own sudden and firm way has a statement to make. . . . The author does not shirk the complicated nature of the problem. Her segregationist is no demon, but any region's ambitious, aggressive politician. . . .

It is said that people are tired of the South and the Southern novel. Yet, I wonder where else in this country past history and present social conflict conspire to bring forth so much of the evil in people, so much of the dignity possible in people, so much of the "pity and terror" in the human condition. Looking at people living elsewhere, in bureaucratized passivity and efficiency, in faceless bustle, in cliché-riddled "progressive" comfort or sophisticated but paralysed bewilderment, we can turn to the South in horror and fascination, and on those counts alone, in some hope.

*Robert Coles, "Mood and Revelation in the South," in* The New Republic *(reprinted by permission of* The New Republic; *© 1964 by Harrison-Blaine of New Jersey, Inc.), April 18, 1964, pp. 17-19.*

Shirley Ann Grau's treatment of the psychoanalytic theory that ties obsession with money to the flight from death—a sublimation of repressed body consciousness—goes further than simply to repeat the conventional, reductive view of the moneygrubber as Puritan or ascetic. The most interesting aspect of [*A Condor Passes*] is its implicit argument for Dionysian man. She has centered her narrative on the deformations of sexuality, reflecting the split between body and mind, that are a particular disease of our acquisitive, repressive culture. From an inability to accept death—that is, to live freely in the body—there follows the paradoxical consequence of death in life. The money drive, Grau seems to be saying, is a morbid surrender of the body's creativity to the waste it must become, and we literally cannot "come to our senses" until we acknowledge its neurotic impulse. . . .

Shirley Ann Grau willingly embraces the risk of tedium that lurks today in the nineteenth-century novel form, and doesn't escape it. In technique, *A Condor Passes* duplicates her previous novel *The Keepers of the House,* and with less control: the same agglomeration of theatrical anecdote and sociological observation, the dependence on "life history" to keep the wheels going round; there are even small stylistic echoes of the earlier work. The underlying concerns of the present novel have more amplitude, as I have indicated. Still, they don't save it from running downhill or sounding too frequently like an overwrought journalistic report on characters that are little more than a typology: The Old Man, the Passive Woman, the Aggressive Female, the Male Weakling. These people are not tragic because they remain unaware of their condition. In one passage Miss Grau describes the Old Man's vision of a furry animal inside his mind which he caressed and quieted: ". . .when the body fell apart at last . . . then the animal inside him would find endless doors opening on echoing corridors . . . it would be gone running around the world . . . hiding and running, free, sunlight and dark." Could the Oliver we are permitted to know dream like this? It is the author speaking in his name, the old "literary" voice interposing itself, summarizing "experience" whose texture has not been reproduced.

*Muriel Haynes, in* Saturday Review *(copyright © 1971 by Saturday Review/World, Inc.; reprinted with permission), September 18, 1971, pp. 44-5.*

A compendium of fact and fable woven into a family chronicle, "The Condor Passes" resumes the theme that informed her earlier books; birth, and death. . . .

Shirley Ann Grau's strength (it is somewhat out of fashion) is her ability to write from multiple views. She inhabits, with equal ease, a child in a nursery, a girl on her wedding day, a Cajun on a binge, and the Old Man lying in bed, dying. . . . Despite her novel's tenacity of detail (want to know how to pole a pirogue through a swamp?) it is basically symbolic. . . .

Her novel is a splendid combination of intensely relaxed detail and overarching metaphor. It is not a perfect book, but its faults are minor. If it sometimes seems to wade in trivia, . . . mostly, it soars.

*Annette Grant, in* The New York Times Book Review *(© 1971 by The New York Times Company; reprinted by permission), September 19, 1971, p. 47.*

I cannot say Miss Grau is a second-rate novelist, but *The Condor Passes* is certainly the kind of shoddy novel that sticks to the New Orleans formula; . . . it is poor and predictable. It is tricked out with the embellishments that readers have come to associate with fictional New Orleans —its perverse tycoons, its sexual precocities, fallen-away Catholics, and shabby pseudo-Frenchmen who pass for the aristocracy. . . .

The publisher describes the novel as "huge." It is long but not very deep, and its sprawl is achieved by Miss Grau's meandering through the histories of each character in turn, not dramatizing their experiences but stating that at this point the character is poor, and now he is rich, and now he is on a ship, and so forth. The reader must take her word for it; there is certainly no internal evidence for their wisdom, wealth, or the sensitivities she credits them with.

*Paul Theroux, in* Book World *(©* The Washington Post*), October 10, 1971, p. 12.*

Shirley Ann Grau has kept herself as far out of [*The Condor Passes*] as is consistent with writing it. Feeling and interpretation are just as lively in her as in . . . any other good writer, but she holds them in abeyance, their time will come but not yet. Each incident is given with as much fullness as its participants deserve, but it is surrounded by silence; either it justifies itself or it does not. If the acts and events are not as opulent as they would be in Utopia, so much the worse, they must do the best they can, the novelist is not going to pretend that they are more than they are.

The theme is given in the title. . . .

I can't see that the symbol does anything for the book, and Miss Grau comes back to it at the end for no good reason. . . .

Miss Grau's policy is clear. She is determined to give her characters free range, subject only to the limitations implicit in the nature of things. As for their own natures, they are welcome to do what they like with what they own. So the novel hovers upon questions of property, possession, rights, duties, needs, license. Miss Grau attends to her art with a corresponding sense of law and limitation. She does whatever she can manage with characters, she invents new characters when she feels in need of them. If there is something that her characters cannot reasonably see or feel, her novel must do without it: that she, the novelist, can see or feel it is not enough reason for including it. In short, whatever cannot be achieved by attending to a large family of characters had better be left alone.

Miss Grau works by concentrating on one thing, one character, at a time, and her art is exhilarating in its precision. But she is not exceptionally good when it is a question of latitude. . . . Every episode is vividly illuminated, but there is very little sense of a world and a time between the lights. The public world does not press upon Miss Grau's private people, and we could be forgiven for thinking that it has gone away. The characters have lively relations to one another, and equally lively relations to themselves, but they do not bump against strangers, they are rarely aware of a world going about its alien business, indifferent to the Olivers.

Miss Grau tells us, in each case, what she thinks we ought to know, and nothing more. Her tact is blessed. But she virtually conceals from us, while the novel lasts, the fact that other forms of reality are present, even if we do not see them. She nearly prevents us from knowing those forms of reality which James called "the things we cannot possibly *not* know, sooner or later, in one way or another." In a richer novel we would hear noises which we would not interpret, except in the ordinary way as the buzz of things. *The Condor Passes* is all foreground, very little background, everything is presented in the same degree of lucidity, that is, a high degree. But after a while the lucidity begins to oppress, and I think we would believe more if we were shown less, or if a little public confusion were to assert itself against the private gleam.

*Denis Donoghue, "Life Sentence," in* The New York Review of Books *(reprinted with permission from* The New York Review of Books*; © 1971 by NYREV, Inc.), December 2, 1971, pp. 28-9.*

Women's isolation emerges more sharply as the focus of Shirley Ann Grau's new book of stories, *The Wind Shifting West,* than of her first collection *The Black Prince* (1955). Although few of the 18 stories expand in one's memory with the yeast of excellence, the volume as a whole is satisfying because it consistently and without fanfare delivers her vision of stoical endurance. . . .

Grau seldom strikes a self-pitying note. She's interested in displaying not the sensitivity of her characters, but their strong defenses against despair. She's not fashionable: when she writes a story whose characters are modishly nameless, it seems silly. As a storyteller tracing the shape of loneliness she's quite different from Joy Williams or Joan Didion, whose females can whine with self-destructive masochism, and from Joyce Carol Oates, whose "scenes of passion and despair" erupt with violence. Grau's women are not grotesque in their isolation, but human for coping with it.

The main limitation of the stories, however, also lies in the choice of theme. The characters' dissatisfactions are revealed economically in the opening paragraphs: a tart reply, oppressive heat (many of the stories are set around New Orleans), a man drifting out of sight. The characters themselves seem to understand these details, just as Caroline interprets the wet anchor or the woman driver the acorn. But their frustrations never issue in violence, hardly even in action. No action can take the death out of loneliness. Even revelations are underplayed. Hence the stories are static. . . . Most of the individual stories are very accomplished, but so exiguous, so reduced in expectation, that one feels something's missing. Stories like "No Other Way" are exceptions because they at least suggest the alternatives to endurance.

This diminishment seems quite deliberately chosen, as if Grau were willing to pay its price, for the few stories that try for surprises seem gimmicky or cute—the neat parable of ecological disaster "The Last Gas Station" or "The Lovely April" which, relying on character changes, is too long and ill-proportioned. By the time one puts the volume down, however, one sees the strength that's gone into the rejection of passion and despair. For Grau's characters it's more important to cope with life than to fight against its conditions. Stoic endurance is a conventional female response, but Grau's best stories dramatize why it is better than emotionalism, passivity, or self-destruction.

*Joan Joffe Hall, "Lives Alone," in* The New Republic *(reprinted by permission of* The New Republic; *© 1973 by Harrison-Blaine of New Jersey, Inc.), November 24, 1973, pp. 30-1.*

# H

## HAMPTON, Christopher 1946-

**An English dramatist, Hampton has written several successful plays and has adapted for contemporary productions plays by Babel, Chekhov, Ibsen, and Molière. (See also *Contemporary Authors*, Vols. 25-28.)**

It is probably unfair to fault Mr. Hampton for tedium, since he seems to have deliberately made tedium an element of ["Total Eclipse"], but three solid hours—episode after episode—of alcoholic bickering and teasing and fighting and coupling are too much. . . . There are no heroics, no sentimentality, no justifications in the script, but, unfortunately, there is no life, either, in its action or characters. . . . "Total Eclipse" also shares the weaknesses of most documentaries—those chunks of exposition wedged into the dialogue and the tyranny of chronology.

*Edith Oliver, "Dropouts," in* The New Yorker, *March 11, 1974, pp. 102, 104.*

Hampton . . . fares less than well with *Total Eclipse*, a play about Verlaine and Rimbaud. . . . It is perilous to put great writers on the stage because (a) the parts of the play in quotation marks tend to outstrip the author's verbiage; (b) the biographical facts are too familiar to civilized playgoers; and (c) the lives of great writers tend not to be all that interesting—it is their writings that matter, but these cannot readily become part of a play. To deal with "a," Hampton chose for his principals poets, and so could put their words not only into quotation marks, but also, as it were, into italics, and could assume that they and his prose were modes sufficiently apart to disinvite comparison. To deal with "b" and "c," he picked lives that are not all that well known to Anglo-American audiences, and that were quite unconventional and violent enough to provide dramatic excitement.

Shrewd strategy for a 22-year-old dramatist, [but] still the play—despite its earnestness, literacy, and rapid movement—fails to ignite. . . . And the very scrupulous sticking to known facts and utterances, alas, works against Hampton: enough is known about the subject to curb the fancy, but not enough to flesh out a three-act play. If only he had permitted himself some dramatic license, and invented! Finally, there is no contact, as Hampton presents them, between these poets' lives and their works. We would expect the poetry, if not to illuminate the lives, at least to become illuminated by them; but the two remain obdurately separate entities.

*John Simon, in* New York Magazine *(© 1974 by NYM Corp.; reprinted by permission of* New York Magazine *and John Simon), March 11, 1974, p. 84.*

[The] documentation of the Rimbaud-Verlaine affair in *Total Eclipse* offers not much more than facts. And facts, as someone has said, are fools: they do not themselves reveal truth. If we know little about the background of this "Eclipse," we learn not much more from it than that certain famous French poets were insane wretches given to spoiling their own and other lives.

Quotations from various of Verlaine's and Rimbaud's writings are of no avail: they do not help shape the proceedings to a cogent meaning. Though there is some violence, along with dashes of acrid humor and some tints of local color, there is no genuine dramatic movement in the play.

*Harold Clurman, in* The Nation, *March 16, 1974, p. 348.*

Hampton's achievement [in *Total Eclipse*] is to remind us that the artist keeps reviewing his past and seeing more than an array of completed and incomplete works. He also sees a life that may, in retrospect, seem shapeless or unacceptable to him. Like it or not, he is engaged in the twofold creation of his art and himself. For Rimbaud, the extreme Symbolist, relying on dreams and the unconscious for inspiration, the poet cannot allow his life to accumulate by a series of accidents. He must mold it, and from this purposeful creation art will emerge naturally.

Verlaine, however, is temperamentally unable to lead the bold, unapologetic life Rimbaud tempts him with. . . .

The material of this celebrated relationship is never less than fascinating. But Hampton's dramatic techniques do not seem consistently worthy of it. The play's structure is old-fashioned, if not commercial. It leans unnecessarily on quasi-documentary and explanatory effects, such as the announcement of each scene's place and time. *Total Eclipse* strikes one as being much more dated than, say, *Baal,* for which Brecht, in 1918, found an unorthodox dramatic form that superbly accommodated its Rimbaud-like hero.

*Albert Bermel, in* New Leader, *April 1, 1974, p. 23.*

[A] significant play by an important young writer . . . is [*Savages*, by] Christopher Hampton, one of the best of the young British playwrights. By taking as his theme the hair-raising genocide carried out on the Brazilian Indians of the upper Amazon, Hampton has risked a tricky chemical compound—mixing his gift for sophisticated, mordant irony with the stirrings of his social and political conscience.

If the result of this blend is unstable, it does not lack for power and theatrical effect. In "Savages" history is an obscene juggernaut—its characters are representatives of historical forces rather than real people, and all of them except the Indians come across as selfish, blind, helpless or homicidal. . . .

Hampton attempts, with more success than might have been expected, to turn an act of political conscience into art.

*Martin Kasindorf, "Killing Ground," in* Newsweek *(copyright Newsweek, Inc., 1974; reprinted by permission), September 9, 1974, p. 91.*

What is most noteworthy about *The Philanthropist* is not its smooth and witty writing, nor the unexpected turns Hampton uses when excessive wordiness threatens to strain our attention, but the creation of a character who is usually accounted undramatically flaccid and who Hampton has nevertheless made entirely worth concern.

He is called Philip, a professor of philology, but no fool. The author is at ease with such folk and does not treat the type as an oddball. He neither reveres nor condescends to the man. Theatrically speaking, what is special about Philip is his mild nature, awkward but gracious, kindly without gush, good without self-consciousness; but he has one marked flaw: benevolence to the point of indecisiveness. . . .

We are not urged to commiserate with him; we even laugh at him. Yet we do feel for him, seeing that he lives in the [contemporary] jungle in which his virtues are not apt to win even the most modest prizes of companionship or marriage.

Though constantly engaging, the play is yet immature in craftsmanship. It begins by way of a prologue with a funny but irrelevant *coup de théâtre*, and continues with reams of conversation, amusingly representative of smart talk in educated London circles. At first I thought that what I was to see was a sophisticated version of a Neil Simon comedy. But in the latter half of the play—particularly in the passages where Philip is confronted by the girl who has seduced him only to find him a dud—and then by the girl who gives him up because of his unassertiveness—the evening comes into happy focus. There is later some further over-discursive wobbling but the final moments are perceptive and touching.

*Harold Clurman, "London" (1970) in his* The Divine Pastime: Theatre Essays *(reprinted with permission of Macmillan Publishing Co., Inc.; copyright © 1946, 1948, 1949, 1950, 1951, 1952, 1953, 1954, 1955, 1956, 1957, 1958, 1959, 1960, 1961, 1962, 1963, 1964, 1965, 1967, 1969, 1970, 1971, 1974 by Harold Clurman), Macmillan, 1974, pp. 238-42.*

* * *

## HAWKES, John 1925-

**Hawkes is a masterful American experimental novelist whose nightmare-fiction exhibits what one critic called "a death-haunted vision." (See also *Contemporary Authors*, Vols. 1-4, rev. ed.)**

A surrealist evocation of European despair . . ., [*The Cannibal*] is so irrevocably dominated by . . . enormities that it remains a remote and terrible fantasy, without any of the profound significance of Kafka's fiction. . . .

*The Cannibal* (1949) is a testimony to a small but persistent struggle on the part of recent novelists to break away from the naturalist impasse. It is in a sense a part of the struggle against naturalism; naturalistic only in its surface details, it depends upon such poignant accuracy of particulars for the ground of its persuasion. Its secret lies elsewhere. . . . [It] cuts through both document and discourse, to reach another and symbolic level of meaning.

*Frederick J. Hoffman, in his* The Modern Novel in America, *Henry Regnery, revised edition, 1963, pp. 198-99.*

Each of John Hawkes's impressively dislocated novels has a different nominal locale, yet they all seem to take place in the same timeless decayed and decaying no-land. Hawkes's surreal world is deliberately out of focus, blurred over by a fog of ugly images which we experience vaguely and unpleasantly, like, as his admirers assert, an actual nightmare. Hawkes is something of a naturalist in reverse; where the naturalist gives us the detailed surface of everyday squalid existence, Hawkes gives us with his own psychoanalytic verisimilitude the blurred surface of the workaday evil dream. His work is prescriptively contemporary, related on the one hand to the nightmare world of Flannery O'Connor and on the other to the antinovels of Sarraute and Robbe-Grillet; for all the brilliances of Hawkes's style, the novels seem so many eccentric exercises—an extraordinary game superbly played, but a game nevertheless.

*Jonathan Baumbach, in the "Introduction" to his* The Landscape of Nightmare: Studies in the Contemporary American Novel *(reprinted by permission of New York University Press; copyright © 1965 by New York University), New York University Press, 1965, p. 5.*

"Lunar Landscapes" makes accessible for the first time several hard-to-get Hawkes' items, including six short pieces and all three of Hawkes' novellas. "Charivari," published in 1950, now seems mannered and dated. The story of an aging married couple terrified by the prospect of a child, "Charivari," Hawkes' first work, is a brittle exhibition of technical prowess. "The Owl" and "The Goose on the Grave" (1954) are much fuller and more resonant. "The Owl" is narrated by a Hangman who makes a sacrament of his executions, and "The Goose on the Grave" is an account of an orphan's search for a father in an Italy devastated by war. Both are distinguished by a beauty and precision of language, an uncanny evocation of terror, an intensity of vision as disturbing as a nightmare. No writer in America is more scrupulous, or ruthless, than Hawkes, and none has given us fictions of greater imaginative purity and power. The fictions in "Lunar Landscapes" do not report on experience but provide an experience.

Virginia Quarterly Review, *Vol. 45, No. 4 (Autumn, 1969), p. cxxviii.*

[In his plays,] Hawkes works largely by nuance, suggesting more than he defines, hoping, I suppose, to infect the audience with a sense of uneasiness or dis-ease (with and without the hyphen). The world of his plays, like that of his novels, is one of matter-of-fact grotesqueness in which blood and lust are staples ("Blood and ecstasy, that's the ticket," says Bingo in *The Wax Museum*) and innocence is forever menaced—mainly by its own innate corruption. At one pole—*The Questions*—his work suggests Harold Pinter; at the other—*The Wax Museum*—it suggests Grand Guignol, devised for a theater that has not got around to buying its bloodmaking machine. The action is minimal; the play, in Hawkes, is largely verbal. . . .

The best of the plays is *The Questions*. . . . [The] play's effectiveness—rather like that of Pinter's *The Homecoming*—depends upon an obvious struggle, all the more compelling for not being concretely defined. Hawkes's language in this work is fascinating; seldom ornate, practically descriptive, it remains dry, spare, and yet evocative. Some of its subtlety comes from cleverly manipulated repetition. . . .

The other three plays are not so interesting. *The Innocent Party* [is] less art than aura. . . . *The Wax Museum* is a macabre item. . . . [The] author once described *The Undertaker* as a "farcical melodrama," a generic term which suggests—perhaps without intending to—a certain lightness of intent. In fact, *The Undertaker* and *The Wax Museum,* both of which should play well, come across simply as clever pieces, teasing the serious subjects which underlie them. *The Questions,* by comparison, is a work of dramatic substance.

*Gerald Weales, in his* The Jumping-Off Place: American Drama in the 1960's *(reprinted with permission of Macmillan Publishing Co., Inc.; copyright © 1969 by Gerald Weales), Macmillan, 1969, pp. 208-11.*

John Hawkes's *The Cannibal* deals not with war but with its aftermath. Spitzen-on-the-Dein is indeed an inferno, a city of the living dead. Having no communication with the outside world, it is completely self-contained. Since no one has a watch, it is also existing outside of time. For the inhabitants, the main task seems to be to burn out "the pits of excrement, burning the fresh trenches of latrines where wads of wet newspapers were scattered, burning the dark round holes in the black stone huts where moisture travelled upwards and stained the privy seats." Nearby is a swamp "filled with bodies that slowly appeared one by one from the black foliage, from the mud, from behind a broken wheel."

In this land of barren earth, barren women, and impotent men (the Census taker is out of a job), dying animals abound. A particularly vivid scene is that at the local asylum from which the patients have fled but left behind them frozen monkeys strewn over the grounds: "One of the monkeys seemed to have grown, and frozen, was sitting upright on the bodies of the smaller beasts, tail coiled about his neck, dead eyes staring out through the gates." In this grotesque figure it would appear Hawkes is implying that those who are punished, those who are fixed in Dante's lowest circles of the Inferno are the ones who have returned to animality.

Situations and images continue to recall Dante's Inferno. The characters are, of course, victims, each enduring his own agony, but each is quite capable of victimizing, even torturing others for the sake of his own wretched survival. . . .

[It] is Hawkes's fusion of realistic detail, psychological acumen, and controlled fantasy that constitute his originality.

*Olga W. Vickery, in* The Shaken Realist: Essays in Modern Literature in Honor of Frederick J. Hoffman, *edited by Melvin J. Friedman and John B. Vickery, Louisiana State University Press, 1970, pp. 153-55.*

Many of us talk about black humor as if it were a brand new art form, but remarkable examples of this "new" comedy have been part of the modern American novel for nearly forty years. The legacy of Nathanael West's *Miss Lonelyhearts* (1933) and of Djuna Barnes's *Nightwood* (1937) has been inherited by a score of contemporary novelists, with John Hawkes as a most difficult but representative author. . . .

John Hawkes (with other black humorists), . . . dismisses the concept of a benevolent social norm, with the result that traditional comedy's aim to use laughter as a utilitarian means for social correction is meaningless to him. Lacking a widely accepted standard of behavior, comedy seems strange, and this is one reason why Hawkes's novels are so difficult to accept as comic fiction. He daringly mixes horror with humor, the grotesque with the heroic, creating a complex tone which some readers find hard to handle. To ignore this complexity is to render his fiction simply an exploitation of terror, for the dire events are too obvious to be missed, whatever difficulties the reader has with the humor. Even the reader who sees that Hawkes's fiction concerns itself with comedy is likely to find the novels rough going. Sensing the humor, he may wonder if his horrified response to the action is inappropriate; or, recognizing the terror, he may doubt his original intimations that the novels are indeed comic. When this and similar difficulties appear in the theater, cinema, and other arts at the same time, a crisis takes shape. It is not that humor is dead, but that the traditional forms of comedy have been altered in order to respond more meaningfully to an untraditional world. . . .

Hawkes's fiction suggests at least two reasons why he repudiates traditional comedy's acceptance of a social standard. First, the concept of a standard applicable to a particular society implies stability, an easily accessible norm. But Hawkes and his contemporaries see the world as fractured, chaotic, and lacking stability because of universal violence which can unexpectedly strike at any man. Second, the idea of a social norm suggests a standardization of manners and behavior which is desirable. . . . [This] concept causes Hawkes to despair, for standardization to this degree strengthens the already rampant automation of modern society while, at the same time, it negates individuality. . . .

Hawkes, writing about a fractured world in which correction seems impossible, emphasizes the malignant quality of comedy to point out the pain and absurdity of reality. . . .

In most comic situations typical of Hawkes's fiction, our intelligence and our emotions react with equal force. The heart is not anesthesized, and the result is a laughter which also causes pain. We are horrified while we laugh at the Duke slicing up Jutta's boy (*The Cannibal*), or at Margaret's acceptance of a beating which will kill her (*The Lime Twig*), because these characters, while they perform ridiculous acts and reveal absurd personal defects in the manner of traditional comedy, rarely discover their faults in time so as to be safely reestablished with society.

Hawkes's characters are not stoics. They respond to their predicaments, but their responses are usually at odds with what the reader expects. In many ways his novels are comedies of the inappropriate response. We laugh, as in traditional comedy, because of a deviation from a standard, but Hawkes knows that the standard is in the reader's expectations and not in the novelist's created world. Thus, the reader often experiences horror as he laughs because the humor fails in its traditional role as a measure for correction. . . . His comedy is a product of the contemporary world with all of its potential for violence. Self-awareness in the world of his fiction is usually ineffectual because the terrifying, destructive events remain beyond the character's control whether he realizes what is happening to him or not. . . .

Hawkes isolates his lonely characters so that they must order their own lives. The chaos of reality leaves them with perhaps the only sense of order remaining: private, irrational, comic, often violent fantasies. In such a dreamlike world what appears abnormal to the reader with traditional notions of humor is real and normal to Hawkes's protagonists. . . .

The key to modern comedy is detachment toward violence, for detachment encourages sympathy. Terrifying incidents and grotesque images are meaningless without sympathy for both the instigators and the victims. "The writer who maintains most successfully a consistent cold detachment toward physical violence . . . is likely to generate the deepest novelistic sympathy of all, a sympathy which is a humbling before the terrible and a quickening in the presence of degradation." . . . We are emotionally caught up in the processes of violence because these artists seem to remain uninvolved; the extreme fictive detachment of today's comedy is kin to literary understatement.

What finally confounds the reader and adds to the crisis in humor is modern comedy's ability to suggest hope despite the violence. Laughter, for Hawkes, is, as it has been through the ages, a "saving" attitude, and it is this common emphasis on futurity which most unites traditional comedy with black humor. For while contemporary humor denies the reality of a stable social standard of behavior, it maintains faith in the invulnerability of basic values: love, communication, sympathy. Given a world of fragmentation, self-destruction, and absurdity, Hawkes tries to meet the terrors with a saving attitude of laughter so as to defend and celebrate these permanent values. Thus, modern comedy also functions to expose evil—not the kind of human inadequacy which in traditional comedy is a deviation from a norm, but the very real evil which generates violence and which threatens to annihilate those eternal verities so treasured by Hawkes.

*Don Greiner, "Strange Laughter: The Comedy of John Hawkes," in* Southwest Review, *Autumn, 1971, pp. 318-28.*

[Hawkes] remains one of the new novel's most promising phantasists whose poetic cinematic style states over and over that one thing is suggestive of almost any other. . . . Hawkes's habit is to satirize subtly the convention of the well-made plot, and for a time "The Blood Oranges" reads as if Anthony Burgess' Enderby were rewriting "Swann's Way."

The author's best energies, as usual, are reserved for weaving beautiful word-tapestries of pure suggestion, for placing his action and characters in an extra-dimensional, mythical world. . . . Hawkes's prose is irreducible—its metaphysical and poetic lambency shouts out to be probed and reread until the reader comes to sense that all things are connected through the power of the imagination and memory.

*R. J. Thompson, in* Best Sellers, *October 1, 1971, p. 300.*

John Hawkes's *The Blood Oranges* fails because it is the work of a contemptible imagination. Hawkes has always seemed to me more an unadmitted voyeur of horror than its calm delineator, but in this . . . novel the pretense that what is being described is horrifying is dropped, and we have only the nightmare vision of a narrator unable to see how awful he is. . . .

There is cruelty here that, because unadmitted, is not even palliated by the relish of sadism. . . .

[The] deeply *un*receptive narcissism has so little aesthetic greed, furthermore, or even mere desire to write well, that we find, on almost every page, something like "The sun was setting, sinking to its predestined death," or "And already the seeds of dawn were planted in the night's thigh."

Hawkes has many admirers, which means some will note that I have completely missed the fact that it is all a put-on; some others will suspect I am guilty of all those sins that Hawkes's narrator so cleverly exposes in your ordinary man. So be. But when horror becomes a pastime it should announce itself or at least know itself; when reticence and shyness become the great human vices, then their opposites should be clearly and ably defended; when the man who does not want his wife sleeping around makes her wear a rusty and viciously designed chastity belt, then narrator and author should not imagine it is chastity's fault; when life is insistently joyless it should not be called good, or even particularly tolerable; when people stop mattering to a novelist, the writing will suffer and the writer should stop.

*Roger Sale, in* The New York Review of Books *(reprinted with permission from* The New York Review of Books; © *1971 by NYREV, Inc.), October 21, 1971, p. 3.*

[Four] plays stress Hawkes' obsessive theme—the decline of white Protestant America—a decline riddled with lust and violence. One play, *The Wax Museum,* is set in Canada, and the other three [*The Innocent Party, The Undertaker,* and *The Questions*] in Southern United States, the decay of whose culture has pervaded twentieth century American fiction. The four short dramas are similarly constructed: a shocking confrontation mounts in intensity to an ambiguous finale. Except for *The Innocent Party,* the confrontation is limited to two characters, but at least one of these two plays several roles, for the plays, like Hawkes' fiction, imply that reality consists of improvised motives accumulating into a role. . . .

[*The Innocent Party* dramatizes] a *rite de passage* from solitude to togetherness, though it is left ambiguous as to *who* is together in an adult world where there are no innocent parties. But Jane [a principal character] has also progressed from the innocence of pure experience to the reflection that is art.

*The Wax Museum* is more pointedly erotic, but it too dramatizes a development from solitude to togetherness. . . . An expanded anecdote, *The Wax Museum* uses insidiously grotesque idiom to show how close we are to the wax dummies we create.

*The Undertaker* and *The Questions* were written in that order, and the one is a preparation for the other. The first, according to Hawkes, is a "farcical melodrama" based on the father's suicide in his novel, *Second Skin.* In spite of the provocative (and debatable) genre designation, the play does not modify the meaning of the novel's suicide scene; insistence upon farcical effects of dialogue robs the death of its fictional intensity and mystery.

*The Questions,* on the other hand, achieves intensity because death remains mystery. . . . As in Hawkes' novels, one has the feeling that the truth of fiction emerges through desperate lies. . . . [The] theatrical urgency of Hawkes' play rests upon the relentless crescendo of suggestive questions, which builds the fatal foursome [the characters in *The Questions*] for us, even though we do not know their fate or their final significance. Dialogue alone dramatizes emotion; in the repeated phrase of the Man: "death, grief, anguish, a life of emotional oblivion."

*Ruby Cohn, "John Hawkes," in her* Dialogue in American Drama, *Indiana University Press, 1971, pp. 198-201.*

As a pastoral prose romance Mr. Hawkes' modern instance [*The Blood Oranges*] is faithful to the genre, being replete with extravagant sentiments about free love ("the only enemy of mature marriage is monogamy"), a landscape sufficiently idyllic for his purposes on the eastern shores of the Adriatic, four Anglo-Saxon principals all willing to believe at least in the beginning that "anything less than sexual multiplicity . . . is naïve," and finally a pedestrian pace that confers upon the whole an inescapable air of dullness characteristic of the form. One could poke easy fun at the whole business were it not for the author's sense of dignity and intellectual honesty in contemplating the proceedings; furthermore, as another shield against cheap jibes he has clothed his narrative in astonishingly lyrical and persuasive prose, rare enough in any age and almost a curiosity in this. Full credit should be given for his brave try in a forgotten field. These pages reveal his fluency, technical skill, and high capacity as a literary craftsman, qualities long apparent in his earlier books.

Virginia Quarterly Review, *Vol. 48, No. 1 (Winter, 1972), p. xviii.*

As prose narrative, Hawkes' fiction is a mode of discourse that claims objective truth. There is no mediating poet's voice and lyrical mode, no matter how many poetic technics are employed, to help evoke in the reader the hallucinatory state which the action claims for itself. Hawkes' characters exist in a limbo because his form will not accommodate itself to their fate. Poe impersonated madmen to explore madness, Nabokov impersonates the perverse to explore perversity. But Hawkes' prose refuses to lose its grip on rational, balanced consciousness. Cyril, Hawkes' narcissist in *The Blood Oranges,* can't seem to abandon himself sufficiently to self-love; consequently his voice's intermittent objectivity suggests the author's attempt to provide a standard against which to judge Cyril—or is Cyril less circumscribed than his actions and self-serving rhetoric indicate? This sort of question does not result from fruitful ambiguity; it is rather evidence of a failure to maintain a tone and perspective which would permit coherent reading and imaginative response. In *The Beetle Leg,* it is flawed Faulkner rather than Nabokov manqué; but the effect is the same: there is no mythy mind to contain both the characters' mundane reality and their urgent, fantastic spirit-life. So both are asserted and juxtaposed, unwedded by a compelling and convincing narrative style. The work, no matter how artfully conceived and carefully constructed, lacks the shape with which Faulkner's tone endows his implausible plots.

I'm saying that Hawkes is basically not a good storyteller. When I read, I want to be beguiled, carried along on some viewless wings; I don't want to see the machinery or be continually prodded back into judgment. So if writing the "experimental novel" entails the loss of narrative moxie, I'm against it. If it means trying what hasn't been done successfully before, one has to ask at some point whether there isn't a reason for previous failures. Before I tested myself against Hawkes, I thought I was a literary liberal. Now, while saddened by my limits, I have the conservative's renewed faith in the existence of law if not the necessity of convention.

*Bob Tisdale, "The Flesh Made Words," in* Carleton Miscellany, *Fall/Winter, 1973-74, pp. 104-07.*

John Hawkes' sixth novel, *Death, Sleep & The Traveler,* cat-footed, makes the first five seem heavy. It walks on psychic eggs, sucks them, leaps off. Not a whit too much or little, nothing too violent or tame, almost nothing too obscure or obvious . . . sophistication could not go further. Clear and impeccable, free of the infra-realism and dream-sogged surrealism of the first books, composed in time-shifting short sequences, each with the throaty resonance of a vibraphone key, each with its soft psychic percussion, in a style at once deliberate and delicate, it is an esthetic performance of the first order. "I'm trying to hold in balance poetic and novelistic methods," Hawkes once said, and in the combined compactness and elaboration of the new book the scales hold.

The plot is minimal. A little love, a lot of guilt. Failure. The body betraying its prehuman origins; the sharking jealousies of dreams. . . .

The story is refracted from dozens of disjunct anecdotes as if from the shattered glass face of a clock, and superbly instances what Kenneth Burke calls formal eloquence: the appropriation of surprise and suspense by the sentence, the image, the contrast, the variation, the nuance.

The poise and tension of the narrative spring from the opposition of its matter and method. Disturbed by the "diving and rising monsters of the deep," by *eventualities,* its tactic is to take narrative stills. On the other hand, terrified by immobility—the throbless engine or organ—it scatters itself through nine years and on sea and land as if leaping to omnipresence. . . .

Yet for such superior adequacy of language as this novel boasts, the price runs high. The narrative *encases* life in its own perfection. Its ruthless detachment makes life itself academic. Though psychological unpleasantness greases the scenes—enticing, repelling the reader onward—the syntax commandeers the greater response. The medium subdues the message. Memorable, brilliantly "overexposed" as the best scenes are, they remain with you, not in you. The book imposes its curious pedantic beauty, then recedes like a hollow.

Hawkes is not merely cold to life, he punishes it. While his narrators and Hawkes himself in interviews could not be more indulgent of Psyche, his imagination runs toward her like fire and his books end in a smolder of peace. In *The Blood Oranges* . . . Hawkes fought it out with his demons and lost. . . .

Since his third novel, *The Lime Twig,* Hawkes' fiction has dwelled upon not only sexual guilt but also the guilt of the artist as such—the dreamer whose dreams leave life untouched, the spiritual Narcissus. The new book sours on marriage and sexuality (Ariane excites Allert most when masking her loins with a goat's skull), as well as on myth, dreams, pornography—*representations* of sexual life. In Allert's preoccupation with sexual tableaux, in Peter's and Ursula's view of him as a fetus dreaming rather than living his life, in Ursula's charge that, with his destructive unconscious, he would wrap her (she who is "perpetually moist") in a rubber sheet, as in his mortification when, watching the self-fellatio of two male bats, he is charged with the practice himself, Allert blends with the novelist. Both together hoist the words that unconvincingly close the book: "I am not guilty." To be sexual *and* an artist is to be doubly criminal. For Hawkes there is only the "beautifully barren" island of Pan's mournful goats and the mournful music of Pan's flute. Guilt being inescapable, his novels mourn themselves.

*Death, Sleep & The Traveler* is a beautiful achievement, unique and elegant in form, brilliantly judged, and likely to endure as a small classic. To be sure, Europeanized, Bergmanized as it is, it may not seem *our* classic, except in being an intense romance and (what for us is hardly separable) its Puritan backlash, its ambivalence toward the raw stuff of life.

*Calvin Bedient, "On Cat Feet," in* The New Republic *(reprinted by permission of* The New Republic; *© 1974 by The New Republic, Inc.), April 20, 1974, pp. 26-8.*

John Hawkes is a prince of the middle-aged avant-garde. His earliest books had the character of a brisk and slightly improvised tour through the surrealist region of mind: they were indeed, wrote an admiring Leslie Fiedler, the personal chronicle of this novelist as he "pursued through certain lunar landscapes (called variously Germany or the American West or Italy) his vision or horror or baffled passion." During much of the 1940's and 1950's Hawkes seemed to dwell in polite obscurity. A late-blossoming flower in the tradition of naive modernism, he could scarcely have hoped to create the "shock of recognition" that comes only for writers in proper season. Yet his reputation has grown in recent years, there have been signs of a modest vogue, and his publisher, now as in the past associated with the meretricious as well as the legitimate side of all that is new, has advertised "Death, Sleep & The Traveler" as a masterpiece. . . .

["Naive modernism"] is a name for the technique of dissociation and the more generalized off-realism that one discovers in Hawkes at every turn and without any particular stress on dramatic effect. It entails a reduction of something profound: ideas have become received ideas, and a licensed habit of thought no longer has to submit to the rigors of imagination. Hawkes is a writer who has never quite realized that words are the daughters of earth, that they are around to do a job, and that unless they are made to serve they will drain life from the most colorful of fictions. . . .

"Death, Sleep & The Traveler" ought not to be judged as a main feature of the Hawkes canon. It has one memorable scene in which a goat's head becomes a temptation to sexual violence. But "The Lime Twig" had a great many similarly haunting details and managed to arrange them almost symphonically. Hawkes has certainly written better things. Yet the thinness of his latest production reminds one of the relative thinness of all his work. Why have artists of undoubted genius like Saul Bellow and Flannery O'Connor numbered themselves among his allies? Perhaps because they sense he is trying to do much that they have succeeded in doing. Surely, Hawkes has the rhythms of a great novelist but not the revelations, the cunning required to be a great prose stylist without the calling.

*David Bromwich, in* The New York Times Book Review *(© 1974 by The New York Times Company; reprinted by permission), April 21, 1974, pp. 5-6.*

Mercifully, John Hawkes's writing has moved out of the clotted obscurity of his early novels toward a sort of clarity. Clarity of a sort: one doesn't want to press the point too far. *Death, Sleep & The Traveler* . . . doesn't have a graceless sentence in it, and it is full of luminous scenes, but I wouldn't pretend to be wholly clear on its events, let alone their significance. . . . In reading this novel, you are well advised to heed the remark of Allert's wife, Ursula, who asks, "How can you tell the difference between your life and your dreams?" . . .

A lovely quotation appends itself to John Hawkes's public life now, from a review by Thomas McGuane of his last book in the New York *Times* Book Review, McGuane said that Hawkes is "feasibly, our best writer," which means, I guess, we could make him our best writer if we tried. But no, I don't think we can. At *its* best, *Death, Sleep & The Traveler*—stripped to a minimum of social detail, purposefully remote and ambiguous—is a gesture at essentiality, and its larger pomposities are lent an edge by sly wit. But a certain genuine pomposity remains, the arrogance of minimalism. Hawkes's work seems to me too narrow, gamelike, self-protective to justify the formidable claims that are made for him.

*Richard Todd, in* The Atlantic Monthly *(copyright © 1974 by The Atlantic Monthly Company, Boston, Mass.; reprinted with permission), May, 1974, p. 130.*

When we read Hawkes, we expect to be startled, if not assaulted, by the density of maddening details.

I stress assault. Hawkes not only writes about violent, insane actions—can they ever be *clearly* motivated?—but he deliberately puts us into his novels as he violates our rational, waking conceptions. . . . His novels deal with dream-like deformations, meaningless violations; they also mirror these themes (or, better yet, images). Their structures reflect their ideas—they are, therefore, "self-contained," nocturnal, and claustrophobic. . . .

Although Hawkes writes a maze-like work [*Death, Sleep & The Traveler*] about maze-like reality, he surely does not remain a passive creator. *He delights in his maze.* He shapes it so cunningly that although it resists thematic analysis, it remains a unique construction. There are many dreams . . . which dazzle me. There are the recurring, brilliant images of water, mirror, and animal. I realize that I am unsure of events . . . but I am confident that this fiction (about fictions) will continue to enlighten me for a long time. In reading it I meet "various unfamiliar shadows," "psychic sores," the batlike terrors of sleep. I appreciate the cleansing anxiety it provokes. I accept its wise violations. I am, consequently, very grateful to Hawkes.

*Irving Malin, in* Commonweal *(reprinted by permission of Commonweal Publishing Co., Inc.), May 3, 1974, pp. 221-22.*

Two major elements from Hawkes's earlier work are missing from [*Death, Sleep & The Traveler* and *The Blood Oranges*]: violence and the memory of World War II. The psychic and physical wounds of war and a brutal violence lent a kind of horrible truth to Hawkes's original surrealistic material. The horror gone, much of what seemed significant truth is gone, too—the truth about human nature reflected in a world created by a writer fascinated by the grim heritage of global holocausts.

The war being fought in Hawkes's last two novels is a sexual one. It is an ugly war, but strangely empty and mechanical; [in *Death, Sleep & The Traveler,*] Allert's pornography collection is boring, even to him. Hawkes writes not about love but about sex. . . .

Through Allert's dreaming mind, Hawkes takes us where we've been with him before: funeral processions and coffins, death and decay, a violent struggle to re-enter the womb, memories of a childhood confused by a conflict of sexual identity. Allert escapes into dreams and Hawkes runs right along with him, a copy of Freud clutched under his arm. Allert spends as much time dreaming his fantastic dreams as he does leading his pointless life. Hawkes spends as much time describing these dreams as he does fleshing out his sketchy characters. Dreams explain and come out of daily life; Hawkes becomes so involved in thinking up dreams for his hero that he forgets to give anyone the life that inspires them. . . .

Hawkes sending Allert on his voyage is an author in search of a myth. Although he does not succeed in finding a resonant myth, his excursion into questions of insanity raises welcome echoes of the surrealism that characterized his earlier work.

More than twenty years ago Albert J. Guerard praised the surrealistic qualities in Hawkes's writing, but predicted that Hawkes would change from a surrealistic to a realistic writer. Sadly, Guerard was right. Despite details and careful descriptions, Hawkes's new realism is not real. In his earlier work people were grotesque types who lived in an anti-realistic world, but they were interesting and unique. Now Hawkes writes about such things as human emotions and psychological motivations, yet his people remain flat, his style heartless. Cyril in *The Blood Oranges* and Allert in the current novel are large, very fat men, as though Hawkes had to compensate with physical size for what these men lack in substance.

Hawkes does not have the support of a literary tradition, or, one suspects, a personal heritage colorful or varied enough to strengthen the kind of ordinary material with which he deals in *Death, Sleep & The Traveler.* He makes Allert a Dutchman, because without that foreignness he might be too dull a figure—but he cares so little about the authenticity of Allert's Dutchness that he gives him a last name [Vanderveenan] that could never exist in Holland. John Hawkes has proved himself capable before of creating his own literary tradition, a surrealistic style that made his earlier books very special works of American art. It was a pity to see him forsake that talent in *The Blood Oranges* and now in this latest novel. It is disappointing to watch Dali turn into Daphne du Maurier, to watch a good writer handle his material in a new way that makes us wish for the old.

*Celia Betsky, "Author in Search of a Myth," in* The Nation, *May 18, 1974, pp. 630-32.*

Great surrealist artists do not have to yield general truths and in fact, unless they take the care to systematize their insights, rarely do. Brilliant stylists too can take a short-cut to literary success by overlaying their vacuous or thin content with a highly polished sheen of verbal brilliance. These lessons are known by writers as well as readers—and exploited. And John Hawkes is certainly one of America's most knowing writers. The givens of his work, the data he's working up, almost always seem to be his knowledge of the literary work and its devices and never what can give those devices meaning and shape. Each macabre theme or grotesque character has no more life than the shell of intellection from which it was hatched. In "Lime Twig," Hawkes's best book, the inert themes and monstrous characters are, more or less, jabbed into sentience by the orchestral baton of Hawkes. The patterns of behavior and the texture of plot are ingenious, but on a closer look, the material remains threadbare.

The narrator and hero of "Death, Sleep & The Traveler" is Allert Vanderveenan, a middle-aged Dutch voyeur beached on the shores of America and his febrile imagination. He is that most tedious of all literary creations, a narcissist without an object. . . .

All powerful surrealist literature dealt with that tension between the real and the imaginary until finally writers like Nabokov were able to create a world surreal and ordinary at the same time, with an ironic and sad accent on the ephemeral beauty of the workaday. It worked as magnificently as [Hawkes's] pale single-paragraph imitations of it do not. The tension between the real and the imaginary is replaced by a more academic one of the literary and an attempt to spin out original fantasies.

This novel is an academic exercise. . . .

There are a few powerful images scattered through the book but they're like strangers fallen from another level of consciousness. The themes of "Death, Sleep, & The Traveler"—hallucination ("concreteness rotating toward illusion"—the best image in the book), the death urge, repression and frigidity, and an inability to take measure of one's thoughts and feelings of those of others—are not dramatized or embodied but illustrated.

John Hawkes is one of several American writers who enjoy the almost legendary reputation of a "writer's writer." This can usually be translated to mean a writer too far in advance of or in reaction to the current taste to become the object of a general appreciation or understanding. I don't feel this is the case with Hawkes. For me the mystery is not in the falsely ambiguous style or situations of John Hawkes's books but in the existence of the imprimaturs of artists like Saul Bellow and Anthony Burgess.

*Randall Green, in* The Village Voice *(reprinted by permission of* The Village Voice; *© 1974 by The Village Voice, Inc.), May 23, 1974, p. 37.*

The journey [of Allert, the protagonist in *Death, Sleep & The Traveler,*] unfolds as a series of exquisitely drawn, fragmented episodes—a sentence, 20 sentences—that together create the effect of a collection of photographs, both positive and negative images, some sharply focused, others faded or shadowy or dissolved in brilliant light. . . .

[The] terrain is thick with images and symbols that twist and wind and linger in the mind like dreams that won't yield to interpretation, and won't be forgotten either.

John Hawkes, who is the author of *The Lime Twig, Second Skin, The Blood Oranges* and many other books, has been likened to both Nabokov and Kafka; most often he is simply described as original. His prose, highly stylized, is lambent and cadenced, at times humorous, at times enchanting, always sensual and evocative—catching the fragrance of a green wood fire, the feel of a ship pitching and rolling "like a bottle lying on its side in a sea of oil," the intense dry heat of a eucalyptus-scented sauna, the phosphorescence of a night sea.

*Carol Eron, "Prisoner of the Self," in* Book World—The Washington Post *(©* The Washington Post*), May 26, 1974, p. 3.*

John Hawkes writes with dizzying brilliance. His novels yield to the reader like geishas, and ask only that the reader yield in return. Experimental, dreamlike, sensuous, comic, and solid, his novels burn like clean aromatic wood, like a forest of sandalwood on the hearth of the intellect.

*Death, Sleep & The Traveler* is told by its central character, the middle-aged Dutchman Allert Vanderveenan. . . . The scenes flow by with cinematic rapidity, in an apparently capricious but deliberate order that juxtaposes Allert's home life, his shipboard romance, and his dreams. These last are especially remarkable; convincing, revealing, original yet strikingly familiar—as vividly distorted reflections of life as the oiled veins of grotesque musclemen or the reverberations of an electronic piano. The past masters of the evocative dream, Nabokov and Ingmar Bergman, have simply been surpassed. . . .

But dreams that seem real are only the other side of the familiar true coin of any Hawkes novel, the reality that seems a dream. Moments when time stands still, or stretches, or snaps. The superclean heat and eucalyptus of a log-cabin sauna in Scandinavian winter; the bleaching brilliance of a midsummer Mediterranean beach . . .; the smell of the reptile house in the zoo. . . . Hawkes's world shimmers with a kind of dazed but fullbodied sensuality that leaves our nerve-ends ringing.

If Hawkes has a fault, it lies in his dallying with an occasional image that functions solely at the symbolic level. Here he can be heavyhanded. . . .

But these are minor mannerisms. Hawkes's comic sensuality is the product of an Apollonian mind and a Dionysian sensibility.

*Charles Nicol, "In The Dream," in* National Review *(150 East 35th St., New York, N.Y. 10016), June, 1974, pp. 659-60.*

God simply meant from the start that John Hawkes should be a "difficult" writer and that is simply what Hawkes is. He has a habit of putting more into a novel than even the most alert reader can absorb in one reading—and when he is at his best, as in *The Beetle Leg* and *The Lime Twig,* more than most of us can soak up in two or three. All he tries for is [to] make the language do what it hasn't done before and he strains it to the limit. . . .

Hawkes seems to me to be at his best when he is closest to the spirit of the grotesque painters—Bosch to Brueghel to Goya—whose work is so full of the stuff that "black humor" and "surrealism" and "neo-picaresque" are made [of]. . . . The juxtaposed incongruities and monstrosities and enigmatic figures in the paintings have the same effect that Hawkes has, in his earlier writing, where he delights and thoroughly disconcerts his reader all at the same time. I deeply regret that *Death, Sleep & The Traveler* . . . disconcerts me far too little. . . . There is some satisfaction, of course, in knowing that here is at least one Hawkes novel that will make reviewers drop the worn cliché of "nightmare," but much less in having to report that instead of being simultaneously frightened, delighted, amused, and disconcerted I've been doing a puzzle I couldn't completely solve.

*David Dillon, "How Hawkes's Humor Works," in* Southwest Review, *Summer, 1974, pp. 330-34.*

[In *Death, Sleep & The Traveler*] and in *The Blood Oranges*. . ., there is a good deal of unmistakable triviality beneath the glitter of the artful language. I don't think we can complain about the glitter itself, precious as it sometimes seems ("The light of the first stars purled impossibly through the last light of the day"), because the glitter *is* the style, the perfect vehicle for Hawkes's fastidiously upsetting effects. . . .

We can't complain about the pompous and disagreeable tone of all Hawkes's recent narrators (and several of his characters), because their stately and indestructible self-absorption is precisely what allows them to survive in the universe of menace and distress which they inhabit. But the concerns that animate these people—performing and watching intercourse, sharing lovers, swopping wives, collecting pornography, and describing their stilted and rather stale philosophies of life—are surely not the most urgent of subjects for a major novelist, which Hawkes undoubtedly is. Hawkes strikes me as a writer who started out as if he were going to become Kafka and turned into something between Henry Miller and Virginia Woolf on the way. Of course, neither Miller nor Woolf is a negligible figure, and of course I don't mean to suggest that the private life is not a subject for fiction any more, or that Hawkes has to take on the holocaust every time he writes. And of course, *any* subject becomes what the writer makes of it. But still, *Death, Sleep & The Traveler* and *The Blood Oranges,* striking, personal, and assured as they are, remain rather wispy works, have the air of dazzling exercises performed on the edge of nothing. The eerie, luminous images of these two books are lost in almost empty narrative space; great songs in search of an opera; brief poems looking for a play.

*Michael Wood, in* The New York Review of Books *(reprinted with permission from* The New York Review of Books; *© 1974 by NYREV, Inc.), August 8, 1974, p. 41.*

* * *

## HÉBERT, Anne 1916-

**A French-Canadian poet, novelist, and playwright, Anne Hébert now lives in Paris.**

I myself cannot appreciate . . . the poetry of Anne Hébert. [She tends] to run to half-prose strophes that remind me of Paul Claudel—a writer I temperamentally so much dislike that I suppose I cannot do him justice, and so perhaps cannot do [her] justice; just as I am possibly handicapped by my indifference to William Carlos Williams, in appreciating the current work of the English Canadian poets. This kind of half-prose *vers libre,* from Claudel to Paul Éluard, leaves me cold when it is written in France itself, and the language of the poets mentioned above, with its abstraction and its purified metaphors that do not seem to refer to anything in their actual Canadian world, inflicts on me a mortal chill that seems to freeze my very hand and prevent it from turning the page. . . .

The fiction of Anne Hébert does take us into the *maisons seigneuriales* and other recognizable Canadian places, but these, too, are rather stripped. And we are partly in a realm of dream. In *Les Chambres de Bois,* much admired by some, a young girl "of the people" is captured and married by the scion of the local mansion, a somewhat sinister place, which "smells of wet ferns and the cedar wardrobe." Young Michel is a dilettante, who paints a little and plays the piano and indulges himself in imaginings of becoming a concert performer. He has a morbid aversion to daylight. In marrying the flattered Catherine, he is trying to secure for himself something "solid and sweet" to nourish his own anemia. But he can only depress and starve her. . . . (The fact that we never know exactly where the story is taking place is characteristic of one kind of French Canadian fiction. The family life described could hardly belong in any country except French Canada, yet Michel and his wife at one point seem to make a trip to southern France. These old-line French Canadians in their cultural enclave on the North American continent do not always quite know where they are.) . . . They have no visitors, no friends, no children. Poor Catherine does not know what to do with herself. Michel neglects to consummate the marriage till his wife breaks down one day and accuses him of not really loving her. After trying to prove by action that he does, he turns on her as something unclean. . . .

But now something more plausible happens—I mean more plausible from the outsider's point of view: I am not prepared to say that the story told above is impossible. Catherine . . . meets a handsome young man, of whom it is muttered by her servant that he is "heavy and obstinate, a true peasant." . . . They fall in love, and he asks her to marry him. The reader of French Canadian novels, which usually end in frustration, may expect that Catherine's inhibitions will prevent her from divorcing her husband, but after spending a night with the lusty young man, . . . she agreeably surprises this reader by telling her lover that she "consents to become his wife." She . . . gives Michel back his ring and goes to join her lover. In the literature of French Canada, this ending is unusually cheerful. A vibration from *Lady Chatterley* has perhaps now been felt in Quebec.

*Edmund Wilson, in his* O Canada: An American's Notes on Canadian Culture *(reprinted with the permission of Farrar, Straus & Giroux, Inc.; copyright © 1964, 1965 by Edmund Wilson), Farrar, Straus, 1965, pp. 123-27.*

Anne Hébert arrived at her view of poetry through a painful exploration of her own imaginative world, discovering gradually that her personal imprisonment in silence, her sense of isolation and paralysis, was shared by others and was indeed a reflection of a cultural paralysis, a collective vision bequeathed by the past. She came to recognize and reject the past, in the rapacious kings who, in "Le Tombeau des rois", propagate themselves through her; in the wraith-like Michel, who secludes his bride in the closed rooms of the novel *Les chambres de bois* and cannot bring himself to consummate their marriage; in *La grande Claudine,* the bitter, puritanical and fierce jailor to her son François who begins the story "Le Torrent" by saying, "I was a child born dispossessed of the world."

For Anne Hébert, rejecting the old vision and going on to

articulate a new, was again a liberation and a birth into the world. It was a living demonstration of the transforming power of the word. . . .

Anne Hébert managed to effect an imaginative revolution without cutting herself off entirely from her cultural heritage. She re-interpreted the Christian tradition of her province giving new stress to the *incarnation* of the Word, to the figure of Adam making articulate the Word incarnate, naming and praising the world, to the communion of all life realized in and through the word. And this was doubly possible because she could see in the religious experience defined in these theological concepts the analogy to her experience of poetry. . . .

The poet is not, she protests, the rival of God; but a witness to His grace. Perhaps she would concur with Coleridge in saying that the imagination is the repetition in the finite mind of the infinite "I am". Certainly it is difficult in Miss Hébert's view not to see him as the rival of the priest.

*D. G. Jones, "Myth, Frye and Canadian Writers," in* Canadian Literature, *Winter, 1973, pp. 14-16.*

I don't know how large a sum Miss Hébert received [with the Prix des Libraires, awarded for her novel *Kamouraska*] but I hope that it was substantial enough to permit both the purchase of Aristotle's "Rhetoric" and leisure time in which to underline those parts which stress the three directions which any discourse may take: rhetorical ethos, pathos, and logos with their accompanying emphases on the speaker's virtue, the audience's emotions, the discourse's coherent arrangement, respectively. . . .

In the midst of a consideration of a twentieth-century novel it may seem quaint to resurrect elements of classical rhetoric. Nevertheless, though classical rhetoric's consideration of the direction of a speech did not include the structure of novels, it does not seem irrelevant to demand of a novel that a narrator's emotional involvement both in herself and in her attempts to provoke emotion in the reader square in intensity with the theme and with the structuring of that theme through plot.

*Frank L. Ryan, in* Best Sellers, *August 1, 1973, p. 199.*

Gwendolyn Moore's translation [of *The Torrent*] is faithful, but too literal. The ghost of the French syntax lurks behind all her sentences and besides *certain* and *parfait*—those two *bêtes noires* of all translators—entire phrases, such as *un édifice parfait de regularité,* are given their exact English equivalents.

*The Torrent* deserves better than this awkward translation into peculiar English. The stories are all carefully worked miniatures which outline the boundaries of Hébert's artistic world. It is a limited one, in which humans struggle more with themselves than with social forces outside their control. But what Hébert loses in breadth, she gains in depth.

*Brian Vintcent, "Hébert in Awkward English," in* Saturday Night, *February, 1974, pp. 34-5.*

## HELLMAN, Lillian 1905-

**Ms Hellman is a prize-winning American dramatist. Most of her plays are set in or near New Orleans. (See also *Contemporary Authors*, Vols. 13-14.)**

In *Toys in the Attic,* Miss Hellman has picked up the sword of judgment many playwrights of the period have laid aside and wields it with renewed vigor. But this time, compassion guides her hand so that she performs surgery on her characters instead of summarily decapitating them, and she gives some heed, too, to the pathos of misunderstanding and the power of circumstance. The reach of compassion in the play extends even to an unseen character, a woman whose hatred for an unscrupulous husband and desire to get away from him at all costs lead her into a shoddy scheme for mulcting him of a small fortune in exchange for a piece of swamp land he needs for one of his speculations. This woman, who never appears on the stage although she is in league with the young hero of the play, Julian, is made as real as any character on the stage. . . .

Miss Hellman displays controlled artistry in this work. It contains excellent dialogue, incisive characterization, and a mature understanding of human attitudes, relationships, and drives. Even the faults of the play seemed contributive to its powerful effect. The first act is undoubtedly somewhat slow and meandering, but Miss Hellman has prepared us suspensively with this act for the mounting passions and tightly coiled spring of doom to be found in the rest of the play. . . .

It is the special merit of Lillian Hellman's work that dreadful things are done by the onstage characters out of affectionate possessiveness, rather than out of ingrained villainy. Although the author's corresponding view of life is ironic and is trenchantly expressed, there is no gloating over human misery, no horror-mongering, no traffic with sensationalism in *Toys in the Attic*. And, unlike some well-known contemporary playwrights here and abroad, Miss Hellman has proved once more that she can deal with human failure without falling in love with it herself. She remains admirably sane in the midst of the ugliness and confusion she so unerringly exposes. Although she looks at life steadily and unsentimentally, she does not advertise herself as a flinty cynic or hopeless nihilist.

*John Gassner, "Lillian Hellman's 'Toys in the Attic'" (1960), in his* Dramatic Soundings: Evaluations and Retractions Culled From 30 Years of Dramatic Criticism, *edited, with an introduction, by Glen Loney (© 1968 by Mollie Gassner; used by permission of Crown Publishers, Inc.), Crown Publishers, Inc., 1968, pp. 481-84.*

Restraints against theatrical pathos or satire are continuous but never predictable [in *Pentimento*], and disclaimers that begin "I don't remember" or "I don't know when I understood" precede any authoritative assurance of knowledge about anything. This is a kind of Faulknerian technique, though it is too instinctive to be called that, and to an extraordinary degree it makes the reader eager to accept whatever is finally confirmed, eager to be released into some extremities beyond that, into emotions and speculations on the other side of the words.

Behind Hellman's style is a strength so assured as to allow all of her subjects the fullest and freest working out of quite individual destinies. . . .

Efforts to determine, in relation to any given person, those limits of closeness which are sometimes the precondition of love can be felt in the wonderfully exploratory, tentative quality of Hellman's prose. . . .

[The] kinds of submerged continuity, the marvelous inner sense of connectedness, the ability to bring disparate things together . . . is the special genius of this book, with its subtle yet intensely clarified grasp of possible analogies between quite different places, different people and different times. . . .

*Pentimento* provides one of those rare instances when the moral value of a book is wholly inextricable from its immense literary worth, where the excitations, the pacing, and the intensifications offered by the style manage to create in us perceptions about human character that have all but disappeared from contemporary writing.

*Richard Poirier, in* Book World—The Washington Post (© The Washington Post), *September 16, 1973, pp. 1, 4-5.*

It is now apparent that *An Unfinished Woman* was the beginning—a try-out, if you will, and more hesitant than arrogant—of a new career for Lillian Hellman. Her . . . memoir, *Pentimento: A Book of Portraits*. . ., is its realization. Approaching 70, she has developed a way to do autobiography perfectly suited to her special strengths, and has written a totally absorbing and marvelous book that is, in its coherence and control and electric passion, a masterpiece on the order of her very best plays. What seemed unfinished or ungenerous in the first book is explored and resolved here. To hitch an examination of friends and memories, an analysis of intense feelings, an intention of scrupulous but focused honesty and accountability, to an engine of calculated dramatic rise and fall and suspenseful force is a risky venture; but this train fairly roars. . . .

[One] of several main themes that run through the book [is] how one saw, sees, recovers, integrates the past. . . .

*Pentimento* is . . . a work of extraordinary richness and candor and self-perception, and triumph enough considering the courage such a book requires, a courage that lies, Lillian Hellman shows by example, far deeper than one is usually inclined to credit.

*Eliot Fremont-Smith, "Lillian Hellman: Portrait of a Lady," in* New York Magazine *(© 1973 by NYM Corp.; reprinted by permission of* New York Magazine *and Eliot Fremont-Smith), September 17, 1973, p. 82.*

The dramatic quality is everywhere evident [in *Pentimento*], not only in the background of social intrigue before which many of these lives are enacted, but rather more importantly in the author's exquisite sense of timing, a kind of poised power over the units of scene that few writers of fiction possess. But there is also the extraordinary gift for the precise detail, which is a fictional quality, and then again, for the often comically explicit detail. . . . She seems always to find precisely the right word, the right combination. . . .

[She] writes what seems to me a prose as brilliantly finished as any that we have in these years.

*Mark Schorer, in* The New York Times Book Review *(© 1973 by The New York Times Company; reprinted by permission), September 23, 1973, pp. 1-2.*

It would be pleasant to report that Hellman writes her memoirs in the same forthright, energetic fashion as she apparently lived her life. Alas, not so. Four years ago, she published a quirky, episodic volume called *An Unfinished Woman*. Her new book [*Pentimento*] covers different material in the form of portraits of people whom she loved at one time or other, plus a chapter about life in the theater and an anomalous, charming piece about a snapping turtle. . . .

It is a rather sad irony that the book should be called *Pentimento,* an artist's term for an old image that reappears through later repainting done on a canvas. Singular and moving memories flicker everywhere, but few emerge clearly. . . .

The writing often recalls Gertrude Stein's stonier prose—obdurate, flat and mannered. Hellman is a virtuoso of ellipsis, a quality that doubtless served her well as a dramatist. In *Pentimento* she seems to take pride in leaving out connectives, or capping a half-told tale with a brief coda, unrelated except for the faintest resonance of tone.

*Martha Duffy, "Half-Told Tales," in* Time *(reprinted by permission from* Time, The Weekly Newsmagazine; *copyright Time Inc.), October 1, 1973, pp. 114-16.*

All well-made memoirs have holes in them, holes where large areas of experience have been cut away. Either the author is unwilling to write about parts of his life, or he perceives these parts as digressions and knows that to pursue them would be to distort the design of the whole. Lillian Hellman's memoir "An Unfinished Woman" was just such an artful book. . . . Her emphasis [in *Pentimento*] is on the memoir as narrative art. . . .

Hellman, as a playwright, was a remarkably strong storyteller; she sustains that difficult art throughout this translation into a different, perhaps equally demanding genre.

*Peter S. Prescott, "Leftover Life," in* Newsweek *(copyright Newsweek, Inc., 1973; reprinted by permission), October 1, 1973, pp. 95-6.*

The portraits in [*Pentimento: A Book of Portraits*] seem to be tied in with a search for self-understanding. As Miss Hellman sorts out her memories and her conflicts, she reconsiders her relationships and we see her edging toward a Chekovian moment of truth. But she never quite makes it for she is a scrupulous editor. . . .

It is all very complex, interesting, exciting, and just a little sad. Not too much so, for throughout she displays with the brilliance of hindsight, a delightful sense of buoyancy toward the seemingly unaccountable vicissitudes of her life.

*Clara M. Siggins, in* Best Sellers, *October 1, 1973, p. 303.*

Lillian Hellman has found her richest subject—the study of herself—and her true *métier* as a writer of very good prose. . . .

*Pentimento* extends the recollections she commenced in her first book [*An Unfinished Woman*] and demonstrates even more persuasively that nothing in the polychrome brilliance of her life is quite so interesting as the fierce-spirited, impetuous, loving, ambivalent woman at its center. . . .

*Pentimento* is a triumphant vindication of the stories the author threw away in her twenties because they were "no good." These complex, controlled narratives profit from the dramatist's instinct for climax and immediate, sharp characterization; but they have an emotional purity her plays have generally lacked. Self-scrutiny has replaced moral fervor, to the benefit of art. In *An Unfinished Woman,* Hellman admitted wasting too much time trying to find "truth" and "sense" in the world. However, her private and public history during a period of troubling contradictions—her recklessness, her ardor, even her confusions—personify much of the real truth about it.

*Muriel Haynes, "More on the Unfinished Woman," in* Ms.*, January, 1974, pp. 31-2.*

*Pentimento* is not, as American reviewers have unwisely said, a marvel and a masterpiece and a book full of perceptions about human character. It is, rather, a collection of sketches of a fairly familiar kind, which blend real people known to history and Lillian Hellman, like Tallulah Bankhead and Sam Goldwyn and Dashiell Hammett, with people known only by their Christian names in the book, who may be real or partly fictionalized. It is not 'a masterpiece on the order of her two best plays' (nor are her best plays masterpieces, but well-ordered and well-executed middlebrow pieces about the Problem of Lesbianism, the Dangers of Nazism, etc.), but a work containing many slabs of prefabricated near-Hemingway, which ambles around any given subject in a way that owes much more to casualness than to art.

Yet when one has gone so far so disobligingly, it has to be added that the personal effect Lillian Hellman produces through this book and 'An Unfinished Woman' is one of charm and candour. A lot of the writing may be secondhand, but she is original. She may make the real figures of her youth seem highly fictional, but what never fails to come across is the excitement with which she responds to them.

*Julian Symons, "Drunk, But Not Disorderly," in* London Magazine, *August/September, 1974, p. 137-38.*

* * *

## HIGGINS, George V(incent) 1940?-

**Higgins, a criminal lawyer and an assistant U.S. attorney, is now becoming an important crime novelist.**

After the flood of books in recent years that have made crime seem either the epitome of glamour and adventure in modern life, or else just one huge joke, this first novel ["The Friends of Eddie Coyle"] by—of all people—a U.S. District Attorney, comes as, among other things, a relief. There is nothing glamorous or humorous about Eddie Coyle, and nothing remotely adventurous about the life he leads. It is seamy; it is drab. . . .

Flat, toneless, and positively reeking of authenticity. Higgins tells the story of Eddie and his friends through dialogue; and he tells it swiftly and well. Characterization is at a minimum. All of Eddie's friends . . . seem not so much individuals as facets of the same personality. Rather than a weakness, I suspect that this may well be Higgins's main point.

I don't know what kind of lawyer George Higgins is, but I know now that he's a writer. With "The Friends of Eddie Coyle," he's given us the most penetrating glimpse yet into what seems the real world of crime. . . .

*Joe McGinniss, in* The New York Times Book Review *(© 1972 by The New York Times Company; reprinted by permission), February 6, 1972, pp. 7, 22.*

George V. Higgins won't like the way reviewers are going to scrawl "genre" all over ["The Digger's Game"]. He told an interviewer he doesn't think he's writing crime stories. He says he's writing "about people, a number of whom have a tendency to break the law." He's right. But most reviewers are unredeemable pigeonholers, and there is probably no way to stop them from winging "The Digger's Game" toward the slots marked "Crime Novel" and "Underworld Fiction." (His own publisher is already guilty.) This categorizing is unfortunate, for Higgins has done more than write a fast, gripping story about Boston's underworld. He has created in the Digger a deeply touching character who can make you weep with laughter and with sorrow and, one way or another, would be equally moving if he were out of crime and struggling for survival in a bank or an automobile factory. . . .

As in "The Friends of Eddie Coyle," Higgins's first novel, the dialogue here is perfect. The descriptive prose is something else again. There's not much of it, but what there is reads like Dick and Jane. Perhaps Higgins, like the Digger, knows his limitations and is trying unsuccessfully to keep things simple and stay out of trouble. Or maybe he's trying for low-key, throwaway drama. In any case, the effect is boring at first, then annoying.

*James Mills, in* The New York Times Book Review *(© 1973 by The New York Times Company; reprinted by permission), March 25, 1973, pp. 2-3.*

This book [*The Digger's Game*], the most inneresting thing is the grammar. They don't dig, you remember Sister Aloysius used to call them, subordinating conjunctions. You need a subordinate clause, you write is like that, hack it? What the ----, they don't write it, they say it. This Higgins, works days as a Mass. assistant DA, he writes it down nights. He writes a book before, *The Friends of Eddie Coyle,* I didn't read it, it sells like strawberry-flavored muffin. Think I'm kidding, there ain't no such thing, you read this new book. Open your eyes. Course there's more about money than muffin. This Digger Doherty, brother a priest, he don't cheat on his old lady, not since the last time. Must be the only guy ever come back from Vegas without getting laid. Dropped eighteen K there. His brother, he don't want to stay in an old priests' home when he retires, thirty big ones he gives the Digger, is all. Digger, he done a job for the rest. The book ends, he's off to San Juan with the old lady leaving the four kids home, don't know this guy Harrington's singing to the FBI. Some guys, they fall down in a jewelry store, they come up covered in crud. The other hand, there's this Greek shoots Torrey, the muffin man, fixing to shoot him. One chapter, you got these guineas, like in *The Godfather,* they speak grammar the way Sister Aloysius down to St. Joseph's taught us. Rest of the chapters, there's a bunch of Micks like you, me, and the Greek. Way I figure it, long as Higgins can stand to write like this, they're goin' to keep reading. Better than knocking over a bank, anyways. Me, I read maybe one, maybe two more, then I start getting pissed off.

*Vivian Mercier, in* World *(copyright © 1973 by Saturday Review/World, Inc.; reprinted with permission), March 27, 1973, p. 57.*

George Higgins, I submit, is the most hard-boiled of American crime novelists. Hammett, Chandler and Macdonald stuff their fiction with commendable quantities of death and realism, but their private operators—cynical vigilantes who wearily consider our corrupt species as it sinks into affectlessness and avarice—are essentially romantic, more than a little sentimental. Higgins, by contrast, writes comedies about the peculiar claustrophobia of the life of organized crime in Boston. He forgoes sentimentality, private eyes and innocent victims to write exclusively of criminals who work on each other in a community where sin is less talked of than are mistakes: presumptuousness, a change of allegiance, a falling off from competence. When his hoods philosophize, as they are ever ready to do, they impress us with the brevity of inarticulateness. . . .

Higgins's novels bear two unmistakable identifying marks: first, they are told almost entirely in a dialogue so faithful to the fractured syntax of the characters that we must strain to figure out what is going on; second, the narrative, the criminal design, winds twistingly around a series of set pieces in which the action is suspended, often for chapters at a time, while the gangsters talk about sex and marriage, their weight and root-canal work. To these people the banal frustrations of life are more important than the taking of it. This is a fine comic device, and Higgins's stylized stories are the most entertaining of their kind.

*Peter S. Prescott, "Talking Shop in the Mob," in* Newsweek *(copyright Newsweek, Inc., 1974; reprinted by permission), March 25, 1974, p. 99.*

Higgins is not what he seems to be. Melvin Maddocks tagged him "a new boss of bullet-lettres," but he is really a local-color novelist wrapped in a crime writer's hide. Imagine Sarah Orne Jewett fresh from a Dorchester brothel or John Millington Synge exiled to Charlestown, and you have classy literary equivalents for Higgins' kind of writing. To distant readers his revelations of life among the Boston lowly must have some of the fascination attached to exposés of Parisian apaches or New York mafiosi; but for readers who come from Boston themselves, the experience is more complex. . . .

It's Boston all right, mentally and physically, and those who have been there can echo George Bernard Shaw's description of *Ulysses* as "a repulsive but accurate picture of Ireland." Higgins has now exploited this world for three novels. His forte is the small-time criminal off duty, rapping with his wife and his fellows, and Higgins develops their monologues almost ritually. When the coster isn't jumping on his mother, we are told, he loves to lie a-basking in the sun; but in Boston, hoods spend much of their time worrying—about money, about their wives, about how their kids are turning out, about bills to pay and cars to buy and deals to arrange—and the rest of their time they reminisce about former jobs and old associates and incredible encounters with wondrously expensive and skillful whores. Higgins evokes clearly a bleak and continually changing world: kids grow up, customs change, new men take over from the dying or incompetent old men, power changes hands, deals succeed or fail, and most of this happens among stupid and cornered people. . . .

Higgins' world, however, is a very hermetic one. We so seldom see ordinary citizens that they come as a surprise when they appear; we don't even see many policemen; we are locked into the milieu of petty crooks who take their orders from invisible authorities—ultimately from the Providence of the Patriarcas—and who perform their violence among themselves. . . .

The action is almost tangential. The characters exist primarily to deliver their long monologues (one, on stealing and disposing of dogs, is a fine Faulknerian comic piece), and when they finally turn to action in the closing chapters it's almost a disappointment.

After three novels, it becomes apparent that Higgins is dealing with dangerous material. His mode is realism, and his topic is the banality of evil; the result too often is banal reality, as Paddy Chayevsky demonstrated a few years ago. One thinks again of Shaw on *Ulysses*: "a fidelity so ruthless that it is hardly bearable." But of course the reader of crime novels knows that Higgins has a special place, and he will read all he can. It's a mistake not to.

*J. D. O'Hara, in* The New Republic *(reprinted by permission of* The New Republic; *© 1974 by The New Republic, Inc.), March 30, 1974, pp. 26-7.*

When George V. Higgins's first novel, "The Friends of Eddie Coyle," made its debut two years ago, it was clear that Higgins had broken new ground in tapping the perennial lodestone of crime novels. Higgins . . . displayed unique virtuosity in exploiting an uncanny ear for the argot of the underworld. His ability to capture its textures and rhythms in fiction without losing authenticity immediately established him as an impressive chronicler of the life style and mores of the small-time hoodlum for whom crime is the only thing that does pay. Moreover, for those of us who are aficionados of the genre it was a rare example of a member of the law and order establishment probing without pious conclusions or clinical transparency the behavioral and mental sets of the petty thief and murderer.

Higgins's second novel, "The Digger's Game" . . . turned out to be not quite so cohesive as "Eddie Coyle." Nonetheless, it was another engrossing and original portrayal of criminals and the peculiar crosses they have to bear. Once again, an integral part of the writing was the tough, realistic, right-on-target dialogue of the underworld.

Now, along comes "Cogan's Trade." . . .

The fascination of the book is not the heist itself, but the unclocking of the *modus operandi* of a particularly nasty segment of society. There are absolutely no good guys. None. And in this particular jungle there are no innocents. He who gets hurt deserves it in one way or another. Is that perhaps the cop in Higgins coming out?

In addition to the usual burdens, this novel also must suffer the inescapable baggage of comparison with its two predecessors, the more so because of the continuity of subject matter. "Cogan's Trade" uses to excess what dazzled us in the first two. The argot takes over so completely that the first third of the book is practically impossible to understand without benefit of prior exposure to the other two novels and/or a really first-rate dictionary of slang.

This is a pity, because reader perseverance ultimately is rewarded with yet another special portrait of a world of petty professionals that is often as funny as it is frightening. Indeed, midway there is a cool-*cum*-zany description of the exigencies of dognapping (as opposed to kidnapping) that uses the jargon to perfection. Until then, we are slogging through a foreign country where the language is not easy to pick up, even if we've read the earlier works. The flaw in "Cogan" is that there is not enough of our mother tongue to keep confusion at bay.

Argot aside, there are other aspects of the underworld that I, for one, would like to see Higgins turn his perceptive eye to exploring more fully. One is the role of women. In all three books women are shadowed background; passive participants, either whores or faithful wives. . . .

Another is the role played by prison. Higgins makes much peripherally of prison as a communications channel, a mainline medium useful in setting up the next job. The correctional institution is as much a recruiter for the big caper as a place of punishment. But the treatment is oblique, and the players are only seen on the "outside."

For all its flaws, "Cogan's Trade" extends Higgins's cultural digs into the seamy nether-world of the savage seventies. Time now to turn his not inconsiderable talents to another part of the jungle.

*O. L. Bailey, in* The New York Times Book Review *(© 1974 by The New York Times Company; reprinted by permission), March 31, 1974, p. 10.*

George V. Higgins is the master stylist of the current generation of serious thriller writers. In fact, the reader can lose his way in a Higgins novel unless the premise of style is accepted. Like James Joyce, Higgins plumbs and replumbs one geographic locale. His Dublin is the dark underside of Boston and its suburbs. Like Joyce, Higgins uses language in torrents, beautifully crafted, ultimately intending to create a panoramic impressionism. The plot of a Higgins novel—suspense, humor and tragedy—is a blurrily perceived skeleton within the monsoon of dialogue.

*Cogan's Trade* is as remorselessly inevitable as Higgins's two earlier novels, *The Friends of Eddie Coyle* and *The Digger's Game*. . . .

As a novel, *Cogan's Trade* is a brilliant exposition of Higgins's Boston underworld as the flip side of all respectable lives of desperation. As a thriller it is that taut story whose drama is heightened by our own understanding of how it has to end.

We know what's coming. We don't know who will be blasted into eternity or what logic will finally prevail. But George Higgins reminds us all over again that the passage from here to the finale is an erratic and inconclusive journey whose meaning is only known in its final arrival—if at all.

*Roderick MacLeish, "Improper Bostonians," in* Book World—The Washington Post (© The Washington Post), *March 31, 1974, p. 3.*

Higgins is a miniaturist, and at his best a Fragonard of the nefarious. But in *Cogan's Trade* he is not quite at his best. He spends too much time away from his strongest character and sputters four-letter words until some pages read like excerpts from a washroom wall. Talk is his forte, and the talk in this book is uninspired. But the action is sharp, and Higgins provides some hilarious glimpses of the home life of the North American gorilla—one thug is on cortisone for colitis, another takes a contract because his wife needs some root-canal work. Cogan himself is a memorable meanie, easily the reptile of the month.

*Brad Darrach, "Reptile of the Month," in* Time *(reprinted by permission from* Time, The Weekly Newsmagazine; *copyright Time Inc.), April 1, 1974, pp. E4, 87.*

*Cogan's Trade* is 90 per cent dialogue; there can't be 15 pages of narrative in 200, unless you add up the "he saids." . . . It's authentic yet, excuse me, it's the same authentic. Some authentics in this world, even hoods, use complete sentences, but you couldn't tell from Higgins. There are eight or ten characters in *Cogan's Trade* and it's all one guy. . . .

Higgins' narrative . . . gets inserted on special occasions like a table leaf. . . .

But you're inclined to forgive. Higgins' monologist, all dozen of him, is a funny man. . . . *Cogan's Trade* has the effect of a well told elaborate dialect joke. . . . This isn't exactly news; it's Higgins' schtick, he's been at it since *The Friends of Eddie Coyle*. A Higgins book is predictable. . . .

*Cogan's Trade* has a governor on it. The words are reproduced with stereophonic high fidelity, yet the people don't talk to each other. They explain, yes; but they can't persuade or beg or cry out. . . . Higgins can't manage emotion or conflict, and it hamstrings him.

The plot is an erector set with maybe seven pieces: scaffolding for conversations. Higgins can educate. He knows the etiquette of contract killing and dognapping. You will have fun with *Cogan's Trade,* crime seems to improve the sense of humor. But Higgins is in jeopardy. A sweet trick can become addictive. He'd better go cold turkey, write something very different, very fast, even under a pseudonym. One *Cogan's Trade* every year for 30 years is a life sentence, not an oeuvre.

*D. Keith Mano, "Boston Laconic," in* National Review *(150 East 35th St., New York, N.Y. 10016), June, 1974, p. 655.*

Mr. Higgins [is] the Balzac of the Boston Underworld. . . . [*Cogan's Trade* documents] shallow, scummy lives, but they are presented seriously, at their own level, and without a trace of condescending irony. The ideal form for the occupational novel is dialogue, and Mr. Higgins has become the finest dialogist of our time. His anxious characters gossip about cars and women and money and food and dentistry and gambling and raising children and the troubles of marriages that must be sustained through long prison sentences, and the talk—full of elisions, interruptions, obscenities, doublings-back, pauses, ruminations, interior quotes, repetitions, and incomprehensibilities—touches us with a thrilling intimacy. In his field, George V. Higgins is now in competition only with himself, and this, his third novel, is also his best.

The New Yorker, *June 24, 1974, pp. 103-04.*

* * *

## HIGHSMITH, (Mary) Patricia 1921-

**Ms Highsmith is an American-born novelist now living in France. Low-key, realistic, and carefully wrought, her tales of murder are terrifyingly plausible. (See also *Contemporary Authors*, Vols. 1-4, rev. ed.)**

It is difficult to find ways of praising Patricia Highsmith that do not at the same time do something to diminish her. To say that among crime writers she is extraordinarily subtle, wise and complicated is by now a reviewer's commonplace. With each new book, she is ritually congratulated for outstripping the limitations of her genre, for being as much concerned with people and ideas as with manipulated incident, for attempting a more than superficial exploration of the psychopathology of her unpleasant heroes—for, in short, exhibiting some of the gifts and preoccupations which are elementarily demanded of competent straight novelists. She is the crime writer who comes closest to giving crime writing a good name.

And this is not a contemptible niche. In a field where imitative hacks and dull formula-mongers abound it might seem easy enough to achieve some measure of distinctiveness, but Miss Highsmith's distinctiveness is of a special kind: it has to do not with strategies but with sensibility. From her first novel, *Strangers on a Train,* right through to her latest [in 1971], *Ripley Under Ground,* she has persistently used the crime story as a means of revealing and examining her own deepest interests and obsessions. . . .

In *Strangers on a Train* Miss Highsmith demonstrated a fairly conventional moral attitude towards her characters—Bruno and Guy both meet sticky ends, and although (in the case of Guy, at any rate) one can hardly detect any overt condemnation, there is throughout the book a clear suggestion that the only possible outcome of all this is a disastrous one. With Ripley, she has a clear affection for her hero; he is the least sinister of her murderers. Miss Highsmith has often been accused of carrying her identification with her psychopathic characters to the point where she actually seems to be preferring their interesting evil to the mediocre virtue of their victims. In a sense this is true, but only in the Milton-preferred-Satan sense. One of Miss Highsmith's most remarkable gifts is her ability to chart the moral consciousness of the immoral; her killer heroes *do* have consciences, they do tend obsessively to examine and question their behaviour, but at the centre of even their most intricate self-interrogations there is a crucial blankness, a missing ingredient, an impassable limitation, and it is this that makes it possible for them to kill. Nearly all Miss Highsmith's murders are conducted in a chilling, dead-pan fashion, with the murderer seeming to view what he is up to as a mere job of work, to be done with neatness and efficiency—it might seem squeamishly obliging of her that few of her murder victims feel pain when they are killed, but this is really just another of her ways of signalling the killers' deadly anaesthesia. . . .

[A] general susceptibility to received formulas (and not just the received formulas of crime writing) does tend to pervade her work and to render it persistently uneven. The strenuously touristy employment of foreign settings, the slackly contrived coincidences, the slovenly dealing with minor characters, the often effortful knotting of loose ends —much of what seems mechanical and manufactured in Miss Highsmith surely derives from *her* awareness that what she is writting is; finally, just another crime book. To say merely that it never is quite that is certainly to cheat her of the tribute that her gifts deserve, but until she does break out in some complete and ambitious way she will go on cheating herself.

*"The Talented Miss Highsmith," in* The Times Literary Supplement *(reproduced by permission), September 24, 1971, pp. 1147-48.*

The writer who fuses characters and plot most successfully is Patricia Highsmith. . ., the most important crime novelist at present in practice. . . . Perhaps it should be added that Highsmith is an acquired taste, which means a taste that some never acquire. . . .

Most of Highsmith's books have their origin in some sensational idea. In her first novel, *Strangers on a Train* (1949), a young man who meets another on a train proposes that each of them shall murder a person whom the other wishes to see dead. Since neither killer will have any connection with his victim, there is no reason why these should not be "perfect murders." In *The Blunderer* (1954), a clumsy amateur killer sets out to copy a crime committed by a more professional one and finds himself being pursued by the murderer. Such tricky plot devices are often used by very inferior writers. . ., but in Highsmith's hands they are starting points for profound and subtle character studies. She recurs often to the attraction exerted on the weak by the idea of violence. In *The Two Faces of January* (1964), when the emotionally footloose Rydal Keener sees the petty crook Chester MacFarland kill a man, his immediate reaction is to attach himself to Chester and his wife rather than to report the affair to the police. In the opening scene of *Those Who Walk Away* (1967), Ray Garrett is shot at and wounded by Coleman, but again his reaction is to link himself more closely to the would-be murderer rather than to attempt to escape from him. It may be said that this is not true to "life," but this means only that it is not the way most people would behave. It is true and convincing in the life of Highsmith characters, who find themselves linked to each other by the idea of crime. There are no more genuine agonies in modern literature than those endured by the couples in her books who are locked together in a dislike and even hatred that often strangely contains love. . . .

Without being directly concerned with politics, Highsmith implicitly suggests that in a society where most people are imprisoned within the mechanisms of organizations, social groups, or families, criminals are potentially free. Her heroes are therefore often criminals, heroic in the sense that they are the most likable people in the story. . . .

But it is not the ideas behind her books so much as the intensity and skill with which they are presented that make her such a rewarding novelist. The original ideas on which her plots are based are sometimes far-fetched and in her early work much marked by coincidence, but she treats them with an imaginative power that gives the problems of the criminal hero a terrifying reality. Her settings—Venice, Crete, Tunis—are chosen with care. In strange surroundings her characters become uncertain of their personalities and begin to question the reasons for their own conduct. She has a professional ability to order a plot and create a significant environment, but what takes her books beyond the run of intelligent crime stories is the intensity of feeling brought to the central figures. Violence is necessary to her, because the threat or actuality of it produces her best writing, and the problem she faces in relation to its use is a way of coordinating sensationalism of theme with subtlety of treatment as she has not always been able to do in the past. The deadly games of pursuit played in her best novels are as subtle and interesting as anything being done in the novel today.

*Julian Symons, in his* Mortal Consequences: A History—From the Detective Story to the Crime Novel *(copyright © 1972 by Julian Symons; reprinted by permission of Harper & Row, Publishers, Inc.), Harper, 1972, pp. 182-84.*

In the chilling, clinical presentation of a wholly twisted world Miss Highsmith has managed an achievement—the creation of an ambience—perhaps superior to that of the early Eric Ambler novels.

But there is something else about her work, which came over even more strongly in conversation than it does on the printed page. Miss Highsmith is an excellent hater, and however patiently she unravels the criminal motivations of her characters, and with however much sympathy she delineates them, there is a powerful rage for justice always to be sensed just beneath the surface. "I hate," she said, "the Mafia above all" and, in *Ripley's Game* there is a clear distinction drawn between different kinds of baddie, different kinds of evil. Her instinct seems to be that, the normal world—the world of good policemen, good detectives, good heroes—being unable to assert itself against the underworld, the underworld itself must find some way of keeping order. And behind the perception lies another awareness that dominates her books—the awareness of nemesis. As in a tragedy events seem to acquire a momentum of their own, so that as the villains weave their webs, the reader can sense an approaching, impersonal doom. The extraordinary power and intensity with which this sense of doom and nemesis is sustained throughout a book is the most distinguishing mark of the Highsmith creation, probably the most consistently excellent body of work of its kind produced since the war.

*"Crime Compendium," in* The Spectator *(© 1974 by* The Spectator; *reprinted by permission of* The Spectator*), March 23, 1974, p. 366.*

It is some years since, in *The Talented Mr. Ripley,* Patricia Highsmith created her monstrous paranoiac Tom Ripley, who reappears yet again in *Ripley's End,* to satisfy his megalomaniacal *ego* by perpetrating a string of unnecessary, messy and sadistic murders and destroying the body and soul of a casual acquaintance, Jonathan Trevanny, who is already dying of an incurable disease, and whose only offence is the complete moral gutlessness which makes him a suitable toy for the odious Ripley to amuse himself with.

In her first novel, *Strangers on a Train,* Miss Highsmith handled a brilliantly ingenious plot with psychological insight and a craftsman's mastery of words. The craftmanship is still there, but something very sad is happening to the talented Miss Highsmith, and unless she hardens her heart and puts an end to her horrible brain-child, for whom she appears to have conceived an inexplicable affection, the fate of Baron Frankenstein will be hers also.

*Tony Henderson, in* Books and Bookmen, *May, 1974, p. 84.*

* * *

## HILL, Susan B. 1942-

**Ms Hill, an English novelist, is considered a brilliant stylist. (See also *Contemporary Authors*, Vols. 33-36).**

Coming hard on the heels of Susan Hill's very considerable achievements in her most recent work, one expects great things from [*Strange Meeting*]. In many respects one gets them: the hard-edged prose, the painstaking detail, some aspects of the portrayal of Hilliard, and many of the minor characters. But the book has inbuilt defects that make it, in the final analysis, a failure. David Barton, everyone's golden boy, is neither credible nor sympathetic, despite heroic efforts to make him so; his family, who write him heartwarming letters and are frank and open and loving with one another, might have stepped from the pages of the late Godfrey Winn. The portrayal of the war is vivid but televisual. . . .

The radical weakness is, perhaps, a failure to realize any of the attitudes that people must have had in the situation at the Western Front.

*Diane Leclercq, in* Books and Bookmen, *January, 1972, pp. 61-2.*

A novel about the love between two men, "The Bird of Night" is by one of Britain's most gifted novelists. . . . This novel is sombre and wholly persuasive, and it gives insights into the dazzle of insanity that even a very good biography . . . fails to do. . . .

There are very few novels concerned with madness that are as compassionate or informed as this one. . . . It is also a calculatedly anti-academic novel, which is a very different thing from an anti-intellectual one. It is an affirmation of the intellect, of creativity and the generous mind; it is written with enormous skill and an absorbing and often heart-breaking intensity.

*Paul Theroux, in* The New York Times Book Review *(© 1973 by The New York Times Company; reprinted by permission), May 27, 1973, p. 16.*

Christianity does not feature much in fiction these days; but the truth is that there are still many people who find that certain experiences can be grasped only with the help of religious symbolism; and for these people, some kind of existential Christianity means a great deal, especially in times of crisis. The heroine of Susan Hill's new novel *In the Springtime of the Year* does not question the specifically Christian aspect of her experience; it is hardly rationalized, but deeply felt. Like everything else in this short, accurate book, it seems true: people are like that.

*Isabel Colegate, "A Year's Grief," in* New Statesman, *January 25, 1974, p. 121.*

*The Bird of Night* is . . . a triumph of the novelist's art. . . .

*The Bird of Night* lacks all those elements that automatically stamp a new novel as "profound" or "important," and worth noticing. What it has instead are qualities rarely found in contemporary fiction and apparently not much valued, which is a pity. It is a thoroughly *created* piece of work, a novel wrought of language carefully designed to tell a story drawn, not from the surface of the author's life or fragments of her autobiography, but from the heart of the imagination. . . .

What is remarkable about the book is the convincing portrayal of Francis both as poet and madman. Susan Hill gives us none of the poetry, only journal entries, indications of books read, scraps of worksheets and Harvey's analyses, but it works—with a little exercise of the reader's imagination. Francis Croft exists as a poet. . . .

She is even more successful in her depiction of madness. Nothing here of any grand romantic notions of artistic frenzy, only a recurrence of terror and pitiful loss of control as Francis is overwhelmed again and again by furies he cannot understand. . . .

Susan Hill does not vulgarize her conception of the poet by larding her book with psychiatric theories of the relationship between creativity and what the ancients called the divine frenzy. Both exist as mysteries, visitations to be endured, two-sided gifts of the imagination not amenable to reductive explanation. . . .

This careful shaping of material to make its effect with the utmost economy, adhered to and practiced by such modern masters as Gide, Woolf, Colette and Pavese, seems to have fallen into abeyance, and it is good to see it once again employed with such great skill.

*Michele Murray, "Restorations-1," in* The New Republic *(reprinted by permission of* The New Republic; *© 1974 by Harrison-Blaine of New Jersey, Inc.), February 16, 1974, pp. 23-4.*

"In the Springtime of the Year" is a book like a handmade quilt. It is traditional, well-stitched, moves slowly towards completion, and is intended, at least partially, as a comfort against the cold. It speaks of home truths, of rituals, of long-established ways of life and of a sense of sharing. Like a quilt, too, it is somewhat abstract, somewhat geometrical, concerned less with departures from the norm than with "the pattern of things," a phrase which recurs with variations throughout the book. Unlike quilts, however, it is of a genus currently unfashionable; one way of saying this is that it is written in a romantic mode, in which absolute goodness is both possible and meaningful, rather than in the prevelant 20th-century ironic mode, in which it is not. . . .

[Despite] lapses into simplemindedness, "In the Springtime of the Year" justifies itself by the intensity of those things it does well: moments of genuine feeling, moments of vision. It is less a novel than the portrait of an emotion, and as this it is poignant and convincing.

*Margaret Atwood, in* The New York Times Book Review *(© 1974 by The New York Times Company; reprinted by permission), May 5, 1974, p. 7.*

Like a hawk circling closer and closer to its prey, English writer Susan Hill has come closer and closer to the subject that dominates her newest novel [*In the Springtime of the Year*]—grief and death. *Strange Meeting,* her novel about World War I, ends with the death of one young soldier and the mourning of his friend; *The Bird of Night* is not only about madness and genius but is also about Harvey Lawson's love for Francis Croft and his long years of mourning after Francis' suicide. Her collection of stories, *A Bit of Singing and Dancing,* published only in England, makes her concern more explicit, for each of the 11 stories treats openly of love, loss and grief between oddly assorted couples. She is drawn to old people and to outcasts—retarded children, deaf-mutes, faded middle-aged bachelors and spinsters still waiting for life to happen to them—and handles sympathetically settings rarely used in contemporary English fiction: deep country and seaside villages when the vacationers have left.

In her new novel, *In the Springtime of the Year,* she has chosen to limit herself to the most naked manifestations of love, death and mourning, drawing on what is apparently a personal experience. . . .

Susan Hill has already demonstrated her mastery of character-drawing and fictional technique in her earlier novels, but *In the Springtime of the Year,* with its deliberate stripping away of almost all the elements of conventional fiction, represents a remarkable advance in what is turning out to be a considerable *oeuvre* for such a young writer. . . .

By looking closely at both setting and character and by putting down what she sees in exact and restrained prose, she has succeeded in transforming the shapeless emotion of grief into a shapely and successful work of art whose affirmation of a world "where all manner of thing shall be well," signals yet another triumph by an artist who, in her quiet, steady way, is fast becoming one of the outstanding novelists of our time.

*Michele Murray, in* The New Republic *(re-*

*printed by permission of* The New Republic; *© 1974 by The New Republic, Inc.), May 18, 1974, p. 24.*

Susan Hill . . . has produced a few small masterpieces, but all her work is distinguished by a notable absence of incessant autobiography or intermittent *romans-a-clef,* and the presence of a powerful imagination. Her subjects are more often men than women, usually society's outsiders by virtue of their strangeness, loneliness, secret longings, or bereavements. Always they seem, as in her collections of stories, *The Albatross* (1971) and *A Little Bit of Singing and Dancing* (1973), to be epics diminute, great subjects and objects looked at through the wrong end of the opera glass. They are stories about hope and despair, loneliness and disillusion, rejection and acceptance, told in a series of spare, tight, closet scenes, and leading into a world of feeling, meaning, implication.

Her approach is to use great concepts and reduce them to such barren, sparse detail that they slip past the reader's attention at first, seeming to be trivial, almost unworthy. But they return to claw at the mind, demanding with stunning force to be remembered, especially in her short novels, *The Bird of Night* (1973) and *Strange Meeting* (1971), two works which established her reputation in England but were hardly noticed here.

Hill's stock-in-trade is the human colloquium. She posits two persons in curious often lopsided tension with one another. . . . Almost always it is a simple (or seemingly simple) duality. Yet the result is a revelation of human worth, disclosed at painful moments of encounter or abandonment. She promotes simple connections made more poignant and meaningful by their oddness, or what the world thinks of as odd.

In *In the Springtime of the Year,* she has even refined her method. A 21-year-old solitary girl has just lost the only thing in her life of any value to her, her husband. . . . Hill chronicles the first year of her loss with lean detail. . . .

On rereading, the slow, almost liturgical progress of this account of a year's sorrow becomes more impressive. But still, its very brevity, its studied reduction to the lowest possible denominator of description and plot, makes me think that Susan Hill has tried to extend beyond the normal length what might have been a powerful short story. It is not true that nothing happens in it, as one reader said. A great deal happens, but it happens in too compressed and linear a fashion; it lacks the texture and richness of the experience of a full novel. The work shows very little advance, to my mind, of her talent, merely an extension of it into a rather narrow corner. . . .

I suspect Susan Hill has . . . the capacity to become, with the expansion of her form and her scope, an important writer.

*Doris Grumbach, "Can Spring Be Far Behind?" in* Book World—The Washington Post (© The Washington Post), *May 19, 1974, p. 7.*

There are so many extraordinary things about Susan Hill's writing and about her success, that I hardly know where to start. Is it not almost past belief that a serious writer should achieve such success in our age, when there is nowhere in her work a whiff of petrol fumes and diesel oil or of any of today's smelly superficial problems (wages and prices, industrial disputes, economic growth, political strife, racialism, technological advance, environmental planning, moral permissiveness, sex, sex, sex, abortion, women's liberation, violence, hi-jacking, juvenile delinquency, mugging, vandalism) but instead a concern with such fundamentals as life and death, the need for love, the absence of it, fear, longing and the death of hope? And also: a most sensitive and receptive awareness of life and of things outside man himself: of animals, birds, of woods and fields, of the sea and the shore, of shells, razors, conches, mere pebbles in the sand. And is it not extraordinary that she should be able to turn her back on the contemporary scene and to treat of these things, mainly in settings atypical of our age (sleepy seaside resorts in the winter, fishing villages, the remote countryside) yet avoid sentimentality and escapism, indeed convince the reader that these are the important things, these are the things that really matter? (I have stopped watching television since I started to read more and more of Susan Hill.)

There is also the extraordinary effectiveness of her prose style. . . . [The] most striking feature of this prose is its ability to achieve the most telling effects, to rouse the most powerful emotions, especially of pain and pity, by the use of plain words. At times, especially when reading the splendid short stories in *A Bit of Singing and Dancing,* I have gone back to a particularly moving passage the following day, to investigate the prose which had created this effect—at times it had been like listening to music. But a careful examination (with a magnifying glass, as it were) did not reveal any special *individual* feature, any specifically *literary* use of words, to explain the effect achieved. No, this is prose which resembles a length of first-quality material: no purple patches; no patches of any kind: good all through. . . .

[Yet] another extraordinary feature of Miss Hill's writing, extraordinary that is in the age in which we are unfortunately obliged to live: this prose is so civilized, controlled and *well-mannered.* It is not prissy, except where the characters it has to portray are that, as in the early novels particularly. No, not prissy, but polite, under control, considerate to the reader—and no less powerful for being so either. . . .

Her insight is unusually penetrating, her compassion unusually sympathetic, her grasp of her subject-matter and her deftness in handling it a delight. . . .

[Susan Hill] is so good she amounts to a phenomenon in our age and is far better, anyway, than anything we deserve. To read Susan Hill is to enrich the spirit. In how many places can one do that today?

*James Brockway, "Old as the Hills," in* Books and Bookmen, *June, 1974, pp. 30-3.*

* * *

## HIMES, Chester 1909-

**Himes is a Black American novelist and detective story writer now living in Spain. He is best known for the nine Harlem crime novels in which the so-called "tough-guy" detective novel was adapted to explore Black experience in America. (See also *Contemporary Authors*, Vols. 25-28).**

Chester Himes, in his two psychological novels, *Lonely Crusade* and *If He Hollers Let Him Go,* bears the imprint of Richard Wright's psychological probing. But Himes lacks Wright's intensity. . . .

[He also] shows the influence of . . . James Cain . . . who . . . wrote *Past All Dishonor* and *The Postman Always Rings Twice*. . . . [Like Cain in *Butterfly*, Himes] describes industrial conditions. There is a similarity as to style and the psychological presentation of characters. . . .

*Lonely Crusade* . . . [develops] . . . a thesis similar to that of *If He Hollers Let Him Go*. Himes exhibits, nevertheless, a more advanced conception of his medium. He uses the steel cage technique, that is to say, the Negro is in a steel cage on the economic level with whites in control of the wealth. Himes is consistent, and his themes deal with materialism and communism. . . .

Himes' forte is the psychological novel, and his projected narrative and characterizations are convincingly done. . . .

The protest novels by Negro authors, such as *Lonely Crusade* by Himes, say that the Negro is proud of his American heritage for the most part. He continues to point out in effect that by choice and birth he will remain a part of the American scene. He seeks an improvement of his condition nonetheless. Rejection of a contrary system and faith in the efficacy of the American experiment from the basis of his protest. . . .

*Lonely Crusade* is a novel in which Himes paints a distasteful picture of the Communist party activities in America according to Lee Gordon's experiences. His book is tantamount to a Negro writer's complete estrangement from such a conflicting ideology.

*Carl Milton Hughes, in his* The Negro Novelist 1940-1950, *Citadel Press, 1953, pp. 68-76, 256-60 (in the paperbound edition, 1970).*

Should the books of Chester Himes . . . be classed as police novels? It is certainly hard to know what else to call them, and his black detectives, Coffin Ed Johnson and Grave Digger Jones, make an exhilarating black comic comment on the activities of all other policemen. From *Cotton Comes to Harlem* (1964) onward, Himes has recorded the activities of these fierce thugs in a world more thuggish still, in rattlingly vigorous prose, and with equal feeling for violence and for comedy. Coffin Ed has been quick on the trigger ever since a glass of acid was thrown into his face by a hoodlum, and when we first meet Grave Digger he has been off duty for six months after being shot up, although, "other than for the bullet scars hidden beneath his clothes and the fingersize scar obliterating the hairline at the base of his skull where the first bullet had burned off the hair, he looked much the same." The humans among whom the detectives move are credulous, lecherous, treacherous, greedy, and savage.

*Julian Symons, in his* Mortal Consequences: A History—From the Detective Story to the Crime Novel *(copyright © 1972 by Julian Symons; reprinted by permission of Harper & Row, Publishers, Inc.), Harper, 1972, pp. 207-08.*

Himes, himself, as explorer of black experience represents a considerably alienated sensibility, a fact which is only partly obscured for [*Black on Black: Baby Sister & Selected Writings*] by the sheer quantity of alienated black writing produced in the 1960's and 1970's. In addition, Himes is extremely individual, a writer of many parts although frequently all parts do not come together in a single piece. Yet his examination of black experience in America has created a place of its own. Lately, he also stuck to his own path in the first volume of his autobiography, *The Quality of Hurt* (. . . 1972), and there is little doubt that his detective stories, notably *Cotton Comes to Harlem* which was made into a film, provided some inspiration for the current spate of hardboiled black movies.

In his confrontation with the black experience, it is tempting to see his hardboiled approach (touched often with sentiment underneath) as his strongest strain. He seems to incorporate both the James M. Cain type fiction with the rebellious hero, made famous by Richard Wright in the novel *Native Son* (1940). In *If He Hollers Let Him Go* (1945), his first novel, Himes pitted a tough but frustrated hero of black middle class status against relentless racism of a war-time shipyard. In *Lonely Crusade* (1947), he involves the same general type of hero in a struggle with Communist ideology, interracial sex, and racial discrimination. In *Cast the First Stone* (1952), he took advantage of a knowledge of prison gained from serving 7½ years of a 25 year sentence for armed robbery; however, the book is about white characters. In *Third Generation* (1954), he gave an often tender and searching exploration of his own pathos filled family background, and in *The Primitive* (1955) he explores again the high tensioned and frustrated black hero of middle class status, in relationship to general suffering, violence, sex. Afterward come a long spate of detective stories in the hard-boiled vein.

The contents of *Black on Black* thus represent the shorter pieces which Himes was also doing. His stand-out pieces often reveal a gutted black life, although he ranges into lugubrious humor, the whimsical, the satirical, and the character study. There is no illusion about a black life wired in as moral beneficiary of the larger society. . . .

Himes reports that the French critics who read *Baby Sister* called it a Greek tragedy. The scenario has no gods, no suggestion of the viability of transcendent values. What it has is *inevitability* and *fate*. . . .

To make his point, Himes has stripped the resources from the black experience—perhaps a bit further than warranted. . . .

Perhaps in an acted version, the scenario would reveal moments of poetry. Read, it confines itself to naturalistic shocks which further violate the humanity of the black experience. Although one can see the advantage of keeping Baby Sister relatively inarticulate regarding her yearnings, it would seem that the author could give her more mental suggestiveness than the statement in which she wishes people would stop looking at her as if she had no clothes on. . . .

All in all, [the stories] show considerable range and skill on Himes' part, but do not give the definitive evidence of the range of emotion, feeling, and search which the novels afford. The novels remain indispensable for a full understanding of Himes' talent.

*George E. Kent, "Rhythms of Black Experience" (reprinted by permission) of* Chicago Review; *copyright © 1973 by* Chicago Review), *in* Chicago Review, *Vol. 25, No. 3, 1973, pp. 76-8.*

* * *

## HOCHHUTH, Rolf 1931-

**Hochhuth, a German-born dramatist now living in Switzerland, is well known for his controversial and much-censored play, *The Deputy*. (See also *Contemporary Authors*, Vols. 5-8, rev. ed.)**

[Rolf] Hochhuth's tendency to make the individual accountable for the failures of the institution is a heritage of his German idealism, an influence which can also be seen in the shape and substance of his play. *The Deputy* is written in the ponderous heroic style of Schiller, full of vaunting speeches, generous sacrifices, and externalized emotions—angry confrontations dominate each scene, the verse pitches and rolls, and indignation keeps the tone at a high boil. As for the characters, they are larger than scale, and, therefore, not always very convincing. When the author permits himself artistic license, he can create an interesting and complex individual—the Doctor, for example, whose fatigued cynicism, experimental cruelty, and intellectual arrogance make him a figure of absolute evil, a creation worthy of Sartre or Camus. But more often, Hochhuth's characters are members of a cardboard nobility.

*Robert Brustein, "History as Drama: 'The Deputy' by Rolf Hochhuth, Adapted by Jerome Rothenberg" (1964), in his* Seasons of Discontent: Dramatic Opinions 1959-1965 *(© 1959, 1960, 1961, 1962, 1963, 1964, 1965 by Robert Brustein; reprinted by permission of Simon and Schuster, Inc.), Simon & Schuster, 1965, pp. 204-07.*

Though there may be doubts as to the merit of Rolf Hochhuth's *The Deputy* as a play, there can be no question as to the absorbing interest of its material. The blunt fact is that I found myself so intent on the subject that I very nearly ceased to concern myself with the performance as an evening in the theatre. . . .

It is nonsense to maintain that we see and judge plays entirely in the light of their "creative" values. If we have no personal relation to a play's human content we are not likely to understand it at all or care anything about it. Imagine a person incapable of passion at a performance of *Romeo and Juliet* or *Tristan und Isolde*. True, there would still be the language of the one and the music of the other, but even these would lose their affective force for such an auditor. He might well ask, "What's all the excitement about?" . . .

We always hope for and seek perfect unity between form and content in a work of art, but I suspect that complete "Apollonian" detachment from the sources of an artist's inspiration—the living matter which generates his work—is even more foreign to relevant judgment in the arts than is complete identification with those sources. . . .

An evaluation of *The Deputy* at this moment is difficult, to begin with, because while it was written as a Schiller-like epic drama—the published text would take more than six hours to perform—each of its versions has had a different translator and has been staged and cut by a different director. Even more taxing to strict criticism, an ambiguity in the dramatist's motivation has led to a confusion in the audiences' reception of the play everywhere.

Apparently Hochhuth set out to write a dramatic "poem" on the existentialist question "Why should a young Jesuit priest, martyring himself on behalf of the Jewish victims of Nazi savagery, cling to his belief in God when all the evidence of his actual experience contradicts any rational justification for such faith?" But this theme was lost sight of in the development of the work because the author was carried away by the more burning question of why the Christian world—embodied in its most organized Church—failed to protest the blackest crime in history: the systematic slaughter of six million Jews between 1941 and 1944. The outraged moralist and historian in the author superceded the religious artist.

The climactic scene of the play becomes, therefore, the one in which Pope Pius XII (Pacelli) refuses to denounce the Nazi action against the Jews or to abrogate the Concordat between Hitler and the Church. It makes the play appear to be primarily an attack on the Pontiff and, by extension, on the Catholic hierarchy.

This is a distortion of the play's significance and value. It should not be construed as anti-Catholic. Even the Pope's role in the dramatic context should not be considered central. The play's real protagonist is Father Fontana, whose tragic outcry and assumption of Jewish martyrdom lie at the heart of Hochhuth's message. What the play tells us is that we all share in the guilt of those years, for none of us acted with sufficient vigor, none of us protested bitterly, clamorously, specifically enough. The governments of Britain and France, to go no further, are as open to the play's accusation on this score as was the Church's chief deputy.

If the audience misses this point, its failure is largely due to a weakness in Hochhuth's dramatic thinking, his inability to bring the play's larger issue and the detail of its scenes into focus. Father Fontana is less vividly and convincingly drawn than are his more compliant fellow clerics. Yet, despite these grave defects of dramatic statement, it would be false to deny the play's hold on our attention or its power to stir.

*Harold Clurman, "Rolf Hochhuth: 'The Deputy'" (1964), in his* The Naked Image: Observations on the Modern Theatre *(reprinted with permission of Macmillan Publishing Co., Inc.; copyright © 1958, 1959, 1960, 1961, 1962, 1963, 1964, 1965, 1966 by Harold Clurman), Macmillan, 1966, pp. 80-2.*

By far the most celebrated of all the works of art which take up the same functions of historical memory served by the Eichmann trial is *The Deputy (Der Stellvertreter),* the lengthy play by the young German playwright Rolf Hochhuth. Here we have a work of art as we ordinarily understand it—a work for the familiar theater of 8:30 curtains and intermissions, rather than for the austere public stage of the courtroom. Here there are actors, rather than real murderers and real survivors from hell. Yet it is not false to compare it with the Eichmann trial, because *The Deputy* is first of all a compilation, a record. Eichmann himself and many other real persons of the period are represented in the play; the speeches of the characters are drawn from historical records.

In modern times, this use of the theater as a forum for public, moral judgment has been shunted aside. The theater has largely become a place in which private quarrels and agonies are staged; the verdict which events render upon characters in most modern plays has no relevance beyond the play itself. *The Deputy* breaks with the completely private boundaries of most modern theater. And as it would be obtuse to refuse to evaluate the Eichmann trial as a public work of art, it would be frivolous to judge *The Deputy* simply as a work of art.

Some art—but not all—elects as its central purpose *to tell the truth*; and it must be judged by its fidelity to the truth, and by the relevance of the truth which it tells. By these standards, *The Deputy* is an important play. The case against the Nazi party, the SS, the German business elite, and most of the German people—none of which is slighted by Hochhuth—is too well known to need anyone's assent. But *The Deputy* also stresses, and this is the controversial part of the play, a strong case for the complicity of the German Catholic Church and of Pope Pius XII. This case I am convinced is true, and well taken. (See the ample documentation which Hochhuth has provided at the end of the play, and the excellent book by Guenter Lewy, *The Catholic Church and Nazi Germany*.) And the importance, historical and moral, of this difficult truth at the present time cannot be overestimated. . . .

It is the whole point of Hochhuth's play that he has barely transformed his material. Unlike the plays of Shakespeare or Schiller or Brecht, Hochhuth's play stands or falls by its fidelity to the complete historical truth.

This documentary intention of the play also indicates its limitations. The fact is that as not all works of art aim at educating and directing conscience, not all works of art which successfully perform a moral function greatly satisfy as art. I can think of only one dramatic work of the type of *The Deputy,* the short film *Night and Fog* by Alain Resnais, which satisfies equally as a moral act and as a work of art. *Night and Fog,* also a memorial to the tragedy of the six million, is highly selective, emotionally relentless, historically scrupulous, and—if the word seems not outrageous—beautiful. *The Deputy* is not a beautiful play. Nor does one necessarily ask that it be. Nevertheless, since one can assume the immense interest and moral importance of the play, the aesthetic questions need to be faced. Whatever *The Deputy* is as a moral event, it is not playwriting of the highest order.

*Susan Sontag, "Reflections on 'The Deputy'" (1964), in her* Against Interpretation and Other Essays *(reprinted with the permission of Farrar, Straus & Giroux, Inc.; copyright © 1961, 1962, 1963, 1964, 1965, 1966 by Susan Sontag), Farrar, Straus, 1966, pp. 124-31.*

[Hochhuth] is perhaps the most traditional, the most tradition-conscious, of all modern dramatists, far less of a revolutionary than Brecht, far less daring than Ionesco or Beckett. His models are Schiller and Shaw. His aim is to explore the human condition on the basis of verifiable human reality and to penetrate to the tragic core of man's plight on earth. . . .

In trying to write his two tragedies of twentieth-century man, Hochhuth has stirred up a series of gigantic wasps' nests. In each case the wild rumors and debates that preceded the performances of his plays provided them with publicity that must have been the envy of all public relations men. In fact, this kind of controversy made it irrelevant—from the commercial point of view—whether the plays were good or bad. By the time they opened they were bound to run on sheer news value. . . .

Since the documents that [Hochhuth] maintains would prove or disprove his case will be locked away for another fifty years, it might follow that aesthetic and critical judgment on *The Soldiers* would have to be suspended till then. But that is clearly absurd. The question is not whether the facts are as they are depicted in the play but whether, in the play, they are wholly *convincingly* depicted. Had Hochhuth concentrated his tragic conflict on an event that is known to all—for example, the Mihajlovich tragedy—it would have been far easier for him to achieve this basic requirement. As it is, *The Soldiers* is somewhat encumbered by the author's excessive need to provide documentation, and by the fact that the documentation can never be wholly conclusive.

Nevertheless, Hochhuth's achievement is already very considerable. He has written only two plays up to now, but he has created a larger immediate and visible impact than any other contemporary dramatist. This in itself must be regarded as a boon for the theatre as an institution and as an art form. For it proves that, even in the age of mass media (or especially in an age of mass media), the theatre still is a forum for the airing of moral problems, for intense political and social debate. He has also, in an age of experimentation and a multitude of fascinating but recondite eccentricities in the theatre, drawn attention to the fact that there is still a lot of life in the traditional mainstay of the stage: large-scale, historical tragedies in verse, basically of exactly the same type as Shakespeare, Strindberg, or Shaw. It would have been difficult, before Hochhuth came along, to believe that plays of such venerable lineage could start riots in the streets outside playhouses. . . .

[There] can be no doubt that Hochhuth can create character, that he can even perform the very difficult feat of making "great men" like Pius XII or Churchill wholly believable on the stage. His idealism, his savage indignation about the evils of his time, shines through Hochhuth's dialogues and gives them real fire and poetic force. He is anything but a *documentary* playwright. He is a very impressive, traditional historical dramatist.

*Martin Esslin, "'Truth' and Documentation: A Conversation with Rolf Hochhuth" (originally published in* The New York Times Magazine, *November 19, 1967), in his* Reflections: Essays on Modern Theatre *(copyright © 1961, 1962, 1963, 1966, 1967, 1968, 1969 by Martin Esslin; reprinted by permission of Doubleday & Co., Inc.), Doubleday, 1969, pp. 127-38.*

Initially banned in London, but eventually produced even there, Rolf Hochhuth's *Soldiers* stirred nearly as much controversy in some quarters as his earlier condemnation of Pope Pius XII in *The Deputy*. It was easy to see why—provided you were British, but more difficult otherwise.

*Soldiers* is in many ways superior to *The Deputy* (which is far from saying it is a really good play). But, like the latter, it is unlikely ever to be discussed primarily in those terms. For better or worse, Hochhuth has a way of making "technique" seem somewhat irrelevant. Whether or not one happens to agree with him, his concerns are a far cry from the soporific concerns of Broadway and his seriousness as an involved, even a tortured, participant in the life of his time is beyond dispute.

In *Soldiers* Hochhuth comes to grips with one of the greatest figures of our time as he confronts two of the most overriding questions of that time. The man is Winston Churchill; the questions, the morality of saturation bombing of civilian population centers and the extent to which the demands of war or other political necessities justify acts that, in the normal course of things, would be termed immoral. Both in their specifics and in extension they have as much relevance today as they did at the time *Soldiers* supposedly takes place. . . .

Here, as was not the case with his depiction of Pius XII, Hochhuth permits Churchill the integrity of his motives, though he strongly questions the reasoning and consequences attendant upon them. He renders the prime minister as a blend of the heroic and the tragic (tragic in the Hegelian sense that both parties to the conflict must be right). Tragic, then, because of the rightness of his intentions in placing the interests of humanity above those of a quixotically, if not diabolically led, nation and because the innocent civilians who died in the firestorms of Hamburg and other cities possessed a *right* to live. And, he suggests, tragic also because the Poles, who provide the second theme of the play, were right in their demand for justice, while Churchill, on a quite different level, was right in acquiescing to Stalin's demands.

In an interview with Martin Esslin, Hochhuth observed: "I don't agree with those dramatists like Dürrenmatt who proclaim the end of tragedy on the grounds that the day of the individual is past forever, that nobody is responsible any more. Those people forget one thing: the number of individuals who *did* achieve something has always been very, very small, throughout history." . . .

Whatever one may think of Hochhuth as a playwright, it would be impossible not to acknowledge that he has employed the theatre as an arena in which the great moral issues of our time can be raised. . . .

If that is the playwright's obligation—and it would certainly seem to be one aspect of it—perhaps it is the audience's to react, not with outrage at the challenge to myths (or realities) long considered inviolable, but with concern at questions that seemingly have no answers but someday must find them.

*Catharine Hughes, "'Soldiers'," in her* Plays, Politics and Polemics, *Drama Book Specialists, 1973, pp. 117-24.*

Hochhuth's theme [in *The Deputy*] is clear and hammered home in scene after scene: Pius XII, with an enormous bank of moral and spiritual credit to draw upon, should have condemned the Nazi atrocities against the Jews. Not to do so was to default not only on his role as the Vicar—the Deputy—of Christ on earth and leader of the most unified religious force in the world, but also on his role as a human being in a position to save other human beings at a time when he alone might have affected their fate. Pius "spoke," Hochhuth acknowledges, but in words that were so deliberately generalized, so hollow and equivocal, that Hitler felt no need to listen. He said nicely, in the carefully couched, fussily diplomatic pronunciamentos at which he was skilled, what should have been said in terms that would stir moral and emotional indignation. . . .

Almost inexplicably, Pius did not speak; it is a fact and a completely valid subject for drama. The problem of *The Deputy* lies elsewhere—in Hochhuth's failure to acknowledge the moral complexities involved, his willingness to present his characters as not merely indifferent but altogether unaware of the human and spiritual dimensions of the question. Pius may have been precisely the cold and prissily unfeeling businessman-diplomat that Hochhuth presents. But to make him superficial, to exaggerate his concern with finances, the supposed menace posed by "the Russian colossus," and the necessity of his own role as mediator to a point bordering on caricature is unconvincing not only historically but dramatically.

One of the curiosities of *The Deputy* is that Hochhuth seems simply not to care about the inner workings of his "villain," about the *why* of his action. Nor, oddly, does he seem notably more interested in the motivations of most of the others. They are viewed almost exclusively in the light of their attitude toward the pope, on the one hand, and as one-dimensional automations on the other. Having decided there was no room for uncertainty, that it simply was not possible, Hochhuth will not permit it in his characters either. . . .

It can, of course, be argued that Pius XII and Ricardo . . . are intended not as characters but as figures in a modern morality, vehicles for moral outrage and compassion on the one hand and inhumanity and evil on the other. But to suggest, as one critic did, that Hochhuth "does not have to understand" his character "because he does not have to forgive" him is hardly valid. Perhaps he does not have to forgive him—forgiveness is something beyond a human prerogative—but given the nature of the play, he does have to convince the audience. And to achieve this, it is more effective to acknowledge that there were areas of uncertainty and to respond to them than it is to deny their possibility. . . .

If, in the end, *The Deputy* still manages to move us, to be one of the most significant dramatic works produced in the 60s, it is despite its essentially simplistic characterization, failure to explore motivations, and the ponderousness of its free-verse form. It forces us to face once more the question of power and responsibility—and perhaps the question of Grace—and to face it in terms of an event that to this day almost defies the imagination.

*Catharine Hughes, "'The Deputy'," in her* Plays, Politics and Polemics, *Drama Book Specialists, 1973, pp. 127-38.*

## HOLUB, Miroslav 1923-

**Holub, a Czech, is a pathologist and a poet. His verse often employs scientific images. (See also *Contemporary Authors*, Vols. 21-22.)**

Miroslav Holub is a curious mixture, perhaps a unique one: he is one of Czechoslovakia's most prolific and original poets and also a distinguished scientist, a clinical pathologist who has travelled widely on both sides of the Iron Curtain, researching and attending scientific congresses. So far his publications include eight books of poetry, two travel books and twenty-five learned papers on pathology; he also edits a Czech popular science magazine. . . .

All Holub's technique is concentrated on the exposure and analysis of reality. He speaks fluent English, reads widely in it and claims to have derived his free verse forms from William Carlos Williams. But the results are very different. Williams used his simple, stripped-down forms for two purposes: first, to achieve an American accent and rhythm, which had nothing to do with the traditional British iambic pentameter; second, in order to make the rather simple perceptions and objects of his poems come out clear and strong. Complexity was not his *forte*, and when he attempted it the result, as often as not, was muddle. Holub, in comparison, is intellectual, sophisticated. . . .

[His] technique is that of the early abstract painters: he reduces the confused uneasy situation to its bare elements, and then reassembles it so that the complexity is somehow clarified, validated by an ironic compassion. He uses free forms so that they won't get in the way of what he has to say. They allow him complexity without padding. And this is as it should be for an intellectual who has no taste for abstractions. In his poetry, as presumably in his science, he continually insists on probing below the surface of received, everyday experience to reveal new levels of meaning, to lay bare new emotional facts. It is as though his poems and his researcher's microscope worked in the same way, and towards the same end. . . .

The source of his strength is his subtle, critical acceptance of the realities as they are, his refusal either to shut things out or to praise them simply because, like Everest, they are there. His poetry is based finally on an unsentimental, probing, compassionate, witty sense of the modern world.

*A. Alvarez, "Miroslav Holub" (originally published as the "Introduction" to* Miroslav Holub: Selected Poems, *translated by Ian Milner and George Theiner, Penguin, 1967), in his* Beyond All This Fiddle: Essays 1955-1967 *(copyright © 1968 by A. Alvarez; reprinted by permission of Random House, Inc.), 1969, pp. 133-41.*

The Czech poet and distinguished pathologist Miroslav Holub seems to have survived both freezes and thaws by quietly keeping his eye to his microscope. Like other doctor-poets—Gottfried Benn and William Carlos Williams, whom, suprisingly, he has read, come to mind—Holub writes a delicately tense, finely observed line. He required of every poem that it be acid and dry and as fine as watchworks. His comments are intelligent rather than wise or ironical; he speaks from the solicitude of a man who knows death too intimately not to value life as an absolute gift. He is like Klee in his imagery, marrying a clear seriousness with a stylized whimsy. . . .

*Guy Davenport, in* The Hudson Review *(copyright © 1968 by The Hudson Review, Inc.; reprinted by permission), Vol. XXI, No. 3, Autumn, 1968, p. 571.*

*    *    *

## HOPKINS, John 1931-

**A British dramatist and screenwriter, Hopkins has written over fifty television scripts.**

Although [*Tangier Buzzless Flies*] is supplied with a full complement of more or less stalwart heroes, a bit battered and careworn by the desert life they pursue in north Africa, the central interest here lies in the Sahara itself, its heat, sandy wastes, and filth, along with the Moslem resignation to fate accepted without question by its inhabitants, hardly able in any event to lift themselves out of the lethargy and indolence induced by their habitual dependence upon hashish. Men and women appear and fade away in these pages and are in fact hardly distinguishable one from the other in a society where differences in sex become matters of little importance. Story is of no consequence to the author. He is content to outline his characters with some sharpness, emphasizing always the futility of their lives. What counts above all is the Sahara, ever shifting, inevitably concealing even the graves of men whose lives were lost in their feeble attempts to conquer it.

Virginia Quarterly Review, *Vol. 48, No. 3 (Summer, 1972), pp. xcviii, c.*

John Hopkins' "Find Your Way Home" . . . is a good play—indeed, for the first two of its three acts it is a *very* good play, and only in the last half hour or so does it begin to falter and break up, not because the playwright lacks invention or stagecraft but because he cannot bear to stultify himself in order to provide a tidy ending. He is an artist and not an actuary, and the lulling serenities of double-entry bookkeeping are not to be applied to the messy hodgepodge or heartbreak. Having pitched his characters headlong into an entanglement from which there can be no quick and orderly withdrawal, Mr. Hopkins must bring his curtain down upon an ambiquity; it is an ambiguity "just like real life," as some kindly soul is bound to say in these circumstances, but real life and a work of art have very little to do with each other, and we are right to feel that the playwright has failed us, however honorably. Impertinent and schoolmasterly though it may sound, I wish Mr. Hopkins to continue working on his play.

The plot of "Find Your Way Home" can be summarized as a triangle with trapezoidal tendencies. . . .

The title of the play hints that at some point in its composition Mr. Hopkins may have intended the husband to return to his family; given the character as now written, this would be not only implausible but a ludicrous repetition of an action that has already taken place before the play begins. Myself, I believe the play can end well only with the death of one or the other of the lovers; maybe it is just as well that it is Mr. Hopkins' play and not mine.

*Brendan Gill, "Views of Home," in* The New Yorker, *January 14, 1974, p. 58.*

*Find Your Way Home* is the most outspoken and honest play about homosexuality that has ever appeared on Broadway. Yet nothing is said or done onstage in order to titillate an audience of either gays or straights. British Playwright Hopkins makes three serious points and makes them well. The first of these affirms what Diana Trilling has written of D. H. Lawrence: "The sexuality which Lawrence celebrated was mating. What the present generation means by love-making is coupling." Alan and Julian make love in Lawrence's sense. Secondly, Hopkins shows how heavily attitudes toward homosexuality are socially conditioned. If Alan were leaving his wife for another woman, she would be dismayed but resigned. It is the social stigma and the half-sniggering, half-pitying gossip of friends and acquaintances that disturb her so deeply.

Hopkins' third point—and it is the lesson of so great a writer as Proust—is that love is indivisible. Whatever its form of expression, the essence of love never differs. Hopkins never makes any of these points as didactic arguments. They are implicit in his play and made explicit by a fine cast.

*T. E. Kalem, "Odd Man In," in* Time *(reprinted by permission from* Time, The Weekly Newsmagazine; *copyright Time Inc.), January 14, 1974, p. 44.*

John Hopkins is fully aware of the dramatic potential in his love triangle [in "Find Your Way Home"], but he kills it off quite neatly through the play-writing sin of excess. The play's language is not only the most sexually graphic Broadway has ever heard, but is often too strong for these characters, who are overdrawn in more serious ways. It is not enough for the boy lover to be vulnerable and sensitive. . . . But Hopkins makes him a neurotic of morbidly delicate sensibility, prone to hysteric behavior that robs his character of its reality.

*Marilyn Stasio, in* Cue *(copyright © Cue Publications, Inc., 1974), January 14, 1974, p. 17.*

If you believe, as some gay activists do, that homosexuals and heterosexuals are two utterly different breeds of people, that a gay soap opera is an insult, because homosexual reality can only be degraded by being forced into the rigidly hetero conventions the concept "soap opera" implies. If on the other hand you believe, along with civil libertarians and a different set of gay activists, that homosexuals are exactly like heterosexuals, except in terms of the gender they prefer to have sex with, then a gay soap opera is probably a double insult, because it means somebody is taking advantage of and sensationalizing a natural part of human life, and attaching an unhealthy stigma to its practitioners; rather like racism. If on a third vestigial hand you believe, in company with Joseph Epstein and a few other escapees from the Dark Ages, that homosexuals are twisted things accursed by God, then you certainly aren't going to enjoy a soaper which presents homosexuals as sympathetic characters entitled to a chance at happiness like everybody else.

Since I can't imagine the existence of any attitude towards homosexuality other than these three, the first thing that puzzles me about "Find Your Way Home" is why the hell John Hopkins bothered to write it; by putting the wrong form and subject together, he's stacked the cards against himself on all fronts, and written a play that nobody can possibly enjoy. I suppose, of course, there are still people who don't believe homosexuality exists—that's a possible fourth attitude—but, unless they enjoy being alternately offended and bored, I doubt that they're going to care much for it either. Maybe they can watch it as a sort of horror movie—a physiological "Invasion of the Body Snatchers."

I'm assuming in all this that Hopkins knows he's writing soap opera; he writes for British television, and the other plays of his I've read are in the same genre of flat-spoken middle-class anguish, enriched by one kinky device per script. On the other hand, you hear rumors that the piece is autobiographical and, while it certainly is an impersonal piece of writing, it's possible that Hopkins knows as little about himself as he seems to know about human sexuality, dramatic structure, and the representation of reality on the stage. He writes from deep within the soul of the stuffy-Englishman cliche—an author who hasn't yet been introduced to his own id, let alone to his characters. How can you take seriously a writer who tackles this subject without apparently knowing the difference between promiscuity and prostitution, between active and passive sexual roles, between the Gutenberg—and the television generations?. . .

If the dialogue weren't so wooden and interminable, and the big entrances and climaxes so awkwardly set up and telegraphed, it would be an ideal play for classes in Victorian Drama.

*Michael Feingold, "Some soap, some hope," in* The Village Voice *(reprinted by permission of* The Village Voice; *© 1974 by The Village Voice, Inc.), January 17, 1974, p. 62.*

I can't think of a living playwright so relentless about pursuing a point, so unafraid of repeating himself or lapsing into melodrama, so apt to take dramatic overkill into the megadeath bracket. . . .

I'm not exactly claiming Hopkins a place in the theatrical histories as the O'Neill of the garden gnomes; but I do think he has some of the same vices, some of the same virtues and, as with O'Neill, it is often hard to separate one from the other. He builds some pretty rugged and unwieldy dramatic structures, so to speak, but the foundation is usually sound. He has observed, thought, and felt. The relentlessness, the excess is his way of expressing his involvement with his characters, and without it there would be no play. And that, for all one's reservations, would be a pity.

*Benedict Nightingale, "Talking to Ourselves," in* New Statesman, *May 10, 1974, p. 670.*

Hopkins plainly feels that his painstaking documentation of the minutiae of suburban life [*Next of Kin*], his profound discovery that a great many family relationships are less cordial than they may superficially appear and, of course, that ostensibly virtuous citizens can have some fairly grubby sexual secrets are sufficiently fascinating in themselves to allow him to dispense with the tedious business of tying up the odd loose end.

I daresay you have news for him. . . .

*Kenneth Hurren, "Kenneth Hurren On Questions Without Answers," in* The Spectator *(© 1974 by* The Spectator; *reprinted by permission of* The Spectator), *May 11, 1974, p. 579.*

* * *

## HUGHES, Ted 1930-

**Hughes is one of England's most important contemporary poets. His bold, tough poetic rhythms and his obsession with primitivism and animal violence are best known to readers of his wholly original "Crow" poems. (See also *Contemporary Authors*, Vols. 1-4, rev. ed.)**

At his worst [Hughes's] poems say "TAKE THAT!" He seems to boast that he can swallow more gore and nothingness than anyone else on the block. Over and over in his first volume, "The Hawk in the Rain," he sneers at human weakness; it is as if Death itself, salacious for fear and violence, had written these pitiless poems. . . .

For the most part, only animals tug him to admiration; they release him for fire-fine empathy. His pike, otters, tomcats, pigs and dragonflies lend him their appetites, their guiltless desire for more. "Veterans of survival," they hearten him. . . .

Then in "Wodwo" the human frailty of the first volume and the animal viciousness of the second snap together, and Hughes's animals learn to weep. . . . So it is that Hughes rounds to human weakness through the struggle, the hot solace, of the dumb beasts. He articulates in them his own apprehensions; they bear him blindly, prevent him from articulating himself away.

Crow adds comic stridency to this synthesis, gives Hughes the nucleus for innumerable farcical black situations, opens his poetry philosophically and dramatically. Greedy and indestructible as Crow is, he also incorporates the world-belittled human figures of the early poems, and Hughes treats him with a strained, disgusted compassion. Crow is a figment of genius, as impudently alive as Bugs Bunny or the Road Runner, yet a kind of philosophical kit. Through Crow's jump-gap poles of automatic appetite and mental quivering before the steaming horror of Creation, Hughes joins the twin nihilistic themes of the century—the Id and the Void—with witty and enormous invention.

Yet "Crow" suffers from being part of the thinning tail of modernism. It has so much to outshrill, its derisive and despairing stances are so familiar, that it seems more noise than news. Only its last-gamble dependence on the will to live and its cartoonizing of poetry and philosophy prove bold. Jaggedly exciting as the volume is, clever, resourceful, relentless, its gusto is achieved at the expense of the verbal subtlety, the poignant empathy, the mystery, of the earlier poems—poems with living, nonconceptual subjects, not flattened themes. "Crow" bangs with the tin of Hughes's will; for all its metaphysical gaping, it lacks the lifting note of wonder.

A large welcome, then, to this gathering ["Selected Poems 1957-1967"] (selected by the poet himself) of most of the early poems. . . .

Hughes's great talent is for a dramatic grip of language, dead cold but bleakly pungent, felt from within his own or his subjects' root-tip attachment to life. His style is emotionally dry, yet burns. It ascetizes imaginative magnificence.

*Calvin Bedient, in* The New York Times Book Review *(© 1974 by The New York Times Company; reprinted by permission), January 13, 1974, pp. 3-4.*

For Hughes, the violence of nature—what Yeats called its "murderous innocence"—seems to be the essential and universal human condition. His best poems are characterized by stark presentation, sharp definition, a peculiarly masculine energy. "Wind," for example, presents the poet's reaction to a storm on the Yorkshire moors. Hughes bombards us with images of urgency and terror: "Flexing like the lens of a mad eye . . . the brunt wind . . . flung a magpie away" and, later, shook the house so violently that it "Rang like some fine green goblet in the note/That any second would shatter it." Finally, the perspective shifts to the human response to this holocaust . . ., a powerful rendering of the sense of human impotence when confronted with the unpredictable violence of nature. . . .

[It] is often said that Hughes's violent nature imagery is symbolic of a dark descent to the depths of the unconscious, to a mysterious interior world of being. His animal poems—like "Otter," "Horses" and "Pike"—are frequently called Laurentian. But there is, in fact, little resemblance between Lawrence's great poems of animistic projection like "Bat" and "Fish"—poems in which the self merges with an alien identity—and a Hughes poem like "Hawk Roosting," which . . . has no meaningful reference to any conceivable human situation.

I would argue that Hughes's peculiar evasiveness, his unwillingness to unmask the "I," is increasingly becoming a limitation in his verse. . . .

The seemingly endless violence becomes tiresome. Indeed, *Wodwo* manifests an increasing sense of strain, of trying to say something new without finding the necessary means. . . .

Hughes becomes increasingly remote; his animals become, more and more, the means by which the poet gets out of the poem, by which he avoids the complexity that results when the self confronts its world. In his most recent book, *Crow*, the effacement of self is completed. By adopting the Crow persona, the poet can be as devastating as he likes, confronting us with the demonic image of a world destroyed by atomic ash in which the jaunty, unkillable Crow is the Last Survivor, without disturbing our serenity. Thus we can chuckle at Hughes's wit, as when Crow is asked, "But who is stronger than death?" and replies, "Me, evidently," without being involved or troubled.

The later Hughes is, in short, at the opposite pole from the poet of *Leaves of Grass* who announced, "I am the man, I suffer'd, I was there." In Hughes's poetic universe, the relation of the individual to the hostile, amoral violence that surrounds him remains obscure. I long for him to shed the carefully contrived mask, the pose of cynical witness to storms, murders and lonely deaths. For there can be no doubt that few contemporary poets—whether British or American—can rival Hughes's technical resourcefulness, his verbal facility, his acuteness of observation, his perfect ear.

*Marjorie Perloff, in* Book World—The Washington Post (© The Washington Post), *February 10, 1974, pp. 1-2.*

Ted Hughes' *Crow* (1971) was the best book of poems by an English poet in many years. . . . *Selected Poems 1957-1967* . . . will show you how he got there. Taken from his three previous books, *The Hawk in the Rain* (1957), *Lupercal* (1960) and *Wodwo* (1967), these poems march steadily into the darkness behind the darkness until they reach Crow's monstrous and monster-filled world. . . .

To read Hughes is to be surrounded by cold and maniacal eyes and jaws. And stones. His cold landscape is jammed with giant crabs, horses, apes, jaguars, whales, dinosaurs, moles, bulls, hawks. As his poems evolve it becomes clear that it is not these beasts' dignity or grace or even fierceness that grips him but their bloodlust, and their pleasure in bloodlust. . . .

The leap Hughes makes in *Crow* is to make this animal violence an intricately worked-out metaphor for man's totality: his civilization, his psychology, his myths and his ultimate "meaning.". . .

Hughes' style changed through the years: he began as a skilled rhymer with precise metrics, working toward carefully modulated off-rhymes. . . . Gradually the style became looser and more dynamic, idiosyncratic and unpredictable, the style of *Crow*. . . .

As a description of his own inner landscape, which we all touch on somewhere, Hughes' poems are completely compelling; but as a description of reality they suffer from "tunnel vision," even in *Crow* where he pushes past despair into something like defiance. After all, even *King Lear* has *some* bright spots.

*Peter Meinke, in* The New Republic *(reprinted by permission of* The New Republic; *© 1974 by Harrison-Blaine of New Jersey, Inc.), February 16, 1974, p. 32.*

*Crow* is the crux. It is deplored as heatedly as it is admired. His attitude to his "black" subjects is condemned as vampiric, Gothic, horror-comical. At the same time, he is said to be a neo-Georgian.

One reason why his later work has been deplored on certain sides is that it is held to have been governed, more and more, by considerations of performance and delivery. Many of these poems are inventories, speeches, tablets of stone, commandments—though they are not the kind of commandments that his readers would know how to obey. They are incremental as well as elemental. They are oratory and liturgy. Thomas's *Eighteen Poems,* whose themes are not all that remote from those of *Crow*, did well in delivery too: but they do better on the page, and are more memorable if only because more melodic, than some of *Crow,* and appear to represent a different case, incantations though they are. Difficult though some of the *Crow* poems are, they have proved acceptable to a generation that wants its poets to climb onto the stage. . . .

I would agree that stretches of *Lupercal* and *Wodwo* seem to reveal a state of exhaustion. They are a trough, as are parts of *Crow*. The increments don't always add up; the oratory can be very confused. I don't think it is possible to detect many *ideas* in his poems myself, but what there is here of the kind of thing that poetry critics call ideas can be unpersuasive and perplexing. There are later poems, present in this selection, which look willed and incoherent when set beside "The Little Boys." He is wrong to prefer them.

Nevertheless, there has been a failure to discriminate within his later work on the part of those who dislike it. Certain of the *Crows* are marvelous: "Crow's Account of the Battle," "Crow's Theology." In "A Childish Prank," grown-ups are "lying about" again, as in "The Little Boys": *"Man's and woman's bodies lay without souls."* This time, though, there is theology, and even for those who don't like theology, a more engrossing point is made. Gothic though it is, "Crow's Account of St. George" is another very good poem: it is of the order of, and is no less richly deliverable than, the Border ballad "Edward."

Early and late, his poems have been engaged in the depiction of instinctual life, and of the death-dealing behavior of fighters and predators, and this has been done in a context which includes a hostility to human participation in such behavior, which includes a desire for peace. His Crow is involved in this drama in an ambiguous way, being both predator and victim. This crow is not a crow as his early jaguar was a jaguar. His exploits are deeply anthropomorphic. He is a very sardonic bird. . . .

A children's story of his, *The Iron Giant,* bears a rather strange relation to his poetry, in that one or two of the themes and incidents of the poetry are revived as endearing fiction. There are little, faint counterparts of some of his most thunderous effects; and cartoon versions of some of his worst monsters for adults. . . .

At the beginning of the book, the boy is fishing, and the scene is like a version of the scene in "Pike," where the poet, fishing, feels threatened by the life in the pond. "It was growing too dark to fish," the boy decides. "Past nightfall I dared not cast," the poet writes. There are owls in both cases, and a hush. Both the boy and the poet sense that they are being watched, and they are both afraid. Then the boy sees the terrible Iron Giant clambering over the horizon. I conclude that Ted Hughes was so interested in fear, and in the adolescent memory which may be recaptured in these scenes, that he had no compunction about repeating his finest evocation of the frightening in terms of a standard episode from a children's book.

*Karl Miller, "Fear and Fang," in* The New York Review of Books *(reprinted with permission from* The New York Review of Books; *© 1974 by NYREV, Inc.), March 7, 1974, pp. 3-6.*

Hughes, though generally acclaimed as Britain's leading poet, gives no quarter to his readers, and his critics give him little in return. His obsession with the bleakly non-human in *Lupercal* and *Wodwo* seemed spent, and his readers looked forward to a new departure. But, continuing his immersion in the primitive, and extending the shadows of his temperament to the full, he published *Crow,* which is resolutely contemporary and shuns the detached control of the typical Audenesque lyric. Indeed, *Crow* challenges the very notion of lyric, for while the individual "songs" have their own emotional shape, it is through imaginative participation in the world of this at once primordial and apocalyptic beast that we can arrive at an estimate of its final worth. Like other contemporary book-length poems, such as Kinnell's *The Book of Nightmares* and Hill's *Mercian Hymns, Crow* demands to be read in full; only in bulk does the blackness of its humor and the redness of its blood appear in the proper light. But to read the book as a unit makes some readers feel battered past tolerance, while others find the work pretentious or puerile. . . .

Someone complained that despite the myriad references to blood, Hughes never convinces us that he has ever seen any. That is witty, but beside the point. The real difficulty is in the relation between the poem and its presumed audience. Persons accustomed to reading neo-metaphysical poetry, or requiring to know whether a poem is an allegory or a realistic "picture," are not well-equipped to face the impurities of *Crow*'s mode. In that poem, agony and broad comedy readily commingle, and we are deprived of any comforting tradition of discourse to guide or relieve our attention to tone. The poem survives by its own manic energy, or it fails utterly.

*Charles Molesworth, in* The Nation, *March 16, 1974, pp. 346-47.*

Hughes is undoubtedly, unfortunately, one of our finest poets still young enough to have an artistic future. As talented and serious and lyrical as one could wish, there is something dry about his brutal anguish. The flights of his bat-winged pegasus are [so] carefully calibrated . . . that the feeling of an almost indifferent depression that one gets from reading him comes more from a response to his technique than his "message." And yet it is for his technique that perhaps he should be read, since his hothouse violence is more often than not ludicrous.

Virginia Quarterly Review, *Vol. 50, No. 2 (Spring, 1974), p. lvii.*

Hughes has long been fascinated by the manner in which life sustains itself in the face of death. Prior to the appearance of *Crow* (1970), a number of his poems explored the behavior of animal-predators, for whom the energy-requirements of the blood constitute "the belly of logic." With instinctive ruthlessness these animals hunt and seize living food. . . . Despite their ferocity, however, the predators too are at the mercy of the organic cycle. . . . With death as a constant threat, violence matters less than vitality. Survival in Hughes's Darwinian realm calls for remarkable strength, alertness, and stamina, such as that of the hawk in "The Hawk in the Rain". . . .

In contrast with this animal vitality which opposes death, contemporary man appears to Hughes deficient in will, stamina, and vigor. While permitting advances in civilization, the eradication of certain threats to man's existence has simultaneously encouraged a general relaxation and softening which the poet regrets, particularly since he associates passivity with death. . . .

To convince himself of the persistence of life, Hughes must ultimately abandon mortal individuals and turn to the foundation of existence, immortal energy itself. This he has done in *Crow,* in which the legendarily persistent scavenger bird becomes the mythological embodiment of energy and is endowed with appropriate physical attributes. . . . [Living] energy is inseparable from change, as Crow dramatically demonstrates by being repeatedly mangled, dismembered, and blown to pieces. Like the atom Crow not only survives such endless transformations but thrives upon them to triumph in his combat with death and inertia.

*Julian Gitzen, "British Nature Poetry Now," in* The Midwest Quarterly, *Summer, 1974, pp. 323-37.*

* * *

## HUXLEY, Aldous 1894-1963

**Huxley was a British-American novelist, essayist, critic, poet, and playwright. Trained in medicine, he was always interested in science; later in life he turned to mysticism and was preoccupied with the occult. His vast learning and searching intelligence are apparent in all of his forty-five books.**

*Point Counter Point* with its counterpointed narratives might be described as a multiple 'novel of ideas'; while *Eyeless in Gaza* hardly belongs to the original genre at all. The conversion theme of this novel demanded a more complex analysis of character and a narrative which stretched over four decades, neither of which could be accommodated within the basically static structure of the 'novel of ideas'. The result was Huxley's most ambitious experiment in form; it contains some of his highly developed characters, and, in spite of the copious notebook extracts, it can hardly be dismissed as a lengthy essay with added entertainments.

The utopian novels, *Brave New World* and *Island,* deserve special mention as they both carry a heavy burden of exposition. This, in itself, does not necessarily point to failure: the 'novel of ideas' by its very nature allows for a large measure of expository material. Perhaps the only criterion we can apply is that the exposition should be lively and that it should be tempered by a measure of dialectical opposition. *Brave New World,* which originated as a parody of the Wellsian utopias, is largely satirical and the expository material never loses its incisive quality. *Island,* on the other hand, as the portrait of an ideal society, offers little scope to the satirist—here the community itself is the norm and only such a peripheral character as the Rani of Pala, a Madame Blavatsky figure, allows for true Peacockian caricature. Further, the savage in *Brave New World* supplies a dialectical opposition which Will Farnaby totally fails to provide in *Island*. As a result the ideas lack the dramatic qualities they possess in the earlier novels. This is not to say that *Island* is completely without merit as a 'novel of ideas'; it is redeemed to a large extent by its sheer intellectual density and the wealth of ideas which it has to offer, but it is the one major novel to which the criticism of 'a lengthy essay with added entertainments' might fairly be applied. In conclusion, it must be said that it is not the least of Huxley's achievements that he has revived an outmoded form, to which only one major English novelist had previously aspired, and blessed it with the touch of his genius. Under Huxley, the 'novel of ideas' has approached the status of a major art form. (pp. 14-15)

*Eyeless in Gaza*, Huxley's single complete expression of the conversion theme, his first novel to restore the meaning, stands central to his work as a whole. Everything he wrote earlier is in a sense preparatory, everything subsequent a tailing off, except for the final utopian vision of *Island*. After *Crome Yellow* the theme of moral regeneration, leading to Anthony Beavis's conversion, is latent in all the novels of the nineteen-twenties. (pp. 19-20)

The search for a more desirable way of life is clearly the most important single theme in Huxley's novels. What distinguishes Huxley's work from that of other moralists is the treatment of this theme within the framework of the 'novel of ideas'. The idea of conversion, for example, is central to both *Eyeless in Gaza* and Tolstoy's *Resurrection* but it is clear that apart from their parallel themes the two works have little in common. It is not just that Huxley's form and characterization owe nothing to the nineteenth-century novel, the whole moral climate has changed. In the eighteen-nineties, Tolstoy could appeal to what was still a traditional morality: to Nekhlyudov, at grips with the problems of a stricken conscience and the Tsarist penal code, Christianity was still a powerful moral force. For Anthony Beavis, no such traditional morality existed: science had made Christian dogmas intellectually unacceptable and if the findings of science were true not even the basis of a humanistic morality remained. The challenge to moral values, then, as it appeared to Huxley in the nineteen-twenties, was substantially an ideological one, a matter of dialectic in which the appeal is to the intellect rather than the emotions. (p. 22)

There is little doubt that when *Point Counter Point* was written, Huxley was a confirmed convert to [D. H.] Lawrence's ideas and the novel with its sympathetic portraits of Frieda and Lawrence as Mary and Mark Rampion is in many respects a tribute to their friendship. Huxley's debt to Lawrence was further acknowledged in *Do What You Will*, the volume of essays published in the same year. To what extent Lawrence actually caused Huxley to deviate from his original path is a matter of argument. The strong anti-clerical element prevalent in Huxley's writing at this time was undoubtedly the result of Lawrence's influence; on the other hand, Lawrence merely reinforced Huxley's growing distrust of intellectualism, and *Point Counter Point* and *Brave New World* represent Huxley's most concentrated attack on the scientific attitude and its effect on the modern world. (p. 78)

While it is profitable to compare, say, *Brave New World* with *Men Like Gods* and *The Shape of Things to Come*, it is worth noting that none of Huxley's novels have yet fallen into the ranks of literary curiosities. His novels have always been something more than mere vehicles for the popularization of ideas; and, although the polemical element is never totally absent from his work, it is almost invariably subordinated to the wider demands of his art. That his interest in the novel declined towards the end of his career is indisputable, but this is no reason for our dismissing him as an inferior talent. (p. 213)

All of Huxley's major novels, with the exception of *Island*, are conceived as ironic structures. The death of Grace Elver in *Those Barren Leaves*; the isolation and suicide of the Savage in *Brave New World*; the discovery of the senescent Fifth Earl in *After Many a Summer*, all provide the final twist of the screw, the ironic reversal which is the characteristic of Huxley's art. Even in *Island*, the least ironic of Huxley's novels, the forces of reason are crushed at the very moment of Will Farnaby's conversion, a piece of super-added irony that caused at least one critic to lose his bearings. What, however, distinguishes Huxley's art is the breadth of his ironic vision, the intensity of the viewpoint which it provides. Nothing is spared, nothing assumed or taken for granted. No one since Swift—certainly not Peacock, to whom Huxley's satire owes a great deal—has viewed the totality of human activity with such complete scepticism. (p. 214)

The weaknesses in Huxley's novels can almost always be traced back to his failure to find an adequate correlative for the presentation of 'goodness'. It is perhaps debatable whether a writer who is primarily an ironist and a satirist should in fact try to explore the more positive aspects of human nature. His appointed task is to tear away the mask of human pretensions, to shock us into awareness; if he momentarily drops the cloak of irony, he takes the risk of either lapsing into sentimentality or becoming merely a propagandist. It must be admitted that Huxley's attempts at moralizing bring him dangerously close to failure on both counts. In the early novels, whenever irony is absent, he is betrayed into sentimentality. The Emily episode in *Antic Hay*, with its recurrent references to wild flowers, 'barrel-bellied ponies' and the 'twiddly lanes of Robertsbridge', is at its best an unhappy interlude. What must be considered the most ineffective chapter in *Point Counter Point*—one which must have caused Lawrence considerable embarrassment—is that describing the early life of Mary and Mark Rampion, an impossibly idealized version of Lawrence's meeting and courtship of Frieda. These lapses into sentimentality disappear in the later novels although the brand of 'goodness' exhibited by Brian and Mrs Foxe in *Eyeless in Gaza* might give some readers a moment of uneasiness. (pp. 225-26)

Huxley never really solved the problem of placing 'goodness' within a novel of this kind. It is indicative of his failure that the redemptive characters, the exemplary figures of Gumbril Senior, Rampion, Dr Miller, Propter and Bruno Rontini, all stand outside the ironic structure of the novel. Unlike the redemptive characters of E. M. Forster, they are largely powerless to influence events and share no significant part in the action of the novel. (p. 226)

The theme of moral regeneration which plays an important part in Huxley's novels also demands an active demonstration of 'goodness' and once again we find Huxley involved in problems of a formal nature. In the early novels the mood of disenchantment predominates and, except for Calamy's precipitant conversion in the final chapters of *Those Barren Leaves*, the moral and satirical elements are for the greater part in harmony. In the later novels the theme of moral regeneration appears and this becomes a secondary principle of organization. As we have seen the theme of conversion is largely autobiographical; it begins in *Antic Hay* and reaches a climax in *Eyeless in Gaza*. As the theme develops so the problem of form becomes critical, the 'conversion episodes' trying to impose themselves, as it were, on the ironic structure of the novel. The formal weaknesses in Huxley's novels belong almost entirely to his failure to reconcile the two opposing elements. (p. 228)

*Island*, the least ironic of the major novels, is the least typical, the least Huxleyan. As a synthesis of ideas it is impressive by any standard, nevertheless it remains the one work which clearly approaches failure. Huxley's art depends above all on a dialectic of ideas, a dialectic engendered by the major ironies inherent in the human condition. This dialectic is absent in *Island* and in consequence, the sense of urgency present in the earlier novels, is lacking. Here the utopian theme could not be treated ironically; thus the situation presents basically the same problem Huxley faced earlier, the portrayal of goodness, only this time on a larger scale. It is significant that the utopian Palanese are the least effective of Huxley's redemptive figures; they fail to emerge as individuals and their virtues are expounded rather than lived. The failure to provide an adequate core of dialectic can be attributed to a great extent to the sketchy characterization of Farnaby. Will Farnaby, whose antecedents lie in Chelifer and Anthony Beavis, is an ineffective foil to the Palanese; as a world-weary Gulliver among the Houyhnhnms, he is too quickly charmed by the superior virtues of his hosts; as a result whatever conflict might have centred on his conversion is immediately lost and with it the dialectic which might have provided a backbone to the novel. (pp. 230-31)

Huxley's inability to animate the ideas in *Island*, to provide a central point of conflict lies not so much in the fact of his conversion, but in the nature of the conversion itself. Mahayana Buddhism, as Huxley insists, is a way of looking at life which reconciles opposites: 'the blessed experience of Not-Two'. In brief, it dissolves the opposing elements which lie at the heart of the ironist's vision: man as a product of his genes and his glands; man as a creature of sensitivity and suffering. To the Mahayanist, 'Born under one law, to another bound' is not a theme for ironic commentary, but merely a distorted vision of reality. It is impossible to be an ironist without being a dualist at the same time; irony depends for its strength on the co-existence of two irreconcilable sets of ideas and this is inimical to the whole concept of Buddhist thought. The point is worth emphasizing because this kind of reconciliation is rare in Western thought; dualism is in fact the basis of Western culture, and it was within the framework of a dualist philosophy that Huxley created his major work. . . .

The harmony which Huxley achieves as a moralist in *Island*, then, was gained at the expense of his ironic vision. Farnaby, of course, remains attached to the old way of life as his Mescalin experience illustrates; but his cynical asides, the puppet figures of the Rani and Colonel Dipa—these are little more than left-overs from the earlier novels. The ideas remain, ideas which . . . provide an important closing chapter to Huxley's development as a moralist, but the unifying factor has gone; what is left is certainly a novel with ideas but one which rightly belongs to the province of the essayist rather than the novelist. The history of Huxley's decline as a novelist is in effect the history of his decline as an ironist and his failure to find an alternative form. (pp. 232-33)

*Peter Bowering, in his* Aldous Huxley: A Study of The Major Novels *(copyright © 1969 by Peter Bowering; reprinted by permission of The Athlone Press of the University of London), Athlone Press, 1969.*

Whether Aldous Huxley has been a force for good or evil, whether he is an artist more noted for his contributions to the novel of ideas or for the ideas themselves, whether he is chiefly a romantic or a neoclassicist—on these questions, critics have not agreed. He has been called a frustrated romantic by [David Daiches in *The Novel and the Modern World*]; he has been attacked because he has joined Freud, Jung, Adler, and Lawrence "to sow distrust of reason, and to represent it as a mere tool of the unconscious [by C. E. M. Joad in *Return to Philosophy*]. His view of life has been characterized as "essential sterility" [by Millett, Manly and Rickert in *Contemporary British Literature*], and his embracing of mysticism has been called "the rationalist's substitute for suicide" [by Edwin Berry Burgum in *The Novel and the World's Dilemma*]. But Huxley has had his defenders, too. His description of the modern world has been hailed as "far more honest and decent than the early Victorian age depicted in Bulwer Lytton's *Pelham*" [by Morris R. Cohen in *The Faith of a Liberal*]. Similarly, "despite the temptations which beset a successful author," he never "seriously compromised with his intellectual integrity" [Jocelyn Brooke in *Aldous Huxley*]. . . .

Wherein then lies the value in giving serious consideration to Huxley? Precisely in his being able to articulate the intellectual and moral conflicts being fought in the collective soul of the twentieth century. D. H. Lawrence would express his reactions viscerally but failed to look through a microscope, as Huxley reminds us. James Joyce could disentangle himself from the nets in which he felt caught, but he did not seem aware of the oases to be found in Eastern meditative systems. E. M. Forster knew of passages to other cultures but preferred to regard art as self-sufficient rather than as catalytic. Virginia Woolf knew the agony of private torment but did not realize the healing that can emerge from societal involvement. It was Huxley of all these twentieth-century English writers who best reflected and coordinated the divisions of the modern world; he best expressed its *Weltanschauung* in its most universal sense. Thomas Henry Huxley, Aldous Huxley's grandfather, was called "Darwin's bulldog" because he so tenaciously clung to and advocated Darwin's theories; similarly, Aldous Huxley may become best known for being both an observer of and a contributor to the shifting values of our world.

That Huxley's works have always demonstrated a search for values can be shown by an analysis of his works from the very beginning. The novels published in the 1920's (*Crome Yellow, Antic Hay, Those Barren Leaves,* and *Point Counter Point*) were all concerned with showing how some of the traditional sources of value—religion, love, family life—were absent from the postwar generation. Most readers thought these books to be cynically entertaining and did not see their essentially moral undercurrent. (pp. 4-5)

He attacks the growing preoccupation with hedonism, materialism, technology, and false intellectualism in *Brave New World* (1932), *Eyeless in Gaza* (1936), *After Many a Summer Dies the Swan* (1939), *Time Must Have a Stop* (1944), and *Ape and Essence* (1948). He considers alternatives to materialism: mysticism (*The Perennial Philosophy*, 1946), an intelligent application of science (*Science, Liberty and Peace*, 1947), and a fusion of mysticism and science (*Island*, 1962). Occasionally, as in *The Doors of Perception* (1954) and *Heaven and Hell* (1956), he endorses the use of hallucinogenic drugs as a means of heightening one's spiritual and aesthetic awareness. *Brave New World Revisited* (1948) considers "the subject of freedom and its enemies." Even in books that are purportedly biographical, there is evident concern with moral directions; when he writes about the life of Father Joseph, adviser to Cardinal Richelieu, he deplores the evil mingling of spiritual and material values—saying, in effect, that Caesar and God cannot be served simultaneously. Similarly, in *The Devils of Loudun* (1952), he impregnates the biography of a seventeenth-century monk with meaning for this century. The life of Maine de Biran, the eighteenth-century French philosopher, occupies about half of *Themes and Variations*, but here again, as with the other subjects found in this 1950 volume, Huxley's observations are tinged with moral implications. (p. 7)

Huxley . . . prefers to consider his characters as states of being rather than what E. M. Forster would call "round characters." It is no wonder then that his characters can be classified under so many "humors." First, there is the intellectual who has developed his mentality but pathetically neglected the emotional and physical sides of life—people like Philip Quarles (*Point Counter Point*), Denis Stone (*Crome Yellow*), Bernard Marx (*Brave New World*), Shearwater (*Antic Hay*), Anthony Beavis (*Eyeless in Gaza*). Then there is the sardonic cynic—people like Spandrell (*Point Counter Point*) and Mark Staithes (*Eyeless Gaza*). There is the promiscuous female—characters like Mary Thriplow (*Those Barren Leaves*), Mrs. Viveash (*Antic Hay*), Lucy Tantamount (*Point Counter Point*), Lenina Crowne (*Brave New World*), and Virginia Mauncipie (*After Many a Summer Dies the Swan*). The mystic began to appear in the novels of the 1930's—characters like Mr. Propter (*After Many a Summer Dies the Swan*), Dr. Miller (*Eyeless in Gaza*), and Bruno Rontini (*Time Must Have a Stop*). Other characters of humors could be listed to make the point that most of Huxley's characters are used to illustrate the values (or more often, the lack of values) of certain ways of life. (p. 8)

Despite his inclusion of a mystic character in all his novels beginning with *Eyeless in Gaza*, it is revealing that the characters who most closely resembled Huxley in those novels (people like Anthony Beavis in *Eyeless in Gaza* and Sebastian Barnack in *Time Must Have a Stop*) were not the mystics but those Hamlet-like individuals who were frozen into inaction by their excessive cerebration. The mystic characters, it would seem, typified the person whom Huxley would have liked to emulate. He still remained the person who found conflict between his ideals and reality; who preferred to detach himself from the torrent of life's paradoxes. . . . (p. 18)

Basic to any interpretation of Huxley's quest for values is an understanding of Huxley's conception of reality, for therein lie the causes for his seeming inconsistencies, his sardonic irony, his rejection of many of the traditional sources of meaning in life, his plunge from the fetters of self, time, and space into self-transcendent mysticism, and finally, his attempt in his last novel (*Island*) to attain heaven on earth by embracing the knowledge of science along with the wisdom of religion. . . .

Huxley's search for reality assumed three seemingly different directions. Until the 1930's, Huxley's books (both fiction and nonfiction) examined a world in which the traditional sources of value (Judeo-Christian religion, patriotism, the conventional frameworks of private and public morality, the "progress" concept derived from the findings of science) were either replaced by a moral vacuum or else privately violated while publicly espoused. Such books as *Crome Yellow*, *Antic Hay*, and *Point Counter Point* indicate Huxley's disillusionment with Western society. In the second stage, approximately from the publication of his *Eyeless in Gaza* (1936) through *The Perennial Philosophy* (1945), Huxley tried to embrace the reality offered by mysticism, especially that preached by Buddhism. Then, in the last decade and a half of his life, Huxley tried to incorporate Buddhism within the framework of science (pp. 27-8)

Let us briefly review the path Huxley took before he embarked on the road to the ultimate reality as revealed by mysticism. He first found objective reality (the world of matter as measured and interpreted by science) both ugly and incomplete. Subjective reality (as explained by most philosophies of the Western World) he found equally objectionable because in most instances these philosophies were merely rationalizations of basic ugliness and selfishness. On the question of teleology, he found little to write about. On the problem of causality, he felt that hereditary and environmental forces are influential; at the same time, he believed, or at least hoped, that an assertion of will can do much to combat the determinism of heredity and environment. Looking at history, he found that the mistakes of the past tend to be repeated. This concept of reality led Huxley first to a kind of bitter cynicism. . . . Even the mystics found in Huxley's early works are somewhat cynical. Mr. Propter, in *After Many a Summer Dies the Swan*, tells Pete: "Most of the things that we're all taught to respect and reverence—they don't deserve anything but cynicism" (p. 97). It was almost inevitable, therefore, that the vacillations from despair to hope, from hope to cynicism again, vacillations which both objective and subjective reality engendered in Huxley, should yield to an attempt to find an absolute reality. This absolute reality Huxley found synonymous with the divine reality, or the divine Godhead. "Ultimate reality is at once transcendent and immanent. God is the creator and sustainer of the world; yet the kingdom of God is also within us . . ." (*Grey Eminence*, p. 59). It is characterized by self-transcendence, that is, by a negation of the world of the ego, of animal desires, or carnal and material aspirations. The philosophy of this absolute reality is the perennial philosophy. . . .

This self-transcendence and loss of personality is the only effective cure for a world suffering from idolatry, stupidity, and cruelty. In the ultimate reality, we can find true salvation. This attainment of the divine Godhead, Huxley felt, can be facilitated by a strong determination to do so. (pp. 36-7)

Selfhood, time, space—these are the obstacles to attainment of self-transcendence. And yet, unless we achieve this state, Huxley warned us in *Themes and Variations*, we are slaves to sorrow, wars, barbarism, futility. . . .

Huxley did not believe that very many people are capable of achieving this self-transcendence, although there has always been yearning for self-transcendence because human beings are tired of themselves, their dreary lives, and their responsibilities. (p. 38)

Despite Huxley's passionate belief that the divine reality is the only reality that can bring salvation, he was sufficiently pragmatic to recognize the limited appeal of such a philosophy of reality for most people. With the exception of the people in *Island*, all the mystics in his novels are, significantly enough, either old or else completely without any family responsibility. (pp. 38-9)

Possibly because Huxley realized that the life of self-transcendence could not be attained by very many people if will power were the only means utilized, Huxley began experimenting with certain drugs like mescalin. He found that the mystic euphoria could be reached not merely by a saintly self-transcendence, but by the taking of these drugs as well. Consequently, the books he wrote during the last decade of his life (*The Doors of Perception*, *Heaven and Hell*, *Brave New World Revisited*, *Island*, and *Literature and Science*) show an increasing respect for science as a means of ordering the chaos of reality into a sane existence. In the utopian society of Pala that he created in his last novel, *Island*, chemistry, physics, physiology, and other sciences are no longer satirized as they were in *Brave New World*. There is still, however, an occasional cynical echo from Huxley's early period. (pp. 39-40)

It should be fairly obvious, however, that Huxley's return to science and religion does not mean that he finally succeeded in his quest for truth. (p. 40)

Huxley began by trying to attain "Shanti." He ended by embracing the hallucinatory bliss of "*moksha*-medicine." On his pilgrimage to reach the shrine of understanding the ultimate reality, he ended by embracing not reality but an escape from it. (p. 41)

Although Huxley has offered many suggestions to effect an ideal government and the establishment of peace, what underlies all his statements for reform is a current of pessimism about the ultimate efficiency of any attempt to ameliorate the evils of our society. This undercurrent of pessimism is perhaps responsible for the paradoxical juxtaposition of offering a cure in one book, and then satirizing it in the next. For example, although he will advocate the creation of bridge-builders to bring about a better understanding of the various countries and philosophies in the world, he will satirize such a bridge-builder as De Vries in *Time Must Have a Stop*. Similarly, although he mildly favors the establishment of a world government, he will say, in *The Perennial Philosophy*, that what is needed is more decentralization. . . . (p. 114)

Despite the lack of finality and absolute certitude in the reforms he suggests, the impression that clearly emerges from the reading of his works written prior to *Island* is that government per se cannot possibly serve as a source of permanent value. . . . (p. 115)

Little wonder that Huxley tried to resolve the mess of human problems by detaching himself from them; consequently, his penultimate solution for the problem which a consideration of government, war, and peace engenders is a life of mystical nonattachment and a striving for a unitive knowledge and love of God. (p. 116)

Whatever else Aldous Huxley may have been, he was not a romantic, at least not a dedicated one. The romantic preoccupation with love and Nature is manifestly absent from his writings. . . .

From his earliest novel, *Crome Yellow*, to his last, *Island* (in spite of his attempts there to preach the yoga of love), sexual relationships are never considered a source of value. His comments about love in his nonfiction works likewise treat physical love disparagingly. With the exception of several artifically delineated happy marriages in *Island*, there is not a single love affair in all of Huxley's novels that is successfully and satisfyingly consummated; the marital and extramarital relationships all lead to pain or frustration. (p. 119)

Up to the time that he embraced mysticism as a way of life, Huxley had been grappling with the problem of sex and love and had come up with no satisfying solution. (p. 128)

In Huxley's novels, Nature is almost completely absent; to this extent, he might be called an urban novelist. He is primarily concerned with the life in the cities, the sophisticated conversations held in drawing rooms. Nearly all his characters are members of the upper classes and of the genteel professions. There are no laborers or rustics in his works; his dialogue never has the Hardy earthiness; his characters speak aphoristically. The forces of Nature play no significant role either in the setting or the characterization of his novels. And yet, in a sense, Huxley does analyze Nature as a source of value: he first attacks the romantic conception of Nature which seeks to find in Nature the source of wisdom and beneficence; he also warns us that if we are to continue the callous exploitation of Nature's resources, then we are faced with a far graver crisis than the political struggle of opposing ideologies. (p. 133)

Huxley's objections to the encroachment of applied science upon our lives are twofold: first, applied science, he argues, has intensified standardized mediocrity and the loss of attention to intellectual and spiritual values; second, the technology of the scientist has contributed to the destructiveness of war and to the diminishing of individual freedom. (p. 144)

Has science, then, no value for man? Huxley tries to work out a kind of conciliatory compromise which would maintain the contributions of science in helping to solve man's ecological problems while it would also tend to eliminate some of the evils that an uncontrolled technology would create. He wants scientists to be more actively responsible for the technological improvements they help to bring into existence; in other words, he wants them to be morally responsible for their actions or, as has been the case in the past, for their lack of active protests against producing more destructive weapons of mass annihilation. He also wants people to recognize the fact that the advantages of technology also bring with them disadvantages. (p. 149)

In his evaluation of science as a source of value, Huxley assigns to science the same function he did to the arts: facilitating the apprehension of the nature of ultimate reality. Science, like the arts, should never become an end in itself; both science and the arts should not be worshiped as ultimately divine entities. Science and technology, unless carefully controlled, can cause many evils: increased mediocrity, rising unemployment, and the barbarisms of warfare and totalitarianism; science and technology can, however, help man wisely use the earth's natural resources and can even aid him in achieving "the end and ultimate purpose of human life: Enlightenment, the Beatific Vision" (*Doors of Perception*, p. 73). (p. 151)

His search for ultimate answers led him, in his examination of religion, into all kinds of paradoxical complexities which were not resolved very clearly in his works and into all kinds of generalizations which have little meaning when subjected to detailed scrutiny. For example, he will sometimes speak of Christianity or Judaism as if they were monolithic entities. Furthermore, when he talks of Buddhism, Confucianism, Hinduism, or Mohammedanism, he does not consider the evolutionary changes that have been incorporated into these beliefs so that when he makes criticisms about them, one is not sure, for example, whether he is castigating the Mohammedanism of the late Middle Ages or the Mohammedanism of today. . . .

There are other difficulties besides trying to find specific meaning in the welter of generalizations one finds in Huxley's comments on religion. There is the difficulty in trying to grasp Huxley's attempts to reconcile religion with philosophy, aesthetics, ethics, and government. There is also the problem of endeavoring to find a relationship between religion considered as a metaphysical concept and religion considered as ritual and as a practical guide to mundane problems. (p. 154)

He found little to admire in the religions of Judaism, Christianity, and Islam. He blamed Judaism for narrowness of vision and excessive preoccupation with material success; he castigated Christianity for its cruel oppression of heresy, its occasional hypocrisy, its failure to object to the existence of wars; he criticized Islam for its pessimism and fatalism. It should be remembered, however, that what he was specifically rejecting in these three religions was the nonmystical element; wherever he found elements of mysticism, as he did in the Book of Ecclesiastes; in the writings of such mystic Christians as St. Augustine, St. Bernard of Clairvaux, Meister Eckhart, Walter Hilton, William Law, St. François de Sales, Thomas Traherne, and others; in the Sufi books of Islam, he accepted their teachings of contemplation, renunciation of worldly preoccupation, and the practice of love. It is, therefore, not so much religion itself that he was rejecting but what he felt was the perversion of the religious essence. (p. 163)

Essentially, then, Huxley's religious quest has been paradoxical and tortuous. He began by mocking and rejecting the Judeo-Christian tradition (though accepting its occasional manifestations of mysticism), flirted temporarily with the Lawrentian doctrine of instinctive living and "blood consciousness," changed to contemplative investigation, turned to the East for further illumination, and died in the West trying to balance, in an uneasy syncretism, the Caliban of Western science with the Ariel of Buddhist mysticism. One is saddened to observe that the religious syncretism turned out to be a synthetic product, that his metaphysical quest ended with a pharmacological solution. (p. 174)

[Since] man lives in many compartments, Huxley also compartmentalized himself. His spiritual self sought value and meaning by turning ultimately to a unitive knowledge and love of God; his societal self realized that man does not live by spirit alone, and thus he wrote frequently about society's need to adopt rational and scientific approaches for its many problems such as an inadequate supply of food, overpopulation, and the threat of man's extinction by war. The inner search and external quest thus formed the two foci of his elliptical journey through life. It was a journey well taken. (p. 183)

*Milton Birnbaum, in his* Aldous Huxley's Quest for Values *(copyright © 1971 by The University of Tennessee Press, Knoxville), University of Tennessee Press, 1971.*

The man who emphatically considers that Huxley attempted the novel proper with only an essayist's gifts is likely to be overlooking Huxley's positive aesthetic achievement. To think of Huxley simply as a satirist is to limit understanding of the purpose of his various devices. The term, 'novel of ideas', is accurate, but needs qualification and should not be allowed to impose the suggestion of a dwarfish offshoot of a grand phenomenon.

Very often, indeed, critics have argued that Huxley ought to have been doing this, that, or the other, instead of holding to his own peculiar course, and the fact that he openly took navigational directions from so many forerunners might sometimes have aided misunderstanding. His technical borrowings are numerous and they range over several arts, but they combine in every novel to form a new, Huxleyan whole. (p. 11)

One peculiarity of Huxley's fiction is the combination of the aims of the generalizing philosopher and the artist. He normally causes his language, his characters, his plots, his structures to signify richly rather than attempt to reproduce the exact multifariousness of personal experience. Particulars of persons, emotions, situations are often presented very clearly, but used (implicitly or explicitly) to illustrate generalities. (p. 14)

[For] Huxley the composition and disposition of characters are features of form. The characters are figures in landscapes, aesthetic components as well as arguments. Both major and minor characters have—quite realistically—clear features and accoutrements which bear out their natures, but, since they are for the most part comic figures (figures, that is to say, conceived in a comic mode even when they are not actually funny), they continually voice characteristic sentiments, and lack both inconsistency and the less obviously revealing surface of real-life conversation. (pp. 15-16)

The fact that Huxley's own people are personalities 'in the old sense of the word' is again a feature of the curious amalgam of the ways of science (or philosophy) and art. Huxley was interested in the classification of human beings, in the Galtonian, Jungian and Sheldonian categories especially, and he was keenly interested in the broad highways of response to experience. He regularly portrayed hedonists, for example, or cynics, because he wished to question the validity of their responses. Thus, while knowing all about the modern, 'atomized' personality, he yet tended to portray the contours of an individual's consciousness, and to align these contours with physical features, as if he believed that such a procedure is perfectly proper to a work of art, especially when that work includes mention of the true complexity of consciousness. It is safe to say that Huxley knew more about post-Bergson notions of the mind and more about the later developments of scientific psychology than most modern authors, but he did not regard such knowledge as necessarily replacing knowledge gained from the old, unprofessional psychologists, and all was grist to his mill. (p. 17)

It is hard to think of any other modern English writer so much possessed by death as Huxley. Death in his novels is often not so much a finale or a departure which produces its effect upon other characters; it is also a fact and a process to be contemplated in itself. Even in *Crome Yellow* Denis climactically thinks of suicide, while Sir Hercules and his wife actually kill themselves. Not many authors, one imagines, would in such a context include the business of severing the artery with a razor. In *Antic Hay* the Monster dies on the same evening that Lypiatt considers killing himself. Frequently the death is a climax and a turning-point. In *Point Counter Point* the deaths of little Phil and Webley occur, as does the death of Grace Elver in the present novel, just before the close, thus modifying all that has gone before and casting a shadow forward over the conclusion. By the time we close the novel old John Bidlake is about to die and Spandrell has been shot. In *Eyeless in Gaza* the details of the death of Brian Foxe (there are, of course others) are withheld until nearly the end; in *Time Must Have a Stop* the early farcical death of Eustace Barnack—followed by his revelations of life beyond the grave—is balanced by the later saintly death of Bruno Rontini. *After Many a Summer* reflects Huxley's preoccupation more concentratedly and obviously than any of the other novels. Just as characteristically Huxleyan is the car-accident and the mutilation of Katy Maartens in *The Genius and the Goddess*. In *Brave New World* the death of the Savage is the denouement, while earlier the act of dying has, for serious satirical purposes, been transformed into a painless event. In *Island*, too, the death of Lakshmi takes place with a minimum of pain, but this time a straightforwardly serious recommendation is being made. It is hardly necessary to comment upon the malformations of *Ape and Essence* or the descriptions of decrepitude, torture and death in two non-fictional works, *Grey Eminence* and *The Devils of Loudun*. (p. 69)

The half-way mark in Huxley's writing career, from *The Burning Wheel* (1916) to *Island* (1962), comes in 1939 when *After Many a Summer* was published; and in a valuable as well as a merely chronological sense *Eyeless in Gaza* represents the close of the first period. We have so far examined the variety of techniques which Huxley used to make sense of his experience, but from now on, excluding *Ape and Essence*, we shall be observing degrees of success in the techniques used to disseminate certainties. (p. 137)

It seems possible that between *Crome Yellow* and *Eyeless in Gaza* Huxley overlooked no alternative to the perennial philosophy and no loophole in the arguments for it. But [*Eyeless in Gaza*] is also a considerable literary feat because it pushes the novel of ideas as far as possible in the direction of the novel proper without losing the distinctive characteristics of the former or dealing less than ably with the requirements of the latter. (p. 138)

*The Genius and the Goddess*, a *nouvelle* of about thirty-thousand words, is for the most part in the guise of a piece of oral narration by a man who played a leading role in the events which he is now describing. This device should be seen first of all as yet another answer to a problem which Huxley had by now been faced with for some twenty years, the problem of how to pass on certainties without fracturing the work. He evidently felt the need to incorporate into his later fictions his own commentaries upon the actions. Take away Mr Propter, for example, and no one could make of the remaining events and characters of *After Many a Summer* what Huxley wished us to make of them. But in that novel the commentary and the action are more clearly separated than Huxley seems ever again to have regarded as satisfactory.

Now in *The Genius and the Goddess* the fictional element and the essay element are at one, though this has been achieved by minimizing the dramatic element. (p. 192)

*Island* is not a hotch-potch of proposals for the good life casually attached to an indifferent story, but a structure in which one's appreciation of each item is enhanced, directly or indirectly, by knowledge of many other items.

In this way the novel is a structure of close inter-relationships, and only the most trivial steps in the story are superfluous to Huxley's didactic purpose. If Will Farnaby has a bad fall, this is so that we can be shown how to deal with physical shocks; if a praying mantis comes on the scene, this is so that Will—and therefore the reader—can be taught in the final chapter how to accommodate even the apparently gratuitous horror of the mantis. Murugan is presumed to be homosexual solely to emphasize by contrast the wisdom of normal Palanese upbringing and the native methods of training in sexual activity. The Rani's theosophy constitutes both a touch of satire for our entertainment and an illustration of false spirituality. Vijaya is given physical strength partly in order to show how strength need not lead to bullying or contempt for the frail. Conversely, the *maithuna* instructress, Mrs Rao, is plump and 'very stupid upstairs' because it is necessary for us to realize that such traits need not be disadvantages. In particular, the concluding deaths of Lakshmi and Dr MacPhail occur so that the reader, having been 'trained', so to speak, by the earlier sections of the novel in a mode of acceptance of such experiences, can properly accept them.

In the foregoing remarks there are implications that some of the effects of *Island* are cumulative, and it is true that the closing chapters form a climax, not simply in the usual sense that a sequence of events bears fruit, but also in the unusual sense of a fusion and heightening of all the preceding ideas. And these ideas form a summit towards which Huxley can now be seen to have been struggling (often without knowing his direction) since at least 1920. (p. 214)

[Complex] emotions, of whatever strength, inform the novels, and it is for these emotions that Huxley in inventing his various devices, including the larger structures, found 'objective correlatives'. At one end of the sequence, the design, the incidents, the people and the language of *Crome Yellow* make up the formula for a particular compound of feelings, including sadness; while, at the other end, *Island* expresses bereavement. Neither the intellectual ideas which the novels are so full of, nor the technical ideas which Huxley thought up or adapted are merely sportive. He had an exceptional capacity for using ideas creatively, as expressive of the whole man. In this way, the tricks of *Eyeless in Gaza* should be recognized as reflecting full-blooded concerns with time, death and spiritual rebirth; and the fantastic effects of *Ape and Essence* as methods of organizing a mood of defection into a countervailing hope of change through the very carnality gross representations of which have helped to express the dejection. *Brave New World* is as much about personal problems as it is about problems of society.

One detects in Huxley's writings—alongside the Pyrrhonism which he gives to Philip Quarles and the searching for non-attachment which he gives to Calamy, Anthony Beavis and Sebastian Barnack—a kind of Stoicism arising from a conviction that, since the individual is a tiny fragment of the cosmic process, it is bad to 'make a fuss' about personal feelings. Instead of having an inclination to rage or repine about any shocking feature of the human condition, he continually recommended, either by direct statements or implicitly through his manner, a mixture of insouciance and intellectual honesty. But Huxley's emotions, though stoically restrained, never appear to have been evaded in the fiction, so that even *Brave New World*, the novel in which ideas seem most flagrantly to crowd out feelings, owes its distinction not only to its celebrated ingenuities but also to emotional pressures which, we can be sure, produced the main ingenuities, and which are amply (though inconspicuously) expressed by construction and style. (p. 225)

*Keith M. May, in his* Aldous Huxley, *Paul Elek Books Ltd., 1972.*

Aldous Huxley never again wrote as badly as in *Eyeless in Gaza*. . . .

As a writer of fiction, Aldous Huxley made an impact which is likely to be felt longer than that of many better writers. This is not to say that the lessonless *Point Counter Point* and the wearisome *Eyeless in Gaza*, both forgotten today, are likely to be rediscovered and hailed by future generations. But *Brave New World* is still remembered and is likely to be for long, is spite of its Wellsian beliefs, in spite of the disastrous parable of the erudite Red Indian who represents the traditional world, in spite of the over-insistence.

As a writer of fiction, Huxley was far too imperfect a craftsman to be described as 'great'. If you want to be sure of that, read another didactic novel with aims similar to Huxley's, *Candide*. . . . Reading [Huxley's] books, one may often have the impression that he was an essayist forced [by his need for money] to express himself clumsily in novels.

Certainly he was a very remarkable essayist. His essays are almost all very good, and the bad ones belong mostly to his later years. . . . Whatever his theme, light or grave, his touch as an essayist was exquisite.

His spiritual and political philosophies were not separable. They were both concerned with an absolute morality based on biological considerations of the means needed to preserve the human race, and the merits of mystical pacifism. His influence on opinion in these respects was massive for a short time.

As a Huxley, he revered science, and though he was the first to protest against excessive scientific claims, he was averse to non-scientific ideas. His admiration for mysticism was to a great extent based on the view that the reality of the mystical experience is open to rational deduction. He did not give any attention to the doctrine of original sin. In a world dominated by Hitler and Stalin, he still could not but believe in the efficacy of persuasion alone. He saw equal impropriety in authoritarian war-mongering and the (unhappily inadequate) efforts of the civilized part of the world to resist. 'Only connect,' he might have said, as did E. M. Forster, another brilliant but bewildered thinker.

*Christopher Sykes, "Aldous Huxley and Original Sin," in* The Listener, *November 1, 1973, pp. 601-02.*

Huxley ends up focusing most of his satire at the point of balance where humanism and aspiration, body and soul, split. His work is comedy of ideas in a universe thus dichotomized between intellect and passion; what, though, is clear is that he recognizes that he himself is one of the order of persons he is satirizing—the new artist-intellectuals—and this induces narrative unease and even guilt, though it is of course essential to the sense of compelling honesty in his books. But it is also evident that his work arises in a very specific social milieu and the unease has a decided historical location. [*Chrome Yellow*, *Antic Hay*, *Those Barren Leaves*, and *Point Counter Point*] are very much *about* the twenties; Huxley writes them about and for a world in which his own sources in culture and art are insecure. The world is in a bewildering disorder; intelligence and reason alone cannot save it, but stand, with several of his heroes, bewildered before barbarism and passion. . . .

Huxley's novels are largely novels of inaction, for his scrupulous, devastating analysis usually produces in the central characters a masochistic withdrawal from action. At the same time, the novels turn on the emptying out of the centre from any dream, hope, or institution, and hence have an apparent air of cynicism, a suggestion of universal failure.

But what is so very Huxleyan about these books is that the author's own cynicism and detachment are very much part of the matter for analysis. The embarrassment of the novelist's feeling that his own ideas and assumptions are themselves a sterile or incomplete view of life comes out most clearly in *Point Counter Point*, where the writing of novels of ideas becomes part of the theme, and where the character of Philip Quarles is the novelist's self-surrogate. But this element runs through all the twenties novels, starting in *Chrome Yellow* with the figure of Denis, the sensitive writer conscious of the loss of a real infinite to feed upon. . . .

[For] Huxley the modern is a species of evolution as well as a matter for excellent comedy and farce, and so his world of parties, free love, adulteries, revolutionary and reactionary passions, and the boredom of 'disillusion after disillusion' is an intense experiencing of the times. The cultural and moral passions both expose and are exposed by the new freeing of repressions, the new sorts of men and women, the new freedom, but also the new anarchy of the post-Freudian as well as the postwar universe. The artist, here, is deeply implicated in the modern not only as an art form but as an enveloping experience. 'Living modernly's living quickly,' says Lucy Tantamount in *Point Counter Point*. 'You can't cart a wagonload of ideals and romanticisms about with you these days.' Huxley's fictional world is one in which this may produce a sense of yearning loss, but one in which the view is taken for granted. If the consequence is that intelligent man is left in a comic predicament, in an historical void, Huxley sees that as inescapable—such is the contemporary historical acceleration. The result is hardly cynicism but a complex blend of involvement and disgust. He is satirically savage, but not satirically secure; his novels are a continuous, tentative intellectual inquiry into new forces as well as a display of ironic detachment. Indeed, the desperation and absurdity of the characters is not at a total distance; it touches the novelist as well.

*Malcolm Bradbury, in his* Possibilities: Essays on the State of the Novel *(copyright ©*

*1973 by Malcolm Bradbury; reprinted by permission of Oxford University Press, Inc.), Oxford University Press, 1973, pp. 151-53.*

# I

## IGNATOW, David 1914-

**Ignatow, an American poet, employs a deceptively simple poetic language to reveal the dreams and agonies of city-dwellers. Many of his poems are about New York, the city in which he has always lived. (See also *Contemporary Authors*, Vols. 9-12, rev. ed.)**

Ignatow does almost completely without the traditional skills of English versification. He makes no effort to assure his lines rhetorical effectiveness; the import of each poem is thus far too dependent upon *what* is said, given in a low, gentle, spell-breaking murmur. At his best, however, Ignatow often seems a real primitive, with the small, serene vision of the Douanier Rousseau or of Bombois. His narrative gift appears to me to be worthy of encouragement, and I look forward, queerly, since concision and concentration are integral to Mr. Ignatow's successes here, to longer work. . . .

Ignatow's poems . . . rank with the most authentic now being written. What gives them their unique power is a kind of strange, myth-dreaming vision of modern city life, and the ability to infuse the décor of the contemporary city with the ageless Old Testament fatality of death and judgment: to make the traditional moral issues of the race *count* in an environment where seemingly they have ceased to, and to give them a fitting dramaturgy of symbol and image which not only brings the reader into the situations Ignatow writes about, but makes him subject to the same unchangeable laws: judges him, doesn't let him get away untouched. There is no obvious brilliance of language; in Mr. Ignatow's use, words are merely a vehicle for recounting what happened: what happens. The dramatic impact of each poem hits you foursquare, always convincingly, and the whole thing, the incident, the judgment, is what you remember. Mr. Ignatow's is a "total poetry" in a different sense from that in which the term is ordinarily used; not like that, say, of Hopkins or Dylan Thomas or Mallarmé. Rather than being word-oriented, it is an inspired and brilliantly successful metaphysical reportage, with an "I-was-the-man" authority that shakes the involved beholder to his bones.

*James Dickey, "David Ignatow" (1961), in his* Babel to Byzantium *(reprinted with the permission of Farrar, Straus & Giroux, Inc.; copyright © 1956, 1957, 1958, 1959, 1960, 1961, 1962, 1963, 1964, 1965, 1966, 1967, 1968 by James Dickey), Farrar, Straus, 1968, pp. 25-8.*

In what is the best poem in [*Rescue the Dead*], a three line epigraph, David Ignatow announces a new course, a new thrust in his poetry: "I feel along the edges of life / for a way / that will lead to open land." He doesn't find the open land in "Rescue the Dead," but he does come closer than ever before by looking away from the almost surreal urban landscape of his earlier work and into himself, the inner landscape of pain, suffering, and the dark joy of love. It is a bleak, cold world that David Ignatow lives in, but in these new poems he finds a strength to endure even as he seems to deny as strongly as ever the idea of prevailing, of really finding open ground. "If I live through the night," he says in one poem ("The Hope"), "I will be a species / related to the tree / and the cold dark." A faith in a silent God, in love, in some inner force that will struggle to endure, these impel Ignatow's inner journey. If he cannot sing the dawn, he is able to know the night, write a strong poetry of that knowing, and perhaps even rescue the dead from the dark. The result is his best book of poems.

Virginia Quarterly Review, *Vol. 44, No. 3 (Summer, 1968), pp. ciii-civ.*

What can you say about a poet who has written consistently excellent poetry for almost thirty years, and whose best work, as it should be, is always his most recent? Ignatow has been ignored by the anthologists, probably because he has never fit into any of the various "schools" of poetry. In the 50's he was neither a beat nor an academic, and in the 60's neither a Black Mountain, "deep image," or New York poet. Hopefully, the publication of *Poems 1934–1969* will help make him as well known as he should be. Ignatow's work is a product of deep and often critical emotion, intelligence, spontaneity, and craft. None of these is previous to the others; all are subsumed by a completely individual voice whose language is a perfect mouth—wholly responsive, immediate, and personal. His poems are aesthetically impeccable, almost in a self-sufficient way, but they have the immediacy and the impact of a person speaking directly to you. . . . For all of its sense of reality, this is a deeply mysterious poetry. Its mystery is, of course, man; which is to say, David Ignatow, and also the reader. I've never read a poetry in which there is such a direct and immediate interplay between the poet and the reader. Ignatow's poems have a quality of reciprocal honesty on both sides of the words, a clean pure fear like cold water which is almost a kind of hope, and which exists in Ignatow's heart and in the heart of the reader. It's this quality which gives Ignatow's words their edge, their austere precision, as if you were reading them always for the first time, no matter how old the message is. And it's this quality which makes Ignatow's work some of the very best, if not *the* best, as well as some of the most frightening, being written today. . . .

*John Vernon, in* Western Humanities Review, *Spring, 1971, pp. 196-97.*

The wide span of years covered by David Ignatow's collection [*Poems 1934–1969*] surprised me. I suppose most people think of him as I always have, as a poet of the 'sixties, for it was in those years that the Wesleyan poetry series brought to his work the wider audience it now has. It is evident from this book that Ignatow is one of those rare writers who begin somewhat out of step and end up decades later sounding unquestionably contemporary. The times have had to catch up with him. His language, which is without ornament and brutal in its honesty, does not date. Ignatow is a master of that tough urban tone that derives ultimately from William Carlos Williams. It must be granted, too, that he has at times the characteristic defects of such a style. Among the large number of poems presented here, a fair amount are simply very raw slices of life or flat-sounding aphorisms. . . .

The problem is not that the language is so direct—that is one of Ignatow's chief assets—but that a photographic description has taken the place of an imaginative engagement with the subject. But this is a drawback which Ignatow is usually able to overcome, particularly in his later pieces. While his language has remained unsparing, his anger and his sense of absurdity have grown sharper. Now he denounces what he sees by means of a kind of deadpan fantasy. . . .

Ignatow should be read for the power of his indictments, and for his pure lyric moments, which emerge like dandelions from the cracks in sidewalks. . . . Reading this book from beginning to end we can chart the growth of awareness in a deeply civilized man who has forced himself to speak the truth amid the wreckage of civilization.

*Robert B. Shaw, "Poets in Midstream," in* Poetry *(© 1971 by The Modern Poetry Association; reprinted by permission of the Editor of* Poetry*), July, 1971, pp. 228-33.*

Ignatow speaks of the world in which a man, if he cannot provide for his family very well, is not a man. He has no books, papers, rationalizations, or arguments to run to. He has only a world of mean bosses, petty customers, and a poor life. . . .

Ignatow talks about a reality few poets perceive, the world where books will *not* help to mitigate the pain. Perhaps it is precisely that workingman's view of the world (I do not wish to imply here that Ignatow's writing is uneducated and without literary content, but simply that the surface of the poem is always that of the mild-mannered, neatly and inexpensively dressed workingman of the city) which may account for the fact that David Ignatow does not receive the attention he deserves from the literary establishment, is not given national prizes. That establishment, even the avant-garde, is filled with bookish people like myself who, even if they have had to live in the workaday world, almost never think about it, escape from it as fast as they can, and in some ways never "sully" their poetry with it.

How brave of David Ignatow to talk about these things and attempt to make poetry from them. Surely that is the object lesson of Williams's own lifework, though he luxuriously had a more interesting and rewarding life to choose from. When Williams eats the delicious icy plums in his refrigerator he can transform the note he leaves to his wife into a metaphysical love poem. Ignatow's icebox is more likely to have rotten apples in it. . . .

I suppose it is unusual that I who love complex, ornate images, the music of dream poems, and long discursive narrative argumentative poems should find David Ignatow's poetry so attractive. But there is an honesty, a wholeness of vision, and a simple humanity in the work which I am drawn to.

*Diane Wakoski, "Working Poet," in* The New York Review of Books *(reprinted with permission from* The New York Review of Books; *© 1971 by NYREV, Inc.), December 30, 1971, p. 26.*

There is [a] strong feeling in *Rescue the Dead* that the poet is at odds with himself for, among other things, being in love and having an occupation. The division between the two selves—the one wanting absolute freedom and the one functioning in society—provides subjects for several poems. Whichever "self" is chosen, the person behind the poems is unhappy.

Other poems exploit the bizarre, cruel, and sad. The sequence of three "Ritual" poems offers a vision of humanity as confused, purposeless, and vicious. One asks after suffering through the atrocities in this sequence, why live at all? Its closing line, "for to live is to act in terms of death," is in a curious relationship to the volume's epigraph: "I feel along the edges of life/ for a way/ that will lead to open land." So far (nearly halfway through *Rescue the Dead*), Ignatow has not found it, and I am beginning to think this is one of the most depressing collections I've run up against.

*Ronald Moran, in* The Southern Review, *Vol. 8, No. 1, Winter, 1972, p. 251.*

Ignatow's poetry owes its success to the Cold War as Wordsworth's did to the French Revolution. The national hostility meshed with Ignatow's harsh intuitions about father and wife, and about day-labor in New York City; it emblematized his rage and helplessness aging toward death. His short, aggressive poems emerge from a mind he compares to an armed camp and a fortified tank. They often begin with some violent assertion or mad conceit, play with it a moment, then conclude abruptly, like the fist-fights they often carry as metaphors.

Because Ignatow trusts his own whims and keeps his lyric voice steady, even the most hyperbolic wit seems reasonable, as reasonable as the newspaper stories we train ourselves to read without flinching. Except that somewhere in our souls we *do* flinch, and Ignatow's poems are aimed at that human response.

*Laurence Goldstein, in* Michigan Quarterly Review, *Summer, 1972, p. 214.*

Starting out as a youngster in the Thirties, [Ignatow] has produced steadily. Slowly he has gained recognition, and after the early years of struggle, wretched jobs, yearning for response, he has been received with a certain respect by his fellows and has in consequence been awarded fellowships, grants, and invitations to talk about poetry in one academy or another. But as far as the greater public is concerned, the name-dropping public not only of the coffee table and the book club but of the exam room (Name 3 Major American Poets, beat, black, breast-beating), his name might as well be Ignoto as Ignatow. . . .

The Ignatow of these poems [*Poems 1934–1969*] is very like a man in a Malamud novel—no, more like someone in a Bellow novel. I do not mean that formally he is at all like either of those writers; I mean rather that he comes to exist for us as one of Bellow's people comes to exist for us, in Chicago or on the Upper West Side, uniquely and centrally American in the way that urban Jews have come to be taken as representative Americans.

*Harvey Swados, "David Ignatow: The Meshuganeh Lover," in* American Poetry Review, *May/June, 1973, pp. 35-6.*

In some ways it seems presumptuous to "review" the notebooks of David Ignatow. The book represents, it *is*, a man's whole life. . . . There is so much unhappiness, frustration, emotional starvation, literary uncertainty reiterated in the book that at first, certainly, I found it unbearable. The *cri de coeur* not only reached me; it deafened me, at first, to the singularity of Ignatow's achievement.

My first thought was indeed that Ignatow has no humor, no associates outside business and his family, no subject matter in the actual world outside this anxious round, no magic, no fantasy. And Ignatow is indeed all too strikingly a man of feeling, living in a world of feeling. The burden of so much "feeling"—by which I also mean the generality and conventionality of many emotional reactions to his hard life—the problem (and so one to us) of a man living in what is too often exclusively a *world* of feeling—this can be overwhelming in its reiteration, and Ignatow certainly relies upon reiteration in order to make himself heard—by God, by the reader, by anyone out there in the silent dark that often surrounds him.

The trouble with having so much self-inflicted feeling, the trouble with *any* mental world too much pressed down with conscious "feeling," is that in our tightly organized mental hierarchy feeling seems to have no "solution," as indeed Ignatow is the first to complain in these pages. If "poetry makes nothing happen," as a much cooler customer than Ignatow said, too often the emotion that goes into poetry is not *happening*. It is just there, stuck on the page like a man's academic credentials. And when the emotions *are* happening, as in Ignatow's notebooks and better still in his poetry, the reader minds getting caught up, shaken up. Too vulnerable oneself, afraid of the assault, I found myself at first recoiling not so much from "emotion" as from the sometimes numbing consistency of Ignatow's writing, the repeated unrelieved quality that he brings to his notebook. . . .

So all this presents an amazingly tight, rigorously severe and punishing picture of a man just held in thrall, of a man who feels that his life is not his own, of a classic compulsive, tragically internalized Jew. Ignatow is beset even by efforts that seem to present no redemption, and unlike so many with his problems, he does not even have conventional intellectual access to these problems. Neither Marx nor Freud nor any other messiah of intellect comes into this record with a helping hand.

Yet *The Notebooks of David Ignatow* become, after the first shock of much unrelieved suffering, a fascinating, even haunting book. . . .

Many of the passages are clearly arguments for a poem, a poem seems to get itself secretly written in the course of many a notebook entry, and the passages succeed each other, as Ignatow's poems regularly do, by falling into the same cadence, manner, issue. This desperate sincerity, this sometimes unbelievable humility of manner, is Ignatow's witting or unwitting way of making something of his life. Largely, I would guess, on the basis of what Santayana called "animal faith," or the sheer intuition that can present itself to a writer by the nature of his experience; that the experience alone will bring him home to the form he needs in order to redeem his experience in the form of art. . . .

What impresses me . . . is the fact that with passage after passage of . . . homely, sometimes touchingly unreal, attempts to reason his "suffering" out, the important thing is the spell his life has on him and so on the journal-like continuum of moods, laments, startled observations, accidents and near-catastrophes that has put his life into his poetry. In Ignatow's *Poems 1934-1969* we really get a *book*, put together from single poems, rather than a selection of poems. The poems in this book are amazingly uniform in quality, but they make a book, they become a successful long poem that could have been called *New York* and is indeed a better long poem than *Paterson*. Precisely because of Ignatow's docility, the modest, the sometimes unbearable self-denial, of the city poet who has come out of so much suffering, and is so much up against it still that line after line is really an attempt to propitiate the Gods.

*Alfred Kazin, "The Esthetic of Humility," in* American Poetry Review, *March/April, 1974, pp. 14-15.*

*Notebooks* is the diary of a search for hope, uncompleted, but unabandoned. . . .

What distinguishes *Notebooks* . . . is its lethal honesty, its awareness that self-revelation in any book is only as valuable as the light it throws on human problems. . . . What makes the book both fascinating and painful is its power to force the reader down through a series of increasingly demanding levels.

Circumstance is the first level: the bafflement, anger, violence and periodic despair of a man who knows he is a fine poet, and who feels that everything . . . has conspired to thwart his very nature, let alone his poetry. This is such an important aspect of the notebooks that it might easily be mistaken for their core. . . .

But below this level is the question of poetry itself, its nature, its justification. Ignatow is cold toward poetry-as-artifice, poetry-sufficient-unto-itself, poetry-as-personal-therapy. . . . Poetry must be an open door, must be rooted solidly in a sharing, a reinforcement of mutual understanding. . . .

He wants his poetry continually flexible, constantly responsive to the nuances of the outside world, of that reality that "withers quickly without constant delicate attention."

But even at this point, an important—the most important—level has not been reached. The circumstantial struggle, the esthetic struggle, are preparatory to the final effort, that of forming a total life, a total human being. Again and again Ignatow stresses that the grim fight for survival must be in the interest of the ultimate establishment of a serene and voluntary order. "I want my life on the level of ceremony and innocence."

*Josephine Jacobsen, "Drama of Hope," in* The New Republic *(reprinted by permission of* The New Republic; *© 1974 by The New Republic, Inc.), June 29, 1974, pp. 26-7.*

* * *

## IONESCO, Eugene 1912-

**Ionesco is a Rumanian-born French dramatist associated with the Theatre of the Absurd. His essentially comic plays nevertheless most often take the form of nightmares, in which his main themes—loneliness and isolation of the individual—are developed in intentional *non sequiturs* and grotesque metamorphoses to the point of paroxysm and unbearable psychological tension. (See also *Contemporary Authors*, Vols. 9-12, rev. ed.)**

The first thing that strikes me about Ionesco's work is its theatricality. What Ionesco does is to take ideas which are now in the air—some people would say à la mode—and make arrestingly vivid stage images of them. The effect in general is usually macabre and witty while the writing is both sprightly and sharp with overtones of pathos. . . .

Attentive spectators will find [his] plays understandable. . .if they do not seek to grasp every word in a literal or information-bearing sense. What must be followed is what the eyes take in (for example, the weird clock in *The Bald Soprano*) and the *line of action* in each scene. The form of the plays rather than the details of each speech carries most of the message. The speech is understandable too, but in a suggestive or "symbolic" rather than a strict sense. The whole is related to meaning as we know it in contemporary painting and in modern verse. What is mainly to be noted in such a play as *Jack*, for example, is that traditional scenes from bourgeois drama with almost conventional action (the mother entreats, the sister reasons, the father moralizes, the boy protests, the would-be in-laws storm, the boy begins to yield, the bride cajoles, love scenes ensue, etc.) are transformed into grotesqueries by the author's thematic intention and poetically stylized dialogue. . . .

Ionesco utters his truth in specific stage terms which are startling and often brilliant. What he has to say, moreover, is justified by the routine of our daily living. The lack of spiritual content in our civilization has been the major outcry of European drama since Ibsen. Ionesco has carried this idea to the climactic point of savage caricature.

*Harold Clurman, "Eugene Ionesco: 'The Bald Soprano' and 'Jack'" (1958), in his* The Naked Image: Observations on the Modern Theatre *(reprinted with permission of Macmillan Publishing Co., Inc.; copyright © 1958, 1959, 1960, 1961, 1962, 1963, 1964, 1965, 1966 by Harold Clurman), Macmillan, 1966, pp. 83-5.*

Ionesco is a formidable parodist, a sardonic sceptic, and an almost irrepressibly gay nihilist; he is as effective in comedy as in pathos. He is capable of challenging reflection while outraging sensibility or tickling our funny bone with his clowning, and of depressing and amusing us almost in the same breath. The fact that thus far all his successful plays have been less than full-length pieces only strengthens the impression that in Ionesco we have had a major theatrician but a decidedly minor writer. We may be sure that this opinion, far from perturbing Ionesco, would actually please him. He would be fortified in his opinion that theatre is "what cannot be expressed by writing literature."

*John Gassner, in his* Theatre at the Crossroads: Plays and Playwrights of the Mid-Century American Stage *(copyright © 1960 by Mollie Gassner; reprinted by permission of Holt, Rinehart and Winston, Publishers), Holt, 1960, pp. 261-62.*

[*Rhinoceros*] was originally a short story; it is overlong as a three-act play. Its apparent point is made at least three-quarters of an hour before its final curtain. I speak of an "apparent" point because there is something more in the play's message than is contained in the symbol of men who turn into rhinoceroses—the comedy and terror of conformism. For the play, despite the central figure's ultimate defiance of bestiality, is essentially anarchistic, bitter, very nearly hopeless.

The rational mind and logic are absurd, Ionesco tells us; they have little relation to the truth (which is the chaos) of life. Intellectuals are fools. Most organized radicals are not only clowns but robots—ready under pressure to swing from extreme Left to extreme Right. The conventional middle-class gentleman is a moron; the smooth little subaltern of the business community is a fraud; favored hirelings of the *status quo* are grotesque; the sweet young thing whom we regard as the sweetheart of the world is spineless. Ultimately, they all turn into monsters of blind energy, cruel forces of destruction.

A little man—confused, uncertain, without direction except for some nameless grace of disposition—will resist, though he too is probably doomed. (He acknowledges that the person who wishes to remain an individual always ends badly.) Destined to defeat or not, he does resist—all by himself—which may be described as a *pathetic* absurdity. In almost all the other Ionesco plays the counterpart of Berrenger (the helpless "hero" of *Rhinoceros*) is always done in by the Monster—the mysterious Evil which dominates all. In this sense *Rhinoceros* may be said to mark an "advance" for Ionesco, a stirring of conscience against complete despair, an anguished sign of protest against surrender.

Philosophically this is an unsound, as well as an unsatisfactory, position. Humanly, it is quite understandable: many people the world over feel as Berrenger does, both lonely and afraid of others. . . . Ionesco's merit as an artist is that he finds theatrically telling means to reflect this contemporary fright. His plays are brilliant statements for the stage; his, therefore, is an authentic and original theatre talent.

*Harold Clurman, "Eugene Ionesco: 'Rhinoceros'" (1961), in his* The Naked Image: Observations on the Modern Theatre *(reprinted with permission of Macmillan Publishing Co., Inc.; copyright © 1958, 1959, 1960, 1961, 1962, 1963, 1964, 1965, 1966 by Harold Clurman), Macmillan, 1966, pp. 85-7.*

What is Ionesco's accomplishment? Judging by the most exacting standards, he has written one really remarkable and beautiful play, *Jack, or the Submission* (1950); one brilliant lesser work, *The Bald Soprano*, his first play (written 1948-49); and several effective short plays which are pungent reprises of the same material, *The Lesson* (1950), *The Chairs* (1951), and *The New Tenant* (1953). All these plays —Ionesco is a prolific writer—are "early" Ionesco. The later works are marred by a diffuseness in the dramatic purpose and an increasing, unwieldy self-consciousness. The diffuseness can be clearly seen in *Victims of Duty* (1952), a work with some powerful sections but unhappily overexplicit. Or one can compare his best play, *Jack*, with a short sequel using the same characters, *The Future Is in Eggs* (1951). *Jack* abounds with splendid harsh fantasy, ingenious and logical; it alone, of all Ionesco's plays, gives us something up to the standard of Artaud: the Theater of Cruelty as Comedy. But in *The Future Is in Eggs*, Ionesco has embarked upon the disastrous course of his later writings, railing against "views" and tediously attributing to his characters a concern with the state of the theater, the nature of language, and so forth. Ionesco is an artist of considerable gifts who has been victimized by "ideas." His work has become water-logged with them; his talents have coarsened. In *Notes and Counter Notes* we have a chunk of that endless labor of self-explication and self-vindication as a playwright and thinker which occupies the whole of his play, *Improvisation*, which dictates the intrusive remarks on playwriting in *Victims of Duty* and *Amédée*, which inspires the oversimplified critique of modern society in *The Killer* and *Rhinoceros*.

Ionesco's original artistic impulse was his discovery of the poetry of banality. . . . By extension, the discovery of the poetry of cliché led to the discovery of the poetry of meaninglessness—the convertibility of all words into one another. (Thus, the litany of "*chat*" at the end of *Jack*.) It has been said that Ionesco's early plays are "about" meaninglessness, or "about" non-communication. But this misses the important fact that in much of modern art one can no longer really speak of subject-matter in the old sense. Rather, the subject-matter is the technique. What Ionesco did—no mean feat—was to appropriate for the theater one of the great technical discoveries of modern poetry: that all language can be considered from the outside, as by a stranger. Ionesco disclosed the *dramatic* resources of this attitude, long known but hitherto confined to modern poetry. His early plays are not "about" meaninglessness. They are attempts to use meaninglessness theatrically.

Ionesco's discovery of the cliché meant that he declined to see language as an instrument of communication or self-expression, but rather as an exotic substance secreted—in a sort of trance—by interchangeable persons. His next discovery, also long familiar in modern poetry, was that he could treat language as a palpable thing. . . .

These discoveries of the poetry of cliché and of language-as-thing gave Ionesco some remarkable theatrical material. But then ideas were born, a theory about the meaning of this theater of meaninglessness took up residence in Ionesco's work. The most fashionable modern experiences were invoked. Ionesco and his defenders claimed that he had begun with his experience of the meaninglessness of contemporary existence, and developed his theater of cliché to express this. It seems more likely that he began with the discovery of the poetry of banality, and then, alas, called on a theory to bulwark it. This theory amounts to the hardiest clichés of the criticism of "mass society," all scrambled together—alienation, standardization, dehumanization. . . .

Compared with Brecht, Genet, and Beckett, Ionesco is a minor writer even at his best. His work does not have the same weight, the same full-bloodedness, the same grandeur and relevance. Ionesco's plays, especially the shorter ones (the form for which his gifts are most suited), have their considerable virtues: charm, wit, a nice feeling for the macabre; above all, theatricality. But the recurrent themes—identities slipping out of gear, the monstrous proliferation of things, the gruesomeness of togetherness—are rarely so moving, so appalling, as they might be. Perhaps it is because—with the exception of *Jack*, where Ionesco lets his fantasy have its head—the terrible is always, somehow, circumscribed by the cute. Ionesco's morbid farces are the boulevard comedies of the avant-garde sensibility; as one English critic has pointed out, little really separates Ionesco's whimsy of conformity from Feydeau's whimsy of adultery. Both are skillful, cold, self-referring. . . .

Disgust is the powerful motor in Ionesco's plays: out of disgust, he makes comedies of the distasteful.

*Susan Sontag, "Ionesco" (1964), in her* Against Interpretation and Other Essays *(reprinted with the permission of Farrar, Straus & Giroux, Inc.; copyright © 1961, 1962, 1963, 1964, 1965, 1966 by Susan Sontag), Farrar, Straus, 1966, pp. 115-23.*

The meaning of [Ionesco's] plays is never explicit. His work is characterized, instead, by what may be termed a purposeful vagueness. His plays, in other words, are full of possible meanings, but void both of specific polemic purposes and of solutions. Ionesco is not committed to a point of view because he realizes that all points of view are useless. His plays are demonstrations of the incongruity between the human condition and the human being's desires. As such, they are true tragedies, for tragedy, as Ionesco himself points out, lies in the unbearable. His plays are "demystifications." They strip the veils off man's everyday actions and expose the unbearable, tragic impasse beneath. Reality is tragic, Ionesco tells us, and it will always remain so, no matter what form the masks take. Committed playwrights, such as Arthur Miller or Bertolt Brecht (Ionesco's particular bête noire), are merely attempting the contemptibly superficial task of changing the masks. . . .

Ionesco's first play, *The Bald Soprano* (La Cantatrice Chauve, 1950), was the ground-breaker for the current avant-garde tradition on the stage. It illustrates, first of all, the dramatic technique which the avant-garde derived from Antonin Artaud; but, more important still, it illustrates the basic philosophical premise on which the whole avant-garde drama is based. This philosophical premise, the importance of which cannot be overestimated in a study of the avant-garde drama, is the concept of the absurd in human affairs. . . . Ionesco concentrates mainly on showing his audiences the mutual isolation of human beings and the meaninglessness of the daily actions which constitute the major portion of their existence on earth. . . .

Ionesco uses the device of nonsense speech as a means of showing one aspect of the absurdity of everyday life through the breakdown of semantics. Since everyday life, whether absurd or not, depends for its coherence entirely on the coherence of speech patterns, it follows that if our speech patterns are absurd, everyday life in general is absurd *as far as we are concerned* (it is possible that to an individual the world does not appear absurd, but since he has no means of communication with other people except through intrinsically senseless speech patterns, it follows that his view is actually nonexistent in practice). Even if the world appears ordered and coherent to *everyone*, Ionesco is saying, it is still absurd because each person is trapped inside his own individual cell by the inadequacies of his means of communication. The only possible type of communication is the indirect method of paradox. . . .

We can see from this examination of Ionesco's plays that the main themes of his early plays (1950-1953) are (i) the paradox of the isolation of the individual in the midst of his fellows; and (ii) the paradox of the ultimate meaninglessness of actions, which, taken together, constitute the sum of human existence. In the plays of his second period (*The Killer* and *Rhinoceros*) Ionesco abandoned the view of pessimistic fatalism in which man is a helpless puppet futilely and despairingly hammering against incomprehensible forces that always overwhelm him. Instead of the doctrinaire determinism which he derived from Antonin Artaud, Ionesco gave man a certain amount of free choice within the context of his temporal life. . . .In his latest (and probably last) phase, Ionesco has openly become an intensely personal writer. *The King Dies* and *The Aerial Pedestrian* are about Ionesco's preoccupation with his own finiteness.

*George Wellwarth, "Eugene Ionesco: The Absurd as Warning," in his* The Theater of Protest and Paradox: Developments in the Avant-Garde Drama *(reprinted by permission of New York University Press; copyright © 1964 by New York University), New York University Press, 1964, pp. 261-62.*

The chief limitation of Ionesco, about which many critics agree, is his failure of growth, partly because of the inability of the absurd to be extensive. Yet, within these handicaps, Ionesco has occasionally provided some interesting theater.

*Harry T. Moore, in his* Twentieth-Century French Literature Since World War II *(© 1966 by Southern Illinois University Press; reprinted by permission of Southern Illinois University Press), Carbondale: Southern Illinois University Press, 1966, p. 155.*

[The] very spontaneity [of Ionesco's plays], the very freedom with which he allows characters and situations to take shape, constitutes the basis and source of their purity of form: plays like *The Chairs* or *The Lesson* are enjoyed by their audiences as above all formal patterns of great simplicity and perfection. His own experience has convinced Ionesco that the spontaneous reproduction of the *structures* of the subconscious imagination is bound to emerge in the form of structurally satisfying patterns. . . .In other words, if a play represents the process by which the author's inner, subconscious conflicts are brought into the open and sublimated by being externalized, the very fact that this externalization has taken place implies that the conflicts have reached a state of equilibrium and will therefore, necessarily, already appear in the shape of a balanced pattern that unifies the contradictions and as such has significant form. . . .

Far from being a showman, a seeker of the limelight, a clown full of gimmicks, as he is so often represented in the popular press, which is characteristically apt to misunderstand and misinterpret the vagaries of a creative personality both difficult and complex, Ionesco . . . [is] an artist of uncompromising purity who fully recognizes the precariousness of a creative personality dependent on the workings of forces outside his own control, and he boldly confronts this dilemma of the creative process.

*Martin Esslin, "Ionesco and the Creative Dilemma," in his* Reflections: Essays on Modern Theatre *(copyright © 1961, 1962, 1963, 1966, 1967, 1968, 1969 by Martin Esslin; reprinted by permission of Doubleday & Co., Inc.), Doubleday, 1969, pp. 115-26.*

# J

## JACOBSON, Dan 1929-

**An English novelist, short story writer, and essayist, Jacobson was born in Johannesburg. His skillful fiction explores problems of identity and environment in South Africa. (See also *Contemporary Authors*, Vols. 1-4, rev. ed.)**

It is difficult to refrain from expressing awe and some genuine admiration for a panoramic novel of the intricacy and scope of Dan Jacobson's *The Beginners*, even though admiration must be heavily qualified. Beginning with the journey of Avrom Glickman from Lithuania to Cape Town and concluding with the birth of his great-granddaughter in a London hospital more than fifty years later, the novel embraces the growing pains, the cultural and religious anxieties, and the destinies of three generations; hence Mr. Jacobson is obliged to deal not only with the baffling subject of South African politics during the first half of this century, but with Naziism, Zionism, technological innovation, mass communications, and cultural dislocation in all its multitudinous forms. . . .

[The] best moments in a novel of this prolixity only reinforce the feeling that the whole is distressingly less than the sum of its multitudinous parts. . . .

There is, unhappily, no . . . formal cohesion in *The Beginners*, though Jacobson's efforts to achieve dramatic unity are clearly apparent. First, he has assigned Joel Glickman the appropriate leading role in the Glickman theatricals: his insecurity, restlessness, questioning, and peripatetic youth do establish some sense of continuity in the novel's labyrinthine progression, but Joel himself is too weak a character (though strong enough as a man) to carry the entire production. Jacobson stands apart from the novel in an anonymous role undoubtedly necessary if he is to manage a book of such encyclopedic scope, but as a result his characters never achieve the vividness they deserve, and feeling is repeatedly drowned by chronology and history. . . .

Mr. Jacobson . . . has given an abundance of insight, compassion, architecture, chronology, and faultless prose—everything, indeed, but the compelling and unifying vision which might have made *The Beginners* a novel worthy of his talents.

*David Galloway, in* The Southern Review, *Vol. IV, No. 3, Summer, 1968, pp. 850-52.*

Novels, taken individually, are all right. You can get them in your sights and pick them off one by one. What worries me is that quite different collective monster, the Novel. Every novel that appears should, under examination, make clearer the nature of the whole massive, tentacular growth. What it actually does is to show a structure constantly changing and re-arranging itself, as far from being a containable entity as the inchoate, invisible mass that destroyed Hugh Morgan in Ambrose Bierce's classic—and aptly-named—horror story, "The Damned Thing." . . .

The Wonder Worker [uses a deliberately fragmented narrative]. Having been comically conceived and delivered, Timothy Fogel is allowed to remain partially a concept, the vehicle for a parable about the Novelist as creative artist, whose freedom, for which Joyce worked, is still a point of discussion today. In this ironic structure the novelist creating Timothy Fogel becomes a mental patient, his writing dismissed as "graphomania." It adds up to a kind of commentary on the Novel, a mental block to be flushed out of the author's imagination, rather than a novel in its own right. Underlining that this is a work of theory, in the closing paragraph the patient goes Time Traveling: "I know what I'm doing. Writing down descriptions of places I have never visited, people I have never met, deeds I have never done. I am a free man."

Must freedom and sickness go together in the Novel, writing become graphomania, structure the obsessive dot-joining of paranoia, the private exploration destroy the public novel? Or will the cloudier shades of [Pynchon's] *Gravity's Rainbow* one day seem as clear and universal as the struggle between good and evil in Tolkien's hobbit world? That's the rub (and the reward) with the Damned Thing: you can never get a straight answer out of it.

*Clive Jordan, in* Encounter, *February, 1974, pp. 61, 65.*

*The Wonder-Worker* is a Double Diamond of a book in that it claims to work wonders but fails to live up to its claim. Dan Jacobson writes economically and vividly, but what he is creating is a fantasy so contrived and in the worst sense 'literary' that I felt his considerable skill and sensitivity were in this instance almost wholly wasted. . . . The book has a flavour of stale Nabokov. I shall go back to Jacobson's short stories to be reassured of his talents.

*John Mellors, in* London Magazine, *February/March, 1974, p. 136.*

Dan Jacobson built a small but solid reputation dealing with what he knew best: the politics and heartbreak of *apartheid*, the sour loneliness of race supremacy, and love shattered by cultural collision, and the moral and intellectual conflicts of exile. . . . Three years ago after the tread on these original themes had begun to wear a little thin, Jacobson seemed to take a fresh fictional start and produced his best novel. Called *The Rape of Tamar*, it was an ironic retelling of the Old Testament scandal about King David's daughter whose half brother assaults her and dies for the offense. The links between *Tamar* and *The Wonder-Worker* are stronger than they at first appear to be. Sexual obsession, the disintegration of a family, the linkage between love and hate are evident in both. But where the biblical background of *Tamar* lent grief and madness some heroic grandeur, Jacobson's new book is furnished with the banalities and trivia of contemporary life. . . .

*The Wonder-Worker* seems to be yet another modern parable of total cultural disintegration. The crazed narrator's inability to write down his novel is actually a failure of language, which is man's unique gift and the carrier of his common humanity. Both the narrator and his character Fogel are isolated shards laboring under the illusion that they are wholly formed vessels. But what could well have been an academic exercise is redeemed by compassion and craft. It makes for a pathetic but telling tale.

*R. Z. Sheppard, "Deep Cleavage," in* Time *(reprinted by permission from* Time, The Weekly Newsmagazine; *copyright Time Inc.), March 25, 1974, pp. K-13, 90.*

[*The Wonder-Worker*] is like a knot, admirable for both its serene deceptiveness and its faithful service to that hoary literary genre in which a madman tells his tale, pleading, justifying and embellishing his life. Dan Jacobson is crowding Vladimir Nabokov on his home court here, and does it with finesse: he warns us what he is up to and still tricks us; what we learn at the end forces us to reconsider every stage of what preceded it. And when we have done, we have assisted at something more than a game, for Jacobson is concerned with freedom, with what happens when a man attempts to transform his own life into a work of art.

*Peter S. Prescott, "Diary of a Madman," in* Newsweek *(copyright Newsweek, Inc., 1974; reprinted by permission), April 1, 1974, pp. 75-6.*

In a healthy cultural atmosphere, it would mean a great deal to say that Dan Jacobson upholds the tradition of craft in writing with this small but impeccably ordered and paced study of madness ["The Wonder-Worker"]. As things stand, however, which is crassly, I hesitate to tell the truth about Jacobson's 10th book; for to say that it is complex, not easily summarized, cannot be imagined as a movie, will certainly not appeal to people looking for a good read, those unencumbered with respect for subtle weavings of perception in fictional form—to say this is to consign this fine novel to quick if honorable obscurity. . . .

[Jacobson] has written a psychological detective novel that poses the question "Did the narrator murder a woman just as Timothy murdered Susie?" But that is a minor question, a secondary aspect of the book. We are witnessing more than an attempt to pass off the events of a possibly real crime on an imaginary character. The narrator is transmuting his own madness and ultimate breakdown into another person's style of mental turbulence.

Jacobson, in other words, employs one of his characters, his narrator, to create the other. And we can truly marvel at the painter's skill that he uses to make each man real.

*Raymond A. Sokolov, in* The New York Times Book Review *(© 1974 by The New York Times Company; reprinted by permission), April 21, 1974, pp. 4-5.*

In [*The Wonder-Worker*] Mr. Jacobson takes as many liberties with point of view as his schizophrenic protagonist does, but no matter: Timothy Fogel is an endearing schizophrenic and, moreover, an interesting man. The novel lacks the force and momentum of that experience which shapes the life of a whole character; writing about madness from the inside has always had its pitfalls in that regard, and Mr. Jacobson's work is no exception. All of which makes it more remarkable that his novel should be such a pleasure to read anyway, so rewarding is Mr. Jacobson's prose, so deeply rooted is the wit in every cadence and observation here. There are few writers in English who can capture a scene, an ambience, in three or four relaxed and authoritative sentences in the way that he does, for example, in a description of the Thames embankment at the end of the working day. The vitality of his prose is such that it informs with its own intelligence everything it lights upon. That is why it is possible to have no deep concern for Mr. Jacobson's protagonist, Timothy Fogel, and yet to read everything that happens in the novel with voracious interest.

*Dorothy Rabinowitz, in* Saturday Review/World *(copyright © 1974 by Saturday Review/World, Inc.; reprinted with permission), May 18, 1974, pp. 27-8.*

Most of Jacobson's stories are about South Africans, particularly South African Jews, who live in such a troubled, ambiguous relation to the larger society that their visceral apprehension of danger is too overwhelming to be articulated. Toward the blacks, whom they guiltily employ and exploit, Jacobson's characters feel a truculent, helpless shame; toward the Dutch Afrikaaners, they feel a wary, frightened disdain; and toward the English South Africans—the part of the population with whom they are most closely associated—they seem envious, eager to be liked, and eager to be like them. It is in each case a hopeless proposition, as Jacobson's stories demonstrate. Immigrants from the *shtetlach* of Russia and Lithuania, Jacobson's "beginners" brought with them the sad baggage of superstition and legitimate fear, and their remarkable, unexpected success in a raw, threatening unsettled land only reinforced the terrible, familiar conviction that the known may be bad enough, but it is at least *known*. Of course, South Africa is hardly a place where intimations of dread can be thought of as paranoid; still, the rules and conventions accepted by the Jewish middle class represented here seem exceptionally rigid, the possibilities correspondingly limited, and the punishments disproportionately dire.

Such a sense of harshness and constriction is in great contrast both to the feeling that Jacobson conveys of the land itself—vast, open, and surprisingly beautiful—and his tone as a storyteller. His manner is direct, casual, and deceptively simple. It's as if Jacobson were taking the reader out for a pleasant, ambling narrative stroll, and he is so deft that it often seems as if he were merely the medium, the vessel for the story being recounted. Still, these are largely stories of youth, of reminiscence, of a time and place to which the author-narrator cannot or will not return. Probably no writer can go on endlessly using the material of his youth, but it is bound to become a sharper, more immediate dilemma for someone cut off from the ongoing life of the country where he grew up. . . .

[The] genuinely difficult, perhaps mystically puzzling phenomenon—how is something—an event, a life, a world—created, re-created, actually imagined, emerges as Jacobson's real concern in *The Wonder-Worker*. It is what the novel is about, and it is, in the highest sense, terrifying. . . .

If the characters often seem somewhat attenuated, it is because they are really secondary to Jacobson's purpose. The substance of the novel is the working out of the creative process itself, and in order to achieve his end, Jacobson has relied on language. The voice is spare, hard, brilliant, and though it is often exquisitely lyrical, it is never lush. It is always precise, and precisely dizzying: Jacobson is leading us, forcing us into that peculiar, unsafe region of the mind where out of memories, dreams, simple fragments of observation and inexplicable distortion, something new, something other than ordinarily recalled or observed reality, is born as a separate entity, achieving its own necessarily mysterious integrity. It is true that both art and psychosis transform experience, but as this book succeeds in demonstrating, only one endures.

*Johanna Kaplan, "Re-Creation" (reprinted from* Commentary *by permission; copyright © 1974 by the American Jewish Committee), in* Commentary, *June, 1974, pp. 94-6.*

Alternating with the narrative [in *The Wonder-Worker*] about the life of Timothy, wonderworker, the journal of the narrator himself shows us a young man who is confined, evidently for nerves, in an elegant sanitarium definitely in "Magic Mountain" country. Timothy's history from drably comic beginning to young manhood is indulged in rather than told; the author takes a particularly sadistic interest in his hero's pain. . . .

Timothy's dreams erupt finally in a psychotic episode in which he kills Susie, and at this point the narrator, whose surroundings have been getting increasingly shabby and sounding more and more like Bellevue, merges with him. . . .

Jacobson's twinned plan derives from "Pale Fire," but instead of the wonderfully interlocked narrative puzzle of Nabokov's masterpiece, it is arranged like a "V"—two separated lines nosediving finally into a frightful and confused moment of failure. Thus Jacobson makes his dramatic crux out of what has most meaning for the psychotic mind—not reality but the fact that the conflicts which caused the dangerous split are masked. But however awful the crushing moment is for the psychotic who can no longer hide from himself, this is not what represents reality for everybody else.

In a sense, without making saints of them, Nabokov's perversely illuminated characters endure the consequences of near psychotic vision because it happens that by putting on their doomed masks they see more of reality than they would otherwise. Timothy and his narrator show us less than reality by taking the masks of psychotic vision at face value. Jacobson has undershot a great tradition and his story of drastic human collapse remains incomplete because its roots are hidden from our understanding.

*Martin Washburn, in* The Village Voice *(reprinted by permission of* The Village Voice; *© 1974 by The Village Voice, Inc.), June 13, 1974, pp. 35-6.*

One must admire a writer like Dan Jacobson who suddenly decides in mid-career to move in a new direction and to set new creative problems for himself. One must admire him even more when his efforts result in successful, striking work. After producing for years extremely well written and penetrating "traditional" stories and novels dealing with his native South Africa (*A Dance in the Sun, Evidence of Love, The Beginners*), Jacobson wrote *The Rape of Tamar* (1970) which retold, in a subtle, elliptical manner, the story of the attack upon King David's daughter, Tamar, by her brother Amnon. . . .

In *The Wonder-Worker*, Jacobson's fascinating new novel, the reader must again [as with *The Rape of Tamar*] work to separate fact from fiction, though here his task is much more difficult, and he can only hope to achieve partial success at best. . . .

The narrator's real life remains vague, as does that of a novelist, a wonder-worker, who has transformed his life into art. Jacobson's book . . . can be read on two levels—as an account of a mental patient trying to come to terms with his troubled life by placing it at a safe distance, in the form of a fictionalized memoir, and as an account of the creative process through which fiction is produced.

The one problem with Jacobson's novel is that the shadowy Timothy, though a haunting figure, is almost as much a mystery at the end of the book as he was at the beginning, and we are left with two abstractions, the creator and his creation. Still, *The Wonder-Worker* is a superbly written novel by an author of exceptional talent and taste. Unlike the host of other writers who flood the market each year with self-indulgent accounts of breakdown and madness, Dan Jacobson has aimed higher and has produced a thoughtful, stimulating, and quietly frightening work.

*Ronald De Feo, "The Act of Transformation," in* National Review *(150 East 35th St., New York, N.Y. 10016), June 21, 1974, pp. 711-12.*

Now on the verge of middle age, the transplanted South African Dan Jacobson has produced eleven books; in his latest, "The Wonder-Worker" . . ., he has again advanced his mastery of craft, and created in fewer than two hundred pages a kind of miniature masterpiece, all the more powerful for its brevity, for its pregnant pauses and silences, for the extraneities that are left out. "The Wonder-Worker" is—in part because of its compression—not an easy book. I have read it twice—both times in rapt admiration for the author's gift of language, amounting to perfect pitch, and for his fierce imagination—and I am still not sure I have penetrated all his artful ambiguities. Nonetheless, I feel rewarded: in this book Jacobson has anatomized schizophrenia and brought it to frightening life.

*L. E. Sissman, in* The New Yorker, *June 24, 1974, p. 101.*

What would one say of a writer who has transformed every daily occurrence, every common sight, by an imaginative inversion, into words which make one gasp at one's previous complacency of acceptance of the world-as-we-think-it-is? The world made anew—this is the writer's dream, and in *The Wonder-Worker*, Dan Jacobson has achieved it.

This taut, telling, stylistic advance is a very exciting development in a writer who used a beautiful descriptive prose from the first, but who now brings an originality of vision and a philosophic confidence to his masterly grip of words. . . .

The plot itself is appropriately faceted, presented with great subtlety, and not easy to understand completely. . . .

This novel about Timothy the miracle-worker has [an] unresolved dream-like quality. If a writer's purpose seems obscure, one can "accuse" him of the fault of lack of clarity, or one can humbly admit that the fullness of his intentions escapes one. I will take the latter course, and say too, that this is no criticism of this breathtaking book.

*Margot Lester, "Unresolved Obsession," in* The Jewish Quarterly, *Spring-Summer, 1974, p. 64.*

Dan Jacobson's [*The Wonder-Worker*] depends upon detection, while not being a detective story, and . . . it asks to be considered in the light of the Gothic tradition.

That in itself may be a surprise. Jacobson's earlier fiction, which I greatly admire, was not such as to lead people back to, or persuade them to persist with, an attention to the Gothic modes. Together with his critical writings, it might be thought to inculcate a respect for stories that are straightforwardly told and rationally pondered, and a distrust of those authors, Gothic and otherwise, who believe that fiction should continuously reflect on the manner of its telling and should interrogate and explore the author's relationship to his subject matter, of those authors who believe in making a mystery or a multiplicity of the consciousness that informs the tale. His earlier works—I am thinking of certain short stories, of the marvelous novella *A Dance in the Sun*, and of his enjoyable comedy about the ploys of two dealers in a South African mining town, *The Price of Diamonds*—were, in this sense, unsophisticated.

His last novel but one, however, *The Rape of Tamar*, brought a change of tune. Here was a work with a Biblical theme and a narrator who used a modern idiom and seemed keenly attentive to the presuppositions of an audience centuries-remote from the events recounted; there appeared to be two levels of experience—that represented by his Biblical persons and that represented by the ironic retrospect which invested them—and the narrator's complex relationship to his theme appeared to be a main source of interest. It was some time since Mr. Jacobson had left South Africa for London, thereby losing touch with the people and places of his first fictions, and there may be those of his readers who suppose that the change I am discussing was produced by habituation to a new environment, that of the Anglo-American big city, and to the sophistication and artifice that were esteemed there. This seems too sweeping a view, but it is not one which would immediately be canceled by an acquaintance with his new novel, *The Wonder-Worker*.

Here, too, he is more metropolitan than "simple." The novel is equipped with facets, like one of the precious stones to which he is drawn, and is cut so as to gleam with a light which might seem to call for spectroscopy as well as criticism. . . .

Those who do not take to doubles and detective work may not respond to the excellence of each of [the] twin narratives [in *The Wonder-Worker*], and they may refuse to see in its equivocations a gifted contribution to a sometimes preposterous genre [Gothic fiction] which has also spoken movingly about delusions of grandeur.

*Karl Miller, in* The New York Review of Books *(reprinted with permission from* The New York Review of Books; *© 1974 by NYREV, Inc.), July 18, 1974, pp. 14-15.*

In the tradition of refined gothicism, [*The Wonder-Worker*] is full of ambiguity and odd, unspecified connections between narrator and subjects. . . .

Like James's [*The Turn of the Screw*], *The Wonder-Worker* relies on the reader's deepening curiosity about not only the subject but also certain mysteries arising from the narrator's perceptions—that sort of thing rather than the special effects of popular gothicism. The strangeness in the tale arises not from a rotating head or a super-charged vomit scene, as in *The Exorcist*, but from the truer darkness of the mind in conflict with itself.

*Speer Morgan, "The Turn of the Screw," in* Rolling Stone *(© 1974 by Straight Arrow Publishers, Inc.; all rights reserved; reprinted by permission), September 26, 1974, p. 105.*

* * *

## JHABVALA, Ruth Prawer 1927-

**Ms Jhabvala, a German-born novelist writing in English, has lived in India since 1951. Her fine novels examine contemporary intellectual, political, and social life in India. (See also *Contemporary Authors*, Vols. 1-4, rev. ed.)**

It is not often given to one to come, unprepared, upon a true and original talent. The recognition in such an encounter must always have something large and unsettling in it: And yet, there is a certainty about these things, an obviousness that seems to have leapt at one from the first page. From the outset of this novel of travelers in India [*Travelers*], the realization that there is an immense literary achievement at hand grows steadfastly upon the reader, and one is no more than a quarter of the way through the work when that realization becomes a certainty. It is, simply enough, the story of Englishmen and Indians, both of the well-born and the moderately poor sort, whose lives become tangled up in the course of their travels. The art that has arranged their meeting is subtle, perhaps negligible. . . . It is a story of random, endlessly impassioned encounters, a novel of caste and class so truly observed and so wittily reported that one must go a long way back to E. M. Forster to find the social novel that compares with it.

*Dorothy Rabinowitz, in* World *(copyright © 1973 by Saturday Review/World, Inc.; reprinted with permission), June 5, 1973, p. 66.*

Ruth Prawer Jhabvala's novels of the contemporary Indian scene have for some time now been earning her a considerable reputation in England. The case has been different in America. Whether it is that India can never be quite the subject of interest to Americans it seems, eternally, to be to the English or whether it is that the leisurely play of character and observation native to this sort of sensibility falls on resisting ears here (I do not for a moment believe it), or some other thing, it is hard to tell; but she is much less known in this country. "Travelers" is Mrs. Jhabvala's 10th work to be published in America, the sort of novel that establishes itself, from the first pages, with that peculiar assurance it is sometimes given to a ripened art to have. (In considerable measure, that assurance has been there right along, notably in the story collections, "An Experience of India," "Stronger Climate," "Like Birds, Like Fishes.")

How does one know when one is in the grip of art, of a literary power? One feels, among other things, the force of personality behind the cadence of each line, the sensibility behind the twist of the syllable. One feels the texture of the unspoken, the very accents of a writer's reticence. . . . The quiet power is what strikes one in "Travelers" right off. . . .

Mrs. Jhabvala's subjects are Indian, but there is an international standard for progressive social activity of the sort recorded in these pages, and Mrs. Jhabvala may well have brought off the finest literary rendering of it in this peculiar century of ours. . . .

Given a hint of its background and of its Anglo-Indian theme, it is easy to mistake "Travelers" for a sociologically weighty book. It is a weighty book all right, in the way that psychological richness is always weighty. As for the sociology, there is not trace of it, except for the sort that comes naturally and implicitly to any novel worthy of the name. Mrs. Jhabvala's art is high comedy, woven in the most sober fashion into the characters of her protagonists. That comedy is in their very nerve and bones, but the lives they are aware of, the lives they have, are another matter: the life they know, each of them, is full of a terrible seriousness. . . .

Mrs. Jhabvala's power as a novelist is compounded of an extraordinary mixture of sympathy, economy and a wit whose effects are of the cruelest sort: the sort that appears to proceed, not from any malice of the novelist, but from the objects of her scrutiny. One always knows what the objects of Mrs. Jhabvala's scrutiny think of themselves; there is not better definition of character in fiction. Her characters are forever jumping up in the middle of conversations to say, "You understand nothing!" She knows the quick, inner ear that judges its words and finds them wanting at the same instant they are spoken, and the impulse that shifts that judgment to another. No reader is asked to stop while she explains. "He who understands, understands," goes the Hebrew proverb, and so says the spirit of the work here; not many things profit literature so much as that spirit, in the hands of true sensibility. That Mrs. Jhabvala has: that and an extraordinary ear for language, for the peculiar idiosyncrasies of speech, here put forth shrewdly, lightly.

The way things sound is no small part of the way things are. There is another sort of recording she does, one of a deeper sort perhaps. The infirmities of her characters take them where we find them, take them, indeed, to ludicrous places and conditions of being. But there are limits to their frailties, stuff in the least contentious of them that rises, unexpectedly to take issue with things when need be. It is the sort of psychological movement that is given only to masterful fiction to produce. Altogether a work like "Travelers" does not come along very often: "Travelers" compares well with the best social novels in contemporary fiction. The reader who takes it up will encounter for himself the wit and the grace of mind that lies at the core of it.

*Dorothy Rabinowitz, in* The New York Times Book Review *(© 1973 by The New York Times Company; reprinted by permission), July 8, 1973, pp. 6-7.*

Does anyone ever write *small* novels about India? Ruth Prawer Jhabvala does, bless her. Small, I mean, in the way that Jane Austen's novels are small—subtle, concise, and magnificent. Neither Austen nor Jhabvala feels obliged to cram into one novel everything she ever felt or thought or saw: but by focusing the brilliance of their absolute attention on one small piece of human frailty, glory, or folly, they convince us—without This-Is-the-Meaning-of-Life pomposity—that in fact they understand everything, that life is exactly as they say it is and could be no other way. . . .

What the women in *Travelers* have in common—whether their avowed needs are spiritual or fleshly—is the need to obliterate their own personalities, to be ravished (by God or man), to submit, to be overcome, to be submerged, to throw themselves away. . . .

In this beautifully structured novel, spirituality and carnality, mysticism and decadence, crisscross; the one partakes of the other. Jhabvala—unlike most Westerners who, once they set foot on Indian soil, need to choose, define, declare (and are cornered and hardened by their definitions)—is comfortable with ambivalence and ambiguity. She doesn't come down heavily for either mysticism or logic, East or West, cause-and-effect or Karma. Jhabvala knows that neither the East nor the West has cornered the market on venality—or, as far as that goes, on goodness—and she knows that people can be as emotionally straitjacketed by repudiating reason as by fanatically adhering to logic. *Travelers*, superb in its characterizations of both Indians and Westerners, is remarkable for its absence of moralizing. If there is a moral at all, it is that if your "Self" is in trouble in Dayton, it's not likely to be in any less trouble in Benares.

*Barbara Grizzuti Harrison, "We're Off to See the Guru," in* Ms., *December, 1973, pp. 28, 31.*

The comparison [of *Travelers*] with *A Passage to India* is inevitable. . . . [Like the characters] the dramatic situations in Ruth Jhabvala's fine novel are familiar—the deceptions, the misunderstandings, the bad decisions that are made when people attempt to live by theories and abstractions—and all of these cause her characters to flail about exactly as Forster's did.

Fundamentally, though, the two books are not alike. The individuals of *A Passage to India* stepped gingerly towards each other, testing the relation between language and race. (For, in the last analysis, the only force that could overcome the obstacles to friendship and love between Englishman and Asian was the power of the Word.) Mrs. Jhabvala's "travelers," on the other hand, communicate not out of any positive desire, but merely from their need for escape. They act only to conquer boredom and restlessness. Yet every effort fails. . . .

The form of the novel reflects the characters' emptiness. *Travelers* is composed of numerous short sequences . . . that turn the experiences of life into little more than a series of impressionistic dots. Mrs. Jhabvala is obviously less concerned with the significance of human existence *in toto* than with the quality of endurance.

Indeed, she pursues that concern in an almost clinical manner. Occasionally, the book reads like a controlled experiment, in which the author, by clearing away any possible limitation on her characters' lives (the kind that comes from poverty or imminent danger), allows them to examine the consequences of their freedom, to investigate the nature of their daily existence. From this perspective, *Travelers* is not a novel about India at all—it could have been set anywhere.

*Francis Levy, "A Passage to Nowhere," in* The New Leader, *February 18, 1974, p. 19.*

Mrs. Jhabvala cannot help but bring a Western, as distinct from a Westernized or Western-educated, sensibility to bear upon the Indian scene. Where she differs from eminent English writers about India, such as E. M. Forster, who serves as a frequent point of reference in her stories, is in her indifference to exoticism, her complete lack of condescension, the extent of her involvement which lies at a deeper and more visceral level than that of virile friendship, and the fact that as a woman with a family she has fewer lines of retreat open to her. . . .

[The] early works belong to the honeymoon period of her encounter with India . . . when her contacts with Europeans were apparently minimal. Here, whatever the inner strains and stresses, the Indian family dominates, wrapping its members in a loving, protective cocoon.

Food plays an enormous part in a land where so many die of starvation every day. It figures as a token of love given and received. The preparation of the loved one's favorite dishes almost resembles a spiritual rite, or at least signifies participation in a powerfully vital and sensuous culture. . . .

Throughout her books, the more extensive a European's knowledge of Indian poetry or ancient monuments or sacred texts, the less genuine his understanding of India and her people will be. It is not through the intellect or the will that India can be understood, she would seem to be suggesting at this point, but through intuition, rather as if what is at stake is a faith, not a continent, to be affirmed in declaring 'I believe because it is absurd.'. . .

Where in *Esmond in India* it looks as though the author were trying to suppress the promptings of her critical spirit through her open dislike of Esmond himself, later on criticism of India will become more insistent and will be conveyed through a woman who, while foolish, affected, absurd in her vehement exaggeration, is also pitiful and portrayed with considerable sympathy: Etta in *A Backward Place* (1965). In that fine novel, the dialectic of love and loathing for India, or of submission versus resistance to its power, assumes a far more subtle form. It is no longer shaped by the author's struggle against one of her characters, but is embodied in two women, Judy and Etta, who may be taken to represent in some degree the conflicting inner responses of the novelist. . . .

Through Etta, the novelist is able to project all the European's exasperation with Indian immovability, incarnate in Mr. Gupta. . . .

Although as a novelist Mrs. Jhabvala's primary concern is naturally with personal relationships, nevertheless the larger political and social scene is by no means neglected. In her work, we find that the noble and disinterested leaders who went to prison and sacrificed everything in the struggle for independence, are now outpaced by the smooth, busy, self-interested political talkers, who guiltily suppress twinges of social conscience when their own comfort and position are at stake. Nor does the author forget those courageous and gifted young men, like Narayan in *Esmond in India* or Sudhir in *A Backward Place*, who leave the fleshpots of Delhi in order to work as doctors in the jungle or as teachers in remote outposts. For such rare spirits as these (acclaimed in word but secretly despised by the status-seekers and the social and political climbers), and for the devoted doctors and social workers among the foreign missionaries, her admiration is manifest. . . .

The novelist's satire does not spare the charitable female do-gooders who are prepared to resettle a colony of slum-dwellers further out of town, whence they will have a longer journey to work, just as elsewhere her satire does not spare the self-important ladies who promote performances of Ibsen in Hindi. Such culture-mongering is seen as maddeningly irrelevant in the face of India's vast problems. And these problems are so overwhelming that there is a perfectly natural tendency for some to lapse into apathy, indifference or sensuous self-indulgence; while others engage in abstract or high-flown talk that commits them and their hearers to nothing, but makes them all feel better. . . .

With the publication of two impressive collections of short stories, *A Stronger Climate* in 1968, and *An Experience of India* in 1971, to be followed in 1973 by a novel of high accomplishment, *Travelers* (known in England as *A New Dominion*), Mrs. Jhabvala's tone perceptibly darkens. One of her ways of conveying the increasingly oppressive weight of India is through contact with its spiritual or religious manifestations. . . .

Images of violence, fear, servitude, isolation, imprisonment and disgust, recur in Mrs. Jhabvala's later fiction:—the respectable woman among the beggars on the Bombay waterfront who "spoke English and hadn't eaten for three days"; the woman who looks like an ordinary housewife, imprisoned behind the iron bars of the nursing home opposite; the English wives like birds trapped in the cage of Indian family custom. Now it is an Indian lady who, with ill-concealed distaste, wipes her hand on her sari after a European gentleman has kissed it. To the mutual incomprehension of Indian and European is added mutual recrimination or revulsion.

It is no longer her European characters like Esmond or the elderly Boekelman in the story, *The Man with the Dog*, who let fall the insulting cry, "Monkeys! Animals!" but Mrs. Jhabvala herself who can speak of living "on the back of this great animal of poverty and backwardness," in the shattering candor of her confession entitled *Myself in India*. . . .

[What] is involved here is the confrontation between two of the strongest spiritual impulses in the world. Sometimes Hinduism seems to be expressing just those wild primordial urges which the austere intelligence of Hebraism both feared and served to contain. At other moments it encourages extreme ascetic practices which Judaism has never favored. Only in Cabala, itself frowned upon by those who follow the mainstream of Judaism, may points of contact common to many diverse forms of mysticism be found. Yet how systematic even the secret doctrine appears when contrasted with Hindu mysticism!. . .

Unlike many of the European characters in her books, Mrs. Jhabvala did not come to India seeking spiritual solace or enlightenment. Such people she largely regards as self-deceivers. One has the impression, rightly or wrongly, that religion did not bother her very much until she came into contact with Indian spirituality. . . .

[We] are left with the disturbing glimpse of Mrs. Jhabvala living as a near recluse in Delhi, reclining in her air-conditioned room with all the blinds drawn, like so many of her female characters whose nerves have been shattered by too long a stay on the continent of Circe. Dismayed by India, no longer at home in Europe, she envisages ultimate defeat.

*Renee Winegarten, "Ruth Prawer Jhabvala: A Jewish Passage to India," in* Midstream, *March, 1974, pp. 72-9.*

Jhabvala brings to her work a sure sense of characterization and dialogue, and to this she adds a zest for getting down just the right detail that will reveal in miniature the larger world to which her prose only alludes. [*Travelers*] is a series of short sketches—perhaps impressions would be more accurate—of the sort of people that have been thrown to the surface as a result of the social and political upheavals of the Independence era. We are presented with marvellous cameo studies. . . .

The dramatis personae move within the framework of a plot that is like a slow train in India: there is the noise and confusion of the departure, the appalling heat and monotony of the countryside, and the fatigue of a midnight arrival, all of which provide illusion of a journey. But it is only an illusion for all that. And this I think is what Jhabvala is trying to tell us: we are all travellers on a train going nowhere. We come, we go and only India remains.

*Laurence S. Fallis, in* Books Abroad, *Vol. 48, No. 2, Spring, 1974, p. 419.*

* * *

## JONES, David 1895-

**Jones is an Anglo-Welsh poet-novelist and watercolor painter. Interest in his complex and beautiful work is now being renewed. (See also *Contemporary Authors*, Vols. 9-12, rev. ed.)**

I do not think that David Jones is a Modern Master by Professor Kermode's standards, but I have a feeling that his poems and his paintings will continue to give delight long after anyone has ceased to worry whether he is "modern" or not. Perhaps I need not remind readers that T. S. Eliot considered his *In Parenthesis* a work of genius, while Auden has described *The Anathemata* as "very probably the finest long poem written in English in this century." *The Tribune's Visitation* . . . is a much shorter poem, and like some earlier pieces of his, such as *The Wall* or *The Fatigue*, is concerned with the troops of the Roman garrison in Palestine in the earlier decades of the First Century A.D. The poem testifies once again to its author's extraordinary gifts. . . .

*R, in* Encounter, *February, 1970, p. 33.*

Few authors require explication as David Jones does, and he has recognized this and become his own best explicator. He has discussed his literary and visual work at some length and on many occasions, notably in the pieces brought together in *Epoch and Artist*, and has written generously and informatively to private inquirers. While, mercifully, there is still nothing like a David Jones industry, he has been the subject of a fair number of notes, impressions, lectures and articles, whose burden, rightly, is that he is among the most important creative artists of the past fifty years. . . .

It is unlikely that David Jones can ever become a popular poet, even as author of *In Parenthesis*. Where can he fit into, much less belong to, the contemporary "poetry scene"? No man was ever less trendy, less with it. It is, of course, a triumph of impercipience to consider him as not interested in today's man and today's world because he assumes we have read the *Gododdin* and the *Song of Roland*, Geoffrey of Monmouth, Malory and the *Mabinogion*, and (almost worse) the Authorised Version and the *Dies Irae*. His work insistently provokes the questions: What are we? From what are we come? What shall become of us? But poetry, he tells us, must be rooted in a tradition and is not merely the creation of a private world. "I believe that there is, in the principle that informs the poetic art, a something which cannot be disengaged from the mythus, deposits, *matière*, ethos, whole *res* of which the poet is himself a product." He is a poet unparochial in time. . . . The "Celtic" aspect of David Jones's work is not eccentric but central. Without it, as without sign and sacrament, what would remain?

*"A Poet Unparochial in Time," in* The Times Literary Supplement *(reproduced by permission), August 20, 1971, p. 986.*

[The] genre [of *The Anathémata*] remains in question, as does that of *In Parenthesis* (1937), which has been called epic, novel, poetry, prose. Curious readers would do well to attend to Prufrock's "Do not ask 'What is it?'/Let us go and make our visit." *The Anathémata* is circular, like its epigraph's calcined wall before which, on a dark and stormy night, a tale-teller relates a story set on a dark and stormy night. Veins of light interrupt the darkness. Individual examples are not readily detachable because of the organic nature of Jones's work. Among the best is the passage wherein the two apostles, preparing for the first Eucharist, decorate "with the green of the year the cross-beams and the gleaming board." Another, showing the rapport between art and sacrament, a favorite tenet of David Jones, represents the cave-paintings in southern France which date from before 20,000 B.C. . . .

The uninitiate . . . may will wish away some of the Welshness of *The Anathémata*, but it is part of the cost. Those who value the sacred (and to Jones everything is so) will be willing to pay the price. Deemed an anachronism by some, a prophet by others, David Jones in his eighties stands forth in dignity as celebrant of Calvary's *mysterium*, for him "the supreme fact, not the supreme fiction.". . . Granted his *donnée*, this artist, more Merlin than the Virgil to whom he is often compared, offers himself as spokesman for a culture that may well be not only "past and passing" but "to come."

*Sister Bernetta Quinn, O.S.F., "David Jones," in* Contemporary Literature *(© 1973 by the Regents of the University of Wisconsin), Vol. 14, No. 2, Spring, 1973, pp. 267-70.*

David Jones is not an essayist or literary critic by nature, nor is he a systematic thinker. His approach is intuitive and eclectic. He proceeds by association, and because he is widely read in non-literary matters, but not a conventional man of letters as regards English literature, what he has to say is often unexpectedly illuminating, especially where it glosses his own writing. . . . [He] can illustrate the relevance of the early periods of our own and other literatures more vividly and cogently than many readers and teachers of post-Renaissance literature seem able or willing to allow. His power to communicate stems from his intense curiosity about the precise details of innumerable things ranging over the whole of Western culture. . . .

In our society nowadays there is an increasing sense of alienation from first-hand experience. . . . In David Jones's writing this diminution of experience is keenly felt. His own preoccupation with the contactual reality of what is made rather than manufactured, with the particular artifact or poetic word or ritual act, is an attempt to keep the channels of communication open, however clogged they have become with the silt of forgetfulness and scholarship. In an age of fragmentation and specialization his work can be seen as an heroic attempt to piece some of the fragments together again.

*David Blamires, in* Critical Quarterly, *Autumn, 1973, pp. 285-86.*

Much poetry today is characterised by emotion without intellect and fancy without imagination. (Ted Hughes's *Crow* is an obvious illustration of what I mean.) It is David Jones's unique imagination which most distinguishes his work from that of his contemporaries. This esemplastic power, to use Coleridge's phrase, illumines every page of *The Sleeping Lord & other Fragments* bringing unity to seemingly diverse material. It is the same quality that closely knits together both his writing and painting, which is all *one*, from his earliest drawings and from *In Parenthesis*, to his most recent poems. This singleness of texture is present in the work of most major artists, but it is I think more marked in David Jones than in any other poet.

A second quality which sets David Jones's poetry apart from that of most poets now writing, from Robert Lowell to many lesser talents, is his realisation that the artist must be dead to himself if he is to create work of permanent value.

*William Cookson, "Two Distinctions," in* Agenda, *Autumn-Winter, 1973-74, p. 31.*

The writer's material, which is words, is continually renewing its resistance and there must be a continual alteration in balance between the degree of resistance that stimulates and that stultifies; but today language is undermined from a new direction and it must fight for its life. It is not resistance, still less renewal, but rejection that it faces, along with art and religion and myth. The first great feat of mankind, greater than the feat of fire or of artefact, was language. It is argued, probably correctly, that neither fire nor artefact would ever have come about without language. From crude beginnings it seemed capable of almost infinite refinement growing more exact and subtle; but now it is said that thought has gone too far for language and has evolved a new means of expression that is more elegant and more exact—mathematics. The simple calculations of the first mathematicians are, to present-day mathematics, as the cries and grunts of primitive man to the *Tractatus Logico-Philosophicus*.

We may expect mathematics to develop much farther; it is at least as capable of development as the language of words, and may even become a vernacular necessary for the small change of daily intercourse, while language as we know it survives, a fossil without function, an intricate bony arabesque enclosed in the strata of an historical deposit. God willing that time is still a long way off; but there are enemies nearer home whose mode of attack lies in their attitude to words and their manipulation—words sapped and regimented in grey prison uniform answering by numbers to the command of the linguistics man, and those who feed the computers in the child-like faith that by some mysterious process, a trivial question can elicit a profound reply. My fear is that this pseudo-scientific paraphernalia will dazzle the understanding of ordinary people so that we grow strangers to our own imagination (imagination itself is almost a lost word these days) till we find outlandish and superfluous the poet's use of words.

It is against this, this short-term cheapening, and long-term rejection of language, that I see David Jones's work. "He guards the *signa*" like the cult-man at the beginning of *The Anathemata*; he guards, not by standing still, or raking back over the past, but by moving forward; for if his memory is ranging back to the folded strata, in his acts he is stepping out onto the new territory.

We have become numbed, anaesthetized to the power and purpose of words and require to be jolted awake, to feel their recessions and transformations. This is exactly what David Jones has done in *The Anathemata*, in the inscriptions, and again in *The Sleeping Lord* where juxtapositions of English, Welsh and Latin give, not only an incomparable richness of texture and of reference, but also give words the life of icons, "images not made with hands". Like James Joyce's *Anna Livia* he forces us to see all around words as though they were a three-dimensional object, a live animal, not the animated corpse of the linguistic manipulators.

*N. K. Sandars, "Some Thoughts Arising From David Jones's Latest Published Works," in* Agenda, *Autumn-Winter, 1973-74, pp. 36-44.*

David Jones shows the reality of our history, something we are not able otherwise to catch together into words. . . .

David Jones has not interpreted history as choice, no one is more conscious of *tempora pessima, hora novissima*, but no one has illuminated so searchingly what it was to suffer the modern history of mankind. He drew light from a great distance, both in *In Parenthesis* and in *The Anathemata*, in such a way that one would wish to have been the suffering creature of his poems as one would wish to have been Hector in the Iliad. Tolstoy's solutions are personal and intellectual, even chauvinistic, but David Jones does in retrospect for our fathers what epic poetry might do; using terrible colours, scorning what is not genuine, he dignifies mankind.

His sense for what is genuine is not simply an artist's integrity or an innocent eye, though he does have these qualities as well. It is rather a sense of what is irreducibly real. At the moment of development of ancient religion in which the gods become united and consciously responsible for every story, which is also the moment of the unification of plot, the gods are immediately in the dock to be judged by mankind. A poem, that is an emotionally charged intelligible unity of language, whose subject is war and which is monotheistic, must inevitably be terrible. Indeed it is likely enough that its unity and its religion are inseparable. At a passionate level there must be a God invented in such a story, otherwise the blackness would not be enough. The same is true in the whole range of prehistory in *The Anathemata*. In that poem David Jones's sense of realities is so striking that he has become the greatest archaeological poet, he has shown the reality of the origins of mankind in a poem that has the breadth and coldness of real dawn. He is more specific and less fragmentary than St. John Perse, he is more passionate and articulate about geology than Auden. The mighty achievement of this poem depends as much as his war writings on the irreducible reality of what he talks about.

The trappings and the dimensions of these poems, the Welsh and the liturgical elements and the many strange and moving references to his repertory of knowledge, are always to show something real. When his poems are understood they are naked in the way a wood of trees might be. There are few poets so rich and so underdecorated. . . .

He uses the whole backward and abyss of time. He is not dictated to by conventional historical time, but things are present or not to him in a single densely woven tapestry. . . . David Jones's poetry is too serious to be called pessimistic. Its time-range is too vast for it to be afflicted by its own darkness. His visions of the green world and the mountainous world are not everlasting but do propose courage. It is interesting that he takes courage more for granted than most writers today, whether in his great lords, his Romans or his infantrymen. As a poet and as a historian he proposes an instinctive virtue. What is everlasting in his poems is the decent riff-raff of Britain, of modern war, and of the Roman Empire. They speak and they suffer the same fate. "But for all the rest there was no help on that open plain.". . .

There are many subjects he has not dealt with, probably because of the primacy in his imagination of the first world war, later of its reflections in Welsh, British and Roman history, and of their reflections back on it. His singular and admirable attitude to the Catholic church is part of the same searching glance. It is also something more, since he has believed that at this point history is directly penetrable and has a single meaning. His appeals to myth and to ritual language are always made on the assumption that here also is an area of reality, indeed the master-meaning of many signs. Words like allegory and symbol are inadequate to his usage, and to use words like sacrament may be *obscurum per obscurius*. There is evidently a strong element of realism in his religious views. They may be close to what in him created his poetry, or they may be its precondition.

*Peter Levi, "History and Reality in David Jones," in* Agenda, *Autumn-Winter, 1973-74, pp. 56-9.*

The past of man is something continuous, and one can never be certain that it is really past, and not present or even more disconcertingly, future. Part of the excitement communicated by David Jones's poetry is the ambiguous position in which he puts his readers, disturbing their neat and safe chronological proprieties and the pedants' division of culture and creed. . . .

Perhaps it is not for nothing that "deposits" is a favourite word of his, both in poetry and in prose. "Deposits" are an essential part of his poetry. . . . It is a significant and revealing word. Deposits may imply a slow historical process of accretion, stealthily forming silts, slow strata, the layers of a pearl; or again, they are the man-made caches and hoards—hidden treasures; votive, ritual and foundation deposits, and the last great deposit of all, the body in burial. . . .

To words themselves he applies a process of inspired nuclear fission. As you read, the simple-seeming syllables, in the context of their deposits, explode in a radiant and beneficent blast of highly charged meanings, associations and what the seventeenth century liked to call "correspondences". As a bard should, he displays his word-hoard, but the words are radio-active with history. Some of the scintillations may miss us, but enough hit their target to start up in ourselves a chain reaction of generated excitement. The words themselves will never be the same to us; they have been enriched historically until each is a piece of history itself.

*Stuart Piggott, "David Jones and the Past of Man," in* Agenda, *Autumn-Winter, 1973-74, pp. 60-3.*

At the centre of David Jones's concerns lies his belief in a break in the Western cultural tradition, which, becoming obvious first towards the beginning of this century, has ever since threatened the power of the community to provide for its members that spiritual sustenance to which Simone Weil adverts, and the primary object of his writings is to attempt to restore some of the tradition's continuities.

The cultural tradition which David Jones has been trying throughout his work to recreate is that of the Island of Britain as a whole, whose various origins, Celtic, Imperial Roman, Western Christian and Saxon, appear there in the form in which the poet himself, by birth, upbringing and conversion a product of the composite tradition, experiences them. Whereas in *In Parenthesis* Jones uses a single major theme, the ideal of comradeship in arms from Aneirin through Malory to Shakespeare, in an attempt to give sense and meaning to the terrible waste of the Western Front, in *The Anathemata* he is concerned much more to recall and celebrate a whole tradition which threatens to slip through his fingers: "one is trying to make a shape out of the very things of which oneself is made"—by a re-presentation or *anamnesis* in imaginative form of what the traditions mean to "a Londoner, of Welsh and English parentage, of Protestant upbringing, of Catholic subscription". But although readers from different backgrounds can respond in general terms to his vision of a tradition under siege from the forces of megalopolitan anonymity, it is less easy to see the world of *The Anathemata* as embodying a real cultural tradition through which contemporary man might experience his identity. This is in part because, fortunately or unfortunately according to your point of view, the political unit Britain is not a cultural unity, but in part also because David Jones's Island of Britain is a projection of his imagination, a vehicle for his views on art, sacrament, history and the nature of man—much as the Arthurian world is for Malory's ideals of chivalry and loyalty—and in part because the impersonality of the writing withdraws the poem from the immediate world of experience and sensation. The idea of a tradition is there, but there is little explicit sense of either the context or the effect of the loss of tradition, still less of how the loss may be made good.

*Nicolas Jacobs, "David Jones and the Politics of Identity," in* Agenda, *Autumn-Winter, 1973-74, pp. 68-75.*

David Jones, whose first drawings were exhibited when he was a child in 1903-4, speaks, whether in words, water-colours, or inscriptions in opaque water-colour, with an authority and beauty which run counter to our habitual modes of perception. His major writings, *In Parenthesis* and *The Anathemata*, share with the water-colours the paradoxical qualities of a crowded airiness, a nervous linear structure overlaying a rich wilderness. His concern with idea and belief is matched to an equal care for the words that must define the particularities of the world's creatures, and so *In Parenthesis*, a palimpsest where the Great War is fought in a dimension which includes all the wars that prefigured it, gives too the most exact picture we have of the actual conditions on the Western Front.

In his collected essays, *Epoch and Artist*, Jones has recorded his belief that man's nature is to make signs to 'give otherness to the particular'. Man is the 'sole inhabitant of a tract of country where matter marches with spirit', and art in the widest sense, that of a gratuitous making over and above the utilitarian need, is his 'distinguishing dignity'. Our language of signs, whether expressed in the making of a birthday cake or the wearing of a rose in the buttonhole, links us together in a web of past and future commemorations and celebrations. . . .

Although Jones may call his works variously a 'fragment', a 'writing', or an 'attempted writing', such terms are not confessions of failure; they describe accurately those things which provisionally satisfy him as parts of his personal, cultural or racial inheritance that he has objectified, tentative parts of a unity whose whole will always elude him. None of his makings are discrete; they must be seen in their relationships to each other. The formative personal experiences, the Catholicism, war service, months in Palestine, make for individuality but never egocentricity. The inclusiveness of his imagination and the singularity of his word-choice may daunt the reader, but the works bear reading and re-reading as the poet is followed on his long quest through 'vast, densely-wooded, inherited and entailed domains'.

*The Sleeping Lord* gathers together poems which have appeared in magazines over the last 20 years, but which have been worked on for longer still. The central concern is with Rome and her hegemony in the first century AD, but the scholarship and exactitude with which Jones explores this world serves neither a nostalgic nor archaicising imagination. Through the heightened, demotic voices of the soldiers, their idioms recalling those of the war Jones served in, implicit correspondences are made between that historic period and our own. Rome, 'the flat palm that disciplines the world', the bringer of peace and order to her subject peoples, is a symbol uniting timeless contrarieties. . . .

*The Sleeping Lord* is perhaps the best introductory volume to Jones's work; the contours can be seen most clearly here, and the textures, though rich, are less elaborate than in *The Anathemata*, since there is an open, dramatic quality running through the book. The richness of his vocabulary is not, as can seem with Auden, material for an erudite flirtation with the reader. His poetry builds by accretion, not by reduction to synonyms. A 'father' is not the exact equivalent of a 'pater familias'; a 'tump' is not the exact equivalent of 'hill'. David Jones is not content to see language beaten to the world-floor; he both takes words back to their origins and sets them glowing in new contexts.

*Peter Scupham, "Textures and Contours," in* New Statesman, *May 24, 1974, pp. 734-35.*

* * *

## JONES, Madison 1925-

**Jones is an American novelist and short story writer. (See also *Contemporary Authors*, Vols. 13-14.)**

Guilt and retribution as fictional themes continue to haunt Mr. Jones [in *An Exile*] as he studies the disintegration of blameless character in a middle-aged man when he is abruptly confronted with a temptation he finds himself powerless to resist. Principal actors in the ensuing drama are few and sharply drawn; action is swiftly progressive; and suspense is once again, as in the author's previous novels, handled with incomparable adroitness. Not many present-day writers are able to evoke an atmosphere of terror so overwhelming, nor to conjure so artfully a sense of anxiety and dread. Impact is here heightened by the very brevity of the narrative. Few readers will be able or disposed to forget this simple tale of plain folk caught up by irresistible forces and hurled to an inescapable doom.

Virginia Quarterly Review, *Vol. 44, No. 1 (Winter, 1968), p. viii.*

We cannot but feel indignant . . . when a towering achievement like [*A Cry of Absence*] is saluted only by the odd and usually obscure reviewer. Though unqualified to do it justice, I feel obliged in this situation to attempt at least to call attention to its true stature. For *A Cry of Absence* is an authentic, pure, and deeply moving tragedy. Sophocles, Racine, Ibsen; in the novel, Flaubert, Hardy, Faulkner—these are the company it keeps and the comparisons it invites. In its dignity, integrity, and somber power it is a reproach to many of us for frivolity: for liking, for instance, such novels as Walker Percy's *Love in the Ruins*, so attractive and funny and entertaining, but finally so disappointing because incoherent and full of loose ends—things implausible or unexplained or meaningless. *A Cry* has, in contrast, the order and economy of the greatest art: there is no detail that is not essential, significant both in itself and in relation to the work as a whole. . . .

Jones's novel is a triumph of tact as well as integrity; there are no wrong notes, and every detail is fully dramatized and completely functional. Each one is necessary to the central action at the same time that it reveals the nature of the characters; each is historically typical, and each also functions on a symbolic or mythical level.

This spareness and economy of means make the reader think of Greek tragedy, as does the action itself, as austere, powerful, and inexorable as any in Greek drama, and as evocative of both pity and terror. The book is full of suspense, too, in exactly the Greek way: not so much as to what will happen, since the pattern of external events is foreseen very soon, but as to how and why it will happen in terms of character. . . .

This novel differs from many recent ones in that its fictional world is emphatically a moral one. And it is satisfying—aesthetically, intellectually, and morally—because it is complete and coherent. . . . It is, in my opinion, a major work of art.

*Monroe K. Spears, "A New Classic," in* Sewanee Review *(reprinted by permission of the editor; © 1972 by The University of the South), Winter, 1972, pp. 168-72.*

*A Cry of Absence* [is Madison Jones'] fifth novel and one of the best to come out of the South in recent years. It is the story of a vaguely aristocratic woman who lives in a small town and discovers that one of her two sons is guilty of the brutal murder of a black civil-rights activist. That is good, solid, "Southern" material, but there is nothing imitative or anachronistic about the novel. Jones movingly portrays the gradual destruction of the curtain of illusions with which the woman has surrounded herself, the desperation with which she clings to "family" against the proof of its corruption. In *A Cry of Absence* we see the white South in its last sad flailings against the inevitable. Place, community, and history all figure in the novel, but in the changed situation of a South facing up to its moral obligations.

*Jonathan Yardley, in* Partisan Review *(copyright © 1973 by Partisan Review, Inc.), Vol. XL, No. 2 (Spring, 1973), pp. 291-92.*

## JONG, Erica 1943?-

**Ms Jong is an American poet and novelist, best known for the quasi-autobiographical novel, *Fear of Flying*.**

Jong's best verse comes from . . . writing about men and women in a memorable vein of lightly mocking comedy. . . .

[In *Half-Lives*] Jong writes in a serial mode, in which five lines, or five stanzas, will all begin with the same phrase, . . . and because her subject is nearly always some form of the double-bind or the Laingian knot, the poems need to be seen whole. The form of iteration, though, threatens to hem her in; there are, after all, other figures of speech besides anaphora. Inside her rigid frames of syntax, a playful metaphorical mind is at work, busy in plentiful invention of little fables. If the whimsical and the bitter sometimes become the petulantly cute, there are nevertheless biting poems about women's feelings, and clever women's half-unconscious stratagems of desirability. . . .

The tone is authoritative, knowledgeable and diagnostic; it admits of no appeal; *de te fabula*, it says to its women readers. I can't quite imagine what it says to its men readers.

*Helen Vendler, in* The New York Times Book Review *(© 1973 by The New York Times Company; reprinted by permission), August 12, 1973, p. 6.*

Erica Jong's best poems (in "Fruits and Vegetables" and "Half-Lives") are quick tempo fables of sexual appetite vs. inhibiting intelligence. The woman in them would like to be a bawdy free spirit, but she drags a ball-and-chain with her: "I fall in love as a kind of research project." Jong can be sharply funny, as in her "Seventeen Warnings in Search of a Feminist Poem". . . .

Her besetting liability is cuteness—a willed abandon and rehearsed tossing of the hair. With exuberant, sometimes unconvincing bravado, her poems record her effort to change herself from the serious, studious girl she once was. . . .

Erica Jong isn't, so far, a good novelist. After a nervy, arresting take-off, she pads out "Fear of Flying" with lengthy, quasi-autobiographical detours . . . and limps home to a pat landing. Yet her book has plenty of energy, some good (and some terrible) wisecracks and a generous showing of distinct, determined talent.

*Walters Clemons, "Beware of the Man," in* Newsweek *(copyright Newsweek, Inc., 1973; reprinted by permission), November 12, 1973, p. 114.*

Erica Jong's first novel, "Fear of Flying," . . . feels like a winner. It has class and sass, brightness and bite. Containing all the cracked eggs of the feminist litany, her soufflé rises with a poet's afflatus. She sprinkles on the four-letter words as if women had invented them; her cheerful sexual frankness brings a new flavor to female prose. Mrs. Jong's heroine, Isadora Wing, surveying the "shy, shrinking, schizoid" array of women writers in English, asks, "Where was the female Chaucer?," and the Wife of Bath, were she young and gorgeous, neurotic and

Jewish, urban and contemporary, might have written like this. "Fear of Flying" not only stands as a notably luxuriant and glowing bloom in the sometimes thistly garden of "raised" feminine consciousness but belongs to, and hilariously extends, the tradition of "Catcher in the Rye" and "Portnoy's Complaint"—that of the New York voice on the couch, the smart kid's lament. Though Isadora Wing, as shamelessly and obsessively as Alexander Portnoy, rubs the reader's nose in the fantasies and phobias and family slapstick of growing up, she avoids the solipsism that turns Roth's hero unwittingly cruel; nor does she, like Holden Caulfield, though no less sensitive to phoniness, make of innocence an ideal. She remains alert to this world. . . .

As a creator of scenes and characters, Mrs. Jong is at her best in the present. . . . Here, comedy becomes satire and distress becomes drama. The prose flies. Throughout, the poet's verbal keenness rarely snags the flow of breathy vernacular; a few false shifts of tone, an occasional automatism of phrase . . ., a few clammy touches of jargon insignificantly mar a joyously extended performance. The novel is so full, indeed, that one wonders whether the author has enough leftover life for another novel. Fearless and fresh, tender and exact, Mrs. Jong has arrived non-stop at the point of being a literary personality; may she now travel on toward Canterbury.

*John Updike, "Jong Love," in* The New Yorker, *December 17, 1973, pp. 149-53.*

[*Fear of Flying*] attempts to explore the female predicament, but the world, the real world, is so strained through the sensibilities of the author that we don't believe in it—and therefore can't appreciate the predicament. The characters exist only in the author's mind, and have been swiftly categorized there in terms of what they stand for. What counts about them is whether or not they have a liberated consciousness and how they feel about the heroine.

There are pitfalls in the *dear diary* genre. Its personal, almost editorial, tone gives the author too much opportunity to tell us about her attitudes. She has no need to re-create experience—all she has to do is tell us about it. So her book becomes a reformist tract on the one hand and on the other a highly personal account of one woman's reactions, digestion and tastes. There is no artistic distance between the author and her subject, and hence no objectivity. We don't know what she's like; we only know what she thinks she's like. We learn nothing about the world, only about how she feels. The action all takes place in the mind of the author-protagonist, or in this case her not-so-private parts.

The cause of women's liberation has given rise, thus far, to a good deal of *dear diary*, a kind of literature that by its nature can do little to advance the ideal goals of the movement. The genre's narrow focus makes liberation unattainable. It expresses the author's indisposition to get out of the prison of herself.

*Ellen Hope Meyer, "The Aesthetics of 'Dear Diary'," in* The Nation, *January 12, 1974, pp. 55-6.*

At moments, [*Half-Lives*, a book of poems] seems obsessed—with sex, with death, with solitude and missed connections—and there is an occasional uneasiness that the extraordinary energy of this poet might suddenly turn in and begin devouring itself. "Your own mouth will eat you / if you don't watch out," she warns in *Chinese Food*. Indeed, her energy is voracious, and images of food, eating, hunger are scattered everywhere in the book, making a powerful central metaphor that shapes a haunting, energetic vision. . . . The cry of 'hunger' is elemental in this book, but too steady to need labored emphasis: the hunger is for wholeness, the appetite for being alive. Roethke provides the epigraph: "The notion of emptiness generates passion"; and to the end of the book this generous talent takes possession of virtually everything that comes its way, lovingly, aggressively, honestly. Erica Jong doesn't have much use for the kind of "delicacy" that comes from concealment, yet even these poems show a raw edge, their revelations are clear and earned.

These poems are savvy and savage, full of tenderness, but guided by a tough, resilient spirit. This is especially so in the many poems here about being a woman, about the terrible beautiful difference it can make. The feminism of these poems is deeply engaged, not with political style or public posture, but with the radical and intimate anguish of trying to be a whole human being. . . .

Even though it is uneven, with some poems a little slapdash and hurried, [the book] is not brilliant dabbling by a long shot, but a nimble craft aiming not for elaborate structures, but trying to keep pace with a quick and penetrating vision. Jong imagines with a wholeness that does not shy away from the passions of emptiness, and with a vigor very much in touch with world, body and a consciousness neither content nor deceived by a desire for a whole life.

*Leroy Searle, in* Poetry *(© 1974 by The Modern Poetry Association; reprinted by permission of the Editor of* Poetry*), March, 1974, pp. 363-65.*

[*Fear of Flying*] has a helplessness, a vulnerability that makes it very likable, and in some backhanded way successful. The flaws in the writing parallel the heroine's mistakes in her life—indeed *are* her mistakes reappearing in another form, since she is revisiting her life in the writing, compounding her (usually generous) errors the second time around. And then at the risk of sounding like a man who'll forgive anything for a couple of wisecracks, I must say there are some very good jokes in this novel: "Think of those Egyptians who built the pyramids, for example. Did *they* sit around worrying about whether they were Equal Opportunity Employers?" "He was a medievalist and before you could say 'Albigensian Crusade' he'd tell you the story of his life." I particularly like the subtle insinuation of "the first of my many psychiatrists, a short doctor whose name was Schrift."

*Michael Wood, in* The New York Review of Books *(reprinted with permission from* The New York Review of Books; *© 1974 by NYREV, Inc.), March 21, 1974, p. 20.*

With such continual and insistent reference to her cherished valve, Erica Jong's witless heroine [Isadora Wing in *Fear of Flying*] looms like a mammoth pudenda, as roomy as the Carlsbad Caverns, luring amorous spelunkers to confusion in her plunging grottoes. . . .

Isadora is also a feminist, interlarding her memoir with grim quotations from Sylvia Plath and Anne Sexton, and tendentious ones from Freud and Rudolf Hess. She says she 'wanted to write *War and Peace* or nothing,' and having chosen the latter, seems to have settled for the ambition of being gamahuched from here to eternity. But there are problems: 'the big problem was how to make your feminism jibe with your unappeasable hunger for male bodies. It wasn't easy.'

This crappy novel, misusing vulgarity to the point where it becomes purely foolish, picturing woman as a hapless organ animated by the simplest ridicule, and devaluing imagination in every line . . ., represents everything that is to be loathed in American fiction today. It does not have the excuse of humour, nor is its pretence to topicality anything but tedious. That it was written with a grant . . . from the National Endowment for the Arts should surprise no one already familiar with the ways American money is used, though is ample justification for any of us to refuse paying his taxes this year.

*Paul Theroux, "Hapless Organ," in* New Statesman, *April 19, 1974, p. 554.*

*Fear of Flying* has pulled far ahead of the pack in the race for the "women's novel of the year" award. And it probably will win, for the author sees in life precisely what the women's movement has told her to see. She finds drama and significance in exactly those places—and only those places—where the movement claims it exists. . . .

The prose style is snappy—super casual—rather like a precocious teenager's diary. It's a highly readable novel, but remains to the end no more than a slight amusement, for the author has no perspective about the things that happen. She simply spills it all out. Nor does the book dramatize any real development. In the end Isadora Wing, the heroine, has outgrown her longing for the "zipless f---" which, I suppose, is progess of a sort. But hardly worth a book.

*Patricia S. Coyne, "Woman's Lit," in* National Review *(150 East 35th St., New York, N.Y. 10016), May 24, 1974, p. 604.*

Passionately indiscreet amd indiscriminate, [*Fear of Flying*] is hardly a novel at all, but a series of furious escapades, loosely tacked together as parts of Isadora Wing's unfinished quest for something called "the zipless fuck." . . . Its particular kind of liberated bawdy, its greed for experience and stentorian humour belong to a tradition of the novel for which the cultivated social ironies of 19th-century fiction have never really existed. It works on the premise that since literature is notably short of picaresque heroines—where are the female Tom Jones?—their invention requires the writer to start from scratch. *Fear of Flying* brings the history of the Women's Novel up to about 1720. . . .

In England, Mrs. Jong has managed to enrage several of her male reviewers: Martin Amis in the *Observer* and Paul Theroux in the *New Statesman* ("this crappy novel . . .") were both driven to apoplexy by *Fear of Flying*. They were clearly galled by the prospect of this woman who, because she is a woman, seems to feel entitled to take the net down before starting the tennis game. No man could get away with quite that calculated artlessness, or blowsy innocence, so why should she? But get away with it she does. Her appalling heroine (reading the book is like being locked in a lift with a woman who tells you her life story twice over, rapes you, and stops you reaching for the Emergency button) has a crude genius for reality, its quantity rather than quality. She persuades one of her existence by brute force, and she will not be budged.

What is more, if she *is* a monster, she is botheringly close to the insatiably willing dream-girl of male fantasies and male fiction.

*Jonathan Raban, in* Encounter, *July, 1974, p. 76.*

* * *

## JUST, Ward 1935-

**Just, an American, writes novels of politics. (See also *Contemporary Authors*, Vols. 25-28.)**

[*The Congressman Who Loved Flaubert and Other Washington Stories*], modest though it is, constitutes perhaps the one intrinsically successful work of fiction about our capital city. It might, drably but accurately, have been called *Government*, a thought I offer only because I am anxious to see this book replace that old dog *Democracy* as the standard fictional text about Washington. If *Democracy* ever had anything going for it, besides the Adams name, it was only a certain sense of subject. Henry Adams was too perceptive a man not to know where the game was to be found, but he was not a novelist, and all he could really do with the game was locate it.

Ward Just has done more. There are only nine stories in the collection, but they are expertly spread and highly focused. . . .

It is not easy to integrate a body of stories, which will have been written at various times, in varying moods, about a diversity of subjects. Just transcends this problem, and does it essentially through tone: the collection as a whole has an impact far greater than even the best of the stories would have, taken alone.

Indeed, it is the controlled, informed, but always impersonal tone of the prose which makes this book the triumph that it is. Many books have been written about Washington, some of them by fine writers. Many of them have been excellent in detail, but all of them have failed, it seems to me, to convey the ambiance of the city. I suspect these failures have something to do with the nature of political narrative itself, with its constant tendency to shade into melodrama. Yet the ambiance of Washington is not passion and melodrama; it is, first and last, control and impersonality. In these tones, or tones very like them, life is lived here, and decisions made, and a nation governed, more or less. Of course, high dramas occur and the passions that go with ambition come into play constantly, but the tones of these passions and dramas seem to vanish almost as they are uttered; they do not, I think, permeate the lives of the secretariat. The antecedent to the tone which Just has employed is the tone of the Michigan stories of Ernest Hemingway; applying it to Washington was a highly effective choice because it is the perfect tone with which to dramatize the kind of inhibitions of spirit which the bureaucratic life requires.

*Larry McMurtry, "Just So Stories," in*

Book World—The Washington Post (© The Washington Post), *July 22, 1973, p. 3.*

Just is an admirer of Ernest Hemingway, and there is something of the tone of the early Hemingway stories in "The Congressman Who Loved Flaubert." The nine stories are polished, sophisticated, understated and possessed of near-perfect dialogue and absolute authenticity. Each fact stated suggests 10 facts known but unstated—Hemingway's tip-of-the-iceberg theory of writing. But the analogy should not be pushed too far, for Hemingway was drawn to external dramas—hunting, boxing, skiing, war—and Just writes of the more muted, internal dramas of political life. Hearts break in Just's stories, but no blood is shed. . . .

Violence and sex are always offstage. A bloody coup in Africa is seen through the indifferent eyes of a desk-bound C.I.A. bureaucrat in Washington. The Vietnam war touches an ambitious Congressman only when a visiting schoolgirl whispers that her brother died there. A Vietnam war hero tries to explain to an interviewer what it was like to kill but can't find the words. Public men prove to be private men, their dramas as secret as cancer.

*Patrick Anderson, in* The New York Times Book Review *(© 1973 by The New York Times Company; reprinted by permission), August 26, 1973, p. 22.*

To say that *Stringer* is one of the best novels to come out of Vietnam may seem a limited compliment, but at its best the book is very good indeed. . . .

The novel deals with a number of themes, but chief among them seems to me the debilitating effect of a cold, faceless, mechanical institution—in this case the Army—on those who must carry out its programmed, computerized policies. . . .

*Stringer* is most effective in the Vietnam scenes, less so in the flashbacks to Stringer's college years and his brief, unsuccessful marriage. Too, the novel's construction is rather shaky—the transition from the jungle to the hospital is somewhat confusing. But overall, this is a work of intelligence, skill and tightly-controlled passion.

*Jonathan Yardley, "Prisoner of War," in* Book World—The Washington Post (© The Washington Post), *March 10, 1974, p. 3.*

Just . . . author of a superb collection of short stories, "The Congressman Who Loved Flaubert," obviously admires Hemingway. His clean, sparse, muscular prose evokes the tensions and suspense of men at war. [*Stringer*] is easily the best of the handful of novels to have emerged from the Vietnam war.

*Arthur Cooper, "The Insane War," in* Newsweek *(copyright Newsweek, Inc., 1974; reprinted by permission), March 11, 1974, pp. 83-4.*

In *To What End: Report from Vietnam* (1968), as in [*Stringer*], Just sees our Indochina entaglement in terms of a script that might have been written by Pinter or Beckett. The earlier book pictured the war as an East Indian theater of the absurd in which violence rolled on "without plot, rhyme or reason." Particularly frustrating, marine Gen. Lewis Walt told Just, was the inability of the US soldier to know who were his friends, who his enemies. The upshot: a paranoia that hit all the ranks. "Madness in Vietnam," declared Just, "became infectious and somehow normal." Paranoia and even suicidal madness play a role in *Stringer* and what emerges is the existentialist theme of human beings pinned down in an absurd and meaningless world. . . .

For readers tired of war and Watergate and other long-standing irritants, *Stringer* may pass as a novel designed to keep us from forgetting, but belaboring a point we all know. Just is a low-profile author, however, and his novel is less an antiwar story than an examination of the ironies growing out of the Vietnam imbroglio. In his nonfictional *Military Men* Just tried to give the army its due, pictured its officer corps as an aristocracy that nevertheless encourages merit, praised West Pointers and other professionals who battled the system, and puzzled over the motives that seduced them into a career where being bookish and introverted made you an oddball and insider-outsider. . . .

Stringer, who fills nearly the whole frame of the novel, is the true existentialist hero in his skepticism and in the sad wisdom that gives him at 35 an air of venerable age slightly modified by his profanity. . . .

Stringer is believable—even his crankiest nihilistic remarks sound like a voice of our times—though future readers may dismiss him as a literary fancy along with the gentleman-heroes of Booth Tarkington and Richard Harding Davis. On the other hand, the minor figures of the novel are blurred, Just having neglected his short story writer's ability to nail down a character with a single descriptive or analytical sentence. *Stringer* is nevertheless an advance beyond Just's earlier books in its suspenseful storytelling, its evocative style, and its refusal to follow up the smartness and flippancy that brought minor fame last year to his *The Congressman Who Loved Flaubert and Other Stories.*

*James Walt, in* The New Republic *(reprinted by permission of* The New Republic; *© 1974 by The New Republic, Inc., April 6, 1974, pp. 27-8.*

[*Stringer* is a] beautifully written but maddeningly obscure novel—allegorical, sentences loaded with symbols planted as carefully as antipersonnel mines, a deceptively simple plot that moves from apparent reality through insanity into what seems to be an updated version of Sartre's existentialist hell. . . . The last third of the novel is set in a nameless capital where Stringer, captured, tries to make sense of his senseless past. The capital may be a real place. Or it may be hell. Or, God forbid, it may be heaven. But that's the problem with *Stringer*. You can interpret it any way you want. It will be read as a novel about Vietnam, especially since Just was *Washington Post* correspondent there for 18 months. But Just, born like Stringer in 1935, seems most interested in explaining not the war itself, but rather how his generation viewed itself in relation to that war, a job he could do more effectively by writing about his own journalistic experiences.

*John R. Coyne, Jr., in* National Review *(150 East 35th St., New York, N.Y. 10016), April 26, 1974, p. 494.*

It is apparent that Mr. Just intends *Stringer* as a statement about both life and war . . ., but he can't seem to make himself clear. His failure, however, is no more than that; he is an excellent writer, and he has given us a novel that, though ultimately enigmatic, is otherwise a splendidly observed adventure.

The New Yorker, *May 27, 1974, pp. 105-06.*

A certain vagueness about the title character [Stringer] raises the suspicion that this tough novel about an American guerrilla-warfare expert who cracks up in an Asian jungle may be a parable of the American Viet Nam disaster. Indeed, it might be entitled *The Gray Badge of Pragmatism. . . .*

Novelist Just finesses most of the moral and artistic questions that could be asked about his book and his character's situation. The reader will find himself wavering between conflicting assessments: the story is really a disturbing piece of surrealism or it is a neat con job. The compromise view—that the book is a bit of both—leaves Ward Just (author of *The Congressman Who Loved Flaubert*, an excellent collection of several stories published last year) as one of several promising American writers now creeping up on the big novel.

Time *(reprinted by permission from* Time, The Weekly Newsmagazine; *copyright Time Inc.), July 8, 1974, pp. E3, 82.*

# K

## KERRIGAN, (Thomas) Anthony 1918-

**Kerrigan is an American-born poet and translator now living on Mallorca. (See also *Contemporary Authors*, Vols. 49-52.)**

Kerrigan is the moment's epicure, therefore its elegiast. . . .

Kerrigan's views are seldom tentative: praiser of the moment, he also makes his mind up about it, and has a critical, passionate bias to pin it to. Making up your mind is risky though; may be damned for every error, and in poetizing the risk is greater than it would be in the moral-religious sphere simply because (if one is not rhapsodizing or improvising) one has the time to reseize the moment, many moments, and make something of them—a poem if possible, an epitome of the self. Judgment is most severe, severer than the fantasies of religious practice, in my opinion, unless you are the karmic ribbon clerk computing every ell of error, or the Grand Sinster of Sinai whose votaries keep tabs on every nanosecond of vagary. Kerrigan's poetry therefore relies on the perceptions of a mind that has studied the real places out there, the scenes we should enjoy if we came to stand where in memory he stands. Dublin, Chicago, Barcelona, Paris, the galleries of the early twentieth-century painters, whose forms he sometimes contemplates by translating their essential ideas of structure into attitudes about people or music or building—but always arriving at something that he can say very succinctly. And his mind also reveals itself, not as an intellectualizing apparatus, of which there is a great surplusage these days, but as the thinking portion of a singular person.

Kerrigan's complex responses reflect a world measured, understood, and largely relinquished to its own chaos of unimportance in favor of a few, but discriminating choices: the woman, in whole or in part: her hair, her eyes, a breast, a thigh; the wind in a certain place; the light in Muslim North Africa; streets built in other times, a quiet square in Dublin. . . .

[*At the Front Door of the Atlantic* is] a bagful of lyrics made like Arp's or Miro's objects out of such natural jetsam as is both ancient yet brand-new, held in the knowing hand and turned to be seen by the canny eye in such ways as to render it presently mysterious, yet also plain enough indeed to the delighted inspection. . . .

Kerrigan has taken for his flight kit fossilized relics from those places in the old world that still recall manly and womanly human ceremony, fringe civilizations, Irish, Spanish, Greek. Still, someone has to stand for something somewhere. And stand firmly, if modestly, without the adolescent feverishness over the poetic of, say, some of the later, wordy James Dickey. There poems, densely wrought and distilled from thought, are a prelude to the silence that is also the form of poetry; not speechlessness, but the thinking presence of a man who knows how to wait and work, and to make poems that have to be read again. . . .

*Jascha Kessler, in* Parnassus, *Fall/Winter, 1973, pp. 223, 225-27.*

* * *

## KESSLER, Jascha 1929-

**Kessler is an American short story writer, poet, critic, novelist, and playwright. (See also *Contemporary Authors*, Vols. 19-20.)**

Jascha Kessler's collection of stories [*An Egyptian Bondage, and Other Stories*] attempts a new bridging of two worlds, the actual and the hallucinatory. Here the exactness of tone is everything—or should have been everything; if the stories sometimes tend to reach too far for too little, or for too little that is defined, they are never without interest. That is not a backhanded compliment; the interest comes repeatedly as a surprise, and even the most tenuous of the stories keeps poking around inside one's head long after the book is done.

*Eliot Fremont-Smith, in* The New York Times *(© 1967 by The New York Times Company; reprinted by permission), November 10, 1967, p. 45.*

The stories in Jascha Kessler's collection, *An Egyptian Bondage* . . .; read as if they were out of an earlier era, and a luckier one. Frank, subjective, bristling with provacation, they are quite unlike the dim and arbitrary cavalcade of fiction that glides through the quarterlies. Though their style is luxuriant, it remains in service to the plot, in contrast to the language of the '60s which, no sooner liberated, starts possessing its creator like some whirling dervish. Jascha Kessler's subject is often work, as it loomed in our anxieties in a period when a good job was hard to find and usually desperately needed, even by teen-agers. The more we prosper and assume the availability of jobs, the less attention our fiction directs toward this absorbing segment of life. But these stories involve us from the start by their curiosity about it, especially about the middle-echelon service jobs that ferment discontent from above and below. Caddies, delivery-boys, hotel stewards, fund-raisers—these men-between make up the cast of *An Egyptian Bondage*.

*Isa Kapp, "Versions of Initiation," in* The New Leader, *February 12, 1968, pp. 20-1.*

Kessler is an old-fashioned contemporary. This is not condemnation with faint praise but a salute to one who rejects obscurantism as a matter of principle. His classical orientation and esthetic sensibility give the poems [in *Whatever Love Declares*] a substance that requires close reader attention. Yet they speak of everyday things, love, family, the landscape, all within a framework of mildly philosophical argumentation spiced with pessimism and perhaps a little guilt. The poems are temperate but strong and honest.

*Jerome Cushman, in* Library Journal *(reprinted from the March 1, 1970, issue of* Library Journal, *published by R. R. Bowker Company, a Xerox company; copyright © 1970 by Xerox Corporation), March 1, 1970.*

Kessler . . . celebrates through his own life, the mystery of birth and love and death. . . .

Kessler is a complex and sentient writer, no mere observer. He is both the experiment and the experimenter. His materials [for the poems in *Whatever Love Declares*] come from life felt, and penetrated for meaning, with the lens of satire, invocation and elegy. He has the gift of evocation as well—not only in personal experience, but in the relationship of abstraction and life. . . .

Perspective is Kessler's quest. A fix on himself and his life, not solely the personal history, but the times in which he lives.

*Robert Kirsch, "The Book Report," in* The Los Angeles Times *(copyright, 1970,* Los Angeles Times; *reprinted by permission), March 13, 1970.*

Jascha Kessler's *After the Armies Have Passed* . . . is a collection of poetry which speaks eloquently to our condition and evokes as well those responses beyond words which are the measure of a poet's gift to us. . . .

It is a measure of Kessler's work that he never offers the easy prescriptions of instant solutions. His experience is individual; his evocation universal. As a poet he is not readily cataloged. He celebrates the private voice, the individual history. And yet its overtones seem to have resonance in us. . . .

The secret theme is love, not the facile illusion of love which salves and redeems, but the complex connection between one human and another, man and woman, man past and woman past, parent and child, teacher and student. Redemption, salvation, change, growth are never easy matters for people shelled like tortoises wandering, "fitted for the lives we lead—/these beaks, these strong legs for our shells."

But in the end, as in "Surfer in Winter": "There's never someone else,/There's only you alone./If it's right and you're right,/you're walking on water, coming in from the sea/as if you were just born—/though you never reach shore."

*Robert Kirsch, "The Book Report," in* The Los Angeles Times *(copyright, 1971,* Los Angeles Times; *reprinted by permission), December 8, 1971, p. 19.*

* * *

## KINSELLA, Thomas 1928-

**Kinsella is an Irish poet, now living and teaching in America. John Montague called Kinsella "an intellectual troubador, his desire to sing increasingly crossed by a need to explain." (See also *Contemporary Authors*, Vols. 17-18.)**

Thomas Kinsella shares with his elders . . . a savage and nostalgic dismay at the present state of Ireland and of the world, with all that is implied for the subjective life in that dismay. But his work has been more closely assimilated than theirs to the new tendencies that he resists, and he resembles the younger urban poets of England and America the more by that token. I do not mean that this gifted poet lacks a voice of his own. Quite the contrary, he seems to me to have the most distinctive voice of his generation in Ireland, though it is also the most versatile and the most sensitive to 'outside' influences.

*M. L. Rosenthal, in his* The New Poets: American and British Poetry Since World War II *(copyright © 1967 by M. L. Rosenthal; reprinted by permission of Oxford University Press, Inc.), Oxford University Press, 1967, pp. 283-97.*

[In Thomas] Kinsella's case the poem is totally immersed in a pre-existing vision of life, in an emotion generated through the ordeal of living. This is something entirely different from the pursuit of the subjective which . . . is nothing more than a conscious literary strategy. Kinsella is an immensely accomplished poet, in perfect control of his craft; but in reading him it is the impact of the experience in his poems that moves one rather than the technique of them, though it is, naturally, only through the technique that the experience becomes available. . . .

Thomas Kinsella is one of Ireland's two or three most important poets, though his poetry is no more obviously Irish than that of Denis Devlin.

*Marius Bewley, in* The Hudson Review *(copyright © 1969 by The Hudson Review, Inc.; reprinted by permission), Vol. XXI, No. 4, Winter, 1968-69, pp. 723-25.*

Taking risks within the boundaries of the prevailing conventional wisdom in poetry doesn't require a lot of courage. The wind really begins to blow cold when the poet sets off obstinately on his own path, away from easy fashionableness, ignoring all the pressures to conform, and devotes several years to writing the kind of verse he wants to, instead of what he is nudged or bullied into writing. It's no surprise that the recent work of the Irish poet, Thomas

Kinsella . . . has not been eagerly received. *New Poems 1973* . . . [is a] weird, and yet magnificently weird, [testimony] to a resolve to write directly out of a store of deeply personal material without worrying about the public reception. [It makes] odd and enthralling reading. . . .

There is scarcely one tidy, rounded poem in the book; but whole passages inside poems stand out with an ornate, eccentric splendour.

*Alan Brownjohn, in* New Statesman, *November 9, 1973, pp. 694-95.*

The Irish poet Thomas Kinsella has loosened up since his stricter forms in 1968's "Nightwalker" collection. His title poem, "Notes from the Land of the Dead," is a group of autobiographical pieces, mostly in the graveyard tone. . . .

I read this book twice, the title sequence three times. For some reason Mr. Kinsella's verses do not quiver like arrows in my brain. I want to be picked up and shaken! My head shoved under cold running brookwater. Ice creeping up my back and scalp. I want to watch a page fill with spiritual light as cold and passionate as the dawn. I prefer almost anything to pits, ectoplasm, hags, graves. I don't see how Kinsella can be so ballsy about murdered demonstrators, but fall into such literary vaporings about childhood.

*Donald Newlove, in* The Village Voice *(reprinted by permission of* The Village Voice; *© 1974 by The Village Voice, Inc.), March 14, 1974, pp. 27-8.*

"Notes From the Land of the Dead"—mere "notes." Ireland's best living poet has brooded himself to pieces. His passion survives in poetic piecing alone. The passionate, he says, "might find it maddening." But "passionate" is in quotation marks that squeeze the word to sand. . . .

We have learned that poetry will put up with almost anything, except stale imagination. Lowell and Kinsella alike break the knees of thematic development; their poems fall on the world. Not long ago—above all in "Nightwalker," "A Country Walk," "Downstream," "The Shoals Returning"—Kinsella's bore the very passion they sought, like "bdellium, seeking the pearl in its own breast." But here among the dead, the Irish of whom he has finally despaired (apart from the public poem "Butcher's Dozen," he is no longer brilliantly angry), here among "a few/tentative tired endings over/and over," his poetry scatters "in a million droplets of/fright and loneliness . . .". . . .

The truth, however, is that Kinsella can hardly write a worthless poem. His style is an almost constant pleasure—meticulously bevelled crystal with a glinting edge. Let him break off, dismantle "let out/the offence simmering/weakly/as possible/within," let him even "dream," his tensions, his timing, his selectivity, are elegance itself: "the passion is in the putting together." The poems coalesce through the surface tension of their style alone, are "random,/persistent coherences." Moreover, his concentration ferrets, and even the poems reduced to "a few simplicities go/burrowing into their own depths." You may indeed "find it maddening," but the more you read the poems the more they impose themselves as passionately delicate constructs. You listen and seem to hear, from something falling, tiny silvery strings, plucked as if by the air itself.

*Calvin Bedient, in* The New York Times Book Review *(© 1974 by The New York Times Company; reprinted by permission), June 16, 1974, p. 7.*

* * *

## KNOWLES, John 1926-

**Knowles is an American novelist and short story writer. His particular achievement has been his sympathetic examination of the problems of young adults in the Fifties and Sixties. (See also *Contemporary Authors*, Vols. 17-18.)**

For an excellent case of mechanical neatness and righteousness, consider John Knowles's little sermon *Indian Summer.* Like everything Knowles has written, despite his protestations, the book is a carefully constructed little machine. . . . Only twice in *Indian Summer* does Knowles fall into writing like a novelist. He has a splendid scene in Kansas, in which Kinsolving takes up a crop-duster biplane and behaves gloriously like himself—doing stupid things, nearly killing himself, and smashing all the countryside; clumsily realizing it's stupid and dangerous but delighting in it anyway, making comically sober but ridiculous observations to himself which Knowles, in the ecstasy of honest inspiration, allows to stand. The other fine moment in the novel is one in which Kinsolving first meets his brother Charley after four years.

*John Gardner, in* The Southern Review, *Vol. V, No. 1, Winter, 1969, pp. 127-29.*

I lost myself in *A Separate Peace.* I identified with Phineas, and I indulged fantasies that would have made even Leper Lepellier stand up and take notice. The book became my bible, a chronicle of the lost tribes of preppies who underwent the torments of youth in search for the promised self. Now, as a college student, I have read John Knowles's new novel, *The Paragon,* and experienced that same ecstasy of identification and understanding that I derived from *A Separate Peace.* For once again Knowles has created a realistic and sensitive portrayal of the confusing and sometimes terrifying predicaments of youth.

*S. Alexander Haverstick, in* Saturday Review/World *(copyright © 1971 by Saturday Review/World, Inc.; reprinted with permission), February 13, 1971, p. 31.*

John Knowles' first published novel, *A Separate Peace,* now a decade old, is a minor but very nearly perfect piece of work: a tight, cohesive account of the corruption of innocence that is not merely the finest "prep-school novel" but a genuine work of art. Such early success, however, has its all-too-familiar pitfalls. Since *A Separate Peace* Mr. Knowles has been foundering—writing with characteristic grace and intelligence, but groping uncertainly for new subjects and themes.

The uneasy process continues in *The Paragon.* As it happens, I like the novel very much, finding it engaging, amusing and thoughtful. But for all its considerable charm, *The Paragon* doesn't quite come off. It is too derivative of *A Separate Peace,* echoing it in setting, dramatis personae, mood and theme. It is also inherently false in tone, for it is a sixties novel in a fifties setting, with resultant credibility problems that greatly weaken it. . . .

*A Separate Peace* may be a miniature, but it is a wholly realized work of art in which a world is created and made believable. *The Paragon* attempts to re-evoke that world but ultimately lapses into imitation.

*Jonathan Yardley, "A Novelist Groping," in* The New Republic *(reprinted by permission of* The New Republic; *© 1971 by Harrison-Blaine of New Jersey, Inc.), February 13, 1971, pp. 27-8.*

John Knowles, though belonging to an older generation, speaks in [*The Paragon*] for the young, or at least for the offspring of middle- and upper-income Americans. Far more effectively and lucidly than Charles Reich in *The Greening of America,* he describes their rebellion and their disillusionment with their parents, the corporate state, the lily-white suburbs, the ecological mess, and the country's military madness. He understands their doubts. He catches their enthusiasm. He sympathizes with their hunger for genuine love and the opportunity for self-expression. Nor is he an academic hippie offering vague protest and a world of inaction held together by a kind of abstract affection. His heroes, both in his latest novel, *The Paragon,* and the earlier *A Separate Peace,* are hopeful activists, eager to contribute to a new society in their own way. . . .

Knowles's style is gentle and unaffected, yet direct and firm. There is an acerbic tone to his treatment of Yale, an ironic bitterness which catches this same mood in his characters. He has shifted skillfully from depicting the naïveté of his prep-school characters in *A Separate Peace* to dealing with the newly acquired cynicism of college sophomores. . . . Perhaps he is rather in the tradition of Samuel Butler's *The Way of All Flesh* with its strong anti-parent bias and its sympathy for children and young adults, though Knowles's literary technique and the world he elects to write about are far removed from Butler's. In any case *The Paragon* is an admirable novel. It deserves to have the same reputation—and will probably show the same power to last—as *A Separate Peace,* the book that made its author's reputation.

*Peter Rowley, "Power to the Partial People," in* The Nation, *May 3, 1971, pp. 569-70.*

"Where'd you get the butler? . . . Out of some murder novel?" John Knowles has a character ask midway through *Spreading Fires,* as if to warn that the fictional possibilities inherent in the first half of this new book . . . will not be realized in the second half, but will dissipate in pulp tale tackiness. . . .

That these characters have been invested with so little inner life that they appear to be pulp fiction puppets is disappointing since Knowles, notably in *A Separate Peace,* has revealed an understanding of emotion and a sensitivity to the psychological struggles between love and enmity, between loyalty and freedom, between the need to accept guilt and the need to be absolved from it. He still knows about emotion. . . . But statements about feeling don't show what characters feel as they interact with one another. Had Knowles developed the relationships for which the foundation is laid in the first half of the novel . . . [he] might have sparked the emotional conflagration suggested by the title. Undeveloped, the characters are wet kindling. Instead of *Gotterdammerung* we get Alfred Hitchcock in the second half. . . .

The symbols and imagery of *Spreading Fires* are more imaginative than the characterization, but tend to be contrived; rather than emerging from the narrative they are tacked onto it. References to Catholic liturgy do emerge from the Lucases' religious heritage, but accompany no genuine crisis of faith or identity. . . .

Despite flaws which make *Spreading Fires* a failure in terms of serious fiction, the novel has some attractions. The style is brisk, the Mediterranean setting is beautifully rendered, the plot is fastpaced and entertaining. And there is some subtle word play. . . .

Why a novelist of Knowles's talent would want to write even superb potboilers is beyond me, and I hope his next novel is more ambitious.

*Wayne J. Henkel, in* Book World—The Washington Post (© The Washington Post), *June 23, 1974, p. 2.*

As a novelist, John Knowles has long been fascinated with the treachery that lurks in the heart of man. In *A Separate Peace,* his now classic account of a teenage friendship, Knowles explored hauntingly our inner urge to destroy. In *Spreading Fires,* he probes still further, this time into the viscera of a deranged soul, finding guilt and madness there in contagious proportions. . . .

The tale is told in a clean, unobtrusive language that belies the insidious nature of Knowles's argument. But Knowles simply fails to convince us, with his social morality and his contrived implications, that evil and sexual longings lurk inexorably in his characters' souls. His novel is less an argument for the infectiousness of paranoia, suspicion, madness, than it is for the deep-running fear of being displaced, for the human hunger to belong, to be part of a family, that sent Neville [the "cheerless, reclusive British-Canadian" protagonist] askew.

*Susan Heath, in* Saturday Review/World *(copyright © 1974 by Saturday Review/World, Inc.; reprinted with permission), June 29, 1974, p. 18.*

Although it was hideously overpraised for the doubtful virtue of being full of restraint—a rare virtue in an age when novels have their pretensions sticking out a mile, but hardly something to make a reader keel over with admiration—John Knowles's "A Separate Peace" remains a novel in miniature, very clear but not very ambitious. It was the work of a literary apprentice who showed himself to have greater range in subsequent novels, "Morning in Antibes" and "Indian Summer." My own favorite is "Morning in Antibes" (a choice [that "Spreading Fires"], with the same setting, does nothing to alter). It is a strange mixture of a foundering marriage and the central character's friendship with an Algerian refugee, saying little about the marriage but telling volumes about the way sympathy of a political and personal kind is generated. In that book, the Riviera was a hothouse of steamy air and unexpected blossoms. In "Spreading Fires" Mr. Knowles's Riviera is again exotic, but here it's hard to keep from thinking that it's really only expensive, and that if you had enough money you could go to pieces there, too. . . .

It is possible to believe in [the novel's] *ménage,* and Mr. Knowles's portrayal of Americans being driven to distraction by [their] cracked, domineering servant has just the right touch of malice; but the novel is too slight a thing, too hastily worked out. . . . Attempting to be allusive, Mr. Knowles is sketchy.

*Paul Theroux, in* The New York Times Book Review *(© 1974 by The New York Times Company; reprinted by permission), July 14, 1974, pp. 4-5.*

* * *

## KONRÁD, György 1933-

**Konrád is a Hungarian social worker and novelist. He is known to Americans as George Konrád.**

Beneath the lowest rung of society live the speechless. They are the broken and deranged, the flotsam and the *lumpens,* all those helpless people who have signed a separate peace with reality and now choose not to confront regulations, skills, responsibilities. . . .

Modern literature has noticed them not as "cases" but as creatures. . . . [Never,] to my knowledge, have they been evoked with such intimate authority and grating clarity as in "The Case Worker," a brilliant first novel by a new writer from Hungary. With this one book George Konrád, himself a social worker in Budapest, strides to the forefront of contemporary European literature. . . .

It is a powerful book, and it gains its power from Konrád's gift for the vignette, the suddenly snapped picture, as if taken through a slightly overfocused camera. The graphic prose carries one from paragraph to paragraph, with no expectation of pleasure or accumulation of suspense, yet a need to share in the fated journey of a mind seeking to reach its limits.

Necessarily, there are losses in this kind of fiction, and the very success of this novel helps to define them. The vignette, the prose snapshot, the virtuoso passage cannot yield us that experience of a sustained narrative that Lionel Trilling has described as "being held spellbound, momentarily forgetful of oneself, concerned with the fate of a person who is not oneself but who also, by reason of the spell that is being cast, is oneself, his conduct and his destiny bearing upon the reader's own." No; in reading "The Case Worker" we are not held spellbound, we are not forgetful of ourselves, since the author is trying for other effects—the effects of a kind of ratiocinative blow, almost a cringing before the extreme possibilities of existence. But what saves the book from mere shock is that Konrád believes overwhelmingly in the moral significance of other people's experience, and writes out of the conviction that the world, no matter how terrible, is still the substance of our days.

The materials of this book are of a kind that in recent years have often become the special property of documentary movies—we have even been told that the old-fashioned printed word cannot match the film for vividness. But "The Case Worker" shows, if anyone doubts it, that language remains the greatest of human powers, with unrivaled capacities for evocation, parallel and echo. A notable debut, a remarkable achievement, and a vindication of the word.

*Irving Howe, in* The New York Times Book Review *(© 1974 by The New York Times Company; reprinted by permission), January 27, 1974, pp. 1, 24.*

A grim talent of Eastern Europe has emerged: one who has the ability to invest the sinister with a fool's cap without diminishing its horror or our humanity. Konrad is now under surveillance, probably for being talented enough to describe reality. Well, you can say this about the Iron Curtain countries: they certainly know who their best writers are.

*Martin Washburn, in* The Village Voice *(reprinted by permission of* The Village Voice; *© 1974 by The Village Voice, Inc.), February 28, 1974, p. 23.*

For ten years, the middle-aged, middle-echelon bureaucrat in a contemporary Budapest child-welfare organization who is the narrator of this scathing first novel ["The Case Worker"] has listened to his "clients'" grotesquely similar, "massive, tentacular, and incurable woes"; he has said "Have a seat, please," some thirty thousand times, he speculates; and he has swept so much pain and remorse off his desk with a bang of his rubber stamp that he feels like "a surgeon who sews up his incision without removing the tumor." The narrator takes us through the encounters of a typical, depressing, frustrating day, through his nightmare-like store of memories of past cases, and, at one point, through a fantasy he entertains about shedding his bureaucrat's armor, leaving his family, and caring for an idiot five-year-old whose parents have recently poisoned themselves. The language is straightforward and utterly unsentimental, which makes the incurable illnesses, perversions, cruelties, lies, and social injustices he describes on page after page all the more shocking. Pity and loathing tug at the case worker (and at the reader) with equal force. The case worker's task—patching up the injuries that the wretched inflict on each other, and especially on their children—is, of course, comically Sisyphean, obscenely unaccomplishable. Such raw human suffering as is depicted here is infrequently the subject of works of fiction, and even more infrequently the theme of a writer as skilled, brilliant, and willing to take risks as Mr. Konrád. This is an almost unbearable book to read, but it should not be missed.

The New Yorker, *March 11, 1974, p. 134.*

At first glance, there doesn't seem to be anything either absurd or particularly Eastern European about *The Case Worker,* a stunning first novel by George Konrád, a young Hungarian writer (in a translation by Paul Aston).

For these precise and dispassionate accounts of the most horrendous forms of degradation and suffering have also become something of an Eastern European specialty—if only because they *are* so simple and straightforward, and never sensationalist or self-indulgent in the Western manner. (In reading Konrád's book, one thinks inevitably of Jerzy Kosinski who in his terse tales of human perversity has also drawn on his Eastern European experiences.) But Konrád, though he himself worked as a superintendent in a child welfare agency and has, like Kosinski, a background in sociology, is not merely a dispassionate observer and recorder. . . .

What makes Konrád's book a remarkable achievement—what transforms the sociological content of his work into art—is that he succeeds in revealing, with his physical descriptions even more effectively than with the actual case histories, the true state of his clients. . . . Konrád, almost in the manner of the French *nouveau roman,* constructs a world of precisely observed objects—but his objects speak, and their tales of woe remain vivid.

The only other examples of Konrád's stylistic departure from his clinically concise narrative are his occasional anguished outbursts. But even in the searing parallel sentences of these prose poems, we find no rhetorical exaggeration, only an intense concentration on fact, a mixture of impassioned plea and ironic understatement. . . . Konrád's novel is not only an artistic *tour de force,* it is also a moral triumph—a book without despair is not altogether despairing.

*Ivan Sanders, in* The New Republic *(reprinted by permission of* The New Republic; *© 1974 by Harrison-Blaine of New Jersey, Inc.), March 16, 1974, p. 26.*

* * *

## KOPS, Bernard 1926-

**Kops, an English playwright, novelist, and poet, is well known for his novels of East End Jewish life in the Thirties. (See also *Contemporary Authors*, Vols. 5-8, rev. ed.)**

*The Hamlet of Stepney Green* and *Enter Solly Gold* are opposite sides of the same coin. In the former, Kops takes himself seriously and fails; in the latter, he does not take himself seriously and succeeds. It is as simple as that, and the lesson for the Jewish playwright is inescapable. The Jew is apt to be extremely emotional and to have a sharp, self-critical sense of humor. Extreme emotion is dangerous on the stage at the best of times. It is successful only when it is entirely impersonal and objective, as in Shakespeare and in the Greek drama. The Jewish form of emotion, as portrayed by Kops, is, however, strictly of the breast-beating, mea culpa type, sung solo with wailing-wall chorus obbligato; and this makes for embarrassed rather than sympathetic audiences. Another drawback to Kops's serious plays is that serious plays require some sort of philosophical orientation. When a man writes a serious play he has to take a definite position with respect to his view of reality. Now, Kops, though a first-class humorist, is anything but a thinker. He feels that the world is really a wonderful place and that everything would be all right if people would only jiggle around flapping their arms and smiling through. To Kops reality is one long, manic vaudeville act.

*George Wellwarth, "Bernard Kops: The Jew as 'Everyman'," in his* The Theater of Protest and Paradox: Developments in the Avant-Garde Drama *(reprinted by permission of New York University Press; copyright © 1964 by New York University), New York University Press, 1964, pp. 244-48.*

The talented English playwright and poet Bernard Kops, whose development as a novelist has been an intense, protracted effort to bring his gifts to full maturity, has achieved that goal with his fourth and latest novel. *By the Waters of Whitechapel* . . . is an enormously funny, macabre, and affecting account of how a pathetically trapped man wins freedom at the paradoxical cost of assuming the role of self-jailer. Kops writes here with greater artistic discipline and more stringent concern for the necessary precision of poetic language than ever before. He has attained a toughness of vision that enables him to evoke significant compassion rather than a mawkish sentimentalism such as that which mars some of his previously published writing, especially his first novel, *Awake for Mourning* (1958).

Kops deals again with material explored by him in drama and fiction—the past and present of Jewish immigrants in London's East End slums. Fortunately, he has reperceived these potentially redundant characters. They have been invested, accordingly, with a unified clarity, sympathy, and significance that elevate *By the Waters of Whitechapel* above the currently omnipresent kind of novel in which ethnic experience is opportunistically trotted forth as almost wholly vaudeville frolic, obsessively castigated as almost entirely traumatic nightmare, or otherwise reduced to misleading caricature.

The American novelist whom Kops most resembles is Bernard Malamud. The latter's career has also been marked by consistent literary experiment; his work contains a similarly deep vein of fantasy. . . .

Kops has not yet demonstrated the intellectualism distinguishing Saul Bellow. It is probably mere coincidence that Bellow's recent *Mr. Sammler's Planet* and Kops's second novel, *Yes from No-Man's-Land* (1965), both employ the imminent death of an elderly Jew as a means for bringing characters together for fruitful interaction.

*Brom Weber, "Half Ham, Half Hamlet," in* Saturday Review *(copyright © 1970 by Saturday Review/World, Inc.; reprinted with permission), May 2, 1970, pp. 29-30.*

Bernard Kops is no tyro. He has published poetry, novels, plays, an autobiography. Now comes another novel [*The Passionate Past of Gloria Gaye*] and I'd like to be able to welcome it. Alas! . . . Mr. Kops has opted neither for fact nor fantasy, but for an injudicious mixture. Somehow, they don't mix or at least not the way Mr. Kops tries to mix them. Yet it cannot be denied that bits of the novel are really funny.

*Robert Greacen, in* Books and Bookmen, *December, 1971, p. 66.*

It is easy to understand that, once having invented the enterprising Simon Katz, there really must have seemed to be very little else the author needed to do. Simon Katz, with his almost limitless capacity for self-delusion. Simon Katz, with a long lifetime of living off his wits behind him and a wardrobe of disguises to prove it—Ascot toff, funeral mourner, blind man, American tourist, rabbi, street photographer, suicide in shabby macintosh. Simon Katz, at sixty-nine still with his insatiable third leg, indignantly demanding cut prices for old age pensioners. Simon Katz with his cat called Nasser, something to kick whenever he feels like it. Simon Katz living alone in a derelict Soho house with the sepia photograph of his long-dead wife, there to admonish him when his courage falters, to give him strength to resist his long-suffering stockbroker son's ten thousandth plea that he should 'settle down'. . . .

There, then, Simon Katz must have been, in his author's affectionate eyes a promising contender for a place in literature's already over-crowded gallery of lovable rogues. And out Simon Katz was sent, his *'Oy-oy!'* honed to a fine cutting edge, to storm the bastions of respectability wherever they might be situate. . . .

Simply to invent Simon Katz was not, after all, enough. He is not—no man could be—strong enough to carry the sometimes unfunny, sometimes implausible, sometimes downright grubby situations his author rather cursorily devises for him [in *Settle Down Simon Katz*]. And his supporting cast, who might have helped him out, are given the sort of stock walk-on parts only very out-of-work actors would be seen dead in.

Even more seriously, the author's unquestioning love for his hero leads him into a fundamental carelessness—he never tells us how we, who do not know Simon Katz quite as well as he does, are meant to regard him. With affection, naturally, but with what else? Are we meant grudgingly to admire him, or feel sorry for him, or think him really rather horrid? In this we get no help: the writing zooms disconcertingly from crude farce, through tear-jerking pathos, and on to the cynical objectivity of the green-toothed layabout who comments on Simon's technique when swindling the ticket collector with one scathing word, *'Puny!'*—which is what it undoubtedly is.

The reader is sadly tempted, in the absence of any other firm direction, to extend the word to *all* Simon's techniques, and indeed to Simon himself. Which is a pity. With just a little more help from his author, just a little more *effort,* he might easily have been right up there with Ron Moody. I mean, Fagin. No, I don't, I mean Ron Moody.

*D. G. Compton, in* Books and Bookmen, *September, 1973, p. 82.*

* * *

## KOTLOWITZ, Robert 1924-

**Kotlowitz is an American editor and novelist. (See also *Contemporary Authors*, Vols. 33-36.)**

Robert Kotlowitz's "Somewhere Else" is a first novel of tense, dry brilliance, remarkable for the immensity of its scope and the individual power of its characters. . . .

"Somewhere Else" is a bitter, beautiful book, unsentimental about the tragedy of caring too much and the greater tragedy of not caring at all.

*Josephine Hendin, in* The New York Times Book Review *(© 1972 by The New York Times Company; reprinted by permission), November 5, 1972, p. 4.*

[It] takes a certain amount of *chutzpah* to challenge such a master as Isaac Bashevis Singer on his home grounds. But Kotlowitz hasn't fallen far short of the masterly achievement of *The Family Moskat* and he has done better than Singer did in *The Manor* and *The Estate* in telling what is essentially the same story, of the breakup of the traditional *shtetl* life of the isolated Jewish communities in Poland under the impact of modern ideas and the technology which made transmission of those ideas so easy.

*Michele Murray, "Old Wine in a Bright New Bottle," in* Book World—The Washington Post (© The Washington Post), *November 12, 1972, pp. 4, 10.*

The journey from Lomza to London, in the period just prior to the First World War takes a rabbi's son the way of many a classic novelistic journey. [In *Somewhere Else*] Mendel is the young man from the provinces out to confront the great world, his province is a *shtetl* in Poland, and his journey from there to a larger world is the matter of which great novels once were made. . . . It is not Mendel alone we are given to know here, but the generation before him, in whose descendants an ineradicable ancestry will continue to assert itself in every generation, albeit in the disguises that the changing times dictate. There were irresistible pressures that caused the inhabitants of the *shtetl* to leave. *Somewhere Else* is about that as well, but it is primarily about character, the one true business of the novelist above all others. The nature of the characters drawn here is such that one willingly pursues them in the meanest details of their lives. For here is that thing one had not ever hoped to see again—a novel in which a milieu is created with a novelist's loving and discursive relish for detail. There is that charm here that comes of the lingering and sympathetic attention true writers confer on their characters. Indeed, the East European milieu Mr. Kotlowitz has caught in this book is of that immediacy which catches at the memory, which reminds us that this is what a novel once was, at its best.

*Dorothy Rabinowitz, in* World *(copyright © 1972 by Saturday Review/World, Inc.; reprinted with permission), November 21, 1972, p. 62.*

Robert Kotlowitz's first novel tells a story which in its every aspect is commonplace. The description of Lomza, the Polish *shtetl* at the turn of the century where the novel begins and to which its title alludes, is commonplace; and Mendel's journey from Lomza to London, the odyssey of a young Jew in search of a larger, more cosmopolitan, and hospitable society, is equally commonplace. But Kotlowitz, through his aesthetic distance from the material and a rare mastery of the novelist's craft, transforms common facts and events into a novel uncommon both for its elegance and for its honesty.

The extent of Kotlowitz's achievement is all the more remarkable in light of other recent attempts to evoke Jewish life in Eastern Europe before the Holocaust and the near-universal failure of such attempts to come to terms with *shtetl* life in its essence. More than any other force, the *shtetl* created and determined the modality of all subsequent Jewish culture in the Diaspora. Significantly, however, efforts to capture it in fiction have either tended to emphasize the grotesque and the demonic side of its religious life, as in the novels of I. B. Singer, or have succumbed to a pervasive sentimentalism marked all too often by ignorance and unimaginativeness.

By contrast, Kotlowitz strikingly succeeds in recreating *shtetl* life precisely because, in his utterly unsentimental way, he takes the *shtetl* for what it was—neither the best nor the worst of all possible worlds. . . .

As a triumphant acknowledgment of the sublime ordinariness and persistence of Jewish life, *Somewhere Else* is nothing less than its author's celebration of his own, and our, roots.

*David Stern, "Odyssey of a Jew" (reprinted from* Commentary *by permission; copyright © 1973 by the American Jewish Committee), in* Commentary, *January, 1973, pp. 102-03.*

* * *

## KUNDERA, Milan 1929?-

**Kundera is a Czech novelist and short story writer whose work has been banned since 1967 in his own country, where he now lives without the right to teach or to travel abroad.**

["Life Is Elsewhere"] concerns the efforts of a young poet, Jaromil, to discover his own identity and his role in the turbulent events of the 1948 communist seizure of power. The work, being built entirely around this egoistic, arrogant, yet strangely appealing youth—he is the only character in the book with a name—traces the hero's efforts to escape from his middle-class background, and especially his mother's influence, his attempts to develop first in the field of painting and then of lyrical poetry, and his humorous yet sad love affairs. This last element, so familiar to us from Kundera's previous works, assumes a new dimension: an innocent joke, a mere white lie leads directly to the heroine's arrest and imprisonment and the final disintegration of Jaromil as a moral person. Constantly identifying himself with the great poets of the past, Rimbaud, Shelley, Keats, Mayakovsky, in the end he becomes nothing more than a police informer.

The last chapters are packed with bitter irony and display the author's unique ability to make bathos just a shade more tragic than comic. Jaromil's search for a *real* life leads him to a banal and humiliating death, a death which no one troubles himself about, except his doting mother, from whom he has tried to escape ever since boyhood. Her proud declaration, "Everything he has done has been for the working class," is as misplaced on her bourgeois lips as is his act of informing in order to be morally *arrivé* and his girlfriend's act of lying in order to win his love.

Along with Pavel Kohout, Milan Kundera is perhaps the most important figure writing prose in Czechoslovakia today. However, unlike Kohout, he has taken an extremely apolitical stand. In "Life Is Elsewhere" there is only one small hint of the "Prague spring" and its aftermath—the mention of a young martyr (obviously Jan Palach). Many more words are devoted to the 1968 events in Paris. This is not perhaps all that surprising; at present for the intellectuals of Czechoslovakia, life must clearly be elsewhere.

*Robert Porter, in* Books Abroad, *Vol. 48, No. 2, Spring, 1974, pp. 397-98.*

*Life Is Elsewhere* . . . is an altogether extraordinary work, complex, chilling, and brilliantly executed. . . .

In his savagely satiric narrative Kundera zeroes in on the romantic sensibility, which, as he defines it during the course of the novel, emerges as an attraction to abstract and absolute systems of faith that enable the believer to "transcend" the bewildering and exhausting exigencies of a fully selfconscious, mature, and moral life. [The] passionate desire [of Jaromil, the protagonist,] to see the world "transformed" is rooted in self-hatred; it is a violent impulse, and one that easily accustoms itself to the straightforward brutality of political tyranny. Kundera has himself witnessed dramatic historical demonstrations . . . and it is, perhaps, the severity of his experience that makes his voice as disciplined, powerful, and uncompromising as it is. The final wonder is that he has so masterfully succeeded in transforming political passions into a disinterested work of art. *Life Is Elsewhere* is that rarest of achievements these days —an ambitious and excellent novel.

*Jane Larkin Crain, in* Saturday Review/World *(copyright © 1974 by Saturday Review/World, Inc.; reprinted with permission), July 27, 1974, p. 25.*

Kundera, who is a magnificent short-story writer and a reasonably good novelist (I am going on the evidence of "Life Is Elsewhere"; [Philip Roth, in his introduction to "Laughable Loves," expresses] a high opinion of "The Joke"), depends for his effects on the ridiculous strictures set up by a Socialist government. You have first to assume that the hacks in the Czech Government believe they have created a Socialist paradise; after that, everything they do is funny. A writer who keeps his sanity long enough to ridicule his oppressors, who has enough hope left to make this ridicule into satire, must be congratulated. And Kundera's humor is impossible elsewhere. One can't imagine his particular situations growing out of anything but a combined anger and fascination with the cut-price Stalinists who have the whiphand in Prague, "that city," he says, "of defenestration . . ." . . .

"Life Is Elsewhere" is a small achievement next to "Laughable Loves," the stories. Roth finds them "Chekhovian." I think he's wrong, but this is a measure of his enthusiasm, not a critical judgment, and I would be very surprised if a better collection of stories appeared this year.

*Paul Theroux, in* The New York Times Book Review *(© 1974 by The New York Times Company; reprinted by permission), July 28, 1974, p. 7.*

The stories in "Laughable Loves" are buoyantly energetic and virtuosic, a leap forward from the sturdy, rather morose realism of "The Joke." The politics here is sexual: male dominance and impotence, role-playing and fantasizing detonate with startling effect. . . .

"Life Is Elsewhere" is a remarkable portrait of an artist as a young man. The brief life of the lyric poet Jaromil, dead of pneumonia before he is 20, is dominated by his Maman, who had first wanted to name him Apollo (meaning "fatherless"). Observing that lyric poets generally grow up in homes run by women, Kundera laces his story with mock-heroic parallels from the lives of Esenin and Mayakovsky, Rimbaud and Baudelaire, Hölderlin and Lermontov, Keats and Shelley. . . .

Jaromil is a deluded and tragic-farcical figure, his mother a pathetic gorgon. Kundera's achievement is to engage our sympathy in their misadventures instead of inviting our contempt. "The genius of lyric poetry," he says, "is the genius of inexperience. . . . We can scoff at the poet's lack of maturity, but there is something amazing about him, too." Kundera's anatomization of the creative process is both tender and unsparing.

*Walter Clemons, "Sexual Politics," in* Newsweek *(copyright Newsweek, Inc., 1974; reprinted by permission), July 29, 1974, p. 72.*

Until now, Milan Kundera has been associated here solely with his sardonic but straightforward protest novel, *The Joke,* published in 1967 as part of the campaign against government repression which culminated in that brief bloom of freedom, the Prague Spring of 1968. *The Joke* dealt with the severe punishment meted out to a university student who playfully rewrote some Stalinist slogans for his politically humorless girl friend, but it had some desperately unfunny consequences for its author. As Philip Roth notes in his generous introduction to the American edition of *Laughable Loves* . . ., Kundera's volume of stories, he has been expelled from the writers' union and fired from his teaching job . . .; he is prohibited from traveling in the West; his books are barred from Czech libraries and bookstores; his plays may not be produced; and he is being financially victimized by a tax, aimed specifically at dissident writers, that confiscates more than 80 per cent of the considerable royalties his work earns outside of Czechoslovakia.

Yet a Western reader unfamiliar with *The Joke* and first encountering Kundera's quirky talent in his stories or the simultaneously published American edition of his novel *Life Is Elsewhere* . . . must feel only shock and perplexity at the political treatment he has received. The corrosive irony of *Laughable Loves,* for example, touches barely at all upon politics; it is directed almost entirely at the characters' sexual foibles. In fact, Kundera's essential attitude toward sex and women—part acid amusement, part *macho* contempt—is strikingly like that of his American admirer, Roth. . . .

Occasionally the setting and mood of a story offer Kundera exactly the scope he requires for his comic scrutiny. But more often, . . . his psychological and dramatic insight is undeveloped, and a nattering repetitiousness reduces the whole project to tedium.

A somewhat similar failure is evident in *Life Is Elsewhere.* . . . On one level, this is a comic story about the delusions of a mediocre poet doomed from birth to be the consuming obsession of his stupidly self-pitying and resentful mother. Kundera's portrait of the monstrous child-eating stage Mom is superb, yet it is difficult to understand what he intends with the foolish and insipid poet-hero Jaromil. In episode after unoriginal episode, Kundera ridicules the spineless mama's boy as he tries, in childhood and adolescence, to lose his virginity. His awkward attempts, one need hardly add, are painstakingly documented.

On another level, however, *Life Is Elsewhere* describes the aspiring poet's effort to identify the lineaments of his literary persona. . . . In the midst of his protagonist's pilgrimage of immaturity, Kundera contemptuously intrudes his own ambiguous commentary on the weakness of lyrical poetry, "a realm in which any statement is immediately accorded veracity." But since he consistently emphasizes Jaromil's abysmal lack of talent, Kundera's fundamental meaning is indecipherable. Is the book an attack on the romantic poet's unspeakable ego, with its treacherous confusion of poetry and politics? One can only make a half-hearted guess, for in the end *Life Is Elsewhere* remains an unenticing mystery, overweeningly arch and coy, a long-winded and unamusing joke without discernible point or punchline.

Kundera reminds us, particularly in his stories, that sex under socialism can be as awkward, funny, delicious, and humiliating as its decadent-capitalist counterpart. . . .

*Pearl K. Bell, "Sex Under Socialism," in* The New Leader, *August 5, 1974, pp. 16-17.*

It is clear now to thoughtful members of the literary *apparat* that a critic who praises an Iron Curtain writer does so at considerable risk to his reputation as a subtle fellow. . . . The message is stern: under an oppressive state, all artists may be persecuted, but not all those persecuted are artists.

Thus the case of the Czech comic novelist Milan Kundera comes up at a time when to be persecuted in Czechoslovakia is not a clear advantage. . . .

There is a Czech tradition of satirizing mindless officialdom that goes back to Kafka's *The Trial* and Jaroslav Hasek's *The Good Soldier Svejk.* But this is not Kundera's main theme, and there is no reason to think that his work would be wholly different if his country's absentee landlords were still the Habsburgs, not the Soviets.

[*Life Is Elsewhere*] is a sly and merciless lampoon of revolutionary romanticism, and it deals with lyric poetry as a species of adolescent neurosis. The hero is an unpleasant young man named Jaromil, whose every childhood uncertainty has been marveled at by his crazed mother as evidence of an artistic soul. Out of resentment of her coarse husband, who hung his smelly socks on her beloved alabaster statuette of Apollo, this monstrous mother determined to make her infant son a poet.

Jaromil indeed becomes a poet. . . . The genius of lyric poetry, Kundera observes, "is the genius of inexperience. . . . We can scoff at the poet's lack of maturity, but there is something amazing about him too. His words sparkle with droplets that come from the heart. . . . These magic dewdrops need not be stimulated by real life events. On the contrary, we suspect that the poet sometimes squeezes his heart with the same detachment as a housewife squeezing a lemon over her salad."

In this way the romantic prose becomes reality, and a necessary part of this reality, Kundera cheerfully demonstrates, is that the poet be an utter ass. The novelist is not shy about invoking the names of such famous poetic asses (as he sees them) as Rimbaud, Keats, Shelley and Victor Hugo. . . .

Kundera commits some of the funniest literary savaging since Evelyn Waugh polished off Dickens in *A Handful of Dust.* Running through it is some wonderfully comic sexual burlesque. . . .

[An] amused look at eroticism is the business of the story collection *Laughable Loves*. The book is light, wry and wise. . . .

Kundera's tone in these stories and the novel is that of a detached observer who lifts an eyebrow now and then in mock surprise at the world's absurdities. As Roth suggests in his introduction [to *Laughable Loves*], this ironic detachment is a natural refuge for a writer who must endure the repressive pieties of a police state. It is also a pose achieved at considerable cost. He cites a remark the author makes in one story, that "a man lives a sad life when he cannot take anything or anyone seriously." The reader is meant to see the lifted eyebrow and to smile. Then he is meant to see the sober truth of the statement behind its mockery. Then the mockery behind that sobriety and so on. What lies deeper, the mockery or the truth? It is a rare comic writer who can raise the question, and Kundera is one.

*John Skow, "A Handful of Lust," in* Time *(reprinted by permission from* Time, The Weekly Newsmagazine; *copyright Time Inc.), August 5, 1974, pp. 82, 84.*

The life and death of a lyric poet form the narrative of *Life Is Elsewhere*. But there is an argument about the role of poetry that is peculiar to Czechoslovakia and forms the real background to this terrific satire. Milan Kundera, who made his own transition from poetry to novel-writing, is one of the deadliest exponents of the argument that there have been too many poets, too few novelists: too much romantic narcissism and too little sober illustration of what is within the capacity of the human animal and what is not. An editor in *Life Is Elsewhere* suggests, in exasperation, that Czechoslovakia should export its surplus poets: "They could give a valuable boost to developing countries. In return for our poets, we'll get the bananas or electronic instruments our economy needs.". . .

It is a subtle, highly constructed satire. It is also heavy with literary reference: Kundera evokes Keats. . . . Scenes from the lives of Shelley, Rimbaud, and Nerval are briefly switched on like amplifiers. There is a little too much of this showmanship: the novel, which seems to me even better than the famous *Joke,* does not need these allusions.

*Neal Ascherson, "People in a Trap," in* The New York Review of Books *(reprinted with permission from* The New York Review of Books; *© 1974 by NYREV, Inc.), August 8, 1974, pp. 14-15.*

It takes a writer of Milan Kundera's caliber and integrity to show that the relationship between art and politics is far more intricate than dogmatic party hacks would make one believe.

*Laughable Loves,* a group of delicate studies of the absurd erotic games people play, *was* deemed publishable in Kundera's native Czechoslovakia, while *Life Is Elsewhere,* a novel depicting a private tragedy against a broad historical-political background, was not, which only goes to show that fiction dealing with a highly subjective, atypical, even bizarre reality is still considered less dangerous in an authoritarian society than the *wrong* kind of political novel. Of course even the stories contained in *Laughable Loves* seem apolitical only on the surface. In many of them, sexual experimentations and strategies become metaphors for personal and political freedom. For example in . . . "The Golden Apple of Eternal Desire," even the protagonist's seemingly harmless hobby of keeping a file on candidates for future amorous adventures—he carefully "registers" promising "contacts" in his notebook—appears to reflect the political climate of a country whose government for years kept confidential files on just about everyone, and where surveillance was a fact of daily life.

The ambiguity of individual identity is a major theme in these stories. The players of amorous games slip into roles with great ease; one Pirandellian disguise follows another, and we are again subtly reminded that a society that has produced millions of "instant" Communists actually encourages pretense and hypocrisy. . . .

Politics—sexual politics, to be precise—becomes [a] more conspicuous feature of Kundera's novel, *Life Is Elsewhere,* although it would be an oversimplification to label the work a political novel. (It could just as easily be called a novel of education or an artist novel.) . . . Fortunately Kundera resists the temptation of fashioning a glib satire out of his story. For one thing, [its] theme of "momism," not an unfamiliar one to American readers, is treated with finesse and humor. Kundera has considerable compassion for "Maman" and he obviously couldn't care less about Freud. . . .

Kundera is brutal in exposing Jaromil's mediocrity and crass opportunism, but he also has his anti-hero express some rather profound ideas about revolution and revolutionary art. With a tenderness that mocks his own irony, Kundera suggests that propaganda literature can also be deeply felt, and that the Stalinist period in Czechoslovakia "was not only a terrible epoch, but a lyrical one as well: It was ruled by the hangman, but by the poet too.". . .

Kundera's fiction does not always make for absorbing reading; the plot meanders, many characters don't come alive, the mock-serious, fussily bureaucratic tone becomes tiresome. But Kundera insists on this style, on his dizzying juxtapositions and digressions. Like some of the great Czech filmmakers who emerged in the '60s, he is uncompromising in his adherence to a highly personal artistic vision. . . .

As we said, these two works, though intensely political, also transcend politics, just as Kundera's previous novel, *The Joke,* was much more than what its American publisher claimed it to be: an exposé of "the brutal regime in Czechoslovakia today." Nevertheless, in reading Kundera's fiction an understanding of time and place is crucial. "How sweet it would be to forget History," says the author wistfully in *Life Is Elsewhere.* He can't, and that in a way is what these two books are about.

*Ivan Sanders, in* The New Republic *(reprinted by permission of* The New Republic; *© 1974 by The New Republic, Inc.), September 7, 1974, pp. 23-4.*

# L

## LAMMING, George 1927-

**Lamming, a Barbadian novelist, created San Cristobal for the setting of two of his novels. His fiction is praised for its powerful and poetic prose.**

[*Of Age and Innocence*] is a novel which somehow fails, I feel, but its failure tells us a great deal. The novel would have been remarkable if a certain tendency—a genuine tendency—for a tragic feeling of dispossession in reality had been achieved. This tendency is frustrated by a diffusion of energies within the entire work. The book seems to speak with a public voice, the voice of a peculiar orator, and the compulsions which inform the work appear to spring from a verbal sophistication rather than a visual, plastic and conceptual imagery. Lamming's verbal sophistication is conversational, highly wrought and spirited sometimes: at other times it lapses into merely clever utterance, rhetorical, as when he says of one of his characters: "He had been made Governor of an important colony which was then at peace with England." It takes some effort—not the effort of imaginative concentration which is always worthwhile but an effort to combat the author's self-indulgence. And this would not arise if the work could be kept true to its inherent design. There is no necessary difficulty or complexity in Lamming's novels—the necessary difficulty or complexity belonging to strange symbolisms—and I feel if the author concentrated on the sheer essentials of his experience a tragic disposition of feeling would gain a true ascendancy. This concentration is essential if the work is not to succumb to a uniform tone which gives each individual character the same public-speaking resonance of voice. I would like to stress a certain distinction I made earlier once again. In the epic and revolutionary novel of associations the characters are related within a personal capacity which works in a poetic and serial way so that a strange jigsaw is set in motion like a mysterious unity of animal and other substitutes within the person. Something which is quite different to the over-elaboration of individual character within the conventional novel. And this over-elaboration is one danger which confronts Lamming. For in terms of the ruling framework he accepts, the individuality of character, the distinctions of status and privilege which mark one individual from another, must be maintained. This is the kind of realism, the realism of classes and classifications—however limited it may be in terms of a profound, poetic and scientific scale of values—the novel, in its orthodox mould, demands. Lamming may be restless within this framework (there are signs and shadows of this in his work) but mere extravagance of pattern and an inclination to frequent intellectual raids beyond his territory are not a genuine breakthrough and will only weaken the position of the central character in his work. He must school himself at this stage, I believe, to work for the continuous development of a main individual character in order to free himself somewhat from the restrictive consolidation he brings about which unfortunately, I find, blocks one's view of essential conflict. This becomes a necessity in terms of the very style and tone of his work. He cannot afford to crowd his canvas when the instinctive threat of one-sidedness is likely to overwhelm all his people and in fact when this one-sidedness may be transformed into a source of tremendous strength in a singleness of drive and purpose which cannot then fail to discipline every tangential field and exercise.

*Wilson Harris, in* Modern Black Novelists: A Collection of Critical Essays, *edited by Michael G. Cooke, Prentice-Hall, Inc., 1971, pp. 36-7.*

Though in *Of Age and Innocence* George Lamming bluntly calls his fictional island, San Cristobal, "an old land inhabiting new forms of men who can never resurrect their roots and do not know their nature," it is obvious as of his next (his fourth) book, *Season of Adventure,* that he is committed to his characters' at least trying to discover their roots and natures. Some sort of reconciliation to or rectification of the terms of the past occupies a central place in his later work. His recent novels, *Water with Berries* (1971) and *Natives of My Person* (1972), all but willfully pursue the theme of history in light of a possible reconciling or purged condition. At the same time, violence and irony, perhaps alternative manifestations of an intense but diffident personality, mark the major amplitudes of his vision in these works. This is not to forget that some degree of violence and irony appears even in his maiden work; indeed his portrayal of these features in *Of Age and Innocence* (1958) is virtually prophetic, rather than merely fashionable, and his imagination of "a really great, constructive chaos" (*The Emigrants,* 1954) anticipates the rhetoric of Frantz Fanon et al. But there remains a suggestion, in *Natives of My Person* and *Water with Berries,* that the violence may spring from intention no less than the pursuit of history, and so it falls in danger of losing its natural character for a contrived or literary one. Its literary character is if anything neo-Gothic—including touches of pornography, the Gothic of our time—and the resuscitation of Gothic potentially interferes with the resurrection of roots. On the surface this seems an altogether different irony from the one Lamming so neatly wields in these novels, which both end with people waiting in ignorant devotion and hope for a millennial coming: the irony of existence between two worlds, one presumably dead, the other hopefully not powerless to be born. But perhaps they are at bottom states of each other, if Lamming's journey into history or by analogy his characters' accumulated life stories exert a force that is more inert and crushing than revelatory and transforming. It is certainly striking that the more explicit and resolute his characters' motives become, the more problematical their existence, and the more their consciousness of the influential past grows, the more they are paralyzed, or at best frustrated in the present. The inexplicable and almost unbearable waiting to act that marks the beginning of *Natives of My Person* swells to take up virtually all of *Water with Berries,* creating a feeling of enormous arrest that may be at once the seedbed and antithesis of the melodramatic action. To look clearly to the past makes ordinary living a suspended activity, passing in an obscurely portentous, volcanic strain (the historical novel becoming a mode of presentiment).

Only two of the novels—the very first, *In the Castle of My Skin,* and the fourth, *Season of Adventure*—manage to escape this malaise of tendentiousness, and though the gothicizing mood obtrudes in the latter, they stand as Lamming's most satisfactory, if not his most redoubtable, achievements. . . .

[There] are indications that, even in *Season of Adventure,* Lamming is driven by a nostalgia—that intimate version of the passion of origins—for what he was, as writer and as character, in *In the Castle of My Skin,* though it would make no more sense for him to repeat that book, however ingeniously disguised, than for Wordsworth to have repeated *The Prelude.* Its centripetal and yet radiant vision, its indissoluble mixture of autobiographical urgency, political and social history, cultural evolution, and philosophical evaluation made it an epiphany, an epoch in British Caribbean literature when it appeared in 1953; it is surely too soon for another. Besides, the novel remains as redolent of the West Indian character and context as Octavio Paz's *The Labyrinth of Solitude* of the Mexican, and defies duplication. That needs to be accepted. But recurrently, as in *The Emigrants* and *Season of Adventure,* an occasional "I" pipes in to confess a feeling of dissociation, of unreason and the unreality of everything save a primary youth or the ubiquitous and amorphous appeal of death. Partitions and separations and disappearances make up the leitmotif of *The Emigrants,* despite its explicit attempt to conjure up one West Indies. . . .

*Natives of My Person* and *Water with Berries* represent Lamming at that critical point, in any artist's career, where he is at once freely indulging his powers and obeying the dictates of his vocation. . . . Both novels exhibit at the outset the idiolectal scene-setting that has marked his work after *In the Castle of My Skin,* with overhanging clouds and an uncomfortable sense of restraint and dark expectancy. And there is, as they conclude, the same unraveling and wearing through of the skein of hope and ambition and vision that seem characteristic as of the writing of *The Emigrants* (*Season of Adventure* makes a provocative exception). And along the way the same calculated testing of the centrifuge of personality and event, of the reader's concentration and the work's coherence, and the same investigation of a perverted idyllicism, the *locus amoenus* gone rank, that we find from *The Emigrants* forward. . . .

[Each] repetition, as it were in a spiral of engagement, reaches a new plane and angle of intelligence. What is peculiar to *Natives of My Person* and *Water with Berries,* appearing in quick succession after a silence of some years, is a systematic approach to an ideal of beginning again, in what should perhaps be called an applied apocalyptic vein. Surely it is the reluctance of revelation, and not a wanton caginess, that makes Lamming so ration the details of the new worlds aborning. The reader, at least in the case of *Natives of My Person,* a more remote but also more plausible story than *Water with Berries,* accepts the stately pace, the gravidity of the narration as part of a process of initiation into the mysteries of founding a new and ultimately humane colony in the New World, to expiate the vicious finding of that world before. (Besides, secrecy is politic.) The very simplicity of the goal makes it portentous, the danger of the undertaking makes it ominous, the chemistry of the participants makes it precarious. . . .

*Water with Berries* . . . ends with a Beckettian expectation of what will renovate the world by redeeming its history. The specific plan in this case is political revolution, or taking it to the world, rather than sailing away. But if in *Natives of My Person* we become spectators of remote events of which the actors are mutually aware, in *Water with Berries* we are made privy to a history of which the revolutionaries' leader, Teeton, learns along with us, and through which the actors themselves proceed in hectic isolation. Perhaps this history justifies the revolution, but it must do so *ex post facto* as far as the novel is concerned. . . .

An atmosphere of secrecy, both physical in terms of hiding or inaccessibility and spiritual in terms of reticence and dissimulation, is crucial to *Natives of My Person* and *Water with Berries.* In light of the strong action of the books it makes for a fascinating paradox, the furtiveness of the sensational. But it goes deeper, and begins to suggest that Lamming himself is struggling with an impulse to keep things *in pectore.* And that is a dismal paradox in a novelist. The Prospero-Caliban relationship (for no good reason, but these things don't wait for one) has enjoyed a certain currency among West Indian *literati* as an image of their place in English literature. Well, bluntly, the Caliban idea was always self-indulgent and senseless, and if now the Prospero idea is coming to the fore, it is bootless and requires a birch more than a wand.

*Michael Cooke, "A West Indian Novelist," in* The Yale Review *(© 1973 by Yale University; reprinted by permission of the editor), Summer, 1973, pp. 618-23.*

* * *

## LAVIN, Mary 1912-

**An Irish short story writer and novelist, Mary Lavin is con-**

**cerned in her fiction with the despair and frustration of lonely people. (See also *Contemporary Authors*, Vols. 9-12, rev. ed.)**

*Affinity* is the key word that, without announcing itself as a word, suffuses the mind of at least one reader when he lives within the stories of Mary Lavin. Maybe, it is more of a quality than a word: it is not nailed to a page in a dictionary; rather, it emanates from people in relationship with nature, with houses, with (rarely) the ways of cities, with, above all, each other—with all of these, in fluent conjunction. It also includes its opposite, for, through her tender irony, Mrs. Lavin causes loneliness itself to be a quality that does not categorize, but, rather, runs through, human kind. Contrast may often provide her dramatic effect; but unity is her theme.

No story in *In the Middle of the Fields* could illustrate this point with more beautiful firmness than "The Cuckoo-Spit." As in all of her narratives, the subject is simple, almost banal. She is not an author who has to prop up mediocre writing and lack of insight with off-the-trail excursions. Nor does she over-decorate simplicity. Even investigation is not her main interest. It is a hovering empathy that is her chief effect. She darts from character to character—centering, for emphasis, on one, but being all of them. . . .

There is a quality of genuine refinement which is native to Mrs. Lavin's work, and unforced. It establishes the tone. . . .

Surely, though, the big test for an author of Mrs. Lavin's stature is the taking of some of the drab constituents of life and, basing her story on one character yet moving from individual to individual, finding new insights into known human traits, new understandings. This is found in her story "One Summer." There is no apology for human weakness or attacks upon it. Again, there is empathy. But there is also a new look at the bared ironies of the human state, no comment made, but a suggestion of understanding acceptance, as of a kind helpfulness before the dying, a thoughtful pause in hopeless movement, a stillness which is an action in itself, an acknowledgment of union. . . .

Mrs. Lavin's plotting is so simple that it can almost be predicted: it is essence for which she is looking, with which she identifies herself; and it is the typical in which she finds it. . . .

The country and nature and its characteristic parts play a large role in these stories; but they do not obtrude, take over, become a character or a rhetorical flourish on a banner or (much worse) all of these, as they tyranically do in the case of some Southern writers of the United States. They are established in a phrase, in a delicately suggestive human relationship. . . . Very, very rarely is there overwriting. . . .

[This] is . . . a volume of stories whose delicacy of perception is matched only by firm control of situation and theme. Here is contemporary and honest storytelling, honorably unanxious about demand and successfully committed to greatness.

*John Hazard Wildman, "Affinity–and Related Issues," in* The Southern Review, *Vol. VI, No. 2, Spring, 1970, pp. 515-19.*

The thing about Mary Lavin is that she knows how to start. Contrary to popular conviction, a tremendous number of people know where to chop it off—too many, in the short story: they write without conviction, but with excessive craftsmanship. . . . Only they never got anything started in the first place. They pretend inscrutability. And hope.

Not so Mary Lavin. She gives at once the impression of knowing what she is going to do, having been caught up in one of those human entanglements which are not "way out," which we ourselves recognize as going on about us. Only she finds that which eludes us or which at least leaves us mentally and spiritually tongue-tied, so that we can formulate it neither to other people nor (more hopelessly graspingly) to ourselves. She can, and does. Typically, the prime matter is tenderness. We feel that she recollects in tranquillity, has it eventually all there, and talks it into her typewriter. . . .

So simple it is to begin a great short story—when you know where you are going. . . . There is Wordsworthian simplicity, without the leech-gatherer bent double under his load of pompous pantheism. . . .

Mrs. Lavin is the short story writer of our times who is capable of viewing philosophically, in the wide sense of the word, the relationship between life and death without being prosy or melodramatic. She knows that the two go together. She knows that in life we must always take life. In "A Tragedy" she pretends to give us a choice between loneliness and life on the one hand and death on the other. But she gives us no choice, and we don't want one. Life is potentiality, she insinuates, even on its loneliest, most nearly sordid, terms. And in "A Pure Accident," her fine study of a bulky, sad, pathetically, mentally foolish priest, she avoids easy brutal caricature. Instead, she shows her usual firm, restrained but genuine tenderness: here, too, even on the grubbiest level, life has its potentialities. . . .

[She] is never overwhelmed by anything. Life for her is always examining and finding, within the suggestive guidance of a large Catholic conception. Within Mrs. Lavin's stories, there is a cosmic awareness, something of grandeur.

*John Hazard Wildman, "Beyond Classification–Some Notes on Distinction," in* The Southern Review, *Vol. IX, No. 1, Winter, 1973, pp. 233-42.*

There is an unrelenting, nearly fevered side to Miss Lavin's short stories, for they are about nothing so much as the probing of one mind by another. That sort of thing does become oppressive in her work from time to time, but never enough to diminish seriously the art of her stories. Her characters are always nagging but interesting. There is a sadness in the view they have of their lives, which seems not out of place, given those lives. They are full of that hopelessness that is the underside of wild ambition; their relationships are tainted by a general disappointment with things but are moved forward by spurts of hope just as surely. Miss Lavin is an expert reconnoiterer in this sort of territory. . . .

[Suspense] is what keeps Miss Lavin's stories afloat when they are in danger of being weighted down by sensibility. . . .

There is a kind of scholarly ascetic type among the Irish that Miss Lavin knows well and punishes roundly. It is her capacity to create characters whose fate seems both just and terrible that puts her among the better practitioners of her craft.

*Dorothy Rabinowitz, in* Saturday Review/World *(copyright © 1973 by Saturday Review/World, Inc.; reprinted with permission), September 11, 1973, p. 44.*

If anyone is interested in encountering great art, then let him turn to the breathtaking title story of Mary Lavin's new collection, *A Memory and Other Stories*. Mary Lavin is a superb writer, and to one degree or another the other four stories in the book are worth your careful attention, but inevitably they suffer from being placed in the same volume with "A Memory."

It is a story of the utmost simplicity, without effects. Dialogue is sparse. Most of the action is interior. . . .

Mary Lavin never raises her voice. Her illumination in this story, as in her others, is invariably quiet. Ireland, her country and the setting of most of her stories, is a country of omissions, repressions and silences. . . .

Certainly the subject matter of Mary Lavin's art has been determined by the landscape of Ireland. Its other writers tell us as well of its life-denying ways, the slow oozing away of lives, the bitterness that fills up the emotional world as the fog does the physical one. And from James Joyce's *Dubliners* down through the work of Liam O'-Flaherty, Frank O'Conner, Sean O'Faolain, Bryan MacMahon and a healthy handful of others, we have been introduced to the tyrannical old fathers and mothers, the ardent young priests and the arid old ones, the laughing girls soon to cry and the lovers who will find their only joy in death. For a small country with a difficult history, its literary harvest has been astonishing; notoriously, it is a land of great talkers where the artistic impulse is channeled almost exclusively into literature and theater.

Even in such company Mary Lavin stands out by the quality of her art. It goes without saying that she writes well in a graceful style that calls little attention to itself, but she is neither a stunning stylist nor an innovator. Her triumph is her vision of life and her attitude toward her characters, and it is these that turn "A Memory" into a great work of art. No matter how reprehensible her characters are, no matter how much suffering they have caused, she does not grow at their expense or hold them up to us for shared contempt. It sounds old-fashioned, and perhaps it is, to speak of a writer's humanity in an age when parody, black humor and self-conscious despair dominate fiction, but so be it.

*Michele Murray, "Human Voices Wake Us," in* Book World—The Washington Post (© The Washington Post), *September 30, 1973, p. 3.*

[One] can only celebrate the attention finally being given in her natal land to this most polished and Jamesian of Irish storytellers. With the septuagenarian Sean O'Faolain, who is a decade older, [Mary Lavin] stands presently as the class-of-the-field in the cameo genre which Irish writers have graced and dominated for a half-century.

Her territory [in *A Memory and Other Stories*] is again the resurgent human heart that wrests victory from the piquant melancholy of worldly circumstances that weigh it down. Her stories, like Henry James's, build outward from cluttered narrative occasions toward "the distinguished thing," the still-point of special, sad, and bravely encountered understanding.

*R. J. Thompson, in* Best Sellers, *October 1, 1973, pp. 293-94.*

"A Memory and Other Stories" is Mary Lavin's fifteenth book, and her thirteenth collection of short stories. She has long been recognized as one of the finest of living short-story writers. Uninterested in formal experimentation, she has concentrated her genius upon certain archetypal or transpersonal experiences as they touch—sometimes with violence—fairly ordinary people. The five stories in this collection emphasize the universality of certain experiences —love, self-sacrifice, the need to relinquish the world to those who follow us—but never at the expense of the particular. Mary Lavin's ability to transcribe the physical world, especially the green damp world of rural Ireland where many of her stories are set, is as remarkable as ever. She rarely strains for metaphors, yet her prose is "poetic" in the best sense of that word; if her people talk perhaps more beautifully than might seem credible, that is what art is all about.

*Joyce Carol Oates, in* The New York Times Book Review *(© 1973 by The New York Times Company; reprinted by permission), November 25, 1973, p. 7.*

According to John Braine's recent sensible-absurd anti-Anti-Novel handbook *Writing a Novel,* what masterpieces do is penetrate to the heart of the human condition. And 'once a reviewer uses the phrase [the human condition], you're home and dry.' The second volume of Mary Lavin's stories—justly celebrated for celebrating provincial Irishness—demands, like the first volume, every tribute about penetrating to the heart of the human condition the critic might muster. Her intense preoccupation with the lovingly charted detail of the narrowest of Irish and Catholic lives expands magically to catch the widest kind of humanity. The comparison with Turgenev that 'An Akoulina of the Irish Midlands' invites, is thoroughly just and applicable to the whole collection.

*Valentine Cunningham, in* New Statesman, *July 5, 1974, p. 23.*

* * *

## LAYE, Camara 1928-

**Laye, a native of Guinea, is a novelist and short story writer writing in French. He is considered a leader in contemporary African literature.**

In *The Dark Child* Camara Laye shows his understanding and respect for African traditions, and in *The Radiance of the King* he makes this tradition work on a stranger.

In *The Dark Child* Camara Laye shows the new spirit of French West Africans towards tradition. He did not consider his African childhood as something remote, primitive, something to be ashamed of. On the contrary: looking back on it from a distance, and having learned the technical skills European education had to offer, he discovered these skills had been animated, and had been more closely related to man, in his native civilisation. . . .

[*The Radiance of the King*] is full of symbolism. It is usually considered as an ingenious allegory about man's search for God. But I think that the book cannot be seen in this sense only; it is ambivalent, even multivalent, as Sénghor says of all African art. Clarence, a European, finds himself without the help and support of his countrymen in an African environment. He is without money, without hope of outside help. He is thrown exactly into that position in which many Africans often find themselves in the European world. He has to conform. And thus he gradually becomes initiated. The whole book can be considered as a lesson in African wisdom. . . .

Noaga and Nagoa, the two boys who accompany Clarence all the time, are neither good nor bad. At any time they take their chance; they steal where there is an opportunity. Clarence is often worried about them, at times he is shocked, at times compelled to admire. They never consider life too seriously. There is no question whether they are to be redeemed by the King or not. "Tomorrow we go with the King," they say. Their redemption is not a question of good or evil, they cannot be rejected by the King, because already they live life as a unity. Clarence on the other hand can only be redeemed after he has learned that his moral problems are not essential. This is one of the strongest arguments against the Christian interpretation of the end of the book. . . .

The end of the novel, often misunderstood, means that even the white man in Africa can be redeemed and accepted when he shows his will to learn and not only to teach. And that Camara Laye in all his lessons does not consider the African way of faith and redemption the only one imaginable and superior. He wants to say that it is the only right way for Africa and that it is of equal value with an other way of mankind.

*Janheinz Jahn, "Camara Laye: Another Interpretation," in* Introduction to African Literature: An Anthology of Critical Writings from "Black Orpheus," *edited by Ulli Beier, Northwestern University Press, 1967, pp. 200-03.*

Camara Laye has employed symbolism as an extremely positive medium. . . .

The fact that his characters are likeable and like each other is crucial to the positive quality of Laye's symbolism. . . . While we do observe the terrors and degradation to which human flesh is heir, we are concerned in [*Le Regard du Roi*, translated as *The Radiance of the King*] with far more than a mere psychological morass. Instead of being asked to remark with horrified surprise that human beings are more vicious and malicious, that the individual is more completely ostracized than we had suspected, we are constantly startled by the opposite discoveries: that in spite of all the obstacles in the way of human relationships, men do make contact with each other.

The characters say what they really think and what they really feel. Laye uses the style he has adopted to eliminate social convention and formal restrictions which obscure in every-day relations the truth that is in each heart. But this frankness does not lead in Laye's world, as one might expect, to anger or resentment. When the characters learn what other characters are actually thinking about them, this does not engender a sullen animosity or a self-defensive counter-attack. Rock-bottom truthfulness leads to a plain answer, and so the statement of what in our actual society is concealed by pseudo-politeness and cynical pretence, becomes the route to real communication. . . .

[If] human beings are likeable, and illogical human behaviour can be as surprisingly attractive in its ramifications as unattractive, and if the symbolic method here reveals to us not so much the primitive bestiality of humanity but rather its unexpected niceness in many situations, then it is easy to understand how Camara Laye is able to use this mode to examine the positive potentials of the extremely complicated pattern of existence which human beings have presented to them. . . .

*The Radiance of the King* is a very serious work but it is the opposite of tragedy. Clarence questions the whole basis of his existence. He doubts his own worthiness, but these doubts prove to be unfounded. The exact nature of what Clarence doubts about himself is, I think, of great interest. The book raises the question of how one human being justifies his social existence among other human beings. . . .

[Though] the racial issue finds a place in the whole pattern, colour is primarily used in *The Radiance of the King* as a symbolic representation of man's individual separateness. Certainly the racial issue is resolved as part of the larger harmony which is achieved. Because he learns to accept both his environment and himself, Clarence is himself accepted. This is narrowly relevant to the white man's need to accept his relationship to humanity as a whole; but it ultimately portrays the universal necessity for every man, whatever his colour, to come to terms with his total environment—and, again, with himself. . . .

Camara Laye seems to escape from all the preconceptions belonging to most of our approaches to the subject of religion, and genuinely to make a reassessment. He asks crucial questions with a refreshing openness—such questions as: What is an adequate god figure? What is the relationship between the human and the superhuman? What are we to understand by worthiness? And, as I say, I believe he has got as near as anyone to free himself from preconceived assumptions.

The book is, of course, cast in the form of a quest—a spiritual quest; though there is nothing pompous, ponderous or moralistic about it. In some senses it is a picaresque novel: it is a journey book like Henry Fielding's novels or *Mission to Kala*. But it is a specific journey, a search. And the search might be compared to the quest for the holy grail—the great myth of early Christendom. The book is profoundly religious yet genuinely without any established dogma; and in this it is very much a book of the twentieth-century world as a whole; a book which perhaps had to emanate from Africa because Europeans cannot escape from the obsessive religious patterns which they are involved either in accepting or rejecting. . . .

*The Radiance of the King* withdraws from all convention, cliché and sentimentality, and yet is not afraid of using fundamental words, like love, in their full sense. Camara Laye is concerned to re-establish a true link between the idea of love and the idea of religion. . . . The concept of love with which Camara Laye is concerned is the monopoly of no particular religion and no particular race. It is, after all, a white man who is accepting the absolute appropriateness of a black god figure, but within a pattern of symbolism which finally frees us from the limitations of colour and the limitations of race.

*David Cook, "The Relevance of the King in Camara Laye's 'Le Regard du Roi'," in* Perspectives on African Literature, *edited by Christopher Heywood (copyright © 1971 by University of Ife; published in the United States in 1971 by Africana Publishing Company, a Division of Holmes & Meier Publishers, Inc. and reprinted by permission), Africana, 1971, pp. 138-47.*

[A] "trapped" portrayal of the African who has been assimilated, and then found it impossible to accept his own traditional culture, has played a part in a number of . . . significant Francophone African works: . . . [including] Camara Laye's autobiography, *L'Enfant noir (The African Child)* (1953). . . .

[It] is with Laye that the picture of the "assimilated" novelist takes on its most significant twist: the négritude novel. Usually négritude is thought of as a poetic movement, but in the works by Camara Laye, African cultural values have been so thoroughly woven into the novel's form that the result is a kind of assimilated presentation of African values, African traditional life: négritude. The result is a much more unified introduction of anthropological materials into the texture of the novel itself, rather than the inclusion of ethnographical background in isolated passages. The African cultural values have been so deftly handled in the works of Camara Laye that the reader is almost unaware that they are there. It is this use of what I call "assimilated anthropology" that, I believe, is the major distinction between the Francophone African novelist and the Anglophone African novelist, for the Francophone writer has remained much closer to the French classical tradition, changing the novel in fewer ways than his Anglophone counterpart, and, as a result, has produced a more intellectualized concept of African traditions, values, and life. . . .

*L'Enfant noir* is undoubtedly one of the most significant works by an African writer and certainly the most readable autobiography by a writer from tropical Africa. It is also, I feel, an illustration of Laye's early attempts at unifying cultural materials into a coherent artistic achievement. Anthropological materials are introduced into the narrative, yet, for the most part, they are left unexplained. Laye wants the reader to accept them at face value, and admits that he often has no explanation for the unusual happenings he has recorded. . . . The clear, matter-of-fact tone records incident after incident in the child's growing awareness of the Islamic/animistic world around him. By the end of the narrative, the reader feels an immense sense of personal loss at a way of life which has rapidly come to a halt. *L'Enfant noir* is a beautiful account of traditional African life, as delicately wrought as a Dürer engraving, a detailed tableau of the paradise Laye knew in his youth and later lost.

*Dramouss*, Laye's third book, published in 1966, is a sequel to *L'Enfant noir,* and the most striking element, that immediately jolts the reader, is the harshness of the book when it is compared to Laye's first work. The softness, the sense of oneness and wholeness expressed in the earlier book is missing in *Dramouss,* which is ostensibly concerned with Laye's life in France and his return to Guinea after living several years in Paris. Laye's interest here is in politics in post-independent Guinea—in the failures of the African regime to live up to the pre-independence promises. As such, this work moves beyond the sense of the personal, which was so vitally important in *L'Enfant noir,* to a concern with problems of nationhood, nationalism, and political charlatanism, resulting in one of the most scathing commentaries on African political institutions written by a Francophone African writer. The publication of *Dramouss* also led to Laye's forced exile from Guinea to Senegal.

*Le regard du roi (The Radiance of the King)*, which was first published in 1954, is, in the view of several critics of African literature, the greatest of all African novels. The novel has won this distinction, it seems, because of Laye's ideal assimilation of African materials into the novel form. As has so frequently been the concern with African novelists, Laye too is outwardly at least concerned with the conflict between African and Western civilization, yet his treatment in *Le regard du roi* is unlike any other we have seen. His main character is not African but European, and instead of recording the conflicts that an African encounters in his exposure to the West, Laye, in this lengthy novel, has reversed the usual pattern and presented a European and his difficulty in coming to grips with Africa. Laye's story goes far beyond this, however, for it is not simply a confrontation which ends in confusion or tragedy, but a story which begins in chaos and ends in understanding, grace, and beauty. The white man may be the protagonist, but Africa is the antagonist. It is the hero's ability to comprehend the magnitude and the complexity of the African experience—to realize that his own culture has little significance at all—which leads us to a basic aspect of what Senghor has seen as the final evolutionary stage of cultural syncretism—"reformed négritude," a kind of world culture which embodies the best of all cultures. Instead of being destroyed in the process, or trapped forever between two cultures like Medza in *Mission terminée,* Laye's hero becomes assimilated into the African culture and through this process achieves salvation. . . .

[The] final paragraphs of *Le regard du roi* constitute one of the most beautiful passages in all African literature. The reader coming upon this ending for the first time cannot help being deeply affected, deeply startled. . . .

If Laye spells out his meaning a little too clearly at the end —and I do not believe that he actually does—this, too, as the reader thinks back over the entire novel, may be interpreted as part of a wider fabric textured with ideas of grace and salvation which are present almost from the very beginning of the narrative. There are any number of indications throughout the story that death can be the only fulfillment for Clarence, a final union with the king and Africa. The only major differences I see in Laye's *Le regard du roi* when it is placed next to Anglophone African fiction are an absence of direct transformation of oral literary materials into the text of the story, and a more limited sense of the situational aspect of African fiction. Nevertheless, it can be argued that Camara Laye's *Le regard du roi* is of all African novels that which fits best into the situational category, since Clarence, who is archetypal of Western man in particular, is symbolic of everyman and his difficulties in adjusting not only to a different culture, but to life itself.

*Charles R. Larson, "Assimilated Négritude: Camara Laye's 'Le regard du roi'," in his* The Emergence of African Fiction, *Indiana University Press, 1971, pp. 167-226.*

*L'Enfant Noir* [*The African Child*] is the story of young Camara Laye in the background of upper Guinea where he lived with his family and friends. It's a very self-centred novel. One is surprised to see that there is nothing in that novel which comes from outside; there is no influence of the conflicting cultures in the background which must have existed in Conakry at the time. There is no shock of impact between the consciousness of the child and his environment in Laye's relationship to his surroundings. His psyche is very much a product of the young boy's growing up in a very well organized traditional society. The main issue flowing from this is a criticism that Camara Laye has not at all dealt with the problems created by the French system of colonization. . . .

And yet somehow, one would have thought that the novel *L'Enfant Noir* by its very closed atmosphere, by the fact that it excludes all talk about a foreign culture, by the fact that there isn't a single European in it (there are no elements of antagonism, culturally speaking), would be the strongest justification for Negritude and for its advocates to welcome the book in that it states that there is a stable society existing independent of Western influences and in that it demonstrates that. This is a viable system: the society within itself caters for every aspect of the social life of the village.

*L'Enfant Noir* is followed up by Camara Laye's second novel *Le Regard du Roi,* which is translated as *The Radiance of the King*. Here we meet Clarence, a European who is bankrupt—and this, for a white man in Africa, is a terrible thing to happen. He finds that he hasn't any means of earning a living, and the only hope for him lies in working in the court of the king. But this is not as easy as one would have thought, because every task has its spiritual significance. Being a foreigner, he finds that he has not got the understanding, the feeling for simple tasks like, for example, being a drummer. . . . He has to adapt himself to a new society, a society which does not need him in any way, a society whose conceptions of life, of the value of life and the values in life are completely different from his own. In the end, Clarence's search for the king with whom he hopes to hold an audience becomes an obsession. It's the mirage which lures him on through dark forests with people he doesn't feel anything for, with people who do not understand him. . . .

This is a very significant part of Camara Laye's thought if we follow it from *L'Enfant Noir*. There is this very dense atmosphere of self-sufficiency in his traditional African location. We feel that the European is shocked by the fact that there is a self-sufficient society and that he has to conform to *it* within its limits if he is to survive. . . .

Camara Laye's third novel *Dramouss* [translated as *A Dream of Africa*] which has just come out, is mainly a diatribe against the political errors of President Sekou Touré, and I don't think it concerns us very much here. We can see his first two novels are a very positive assertion of his own identity. He lays open a challenge to anyone who is foreign to it to accept this identity for what it is, to try to understand it, and then to seek to merge the two—as when Clarence is finally received by the king.

One could suggest that Clarence is going to be absorbed into the society. That could mean Western civilization is going to be absorbed into Africa—which I rather doubt—or that the spiritual development of a being is the ultimate factor in juding humanity, and not race, colour, religion or political ideology. I think it would mean more likely that Camara Laye did not talk about hunger just accidentally. He meant, probably, that there is a lot that is complementary between the two cultures. Unless one is prepared to see the African traditional heritage for what it is, as something separate, independent, self-sufficient, and, unless from that point of view, one tries to understand, and cooperate with, the African, unless this is done, there is no hope of there ever being a fruitful meeting point between the two. From the point of view of assimilation, it is suggested that there should be an assimilation in reverse. The European has to become, to a certain extent, a part of the African society in order to understand it; whereas in the actual political situation, the African has always had to become a part of the European mainstream in order to understand it and create the synthesis, the balance.

*Jeannette Macaulay, "The Idea of Assimilation: Mongo Beti and Camara Laye," in* Modern Black Novelists: A Collection of Critical Essays, *edited by Michael G. Cooke, Prentice-Hall, Inc., 1971, pp. 132-41.*

* * *

## LEVINE, Philip 1928-

**Levine is an important American poet. (See also *Contemporary Authors*, Vols. 9-12, rev. ed.)**

[In *Not This Pig*] I found nothing to excite me and a good bit to make me gloomy. I think both the themes and the devices are pretty dull stuff. The business of sharing the deprivations of one's fellow man, and then discovering in a poem that one has thereby become the fellow man's brother—this seems to me such a commonplace . . . that it can only be successfully reiterated in some kind of prosodic *tour de force*. The necessity of exploring the Jewish heritage and laying it both against one's life as a person and a father, and against one's exposure to the country that built the death camps, I can certainly understand; yet it leaves me sympathetic but cool. The indefatigable concern for the squalor and pitiableness of the human condition—with a mild sermon on the need for dignity despite all—seems to me here to serve no other function than to display the poet's good eye.

And Levine does have a good eye; I don't mean to suggest this is a bad book of poems. It is simply too flat to be long remembered. Ten minutes after the event is described, the event has vanished from the reader's mind; no image, no picture, no cadence, no fancy survives. Most of the poems come visually alive in the reading, then black out when the page is turned—partly, I suppose, because of the relentless syllabics-in-sevens, partly because of the consciously negative quality of the poems' statements, a sort of no-bird-sang effect done over and over in what is apparently intended to be a dramatic effect but fails, for me, to connect with the thrust of the poetry. And I respond in the same stolid way to the frequent occasions when the poem suddenly reaches outside itself to a vignette of Nature; I take it Levine wants to use the Natural as a correlative, but I have the strong feeling Nature could as often as not be excised without damaging the poems.

*Robley Wilson, Jr., "Five Poets at Hand," in* The Carleton Miscellany, *Fall, 1968, pp. 117-20.*

Philip Levine quietly has become one of the most interesting poets writing today in America. I say quietly, because Levine's poems do not contain many fashionable gestures. He never picked sides in the round robin of public quarrels which enlivened the poetry scene during the 1960s (New York Poets versus Black Mountain Poets, Deep Imagists versus Academic Poets, etc.) Instead, in his earlier books, *Not This Pig, Red Dust* and *Pili's Wall* he worked to develop a strong, precise language, expressing moments of illumination and compassion, expressing too the bass-tones of suffering and vulnerability which the emotionally open life must experience. In common with the best insight of many contemporary poets, Levine has learned to focus intensely on the "correspondences" which bind together different orders of experience. Stones and forests, the conflagrations of poverty, the Spanish landscape, the inhumanity of urban America, are yoked together into a structure of revelation which becomes the real subject matter of Levine's poetry. Not urban poverty alone, and not the mysteries of pastoral quietness, but the groundswell of understanding, the sharp, often dark energy which they share. The title poem of his most recent book, *They Feed They Lion,* is an example of the power which sweeps through the best of these poems. . . .

An energy of despair rises in the poem, ominous yet expansive; deadly, yet almost joyful. The voice of the black poor chants a language of apocalypse. "They Lion" feeds on suffering, and grows; not only human suffering, but the suffering of grass and stumps and gutted cars. The effect of Whitmanesque accumulation building from image to image creates a fraternity of darkness; the animate and inanimate worlds speak together in a single chant. "They Lion," etched more deeply by Levine's dialectal spelling, is a brother of Yeats's "rough beast" slouching toward Bethlehem; it is a mockery of St. Mark's biblical lion. When it comes, man and the earth will be devoured by one hunger.

*They Feed They Lion* sustains throughout a mood of mature, tough vision, in which the suffering of the earth, the suffering of man, the anxiety of inward failure, mingle to create a strangely literal Apocalypse, without chest-beating or the glamour of surreal imagery. Levine's phantasmagoria is real. . . .

Where *They Feed They Lion* fails, it is because Levine has a tendency to outrun his own vision. When he cranks up the intensity of his language, the sense of mystery becomes strained, and one feels a sort of exoticism in the imagery. A number of poems are simply too long, going through the motions of language when their actual strength has dwindled ("The Cutting Edge," "Saturday Sweeping," "Salami," etc.). But these are small blemishes. There remains so much good poetry in *They Feed They Lion* that it is without a doubt Philip Levine's best book, and one of the finest I have recently read.

*Paul Zweig, in* Parnassus, *Fall/Winter, 1972, pp. 171-74.*

Levine is an unsettling poet. I never open his books without a feeling of apprehension—expectation, yes, but also that strange marginal maidenly reserve that wants not to be startled. But Levine is startling because, for one thing, you never know from which direction he will attack. . . . Writing of Detroit's downriver suburbs, writing of the Spanish countryside, Levine evokes a personality that is ghostly, stunned, perplexed, trying to know itself but realizing that he, himself, is somehow being created, like a poem. . . . Yet what is curious about him is the sense one gets that he is in control of his poetry only at the point at which it becomes verbal, and perhaps even visual; the energy of the poetry itself comes from some impersonal, chaotic, probably very frightening dimension Levine cannot control but must not resist. . . .

Levine's unclassifiable poetry weaves violent and not-to-be-softened images in and out of a single sensibility's monologue of awe. The poems move back and forth from a mystical affirmation of the earth to a fragmented, carelessly questioning consciousness that excites us, sometimes against our will, with the prospect of a good fight. My first impulse is to say *He should write novels!*—but my more reasoned instinct is *He has no need to write novels. . . .*

In one of her essays Flannery O'Connor, shortly before her death, made the enigmatic statement that for many of "us," the future would lead away from the novel and into poetry. Surely Levine's poetry is the sort of thing she had in mind: brooding, musing, angry, alarming.

*Joyce Carol Oates, in* American Poetry Review, *May/June, 1973, p. 55.*

Philip Levine's new poems in *They Feed They Lion* depict a hard world—hard in the sense of being both unyielding and difficult. It is a world filled with stones, and stones recur as images in poem after poem. Indeed, the book's first line is "River of green stone," and two pages later is a poem about a "green rock." It is as though Levine, by comparing rivers to stone and giving stone the color of grass, were insisting that little on this earth is soft and comforting. . . .

But, unlike many sophisticates who in recent years have embraced a rural life, Levine does not find much solate in nature. . . .

Most of the poems are written in short, unadorned lines. They are compact, and at their weakest tight-lipped: some of the narrative incidents in such pieces as "The Angels of Detroit," "Thistles," and "Dark Rings" are so compressed that they lack emotional resonance. Yet the absence of rant helps make the best of them powerful, particularly the startling poems in which Levine, going beyond saying that the world is a tough place to live in, points out that it can be positively brutal. . . .

By mingling blossoms with an awareness of inevitable aging and by seeing life and breath as a perpetual giving and taking, Levine achieves a calm resolution, yet one devoid of easy sentimentality and consonant with his flinty perceptions throughout the book: nothing, he keeps saying, is ever easy.

*Jack Anderson, "Flinty Perceptions," in* Prairie Schooner (*© 1973 by University of Nebraska Press; reprinted by permission from* Prairie Schooner), *Summer, 1973, pp. 181-83.*

Philip Levine has . . . an utter scrupulousness of observation. His poems are personal, love poems, poems of horror, poems about the experiencing of America, which instead of simply representing the objects and the "scene" concentrate on the physical body experiencing these things. . . .

Awareness of the outside world as a threat to the individual perceiving it is the subject of many of his poems. . . .

The object seen, in order to be seen, is dependent on the body that perceives it. Since, without that witness, there will neither be seer or thing seen, then the act of seeing is a reminder of death, a threat of murder almost. In some of [the] poems [in *They Feed They Lion*] Philip Levine seems to see life and death interlocked—in fact more than that, as a perpetual collision of the killed with the killer. Some of his poems are about accidents, and they give a sense of this coitus of life with death as though the accident were a metaphor for living. Reading these poems one feels in the presence of a strange, alarming, and irrefutable way of seeing things. At the same time they contain observations which are pleasurable very much in the manner of James Schuyler's poetry.

*Stephen Spender, "Can Poetry Be Reviewed?," in* The New York Review of Books *(reprinted with permission from* The New York Review of Books; *© 1973 by NYREV, Inc.), September 20, 1973, pp. 8-14.*

Philip Levine's first book of poems (*On The Edge,* 1963) was remarkably good. It demonstrated an already accomplished poet whose strong voice moved through the mostly traditional verse with intelligence, confidence, and an uncanny power to unsettle. Its theme was "the loss of human power" and "the gradual decay of dignity"; its mood was one of almost unremitting pessimism. . . . Since that first book Levine's pursuit of his central theme has worked a big transformation in his style. . . .

Levine risks a lot with his new poetry; and when his vision is wholly private, then lines, images, sometimes entire poems fail to communicate; sometimes a flat and predictable language seeks automatic response. But when he focuses on the private pains and social ills of others, his best poems oblige us to cry with him. *They Feed They Lion* is not a comforting experience. More important, in its compassion, its skill, and its rare power to disturb our dulled attentions, it is a necessary and a valuable one.

*Alan Helms, in* Partisan Review *(copyright © 1974 by Partisan Review, Inc.), Vol. XLI, No. 1 (Winter, 1974), pp. 151-53.*

The poetry of Philip Levine, from *On the Edge* (1963) to his two latest collections, *Red Dust* (1971) and *They Feed They Lion* (1972), has always displayed technical skill, a dexterous handling of both formal and, more recently, informal modes, and a command of the resources of diction and rhythm. Yet these aspects of technique seem in a way secondary, absorbed as they are by a central, driving intensity peculiar to this poet's approach. Such intensity leads him to a relentless searching through the events of his life and the lives of others, through the particulars of nature as these signify something about the processes of living, the states of existence, in order to arrive not at Eliot's transcendence, Roethke's "condition of joy," or Whitman's ideal of progress and brotherhood (though the sharing of suffering and the common ties of humanity are basic to Levine's attitude) but to the sort of awareness suggested by Yeats' phrase, "the desolation of reality," an unflinching acquaintance with the harsh facts of most men's situation which still confirms rather than denies its validity. . . .

Levine's early poetry is taut, sharp, formal but gradually alters to accommodate his desire for greater freedom in line length and overall construction. A prominent theme of his first book is the reversal or defeat of expectations. Put another way, it motivates a struggle on the poet's part to view life stripped of the vestiges of illusory hope or promise, a type of hard spiritual conditioning which helps to engender his fundamental responsiveness to the dilemmas of the poor, embittered, failed lives of the "submerged population" (the late Frank O'Connor's term) in modern society, a responsiveness that accounts for much of both the energy and the deep humaneness of all his work. A firm grip on existence itself takes priority for Levine from the start, though with it necessarily comes an acceptance of pain and the admission that failure, defeat, and imperfection—but not surrender!—are unavoidable in men's affairs. . . .

Committed to a fallen, unredeemable world, finding no metaphysical consolations, Levine embraces it with an ardor, anguish, and fury that are themselves religious emotions. . . .

Rich and complex though they usually are, the poems of Levine's first two collections are relatively direct, proceeding by certain logical, sequential, narrative, or other means, which provide the reader with support and guidance. Levine never altogether abandons poems of this sort, but even in *Not This Pig* he begins to widen his fields of exploration to include experiences which manifest themselves in irrational, dreamlike, fantastic, or visionary forms, and doing so variously in such poems as "The Rats," "The Business Man of Alicante," "The Cartridges," "The One-Eyed King," "Animals Are Passing From Our Lives," "Baby Villon," "Waking an Angel," "The Second Angel," and "The Lost Angel." These pieces prepare the way for the surrealist atmosphere of *Red Dust,* the elliptical, disjunctive composition evident there, and further visible in portions of *They Feed They Lion.* Levine has cited the

Spanish and Latin American poets Hernandez, Alberti, Neruda, and Vallejo, in addition to post-war Polish poetry, as having presented new possibilities available to him. The freedom, vigorousness, metaphorical and imagistic daring of these poets plainly has had a tonic effect on Levine's more recent writing, releasing him to new boldness and strength.

So, by any but a narrow or restrictive view, Levine's latest books must be judged extraordinarily successful, exhibiting an access of inventiveness and vision. . . .

Two . . . amazing and powerful pieces, "Angel Butcher" and "They Feed They Lion," . . . [achieve] a climactic level of prophetic vision; the latter poem is dazzling in its syntactic, linguistic, and dramatic invention, its use of idiomatic effect. But both poems need to be read in their entirety and are too long for quotation here. It remains now simply to say for the purposes of this brief commentary that Levine's poetry, praiseworthy at the start, has developed by momentous strides in the past decade. His new poems make it impossible for him to be ignored or put aside. He stands out as one of the most solid and independent poets of his generation—one of the best poets, I think, anywhere at work in the language.

*Ralph J. Mills, Jr., "'The True and Earthy Prayer': Philip Levine's Poetry," in* American Poetry Review, *March/April, 1974, pp. 44-7.*

*1933* is Levine's most beautiful accomplishment so far. He is one of those poets whose work is so emotionally intense, and yet so controlled, so concentrated, that the accumulative effect of reading a number of his related poems can be shattering. If only most non-creative critics knew how difficult it is to write like this!—and what a miracle it is, in fact, that private emotion should be communicated on so dramatically transpersonal a level. Levine's "Letters For the Dead" in this volume, as well as the title poem, are works that, though based on his own experience, speak to us all—painfully, beautifully; like much of Levine's work, they really cannot be quoted except in their entirety. (This will be a difficulty serious critics will have with Levine—his artistry is such that only a complete poem represents him, and his books are so intensely unified that only the complete book represents him . . . so the best thing to do is simply buy and read his books. . . . I really think he is extraordinary, a visionary of our dense, troubled, mysterious time. The grittiest and most brutal of his poems is, to me, an experience I would not hesitate to call ineffable.)

*Joyce Carol Oates, in* The American Poetry Review, *May/June, 1974, p. 44.*

* * *

## LEZAMA LIMA, José 1910-

**Lezama Lima, one of Cuba's foremost poets, is also a novelist and essayist. Since the publication of *Paradiso,* however, he has not enjoyed the favor of the Castro régime.**

Twelve of Lezama Lima's best essays taken from *Analecta del reloj* (1957), *Tratados en La Habana* (1958) and *La cantidad hechizada* (1970) are included in [*Introducción a los vasos órficos*]. The inherent difficulty and hermetic nature of most of them may make the unwary reader wonder if the volume is a literary hoax conceived in the manner of the diligent weaver's cloth in "The Emperor's New Clothes." However, while Andersen's famous tale is based on an invisible and ultimately non-existent, exquisitely fine, imaginary fabric which everyone pretends to see and admire, Lezama Lima's essays are spun in a visible, ornate and carefully woven prose which may well appear to some readers to lack intrinsic meaning. In any case, *Introducción a los vasos órficos* is an experiment with language that aims to generate emotion through language, as both tool and finished product. Lezama's creative goal is thus supremely ambitious: language as a spinning wheel and a loom, as well as an intricate, fascinatingly rich fabric.

*Klaus Müller-Bergh, in* Books Abroad, *Vol. 46, No. 3, Summer, 1972, pp. 457-58.*

[In *Paradiso,* Lezama] has backslid . . . into Borgesian labyrinths of "innumerable mirrors that populate the universe" and into a prose larded with oblique and recondite allusions to almost everything from the species of lungfish through Plato, Aristotle, and Aquinas, a prose decorated with student rhetoric about Mallarme, Hegel, Nietzsche, Augustine, Kafka, Odysseus, the Book of Hours of the Duc de Berri (a prose counterpart of the racial salad of the characters—Cuban, Spanish, English, French, Basque, Indian), a prose often as unreadable as this sentence.

These philosophical, theological, mythological, and historical materials are brought to bear on events in order to squeeze from them a non-consequitive truth—a process that encourages lush elaborations not only of knowledge but of words and images, especially those metaphors that by joining two things irrationally evoke a meaning uncontaminated by cause-and-effect: "the President crossed the ballroom like a nicety on the lid of a cigar box." Whether we trace it to Joyce's purple passages ("Ineluctable modality of the visible: at least that if no more, thought through my eyes") or, as Lezama does, to "a revival of Gongora and the baroque," this complexity should be capable of delighting us: Guillermo Cabrera Infante demonstrated the Cuban facility in this style to English readers in his *Three Trapped Tigers* several years ago.

But Lezama plays the games with a difference. . . .

Many . . . semi-intelligible passages are foistered on the characters. As a result they all resemble each other, and their identities are merely verbal. What one says of another is true for all: "He says so much about himself aloud that when his words are extinguished he seems to be a phantom, he's no longer there, he's a cloud's tail." The publishers hint that the novel is autobiographical, but this is surely Lezama's little joke; there's not enough reality here to flesh out even half a life. The publishers also say that the Castro regime has been petulant about the absence of its favorite revolution and the presence of extensive homosexuality. But both absence and presence are obscured in such fog that the objection seems ill-aimed. A novel so often unintelligible needs no further criticism. Down with such decadence, Cubans; raise high the sackcloth banners of socialist realism!

*J. D. O'Hara, "From Cuba–Without Life," in* Book World—The Washington Post (© The Washington Post), *April 14, 1974, p. 2.*

Gregory Rabassa has bravely and helplessly translated [*Paradiso*]. Helplessly, because nothing short of a major re-creation in English—something quite different from Rabassa's patient rendering of the Spanish words on the page—would have made this cluttered and stilted text really available to us.

It is not a question of the translation's missing nuances of the original, losing flavors or marginal meanings. The whole pompous, self-conscious march of the Spanish simply comes out as comic or laborious in English, and I should say at once that I am not convinced that *Paradiso,* even in Spanish, is the masterpiece that many people take it to be. It is rather, I should say, subject to correction or persuasion by readers who could make me see the text in a different light, a weird and gleaming literary freak, a collapsed monument, a grand, failed landmark sunk in the sands of its author's colossal self-indulgence.

Baroque is the word that keeps coming to mind. Lezama Lima has written brilliantly on Góngora, and a character in *Paradiso* describes the baroque as "what has real interest in Spain and in Hispanic America." Alejo Carpentier, a distinguished Cuban novelist of Lezama Lima's generation, has said that Latin American art has always been baroque, from pre-Columbian sculptures and codices through colonial cathedrals to the anarchy of contemporary prose. Admittedly Carpentier is offering an oblique defense of his own difficult and ornate style (seen most clearly in *Siglo de las Luces,* translated as *Explosion in a Cathedral*), and his sense of the baroque is not at all the same as Lezama Lima's.

Nevertheless, these tastes and these comments point to a large and simple distinction between Cuban novelists of this century and other Latin Americans. The major modern novels of the subcontinent—Cortázar's *Hopscotch*, García Márquez's *A Hundred Years of Solitude,* Donoso's *Obscene Bird of Night*—are metaphors for a vast, encompassing unreality. The narrative games and the drifting characters in the Cortázar, the narrative tone and the little town in García Márquez, the fabulating narrator and the crumbling old convent in Donoso—any Latin American will recognize these conjunctions as versions of his daily experience of the world. This is not the unreality of North America, which is a matter of anxiety, of constant fear that tomorrow will arrive before today is over; it is not the unreality of Europe, which is a question of rotted structures, of buildings and institutions standing there (for the moment) with nothing holding them up. Unreality in Latin America is a sense of the world as a charade, some sort of game or fiction for which history insists on recruiting innocent people as both actors and audience—a sense of having to sit through an omnivorous, unending melodrama.

But then in Cuba, to return to my distinction, this unreality is so extreme, and so extremely enjoyable, that metaphors are not even sought for it. The unreality is taken as a license, as a gambling permit for poets, and a modern form of the baroque is the result, a proliferation of language which simply leaves reality to its own devices—except in the case of Carpentier, who adds to the unwinding historical melodrama a profusion of exotic, oddly named natural objects, a dazzling, unreal display put on by tropical reality itself. In this sense, then, not only Carpentier and Lezama Lima but younger Cuban writers like Cabrera Infante and Severo Sarduy are baroque artists, and it is no accident (to borrow a cagy phrase) that some of Joyce's most faithful and talented imitators are Cubans.

Joyce, of course, even in *Finnegans Wake,* didn't leave reality to its own devices, and is perhaps to be regarded as an instigator of the baroque in others, a writer who opened up new technical territories. Lezama Lima, on the other hand, is a prophet of the baroque who never quite descends to the technical—or rather who inserts a single baroque technique into an otherwise stodgy and classical manner. To put it crudely, his imagery is baroque while his syntax remains unremittingly academic. . . .

Lezama, as he says of one of his favorite characters in the novel, can't live without similes, and yet the similes he chooses are all fussy and self-advertising, mere gesticulations that never come together into that intense and intricate decorative fabric which is the mark of the successful baroque. And apart from its similes and periphrasis, Lezama's language is arch, cumbersome, and mercilessly solemn. Here is the university: "The classes were tedious and banal, open assignments were broadly simplified, and there was no extensive offering of quantitative material from which a scholar might extract a functional knowledge to apply to reality and satisfy immediate goals."

Here is a son responding to his parents' accusation that he won't talk to them: "It's not that I don't want to talk to you, but things have happened and you don't talk to me, you will always remain silent in an unfeeling muteness. Certain zones of our everyday relationship have become mute." Here is a poet thinking about his craft: "When his vision gave him a word in whatever relation it might have to reality, that word seemed to pass into his hands, and although the word remained invisible, freed of the vision from whence it had come, it went along, gathering a wheel on which gyrated incessantly its invisible modulation and its palpable modelization; then between intangible modelization and almost visible modulation, he seemed finally to be able to touch its forms, if he closed his eyes a little." I repeat that such passages are neither exceptional nor incidental, and that Rabassa is in no way to blame for their unfortunate comic flavor, which is only slightly less striking in Spanish.

Lezama himself doesn't appear to lack a sense of humor, and he writes at times as if he knew what irony was. But he has found no literary form for either irony or humor. Narrator and characters alike in *Paradiso* all speak in the same lofty, abstract, erratically imagistic, stylistically undifferentiated jargon that I have illustrated above, and while it would be absurd to think that Lezama is aiming for ordinary realism, for an imitation of the sounds and surfaces of ordinary life, the text does make disconcerting references to itself. People remark on the strange language others are using, are abashed at their own loquacity. Yet the language that causes the surprise is no stranger than the language which registers the surprise, and abashment at a loquacity that is a regular, if not an uninterrupted, event hardly makes any sense.

People are repeatedly *said* to be speaking ironically, yet there is nothing but the author's assertion to make that irony accessible to us. We can't read it in the tone of the supposedly ironic speech, since that tone is indistinguishable from the tone of the rest of the book. . . .

*Paradiso* is an enormous act of creative memory, a genealogical excavation, a digging up of long-dead family members to find them encrusted with fantasies and associations which belong properly to the excavator—as well as with such of their own attributes as the excavator can recall or intuit. It is a slow entwining, as Lezama says about the habits of thought of one of his characters, a rich complication of the past, a world of aunts, uncles, grandmothers, exile, rebellion, school, university, repeated sudden deaths, the discovery of sexuality, and long discussions of Nietzsche and the Church Fathers. It is a huge poem in prose, a personal mosaic of Cuban history, and has more than one point of resemblance, *mutatis mutandis,* with Mann's *Magic Mountain.* Its total effect is more impressive than the effects of any of its parts, and for Latin American readers and writers, it is now *there*—like the Alps, in or out of Mann's novel.

And yet, it seems to me, it is a garish, Alpine sideshow rather than a real mountain, a curiously timid and reactionary work hiding behind the skirts of an apparent boldness. It is less a modern novel than a garrulous, old-fashioned treatise about a modern novel which hasn't been written yet (or at least not by Lezama Lima); and the reasons for this state of affairs are fairly clear. It is a novel written by a certain kind of poet, with all that kind of poet's slavish devotion to the belief that only images matter. All the riches and invention in *Paradiso* have gone into its figurative language, leaving tone, syntax, and the whole craft of prose to fend for themselves. Four hundred and sixty-six pages of writing by a man who doesn't care enough about the form of writing he has chosen guarantees an astonishing monotony, a clanking commitment to the most unimaginative prose cadences—almost a record of stamina for staying so long on the wrong bus.

*Michael Wood, "Purgatorio," in* The New York Review of Books *(reprinted with permission from* The New York Review of Books; *© 1974 by NYREV, Inc.), April 18, 1974, pp. 14-16.*

There is scarcely a line in [*Paradiso*] that could be mistaken for anyone else's writing—or for prose in any familiar sense of that word. The skilled translation alone must have been a monumental task. Depending upon your taste or tolerance for elaborate diction, you will find Lezama's style either intoxicating or repellent, but you will not have a neutral reaction to a sentence such as this one, chosen because it is typical: "When we lift our faces he is no longer there, he is in the whirlwind of his joy, there to attract us again like a firefly, a geometric point, the eyes of a cat, the look of a mother, to converge in the night on a tree, a blackboard, a bedroom, on the unchanging ground in front of the lowered eyelid."

Lezama's language is reckless, voluptuous, sly and unrelentingly sexual. Those scenes in the book that are literally sexual (and there are many juicy heterosexual and homosexual interludes) are no more charged with bristling erotic energy than any other moment. At every point words are courting or stroking or probing the banal facts of everyday life (the stated intention of "Paradiso" is to portray "as closely as possible the daily life of a Cuban man and his family"). . . .

Lezama not only has the power to create absorbing and memorable images; he has also placed these images into a vast network of philosophical and mythical significance. Like Proust he is intent upon defeating time and submerging it into the eternity of art, but Lezama has recaptured the historical as well as his own personal past. Lurking just beneath the surface of his prose, and sometimes breaking through it like leaping dolphins, are references to the great hermetic traditions of Egypt, Europe, Asia and pre-Columbia America.

His central vision is of a spiritual unity that preceded terrestrial multiplicity—a unity that is reconstructed in the final pages of "Paradiso." Seen in this light, his bizarre metaphors turn out to be parabolas that trace the hidden correspondences between visually rhyming things that only appear to be unrelated (the glowing tip of a cigar and a distant star, for instance). The tale of a boy seeking his father and finding wisdom becomes a parable in which Adam attempts to regain Paradise. . . .

There are many readers in the United States who have a mystical turn of mind and a few, I suppose, who also have the inclination and erudition to track down "Paradiso's" allusions to Pythagoras, Plotinus, St. Augustine's "De Musica," Goethe's "Wilhelm Meister's Apprenticeship," Rimbaud's "Illuminations" and Lao Tzu's "Tao Te Ching." I am not one of those readers. For me, the proof of the greatness of "Paradiso" is that for the last two weeks I've been walking around New York seeing things through Lezama's eyes. When I went past an office building in Midtown I stopped to watch goggled men slowly sweeping flaming acetylene torches across the cracks between stone slabs of a huge, windy plaza. Instantly they became angels performing a sinister task—regretfully, sadly.

*Edmund White, in* The New York Times Book Review *(© 1974 by The New York Times Company; reprinted by permission), April 21, 1974, pp. 27-8.*

By all accounts [Lezama Lima] is . . . an immensely erudite poet.

"Paradiso" has no discernible story. The narrative can best be described as a complex web of experiences. Caught at the center of the web is the hero, José Cemí (note the initials). Embedded at various other points are Cemí's parents, grandparents, aunts, uncles, and school friends. On the outer filaments there are Indian soothsayers, Mexican troubadours, insolent domestics, octoroon prostitutes, secret homosexuals.

At its best "Paradiso" has the "leaps of imagination" which have come to be associated with the best contemporary Spanish literature. In one vignette a malodorous blue cloud escapes from the armpit of a traffic policeman and lodges itself in the armpit of an innocent, passing salesman. This nearly ruins the salesman. For merchants are suspicious of salesmen who have vile-smelling blue clouds hovering under their arms. Countless baths cannot drive away the cloud and the salesman begins to lose his wits. When the traffic policeman is finally able to reclaim his awful stench he does so with a mixture of pride and tenderness. To him the cloud is a beautiful, runaway child—an intimate and inseparable part of his being. This is a fine conceit. But unfortunately, moments such as this are rare. . . .

The problem with "Paradiso" (though some will consider it the book's charm) is Lezama Lima's stilted (or baroque) use of language. Characters do not die, they are spirited off to "Persephone's gloomy vale." Nietzsche, Zeus, Cranach, Shakespeare, Hecate, Cagliostro, Cellini, and even the likes of poor Stavrogin are constantly being dragged into the prose. The fiction ends up being strangled in direct proportion to Lezama Lima's allusiveness. Put another way, the reader feels he is not in Havana so much as he is visiting a cultural jumble sale.

For every luminous, tropical moment there are hundreds such as this: "The essential characteristic of Diaghilev was his spermatic ability to agglutinate."

If there is any point at all to fiction, it is to unmask culture —not merely recapitulate it.

*Jack Friedman, in* The Village Voice *(reprinted by permission of* The Village Voice; *© 1974 by The Village Voice, Inc.), April 25, 1974, pp. 23-4.*

José Lezama Lima, Cuba's major poet, wrote *Paradiso* to render "as closely as possible the daily life of a Cuban man and his family," a statement that has no connection with the novel I have just struggled through, although *Paradiso* does follow a character named José Cemí from childhood through school days. . . .

*Paradiso* can pass as no one's daily life. Lezama, a name some Americans know from a quotation Cortázar uses in *Hopscotch,* is a disciple of the baroque poet Góngora and a remarkably wide reader (he is a leading critic in Cuba) who has assimilated the total recall of several lifetimes worth of serious reading. In *Paradiso* he seems to have two main purposes: to dumbfound us with his erudition and to extend Góngora's euphemisms into a baroque novel. He succeeds in both, but the novel is impossible.

*John Alfred Avant, in* The New Republic *(reprinted by permission of* The New Republic; *© 1974 by The New Republic, Inc.), June 15, 1974, p. 27.*

* * *

## LIEBERMAN, Laurence 1935-

**Lieberman is an American poet and literary critic. (See also *Contemporary Authors*, Vols. 17-18.)**

"The Osprey Suicides" is globe-hopping, frantic and protean, but it is also slow and domestic. Many of the poems convey the feeling of constant danger; man is soft flesh pitted against sharp coral, biting fish, against the smack of waves, the pull of undertow, the rip of lightening. But other poems come home to things comfortable and familial, as familiar as the twisted sheets of an unmade bed, or as warm and fetal as that bed filled with children and husband and wife. . . .

It is in part three, "The Osprey Suicides," and more particularly the title poem itself, that Lieberman excels. He outlines America's peculiar state of despair, its ill-planned land development, its air pollution, its people's specialized professionalism.

His images become raw and vicious. His protests do not have anything to do with those ugly, touchstone words "ecology" and "conformity," but rather with poetry, with the exclusion of poetry from our lives, and the cheapening of our spiritual values.

The American is not a majestic eagle and never has been. He is a plucky osprey who dares too much always, even to the point of self-destruction. The osprey and the American have been driven a bit mad, their conduct is unnatural, their acts sometimes reprehensible.

But Lieberman can look at the scene, shake his head and, as it has been done so many times in our poetry, come up with an affirmative statement.

*H. Leslie Wolfe, "Lieberman's New Poetry —Fresh Voice from Midwest," in* The Daily Illini, *May 17, 1973.*

"Composition," wrote young Delacroix in a letter to a friend, "gives wisdom and steadiness to a terrain shaken and set on fire by volcanoes. There lies the integration that alone makes for greatness."

*Composition,* in a reading of the word that transcends even this dignity, is the embracing magnitude that endows Laurence Lieberman's second volume of poems [*The Osprey Suicides*] with total integrity. This must be recognized promptly, for the attribution to Lieberman of "Whitmanesque" length and breadth might dissipate from the start any thought of compositional integrity. If, in poems appropriate to the comparison, he is indebted, he has revised the apostolic creed with the very disciplines customarily shunned by those who rehearse it. Lieberman may be easy to read carelessly since, when he is most energetic, he seems to write breathlessly; from the appearance of his poems on the page—long, long strokes and short choppy ones; dots and dashes, peristaltic passages muscled with alliteration; indented short-step blocks like ziggurats; hyphenated gerunds and tandem modifiers ("flipper-flapping," "wind-whipped," "love-sucking") and so on—you might infer a freeform improvisation irresponsible to detail or coherence. So many blinding sequences in his submarine or up-in-the-air poems dispute the inference that I'm faced with an embarrassment of splendors to show off. . . . Any assistant professor will assure you that syntactical virtuosity is not the only wear. What *is* valuable to emphasize is the fantasy with which this poet invests knowledge.

Something further. Composition, I have stressed. *Orchestration* would be the more fitting term, to be applied beyond the single, devastating poem. We have only begun to read Lieberman when we applaud such episodes as *phenomenal* exercises. His book, containing a quantity of poems in unrelated styles, subscribes to a comprehensive metaphor, with consistent, undulating motifs: the creative struggle of the poet towards *communion,* undergoing seasons in hell, assuming protean shapes to elude the insistent agonies of self-consciousness, exploring the depths, scanning the ether, stalled in the halfway region of domestic hope and alienation, a place as weird in its way as the lobster cave of that appalling *tour de force,* "Lobsters in the Brain Coral." Take my program notes on trust, common reader, but if, usually, you "dip into" a book of poems, break the habit for Lieberman: read this "collection" as if listening to a concerto—from beginning to end. . . .

Brave and inexhaustible voice—more often than of Whitman he reminds me of Hopkins, having, it is true, the same tendency to become hypnotised by his own homographs. This is my only reservation, a small one. Lieberman is a Heracles among American poets.

*Vernon Young, in* The Hudson Review *(copyright © 1974 by The Hudson Review, Inc.; reprinted by permission), Vol. XXVI, No. 4, Winter, 1973-74, pp. 729-31.*

* * *

## LIND, Jakov 1927-

**Lind is a Viennese novelist and short story writer living in England. His brilliant fiction—and especially his keen sense of "gallows humor"—has reminded critics of work by Kafka and Grass. (See also *Contemporary Authors*, Vols. 9-12, rev. ed.)**

Lind writes like a devil (and don't forget that Lucifer was an angel), and he deals with the contemporary nightmare at its most desperate. As in *Soul of Wood,* his first book of short stories, Lind's actual material in his novel *Landscape in Concrete* is the Third Reich near the end of World War II. But the overtones are far-reaching. Lind's landscape is as violent, as unstructured as any modernist would wish. Yet there stands behind the lunatic horror a viewpoint, not summed up, only hinted at in imagery and allegory. It lends to Lind's picture of the abyss the stature of prophecy. . . .

One of the extraordinary dimensions Lind brings to our understanding of the German nightmare is the element of fantasy. We have learned the hard lesson that very real dead bodies may be the result of unreal but driving inner fantasies. In tapping them and in relating them to human experience, although in the extreme, Lind is connecting us all to the violent horror in which our century's drama has taken place. Our idealistic ambitions and our passions have led us into hell, Lind seems to be suggesting. And by presenting ambition at its most extreme, as well as the wildest fantasies of murder and sexuality, in the cold light of realistic action, Lind is speaking directly to his reader: *hypocrite lecteur, mon semblable, mon frère.*

To this end Jakov Lind's style serves him as an extraordinarily flexible instrument. The wildest flights of poetry are followed by passages of plain prose, like a dash of cold water in the face. . . .

*Landscape in Concrete* is a mad, brilliant book that calls to mind Emily Dickinson's phrase "zero in the bone". In presenting one of the most piercing pictures of the nihilism of this century, Lind has gone beyond nihilism. (It is no accident, by the way, that his hero is fond of quoting Nietzsche.) God is deaf (or dead) in Lind's world, and Man is in imminent danger of turning into stone. But his man is a meaning-seeking animal. And in his own wild way he has not stopped seeking. Destined by his family tradition to create beautiful things out of precious metal, he destroys instead. Yet the other possibility is always there, and it makes this not merely a startling and shivery book but a valuable one.

*Daniel Stern, "A Contemporary Nightmare," in* Saturday Review/World *(copyright © 1966 by Saturday Review/World, Inc.; reprinted with permission), June 25, 1966, pp. 25-6.*

With "Soul of Wood," a collection of short stories . . ., Jakov Lind took his place among the important writers of postwar Germany. In the seven extraordinarily inventive stories of that volume he revealed an imagination obsessed with the horrors and the ultimate absurdity of human existence. Some critics compared him to Günter Grass, Gustav Meyrink or Franz Kafka; others found deficiencies in craftsmanship; but no one could deny the authenticity of his vision and the savagery of his assault. Lind writes the way an existentialist philosophizes, with no attention to canons and conventions. In another age, Lind, brilliant and untutored, would have been proclaimed an original genius. . . .

Central to "Landscape in Concrete," it would seem, is the idea that men, whatever they do, enact a barbaric ritual demanding violence and death. References to Christ, Faust and Nietzsche underscore the allegorical structure of the work, and a wealth of symbols, some obtrusive and some very subtle, raise it far above fashionable variations on the theme of *angst.* It would be too easy to regard this novel as one more account of the perversity of the Germans. Theirs was the deed, but the questions raised by it have not been answered. Nazi Germany, Lind implies, and with brutal power, is a metaphor of universal validity.

*J. P. Bauke, "There Is a Plague Called Bachmann," in* The New York Times Book Review *(© 1966 by The New York Times Company; reprinted by permission), June 26, 1966, p. 4.*

The same surreal atmosphere and wild imagination of Lind's first book, *Soul of Wood,* is evident in *Landscape in Concrete.* In *Soul of Wood,* the physical regeneration of the crippled Jewish youth, Barth, and his life tenacity may be interpreted as the symbol of the Jewish people. Complementing this, in *Landscape in Concrete,* the gigantic German soldier, former goldsmith Bachmann (Bach plus Mann, an ironic fusion of German culture's great names?) may represent the German who, despite appreciation for culture and civilized refinements, slavishly submits to evil. . . .

Each scene is a surprise, rich in comic and savage invention, each told in Lind's succinct prose.

Neither Jews nor concentration camps appear in *Landscape in Concrete*. But these precisely are the moral burden of Lind's imaginative novel whose central scene is a symbolic metamorphosis of the genocide.

*Curt Leviant, "The Landscape of Jakov Lind," in* Congress Bi-Weekly, *November 7, 1966, p. 29.*

"Ergo" lacks almost all objective correlatives: the breakdown of European morality that Nazism precipitated has not, in Lind's view, been restored by the defeat of Hitler. Madness cannot be cured by force of arms, as the Anglo-American naiveté imagined; you cannot fight your way into people's minds. When Lind examines the way things are today, he finds no society worth anatomizing; he finds only a stratification of paranoid and psychopathic obsessions. He rips off the careful patches that have been so solemnly applied to the face of Germany and, somewhat gleefully, reopens the ulcers underneath.

In fictional terms, the consequences of his attitude are less than convenient or comfortable. "Ergo" is no easy read. There is, in a sense, neither prose nor dialogue in the book, nothing on which the reader can rely. The thing is unloaded in a curious amalgam of ranting confessions. Like Günter Grass, Lind can get to grips with his material only through the creation of grotesques. No normal person exists in his vision. . . .

"Ergo" is less a novel than a case history, an attempt to explain an insane condition. It is often incomprehensible because the writer has no access, or denies himself access, to any common language; he can proceed only by analogy: his meaning is revealed in his meaninglessness.

Lind's determination not to falsify his vision leads him to be false to the notion of the conventional novel. This is, of course, an increasingly common predicament (it is to be observed in many novels by Negro writers who have become disillusioned with the "consensus" which the English language, metaphorically, represents), and while I sympathize with the esthetic schizophrenia which it induces, I cannot myself believe that English is a burnt-out medium. Moreover I cannot, with all the goodwill in the world, accept that books as opaque and as unrewarding as "Ergo" can long continue to have it both ways: to claim the status of fictional art without allowing the reader some foothold on their surface.

*Frederic Raphael, "With Furious Contempt," in* The New York Times Book Review *(© 1967 by The New York Times Company; reprinted by permission), October 22, 1967, pp. 8, 60.*

Two books, *Soul of Wood* (1962) and *Landscape in Concrete* (1966) have sufficed to establish for Jakov Lind a most enviable reputation. Influenced distantly by Franz Kafka and very immediately by Günter Grass, Lind's imagination shows the bloody marks of the Hitler era. [Written] from London, his two books have centered more about the evil of executioners than the sufferings of victims. Nor is Lind one-sided in the treatment of Nazi crimes. In the title story of *Soul of Wood* he deals with the curiosities of evil, while in *Landscape in Concrete* he stresses its banality. . . .

The author's vision is that of a man who can no longer weep over humanity but only laugh over its cruel and ludicrous ways. "Soul of Wood" deals with the machinations of an Austrian male nurse to whose care deported parents entrust the welfare of their crippled child. As a reward, they offer him their apartment. He in turn abandons the crippled youngster on a mountain top and sets off to negotiate for the sale of the apartment to a Nazi bigwig. The latter has him committed to an insane asylum where two maniacal doctors, in deadly competition with each other, seek his services as a spy and informer. With the end of the war, the crippled Jewish boy, miraculously alive, is needed by all as proof of their good-will toward Jews. Lind's irony is skillful in this story as, indeed, in most others.

*Lothar Kahn, in his* Mirrors of the Jewish Mind: A Gallery of Portraits of European Jewish Writers of Our Time, *A. S. Barnes, 1968, pp. 231-32.*

What comes out of Mr Lind's attempts to describe, enliven and justify his wanderings in a stricken postwar Europe is, unfortunately, a book [*Numbers*] which readers moved and entertained by *Counting My Steps* might well prefer to forget. The instinct for survival which carried him through the horrors of war is not positive enough to make these peacetime experiences either creditable or interesting. Mr Lind the husband becomes, in turn, father to a child whom he periodically abandons, and then the sexual conqueror of a long series of women of all nationalities during his restless European travels. He briefly trains for the stage, works spasmodically in a usual range of unsuitable jobs, and justifies his sad, picaresque jaunt with vague reference to the obsession of the writer in him with freedom. . . . The moral of this brief and banal let-down might be that the more candid and revealing increasing numbers of people are, the less absorbing the whole process becomes; in literature as in life.

*"Over-Exposed," in* The Times Literary Supplement *(reproduced by permission), March 9, 1973, p. 261.*

In [*Soul of Wood* and *Landscape of Concrete*], the first a collection of short stories, the second a short novel, Lind established a prose style somewhere between Kafka and Günter Grass that allowed him to recreate the banality and terror that were the twin components of the German catastrophe. Lind is at his best as a chronicler of nightmares and knew the historical one firsthand. . . . Europe in the age of the cannibal was Lind's hard-won subject, and in his early books of fiction he recorded it in the most bizarre throes of its derangement. . . .

In his fictional books he had found highly original expression for such visions, but as he retreated from fiction and went back over the same ground of his war-time experiences in the form of first-person autobiographical narrative, the writing seemed lacklustre and without force. *Counting My Steps* was not a strong book, although some of its more unusual character sketches and anecdotes remain memorable. *Numbers,* its sequel, was even less impressive. In part, but only in part, the relative weakness of these two books may be owing to the fact that they were among the author's first writings in English; yet form was a more crucial factor than language, for while fantasy allowed Lind to relate his experiences from the built-in concealments provided by story, autobiographical narrative demanded a more naked exposure of the self. And the self, or several selves that Lind had put on and put off . . . he did not much like.

As his writing turned inward, it tended to turn brutal, this time not so much to reflect the brutality of outward circumstances but, more painfully, to register feelings of an inner self-loathing. . . .

If the two previous installments of Lind's autobiography indicated a weakening of resources and a general confusion of aims, this third volume [*The Trip to Jerusalem*] carries us all the way into silence. And not the silence of the beatific vision, as the author would have it, but the silence of empty cisterns and exhausted wells. . . .

The wrenching quality of Jakov Lind's writing grows out of [a] fundamental contradiction, and its note of stymied pathos results from his inability to resolve the split between his felt will towards Jewishness and the triviality and self-mockery with which he treats the subject. Ambivalence is too weak a word to indicate the weight of sadness and frustration that characterizes Lind's opposing self. . . .

*Alvin H. Rosenfeld, "Jakov Lind and the Trials of Jewishness," in* Midstream, *February, 1974, pp. 71-5.*

It is the minor, the apparently irrelevant, the easily overlooked detail which stays with [Jakov Lind]; and this is one of [his] charms—and strengths—as a writer: to say much in deceptively casual ways. *The Trip to Jerusalem* is full of hints and nuances which accurately capture the sincere confusions of its author; it is occasionally rather moving and, just occasionally, wise, in a sly and humorous fashion. But it is all somewhat whimsically small-scale, and tantalizingly incomplete. One wishes that a writer of his background, intelligence and discernment had gone much more thoroughly to the heart of things, and given us his fullest possible picture of how Israel looks to a brilliant, articulate, yet not entirely committed, Occidental Jew: in other words, his own frank and explicit answer to the perennial Israeli question of the visitor, "*Nu,* what do you think?"

*"The High Way Home," in* The Times Literary Supplement *(reproduced by permission), July 12, 1974, p. 745.*

* * *

## LIVESAY, Dorothy 1909-

**Ms Livesay is a major Canadian poet. (See also *Contemporary Authors*, Vols. 25-28.)**

Dorothy Livesay begins the foreword to her *Collected Poems* with the statement: "These poems written between 1926 and 1971 create an autobiography; a psychic if not a literal autobiography," and thus directs our attention rather to the personality than the philosophy of the collection. We are not, it seems, to look for an intellectual schema; we are not to think of the poet as a teacher in the way that we think of Yeats, or Stevens, or Pound; we are not to expect the vatic, the prophetic, the oracular: we are simply to take the poems as the story of a life, its passing thoughts, its occasional intensities, its doubts, its confusions, its sudden clarities.

The book certainly seems to be of this kind. There are many occasional poems, many anecdotes; the language is frequently a little pedestrian, a little too casual, so that we feel the poet's modesty may have led her to accept small returns rather than labour for masterpieces. Many of the images are commonplace; many of the cadences are tired and predictable. A good many poems would be improved by cutting; some miss the target completely. The dramatic poems are often marred by conventional rhetoric. . . . Lapses of this kind might well destroy one's faith in a poet of less obvious integrity, but Dorothy Livesay's work reveals such passionate honesty of feeling, and such consistent moral courage, that even the grossest defects become, like those of Thomas Hardy, curiously endearing. It is as if the poet were more concerned with the poem itself than with the reputation of the poem, more concerned to spell out the thought and feeling in simple and direct ways than to labour after an elegance of sophistication that might pervert the meaningful into the marmoreal. This is clearly an honest book. . . .

It might even seem that in stressing Dorothy Livesay's honesty I am damning the book with the faintest of praise. Such is not my intention; I am concerned only to suggest that the stylistic defects appear to derive from the same cause as the poetic excellence: an integrity of feeling that distrusts the straining after rhetorical effects, and seeks to explore the texture of human experience in "a selection of the language really used by men".

Such language must necessarily include the platitudes, the clichés and the stock expressions of current speech as did the language of Wordsworth, and it must, like the language of Wordsworth, attempt the impersonation of the unsophisticated memorialist, and the innocent visionary. Dorothy Livesay's poetry is capable, not only of Wordsworthian leisureliness with its attendant subtleties and longueurs, but also of the gnomic clarity which illuminates the Lucy poems, and which is characteristic of those later romantics, Emily Brontë and Emily Dickinson, whom Ms. Livesay celebrates in one of her poems. . . .

After 1956 the earlier prolixity and syntactical disarray seem to have been almost entirely conquered. The punctuation remains arbitrary on occasion, but the poems have a new force and clarity, a new directness and sense of form. . . . In this section of the *Collected Poems* the passion and the poetry fuse, and the later poems are equally deft and poised and strong. It is as if all the honesty, the sincerity, the courage, of the earlier poems have now come together with a real concern for poetry as an art. The descriptions are more vivid than before, and the technique is more assured.

*Robin Skelton, "Livesay's Two Seasons," in* Canadian Literature, *Autumn, 1973, pp. 77-82.*

Because Northrop Frye did so, most of Livesay's critics have labelled her an imagist, but the label is, for me, too sweeping. Certainly Livesay was influenced by the imagists; her affinities to H.D., both in quality and method of expression, are obvious, and have been noted by the critics. But there is much more to Livesay's poetry than her imagism. For me, she is primarily a lyricist, a poet who is deeply concerned and committed to the interaction and fusion of sound, rhythm, and expression in poetry. She has said that "song" (sound) and "dance" (rhythm) are the roots of poetry, that she is "always hearing this other beat behind the ordinary spoken language and I'm always hearing the melody". This is the ingredient which usually distinguishes poetry from prose, but occasionally there are prose writers who focus in on the sound and rhythm of their words; Virginia Woolf was one who did this. Margaret Laurence does it. And so does Dorothy Livesay. . . .

Livesay, the poet, is tremendously aware of the effect which word music can create; she has transferred this aspect of her poetry to her prose. And the best sections of [*A Winnipeg Childhood*] are those in which sound and idea merge with image into a wholeness of expression. . . .

Livesay's perceptions of the reality of existence—that is, of people trapped and alone in their own minds—is evident in many of her poems, and is the main theme to these stories, presented and structured like the processes of the mind. *A Winnipeg Childhood* proceeds in flashes of vision and memory, the most obvious example of the mind working. And the stories express the frightening sense of separateness, and of the ultimate uselessness of communication. . . .

Dorothy Livesay [has] moved through her life, looking for certainty, yet recognizing that it is impossible. She realized in her poetry that the process of living results in the endless creation of new myths; many of her poems express an awareness that the humanitarian belief in life, in its unconquerable onward rush and in its possibilities for betterment, can become, in fact has become the new myth.

*Donald Stephens, "Words and Music," in* Canadian Literature, *Spring, 1974, pp. 93-5.*

* * *

## LOWELL, Robert 1917-

**Lowell is one of America's foremost contemporary poets. One of the most striking qualities of all his work has been the intensity of his moral and political concern for American civilization. He is also a playwright and the author of a book of "imitations." (See also *Contemporary Authors*, Vols. 9-12, rev. ed.)**

[Lowell's] poems have been offered to us, over the years, in several contexts. For a few years we were advised to consider him a major Catholic poet, and this gave us—depending upon our attitude to Catholicism—either a stick with which to beat the poems or a pilgrim's staff to help us reach them. Either way it was a temporary facility. We have also been told to think of the poems, especially the early ones in *Lord Weary's Castle,* as acts of violence directed against all the forces of constriction wherever the poet feels them—especially those associated with his own New England ancestors, guardians of a deadly law. This has now become critical orthodoxy in regard to Lowell's poems, and we tend to grasp it, on the principle that recommends any port in a storm. But I think we have settled down too easily. It is not very difficult to make a few generalizations about the New England ancestors, accurate or not, but there is very little evidence in the poems to support the sentimental image of a tender poet wounded and darkened by his membership in a great dark family. The occasions that incite those poems are invariably immediate, personal; we don't need to go back to Plymouth Rock.

*Denis Donoghue, in his* Connoisseurs of Chaos: Ideas of Order in Modern American Poetry *(reprinted with permission of Macmillan Publishing Co., Inc.; © by Denis Donoghue, 1965), Macmillan, 1965, p. 150.*

[What] Tate meant [in his introduction to *Land of Unlikeness,* Lowell's first book,] in calling Lowell "consciously a Catholic poet" is that Lowell has consciously chosen a position of aesthetic involvement which can merge the techniques of religious vision with those of artistic vision. Behind this choice is the belief that God, not man, is the measure of ultimate reality and that what is important about man is not his achievements but his soul, his likeness to God. In such a relationship the function of the poet, like that of the prophet, is to reveal essential reality to the world which may have lost sight of it. He is no longer the imitator of life in the Aristotelian sense; he is the illuminator of Joyce's *Portrait* or Dante's *Divine Comedy*. . . .

Like Dante, he seems to take his heroes and epic events from Vergil, Lucan, and Ovid, and like Dante, he merges these heroes and events into a structure of Christian morality. The result is not always happy, for, as a poet, he can develop modern counterparts to Aeneas and still be forced to condemn them theologically. Ulysses, for instance, ends up in Dante's *Inferno* in the circle reserved for evil counselors. In addition, there is a whole realm of twentieth-century experience which Lowell seems not able to examine—or to examine only with distortion—because there are no exact classical parallels. (p. 19)

[With his second volume, *Lord Weary's Castle,*] his view of salvation has become narrower. It is now more completely allied with the contemplative tradition and seems to consolidate into one step the various separate ways to salvation suggested in *Land of Unlikeness.* No longer can one augment baptismal likeness to God merely through a complete faith in Christ or an avoidance of war or a belief in the power of prayer or an ability to value worldly goods at no more than their price or by Catholicism. One must go beyond these means into the contemplative life. (p. 47)

In the closing pages of *Lord Weary's Castle,* beginning with such poems as "Between the Porch and the Altar" and "After the Surprising Conversions," a new direction in Lowell's poetry appears. The direction manifests his reading of Friedrich Nietzsche and relies frequently on the run-on couplet and monologue devices of Robert Browning. It examples a change from the epical to dramatic and narrative forms [Mazzaro is referring to the three basic positions of aesthetic involvement defined by Joyce in the closing chapter of *The Portrait of The Artist as a Young Man*] and carries beyond Lowell's next volume of poetry, *The Mills of the Kavanaughs* (1951), into parts of *Life Studies* (1959). . . . The new direction, then, may be seen as an attempt to expand the range of poetry so as to include both plot and character. But to do so successfully, Lowell must also increase his range of character and action beyond the limited mysticism demanded by his current means of salvation. (p. 61)

Lowell's poetry at this time does seem to be of its own direction committed more and more to the vitality and credibility of its characters rather than to the force of its ideas. (p. 62)

In *The Mills of the Kavanaughs* Lowell's interest in plot and character prompts seven new poems, all primarily human, time-possessed, and definite. Ranging into the "longer poem" category, they complete the disintegration of the anagogical level in Lowell's poetry and, at the same time, provide more diversification in his characterizations. The realization that his basic poetic vision relied heavily on sensuous detail, that he was unable to develop, as Dante had, a new way of looking at things, that his interest was in the active rather than the contemplative life, or that drama is basically anthropocentric rather than theocentric may account for this disintegration. In any case, the disintegration provides for the inclusion of new ideas and personages neither interested in nor capable of understanding the structure of religious contemplation. Having emerged, these voices receive a sympathy and understanding not often shown previously by the poet. (p. 74)

*Life Studies* (1959) continues Lowell's noncontemplative pursuit of plot and character and marks further changes in the religious concepts and structure behind his poetic style. . . . Man is constantly compared to creatures of habit, suggesting the loss of free will and the determinism of the obliterated spiritual purpose inherent in Anne Kavanaugh's final acceptance of death. In addition, with this acceptance of death and man's subsequent loss of spirituality, the automatic exclusion of contemplation as a means of regaining God's likeness leads to the elimination of minutely realized detail indicative of meditational poetry. These details, which once contributed to Lowell's inverted baroque style, were important only as they led to an escape theology and, as in the case of "The Mills of the Kavanaughs," could prove cumbersome to the other facets of a poem's meaning. Their elimination results in an overall simplifying and tightening of techniques in Lowell's new character portrayals, but not to any lessening of his pessimistic world view. (pp. 88-9)

Simultaneous with these changes and perhaps as a justification of them is the appearance of a new, worldly aesthetic deriving much of its framework from the aesthetic ideas of Ezra Pound, particularly his definitions of style and culture in *Guide to Kulchur* (1938), but still preserving Lowell's own desires for an ideal, all-inclusive poetry. Style, for Lowell, becomes now a matter of "so knowing words that one will communicate the various parts of what one says with the various degrees and weights of importance which one wishes," and culture "is what you can pick up and/or get in touch with, by talk with the most intelligent men of the period." (p. 89)

Still it would be deceptive to conclude that the colloquial tone and the idea of culture, the imagery and the loose metrical structure of the poems in *Life Studies* are simply derivative. In the *Cantos* Pound transforms culture into talking; in these poems Lowell does not. . . .

[Behind] the poems of *Life Studies* and the techniques of both Lowell and Pound lie epic visions which incorporate three common important principles: communication, history, and love. (p. 90)

[Although] the morality is the same, religiously Lowell has changed to a position which not only portrays but understands aspects of the active life. The contemplative threads and now the archetypal framework of meditation have been eliminated. What he keeps is a fluid, adaptable style which places communication and diversity of character above all else. But behind this lurks a tendency to view such diversity as a lack of spirituality and to picture people in animal images. Lowell needs to take a new look at himself, and in the final section of [*Life Studies*] the effect of this look is a long smoldering break with Joycean ideas. (p. 103)

*Jerome Mazzaro, in his* The Poetic Themes of Robert Lowell *(copyright © by The University of Michigan 1965), University of Michigan Press, 1965.*

I think the real and radical importance of [Lowell's] best . . . poetry [is that it] does not create a world of its own in its age, but looks out.

Lowell's poetry looks out in an unexpected direction. It yearns towards non-existence. If a poetry can be said to have the death-wish, it has it. As his poetry has transformed itself it has perfected a capacity for self-extinction. The words of the early poems lie about helplessly, turgid and swollen: the words of the later ones achieve a crispness of cancellation, leaving behind them only a kind of acrid exhaust smell. A lot of *poets,* no doubt, have had a death-wish, but none have entailed it by method on their poetry—their poetry is on the contrary an insurance against the extinction they may personally seem to crave. . . .

It is Lowell's achievement to have successfully alienated *the poem itself,* to have made it as unaware of us as the suicide caught by the camera flash. And this seems to me the real thing. It gives *Life Studies* and many of the later poems their quality of nicking the advanced edge of time, the moment that burns us before the unmeaning future and the numbed unordered past. . . .

Lowell's most ambitious attempt to create a prophetic myth of the American past and present—*The Mills of the Kavanaughs*—is a complete and incoherent failure. He has written no open public prophecies, no *Waste Land* or *Second Coming.* And one must emphasise . . . that the notion of him as 'important' in that way is quite misleading. He is not a prophet, but his best poems are in themselves prophetic indications of a state which may be becoming increasingly common in Anglo-American society, the state in which traditional 'feelings' are ceasing to exist, or to have their traditional status assumed—the state in which more and more people come to have knowledge of, even to desire, the symptoms of clinical alienation.

It is this state which Lowell catches, in himself and others. But the 'others' are in fact usually himself, for . . . one cannot project madness. . . .

In [his "imitations"] Lowell still seems to be attempting . . . the rhetorical and explanatory side of his poetry which is also its weakest side. However much he is expected to be in America he simply is not a poet of the 'big bow-wow'—he is a big poet who cannot write 'big' poems. Unquestionably his best poems to date are the most seemingly trivial ones, poems which find their precision and their weight in the slightest context; and when he moves us, as in such a poem as *Man and Wife,* he does no unexpectedly and as it were unmeaningfully, as Dryden does in his *Epistle to Congreve*. In an age when destruction and madness oppress the poet, like every other citizen, Lowell has learnt not to write about these things but to take them on; and he has taken them on with brilliant success and logic in terms of a style which can perfectly *be* its own alienation, if it can be little else.

*John Bayley, "Robert Lowell: The Poetry of Cancellation," in* London Magazine, *June, 1966, pp. 76-85.*

As we read *For the Union Dead,* we realize that two intellectual traditions, both bankrupt, have come together in the book. One is the entire string of intellectual longings represented by the history of the *Partisan Review*. The *Partisan Review* writers never broke through to any clear view of modern literature or politics. Their insistence on the value of alienation, their academic notions of modernism, are dead, like fatigued metal.

Phillip Booth foolishly compared Lowell to Whitman in his review, but Lowell's book embodies exactly what Whitman was fighting against. *For the Union Dead* has a peculiarly stale and cold air, instantly recognizable. It is the air of too many literary conversations, an exhausting involvement with the Establishment.

Since the ideas behind the book are decrepit, Lowell has no choice but to glue the poems together with pointless excitement. The persistence of bodiless excitement derives from a second bankrupt tradition which is centred on the notion that an artist must never be calm, but must be *extreme* at all costs. This destructive notion, a bourgeois notion, flows from both right wing influences on Lowell, like Tate, and left wing influences like the *Partisan Review* writers.

Lowell has always had a poor grasp of the inner unity of a poem. In *Imitations* he inserted violent anal or explosive images into quiet, meditative poems—his translations of Montale for example—without realizing that the sensational images had destroyed the inner balance of the poems. In *For the Union Dead* he does the same thing to his own poems. . . .

*For the Union Dead* is something rare, a book of poems that is a melodrama. . . .

Men write melodrama when the ideas available to them are dead. Lowell tells us that modern life makes everyone nervous, that we shouldn't support South American generals, that gods seem less real as we grow older. The ideas Eliot and Stevens put in their poems had size and vigor; Lowell's ideas are banal and journalistic. They have no life of their own, and are painfully incongruous in poems intended to be on the highest level. . . .

What Lowell is doing . . . is counterfeiting. He is counterfeiting intellectual energy, pretending to be saying passionate things about tyrants and hangings, but in fact he gives only a series of violent words set next to each other; the indignation is ersatz. . . .

*Robert Bly, "Robert Lowell's 'For the Union Dead'," in his* Sixties #8 *(copyright © 1966 by Robert Bly; reprinted with permission), Sixties Press, 1966.*

[The] stereotype of Lowell as the confessional poet struggling for identity is only half true. The forces of darkness that swell in his mind and those that aggrandize the world are often the same: the history of his personal salvation cannot be separated from the social and political destinies of his countrymen. . . .

Lowell's ambivalent attitude to the Puritans is central to an understanding of his poetry. Although he repudiates them intellectually, he is at home with their buffetings and morbidity. From them he takes or rather corroborates the habit of self-examination and the strenuous burden of their, at times inexplicable, guilt. They are the injectors of a foul self-righteousness into the national life; they are carved in the heroic mold but are mean-spirited (the poet, self-castigating, sees himself as the inheritor of a "poor bred-out stock"); they are visionaries but theirs is a carrion vision. . . .

The Puritans wrestled with the devil, with the powers of blackness, and this drama, spelled out in their theology and acted out in the colonial experience, intrigues Lowell. The serpent is an omnipresent figure in the gardens of his America. Evil is double-dealing, vital, corporeal; it inflicts a lasting isolation. . . .

Lowell excels at funerary art, at epitaph-making, and in the elegaic sequence "In Memory of Arthur Winslow," the finest poems in *Land of Unlikeness,* he mingles his Gothic religiosity with ambiguous pride in his birthright and discomfiture at the Puritan heritage—even if his ancestors had not burned any Salem witches like Hawthorne's. The weight of his ancestors is heavy; they speak to him from the grave of loss: loss of power, loss of a secure selfhood, loss of grace. . . .

Notwithstanding his God-intoxication, his Edwardsean belief that God is glorified by Man's dependence, Lowell cannot shake free of his confusions and overwrought crises to write simply about the things that matter to him: his boyhood, family, and Americanness; his sense of engulfing chaos. It is not a matter of insincerity—Lowell believes that he believes and that he is unworthy of grace—but poetically his Catholicism is probably responsible for the Baroque embellishments of his language, for a feigned knowledge and contrived emotionalism, whereas his Puritanism, as in "Children of Light," calls forth a spare, stark language and a relative fidelity to his emotions. . . .

The world of Lowell's poems is a world of wonderful particulars. The qualities most conspicuously missing in his verse are not hard to locate: joy and jubilation certainly, in Stevens' phrase, "the rotund emotions". . . . But Lowell has what no other American poet writing today has: scale, featly energy, inventiveness. His singular achievement does honor to his ancestors and to his predecessors in the American tradition: it illuminates the moral history of our time.

*Herbert Leibowitz, "Robert Lowell: Ancestral Voices," in* Salmagundi I, *Fall-Winter, 1966-67.*

It would appear that the domain of Robert Lowell's *Imitations* is public rather than private in character [and that] . . . Lowell, like Pound and Eliot, has employed a mode of translation to enact a repertory of "personae" native to his irascible and inquiring genius; that what we have is, in fact, not an anthology of European poetry, but a species of dramatism: an artist's mimicry of other artists. . . .

The "one voice" "running through many personalities, contrasts, and repetitions" is unmistakably the voice of Robert Lowell—the most eventful and passionate voice of our epoch, whose voracity matters because it helps to give character to our century. Its impersonations, collapses, reassertions are never parasitical in the morbid sense of enacting flights from the poet's responsibility, or providing lines of least resistance in a peripheral struggle for existence.

On the other hand, little is to be gained from rushing to the defense of the *Imitations* with toplofty disclaimers which pay the poet the dubious compliment of removing him from the imputation of translation entirely. . . .

It is to be hoped that with the passing of time and the channelization of a sensibility which hindsight now shows to have been constantly "histrionic," Lowell will continue to leaven the integrity of his translation. Ultimately, there should be no need for him whatever to remove himself from the rank and file of translators as such, or work in a special aura of privilege, in the name of "imitation." I say this without much hope that translators are ever any the wiser for having translated for a decade or a lifetime, or that they can ever hope for Adam's dream, who "awoke and found it true."

*Ben Belitt, "'Imitations': Translations as Personal Mode," in* Salmagundi, *Winter, 1966-67.*

[Robert Bly's] review [of *For the Union Dead*] disregards almost entirely the integrity in Lowell's dealing with the teleological problems of his vision and launches an attack into his failure to form an acceptable, practicable socio-political program. Bly extends this failure generally to writers whom he groups about *The Partisan Review*. . . . The disappointment might have been less had Bly disregarded *The Partisan Review* altogether and proceeded along lines suggested by Ralph Waldo Emerson's "Self-Reliance" that the failure to believe in one's values makes for a literature and a life whose excitements can only be pointless. He might have then seen that Lowell's current message to a post-Christian world is precisely the portrayal of fatigue, decrepitude, and pointless excitement. . . .

The means by which Lowell seems to come to grips with the substance of his vision . . . is twofold. First, having gained in the interval distance from his once Christian convictions, he is able now, for the purposes of his art, to sustain perspectives in which he does not necessarily believe. He is able to do so because in an age of overkill such perspectives evoke nightmare visions of a world either destroyed by continuing its wrong idea of a struggle for existence or else reduced to an equally destructive sado-masochism in the drive by its populations to prove their existences through their powers to inflict and endure pain. The real fears of both prospects in the absence of a constructive alternative contribute to Lowell's ability to make them visible, human alternatives rather than mental hypotheses. Moreover, he is able to strengthen his distance from them by adding to the outlines of the masks he formed elements which either so repulse his nature that they preclude his sympathy or so work to reinforce his initial antipathy that they provide complementary, supporting arguments. . . .

Next, the effect in Lowell's poetry of this gained distance is a temporary acceptance of an ironic view of life similar to that which began his career. Then, the intensity of a Christian vision in a world of perverted Christianity on the verge of the Last Judgment turned the irony into a source for invective and satire. Now, as his protagonists lack the grace for meaningful action, the irony results in a picture of the combined futility and absurdity of weighing the minimal actions which man can muster against an irresolvable purpose. Time and again these actions turn into a mockery of the protagonist as Lowell ends his poem by evoking a Schopenhauerian future. This future, if it will not solve the problems of meaning raised, will at least distance them into some perspective that perhaps may overcome their pain as time is reputed to heal all wounds. Thus, what begin as basically personal and ontological poems evolve into seemingly didactic, impersonal observations which record simply the biding of time.

The movement to these final observations with their releases from the bondage of the present by the acceptance of this Schopenhauerian will recalls structurally the release or escape to God in the contemplative poems of Lowell's initial volumes. A similar pattern of vividly constructed scenes which start off the contemplation which, in turn, proceeds to annihilate and escape the scenes is established. However, whereas the pattern of this annihilation in the contemplative poems followed a progression of humility (self-knowledge) to love (knowledge of others) to contemplation (knowledge of God), the pattern now seems to flow from egoism (the impulse toward one's own good) to malice (the impulse toward others' woe) to compassion (the impulse toward others' well-being). This last impulse, under the guise of Christian charity, is probably Lowell's strongest link with the past. . . .

In concert, the poems reveal that man is somehow at odds with the structure of his world and ill-equipped to create permanent new structures without some sort of absolute purpose. On the basis of the purposes suggested by any of the perspectives left after Christianity, Lowell advocates a preservation of Christian charity or Schopenhauerian compassion as basic to all social reform since it establishes the spirit for law. On this spirit rather than on law or social institutions, Lowell bases his socio-politics. Thus, the few specific references which he makes to social and economic reform are principally to structures which have been outdistanced rather than to structures which should come into being. . . .

Lowell may no longer be able to see the true city of the religious mystic or even of the romantic, he can still tell the Vanity Fairs along the way. He may no longer be the conscientious objector crying out against the evils of war in *Land of Unlikeness* and *Lord Weary's Castle,* or the Arnoldian in "The Mills of the Kavanaughs" and *Life Studies* struggling with a belief in personal relationships which gives out in *For the Union Dead.* Nevertheless, he has still not lost faith with human concerns, nor with history, or rather faith with the inevitable will, which for him is now the reality of the future.

*Jerome Mazzaro, "Lowell After 'For the Union Dead'," in* Salmagundi, *Winter, 1966-67.*

From the first Lowell's poetry has had an inner force bespeaking his great native gifts. It has put him in the class of wonder boys, along with poets like the early Auden and Dylan Thomas who, however idiotic they may sometimes look in other respects, were simply unable to write a trite or flaccid line. . . .

In each stage of his poetic evolution, Lowell has written a few poems that seem to me extremely fine, and he has also written poems that seem to me mannered, pointless, incomplete, and obscure. Indeed, try as I may—and I have tried again and again over the years—some of his poems, particularly his earliest and then again his latest, remain incomprehensible to me, as dark and profuse as a pot of Bostonian whistleberries. Moreover, I cannot escape the feeling that some of this obscurity has been purposely, even crassly laid on. For me, this is the single largest detracting element in his work. . . .

Lowell's defect is a temptation to mere appearance, to effects, trappings—to the extraneous. And it arises, I believe, from a discrete imagination, i.e., an imagination which works best in disjunctive snatches. I suppose some people would call it an analytic, rather than a synthetic, imagination. His problem as a poet during the past fifteen or twenty years has been to continue digging deeper toward his essential theme, while at the same turning, if it is possible, his defect into an advantage. . . .

Lowell's methods are distinct from those of Ezra Pound. This is a distinction we must be careful to draw, I think, because Pound's methods have become so much second-nature to us all that they blur our recognition of the principal fact about the two poets, viz. that the historical gulf separating them is enormous. . . . Pound's work, in effect, is an Arnoldian criticism of life on a very grand scale, which is only possible because the critic looks out from the secure bastion of his own personality founded on a stable scheme of values. Lowell, on the other hand, is a poetic ego without fixtures: in a sense neither being nor becoming, but a sequence of fragments, like the individual frames of a movie film, propelled and unified by its own creative drive. This does not mean that Lowell's work lacks values; his poems are as strenuously moral as anyone's. But his objective is not critical, nor even broadly cultural; it is personal; and the moral elements of his poetry are used, not as precepts, but as the hypotheses of an experimental venture in self-validation. In his autobiographical work, both translations and original poems, Lowell employs many of Pound's devices, perhaps most of them, but his ends are his own—and this makes all the difference. . . .

Why has Lowell moved progressively away from the simplicity of *Life Studies* toward a new formalism? . . .

No doubt [various] reasons . . . are at work. But the result is a too great concentration of effort upon the verbal surface—to my mind very unfortunate. We now have poems which are compositions of brilliant minutiae, like mosaics in which the separate tiles are so bright and glittering that we cannot see the design.

*Hayden Carruth, "A Meaning of Robert Lowell," in* The Hudson Review *(copyright © 1967 by The Hudson Review, Inc.; reprinted by permission), Vol. XX, No. 3, Autumn, 1967, pp. 429-47.*

What Robert Lowell has done in his poetic translations, which he calls "imitations," is to return to the medieval mode: to retell a poem as though it came from some communal stock of plots or *topoi* in his own terms. One difficulty with this is immediately apparent. The medieval poet drew on stories that were vaguely but widely known, and his hearers or readers expected both a certain fidelity to and a certain variation on the themes. This poet-translator was dealing with stories in verse, and long story poems lend themselves to such "retelling": more or less following an outline while improving on some particular, embellishing a detail. But when poetry becomes predominantly lyrical and highly personalized, there is no story line to cleave to: everything is in the imagery, prosody, diction, sound. You render these—to the extent that you are able—or you render nothing. . . .

The begetter of Lowell's imitations is, without question, Pound, and particularly the Pound of the versions from Propertius. But though I am no great admirer of Pound's Propertius (and even less of such jesuitical champions of Pound's Propertius as Hugh Kenner), I cannot be wholly unmoved by Propertius's Pound, that is to say, by what Propertius brought out in Pound. But it is precisely because Pound was able to ignore his original so sublimely, and because Pound is a great enough poet in his own right, that the damage to Sextus Propertius becomes an homage to Ezra Pound and English free verse. Lowell, however, is not that free from his models, nor has his free verse the energy and variety of Pound's. It is the neither-fish-nor-fowlness of Lowell's imitations, plus all the red herring they contain, that makes them perverse as translation and unpalatable as poetry. And though there may be only a tenuous connection between literature and morality, there seems to me to be a more demonstrable one between this kind of translation and immorality.

*John Simon, "Abuse of Privilege: Lowell as Translator," in* The Hudson Review *(copyright 1968 by The Hudson Review, Inc.; reprinted by permission), Vol. XX, No. 4, Winter, 1967-68, pp. 543-62.*

*The Old Glory* is [a] disappointment. Whatever one thinks of Lowell as a poet it ought to be obvious that his subjects are limited and his manner is nearly always violent. Both conditions would suggest that Lowell's talents are best suited to the short poem and not to the verse drama; and for me the best writing in Lowell is to be found in the short poems such as "The North Sea Undertaker's Complaint," "Water," "Caligula," and "The Severed Head": on the other hand none of the plays seems successful to me, and one of the reasons may be that Lowell has developed skills for writing short poems which are not suited to longer works. The main difficulty, however, is that Lowell's plays inescapably invite comparison with their sources, with the result that Lowell comes off rather badly. Two of the plays are based on tales by Hawthorne and the third and best play, *Benito Cereno,* on Melville's short novel.

*Kenneth Fields, in* The Southern Review, *Vol. V, No. 2, Spring, 1969, p. 574.*

I suspect that the complaint one sometimes hears about nothing happening in Lowell's plays has less to do with stage action than it does with characterization. . . . [The] characters in Lowell's plays . . . do not climb off the page, as do Uncle Vanya and Big Daddy and George and Martha. Even on stage, they can suggest men, down to the details of thought and gesture that make individuals, without quite becoming men. In part, this is because Lowell's plays are not in the realistic tradition. Yet, I am not faulting Lowell's characters because they are not true-to-life, as the cliché has it, but because they lack theatrical validity. They are somewhat hedged in by his virtues—his intellectuality, his irony, his sense of language, his emphasis on theme, his preoccupation with the major concerns of our or any time.

*Gerald Weales, in his* The Jumping-Off Place: American Drama in the 1960's *(reprinted with permission of Macmillan Publishing Co., Inc.; copyright © 1969 by Gerald Weales), Macmillan, 1969, p. 179.*

Lowell has been in and out of mental institutions as well as jail. . . . It is interesting that Lowell mentions Catholicism in . . . poems about both lunatic and criminal: they are all Outsiders. . . . Lowell's poetry, his lunacy, his felony, and his Catholicism all conspired in his revolt against the heritage of the Puritan Fathers. But he is a puritan, a father, a patriot and WASP citizen, descendant of the Mayflower, at the same time that he contrives his revolt. . . . These are the roots of the tensions that animate his poems. They reach deep inside the American conscience. (p. 25)

The revolutionary energy of which *Life Studies* was a center was exactly [as Eliot wrote in "A Talk on Dante," *Kenyon Review,* Spring, 1952] "to make poetry out of the unexplored resources of the unpoetical"—including the private, homely, or indecorous, or even the prosy minutiae of the poet's own life. I have heard it maintained that the real innovation in *Life Studies* was not so much to treat the everyday as to use the poet's own personal history as subject, *contra* Eliot's influential conception of the impersonality of poetry. But this is to take a very narrow view of Eliot's idea, as well as of Lowell's poems. Eliot did not mean that the personal should be avoided, only that it should be transformed; and Lowell's treatment of autobiographical material, in Pearson's words [in *The Review,* March, 1969], "was not making his poetry more personal but depersonalising his own life." (pp. 38-9)

*Life Studies* channeled a flowing together of currents long waiting to be combined. Its antecedents include, I believe, not only the work of William Carlos Williams and Allen Ginsberg, but also *Prufrock and Other Observations,* to mention only the earliest of Eliot's poems. And its theory can be found in [Eliot's] famous essay on "The Metaphysical Poets," whose incidentally lofty distinction between the poet and the ordinary man may have thrown half a century of readers off the real track: "When a poet's mind is perfectly equipped for its work, it is constantly amalgamating disparate experience; the ordinary man's experience is chaotic, irregular, fragmentary. The latter falls in love, or reads Spinoza, and these two experiences have nothing to do with each other, or with *the noise of the typewriter or the smell of cooking*; in the mind of the poet these experiences are always forming new wholes" (italics mine). (p. 39)

*Lord Weary's Castle* is a book of lyrics in the grand manner. By way of a lyric ambivalence that is dramatic and universal, it engages themes as large as Milton's and Shakespeare's. At the same time, it is an intensely personal book: the problem of evil is brought all the way home; the monster finds his tongue in colloquial speech. (p. 54)

Lowell's descent from the high style of *Lord Weary's Castle,* through the dramatic but still elevated monologue, "The Mills of the Kavanaughs," to the low style of *Life Studies* and after, enacts a movement of the pattern [Geoffrey] Hartman describes [in "Structuralism: The Anglo-American Adventure," *Yale French Studies,* October, 1966], and corresponds to a profanation of the sacred. The development of Lowell's style recapitulates, by analogy, the pattern of mythic descent, the *descensus Averni,* required for the renewal of the seasons. The project of renewal is familiar in both myth and poetry. (p. 69)

The cycle of the *Notebook* is a paradigm of renewal. Renewal of his life, renewal of his work, was the special need that governed the book's inception. (p. 140)

Behind the breaking and re-establishing of illusion, behind the artifice of the autobiographical awareness, and implicit in the equation of the life with the writing, of the body of the poet with the corpus of his work ("this open book . . . my open coffin"), is the figure of the circle. The *Notebook* is bound by the circle of a year, and its parts reflect corresponding cycles of all sorts: the "invisible/coronary," crowning and circular network of the bloodstream; the cycles of the earth's waters, through the rivers, to the ocean, and back again across the sky; the paths of the stars; the cycles of human and animal conflict and generation, mindful and mindless, mythic and historical; the pattern of the seasons, the year. These are not the subjects of the poems, but implicit and traditional clues to their coherence. The awareness of their fabric brings together, in a single thought, poetry, "the little myth we make," and history, "the big myth we live, and in our living, constantly remake." Not only is there no contradiction; poetry and history validate each other. (pp. 151-52)

*Philip Cooper, in his* The Autobiographical Myth of Robert Lowell, *University of North Carolina Press, 1970.*

Lowell shows affection for individuals in his family history but he is obliged always, even when he is not raging at the hypocrisy and determined brutality that gave New England birth (as in 'Concord') to 'place' them—and thus diminish them—because they do not meet the terrible standards set for the 'unblemished Adam'. This critical alienation from his heritage has had profound effects on Lowell, for it has meant that the New England and family material which forms so great a part of his work, is never or rarely central to the ambition and drive that characterises his best as well as his weakest poetry. It is not so much, indeed, that his disdain and disgust come between him and quotidian experience (no modern poet uses the *bric-à-brac* of life more richly or rewardingly) but that they come between him and a just judgement of experience: common sense alone would revolt against so total a claim that the historical and individual activities of men were so profoundly against the grain of the search for God which New England believed characterised its history and which Lowell has said dominates all poetry. But Lowell could not, in his earlier work, achieve a morally balanced understanding of the strengths and frailties of men because of the religious demons that whipped him on in the search for the loudest possible religious affirmation. (pp. 18-19)

[An] inherent violence—moral in appearance, probably partly psychological in origin—is inseparable from Lowell's work at its fullest stretch. Secondly, though this violence is highly personal—even his religious views were nearly heretical—the true ambition of the poet is public; that is, he burns to judge men and affairs against an immutable and objective standard. The work is public, too, in a more obvious sense, in that much of it deals with the world of politics and public affairs. (pp. 23-4)

Occasionally—and most particularly in *Life Studies*—Lowell uses a symbolism too private, too inexplicable to bear the weight of emphasis he puts on it; he never falls victim to the counter-vice of neurotic over-explanation. A great source of strength has, of course, been his close study of the poetry of other times and languages, which bears fruit in the *Imitations*. The great courage of Lowell, however, is shown in his determination to judge experience, from which he rarely relents, and to judge it—as the whole corpus of his work, particularly in its intricate system of reference to history shows—by objective and immutable rather than contemporary and personal standards. In him the ambition is devised which was natural to the eighteenth century: but it is there and it forms the link with the great tradition of public poetry. (p. 36)

Lowell [eventually] abandoned religion as the source of an independent system of moral reference and evaluation to put against quotidian experience in his verse. The trouble with his religious structure was, of course, precisely its failure to provide him with—or his failure to find in it—a wide and flexible system of values. (p. 44)

The inadequacy of both poetic forms and religion as life systems left Lowell with only New England and, in a wider sense, America, as subjects. In small domestic poems (notably in *For the Union Dead*) and in wry moments of affection for his ancestors, Lowell achieved a certain balance, a momentary tranquillity. But fundamentally, perhaps because he was still struggling to free himself from its theology, he found more to hate than to love in his own history. New England and his hate threatened also to swallow him up, because his own attitude of total condemnation was as inhuman as what he was attacking, his own total condemnation of the self-righteousness leading to injustice of historical New England culture was ultimately destructive.

Lowell was left with himself, with the richness or poverty of his own nature and personality, which he lacerated in search of truth in *Life Studies*. This unrelieved focus—of, say, 'Skunk Hour'—could not long be maintained without madness. Lowell was left with two resources. One was the private and obscure world of historical analogy of 'Falling Asleep over the Aeneid': but this is always ultimately incomplete and unsatisfactory because . . . we can only see that there is some analogy, not what it is. Nevertheless, though flawed, work in this vein is impressive, if neither wholly satisfactory nor commensurate in achievement with Lowell's ambition. The other resource was the *Imitations*, the one mode of work which has remained constant throughout Lowell's development. If only because they are so consistent a resource for the poet, I believe the *Imitations* have been insufficiently attended to. (pp. 45-6)

The imitations . . . represent a deliberate apprenticeship on his part, a cultivated vocation for poetry, enjoying a separate existence—an educational existence—from his own work.

It seems to me that this concern is ultimately self-critical and represents the sense in which Lowell's devotion to the craft of poetry is pure, disinterested, concentrated and objective, the sense in which it is separate from and standing above the egocentric non-poetic and anti-poetic tendencies that intrude so frequently into his own original work. The pursuit of the imitations reminds us of the extent to which Lowell's triumphs are triumphs of will. There is a sense, of course, in which poetry and literature generally can be thought of as enjoying a separate existence—an existence on a different moral plane—from the human experiences, with or without order, on which it draws for substance and sustenance. The cultivation of such a belief is, however, dangerous, because it may tend to separate the poet from human nature, separate him from the human concerns of his species. This is a danger Lowell has often met and often fallen victim to; nonetheless, in the end, the failures that resulted from his falls may have well been worth the achievements purchased by his deliberate dedication. (pp. 206-07)

*Patrick Cosgrave, in his* The Public Poetry of Robert Lowell *(copyright © 1970 by Patrick Cosgrave; reprinted by permission of Taplinger Publishing Co., Inc., and Victor Gollancz, Ltd.), Taplinger, 1970.*

In *Life Studies,* which marked the beginning of what has been called confessional poetry, Lowell's techniques of self-discovery exclude myth; he concentrates on the personal and intimate episode, and his language is direct and sometimes colloquial. Important as this volume is as an expression of Lowell's new voice and his growing power to elicit from the absurd remark or the pathetic incident a link to the deepest levels of human suffering, and vital as it was in influencing younger poets, such as Sylvia Plath and Anne Sexton, it represents only one phase of his development as a poet. Lowell has gone on in later works to combine the mythical method of his early poetry with the direct and sometimes shocking psychological revelations of *Life Studies* and, in so doing, has reached beyond the compulsive inner probings of that book for a deep and intimate knowledge of human feelings as they are manifested in the larger realm of natural, social, or political life.

*Lillian Feder, in her* Ancient Myth in Modern Poetry *(copyright © 1971 by Princeton University Press; reprinted by permission of Princeton University Press), Princeton University Press, 1971, p. 408.*

The sequence [*The Dolphin, History,* and *For Lizzie and Harriet*] records the poet's change from one life and marriage in America to a new life on new terms with a new family in England. This shift in geography and emotion is set down in fourteen-line poems of such stunning technical power and control that their art and skill go almost unnoticed. Lowell's long training in classical forms has enabled him here to produce verse which at its best is beyond the powers of any other living poet including Auden. The poems move out into a new and enlarged sensibility where the matter-of-fact joys of life are recognized and accepted, holding in balance the old demons, time and death. Lowell has left behind him the liabilities of worn-out emotions and narrow insatiable concerns and brought his poetry at last with certainty to the high open ground of greatness.

Virginia Quarterly Review, *Vol. 49, No. 4 (Autumn, 1973), p. cxxxviii.*

Robert Lowell's career has exemplified in every phase [a] perspective which I have identified as "modern"—the thrust towards ever-more-direct confrontations with time. Both *Land of Unlikeness* and its impressive sequel, *Lord Weary's Castle,* reinvigorate conventional forms while courting a future of apocalypse. Filtering his vision of contemporary America through the context of a sordid American tradition, Lowell achieves tremendous power by an almost total rejection of the present. The apocalypse follows hard upon the sins of America's past, and the poet treats the time from which he prophesies as minimal. The violence of language and tone in Lowell's early poems suggests that the poet-prophet behind them already finds himself surrounded by the sparks of the "fire next time," after which there will be no next time. . . .

Although the two earliest volumes of Lowell's poems present themselves as poetry of vision, Lowell substitutes for this a poetics of revision in subsequent work. On the most basic level, even *Lord Weary's Castle* is a revision of *Land of Unlikeness.* A passage from "Cistercians in Germany" (*Land of Unlikeness*) is rewritten to form the ending of "At the Indian Killer's Grave" (*Lord Weary's Castle*); poems like "The Quaker Graveyard in Nantucket" provide *Lord Weary's Castle* an air of completeness which *Land of Unlikeness* lacked. But the varieties of revision embedded within both early volumes come to represent, in the later work, both an embryonic subject and a means for the continuation of the poetic enterprise. When Lowell borrows—or "steals"—from Thoreau, Melville, or Milton in "The Quaker Graveyard", he has already begun to reach beyond the simplest interpretations of Pound's command, "Make it new," and has pointed to a self-conscious treatment of literary works as existing and enduring objects—objects which endure largely through their capacity to change under the pressure of the perceiving consciousness. Just as Eliot's "Animula" and "Marina" simultaneously assert the continued existence of Dante's verses and Shakespeare's *Pericles* and also explore a road not taken by the earlier poets, so Lowell's "The Quaker Graveyard" establishes itself through revision, seeing again.

Imitation—seen as a repetition constituting re-vision—is not Lowell's attempt to supplant all previous literature. Rather, it represents his recognition that poetry documents the movement of consciousness—which can only be living—upon the objects of consciousness—which have an observable existence but no living consciousness. In the eyes of Lowell-as-poet, all previous literature exists initially as an aggregation of enduring objects and, eventually and significantly, as an index to a once-living consciousness which can be renewed by an altering re-vision. If Emerson and Stevens directed their attention to the consciousness acting upon the objects of the world, Lowell constructs an imaginative order in which the new poem may openly take those very acts of consciousness as objects for a new subjective creation. . . .

Even in *Life Studies,* the book which has repeatedly been regarded as the poetic autobiography which instituted the contemporary school of "confessional poetry", Lowell was writing a very peculiar sort of confession, because the disjunction between the Robert Lowell writing in the present and the past Robert Lowells which he describes immediately introduces a disjunction between Robert Lowell and other subjectivities external to him. The effort to recapture his own past selves tends to accompany an effort to recapture other past selves.

What initially appear to be the most intensely personal, unborrowed poems in *Life Studies,* poems about Lowell's struggles against madness and the collapse of his first marriage, frequently rely upon complicated movements of the Lowellian speaker into and out of the consciousness of various literary characters. . . .

In *Notebook: 1967-68* (1969) and *Notebook* (1970), the problems inherent in Lowell's allusive techniques have been multiplied, and they have, I think, been met less successfully than in *Life Studies, For the Union Dead,* and *Near the Ocean.* The two editions of *Notebook: 1967-68* gesture compulsively toward the world of experience beyond the poems, and *Notebook* compounds the self-conscious inadequacy of these gestures with an additional appeal to temporal process. . . . Each poem is less an entity than a reminder of the existence of the others; individual poems—and individual words—undergo devaluation in the notebooks. . . .

Lowell's obscurity in the notebooks is the obscurity of a poetry which sets out, through a poetical recasting of a traditional Hegelian view of historical time, to make nonbeing increasingly tangible with the passage of historically poeticized time. In Hegelizing his poetry, Lowell attempts to yoke the passage of personal historical time with a growth analogous to the development of the phases of World-History. . . . Through the poeticized personal history of the notebooks, Lowell clearly struggles to reconcile a language of representation—which represents the world of historical time—with a language of self-consciousness or spirit—which represents the eternity beyond duration. Poetry is his mode of confronting historical time, but poems are not properly objects of historical change, because literary works are (in some sense) intended to endure. In subjecting his poems to historical time by linking them to temporal schemata and by discarding them in progress, Lowell incorporates his own words, his own poems into a language of representation which marks duration. Although some such incorporation seems inevitable in any poetry striving for self-consciousness, Lowell's minimalization treats everything under the rubric of representation and historical time as mere rubble to be stared through. . . . Lowell frequently and finally stakes the poetry of the notebooks on the possibility of wresting a spiritual autonomy from the flux of historical time. But one finishes each of the volumes, *Notebook: 1967-68* and *Notebook,* with a sense of the triviality of historical time and a Satanist's question—Can there be an eternity which is not in love with the productions of time?

*Frances Ferguson, "Appointments with Time: Robert Lowell's Poetry through the 'Notebooks'," in* American Poetry Since 1960: Some Critical Perspectives, *edited by Robert B. Shaw (reprinted by permission of*

*Dufour Editions, Inc.), Carcanet Press, 1973, pp. 15-27.*

In *For the Union Dead* (1965) Lowell's extremes are his familiar ones, of paradise and purgatory; 'We know how the world will end', he writes, 'but where is paradise?' Those moments of nostalgic recall that so beautifully flare up in poems like 'Old Flame' or 'The Lesson' have only the power to hurt; it is in spite of love that we are 'wild spiders crying together' who are doomed to nuclear extinction, who must crack up or hit the bottle, or cling in desperation to the imagery that can merely measure our predicament. . . . The relaxed, digressive sadness of *Life Studies* is tightened up into a sustained, but never hysterical, alarm.

There is no other poet writing at the moment who can match the dense visual accuracy of Lowell's best work; his concentration is insistently upon 'the stabbing detail', his intense demand is always for 'the universal that belonged to this detail and nowhere else'—nothing is inertly factual, nothing is neurotically corrupted; there is fever, but no delirium. By an immensely subtle process of reverberation, his images seem to seek each other out, not to be wise so much as to be confirmed in tragedy, and they are interpenetrated in a structure tight enough to encompass their full range of connotation without any loss of urgency. In the title poem, for example, there is the minimum of actual comment; what seems at first a local scandal is intensified —without the reader really having noticed how—to reveal itself as a profound upheaval in the whole of nature, an 'earthquake', a dinosaur that eats into the heart of America, a nuclear explosion. What really impresses, though, is that even with this much evidently conscious shaping it still comes over as a deeply personal lament for those American images, both private and public, that have meant most to the poet and that are now braced for extinction. Lowell has fought hard to rid himself of Boston, but has returned to it time and again, probing nearer every time towards what he sees as the root of its, and America's, corruption, from the apocalyptic pulpitry of his early poems through the movingly ambivalent elegies of *Life Studies* (1959). In this . . . book it seems much less the private burden of a Mayflower aristocrat, and much more a richly emblematic means of giving voice to the sort of anguished perceptions about modern America that could only spring out of a deep involvement in what Boston can still, if feebly, point to as its failed historical mission.

*Ian Hamilton, in his* A Poetry Chronicle *(reprinted by permission of Faber and Faber Ltd.), Faber and Faber, 1973, pp. 11-13.*

After publication of *The Mills of the Kavanaughs* (1951), a book many regard as a failure, Robert Lowell stated it was difficult for him to find a subject and a language of his own. But by 1959 it was obvious he had found his subject—himself. And the more personal material gave rise to a more personal style, a style modeled upon Lowell's own voice, freed from the early echoes of Hart Crane, Eliot, and Tate, freed from all packed and baroque mannerisms and iambics. If Lowell's earlier work can be summarized as an attempt to reconstitute American history and the Christian experience, these later poems are an attempt to reconstitute his family history and personal experience. And his style changed as radically as his subjects. It is almost as if the abandonment of rigid Catholic dogma tripped a loosening in his own work. . . .

*Life Studies* . . . began as prose. Its intention was to communicate personal history. With their free metrics, there is about the poems a great deal of the accessibility of a prose autobiography. Surely they are the most readable of all Lowell has written.

Readability, however, is not to be confused with ease of composition or ease of comprehension. . . .

This is a poetry of self-discovery and fact far removed from the fiction and melodrama of *The Mills of the Kavanaughs* and the religious allegory and ideology of *Lord Weary's Castle* (1946). One should by no means assume that every statement in *Life Studies* is factually autobiographical. But Lowell's inclusion of the long prose piece, "91 Revere Street"—labeled "An Autobiographical Fragment," and presumably what remains of the autobiography he attempted in prose—confirms that the poems are indeed autobiographical in intent. As never before in Lowell's work, the *persona* gives way to the person, fiction to fact. . . .

While working out his personal salvation in these poems, Lowell in no way exhausted the confessional mode. . . . Lowell continues to define the moral and intellectual passions which distinguish man as a social being, and his poems perform a civilizing function in an increasingly barbaric world. Looking inward, Robert Lowell continues to find images valid for the outward world, and powerful enough to illumine it.

*Robert Phillips, "Robert Lowell: Free-Lancing Along the Razor's Edge," in his* The Confessional Poets *(copyright © 1973 by Southern Illinois University Press; reprinted by permission of Southern Illinois University Press), Carbondale: Southern Illinois University Press, 1973, pp. 18-44.*

[Lowell] shares with Eliot a sense of the decadence of New England culture and a Puritan preoccupation with death and the problem of personal salvation. These qualities strongly mark such early poems as "Colloquy in Black Rock" and "The Drunken Fisherman." In both, Lowell develops themes and images reminiscent of Eliot's *Waste Land* story of the Fisher King, within the metrically regular forms favored by Ransom and the New Critics. . . .

More recent poems, beginning with those of *Life Studies* (1959), reveal a shift away from his early models. In keeping with the trend of the times, the poems are in metrically freer forms. The habitual self-questioning and self-analysis, which have given Lowell a place among modern "confessional" poets, are carried on, but in an autobiographical rather than religious context. Some of the pieces, like the long prose narrative of Section II, "91 Revere Street," explore the writer's introverted childhood and painful family relationships. They are suffused with a sense of alienation and sickness. . . .

An oppressive sense of general corruption (a link with Eliot) is perhaps the most distinctive quality of all Lowell's poetry.

*Walter Sutton, in his* American Free Verse: The Modern Revolution in Poetry *(© 1973 by Walter Sutton; reprinted by permission of New Directions Publishing Corporation), New Directions, 1973, pp. 157-58.*

With a few grave reservations, I find *History* a more satisfying book than *Notebook*. Despite some beautiful interweavings of past and present, public and private (such as the old "Charles River"), *Notebook* was often pointlessly haphazard in its organization. Swamped with irrelevant context, many poems turned obscure or merely anecdotal, that shine with intellectual depth when clustered around common themes: early religions, Romantic melancholy, the anti-war movement. The chronological sequence usually seems natural and dramatic, though there are a few dry stretches, particularly toward the beginning, where Lowell lays too many of his old translations on the Procrustean bed of his new sonnet. (Although some of the new renderings—notably Rimbaud—are both more faithful and better poetry.) A more severe misjudgment is the transplanting of previously successful personal sonnets onto unlikely historical figures—Cassandra, Antony.

After many comparisons, I found the overwhelming majority of Lowell's specific revisions to be in the direction of clarity, proportion, and metrical grace. There is less eccentric speech and syntax, and what remains is correspondingly more telling. For many poems—"Dawn," "The Good Life," "Death and the Maiden," and "Memorial Day," to name only four—placement and revision together make up the leap to greatness. . . .

*History* is a darker book than *Notebook*—perhaps because a countervailing mystical tendency is sequestered off in the accompanying personal volumes; or because the chronological order contributes a double sense of repetition and inexorability. Chillingly and majestically, *History* tells the 20th Century's story of the short road man has travelled, not the 19th Century's story of the long. Everywhere we look we see the awesome dominion of sex and death, the crudely escapist element in the more complicated human enterprises: power and thought, primitivism and transcendence. It is a paradox of genius that Lowell makes so many subjects so interesting to us, when they show him such a painful sameness. . . . [The] Lowell of *History,* like Prospero, renounces his power to spin private worlds, to make symbol win over fact. The choice is hard to love, particularly for admirers of the younger Lowell's grandeur and momentum; but it is impossible not to respect.

*Alan Williamson, "'History Has To Live With What Was Here'," in* Shenandoah *(copyright by* Shenandoah; *reprinted from* Shenandoah: *The Washington and Lee University Review with the permission of the Editor), Winter, 1974, pp. 85-91.*

What is most remarkable about Robert Lowell's *The Dolphin* is its continuous reflexive preoccupation with the problems of self-definition in poetry—problems necessarily elided in order to produce Lowell's great work of self-objectification, *Life Studies.* In *The Dolphin,* Lowell suggests that a writer can approach, but never quite reach, the limit at which self-analysis ceases to be in some sense self-flattery. . . . But the desire to overcome this limit obsesses Lowell on every page of *The Dolphin*. . . .

Adrienne Rich [in *APR,* September/October, 1973] complains of *Notebook* and *History* that "this is poetry constructed in phrases, each hacked-out, hewn, tooled, glazed or burnished," and yet, at the same time, that "at the moment when you thought Lowell was about to cut to the bone, he veered off, lost the thread." These apparent flaws seem to me the result of a deliberate, peculiar honesty in Lowell, in which he uses his own tendency to excessive (or old-fashioned) formal definitiveness in order to clarify the limits of the reality people can bear, the perpetual element of self-consciousness in consciousness. To put it differently, he is attempting to represent action and reaction in his own psyche, to let each mood or insight attempt to become absolute and self-sufficient, to isolate or glaze itself, only to fall before the succeeding one. The great majority of lines are end-stopped, and turn on the lines preceding with a disruptive, sometimes an ironic, force. It is like watching a film just slowly enough to see the lines between frames; a hard, even irritating, effect, but one with definite advantages for self-inquiry, particularly when contrasted with the "surrealist" styles whose extreme fluidity tends to make of the unconscious—whatever its contents—a Peaceable Kingdom.

In moral as well as in aesthetic terms, *The Dolphin* is Lowell's "I am that I am," in which he declares his independence of the judgments of others without thereby exalting his own, or denying the consequences of his actions: "my eyes have seen what my hand did." The controversial letter poems play an important role in this: by letting his ex-wife appear in her own powerful, cogent words, not in his impressions of her; and by letting those words stand in poems by themselves, with no answering intrusion of his own voice, Lowell makes us feel that she cannot be answered, that there can be no literary, or human, resolution of opposing points of view into a more inclusive authorial one. Lowell even weakens his own voice to avoid excessive authoritativeness; he often ends poems, not with the settled epitome of truth the sonnet tradition calls for, but with a sudden influx of new, fleeting, often irrational emotion. . . .

The quality that is meditated and practiced in *The Dolphin* —a reflexive turning on the self that paradoxically defines the self, casts it into three dimensions—is not unique to Lowell, though his current version of it is perhaps more extreme than anyone else's now writing.

*Alan Williamson, "'I Am That I Am': The Ethics and Aesthetics of Self-Revelation," in* American Poetry Review, *January/February, 1974, pp. 37-9.*

In general I have great faith in developing one's good critical facilities by simply attending to three things: the language on the page in front of you, the purposes of the poet in the individual poem and in a body of poems, and your own emotional response [to] what is being said and how the poet is saying it in the poem. With the last premise goes, 1) some humility, 2) some sense of your own prejudices (perhaps even a discussion of them), and 3) an openness to many kinds of poetic expressions. . . .

But what could make Adrienne Rich [in her review of *The Dolphin, APR,* September/October, 1973] read Robert Lowell's magnificent *The Dolphin* with a better critical eye when what she is angrily denouncing is the poet's own life, his own ill-treatment of women, and his morals? . . .

The poems present a world with a magnificent woman named Elizabeth in it. They present a man who is living as he feels he has to live, even when he knows he has no justification for it, but his own passions. He does not ask for pity. He asks one thing, I think, of the reader. Belief in the poems. They are a mythology with characters named Elizabeth and Harriet and Caroline in it. The myth of the prince, inheritor of a throne, father's favorite, who leaves bourgeois morality behind, adopts feudal values yet struggles with a puritan and (ironically) bourgeois conscience. The poems present this so well. It is, in fact, a beautiful book. And Lowell himself becomes the modern anti-hero. Who can love him? Or even pity him? Yet we admire him. Why? Because he has written the very document that chronicles all this. A beautiful book.

*Diane Wakoski, in* American Poetry Review, *January/February, 1974, p. 46.*

* * *

## LURIE, Alison 1926-

**Ms Lurie, an American, is a witty and intelligent novelist. (See also *Contemporary Authors*, Vols. 1-4, rev. ed.)**

Alison Lurie's . . . novel [*The War Between the Tates*] is the neatest bit of literary kung-fu since we have known that name to call it by: at the end of the book the characters are laid out in rows. Yet at the beginning they seem an amiable, deserving enough lot. . . .

The whole operation is performed by Miss Lurie with great dash and readability, and, up to a point, persuasiveness. But there is one source of ambiguity and unease in the book that seriously limits it. Is Miss Lurie offering this devastating account of some very ordinary middle-class Americans as a mirror in which everyone, herself included, must see a reflection of themselves? Or does she feel them to be an utterly different species from herself, mere objects for her proper scorn and malicious pleasure? We don't know what expression there is on her face as she stands back and contemplates the field of slaughter—and we wonder, in fact, if she does, either.

*Derwent May, "Campus Consciences," in* The Listener, *June 20, 1974, p. 808.*

The ironic elision in the title of Miss Lurie's latest conceit [*The War Between the Tates*] is only the first inkling of its small scale; it is, you might say, a mock-Homeric battle between frogs and mice since the intelligent lady has a fastidiousness which reduces small events to miniature. This fits quite neatly with the romance of her suburban heroes, and I was relieved that there were thin walls between me and their ungainliness. . . .

Miss Lurie wields a relentless prose which it is more than a duty to read. It is a pleasure. She has a solid appreciation of the richness of her own intentions, and both style and construction are realised with a strength and tact that remind one of the finest excesses of the early nineteenth century. With a judicious and ironic use of perspective two or three voices are able to come back to haunt both themselves and the narrative, and it is not the merest coincidence that *The War Between The Tates* should concern itself with the hiatus between the perceptions of each character, that variation which is enough to make and unmake different worlds or what Brian Tate would call "spheres of influence" in the interminable book on the Cold War which he is writing throughout the novel. . . .

The authoress is so invisible that you see her everywhere, her interventions couched in a discreet present tense which is the literary equivalent of pursed lips. . . .

And as the net of her prose, transparent though it is, slowly begins to tighten the protagonists are seen to be the breathless and exhausted creatures which they always were. . . . What *The War Between the Tates* has done is to derive intellectual comedy out of a war between ages and sexes that owes more to Thurber than it does to international politics and the 'urban situation.' It defies contemporary America with lucidity and with charm.

*Peter Ackroyd, "Miss American Pie," in* The Spectator *(© 1974 by* The Spectator; *reprinted by permission of* The Spectator), *June 29, 1974, p. 807.*

For 10 years, Alison Lurie has regularly produced insightful and witty novels about The Way We Live Now, drawing on a large talent for social verisimilitude. In her fifth book, with the effortless grace of a real ironic gift, she has raised The Way We Live Now into the Human Comedy. "The War Between the Tates" is a novel not only to read, but to reread for its cool and revealing mastery of a social epoch; something "light and bright and sparkling," in Reuben Brower's phrase for "Pride and Prejudice"; a near-perfect comedy of manners and morals to put on the shelf next to "Vanity Fair" or "The Egoist."

Miss Lurie has been working steadily toward "The War Between the Tates." I have not read her first book, "Love and Friendship"; the other three are all variations on the same theme and the same device for bringing it to life. Miss Lurie's protagonists are always academics or writers; well-read and well-controlled, thoughtful and successful, people of good taste—and hence people especially susceptible to the Call of the Wild and the perfectly rational processes of self-deception. In each case, their carefully-constructed lives and self-images, glowing with conscious enlightenment, break up on the rocks of the irrational, to which they have been lured by the siren song of sheer sexual energy. The resulting splinters reveal the real nature of the personal material. . . .

"The War Between the Tates" is a thing to marvel at, very nearly all that the novel was meant to be.

*Sara Sanborn, in* The New York Times Book Review *(© 1974 by The New York Times Company; reprinted by permission), July 28, 1974, pp. 1-2.*

"The War Between the Tates" will make [Lurie] famous. Having read it, latecomers will want to search out her academic comedy "Love and Friendship," her sharp-edged Los Angeles novel, "The Nowhere City," and her send-up of sociologists and spiritualist cranks in "Imaginary Friends." . . .

The Tates' domestic war breaks out in the spring of 1969 and continues—with truces made and broken, attacks, retreats, defections and battle fatigue—into the summer of

1970. Ninety pages into the book Lurie rolls out a dazzling piece of equipment: a detailed parallel between events in the Tate household and the progress of the war in Vietnam. This metaphor, of Miltonic grandeur and epic absurdity, ascends from the embattled Tate home and floats over the campus of Corinth University like a majestic balloon. . . .

None of Alison Lurie's earlier books was so cunningly plotted. . . . Lurie is a baleful comic artist; in "The War Between the Tates" she is at her most corrosive.

*Walter Clemons, "Uncivil War," in* Newsweek *(copyright Newsweek, Inc., 1974; reprinted by permission), August 5, 1974, p. 64.*

*The War Between the Tates* is Alison Lurie's fifth novel, her longest and most ambitious, yet it is a sober, witty, modest book, like all her others, better perhaps, very touching in places, no "break-through," for her or for fiction. . . .

In *The War Between the Tates* Lurie cheerfully takes on the standard plot—an ambitious professor, his well-educated wife, their domestic boredom and strain, a student mistress for the husband, futile attempts at retaliation and freedom by the wife, and whenever these figures and actions move into the surrounding community, we have clarity and brightness where others usually have managed murky expositions and cute tricks. . . .

In *The Nowhere City* and *Imaginary Friends* Alison Lurie relied with considerable success on neat and clever plotting; in *Love and Friendship* she assayed a romance with markedly less success. In *The War Between the Tates* she has given herself space for her witty observing, she has kept her plot unobtrusive but timed within an inch of its frail life, and she offers another romance, at least of sorts. Since she herself is older, so are her characters, and sadder, too. . . .

When the characters are asked to play parts of some consequence, . . . and Lurie's method with them still remains the same as it does with the background figures, the results are caricatures that can be embarrassing in their simplicity. . . . [Characters] named Jeffrey, Matilda, and Wendy reappear many times without once being anything but utterers of fantastic sounds. . . . Lurie treats [Brian Tate] throughout with the same cool ridiculing air she gives her background characters, and so he becomes a bloated oafish weight around his creator's neck, and she does nothing to relieve herself of it.

*Roger Sale, "The Way We Live Now," in* The New York Review of Books *(reprinted with permission from* The New York Review of Books; *© 1974 by NYREV, Inc.), August 8, 1974, pp. 32-3.*

The "Silent Generation," now in its 40s, is like a piece of sandwich meat pressed between the icy slab of its parent's emotional impermissiveness, and the hot toast of the hippie revolution. It has long since become the Garrulous Generation, but those who do the talking have usually identified with the hot side of their lives.

It is the distinction of Alison Lurie's novel [*The War Between the Tates*] that, uncruelly and unsatirically, it is not encouraging about the degree of humanity on either side. . . .

This novel could use more grounding in nature and in a sense of the texture of places as counterpoint to social realities. . . . But the strength of the book is in Lurie's detached ability to describe rather than judge, with results far more devastating than denunciations. While Alison Lurie has been compared to Austen, she seems to me closer in spirit to Colette; though not yet as fine a writer as Colette, she could be, and like Colette she has that inestimable icy warmth which is a literary and human accomplishment of high order.

*Martin Washburn, in* The Village Voice *(reprinted by permission of* The Village Voice; *© 1974 by The Village Voice, Inc.), August 8, 1974, p. 27.*

I imagine Alison Lurie puts on surgical gloves before sitting down at the keyboard of her typewriter. She comes equipped with scalpel, hemostat, forceps, rongeurs. She operates on her characters. Their hopes, illusions, pretensions and rationalizations are tumors to be removed. Whether, after the operation, they will recover or relapse is generally left to the reader to decide. In her four previous novels—*Love and Friendship, The Nowhere City, Imaginary Friends, Real People*—she seems to have wearied of her elegant work and to have gone home before the anesthetic wore off. *The War Between the Tates* is no exception. . . .

Now there are a great many pleasures to be found in *The War Between the Tates*. There is, for one thing, the faultless prose, like an English lawn. One could play polo on such prose, swatting ideas with a mallet up and down the pastoral field. There are brilliant scenes, dozens of them. . . . After the horses have galloped through each scene, Alison Lurie slips back on the lawn, tamps down the divots, smoothes the way for the next chukker.

There is, as we've come to expect from a Lurie novel, a detachment so profound that we might be looking at tropical fish in a tank instead of people in extremis; an irony so heightened that we're embarrassed for her characters and for ourselves; a comedy so grey that it tickles the frontal lobes while chilling the gut. On her turf—the evasions and self-deceptions of our upper middle classes, the strangled cries of artists and academicians—she is masterful and savage. She bends conventional narrative techniques to her scourging purpose; it is surprising that they do not break, that her well made novels can support so much disdain.

And yet *The War Between the Tates* is an annoying book. Alison Lurie is punishing the Tates for their having thought themselves better than other people, "exceptionally handsome, intelligent, righteous, and successful young people." They end up the novel "ugly, foolish, guilty, and dying." Then why was it necessary to drag in the Vietnam war? Analogies between that war and the war between husbands and wives drag through the pages; the metaphor weighs a ton. Containment, escalation, guerrilla warfare, hostages are not so much alluded to as forced down the reader's throat. Even the rapprochement of Erica and Brian is made to occur at a peace demonstration. Yes, adultery is *the* obsession of American novelists, and maybe it has something to do with our finding out that we aren't the perfect children of the Enlightenment that we believed ourselves to be, but, no, our foreign policy is not an extension of our boredom in the bedroom or our loathing of teenaged ingrates or our self-righteousness about marriage vows.

More significantly *The War Between the Tates* is populated by people who are never permitted to experience their own possibilities, cerebral or visceral. Alison Lurie's clamp is on them. . . .

In their different ways John Cheever and John Updike have covered this turf, too: Updike seeking some lyrical equivalent of the joy of discovery and the pain of betrayal, Cheever finding even in our failures a redeeming humanity, sorrow instead of disgust. Alison Lurie refuses to sympathize, and so this marvelously polished, splendidly crafted novel creates an antiseptic space in the mind: no one can live there.

*John Leonard, in* The New Republic *(reprinted by permission of* The New Republic; *© 1974 by The New Republic, Inc.), August 10 & 17, 1974, pp. 24-5.*

If Alison Lurie's novel [*The War Between the Tates*] is a triumph in familial realism executed by the use of an extraordinary, scornful intelligence, it is also a beautiful example of good writing, perfectly suited to what it is saying. The device of sliding back and forth between the present and the past tense, so annoying in the hands of a lesser writer, here suits her purposes exactly. It gives the novel a simultaneous past and present, moving it at crucial moments out of the narrative past and bringing it into the often-painful immediacy of the current moment. Further, her ear for dialogue at every age level is impeccable, from the shrill ingratitude of adolescents to the self-absorbed egoism of faculty members. Every word of the speech she records rings true. So, there is no possible way we can escape the truth of her observations about the discontents and disappointments of their lives; the shock of recognition is absolute.

Lurie has taken a set of ordinary characters, or at least not exceptional ones, submitted them to the strains and battles of time, sex, legal alliances, generation gaps, politics and work: all the ingredients of a popular novel. But her sensibility and talent are so superior that she has given us an artistic work, which every one will read because it is "common" to us all, but which some will perceive to have the crafted look and feel of first-rate work.

*Doris Grumbach, in* Book World—The Washington Post (© The Washington Post), *August 11, 1974, p. 3.*

Miss Lurie writes . . . coolly and wickedly . . . about all the highly contemporary moral, psychological, sexual, and, above all, practical problems her characters are constantly grappling with. Almost everybody in [*The War Between the Tates*] is a victim of crumbling institutions, self-deception, and half-baked ideas, and when she is finished with them there is very little left but bones and hair. But her tone is not exultant—merely matter-of-fact.

The New Yorker, *August 19, 1974, p. 89.*

[When] one gets past the klieglight superlatives [festooning the dust jacket of *The War Between the Tates*] and proceeds to wade through the book itself, one discovers a handful of chestnuts that have seen better days in better hands. Despite [Miss Lurie's] attempts to be as sharp and mercilessly satiric as she was in her earlier, far superior efforts—*The Nowhere City,* with its scathing portrait of Los Angeles, and *Imaginary Friends,* with its unrelenting mockery of sociologists and quack psychics—Miss Lurie has in fact produced her weakest, most tedious work to date. In part this is because of her subject—the human comedy enacted in an American university. . . .

Though Miss Lurie has tried to update the genre with hippies and peace marches and Women's Lib, not to mention an elaborate but unsuccessful metaphor linking domestic strife with the Vietnam War, all these devices sit leadenly on her trite novel like an undigested meal. . . .

Unfortunately, almost all the wit and wisdom in *The War Between the Tates* has the facile glibness and smug complacency of . . . machine-tooled profundity about the ages of man. The characters are predictable in their mediocrity and unimportant in their fatuousness. Miss Lurie at her best is a lesser Mary McCarthy—much lesser because her scorn is consistently blunted by the cliché lineaments and responses of her cartoon people; her icy distaste is entirely out of proportion to their dull insignificance.

For this reason her new book, though stuffed with the sardonic observation that is Miss Lurie's trademark, seems finally without a point of view. Whenever someone—usually a woman—appears in danger of engaging the reader's sympathy, Miss Lurie retreats into a diffuse, unfocused derision that vitiates judgment altogether. Feeling is the enemy, the meticulously aimed jab the means for keeping emotion at bay. Randall Jarrell wrote of the McCarthy-like lady novelist in his book [*Pictures from an Institution*] that she did not murder to dissect, she dissected to murder. Even this repellent but fascinating cruelty is absent from *The War Between the Tates,* for the objects of its homicidal dissection were dead at the start.

*Pearl K. Bell, "The Overblown and the Overlooked," in* The New Leader, *September 2, 1974, pp. 17-18.*

# M

## MacDIARMID, Hugh (pseudonym of Christopher Murray Grieve) 1892-

**MacDiarmid, sometimes called the modern Burns, is a Scottish lyric poet and essayist, best known for *A Drunk Man Looks at the Thistle,* his long poem written in Lallans, the "synthetic" Lowland Scots literary language. M. L. Rosenthal has said that he is one of the least known poets "who can conceivably be called 'great'." (See also *Contemporary Authors*, Vols. 5-8, rev. ed.)**

MacDiarmid's *Collected Poems* represent a massive achievement. Massive in both senses: although a good many pieces have been dropped by the author, the volume still runs to almost 500 pages; and among them is poetry of the first importance.

But it is also an extraordinarily patchy achievement. Like Shelley, who was the last important English radical poet, or like Ezra Pound with whom, despite their politics, MacDiarmid has a good deal in common, he has written far too much. Even the first slight lyrics run on and on. He finds it hard to let a subject be, or to distinguish between what he once called 'The Kind of Poetry I Want' and the kind of poetry he can write.

There are four stages in MacDiarmid's artistic evolution. In the first, he was a sharp but fairly conventional lyricist with hankerings after God. Then, in the mid-twenties, he started writing in Scots. The language he used put him in touch, at least theoretically, with the audience he was after. Though he was not yet in the C.P., he was a fierce Scottish Nationalist and far on the left. The vernacular poems were written for his ideal readers (whom he probably, like most influential poets, created): proletarian, intelligent, hard, witty, a bit battered and wholly un-English. . . .

[His] best work more than makes up for the boredom, clumsiness and didacticism of the bad. He has managed a curious creative amalgam of old and new, uniting great feeling for his country, its traditions and language, with the strengths of the ideal modern industrial man: virile, unaffected, passionate and, like the poet himself, taking both poverty and learning for granted.

*A. Alvarez, "Hugh MacDiarmid" (originally published in* The Observer, *1962), and included in his* Beyond All This Fiddle: Essays 1955-1967 *(copyright © 1968 by A. Alvarez; reprinted by permission of Random House, Inc.), Random House, 1968, pp. 82-4.*

[It] is clearly from medieval Scottish poetry that MacDiarmid inherits his ability to move from lyric to flyting, as well as his grasp of physical reality. In this, he is more lucky than William Carlos Williams, in whose letters we can trace a baffled resentment at that theory of modern poetics which would deny validity to the ordinary details of twentieth century life. There is a careful recording of a pub scene in *The Waste Land,* but *The Drunk Man,* like the Night-town sequence in *Ulysses,* is written by someone for whom it is a natural backdrop. Does this adherence to a national tradition exclude MacDiarmid from the main concerns of contemporary poetry? From Anglo-American, perhaps, but his answer surely would be that he rejoins contemporary literature at a wider point on the arc, with the semi-public racially conscious poetry of writers, like Lorca and Pablo Neruda.

If the early poetry derives from a willed rediscovery of what the schoolbooks used condescendingly to call the Scottish Chaucerians (I may seem to be riding the point but some recent reviews indicate that English critics are still not prepared to pay MacDiarmid the simple courtesy of recognizing the tradition he is working in) the best of his middle poetry often springs from his fascination with the maimed Celtic tradition. I am thinking of poems like "Island Funeral", "Direadh" and above all, "Lament for the Great Music". . . .

[The] central question of MacDiarmid's career [is that] any attempt to concentrate on an aspect of his work tends to be dissipated by "the seamless garment" of his vision, especially in the later poems. Thus *A Drunk Man* sweeps up all the lyrics and doric-ised reading of a particular period, but the first section of *In Memoriam James Joyce* leans back to incorporate stanzas from "In a Caledonian Forest" *(Stony Limits)* and "In the Shetland Islands" *(The Islands of Scotland),* 1934 and 1937 respectively.

This is the kind of thing which annoys critics bloodhounding for development, though it may well be the clue they are looking for. The primary reason for the change, acknowledged by the poet himself, seems to have been a mystical intuition of the universe as a unity of energies. This was always latent in MacDiarmid, whose early books combine poems of marvellously coarse farmyard detail, like "In Mysie's Bed", with glimpses of interstellar space. . . .

But when he attempts an explicit statement, as in "Moment of Eternity", which actually *opens* the *Collected Poems,* the language is too conventional to convince us that he has experienced Ygdrasil rather than a Shelleyan dream. . . . Nor does he come closer in *The Drunk Man* where the visions of eternity are so locally tethered that he can use "the mighty thistle in wha's boonds I rove" to mock the ending of the *Divina Commedia,* the one real failure of taste in MacDiarmid's masterpiece.

It was at some point afterwards, probably during his lonely sojourn in the Shetlands, that his sense of the endless pattern of the universe became overpowering. . . .

Seamless garment or water of life, there is a force in MacDiarmid's later work which often dissipates the contrast and detail upon which, line by line, poetry must depend. And here perhaps one should enter the dangerous but necessary ground of poetic psychology; for the Universe of Light, the poetic equivalent of the Burning Bush seen by Moses in the Old Testament, is only one of the two primary poetic experiences. There is also the Muse, who, even through the medium of someone else's translation doctored into doric, dominates the variety of *A Drunk Man*. . . .

Certainly he has been for many years the most interesting of what John Berryman once described to me as "the outriders" in contemporary poetry, the only one who has sought to reconcile defiant adoption of a local or special tradition with the international claims of modern poetry. When I first discovered *Stony Limits* in the darker shelves of a Dublin library I was dazzled by its variety and energy, and although I think Austin Clarke has transferred more of the skills of Gaelic poetry into English, and that MacDiarmid's later poetry might be more successful if he had learnt, like David Jones, to break the line for emphasis, his *Collected Poems* makes most contemporary work seem thin-blooded. His aggressive masculine pose may seem inimical to sincerity, but it is close to . . . Wyndham Lewis's famous prescription for modern poetry: one knows that it is a man singing, and not a bird.

*Tom Scott, "'Lament for the Great Music'," in* Agenda, *Autumn/Winter, 1967-68, pp. 19-34.*

Hugh MacDiarmid's work has always been rooted in locality; it is as local as the poetry of Wordsworth or Basil Bunting, both in language and in its sense of place, and, because of this, the intelligence that informs it is international in the best sense. While fighting the stupidity of parochialism throughout his life, he has always realized that true internationalism grows out of, and is indissolubly part of nationalism. It is consequently essential that his work is seen in a native, and European setting and not as an appendage to English poetry whose tradition is at least partially alien to that Scotland. . . .

*A Drunk Man Looks at the Thistle* is one of the very few works of modern literature that never tire. There is a huge pressure of tragic emotion behind the words of "private experience at its greatest intensity becoming universal", to use a phrase of T. S. Eliot, set against a background of the night, the elements, and the dereliction of Scotland in the twentieth century. . . .

It is often said that it is impossible for a poet to write well in a language that is alien to him, and MacDiarmid occasionally writes Southern English with an insensitivity that I think springs from its innate foreignness to the tradition to which he is indigenous. It is doubtful whether any poet could be equally at home in both English and Scots. English for a Scot is the language of prose as Latin was in the Middle Ages. Scots, or Gaelic is the language of poetry and the prosiness of MacDiarmid's later poems stems directly from his decision to write them in English.

But, although the rhythm of his English poems is always closer to that of prose than verse, there are times (*The Lament for the Great Music* is a good example) when the ideas *are* "assimilated by the sensibility" and embodied poetically so that the result is magnificent. This occurs in various contemplative poems where the 'philosophy' stems directly from experiences in desolate or lonely places. MacDiarmid's finest later poems often have this sense of place integrating the fragmentation of his curiosity. This is true of the many memorable poems in *A Lap of Honour,* particularly of *Diamond Body,* with its detailed description of sea flora and fauna that has a quality akin to passages of Agassiz which deal with the "intelligence working in nature". . . . At such times a balance is achieved between all the conflicting elements of his poetry and he goes some way to creating a rhythm to express this. . . . [The] sense of "the interdependencies of life", of serenity, and rest, amid a welter of disparate experience, he never excludes, is probably the most moving quality of MacDiarmid's later work. And although often his language only lamely expresses the true seriousness of his vision, I believe that he has written a body of durable poetry both in Scots, and to a lesser extent in English, that "formed by cataclysm and central fires" and of "broken lights", realizes, at least in flashes,

the harmony of that
Which is,
The pure phenomenon
Abiding in the eternal radiance.

*William Cookson, "Some Notes on Hugh MacDiarmid," in* Agenda, *Autumn-Winter, 1967-68, pp. 35-41.*

MacDiarmid was the first Scots poet whose original verse expressed a post-romantic sensibility; and he was the first to be acutely aware of the contemporary world. . . .

*A Drunk Man Looks at the Thisle,* the first major poem in Scots for at least a century, ranged widely over time and space, exploring the fundamental mysteries of love and death and human destiny. In form, the work was a dramatic monologue, a meditation on Scotland, the world and the universe as these appeared to an intoxicated reveller who had tumbled into a roadside ditch while plodding his weary way homeward from the pub. While his drunken imagination reeled and plunged across the cosmos, the hero delighted equally in the gorgeous and the grotesque, the obscene and the absurd, the mystical and the material, finding beauty in the terrible and terror in the trumpery. Abrupt transitions and sudden changes of mood were dictated by the association of ideas in the drunk man's mind, and the poem proceeded by means of a series of shocks of surprise, as the sublime suggested the ridiculous and the ridiculous the sublime.

Bound together by the complex character of the protagonist, who was by turns a satirical critic of Scottish life, a wondering spectator of his own situation, a lover of beauty whose senses were alive to the finger-tips, and a speculator on the mysteries of time and fate, *A Drunk Man* was at once a portrait of the author, a vision of the world, and an exploration of the nature of reality. "A sardonic lover in the routh [plenty] of contraries," MacDiarmid created new and striking harmonies from elements of comedy, satire, farce, documentary, lyricism and tragedy, the range and richness of his personality going far towards resolving the contradictions of experience. . . .

Hugh MacDiarmid, who has restored Scots as a language of the highest poetical art, is the greatest of all Scots makars, and one of the great poets of the world.

*Alexander Scott, "Hugh MacDiarmid and the Scottish Tradition," in* Agenda, *Autumn-Winter, 1967-68, pp. 42-51.*

Some of MacDiarmid's theories strike me as plain daft, although I find others very convincing and all of them stimulating and, in themselves, a fascinating monument to the most fertile mind Scotland has produced in centuries. I am not here suggesting that MacDiarmid is a great creative thinker and, indeed, I have an idea he was thinking as much of himself as Yeats when he put the following quote at the head of a poem addressed to Yeats: 'The philosophical content of his poetry [Yeats's] is neither consistent nor systematic. The poet was not a creative thinker, and his genius drew from many sources and influences, lacking a supreme originality. Here, in fact, is an intellectualism, which stands apart from the classic English tradition.'

One of the strengths of MacDiarmid as a poet has been his ability to build up these intellectual theories in the eclectic manner ascribed to Yeats in the above sentence and, even more important, when he has outgrown them—as a poet—to disregard them as he builds up new or changed theories. He has often enough attacked others for not accepting ideas which he himself disregards in his poetic practice. These theories then, far from being a restrictive influence on his poetry, have been supporting structures for him and which he especially needed as a poet writing in isolation and in the ruins of the Scottish literary tradition. Without much doubt the most fruitful of MacDiarmid's personal theory building has been that which he built in the twenties and which has been important outside his own poetry in that it has produced the Scottish Literary Revival. But for all that, his theories for a renaissance of Scottish poetry were also one of the main cultural supports for his own poetry. . . .

[The] stance taken by MacDiarmid has been beneficial to Scottish poetry and also I think has served his poetry well in that, as with other of his creeds, he used it but was not slow to ignore it when it suited his purpose. As Yeats said 'passionate man must believe he obeys his reason'.

*Duncan Glen, "Hugh MacDiarmid: Supporting Roles," in* Agenda, *Autumn-Winter, 1967-68, pp. 53-8.*

All poets are political, consciously or unconsciously—if we except the purely vegetable: for the poet whose work does not reflect the most vital and yearning involvement with the social forces of his time must be dismissed as not merely inhuman, but anti-human. Quite frequently, too, the poet is the pioneer and pathfinder in momentous political development, blazing and illuminating the trail, the mere politicians hirpling behind, powerful suction that follows in the wake of the advancing *Zeitgeist*. MacDiarmid is such a poet.

He has had a hand in the founding of every Scottish Nationalist movement in existence—as well as one or two no longer extant. . . .

As long as MacDiarmid is connected with it, Scottish Nationalism is a strong disadvantage to anybody who aspires to acceptance by what is loosely but usefully known as The Establishment. A literary man after a title, or a place in the list of a fashionable publisher, or a University lecturer hoping for a Regius professorship may be a Socialist or even a Communist without too much harm to his prospects; as a Scottish Nationalist he would have no chance whatever. . . .

Monetary reform, Nationalism, Social Revolution. Three political ideas, not disparate, but not equivalent either, in all of whose names great and terrible mistakes have been made, but whose objective validity, for us at least, matters less than their value as fertilising influences on the poetry of Hugh MacDiarmid; poetry, that in an inevitable process of cross-fertilisation, disseminates itself into the minds of the people, who may not yet realise that it is one of the few political forces they have anything to hope from. Until they do, let us do our best to honour this great political poet: enjoy his irony and his economics; his passion and his polemics; his tracts and his tendernesses: all gathered together in a mental grip awesome in its tensile strength; and all released at last in poetry the magic of which is inescapable forever.

*Hugo Moore, "Hugh MacDiarmid in Politics," in* Agenda, *Autumn-Winter, 1967-68, pp. 59-64.*

Although not quite right *neoplatonism* most readily indicates the sort of experiences and ideas central to MacDiarmid's work. . . . This is not to say they are all ideas traceable to Plato or Plotinus, or elements of an independent system adopting their terminology, or occasional intuitions now to be set in order with professional rigour. . . .

What makes neoplatonism in logic a system of such subtlety and complexity, the derivation of the Many from the One, is in the experience of the imagination so simple that in art the difficulty is rather to avoid monotony. Simple as they are, the actions of the imagination are not all of equal force or the same direction. To distinguish their vectors is one of the functions of criticism. The margin of error is large: it ought all the same to be permitted to talk about these things.

An attitude of neoplatonism characteristically English is that of aspiration to the One. It is compatible with other attitudes evincing humility but directed upwards: appeal to mistress, obeisance to monarch, praise of God. These attitudes of supplication and subservience coalesce: Spenser's celebration of Heavenly Beauty has the same poetic vector as his flattery of Gloriana. The causes are no doubt social, the experience of ecstasy having been fitted into a system of feudalism where stress was laid on the difficulty and rarity of rising. If we remain inside the European vocabulary of neoplatonism successful union with the One must then be associated with acts conventionally disapproved: adultery, lèse-majesté, blasphemy. The aspiration may consequently, as in Shelley, be complicated by sentiments of revolt, a spurning of the actual condition, or somersault into the reversal of roles where the last becomes first and Punch hangs the hangman.

To escape this implication of the traditionally English but not originally Hellenistic concept the self-deification of MacDiarmid's poetry is perhaps better mentioned in terms of the identification of Atman with Brahman. In comparison with that of the feudalistic English, MacDiarmid's may be regarded as a neoplatonism turned inside out. Instead of a lovesick serf raising himself from the soil to salute the unattainable you have a genial, uncertain and ill-organized centre, occupied by MacDiarmid himself, from where the extremes of reality are contemplated in directions outward and downward. Both his and the English are monentary if not accidental states, owing little or nothing to spiritual exercise and coloured by emotion. The pitfall of the English is pretension, of the Scots, arrogance. As to the process of unification it seems that three stages are distinguishable: a rather disagreeable narcissism where the mind boosts itself without working, a preliminary irritable thrashing about among notebooks and recollections and, after a moment of incommunicable revelation, entry into the stage where the poet speaks *with a monopoly of movement and a sound like talking to God.*

MacDiarmid leaps the gap between One and Many at the price of rejecting the whole of the middle area of existence where the human comedy is played. His abhorrence of the middle was no doubt reinforced by circumstances: a country denuded of much of the apparatus of national life, its civilization reduced to a mockery of its former self or replaced by organs of *the hideous khaki empire*. The *lonely at-one-ment with all worth while* set up as standard in his lines to Doughty implies the rejection of *all the solemn plausibilities of the world* listed in *Lucky Poet*. MacDiarmid's contempt of the world, the recognition that it is *impossible to rise to position or power without a great sacrifice of human values at every upward turn,* the isolation which begins by avoiding contact and ends by destroying it, contains an intense objection to all movements upward. They are seen not only as proofs of ambition or as suicidal separations from reality but as evidence of a view of the world seen from the bottom or edge. Surely nothing less than a theory of metaphysics buttressed by nationalism and communism could have provoked his attack on the dytiscus beetle, harmless bug.

Established at the centre and ignoring the middle MacDiarmid's poetry reaches out to the remote extremities of the real. It is fascinated by the diversity of detail at the fringe. To the egalitarian intellect one thing is as good as another so long as it differs from everything else. (In MacDiarmid a certain favouritism is apparent for things not exactly animate but which under terrestrial conditions attach themselves to human life: landscapes, colours, jewels, viruses.) Hence his collections of particulars: the lists of stones in *The Kind of Poetry I Want* and *On a Raised Beach,* of tree-colours in *In the fall,* of manual gestures in *The Glass of Pure Water,* of languages and the Norn words for movement of the sea in *In Memoriam James Joyce.* Brilliantly as they are written, these catalogues are not, like those of Joyce or Rabelais, games of a mind exulting in its virtuosity and liberation from constraint. They are counterparts to the hymns to intellectual beauty. Reversing the adoration from below of an abstract and monotonous One, MacDiarmid's poetry celebrates the utmost multiplicity of the Many. . . .

MacDiarmid draws on the sciences for knowledge of the detail running in parallel with them without overstepping the boundaries of discourse. Beyond speech lie the symbolical systems of logic, mathematics, chemistry etc. In its description of ultimate detail, MacDiarmid's poetry goes to the limit set by the rational imagination but not further. Unlike some poetry of today, it does not use language in unusual ways in the hope of evoking by magic or chance a part of the reality that lurks in the gaps between words. It retains the expository character which dominated European poetry of the renaissance up to the romantics. *Wovon man nicht sprechen kann, darüber muss man schweigen.*

But though the unsayable cannot be said, its unsayability is sayable—at least up to a point and then one could say the unsayability of *that.* Having come to the end of what it can rationally and verbally expound MacDiarmid's poetry states the impossibility of going further. . . .

To the extent that neoplatonism derives from the experience of a moment its exposition in poetry tends to be either reminiscence or agitation. It depicts the imperfections of the world in relation to a remembered or potential whole. It therefore easily turns to advocacy of change in the sense defended in the *Second Hymn to Lenin.* Poetry of this kind, operating in the area between representation and action, has for essential function not the mere manifestation of meaning but its utterance with conviction piercing enough to persuade others, with the original energy art can canalise but not simulate.

*Kenneth Cox, "Hugh MacDiarmid's Neoplatonism," in* Agenda, *Autumn-Winter, 1967-68, pp. 65-71.*

It is difficult to explain to Englishmen what Hugh MacDiarmid has meant to Scotsmen of my generation. His politics have often been absurd. It is difficult to be patient with a man who could spend his life fighting for Scotland's freedom from England and then turn round and applaud Russia's crushing the Hungarian revolt. In his public appearances—and in some of his prose essays—he often contrives to present an image of a bar-room orator, cantankerous, argumentative and totally unreasonable. But his poetry, and particularly the poems written in the 1920s and 1930s, are another matter. I do not want here to enter into the old argument as to whether the language, Lallans, which he invented for his purpose has any future. The plain fact is that he used it with magical skill to express his meaning. And what he had to say in *A Drunk Man Looks at the Thistle* rang like a bell in my mind.

He taught us that what was now generally thought of as Scottish culture was sentimental and debased; that, through our own neglect, we had lost or forgotten an earlier, truer

Scottish culture; that until we rediscovered it our lives would be empty and unsatisfying. . . .

Most important of all, he showed, like Yeats and others had done in Ireland, that a literary renaissance could point the way to a renaissance of national feeling.

*John Douglas Pringle, "Anglo-Scot," in* Encounter, *November, 1970, p. 32.*

[Like MacDiarmid] Pound and Zukofsky have sought a poetry of facts . . . but neither, I think, has ever quite separated facts from metaphysics. MacDiarmid has his mysticism; and no doubt science itself is founded on undefined faith: but MacDiarmid sees things washed clean of irrelevancies as Darwin did. Suckling poets should be fed on Darwin till they are filled with the elegance of things seen or heard or touched. Words cannot come near it, though they name things. *Their* elegance is part precision, more music. . . .

For MacDiarmid all knowledge is organized by art and centres round it. He has written much about art, mainly about poetry itself, seen oftenest in the light of complex music. Sometimes his writing seems to be largely an attempt to persuade people muddled by economics and politics, enthralled by feats of technology, that their safety lies at last in poetry and music, poetry as music, words that name facts dancing together.

Thus there is no gulf between the great series of MacDiarmid's didactic and polemical poems—*The Kind of Poetry I Want* for example—and the lyrics, ballads and meditations in Lowland Scots which are nearer to types less literate ears can recognize and some of them well on the way already to being as much loved as the best of Burns. In these, the sound is the sense, whatever a man with a dictionary may make of it, as it is in the best of the songs we inherited from Tudor poets as much musicians as poets. It is not for the likes of me to hamper them with comments. They are for ears. Read them aloud. They are not all modulations on folktunes; but if you can follow a pibroch or disentangle a fugue none will fail to reach you.

To say that MacDiarmid reinvented a nation when he wrote *A Drunk Man Looks at the Thistle* is not a very flagrant exaggeration; by now it is almost a commonplace. Since, he has enriched that nation, not only in poems which boarden the original theme, such as *The Island Funeral* or *Lament for the Great Music,* but with others perhaps less accessible but no less valuable based on interests astonishingly wide which have led him to chase knowledge in many sciences and many languages. He has been fertile and generous. The five hundred pages of what is called his *Collected Poems* fall far short of his output. Two new volumes, *More Collected Poems* and *A Clyack-Sheaf,* still leave much work we will not willingly lose sight of unobtainable, to be the matter for future volumes till someone issues the *Complete Poems* we need.

*Basil Bunting, "Thanks to the Guinea Worm," in* Agenda, *Autumn-Winter, 1970, pp. 117-21.*

Much has been said by sympathetic critics of the way in which the Scots tradition of 'flyting' (literary invective) is powerfully apparent in Mr MacDiarmid's work—a comment which the poet has himself endorsed. Sceptically, one might reply that this traditional coverage makes bad temper a matter of rhetoric and abrasive mirth. Certainly, the note of scurrility is frequently sounded by MacDiarmid, often against those who might have been thought to be numbered with him. . . .

*Lucky Poet,* is . . . an intellectual autobiography and challenges comparison with such works as Heine's *Confessions,* or Herbert Read's *Annals of Innocence & Experience.* Without the elegance and wit of the first or the reflection and mental order of the second, *Lucky Poet* is—what it has been called—a veritable rag-bag of a book: a vast compilation of ill-sorted quotations strung together on a thread of invective. Not that there are not interesting things in it. His chapter on *The Kind of Poetry I Want*—a chapter made up of verse and prose—advances Mr MacDiarmid's notion of a *poetics of fact,* introducing us to his theory and practice as a poet of science and technology. . . .

On the television Celebration Programme for Mr MacDiarmid's 80th birthday, Edwin Morgan described him as the most uneven of great poets he could think of. The same lack of self-correction—of artistic and intellectual distancing—flaws this energetic, annoying and carping autobiography. Mr MacDiarmid tells us he regards *Lucky Poet* as his second most important book—his first, and natural, choice being his volume of verse *A Drunk Man Looks at the Thistle.* All of which goes to show that Mr MacDiarmid is much in the dark about himself and his works—just what one would expect of such a volcano!

*Derek Stanford, "Lucky MacDiarmid," in* Books and Bookmen, *October, 1972, p. viii.*

MacDiarmid belongs, with Pound, Joyce, Eliot, to the great beginning of the modern movement. But the lines of that movement were mapped out some time ago, its tendencies and achievements fixed, excluding MacDiarmid. (As William Carlos Williams has often been excluded or undervalued, and I think for the same reasons; Williams has much in common with MacDiarmid.) For one thing, this situation bears out MacDiarmid's own observations about the general ignorance of Scottish culture and its virtual nonexistence in the world. More than that, it shows that in important ways MacDiarmid differed from his fellow modernists, and that his differences aligned him with the future, with struggles which he made central to his life and work but which had not yet appeared to be central to modernism. He now speaks with clarifying force on precisely the issues about which men like Pound, Yeats, Eliot, and Lawrence were most confused and untrustworthy. MacDiarmid is the one major poet in our language (or near it) who has been constantly, authentically, and actively allied with the political Left. It is the struggle to achieve this position, the depth of his grasp of its implications, and finally the richness he brought to it that are described in *Lucky Poet* and embodied in [*The Hugh MacDiarmid Anthology*]. . . .

He is for the working class and was born into it, but he is also in his own words a "high-brow," an intellectual, a writer of "difficult poetry," and he deplores "the philistinism of most of my fellow Communists." He is a national poet, self-appointed; but he has never limited himself to national subjects, and is apt to do so least when he is writing about Scotland; and he is incapable of propaganda. If we consider how often Communists lack culture, intellectuals lack any notion of the just place of labor in human society, internationalists lack an understanding of place and native quality, nationalists lack openmindedness, materialists deny the spirit and spiritualists deny matter, we may realize that MacDiarmid has written and acted with great awareness, thoroughness, and rightness in bringing these fragmentary views together into the "seamless garment" of his vision.

*Richard Pevear, in* The Hudson Review *(copyright © 1973 by The Hudson Review, Inc.; reprinted by permission), Vol. XXVI, No. 1, Spring, 1973, pp. 192-94.*

* * *

## MacINNES, Colin 1914-

**MacInnes is an English novelist and essayist. His mature fiction, eloquent and exuberant, is concerned with youth and racial problems in contemporary London.**

Colin MacInnes is regarded as a sort of voice of the displaced, downtrodden, or misunderstood—the rebel (real or would-be) with a cause. 'Low life' may be regarded as the subject-matter of *City of Spades, Mr. Love and Justice* and *Absolute Beginners,* but there is no attempt to exploit the sensational in the manner of the popular novelist. *City of Spades* avoids showing Negroes as either brutish, innocent or quaint; it is moving and indignant in its presentation of racialism in the London of the fifties, but it is not merely propaganda. The aim of *Mr. Love and Justice* is to show what the world of the prostitute and the ponce is really like and to examine the conventional image of an incorrupt British police force. *Absolute Beginners* is sympathetic to the culture-patterns of teenagers. MacInnes knows the underside of London life, but, strangely, he does not seem to have a sharp ear for its language. Being unable to record faithfully the idioms of Negroes, small criminals and adolescents, he makes up dialects for them out of his head—at least, this is the impression one has when reading him. For all that, his work is psychologically accurate, very enlightening, and full of a real (and quite unsentimental) compassion.

*Anthony Burgess, in his* The Novel Now *(reprinted by permission of W. W. Norton & Co., Inc.; copyright © 1967 by Anthony Burgess), Norton, 1967, pp. 146-47.*

[One] characteristic of [MacInnes's] fiction [is] the focus on outsiders—blacks, the suspect young, those outside the law, and police who twist the law to construct the cage of what they consider to be justice.

One reason for MacInnes's penchant for walks on the wild side is his ceaseless curiosity. He gets around. And it is especially a curiosity about how people spend rather than hoard their lives. . . . There is the thrust of anger in his work, particularly in his accounts of police practices. But coursing through each of the novels is a highly sensate appreciation of being alive, of being able to react spontaneously, whether with rage or tenderness. In writing of the 'curiously dancing quality' in MacInnes's work, a British critic adds that MacInnes 'can't help praising life.'

But another reason for the frequency of outsiders in his fiction is a moral concern. Most who are not outsiders acquire considerable skills in what the American social critic Joseph Lyford calls auto-anesthesia—the ability to exclude from all but the most surface levels of consciousness those who are not like themselves. . . . Around them seethes a great flux of bizarre social groupings through which they proceed, like tourists traversing the casbah, unseeing and unaware. . . .

Oh, they read and see some of what's 'really happening', but with the paper thrown away and the television set switched off, *their* world is still all they really know. One of MacInnes's purposes, then, is to inform. But if he were to use only documentary techniques, he too could be quickly switched off. By getting inside diverse outsiders through an act of the imagination, however, MacInnes makes it much more difficult for his readers to engage in auto-anesthesia. . . .

As a novelist, not a documentator, he created characters who, I expect, kept surprising him, for they are more than social indicators. Strongly rooted in a particular time and place, they took on their own lives.

I am not claiming a position for Colin MacInnes in the pantheon of novelists, but I do submit that he has created a vivid trilogy of London life [*City of Spades, Absolute Beginners,* and *Mr. Love and Justice*] that transcends documentary and all other categories. Zestful and tough, it is self-sustaining in that 'perennial battle between life and living death.'

*Nat Hentoff, "Introduction" (reprinted with the permission of Farrar, Straus & Giroux, Inc.; copyright © 1969 by Nat Hentoff) to* The London Novels of Colin MacInnes, *Farrar, Straus, 1969, pp. vii-xii.*

Colin MacInnes, assiduous annotator of contemporary scenes, has always been determined not to be constrained by the frustrations of real documentation. But exciting as is the licence to make cases you don't have to keep fuelled by hard evidence, it's a dangerous freedom to claim for any form of writing, even the novel. So, though *Out of the Garden* is a heady concoction that actually confirms some of one's worst fears and prejudices about trends in current English politics, its own tendentiousness can be perturbing. . . .

The political emphases of the . . . theme [of *Out of the Garden*] come across with admirable clarity. Alas, however, the novelist isn't happy with this abundant explicitness. The characters' names must join forces with the title to spell things out more loudly. It's just tolerable, I suppose, that the Adamses' juvenile delinquent offspring should be nicknamed Kik and Mas, after the Kikuyu and Masai peoples (their father fought in Kenya) to underscore the observation about Britain becoming the last colony.

But the novel's point about a class-ridden displeasure garden, in which the ex-officer still needs and exploits his ex-sergeant is not just clear but overstated. . . .

Still, this is an occasionally riveting read, with incidental sharp exposures of modish foibles and follies liberally dolloped in for good measure. And it's also—given the necessary caveat about tendentiousness—a set of serious reflections on the relationship of the military to social order in Great Britain.

*Valentine Cunningham, "Displeasure Garden," in* The Listener, *March 7, 1974, p. 311.*

*Out of the Garden,* Colin MacInnes's new novel, is a brilliant treatise on the role of the military in our post-colonial period, using the analytical techniques of Marxism to draw reverse political conclusions. It is enjoyable, intellectually stimulating and almost a good novel to boot. MacInnes's social analysis is appealing not so much for its inherent plausibility as for the logical charm that fresh concepts have when they are cogently but slightly perversely systematised. He is perhaps less perceptive about people.

This failing is compounded by the method of approach. The novel is cast almost entirely in conversation, which at its most extreme becomes Socratic, just a chance for the author to pour his own effervescent ideas through the mouths of his characters. There is, however, such an imperative rhythm to the dialogue that even those most resistant to the novel of ideas will find themselves carried along. This is all the more remarkable considering that the tiny fraction of the writing that is not speech is just sophisticated stage direction.

As well as being a repository of ideas the tale doubles as an extended biblical metaphor: the garden of original guilt being Otranto Towers, the ruined stately home that aristocratic Captain Rattler and his beautiful platonic companion Aspen plan to open as cover for a military putsch and general gun-running. Playing proletarian innocents against these hissing class enemies are Rattler's former Sergeant, Adams, his wife Evie and their two wayward, engaging sons. And, as a thumping afterthought, Evie's card-carrying, mechanical hard-liner of a father is called Angell. There the metaphor should have withered. One salutes the author for working within the discipline of a form but it is a pity that his rather endearing characters should have become trapped in the structure without a chance of growth. . . . Fortunately, the metaphor becomes obtrusive only at the end. Before that a parade of theorems dressed up as witticisms enchants and convinces.

*Timothy Mo, in* New Statesman, *March 15, 1974, p. 370.*

* * *

## MacNEICE, Louis 1907-1963

**MacNeice was an Irish-born English poet, translator, classical scholar, critic, and the author of several plays, many radio scripts, and, under a pseudonym, a novel. MacNeice wrote complex poems characterized by rich and subtle imagery and controlled sardonic wit. He cultivated a deliberately flat language for what Christopher Ricks called "an economic truth-telling which sees the encroachment of disaster without revelling in the apocalypse."**

[MacNeice] is like an ancient catalpa in a London square dazzling with its annual display of blossom the passers-by who are unable to see it. It is time that someone spoke up and said what pleasure his writing has given during the last quarter of a century since he arrived, in full possession of all his gifts, with the first startling lines of 'An Ecologue for Christmas'. . . .

To begin with, he is a classical scholar and so we shall always be able to rely on his grammar, on his lucidity, on mental processes which, if not always easy to follow, obey the rules of thought as practiced by good minds; and he has also a knowledge of prosody.

On the other hand he is not a don, his philosophy has been tested in a hard school; he is not intellectually arrogant which lends an added beauty to his intellectual images; he is a toughminded stoic with a soft spot for hedonism. His weakness is a tendency to fall into flatness and banality, the music giving out and the thought disappearing into clever tricks. At such times he seems to be playing the tortoise to Professor Auden's hare, and this perhaps is what Dame Edith Sitwell meant by referring to his 'inelasticity of rhythm, his verse either sticky in texture or disintegrated, gritty and sabulous'. He has a strong vein of journalism and sometimes seems to be putting the *New Statesman's* 'London Diary' into free verse.

But the toughness and energy of the journalist sustains the poet and philosopher who also draws sustenance from love and nature and travel, and from his local inheritance as an Anglo-Irish expatriate, a product of the Oxford of Auden, Spender, Day Lewis and Rex Warner.

Like Dylan Thomas he managed to write some of the best war-poetry; in fact the books which I enjoy the most, besides his first *Poems*, are *Plant and Phantom* (1941), which includes one of his best love-poems ('Time was away'), and the Irish poems of *The Last Ditch* and of *Springboard* (1944) which also includes 'Brother Fire', 'The Libertine' and 'Prayer before Birth'. And, of course, *Autumn Journal* (1939), where the journalist has helped the philosopher to preserve for ever the uneasy atmosphere of 'Munich'.

*Cyril Connolly, "Louis MacNeice" (originally published in the* [London] Sunday Times*), in his* Previous Convictions *(© 1963), Hamish Hamilton, 1963, pp. 320-23.*

Louis MacNeice's last volume of poems, *The Burning Perch,* went to press in January 1963; he died suddenly in September of the same year at the age of 56. Critics since have generally acknowledged that he was a poet of genius, and that much of his finest work was produced in the three years immediately preceding his death. While granting him his place in the front rank among the poets who came to prominence in the thirties—W. H. Auden, Stephen Spender, Cecil Day Lewis—they have had considerable difficulty in assessing the nature of his achievement. On his death, T. S. Eliot commented that he "had the Irishman's unfailing ear for the music of verse." During his lifetime, however, many readers felt that his ear did indeed fail him, that his rhythms were frequently too easy, and his parodies and imitations of jazz lyrics too flat and mechanical in nature to hold one's interest for long. While he had much in common with his contemporaries, he was, in many ways, totally unlike them. His poems are easy to understand on the surface (seemingly far less complicated than those of Auden or Dylan Thomas), but they present deeper, less obvious difficulties. They appear to be the open, easy expression of an engaging and intelligent personality, but basically that personality, and the poems through which it manifests itself, is not easy to grasp.

*William Jay Smith, "The Black Clock: The*

*Poetic Achievement of Louis MacNeice," in* Hollins Critic, *April, 1967, pp. 1-11.*

The tributes in verse and prose which, since MacNeice's death in 1963, have poured out from the distinguished poets who knew him and admired him document his significance in the history of the poetry of our time. This bulky collection of his works [*The Collected Poems of Louis MacNeice*] demonstrates that he stands apart from most of his contemporaries in the volume of his work. The consistent polish of the poems bears witness to his achievement as an artist. Yet the poetry—perhaps in some measure because of his reputation, perhaps in some measure because of its bulk—disappoints the expectant reader. It impresses, but it fails to excite. There are good lines in abundance, there is accuracy of observation, there is an admirable objectivity, and yet there is all too seldom what we recognize by instinct to be poetry. MacNeice's *forte* was the long personal narrative in verse best represented by "Autumn Journal" and "1953." But personal narrative—autobiography—is a recalcitrant genre; being what it must be, it resists the shaping imagination of the poet, his sense of pace, his ordering of experiences toward a climax. In just these respects MacNeice's poetry comes short of the highest achievement.

Virginia Quarterly Review, *Vol. 43, No. 3 (Summer, 1967), p. cxi.*

[Louis] MacNeice had the luck and the persistence, if not quite all the time he should have had. Without arguing the case, let me assert that [*The Collected Poems*] is the evidence that his work is comparable in seriousness and in wit to his contemporaries—Auden, Edwin Muir and Graves (*not* Spender and Day Lewis as has too often been said). And there are moments in the poems when the personality revealed seems incomparable, like to nothing but itself. . . . The life that beckons from MacNeice's poetry is welcome indeed.

*William H. Pritchard, in* The Hudson Review *(copyright © 1967 by The Hudson Review, Inc.; reprinted by permission), Vol. XX, No. 2, Summer, 1967, pp. 313-14.*

[MacNeice] distrusted all neat philosophical systems, all 'the nostrums Of science art and religion'; he had abandoned his father's Christian beliefs; he regarded the world of scholarship and of museums as an attractive but slightly disreputable escape from reality. . . . Yet, despite his frequently expressed desire to live in the present, his resolve to cease constructing moral or philosophical codes, his longing to throw off the burden of introspection—'I do not want to be reflective any more'—he was never able to abdicate from the responsibility of being a rational, moral creature. He remained all his life his father's son, often indeed weakening the impact of his poems by his tendency to preach a lay sermon, to expound the necessity of decency, courage, endurance. (p. 31)

The coming of war provided MacNeice with a new range of experiences and deeply affected his emotional development. Although his verse undergoes no spectacular change, it gradually alters its character in a variety of ways, becoming less impressionistic and glittering. MacNeice seems now to be more concerned with the congruence of the images in a poem than with their individual brilliance. (p. 35)

In many of the poems MacNeice is haunted by Christian symbols, by the ghost of that Christian morality which he has rejected but not exorcised. (p. 37)

Perhaps the most original achievements in [the] final volumes are those poems in *The Burning Perch* that convey a sense of desolation, of something gone awry, as though one were walking down a staircase where a step is missing, or had entered a room where everything is in order except for some terrifying absence or reversal of normality. These poems crackle with an eerie vitality, and are shaken by the kind of savage mirth that informs some of Bartok's later music. (p. 44)

Few poets have managed to make poetry out of the enjoyment which they have distilled from the minor pleasures of life. A short list of such poets would include Shakespeare, pre-eminent in this as in so much else, Ben Jonson, Herrick, Burns, Byron, Tennyson and Browning. MacNeice belongs to the select company of those who are able to communicate their delight in the minutiae of daily life, the sense of happiness and well-being that springs from good health, mental alertness and emotional vitality. (p. 44)

*John Press, in his* Louis MacNeice, *Longman Group Ltd., for the British Council, revised edition, 1970.*

MacNeice defined a poet as "an ordinary man with specialized gifts". His own gifts were an acute sensory, and especially visual, perception; colour, shape, light and shade, sound, smell, touch and taste, lend to his verse an immediacy closely connected with time and place. For him emotional recollection was bound up with where and when, as in the whole of *Autumn Journal,* in 'Birmingham' and 'Belfast'. He exploited the pathetic fallacy for all it was worth, not as a mere device, but because his experiences were bound up with actual times and places, as we see clearly in 'Solitary Travel', in Canto III of *Autumn Journal* and, above all, in 'Snow'. This external sensory perception was an integral part of the deeper emotional or intellectual feeling he was trying to express. So when he had to try even harder to convey an emotion whose validity he doubted, as in 'Flowers in the Interval', he relied on the association with places both to recall and heighten it. (p. 237)

He knew, and expressed again and again in his poetry, the delights of the senses and he experienced them so fully that he could half deceive himself into believing that they were a "mystical experience" and half way to faith, or belief. . . .

MacNeice came no nearer to a passionate resolution of philosophical or religious conflict than the expression of doubt in 'Didymus', the regression of 'Prayer Before Birth', and the terrible fear that lies at the heart of 'Charon'.

[In this study, we] approached the poetry of MacNeice, expecting to find, as he had himself indicated that we should, a poet in the Romantic tradition, and this indeed we have found. We may compare his achievements with [Marcel] Raymond's definition of the Romantic poet. . . . His primary "form of knowledge" as displayed in his poetry, is self-centred. Every shift of ground, every alteration of emphasis is, in his verse, a contribution to the "metaphoric" or "symbolic" portrait of himself, pored over, again and again, with the nostalgic longing for the moment it embodies. His metamorphoses range from the lonely child, cursed with a lifelong Oedipus complex, the schoolboy and student, then the townsman, the deserted lover, the husband, father, academic and author. The word "enjoyment" is echoed in the use of "mystical" to cover the experiences of the senses. Only when we come to the phrase "a feeling of the universe, experienced as a presence" are we forced to pause. A feeling of the minutiae of the universe, its colour, sounds, touch and smell, was indeed an integral part of his poetry and gives it an immediacy, a sense of heightened reality, that might at first sight satisfy the requirement of this definition, but the pleasure in colour or shape is not enough. It is not "a mystical experience". "A feeling of the universe, experienced as a presence" calls for a transcendental understanding of which he was only occasionally capable, as in the last few poems.

MacNeice remained the prisoner of his childhood. He could never escape the nostalgic chains this placed upon him either as lover or thinker. (pp. 247-48)

A parallel and not dissociated failure lay in his inability to make the intellectual effort either to achieve faith, to deny all belief, or to systematize his agnosticism. This ethical and intellectual weakness led to a certain sentimentality in his approach to social criticism and equally made any firm political attitude impossible. So MacNeice could find neither spiritual faith, political belief, or personal love and understanding to form the basis of his poetry, but relied instead on the conflicts of indecision. In so far as it lacks a passionate attempt to cope with the conflicts that arise from doubt and indecision, the poetry of MacNeice sometimes falls short of greatness. The tragedy is that he could not escape from within himself to wider exploration. (p. 249)

*D. B. Moore, in his* The Poetry of Louis MacNeice, *Leicester University Press, 1972.*

MacNeice, at his best, was always the personal poet, "lover of women and Donegal," responsive to a particular, quotidian world that was "incorrigibly plural." He was also responsive, and knew he was, to the delights of self-pity, and he had the true melancholiac's gift for ironic self-denigration. But he also valued honesty, even when it meant the faithful recording of his own inconsistencies and uncertainties. He was not a thinker, and his efforts to think in verse (as for example in *Ten Burnt Offerings* and *Autumn Sequel*) are his dullest poems—though as Auden remarked, even the dull poems are beautifully carpentered; what he could do best was record feelings, and especially the sad side of feelings—the regret, the melancholy, the nostalgia, the helplessness and hopelessness of ordinary existence in an ordinary world. If he could not think his way to a philosophy or a religion, he could at least *feel,* and sentiment is, in his poetry, a value in itself—a way of affirming the personal life by responding to it. Such a poetry of feeling is always at the edge of sentimentality, but sentiment and sentimentality are not the same thing, and in the best of MacNeice's poems it is honest feeling that we acknowledge. In his *Autumn Journal,* or a typical poem like "Plurality," the world does not make sense, but the feelings about it do. That world didn't change much from the first poems to the last, and neither did the tone of voice; both seem to me to derive from the thirties, and to evoke that time, so that even the poems of *The Burning Perch,* MacNeice's last collection, seem instantly nostalgic of a time long before they were written.

*Samuel Hynes, "Auden and MacNeice," in* Contemporary Literature *(© 1973 by the Regents of the University of Wisconsin), Vol. 14, No. 3, Summer, 1973, pp. 378-83.*

A poetry like MacNeice's which is so persistently dogged by honest doubt, which wavers at such intimate lengths between such dismal opposites, can be expected to have a ready appeal. But to accept this as a full characterization of MacNeice's achievement is to under-emphasize the very gifts which he himself spent so much time suppressing and apologizing for; it is to be too solemn about a poet who could never finally accept that he 'loved the surface but lacked the core'. . . .

It is interesting that in [his] first volume [*Blind Fireworks*] MacNeice constantly treats of visual experience which is unintelligibly (if engrossingly) fluid and confused; he confronts a glittering, opalescent universe in a wholly submissive and amiable manner. Poem after poem opens on a note of tranquil decline; 'the quietude of the soft wind', 'Trains came threading quietly through my dozing childhood', 'In this evening room there is no stir, no fuss', 'The room is all a stupid quietness', 'In a between world . . . the old cat . . . sleeps on the verge of nullity' and so on. It is from a similarly drowsy 'between world' that MacNeice watches his random experience fragment and dissolve. Time passes, the view changes, these poems seem to say. The poet's intrusion on the cycle is marginal, almost photographic, rarely rhetorical or analytic, never profoundly disturbed.

What is charming in these early poems is a fractional immediacy of perception, a developed gift for projecting a momentary visual complex (a gift that made MacNeice wary of grand systems; see the post-war 'Plurality' for an interesting, if leadenly expressed, background to all this) and a passive liveliness to the sheer plenitude and variety of human experience.

It is easy to see how gifts of this kind could be made to seem irresponsible and trivial, but it is in them that one can discover the source of MacNeice's most brilliant passages of social reportage and also of the self-consciousness that enervates such large stretches of his subsequent work. . . .

Throughout the 'Eclogues', the 1936-8 volume, and the best passages (Parts 5 to 8, particularly) of *Autumn Journal* there is a range and accuracy of observation, a lively grasp of the frenetic bored excess of a threatened social order, which are really admirable. Predictably, it is the scope and variety of social experience, the detail of its surface, that delights him; he alternates between moods of jaunty 'bravado in the face of time', of ironic sumptuousness, and of flat, menacing reportage. . . .

[While] the thirties climate matured MacNeice's bright, documentary style it also encouraged the development of his prosy analysis. The problem of his own personal involvement in what he saw could not be evaded and MacNeice became obliged to stand at the centre of his work in a confessional stance that did not suit him but which he never completely abandoned. His doctrine of the poet as extension of the ordinary man was not vanity but a way of burying his personality in the kind of plural activity he could handle. He believed that the poet should remain elastic in his sympathies whatever the pressures on him to propagandize; his reaction against the 'esoteric' poetry of Eliot did not mean that he chose instead a legislating or civilizing role for the poet but simply that he must write out of experience which was generally available and interesting. For this purpose his poetry of appearances could work very well. But the detachment, the range of acceptance which it presupposed was difficult to preserve. Credentials had to be shown, the surfaces had to be probed.

It is in attempting this that MacNeice is at his weakest. The devitalized ambivalence of, say, Parts 2 and 3 of *Autumn Journal* is typical; the conflicts he writes about are real and important ones and his motives are worthy, but the structure of his argument is limp and half-heartedly protracted. One is conscious primarily of an enormous failure of energy. . . .

[It] is never clear if this malaise results from the insoluble issues of commitment that face him, if it is a personal failure in love that causes it, or if it is to be seen as symptomatic of the total uneasiness of the time. . . .

In his war-time poems, MacNeice attempts to synthesize the rhetorical and documentary aspects of his work in a series of anecdotal character-poems ('The Conscript', 'The Mixer', 'The Satirist') but these are too complacently punch-lined, their solutions intrude too glaringly and, worst, they are pale imitations of Auden. The tight, witty accent is largely abandoned and where it is attempted—as in 'Brother Fire', 'Bar-Room Matins' etc.—it seems tricksy and hollow. . . .

It is noticeable that in *Visitations* (1957) and *Solstices* (1961) MacNeice was able to rediscover much of his old concentration and vitality, and to withdraw into the background of his work. In these he is no longer so prone to 'mark the spot/Meticulously in black and white' but is more directly susceptible once more to 'whatever glints'. There are still poems in which he seems to lose his nerve after a riotous first stanza and relapses into frozen paradox but on the whole one senses a welcome access of vigour and invention. This is true also of the volume that was published a fortnight after his death, *The Burning Perch*. His *Budgie* once more attitudinizes entertainingly; that it does so on a burning perch is not ignored but nor is it laboriously overemphasized. Throughout the book the old paradoxes are seen to be inexorable, and thus nonsensical or terrifying, or both; undebatable finally, but still to be spoken of. . . .

*Ian Hamilton, "Louis MacNeice," in his* A Poetry Chronicle *(reprinted by permission of Faber and Faber Ltd.), Faber and Faber, 1973, pp. 30-6.*

* * *

## MAILER, Norman 1923-

**Mailer, an American, is a novelist, essayist, social critic, and film-maker. He is one of America's most controversial and most visible literary personalities. (See also *Contemporary Authors*, Vols. 9-12, rev. ed.)**

Mailer's radicalism is of an indeterminate sort, the kind that expresses itself preëminently, perhaps, in images and fictional constructs rather than in abstract schema. . . . [His] dislike [for any kind of collective action] lies at the heart of his first novel and has often been interpreted as making his critique of capitalist society an entirely negative one; nevertheless *The Naked and the Dead* is a radical novel which affirms and does so within its own logic as a literary work.

Mailer's novel has a number of faults, not the least being that it sounds at times like a pastiche of the novels about World War I. The echoes of Dos Passos, another individualist rebel, are especially insistent: the interchapter biographies in *The Naked and the Dead* combine the techniques of the biographies and the narrative sections in *U.S.A.*, and the fact that all of these individual soldier lives are thwarted and stunted by a sick society seems clearly reminiscent of the social vision at the base of the trilogy. . . .

If, as Mailer himself has stated, the book "finds man corrupted, confused to the point of helplessness," these qualities particularly express the personality of that key figure, Lieutenant Robert Hearn, a confused liberal intellectual who, like the middle class in Marxist theory, is caught between the hammer and the anvil of great antagonistic forces. In him Mailer skillfully fuses form and content, for Hearn partakes in and thus links both of the power struggles which operate simultaneously in the book, in each holds a kind of ideological middle ground, and in each is defeated. In order to understand Mailer's radical purpose, however, it is necessary to see that the same alternative to defeat exists in both struggles. . . .

Mailer seeks to demonstrate the inability of power moralists to manipulate history in opposition to mass will. If *The Naked and the Dead* is taken as the accurate sum of all its parts, it must be considered, as Mailer himself has declared, a positive and hopeful book rather than a negative and pessimistic one. . . . More skillfully than most radical novelists Mailer has solved the problem of the ending which with artistic inevitability affirms the author's belief. Incident flowers organically into idea.

*Walter B. Rideout, in his* The Radical Novel in the United States 1900-1954: Some Interrelations of Literature and Society *(copyright © 1956 by the President and Fellows of Harvard College; excerpted by permission of the publishers), Harvard University Press, 1956, pp. 270-73.*

The price of success for the best of our writers is the recognition of a special and unredeemable failure. The career of Norman Mailer, though mostly exceptional, is a case in point. His first novel, *The Naked and the Dead* (1948), was overpraised for reasons having little to do with its achievement into an extraordinary popular and literary success. At twenty-five, Mailer had written, he was told, that mythic slouching beast of our popular criticism, the great American novel. Influenced by Dos Passos and Hemingway, *The Naked and the Dead* is an amibitious, panoramic, powerfully rendered realistic novel which only occasionally transcends the meaning of particular experiences—the charged raw materials of the war itself. What the novel does brilliantly is evoke the experience of war: the heat, the wet, the odors, the fear, the stupidity, the waste, the degradation, the unmitigating and unredemptive nightmare of the battlefield. As is often the case with antiwar novels, however, the impulse of *The Naked and the Dead*—its secret fascination with the violence of war—subverts the liberal high-mindedness of its intention. In the chaotic universe of war, the power drive of Mailer's villains, Croft and Cummings, seems a more positive virtue than the uncommitment of Red, the humility of Goldstein, the innocent liberalism of Hearn, or the weakness of the others, the naked and the dead.

If Mailer avoids the trap of self-imitation in his later two novels, he avoids it at the exorbitant risk of testing, with the odds contrived against him, the durability of his talent. Both *Barbary Shore* (1951) and *Deer Park* (1955) are adventurous failures, quixotic attempts at redefining the possibilities of the task. While *The Naked and the Dead* is not nearly as good as its reputation, *Barbary Shore* and *Deer Park* are not nearly as bad as theirs. Much of *Deer Park,* in fact, is Mailer at his best. Marion Faye's dope dream, the shrill Hollywood parties, the love-making of Elena and Eitel are as charged with the energy of insight as almost anything in contemporary fiction; yet other parts of the novel, especially Sergius's hallucinatory dialogue with God at the end, are incomparably, embarrassingly indulgent. It is Mailer's peculiar exhibitionistic gift to be from one moment to the next either better or worse than anyone. As with *The Naked and the Dead* and *Barbary Shore,* the point of view of *Deer Park* is not so much ambivalent as vaguely defined. What is being satirized in the novel? What is Mailer affirming? Does it matter? *Deer Park* is a curious failure; it is an alternately impressive and atrocious serious novel.

In recent years Mailer seems to have emerged as a more significant essayist than novelist—along with Baldwin, the most apocalyptic of our literate journalists. It is ironic that Mailer wrote the essays ostensibly to keep himself in the public eye while he was working on an ambitious ten-volume novel, "the longest ball ever to go up into the accelerated hurricane air of our American letters." Instead of the ten-volume marvel, we have a new one-volume novel from Mailer [*Deer Park*] . . . which is, if such a distinction is still possible, Mailer's most embarrassing performance to date. Yet one still believes in him. For all his posing and chest-thumping, his success-mongering and clownish self-parody, he is an authentic talent, capable at his best (as in the story "The Man Who Studied Yoga") of touching the very deepest nerves of contemporary experience. Mailer remains now, as after the publication of his first novel, a potential major novelist who has not yet written a major novel.

*Jonathan Baumbach, in the "Introduction" to his* The Landscape of Nightmare: Studies in the Contemporary American Novel *(reprinted by permission of New York University Press; copyright © 1965 by New York University), New York University Press, 1965, pp. 9-11.*

Listen to Mailer and he'll tell you that no one makes the American idiom move and liberate as well as he. We need not argue whether that confidence is misplaced in principle for *Why Are We in Vietnam?* has plenty wrong in plain fact. There is, first, the intellectual pitch: as we read about some Texans bear hunting in Alaska, we learn why we are in Vietnam. Mailer's politics, thus, are rather like those of *Doctor Strangelove* in their really simple notion that what's wrong is that we have let people from our west run the country. You can tell them by their accents, and if Mailer's teen-age narrator doesn't call them "preverts," he's got all the other names. . . .

*Why Are We in Vietnam?* participates in every American myth about America; every gesture asks that it become a staple in our textbooks because it fits in most of our more obvious conceptions of ourselves. That's not all that's wrong with it, but it is enough.

*Roger Sale, in* The Hudson Review *(copyright © 1968 by The Hudson Review, Inc.; reprinted by permission), Vol. XX, No. 4, Winter, 1967-68, pp. 669-70.*

*The Deer Park* has some virtues, primarily comic ones . . ., but it finally fails as a play because Mailer is neither content to work in abstractions (however nonrealistic his play's form) nor able to create the characters that he otherwise needs. This weakness may be the result of his conscious attempt to avoid conventional plot, to write, as he says in the Introduction, a play that "went from explosion to explosion . . . from one moment of intensity or reality (which is to say a moment which feels more real than other moments) to the next—a play which went at full throttle all the way." Without the "dramatic scaffolding, connective tissue" that he cuts away, an audience comes to the scenes lacking the emotional freight that the characters presumably carry, and although they will not find it difficult "to fill the spaces" (there is exposition enough), the scenes are likely to remain dull and flat. . . . Too many of the explosions are pure disquisition, not interesting enough in its own right and, because of the problems in characterization, not dramatically compelling as argument in which ideas become weapons.

*Gerald Weales, in his* The Jumping-Off Place: American Drama in the 1960's *(reprinted with permission of Macmillan Publishing Co., Inc.; copyright © 1969 by Gerald Weales), Macmillan, 1969, p. 221.*

What are the requirements for reading *Why Are We in Vietnam?* None. I offer, nonetheless, a small exercise in hurtful meditation. Let us recall one or more of these:

1) The liquids of love.
2) A pimple invisible beyond adolescence.
3) Adrenalin, vintage a few seconds.
4) The aroma of our burial urn.
5) Sweat gathering in the palm of the hand.
6) An animal with yellow or green eyes.
7) America now.

Norman Mailer has never been to Vietnam. Neither have I. Fact and fiction have now become the same, and they require from us a new consciousness. The novel as history, history as fiction. Precisely Vietnam.

Obscenity is crucial to this novel.

Obscenity repels us first, then it disturbs. When we say that it bores us—how debonair!—we try to keep ourselves intact. We are, after all, what we are because we have transformed outwards its demands.

Obscenity is protest. We are right to fear it; vengeance befouls its breath. The return of the repressed. Obscenity begins as protest, ends as assault. Afterwards, release.

Obscenity reminds us of corporeal experience. Unheroic man, clowning between food and excrement, blood and semen. This is the comic element.

Obscenity celebrates; there is sacramental power behind its reductive rage. Nothing merely personal, nothing perishable. The force of obscenity moves the stars.

Obscenity reaches for the root of language, clutches the mystery. When the thick sap rushes upwards, symbols explode. This is also the force of obscenity.

Obscenity, Henry Miller says, seeks "to awaken, to usher in a sense of reality. In a sense, its use by the artist may be compared to the use of the miraculous by the master."

Obscenity, in Mailer's novel, repels and releases. Does it also constrict? Rarely. Its spirit is genital, procreative. . . .

It takes an America lover to recognize another. Mailer is a deep lover of America. Anyone who cannot see this may be hiding something worse than treason from himself. . . .

America as scavenger. Why are we in Vietnam? . . .

The language hops and bops, a new, obscene, metaphysical language full of wit, conceit, learning, defiance, misery, insight and self-delight, hallelujah and hallucination, maddog viciousness, full of smell, full of touch. Mailer knows that the hierarchy of senses tumbles from sight to hearing to taste to smell to touch—the more primitive, the more ineluctable. The senses are here. This is why the language rarely lapses into anti-language, neon color, or stroboscopic sound. . . .

Revolution is no longer radical enough.

The imagination is the teleological organ of evolution. It predicts and fulfills change. At the center of every fancy, a fact waits to be born.

Your violence: the ultimate resource of your enemy.

Creation is the masterwork of Eros, and its Form is Change. Metamorphosis is paedamorphosis.

Guilt: the obscene debt we owe our ancestors. Guilt is to responsibility what onanism is to love.

Choose Life. But choose Death over Immortality. Evil is the flower of Immortality as vampires and werewolves know.

Silence: the alteration of consciousness.

*Dear Norman:*

You said there were Barons and Counts among men. I said there is Faustian and there is Orphic heroism. We can agree on "the aristocracy of achieved talent," and the enhancement of life in its struggle with itself. But the warring vision can have its snobberies too. The sweat or blood we shed waters the laurel tree from which leaves are taken to crown prettily our head.

More: the time has come for man to break the syntax of his dreams, and speak a language stones and gods can hear. Harlem and Dallas are not the same though every night they meet secretly in our dreams. The stones are dumb to their converse, and the gods yawn.

Who knows but at the silent, magnetic Pole America still waits for Columbus to be born?

Sincerely yours,
Ihab

*Ihab Hassan, "Focus on Norman Mailer's 'Why Are We in Vietman?'," in* American Dreams, American Nightmares, *edited by David Madden (© 1970 by Southern Illinois University Press; reprinted by permission of Southern Illinois University Press), Carbondale: Southern Illinois University Press, 1970, pp. 197-203.*

Norman Mailer's use of the word "existentialist" has become by now something of a running joke, or owlish put-on. Since he has coupled it with every conceivable school of noun, it is impossible to tell precisely what he means by it. But if it has something to do with making yourself up as you go along, then it may be the right word for him after all.

Until recently, I had supposed that the one link between his various identities was the wish to be a genius in each. "Genius or nothing" has been his proposition—the greatest whatever, novelist, playwright, moviemaker of his generation, nation, universe (depending on his *afflatus* that day): not simply the most talented, although he uses the word a lot, but something beyond talent. In his acting roles, he has used the names Pope and King; but transparently, the one he was groping for shyly was God. . . .

Rolling with the times is part of what being a genius is all about. American writers are especially prone to think of themselves as spokesmen for their generations, so that the line between prophet and journalist is a blurry one at all times.

Thus it is no accident that Mailer wrote the first big war novel, subsequently managed to hook himself on to both the Beat Generation and the French Existentialists, jumped off in time to catch the Negro express, elbowed briefly to the front of the Peace Movement, worked Viet Nam into the title of a novel (an almost infallible sign of charlatanry) and caught up with the movie fad, all in no time at all. And who is the first writer to tell us about the moon? This is just an abridged survey. In between he wrote a play, which he considered the most exciting theatrical event since World War II; then, having established his genius one more time, he left the form behind. Who goes to plays anyway?

An opportunist? Of course. Prove to him that there's anything wrong with that. In personal style, he is the greatest of the businessmen-adventurer writers. I have seen him pull out a wad of notes to bet on some trifle, then plunge the notes into a wine glass to prove his ascendancy over money. Mailer is not a primitive in this respect, but a conscious follower of tradition. His old crony, Seymour Krim, recently accused him of introducing crassness and success-worship into American letters. But in fact, Scott Fitzgerald could have written the same about Hemingway, and Edith Wharton could have written the same about Scott Fitzgerald. Here as elsewhere, Mailer is not always the innovator he appears. . . .

The question for us is not why Mailer keeps shedding his skin, but whether it has been good for him. In terms of artistic production, his career is a disappointment so enormous that it almost begins to look impressive. He had the makings of a first-rate naturalistic novelist, but veered from that, either because it was too easy, or because the jig was up with naturalistic novels; and he has not lingered long enough in any other form to master it. When he does do something outstanding now, as in parts of *Armies of the Night,* it will usually be found to be in the old naturalistic mode. His descriptions of persons and places are demoniacally acute. But he gains no help from the forms themselves. His movies are just like his speeches, his play was just like his novels; the necessity of being a genius flattens them all out indiscriminately.

Mailer rejects, like Lucifer, the principle that to be great you must first be good. In his famous novel, *The Naked and the Dead,* he did try simply to be better than his rivals, to win within the rules. But he has not allowed that to happen lately. He has produced work for which words like "good" or "bad" are simply irrelevant. Mailer has some intelligent ideas about art, yet artistically his later work is slapdash and even amateurish. His novel, *An American Dream,* is gawky and improvised; his play, *The Deer Park,* hard-breathing and stilted. Submission to form requires some minimal self-effacement, and Mailer can see no point in writing if not to advertise. It is inconceivable that he would ever write something anonymously—or write a single page without announcing his presence. Naturalistic novels were too anonymous and he dropped them. Good movies are anonymous too, so he makes bad ones. Good actors are anonymous, so he comes on as a ham. "Greatness," as Orson Welles has shown, can actually war with goodness; genius can obliterate talent. . . .

His feats of introspection began to treat wider and wider sectors of experience. His strategy was to become the subject he wanted to write about—a cop, a politician, a burned-out romantic—and then simply to write about himself. Without taking his eye off Mailer for a minute, he became a first-rate reporter.

This imaginative projection requires colossal nervous exertion. And Mailer seldom cheats. He may be a chameleon, but he is a sincere one. He really *does* turn into those things. To do so, he surrenders trappings of Self that other writers cling to; although he talks about himself relentlessly, he is quiet about his origins, his parents, his childhood, anything that would nail his ego down to specifics and keep it from reincarnating. He has passed the ultimate test of sincerity. Lots of bright well-behaved boys have toyed with romantic insanity, but Mailer actually got there. It cannot have been easy for a mathematics prodigy and "nice little Jewish boy from Brooklyn" to turn into an authentic wild man, but he did it—up to a point. That is, he takes turns being crazy and being sane. . . .

His gravest handicap is that his worst moments are often his most genius-y, and he sometimes seems to cultivate them for just that reason, though the critic in him must know better. His foolishness can seem, at times, too calculated, a sane man trying his damnedest to be crazy. (Everybody knows that geniuses are crazy, don't they?) In my darker moments, I sometimes wonder whether Mailer is crazy at all. His clipped speech and watchful eyes suggest that the frenzy may be the fruit of calculation. But even if so, he has been true to its demands, has laid the pressure of occasional madness on his brain and has got some fine writing moments out of it, as well as some passing bad ones.

If he just forgets about masterworks and sticks to the rather special art of direct self promotion, his future will still be interesting. Because he gives himself unstintingly, opening his lungs to experience with a romantic willingness that comes close to being noble. Also, from our less exalted point of view, a weather vane with that kind of accuracy is something to prize. Watch Mailer: if he turns to contemplation, buy a prayer mat; if he stays with politics, expect huge voter turnouts. As Mailer goes, so goes the nation. That is the form his genius takes.

*Wilfrid Sheed, "Genius or Nothing: A View of Norman Mailer," in* Encounter, *June, 1971, pp. 66-71.*

Mailer's position [on women, in *The Prisoner of Sex*] is similar to that of the antibellum slaveholder. If they recognized the validity of criticism, they must give up the psychological and material advantages gained from slavery, or live openly as hypocrites. They chose to construct an elaborate defense based on putative differences between blacks and people. Mailer's sentimental, romantic premise, and the "conclusions" he draws, are the same self-serving stuff. His response to feminism is summed up in a book about himself, opening with the easy assertion that he could do it—be a housewife—no sweat! and ending with the equally silly statement that to be allowed "free search" to look for "that one man in a million" (Tin Pan Alley would blush) is what women's liberation is about!

*Helen G. Hill, "A Prisoner of Sexism," in* Mediterranean Review, *Fall, 1971, pp. 48-50.*

That Norman Mailer's *The Armies of the Night* (1968) straddles [the] boundary [between fiction and reportage] is very clearly advertised by its subtitle: 'History as a Novel —The Novel as History'. The first part . . . is, in Mailer's words, 'nothing but a personal history which while written as a novel was to the best of the author's memory scrupulous to facts'. It is distinguished from a straight autobiographical narrative primarily by the fact that Mailer writes about himself in the third person, thus achieving an ironic distance on his own complex personality which is one of the chief delights of the book. . . . This self-irony enabled by the third-person narrative method also licenses Mailer to describe his fellow-participants . . . with a mischievous candour that might have seemed impertinent in a conventional autobiography, and to indulge in a good deal of prophetic cultural generalization about America which, like 'ideas' in a novel, we judge by their plausibility, rhetorical force and relevance to context rather than by the stricter criteria of logic and verifiability. . . .

It is less easy to describe the narrative principles of the second part of *The Armies of the Night,* partly because Mailer himself seems confused about them. When, at the beginning of this section, 'The Novel as History' he speaks of 'the novelist . . . passing his baton to the Historian', he seems to mean that the narrative method of Part I, in which events were seen from one, limited point of view, in the manner of a Jamesian novel, will be exchanged for the method of the historian, who assembles and collates data from various sources and presents a coherent account of a complex sequence of events.

> The mass media which surrounded the March on the Pentagon created a forest of inaccuracy which would blind the efforts of a historian; our novel has provided us with the possibility, no, even the instrument to view our facts and conceivably study them in that light a labour of lens-grinding has produced.

I take this to mean that, both for the writer and for us the readers, the research into the self that is carried out in Part I has exposed and purged the inevitable bias of any human report. Thus the 'novel' has given the 'history' a unique kind of reliability. About half-way through Part II, however, Mailer abandons this claim . . . [and] announces that Part II 'is now disclosed as some sort of condensation of a collective novel. . . . Mailer thus claims the freedom to enhance his narrative with vivid invention. . . . [He] uses to advantage a novelist's gift for caricature by violating the rules of modern historical method (though the convention is a very familiar one in classical historiography).

*The Armies of the Night* implies no disillusionment on the author's part with the novel as a literary form: on the contrary, it reaffirms the primacy of that form as a mode of exploring and interpreting experience.

*David Lodge, in his* The Novelist at the Crossroads *(© 1971 by David Lodge and used with his permission), Cornell University Press, 1971, pp. 10-12.*

Mailer's sense of self is of a multitude of selves, constantly interacting, seemingly contradictory, each of them feeling like an embattled minority. He is, in his view of it, like a composite of America, and it is not surprising that his birthday celebration should be thought a fit occasion for announcements of national importance. Just as there is no single self who is Mailer, but rather a dialectically-active, even punishing play of selves, so there can be no discrete separation of occasions, and a birthday is a political, sexual, familial, social and literary event all at once. He is a writer who cannot ever see one thing except in dialectical opposition to, or in some circuitous relation with, a multitude of other things. He is concerned always with secret sources of power, and with that paranoia which precisely traces out the hidden webs of connection between public life and private obsessions. The effect upon his style is to open his paragraphs to a great variety of tones and vocabularies, each modifying and competing with the others. . . .

Mailer has become of late so predictable and mechanical and repetitious in his use of polarities—nature and technology, God and the Devil, obscenity and concept, sex and death—that he has not yet earned the right to be called what he called Lawrence: 'a cauldron of boiling opposites.' He has not yet grown to the dimensions of his ideal 'Novelist'.

But it would be unfair to one of the great living masters of our language merely to criticize him for not meeting such nobly high self-imposed standards. The urgency in Mailer for some coherent system is evidence, indeed, of how much chaos he is willing to imagine and willing to engage. His conduct in public or on TV is one aspect of this: a refusal to act only in obedience to some predetermined pattern or to the demands of a particular medium. He won't stick to a prepared text if, inside, he is simultaneously responding to what might be called a sub-text. If this Mailerian quality has at last become predictable, we can nonetheless be grateful for the liberating motive behind it.

Now at a crisis in his career equivalent to the early period of exhaustion after *The Deer Park,* Mailer is uniquely situated to escape the trap that often turns American writers into imitators, and finally into unconscious parodists, of themselves. His situation is unique because some of his most brilliant work is literary self-criticism. In *The Prisoner of Sex* there are already hints of a healthily negative assessment of where he is, of boredom with characteristic and familiar ways of doing things. Finally, he is even at 'war' with his own achievements, and out of this may emerge still other, different forms for himself, for contemporary life and for our language.

*Richard Poirier, in* The Listener, *November 8, 1973, pp. 626-27.*

I think [Norman Mailer] has great histrionic gifts. Now, that's a bit snide, and I don't want to be snide. In a different climate he probably would have been a first-class semirealistic novelist of the type of Victor Hugo or parts of Dickens. But he's been seduced by all the apparatus of modern media, journalism, and everything else. Money is a bit too easy to make from that. I'm perfectly prepared to believe that Dickens in modern America with *his* particular histrionic talents would have found easier ways of making a fortune than by writing novels.

*C. P. Snow, in "A Conversation With C. P. Snow," by J. Robert Moskin, in* Saturday Review/World *(copyright © 1974 by Saturday Review/World, Inc.; reprinted with permission), March 6, 1974, p. 20-2, 47.*

Mailer is concerned to poke around in our collective (and, to him, always menacing) unconscious, and to suggest [in *The Faith of Graffiti*] a variety of occult or free energy connections. (Jung and Reich live on in Mailer.) Thus the motivations and sources of . . . graffiti are not simply the obvious ones—the drabness of the slum, the Latin urge to colorful display, the *macho* lure of physical risk and danger, the human desire to make one's surroundings one's own and leave one's mark upon them, the stylistic influences of comic books and TV ads—but include, for instance, possible secret emanations across time and distance from all art, cave to Pop. . . .

Mailer . . . is not really interested in visual aesthetics (for mundane example, whether colorful curlicue signatures enhance bleak buildings—or handsome subway cars), but rather, and as always, in the enticement, the thrall, the dread, the value, and the metaphysics of risk alone. This is a central and recurring theme in Mailer's work, and . . . in exploring and celebrating risks he advocates illegal or destructive or antisocial action without regard to consequences. The attacks tend to be simplistic, and Mailer's responses tend to be evasive: interestingly, the evasiveness —at times sly, at times clownish, at times brilliantly glancing off the point—is often the meat of his entertainment. . . .

There is a notion abroad that writers are overpaid. They are not. Nor is Mailer. He is a star, a celebrity; he is also one of the very best, most imaginative (yes, riskily imaginative), and accomplished writers working anywhere in the world today. He makes less than many stars in other fields (sports, rock), less than many writers of negative quality, and less than many executives of newspapers and news magazines that apparently begrudge his, or any really good writer's, making more than a minimum wage.

*Eliot Fremont-Smith, "Mailer on the IRT," in* New York Magazine *(© 1974 by NYM Corp.; reprinted by permission of* New York Magazine *and Eliot Fremont-Smith), May 6, 1974, pp. 97-8.*

Of course the Norman Mailer we all know and dislike is simply not the same man who wrote *The Naked and the Dead* when he was 25. Its young, likable author was a modest Harvard graduate and war veteran who didn't even want *Life* to take his picture because his novel was supposed to stand by itself (perhaps a typical attitude for a young literary man of the time, but still praiseworthy). The text's the thing—and the text, even if it seemed a pastiche of Dos Passos, Farrell, Hemingway, and even Fitzgerald, was often brilliant. Its faults were the faults of a very young author, an author who showed unlimited promise. Now Mailer has outlived that promise. He is more than twice as old, a noisy hack writer who occasionally hits a good streak. How did he lose so much?

First success went to his head; then failure. His second novel, *Barbary Shore* (1951), never really finds an appropriate way to handle its subject; a crude allegory with little logic and no characterization, it is probably the worst novel ever written by an up-and-coming young writer. . . .

Mailer must have eventually realized how bad *Barbary Shore* really was—or why would he have basically rewritten it as *The Deer Park* (1955)? . . . Still, the incredibly clumsy *Barbary Shore* was written to argue a view, while *The Deer Park* seems written primarily for the continuing market in melodramatic Hollywood novels; if its supporting cast holds up better than most, its hero has the hopelessly adolescent reek of third-rate fiction. . . .

Mailer had not been able to handle success; now he couldn't handle failure. He had already turned to the drugs, savagery, and overwhelming megalomania that made all his writing of the late Fifties so vulgar, so blatantly obvious, so dull—culminating in *Advertisements for Myself* (1959). Afterward he began to improve, and there was a four-year period between 1964 and 1968 when it looked as if Mailer would amount to something after all. During those four years he published his best work, *The Armies of the Night* (essentially a personal memoir of the march on the Pentagon), as well as some noteworthy shorter articles and two idiosyncratic novels, *An American Dream* and *Why Are We in Vietnam?* . . . I find [*Why Are We in Vietnam?*] derivative in style, unconvincing in tone and locale, and especially unappetizing because it intends to be comic and Mailer's sense of the comic is, in every sense of the word, crude. . . .

[Surely] the greatest of all unimportant mysteries on earth is why some people praise Norman Mailer's style; Mailer is an extremely sloppy woodsman flailing away at the tree of art with a dull axiom.

*Charles Nicol, "Studying the Sloppy Woodsman," in* National Review *(150 East 35th St., New York, N.Y. 10016), June 21, 1974, pp. 710-11.*

The whole first phase of [Mailer's] public performance, lasting up through 1967, was rife with a basic, if somehow friendly, warning: don't believe all this in too simple a way, he was saying—we are all involved in an illusion. The author was pointing toward a second stage in his public career, a stage in which performer and audience together might examine from a special angle this curious relationship between a culture and its heroes. *Why Are We in Vietnam?* in 1967, brought the first major phase of his career, the celebrity phase, to a conclusion. His endless array of faces had by this time marked him the Lon Chaney of American letters, and his celebrity lore, rich in the rhythm of personal disaster counterpointed by victorious recovery, began to take on the resonance of legend. As if to mark a point, he was that year even elected to the American Academy of Arts and Letters, but the really significant new development took the form of two *cinéma vérité* movies, *Wild 90* and *Beyond the Law,* in both of which he functions simultaneously as director and star. In accepting this duality of role, Mailer introduced into the apparently already completed compound of his public formula a radically new element: he introduced detachment. . . .

When Mailer, the director, stood back and, as it were, joined the audience in viewing Mailer, the figure on the screen, he established a perspective hitherto unheard-of in the career of an American public figure. It was the detached perspective which identified his central narrative device in *The Armies of the Night* and *Miami and the Siege of Chicago,* both published the next year, and of the two nonfiction narratives that followed these: *Of a Fire on the Moon* in 1970 and *The Prisoner of Sex* in 1971. It is again central in the huge third movie, *Maidstone,* shot in 1968 and two years in the cutting. In the third-person device we stand back with Mailer and critically analyze the character and actions of the hero, one "Norman Mailer," an artificial construct whose composition invites and promises to repay careful study. It is a construct which, as a matter of record, had mightily stimulated the public imagination over the previous decade, and a detached analysis of how the thing operated would necessarily tell the student much about this matter of the culture's imaginative needs.

Of the many things that differentiate between Mailer and the two public writers who came before him [Fitzgerald and Hemingway], perhaps the most crucial is that he was trying to make the public do something importantly different—he was not so much trying to establish the importance of art and the artist in the public imagination as he was trying to create self-recognition in that imagination. Consciously or otherwise, Mailer in some way perceived that things had reached the point at which a new set of Great Profiles would no longer serve the imaginative needs of the individual in the culture, perceived that just as the star system in Hollywood had died out, so had the public's capacity to find surcease in simple fantasy. What the imagining individual in the culture needed now was the experience of standing back and watching himself imagine, to become conscious of the needs revealed by his dreams, and to know clearly the significance of those needs. It was hardly the destroying of illusion that Mailer was after—illusion is the artist's gold—but rather a conscious awakening to the fact and function of illusion in our lives, and a consequent sophistication that might keep us from the danger of cultural self-deception. To this end he began disassembling his "self," showing the pretentious clown, the seeking reporter, the bewildered student of technology, the once-confident sexolog lost in the mazes of the mystery, the cop, the crook, the movie maker who wants to be president. All are shown in the detached light of analysis, and the point of the analysis is to teach the audience that all of these figures were created to feed that audience's appetite for fantasy. Mailer has begun disassembling himself, and he is doing it yet, doing it in so intricate a way as to defy a simple prophecy of how it will all turn out. But it is at least clear that it is the process of creation, not the product alone, that he wants to bring into the light, and it is just as clear that in so doing he is forging a legend for himself that our imaginations will not easily let die.

*Robert F. Lucid, in* American Scholar *(copyright © 1974 by the United Chapters of Phi Beta Kappa; reprinted by permission of the publishers), Vol. 43, No. 3, Summer, 1974, pp. 464-66.*

* * *

## MALRAUX, (Georges-)André 1901-

**A French novelist and a critic and philosopher of art, Malraux has unceasingly pursued the possibility of the individual's transcendence of his mortal fate, his triumph over silence and death, and his subsequent ennoblement. He sees Art as man's dynamic search for absolutes. His fiercely intelligent novels of ideas are considered among the world's most important contemporary work. (See also *Contemporary Authors*, Vols. 21-22.)**

Malraux's techniques depart radically from those common in France. His themes are universal: human suffering, human solitude, humiliation and human dignity, the constant imminence and irrevocability of death, the inanity of life. His heroes are rarely French: Perken, Kyo, Kassner, Garine, Manuel, and Vincent Berger are either people of indefinite origins, or of mixed blood, or foreigners. And the values Malraux deals in are perhaps less remote from us than from the French. Action and violence are not radical departures for us, at least in literature. (p. viii)

Malraux is a writer whose ideas are as important as his emotions. His novels are a product of both intellect *and* sensibility and, even more, of a need to establish an equilibrium between intellect and sensibility with respect to . . . "the political problem." For the central, crucial experience of Americans and Europeans alike has been the familiar political choice between passivity and revolution, and Malraux's name is high on the list of writers who moved away from democratic capitalism in the 'twenties and 'thirties, only to move back again. . . . His novels had their first and greatest success as the work of the most distinguished of French fellow travelers. They are nourished by the imperious need he felt to clarify his experience by transposing it into art; their special excellence lies in his ability to feel the relations between politics and the characteristic ideas, preoccupations, apprehensions, and anxieties that torture our time. (pp. viii-ix)

Critics like those of the British *Scrutiny* group deny that Malraux's six fictions may properly be called novels at all. In one sense they are right. Certainly these hurried stories, often overpopulated, always embarrassed by the size of what they try to contain—hard, brilliant, nervous, and closely related to drama as they are—are the antithesis of the kind of narrative which is defined by the unhurried thoroughness of its method. They are not patient, massive, rich; they seem to be deficient in Ortega's "thick texture of life." Malraux's fictions do not "create a world" of their own so much as they illuminate the hidden nature of a world which already exists. They mean to "reveal reality," as Lionel Trilling thinks a novel should, but to reveal it in flashes, with great demands upon the visual imagination of the reader as well as upon his comprehension, and probably not at all in the way that Mr. Trilling has in mind. Yet such strictures merely make it clearer than ever that what Malraux tries to do with fiction requires a special form—one, precisely, which will permit establishing a balance between sensibility and intellect.

Malraux rather luxuriates in the epithet "intellectual" and clearly delights in ideas. But "intellectual" does not have to mean "philosopher." We grant the title of intellectual to a man if "ideas mean a lot" to him, if what he does betrays his preoccupation with them. His ability to align them in the form of rational discourse is not what makes him an intellectual.

Only by such a definition can Malraux be counted among the intellectuals. His ideas are deeply felt but not, properly speaking, *thought*. Rarely has he chosen—or perhaps been able—to develop them discursively. When he tries to do so, as in the books on art, his prose does indeed have unity, but not because it develops a rectilinear argument. It owes such unity as it has to the fact that every paragraph is related, if not always to the paragraphs adjacent, to the eternal, unchanging preoccupations of his mind. The style is oracular; ideas are juxtaposed to other ideas with scant attention to those little matters of conjunction and subordination which make such a difference to the reader. The parts of *The Psychology of Art,* for example, were so far out of rational order that the new version, *Les Voix du silence,* is an improvement less because of its added materials than because of its superior clarity and coherence. So long as *The Psychology of Art* succeeds as well as it seems to be succeeding now in making readers aware of the significance of styles in art and of the relations of various arts to each other, the weakness in its structure is not fatal. It is merely a detriment, and hardly important to us here. What is important is that when we look back to this "intellectual's" novels after reading the art books, we see that the novels are incoherent in just the same way.

The logic of the stories—of situation and circumstance and inevitable outcome—invariably leads in one direction, to one conclusion, and the conclusion is invariably unpalatable. *La Tentation de l'occident* (which happens not to be a novel but which contains an implicit story) demonstrates the inanity of Occidental life; *The Conquerors* demonstrates the absurdity of *all* life, East or West; *The Royal Way* presents the final ignominy of death; *Man's Fate* illustrates our inability to rise above the human predicament and our inability this side of death to achieve a fitting dignity. And so on, with the exception of *Days of Wrath,* through the whole Malraux canon. Malraux does not reject these conclusions—how could he?—but he turns their logic, juxtaposing to them some picture, figure, image, or poetic symbol which affirms, oracularly, the opposite of what the rational discourse affirms. Thus in *Man's Fate* the manner of Katow's death makes the reader forget how thoroughly both he and Katow are subject to human bondage. The technique here is the technique of the art books: it consists of omitting links—of not setting down, for example, a reason why Katow's behavior as he goes out to be burned in the locomotive is at all relevant to what we have seen, for several hundred pages, to be man's fate. But in the art books we call this incoherence a defect and in the novels we call it an artistic technique. His craft is a craft of ellipsis. (pp. ix-x)

Malraux's . . . characters . . . are motivated by inner, obsessive drives, and what most frequently obsesses them is an idea. A given character acts as he is forced to by his attitude toward death, sex, human dignity, power, liberty, or something similar. He appears at once as an individual and as the incarnation of his special drive. Thus he becomes easy to label: Garine is The-Man-Haunted-by-the-Absurd, Hong is the Terrorist, Gisors is the Paralyzed Intellectual. Such labels reek of allegory, and it is a tradition of Western literature that allegory should teach a lesson.

But looking in Malraux's novels for *clear* lessons is as fruitless as asking them to be conventional novels, and extracting theses from them is like extracting theses from Shakespeare. The mere fact that he returns to worry the same old ideas, twisting and turning them over and over, should be a warning. As a matter of record, he is a man of a very few seminal ideas, though [a] few are important [and to] them he comes back like the dog in the Bible: *Les Noyers de l'Altenburg* and *The Psychology of Art* take up again themes already present in 1925 in *La Tentation de l'occident*. In view of the technique of ellipsis which is natural to him, we have to accept the fact that the novels are extremely slippery documents on what, at the time of writing, Malraux *thought*.

They are excellent documents on how he *felt*—which is to say that his work should be treated primarily as the work of a poet. It is dramatic poetry by an intellectual, for whom ideas become themes. (pp. xi-xii)

The poetry of the novels . . . rises out of the tension created by Malraux's craft of ellipsis. The logic of events in his novels is opposed by the magnificent picture of the human individual, placed *in extremis* by the events, which he juxtaposes to the logic. For this juxtaposition to be plausible, obviously, the character involved has to be of a certain size. (p. xii)

Politics is only one of the contexts in which man's nature stands out with great clarity. Malraux makes anthropology another. . . .

[No] serious treatment of Malraux's work can avoid anthropology, because *Les Noyers de l'Altenburg* not only identifies its hero with a mythic type dear to cultural anthropologists, but also contains a specific invitation to the reader to look back and find the fundamental mythic experience recurring in Malraux's previous books. With this much to guide a rereading, at least three of the earlier novels turn out to have characters in them who have undergone the same experience. And when, after the novels, we re-examine the legend of Malraux's life of action, it becomes clear that the hero of the legend has had the experience also. (p. xiii)

Critics have always been tempted to read *The Conquerors* and *Man's Fate* as though these novels were eyewitness accounts of the events they describe. They know that there is much autobiography in *The Royal Way, Man's Hope,* and *Les Noyers*. They assume that there must be autobiography in the other novels (except *Days of Wrath*) as well. They speak of Malraux as *"le témoin capital"* and allow the words to imply that the witness was always physically present. The transition from such assumptions to the belief that *all* of Malraux's books involve an element of journalism is easy.

Now "eyewitness" (or "journalist") is not necessarily a term of disparagement. But to treat as a kind of reporting these novels which are actually built not of historical but of imagined action is to fail to recognize the *nature,* if not the quality, of Malraux's achievement. If we know that the ferocious violence of *The Conquerors* and *Man's Fate* is in these books *because Malraux's fictional world needs to be violent to be complete,* and not just because he saw torture, suffering, and death while he was in the Orient, we know something decisively important about his peculiar originality as an artist. (pp. 9-10)

His first novels are dark with the apprehension of death and sad with the vanity of life, and haunted by the inevitable, tragic defeat of man's attempts to impart real meaning to what he does. They contain hardly a hint that in some way life may acquire meaning through the fraternity of revolutionary action and sacrifice. This suggestion will come in 1933, in *Man's Fate*. (p. 34)

Malraux has never written a book in which violence has not been an element of man's fate. His novels need it so that whatever acts the hero is forced to perform will have the necessary quality of decisiveness: what he does must be irremediable. For most of his protagonists a life of violence is the only satisfactory one. Violence provides them a field where action is possible despite their feeling of rupture and separation from their fellows. (p. 56)

These acts of violence are closely associated with the technique of ellipsis which is a permanent aspect of Malraux's writing. They form a part of the corrective picture in which he juxtaposes to the evidence of man's weakness the poetic proof of his tragic stature. (p. 57)

One may well agree with Marcel Savane's judgment [in his *André Malraux*], that *Man's Hope* will endure into the twenty-first century as one of the best revelations to later readers of what it meant to live in the twentieth. But if so, it will survive more by its value as a document than as a piece of literature, and by its appeal to the comprehending intellect rather than to the emotions. Its confusions, its loose ends, its diffuseness, may even increase its documentary interest. In its consciousness of what the fighting was about, *Man's Hope* towers above the book that is inevitably compared with it, *For Whom the Bell Tolls*. But Hemingway's book has the tight unity, the coherence, the constant emotional tension, and the finish, that Malraux's does not. The difference is that Hemingway intended a novel while Malraux intended a novel and something more. The books are thus not entirely commensurable. If Malraux's book outlasts Hemingway's, all that will be proved is that novels are not necessarily the most durable of books. (p. 125)

*W. M. Frohock, in his* André Malraux and the Tragic Imagination *(reprinted with the permission of the publishers, Stanford University Press; copyright 1952 by the Board of Trustees of the Leland Stanford Junior University), Stanford University Press, 1952.*

As a twentieth-century thinker, [Malraux] has illuminated his way through his investigations with his own intense, blazing light; his aim from youth has been to apply a half-dozen key ideas he selected at the start to the decoding of civilization and what he calls its great myths, meaning all its dominant invisibles, such as religions, systems of ethics and political faiths, and to make his report on man—on his singularity, his scope, the condition and the meaning of his life, and his tragedy (happiness has not been one of his studies)—using himself as creator, artist, fighter, witness, critic and microcosm. For the French, his genius lies in his rare intelligence, in his quintessentially French gift for complex ideas, in his capacity for formulation, for creative, unconventional deduction, and in the subtle perceptiveness of his thinking, often more lucid than logical. They feel that, unlike those of most creative thinkers, his intelligence and his emotions are equal—and both present in almost superfluous quantities. He has arrived at his eclectic erudition by a private way, choosing and studying, as he has proceeded through life, only what has fascinated him. His mind, now richly overloaded, seems to be divided into compartments, in each of which he functions separately. His novels are built on a world scale, achieved in part by the omission of women, since his male characters, depicted in fatal international, martial or political crises, are elevated above the domestic, the daily and the ordinary, and thus above the interferences of love.

*Janet Flanner, in her* Men and Monuments *(copyright © 1947, 1951, 1954, 1956, 1957 by Janet Flanner; reprinted by permission of Harper & Row, Publishers, Inc.), Harper, 1957, pp. 56-7.*

Twentieth-century Western man, according to Malraux, is deprived of God, and many values once worth fighting for, were there a God, have now also disappeared. (p. 7)

If Malraux were to be classified in any known category in regard to his religious position, he should be called what he says he is, an agnostic, but (something he does not say) bred of postulatory atheism. This atheism . . . is the only position compatible with his belief in the autonomy of man. (p. 11)

Christianity is, for Malraux, the first religious rupture with the absolute. . . . The result is that Western man is delivered into the individualism that finally played him false.

It would seem, then, that the Incarnation, for Malraux, finally ended in the triumph of man over God. To teach a man his worth as a man, because God thought him worth the price of His own Son, encouraged man's pretensions; and in man's gradual awakening God recedes into the world of dreams. (p. 20)

With the demise of the absolute, enter *le destin, l'absurde,* and *l'angoisse. Le destin* is Malraux's word for all that we cannot escape and crave to escape: it is fatality, necessity, all the forces of deriding determinism. (p. 23)

The impact of destiny for Malraux is coincident with the resurgence of the irrational as a force in life. (p. 24)

What has brought on this fascination with the irrational? Precisely the crumbling of any mental structures able to make sense out of life. (p. 29)

The *condition humaine* is a word, a cry, with no recourse to philosophical arabesques: man cannot live according to his hopes. (p. 33)

[As Kurt F. Reinhardt wrote in *The Existentialist Revolt,* "if] the object of anguish could be . . . determined, man might be able to rise in defense, ward off the danger and regain his security." It is more the sense of the nothingness of things in our regard, the deception in formulas, that brings on the anguish; and in it all is what one might term the modern mystery of negation. (p. 34)

When all the poetry is stripped away and all the modern descriptions of *destin* are reduced to their quintessential element, there emerges the oldest and most recurrent of human themes: that the immortal will ever be stranger amid the mortal, that the finite cannot ever be filled except (paradoxically) with the infinite, that unhappiness is precisely not having what we are made for, and that happiness, even now, is only partially attainable, and that precisely in being sure that we are on the way to what we are made for. It could be that Malraux and other moderns say this better than it has ever been said, but one is annoyed with the suspicion that they frequently prefer the saying of it all to the solving of it. (p. 36)

Except in *Le temps du mépris* Malruax has never presented a straightforward theme; he would seem unable even to leave unsaid the things that contradict his chief lines of thought. A man of deep human sympathy first, he seems to find enough justification in the pattern of tragedy to publish books that are emotionally disturbing and intellectually unclear. He repudiates the great intellectual who is interested in absolute truth and the complexity of things. "He is . . . anti-Manichean by definition, by nature." Malraux is not an intellectual of that stripe; addicted to a message of action, he thinks that "all forms of action are Manichean . . . every true revolutionary is a born Manichean" [*L'espoir,* p. 279]. It is as though Malraux, long passionately believing in man, knows only too well that that belief will always be a bittersweet thing: an absolute humanism must necessarily be pregnant with tragedy. (p. 88)

Malraux has long abandoned violence and individualism; and as his thought has developed, it has passed from the nobility of the individual to the fullness of fraternity. Now [with *Les noyers de l'Altenburg*] it is going to fan out over history until it formulates an eloquent appeal to belief in mankind. (p. 99)

Malraux's thought, from *Les noyers de l'Altenburg* on, becomes more and more difficult to unravel because he continues to talk to his reader in the same concrete, poetic terms that belonged quite naturally in the novels, but which, when he becomes "doctrinal," render the thought that much more impenetrable at first reading. Were he, of course, to become philosopher-sans-poetry in his direct discourse, he would lose much of his force; but the reader sometimes pines for some straight, prolonged explanations instead of flashes of intuitions in fiery language. (p. 106)

Malraux, among moderns one of the most sensitive to the discoveries of archeology, ethnology, and history, has, surprisingly, seen in the intrusion of historical consciousness into modern man another, and the latest, *destiny*. It is essential that we understand which concept of history he considers a new imposition of fatality on the modern mind. . . . [History] is either a progress, or it is a meaningless series of accidents, the only constant being that there are always civilizations.

Malraux is convinced that the "progress" idea has no play today. It is the meaninglessness of history which now weighs on us. With the death of the absolute and the rejection of any Christian meaning to history, we have plunged back into time, and come up with the poignant discovery that civilizations are unrelated, that they play their appointed time and lapse into nothing. We are now obsessed, not with man's permanence, but with his dissimilarity [*dissemblance*]. (pp. 119-20)

For Malraux man is always an accident of the universe, and there are always the age-old questions of death, old age, and all the forms of destiny, including the twentieth-century form, which is historical determinism.

It is the modern artist's fundamental acceptance, along with all thinking men of this age, of the fact of destiny that has driven him to an interest in what seems "fundamental" art (that of the insane, of children, of "popular" art) and in "savage" art. The modern artist, engaged in a conflict between the supreme value that he sees in art alone and what to his eyes are pseudovalues, usurpers, thinks he finds a kindred soul in the artist of the night, of the stars and of blood. The world of destiny is a cold, hard, unavoidable fact, and the "devil" now exists again; and the honesty of the arts that accept this fact, or portray it, is a world the modern artist understands. (pp. 193-94)

Art is a chorus of the past, of other men drowning out the voice of the same destiny that crowds us. We are united with all the effort of the past, through art, to resist destiny, to make it man-sized, to give at least an ephemeral importance to life, because it is in this resistance to destiny that man is at his noblest. Thrilling to the chorus of art, we sense the possibility of "the first universal humanism" in history. (p. 200)

Malraux's enthusiasm for art is sincere. He means desperately to move us to turn to it to find a new belief in man. His sincerity will gain disciples. But culture will never be a universal religion. (p. 216)

Malraux has come far. The thirst for action, because of the value of courage in accepting the absurd, yielded early to action for estranged, humiliated mankind, which in turn engendered a faith in mankind that sent Malraux hunting mankind's great moments in art. There it is that he finds the rebuff to the "meaninglessness of history," and in the autonomy of the artist Malraux sings of a valiant *anti-destin*. (p. 222)

*Edward Gannon, S. J., in his* The Honor of Being a Man: The World of André Malraux, *Loyola University Press, 1957.*

Malraux is that *rara avis*, the genuine political novelist. Like [D. H.] Lawrence he has not confined himself, in life or in literature, merely to fiction. And his ultimate work is a critique of art whose vision surpasses, strangely, the achievement of his novels.

In *La Condition Humaine*, as the title comes to suggest when set against the novel, action at once illustrates and incarnates idea: motive and act, attitude and character, will and destiny, become one under the purgative extremity of a revolution. . . .

The coherence of Malraux's idea is fictive enough to be independent of any specific communist platform. His fictional vision, while inseparable from its leading political idea, has a temper and incisiveness unattained by even such perspicuous communist parables as Aragon's *Voyageurs de L'Impériale*.

In *L'Espoir* the vision of a purpose underlying individual destinies is made too explicit. Random documentation in this novel supplants the diversified analogies of *La Condition Humaine*. In an earlier novel, *Les Conquérants*, Malraux casts his burden of social idea not so much in the plot —otherwise similar on a simpler scale to the situation of *La Condition Humaine*—as in the character Garine. In China, where Garine has come for just this vision of pure action, he finds politics as existential as Malraux would have them. But the vision of reality is still fictive. And Garine's notion, "beyond good and evil," is nonetheless a moral idea, the end of a soul-searching, opposed in the novel to the mindless power functionalism of Garine's antagonistic henchman, Borodine. . . .

For Malraux, fiction is an unparalleled instrument for mirroring the elusive nature of the historical process.

*Albert Cook, in his* The Meaning of Fiction *(reprinted by permission of the Wayne State University Press; copyright © 1960 by Wayne State University Press), Wayne State University Press, 1960, pp. 175-77.*

Better than any other figure of his epoch, Malraux anticipated and crystallized the postwar Existentialist atmosphere that has become associated with the names of Sartre and Camus. Man's irremediable solitude; his absurd but unquenchable longing to triumph over time; his obligation to assume the burden of freedom by staking his life for his values; his defiance of death as an ultimate affirmation of "authentic" existence—all these Existentialist themes were given unforgettable artistic expression by Malraux long before they became fashionable intellectual catchwords or tedious artistic platitudes. Indeed, the genesis of French Existentialism as a full-fledged cultural movement probably owes more to Malraux than to Heidegger, . . . Jaspers, [or] Berdyaev. . . . For it was Malraux, through his novels, who shaped the sensibilities that then seized on doctrinal Existentialism as an ideological prop. . . .

Up to the beginning of the Second World War, Malraux was the radiant symbol of the free liberal intellectual who had dedicated his life to the Communist Revolution and the struggle against fascism; and the focus of critical interest in his novels was their political content. But the Communists were never too happy about Malraux as an ally—and with good reason. For Malraux's heroes were never simply engaged in a battle against a particular social or economic injustice; they were always somehow struggling against the limitations of life itself and the humiliation of destiny. . . . [What] makes *Man's Fate* the greatest of all novels inspired by revolution, what gives it a poetic resonance invulnerable to changing political fashions, is precisely that Malraux was able to experience the revolution in terms of man's immemorial longing for communion in the face of death. . . .

The whole purpose of *Man's Hope* is to portray the tragic dialectic between means and ends inherent in all organized political violence—and even when such violence is a necessary and legitimate self-defense of liberty, justice, and human dignity. Nowhere before in Malraux's pages have we met such impassioned defenders of a "quality of man" that transcends the realm of politics and even the realm of action altogether. . . .

It is this larger theme of the "quality of man," a quality that transcends the ideological and flows into "the human," which now forms the pulsating heart of Malraux's artistic universe. To be sure, Malraux does not abandon the world of violence, combat, and sudden death which has become his hallmark as a creative artist, and which is the only world, apparently, in which his imagination can flame into life. *The Walnut Trees of Altenburg* includes not one war but two, and throws in a Turkish revolution along with some guerrilla fighting in the desert for good measure. But while war still serves as a catalyst for the values that Malraux wishes to express, these values are no longer linked with the triumph or defeat of any cause—whether that of an individual assertion of the will-to-power or a collective attempt to escape from the humiliation of oppression—as their necessary condition. On the contrary, the frenzy and furor of combat are only the somber foil against which the sudden illuminations of the human flash forth like the piercing radiance of a Caravaggio. . . .

No writer in modern literature can compete with Malraux—at least not with the Malraux of [the] final scene [of *The Walnut Trees of Altenburg*]—in evoking so poignantly what Wordsworth called "the still, sad music of humanity." And this music, despite its stillness and sadness, never ceases to sound in Malraux's novel above the roar of battle and the tumultuous march of the centuries. Malraux manages to wrest an affirmation of an absolute value in man out of the very teeth of the experience which—for example, in Sartre's *La Nausée*— had resulted in Antoine Roquentin's frightening vision of man's absorption into the world of brute materiality. The disclosure of the contingency of existence had led Sartre to portray man himself as a futile excrescence on the blank surface of things; and despite the role that liberty plays in his philosophy. Sartre has not yet succeeded (it is dubious whether he ever will succeed) in transcending the hopelessness of *La Nausée* by any equally powerful artistic expression. Indeed, one wonders whether Malraux's *The Walnut Trees of Altenburg*, consciously or otherwise, might not have been intended to meet the challenge of the vision of man proposed in *La Nausée* (which after all appeared in 1938, and which Malraux very probably would have read).

However that may be, there is no doubt that Malraux has managed by the sheer force of his artistic genius to extend the bounds of Existentialism in an extremely significant fashion. Even when Existentialism is determinedly atheist, as in Heidegger or Jean-Paul Sartre, the movement as a whole has drawn its image of man from the tortured cogitations of Kierkegaard; and that means from a Christianity which emphasizes the fallen nature of man and all the dark and gloomy aspects of human existence. Malraux, on the other hand, might be said to have created—paradoxical as it may sound—an Existentialism of the Enlightenment. For in reading *The Walnut Trees of Altenburg* one thinks of Kant rather than of Kierkegaard—not, to be sure, the Kant of *The Critique of Pure Reason* but the Kant who, in *The Critique of Judgment*, defined the "dynamic-sublime" as man's consciousness of the final inability of the power of nature, however menacing it might be, to force him to surrender his humanity. Malraux's image of man is therefore "sublime" in the strict meaning given that term by the greatest mind of the Enlightenment. And Malraux has performed the remarkable feat, unique in our time, of projecting this image both on the highest level of cultural achievement (through the symbol of the artist as creator in his books on art) and, in *The Walnut Trees of Altenburg*, as equally embodied in the simplest and most unself-conscious human response.

*Joseph Frank, "André Malraux: The Image of Man," in his* The Widening Gyre: Crisis and Mastery in Modern Literature, *Rutgers University Press (New Brunswick, N.J.), 1963, pp. 105-30.*

[The] surprise occasioned by Malraux's art studies was due of course . . . to an inattentive reading of [his] novels . . ., and to popular ignorance of Malraux's several interrelated careers. It is now clear . . . that there is an astonishing unity to everything Malraux has written, one is inclined to add everything he has done, since his first significant book, a sort of epistolary novel bearing the Spengler-echoing title *La Tentation de l'Occident (The Temptation of the West)* in 1926. A main element of that unity has been a persistent preoccupation with art—with works of art and the cultures they comprise and express—and with the role of art in a generally "absurd" universe. It was Malraux who, in *La Tentation de l'Occident*, introduced the word "absurd" into the modern philosophical vocabulary in a contention that, to the eye of modern man, the universe appeared fatally bereft of meaning, because of the loss of compelling and explanatory religious belief and, with it, the collapse of any direction-giving concept of man: because of the successive "deaths" of the idea of God and the idea of man. Most of Malraux's novels have been symbolic assaults upon history, in an endeavor to wrest from history a persuasive definition of human nature and a dependable guide and measure of human conduct; while in his life Malraux has been committed to intensive action and to what Gaëtan Picon calls "the myth of the great individual" as sources, perhaps of insight, but certainly of compensation. But he has also and ever more strenuously been committed to the great art work as performing, more satisfactorily yet, these same functions. If Malraux evidently still believes in the efficacy of the master, he believes even more in the saving power of the masterpiece.

The play of these terms—man, the absurd, action, history, and art—has been constant in Malraux's writing from the beginning. But before criticism could explore their use, it had to get beyond a prior misapprehension—namely, that Malraux was primarily a chronicler of contemporary revolutions, a skillful journalist of the political and economic upheavals peculiar to his age. (p. 2)

[Leon Trotsky] felt that *Les Conquérants* was itself a work of considerable art and made some acute and generous observations about its beauty of narrative. But he felt that the author's revolutionary passion was flawed; that Malraux's effort to give a faithful portrait of insurrectionist China had been (in Trotsky's word) corrupted, both by an "excess of individualism" and by "esthetic caprice." Even in retrospect, the charge (which Trotsky supported with considerable and pressing detail) is not without substance and pertains to a wider problem: for there has always been a sort of murky imbalance between Malraux's political affinities (the presumptive ones in his novels and the actual ones—Communist and then Gaullist—in his life) and his stated or implied beliefs about literature. Nonetheless, Malraux had reason to say, in answer, that his book was not intended and should not be judged as a fictionalized chronicle, and that, in effect, it was just the individualism and the esthetics that made it a novel. As to the former, the book's stress was placed "on the relationship between individual and collective action, not on collective action alone." As to the latter, Malraux made the crucial remark that the novel was dominated, not by considerations of doctrinal loyalty and historical inclusiveness, but by the vision, the way of looking at things—in Malraux's French, by *"l'optique"*—proper to the novel as an art form. The entire critical "problem" of Malraux—the "Malraux case," as some French commentators have called it—lies, implicit but bristling, in this early exchange.

Still . . ., it became generally agreed that Malraux . . . was *the* novelistic historian of the great social agitations of the century. (pp. 2-3)

Malraux's main characters really are protagonists: that is, etymologically, primarily combatants. What they do about the human condition is to take arms against its historical embodiments; and they will go to the ends of the earth to seek them out. . . . In short, and the commonplace is worth repeating since it applies more unequivocally to Malraux than to any other modern novelist, Malraux's heroes make their test of life in those places and times where human experience is most intensified, where indeed it has become most decisively embattled.

But as they do so, we move with Malraux into perplexities which, if not wholly philosophical in nature, are at least sources of logical anxiety. Time and again, Malraux has implied that it is in *action* that the strongwilled individual may hope to find not only assuagement but revelation. (p. 4)

Malraux's dilemma, if dilemma it be, is caused in part by the very subject—contemporary historical violence—which he has been brave enough to deal with. When, as in *La Condition Humaine,* he remains faithful to the historical outcome of the struggle, he concludes with a disaster which is not, *within the novel,* invested with any particular significance. But when, as in *L'Espoir,* he shapes historical fact to his fictional purposes (by concluding with the Loyalist victory at Guadalajara), he suggests an outcome and a meaning other than those history was already bleakly providing. . . . Malraux has not felt or envisaged the civil wars he has participated in as genuine tragic actions—not, at least, on any scale beyond that of a few driven and defeated individuals.

The importance, indeed the artistic and spiritual "value," of those individual destinies should not be minimized. It is true, as several critics have noticed, that there are no really evil figures in Malraux's novels: no persons who either are evil through some private wayward impulse or who represent the force of some evil principle in the universe. But it is not true . . . that Malraux has never created a character who "changes and really grows." Malraux does not concentrate his narrative on the change and growth of an individual psyche with the patience, say, of a Flaubert or a Proust. Change, in Malraux's fiction, is a regular phenomenon, but it occurs spasmodically, with earthquake speed and shock, and almost always during moments of greatest intensity. (pp. 5-6)

*La Condition Humaine* has, of course, been Malraux's most wisely admired novel, and it is no doubt his major contribution to the history of literature in his generation; beyond that, and beginning with the title, it is so impressive and enduring a challenge to its own content that it is likely to endure long after that revolutionary content has ceased to agitate the minds of readers. But the work of Malraux's which best fulfills the requirements of art—in Malraux's terms or anyone else's—seems to me to be *Les Noyers de l'Altenburg*. . . . (p. 9)

*R. W. B. Lewis, in his "Introduction" to* Malraux: A Collection of Critical Essays, *edited by R. W. B. Lewis (copyright © 1964; reprinted by permission of Prentice-Hall, Inc., Englewood Cliffs, New Jersey), Prentice-Hall, 1964.*

More than simply a duality of interest, all of Malraux's work presents an essential play between an action and its perspective, between the present and the eternal, between the loss of oneself in the moment and the recognition of oneself in terms of one's whole destiny. And this duality endures however violent the changes in ostensible subject matter or in genre. Or one might put it that the underlying subject matter itself never changes, and in his first works as in his last the same issues dominate: there is an obsessive and consistent investigation of the place of the private individual in historical time, the place of the individual passion in the overwhelming and unintelligible rush of events. And beyond the historical query lies a metaphysical one, distinguished not by its intellectual form but by its felt presence and insistence, a dramatization of the human demand to know something of its place in the pattern of things beyond itself, to relate the very course of human history to some intelligible feature of the structure of things. In so far as Malraux can be called a philosophical novelist it is not on the grounds of theories he presents, but of philosophical queries which are dramatized by the lives of his characters, or later, analogous queries which other men have, however dimly, formulated in the world of art. (pp. 4-5)

On the whole, the action of Malraux's heroes accomplishes little: revolutions fail, projects are abandoned, no course of affairs seems to work towards any decisive conclusion. Rather it is the style of the man, the unique human quality displayed that is of ultimate value. . . .

[Two] elements seem to work side by side: the concentration on episodes involving the psychological moment of truth, and the selection of those stylized and expressive features of human behaviour that are intrinsically dramatic and psychologically revealing. Added to an extraordinary sense of movement they produce the often noticed 'cinematographic' quality of Malraux's novels—'cinematographic' in the sense of moving from image to image, rather than from event to event—where it is the flow of images that controls the narrative. But even if deprived of that sense of movement the individual fragments exist as 'stills' and are perhaps more interesting as isolated images: in a way Malraux's technique is better described as the careful arrangement of psychological snapshots. (p. 9)

Malraux and his predecessors share two notions which are profoundly conjoined. One is the view of 'style' as being the most important means through which the expressive powers of art work; the other is of the subordination of 'speaking', that is of ordinary conceptual thought, to the deeper revelation obtained through the mysterious logic through which a style unfolds itself. 'It's not the style, but the stuff, that stupefies'—to invert a mnemonic slogan. And Malraux has from the start been excited by the obscure world of evocation lying behind the great works: Claude says in *La Voie Royale,* 'What interests me most in works of art is their deeper life, the life made up of the deaths of men.' (p. 25)

His particular gift is that of giving dramatic intensity to the facts of the human situation, and of showing the impact of that situation on what we can see of man's nature and creative powers. He is above all the spiritual chronicler of the human revolt, and his also is the artist's double rôle of actor and commentator. For him, the fact of man's presence and dignity can only be given a dramatic instantiation, a *picture* of that presence with its many resonances, but not a rationalization. By creating his own values what does man create? By asserting his humanity against the void what does he assert? These questions remain to trouble Malraux —as to trouble any form of humanism. But perhaps the most specific and immediate contribution of existentialist humanism, and of Malraux's in particular, is to give us a more profound and dramatic sense of human reality in the face of the void. (p. 74)

Malraux's humanism is based on a highly personal and intensified form of a concept at least as old as Aristotle's notion of the superiority of the contemplative man. It was a commonplace of the ancient world that reflective intelligence based on the power of speech, the fact of self-awareness and the power of expressing it distinguished the human creature and ennobled him, and gave him the closest thing to kinship with the gods. However, there is nothing in Malraux which suggests either the neatness or the assured rationalism of ancient psychology. The whole background of Malraux is overwhelmingly romantic, and he shares the romantic presupposition of a human self, infinite in its capacities and creative powers, and capable of incalculable transformation through the will. The heroism of man, as it was for Nietzsche, is the fulfilment of a will. In Malraux's career, the will has taken two forms: the *political will,* whose essential features are commitment and action, and the *rhetorical will* devoted to an indirect creation through the powers of human expression. And of course it is a short psychological step from 'willing' to 'choosing', the essential existential act. (pp. 75-6)

The most suspect element in Malraux has always been the 'fascinateur' or 'prestidigitateur'—the magical but meretricious juggler of glittering words, striving for a spell, producing a panoply of effects without certainty of substance. . . . And for him there may well be some profound connection between the importance of the created thing and the depth of mystery that surrounds it. (pp. 77-8)

*William Righter, in his* The Rhetorical Hero: An Essay on the Aesthetics of André Malraux, *Chilmark Press, 1964.*

[Malraux] clearly belongs to the 'heroic' tradition in French literature, running from Corneille through Stendhal and Barrès to the present, with its roots in epic, and powerfully reinforced in the nineteenth century by the symbol—or the legend—of Napoleon. (p. 204)

Stendhal is a direct antecedent of Malraux the novelist. The main link is . . . energy, or the quality which since Schopenhauer and Nietzsche has usually been called will; and its expression in fictional terms, the theme of ambition, in which the protagonists test their energy in a situation involving struggle. In Malraux's case the ambitions are much more grandiose than the usual purely social aims, metaphysical in their challenge to destiny or worldshaking in their attempt at political revolution; yet ambitions they remain. But, above all, both men try to create their own fictional world. (pp. 204-05)

The creation of a personal fictional world is the link in common between Stendhal, Malraux, and Dostoevsky, who can probably be regarded as the strongest fictional influence on Malraux. Dostoevsky's characters are also largely projections of his own personality, and his novels add up to a vision of the world, not an attempted copy of it (and, once more, some readers refuse the vision utterly, in the belief that human beings are just not like Dostoevsky's vision of them). But whereas Stendhal's writing is constantly shot through with irony, both the other men are writing at a high pitch of seriousness and self-consciousness from which irony and humour of the normal kind are usually absent. It is this frenetic intensity which unites Malraux most closely with Dostoevsky, together with treatment of characterization, in which there is little psychological analysis of the traditional type, but instead ample illustration of psychology in action, if possible violent action; that is, insights into human behaviour rather than explanation of it. Also dialogue is the favourite narrative mode of both men, while they each use imagery in the same way, to intensify emotional appeal; much of the content of the imagery—insects and reptiles, inspiring horror and disgust —is also similar. There is something of Dostoevsky in Malraux from the mid 1920s onwards—the theme of an exhausted Western material civilization in need of spiritual regeneration in *La Tentation de l'Occident*—but the influence becomes overt in *La Condition humaine*. (pp. 205-06)

The greatest individual influence on Malraux's life and work has been Nietzsche; from *La Tentation de l'Occident* onwards the idea of will pervades his writings, and, indeed, his whole life is a brilliant example of Nietzsche's ideal of 'giving style to one's character', and of heeding Nietzsche's call: 'Dare to lead the life of tragic man, and you will be redeemed.' . . . Perhaps a caveat about Malraux's use of ideas should be entered at this point. He has been widely taken by enthusiastic critics not only as an original philosopher, but also as a man of encyclopedic and exact knowledge in the field of history of ideas; and he has not disclaimed this.

In fact it is unlikely that he has ever made a detailed study of any philosopher. . . . [It] seems clear that Malraux's gift is for seizing on individual ideas and expressing them in dazzling formulae, rather than for systematic study and analysis. (p. 211)

Ultimately Malraux's adherence to Nietzschean attitudes may prove to have been a mixed blessing. The German's ideas have in the past proved more dazzling to the young than seductive to the mature, and it is possible that Malraux, while owing much of the intellectual and metaphysical weight of his earlier novels to him, has remained too close to Nietzsche to progress artistically much beyond the attitudes of his twenties and thirties. Whereas Stendhal and Dostoevsky primarily inspired Malraux to create novels, Nietzsche's influence seems to have made him want to cast himself in the role of sage, seer, and philosopher, without his having the full equipment—or originality—to succeed in it. In my own view, at least, Malraux's best work is in his novels, and when ideas have become ends in themselves, rather than creative material like any other, the final impact of Malraux's work is weaker. (p. 217)

[Malraux] himself, notably in the preface to *Le Temps du mépris,* has attempted to assimilate his work to the tragic mode; more recently certain critics have tried to formulate a new definition of tragedy, specifically in terms of man's fight against the absurd, using Malraux as a key example. Certainly, if we define tragedy as man's assertion of his dignity by a necessarily unsuccessful struggle against his destiny in an absurd world, cut off from all transcendental redemption, it is obvious that much of Malraux's work—art philosophy no less than novels—fits very well. Clearly confrontation with the absurd leads ultimately to death, and automatically irony of fate and a kind of tragedy will result. Yet it is just this automatic quality which casts doubt on the definition, and there is a slight suspicion of circularity in the argument. (p. 238)

If Malraux's works are judged on their effects, not on their correspondence to a theoretical definition, my contention would be that only *La Condition humaine* comes near to anything properly justifiable as tragic, despite greater superficial pretensions in *Le Temps du mépris*. The fundamental optimism kills the tragic in the later novels, while Perken's death is too melodramatic and Garine's situation too confused fully to justify the claim. It is also, perhaps, too easily assumed that the novel is the natural inheritor of the tragic mode formerly embodied in the drama. The belief that the novel should deal primarily with 'metaphysical' subjects, and in particular 'man and his destiny', is currently powerful; but it is none the less a survival of the nineteenth-century view exemplified in Arnold's literary criterion of 'high seriousness', itself a Romantic survival. It is a tenable position, but is open to the criticism that the novel has not, for much of its history, confined itself to—or even especially interested itself in—'metaphysical' themes; and that, if this criterion is applied now, the novel is restricted to only a part of the full richness of life. (pp. 238-39)

Malraux's appeal seems, in the main, to spring from the combination of contemporary (political) topics with metaphysical preoccupations. (p. 242)

Ultimately it is as a poet that Malraux is best considered: a poet in the widest sense. Although he uses ideas extensively, as we have seen, they are, if penetrating, usually not original, and the contrast with Sartre immediately brings out the fact that Malraux is little of the analytical thinker, and that his gift is much more for conveying ideas by pithy —poetic—formulations. What matters is not that he has developed a theory of modern tragedy, based on the necessity yet impossibility of self-transcendence in a godless world. . . . What matters in Malraux is that he has expressed his own feeling of restless anguish in the face of a meaningless world, in novels which succeed in conveying this powerful vision to the reader. His ideas are less a philosophy than a *Weltanschauung* [it is of course arguable that all popular philosophy must be *Weltanschauung*], and, although this attitude to life may form the basis of his works, their value does not depend on it. (p. 244-45)

[The] internal difficulties and contradictions of Malraux's ideas dissolve when he is looked at as a poet. (p. 245)

For myself *La Condition humaine* is Malraux's finest contribution. I find it impossible to see the Surrealist works as other than trivial and imitative; and, although *La Voie royale* foreshadows his later novels, Malraux has not succeeded in detaching himself from his subject-matter, which remains confused, nor in freeing himself from adolescent attitudes. In *Les Conquérants* the use of the revolutionary struggle gives him more adequate material to treat, but he is hampered by his first-person narrator and by the lack of harmony between the comparative success of the revolutionary movement and Garine's personal failure as he sinks into disease and disillusionment. Again, there is some confusion in the novel and its effect on the reader tends to be blurred. In *La Condition humaine* Malraux contrives to integrate a number of different elements, and above all, by choosing a historical episode which inevitably ends in disaster for nearly all his principal characters, an aura of tragedy is lent to the novel. As we have seen, Malraux's conception of the tragic side of life derives largely from Nietzsche, and more generally from loss of transcendental religious belief; and this modern view of the essence of tragedy has perhaps nowhere been more powerfully expressed than in this novel. Elsewhere Malraux tends to use his novels to affirm values, but here in the various characters—his richly drawn ones—there is a genuine search for them: a complex situation is probed for its profound significance, rather than an artificial one constructed to demonstrate values which precede the conception of the novel. And also *La Condition humaine* is emotionally richer than the other novels: the themes of love and compassion are more sensitively treated. . . . Fundamental poetic symbols—the sun, stars, earth, and trees—are finely presented, but the balance between the poetry and the ideas remains uncertain, and subjects outside Malraux's major preoccupations are very cursorily handled. . . . If the primary function of the poet is to absorb experiences from life —either his own or others'—to transform them into an acceptable form that he can communicate meaningfully to the reader, then it is in *La Condition humaine,* I should maintain, that Malraux has succeeded most richly. (pp. 248-50)

*Denis Boak, in his* André Malraux *(copyright © 1968 by Oxford University Press; reprinted by permission of The Clarendon Press, Oxford), Oxford University Press, 1968.*

In Malraux, a harmony between the human and cosmic cycles often serves to set the tone and create the physical atmosphere for a human adventure unfolding on earth against the canvas of the cosmos, and in time against a backdrop of eternity. The stars, the constellations, the moon, the sun, and the earth play prominent roles in suggesting an interplay between the hero's inner world and other elements in the created universe. The various time cycles—the day, the week, the month, the season, the year, the generation, and the epoch—often govern both the structure of the works and the evolution of the heroes.

As early as *Lunes en papier,* his first published volume, Malraux's vision of the world in terms of the cycle is compounded of anguish and hope, for the cycle implies not only a beginning and an end—or death—but also the idea of resurrection and renewal. . . . close association between life and death as part of a continuous cycle of creation is a recurring theme in Malraux, one which governs his vision of both human life and civilizations.

The Malraux cycle has two movements: one winds from death to new life and the other from death to resurrection after the passage of centuries.

Malraux's overall vision is one of creation in continuous progress. In accordance with this vision, change emerges as the new "absolute," with a consequent rejection of all closed systems and an emphasis on the relativity of all human knowledge and values. Malraux enjoins man to remain unreservedly open to the infinite possibilities of human destiny as the creation of man by man continues with the unfolding of the human adventure in time.

The cycle of constant flux as the scheme of things is at the heart of Malraux's tragic humanism, at least insofar as the flux is in direct opposition to man's perennial yearning for eternity and stability. Awareness of the impermanence of both human life and human values, including the succession of absolutes man has set up in an attempt to defy destiny, engenders the sensibility of the absurd, which is the point of departure of Malraux's hero.

For Malraux's early heroes the cycle represents a wheel of fate, an order of life over which man has no control and to which he must submit. When consciousness of the absurdity of this state of affairs becomes acute, it leads to a violent eruption out of the historical cycle into which the heroes are born—to a rupture between the heroes and their world.

It is this sensibility of the absurd that fires Malraux's imagination and leads to his relentless drive to transform the absurd into the significant by illuminating the past achievements of man, by forging for him a new *raison d'être* in the rapidly changing world of the present, and by opening a vista to a future which man himself must fashion.

More and more Malraux sees man as a being who must make history rather than submit to it, and here the ethical aspect of his work flashes into focus. He envisages man making history directed toward a definite goal: the promotion of the dignity of all men everywhere. The vision extends far into the future—perhaps beyond the human adventure.

The cycle which begins as the source of the hero's anguish gradually becomes the source of his hope. To an ever-increasing extent the hero regards himself not as a victim of the flux but as an active participant in its creation and perpetuation. Effecting change becomes a creative act, an outlet for man's creative potential, the *sine qua non* of progress. In Malraux, absurdity is transformed into significance as both the man of action and the artist contribute to the formation, transformation, or elaboration of the civilization of the epoch into which they are born.

Consciousness of imminent death—the end of the human life cycle—is the source of man's greatest anguish. (pp. 2-4)

If the final vision is still one of tragedy, it is the tragedy of Malraux the agnostic, haunted by the obsession that time, and with it the human adventure, will eventually come to an end, and that all the effort and striving of man's earthly existence might some day prove to have been in vain. But there can be no doubt that Malraux continues to see his world through "a Christian grating"; religious terminology and numerology occur throughout his works, beginning with the seven deadly sins in *Lunes.* If the vision is a Christian one, it is darkened by the doubt of an agnostic who envisages time flowing "certainly toward death" and only "perhaps toward eternity." The interpenetration of time and eternity definitely exists in Malraux; it occurs in those moments when man's creative spark is kindled into activity—either artistic or heroic. It is experienced by the artist especially when he discovers a new "truth," and by the hero particularly after a direct confrontation with Death, over whom he emerges victorious. Malraux beckons contemporary man, alienated from God, to seek this spark—his link with the divine—within his own being. (pp. 4-5)

His focus is directed to what men of all ages and regions have in common, rather than to what differentiates one man from another. His concentration is centered on man's *misère* and on his *grandeur,* and on his capacities for good and evil. As a compound of *misère* and *grandeur* Malraux's fundamental man is Pascalian; in his capacity for good and evil, he is Augustinian. In terms of his human condition, which involves him in a struggle between the opposing forces of human nature both within his own being and in the world, he is a combination of both: his life is a compound of anguish and hope.

Malraux's view of the human adventure unfolding in time bears much in common with St. Augustine's theory of human history as an endless struggle between the forces of good and evil or between the "City of God" and the "City of Earth" inhabited by the descendants of Abel and Cain respectively. Both Malraux and St. Augustine conceive of man's temporal existence in terms of one grand cycle (within which there are innumerable secondary ones) beginning with man's fall from a state of innocence. They do, however, differ as to where and how the cycle will end. Neither deems it possible to penetrate the ultimate meaning of human suffering and striving. (pp. 7-8)

Malraux's literary creation as a whole embodies the hope that man will ultimately remember that the purpose of his sojourn on earth is to destroy Satan, the task forgotten by the seven deadly sins of *Lunes.* Foolishly they destroy Death, and with her the cycle of creation (in which the role of death is just as important as that of life—the one flowing endlessly into the other), leaving Evil, or Satan, rampant without the possibility of change and renewal as the means by which the creation or redemption of man by man may be completed in history. Malraux's hope is focused on Pascal's *homme-grandeur*; his aim is to awaken man everywhere to a consciousness of a *grandeur* hidden in the deepest recesses of his soul, to a divine spark ever-ready to be kindled into creative activity. This activity includes all acts that serve to defy a destiny imposed upon man; it comprises any action that manifests man's freedom in terms of a refusal to submit to forces denying his dignity or to a world offering no outlet for his creativity. (pp. 8-9)

Life is movement—creation in perpetual progress. Malraux does for man throughout the ages what Montaigne does for the individual: he urges him to remain open to the infinite possibilities of his destiny. To man's quest for stability, Malraux opposes the cycle of constant flux without which the evolution of man would cease before the creation of man by man could be completed.

If Malraux's vision begins with his fundamental man as a combination of Pascal's and St. Augustine's, his ultimate hope is that *l'homme-grandeur* will triumph. If, in the world of the twentieth century, the evil in man finds full expression, and if "man against God" has become "man against man," there emerges from Malraux's works the nascent hope that "man against man" may, in the not-too-distant future, become "man for man."

Malraux's complete *oeuvre* spans the whole of man's earthly existence, from the dawn of recorded history to a glimpse of the end of time. Viewed in their entirety his works constitute an epic of man. (pp. 9-10)

As we venture into Malraux's fictional world, which runs parallel to the real world in that each novel centers around one or more of the crucial events of the first half of the century, we are increasingly convinced that Malraux's literary creation as a whole is dedicated to the penetration of the mystery of man living in a universe where everything, including man, is subject to the relentless cycle of flux from life to death.

The evolving contemporary setting of the novels destroys the comforting sense of tranquility provided by the traditional novel. It transmits to the reader an underlying mood of uncertainty and anxiety which emanates from characters embarked on a quest for meaning in a restless, turbulent world.

If the volumes on art reveal how men of distant ages and places have defied the implacable cycle of time which flows "certainly to death and only perhaps to eternity," Malraux's fiction—his novels in particular—enables the reader to witness contemporary man as he renews the age-old struggle against time and death. Malraux's seven novels are set forth as an organic unity; the first, *La Tentation de l'Occident,* discloses the crises and prepares the setting for the struggle which engages the heroes of the other six. The six full-fledged novels, which are presented as a "divine comedy" in an existential setting, form a cycle based upon an analogy between contemporary man's quest for identity and the spiritual journey of "everyman." It is a journey that begins with the hero's descent into hell (the prison of the self no less than that of the world) and ends with his intimation of a far-off Earthly Paradise. If there is tragedy in the implication that the "journey" or cycle will have to be repeated by each man and each generation throughout the course of human history, there is also the hope that progress is being made toward the ultimate creation of a world society where men may live in peace and dignity.

Thematically speaking, the cycle winds from the hero's discovery of the tragic finality of death to his rediscovery of the secret of life; as the two ends of the cycle meet, both life and death are viewed as parts of the incessant cycle of creation. This accounts for the recurring close association of the two concepts in Malraux's imagery and thought, not only in the novels, but in his works as a whole. (pp. 10-11)

*Violet M. Horvath, "Introduction" to her* André Malraux: The Human Adventure *(reprinted by permission of New York University Press; copyright © 1969 by New York University), New York University Press, 1969.*

Like Trotsky and T. E. Lawrence, Malraux exemplifies the problem of the intellectual as a man of action. "For a thinker, the revolution's a tragedy," he writes in *Man's Hope*. "The path that leads from moral standards to political activity is strewn with our dead selves. Always there is the conflict between the man who acts and the conditions of his action." Malraux's fictional heroes reflect his own life: a trial by ordeal that attempts to affirm "authentic" existence through an obsession with the metaphysical questions of time and solitude, freedom and destiny, anguish and humiliation, suicide and death. His characters lead a symbolic existence at a high level of self-consciousness. Behind them stand the example of Rimbaud (whose suppurating leg wound is suffered by Perken in *The Royal Way*) and the philosophy of Nietzsche (who appears in a moment of lucid madness in *The Walnut Trees of Altenburg*). . . .

What is so impressive about Malraux's life, however, is that his sensitive idealism was never defeated by his failures and he was always on the right (in our century, too often the losing) side. He *did* bring moral standards to political activity, he projected his brilliant intellect into a number of ambitious and exciting art books through which he revealed a new way of seeing art, both individually and contextually; and he wrote three first-rate novels: *Man's Fate, Man's Hope* and the little known but rich and moving *Walnut Trees,* with its superb evocation of Malraux's great theme of the virile fraternity. Malraux, who has just published his eighteenth century studies of Laclos, Goya and Saint-Just in a single volume, *Le Triangle noir,* and is halfway through the second volume of memoirs, is certainly one of the most creative intellects of this century. "In the menstruum of this man's wit," as Emerson said of Goethe, "the past and the present ages, and their religions, politics, and modes of thinking, are dissolved into archetypes and ideas."

*Jeffrey Meyers, in* Commonweal *(reprinted by permission of Commonweal Publishing Co., Inc.), December 11, 1970, pp. 280-81.*

[The] "formalist" critics, who are attracted by the textural complexities of the inheritors of Flaubert and the French symbolists, have ignored Malraux and left him to the historians of literature and to those intent on defining the stages of a *Geistesgeschichte*. . . .

Therefore, while the other phases of Malraux's achievement have been amply documented, there is still something left to be said about his methods as a novelist. . . . Malraux has systematically acquainted us with his literary forebears and with his likes and dislikes. Thus we know what he thought of Flaubert, the darling of the formalists: he considered him more and more a "pale reflection" of Balzac. . . . The hectic pace and staccato rhythm of Malraux's novel [*Man's Fate*] is very different from the calm, leisured pace and almost still-born movement of Flaubert's [*Madame Bovary*]. Flaubert's *coupes,* which make his sentences drop unexpectedly at the end, offer a tight coherence unrelated to Malraux's "stylistic abridgements" and what Frohock [in *André Malraux and the Tragic Imagination*] called "craft of ellipsis." In one way, however, *Madame Bovary* and *Man's Fate* try for a similar effect: simultaneity. Flaubert uses his intermittent *tableaux,* we have been told many times, to slow down the forward movement of his novel and to offer the sense of juxtaposition we get from looking at a painting. *Man's Fate* also thrives on the illusion (and that is all it can be in literature) of simultaneity; it offers a modified example of what Joseph Frank . . . has christened "spatial form."

We must qualify. The famous *comices agricoles* scene in *Madame Bovary* is pictorial and has a Bruegel-like density. . . . [Scenes] in *Man's Fate,* have a Goyaesque fluidity. (Malraux himself would appreciate this distinction and would want to be entirely on the side of Goya.) What I am saying is that there is a more restless, chaotic side to the Malraux scene than to the Flaubertian one.

*Melvin J. Friedman, "Some Notes on the Technique of 'Man's Fate'," in* The Shaken Realist: Essays in Modern Literature in Honor of Frederick J. Hoffman, *Louisiana State University Press, 1970, pp. 128-43.*

In Malraux's novels, as in his writings on art, the personification of man's ineluctable defeat holds the center of the stage, setting the tone for a variety of lost types who gesticulate in an atmosphere of glamorous resignation. And by the side of his hero, Malraux himself, in the guise of a man enacting Man, has played his part in the major situations of the past forty years.

Thus while Malraux is both an artist and a theoretician, he is above all a protagonist. He speaks as a character seeking to give his own stamp to the historical drama in which all who live in this epoch have taken part. He has striven to bring his art and his thought into play with actual events. His ideas have been both instigators of real actions and their verbal accompaniment.

Since Malraux's writings are part of his total performance, they ought to be interpreted in the light of it. Words like "Man," "Action," "Solidarity," "History" take their meanings from the use to which he has put them within the framework of contemporary conflicts. . . . To discuss Malraux's theories and fiction apart from what their author has been doing, including the doing of his words, is like discussing a character in a play by analyzing his dialogue without paying attention to his part in the plot. Perhaps a special kind of historic-dramatic criticism is needed to deal with a writer who has intended not only to capture our attention as an artist but to change our lives as a political force. . . .

Typical Malraux criticism, however, . . . treats Malraux as a philosopher and poet of human destiny, whose part in the history of the drama of our time is no more relevant in evaluating his work than might be the fact that an author had been employed in a bank. . . . Apparently, the way to read Malraux's novels is to treat the historical situations in them as mere pretexts for the display of a higher conflict. . . .

I [have wondered] where . . . these critics [were], both the Americans and the Europeans, during the events to which Malraux's novels were a response, and what . . . their own response to those events [was]. . . .

Aesthetically perceptive, and engaging in speculation on a high level, [their] pieces are manuscripts found in a bottle—as if their authors had been living in another century than the one which Malraux has been agitating with such fervor. They apprehend the drama in his writings but not his writings in the drama of the time. . . . Has detachment from current history become part of the "discipline" of literary criticism? . . .

It is symptomatic that though Malraux is a voluminous author, the same passages are chosen by critic after critic to illustrate the wide span of his thought. . . .

Some of Malraux's commentators cling more persistently to his abiding truths than does Malraux himself. [For example], . . . Malraux confessed that "little of what I dramatized in *La Condition Humaine* holds true." . . .

In sum, the problem in current criticism of Malraux is not lack of awareness of his qualities, but a persistent tendency to falsify the scale of his achievement through stringing his writings upon the lofty scaffolding of the issue of human destiny. . . .

After a glimpse of the specific content of Malraux's notions of fate, action and history, it seems obvious that criticism of Malraux ought to begin by dismantling his verbal screen of "the human condition" in order to get at what is actually reflected in his texts. . . .

[In] Malraux's novels the characters find themselves engaged in actions already in progress and which they cannot affect. The ready-made event calls for the ready-made actor—the formula of melodrama. In Malraux the "great act" of history is enacted by a cast of melodramatic types with the whole of humanity for their audience. Indeed, consciousness of this audience is an essential motive in their performance as men of destiny. . . . In Malraux's thinking, action constantly blends into acting: with historical script in hand, the only problem is which part to play and how to play it. . . .

The trouble . . . lies in his corny idea of the great role. Malraux will have nothing to do with anyone less than a god or a hero—and the god must be dying and the hero hopeless.

*Harold Rosenberg, "Actor in History," in his* Act and the Actor: Making the Self *(copyright © 1970 by Harold Rosenberg; reprinted by arrangement with The New American Library, New York, New York), New American Library, 1970, pp. 152-69.*

For Malraux, religion is not dead. He is ready to admit that this terrestrial life may be succeeded by another. What he insists upon, however, is that no human society any longer treats Christianity as a life-giving force. Man has emancipated himself. Upon him alone individually now lies the task of replacing a discarded providence.

In short, politics in *La Condition humaine* as in *Les Conquérants* is background. It furnishes the context in which the characters grapple not with political systems but with life itself. There is no question of weighing the validity or invalidity of communist arguments. The whole point lies in the power of communism as a faith, whether the faith is valid or invalid, to quicken its converts into more intense living, into a sharper self-consciousness. . . .

In reading *L'Espoir* the reader is not to worry over the ultimate defeat of the republicans or about the true worth of their claims; he is not to worry about what he may have read of the divisions among the republican politicans, divisions which the novelist honestly refers to in passing and which Don Salvador de Madariaga, for example, has dwelt upon. The reader has to let himself be carried away by the strength of conviction, the fanaticism even, with which the protagonists in their losing struggle wage their sectional battles, see to the wounded, collect prisoners, and so on. For although it is impossible to underrate the fervor with which Malraux himself espoused the aim of the Spanish republicans, neither politics nor any political creed is at the center of the novel. As in *Les Conquérants* and as in *La Condition humaine,* the prerequisite of the drama is not the validity of a political ideology but the power that such an ideology can exert over its adherents, rousing them to more intense living. In reality Malraux is no politician in the accepted sense. He is a social philosopher, a writer anxious to bring home to his readers the excitement of being faced with the infinite potentialities of actual life. . . .

Malraux has organized, edited, and partly written a remarkable and now widely known series of art books. They are books filled with reproductions of works of fine art. They have been a notable publishing success. They constitute one more indication that the reason Malraux has been preoccupied with political creeds and with actual political struggles is that the best political regime in his view is one that allows the widest opportunity to as many human beings as possible for each to make something of his one life and its infinite potentialities. Logically, of course, those he labels fascists can find in their cause as much as those he calls communists or those he calls patriots can find in theirs. Ultimately what particular cause is embraced cannot in this respect matter. But he invariably writes with the bowels of compassion. He writes in favor of the emancipation of the oppressed and the release of those under an invader's heel. . . .

[Since] the war Malraux has produced his book on Goya and on those works of Goya's that are gathered in the Prado. It is called *Saturne* (1950). The choice of painter was not fortuitous. Goya reacted with his whole being against the presence on Spanish soil of Napoleon's soldiery even as Malraux was unable to stomach the presence of Hitler's troops in France. So it is that the novels are invariably related to the experiences of an author who has himself lived to the full. Quite possibly there are readers persuaded in advance that the politics must be wrongheaded. After all, every question has two sides. But any such refusal to agree is irrelevant. What matters in the novels is the evidence of the generous human impulse which they contain. Let me insist again that the political element, although it figures so largely, is background. In front of that background are various human figures face to face with the task of each shaping his own destiny unsustained by religious faith and, as the price of his autonomy, constantly face to face with the gravity of death.

*Montgomery Belgion, "André Malraux (1901- )," in* The Politics of Twentieth-Century Novelists, *edited by George A. Panichas (reprinted by permission of Hawthorn Books, Inc.; copyright © 1971 by The University of Maryland; all rights reserved), Hawthorn, 1971, pp. 174-88.*

Trotsky admired what he felt were the purely literary virtues of Malraux's first novel, *The Conquerors,* but faulted Malraux and his hero Garine for not understanding the true nature of revolution. . . .

If Malraux espouses no orthodox program of revolutionary behavior, his characters do act within a context of shifting and provisional attitudes toward the historical process—the great sweep of events and the power which seems to impel them. Garine, although obsessed with the idea of revolution, is no *apparatnik.* What drives him to action on behalf of the revolutionary movement is richly contradictory, that is, fundamentally confused and *human*. . . .

Garine's attachment to the life of action is undercut by a pervading inner anguish. Knowledge may be evaded in deeds; the symptoms of a diseased subjectivity ignored or suppressed in the heat of battle. But Garine's individuality, which he offers to the objective force of History, paradoxically enlarges and mounts as he seemingly succeeds in bending events to his will. Through sudden executions of brutal policy, acts of instant justice, and brilliantly intuitive strategy, Garine actually brings the revolutionary action to the point of success. As he succeeds, his inner doubt and confusion mount; he is ill with fever and will eventually die of it. His illness is a given of the novel but Malraux heavily suggests that it issues from an existential despair. . . .

*Man's Fate* enlarges and deepens the thematic concerns of *The Conquerors*. . . . The theme of *Man's Fate* is the tragic discrepancy between human intention and historical outcome; between what man's will attempts with all the passion of intellect, feeling, and desire and what emerges in "the desolation of reality." Kyo, who is not so much spokesman for Malraux's position in *Man's Fate* as his mediator among a number of positions, opts for will, albeit with a certain amount of caution. . . .

The tension between the fatalism of history and "the activity of men in pursuit of their own ends" sustains both ideology and structure in *Man's Fate*. . . .

*Organized apocalypse* [a phrase from *Man's Hope*] might conceivably define the successful work of art where inchoate elements of raw experience are ordered into significance by ethical and structural control. But *Man's Hope,* Malraux's full-scale attempt to render the historical immediacy of the Spanish Civil War, strikes me as a disorganized apocalypse. It is Malraux's most ambitious fictional work, Tolstoyean in its sprawling proportions and ideological scope. Apparently Malraux tried to tell us everything he observed, everything he felt, everything he *did* (for he was part of the action) in Spain. Malraux also intended the book to speak for the Loyalist cause; it was meant to influence the course of history in a way fervently desired by men and women opposed to fascism. Unfortunately, *Man's Hope* is disappointing as a novel and largely unconvincing as a work of special pleading. . . .

*Man's Hope* moves with history as it happened, a book so close to events that it develops a coy attitude of busy self-consciousness. It is filled with what William Empson calls "the hearty revolutionary romp," an embarrassing sentimentality about comradeship in arms couched in stiffly unreal dialogue. . . .

Immersed in action and event *Man's Hope* never develops functioning protagonists—characters who speak and act for themselves, out of individual will and inner struggle. . . .

Malraux took too many risks in *Man's Hope*. He assumed the stability, humanity, and efficiency of the Communist leadership. He tried to outguess History or perhaps outshout it. . . . He largely forsook the structural conventions of plot and character and tried to create a fictional world out of episodes, tones, moods, and pages of brilliant writing. He tried to write a book about a political conflict from a partisan stance and hoped the book itself would become part of the action and help summon the democratic world to the aid of Loyalist Spain. Parts of *Man's Hope* struggle free of its ideological and structural shackles; but a book so conceived and written was doomed as was the cause it so desperately espoused. . . .

Action, blood, and fate stand as rubrics on every page of Malraux's novels. While some have called Malraux's espousal of revolutionary causes instances of political opportunism or adventurism, his commitment to action hurled a challenge across "the metallic realms of the absurd." To be sure, Malraux was afflicted with that *amor fati* which in Spengler means submitting to historical necessity and those historical forces poised to destroy man's freedom and man himself. . . .

Even though early in his career Malraux urged the refutation of Spengler, he was obviously caught up in his ideas. Malraux accepted the fatality of History and Spengler's closed, organic view of culture. Every culture had its spring, summer, autumn, and winter; no culture can escape its final dissolution any more than man can resist the change of seasons. Man as an individual, then, is the helpless victim of historical process.

*Harvey Gross, "André Malraux," in his* The Contrived Corridor: History and Fatality in Modern Literature *(copyright © by The University of Michigan 1971), University of Michigan Press, 1971, pp. 124-54.*

Malraux has been not so much the privileged spokesman of the real world as the tormented visionary looking beyond the present struggles of men to the permanent tragedy of "Man": not so much the novelist of history, in fact, as the poet of what he everywhere calls "destiny." (p. 17)

Malraux's essentially antihistorical vision tends ironically to depend for its force upon the force of history itself. It is significant that in the three novels which he privately regards as unsuccessful—*La Voie royale, Le Temps du mépris,* and *Les Noyers de l'Altenburg*—he was operating without the pressure and the prestige of the revolutionary situation. Even so, he everywhere bends the novel of history to the poem of destiny. (p. 19)

The post-Nietzschean adventure of the first phase of Malraux's writing runs into an impasse. The real "destiny" of the adventurer is his very elevation of his own estrangement into a false and separatist notion of Destiny. His "authenticity" is alienation; his "lucidity," self-deception. In these circumstances, his relentless implementation of his own will "beyond Good and Evil" reveals him as a kind of noble image of Fascist man, attempting to resolve despair in a violent imperializing dream. And yet for Malraux as a writer the very representation of the New Man, and of his defeat, was something of a moral achievement and a clarification. In . . . *La Condition humaine,* he [attempted] to find values meaningful for all men, whether they be heroic and 'authentic' or not. (p. 59)

To the Anglo-Saxon mind, Malraux's search for "fundamental man" may look like eccentricity or pretentiousness of quite continental proportions, even though the "fundamentality" of man is arising in different terms today as a problem for a variety of intellectual disciplines, including linguistics—there is, indeed, a certain "prestructuralist" quality about the Altenburg debate in [*Les Noyers de l'Altenburg*]. Nevertheless, the idea of the need for a notion of "fundamental man" was obviously the axis of Malraux's work from the beginning. Arguing in his early diagnosis of Western civilization that man was "dead," after God, he suggested that civilization could only be founded afresh on a new idea of man himself: in effect, on something as firm and suprahistorical as the Christian idea of the soul. Yet this was in practice impossible in that the individual, that "monster of wish-fulfillment," could know neither himself nor others. (p. 106)

The major writer does not so much give "answers" as project the "questions" in such a way as to bring out the final mystery of the human situation. The weakness of the "novelist of ideas" is that his works tend to die along with the ideas themselves. The strength of Malraux as an imaginative writer is that—in accordance with his own coherent and objectively quite important aesthetic of fiction—he is essentially a novelist who enacts the extreme situation in which the "ideas" of the character come sharply up against an ultimate ontological mystery. And what gives his best fiction its peculiar intensity and poignancy is less the dramatic historical moment itself, whether it be a turning point of the Chinese revolution or of the Spanish Civil War, than the coincidence of this with a boundary situation at the metaphysical level. (p. 153)

*Cecil Jenkins, in his* André Malraux *(copyright 1972 by Twayne Publishers, Inc.; reprinted with the permission of Twayne Publishers, a Division of G. K. Hall & Co.), Twayne, 1972.*

* * *

## MAURIAC, François 1895-1970

**Mauriac, a French Roman Catholic novelist, playwright, poet, essayist, scenarist, and journalist, won the Nobel Prize for Literature in 1952. His novels, according to one critic, offer us "a theology of the passions—or, more exactly, the opposite of a theology: a demonology." (See also *Contemporary Authors*, Vols. 25-28.)**

[What is] surprising, as we re-study Mauriac, is the now apparent fact that much of his thought and insight corresponds to the work of existentialist philosophers. Both they and he search out the unauthentic, the complacent illusion, the fear of honest confrontation in human experience. They and he are obsessed with the isolation of the human person in an alien universe. Correlative is the disillusionment seemingly inevitable in human love.

Seen in retrospect, however, the existentialist motif most evident in Mauriac's writing is the working-out of the search for self-knowledge and self-realization. . . .

For Mauriac, the world is indeed a somber place, but not for the reason that evil is an inherent and undefeated force therein. Rather does Mauriac center on the paradox rooted in man: the inviolable nature of his person as a unique human being with a destiny he alone can achieve and the inescapability of his fulfillment without surrender to Someone transcending himself. The sacredness of the human person is acknowledged first and recognized by the individual as he looks at himself in the light of the truth. . . .

Certainly we find often in the novels of Mauriac shallow and complacent Christians carefully cushioning themselves from the shock of self-recognition. Sometimes we see them in another aspect—that of those who attest their self-knowledge, but who refuse the gift of themselves, serving only their ego, in a monstrous parody of life. It is on these individuals that Mauriac is especially harsh in judgment. . . .

Seldom does Mauriac choose to show us those who, recognizing themselves for what they are, give themselves fully to God in service, carrying on with Him a dialogue of love. Self-knowledge and self-realization here become reciprocal in growth. Mauriac usually portrays these rare persons as unattractive or misunderstood, perhaps to emphasize how little the approval of others is necessary for their peace or joy. Their common quality in Mauriac's work is a great-hearted generosity with which they freely offer their lives or their ambitions or their sufferings that others may live.

*Sister Anita Marie Caspary, "Introduction" to her* François Mauriac *("Christian Critics" series), B. Herder, undated, pp. v-x.*

[Mauriac] is concerned not with outward appearances, but with the heart; not with neat artistic designs executed as an end in themselves, but with words as a means of testifying to the Word. Reality is the aim of his fiction—a reality whose drama is heightened because it is played against an eternal background. . . . To restore to the flesh its mystery and to speak truly of the heart Mauriac has risked everything.

*Neville Braybrooke, "The Seventh Skin: The Novels of François Mauriac," in* Blackfriars, *October, 1954, pp. 430-38.*

Although a Christian view of life brings with it a sense of drama that may be propitious to the writing of a novel, the novelist, if he is to succeed as such, must still graft this onto a personal vision of life—thus necessarily revealing his own imaginative powers and limitations. As good a novelist as Mauriac is haunted by this problem. There is no doubt that his work suffered at times from his ambiguous attitude toward his own creations. A humorless pathos pervades his tone when he bids us look upon the—to him fearful—creatures of his own imagination. Why should an author have so much trouble accepting the stories he invents? Mauriac's bad conscience occasionally makes us uncomfortable, and whenever it protrudes, it tends to destroy the integrity of his fictional world. (p. 99)

[According to] Mauriac, . . . man [is] condemned [by fate] to wander unsatisfied on this earth, exiled from the love of God that alone gives meaning to man's relationship with the Creation. Human beings therefore attempt to satisfy their inner void—a void that can be filled only by God—through the spiritual and physical possession of their fellow beings. . . . As Mauriac sees it, the novelist, like the priest, is deeply concerned with the fate of human beings; but unlike the priest, he uses them for his own ends, like a Mephistopheles in disguise. . . . But the particular atmosphere of the novel comes rather from an imaginary inner landscape that Mauriac seems to carry in his mind both as a memory and as an image of remorse. . . . (p. 114)

This inner landscape pervades Mauriac's novels, imposing a strong and simple pattern and carrying its own recognizable atmosphere. . . . His imaginary land can . . . seize one in a glacial grip, but never can it give relaxation or temporary comfort. There is a terrible beauty in it, an alien, disquieting beauty, that generates disaster. . . . (p. 115)

The story that Mauriac tells is the story of individual solitude and hunger, a spiritual hunger that springs from the deep realms of the subconscious where our hidden aspirations, lusts and frustrations lurk. The plot is less a succession of events than the welling up of this secret inner life; this life breaks through to the surface and then subsides, sometimes becoming perceptible in an action, more often simply in the modifications it imposes on the relations of the central character to those around him. There may be no external evidence of a life thus led in secrecy, merely a dramatic heightening of the atmosphere. . . . Mauriac's novels are sustained by the brilliance of their tense atmosphere. But they can stand no dilution, and dilution for moral purposes is the pitfall that Mauriac finds difficult to avoid. (pp. 116-122)

*Germaine Brée and Margaret Otis Guiton, in their* An Age of Fiction: The French Novel from Gide to Camus, *Rutgers University Press (New Brunswick, N.J.), 1957.*

In the wake of Pascal the fundamental fact of human life is, for Mauriac, the collision of the Christian ethic with the inclinations of nature. The Christian is committed to a perpetual struggle. The concupiscence of the flesh and the pride of life are twin rivers of fire which he must breast. The whole nobility of man consists in vanquishing his nature where God demands that it should be vanquished. (p. 16)

His many gifts of style, his amazing sensuous awareness, must, in any critical evaluation of the French novel in the twentieth century, be subordinated to the fact that it was his undeviating practice to impregnate the novel of naturalism with the agitated Pascalian concern with sin. (p. 17)

Many of Mauriac's readers, even those inclined to sympathize with his basic view of life, have been repelled by what they feel is the harshness of his vision. . . . [But the] true force of Christianity does not lie for him in its power to exempt man from suffering but rather in its ability to give meaning to suffering. . . .

Obviously, the omnipresence of spiritual struggle has given to Mauriac's novels their identifying character. . . . Although man, in Mauriac's view, can never escape his sense of divine filiation, his earthly pilgrimage is fixed in an environment which openly conspires with the inclinations of his physical nature. The earth from which he springs bespeaks the pagan deities rather than the Christian God. This paganism which looms large in all of the novels is not necessarily sinister, although always potentially so. Mauriac, as a Catholic, finds the conflict of earthly-inspired passions and grace inescapable. As a poet whose senses are keenly alert to the aching beauty of the universe he knows that myriads of his fellow men treasure a nostalgic attraction to that beauty. (pp. 19-20)

[The] particularization of the Mauriacien drama [is] the fact that in the internal struggle which rends man's soul the external universe participates on the side of the carnal inclinations. Because the struggle is internal, the actions of Mauriac's novels are uncomplicated and the settings are, for the most part, in the village or countryside. Strangely, on the pavements of the great city the drama of the flesh is muted. (p. 21)

Following [Maurice] de Guérin, Mauriac is a poet-novelist smitten with the beauty of the physical universe, yet never losing contact with the mysteries of the human heart which are inextricably bound up with that universe. For him it is at once man's burden and his glory that he cannot identify himself with the earth to which he is so deeply attracted. Human life is basically tragic, the tragedy lodging in the circumstance that man, a creature of two worlds, cannot rest in the one nor apparently attain the other. The struggle to reconcile the two worlds, as befits tragedy, always ends in failure. (p. 22)

*Michael F. Moloney, in his* François Mauriac *(copyright 1958 by Michael F. Moloney; reprinted with permission of The Swallow Press, Inc.), Swallow Press, 1958.*

A theme pervading many of the novels of Mauriac and providing a key to his view of human life and love is the concept of the essential isolation of each human being. . . . To suggest, however, that Mauriac's treatment of isolation is comparable to the existentialist concern with "estrangement" would be thoroughly to misunderstand him. For Mauriac, the isolation of the human person most frequently parallels his conviction of the futility of human love in attempting to possess another. But this dual theme is a distortion unless it is seen as supplementary to the thesis, central to Mauriac, that love of God alone can truly penetrate the "secret city" of the human heart. . . .

The notion that human love is a betrayal, that the creatures we think we love do not actually exist at all but are merely reflections of ourselves whom we seek in the blind desire for union with the "Other" is the theme of *The Loved and the Unloved*. . . .

Perhaps the best material for the analysis of Mauriac's treatment of human isolation is found in the novel *The Desert of Love*. . . . In this novel, the theme that God alone will satisfy the human heart is fundamental and is found in the structure of incidents as well as in the commentary of the basic voice. . . .

The concept of the sphere, the planet, visualized as a microcosm self-contained and associated with other bodies in a gigantic but uncommunicative system, is Mauriac's most frequently chosen image of isolation in *The Desert of Love*. . . .

In *The Desert of Love*, Mauriac draws the major theme—that Divine Love is man's only fulfillment—in bold outline. [To] describe the various aspects of human isolation as a secondary theme he employs chiefly a wide range of imagery. By his skill in the use of this technique, Mauriac implies delicately but unmistakeably that human isolation is viewed by him only against the background of God's ability to satisfy the lonely human heart.

*Sister Anita Marie Caspary, "The Theme of Isolation in Mauriac's 'The Desert Love'," in* Twentieth Century Literature, *October, 1961, pp. 107-13.*

If the French critics of 1930-45 had been asked which novelist, in their estimation, was the most likely to outlive the wreckage of time and to rank next to Proust in greatness, more votes would probably have been cast for Mauriac than for any other living French writer, his rivals being Malraux, Giono, and Bernanos, probably in that order. Mauriac's eminence remained comparatively unrecognized in English-speaking countries, long after his election to the French Academy in 1933 and even after the Nobel Prize had been bestowed upon him. . . .

If the factors at work at any time in life and in art may be grouped into the conflicting forces of tradition and of experiment, Mauriac seems to rank with those novelists who have shunned the loudly advertised paths of experimentation. At a time when the *roman-fleuve* appeared as the order of the day and when juggling with the old-fashioned structural unity and with the continuous flow of time had become the first gesture of a writer asserting his modernity, Mauriac chose to compose isolated novels, strictly organized, with few of those contradictions and violent plunges into the unconscious that other Frenchmen took as evidence that they lived in a post-Dostoevskian era. . . .

Mauriac's fiction has been charged with monotony. It moves in a world that indeed is, geographically and socially, narrowly limited. It revolves around the same perennial obsessions with money, property, the enticements of the flesh, and the wages of sin. Within these confines, however, it explores in depth. What is more, it conjures up that diseased and haunted world, and gains in vivid intensity what is sacrificed in diversity. . . . He writes because he must rid himself of the obsession of his characters and endow with shapes and sounds the desolate world that he carries within his imagination. . . . His novels move swiftly to a relentless denouement. Indeed, their tension is so feverish that they could hardly last longer without becoming painful to the reader. . . .

The advantage derived by Mauriac from his Catholic conception of the world are to perceive life as unceasingly torn between contrary forces and to picture man as restlessly preyed upon by the powers of Evil. Christianity, says Mauriac, enters into souls in order to divide them. The world is an arena for the struggle in which the Devil fights against God, vice against virtue, the animal part of ourselves against the call of the spirit. To the honest observer, virtue is not triumphant, as it may be in edifying novels; nor can vice win in the end, for that would be a denial of Providence. Thus a conflict is perpetually being waged. Man finds in his own ability to doom himself the very proof of his freedom. He revolts against God; but the life he makes for himself is, but for a few unreal moments of bodily and sensuous exultation, afflicted with an oppressive sense of dereliction.

Life assumes a significance to the Catholic novelist, in contrast with the naturalist author in whose fiction one felt only the slow, meaningless gnawing of an average existence, abandoned to forces of heredity, environment, and instinct. The Catholic novel portrays a struggle, with an end at least dimly perceived, sometimes attained with the help of divine grace. Sin also takes on a significance. . . .

Mauriac's originality as a novelist lies in his Catholic vision of the world, in his analysis of love and especially of middle-aged women and adolescents led by a love affair to explore the bitter depths of love. It lies, too, in his craftsmanship, which, conscious and subtle as it is, contrives to leave in the novel the element by which it is most likely to challenge time—poetry.

*Henri Peyre, "François Mauriac," in his* French Novelists of Today *(copyright © 1955, 1967 by Oxford University Press, Inc.; reprinted by permission), Oxford University Press—Galaxy, 1967, pp. 101-22.*

Mauriac was a great "Catholic novelist," but there has been a great shift in Catholicism in recent years; we are no longer so eager to appropriate, to claim, to elevate all things Catholic. . . . To be specific. The United States was never very hospitable to a certain strain of Catholicism and its literary expression. It was not simply the puritanical or Manichean aspects of Mauriac which put American readers off, for America has its own literary tradition of puritanism. But it is a Protestant puritanism, a tradition in which Hawthorne is a central figure, but a tradition which could accommodate, make sense of, a writer like the Calvinist Gide. Not, however, the Pascalian Mauriac, who knew on what side of the wager he was forever committed. . . .

What did we lose with the passing of Mauriac? When the inevitable reassessment takes place—which in the case of an old man begins even before his death—what will his achievements amount to? *The Kiss of the Leper, Genetrix, The Desert of Love, Thérèse Desqueyrous*—these *récits,* clear as a stream and diamond-hard, are peaks among his books, nearly 100 in number. Almost more intensely than one can bear he has here exposed some of the cruel burdens that one person can impose on another, the tension between the flesh and a special kind of spirituality, the ravages of aging, the dissimulations of love. These artistic achievements I take to be secure, to be able to withstand, as well as any literary production which France has produced in the first half of this century, the waves of fashion and the ravages of time.

But in addition to being the creator of these works Mauriac was one of those persons one can best refer to as a presence. One knew he stood for a certain quantity and could gauge an event better by his reaction to it. He was a Catholic of a clearly defined tradition and a severe style. Never did he try to bend or yield to opposing ideas or trends. He took them full on and dealt with them full force. . . .

A number of contemporary writers have been intent on showing us how miserable we are, and they have gone noticeably further than Mauriac in depicting certain aspects of our degradation. But Mauriac had a right to say, just as he had a need to argue, that he did not "fake reality." But for him reality included the greatness of the human spirit. He gave weight and dimension to these words. It is one measure of his achievement that we can, in speaking of Mauriac and his work, use these words without embarrassment.

*James Finn, "François Mauriac," in* Commonweal *(reprinted by permission of Commonweal Publishing Co., Inc.), December 25, 1970, pp. 320-24.*

[Despite his decision to cease working as a specifically Catholic novelist,] the first work of Mauriac's new period, *The Desert of Love* in 1925, is a "Catholic novel" in a far more essential way than his earlier works. Explicitly religious background has duly been excised, but the principles behind the action have a moral and theological depth greater than any he had previously explored. *The Desert of Love* shows more than creatures overcome by greed or possessiveness. It depicts them drawn by a blind longing for good, which they cannot understand and which they distort, but which also touches them inescapably. *The Desert of Love* expresses a different side of Mauriac's Jansenism: emphasis on supernatural grace. . . .

*The Desert of Love* reveals itself as a "Catholic novel" long before the Catholic ending in Maria's conversion, for the whole story depends on the Catholic idea that human beings seek the love of God behind all earthly loves. Nevertheless, *The Desert of Love* is not a depiction of the Catholic community. For most of her life Maria is not a believing and practicing Catholic, and Raymond is never one. *The Desert of Love* falls, therefore, into the older category of Catholic writing practiced by Huysmans, which was characterized primarily by opposition to the non-Catholic environment. But in 1932, when Mauriac began a new novel, *Vipers' Tangle,* and was ready to resume writing as a specifically "Catholic" novelist, he returned to the setting of the Catholic rural community of Les Landes, which had been the background for *Genitrix* and *The Kiss for the Leper*. Mauriac had learned a great deal from such ostensibly non-Catholic books as *The Desert of Love*. In his new novel he once more opposes grace to natural depravity but occasionally emphasizes freedom of choice. He also brings Catholics and non-Catholics into confrontation. Catholics and non-Catholics are equally recipients of grace, which they distort to varying degrees. The result is more powerful drama, in which there is an abundance of struggle, both internally in the mind of the protagonist and externally between the characters. *Vipers' Tangle* is a subtle work, easy to misinterpret. . . .

*Vipers' Tangle* is, however, more than an attack on corrupted Catholicism. In this book corruption of man's faith is depicted as a reflection of a metaphysical corruption at the root of the world. The land itself is under a shadow. The rain that should nourish the vines also beats them down. A flaw at the heart of the universe has estranged it from God, as Catholics have been estranged from true belief. In this sense, Mauriac's attack on the degenerate Catholicism of the bourgeoisie of Les Landes is even more profoundly Jansenist than the theme of *The Desert of Love*.

There are at least two possible readings of *Vipers' Tangle*. One is to see Louis, the dying miser, simply as a villain who reforms, a sort of Harpagon who receives grace. Mauriac's neoclassical orientation makes this interpretation tempting, but it not only overlooks the metaphysical depth of the book but also destroys its unity. Avarice thus regarded is simply a universal vice, and the book's attack on the Catholic middle class becomes alien to the main point. A different reading, which I believe to be the only correct one, is to see the novel as an exposé of the Catholic middle class, whose victim is Louis. Shunning Louis because he is a freethinker, Louis' wife from the first years of their marriage forms a cabal against him with their children. If a child ever climbs into Louis' lap, she is quick to call it away. Denied love by his wife and children, Louis turns to his peasant passion for property as a love-substitute. Louis, therefore, is not so much a villain who reforms as a victim who forgives. In this reading, the book's unity is inviolate. It is a single thrust against the blasphemous false piety Mauriac so detested—and yet (here is the subtlety of this Jansenist drama) this same false piety becomes the source of Louis' redemption. Grace is so powerful that it can use evil itself as a source of light. . . .

The recipient of grace must be shown as free to cooperate or refuse, as Louis was free in the sections where he was remembering Marie, if the reader is to feel any sense of continuous conflict. Bernanos and Graham Greene are experts at sustaining this kind of tension. Mauriac regrettably is not. One must conclude that at most periods of his life he simply did not believe in it. Mauriac was typical of French Catholics with strong Jansenist orientations. All his work reflects the community to which he belonged. The faults he saw in French Catholicism and opposed so vehemently ironically never included its Jansenism. . . . The bleakness of Mauriac's work comes not only from his Jansenist view of natural depravity and his antipathy toward a profit-oriented world, but is caused also by his complete separation of the world of God from the world of man and the inaccessibility, even to the author's prose, of the former.

*Gene Kellogg, "François Mauriac," in his* The Vital Tradition: The Catholic Novel in a Period of Convergence, *Loyola University Press, 1970, pp. 39-52.*

[In] his Christian faith Mauriac has been possessed of a great hope which pierces the shadows he has described. He feels that his characters differ from others in fiction because they have a soul. "Any writer who has maintained in the center of his work the human creature made in the image of the Father, redeemed by the Son, illumined by the Spirit, I cannot see in him a master of despair, however somber his painting may be." And if Mauriac is obsessed by evil, he is also obsessed by purity, by childhood. He regrets that critics have not observed the important role that children play in his works. "They see the vipers of my novels, they do not see the doves which nestle there also in more than one chapter, because with me childhood is the lost paradise and leads to the mystery of evil." (p. 49)

Throughout Mauriac's work we [can observe] three predominant themes, all of them present also in the personality of this most subjective of writers. First, there is the essential element of tension and conflict: sometimes between Cybele and God, passionate and pagan love of nature versus religious faith; sometimes between God and Mammon, worldliness and sensual passion combating the desire for purity and saintliness. Second, we have the desperate loneliness and solitude of the individual, unable to communicate with others, even those most beloved. We recall in this regard Mauriac's own admission that "desert of love" might well serve as title of his entire work. Third, there is the flagellation of bourgeois smugness, social conformity, and lack of true Christian compassion, a theme first appearing in the early *Préséances* but cropping up in most of the later works, particularly in that savage *Noeud de vipères*. (p. 158)

There can be no doubt of Mauriac's pre-eminence as an analyst of human motives and emotions and as a creator of characters who stand out in our memory long after we have closed the books in which they appear. From his earliest childhood Mauriac was possessed by curiosity for penetrating into the innermost recesses of those around him—family, comrades, servants, indeed all with whom he came in contact. In twenty novels he was able to return again and again to this rich storehouse of his youth, modified and transfigured by emotions coming from the least noble aspects of the writer's own depths. It is no coincidence that each great novel of Mauriac is called up for the reader by the memory of at least one impelling character who lives on with a life peculiarly his own. (p. 162)

*Maxwell A. Smith, in his* François Mauriac *(copyright 1970 by Twayne Publishers, Inc.; reprinted with the permission of Twayne Publishers, a Division of G. K. Hall & Co.), Twayne, 1970.*

In February, 1939, when Mauriac had already been at the top of the tree for a good many years and Jean-Paul Sartre himself still had a very long way to go, Sartre took a savage swipe at the novelist. "God", he said, "is not an artist; nor is M. Mauriac. . . ." Whatever Mauriac's final rating, nothing could have been further from the truth. He was an artist to his finger-tips and one of the most versatile writers of our time: poet, novelist, playwright, biographer, autobiographer, hagiographer, critic, essayist, author of religious treatises and a mass of miscellaneous writings who eventually became, like Sartre, a fierce political commentator. . . .

The family is the centre piece in most of the novels. It presents a united front to the stranger. The reality is very different. . . .

The only characters who really win our sympathy are the youthful sinners itching to hop into bed with one another, or the young innocents pursued by some lecherous middleaged female. The youthful sinners enjoy Mauriac's sympathy too. For he is not so much the Catholic novelist as the Catholic sex-novelist who is much more interested in seduction than conversion. . . .

The atmosphere of violence, which permeates the novels, is intensified by the landscape. Mauriac appears as a man who was deeply rooted, physically as well as socially and psychologically, in his province, whose roots thrust down into the very soil. He extracts a grim, dry, gritty poetry from what he calls "this silent empty country", "this land of cinders" or, in the last novel of all, "this arid anguished land with its bleeding pines". It is a country of pines and vines and sand whose inhabitants live in a perpetual state of tension, sniffing the air, glancing at the skies. They fear the torrid heat which brings the forest fires that destroy the precious pines and the storms which wreck the vines—both a threat to their cherished prosperity. . . .

Racine was almost certainly the greatest single literary influence in Mauriac's novels. They had a good deal in common as writers. They both display the same ruthlessness, the same preoccupation with the family feud, with violence, and hatred, with formidable women, and show the same fondness for the word "prey", meaning the victim of a highly aggressive sexual pursuer. There is a family likeness, too, in the characters. Some of Mauriac's characters turn up or are mentioned in more than one novel, but that is not the real point. The majority of them reveal the same sort of psychological resemblances among themselves as Racine's. What is even more striking is the form. At their best Mauriac's novels possess the same brevity, the same tightness of structure, develop with something of the same certainty and pace as Racine's tragedies. It was when this influence was at its height in the 1920s that Mauriac produced what still seem to me to be his finest novels: *Le Baiser au Lépreux, Genitrix, Le Désert de l'Amour, Thérèse Desqueyroux, Destins* and (with reservations) *Le Noeud de Vipères*. . . .

It is particularly sad that Mauriac should have died when he did. He not only made a remarkable come-back last year by producing at the age of eighty-three the best novel that he had written for over thirty years: he had signed a contract to write two more. . . .

Mauriac was a greatly gifted man who excelled in many fields. At the same time, we have to admit that his gifts as a novelist were limited. His world is a circumscribed world; he confines himself to one corner of society and one set of problems. He probes deeply, but does not possess the range or the weight which stamp a man as a master. The provisional verdict should perhaps be: a very distinguished novelist whose work may well outlast that of most of his contemporaries.

*Martin Turnbull, "François Mauriac," in* Encounter, *February, 1971, pp. 46-8.*

* * *

## McCARTHY, Cormac 1933-

**McCarthy is an American novelist. (See also *Contemporary Authors*, Vols. 15-16.)**

Incest and murder in the backwoods of East Tennessee sometime during the nineteenth century are principal ingredients in the witch's brew concocted by [McCarthy] in a second novel [*Outer Dark*] artfully designed to prickle the skin and tighten the scalp of any susceptible reader. Three sinister embodiments of evil cast their malignant shadows from time to time while brother and sister search for each other and the sickly infant born out of their unnatural union in an atmosphere redolent of unmentionable horrors that frequently materialize as sin but no redemption, crime but no punishment. Had Mr. McCarthy given more of a philosophical cast to his tale of terror so that the torment, suffering, and anguish might have a meaning more real than apparent, his narrative would have possessed a significance all its own, quite apart from its merits as a bravura piece.

Virginia Quarterly Review, *Vol. 45, No. 1 (Winter, 1969), p. viii.*

"Child of God" . . . demands its reader's attention from the opening sentence and is composed of brief fragments, but Cormac McCarthy's skill as a writer is not supported by a grasp of his narrative as a whole. . . .

The scene is ostensibly Tennessee, but more nearly a caricature of a Faulknerian landscape: a place that lends itself to incest, murder, necrophilia.

McCarthy is a brilliant writer who can, in a page or two, create a blacksmith Kipling would admire, a man who explains in words close to poetry how to beat and hammer an old ax to make it new again. McCarthy can, in a few paragraphs, write about a boar pursued and killed by hounds as if the subject were fresh, and yet against the brightness of these scenes his protagonist lumbers in silhouette. . . .

This novel, according to its jacket blurb, "explores the limits of human degradation." Unfortunately, it explores nothing at all. Certain acts—a brain-damaged child, for instance, chewing the legs off a robin—are presented to us in McCarthy's admirably distilled prose from which all emotion has been pared away. But there is no resonance, no perspective in attendance, and these isolated episodes, left unconnected on our laps, fade from our memory even before the book is finished. Cormac McCarthy is a good writer confronted with a difficult subject; the pity is that he seems to have retired from the field before he engaged his narrative.

*Peter S. Prescott, "Dangerous Witness," in* Newsweek *(copyright Newsweek, Inc., 1974; reprinted by permission), January 7, 1974, pp. 63, 67.*

It seems to be true in fiction—and it may be in life—that there are characters so flattened by fate before they crawl into our view that they exist beneath the reach of tragedy. Cormac McCarthy's child of God, Lester Ballard, is such a character. . . .

Harsh words constitute the novel like bumps of dirty ice, and harsh scenes stud it, some quite effectively repulsive. . . . But the carefully cold, sour diction of this book—whose hostility toward the reader surpasses even that of the world toward Lester—does not often let us see beyond its nasty "writing" into moments we can see for themselves, rendered. And such moments, authentic though they feel, do not much help a novel so lacking in human momentum or point.

Its hopefully suggestive title implies that Lester warrants our attention because he is a child of God and because, therefore, he is "much like yourself perhaps," as the author timidly posits. But Lester is not demonstrably connected to the rest of us in a way reached without straining, and he is not, either, connected to himself. . . .

Nor is the novel a "horror story," calculated to make us shudder. But even if that were its intention, it would not be more successful than it is as a statement about cruelty, isolation, inhumanity, etc. It is too self-contained for significant effectiveness on any level. . . .

What we have in "Child of God" is an essentially sentimental novel that no matter how sternly it strives to be tragic is never more than morose.

*Richard P. Brickner, in* The New York Times Book Review *(© 1974 by The New York Times Company; reprinted by permission), January 13, 1974, pp. 6-7.*

McCarthy is perhaps the closest we have to a genuine heir to the Faulknerian tradition. His prose sounds and feels like Faulkner's and his themes are similar to Faulkner's. Yet he is not merely an eerily skilled imitator. His novels have a stark, mythic quality that is very much their own, as *Child of God* stunningly demonstrates.

To continue the parallel with Faulkner (though I do not wish to belabor it), McCarthy's novels occupy not the country of *Absalom! Absalom!* but of *As I Lay Dying.* They are about hard country people struggling to stay alive, and a central character is the hard, wooded countryside itself. Their people are, if literate at all, barely so; their landscape is beautiful but rough; their mood is dark, yet broken by bright flashes of humor and lovingly drawn descriptive passages. . . .

The sordid material of Lester Ballard's tale becomes more than an exercise in southern grotesque because of McCarthy's artistry. His prose is lean, packed with vivid imagery, building its own force and intensity; the quasi-Faulknerian excesses that mar some passages of *The Orchard Keeper* and *Outer Dark* are almost totally absent here. The narrative, which alternates between the author's voice and those of the hill people, is tense, adroit and economical.

What makes *Child of God* an unusual and remarkable book is that McCarthy succeeds in making Ballard a sympathetic character. That may seem improbable, considering the crimes Ballard commits, but his is a story about a man who loses everything yet carries on, hanging on to life. It is the old Faulknerian theme of endurance and persistence, here seen in new light and brilliantly explored. There are moments when Ballard becomes as *human*, a real child of God, as any among us. . . .

[Somewhere] deep in Lester Ballard, beneath all that anger and outrage and despair, there is love and yearning. It is that which makes his story so poignant and, in the end, surprisingly and affectingly universal. *Child of God* is an extraordinary book.

*Jonathan Yardley, "Alone, Alone, All, All Alone. . .," in* Book World—The Washington Post (© The Washington Post), *January 13, 1974, p. 1.*

*Child of God* [is] a reading experience so impressive, so "new," so clearly made well that it seems almost to defy the easy esthetic categories and at the same time to cause me to thrash about for some help with the necessary description of my enthusiasm. Cormac McCarthy is a Southerner, a born storyteller (to judge from this, the only one of his three novels I have read), a writer of natural, impeccable dialogue, a literary child of Faulkner. His third novel resembles, in a small way, *As I Lay Dying*, but in other ways, it is related to very few things you may have read before. . . .

[The] lack of contrast between the rotting victims and the details of Ballard, child of God's life is the *subject* of this extraordinary quest-novel. In less than 200 pages, the journey from death-in-life to death-in-death, from the hunted to the discovery of the hunting, from the unnatural to the natural and even supernatural, from fury against life to fury against the living, is accomplished in rare, spare, precise yet poetic prose. It is played out, always, or resolved might be better, in the presence of sometimes cruel, sometimes beneficent Nature, in what Faulkner called "the travail of man within his environment". . . .

Again like a child of Faulkner, McCarthy is capable of black, reasonable comedy at the heart of his tragedy. . . .

In McCarthy's eyes there is a holy alliance between the madness of Ballard and the wet, cold confusion of his surroundings, the "disorder in the woods, trees down, new paths needed. Given charge Ballard would have made things more orderly in the woods and in men's souls." The natural world and the world of violence and madness are united in Ballard. . . .

About Lester Ballard there is no prehistory, we know almost nothing we have not been able to watch, like voyeurs perched somewhere above him in his Tennessee hills. We never come close to understanding him or the cutting, touching, harsh beauty of his landscape: both are equally immune to our comprehension. . . . Cormac McCarthy has allowed us direct communion with his special kind of chaos; every sentence he writes illuminates, if only for a moment, the great dark of madness and violence and inevitable death that surrounds us all.

*Doris Grumbach, "Practitioner of Ghostliness," in* The New Republic *(reprinted by permission of* The New Republic; *© 1974 by Harrison-Blaine of New Jersey, Inc.), February 9, 1974, pp. 26-8.*

Cormac McCarthy's *The Orchard Keeper*, an impressive, complex debut, was a recipient of the William Faulkner Foundation Award. Contrary to rumor, this annual prize is *not* bestowed upon first novels which best mimic the South's greatest master. But to its misfortune, *The Orchard Keeper* bore countless comparisons to Faulkner's novels. The story, chronicling young John Wesley's friendship with his father's murderer, echoes the major Faulkner themes: the criminal as hero, the interplay of language, memory and myth, and the overriding problem of survival.

To admire and emulate a master is not a fault; and the fact that Southern writers continue to be influenced by Faulkner should now be a dead issue. *The Orchard Keeper* suffers less from its Southern origins than from its Irish excesses. McCarthy takes an intriguing, basically linear plot, splits it into three separate strands, and, by means of a lush coating of language gives his story an unnecessary "poetic" facade. He approaches his theme with caution, using language as a distancing element, the perfect equivalent to the novel's narrative technique where strict chronological order is relinquished for a mistier interweaving of events. Ostensibly, the story takes place in the Tennessee hill country during the Depression years, but McCarthy's prose allows little period detail to emerge. McCarthy wishes to describe rather than to relate. Everything is highly "imagined" and all natural events read like eulogies to some great Cosmic spirit. . . .

*Outer Dark,* McCarthy's second novel, begins in the teeth of an incestuous affair that is thick with Gothic atmosphere. It matters little that we are in an unspecified region of the South during an unspecified period of time. The terrain is lean and uncluttered. There are few modern objects in sight, and the stage is set for the passions of a morality play. . . .

*Outer Dark* is an exceptional advance over *The Orchard Keeper*. The language is less florid, and McCarthy squarely faces the Faulknerian overtones, thereby avoiding the suppressed violence of *The Orchard Keeper*. The three men who ransack and murder are a brilliant device; a mad variation on the Magi, they skim about the perimeter of the tale and eventually bring the work to its justifiable conclusion. The creation of landscape is McCarthy's finest achievement. By some magical combination—leaving the locale unspecified but investing it with a fairy tale quality—the land has a disturbing quietude where actuality turns ever so gently into myth without sacrificing the necessary reality.

With *Child of God*, language is a blessing. McCarthy is not beyond an occasional flourish, as in this purplish depiction of urination: "The man stands straddlelegged, has made in the dark humus a darker pool wherein swirls a pale foam with bits of straw." But in general the prose is pared clean. . . .

The novel is thinner, less full-bodied than either *The Orchard Keeper* or *Outer Dark*; this has little to do with length. Faulkner knew when to let his criminals lie still among the shadows and have the citizenry of Yoknapatawpha County capture center stage. There is no corresponding reality against which to pit Lester's violent world. Early in the work McCarthy had interjected brief passages in which the townspeople mulled over the myth and actually of Lester Ballard, but he dropped the device quickly, to the book's detriment. *Child of God* is a swift exciting read, but we are left with only incisive images strung along a thin plot line, the why and wherefore unexplained.

*Child of God* will perhaps be looked upon as a bad novel written by a good writer, and this would be regrettable, for *Child of God* marks a progression in McCarthy's career. He has learned restraint. The "old themes" live on in him, but his South is not rendered with the precision of a realist. He has taken realism to the province of folk myth.

*Robert Leiter, in* Commonweal *(reprinted by permission of Commonweal Publishing Co., Inc.), March 29, 1974, pp. 90-2.*

Necrophilia, incest, transvestism, rape, and murder are some of the scabrous subjects incorporated in [*Child of God*] laid in the mountains of East Tennessee, but the author recites the horrendous proceedings with at least a simulacrum of decency by stating the existence of such situations without dramatizing them to excess, thus conferring upon his narrative a seriousness of purpose somewhat at odds with the nature of his material. What the author has done with his half-demented antihero is view him objectively without passing judgment upon him to any marked degree. Here it is, take it or leave it, the author seems to say, it may all be inherently repulsive, true enough, but this is the way things are among these people in this part of the country.

Virginia Quarterly Review, *Vol. 50, No. 2 (Spring, 1974), p. lvi.*

Cormac McCarthy's *Child of God* . . . may be as remarkable for what it avoids as for what it achieves, but it's remarkable all the same. The word necrophilia has real referents in the world; no reason why it couldn't be a subject for fiction, and so it is in this tale of Lester Ballard, a hermit in the Tennessee hills who specializes in surprising lovers, murdering them, and making off with the female corpse. McCarthy's accomplishment is not to account for this insanity—we learn almost nothing of Ballard's past—nor to enter for very long the demented mind. Instead he composes a scene, in which it is possible to place horror without being gratuitously grotesque or—a worse possibility—inadvertently comic. He writes a lean prose alive to the natural world, speech, and to the tenuous civilization that fails to contain Lester Ballard. And he continually suggests that the worst depravity is not inhuman, merely the far end of the continuum on which we live. A *tour de force*. But an arresting novel.

*Richard Todd, in* The Atlantic Monthly *(copyright © 1974 by The Atlantic Monthly Company, Boston, Mass.; reprinted with permission), May, 1974, p. 128.*

[In *Child of God,*] Lester Ballard destroys and is destroyed, but we have not a clue as to why. It is as if the author thinks his character is beyond scrutiny—possessed of a nature and a destiny that lead to the impersonal collisions of the Oresteia, rather than the exchanges and confrontations of our contemporary theatre; it is as if only when we learn to accept the mysterious and the terrible judgment of the gods do we come close to what wisdom is allowed us. . . .

Cormac McCarthy resembles the ancient Greek dramatists and medieval moralists—a strange, incompatible mixture: Ballard blind to himself and driven by forces outside his control, and Ballard the desperately wayward one whose vagrant life is one day to be judged by God. Strangers like Ballard, errant outsiders who bewilder and sometimes brutally assault a community, remind those who shun them that a "child of God" can inexplicably become, in the imagery of ancient Greece, an instrument of the gods. Cormac McCarthy does not know why some men are haunted Ballards, while others live easily with kin and neighbors. He simply writes novels that tell us we cannot comprehend the riddles of human idiosyncrasy, the influence of the merely contingent or incidental upon our lives. He is a novelist of religious feeling who appears to subscribe to no creed but who cannot stop wondering in the most passionate and honest way what gives life meaning.

His characters are by explicit designation children of Whoever or Whatever it is that we fall back upon when we want to evoke the vastness and the mystery of this universe, and our comparative ignorance and uncertainty. His task is ambitious and enormously difficult—to tell his readers that we are not as knowing or in control of our lives as we assume. He cannot yet affirm with confidence life's possibilities. From the isolated highlands of Tennessee he sends us original stories that show how mysterious or confusing the world is. Moreover, his mordant wit, his stubborn refusal to bend his writing to the literary and intellectual demands of our era, conspire at times to make him seem mysterious and confusing—a writer whose fate is to be relatively unknown and often misinterpreted. But both Greek playwrights and Christian theologians have been aware that such may be the fate of anyone, of even the most talented and sensitive of human beings.

*Robert Coles, "The Stranger," in* The New Yorker, *August 26, 1974, pp. 87-90.*

* * *

## McCULLERS, (Lula) Carson 1917-1967

**Mrs. McCullers was a Southern American novelist, short story writer, and playwright. Death, sacrifice, withdrawal, and the failure of love were the principal themes of her gothic fiction. Her work is considered among the most important of her generation. (See also *Contemporary Authors*, Vols. 5-8, rev. ed; obituary, Vols. 25-28.)**

Mrs. McCullers is "romantic". . ., but she does not strain for beauty. She is natural in detail and diction ("gang," "hard," "sweat"), yet at the same time she conveys the transcendental, the philosophical (music of the wide sky). She concentrates on—and makes us feel—*pain.*

*Irving Malin, in his* New American Gothic *(© 1962 by Southern Illinois University Press; reprinted by permission of Southern Illinois University Press), Carbondale: Southern Illinois University Press, 1962, p. 157.*

In the fiction of Carson McCullers I believe that we can observe the effort to arrive at the objective externality of myth by placing the most extreme demands on that very subjectivity which is its opposite. The effort is not always successful and sometimes it is only partial, but, except for most of the short stories, her least impressive work, it is almost always there.

*Mark Schorer, "McCullers and Capote: Basic Patterns," in his* The World We Imagine *(reprinted with the permission of Farrar, Straus & Giroux, Inc.; copyright © 1948, 1949, 1953, 1956, 1957, 1959, 1962, 1963, 1969 by Mark Schorer), Farrar, Straus, 1969, p. 275.*

*Member of the Wedding* is not an admonitory novel. It is descriptive, showing what occurs to people who happen to be born into life. There is nothing we can "do" to modify that life in its basic characteristics and hence we must content ourselves with separateness and the peculiar freedom that accompanies that separateness. This does not mean that our condition denies us the warmth of human love and understanding. The heart, as Miss McCullers suggests in the title of her first novel, is a "lonely hunter." But as Frankie says, there is a connectedness between people which she cannot explain, which indeed is beyond the human being to explain, and that connectedness is illustrated in the scene following the discussion about the inescapable loneliness of humans. Frankie, nervously confronting a deep and important truth, sits for comfort on Berenice's lap; little John Henry leans against her ample hip. In the dusk of the kitchen they all begin to cry, and all for a different reason. For all their differences, however, they are in one sense united. The scene dramatizes the sad fact of human existence—the impossibility of ever filling up consciousness without turning it into something else, the necessity of remaining separate, and, most important, the beauty of sharing these human deprivations. Their weeping is like their singing: ". . .their three voices were joined, and the parts of the song were woven together." People's lives are like this song and this weeping, each separate strand contributing to a whole and deriving from that whole a satisfaction missing without the others. If the condition of the human being is to "lack," he can share that condition with others through love. Metaphysically, it is the actual entity committing himself to his society as an element of his individual satisfaction. As a child, this is not good enough for Frankie. She demands absolute communion. As an adult, suggests McCullers, she will learn that this is the way we fulfill ourselves.

*Jerry Bryant, in his* The Open Decision *(reprinted with permission of Macmillan Publishing Co., Inc.; copyright © 1970 by The Free Press, a Division of The Macmillan Company), The Free Press, 1970, pp. 248-49.*

While there are no significant successes among the stories, essays, and poems in *The Mortgaged Heart,* they help to round off Carson McCullers's literary career. She showed her talent early and developed rapidly. . . .

The essays complement the early stories and Mrs. McCullers's later work by underscoring her movement away from personal reminiscences to larger social commitments; themes of loneliness, spiritual isolation, and universal love; obsession with the mystery of Time; youthful attraction to the theater and music, and to James Joyce, Walt Whitman, and Faulkner.

*Thomas A. Gullason, in* Saturday Review *(copyright © 1971 by Saturday Review/World, Inc.; reprinted with permission), November 13, 1971, p. 64.*

In a sense [*The Mortgaged Heart*] is a writer's dream—to have everything one ever wrote, including a rough outline for a novel, published. What more could an artist hope for? On the other hand, for a perfectionist like Carson McCullers, who rewrote over and over again until the gem was sufficiently polished, it might have been a horror. . . .

Her dramatic sense of detail was there from the beginning in character sketches and evolved to maturity in her later stories and essays. The essays are remarkably lucid prose. Worth the price of the book are the seven brief essays on "Writers and Writing." . . .

Some of her early stories prefigure later fuller characterizations. Noticeable is the constant use of an adolescent in her stories. . . .

Carson felt all good prose writing has an element of poetry as well. Her own prose is better poetry than the nine poems included here. It would have honored the author's memory to have left them buried in a bottom drawer somewhere.

*Jeanne Kinney, in* Best Sellers, *November 15, 1971, p. 371.*

The importance [of *The Mortgaged Heart*] comes from the rare opportunity it affords us to study the growing-pains of genius. All the seeds of her later work are in these early exercises. She herself saw the unity of her vision and characters: In "The Flowering Dream," reprinted here, she comments: "Spiritual isolation is the basis of most of my themes. My first book was concerned with this, almost entirely, and all of my books since, in one way or another. Love, and especially love of a person who is incapable of returning it or receiving it, is at the heart of my selection of grotesque figures to write about—people whose physical incapacity is a symbol of their spiritual incapacity to love or receive love—their spiritual isolation."

This theme and these characterizations are fully evident in Mrs. McCullers' work, from the earliest story ("Sucker", written when she was seventeen) to the latest ("A Hospital Christmas Eve," published after her death). Carson McCullers was one of those fabulous originals who from the first are gifted with a voice and a vision, whose immature works are as purely original as the later achievements. . . .

Everything here has its own peculiar beauty, perhaps more casual than that of the achieved work, but also sometimes more adventurous, less self-conscious, and occasionally more moving. There are whole stories lying undeveloped in some of these pieces the impact of which most writers can never approach. We are thinking of the story of Lester, in the essay on loneliness; of the protagonist of the fragment, "The Orphanage"; and of others. . . .

Tracing the trajectory of her talent from these early stories to late, first book to last, we see the map of an artistry which fully expressed itself at a young age. Her last stories and her last novel were not her best. It was her middle period which bore greatness. Had she lived to be ninety, it is doubtful she would have added much that would widen the scope of her work, or improve upon it. Yet *The Mortgaged Heart* reveals everything she wrote to bear some unique gift, the voice of one crying in the wilderness.

*Robert Phillips, in* Studies in Short Fiction, *Winter, 1973, pp. 109-11.*

Carson McCullers was a greater myth-maker than she was a novelist. Her theme was the utter dislocation of love "in our time" and "in our town." Her extreme sense of human separateness took form in deaf-mutes who were also Greek foreigners in the Southern town in which they inexplicably found themselves, Negro doctors maddened by their intellectual isolation, fathers always widowers, and above all a young tomboy who, whether she is too young for sexual love or too odd for it, attributes her own unusedness to everyone else, then projects this "loneliness" against the political terror of the Hitler period and the excessiveness, vacancy, and stillness of summer in the town.

In McCullers what fills the space usually occupied by man-and-woman love is a sensitiveness that charges other people with magical perceptions. She radiated in all her work a demand for love so total that another was to become the perfect giver, and so became magical. The world is so bleak that it is always just about to be transformed. *The Heart Is a Lonely Hunter* (1940) astonishingly comes alive still not only as a virtuoso performance dramatically engaging so many hard solitudes, but also as a novel of the depressed Thirties haunted by the powerlessness of people and the ferocious powers of governments.

McCullers's myth-making power was to fit this obsessive loneliness, this sense of total weakness before real earthly damnation, into the Southern climate, the town in summer, the doldrums of children with nowhere to go. She made many different lacks equal illuminations of the system of life in a Southern town. The bareness, vacancy, inertia seem to come out of the weather; the emotions of solitude flourish crazily in the parched streets; even McCullers's concentration on absolute clarity of style suggests the same still, depressed, vacant atmosphere, produces distinctness as a tragic effect. "In the town there were two deaf-mutes, and they were always together." Unlike the lonelies defeated by convention in *Winesburg, Ohio,* McCullers's girl-children recognize that the town is like themselves. The consistency of her theme absorbed the town into itself, made the immediate landscape hot with silent emotion.

McCullers had the intuition that human beings could be psychic states so absolute and self-contained that they repelled each other sexually. The characters in *The Heart Is a Lonely Hunter* live in another world so insistent as to suggest damnation. They are out of nature. Though she converted this sense of some deep personal unnaturalness into brilliant "atmosphere" (all the more so because her style suggests fright striving for perfect control), the demon of self-damnation, of being utterly locked up, sexually limited, was a subject that fascinated her but which she objectified, as comedy, only once—in *The Ballad of the Sad Cafe*.

*The Member of the Wedding,* her most popular work, turns the Huckleberry Finn of her first novel back into the children's literature of *Tom Sawyer;* it devalues her most familiarly tragic feelings about sex into cuteness: now she imitates Carson McCullers with an eye on the audience. But in the *Ballad,* emotionally the most detached of her fictions, the distrust of sex which runs all through her work expresses itself as a folktale in which the characters are mostly legends, unnatural and against nature. Everything is seen as a fable; there is nothing of that pervasive cry for sympathy which fills up *The Heart Is a Lonely Hunter* like a gas, numbing us.

*Alfred Kazin, in his* Bright Book of Life: American Novelists & Storytellers from Hemingway to Mailer *(copyright © 1971, 1973 by Alfred Kazin; reprinted by permission of Little-Brown and Co. in association with the Atlantic Monthly Press), Little, Brown, 1973, pp. 51-4.*

[The] so-called literature of alienation frequently is so lacerated with hatred and self-pity that it fails to offer any really mature understanding of the phenomena of alienation. Not so with the fiction of Carson McCullers; for McCullers, who made personal alienation the explicit single concern of all her fiction, treats the solitude of the heart with both objectivity and compassion and, ultimately, with an understanding born of the blending of head and heart.

Mrs. McCullers once said of her work "my central theme is the theme of spiritual isolation. Certainly I have always felt alone." In her *The Ballad of the Sad Cafe,* the setting itself serves as metaphor for such spiritual isolation. She begins this novella by establishing the dreariness, lonesomeness, and sadness of a setting which seems "estranged from all other places in the world." . . .

We have the impression that the town itself is a grotesque, warped by its isolation, and that the building, with its cracked appearance, its dilapidated one-sided construction, and its boarded-up facade, might serve as symbol for whatever life remains in it and in the town. For life here is hopelessly inward, separated, and estranged. Selfhood means only confinement in the solitude of one's own heart. . . .

Most studies of *The Ballad* emphasize only McCullers' theme of spiritual alienation and irreparable loneliness; they seem to disregard the fact that aloneness was, for a time at least, actually overcome. But Carson McCullers is very explicit about the achievement of "an air of intimacy . . . and a vague festivity" in the café. . . .

Although . . . the "people in this town were unused to gathering together for the sake of pleasure," they do manage for a time to do so and consequently to escape the humdrum everydayness of their lives and the sense of their own worthlessness. But the effort cannot be maintained; the café is closed and the people retreat once again into their own separateness and aloneness. The convivial nights in the café end ostensibly because Marvin Macy and Cousin Lymon have ransacked the place, carving obscene words on the tables and bringing shame and sadness to Miss Amelia. But I should like to suggest that the café's violent end was already inherent in the consciousness of Amelia and her patrons.

*Panthea Reid Broughton, "Rejection of the Feminine in Carson McCullers' 'The Ballad of the Sad Cafe'," in* Twentieth Century Literature, *January, 1974, pp. 34-7.*

Granville Hicks has written that Mrs. McCullers went downhill after her first novel. With the exception of the brilliant story, "The Ballad of the Sad Café," I would agree. Why the decline? Because her subsequent works depend almost entirely upon the imaginative use of language, and neglect the solid foundation of place. Too many of her characters are like those created by her friend, Tennessee Williams—poetic but shallow. She continued to write about the South even though she did not live there—physically or spiritually. She said Brooklyn was her "real neighborhood," but, as if obligated by birth, she continued to write about unreal people in that fictional town somewhere south of Atlanta and west of Milledgeville. Carson McCullers could not recover the South in her fiction, because she left it before she really understood it. The only novel which approaches a serious exploration of the moral dimension of her characters, *The Heart Is a Lonely Hunter,* she wrote while living in North Carolina. This novel does rest upon a solid foundation of place. Furthermore, it elaborates a correlation between the emotional estrangement of the adolescent Mick and the anomie of those around her—the only instance of a successful correlation of this sort in her works. . . .

If her early years in the South contributed anything to her craft, it must have been, as she said, in terms of language: "I love the voices of Negroes—like brown rivers." Flannery O'Connor, another Georgian who was McCullers' contemporary, could talk about how the "Christ haunted" South made possible the literature of the grotesque, but Carson McCullers attributed the vision of grotesque fiction to the "cheapness of human life in the South."

It is clear that Carson McCullers did not assimilate much of the intellectual and cultural heritage of the South. Her chief difficulties as a writer stemmed from her disregard of her own past. Ironically, this disregard lies at the heart of the fundamental problem she spent her life writing about—the perennially-thwarted search for identity. The early novels and stories were written by a pessimistic young woman who, like her adolescent protagonists, longed to transcend the environment of her frustrated childhood. The last novel came from a less sober, more optimistic McCullers who claimed there was something worth saving in her South. But in *Clock Without Hands* she was unable to identify exactly what she had in mind. If her early familiarity with the South bred contempt, then her exile's unfamiliarity with it bred something worse than contempt—vacuity.

In a larger sense, this discussion about Carson McCullers and the South concerns the matter of cultural symbols which continue to motivate many modern, upwardly-mobile Southern intellectuals. Carson McCullers, let us remember, experienced the South quite differently from writers like Donald Davidson, Allen Tate, John Crowe Ransom, William Faulkner, Walker Percy, and a host of others whose parents and/or grandparents were aristocrats of the Southern mind. She did not inherit a sense of tradition, and the record she left indicates she did not attempt to embrace any tradition. She built her life on the hope that, somehow, Paris or New York would reach down and rescue her from the frustration and stagnation she felt and feared in the South. Unlike many whose lives have been galvanized by this kind of hope, she had the rare misfortune of seeing the hope fulfilled when she was very young—too young, indeed, to know that the fulfillment would be self-defeating.

*Delma Eugene Presley, "Carson McCullers and the South," in* The Georgia Review, *Spring, 1974, pp. 19-32.*

* * *

## McNALLY, Terrence 1939-

**McNally, an American, is a dramatist with a fine comic talent. (See also *Contemporary Authors*, Vols. 45-48.)**

A classic farce in modern (un)dress—that's the very bright idea behind Terrence McNally's new play ["The Tubs"] instead of drawing rooms and ladies' boudoirs, the scene is a male bathhouse; and the inevitable philandering husband . . . dallies with boys instead of dollies. But the structural mechanics are classical—mistaken identity, chase scenes, a network of doors to open and slam. . . . McNally's basic problem is also classical: he has grasped the spirit but not the mechanical intricacies of farce—although a funnier, more serviceable set, and funnier, more personally inventive actors might have been a help. McNally's humor is genuine and often original; its farce outlets just aren't sufficiently mathematical, subtle, or imaginative to sustain what is still a very bright idea.

*Marilyn Stasio, in* Cue *(copyright © 1974 by Cue Publications, Inc.), January 14, 1974, p. 17.*

The non-stop hilarity of Terrence McNally's new pair of one-act comedies ["Bad Habits"] derives from his amused fascination with obsessive behavior. "Ravenswood" is a wacky sanatorium whose wacky director prescribes complete indulgence of such "bad habits" as drinking, smoking, and sexual promiscuity. The second play, "Dunelawn," shows us an equally daffy institution whose daffy director dictates complete abstention from all such practices. The two outlandish institutions accommodate almost every conceivable form of social neurotic, from a cherubic sado-masochist to a monumentally narcissistic show-biz couple. . . . Although both plays are casually structured, the character satire is dead-on accurate, and for all its zaniness has a niceness of logical clarity that is akin to classical farce.

*Marilyn Stasio, in* Cue *(copyright © 1974 by Cue Publications, Inc.), February 11, 1974, p. 17.*

Both [*Ravenswood* and *Dunelaw*, two one-acters produced under the program title, *Bad Habits*] go on a bit too long, and in both McNally succumbs to his chronic weakness, the inability to find the right ending. But this is not the amiably floundering McNally of *Tommy Flowers* and *Whiskey*; this is the McNally of *Next* and *Noon,* at his sick, mean, absurd yet purposive best, vicious crack topping vicious crack in the most demurely trotted-out fashion, like debutantes being presented at Court. For McNally, nothing has been desecrated enough not to deserve another friendly kick in the butt. . . .

McNally, who was once Albee's protégé and disciple, has moved far beyond his now stagnating master, as if he had sucked him dry, and then some. You can call these plays unwholesome, inhuman—whatever you like—but not undazzling or unfunny.

*John Simon, "No Regalia, No Regality," in* New York Magazine *(© 1974 by NYM Corp.; reprinted by permission of* New York Magazine *and John Simon), February 18, 1974, p. 78.*

Terrence McNally is one of the most adept practitioners of the comedy of insult. His two one-act skits entitled *Bad Habits* are the best examples of his writing in this mode. . . .

Both plays aim their shafts at institutions for the treatment of psychological disturbances—"encounter groups." The ills the patients suffer, McNally indicates, are more benign than their cure. Everyone has a right to his "disease," and both the desire to rid oneself of it and the methods employed to heal it are bogus.

I am stating this much more solemnly than McNally does. His plays are spoofs and at times quite funny. . . .

There is, of course, a satiric element in these sketches which sustains and "justifies" them. But there is no real criticism in them: the grotesquerie of the jokes supersedes all. These, in turn, are based on a strain of generalized dislike. The undeclared "message" is: people are no damned good, so let's leave them alone to proceed on their own nasty way—which is, after all, *our* way! The bitterness inherent in this cannot be acknowledged; it is masked as fun and games. We laugh to free ourselves from what is implied.

*Harold Clurman, in* The Nation, *March 2, 1974, p. 285.*

* * *

## MEREDITH, William 1919-

**Meredith is an American formal poet and translator. (See also *Contemporary Authors*, Vols. 9-12, rev. ed.)**

[William Meredith] is the kind of poet who stands looking at the ocean where the atomic submarine *Thresher* went down, meditating, speculating, grieving intelligently. Things of this nature hurt him into poetry, but not poetry of great intensity. Instead, it seems muffled and distant, a kind of thin, organized, slightly academic murmur. One keeps listening for Meredith's *voice,* and is baffled at its being, although one is surer and surer it is there, so consistently elusive. It is not at all to be found in those poems imitative of, say, Frost, such as "An Old Field Mowed for Appearances' Sake," but rather in pieces like "For His Father" and, oddly, in the wonderful translations from Apollinaire, which seem, although faithful enough as translations, really more Meredith's than Apollinaire's. It is better to hear "My glass is filled with a wine that trembles like flame" than to hear, in Meredith's poem *to* Apollinaire, "The day is colorless like Swiss characters in a novel," which presupposes that the reader agrees that Swiss characters in a novel (what novel?) are colorless, that everyone knows they are (I, one shyly thinks, didn't know they are, and keeps one's mouth shut about it), and thereby enters into collusion with a certain ingroup variety of bookish snobbery that is probably Meredith's one outstanding weakness as a writer. But at his best he is a charming poet, cultivated, calm, quietly original, expansive and reflective, moving over wide areas slowly, lightly, mildly and often very memorably.

*James Dickey, "William Meredith" (1965), in his* Babel to Byzantium *(reprinted with the permission of Farrar, Straus & Giroux, Inc.; copyright © 1956, 1957, 1958, 1959, 1960, 1961, 1962, 1963, 1964, 1965, 1966, 1967, 1968 by James Dickey), Farrar, Straus, 1968, pp. 197-98.*

The sparse, undeclamatory quietness of William Meredith's poetry may keep it from getting the attention it should have, but this will not concern the poet, for all these poems [*Earth Walk: New and Selected Poems*] have been brought to a point where they seem like the inevitable, furniture of a solid and warmly-inhabited old house. They are beautifully worked, distinct objects, the language at once exciting and unobtrusive—what keeps them together is a tone wistful and ironic, which gives them the air of events as inevitable to the reader as to the poet.

The Antioch Review *(© 1970 by The Antioch Review, Inc.; reprinted by permission of the editors), Vol. XXX, No. 1, 1970, p. 134.*

It is when Meredith is most devious [in *Earth Walk*] that he is indeed best: sermons, uplifts, sententious dallyings with mortality are not only plainspoken, they are outspoken, and they do not serve to advantage the subtle art, the resilient devices Meredith has accommodated with such determined mildness. They are here, though, the moralizing and the temperance and the terrible monosyllables—*love* and *guilt* and *time* and *heart*, sending their spondaic juices through the verse. . . .

Though he is anything but naive, Meredith has a great gift for innocence, for the recovery of terror and joy which reside in the usual. And it is from the usual that he rises to his moments of the genuinely vatic, not preaching but prophecy, inviting the mediation of the ordinary in its original sense, the sense of participating in an order, so that the poem is an ordination. Meredith is a poet who would single out experience only provisionally, only to remark the more readily on its affinities with other experiences rather than on its ecstatic isolations.

*Richard Howard, in* Shenandoah *(copyright by* Shenandoah; *reprinted from* Shenandoah: *The Washington and Lee University Review with the permission of the Editor), Winter, 1971, pp. 82-3.*

Of the thirty-three poems originally published in *Love Letter from an Impossible Land,* William Meredith has chosen only six for inclusion in *Earth Walk,* rightly discarding the portentous and eclectic rhetoric of much of the early volume, with its recurrent hints of indebtedness to Auden and Spender. Even those few poems that he has retained have been purged of a few touches of artificiality of diction—thus, "Against whose vault is no thing tall" in "Airman's Virtue" has been altered to "Against whose vault nothing is tall." The germ of Meredith's creative development lay rather in a poem like "Ten-Day Leave," reprinted in the new volume, with its simple language, its directness of statement, and its theme of familial rootedness. The road that led away from Auden and Spender led toward Frost. . . .

Like Frost, Meredith portrays a natural landscape of fields and woods, the clearing where "a whippoorwill calls in the dark," the hill where the poet has "planted spruce and red pine." But Meredith's poetry also incorporates the contemporary city where a man's wallet is snatched from him on a stairway by a boy who, running away, "turns a brown face briefly / phrased like a question." And whereas, in Frost, the landscape of farm and countryside has significance as part of an ethical drama, in which man pits his strength and courage against inimical nature, in Meredith the props of the natural scene stand for a deeply intuited consciousness of an identity between our physical selves and the earth we inhabit and are made of. If Meredith's poetry has a signature, it is the tree, which appears over and over again as a literal object in a scene, an emblem, a self, rooted in earth and growing outward to air and sun.

The poet of *Earth Walk* chooses to place himself squarely in reality, conveying to us a sense of the mind's rootedness in a body against whose weight we struggle to raise up decent lives.

*Marie Borroff, in* The Yale Review *(© 1971 by Yale University; reprinted by permission of the editors), Winter, 1971, pp. 284-85.*

William Meredith displays attention to the formal shape of his poems. It is typical that two of his best should be *Notre Dame de Chartres,* a sestina, and *Effort at Speech,* a poem written in sapphics (!) about an attempted mugging. He is often compared with Richard Wilbur for imposing, with considerable grace, the most rigorous formal demands upon his verse. Such writing had a notable boom in the 'fifties, and following the usual sea-change in literary taste is viewed with suspicion now. But it seems unfair for Meredith or Wilbur to be held accountable for the refined disasters produced by their imitators. Meredith's best poems are elegant but not precious, ordered but not finicky, deeply thoughtful but not recondite. He has rendered so stringent a judgment in selecting from his previous poems that it is hard to find any one piece that is not worthy of its companions. The new poems [in *Earth Walk*], I think, form the volume's finest single section and show that Meredith is still making advances at an age when most writers are traveling in tried-and-true ruts. The book is handsomely varied in its subject matter, like an inviting old attic sea chest. Meredith writes about his fighter pilot days, about crows and fish vendors and Persian miniatures, about talking to Robert Frost and translating Apollinaire. . . . These poems express their love most tellingly as they embrace the aging, helpless, or outcast beings of the earth. . . .Time and again Meredith has discovered dignity where other men have ceased to look for it, and given it new life in his poems. I am happy for him that he has seen such things, and for us that he has written them down.

*Robert B. Shaw, "Poets in Midstream," in* Poetry *(© 1971 by The Modern Poetry Association; reprinted by permission of the Editor of* Poetry), *July, 1971, pp. 228-33.*

Most of the poems of William Meredith are so balanced and modest and appealing, composed in so many uncomplicated and civilized ways, so much the sort of poetry appropriate to read on a lazy afternoon, perhaps even to read while listening to Dietrich sing "Lazy Afternoon," that an intemperate spirit might, at times, wonder—no doubt, frivolously—what would happen if Professor Meredith read nothing but Rimbaud or Mayakovsky or—heaven help us—Anaïs Nin? Would the climate in Connecticut change, would there be unruly declamations, moments of fine excess, would one go absolutely out of one's squash? It seems unlikely. William Meredith, a durable, though admittedly minor, poet, has always had a conservative sense of people and place. He offers two mottoes—"The Poet as Troublemaker" and "Iambic Feet Considered as Honorable Scars"—and only the most thoughtless of his readers would ever be hard put to know which of these mottoes was closest to the professor's heart.

In the *New and Selected Poems* [*Earth Walk*] we follow him moving gracefully over the years from the authority of the military life (the Second World War, "the bomb's luck, the gun's poise and chattering") to the authority of the university (for a while it seemed as if Professor Meredith would become the academic poet par excellence) to that, finally, of the suburban and reflective style of his most recent and most successful stage.

If he is really too disciplined and adjusted an individual, too genial, too much the hero of the buried life, harumping among the hydrangea bushes, he is, nevertheless, a poet who knows, deep to his fingertips, what the tiger or the nightingale always forgets, that the dispassionate, domestic, monogamous world has its dramas and sorrows, that rectitude itself can be an adventure, a moral adventure almost as Kierkegaard dreamed, that if "identity is a travelling-piece for some," for the poet, for *this* poet, "here is what calls me, here what I call home." That, within it, "there is no end to the / Deception of quiet things / And of quiet, every-day / People a lifetime brings"; that the common routine, in its diffident way, is a magical contrivance; that the common experience can be a fable, and "yet all of a piece and clever / And at some level, true."

*Robert Mazzocco, in* The New York Review of Books *(reprinted with permission from* The New York Review of Books; *© 1972 by NYREV, Inc.), June 15, 1972, pp. 32-3.*

In Mr. Meredith's [collection entitled *Earth Walk*] (including selections from *The Wreck of the Thresher*) the subject matter at last begins to threaten the prosody all along the line; and the result is a clear, free style which generates excitement. "Roots", reminiscent of Frost at his best, is a conversation between the poet and a country woman, an "eclogue" in which the complexities of mortality are treated in a startling metaphorical matrix which is profoundly philosophical in its implications yet simple and unselfconscious. "Hydraulics" is a sequence of six poems in which the physical principles governing water are put to a variety of imaginative uses; and while in one or two instances the metaphors are ambitious, the poet does not jeopardize their serious intent with a stilted rhetoric. And in "Ten Accounts of a Monogamous Man" and the excellent "Winter Verse for His Sister" the tone becomes surprisingly confidential, the subject matter personal, without sacrificing too much of the aesthetic distance that has always been one of Mr. Meredith's virtues, even when he exercises it to excess.

*Thomas H. Landess, in* Sewanee Review *(reprinted by the permission of the editor; © 1973 by The University of the South), Winter, 1973, pp. 147-50.*

* * *

## MILLER, Henry 1891-

**An American novelist, essayist, literary, art, and social critic, Miller has long been a major influence in world literature. He calls himself "a holy old Untouchable" and he speaks, as Kenneth Rexroth has written, for "Surplus Man to whom the values, the achievements, and the classics of the dominant civilization are meaningless and absurd." His ribaldry and eroticism have made him perhaps the most censored writer of all time. Lawrence Durrell, however, sees in the prose of his autobiographical novels an "Elizabethan quality, a rare tonic vitality which comes from the savage health of its creator." (See also *Contemporary Authors*, Vols. 9-12, rev. ed.)**

I call Henry Miller the greatest living author because I think he is. I do not call him a poet because he has never written a poem; he even dislikes poetry, I think. But everything he has written is a poem in the best as well as in the broadest sense of the word. Secondly, I do not call him a writer, but an author. The writer is the fly in the ointment of modern letters; Miller has waged ceaseless war against writers. If one had to type him one might call him a Wisdom writer, Wisdom literature being a type of literature which lies between literature and scripture; it is poetry only because it rises above literature and because it sometimes ends up in bibles. . . .

Every word he has ever written is autobiographical, but only in the way *Leaves of Grass* is autobiographical. There is not a word of "confession" in Miller. His amorous exploits are sometimes read as a kind of Brooklyn Casanova or male Fanny Hill, but there is probably not a word of exaggeration or boasting to speak of—or only as much as the occasion would call for. The reader can and cannot reconstruct the Life of Henry Miller from his books, for Miller never sticks to the subject any more than Lawrence does. The fact is that there isn't any subject and Miller is its poet. . . .

Miller's achievement is miraculous: he is screamingly funny without making fun of sex, the way Rabelais does. . . . Miller is accurate and poetic in the highest degree; there is not a smirk anywhere in his writings. Miller undoubtedly profited from the mistakes of his predecessors; his aim was not to write about the erotic but to write the whole truth about the life he knew. This goal demanded the full vocabulary and iconography of sex, and it is possible that he is the first writer outside the Orient who has succeeded in writing as naturally about sex on a large scale as novelists ordinarily write about the dinner table or the battlefield. I think only an American could have performed this feat. . . .

What makes Miller unique is his time and place; he is the only American of our time who has given us a full-scale interpretation of modern America, other than the kind of thing we find in the cultural journals. . . .

Miller writes as a poet about the demonic hideousness of New York City, Chicago, the South, or he rhapsodizes when there is anything to be rapturous about. But it is not Art that he cares about; it is man, man's treatment of man in America and man's treatment of nature. What we get in Miller is not a sense of superiority but fury, even the fury of the prophet of doom. . . .

Miller is "irresponsible" as far as official and popular politics go, or as far as common church morality goes, and as far as literary manners go. But he is not a poseur, he has no program, yet he has a deep and pure sense of morality. I would call him a total revolutionary, the man who will settle for nothing less than "Christmas on earth." . . .

Miller calls for an end to revolt once and for all. His message is precisely that of Whitman, of Rimbaud, of Rilke: "Everything we are taught is false"; and "Change your life." As a writer Miller may be second- or third-rate or of no rating at all; as a spiritual example he stands among the great men of our age. Will this ever be recognized? Not in our time probably.

*Karl Shapiro, "The Greatest Living Author," in his* In Defense of Ignorance *(copy-*

*right © 1960 by Karl Shapiro; reprinted by permission of Random House, Inc.), Random House, 1960, pp. 313-38.*

The Miller man, [in *Tropic of Cancer*] and in later books, is in effect the descendant of Dostoevsky's Underground Man, without his nastiness, and of Rilke's Malte Laurids Brigge, without his fastidiousness. Miller's hero even has his feminine ideal, the American girl here called Mona, who recurs in his other books under a slightly different name; and although he marries her, she remains elusive. Yet his hectic devotion to her doesn't stop him from having all those other jubilantly recorded love affairs. . . .

He has been a generally liberating influence upon other writers, for many of his values, particularly his reverence for life and his attacks upon standardization, have been widely circulated and adopted, if only unconsciously. Overtly, his influence is most apparent upon celebrants of rootlessness such as the beatniks, or upon Lawrence Durrell, whose later works are the outgrowth of his early novel, *The Black Book*, which in its turn is an outgrowth of Miller. Durrell says of Miller: "American literature today begins and ends with the meaning of what he has done." Of course to some readers *Tropic of Cancer*, strong language and all, may seem dated, but perhaps to many others the publication of the book here and now will reemphasize its enduring freshness. . . .

Now it must be granted that parts of *Tropic of Cancer* will hammer away at some of the strongest of stomachs, even in this epoch in which so many books are really scabrous. But in the present volume, among other things, Miller projects with gusto some of the great comic scenes of modern literature. There are, for example, the Dijon sequence in which the narrator goes to teach for a while in a broken-down provincial lycée; the last episode of the book, which involves the Miller man and one of his friends and a French family in a crazy farce; and, above all, the scenes describing a Gandhi disciple looking for fun in a Paris brothel. If literary quality is a criterion, these passages run far ahead of any considerations of obscenity; in themselves they guarantee that Henry Miller is an authentic, a significant author whose ripest work has been too long forbidden in his homeland.

*Harry T. Moore, in* The New York Times Book Review *(© 1961 by The New York Times Company; reprinted by permission), June 18, 1961.*

Essentially [this] is what [*Tropic of Cancer*] is: a mirror-image of the testimony which is given at revival meetings. There you can hear about men who got right with God; this man got right with art and sex and the use of his brain and time. Like all converts, he is on fire. Like all converts, he simply will not leave your lapels alone. Thus he is a bit tedious. Because he came fairly late in life to a personally valid ethic, he cannot believe that anyone he talks to has ever done it before him. . . .

Narrative is not his forte; his characterizations are sketchy; his philosophy is jejune. It is in pressing his whole existence against the warm wax of his prose and leaving there its complete imprint that he is at his best—in following every quiver of sentience to its source or destination with phrases that sometimes add up to a gorgeous fabric. . . .

[*Tropic of Cancer*] belongs, modestly but securely, in the American tradition of profundity-through-deliberate-simplicities that has its intellectual roots in Thoreau and continues through such men as Whitman and Sherwood Anderson until, in a changed time, it thinks it needs to go abroad to breathe. Miller stands under his Paris streetlamp, defiantly but genially drunk, trolling his catch mixed of beauty and banality and recurrent bawdry—a little pathetic because he thinks he is a discoverer and doesn't realize that he is only a tourist on a well-marked tour. We see him at last as an appealingly zestful, voracious, talented hick.

*Stanley Kauffmann, "'Tropic of Cancer'" (originally titled "An Old Shocker Comes Home"; copryight © 1961 by Harrison-Blaine, Inc.; reprinted by permission), in* The Critic as Artist: Essays on Books 1920-1970, *edited by Gilbert A. Harrison, Liveright, 1972, pp. 211-16.*

As early as the thirties, Miller decided for himself that either American society was through or he was through with it. He jumped off the bandwagon of "success" (depicted in those great scenes in which he was a personnel manager for Western Union in New York City), went underground to live a bum's life, and to write. Sexual pleasure became both an opiate and a way of protest for him. He is the true ancestor of all the beatniks and hippies, except that he is a most immensely learned, intensely cultivated writer of major stature. To read him, after recognizing all his quirks, traps, and entanglements, is to breathe the air of great literature again. Literally hundreds of ordinary people (his old friends and acquaintances), people from the middle and lower depths of American urban society, caper, throng, prance, and stumble through the pages of his two major works of fiction.

But Miller's view not merely of the American scene but of all modern, progressive, scientific, and industrial life, is basically hopeless if not desperate. As a writer he lives, as it were, on his biological energy and his devotion to thought and art; and it is logical that his scenes of warmth and love and affection center around "old-fashioned" American life, such as the beautiful eulogy to New York's East Side in the first decades of the century. . . .

From Miller descended . . . the beatnik and hippie traditions which, whatever their obvious limitations, provided a liberating force in our literature from the sterile conformity of the fifties. Such writers as Jack Kerouac, Allen Ginsberg, Lawrence Ferlinghetti, to mention only a few, brought our literature out of the bowers of academe back to the streets of life, a life distorted and malformed and "sick" with the modern sickness which the early existentialists first proclaimed.

*Maxwell Geismar, "The Shifting Illusion: Dream and Fact," in* American Dreams, American Nightmares, *edited by David Madden (© 1970 by Southern Illinois University Press; reprinted by permission of Southern Illinois University Press), Carbondale: Southern Illinois University Press, 1970, pp. 45-57.*

Like James, Dreiser, and Fitzgerald, Miller assails the American Dream of permanent wealth and happiness as the automatic reward of individual effort and excellence of character; he joins in the attack on the Dream as a hoax and a fraud. But where the others dramatize the process of belief and disenchantment, where they take account of losses and gains, analyze the social matrix of illusion and credit the desire for success as human facts worthy of compassion, Miller alternates between satire and direct assault. Less the novelist, he reveals himself as far more the moralist, which raises questions about the grounds of his moral fervor.

Since he settled in California in 1944, Miller's moral vision has become a major note in his writing. It is based on a vision of modern society as irredeemable, unchangeable, except through some form of apocalypse or shattering revelation. By "society" Miller means the way of life depicted in the caricature—the style of daily living, rather than the structure of social relations which gives that style a concrete historical setting. Any redemption must find its source outside social relations, that is, outside history. "To live beyond the pale, to work for the pleasure of working, to grow old gracefully while retaining one's faculties, one's enthusiasms, one's self-respect, one has to establish other values than those endorsed by the mob." The "mob" is Miller's indiscriminate label for American "society," the antithesis to which is the "artist." "It takes an artist to make this breach in the wall." . . .

His artists are a life-giving elite. . . .

This redemptive function Miller assigns to his artists is a familiar idea with roots in nineteenth-century antibourgeois sentiment. Miller's artist is often the free bohemian, whose life on the fly is a deliberate slap at the order and routine of respectable life. But he is also something more. With all the eclecticism of Miller's thinking about art, and the important influence of European ideas, especially Surrealism, at bottom he is still attached to the idea of a particularly American function for his artist, or for personal liberation as such. To be sure, the idea does not often reach the surface of his writings, but there are enough clues to suggest that Miller hopes for a specifically *American* redemption—indeed, we discover, a return to traditional or mythic national values. How else are we to understand Miller's description of the present money-getting as a "bitter caricature" of the ideals of "our liberty-loving forefathers"? Or his mention of "a great social experiment . . . begun on this virgin continent" [*The Air-Conditioned Nightmare*]? . . .

The image of the "air-conditioned nightmare" . . . affirms implicitly a "dream" as a measure of judgment. In his earlier books America represented death and destruction of spirit. The American city suffocated him; he needed to escape. . . . *Black Spring*, the most successful of his [books, evokes] both the suffocation and the frenzy of release. . . . The solution is to destroy the old American world in himself, the world of fraud, materialism, gadgetry, the dream turned nightmare, and to die into a new, free being.

But does the new being Miller elicits from his desperate experiences really constitute a rejection of the American Dream? Or is it a translation of the values of the Dream from economic and social terms to psychological and aesthetic ones? To be "immune, great, godlike" remains the goal of his energetic assault upon the world, and in a sense he has freed himself to undertake that assault in a manner which has something in common with the fantasies of urban popular culture—fantasies of escape from conventions of family and work, of personal license in pursuit of pleasure, of "doing you own thing." If the heart of the American Dream is the image of the unfettered man "making" himself by accumulation of goods and credit, assuring a place for himself at the American banquet, Miller has detached the activity from any social end, and celebrated the act of accumulating experiences, especially sexual experiences, as an end in itself. Instead of a duty, life becomes an adventure—but still an adventure of self-aggrandizement and self-creation. By inverting the Horatio Alger style of the Dream, Miller discovers its essence, the desire to have what William James called a "moral holiday" as a permanent condition. "I have no money, no resources, no hopes. I am the happiest man alive." . . .

The flight from history, from social ties and obligations, is the clearest mark of Miller's underlying commitment to an American Dream. The idea of a "history on the side" may have replaced the "castle of pure white spit," but the motive of immunity from time and society remains intact. Not wealth but voluntary poverty, not excellence of character but its exact reversal, become the means toward this immunity. Miller's career, as recounted in his books, can be taken as a quest for ultimate self-transcendence, for the perfect frontier where without any encumbrances the self can feed on the world without distraction.

Once we become aware of these familiar American aspirations in Miller, it is not surprising to discover other elements of the cultural pattern, especially the obsession with memory, the attempt to recapture an idealized past. While Miller rejects history as "meaningless," as a "cancer," his works are obsessed with the past. The personal past becomes a virtual alternative to world history. The pattern completes itself when we encounter passages which can only be described as "pastoral" in their yearning to recapture earlier moments of peace and harmony. . . .

The wild park, the park of the unconscious, which the writer both invokes as theme and employs as technique, is meant to dispel the nightmare of the city. Liberation is expressed in the act of writing, in its putative freedom from restraint. Flow takes the place of plot. The *persona* commands a range of styles—comic vernacular, high-flown prophecy and exhortation, surreal fantasy—but it does not possess any genuine plasticity. It is beyond change, beyond the ability to register experience as anything other than force, energy, impact. The effect is to make voyeurs of the readers, not participants. Self-absorption indulged on a scale of verbal magnificence is Miller's essential form of liberation. His "history on the side" is autobiography in which event and fantasy have identical status. To discriminate would be to falsify the flow, the tangled undergrowth of the "natural park" of the self.

*Alan Trachtenberg, "'History on the Side': Henry Miller's American Dream," in* American Dreams, American Nightmares, *edited by David Madden (© 1970 by Southern Illinois University Press; reprinted by permission of Southern Illinois University Press), Carbondale: Southern Illinois University Press, 1970, pp. 136-48.*

## MILLER, Walter M., Jr. 1923-

**Miller, an American, writes science fiction novels and stories and television scripts. He is best known for *A Canticle for Leibowitz.***

[In *A Canticle for Leibowitz*] we have an epic of time, space, and consciousness. We have a succession of Ends and Beginnings, a concept of human history which stresses the unity of judgment and redemption. Space is the locus of the action, but while redemption is glimpsed in space and time, it is only visible as a suggestion of hope for a future which is beyond the time and space of which we are presently conscious. A notion of man comes through in this story which plays upon his seemingly inevitable tendency to destroy what he creates: "The closer men came to perfecting for themselves a paradise, the more impatient they seemed to become with it, and with themselves as well. They made a garden of pleasure, and became progressively more miserable with it as it grew in richness and power and beauty." . . . Thus we have a suggestion of history as it has been: Man builds his house laboriously, only to bring it crashing down. But out of the holocaust the remnant survives to carry forth the story of man.

But what is the source of the folly in man? What prevents him from building a house that can endure? Miller suggests that superimposed upon man's capricious freedom—the source at once of creative action and the seeming obligation to destroy—is a failure, an incapacity, to use this freedom properly. The freedom which is attained when man attains consciousness of good and evil, when he distinguishes himself from nature and begins to build civilization, carries with it the tendency not merely to ignore nature, but also to manipulate time, that is, to fail to distinguish between the area of existence which falls within man's control and that which does not. When man is aware of the justice which is history's goal—the justice that would exist if man's freedom to choose were exercised correctly—and when he seeks to act in accordance with that justice, his life becomes authentic. But the same freedom that draws him toward justice leads to his embitterment with the space (nature) and time (history) which he is given. And this bitterness impels him either toward despair and inaction or toward an attempt to assert a control over space and time which he does not possess. He attempts to become God, and in doing so forfeits the possibility of authentic manhood. In this context, the suggestion that God alone is the Lord of history is not a summons to human slavishness and subservience, but rather to the fulfillment of man's freedom in justice and love. . . .

Miller, whatever his concern for theology, is always true to the story. His characters happen to be concerned with theological questions, but when they speak they always remain within the context of the story. Thus the theological conclusions are drawn by the characters and not by the author speaking directly to the reader. The theological realities become a part of the story itself.

*Lois and Stephen Rose, in their* The Shattered Ring: Science Fiction and the Quest for Meaning *(© 1970 by Lois and Stephen Rose; used by permission of John Knox Press), John Knox, 1970, pp. 91-4.*

[The] peculiar merit of [*A Canticle for Leibowitz*] is traceable to virtues which are both subliterary and transliterary. For one thing, it is science fiction . . . and its prose while competent is not distinguished. So it is not as "good" as, say, Katherine Mansfield. Yet it is of more moment than Katherine Mansfield. It is also of more moment than the better known sci-fi futuristic novels, *1984* and *Brave New World*. . . .

*A Canticle for Leibowitz* is like a cipher, a coded message, a book in a strange language. From experience I have learned that passing the book along to a friend is like handing the *New York Times* to a fellow passenger on the Orient Express: either he will get it altogether or he altogether won't.

Like a cipher the book has a secret. But unlike a cipher the secret can't be told. Telling it ruins it. But it is not like giving away a mystery by telling the outcome. The case is more difficult.

A good indication of the peculiar nature of the secret is that the book cannot be reviewed. For either the reviewer doesn't get it or, if he does, he can't tell. . . .

To say that the book is a cipher and that some readers have the code and some do not makes it sound like a gnosis, something like Madame Blavatsky's *Secret Doctrine,* which only an elect lay claim to understanding. But it's not that either.

Rather has the mystery to do with conflicting anthropologies, that is, views of man, the way man is. Everyone has an anthropology. There is no not having one. If a man says he does not, all he is saying is that his anthropology is implicit, a set of assumptions which he has not thought to call into question. . . .

At the end of an age and the beginning of another, at a time when ages overlap, views of man also overlap, and such mishmashes are commonplace. We get used to a double vision of man, like watching a ghost on TV.

Or, put mathematically, different ages locate man by different coordinates. In a period of overlap he might be located by more than one set of coordinates. Culture being what it is, even the most incoherent anthropology seems natural, just because it is part of the air we breathe. The incoherence is revealed—and the reader experiences either incomprehension or eerie neck-pricklings—only when one set of coordinates is challenged by the other: look, it is either this way or that way, but it can't be both ways.

The anthropology in *A Canticle for Leibowitz* is both radical and overt. Accordingly, the reader is either uncomprehending, or vaguely discomfited—or he experiences eerie neck-pricklings. . . .

Miller has hit on the correct *mise en scène* for the apocalyptic futuristic novel. The setting is the desert. An old civilization lies in ruins. There is silence. Much time has passed and is passing. The survivor is alone. There is a secret longing in the reader either for the greening of America, vines sprouting on Forty-second Street, or for the falling into desert ruins of such cities as Phoenix. Phoenix should revert to the lizards.

Such is the ordinary stuff of good end-of-world novels, a sense of sweeping away, of a few survivors, of a beginning again. Here is the authentic oxymoronic flavor of pleasurable catastrophe. Shiva destroys, but good things come of it.

But the neck-pricklings, the really remarkable vibes, come from another direction in *Canticle* and set it apart from every other novel in the genre.

For the good vibes here are *Jewish*. The coordinates of the novel are radically Jewish-Christian. That is to say, the time-line, the *x*-coordinate, the abscissa runs from left to right, from past to future. But the time-line is crossed by a *y*-axis, the ordinate. What is the *y*-axis? It is Something That Happened or Something That Will Happen on the time-line of such a nature that all points on the time-line are read with reference to the happening, as before or after, minus or plus. The Jewish coordinates are identical with the Christian save only where *y* crosses *x*.

To apply Jewish-Christian coordinates to a sci-fi novel is almost a contradiction in terms. Because all other sci-fi novels, even the best, *1984* and *Brave New World*, are written on a single coordinate, the time-line. There is a Jew in *Brave New World*, Bernard Solomon, but his Jewishness is accidental. He could as easily have been a Presbyterian or a Sikh. . . .

For Jewish coordinates (I say Jewish because for our purposes it doesn't matter whether the coordinates are Jewish or Christian, since both have an intersecting *y*-axis, and after all the Jews had it first) to be applied to the sci-fi genre is a radical challenge of one set of coordinates by another. It is either absurd—and some reviewers found it so—or it is pleasantly dislocating, setting up neck-pricklings. It is something like traveling to a habitable planet of Alpha Centauri and finding on the first rock: Kilroy was here. Or it is like turning on a TV soap opera and finding that the chief character is Abraham. . . .

The peculiar virtue of the novel lies in the successful marriage of a subliterary pop form with a subject matter of transliterary import. Literature, in one sense of the word, is simply leapfrogged. Katherine Mansfield is bypassed.

*Canticle* is an agreeable battle of coordinates. The eerie neck-pricklings derive from the circumstance that the uni-axis time-line of futuristic fiction has never been challenged before and so has become one of those unquestioned assumptions that form us far more firmly than any conscious philosophy. Miller lays the old coordinates over the uni-axis—like one of those clear plastic overlays in mathematics texts—and the reader experiences a slight shiver, or annoyance, or nothing at all.

When Miller's starship, which leaves the earth in the second holocaust, reaches Alpha Centauri and discovers intelligent beings there, most of the astronauts will ask the strangers the usual uni-axis time-line questions: What is the state of your agriculture? Have you split the atom yet? What about your jurisprudence? Etcetera.

But at least one of the astronauts will be a fellow like Walter Miller and he will ask a different set of questions—questions that, oddly enough, the strangers may understand better than his fellow astronauts: "How is it with you? Are you yourself? Or did something go wrong? Was there a disaster? If so, where do you presently stand in relation to a rectification of the disaster? Are you at a Time Before? Or a Time After? Has there been a Happening? Do you expect one?

When he finishes *Canticle*, the reader can ask himself one question, and the answer will tell whether he got the book or missed it. Who is Rachel? What is she?

*Walker Percy, "Walter M. Miller, Jr.'s 'A Canticle for Leibowitz'," in* Rediscoveries, *edited by David Madden (© 1971 by Crown Publishers, Inc.; used by permission of Crown Publishers, Inc.), Crown, 1971, pp. 262-69.*

* * *

## MISHIMA Yukio 1925-1970

**Mishima was a Japanese novelist, short story writer, playwright, and essayist. He was a youth cult figure in his own country and, internationally, the best-known Japanese literary figure. He took his own life by performing the ritual *seppuku*. (See also *Contemporary Authors*, obituary, Vols. 33-36.)**

Mishima is often compared to several Western writers—Gide, Proust, Balzac, Flaubert, and even Brecht, to make the comparisons seem almost fanciful—but it is impossible to find an equivalent that suggests his work. Like all good writers he takes much from other writers but is finally what *he* is. A sharp observer of a broad canvas of life, he portrays subtly and without sentimentality those often slight but all important moments in life when an event turns our life painfully and irrevocably. In [his] tales he says much about modern Japan, and he can be read for this insight, but he is greater than a country: he finely reveals many of the aspects of the human experience anywhere.

Virginia Quarterly Review, *Vol. 43, No. 1 (Winter, 1967), pp. xiv-xvi.*

Mishima was a Japanese, and Mishima was Mishima. Admittedly, the sexual 'frankness' of his writing may have made us think how Western and how modern he was—in the line of Gide, Miller, even Mailer, even (in his occasional mixing of sex and violence) the Soho porn-shops—and the more so if all we knew of Japanese literature was the *haiku,* that species of verse which is all soul and no body, all refinement and no roughage. His *Five Modern Nō Plays* may have struck us, especially if we were unacquainted with *Nō,* as having something in common with the 'Absurd', though they must also have struck us as rather more interesting than most exercises in that modish mode. As for his concern with the Marquis de Sade—what could be more Western and up to date than that?

In fact, all the time Mishima was intensely Japanese. The determined perversity of *The Temple of the Golden Pavilion,* the fearful consciousness of it all and (to our eyes at least) the final ludicrousness. . . .

Much of [Mishima's most Japanese work] could be thought of as 'Western' because of the 'extreme' nature of the situations and events, just as the mixture in Mishima's characters of obsessive introspection with gratuitous action could be considered distinctively modern. And yet—as I suggested recently in reviewing an obnoxious novel by a young Japanese whom his American publisher described as 'revolutionary' and 'the first truly modern Japanese writer'—Japanese writers of fiction have been modern in this sense for a long time, and 'extreme situations' are no import from the incontinent West! . . .

Possibly Mishima was one of those in whom an intimacy with the literature and the life of the West served to sharpen, intensify and exacerbate his awareness of being a Japanese. . . .

Mishima was originally considered the spokesman for post-war youth, adrift in the Waste Land, and its spiritual problems. At that time the villain of the piece was Japanese Tradition, for traditions had brought the land to madness and then to waste. But 'après-guerre' is now long past, and if the spiritual problems still persist despite everything, isn't that because the only solution is Japanese Tradition? The brilliant young Japanese whom foreigners could really talk with, the darling of American publishers who visited the U.S. as guest of the State Department and *Partisan Review,* yet it seems Mishima knew which way his blood called him. At times the most aesthetic, the most 'decadent' of writers, yet he went in for weight-lifting and *kendo,* he kept fit. He must have known what a thoroughly Japanese end his thoroughly Japanese patriotism could bring him to.

*D. J. Enright, "Mishima's Way" (1970), in his* Man is an Onion: Reviews and Essays *(© 1972 by D. J. Enright; reprinted by permission of Open Court Publishing Co. and Chatto & Windus), Chatto & Windus, 1972, pp. 195-203.*

Mishima, although only forty-five when he died, probably achieved a reputation in the English-speaking world greater than that of any other Japanese writer this century. His novels, from the *Sound of Waves,* through *The Golden Pavilion* to, for instance, *The Sailor who Fell from Grace with the Sea,* have been more widely translated, read, and circulated even than those of novelists such as Kawabata, the Nobel Prize winner, or the late Tanizaki, who is considered by many Japanese as the outstanding novelist to span prewar and postwar years. Other figures on the modern Japanese literary scene, such as Serizawa . . ., have had just as high if not a higher reputation in Japanese eyes. To many in Japan, in fact, Mishima was in danger of becoming a bit of a bore. He seemed to write too much and to try to cover too many literary forms. Moreover his ventures into extremist right-wing politics of the lunatic fringe and his unconcealed sado-masochism alienated many Japanese in all age groups.

Even if he was not, however, typical of modern Japan or was not in Japanese eyes the outstanding genius of his generation, his vitality, his capacity to tell a story and to evoke atmosphere, his insight into the seamier or less rational sides of human character, and his architectonic style made him a writer of great importance not only in Japan but also in the literature of the modern world.

*Sun and Steel,* which was published in Japan some months before his death, clearly pointed the way in which Mishima's mind was moving, and shows that his final and macabre gesture was carefully planned as the histrionic culmination of his life. This slender book can indeed be regarded as his literary testament and is necessary reading for anyone who wants to try to understand the background to his suicide and his outlook in this last period of his life. But the work, which is little longer than an essay, makes no pretence to sum up his life's work or to make a coherent and rational presentation of his overall outlook or philosophy of life or, for that matter, of death. In style it is poetic and evocative and might be better regarded, in part at least, as poetry rather than as prose; Mishima indeed did not like to regard the two as separate forms, and it is perhaps appropriate that the book ends with a poem entitled "Icarus". . . .

While Mishima's attitudes to the sword, the warrior and honour are in the Japanese tradition, his concept of muscle and the physical beauty of the athletic male body seem to owe more to Greek and Teutonic traditions than to Japanese. His approach to death is, he admits, conditioned not merely by what he regards as the heroic attitudes of, for instance, Japanese wartime suicide pilots, but also by a Western-style romanticism and a pervasive feeling of boredom with life.

*"The Warrior's Way Out," in* The Times Literary Supplement *(reproduced by permission), March 12, 1971, p. 297.*

Mishima was the only writer of his generation who knew the classical literature thoroughly and turned to it again and again, not because of any failure of his imagination, and certainly not out of ignorance of European literature, but because he desired to associate his writings organically with the past. His vocabulary too, drawing on the full resources of the Japanese language, was extraordinarily rich and nuanced, as any translator soon learnt to his grief.

Mishima frequently expressed his contempt for authors ignorant of Japanese tradition. Among his predecessors he revered Ogai Mori (1862-1922) who, inspired by the ritual suicide of General Nogi, the hero of the Russo-Japanese War, abandoned a career as a writer in the German romantic tradition to devote himself exclusively to painstaking, historically accurate accounts of virtuous samurai, considering that they represented the essence of what it meant to be a Japanese.

Mishima was also a devoted admirer of Junichirō Tanizaki (1886-1965) who had turned from his youthful fascination with Poe and Baudelaire to create nostalgic evocations of the classical literature. . . .

Finally, Mishima might be said to have been the protégé of Yasunari Kawabata (born 1899), whose devotion to traditional Japan lay in a somewhat different area from either Tanizaki's or Mishima's—the aesthetics of the old garden or the tea ceremony, the indirection of the utterances in the classical literature, and the childlike beauty of the women in the old paintings. . . .

As a writer Mishima had achieved the highest distinction. Not only was he generally recognized as the best Japanese novelist and playwright actively engaged in writing, but translations had spread his fame to many countries. Among the younger writers his only rivals were Kobo Abé and Kenzaburo Oë, both totally opposed to him in literary manner as well as in politics. Among the older writers only Kawabata ranked higher, and he had not written a major work of fiction in ten years. No doubt it was a disappointment to Mishima when Kawabata won the Nobel Prize in 1968, thus precluding his own chances at the prize for years, until Japan's turn came round again. Kawabata, with characteristic modesty, stated at the time of the award that

Mishima, a genius whose like was seen only once in 300 years, deserved the honour more than himself, and perhaps he was right. Mishima certainly wanted this international cachet of approval. The importance of foreign evaluation of his works is suggested by the prominence in his last letters of requests that the recipients assist in making sure that the English translation of his tetralogy would be published in full.

But Mishima must have felt utterly secure about his reputation in Japan. He told me in August, 1970, that he had written enough for one lifetime, and had put into *The Sea of Fertility* everything he had learned as a writer. "When I finish this book I'll have nothing left to do but to die", he said with a laugh, and I laughed too, unable to take him seriously. But Mishima meant it literally, and it must have seemed peculiarly appropriate to die on the day that he delivered to the publisher the concluding installment of his culminating work. It was not that Mishima feared a waning of his creative powers. He knew he could go on writing better than anyone else in Japan, almost without effort. But there was nothing more he wanted to say. He chose to end his career at his peak.

*Donald Keene, "Mishima and the Modern Scene," in* The Times Literary Supplement *(reproduced by permission), August 20, 1971, pp. 989-90.*

Mishima was probably Japan's first truly international novelist. He had a wide knowledge of Western literature, both classical and modern, and yet he knew his own classics better, and his feeling for the Japanese experience was more sensitive, than any writer of his generation. Where, for instance, Abé Kobo's style is marked by a desiccated brevity and a metallic ring, Mishima did more than any postwar Japanese writer to retain the "wetness", the "humidity" of the tradition. . . .

In *Spring Snow,* Mishima reverts regularly to the literary and stylistic techniques of an earlier Japan—the *haiku* poet's use of stereotyped images to set a seasonal background, for instance; the twang of a bowstring and the dull thud of an arrow as images for the cold bite of the winter wind, and "a huge flock of crows perched in the bare branches of the maple", which is lifted almost straight from a well-worn *haiku* poem.

Nowhere before in Mishima's writings is the style quite so dazzling, nowhere does it recall quite so forcefully the rich and resplendent culture of Japan's Momoyama period. Nowhere has Mishima's imagination reached such powerful and complex heights. Some of the passages describing the sea are, in Arthur Miller's phrase, "compressed visions, enormous myths".

*"The Meiji Adventure," in* The Times Literary Supplement *(reproduced by permission), November 10, 1972, p. 1357.*

The Buddhist doctrine of rebirth provides the underlying structure of the first half of Yukio Mishima's tetralogy, "The Sea of Fertility." In fact, the second volume, "Runaway Horses," is the reincarnation of the first, "Spring Snow." To the Buddhist, of course, reincarnation does not mean the continued existence of the same old soul in the new skin but rather the taking up of a previously unrelieved moral burden. And so the second book is the consequence, not the repetition, of the first.

Let me explain. Kiyoaki, the hero of "Spring Snow," is the essence of "elegance"—that is, melancholy ineffectual estheticism. . . .

Isao, the hero of "Runaway Horses," is quite explicitly the reincarnation of Kiyoaki. . . . But whereas elegance, transcended through love, characterized Kiyoaki, there is nothing poetic, languorous or lovesick about Isao. He is the embodiment of "purity," though what Mishima means by that word will shock the Western reader.

Purity is single-minded and irrational. . . . Purity is the special property of youth. It is a form of emperor worship. It is preserved through constant contemplation of death. And purity hungers for bloodshed.

At the end of "Runaway Horses" Isao expresses his purity by murdering a big businessman and then by disemboweling himself—*seppuku,* the samurai's ritual suicide. . . .

All the diverse, incompatible beliefs ever entertained in traditional Japan are treated in these books with respect. The aristocratic cult of poetic perception may have conflicted with the samurai code of military honor. The otherworldliness of Buddhism may have undermined the emperor worship of Shintoism. No matter. For Mishima such tensions are painful but creative; even one of his least attractive characters is capable of experiencing the productive contradictions. . . .

Isao, however, does not feel the double lure of elegance and purity. His only concern is to protect his idealism and to fulfill it in *seppuku*. . . .

Mishima failed to make Isao a character interesting enough to hold our attention. Could it be formulated as a general principle that the closer a character resembles an author's ideal, the less successfully that character is portrayed? George Eliot's Ladislaw pales beside her Casaubon, Jane Austen's Fanny is a cipher beside Emma, Tolstoy's Levin recedes behind Anna. Whether they are self-idealizations or longed-for versions of the opposite sex, these "perfect" characters do not develop; Isao, for instance, is tiresomely static. Nor are such characters motivated; the author's adoration is motive enough.

I suppose writers are no better at showing people they loathe. The most believable characters are generally those towards whom the writer feels a complex affection, who exhibit qualities the author can like but not respect, who do things that evoke not approval but compassion or amusement.

In Mishima's case, the indolent, effete Kiyoaki attracts this oblique admiration and is thereby a fully perceived character. Not so the ideal Isao. . . .

My impulse to speculate about a novelist's intentions may be out of fashion. But I can't help recalling that in Mishima's very early book, "Confessions of a Mask," the erotic and the violent were intertwined into the (for him) sexually provocative figure of Saint Sebastian transfixed by arrows. In Mishima's last work, the tetralogy, the two temptations have been separated, the erotic energies going to Kiyoaki, the violent to Isao. Eros triumphs—and the "pure" Isao behaves like a lunatic when he's not being a bore.

*Edmund White, "Runaway Horses," in* The New York Times Book Review *(© 1973 by The New York Times Company; reprinted by permission), June 24, 1973, p. 3.*

The demons which possessed Mishima were wild-eyed Japanese ones; so his life, his work and his death have a bizarre appropriateness that insists on standing. There is something rashly theatrical about him, a seemingly spurious exoticism his suicide makes genuine, for his death in that way looks like proof of his sincerity. And yet I am left with the feeling that it was the act of a disgusted fanatic, appalling because it was unnecessary, and throughout the first three novels of the tetralogy he knew was his last work, it is hard to avoid looking for clues to his suicide—insights of despair, hysteria, spite or strange joy.

With this third novel, "The Temple of Dawn," a theme is apparent. It is that of reincarnation, the transmigration of souls, a Nipponese rehearsal of Joyce's "met-him-pike-hoses." If one reads "The Sea of Fertility" as an elaborate suicide note, clearly Mishima expects to be back with us in one form or another. I had no idea of this when I read the first volume, "Spring Snow." It struck me as being a great love story . . . decorous and simple.

But "Runaway Horses" introduced the theme of reincarnation . . . and "The Temple of Dawn" continues the cycle. . . .

Hindu and Buddhist texts . . . provide the mystical underpinning for the whole cycle of novels. . . .

To see this, as the publisher does, as a novel showing "Mishima's ultimate understanding of Buddhist philosophy and esthetics" is to misrepresent somewhat "The Temple of Dawn." That whole side of it is disappointing compared with the much subtler portrait of Japan, richly textured situations of undeniable power that will eventually make up four panels of a Japanese screen in the tetralogy. Fortunately, the cycle does not depend on one's acceptance of reincarnation; that breathless relay race with the baton of the psyche being passed from hero to hero seems—at least in translation, and for this foreigner—nothing more than a kind of hopeful gimmickry.

The characters are important enough individually for one to believe in them without feeling obliged to prove or dispute their Buddhist bond . . . [and] seem to me of greater significance than the ponderous itinerary of their souls. . . . The next and last novel in the cycle, "Five Signs of God's Decay," . . . is bound to contain more intense fascinations than this and if it is anything like its predecessors it will make up the most complete vision we have of Japan in the 20th century.

*Paul Theroux, in* The New York Times Book Review *(© 1973 by The New York Times Company; reprinted by permission), October 14, 1973, pp. 6-7.*

The serial publication of Yukio Mishima's last works, a tetralogy called *The Sea of Fertility*, has the eerie effect of making him seem the fastest and most prolific dead writer in history. . . .

Mishima sealed this literary package with his ritual suicide in 1970, when he was only 45. Unlike, say, Ernest Hemingway, who shot himself at 61 in apparent despair over a deteriorating mind, Mishima killed himself in what seemed a gesture of robust if wasteful heroism, the ultimate act of self-control. Since his death was so theatrically deliberate, the temptation is strong to judge the tetralogy as an artistic and philosophical suicide note to the world. . . . It is fascinating and ambitious, but the final message (and literary value) is still difficult to decipher.

The first three interconnected books are extraordinarily good. Mishima uses the Buddhist doctrine of reincarnation to link various characters throughout the 20th century with changing manners, politics and national psychology in Japan. In *The Temple of Dawn*, he also discourses widely and sometimes pedantically about Buddhist theory; that is unfamiliar country for most Western readers. But Mishima's intensely poetic moral sense communicates his own fascination with such subjects.

In *Spring Snow*, the dreamy and aristocratic hero Kiyoaki Matsugae died a vaporously youthful death. He becomes Isao, the fanatic young political conspirator of *Runaway Horses*. In *The Temple of Dawn*, Kiyoaki/Isao is again transformed, this time into Ying Chan, a lovely Thai princess. The witness to all three incarnations is a wonderfully subtle spiritual voyeur named Honda, a rationalist Japanese judge and lawyer. Honda, like a principle of embattled moral intelligence, acts as Mishima's civilized guide through the mysteries of love, death, political tragedy and reincarnation.

If Mishima had written nothing else, his account of Honda's excursion to Benares, the holy Indian crematory site on the Ganges, would be considered a small masterpiece, on the order of E. M. Forster's visit to the Malabar caves in *A Passage to India*. . . .

The combination of filigreed Oriental pornography and slightly cheap *Götterdämmerung* has sometimes been a contaminating tendency in Mishima's work. But the rest of the book plausibly suggests a writer whose gifts amount at least to minor genius.

*Lance Morrow, in* Time *(reprinted by permission from* Time, The Weekly Newsmagazine; *copyright Time Inc.), October 15, 1973, pp. 122, 125.*

Since the revelations generally refer back to events in *Spring Snow, Runaway Horses* suffers if read in isolation from the earlier novel. Mishima's method has something in common with the ancient Nō drama he so admired, with its even, ritualised progress broken by heartrending flashes of insight. Indeed in one key passage it's the mystical effects of the performance of two Nō actors which confirm Honda in his belief that Isao is Kiyoaki reincarnated, the active balancing the passive, 'two superb lotuses, red and white'.

Adulation of the young male is not the only element to recall Oscar Wilde and European fin-de-siècle writers. Mishima's style is lyrical, full-blown, almost over-ripe, yet apt for all these perfect blossoms about to fall. One Shinto ritual, in which girls dance carrying lilies, provokes a cluster of images—lilies, swords, cruelty, beauty—which would have delighted Wilde or Dowson. But Mishima's imagery, almost always drawn from closely-observed nature, has a simplicity, strength and mystical significance generally more reminiscent of D. H. Lawrence. There is also a certain coldness and inhumanity, with human beings themselves seen as part of an austere natural order.

*Clive Jordan, "Last Rite," in* New Statesman, *November 30, 1973, pp. 828-29.*

At a personal level, it is probably impossible for a Westerner to identify with Mishima, whether in life or death, despite the abundant evidence [in *Runaway Horses*] that in him a formidable, self-aware artist was to be found at work until the very end, and despite our folk-memory of the long period in Western Christendom when the chief end of life was thought to be the making of a 'good death'. But the . . . comparison [of Mishima] with [the Japanese Catholic novelist Shusako] Endo shows that divergent missions, tempers and prescriptions may arise from fundamentally similar perceptions. Mishima's and Endo's imaginative responses to the sorry, soggy mudswamp-aspect of contemporary Japan both have the kind of authenticity that the world recognises in Solzhenitsyn on a larger stage. The Japanese writers, like the Russian one, say what their own countrymen do not particularly want to hear, and what the people of other countries can with the best will in the world only overhear. It is a battle honour not to be despised: the inkbrush, after all, is mightier than the kendo stave or the samurai sword.

*Christopher Driver, "The Inkbrush is Mightier," in* The Listener, *February 14, 1974, pp. 215-16.*

The question naturally arises: Is Mishima's tetralogy really of such magnitude as to make this tremendous job of translation worthwhile? Even without seeing the final portion, the answer would appear to be "Yes!" It is regrettable that the English of E. Dale Saunders and Cecilia Seigle tends at times to lumber along; even so, the power of Mishima's portrayal and the richness of his metaphors give this work a stature seldom matched in modern literature.

Virginia Quarterly Review, *Vol. 50, No. 2 (Spring, 1974), p. lvi.*

*Runaway Horses* is one of the few books in which the *weltanschauung* of nearly all its characters so repelled me that I found myself resenting the author's skill and the power of his story-telling technique. Nevertheless, they were formidable talents and must be acknowledged. Mishima, as you might expect from one who tried his hand at directing films, had a strong visual sense. His descriptions of landscapes, plants, weather and the effects of light are masterly. Even at the book's climax when Isao kills the hated capitalist (although, typically, Isao claims to be killing him not for his politics but because he has defiled a shrine) and runs towards the edge of the cliff to commit *seppuku*, there is a vivid description of the terraced tangerine fields through which he goes, and far from holding up the action it seems to increase the tension. *Runaway Horses* is an impressive novel, scenes in which still haunt me, but I hated reading it.

*John Mellors, in* London Magazine, *April/May, 1974, p. 137.*

As in the case of other prophetic novelists, Mishima's best work is not always his neatest and most controlled. His universally admired "After the Banquet," for all its perfect literary manners, is not ultimately so generous as the tiny, diseased "The Sailor Who Fell From Grace With the Sea," nor as provocative as the overwritten and analytic "The Temple of the Golden Pavilion." Like these, his final novel, "The Decay of the Angel," has its pitfalls and its faults. They will be felt, most immediately perhaps in the style—sharp, almost clawing. . . .

The ["Sea of Fertility"] cycle is completed and we can see now what Mishima did with his supernatural notion. Taken together, these four novels constitute an epic, the dynamism of whose characters and action is the classical, if perverse, *amor fati*. No foreknowledge "would keep them from flinging themselves after their destinies." Mishima's epic, however, is not simply a chronicle of failed lives, historical decay and social disaster, nor is it merely a suicide note about spiritual rot. His theme—let us say it aloud—is not reincarnation. His subject is incarnation—in the Western sense, too. His theme (if anything so large as an epic must be said to have one) is the assumption by spirit of fleshy being, hence our engagement in human suffering and our final disengagement from it.

Yes, no doubt those annoying Buddhist and Hindu concepts catalogued for the reader, both in the earlier volumes and in "The Decay of the Angel," might have been better integrated into the moment-by-moment evolution of the drama. But the annoyance they caused there was fruitful. Honda's rational confidence in their significance, and the Western reader's esthetic annoyance at their insignificance, were both ultimately misplaced. When in the last chapter, Honda staggers to confront the last living representative of the lost age of romance, Satoko—once beloved of his friend Kiyoaki, but now the holy Abbess of the Gesshuji—he is overwhelmed. There the author burns holes in even his own assumptions, to say nothing of ours. In the very last pages the entire cycle destroys itself and then turns right around and regenerates itself by contemplating, with a tranquility that is nothing short of ferocious, the questionable reality of its own long, long fiction.

Yukio Mishima's work and his way of death consciously enforced that antinomy: action in the service of an illusion.

*Alan Friedman, in* The New York Times Book Review *(© 1974 by The New York Times Company; reprinted by permission), May 12, 1974, pp. 1-2.*

[*The Sea of Fertility: A Cycle of Novels*] resembles Galsworthy's Forsyte cycle (novels Mishima did not know) and shares with it an artless structure and a nostalgia for the past, an interest in action which verges occasionally into melodrama and a pathos which is sometimes near sentimentality.

The book is held together by its theme, for each of the characters has an inner connection with the others. This connection (avidly observed by Honda who, typically, becomes a voyeur in later life) is simple transmigration. Each is believed to be the incarnation of the other.

This is believed not only by Honda but (as the book makes clear) by Mishima himself. One's surprise at an intelligent author's acceptance of the literal truth of such tenets is lessened as his necessity for doing so becomes apparent.

Mishima was excessively concerned with immortality. He found the outward signs of decay—ordinary aging—disgusting . . . and he kills off his heroes, as he killed off himself, before decay can occur. Reincarnation offers a promise of eternal youth. At the same time it is more than a way of being endlessly alive. It is a way of being always known. As Mishima writes in the third volume: "There are only two roles for humans in this world: those who remember and those who are remembered." . . .

His concerns . . . are not those of an artist but a moralist. In these pages Mishima shows us little; he tells us everything. This is not a book such as his own favorite among his works, *After the Banquet*, one marked with expert observation and ironic understanding. It is moving but it is moving as a cry of pain is moving.

Like all moralists Mishima was a romantic in that he perceived something more pure, more innocent, something higher and better to which he might unfavorably compare himself as he was and the world as it is.

This attitude is as attractive as it is gallantly quixotic. It makes the world seem a simpler place, and a more urgent one. For that reason this long testament will always have its admirers. In it Mishima rushes to establish himself. But Mishima the artist was already established—by the novels which came before this one.

*Donald Richie, "Mishima and the Savage God," in* Book World/The Washington Post (© The Washington Post), *May 19, 1974, p. 1.*

Mishima, the literary genius of Japan's postwar generation, often mentioned for the Nobel Prize, delighted in shock and contradiction. He possessed luminous and fertile abilities: his complete works in Japanese are now being collected in 36 volumes. He was also a master of what Russians call *poshlust*, a vulgarity so elevated—or debased—that it amounts to a form of art. . . .

Mishima's last work, *The Sea of Fertility*, is a four-volume cycle of which *The Decay of the Angel* is the final part, finished on the morning of the author's suicide. Encompassing four Japanese generations and more than 70 years of the country's most complex history, the tetralogy is a daring, not always successful enterprise. At its best it has a brilliant, erratic, lunar clarity. Mishima did not believe in reincarnation, yet the premise of all four novels—*Spring Snow*, *Runaway Horses*, *The Temple of the Dawn* and *The Decay of the Angel*—is reincarnation. The unifying figure throughout is a lawyer-voyeur named Honda, who has devoted his life to tending the various incarnations of his boyhood friend, Kiyoaki Matsugae.

Symbolically, Matsugae's last incarnation—as a preternaturally evil young orphan—turns out to be a fraud, just as modern Japan has turned into a polluted and plastic travesty of its disciplined traditions. *The Decay of the Angel* is nonetheless a wonderfully frigid dance of death in which Mishima, like a Japanese Prospero, gathers all his artistic belongings together. In its austerity it is among the best of Mishima's novels. Perhaps there was something solipsistic in Mishima's terminating both his work and his life simultaneously, making his entire world self-destruct at the same instant. What remain, of course, are his queer, lovely works, like dividends from an insane dictator's Swiss bank account.

*Lance Morrow, in* Time *(reprinted by permission from* Time, The Weekly Newsmagazine; *copyright Time Inc.), June 10, 1974, pp. 92-4.*

Mishima indulged no worries about form: for him fiction was simply a useful means of protesting at the post-war dulling of those traditional Japanese virtues: monarchy, ritual self-slaughter, and the cult of fitness and brute force. In *The Temple of Dawn*, third novel in his final tetralogy *The Sea of Fertility*, Mishima's narrator Honda—whose very name declares the commercialised, yankeefied modernity his author deplores—is a mouthpiece for the nastiest sort of reaction. He's spiritually emasculated, a *voyeur* rather than an actor wielding 'the Japanese sword with its glistening blade so pure and sharp'. But foreign travel and the best kind of reading soon set him to rights. Watching the (attentively detailed) ritual slaughter of goats in Kali worship helps rinse his spirit of modern impurities, and Vico and Nietzsche cheer him up with their praise of 'natural savagery' and their hopes for its renewal. The novel glooms over Japan. . . .

Ironically, Mishima's novels are, of all modern Japanese fiction, most recognisably westernised in tone: the princess, innocent and virginal, is even—shades of Milton—bitten to death by a snake in a garden. With any luck, Mishima's crusade will prove a dud: it'll be terrible indeed for Japan if future events fail to guarantee his relegation to the curio corner of literature.

*Valentine Cunningham, "Bags of Tricks," in* New Statesman, *July 19, 1974, p. 90.*

* * *

## MOORE, Marianne 1887-1972

**Marianne Moore was one of America's finest poets. Her entirely unique body of work is built upon subjects not generally considered the stuff of great poems. Exotic flora and fauna abound; baseball players, virology, musical composition, rare china, meteorology, and a snail appear. Miss Moore examined the world in meticulous detail, but it was not the things themselves that counted so much as the relations. As Sister M. Therese wrote, "she sees all created things in a shining unity." She was once called a "practitioner of beauty, poetry, and healing." Moralistic, truthful, witty, and idiosyncratic, her poems are an affectionate celebration of life. (See also *Contemporary Authors*, Vols. 1-4, rev. ed.; obituary, Vols. 33-36.)**

The technique of Marianne Moore's poems is a national one. She constructs a poem with engineering methods and with the blessed aptitude that American fingers have for mechanics. In her poems one *sees* America, and in seeing *hears*, and in hearing, *feels* America. It is a threefold complex process which is put together with mild good-natured trifles: a sentence jotted from a book, a word from a catalogue, quotations from a tourist guide; an overheard conversation, a memory, a comparison, a returning thought—from all these materials a poem is built. And when it is finished one sees that it is as national as baseball, and is created according to rules that became prevalent in America during the last quarter century.

Yet Miss Moore's art is a personal one. Modern poetry, which had its beginning in America with the magazine *The Little Review*, was a product of spiritual uprootedness and of dissatisfaction. But Marianne Moore made this dissatisfaction homey and familiar. . . . [She] was able to harmonize her poetic quest with the American temperament. Thus Marianne Moore became the poet of contemporary America. . . .

Miss Moore is truly protector of all those hard and so-called "prosaic" words that poets avoid. She comes near to them, breaks them into syllables and in these syllables she finds internal rhymes which do not stifle the effect of the prose in the poem. This is very important, for every poem is, in its raw state—prose, before the poet "does something" with the ore. It is often easy to make two lines rhyme so that prose takes on the formality of poetry. But Marianne Moore does double work. First she perfects the prosaic part of her poem and makes of it good prose; later, she converts the prose into a poem, and because the prosaic element is important to her she does not obscure it with superficial rhythm or with too facile rhyme. Many conventional poems may indeed be poems but they are cheap prose.

Marianne Moore takes simple, commonplace words and elevates them. She shows explicitly that the entire half-million English words are material for poetry. Above all, she loves the dry, essayist words, the speech-like ones, not those words which blatantly sing from within themselves. Often she arranges her difficult words in a distinctive typographical order. She shows that they possess even external grace. After all, books of poetry are printed words and she wants these words to stand by themselves, like Coleridge's picturesque "painted ship upon a painted ocean." Her printed words appeal immediately to the eye before one hears them with the ear.

Moore's rhymes, too, are more visible than audible. They are silent because she does not want to give them complete possession over the line. Her rhymes, like candles, blaze and burn out. She creates the impression of being a difficult writer only because her simplicities are assembled in a complex fashion. Miss Moore writes by association, yet she never offers the dream—only, at once, the interpretation; and the interpretation is full of the phantasmagoria of a dream. Her interpretation scintillates with expertise of the word, and of the second word which combines with the first. She pauses at the smallest trifles, pointing out every detail, which is not only seen but pondered over, and analyzed. When she focuses on something, she says all that can be said about it, all she is capable of remembering. She brings into the least corner the accumulated culture of her time in condensed form. This is her major achievement as a poet. . . .

Miss Moore's poems often fascinate the reader with their unique "tedium." She does not avoid tedium, but rushes directly toward it. The opposite of the tedious is the interesting, the amusing. A line becomes a lightning-rod of a moment that wishes to come and be, but the moment is burnt up and is no more. When one reads Marianne Moore's poems one sees that time is elemental in the poem, that the poem is actually swimming against time as one swims against waves. *Moore's poems exist in living time and not in squandered or past time.*

The humor of Marianne Moore's poetry is comparable to humor in music, in the sense that we say a Haydn quartet is humorous, or Beethoven's Eighth Symphony is full of pranks. It is humor intricately bound to form rather than content. Her humor if often achieved through a quotation meant in all seriousness, yet behind her use of it lies a hidden smile.

*Jacob Glatstein, "The Poetry of Marianne Moore" (originally published in Yiddish in Glatstein's* In Tokh Genumen: Essays 1945-1947*); translation by Doris Vidaver (copyright © 1974 by Doris Vidaver; reprinted by permission of Doris Vidaver), in* Prairie Schooner, *Summer, 1973, pp. 133-41.*

Offhand I would probably have shared what seems a widespread impression that Marianne Moore was admirably qualified, not only by talent but by sympathy as well, to translate the *Fables* of La Fontaine: this impression appears to have been based on a very rapid summing-up of both poets: "Ah, yes—animals." But there is, I find, a great distance between a Moore jerboa and a La Fontaine rat, and because I enjoy some of Miss Moore's poetry a good deal I am sorry to have to say that the results of this cooperation strike me not as merely inadequate or mediocre but as in a positive way terrible. My fine critical hindsight tells me now, what it didn't warn me of beforehand, that Miss Moore has never been a fabulist at all, that her animals never acted out her moralities; that their function was ever to provide a minutely detailed, finely perceived symbolic knot to be a center for the pattern of her recondite meditations; that what she shares with La Fontaine is a shrewdness and delicacy of the moral judgment, but that the two poets' ways of getting there—their *fables*, in fact—are so different as to be opposed. I still feel, with somewhat less conviction than before, that Miss Moore might have got a happier result by setting herself to *tell* La Fontaine's stories in English, for it seems that a critical factor in the failure of these translations may have been an uncertainty about the ideal degree of her dependence on the French: as poems to be read in English, they are irritatingly awkward, elliptical, complicated, and very jittery as to the meter; as renderings of the French they vacillate between pedantic strictness and strange liberty. . . .

Perhaps these are quibbles; I'm sorry if so. And I would give them up instantly if it seemed that the sacrifice of simplicity, accuracy and sense had resulted in some clear gain in the English version; but it was the oddity of the English which in the first place drew my notice. . . .

The general objection, of which the two foregoing objections are specific instances, is that Miss Moore is so often found going the long way around, making complexities out of simplicities, loading lines with detail until they are corrupted in sense or measure, and writing, in consequence, absurdly bad English.

*Howard Nemerov, "A Few Bricks from Babel" (1954; © 1962 by Howard Nemerov; reprinted with permission), in* Marianne Moore: A Collection of Critical Essays, *edited by Charles Tomlinson, Prentice-Hall, 1969, pp. 134-38.*

What . . . is the real gestalt of Miss Moore's formal structures? . . . [In] all but Miss Moore's later poems, the syllabic prosody and attendant devices are so used as to minimize the usual rhythmic possibilities of the syllabic structure, in order to give an effect more nearly approximating free verse, and that as a consequence we must presume the mathematic tone of her poetry is derived from other aspects of her total poetic. . . . [A] certain number of the later poems, still syllabic, represent a departure from this minimization of the usual syllabic effect, while paradoxically developing a tone in which the sense of dry precision is a less important constituent. . . .

The heightened, more lyrical voice of Miss Moore's later poetry is lifted on a combination of a more musical rhythm, and the more intricately wrought pattern of sound which is so apparent in these selections. Peculiarly enough it is in the early poems of Marianne Moore, where the "mathematic" tone is most obvious, that she employs so successfully so many means for reducing the importance of her syllabically determined line. The tone there rises, both in the syllabic and in the free verse poems, from uses of diction and rhythm. . . . It is in the later poems where (though they are without doubt no less precise) the tone desired is not so much one of precise distinctions, nice contrasts, and slight if portentous ironic gestures—it is here that the particular formal qualities of syllabic poetry are heightened by rhythm and euphony to a tone which is paradoxically not happiest in the drawing room, yet more clearly something of "hammered gold and gold enamelling."

*Robert Beloof, "Prosody and Tone: The 'Mathematics' of Marianne Moore," in* The Kenyon Review, *Winter, 1958, pp. 116-23.*

The achievement of Marianne Moore's version of La Fontaine is . . . to have discovered the principles of a badly needed idiom, urbane without slickness and brisk without imprecision. Since Chaucer's fell into disuse, English verse, constantly allured by the sonorous and catachrestic, hasn't had a reliable *natural* idiom that can imitate the speech of civilized men and still handle deftly subjects more complex than the ones whose emotions pertain, like Wordsworth's, to hypnotic obviousness; hence nothing existed for a La Fontaine to be translated into. . . .

That a Marianne Moore crow even in a translation should be unmistakably a crow, not a symbol, is what we should expect from the use to which she puts the celebrated animals in her poems. Her characteristic beast is the only thing of its kind prized for its uniqueness ("an aye-aye is not / an angwan-tíbo, potto, or loris"). . . .

The uncompromising inhabitants of Miss Moore's zoo, cross-bred with the citizens of the urbane La Fontaine's hierarchic animal kingdom, lend to an enterprise endangered by obviousness a jaunty manner of speaking that always arrests and often wholly entrances the modern reader. . . .

When Miss Moore gets preoccupied (understandably) with tucking all the words into the given rhythms and rhyme schemes she frequently produces what may be the neatest solution to this particular crossword puzzle, but is not the best way of conveying the subject at hand in English.

It is often, however, the best way of creating a climate of mind, not heretofore available in English, in which the wit of the Fables can thrive. All convincing translation remains miraculous, but the normal excellence of this one is surprisingly sustained: the work of a deliberate and indefatigable intelligence, which earns its reward when the translator's special diction, personal and by existing literary standards impure, re-creates the French aplomb with an absoluteness no careful reader is going to ascribe to luck.

*Hugh Kenner, "Supreme in Her Abnormality," in his* Gnomon *(© 1958 by Hugh Kenner; reprinted by permission of Astor-Honor, Inc., Stamford, Conn.), 1958, pp. 180-97.*

[Marianne Moore's] poems are not for the voice, she senses this in herself reading them badly; in response to a question, she once said that she wrote them for people to look at. Moreover, one cannot imagine them handwritten; for as Ruskin's tree, on the page, exists in tension between arboreal process and the mind's serial inventory of arms, shields, tables, hands, and hills, so Miss Moore's cats, her fish, her pangolins and ostriches exist on the page in tension between the mechanisms of print and the presence of a person behind those mechanisms. Handwriting flows with the voice, and here the voice is as synthetic as the cat, not something the elocutionist can modulate. The words on these pages are little regular blocks, set apart by spaces, that have been generated not by the voice, but by the click of the keys and the ratcheting of the carriage.

The stanzas lie on the page, one after another, in little intricate grids of visual symmetry, the left margin indented according to complex rules which govern the setting of tabulator stops. The lines obey no rhythmic system the ear can apprehend; that there is a system we learn not by listening but by counting syllables, and we find that the words exist within a grid of numerical rules.

*Hugh Kenner, "The Experience of the Eye: Marianne Moore's Tradition," in* The Southern Review, *Vol. I, No. 4, Autumn, 1965, pp. 754-69.*

One may speak of Marianne Moore's poetic practice very generally as follows: feeling is expressed by concrete images; these are very carefully perceived, and to the extent that the poem pays attention to them, elaborating them for their own sakes with the play of fancy, the feeling is restrained; to the extent that the opposite occurs, in the limited number of instances where Miss Moore uses an image in the mode of the imagination, feeling is unrestrained. . . .

[Many of] Marianne Moore's poems have form—form gained from rhymes, rhythms, and patterned arrangements of lines. But she avoids form that results from the organization of parts—a process in which details are selected, shaped, and ordered to contribute and conform to the whole, such as the faculty of the imagination, the "shaping spirit," would follow. To subordinate particulars to a general picture is contrary to her characteristic practice. . . . When she does subordinate details, she does so to provide a foil for the kind of perception which appreciates them. . . .

By dwelling upon the imagery for its own sake or by proliferating images linked by fanciful association Marianne

Moore achieves the control of feelings, that justly celebrated restraint and classic decency which is perhaps the most superb feature of her work. . . .

The virtuous restraint that results from Miss Moore's use of images, the unassertiveness that comes from the use of quotations and oblique statements is balanced against the form of the poems: for form, says Miss Moore, "is the outward equivalent of a determining inner conviction." Form manifests itself in her poetry as the over-all shape of a poem achieved by symmetries of sounds and meanings and also as the local fusing of these two in the expressiveness of her sound effects. Either of these achievements is, I suppose, a notification of the poet's conviction. . . . [In] general, form which asserts the conviction is by no means allowed to dominate: the instinct which scrambles the feeling through associated images controls likewise the notification of the conviction. All these techniques I take to be caveats and guards indicative of the poet's terrible sense that truth is a high hill, unassailable by the crude advance, and that one "about it and about must go."

*A. Kingsley Weatherhead, "Marianne Moore," in his* The Edge of Image: Marianne Moore, William Carlos Williams and Some Other Poets, *University of Washington Press, 1967, pp. 58-95.*

A woman poet who is also American will find herself measured sooner or later against Emily Dickinson. Few of them may like this, because the comparison will seem invidious on two grounds. Why should women be judged as poets differently from men? And is it fair that competition should be set so high? Emily Dickinson was, at her best, a poet unequalled in American literature. We may admit the complaint and still proceed with the experiment. In judging a woman poet, . . . we think first of the poet, but expect that her endowments as a woman will in certain ways modify what she writes. . . .

Marianne Moore and Emily Dickinson do not stand to each other in a relationship as undeniable as that between Miss Moore and Henry James. I doubt if one who mastered the urbane obliquity of James would care altogether for the abrupt and unceremonious withdrawals into enigma of Emily Dickinson. It has often been remarked that Marianne Moore's style develops out of highly civilised prose. Her sentences are beautifully articulated, more condensed than prose normally is, and with an odd sidelong movement that in prose would probably disconcert; but no one could mistake the element from which they have arisen. Their affinities are with conversation. . . . Emily Dickinson was afraid to converse: she utters a few astonishing words from behind the door and then closes it in palpitation. . . . Emily Dickinson all but abolished prose from her written communications with the world. . . .

And yet, given this all-important distinction between the two poets, their choice of language seems to unite them unexpectedly. Both are incontrovertibly American—or perhaps one should say American of a certain tone and temper which, like much else in the modern world, may be dissolving. They are individual, ironic, and above all fastidious. They place a high value on privacy and know the power of reticence. Their poetry is exact and curious like the domestic skills of the American woman in ante-bellum days. It has the elevation of old-fashioned erudite American talk—more careful in its vocabulary, more strenuously aiming at correctness and dignity than English talk of the same vintage. This is not to confuse the milieux of Emily Dickinson and Marianne Moore; nor to insinuate that both poets stand at a distance from today in a charming lady-like quaintness. What distinguishes them is something very far from quaintness: a practical interest in the capacities of the English language both learned and colloquial, in its American variety. . . .

A characteristic poem by Marianne Moore hovers between the colloquial and the instructed, just as it embodies her own spontaneous thoughts and a mass of felicitous quotation. The tone is equable and gracious, but never intimate: Miss Moore holds herself at a distance. The "I" in her poems is not central and exposed like the "I" in Emily Dickinson's. Rather it appears when comment is needed, or to provide a focus. . . . Almost at once the personal becomes generalized. . . . And her bent for anthologizing, for grafting quotations on to the living stock of her poem, leads also to a tactful self-effacement, for the sake of showing whatever it may be more clearly. Marianne Moore inhabits her poetry as a watchful commentator, much as Jane Austen can be sensed in every line of her novels. The actual incidence of the first person is not to the point. What reveals her throughout is a consistent tone.

The tone derives its authority from a philologist's care. . . . The words have no surprising depths, as they would in Emily Dickinson; but the public forms, as with her, the institution or enterprise, the obligation, are weighted against the private feelings. . . . Everywhere, she actualizes her abstract terms, which may be quotations, by doing what Emily Dickinson did—exposing them to the world of sensation. . . .

Marianne Moore's work houses a museumful of detail, drawn from her own observation, from her reading in such books as *Strange Animals I Have Known*, from art galleries, and from *The Illustrated London News*. She has assembled all these objects and impressions for the imagination to work into a new arrangement. So with language, the specimens of its use for a myriad purposes are presently given their place in a poem. Entering they are changed, it may be in almost imperceptible ways. The English language with all its Latin accretions is perhaps more than any other prone to degeneracy. It has to be kept alive from one era to the next, as indeed do all languages; and the most effective way with ours is that of Emily Dickinson and Marianne Moore—to restore the Latin words to their full rights by engaging them in the common labour of interpreting and assaying experience. They serve mostly to balance and control. . . .

Marianne Moore's emotional pitch and range differ from those of Emily Dickinson. They do not exclude terror . . . or ecstasy. . . . Her essential kinship with Emily Dickinson can be explained partly by the obvious facts that they are both women poets and both American; but it would scarcely add to our understanding of either did we not recognize the common bond of philology. To probe meanings, to read the past history and the present possibilities of words, to modify them by an apt new employment, to keep them adventurous and generative—such has always been the concern of the poet. Marianne Moore and Emily Dickinson have their separate ways of bringing words into prominence, and this essay could enlarge on the emphasis given by Emily Dickinson's dissonant rhymes, and the manner in which Marianne Moore's light rhymes duck to make way for the stress where it is most needed. But the important thing was to signalize what is common to their achievement, and to express gratitude for what they have done.

*Henry Gifford, "Two Philologists" (reprinted by permission of Henry Gifford), in* Marianne Moore: A Collection of Critical Essays, *edited by Charles Tomlinson, Prentice-Hall, 1969, pp. 172-78.*

[Marianne Moore's] poetry, for all its untraditional form, nevertheless reveals full knowledge of the traditions of the past; her technique is firmly rooted in complete understanding of the poet's craft. When she breaks the "rules," she knows *how* to break them, and, even more important, *why* she is breaking them. Thus her poems have an authority of tone, even while they are most daringly experimental. Her emphasis on the "instruction" element in poetry, along with "fascinating" (which she places first) and "stirring the mind," makes her work seem at times to hold a special kinship with the eighteenth century. She admits to the specific influence of eighteenth century prose, especially that of Samuel Johnson and Edmund Burke. . . .

But, though her poetry partakes of the general ethos of the eighteenth century, there is no similarity whatever in form. Nor is it derivative from any other source. A Moore poem is uniquely, unmistakably Moore. She firmly disparages a theory recently advanced, that her poems are planned deliberately to fit into a pre-arranged syllabic count. . . . When her work was first published, Ezra Pound remarked that she must have been reading Laforgue and the French symbolists; actually she read them for the first time in the 1950's. She received no inspiration from the Imagist movement—"I wondered why anyone would adopt that term"—nor from Amy Lowell's polyphonic prose.

Perhaps the poet whose approach most resembles her is Gerard Manley Hopkins. As in his "sprung rhythm," the rhythm of normal speech provides her metrical pattern. . . . The key word is *sound*. . . .

[No] matter how complex the sentence may be, there is never a loss or diminution of sense.. . . . Nor does the poet's insistence upon clarity and precision imply an obsession with the obvious. A Moore poem is subtle, demanding careful reading—sometimes several readings—but it is never obscure.

*Rosemary Sprague, "Marianne Moore," in her* Imaginary Gardens: A Study of Five American Poets *(reprinted with permission of the Publisher), Chilton, 1969, pp. 199-204.*

To be legendary is often to be dismissed. Enduring fame can be a kind of pigeonhole. Marianne Moore's is a pleasant pigeonhole: among critics she is almost universally admired. The unanimity of affectionate respect is, in fact, remarkable; no one whose poetry is being read with close attention could be held in such unvarying esteem. One suspects that, in a curious way, Miss Moore has, indeed, been dismissed. Long since, she has been read, "understood," and accorded a permanent pedestal. She deserves better treatment. Being understood is a condition fatal to further understanding. When Marianne Moore is unanimously acclaimed a technical virtuoso, everything important is left unsaid. She is recognized as a master of surface perfections whose poems are difficult, intelligent, scrupulously accurate and charmingly whimsical. There is at the same time general agreement that they are unemotional. . . . Miss Moore's reputation rests on brilliant surfaces and on charming eccentricities.

The basis for this reputation is understandable. The surface of the poems *is* brilliant. Miss Moore's poetic technique has reached its own potential. One may read such a poem as "The Jerboa" and be convinced that if surface is all, it is enough. But in limiting one's understanding of Miss Moore's poetry to an appreciation of polished surfaces, too much is ignored. How does one explain a poem like "A Grave" by applying to surfaces? One would have to ignore the dark music of feeling that informs that poem; the sacrifice would be too great.

Critics insist on the brilliance of Miss Moore's surfaces and, after all, the surfaces are there. It is Miss Moore who has created them, so part of the insistence, then, must be her own. A polished surface can serve as a concealment. Reflecting light, it can deflect attention from what it conceals. In numbers of Miss Moore's early poems, I think her concentration upon technique, wit, and intellectual hair-splitting serves such a purpose. A young woman's vulnerable feelings hide behind the cleverness. In the poems of her middle years, Miss Moore is less concerned with high polish (although the decreased concern is only relative) but often the content of the poetry is more conventional. In such a poem as "What Are Years?" the feelings expressed, although strongly stated, are those not-very-private ones that any thoughtful person might have in considering human life. The surface may be penetrable because the feelings are acceptably conventional. In the first sort of poem, feeling is controlled by a manipulation of surface fireworks. In the second kind, the feeling itself is a surface. It is ordinary emotion, rationally expressed. Throughout the poetry, from early to late, there is a third kind of poem that interests me most. It not only deals with the content lurking deep under the surfaces but is expressed in images that come from these depths. Such a poem is "A Grave." There are others like "The Plumet Basilisk," "The Fish," "Marriage," and "Sun." These are poems in which the ostensible subject—the surface object—simply will not support the weight of implied concern. Something else, something quite different from the stated subject, is in control of the poem. (pp. 11-13)

Miss Moore's surfaces, then, are not perfected simply for their own sake. It is almost axiomatic that in Marianne Moore's poetry the more glittering the surface, the greater the underlying emotion. The stronger and more frightening the feeling, the more necessary the protection that complexity of surface can provide. In the third category of poem I mention, the surface dazzles. The poems are rooms of mirrors, faceted with imagery that blinds in its brillance. They have an Arabian Nights opulence held tightly in a frame of technical control.

Something peculiar happens intermittently in these poems. In the midst of comprehensibility, rational content suddenly disappears. All at once there is no paraphrasable meaning. Nothing makes sense. One realizes slowly that something else has taken over the poem. The images are no longer images of any *thing* but are, rather, images of feeling. They are molten, coming like lava from the dark place of serpents and gold. The surface has broken and the crazy language of the unconscious mind pours in. (p. 13)

It is these moments when control is lost, these eruptions of feeling, that are for me the greatest pleasure in Marianne Moore's poetry. The surface of the poetry is undeniably brilliant, but it is perhaps the power of underlying emotion that is responsible for its highly-worked perfection. . . .

People who have chosen to see only the surfaces of Marianne Moore's poetry have missed at least half of what is there. In calling attention to technical detail so determinedly they have fallen into the trap the poet, herself, has provided; they have taken her insistence upon emotional restraint as evidence of no emotion. There is enormous restraint, of course, but one should not be misled by it. Only the wildest animals need cages so carefully made. (p. 14)

The confusion of Miss Moore with the Imagists, insofar as it has existed, has been a matter of seeing in similarities of technique an identity of purpose. Marianne Moore has used exactness, concentration upon and detailed description of a particular object in the service of idea and emotion. (pp. 37-8)

Nonetheless, between 1914 and 1920 Marianne Moore had been writing poems in harmony with new theories of modern poetry. Apparently quite independently, she was writing the sort of poetry that Pound and others were saying ought to be written. Use of the exact word and the language of ordinary speech, new and freer rhythms that would accommodate themselves to the content rather than demand accommodation, clarity, and concentration of expression, and the particular image in place of the abstract generalization—all of these innovations were being practiced by Miss Moore as they were being preached by Pound. (p. 38)

Miss Moore prefers the natural to the artificial, innocent honesty to sophisticated obfuscation. When she writes of the various literary people in the poems in *Observations*, it is the artificial pose, the deadening intellection and sophistication that she criticizes. . . . Truth is the plain and clear and simple. It is the honesty of pure color, the lucidity of clear air. (p. 39)

The preference for clarity here is more than a matter of taste. It is an ethic. Deliberate obfuscation is a species of immorality. The use of murky, equivocal expression in literature is evidence of a dishonest mind. This equating of style with moral integrity is a peculiarly modern idea. As a man's character might once have been read in his face, so now it could be found in his mode of expression. Honesty of intention would lead a man to be as accurate in his choice of words and as clear in his syntax as possible. The new emphasis on precision, particularity, and clarity, then, was as much a moral stand as it was a stylistic rebellion. (p. 40)

One thinks of her in connection with Walt Whitman, that most "American" of poets. In both cases being American meant simply being self-reliant, trusting to inward vision rather than received form. Of course, this is no more American than it is Rumanian or Chinese. It is seeing the vision and not denying it. It is an acceptance of oneself. (p. 56)

Most of Miss Moore's poetry is self-centered as, perhaps, all poetry is and has to be. Peculiar to Miss Moore's self-concern, however, is its emphasis on self-protection with concomitant non-involvement and withdrawal. Her concern for others has nearly always been in terms of identification with their vulnerability which, finally, begins to seem more like care for a projected self than real concern for real people. It is possible, then, that the guilt Miss Moore expresses in this poem comes from an acknowledgement of the cowardice of deliberate non-involvement. She has, indeed, inwardly done nothing or, more accurately, has deliberately set out to avoid being involved. Whether there is any validity in the idea of morally involving oneself in a separate question. The point is that for Miss Moore to feel this particular guilt is interesting in light of the persistent theme of a great deal of her poetry. (p. 112)

In many ways Marianne Moore and La Fontaine display such striking similarities in their respective verse that the one seems a spiritual descendent of the other. Their styles are remarkably alike. Syllabic versification and light, unaccented rhyme was Miss Moore's customary mode long before she translated La Fontaine. Both have a liking for precision that exhibits itself in the most delicate shadings of language. Both are possessed of a dry wit and a wry view when observing human nature. Animal subjects what Levin calls the human bestiary, are, of course, common to the poetry of both. The "surgical courtesy" Miss Moore admires in La Fontaine is equally apparent in her own work and bespeaks a philosophy of living as much as a style of expression. Finally, they share an ethical code. The morals of La Fontaine's *Fables* would be wholly congenial to Miss Moore's view of things and, in fact, many of the human values implied in the *Fables* have been more-or-less plainly expressed in her poetry.

For all the similarities, there is at least one major difference between the poetry of Marianne Moore and that of La Fontaine, and it is strikingly evident in the translations. Miss Moore is a poet of the eye first, a poet of the intellect second. La Fontaine is brain first and imagistic only occasionally. His *Fables* are prose written in verse. Miss Moore, on the other hand, does verbal water colors. She has transformed the *Fables*, in translating them, from black and white to bright colors. She has brought metaphor into the translations wherever she can do so without sacrificing the sense of a passage. She is scrupulously careful to imitate La Fontaine's versification but often transforms a line with her own metaphor. (pp. 118-19)

Frequently, in her later poetry, Miss Moore writes a kind of light verse inspired by some current topic that has taken her fancy. A gentle statement of value is usually implicit in these poems. The tone is light and conversational. Armored animals and amorphous fears dwindle away. The things Miss Moore has always valued she values still in these late poems, but her tone of exhortation is gone. (p. 159)

Because, in Miss Moore's poetry, form is synonymous with content it is often a poem's style that first hints at what is going on. As a general rule, the closer Miss Moore approaches to feeling, the more involuted the poem becomes. The connection between images becomes attenuated, the language of the poem becomes ambiguous. In the poetry of observation and intellect the style is considerably more straightforward. The relation of one image to another is, if not obvious, understandable after a little thought. One can understand readily why certain words have been chosen to modify certain others. The style, in short, is available to the rational mind. The poem can be understood intellectually.

The other kind of poem cannot. It must be understood, if that word even applies, by the irrational center within the reader. (pp. 178-79)

We have seen the haunted quality of some of her poems, have wondered why there was such fear and from what source it came. I have suggested that it was the contents of the mind's dark side that threatened beneath the surface of the poetry. How to protect oneself from this unnamed danger has been the obsessive theme of much of Miss Moore's poetry and a variety of armor has been tried. Yet all the time imagination, functioning as image-maker, has been the ultimate armor.

The imagination can go into the place of fears and return with metaphors. It can achieve a purgation without the rational mind's ever having really to know or name the fears that have been touched. Poetry, then, can be like dreams, peopled with old memories and emotions disguised in the crazy imagery of imagination. Dreams protect us. Imagination can protect us, too. It can talk of the mind's obsessive fears in a language of ambiguous metaphor. To face the fears bare of veils would be too dangerous. Yet they insist, persist. They can be looked at slantwise if they wear the costumes of imagination.

Thus, the obscurity and ambiguity that occur in the poems where feeling seems deepest is no accidental thing. Where feeling is deepest, veils are most required. They protect the poet. The obscurity of the imagery is an armor she invents, not as a barrier to the reader's understanding, but as a necessary protection for herself. (pp 180-81)

*Donald Hall, in his* Marianne Moore: The Cage and the Animal *(copyright © 1970 by Western Publishing Company, Inc.; reprinted by permission of the present publisher, The Bobbs-Merrill Company, Inc.), Bobbs-Merrill–Pegasus, 1970.*

Marianne Moore, . . . was (except for Ezra Pound) the last survivor of a group of brilliant experimentalist poets which included, besides Pound and Miss Moore, Wallace Stevens, T. S. Eliot, William Carlos Williams, H. D., and Mina Loy. They changed the course of Anglo-American poetry for several decades and they left a body of verse which, regardless of the place eventually assigned to it by historians of literature, will be a source of perennial fascination for anyone seriously interested in what Yvor Winters has called "forms of discovery"—the attempt by means of language to "discover and embody an increasing extent of reality." These experimentalist poets were radical and adventurous for their time. They wished to make poetry over, to make it new. They were absorbed in problems of technique and each spent a lifetime in mastering the craft of poetry as he understood it.

They thought that modern life was fragmented, complex, and to a great extent incomprehensible and they felt that "modern poetry" would inevitably possess the same characteristics. For many years each wrote for a small, elite readership, although in their later years several of them, including Miss Moore, became well-known pesonalities. Miss Moore, for example, was interviewed on the Today Show by a baffled Joe Garagiola on the subjects of poetry and the Brooklyn Dodgers. As an effort to share common interests the interview was a failure. . . .

Like Emily Dickinson, Miss Moore was excessively timid about publication and her first volume of poems was printed without her knowledge or consent. Each poem she wrote was an autonomous, intricate, symmetrical design put together with immense patience to satisfy the author. Communication, I suspect, was not of primary concern to her. The tone of her verse is usually witty and ironic. The deeper feelings are rarely involved. In the matter of feeling she was almost never false. She did not fail because she did not risk very much. In technique, in her combination of unusual visual, tactile, and sound effects, and in her complicated rhythms she was often brilliant.

*Donald E. Stanford, "Marianne Moore," in* The Southern Review, *Vol. VIII, No. 2, Spring, 1972, pp. xi-xiii.*

The concern for the shaping principle of a given poem, as an organic expression of the writer's perception and thought, is a distinguishing feature of the work of Marianne Moore. Miss Moore's interest in detailed patterns might well suggest a rationalistic belief that the world is susceptible to easy ordering. But the impulse toward order in her poems exists side by side and in tension with a full awareness of irrationality, disorder, and violence as inescapable conditions of life. The mind, she believed, must recognize the intransigence of experience as it pursues, carefully and flexibly, the task of informing its world with meaning. By exploiting imaginatively the very limitations of life and of the metrical patterns she devised, Marianne Moore created poems of unusual freshness and distinction. . . .

Partly because of her economy and restraint, the imagery of her verse gives the impression of a satisfying integrity and independence. Even when it supplies a clearly discernible pattern of metaphoric meaning, the structure of imagery is not symbologically burdened or exploited for ulterior ends. Sometimes, in fact, her poems do not show fully developed patterns of metaphor, and the reader is left with unsolved if not insoluble problems of interpretation. . . .

It is mind understood as the disciplined effort of the intellect and sensibility to achieve a tentative order that is perhaps the most distinctive principle of Marianne Moore's poetry, the expression of a unique, sensitive intelligence, enchanted by the abundance of experience, enchanting as it orders this experience through measured verse (*in + cantare*). A characteristic and abiding concern for responsible thought lies behind her reference in one of her later poems to poetry as a realm "where intellect is habitual." . . . Miss Moore did not believe in the Romantic head-heart dichotomy. To her, the mind was not unfeeling. Nor was it divorced from passion. She was attracted to subjects that dramatize the virtues of a mixture of thought and feeling, civilization and wildness, humane order and passion. . . .

The praise of human love is less common a subject . . . than the celebration of a wildness and disorder that Miss Moore obviously relished for its excitement, its threat of violence, and its challenge to the ordering mind and imagination. To come to terms with disorder as the unforseeable and thus apparently random events of life requires a special poise or "propriety," a word that Miss Moore used as the title of a poem. . . . In human expression, in art, it means a sense of fitness and proportion—of a resistance combined with acquiescence. . . .

*Walter Sutton, "Marianne Moore," in his* American Free Verse: The Modern Revolution in Poetry *(© 1973 by Walter Sutton; reprinted by permission of New Directions Publishing Corporation), New Directions, 1973, pp. 103-17.*

* * *

## MORRISON, Toni 1931-

**Ms Morrison, a Black American, is an editor and novelist. (See also *Contemporary Authors*, Vols. 29-32.)**

Toni Morrison is someone who really knows how to clank a sentence, as the novelist Irving Rosenthal has put it, and her dialogue is so compressed and life-like that it sizzles. And Morrison's skill at characterization is such that, by the end [of *Sula*], it's as if an enormous but too severely framed landscape has been unrolled and inhabited by people who seem almost mythologically strong and familiar; like the gorgeous characters of García Márquez, they have a heroic quality, and it's hard to believe we haven't known them forever.

Yet the comparison can't be extended: Morrison hasn't endowed her people with life beyond their place and function in the novel, and we can't imagine their surviving outside the tiny community where they carry on their separate lives. It's this particular quality that makes "Sula" a novel whose long-range impact doesn't sustain the intensity of its first reading. Reading it, in spite of its richness and its thorough originality, one continually feels its narrowness, its refusal to brim over into the world outside its provincial setting.

As the author of frequent criticism and social commentary, Morrison has shown herself someone of considerable strength and skill in confronting current realities, and it's frustrating that the qualities which distinguish her novels are not combined with the stinging immediacy, the urgency, of her nonfiction. . . . Toni Morrison is far too talented to remain only a marvelous recorder of the black side of provincial American life. If she is to maintain the large and serious audience she deserves, she is going to have to address a riskier contemporary reality than this beautiful but nevertheless distanced novel. And if she does this, it seems to me that she might easily transcend that early and unintentionally limiting classification "black woman writer" and take her place among the most serious, important and talented American novelists now working.

*Sara Blackburn, in* The New York Times Book Review *(© 1973 by The New York Times Company; reprinted by permission), December 30, 1973, p. 3.*

Toni Morrison's [*Sula*] seems to me an exemplary fable, its brevity belied by its surprising scope and depth. . . .

Sula's moral and spiritual entropy is set against the essential mysteries of death and sex, friendship and poverty, and the desperation and vulnerability of man that one encounters in many stories, but rarely so economically expressed. Toni Morrison's narrative contains symbolical and fabulous elements and is laid out in small set pieces, snapshots arranged in a pattern that cannot be anticipated until the author is done with her surprises. There is a great deal of humor here, and a sense of celebration, in spite of deaths by water and fire, of all there is that a man or a woman can lose—husbands, lovers, children, even misery—and all of it is beautifully wrought.

*Peter S. Prescott, "Dangerous Witness," in* Newsweek *(copyright Newsweek, Inc., 1974; reprinted by permission), January 7, 1974, p. 63.*

What gives this terse, imaginative novel [*Sula*] its genuine distinction is the quality of Toni Morrison's prose. *Sula* is admirable enough as a study of its title character, an alluring and predatory woman, and of life in the black section of a small Ohio town; but its real strength lies in Morrison's writing, which at times has the resonance of poetry and is precise, vivid and controlled throughout. . . .

Thus the novel is much more than a portrait of one woman. It is in large measure an evocation of a way of life that existed in the black communities of the small towns of the '20s and '30s, a way of life compounded of such ingredients as desperation, neighborliness and persistence. . . .

Morrison's ideas are striking and inventive, though a subplot involving an off-kilter World War I veteran who celebrates "National Suicide Day" seems to me to be strained. *Sula* is rich in mood and feeling, its humor is earthy and delightful, and its dialogue is especially sharp. Sula Peace herself is a fascinating character, a tough and ruthless woman who nonetheless is possessed by her own private aches and pains.

The most fully realized character in the novel, however, is the community of the Bottom. Toni Morrison is not a southern writer, but she has located place and community with the skill of a Flannery O'Connor or Eudora Welty. *Sula* is an intelligent and intriguing novel—and prose such as Morrison's simply does not come along very often.

*Jonathan Yardley, "The Naughty Lady," in* Book World—The Washington Post (© The Washington Post), *February 3, 1974, p. 3.*

I am madly in love with the book.

*Sula*. Just the name/title rolls poetically off the tongue gently dripping like an ice cream cone on a hot day. The novel itself is a visit to Baskin Robbins where new flavors of ice cream are served up on a smooth pink plastic spoon, care having been taken to secure samples of all the ingredients, i.e., sweets, fruits, crunchies, nuts, nougat goodies. Toni Morrison serves up a marvelous pink spoon sample of credible—sometimes familiar—people; Sula, Nel, Eva (oooooooh, do I know an Eva), Hannah, Shadrack, Ajax (uuuuuh, would I like to know an Ajax), Jude and Plum. It isn't a huge double dip of people. It is served up small and potent so that you take it seriously, roll it around in your mind/mouth, savor and think about it.

The book begins with the now familiar Negro Removal project to make room for the golf course in Medallion City (should we assume Ohio, U.S.A.). There Black folks lived in the Bottom (Black Bottom?).... Two Black girls grow up here: Nel, whose parents "had suceeded in rubbing down to a dull glow any sparkle or sputter she had"; and Sula, who was described by a townswoman as an adult with: "when Sula drank beer she never belched." . . .

Toni Morrison has served up a thought provoking story worthy of her marvelous talent. While waiting eagerly for her next novel I, for one, will view this book as she describes love—"a pan of syrup left too long on the stove and cooked out leaving only its odor and a hard, sweet sludge, impossible to scrape off." The effect of reading this novel is absolutely impossible to scrape off. But then, I don't believe you'll want to.

*Ruth Rambo McClain, in* Black World *(copyright © June, 1974 by* Black World; *reprinted by permission of* Black World *and Ruth Rambo McClain), June, 1974, pp. 51-2, 85.*

A fascination with evil has crept into black fiction, an interest in the lower layers of the psyche of black characters, in their capacity to hurt and destroy. I don't see that this is as yet a "movement," or even that writers like Bullins, Walker and Morrison have by deliberate plan entered these new areas. But when Bullins shows us a cool rapist or that murderous half-rodent, half-bird that slashes to death its would-be protectors; when Walker depicts an ignorant black sharecropper cutting away his daughter's breasts and blasting her with a shotgun; and when Morrison gives us a Sula, we know we are faced with something quite different from Williams' *The Man Who Cried I Am* or Gaines's *The Autobiography of Miss Jane Pittman*—or, for that matter, Barth's *Chimera* or Pynchon's *Gravity's Rainbow*.

It is true that Morrison operates within many of the racial commonplaces. First in *The Bluest Eye* (1970), now in *Sula,* she has staked out an area of the Midwest made familiar to us by Sherwood Anderson, the small Ohio town governed by a rigid moral prudery that dampens spontaneity and twists natural appetites. She focuses on the black sections of those towns and, to the middleclass hypocrisy attacked by Anderson, she adds the racial prejudice of the whites. But this is the weakest strain in her novels, for it is virtually impossible to do anything fresh with a vein that has been mined to exhaustion. We begin to fidget when we see her stacking the deck against such easy marks as the black bourgeoisie and reaching for the heartstrings when describing the humiliation of some proud black soldiers on a Jim Crow railroad car.

Her orginality and power emerge in characters like Sula, that we have seldom seen before and that do not fit the familiar black images.... Against the background of the respectability of black Medallion, Ohio, . . . acts and emotions appear as the trust of some powerful new force, loosening the foundations of the old sterotypes and conventional manners.

Writers like Toni Morrison, like Ed Bullins and Alice Walker, are slowly, subtly making our old buildings unsafe. There is something ominous in the chilling detachment with which they view their characters. It is not that their viewpoint is amoral—we are asked for judgment. It's that the characters we judge lie so far outside the guidelines by which we have always made our judgments. . . .

The feeling I get . . . is not so much that of the familiar literary viewpoint of moral complexity as that of a calm sardonic irony over the impossibility of ever sorting out the good from the bad. This feeling gives *Sula* a portentousness that makes it perhaps an inadvertent prophet, whose prophecy is that all our old assumptions about morality are disintegrating before a peculiarly black assault against them.

*Jerry H. Bryant, "Something Ominous Here," in* The Nation, *July 6, 1974, pp. 23-4.*

There is nothing particularly striking about the black citizens of Medallion, Ohio where *Sula* is set. . . . Despite the mundane boundaries of their lives, Toni Morrison illuminates the complexity of their attitudes towards life. Having reached a quiet and extensive understanding of their situation, they can endure life's calamities and not burn up prematurely, the martyrs of some terrible desperation.... Morrison never allows us to become indifferent to these people. She knows them and we know them too; we have seen them in our neighborhoods and in our churches. They make up our communities. Her citizens of the Bottom jump up from the pages vital and strong because she has made us care about the pain in their lives; and *Sula* is ultimately a book about pain and estrangement.

All the personalities in this story are molded by the quality and the duration of their pain. . . .

Morrison portrays Sula and Nel with an amazing delicacy and lightness of touch. Nothing glares out, instead we reach inside their beings and begin to understand what activates their needs and what motivates their hostilities. The language is always simple and potent. It is both tight and quiet, not overluscious with flowery phrases. This spare quality of the writing blends softly with the languid and familiar tone of the dialogue. A beautiful and haunting atmosphere emerges out of the wreck of these folks' lives, a quality that is absolutely convincing and absolutely precise. These people's tears and hurts are our own; we have watched it happen too often around us to deny them their tragedy. Toni Morrison takes that simple locality and populates that landscape with familiar folks. But these types—like Sula, like Shadrack, like Nel—especially take on a larger and more encompassing importance. They are not limited to their time and space, but reach out to us and take in our pain also. We happen with them through lives, fraught like our own, with all sorts of tragedies and jokes. It is this capacity which distinguishes Toni Morrison's work: she can write so that it rings true to us. She draws in *Sula* a vision of pain that lives in our eyes too.

*Fath Davis, in* The Harvard Advocate *(© 1974 by* The Harvard Advocate; *reprinted by permission), Vol. CVII, No. 4, Special Issue, 1974, pp. 61-2.*

* * *

## MURDOCH, (Jean) Iris 1919-

**Iris Murdoch, an Irish-born English novelist and lecturer in philosophy, is one of the most accomplished of contemporary novelists. Her complicated and tragicomic novels, compelling and intelligent, are concerned with problems of morality—**

**knowing, loving, and being free—in contemporary society. (See also *Contemporary Authors*, Vols. 13-14.)**

[*Under the Net*] is a highly philosophical novel, done in comic-picaresque form. Its subject is the relation of words to actions, and also what makes for good and bad human intercourse; it is hence a good book about virtue though also a good book about contemporary life. Its shape derives from certain events which form a phase in the life of Jake Donaghue, and which are also events in his mind and emotions, involving a deep change in them. Jake is a *picaro* and the action is a quest, which takes the form partly of an illusory comic chase, constantly repeated, involving lockings in and out, cages and masks and disguises and theatres, and partly of a pursuit of home and money, love and wisdom, intellectual clarity and emotional release. The book begins with Jake homeless, jobless, and with only an accommodation-shop address; it ends with these things not greatly changed—after much talk of love Jake is still alone; after much exchange of money, he has still the same low bank balance—but vastly better understood by him. . . .

To some extent Jake is the conventional hero of many fifties novels—the intelligent rebel, the sleeper on other people's couches, the honest man of art poor amid the world's riches—but he is also in a philosophical impasse, which is the theme of the book. His problem is a traditional one of the classless artist; it is there, for example, in the discussions of Ladislaw and Dorothea in [George Eliot's] *Middlemarch*: how much is owed to the aesthetic and the social, with their contesting claims? . . .

The discovery of the ending is a traditional one, one we know from George Eliot or James; it belongs with the historic business of the novel. Still in her way of making the book and reaching the ending Miss Murdoch strikes, or ought to strike, us as an inventor of a very unusual sort. For one thing it is an ending as much philosophic as moral; to encroach on the individuality of others is less a failure in sensitivity or moral competence, as in the tradition, than in knowing truth. Then there is the very playful, inventive aspect of the book; its neat, flexible style has to comprehend both the variousness and literalism of Jake's mind and the decidedly surrealistic fantasies of the novelist, that consort oddly with the philosophical and moral intensity. By *A Severed Head* the contrast between the weighty, scrupulous Jamesian style and the very unJamesian invention and subject-matter becomes a comic strategy.

*Malcolm Bradbury, "'A House Fit for Free Characters': Iris Murdoch and* Under the Net," *in* Possiblitites: Essays on the State of the Novel *(© 1973 by Malcolm Bradbury; reprinted by permission of Oxford University Press, Inc.), Oxford University Press, 1973, pp. 231-46.*

[Iris Murdoch's] plays [*The Three Arrows* and *The Servants and the Snow*] are interesting enough to read, but they have nothing of the density or complexity of her novels. Both are set in deliberately stylised worlds: the first in a vast country mansion in snowy mountains, with a cast of peasants and Gypsies and off-stage wolves; the second in Medieval Japan, with a cast of Samurai, holy men and crown princesses. The themes are familiar: destiny and choice, goodness and wildness, action and contemplation are set against one another; the question of whether or not, God being dead, one should continue to behave as though God existed is discussed, and various Freudian and Christian patterns of love are presented.

But there is a curious lack of resonance. It's not that these plays haven't any action: in one sense they have quite a lot—characters fight, embrace, are beaten, risk their lives, are killed, and all on stage, too. They are plays of ideas, but they couldn't be accused of being static. On the contrary, it is as though the author had tried too hard to provide the audience with something to watch, with not enough sense of what is practically plausible upon a stage. The first play has tableaux with unspecified numbers of servants in a servants' hall: the very best that the mind can visualise is a kind of Gothic Hollywood set with gaping extras. The second demands a mountain temple with a view 'of snowy slopes, snow-laden bamboos etc, and Fujiyama in the farther background. . . . The scene is extremely beautiful. The audience ought to gasp.' Who has ever heard of an audience gasping at a backcloth, except perhaps in the Palladium? And yet, as one knows from her other work, Iris Murdoch is a masterly creator of atmosphere, of scenic effects. Her claustrophobic mansion and imperial palace would have worked beautifully in terms of the novel.

The dialogue suffers from the same sense of effort. The author, intelligent, sophisticated, subtle, has tried to amuse the audience, and to reduce her complex attitudes to aphorisms, with the result that everything sounds rather second-hand. . . .

Somehow, everything that makes Iris Murdoch's novels so compelling is missing from these plays. The stuff has slipped out between the lines of the dialogue. Because the settings are totally fantastic, we miss the exciting, baffling sense of the myths lying behind contemporary culture, the patterns of love and servitude on which modern life is built. There are none of her acute social observations, none of her jokes, none of her ambiguities. All is unambiguous and banal. It is perhaps not surprising that when a writer tries to explain what he did in a certain work, he often makes an interesting work sound both dull and simple, because a real work is its own explanation: and these plays are like explanations rather than embodiments of meaning. . . . Too much anxiety about the audience seems to be the trouble. . . . It is ironic that Iris Murdoch, who is so often accused of gratuitous complexity, should become dull when she takes the trouble to be plain. The kind of writer who can create a difficult, powerful and complex stage-play must find his energy from some quite different source.

*Margaret Drabble, "Gothic Hollywood," in* The Listener, *January 17, 1974, p. 89.*

The most consistently provocative thing about [*The Sacred and Profane Love Machine*] is its title. Apart from being janglingly discursive in its own right, it extends a warm invitation to Miss Murdoch's decriers—to the satirical rogues who might claim that [it] is just an upper-middlebrow version of the earthier *Love Machine* of Miss Jacqueline Susann, dignified in accordance with those two percussive epithets: the motivation orchestrated by someone of a rather more philosophical turn of mind, perhaps, the heartbreak less perfunctorily considered, people going to bed with each other for somewhat better-read reasons, but essentially the same sort of thing. And indeed the present book is particularly vulnerable to such a conceit; persons, symbols and ideas do their usual coming and going, are bound upon the Murdochian ferris-wheel of fire, yet we seem to have only the title's ponderous word for it that they are doing so to much purpose. . . .

That title. It belatedly occurs to you that the epithets aren't meant to be antithetical but complementary—like *The Beautiful and Damned* rather than *The Naked and the Dead*. . . . Perhaps Miss Murdoch's concern is not an easy distinction between two varieties of love so much as a slant on their interdependence. . . .

Such an angle on the book gives a sense of unity which the experience of reading it is unlikely to reproduce. Miss Murdoch is, of course, endlessly acute and insatiably empathetic, and as notes towards a psychology of the upper-middle classes, the book has plain uses. The ingredient it lacks—an ingredient that enriched its predecessor, *The Black Prince*—is a linguistic centre-of-gravity, and without it the book sprawls. Serious literature is, among other things, a pattern of words, and an author's more general procedures will always be reflected in its verbal surface. Just as Miss Murdoch's prose covers all the options, chucking in a dozen careless phrases where one careful word would do, she similarly attempts to evoke and dramatise by sheer accumulation. The book contains as many elegant paragraphs as slovenly ones and for somebody who writes so fast Miss Murdoch writes dismayingly well. But it is bloated, and it sags.

I suspect that Miss Murdoch's huge productivity is, paradoxically, a form of self-defence or self-effacement. . . . Were she to slow down—were she to allow one of those ominous 'silences' to gather, silences such as more tight-lipped novelists periodically 'break'—she would be accepting a different kind of responsibility to her critics and to her own prodigious talents. She would, in short, begin to find out how good she is, that strange and fearful discovery.

*Martin Amis, "Queasy Rider," in* New Statesman, *March 22, 1974, p. 414.*

Miss Murdoch's only concession to modernity is the title of her latest novel [*The Sacred and Profane Love Machine*] reminiscent as it is of pop-groups and the wilder fringes of of fiction. The narrative itself is solidly in the centre, and it breathes heavily over the doings and undoings of some suburbanites who find great difficulty in making means and ends meet. Miss Murdoch's role is that of the literary priest ess, poring over the entrails, the botched job of other peoples' lives. When three or four lives are conceived in sweaty proximity, it is difficult to see them as anything but a mistake—but Miss Murdoch has too much intelligence and style to write a cautionary tale. . . .

Murdoch's protagonists are not, of course, . . . flat and . . . lifeless . . . and they are all more complex than their situations imply. They exist within a series of small frames, all of them looking for permanence or definition and all of them failing. They would be insubstantial, were it not for their bad dreams.

*Peter Ackroyd, "Iris is No Pupil," in* The Spectator *(© 1974 by* The Spectator; *reprinted by permission of* The Spectator*), March 23, 1974, pp. 363-64.*

*The Three Arrows*, set in the imperial palace of an imagined medieval Japan, has scenes of almost Wildean wit and gaiety. . . .

*The Servants and the Snow* is, I hope, the earlier of the plays; certainly it is the weaker in every way. Any play that includes a gypsy in its cast—and one named Patrice, to boot—has a lot to live down, even when not burdened by dialogue like this, from Maxim, the young rebel: "I reject your old blind justice just as much as I reject his meaningless authority. The whole situation here makes me sick to my soul. . . ." To which Peter Jack (half Catholic, half Calvinist?) replies, "You're young, Maxim, and you want things to be perfect, but human beings aren't made for perfection. We have very little goodness in our hearts and yet we have to live with each other." On the whole, I prefer Murdoch when she is improvising the Unchanging Wisdom of the East (Fortune Cookie Division) in the other play. . . .

Better than all this instant wisdom, though, is the campy chitchat of the emperor and his courtiers, who call chess "that horribly intellectual Chinese game" and take delight in a well-turned haiku or love letter. Perhaps, I thought to myself, Murdoch's true vein is comedy rather than the melodrama aspiring to be tragedy that she achieves in these plays and in her later novels—if *The Red and the Green* is in fact typical. Accordingly, I read *Under the Net* for the first time and enjoyed it, up to a point. It isn't as funny as a novel dedicated to Raymond Queneau ought to be, however. . . .

Unlike Beckett, Murdoch has failed to learn the lesson of Buster Keaton. Yeats warned us that Hamlet and Lear, "If worthy their prominent part in the play,/Do not break up their lines to weep." Likewise the comic hero does not break up his lines to laugh: What seems ludicrous to us is life and death to him. The same with the tragic hero: He doesn't weep because he is too involved in his own plight to stand back and enjoy the luxury of being sentimental over it. Either Millie and Yorimitsu and Basil aren't in earnest, or, more likely, their creator doesn't take them seriously enough. It's an understandable attitude in a philosopher—Iris Murdoch used to teach philosophy at Oxford—but if you want to be a novelist or a dramatist, ma'am, you can't afford to seem so bloody detached. Don't feel you have to be so relentlessly clever all the time, either. Be content to be boring once in a while, like George Eliot or Doris Lessing.

*Vivian Mercier, "Two From the Isles," in* Saturday Review/World *(copyright © 1974 by Saturday Review/World, Inc.; reprinted with permission), March 23, 1974, p. 42.*

Iris Murdoch is one of our most admired novelists. When people say they are going to bed with a good book they are almost certainly reading Iris Murdoch. Fine, but fiction might be more than something to occupy the time left over from other activities. As an art form it possesses the power to transform us. Maybe one is over demanding. Perhaps we have no great writers at the moment, only ingenious experimentalists on the one hand and time blotters on the other. Miss Murdoch is a denizen of the latter category, of the serious solid novel. Like a very well-made television series her books are only engrossing for their duration and not too significant after it. The final full stop does of course take some reaching, there are plenty of words and the content is quite busy, but having attained it one experiences no sharp sense of loss which signifies the end not of a good read but of a great book. . . .

It is said that everybody has at least one novel in them and it occurs to me that Iris Murdoch is a writer of this sort who just didn't stop there. Surely she writes too much. Even were all her books successful in their workmanlike way, and perhaps they are, the sheer volume of prattle is a grave aesthetic disadvantage. Clearly she works hard at it with an automaton efficiency, an eager, mechanical sensibility, as if her sole reason for writing were to fill up the top shelf with her works before biting the dust. One encounters less intelligent reasons than this for fictionalising and [*The Sacred and Profane*] *Love Machine* when it does grab you does so as if one were watching a game of chess and suddenly became interested in the fates of the pieces without participating. In fact she is a paperback thriller writer in other clothes. The psychology of her characters though elaborated *ad nauseam* is two dimensional and wooden, they are soap-operatic, uninspired in spirit. The quality of the writing itself is functional and unconceited, imparting little wit, humour or technical interest. Anyone who can write an ungainly line like 'undulating in a circular ballet of quiet orderly prancing' is not going to be famed for the beauty or precision of their prose. . . .

She is the Agatha Christie of emotional worries. She is about as good as it is possible to be within the intellectual ambience of the woman's magazine. She is the perfect novelist to read in bed since when set aside nothing too profound is going to induce unusual insomnia. Why pretend more?

*Duncan Fallowell, "Plotting the Emotional Course," in* Books and Bookmen, *June, 1974, pp. 85-6.*

Iris Murdoch continues to write sophisticated fairy tales. In their search for The Good Life, her characters use art, alcohol, scholarship, religion and, of course, sex and love relationships both homo- and heterosexual. *The Sacred and Profane Love Machine* is a magnificent novel, rich, bold, teasing, highly inventive deeply thoughtful. It is packed with moral observations, aphorisms and paradoxes. . . .

Add a vigorous narrative power which takes you briskly through an intricate plot, and an unfailing fertility in the creation of eccentric characters, and you have another example of the most individual collection of novels, sixteen now, since Dickens. . . . Where this latest book succeeds even more than any of her others since the first, *Under the Net*, is in its descriptions of place—landscapes, gardens, interiors and, in a set piece written with all the stops out, a pool with nubile baigneuses; Proust is not the only novelist to have looked at Vermeer and Monet, and Iris Murdoch is one up in being able to appreciate and make use of the voluptuous nudes of Renoir.

*John Mellors, "Ladies Only," in* London Magazine, *June/July, 1974, pp. 135-39.*

At a time when fiction seems harder and harder to write with any confidence, Miss Murdoch makes it look as easy and natural as breathing. She wears her formidable intelligence with a careless swagger, and her astonishingly fecund, playful imagination looks as fresh and effortless as ever. *The Sacred and Profane Love Machine* . . . adds a glassy new extension to the mansion of her fiction and cannily leaves more room to build on. Part of the joy of reading Iris Murdoch is the implicit assurance that there will be more to come, that the book in hand is an instalment in a continuing work which grows more and more important as each new novel is added to it.

In *The Sacred and Profane Love Machine* she has constructed an intricate honeycomb, a civilisation in miniature, full of interior walls, boundaries, conventions. . . .

With just a few characters, a garden, and three doll's-houses, each with a cutaway wall to reveal their inner goings-on to the audience, Miss Murdoch creates a teeming society, so densely populated and so morally fraught that we are readily persuaded that it is the world. Her fiction, with its compressions, its brilliant stage-lighting and fierce logic, is the wind tunnel in which she tests the morality of her characters to breaking-point. *The Sacred and Profane Love Machine* is really an experiment to see just how far it is possible for a person to keep his own private moral world intact. . . .

Titian's "Sacred and Profane Love" is a puzzle-painting; it inverts our customary notions of "sacred" and "profane", and makes an even darker confusion by using the same model to portray both kinds of love. It masquerades as an illustration of moral conventions, but in fact it collapses them. *The Sacred and Profane Love Machine* does much the same thing. It asserts the necessity of all those boundaries and categories which the characters are heroically striving to keep up; at the same time it invests them with a wilful arbitrariness. . . .

The novel itself moves in a series of stately tableaux, as formal as a sequence of allegorical scenes on a painted frieze. Indeed, the characters have a habit of regarding themselves as if they knew they were acting out an allegory. The terrible arbitrary mess of life is chronicled with a novelist's as well as a moralist's regard for the importance of convention. One or two reviewers have complained of the oddly static quality of this book, but that is very much of a piece with its theme. The operatic conversation, the elaborate scene-setting, the air of something mounted or got-up, like a masque, are like the morals and manners which are the novel's subject, fragile necessities. We are, I think, supposed to feel that they are on the brink of crumbling too. The point is not to give in to those dreams and intimations of the void beneath, but to respond to the brave artifice with which people—and novels—stave off the void. Box hedges, Miss Murdoch seems to say, are very fine and desirable things, but we must remember that we make them, not they us.

More than twenty years ago in her study of Sartre, Iris Murdoch observed that one function of the novel was to preserve our discursive, "thingy" view of the world. Her own novels are amazingly rich in thinginess. It is fairly easy to describe the metaphysics, the theory, on which her fiction is suspended; much harder to convey their thick, bubbling surface of people and events—the human minestrone soup from which she conjures these elegant propositions. She has often been accused of having a style only one remove away from that of the women's magazine—resolutely chatty and breathless, closer in tone to gossip than to literature. There are dozens of passages in *The Sacred and Profane Love Machine* which look like bad, careless writing if you take them out of context. Yet in context they assume an unexpected weight. For meaning in Iris Murdoch arises out of a subtle collusion between the inherently metaphysical and articulate arrangement of the world and the scruffy, frantic, unstylish lives of the people who live in it. The most seemingly disposable words and actions take on significance because, whether we like it or not, the world is a place where everything has meaning, and Miss Murdoch is one of its most alert exegetes. Not a consequence escapes her detective's eye; the frothy, inconsequential feel of her fiction is there to make the act of philosophical detection seem miraculous and hard-won. Just tagging along behind is a delight for the slow-minded reader.

*Jonathan Raban, in* Encounter, *July, 1974, p. 73-5.*

Murdoch is masterful at ripping the masks off her characters, at revealing the true nature of what goes on behind a facade that is ever so British, ever so complacent and proper.

She also disinters a shared sense of fear from the depth of the psyche, exposing the static, staid qualities of English middle-class life for what she believes it really is: pure, unadulterated horror of oneself and others, of the outside world and any internal one, of a life wasted and of existential failure. Terror can destroy the seeming tranquility, mediocrity and level-headedness of simple suburban existence. Violence when it surfaces is lethal, both literally, as in many of Murdoch's earlier novels, and psychologically, as it is [in *The Sacred and Profane Love Machine*]. We live and learn through violence and insecurity, Murdoch seems to be saying to us.

Iris Murdoch does not write novels about many different people, nor does she marshall a varied group of personalities. What she does is to show that people, however frequently and closely they associate with one another, are strangers until they fall in—or out—of love. In the past she often failed because she imposed an artificial design on human interactions instead of presenting a story based in experience, not experimentations. In *The Sacred and Profane Love Machine* she has been able to make her way into that realm of feeling and sensitivity that is vital to the art of the novel.

*Celia Betsky, "'The Sacred and Profane Love Machine'," in* The New Republic *(reprinted by permission of* The New Republic; *© 1974 by The New Republic, Inc.), September 14, 1974, pp. 28-9.*

It's so easy to underestimate Iris Murdoch. I say this knowing full well how much appreciated she is, how dutifully and faithfully her books are reviewed (sixteen novels to date . . ., two volumes of philosophy, two plays). Yet, in the end, she's probably best valued as a good read. . . . With each new [book] the reader settles down, happy to be in the hands of a master—mistress—grateful for the impending pleasure, tossing the thing away at the end unknowingly ungrateful for all the good that *has* been done, all the small favors, all the little technical difficulties solved without impinging. . . .

Actually, if Murdoch has a technical failing it is a small but interesting one, which is that her characters are always having to look into mirrors in order to describe themselves, not to themselves but to us. The old problem of who sees the central observer, which, as I recall, even confounded that old Anglophile Henry James. But perhaps, being Iris Murdoch, in another few novels she'll solve this one too.

*Ann Birstein, in* Book World—The Washington Post (© The Washington Post), *September 15, 1974, p. 1.*

Early in [*The Sacred and Profane Love Machine*] this glittering examination of love's disguises in the London suburbs, Novelist Iris Murdoch introduces Blaise Gavender, a successful psychotherapist whose practice is among the well-to-do. Murdoch's tone is aldous, which is to say it seems to promise an ever-so-dry, Huxleian sort of farce: "He received an early lesson from a patient who always wore gloves because she said she had the stigmata. It was a little while before it occurred to Blaise to ask her to remove the gloves. She had the stigmata, and was later successfully treated for hysteria." . . .

In some ways this is the customary Murdoch blend of incipient farce, domestic tragicomedy and intellectual soap opera. Baroque pratfalls occur as usual, but neither the release of laughter nor the expected snicker of superiority (what odd and frightful people!) follows. . . .

If Novelist Murdoch is not playing for laughs, what is she up to? As the novel's title says explicitly, the author, who looked at love sentimentally in *The Black Prince*, is now coldly exploring its mechanistic aspect. In mockery she has made her central figure a psychologist, who supposedly manipulates the mind's mechanisms and who effects his cures by forming "love relationships" with his clients.

How absurd we are, how the machine crushes us, seems to be Iris Murdoch's [message]. . . . Like a Victorian morality tale done with a light touch, the book leaves its characters either dead of love or diminished by it.

*John Skow, "Uncouples," in* Time *(reprinted by permission from* Time, The Weekly Newsmagazine; *copyright Time Inc.), September 23, 1974, pp. 96, 98.*

# N

## NAIPAUL, V(idiadhar) S(urajprasad) 1932-

**Naipaul, a novelist, short story writer, essayist, and author of travel books, was born in Trinidad and has lived in England since 1950. The winner of several important awards for his fiction, he writes with precision, confidence, and a fine wry humor. (See also *Contemporary Authors*, Vols. 1-4, rev. ed.)**

A travel book by an author of little personality is likely to be plain dull; a travel book by an author with a pronounced personality (like Mr Naipaul) is likely to tell us more about the author than about the country. Heads, the country loses; tails, the author wins.

Mr Naipaul's earlier book on the West Indies hinted pretty strongly at its author's prickly, susceptible nature, the rawness of his nerves, his thinness of skin. In *The Middle Passage* it was the noise, especially in Trinidad, which most obviously tormented him. In *An Area of Darkness* it is the public defecation. . . . There are moments in both books when the reader fears that the author (who has a gift for drawing the reader too into his orbit) is about to be badly beaten up. Mr Naipaul loses his temper with an Indian, and then loses his temper with himself for losing his temper. And, such is the author's absorptive power, somehow the reader feels partly to blame for it. His quick exasperation is tied up with his artist's openness and vulnerability, and unhappily in *An Area of Darkness* (a generalising title!) he is mostly open to spectacles of human degradation or double-think or colossal inefficiency. The sight of a beggar, a human ruin, or 'the starved child defecating at the roadside while the mangy dog waited to eat the excrement', this arouses pity. But what use is pity?—it soon yields to contempt. Contempt must be fought down—but how, except by learning to feel nothing? And out of feeling nothing, nothing can come.

Mr Naipaul agrees with Malcolm Muggeridge (and a number of other Englishmen) that almost the last true Englishmen are Indians. The epigram flatters neither race. Certainly in his sense of personal outrage when, say, someone is trying to cheat him, Mr Naipaul is very much the Englishman, especially the Englishman during his first few days in the mysterious East. . . .

The determination to remain what he was, to preserve his face, is plain and strong throughout *An Area of Darkness*, and sometimes, I suspect, it prevents him from seeing other people for what they were. 'All things uncomely and broken, all things worn out and old. . . .' Mr Naipaul is something of an aesthete, an aristocrat, he has the sensibility of a brahmin, but not the supporting beliefs—or complacency—or callousness. His puritanical honesty, his refusal to be taken in by talk of Indian spirituality, afflicts him like an ingrowing nail. He is hardly ever out of pain. The reader suffers with him. Perhaps that is all we can do in the face of such colossal suffering—suffer a little ourselves, for a very little it will be, relatively.

*D. J. Enright, "The Sensibility of V. S. Naipaul" (1964), in his* Man Is An Onion: Reviews and Essays *(© 1972 by D. J. Enright; reprinted by permission of Open Court Publishing Co. and Chatto & Windus), Chatto & Windus, 1972, pp. 204-11.*

V. S. Naipaul is by now recognized as the most talented of those West Indian novelists who have appeared on the literary scene since the publication, in 1949, of V. S. Reid's *New Day*. Yet Naipaul's true literary stature, and the magnitude of his achievement, are generally obscured by the ultra-traditional guise of his writing, with its Victorian ease and lack of stylistic innovation, and by his reputation as a purveyor of whimsy and patronizing satire. . . .

He does not seek to produce documentary propaganda, but nevertheless sees the act of literary creation as being deeply involved with the desire to produce observations of a quasi-sociological nature. C. L. R. James, the West Indian historian, has drawn attention to such a phenomenon in a different context by talking of a particular feature of West Indian life—the non-political writer devoted to the analysis and expression of West Indian society. Naipaul seems to be cast in this mold. . . .

Naipaul's finest achievement is undoubtedly *A House for Mr. Biswas* (1961). It is the story of one man's effort to overcome the wasteland, the derelict land of Trinidad's East Indian community. . . . The writer's attitude is tender but ironic; there is the inner, sardonic toughness of phrases like "futile with asthma." The impact is attenuated and diluted, yet the tragic undertone to the comic cameo is apparent.

*David Ormerod, "In a Derelict Land: The*

*Novels of V. S. Naipaul," in* Contemporary Literature *(© 1968 by the Regents of the University of Wisconsin), Vol. 9, No. 1, Winter, 1968, pp. 74-90.*

The position of the ironist in colonial society is indeed a delicate one. [George] Lamming [in *The Pleasures of Exile*] can see little that is risible in a society whose history is one of underprivilege. One appreciates his point. The early Naipaul is at times the irresponsible ironist, subtle, but lacking in a sensitive participation in the life he anatomizes. If one says that the exercise of irony precludes sympathy, one is merely defining the limitations of irony, and the limitations of any of Naipaul's work which depends solely on irony. So far one agrees with Lamming.

Satire is the sensitive measure of a society's departure from a norm inherent in itself. Since Naipaul starts with the conviction that such a norm is absent from his society, his task as satirist becomes doubly difficult. Not only must he recreate experience, but also simultaneously create the standards against which this experience is to be judged. This explains the mixture of farce and social consciousness which occurs in [*The Mystic Masseur* and *The Suffrage of Elvira*]. (pp. 122-23)

If in the early farces an absurd world is presented as real, in *The Middle Passage* a real world is presented as tragically futile and absurd. The deeper implication of the first two books is that West Indian society, emerging from ignorance and superstition, is peculiarly susceptible to depredation by the fraud and the politician, and by all opportunists who are prepared to exploit the social unease for their personal ends. That Ganesh and Harbans are treated so genially conceals Naipaul's seriousness of purpose. Ganesh, who poses as the defender of Hinduism while it is politic and profitable to do so, completely rejects Indian dress and changes his name to G. Ramsay Muir once he becomes a successful politician. This change of name and dress is always used by Naipaul to symbolize the acculturation of the East Indian to pseudo-western patterns of life, which is something he writes of with bitterness, despair and regret. One should not be misled by his genial tone to overestimate his admiration for Ganesh, the successful fraud. (pp. 123-24)

[If] the impulse behind *Miguel Street* is similar to that behind *The Mystic Masseur*, the whole tone is more serious. The farce has become a nightmare. Here one finds it difficult to accept Lamming's description of Naipaul's satire as a refuge and escape from experience. If satire is a means of running away, it is equally a means of fighting: an act of bravery, not cowardice; the confrontation of a nightmare, not the seeking of a refuge. (pp. 125-26)

Sometimes one wonders at Naipaul's hypersensitivity and asks oneself whether the neurosis is completely controlled by the irony. Is not this complete acquiescence with Froude that there are "No people there in the true sense of the world," a formula for evading the complex sympathy which the West Indian experience seems to demand? I stated above that what appears to Lamming as a conscious struggle on Naipaul's part to adopt the standards of a "superior" metropolitan culture, is explicable as a too easy acquiescence with European historians; they assumed that the "native" was an inferior animal and consequently failed to look for positives in his society. Perhaps it is easier to see Trinidad as an historical rubbish-heap and a sociological abstraction; easier to see evidence in every observed and carefully chosen detail of some deep-seated social malaise which justifies one's neurosis; easier than to see the country as a vast Miguel Street of individuals, people in a truer sense of the word than Froude seems to have been aware of, each making demands on one's imaginative sympathy, because of the unique history which each has endured. (pp. 130-31)

[Although] one accepts Naipaul's point that protest literature can become a sterile and stereotyped posturing in the name of blackness, one also realizes that protest against the past is a vital transitional stage in the reconstruction of a sense of personality. Naipaul does not realize that in treating the theme of East Indian acculturation, and the reconstruction of the Indian personality in the New World, he is at one with Negro writers who are also trying to reconstruct personality, and is writing a most vital portion of the sensitive history of the West Indies. Naipaul's Mr. Biswas rebels because his society denies him personality and forces him to live with an inferiority complex and a sense of nonentity. Negro writers, in the Caribbean or America, protest because their society annihilated identity. Both in the case of Mr. Biswas and the Negro of the New World, underprivilege is struggling to build its symbolic house against overwhelming odds.

*A House for Mr. Biswas* is more profound than anything else Naipaul has written because, for the first time, he is able to feel his own history not merely as a squalid farce, but as an adventure in sensibility. (p. 132)

*The Middle Passage* relates to the problem of West Indian creative writing, as well as to the writing of West Indian history as an academic pursuit. West Indian history can never be satisfactorily told, he says, because nothing was created in the West Indies, where there is neither achievement, nor a tradition of accepted values. Yet in *Miguel Street* and *A House for Mr. Biswas* he tells a vital part of West Indian history, for the books are a sensitive presentation of the history of underprivilege. The worth of his irony is that it enables him to examine his past without any sentimental self-indulgence. We see Biswas as a full human being who is as weak and contemptible as he is forceful and admirable. Irony enables Naipaul to get down to the bare humanity beneath his history. Because he is dealing with his own personal past, his irony does not preclude sympathy but reinforces it. He is able to answer in terms of creative sensibility a question to which he could find no satisfactory academic answer. (pp. 138-39)

*Gordon Rohlehr, "The Ironic Approach: The Novels of V. S. Naipaul," in* The Islands in Between: Essays in West Indian Literature, *edited by Louis James (copyright © 1968 by Oxford University Press; reprinted by permission of Oxford University Press, Inc.), Oxford University Press, 1968.*

I have always believed that a writer writes one book all his life: whether consciously so or not, his work is of a piece. For this reason the writer is entitled to present as the provisional entity between two covers, which is what any single book is, any combination of writing that *he* sees as that entity. V. S. Naipaul's grouping together of a short novel, two stories and two fragments of a travel diary [*In a Free State*] is not a collection of "occasional" pieces but an entity; and I approach it as contiguous with a personal vision that blazed forth in his magnificent novel "A House For Mr. Biswas" a few years ago.

The free state of the title that Naipaul's people seek is, needless to say, an inner kingdom. But they seek it in their various ways, through the poor, crude, ridiculous instruments which are all that daily life has to offer in the various societies they find themselves in. . . .

To borrow a description from another of V. S. Naipaul's novels ("The Mimic Men"), the black people he writes of are doomed to be "mimic men." They try to find meaning for themselves in the values of a foreign popular culture and are gradually imbued with embarrassment for their own identity, since others fail to understand it.

In the brilliant and shocking funny story in this volume, "One Out of Many"—shocking because what one is seeing is the disintegration of personality, Naipaul is past master of the difficult art of making you laugh and then feel shame at your laughter. . . .

I know of no other contemporary novelist who can deal so devastatingly, yet quietly, with the sensation and terror at the core of ordinary encounters.

This book is not his best work; but it is part of an achievement that I believe in the end will show him to have been a great writer. His limitations? They are perhaps unconsciously expressed in a reflection, in the epilogue to this book, on the unknown tomb artist of Egypt: "Perhaps that had been the only pure time, at the beginning, when the ancient artist knowing no other land, learned to look at his own and had seen it as complete."

*Nadine Gordimer, in* The New York Times Book Review *(© 1971 by The New York Times Company; reprinted by permission), October 17, 1971, pp. 5, 20.*

Many critics have commented on Naipaul's unique gifts, but they have said little about his unique condition. He is, in his own words, "without a past, without ancestors," "without a tradition," "a little ridiculous and unlikely." His homelessness has produced in him a capacity to create characters of tremendous diversity. This is an age of the national writer; it is very unusual to come across a writer who has no national identity, a stateless artist.

Naipaul's concerns remain constant. He writes of fantasy, slavery, power, empire, exile. The condition of rootlessness, a motif in his *Area of Darkness,* is a frequent theme in his fiction; and it is the subject of *In a Free State*. Some of the territory here is new. For the first time, he is writing of an Indian in America; of West Indians in London; British people in Africa. Framed by two personal anecdotes, which serve as prologue and epilogue, the three stories—incidents in three countries—form a sequence and make a large statement about freedom and homelessness, dependency and belonging. The book is Naipaul's most ambitious work, a story-sequence brilliant in conception, masterly in execution, and terrifying in effect—the chronicles of a half-a-dozen self-exiled people who have become lost souls. Having abandoned their own countries (countries they were scarcely aware of belonging to), they have found themselves in strange places, without friends, with few loyalties, and with the feeling that they are trespassing. Worse, their lives have been totally altered; for them there is no going back; they have fled, each to his separate limbo, and their existence is like that of souls in a classical underworld. . . .

The subject of displacement is one few writers have touched upon. Camus has written of it. But Naipaul is much superior to Camus, and his achievement—a steady advance through eleven volumes—is as disturbing as it is original. *In a Free State* is a masterpiece in the fiction of rootlessness. France claimed the Algerian Camus. No country can claim Naipaul. It is a demonstration of the odds against him, but certain evidence of the uniqueness of his vision.

*Paul Theroux, "To be Without Roots," in* Book World (© The Washington Post), *December 5, 1971, p. 22.*

["In a Free State"] is an extraordinarily penetrating book and a disturbing one. . . .

Naipaul writes about the many psychic realities of exile in our contemporary world with far more bite and dramatic havoc than Joyce brought to that stage Jew Leopold Bloom.

In this new book, one of his very best, he has sharpened and tuned, on five different examples of contemporary wandering, his already prodigious sense of fiction. No one else around today, not even Nabokov, seems able to employ prose fiction so deeply as the very voice of exile. If "our" fiction began with the raw merchants settling into their overstuffed interiors, the brilliance of fiction today would seem to depend on a sense of displacement which so many smart American novelists who have never been put to the actual test have already played with in their more theoretical novels.

What makes Naipaul hurt so much more than other novelists of contemporary exodus is his major image—the tenuousness of man's hold on the earth. The doubly unsettling effect he creates—for the prose is British-chatty, proper yet bitter—also comes from the many characters in a book like this who don't "belong" in the countries they are touring or working in, who wouldn't "belong" any longer in the countries they come from, and from the endless moving about of contemporary life have acquired a feeling of their own unreality in the "free state" of endlessly moving about. All travel is an adoptive consciousness—only Ulysses was transported in his sleep. And it is so *much* consciousness, "raised" yet unavailing, that makes one's motion and freedom clash with so many other too conscious egos forever crazily on the move. There is a peculiarly contemporary despair in seeing so much exertion of the will mocked by the lack of tradition, assurance, and moral comfort in which we travel. . . .

Naipaul has never encompassed so much, amd with such brilliant economy, with such a patent though lighthanded ominousness of manner, as in ["In a Free State"]. The volume of detail is extraordinary, and so is the sequence of action parodying the fretful trip by car as Bobby confesses his dream of returning, somewhere, out of the rain, to a warm lighted house. . . .

The sinuous conjunction of the talk between the unloving couple in the car with the sudden sharp treacheries of the road and the weather, and above all the dramatic movement, line by line of landscape and action duplicating the mingled ease, boredom, and anxiety of a long trip by car—all this gives "In a Free State" an amazing tense fullness in all it takes in and suggests of the African landscape, the old "settler mentality," the educated African politicians whom Bobby and Linda discuss and whom we never see, the sheer sweating fear of the English and blacks toward each other. . . .

I suppose one criticism of Naipaul might well be that he covers too much ground, has too many representative types, and that he has an obvious desolation about homelessness, migration, the final placelessness of those who have seen too much, which he tends to turn into a mysterious accusation. Though he is a marvelous technician, there is something finally modest, personal, openly committed about his fiction, a frankness of personal reference, that removes him from the godlike impersonality of the novelist so often praised by Joyce—and so much cherished by novelists like Nabokov who angrily deny that *they* use themselves. Naipaul belongs to a different generation, to a more openly tragic outlook for humanity itself. He does not want to play God, even in a novel. He has associated himself with "history," and does not expect better treatment.

*Alfred Kazin, "Displaced Person," in* The New York Review of Books *(reprinted with permission from* The New York Review of Books; *© 1971 by NYREV, Inc.), December 30, 1971, pp. 3-4.*

[The] sad figure of Mr. Biswas lends itself to a vulgar and comic principle of classification of things and people which gives [*A House for Mr. Biswas*] a conventional centre. In the first place Naipaul's world is one which is devoid of phenomenal and therefore corrosive sensibility. He builds his chronicle around a traditional Hindu family in Trinidad and therefore persuades his readers to identify with an assumption of individual status, of historical context. The inner and outer poverty of Naipaul's characters—while achieving at times memorable pathos—never erupts into a revolutionary or alien question of spirit, but serves ultimately to consolidate one's preconception of humanity, the comedy of pathos and the pathos of comedy. It is this "common picture of humanity" so-called on which Naipaul's work rests. The novel for him, as for many contemporary readers and writers, restricts the open and original ground of choice, the vision and stress of transplantation in the person out of one world into another, the necessity for epic beyond its present framework, or tragedy within its present framework, since the assumption remains to the end a contemporary and limited one of burial and classification, a persuasion of singular and pathetic enlightment rather than a tragic centrality or a capacity for plural forms of profound identity.

*Wilson Harris, in* Modern Black Novelists: A Collection of Critical Essays, *edited by Michael G. Cooke, Prentice-Hall, Inc., 1971, p. 38.*

Wholly original, [Naipaul] may be the only writer today in whom there are no echoes of influences. (p. 7)

[The] act of writing, the capacity for creation, separates those of Naipaul's characters with an active imagination from those who fantasize. (p. 10)

Creation, in Naipaul's terms, involves perception. The ability to assess oneself in one's setting is necessary if a person is to write well or make anything new; detail must be seen, judgements questioned. With these perceptions, the experience of something sighted, arrives a specific calmness which is resolution. In this calmness is the confident detachment which can result in creation: this still moment, which the creator occupies, makes it possible for the experience to be written about, or painted, or sculpted, given its true shape. . . .

The release that true creation offers in completing a man is a point that is often made in Naipaul's work. (p. 15)

Naipaul's heroes are extremely private souls, sensitive about revealing anything of themselves, even to people who are close, to wives and children. (p. 21)

Imagination helps a man to become whole. Fantasy, which is the expression of a perverse hunger, destroys and degrades a man. This idea occurs, with various illustration, in every one of Naipaul's books. It is related to Naipaul's ideas of grief and religion, ritual, empire, slavery and dependency. (p. 36)

The fact of death stuns various of Naipaul's characters into a mechanical bewilderment which is more fantasy than grief. It is almost as if grief is beyond them; they are not whole enough to experience true loss. Their sadness is compulsive utterance. (p. 45)

Rebellion, flight, danger, homelessness, dependency, fame: they are linked concepts in Naipaul's work, and he gives elaborate expression to them in his essays, travel books and novels. Apart from the concept of fame—a significant omission—these are the themes in his most recent novel, *In a Free State*. But the people in this book are quite different from Naipaul's other fictional characters: they do not rise; they are uncreative, vulnerable, terrified, dependent, as unlike the rebellious heroes as it is possible to be. It is a book about rebellion's absence, about resignation, a statement about surrender, with a personal, uncompromising act of assertion—Naipaul's own—in the Epilogue. (p. 118)

*In a Free State* extends Naipaul's ideas of rootlessness and rebellion and the paradox of freedom. The title itself suggests continual aimless movement. The factual Prologue and Epilogue, Naipaul's personal experiences, a traveller's tales, seem to contain a reply to the degradation he dramatizes in the stories. (pp. 123-24)

The action in the Epilogue—it helps to know what Naipaul has seen in *The Middle Passage* and *An Area of Darkness* to understand how huge a gesture it is—indicates that he hasn't surrendered himself; but symbolic action is not enough relief, and temperamentally Naipaul is so different from these characters that it is really impossible for his behavior to serve as a model for them or to draw any conclusion other than, urged by conscience, a man can still make himself a rebel by acting. (p. 125)

*In a Free State* is the first book of Naipaul's in which a fear of death and a preoccupation with failure are considered as being final. In his other fiction—*Mr Stone* is a good example—thoughts of death and failure produce a moment of vision by feeding the imagination with a means of escape. What confounds and isolates the characters in *In a Free State*, liberates and involves Mr Stone. It is his most disturbing book. (pp. 125-26)

What is Naipaul's style? Is it those short single sentences of *Miguel Street*? Can it be found in the long luxuriant paragraphs of *Mr Biswas*, or the lucid short paragraphs of *Mr Stone*, or the heavily-punctuated regrets of Ralph Singh? . . . In each instance Naipaul is making a direct response to his subject, allowing his material to determine his tone. (pp. 131-32)

Compression is Naipaul's forte. . . . [He] is a writer who places little value on coincidence or suspense. He conceals nothing; his ingenuousness, his avoidance of sarcasm, and his humour—a delight that no essay can do justice to—make him very special among writers; there is no one like him writing today. He is odd in other respects: he has no feeling for the theatre; he has never written a play or a poem or an autobiographical novel; he has neither pandered to the popular taste nor offered the cheap comfort of fictional simplicities. It is evidence of the uniqueness of his vision, but a demonstration of the odds against him, that no country can claim him. (pp. 134-35)

*Paul Theroux, in his* V. S. Naipaul: An Introduction to His Work, *(copyright © 1972 by Paul Theroux; published by Africana Publishing Company, a Division of Holmes & Meier Publishers, Inc. and reprinted by permission), Africana, 1972.*

*Miguel Street's* slum dwellers lack education, tradition, culture, and sometimes enough food—but not pride, vitality, humor, free-wheeling imagination, and tenacity. Fortunately Naipaul does not sentimentalize them; they are folk realists about whom he is realistic. . . .

*The Suffrage of Elvira* (1958), . . . [one] of his slighter novels, without any well-developed characters or especial richness of theme, . . . has engagingly idiosyncratic figures, ample comic inventiveness, and the pointed, dead-pan humor through dialogue which is one of Naipaul's most effective and characteristic satirical strategies. . . . *The Suffrage* is a farce, not a realistic novel. . . .

With its amiably unprincipled hero Ganesh in inventive quest of success and its ingenuously admiring narrator, Naipaul's first published novel, *The Mystic Masseur* (1957), is his most delightful effort in pursuit of truth. . . . Naipaul's indefatigable Ganesh from Trinidad is a successful man because he is shrewd enough to know how to turn "fate" to his advantage. Forever proclaiming that destiny has preordained his successes, he is meanwhile creating them for himself. But Ganesh is very much of our times in not taking personal responsibility for his actions. That is really why the narrator follows his career with such interest. . . .

His concern with how men dodge and face responsibility reappears in *A House for Mr Biswas* (1961), a good companion piece to the success story of Ganesh. This is Naipaul's longest novel, an almost painfully specific account of the struggles of a poor Trinidadian to make himself matter. And given every possible disadvantage, from an ill-omened birth into a superstitious, impoverished Hindu family, to a scrawny physique and an ill-advised marriage, to a dangerous naiveté about the ways of the world and apparently irremediable poverty, Mr Biswas succeeds. He achieves nothing without pain and acquires nothing without flaws, but he continues to struggle and manages to die content, at forty-six, in his own house. A symbolic house for Biswas and the reader, the house is mortgaged and badly designed and constructed, but Biswas has achieved possession of it and—as Naipaul is really saying, of himself—justified his existence. . . .

The narrator of his *Miguel Street* (1959) is describing all Naipaul's novels when he says, we "saw our street as a world, where everybody was quite different from everybody else." Naipaul's five novels are peopled by quite singular characters who dwell on a street with universal boundaries. He transmutes the vagaries and quotidian confusions of modern antiheroes into energetic, universalized fiction in the precisely phrased, deftly ironic novels—*The Mystic Masseur* (1957), *The Suffrage of Elvira* (1958), *A House for Mr Biswas* (1961), *Mr Stone and the Knights Companion* (1963), and *The Mimic Men* (1967)—which have earned him his impressive list of awards and honors. . . .

Because, except for *Mr Stone and the Knights Companion*, his novels are set wholly or partly in Trinidad, and he has written two nonfiction books about the Caribbean area, he has gained some reputation as a West Indian writer. Yet Naipaul does not see himself as one. He objects to West Indian writers as inclined to choose "too special" situations, meaningful only to compatriots: any other reader "is excluded; he is invited to witness; he cannot participate." . . .

Granted the particularity of Naipaul's Caribbean descriptions and the vitality of his dialect, seeing him only as a skillful local colorist or regional sociologist underestimates him. Naipaul's novels are about contemporary man and how he manages to survive and sometimes almost flourish. His books are not confined within their local settings nor, for all their explicitly precise detail, are they tied to literal realism: he finds metaphor more expressive. The local settings are convenient to his ideational purposes. As a society "continually growing and changing, never settling into any pattern" . . ., Trinidad invites themes of instability and flux, and as a colonial and emergent nation it provides a good setting for problems of dependency and freedom. The narrator of *Mimic Men* aptly says, "It has happened in twenty countries." . . . The dominant pressures in Naipaul's fictional world derive from man's precarious existence. He has not only to contend with psychic conflict and cultural fragmentation but to exist in a hard world within an indifferent universe. . . . At their best, Naipaul's characters are resilient, managing to transcend nonentity by their stubbornness. Naipaul may not willingly suffer people's pretensions, deceptions, and illogicalities, but he can admire their refusal to be the counters of fate or circumstance. . . .

The elusive narrator [of *The Mimic Men*], whose opinions keep changing under the pressure of his recapturing the past, is a more intellectually and emotionally sophisticated character than Naipaul has created before. His account is not a simple flashback but a process of sorting and regrouping the psychic freight of roughly five periods in his life. . . . Naipaul thus asks far more of his reader with this book than with earlier ones. Singh [the protagonist] being essentially a humorless man, he also dispenses with truly comic effects (in any case, these were diminishing with each succeeding book). Yet one recognizes a familiar Naipaul. . . .

Singh accepts essentially Naipaul's perspective, according to which we neither come from nor return to a universal scheme of wholeness and harmony and should not plan on finding restorative magical light anywhere. We cannot pretend to any sort of mythic consciousness; its time has long since passed. On the other hand, individual cells can and do clump. Even men in cities, as Singh discovers . . ., manage to form meaningful units and, more important, manage to grow into operatively unitary personalities, assimilating change as it comes. Real men, Naipaul says once again, can manage with what is given. . . . Pursuing illusions of a better world on earth is a game for mimic men. One may take an insistence on confronting reality as (provisionally) Naipaul's final stand as a novelist. It does accord with his belief in, and skillful practice of, the novel as an expression of "concern with the condition of men" and "a response to the here and now." . . .

*Harriet Blodgett, "Beyond Trinidad: Five Novels by V. S. Naipaul," in* South Atlantic Quarterly *(reprinted by permission of the Publisher; copyright 1974 by Duke University Press, Durham, North Carolina), Summer, 1974, pp. 388-403.*

* * *

## NIN, Anaïs 1903-

**Ms Nin, an American born in Paris, is a novelist, short story writer, literary critic, and diarist. The beautiful, dream-like prose of her novels has long been admired by young people, for whom she is almost a cult figure; but her reputation is most likely to rest on her remarkable diary, five volumes of which have now been published. (See also *Contemporary Authors*, Vols. 13-14.)**

Over the years defenders of Anaïs Nin—myself included—have maintained that whatever the shortcomings of her books, the diaries, their primal source, would one day establish her as a great sensibility. Now here they are, and I am not so certain. Admittedly, she has left out a great deal. Of the two analysts she was going to (1944-47), only one is mentioned. And at least two Meaningful Relationships are entirely omitted. What she has done is shrewdly excerpt those pages which deal with people well known to readers today. The result is not the whole truth but an interesting *tour d'horizon* of her works and days, loves and hates among the celebrated of lost time, and for me reading her is like a feast of madeleines awash with tea. . . .

At her best, Anaïs Nin can write very beautifully indeed. Suddenly a phrase gleams upon the page: she does notice things, one decides, looking forward to the next line but then the dread flow of adjectives begins and one realizes that she is not seeing but writing. Since she is not a fool, she is aware of her limitations, yet, like the rest of us, she rather treasures them. . . . Not able to deal with other women, she can only write of herself apostrophized. People exist for her only as pairs of eyes in which to catch her own reflection. No wonder their owners so often disappoint her. They want mirrors, too.

*Gore Vidal, "The Fourth Diary of Anaïs Nin," in* Los Angeles Times Book Review, *September 26, 1971 (and collected in* Homage to Daniel Shays: Collected Essays 1952-1972, *by Gore Vidal, Random House, 1972, pp. 403-09).*

*Cities of the Interior* is unmistakably *about* the characters who are portrayed in its pages. However, in comparison with traditional character presentation and development, Miss Nin's procedures appear perverse. Her characters have no last names. Their faces and their bodies are rarely described, even though their clothing is frequently carefully detailed. The reader often does not know where or with whom they live. Their ages are almost never indicated. These characters possess a fluid quality. One can never be certain when or where they will "turn up," and one never receives any explanation of how or why they have changed one set of life circumstances for another. In short, in Miss Nin's work as in Beckett's, everything that would be carefully explained in a conventional "realistic" novel is ignored or merely summarized. Both authors select for emphasis only those details that pierce the core of any character or situation, and they refuse to acknowledge the claims of any other types of material for expression. . . .

Miss Nin's unorthodox approach to characterization permits her to ignore everything that the reader can easily infer for himself so as to concentrate her energy and skill at making images based upon the exposure of the characters' inner lives, their fears, desires, and conflicts; these areas are exposed by more conventional novelists only by means of the stream-of-consciousness flow or by some variation upon it such as the *sous-conversation* recently developed by the French novelist Nathalie Sarraute. . . .

*Cities of Interior* is a collection of distinctly separate but related works of novella length with individual titles: *Ladders to Fire, Children of the Albatross, The Four-Chambered Heart, A Spy in the House of Love*, and *Seduction of the Minotaur*. It is described by Miss Nin as a "continuous novel." The various characters, who are often artists, appear and reappear, now one and now another occupying the central position. The order of the component parts of the "continuous novel" does not at all affect one's comprehension of the whole. The individual novellas can, each one, stand quite alone; as parts of a larger entity, they are interchangeable. This is partly because specific chronological references have been avoided and partly because the transitions linking the novellas are so graceful and so fluid that the reader never feels that anything has come to a definitive end.

The structure of *Cities of the Interior* coincides perfectly with the fluid concept of personality which is reflected in the novel's characters and events. In this dynamic idea of being, the focus is always on the process of becoming, on the Bergsonian notion of personality as constant change. Therefore, the ever-developing and self-modifying structure of the "continuous novel" is the ideal "enclosure," for in effect, it destroys the very idea of enclosure. In such a novel, neither a definite beginning nor an irrevocable ending is implied. New "cities" can always be prefixed, inserted, or added whenever and wherever the author desires. The shape of this novel is never final: it cannot be final within the author's lifetime. The result of the organic quality of *Cities of the Interior* is a fiction that is at once extremely abstract and intensely personal, for insofar as it reveals, in a depth highly unusual for psychological fiction, the various phases of sexual being, it is theoretical; but insofar as it creates memorable personages, it is descriptive and evocative. Here a balance is maintained between the general and the specific, each enhancing the other, as, indeed, Miss Nin herself claims they ought to do. . . .

*Sharon Spencer, in her* Space, Time and Structure in the Modern Novel *(reprinted by permission of New York University Press; copyright © 1971 by New York University), New York University Press, 1971, pp. 16-19.*

*Diary IV* is a subjective, nonacademic, intuitive attack upon objective, established, scientific critics for their prosaic, political, traditional criticism of poetic, psychological, innovative writing. The work belongs to literary criticism and is a valuable contribution in the iconoclastic, prophetic, and creative way of much of Lawrence's writing. . . .

Much has been written of late about the need for a science of criticism; *Diary IV* suggests that what is needed even more is a humanistic philosophy of criticism. And it is at bottom in its suggestiveness that the critical value of the work resides. Nin's insights into specific works are frequently inaccurate: Hemingway and Wolfe are grouped with Dreiser; her critical terminology is limited and occasionally confusing—sometimes "reality" is the opposite of "realism"; sometimes it is synonymous. Her conclusions are often over-simplistic. Nor should one "excuse" these failings on the grounds that she never professes to be a professional. But whatever the limitations of her comments of specific texts, her strength is her challenge to the premises of contemporary critical work. One must consider whether the attack she makes on the critical establishment is sufficiently incisive and challenging to be critically stimulating. I believe it is.

*Evelyn J. Hinz, in* Contemporary Literature *(© 1972 by The Regents of the University of Wisconsin), Vol. 13, No. 2, Spring, 1972, pp. 256-57.*

For five years we have watched unfolding the supreme work of a modern master. Now the fourth installment of Anaïs Nin's *Diary* has been given to us, another stone in the mosaic, another piece in the puzzle. Who is Anaïs Nin? That is the puzzle she offers us. The only certainty we have is that there is no final answer, no solution to the riddle, no end to the mosaic.

The grand theme of the *Diary*, as of all Miss Nin's work, is the mystery of personality. It is not a mystery to be solved, but lived. Personality, for Miss Nin, is not a fixed quantum of habits and conditioned reflexes, nor a standard issue of proper values and opinions, a sort of definitive diploma of the soul; and least of all some basic essence, immutable and eternal. It is rather a fluidity to one's own changingness, a sensitive, delicate sculpting of experience, a quality at once attentive and supple: in short, the controlled flow of one's being in the world.

In this, Miss Nin has proved a faithful disciple of her first great master, D. H. Lawrence. But the quality of her approach is utterly different. Lawrence's intuition has often been called feminine; but in the combativeness of his relationships, the proud isolation of his characters, he is almost grimly masculine. Miss Nin herself pinpoints the distinction: "Lawrence wrote against merging. But it is this merging I love and seek." Not merging as Lawrence described it, with his horror of intimacy, but an exchange of equality, an act of freedom. Not clinging, not dependency, but a feminine ideal of true friendship, true loving.

The search for such possibilities of exchange is the particular theme of Volume IV of the *Diary*. In this book it is a frustrated quest. . . .

[A] bare summary can give little indication of the richness and beauty of Volume IV of the *Diary*. It will be read as an invaluable document on the New York avant garde, as the source material of Miss Nin's own novels, as an apologia for her own poetics. There are passages of deep sweet clarity on the nature of writing, on the relation of experience to art. But above all it is the odyssey of a great woman's life, a life which presents itself to us now as one of the most serious and important of our time.

*Robert Zaller, "The Mystery of Personality," in* Prairie Schooner *(© 1972 by University of Nebraska Press; reprinted by permission from* Prairie Schooner*), Summer, 1972, pp. 181-83.*

Anaïs Nin. A lady whose diaries are considered her major and brilliant literary work. Not her novels, though we could all make a case for the excellence of those books. But they are not what excites us. And I see her as symbolic of Genet and Artaud when they create the play within the play which makes improvised theater possible. I see her in Mailer when he writes the novel within the commentary or Ronald Sukenick when he writes the novel as a novelist struggling to write the novel. I see her in Olson in his essay on projective verse, where the attempt to explain a new notation and syntax becomes organically that explanation; practically leaves off in mid-sentence to become the voice, the poetry of the voice. I see her in Henry Miller writing a real sociological history of the 20th century in the guise of pornography or his comic sexual fantasies. I see Anaïs Nin a symbol for all of this, her spirit prevailing all this time and helping all the serious experimenters to see their own possibilities. Here is a novelist whose unabashed most serious work is her diary. It is the one thing she has written on almost every day of her life. The one thing which is coherent and brilliantly thematic. One almost feels in retrospect that she wrote her fine little novels and stories to justify continuing to obsessively write her brilliant and exhaustive diaries. Almost, that she lived her life so that her diaries would have the range of content and idea and feeling that they do. . . .[Here] we have a fine writer whose diaries *are* her great work of fiction. Whose life becomes an exciting fiction in a way that perhaps none of her invented novels will be. And I don't think it's because the novels and stories are weak but because the diaries are so powerful. And because she allows us to think of the artist as the form-maker rather than the man who trims himself to fit the form. . . .

The delight and surprise of Anaïs Nin's diaries is that they are not indifferent pieces of writing. They [are] full of more innuendo, subtlety, and excitement of character and landscape than we find in most novels. Perhaps we have learned the lesson of the passion of authenticity—that when something actually happens to a writer, he can then use his imagination to reconstruct possibilities for the reader which, unaided by experience, the imagination might not be capable of. . . .

In a powerful novel or story or play or poem, the reader usually gets more of a sense of participation—the formality allowing him to shed his own identity and be a character—than he does reading biographies or letters or histories or diaries. But, for the last few years it has seemed possible only to be involved in literature if we really understood the writer behind it. Sometimes this has created the problem of personality cults. But sometimes it has opened up literature to a wider audience. I think now of Sylvia Plath, a fine poet and indifferent novelist, whose novel became a best-seller because it informed us both about the poet who killed herself, and the magnificent poems which came out of his quirky life. It is ironic to me that the poems, which themselves are/should be the reason we care about Sylvia Plath seem to be poor runners-up for the reader's attention. It's *The Bell Jar* first and then maybe the poems.

I thought of Anaïs Nin's diaries and how unimportant it is to the reader that she was in important places at important times, that the people she was intimately involved with were famous or exciting in their own right. I thought of how she lived each moment and recorded it as a personal experience. Each story has its own integrity as a story. Each character is Anaïs Nin's character. Each comment is an extension of the life led and intelligently thought out. And you know that it is exciting because it is Anaïs Nin telling you, not because of anything inherent in the places or people or events themselves. And it is not Anaïs Nin's personality we care about, though that personality is an index to the haunting complex perceptions of her work. It is the way that personality becomes itself as the writer of the diaries. It is the writing that is important, not the living. But it is living in such a way that the writing becomes an organic extension of the life that makes the writing so powerful.

Do you realize that Anaïs Nin has made all that possible for some of the best writers? . . .

In her diaries, she is the most fascinating woman on earth, taking every perception and event and turning them into poems or stories or part of a history so that the reader becomes as obsessed with it as if he were living her life himself. It is the complete fiction of the personal—not personal fiction. Anaïs Nin has given us new possibilities for making life the real work of art. The new poetry, the new fiction, the new journalism, the new theater: they all owe her an enormous debt. Her work *is* as interesting as she is. And she is the closest thing we have to Venus living among us.

*Diane Wakoski, "The Craft of Plumbers, Carpenters & Mechanics: A Tribute to Anaïs Nin," in* American Poetry Review, *January-February, 1973, pp. 46-7.*

With the publication of her "Diary," of which four volumes have appeared since 1966, Anaïs Nin emerged from partial obscurity and took her place among the successful writers of the day who have a fairly wide and faithful public. The publication of the "Anaïs Nin Reader" signals the fact that her work is now extensive enough to warrant an anthology, helpful both to new readers who wish to learn of her work and sample it quickly, and to those older readers who wish to review her work as a whole. . . .

We have come to expect from a major writer a vision of the world that is uniquely his own. On rereading the passages chosen for this anthology from the novels, stories, portraits, essays and the diary, I felt once again that Anaïs Nin has transmitted to us a significant and singularly personal vision. It is a truism to state that novels are a recuperation of the past. Whereas the writing of a novel is an attempt to fill a void in the life of the novelist, the book itself is not about that void. It finds its axis somewhere beyond the void. Miss Nin gives us the impression of writing in order to find herself and in order to recognize and re-create the world that is hers.

The world that holds her is not the physical world that can be described in words and that changes its form with the corrosion of time. Her inner world of the psyche valiantly resists the attacks of time. The part of her writing that might be called narrative is circular and fragile. She testifies on almost every page to something more important for her than storytelling. It is the delineation of a character—especially a female character—caught in a fascinating labyrinthine reality.

The selections of the "reader" confirm the leading characteristic of Miss Nin's art that has often been rehearsed in print by such eminent writers as Edmund Wilson, Lawrence Durrell and William Carlos Williams, namely, the feminine quality of her writing. The long passage from "Seduction of the Minotaur" (1961) is the kind of text revealing the deep subjectivism of woman, the lucidity about herself she manifests in moments of crisis or distress, and her concern with personal relationships. Yet Miss Nin is far from being a psychoanalyst in her writing. The nature of her characters is brought out by their experiences no matter how inconsequential these experiences appear to be. . . .

The appearance of this anthology ["Anaïs Nin Reader"] coincides, appropriately, with a new phase in the courageous career of Miss Nin when critical studies on her themes and style are being undertaken. Her books, iridescent as they are, do not depend on classical construction. They form a counterpoint of confessions and dreams, in which human personality is described more in terms of symbols than of action.

Her first novel, "House of Incest" (1936),. . . resembles a film-confession of adolescence. All her themes are in it, and many of the major literary influences, which are less visible in later works. Like Rimbaud, she has known seasons in hell. Like Proust, the lover in her novels creates the object of his love. In one of her more recent novels, "Collages" (1964), we find the same fusion of reality and fantasy, of dream and action. Even in the many brilliant portraits of famous people that appear in the "Diary" and in such a work as "Collages," she once more attempts to unite the visible and invisible worlds. In "Collages," the Greek painter Varda's relationship with women is analyzed as a way of speaking of the paintings. Varda's daughter as a child and as a young girl is created out of the writer's imagination. The wonderment of the child figure and the serenity of the adolescent girl are means of making us feel the temperament and the art of the painter. . . .

[A] theme that is central to Anaïs Nin [is] the discovery and preservation of the individual's freedom. It is freedom of the spirit, the ability to turn inwardly and to divest oneself of all counterfeit ideas and sentiments. . . .

Anaïs Nin developed her own language; speaking in terms of a fable, she often ends by exhibiting a truth concealed by the fable. She knows there is a secret reality in each person waiting to be made visible; and, because her unconventional world is not easy to comprehend, she demands the reader's full cooperation. I imagine she would define hell as the absence of authenticity, as concealment. She is the privileged observer, moving from the unformulated intuition to the formulated sentence. The act of writing encourages the birth of awareness in her. Writing is a deliverance from falseness, language the revealer of a particular reality she has sought since age 11 when her diary-writing began.

*Wallace Fowlie, in* The New York Times Book Review *(© 1973 by The New York Times Company; reprinted by permission), September 9, 1973, pp. 26, 28.*

The *Anaïs Nin Reader* is just what is needed now to set the record straight. It demonstrates through its selections that the contributions of Anaïs Nin to the art of fiction are as significant to the literary history of our time as the much heralded diaries. . . .

It is Anaïs Nin herself who makes the most perceptive statement regarding the relation between the two kinds of writing. In her critical book, *The Novel of the Future*, a selection from which appears in the *Reader*, Nin writes:

> The diary, then, was where I checked my realities and illusions, made my experiments, noted progress or its opposite. It was the laboratory! I could venture into the novel with a sense of psychological authenticity . . .

The diarist's fiction, however, gives more than psychological authenticity. Rereading the work as it is presented in the *Reader*—and Phillip K. Jason deserves high praise for his judicious selections—is like taking a journey through a country one has formerly lived in and loved. One realizes one's memory of the first visit was not exact: the reality is more beautiful, richer than one thought. The first selection, for example, is from that early and frequently misunderstood book, *House of Incest*. Suddenly because Anaïs Nin's work *has been*, we understand. We know why we had misunderstood. As Nin comments in critical work already mentioned, "The first misunderstanding about my work . . . was that I was writing dreamlike and unreal stories. My emphasis was on the relation between dream and reality, their interdependence."

Now when we read a passage from *House of Incest*, how clear it all is. We are used to the interdependence between dream and reality; used to the surrealism, to the irony—and to the myth. Here is the opening paragraph of the novel. We read it today without the shock of the earlier reader. It has taken us decades to grasp this new contemporary sensibility:

> The morning I got up to begin this book I coughed. Something was coming out of my throat: it was strangling me. I broke the thread which held it and yanked it out. I went back to bed and said: I have just spat out my heart.

It is this kind of writing, this stunning new awareness of an existential terror that appears time and again in the fiction of Anaïs Nin. . . .

When one reads the excerpts contained in the *Reader* from the novels *Winter of Artifice, Children of the Albatross, Seduction of the Minotaur*, or from the important *D. H. Lawrence: An Unprofessional Study*, from the reviews of Otto Rank or of Dostoevsky, the early preface to Henry Miller's *Tropic of Cancer*, one is impressed with the clarity and essential truth of the writing of Anaïs Nin. It is no small matter that the work that has influenced major writers from the '40s on—in the so-called Underground and along more usual routes—should have emerged with such force from the writer's deep belief in Jung's dictum: "from the dream outward." Anaïs Nin knew the dangers of the closed-in dream. She had written: "Bring me one who knows that the dream without exit, without explosion, without awakening, is the passageway to the world of the dead." But she also knew that the writer who realized the interdependence of the dream and reality would bring "a strong antidote to the incoherence and disintegration of modern man." This is one of the major truths of the poets of our time—American, Latin, European—and it is a major contribution of the novelist-diarist Anaïs Nin, who long ago as a master of the prose poem wrote her "continuous novel" as a City of the Interior. *The Anaïs Nin Reader* contains enough of that novel for the reader to become familiar with one of the most significant literary modes of our time.

*Harriet Zinnes, "Reading Anaïs Nin," in* Carleton Miscellany, *Fall/Winter, 1973-74, pp. 124-26.*

Volume Five, through sensitive editing and a natural development of events in Miss Nin's experience during nine years, is perhaps the most unified and shapely volume of the published diary so far. And it is in some way the most personal fragment, the most mature, the least self-advertising. There is less rambunctious interference with the evangelist's need to save, in the lives of the young, the disturbed and the self-destructive. There assembles before us an increasingly self-defined woman.

*William Goyen, "Portrait of the Artist as a Diarist," in* The New York Times Book Review *(© 1974 by The New York Times Company; reprinted by permission), April 14, 1974, p. 4.*

In forty years Anaïs Nin has produced five novels, several short stories, and a prose poem, all arguing the case for the reality, indeed the primacy, of the inner, emotional life. But the writings that most urgently convey her own exultations and illusions are those secreted in the detailed, near-legendary diary she has kept since the age of nine. The [fifth] volume of these intensely feminine, deeply serious revelations . . . is about the relatively uneventful years 1947-1955. . . .

Throughout, her prose quivers with nervous aliveness as she energetically argues for art and humanity, and displays her unfailing, sometimes unnerving, faith in the Freudian system, emotion, and instinct. Possessed of an acute sensory awareness and a startling intuition, she evidences her vivid writing ability in the quick sketch, the overtone, the nuance. Yet her egoism dominates all, driving her energies inward, until they erupt, transformed into self-idealizations and self-justifications.

Miss Nin withholds nothing, for she is determined to lay bare her own consciousness, tracing the patterns of its deliberate, involuted search for itself. Inevitably, the contours of that private world take on the texture of her own neurosis. Visions of dreams and demons flash through these pages, illuminating her long-suffered strangulation by anxieties, defeats, and sorrows.

In her diary Anaïs Nin has created a retreat—a place, as she says, "to re-create myself when destroyed by living." In the process she has tried to elevate self-contemplation to a high art. But surely only the self-absorbed will be fascinated by this solipsistic quest for healing and wholeness, for they will see themselves in the mirror Miss Nin has held to her soul. And the disenchanted will recognize it as the tiresome work of a querulous bore who cultivates neurosis in hopes of achieving self-realization.

*Susan Heath, in* Saturday Review/World *(copyright © 1974 by Saturday Review/World, Inc.; reprinted with permission), May 4, 1974, p. 52.*

Nin is the champion of the feminine inner life—her material, the unconscious mind, the dreamworld and her own evolving identify. The diaries have been presented as bridesmaids' gifts, sell well in college book shops and suburban shopping centers. But for me, Nin's popularity signifies the perpetuation of a female preoccupation with self at the expense of authentic action in the outside world. Discussions of the diaries invariably divide along class lines, with women less privileged or more openly political than Nin finding her demons either inconsequential or boring. . . .

Nin was in the process of mythmaking. In Diary II she spells out fully her notion of the woman artist as the destroyer of "aloneness," whose art is "born in the womb-cells of the mind." She works close to "the life flow," making articulate the subjective and the unconscious. The woman artist is seen as the crucial link between earth elements—both good and demonic—and what Nin calls man's fatal detachment. Diary V, pervaded by nostalgia and a sense of isolation, adds nothing new. The volume reads as through a haze, as if the writer were looking out from inside a glass bell jar. . . . Diary V is not memorable; I stand with those within the volume who recognize Nin's quality of being not quite there."

*Nancy Hoffman, "Serialized Life," in* The New Republic *(reprinted by permission of* The New Republic; *© 1974 by The New Republic, Inc.), June 15, 1974, pp. 31-2.*

* * *

## NISSENSON, Hugh 1933-

**Nissenson, an American short story writer, is concerned in his fiction with the religious aspects of contemporary Jewish experience in America, Europe, and Israel. (See also *Contemporary Authors*, Vols. 17-18.)**

Nissenson is, as far as I can recall, the only genuinely religious writer in the whole American Jewish group. His fiction represents an attempt to follow the twisting, sometimes treacherous ways between God and man; his stories reach out for Jewish experience in Eastern Europe, in Israel, and in America, in an effort to discover what Jews do with their faith in a God who so often seems conspicuous by His absence. Where other Jewish writers haul in forefathers by their pious beards to provide scenic effect, or symbolic suggestiveness, the introduction of such figures in Nissenson's work is an act of serious self-examination: can the God of the kaftaned grandfather still be the God of the buttoned-down grandson, especially with the terrible shadow of the Holocaust intervening between then and now? . . .

*A Pile of Stones* offers welcome relief but hardly an indication of a change in the current trend of American Jewish fiction. It allows one to hope for more writers who will try in varying ways to observe the Jew as a real human being, but what seems immediately in prospect is a continuing parade of Jews as holy sufferers, adepts of alienation, saintly buffoons, flamboyant apostles of love—in all the twisted, grinning masks of a literary convention that keeps literature from making imaginative contact with reality.

*Robert Alter "Sentimentalizing The Jews" (originally published in a slightly different version in* Commentary, *September, 1965), in his* After the Tradition *(copyright © 1969 by Robert Alter; published by E. P. Dutton & Co., Inc., and used with their permission), Dutton, 1969, pp. 44-5.*

These lucidly conceived small-scale stores ["In the Reign of Peace"] are enlisted in a large enterprise. Not in the sense that they aspire to be novels-in-little, as some short fiction does, mistaking inscrutability for breadth or psychology for an idea, but rather in that they have a subject of uncommon scope. The subject is simultaneously elusive and persuasive: what Christianity means by grace, Zen by *satori* and Judaism by *kavanna*—understanding in the grip of benediction.

Hugh Nissenson, in brief, possesses what can be called the theological imagination. In this he is by no means unusual among American writers generally—the late Flannery O'Connor is perhaps pre-eminent among the fictive theologians, followed by John Updike and, sometimes, George P. Elliott. But the Jews, a people supposedly charged with a predisposition for the spiritual, have up till now given to American letters no single visionary fiction writer, whether major or minor. . . .

Nissenson is an another line. He means to sink into Godhood itself, though tentatively, circumscribed by the notion that the economy of simplicity is the whole of craft. Since he is for the moment alone in his reach, his limitations are unimportant. I think it is a limitation, though, that this second book of stories is no more than a continuation of "A Pile of Stones," his first. Both are short volumes, and, though separated by seven years, they might have made one book without anyone's being aware of any difference in style or movement. But this can be a self-imposed restraint, after all—a corollary of the perfectionist temperament. By and large these are meticulous stories, perfected, polished, as a result often radiant. The strength of Nissenson's prose is not in what he puts in—the clean dialogue avoids idea-mongering, and there is no luxuriant visual or verbal surface to this fiction—but in how he omits.

Still, what matters beyond such questions of density and finish is the power of Nissenson's consuming pre-occupation. He is the first American Jewish writer to step beyond social observation, beyond communal experience, into the listening-places of the voice of the Lord of History. . . .

Not all the stories are this masterly, but each one signifies, sustains, interprets and fictionally enriches a text. Each is a *midrash,* a revelatory commentary. . . .

Only two stories take place in America. . . .This is a deeply curious circumstance; it is as if, in Nissenson's imagination, contemporary America cannot accommodate the profoundly Jewish theme. His stories might almost be recent translations from the Hebrew; some of them suggest a kind of *Sabra* mimicry. One wonders at the implication. There is a Talmudic dictum which observes that when Jerusalem was destroyed and the Jewish people went into exile, so did God. America may or may not count as "exile"; nevertheless for Nissenson, at least in these stories, and for whatever reason, the voice of God is not heard in America.

*Cynthia Ozick, in* The New York Times Book Review *(© 1972 by The New York Times Company; reprinted by permission), March 19, 1972, pp. 4, 22.*

For Nissenson, as for Hemingway, the modern world is defined by war, bloodshed, and dying. The title *In the Reign of Peace* is finally no less ironic than the title of Hemingway's *In Our Time* because each story deals significantly with violence and death. . . . In contrast to Flannery O'Connor, Nissenson does not use violence and death to demonstrate the presence of the miraculous amidst the mundane. His stance, instead, is suggested by the narrator's question at the end of "The Throne of Good": "Is it conceivable that any good can come of it?" Even the intensely religious Uncle Mendel of "Going Up," who believes that "He who keepeth Israel shall neither slumber nor sleep," ends in despair after surveying the carnage of war: "He never sleeps. One forgets. It wouldn't be so bad if I believed He was asleep."

Nissenson's stories place him firmly in the tradition of twentieth-century American realism begun by Sherwood Anderson. Unlike such contemporaries as Stanley Elkin, Thomas Pynchon, and Joyce Carol Oates, Nissenson shuns weird, absurd, and implausible events and characters; he does not write a modern version of the romance in which the ordinary is exploded by the fabulous or in which fact and fiction are inextricably blurred. Instead, he often recalls Hemingway, especially the Hemingway of *In Our Time, Men Without Women,* and *Winner Take Nothing*: thematically, in the stark and unsentimentalized depiction of man's alienation from the traditional sources of comfort and solace; technically, in the weight borne by proper nouns and concrete, factual details, in the stripped syntax dominated by the simple sentence, in the prominence of dialogue, and in the pervasive irony. At his most effective, I think, Nissenson is as good as Hemingway, particularly in the poignant, delicately balanced "In the Reign of Peace" and in the harsh, powerful "Forcing the End." His use of the first-person point of view in "Charity" and "The Crazy Old Man" is as masterful and subtle as in Hemingway's best first-person narratives, "In Another Country" and "Canary for One." Few American writers have been capable of crafting short fiction as clear, forceful, and aesthetically satisfying as the finest stories of *In the Reign of Peace.*

*Donald A. Daiker, in* Studies in Short Fiction, *Summer, 1973, pp. 291-92.*

# O

## O'BRIEN, Flann (pseudonym of Brian O Nuallain) 1911-1966

**O'Brien, an Irishman and a comic genius, was a novelist and columnist. (See also *Contemporary Authors*, Vols. 21-22; obituary, Vols. 25-28.)**

*At Swim-Two-Birds* by the late Flann O'Brien, as the work of a fellow-countryman of Joyce and Beckett, is a piece of characteristically Irish verbal exuberance and can hardly be considered as a representative English novel. Yet its reputation has developed interestingly since it was first published in 1939; it made no impact at all then, but after the book was reprinted in 1960 it attracted a growing circle of admirers, although John Wain, in a masterly analysis of *At Swim-Two-Birds*, has described it as 'the only real masterpiece in English that is far too little read and discussed.' . . . *At Swim-Two-Birds* both contains a novel within a novel, and embodies the idea of a Promethean or Luciferian revolt against the novelist who, as Sartre said of Mauriac, wants to play God. . . . In so far as it is a very funny book, *At Swim-Two-Birds* is more like *Tristram Shandy* than are other twentieth-century novels that juggle with levels of reality. Yet . . . it is also a continuous critical essay on the nature and limits of fiction. In Trellis's story the characters plot against him while he is asleep, at the same time quarrelling among themselves. One of them is the legendary giant Finn McCool, who tells a beautiful but interminable story drawn from Irish mythology, which counterpoints the naturalistic lowlife chat of the others. The narrative is also complicated by two cowboys who had been characters of—or, as they put it, worked for—a writer of cheap Western fiction. . . .

Flann O'Brien's imaginative and verbal exuberance dominates the whole work, which is a magnificent piece of ludic bravura. John Wain, who sees the novel in slightly more serious terms than I do myself, has effectively shown the way in which it is about the culture and destiny of Ireland. . . . The influence of Joyce is, of course, paramount, although absorbed by an original intelligence. In the naturalistic parts of the novel the situation of the seedy young narrator, spending long hours lying on his bed and occasionally drifting into a class at the National University, recalls Stephen Dedalus, while the ribald conversations of Shanahan, Lamont and Furriskey, although rooted in the speech of Dublin, also remind us of stories like 'Grace' and 'Ivy Day in the Committee Room'. And the prevalent encyclopaedism of O'Brien's novel, the collage-like introduction of extraneous fragments of information (a sure way of short-circuiting the distance between fiction and the external world), the tendency to present information in question-and-answer form, all derive from *Ulysses*, particularly the 'Ithaca' section. *At Swim-Two-Birds* is one of the most brilliant works of modern English fiction, which was fortunately given a second chance to establish a reputation. In the 1960s critical opinion, however averse to heavily experimental or innovatory works, has been more inclined to look sympathetically at novels which depart from the established norms of fictional construction.

*Bernard Bergonzi, in his* The Situation of the Novel *(reprinted by permission of the University of Pittsburgh Press; © 1970 by Bernard Bergonzi), University of Pittsburgh Press, 1970, pp. 199-200.*

To attempt a criticism of *At Swim-Two-Birds* is a task I have alternately longed and dreaded to approach. I love it and have always been willing to testify to my love. Yet to discuss it? To do anything more ambitious than merely assert its uniqueness? In an essay published in 1962 I made a passing reference to *At Swim-Two-Birds* as 'a Gargantuan comic novel which makes a simultaneous exploration, on four or five levels, of Irish civilization'. The vagueness of 'four or five' suggests that I wasn't counting the levels very carefully or distinguishing them with much clarity, but what interests me now, looking back, is my untroubled assumption that the book explored 'Irish civilization'. I think so now and I thought so then, but why was I so certain? Partly, I think, for the very reason that it *was* so amusing. Funny writing never really comes over as funny unless it is saying something serious; wild humour in particular, unless it is anchored to the rocks, just floats up into the empyrean and vanishes in a cloud of boredom. As George Orwell noted in connection with Dickens, 'You can only create if you *care*. Types like Squeers and Micawber could not have been produced by a hack writer looking for something to be funny about.' O'Nolan was a desperately funny writer, therefore (I felt) his work must be about something. If it had merely been a romp, it would have been perfunctory and the perfunctoriness would have shown through.

Basically, *At Swim-Two-Birds* is about a man writing a story about a man writing a story. The narrator (he is nowhere named) is a young student, living with an uncle. . . . The uncle is portrayed in comic-satirical vein, though without any real malice, as a lower-middle-class Dubliner, 'holder of Guinness clerkship the third class'. Through the sardonic eye of the narrator, we catch occasional glimpses of the uncle's life. . . . The picture is thumb-nail size (but it is a vivid miniature of the mind and life of that generation of the Dublin petty *bourgeoisie* who would be, say, sixty in 1940: the men who remembered the fall of Parnell, who had been of fighting age at the time of the uprising of 1916. Narrow as they are, seen as they are through a comic lens, these men are given a stiff, provincial dignity that redeems them. . . .

[The] literary method of *At Swim-Two-Birds* combines the nonchalant non-credibility of the story ('a self-evident sham'), the autonomy and indeed rebelliousness of the imaginary personnel, and the frequent resort to borrowing of characters from previous writing or from legend. Except that true to the book's sardonic farcical atmosphere, the 'previous writing' turns out to be itself an invention, and the legends highly fantasticated. . . .

There are [also] . . . a good many things that go over the head of a reader like myself who knows virtually nothing of ancient Irish literature. On the other hand, anyone who has ever looked into the literature of the Middle Ages at all, in any language, can see that another layer of parody is being added to the structure, and that in the main it is affectionate parody. . . .

Without [considering] . . . the envelope-story of the narrator and his uncle, we are . . . operating on at least three levels. The Pooka and the Good Fairy are pure folklore, rendered in terms of outright farce. Finn and his tale of Sweeney come from the ancient heroic world of Ireland. Then we have Furriskey, Shanahan and Lamont, and Mrs Furriskey, who are modern Dubliners of a lower social class than are the narrator's uncle and his friends. . . .

[The] technique of superimposition and palimpsest . . . links this novel firmly with central twentieth-century works from *The Waste Land* and the *Cantos* to *Finnegans Wake*. . . .

O'Nolan was too much of an artist to make [his] points in a crude fashion. The book's impact is total. Its message is conveyed integrally, by everything that is said and done. The ironic flatness of the narrator's style, the uneventfulness of his life, are in utter contrast to the blended parody and lyricism of Finn's recitals, and also to the absurdity of the conversations between Furriskey, Shanahan, and Lamont. The three worlds are sealed off from each other, yet they go on existing side by side. And Ireland? A small, drab, orderly, modern country, haunted by an heroic past, dwarfed by an over-arching imaginative vision, its artist drinking pints of plain as the tourists walk up and down O'Connell Street and the fresh-faced country boys line up to emigrate to New York. Is there, anywhere, a better total description of Ireland than is conveyed in this book? . . .

*At Swim-Two-Birds* . . . seems to me, in these days when modern literature is so intensively studied, just about the only real masterpiece in English that is far too little read and discussed (the two are not always the same thing). . . .

But, after all, it seems to me an impossible thing to describe. So much of it is purely atmosphere, and the atmosphere could only be conveyed by a commentary of the same length as the book. One of the things my description has entirely failed to convey is how the book's allusiveness provides it with dozens of little tap-roots to the Irish literary and social memory. Such things as the literary evening at Byrne's; the structural function of this scene is merely that Byrne, the arbiter of taste, lays down the law that everyone ought to sleep much more, thus providing a link with the two reposeful characters, the narrator and Trellis. But the mere fact that he is called Byrne, given the same name as James Joyce's closest friend in his student days at the National University, gives one's memory a tiny jog, reminding one how near at hand is this crowd of powerful ghosts. And when the narrator, wishing to annoy his uncle by staying in his room for an extra few minutes when he knows the uncle is waiting to see him, opens a book to read a page or two, the book he chooses, and from which an extract is promptly woven into the tapestry of the scene, is Falconer's *Shipwreck,* and again something stirs in us and we remember that passage from Yeats's unforgettable description of his grandfather William Pollexfen: 'He must have been ignorant, though I could not judge him in my childhood, for he had run away to sea when a boy, "gone to sea through the hawse-hole", as he put it, and I can but remember him with two books—his Bible and Falconer's *Shipwreck,* a little green-covered book that lay always on his table.' . . .

[*The Third Policeman*] is, indeed, the perfect second book, showing continuity with the first while at the same time varying the idiom and breaking into new territory.

*The Third Policeman* resembles *At Swim-Two-Birds* in having a narrator who describes the action in a deadpan, uncoloured style; and in exploiting the comic possibilities of uneducated Irish speech; and in juxtaposing the banalities of this speech with the wildest fantasy. Beyond that, we come to the abrupt differences. The four levels of the first book are here reduced to two; the fantastic element, instead of being partly invented and partly made from a *collage* of 'old mythologies from heel to throat', is entirely invented; and the tone has altered. Where the first book was hilarious, elegiac, sarcastic, grotesque, relaxed and genial, the second is tense, grim and threatening. It describes a horrible murder in the first sentence, and in its closing pages it contains an entirely realistic picture of a man dying of fright. In between, the tension is very seldom relaxed. . . .

Neither *The Hard Life* nor *The Dalkey Archive* has the authority and inclusiveness of *At Swim-Two-Birds,* nor the deep, concentrated power of *The Third Policeman.* Both the later books seem to toy with symbolic overtones rather than genuinely incorporate them. They pick their way round the edges of vitally important subjects rather than going hell-for-leather through the middle. And this realization gives us a vantage point to look back on *At Swim-Two-Birds,* noting clearly now its elegiac quality, its sense that the problems posed by time are not soluble; and also on the quietly agonized exploration of the damned state in *The Third Policeman.* If, in his first book O'Nolan came close to Joyce, in his second he anticipated the best work of Beckett. In temperament, he stands somewhere between the two. He is more discouraged than Joyce, less of a Yea-sayer. Joyce's work is bleak but it is not elegiac. It affirms the stature of man. The eighteen hours of Leopold Bloom's life which we follow in *Ulysses* are full of shabbiness, failure, and discouragement, but they are also Homeric. Joyce's purpose in elaborating his technique of literary *son et lumière* was to affirm that his wandering Jewish salesman was no less important than Odysseus. By contrast, O'Nolan's parallels between Trellis and Sweeney, between the bardic feast and the paralytic loquacity of the saloon bar, are parallels of hopelessness. On the other hand, he is not a connoisseur of hopelessness like Beckett, who seems to have cast himself in the role of a vulture, waiting on some dusty branch for the kicking human body to become a nice quiet corpse. The sense of doom, of the curse of meaninglessness laid on all that a man is and does, is brilliantly conveyed in *The Third Policeman,* but it is set within a religious framework and shown as the punishment for taking a man's life, cruelly, for gain. In Beckett's work, the capital crime is simply to be alive; *that* is the stupidity, the evil, the appalling metaphysical *gaffe* for which we are to be snubbed and punished for ever. O'Nolan does not talk in this strain; if he lacks the gigantic affirmative energy of Joyce, he nevertheless has some of Joyce's centrality and sanity.

*John Wain, "'To Write For My Own Race': Notes on the Fiction of Flann O'Brien," in his* A House for the Truth: Critical Essays *(copyright © 1968, 1970, 1971, 1972 by John Wain; reprinted by permission of The Viking Press, Inc.), Macmillan, 1972, pp. 67-104.*

Most readers of Flann O'Brien have been waiting for a translation of his novel in Gaelic, *An Béal Bocht,* and Patrick Power has at last provided *The Poor Mouth,* which appears—at least to one reader who has no Gaelic—marvellously attuned to O'Brien's subtle, peculiarly cold-blooded style. Like [Donald] Barthelme, O'Brien was effortlessly funny, fond of extended, elaborate jokes. *The Third Policeman* and *The Dalkey Archive* in particular, novels in which the intensity begins to flag a bit, are lifted and carried by their conceits: and the present book swings gaily and ruthlessly along by inverting conventional responses to squalor, filth and penury. . . .

Much of Mr. O'Brien's fun—and my guess is that it loses none of its point in the translation to English—consists of parodying the sentimental conventions of earlier Gaelic novels. . . .

*Peter Straub, in* New Statesman, *December 7, 1973, pp. 875-76.*

Allowing for a few exceptions, original and independent-minded writers in Ireland have traditionally been in a position not unlike that of the legitimate offspring in the nest with a cuckoo child—sooner or later claustrophobia, lack of air or lack of food force them out. A hardy bird is the one who remains to make his voice heard in and beyond his stifling home. Flann O'Brien, alias Myles na Gopaleen, alias Brian O'Nolan is one of this rare brood. The protean range of names would seem to suggest a constant need for adaptation and camouflage. . . .

[It] would be unwise to overstate O'Brien's 'Irishness' lest I give an impression of a lachrymose Gael trying to staunch an ebbing culture. O'Brien's reputation stands firmly on his strength as a comic writer, as a compulsive parodist and satirist and a near obsessive punster. There is pathos in his description of his characters and their fates, but their very wretchedness is the springboard for O'Brien's wit. . . .

*Robert Eagle, "Flann O'Brien: Voice in The Wilderness," in* Books and Bookmen, *January, 1974, pp. 46-7.*

Flann O'Brien's sense of humour is like that of a man who cracks jokes about blindness to a party of would-be revellers who have been trapped in a pitch black tunnel for longer than they find comfortable. Even at its most rumbustious his wit has a touch of horror, a cynic's glimpse of a bottomless pit of folly and error. Claude Cockburn, in his introduction to his volume, mentions the disapproval of Frank O'Connor and others toward the likes of O'Brien whose acute lack of respect and sentimentality threatened to undermine all reverence for national pride and patriotic heroism. Politics, religion, the Irish people, drugs, drink and madness are the common themes of this collection, and O'Brien's treatment of them all is uniform—he turns them to farce.

It would be unwise to attempt a summary of any of [the tales in *Stories and Plays*]; like all his plots they are a devilish network of false trails, boutades and caprices which are very engrossing and amusing until you realise that you, the happily detached reader, are not just laughing at the author's butts, you have become one yourself. Seeing perhaps how the work of his mentor Joyce had become a hunting ground for analysts, scholars and in-depth commentators, O'Brien has strewn the path to all sane interpretation with minefields and booby traps.

*Robert Eagle, in* Books and Bookmen, *March, 1974, p. 88.*

* * *

## OLSEN, Tillie 1913-

**Mrs Olsen is a prize-winning American novelist and short story writer. (See also *Contemporary Authors*, Vols. 1-4, rev. ed.)**

The strength of Mrs. Olsen's writing is remarkable, and the Holbrooks' threadbare, famished odyssey [*Yonnondio*] cannot help but arouse shame in those of us who have ever spoken lightly of poverty. This is in no way a treatise on poverty—it is the story of real people who are visibly shackled by having no money at all and by the daily insults offered by the world to their pride. To see the abundance of life and energy in Anna and Jim is very painful, because seeing it means that we are close witnesses to a fierce and almost breathless struggle, as these young parents attempt to make a living for themselves and their children in a world that has no interest in them. There are neighbors everywhere, and on every page a sense of teeming, tumbling life, so that the Holbrooks' struggle and their bafflement are the struggle and the bafflement of multitides. Mrs. Olsen is a most appealing writer, a strange new charmer in the wilderness that is fiction today.

The New Yorker, *March 25, 1974, pp. 140-41.*

Unlike the poor protagonists of some highly praised social realist novels of *Yonnondio*'s period, the Holbrooks' virtues don't give them superior strength, their defeat has no tinge of triumph. . . .

The cadences of *Yonnondio* seem almost a development of the structure of [Rebecca Harding Davis'] "Life in the Iron Mills." Lyrically brutal scenes are followed by pleas that the reader connect these lives with his own. Sentences break off midway; transitions are surprisingly abrupt. But what is a losing struggle with words in Davis is distinctively rhythmic in Olsen. *Yonnondio*, whose language is often achingly beautiful, is an elegy that acts on the reader indirectly by its emotional suggestiveness, rather than by its direct succession of events. The young Tillie Olsen was already an artist, but her vision was only half formed. [Mrs. Olsen began her novel in 1932.] Something central is missing from *Yonnondio*; and, although it may be unfair to judge an unfinished work by normal standards, in this case the finished work might have been similarly unsatisfying. In her youthful enthusiasm for "Life in the Iron Mills," Olsen perhaps didn't realize that Davis saw no redemption for her characters except money. Olsen makes us aware of the Holbrooks' humanity, but *Yonnondio* is an elegy that is as inarticulate as its characters about what is being mourned.

Until the family comes to the city, the novel belongs to Mazie, who at six is already something of a mystic. From her child's view, everything is twice life-size; defeats are more crushing, but even the smallest discovery is an epiphany. When Mazie finds visions in cloud formations, Olsen comes close briefly to Whitman's pantheism. But in the city the ailing mother Anna becomes the focus, and we only glimpse Mazie. This is a serious mistake. If we could experience the novel's cumulative revelation—poverty is final and all-embracing—through the corrosion of Mazie's sensibility, *Yonnondio* would be a success despite its fragmentation, because the possibilities that poverty has negated would be real for us. But Anna doesn't become the central figure until long after she has lost her sense of selfhood. She is wrenching, but Olsen can't lift her out of pathos. The hurt of *Yonnondio* is finally Anna's hurt; and since Anna is insubstantial, the pain is localized.

In Harriette Arnow's *The Dollmaker*, also about a farm family dislocated in a large city, the reader identifies totally with Gertie Nevels, the strongly intelligent heroine. Her ultimate defeat has a tragic meaning because we know what she might have been. *Yonnondio*, never completed in the first place and undefined in its fragments, needs a center like Gertie. Twenty years after *Yonnondio*, when she wrote the stories of *Tell Me a Riddle*, Olsen found characters who could fully embody her vision of hope with hopelessness, of beauty in the midst of ugliness. *Yonnondio* is a failed attempt at that later achievement, and it puts the reader through much pain without the release that fulfilled art brings; but it offers the opportunity to read a flawed but extraordinary early work knowing that its author would later bring her art to completion.

*John Alfred Avant, in* The New Republic *(reprinted by permission of* The New Republic; *© 1974 by The New Republic, Inc.), March 30, 1974, pp. 28-9.*

It is remarkable that Tillie Olsen, who already knew profoundly as a young writer what a great weight poor women carry, had also a deep sympathy for the restlessness and degraded pride of the men. And throughout "Yonnondio," her portrayal of faltering, caring motherhood and fatherhood against the most overwhelming of odds is tremendously moving.

"Yonnondio" soon moves into myth, an odyssey indeed, and its style into incantation. At one point I had the feeling that it should be read aloud by firelight, that it was something very close, for immigrant America, to the myths of origin and wandering that carried the whole inner history of American Indian tribes. But "Yonnondio" moves even beyond this Whitmanesque moment. Its archetypal figures —the shawled women waiting around a caved-in mine, the man slumped on his front porch, "menacing weariness riding his flesh like despair"—deepen into individuals. . . . With this work (as perhaps with the poetry of Sylvia Plath) motherhood must finally be counted among the circumstances that can simultaneously hinder and nourish genius.

The most fully drawn characters in "Yonnondio" are the women. . . .

*Annie Gottlieb, in* The New York Times Book Review *(© 1974 by The New York Times Company; reprinted by permission), March 31, 1974, p. 5.*

*Yonnondio* clearly must take its place as the best novel to come out of the so-called proletarian movement of the '30s. The dogma and stilted characterizations that deform so many of the novels of that period have no place in Tillie Olsen's writing. She is a consummate artist who, in a paragraph such as the following one about the life of a miner, demonstrates just how searingly successful "protest" writing can be: "Someday the bowels (of the earth) will grow monstrous and swollen with these old tired dreams, swell and break, and strong fists batter the fat bellies, and skeletons of starved children batter them, and perhaps you will be slugged by a thug hired by the fat bellies, Andy Kvaternick. Or death will take you to bed at last, or you will strangle with that old crony of miners, the asthma." I know of no work that "bespeaks the consciousness and roots" of the 1930s as brilliantly as *Yonnondio*.

But it would be a terrible mistake to see *Yonnondio* as a work limited to, and bound by, the '30s. Mrs. Olsen's richness of style, her depth of characterization, and her enormous compassion make *Yonnondio* a work which must not —cannot—be restricted by any particular time or period. Its publication simply reinforces what we already know from *Tell Me a Riddle*: Tillie Olsen is one of the greatest prose stylists now writing. One can only think ruefully of what might have been had she not been "denied full writing life"—had those 40 years been hers, and so our, not 40 years of "unnatural thwarting of what struggles to come into being, but cannot." Mrs. Olsen is quite right when she says (again, in "Death of the Creative Process") that a writer cannot be reconciled "for what is lost by unnatural silences." *Yonnondio! Yonnondio!* "The word itself a dirge," wrote Whitman. "Then blank and gone and still, and utterly lost." But now, with the publication of the found manuscript—unfinished as it may be—we can say: At least not that—not utterly lost. *Yonnondio* is a magnificent novel, one to be all the more cherished for the disruption it makes into the unnatural silence of Tillie Olsen.

*Jack Salzman, "Fragments of Time Lost," in* Book World—The Washington Post (© The Washington Post), *April 7, 1974, p. 1.*

Tillie Olsen is miner, archaeologist, and museum-curator for a special and growing collection. Special because in it she disdains her role of culture-bearer, of preserving man's culture, and salvages instead the work, the thought, the dream nearly buried beneath it because it belongs to the poor and forgotten, especially women. All her work—editing, compiling bibliographies of working-class women's literature, essay and fiction-writing—springs from this single goal of reclamation. This involves tireless research and the skill of adjusting our vision so that we can understand and value, *see* what has been neglected before. The process is conservative, the effect insidiously revolutionary. . . .

Some readers may wish the mature Olsen had not refrained, as she did, from rewriting. Olsen began it at 19, and "Yonnondio" is unmistakeably the work of a young author. That was 1932 and the novel has the feel of the '30s and even of earlier work. Since she was 15, Olsen had been carrying around [Rebecca Harding] Davis's story ["Life in the Iron Mills"], and some of that bold and simple compassion, risking sentimentality, is here. And I sometimes feel the lyrical pain of Stephen Crane, but never his detachment. Although the vision of industrial and urban horror feels ancient, the writing is fresh. I like it best for the way it expresses on another level Olsen's life-project of snatching beauty from destruction. The heart of meaning in this book, the key to its rhythm, is the phoenix rebirth of spirit. . . .

I found the misery at first too unremitting to feel. Overwritten or over-suffered—I don't know which to call it. But Olsen is wise about feeling and moves past this. Her last three chapters resume the rhythm of the struggle between the meanings of mine and farm, circumstance and spirit. The deepest impression the book leaves—what keeps it painful but not depressing—is of the intimate knowledge the poor and desperate have of happiness because it is so tenuous. . . .

"Yonnondio" lays the ground for Olsen's later and greater story. "Tell Me a Riddle," which more directly poses the paradox confronting women: that children, who most identify and confirm the values women want to bring to the transformation of the world, most surely bind them away from such action.

*Bell Gale Chevigny, in* The Village Voice *(reprinted by permission of* The Village Voice; *© 1974 by The Village Voice, Inc.), May 23, 1974, pp. 38-9.*

* * *

## ORTON, Joe 1933?-1967

**Orton was an English dramatist. (See also *Contemporary Authors*, obituary, Vols. 25-28.)**

Joe Orton, the homosexual playwright, was brutally murdered at the age of 34 by his roommate—to whom, it turned out, he had left all his money. The latter was unable to collect because (a) under British law, a murderer cannot inherit, and (b) he had committed suicide right after bludgeoning Orton. So the money went to Orton's father, whom the playwright ridiculed in his plays. A man who dies, and undoubtedly lived, a black comedy, should be able to write a good one; still, Orton's first play, *Entertaining Mr. Sloane*, had struck me as too conventionally commercial for the unconventional attitudes it was promulgating as well as ridiculing; nor did it seem to me as entertaining as its title. *Loot*, however, is something else again. Its tone and characters are properly absurd, yet they retain a great deal of authentic London lower-class wryness. . . .

What makes *Loot* a considerable play is its uncompromising yet cheerful rejection of the world. The main targets are Catholicism, i.e., religion; the police, i.e., government; sex, i.e., what we are pleased to call love; people, i.e., all people without exception—stupid, demented, greedy, hypocritical, and vicious: *homo* (or hetero) *homini lupus*. When you think about it, no one—not even Beckett, Ionesco, Genet—went that far. And let no one think it is easy to see the world that blackly and still be as jolly, urbane, even amiable about it as our playwright. Merely writing a play that is calculated to offend almost everyone takes courage; to live on and work in a world such as Orton perceived, requires a good deal more. All this, of course, would be scant recommendation if Orton's writing were not, most of the time, breezily, bruisingly equal to his somberly uproarious vision.

*John Simon, in* The Hudson Review *(copyright © 1968 by The Hudson Review, Inc.; reprinted by permission), Vol. XXI, No. 2, Summer, 1968, pp. 325-26.*

[Joe Orton's *Entertaining Mr. Sloane*]. . .is about four English working-class people whose expectations are wildly fantasized but, all the same, bitterly low in reach. While the slumberous savagery of the action goes on the characters chat to each other in a mixture of genteelisms, crime journalese, pub-brawl insults and desperately repeated pieties lifted from advice columns. . . .

The language of the text is like parquet over a volcano. . . . [It] would be possible (but not exact, I think) to argue that this is actually a highly moral piece. If it shows us people with a knee-high view of life, barbarous infants in genteel grownups' carcasses, there could be said to be an implication that the world should have done a lot better by them. Voltaire also wrote about people who are totally disreputable but issues that are absolutely serious. The young Joe Orton, though . . . , was understandably not yet so sure of what he was doing. Voltaire could shock; so could Firbank, whom Orton admired. But it takes genius to shock. In this text, perhaps, there is only talent, and a strain of the professionally outrageous. There may attach to it, in our heads, the notion that outrageous things ill-done have courage because they repel, but the truth may be that they repel because they are ill-done and not very brave. All the same, the piece is by a young master of artificial diction and ribaldry, a writer whom other writers recognized. Sean O'Casey said cheerfully to me that this was a play to make a man pull his trousers up.

Its trouble is the time's, not Orton's in particular. It can't quite find its own voice. Not only the characters but also the text itself seem to be speaking in quotation marks. Nothing is said directly; everything is on the bias, spoken at a tangent to mock suspect "sincerity." This may be one of the few specifically modern characteristics (cool, for instance, is nothing new; nor is gallows humor). It can impose a terrible load of mannerism on writing, even though one of its causes, paradoxically, is the modern horror of indulging the phony. I believe Orton was a serious-minded man; it is this contemporary problem of utterance that belies his work, this problem of his not seeming to mean a word he says. He would probably have got round it by some technique of his own if life had been halfway forbearing with him. Instead, . . . he has now posthumously left us [the film version of *Entertaining Mr. Sloane*,] a revenge tragedy going on among the antimacassars and the doilies and the ketchup; an analogy of *The Cenci*, but one that has no comprehension of the blasphemous.

*Penelope Gilliatt, "Could-Haves" (1970), in her* Unholy Fools: Wits, Comics, Disturbers of the Peace—Film and Theater *(copyright © 1973 by Penelope Gilliatt; all rights reserved; reprinted by permission of The Viking Press, Inc.), The Viking Press, 1973, pp. 238-42.*

Between his first play, *The Ruffian on the Stair*, produced . . . in 1964, and his sudden death in 1967,. . . [Orton] had not only written two of the new dramatists' biggest commercial successes, *Entertaining Mr Sloane* and *Loot*, but had developed his own unmistakable vision of the world and his own tone of voice as a dramatist—to such an extent that ever after one finds oneself reading actual news stories in terms of a Joe Orton script.

The key to Orton's dramatic world is to be found in the strange relationship between the happenings of his plays and the manner in which the characters speak of them. The happenings may be as outrageous as you like in terms of morality, accepted convention or whatever, but the primness and propriety of what is said hardly ever breaks down. And the gift of Orton's characters for intricate and inventive euphemism, so far from toning down the outrageousness of their actions and ideas, only places it in even stronger relief. Orton was, perhaps first and foremost, a master of verbal style—or of his own particular verbal style. And even during his short public career his mastery of that style may be observed increasing and refining itself. . . .

Like the highly formal language his characters speak, the intricate plots through which they are manoeuvred create a critical distance between play and spectator. One is always aware in Orton that he is using a convention to make his points, even though he himself always insisted that in a very important sense his plays are realistic (the sense, as I understand it, that they embody his observations of what happens within society in the real world and are written in a style which seems to him perfectly natural, however odd it may seem to anyone else). It is a convention suggestive at once of the two surviving genres of truly popular theatre, farce and the whodunnit, both of which require intricate plot and simplified, or at any rate very simple, characterization. It is obviously significant that in later plays he makes the connection explicit; *Loot* is on one level both a whodunnit and a parody of a whodunnit; *What the Butler Saw* is both a farce and a parody of a farce. . . .

What is beautifully kept up in *Mr Sloane*, rather less so in his other plays, is the almost surrealistic dislocation between the most extraordinary and improper happenings and the unruffled propriety of the characters' conversation. The two elements are held in perfect balance. . . .

The play is a comedy of language, but it is also a comedy of manners: the humour derives as much from gradual revelation of character as from the manipulation of spoken words. And formally it is immaculately managed: the clue to its structure is in the title, the meaning of which inexorably shifts in the course of the play from providing entertainment for Mr Sloane to using Mr Sloane as an occasion of entertainment. . . .

It is remarkable . . . that though they seem to start from the material of camp fantasy, Orton's plays manage completely to transform that material into a serious vision of life, which, however, eccentric—and however comic in its chosen forms of expression—carries complete conviction as something felt, something true.

*John Russell Taylor, "Joe Orton," in his* The Second Wave: British Drama for the Seventies *(reprinted by permission of Hill and Wang, a division of Farrar, Straus & Giroux, Inc.; © 1971 by John Russell Taylor), Hill & Wang, 1971, pp. 125-40.*

Orton's dialogue is a collage of the popular culture. It assimilates advertising jargon, the idioms of the popular press, the stilted lusciousness of Grade-B movies. Like the characters in his plays, a poetry is forged from words debased and thrown-away by the culture. His characters do not speak in the refined, heroic language of Osborne and Arden. Orton does something much more elusive and difficult. He adds his own brand of irony to the colloquial. Fantasy finds its way into the sentences of his characters, and their words stand out like banners flagging their dream to the audience if not themselves. . . .

*Entertaining Mr Sloane* is Orton's most naturalistic work, and the piece does not use the stage with full playfulness—a fact that Orton recognized. *Loot* and *What the Butler Saw* work more boldly with theatrical artifice. Orton considered them an advance, a development in which his dazzling capacity to manipulate words was matched with equally startling talent for constructing hilarious stage images. In *Entertaining Mr Sloane*, Orton was toying with farce. Kath loses her teeth and is grovelling on all fours at the play's tensest moment. The cut and thrust rhythm of the play's third act dialogue has a potential for mayhem that never gets beyond the vaudeville of language to movement. . . .

[It] is as a farceur that Orton's reputation continues to grow. He succeeded in taking a frivolous form and turning it to resonant ends. Conscious of the theatre's literary heritage, his plays extend the style and savagery of Restoration comedy into twentieth century life. With farce, his characters move at a momentum which augurs their disintegration. They defy—in both senses of the word—gravity. Orton's farces carried out Nietzche's commandment in *Thus Spake Zarathusra*. 'And when I beheld my devil, I found him serious, thorough, profound, solemn; it was the Spirit of Gravity, through him all things are ruined. One does not kill by anger but by laughter. Come let us kill the Spirit of Gravity.'

Orton waged his war with a clear understanding of his

goals. In the three years before his death in June 1967 at the age of 34, his confidence and technique grew. He offered an audience grotesques which, like the gargoyles on a medieval cathedral, forced the viewer to imagine Hell and redefine Heaven. To him, nothing was sacred; but the fury of his attack, its peculiar combination of joy and horror, was not without a broader spiritual motive. Orton wanted to shock the society and also to purify it. On stage, his characters are performing animals. And, once the beast in every man is faced, then tolerance can more easily replace righteousness. . . .

Critics and audiences are now beginning to recognize Orton's staying power. His style is too unique, his humour too side-splitting, his stage metaphors too accurate for him to be relegated to history's rubbish heap. In showing us how we destroy ourselves, Orton's plays are themselves a survival tactic. He makes us laugh to make us learn. There is a salvation in that.

*John Lahr, in his "Introduction" (© 1973 by John Lahr)* to Entertaining Mr. Sloane, *by Joe Orton, Eyre-Methuen, 1964, pp. 5-10.*

# P

## PALEY, Grace 1922-

**Mrs Paley, an American short story writer, is the author of *The Little Disturbances of Man,* stories whose reputation lived primarily "underground" for ten years and were well known only to literary cognoscenti. She is an expert stylist and is considered by many to be one of the masters of the genre. (See also *Contemporary Authors*, Vols. 25-28.)**

Grace Paley's short stories are often so enjoyably ethnic that one may miss, on first reading, some of the several layers of feelings and meanings that are being transmitted. . . . Paley's writings . . . also reach deeper on a second reading. One has to become used to incongruous malapropisms, the deliberate innocence that conveys double meanings, the tough-kid humor that pretends to hide (but knows it doesn't) a sympathetic heart. [She] often [uses] language in odd, unexpected, vivid, sometimes lurching ways that make one stop and go back, annoyed, provoked, alerted to fresh perceptions. Paley's people, especially her women, are . . . engaged in struggles for self-definition or assertion, impeded as well as propelled by their passions and sympathies.

*Ann Morrissett Davidon, "Women Writing," in* The Nation, *September 10, 1973, pp. 213-14.*

Grace Paley never rambled; she moved swiftly and unerringly, however obliquely, to her goals. Writers told each other about her. During the '60s, between infrequent stories, she surfaced as an antiwar activist. And in 1968 "The Little Disturbances of Man" was formally republished, by a different house than had brought it out the first time—an event almost without parallel in the forlorn history of short-story collections. . . .

Now here is a second collection [*Enormous Changes at the Last Minute*] quieter, more reflective, more openly personal than the first.

*Walter Clemons, "The Twists of Life," in* Newsweek *(copyright Newsweek, Inc., 1974; reprinted by permission), March 11, 1974, p. 78.*

Paley's stories, more often than not, are not really stories at all. Rather, at their best, they are elaborate introductions —through language, not through plot or character development—to a group of people who, like the author herself, believe they deserve the open destiny of life. . . .

Paley, to this day, continues to be what the academics call an "uneven" writer; her successes are intermittent, unpredictable, often unshapely and without wholeness; there is no progression of revelation, the stories do not build one upon another, they do not—as is abundantly clear in this new book—create an emotional unity. On the other hand: Paley when she is good is so good that she is worth 99 "even" writers, and when one hears that unmistakable Paley voice one feels what can be felt only in the presence of a true writer: safe. The darkness is pushed back, solid warmth fills the gut, the universe is re-created in the company of a living intelligence; flesh and blood is on that page; it's good to be alive again. As one of Paley's characters might say: "You could die with the pleasure of it."

Two things in particular mark Paley's work: a deep sense of the ongoingness of life, and an even deeper sense of the New York idiom. . . . When the stories are successful, what is communicated is the ongoing, dream-like quality of the passage of "normal" time—as it surrounds the vividness of remembered feeling. . . .

Paley is the ultimate New Yorker. She is to New York what William Faulkner is to Mississippi. Her pages are alive with the sounds of the savvy, street-smart New Yorker, and every character—regardless of age, sex, or education—knows his lines to perfection. In her extraordinary tone of voice and use of imagery, in the shape and rhythm of her language, is captured whole the incredible combination of shrewdness, naivete, appetite, and insight that is uniquely New York street life; and therein stands revealed in all its rich particularity the essence and emotional meaning of "idiom"; very few writers—and almost no New York writers—have ever managed it; and if that isn't an accomplishment to take one's hat off to, then I am hard put to know what the storyteller's art is all about.

*Vivian Gornick, in* The Village Voice *(reprinted by permission of* The Village Voice; *© 1974 by The Village Voice, Inc.), March 14, 1974, pp. 25, 28.*

When Grace Paley's first collection of stories, *The Little Disturbances of Man,* appeared in 1959, it was clear at once that a fresh writing talent had presented itself. While her subject matter—the frantic life of urban men and women, mostly Jews, in and around the West Village—was hardly new, her style was very much her own. She wrote like the ultimate *yenta,* Molly Goldberg raised to a fine art without losing her roots in oral speech, and the stories she told were splendidly suited to her style, being mostly tales of feminine woe of the kind that would set Molly Goldberg's tongue wagging. . . .

[Even] with the glitter of its style, over which Paley skates like some Olympic champion of language, *Enormous Changes* is a book of losses and failures that add up to one of the most depressing works of fiction to be published in the last decade, hardly a time noted for the prevalence of upbeat writing. . . .

Most of Paley's stories are too short for any plot. They're quick sketches, blackouts, comic monologues spoken in a theater bereft of audience by a voice increasingly desperate for coherence.

Finally though, there isn't any coherence, or nothing more substantial than the style, to which we return in the absence of anything else that will reward our attention.

*Michele Murray, in* The New Republic *(reprinted by permission of* The New Republic; *© 1974 by Harrison-Blaine of New Jersey, Inc.), March 16, 1974, p. 27.*

I can't think of another writer who captures the itch of the city, or the complexities of love between parents and children, or the cutting edge of sexual combat as well as Grace Paley does. . . .

In her last book, "The Little Disturbances of Man," . . . Paley wrote chiefly about herself, her children, her parents, her awful ex-husband and her friends. The horizon is the same here, but bleaker—especially when she writes about her women friends. . . . Paley was among the first women fiction writers to describe in plain words how the world looked from behind a pile of diapers; she was, and is one of the few who also puts in a few cheers for children. The children in her stories, like almost all her characters, are, *Deo gratias,* good *and* bad, in transit, unfinished products, humans. . . .

Many stories, though, including the title one, are marred by fishy, pat endings. I felt that was especially true of "Politics," in which a playground fence wrung out of the city by a group of militant mothers is vandalized the night it goes up by a policeman, and "Gloomy Tune," which ends so abruptly it practically skids off the page. I thought the fine, ironic note sounded a little false and shrill at times, too. . . . I suspect that Paley worries too much and guards, unnecessarily, against being thought too soft-hearted. "Living" and "The Burdened Man" hardly have a chance to get airborne before they end with a wry thump.

Grace Paley has spent a good part of her time and energy in the last decade working, as she herself puts it on the back flap, as a "somewhat combative pacifist"—a vocation for which I have nothing but admiration. Good as the present collection is, however, I suspect that its unevenness reflects the fact that during these past years she must often have felt that her attentions were needed in places far from her typewriter; or, to quote again, "that art is too long and life is too short."

*Lis Harris, in* The New York Times Book Review *(© 1974 by The New York Times Company; reprinted by permission), March 17, 1974, p. 3.*

Grace Paley, as several people have said, is a *regional* writer, the scribe of a local moral and psychological dialect. She writes about New York City in the way that Giono wrote about Provence or George Borrow wrote about gypsies, quietly maps out a whole small country of damaged, fragile, haunted citizens. This would seem to suggest some sort of order and stability and continuity—at least a world which stays put long enough to be fixed in fiction by a writer who publishes a book only once every fifteen years. . . . But the suggestion is deceptive. This country is veined with cracks just waiting to open, as the language of [*The Little Disturbances of Man* and *Enormous Changes at the Last Minute*] is strewn with almost invisible landmines. . . .

Grace Paley's language hovers constantly on the edge of an awful cuteness and whimsy, performs an elaborate balancing act, and for an example of what it looks like when the writer falls off the wire we have only to turn to the back of the jacket of the book, where we learn, in Grace Paley's own words, that she is a "somewhat combative pacifist and cooperative anarchist" and that she writes short stories "because art is too long and life is too short." Unfair evidence, perhaps. *In* the book the writer stays on the wire all right, and the successful act is obviously harder to illustrate. . . .

Grace Paley is occasionally a bit defensive about the breeziness of her writing manner; seems tempted to apologize for it. If you're *not* blind or cockeyed, she implies, you need jokes in order to be able to look out at the cold street. But then if the jokes don't come off, you're left with your thin skin. If they come off too well, you've hidden the street away altogether. And the nagging question keeps returning: what if the world after all could be looked at without the filter of fun?

*Michael Wood, in* The New York Review of Books *(reprinted with permission from* The New York Review of Books; *© 1974 by NYREV, Inc.), March 21, 1974, pp. 21-2.*

Mrs. Paley's new collection [*Enormous Changes at the Last Minute*] is a far cry from the first and memorable *Little Disturbances of Man.* In the intervening time, a tough wit has given way to archness, and coherence has yielded to obscurantism. There has always been a strident ethnicity to her work, and in this regard, happily, her voice has not changed; Mrs. Paley has one of the best ears going for dialect of the inward kind, the sort of thing that confers a painful vitality on stories like "Faith in the Afternoon" or "A Conversation With My Father." These excellent works aside, it is clear in this collection that Mrs. Paley's art has been given over almost entirely to politicized themes and situations, in a fashion that is all too familiar. It is one that appears to have been nurtured in those pleasant regions of political society where one is exposed regularly to the agreement of comrades and partisans, a region in which one becomes habituated to the conveniences of a shared frame of reference. It is not the best sort of nourishment for writing. . . . With the exceptions noted, it would appear, from this collection at least, that an extraordinarily good writer has left off the business of story making and has offered in its place a sort of sociological shorthand—and this . . . in tones which make clear that when one is beset by the apocalyptic vision, the ordinary lives of men and women are beside the point, and there can be neither shape nor coherence to events in those lives. Mrs. Paley is not the first writer—nor will she be the last—to have proved, if proof were still needed, that progressive politics, which advances so many estimable causes, is a downright heavy burden on the art of fiction.

*Dorothy Rabinowitz, in* Saturday Review/World *(copyright © 1974 by Saturday Review/World, Inc.; reprinted with permission), March 23, 1974, p. 45.*

Some of [the stories in *Enormous Changes at the Last Minute*] are mere wisps—a filament of character, a *frisson* of nuance. A few are too fanciful by half. What makes the collection very much worth reading is the author's ardent belief in her characters. Paley finds all her people exceptional, and she describes them with a charge of feeling that is unfailingly seductive.

This kind of *a cappella* writing is a very chancy business. Paley usually succeeds because she is a poised, naturally gifted writer who trusts her own quirky, ironic imagination. The stories—whether two pages or 20—run their courses as cleanly and surely as arrows flying in air.

*Martha Duffy, "Straight Arrow," in* Time *(reprinted by permission from* Time, The Weekly Newsmagazine; *copyright Time Inc.), April 29, 1974, p. 108.*

Mrs. Paley takes a firm stand against gloom—and for several extra-literary reasons that can be discerned in her work. She is naturally cheerful—trite as that sounds—and, in fact, a born comedienne. She is a comforting woman, aware that "hospitable remarks" can make a great difference in the tenor of life. And, having grown up "in the summer sunshine of upward mobility," as she puts it, she shares in the great American dream, the belief that the world *can* be made a better place to live in. But the way the world wags these days, she has a hard time keeping her spirits up. She tries. And the signs of strain are apparent in her lack of wind—she writes *short* short stories and not many of them—in her tone, resolutely airy or ruefully sincere, and especially in her endings, which seem contrived or tacked on. She knows the importance of a last line in a short short story and, skillful as any poet, she knows how to make it ring. But with a strange effect—as if anxious to ward off pain, to avoid the note of finality, or to free the subject from the shackles of grim fact. . . .

Mrs. Paley is right to avoid looking tragedy in the face; she knows where her talent lies. It is, if not for comedy exactly, for virtuoso mimicry. I would guess—though she may rise up and contradict me—that the first thing she has in mind when starting work on one of her better stories is a voice. Definitely not a plot which would keep her to the straight and narrow and cramp her digressions, or a situation or a point of view or even a character, but a voice with a particular ring and particular turns of phrase. Out of this voice grows all the rest. Many of her stories are told in the first person by a speaker who casually reveals everything about himself—or more usually, herself. Others consist largely of dialogue with very little in the way of comment. A native New Yorker, she has an unerring ear for the various kinds of city speech. And she enjoys exploring all the neighborhood dialects. . . .

Dialect in her hands is free of condescending folksiness or the brazen overriding of embarrassment inherent in the racial joke. It is local color, noted and relished and intensified, which serves to paint a portrait. . . .

[She] finds a vocation in glorifying the accents of a now vanished and slightly fabulous Second Avenue and those of the old-age home. Accents that are now dying and no longer of use to her! For the worst enemy in Mrs. Paley's fight against gloom is . . . change—a fact of God—the disappearance of a familiar milieu, the need to find new material congenial to her, new people, new voices. When she comes on as herself, something is lacking, a certain sharpness of focus. It makes little difference whether she speaks in the first person or the third, disguised as someone called Faith or Alexandra, or whether she tells her own troubles or those of her friends and contemporaries. She becomes a mere sensibility, a succession of moods—breezy, anguished, charming, pensive—a writer of memoirs. But dialect offers her a role to play. She steps into it with a sense of release, she invents business, she improvises in character. She becomes an actress.

*Burton Bendow, "Voices in the Metropolis," in* The Nation, *May 11, 1974, pp. 597-98.*

*Enormous Changes at the Last Minute* is a group of very energetic stories. Some are wonderfully clear, extraordinarily authentic, and have an enthusiasm that makes them invigorating reading. Others are moral-ridden fables full of misplaced bile and small pronouncements that hinder and annoy the reader. A few are so very ethnic that they sag in the middle and collect a lot of debris.

When Grace Paley is writing well there is considerable force provided by the striking aptness of speech of her characters describing each other. . . . When she is not smothered by her concern for a very local issue, Paley's writing shows considerable breadth, and she is able to give her characters important freedom. One sits in a tree for an afternoon; another, running for exercise, is able to spend a few weeks at her former family home discovering the new occupants. . . .

As a whole, the book is a fascinating conglomeration of ideas, fears, and limitations. The past is portrayed as chimeric, the present difficult, and the future chancy. One is not completely convinced, however, for the recurrent defects in craftsmanship obfuscate the image Paley would leave with us; and at times the aptness turns to coldness and the freedom she allows her inventions leaves them standing dreadfully still. Yet whatever its faults, the book has panache and the cast are creatures of courage, a rare virtue in modern literature.

*Benjamin Reeve, in* Harper's *(copyright © 1974, by Harper's Magazine, Inc.; reprinted from the June, 1974 issue of* Harper's Magazine *by permission), June, 1974, p. 96.*

Unlike those writers who lost their identity, their sense of humor or the ground they stood on in the '60s, Grace Paley maintains a gallant line of distinction between the world's mistakes and her own state of mind. . . .

She possesses, among female writers, perhaps the strongest sense of fraternity with her own gender. . . . Mrs. Paley also has the knack, so prominent in her first story collection, *The Little Disturbances of Man,* of romanticizing even the weakness and unreliability of men. . . .

Over and over, husbands fly the coop for reasons of their own, but the women do not hold a grudge. They acknowledge that men are magnetic, transient, slippery, and that women's lives are destined to be shot through with a chronic *Sehnsucht* for some ideal man who is not there. In a period when liberationists believe female happiness can be articulated in the form of pragmatic demands, this kindly fatalism alone would make the writer extraordinary. . . .

Readers who take to Mrs. Paley's stories will . . . not do so for their "literary merit" (of which there is sufficient amount) but for her disposition, which is remarkable.

She is, first of all, generous in her estimate of everyone, beginning with her autobiographical heroine, who cherishes a clear and favorable image of herself. Mrs. Paley does not have it in her to practice a sullen art, and seems almost oddly unwilling to entertain an adverse moral judgment or a hostile response. . . .

Mrs. Paley does not like to study sorrow. She can say, with one of her heroines, "I am better known for my hospitable remarks." If at times her general beneficence extends so warmly to herself that she becomes a pushover for her own charm, what could be more therapeutic in this age of self-deprecation?

*Isa Kapp, "Husbands and Heroines," in* New Leader, *June 24, 1974, pp. 17-18.*

*Enormous Changes at the Last Minute* is a selection of the work [Grace Paley] has done in the past fifteen years. Although her narrative voice has become somewhat more cryptic than it used to be, this second volume is essentially an extension of the first [*The Little Disturbances of Man*]; Mrs. Paley's imagination continues to be fired by "ordinary" people fixed in reduced and unremarkable circumstances, living lives sodden with small and unengaging woes, in whom, were it not for Mrs. Paley's literary labors, we might take no interest whatsoever. As her narrator grandiloquently remarks, the point is to "tell their stories as simply as possible, in order, you might say, to save a few lives."

Most of the stories in *Enormous Changes at the Last Minute* reflect Mrs. Paley's highly stylized conception of lower-class, immigrant, or second-generation "ethnic" New York. Plot and action are, to say the least, secondary; the author's concern is primarily with the social milieu, and with the immediate thoughts and feelings of the people she portrays. . . .

By and large, the people in Mrs. Paley's fiction lead lives characterized by an almost surreal psychic isolation and a passivity bordering on despair. Despite statements like, "Everyone, real or imagined, deserves the open destiny of life," Mrs. Paley's "inventions" (as she herself calls her characters) are placed typically in bleak situations where their best hope is to survive, rather than to comprehend, let alone alter, the fate that has been meted out to them. Although there is little active or dramatic suffering, the threat of emotional violence is pervasive—engendered, perhaps, by the narrow horizons under which everyone in the book labors. . . .

Even setting aside the portentous references to overtly political matters—"community action," the inadequacy of welfare stipends, the immorality of the Vietnam war—her stories are suffused with a set of narrow-minded attitudes and assumptions about the nature of experience in modern America that are borrowed wholesale from the communitarian/utopian ethos of the radical Left. Motherhood, the "plight" of women, the relationship between the sexes—virtually any human condition at all is relentlessly politicized in this setting, made to fit smoothly with the thesis of extreme victimization and polarization which is Mrs. Paley's representation of reality.

Such a reductive reading of life inevitably takes its literary toll. The stories have about them a self-conscious and mannered quality that mirrors their refusal to evoke any recognizable emotional or psychological reality. The dominant voice is the authorial one; narration and dialogue both are written in an idiosyncratic and elliptical language, making it seem as if, in addition to their other privations, Mrs. Paley's characters are without the means or the desire to understand anything about themselves or to communicate with one another in any but the most primitive and unrevealing fashion. The plotting in *Enormous Changes* ranges from the incredibly bad to the nonexistent, and the reader often gets the feeling that the author found herself in the middle of a story and then simply ran out of the imaginative energy necessary to complete it.

Mrs. Paley's sense of herself as friend to the friendless is endlessly reiterated in these pages, but the note that sounds most clearly is one of cynicism and condescension, if not of enmity. Her bloodless "vision" of the way things "really" are leads to the minimizing of everything and everybody in her fictional world. Any life would inevitably be larger, more variegated, and more substantial, the scope of its possibility far wider, than Grace Paley even begins to allow in her stories. It is as if what she had set out to do was not to "save a few lives" but rather to kill off any possibility of rendering them imaginatively. In this she has nearly succeeded.

*Jane Larkin Crain, "'Ordinary' Lives" (reprinted from* Commentary *by permission; copyright © 1974 by the American Jewish Committee), in* Commentary, *July, 1974, pp. 92-3.*

* * *

## PATON, Alan 1903-

**Paton is a South African novelist who deals in his fiction with racial problems and the terrors of alienation. He is best**

**known for *Cry, the Beloved Country*. (See also *Contemporary Authors*, Vols. 15-16.)**

*Cry, the Beloved Country* is a great and dramatic novel because Alan Paton, in addition to his skill of workmanship, sees with clear eyes both good and evil, differentiates them, pitches them into conflict with each other, *and takes sides*. He sees that the native boy, Absalom Kumalo, who has murdered, cannot be judged justly without taking into account the environment that has partly shaped him. But he sees, too, that Absalom the individual, not society the abstraction, did the act and has responsibility. Mr. Paton understands mercy. He knows that this precious thing is not shown on sentimental impulse, but after searching examination of the realities of human action. Mercy follows a judgment; it does not precede it.

*Edmund Fuller, in his* Man in Modern Fiction: Some Minority Opinions on Contemporary American Writing *(copyright © 1958 by Edmund Fuller; reprinted by permission of Random House, Inc.), Random House, 1958, p. 40.*

The most famous and one of the earliest novels of forgiveness is Alan Paton's *Cry, the Beloved Country*. This work and *The Story of an African Farm* are the two best-known novels in English—with a South African locale—to readers outside South Africa. Ironically, though Paton's novel has spawned a host of imitations and has been highly praised as propaganda, most contemporary South African writers deny any literary indebtedness to Paton. Yet *Cry, the Beloved Country* is at least as well-written a novel as the many novels which have followed its lead. Today also, Paton's humanism is being attacked as old-fashioned and sentimental. Ezekiel Mphahlele has accused Paton of falsifying human nature because in his view Paton divides people into good and bad and then lays on these cardboard figures a heavy liberalism and a "monumental sermon." . . .

In *Cry, the Beloved Country* the ways of justice and God are mysterious, but in the person of Paton's central character love brings an acceptance that explains nothing while meaning all. (pp. 223-24)

The second half of the novel has had a profound influence on the thoughts of non-South African readers, even if its message is currently being derided by some black South African literary critics. For Paton's novel is the supreme example of the kind of novel of forgiveness which calls for the construction of love on the ruins of tragedy. (p. 225)

If *Cry, the Beloved Country* has been likened to a sermon, *Too Late the Phalarope* can be likened to a lament. . . . Yet the point of Paton's [second] novel is not that Pieter could have been saved by the psychological awareness of others; it is that the South African milieu destroys those who are seeking love irrespective of color. Paton's people are not romantics but people simply open to the fact of experience. Those who accuse Paton of soft sentimentalism should look at his characterization of Stephanie. She is not represented as a heroic or vivacious woman but as a frightened animal, and Paton's attack on the Immorality Act (prohibiting cohabitation between white and non-white) is aimed at its senselessness. Pieter did not love the black girl he slept with. It was a matter of sexual, animal urgency, yet Pieter has to pay for his act with imprisonment and moral denigration. (p. 226)

Paton is the most important force in the literature of forgiveness and adjustment. His popularity and his integrity have made possible a receptivity to a whole new body of work that might otherwise have remained unnoticed. Undoubtedly his work is more significant as propaganda than as literature, but it should be emphasized that his writing is not without literary quality. If his talent lies in his ability to project the fervor and sentiment of his liberal views rather than in his ability to convey full-blooded human beings, it also contains much that is genuinely creative. (p. 227)

*Martin Tucker, in his* Africa in Modern Literature: A Survey of Contemporary Writing in English, *Ungar, 1967.*

*Cry, the Beloved Country* shares that quality of universal interest that always distinguishes outstanding products of the creative imagination. Some readers valued Paton's first novel for the refreshing combination of simplicity and lyricism in its language; others valued it most as a revealing record of South Africa's social and racial situation; and others again, although perhaps fewer in number, valued it for its challenge to their own comfortably sterile Christianity. (p. 22)

In *Cry, the Beloved Country: A Story of Comfort in Desolation,* Paton succeeds to a remarkable degree in portraying a segment of South African life during a brief period immediately following the end of World War II. And he succeeds, to an even more remarkable degree, in endowing this regional portrait with universal significance. He accomplishes this by incorporating into the actualities of South Africa's physical and social setting a fundamental theme of social disintegration and moral restoration. (p. 49)

It is not surprising that Paton wrote *Cry, the Beloved Country* quickly, since he already had all the material in mind. What is surprising, however, is that he wrote it so well. The stroke of genius that produced a unique artistic masterpiece was his hitting upon a lyric and dramatic framework that could incorporate more than the realistic "slice of life" ordinarily offered by novels of social purpose. (p. 54)

Three artistic qualities of *Cry, the Beloved Country* combine to make it an original and unique work of art: first, the poetic elements in the language of some of the characters; second, the lyric passages spoken from outside the action, like the well-known opening chapter; and third, the dramatic choral chapters that seem to break the sequence of the story for social commentary, but which in fact widen the horizon of the particular segments of action to embrace the whole land, as well as such universal concerns as fear, hate, and justice. (p. 55)

Paton's *Cry, the Beloved Country* offers no blueprint for society. What it does objectify is individual recognition of personal responsibility. Such recognition depends on a process of self-discovery. . . . (p. 66)

Paton's collection of short stories [*Tales from a Troubled Land*] seems likely to be the last of his books of fiction; for his career as a creative writer, that began with such promise in 1948, ended for all practical purposes when he was elected Chairman of the Liberal Party in 1956. In attempting to estimate his creative artistry on the basis of the novels and short stories he wrote during that short period, one thinks first of his regionalism. His art is related to South Africa as Robert Frost's is to New England. Both of these writers work within the framework of an external landscape where they know all flowers and shrubs, birds and animals, by their familiar names. As observers of the human inhabitants of these landscapes, both writers recognize the profound aspirations of human personality; and both communicate their insights in language that is fresh and simple, yet vibrant with meaning. While one may appropriately speak of the art of Paton or Frost as *regional,* it would be wholly inappropriate to speak of it as *provincial*—a term that suggests narrow interests or limited intellectual horizons. (pp. 96-7)

While he does not regard his occasional expressions in verse as constituting a claim to the title of poet, Paton has continued, from time to time, to publish poems. . . . These later poems draw almost exclusively on South African life and attitudes for their subject matter. These poems may be classified in three categories: first, some lyric portraits of aspects of African life; second, a few satirical verse commentaries aimed at conventional white South African assumptions and the theory of *apartheid*; third, a number of religious poems. (p. 107)

For some years Paton's literary reputation has rested on two successful novels and a handful of short stories. But the judgment of the future may rank his recent biography of Jan Hofmeyr as a literary achievement equal to the novels and possibly surpassing them. (p. 110)

Paton's personal relation with Hofmeyr helps to make this work a representative example of what the art of biography can accomplish in our age. (p. 112)

*Edward Callan, in his* Alan Paton *(copyright 1968 by Twayne Publishers, Inc.; reprinted with the permission of Twayne Publishers, a Division of G. K. Hall & Co.), Twayne, 1968.*

* * *

## PAZ, Octavio 1914-

**Paz, a Mexican, is a brilliant poet, essayist, and social philosopher.**

Paz has never been one to hold his rhetoric (in prose) on any kind of rein, and I sometimes feel that a very good prose style could be created for Paz if a kindly friend or editor would simply cut out every third sentence he writes. Still, this too is part of being an intellectual in Latin America. There is the constant obligation to keep talking, and one senses that Paz's brilliantly vacuous remarks ("but the differences between civilizations hide a secret unity: man"—that is, human societies are inhabited by human beings) are perhaps a means of bearing the burden without being crushed by it: you take the job, but you don't take it too seriously. Paz has not been bought off by a reactionary government; he has not taken flight into formalism or aesthetics; he has sanctioned neither Stalinism nor terrorism. He has sustained a high critical intelligence where it was desperately needed; and above all, or at least above all *for us,* at this distance from the Latin American scene, he has written major poetry which has been in no way diminished by his onerous, multifarious activities. . . .

*Conjunctions and Disjunctions* is an act of homage to Lévi-Strauss and Norman O. Brown, Paz's try at playing their games with his own deck of cultural cards. . . . Paz's devotion to symmetrical antitheses exceeds even that of Lévi-Strauss and his working principle seems to be that any pair of opposites can be exchanged for any other pair, on the grounds that there are two of them as well. Thus the book begins with a brilliant and witty exploration of a metaphor (taken from Quevedo and Posada) which equates the face and the ass: the face *is* an ass, the ass *is* a face. But then ass and face soon become explosion and repression, the pleasure principle and the reality principle, which in turn are converted into the forces behind, respectively, the ruled and the rulers, jokes and pedantry, ignorance and education, vulgarity and good upbringing, wisdom and prudence, and the relative value systems of the poor and the rich. . . .

Enough? Well, as a matter of fact, all this is "only a variation of the old dichotomy between nature and culture." This is meant to be dazzling but just makes you dizzy, and it is cruelly reductive, a violent crushing of differences into uniformity. . . .

Still, there are good things in *Conjunctions and Disjunctions,* notably an elaborate (and genuinely dazzling) display of the inverse relations between Buddhism and Christianity—the religion that points to disincarnation exalts the body, while the religion that rests on the incarnation of its god denies and transfigures the flesh. As always in Paz, there are wonderful epigrams ("Man's paradises are covered with gibbets") and a humane, urgent lesson is to be found at the end of the intricate allusions and ratiocinations. . . .

*The Bow and the Lyre* is Paz's poetic confession, and is written with an urgency and a care and a tact which none of his later prose works possesses. . . . [The] book communicates a real sense of an arduous inquest taking place, of a man excavating his profoundest assumptions, putting his thoughts together for himself, wherever they come from and whoever may have thought some of them before. Paz's rather meandering habits of mind here correspond to the authentic mystery of his subject: one can only prowl around it, circle its fringes, make occasional intuitive raids. . . .

Certainly here as elsewhere Paz is tempted to simplify, but he resists the temptation remarkably well, and this book is full of fine distinctions. . . . Of Paz's later prose works, only his essays on Duchamp and Lévi-Strauss, and the pages on Breton in *Alternating Current,* have this discreet and luminous intelligence, and we are back where we began. The decline of Paz's prose is the price of being an intellectual in Latin America; of having to talk so much; above all of talking so much in a vacuum, in large, empty, unresponding rooms; of being listened to with servile respect or not being listened to at all. . . .

Oddly enough, Paz, who *believes* in Surrealism, writes very much like Surrealism's antithesis, Paul Valéry, the poet of intricate, debilitating lucidity. Paz puts his faith in love, but devotes his poems to the travails of consciousness. Paz's diction and vocabulary, like Valéry's, are decorous and formal, almost classical. Indeed, Paz's whole work often looks like an extended meditation on Valéry's "*Cimetière marin,*" an offering of the world to the glare of the noonday sun. Yet there is a curious composite effect here. Valéry's Mediterranean landscapes, which are literally taken up by Paz in poems like "Hymn among the Ruins" (set in Naples) and "Ustica" (set in the Sicilian sea), become *Mexican* landscapes too, or at least make miraculously apt analogues for the dry, hot, sun-stricken spaces of the central Mexican plateau. Mexico and the Mediterranean meet in these poems, much as Spanish American and French traditions meet in Paz, and just as Valéry's European bafflement, the predicament of a glittering mind at the end of its tether, joins hands with Paz's Latin American loneliness, his sense of the unreality of everything around him, so that *only* the mind is left, the mirror that devours mirrors.

*Michael Wood, "Dazzling and Dizzying," in* The New York Review of Books *(reprinted with permission from* The New York Review of Books; *© 1974 by NYREV, Inc.), May 16, 1974, pp. 12-16.*

[One] way we ignore South America is by denying it any philosophy, any fund of critical, esthetic or systematic thought—in short, any *wisdom*. Even so vulgar an index as Bartlett's *Familiar Quotations* reflects this neglect by quoting Ortega y Gasset but not Octavio Paz, Yevtushenko but not Neruda. But such wisdom in both its systematic and quotable forms does exist and nowhere more impressively than in the works of Octavio Paz which are a colossal *piñata,* spilling prizes, unexpected and fabulous, stylistic and topical, for any who will crack the books.

(No, not a *piñata,* a *fiesta*—one of Paz's favorite images—where individual aperçus explode brilliantly in throngs of thought.)

At the same time, Paz is cool. He writes as with a diamond-tipped stylus on sheets of clearest crystal and what he writes is incandesced by a lunar imagination streaming in images like moonlight through stained glass: Paz illuminates glowing hues in whatever he writes but always pours through, pure, fine, uncolored by anything but himself.

Like that unpolarized moonlight, whether in poetry or prose, Paz is always inspiring even when not inspired, always novel and always consistent. Sometimes the richness of his production, only partially reflected in [*Early Poems, Alternating Current, Conjunctions and Disjunctions,* and *The Bow and The Lyre*], obscures the dialogue of unity and multiplicity which is both his persona and his theme but any prolonged acquaintance with his work discovers that inhering principle. The title *Conjunctions and Disjunctions,* for example, fits both Paz's general method as well as his specific subject in that book: the differing approaches of East and West to an integrated view of reality expressed in a subtle, erudite choreography of words and notions like Siamese twins: "life with death, sex with spirit, body with soul."

This "binary relation between the *I* and the *Thou*" is again the form and content of the mimetically entitled *Alternating Current,* a small masterpiece of miscellaneous fragments of which Paz writes: "I believe the fragment to be the form that best reflects the ever-changing reality that we live and are. The fragment is not so much a seed as a stray atom that can be defined only by situating it relative to other atoms: it is nothing more nor less than a *relation*. This book is a tissue of relations," so is the best of all Paz's work and *Alternating Current* is among the very best. Ranging over literature, mysticism, eroticism, ethics and politics—with especially charged passages on Cernuda and André Breton—Paz creates a "contrapuntal unity" echoed in his contrary title *The Bow and the Lyre.*

Among these books, *The Bow and the Lyre* is the most ambitious with the least pretense. Here, Paz has worked a poetic of dominion and majesty from sources as diverse as Mallarmé, Whitman and Juan Ramon Jiménez and done it in such a way as to implicate us fully—socially, spiritually and sexually.

The major sections of this book correspond to the phases of that implication. In "The Poem," Paz concentrates on elements of poetry, culminating with imagery containing "many opposite or disparate meanings," which it embraces or reconciles without suppressing, thus providing "the key to the human condition"—just as Paz does. In the second section, "The Poetic Revelation," Paz links the poetic with the sacred by means of wonder which inspires man: "he poetizes, loves, divinizes" under its spell. In the third, "Poetry and History," Paz argues that "man's true history is the history of his images: mythology" and explains surrealism as the poetic attempt to ground society on a poetic, imagistic and, thus, a liberated basis correspondent to a world view. Surrealism, he recognizes, failed and in a section of his epilogue, Paz looks back to the Aztecs whose works of art were literally their religion. . . . In this backward glance, Paz returns us to his originating notion of the image as synthesizing without suppressing. Similarly, we see that Paz's own work fully lives up to his definition of the image in "The Poem" so that his own critique is also his best example.

I say that not forgetting Paz's many poems. . . . Paz is a very good poet but by the measure of his own prose he is not a great one. Yet that judgment in itself is a disjunction. When I view the coolness in his "dialogues of transparencies" as disassociation *toward* sensibility, then I see Paz's verse as the negative charge to his positive prose, his essays as the poetry of prose.

Either way—as well as both—Paz is a great writer who has determined a great subject—*relation*: the universal, existential—and a perfectly adjusted means for expressing that subject—conjunctive units of imagery and grammatical parallelism. If at times you get impatient with his subject or his representation, his praise of the East, his pairs of tugging doubles, you should remember, rephrasing what Hugh Kenner said of G. K. Chesterton, that Paz is not a great writer because he is important; Octavio Paz is a great writer because he is right.

*Ronald Christ, in* Commonweal *(reprinted by permission of Commonweal Publishing Co., Inc.), May 31, 1974, pp. 316-17.*

Though [*The Bow and the Lyre*] is not a new book (the first edition, in Spanish, appeared in Mexico in 1955), it is a book so timeless and so profound that it will always be new. The subtitles read: "The Poem. The Poetic Revelation. Poetry and History," topics inexhaustible to thought, modified by the appearance of each new poet, forever provisional, and forever readdressed. These are "solitary thinkings, such as dodge/Conception to the very bourne of heaven," appearing as aphorism, epigram and prophecy as well as exposition and argument. The torrent of Paz's writing claims assent by passion; the book has the indisputable truth of testimony, and whatever its serviceability as a generalized poetic, it is unquestionably one of the strongest and most eloquent diaries of the poetic process in our century. . . .

Poems are, says Paz, expressions of something lived and suffered; that conviction is balanced by the equal conviction of the peculiarity and opacity of the poetic medium; together, these beliefs ensure that Paz's work is neither an argument for the direct transcription of experience, nor a defense of specious hermeticism. The indispensable participation of the reader, by which the instant of creation is recreated, is not forgotten either, and is in fact raised by Paz to the level of coordinate reincarnation of experience. . . .

For Paz, poetry is a brink, a precipice, an abyss, where, silent before a void, the poet leaves historical time to reenter the time of desire, a time always within us, for which our myths of the Golden Age are only a representation. That entry, made through abandon of props, supports, defenses and hesitations alike, is as accessible, at least in a secondary sense, to the reader as to the poet. In this entry, the rhythm and flow of life are present and sustained, but in a rhythm formed by yearning rather than by fact, a rhythm not describable in the short titles of meters but rather comparable with the long cyclical undulations by which biological movements rise, extend themselves and subside. . . .

The poet's utterance transmutes man and converts him in turn into an image, as Paz's brilliant formulation has it; man himself becomes a space where opposites fuse. In this passage lies the heart of Paz's poetics.

*Helen Vendler, in* The New York Times Book Review *(© 1974 by The New York Times Company; reprinted by permission), June 30, 1974, pp. 23-4, 26.*

Two dovetailed theses [in *Children of the Mire*]: the "creative self-destruction" of modernity, and its dissolution in mass democratic divinations of "the unalterable principle that is the root of change." On the second Paz is hasty, too brief, unpinned. On the first, however, he writes with such lucid density, such dialectical panache, such agreement of scope and precision, such *flings* of the hooks of reference, that his book is an instant classic. There is nothing to compare with it in modern poetry in the Western world—a poetry that, whether Anglo-American, French, German or Hispanic (and this worldly Mexican is fresh and expert on all these and more) is, as Paz says, "one." *Children of the Mire* reveals how high the subject of poetry can rise on the wave of an immense human culture. . . .

Graciela Palau de Nemes, surveying modern Hispanic poetry from Jiménez to the present, concludes that Paz climaxes the gradual rebellion against ancient Spanish morbidity. At home, then, his erotic mysticism may seem new and necessary indeed, though to us it has the thud of Lawrence all over again.

However that may be, where most of *Children of the Mire* has a lookout of breathtaking universality, the conclusion seems to pour from the Romantic steam bath of Paz's *Early Poems*.

This last . . . is a needed complement to . . . *Configurations,* with its later and still better work. Here are the first short pieces in all their weakness of relation, their random piercing beauty; here the first surging long poems, attempting to be, like a river, "a long word that never ends."

And here, it must be said—though the voices in *The Perpetual Present* seem to conspire not to say it—is too willed a Romanticism, however refreshing in a land where the hot wounded days creep "along the length of time" and never finish "with dying." ". . . Let . . . the poem be an implacable radiance that advances/and may the soul be the blackened grass after fire. . . ." Could any poem live up to this? Paz, in mid-poem, will abruptly declare himself out of time, at the "source." But can words reach us from there? Paz never seems to say what he does *not* know. His Romanticism is as direct as a lesson.

Still he is great enough, in his own terms, to show his fissures. He leaps into Romanticism from a conscious void. "Here we are not who are not," he says, envying "a flock of trees drinking at the stream," trees "all there." Paz is Romantic partly in open defiance of the blood "that goes and comes," that "says nothing and carries me with it."

In sum, at his most complete Paz himself represents the modern "dialogue"—Romanticism pursuing the mystical seed puff that jumps away precisely *because* the hand reaches for it; Modernism in its sour irony, its days that never finish with dying.

*Calvin Bedient, in* The New Republic *(reprinted by permission of* The New Republic; *© 1974 by The New Republic, Inc.), July 27 & August 3, 1974, pp. 23-4.*

* * *

## PERSE, St.-John (pseudonym of [Marie-René] Alexis Saint-Léger Léger) 1887-

**Perse, a French poet, won the Nobel Prize for Literature in 1960. He is best known for *Exile* and *Seamarks*. (See also *Contemporary Authors*, Vols. 13-14.)**

Perse composes poems which rely almost as much on their sonorous music as on their, literally, farfetched imagery for a bizarre effectiveness. His adopted name is a key to the character of his poetry, carrying as it does associations with the desert, with the hermit's diet or the fragrance of sherbets in a Persian rose garden and the whiff of sweat and leather from a Persian mount after a lion hunt. And, since "la déesse aux yeux perses," the goddess of the blue-green eyes, was Athene, perhaps the name also suggests wisdom.

*Babette Deutsch, in her* Poetry in Our Time *(copyright by Babette Deutsch), Doubleday, revised edition, 1963, pp. 187-88.*

Saint-John Perse's unexpected collaboration with Braque [*Birds*] began as a poetic meditation on birds and turned into a poem about space and the rapture of the poet. Exile, migrant and navigator of the air, Perse's bird, like the rhapsodist, brings the seasons together. His allegiance to life and to nature is that of the ascetic. Launched on his wings, doubly loyal to air and land, he liberates himself from the "tragic shores of the real," only to reaffirm, through the austerity of flight, a sense of peace and unity achieved at the very frontiers of man. He is a "prince of ubiquity," a creator of his own flight.

The *topos* of the bird is one of the richest and most elusive in Western literature. Soarer of apocalypse or of lyric ecstasy, warbler of songs or predatory circler of the upper spheres, the avian creature has been, in turn, symbol of freedom, pride, creative fancy and Icarian ambition. To the imprisoned spirit it meant freedom and movement. To the spiritually oppressed it represented elation and escape. . . .

Partly a votive poem, partly an *oeuvre de circonstance* (an almost unique occurrence in Perse's production), *Birds* curiously combines impressionistic-essayistic meditations with authentic lyricism. By coincidence, Braque and Saint-John Perse, who came to like and respect each other, were both at work on the bird motif. For his projected series of plates, *L'Ordre des oiseaux,* Braque had chosen an epigraph from Perse's *Amers* (*Seamarks*). When they agreed to collaborate on a de-luxe album, the poet's own text developed, partly at least, into a meditation on Braque's avian order. . . .

[The] themes of space, movement, migration have been permanent themes in Perse's work, ever since *Anabase,* and even earlier in his Antillean poems. The very word *anabasis* suggests, in the original Greek, expedition, travel and adventure, as well as ascension. This exploration is that of the spirit, but it is conceived first of all in topophilic terms: ". . . o seekers, o finders of reasons to move elsewhere. . . ." Roger Caillois, in *Poétique de St.-John Perse,* describes the poet's creation as a "universe of extreme exile." Years later, in his Nobel prize acceptance speech, Perse himself seemed to confirm the notion of a spiritual quest translated into spatial terms. The "great adventure of the poetic spirit" was in his mind related to the "expansion in the moral infinite" of man. It is only appropriate that the Nobel Prize citation should have stressed the "soaring flight" of Perse's poetry. The very titles of his works (*Winds, Rains, Exile, Snows, Seamarks*) suggest the drama of elemental forces played out in space, as well as the proud isolation of man communing with these forces, and, through them, with other men.

The relationship between love and space has perhaps never been more beautifully sung than in Perse's long sea-poem, *Amers* (*Seamarks*). . . . There is in Perse's work, a noticeable freedom from Christian beliefs and from the themes of sin. But more significant than this aloofness from Christian anguish or Christian commitment is the positive mystic bond which Perse repeatedly establishes between the private and the universal. He himself, in a commentary on *Amers,* clearly stated his desire to bring into focus the integrity of man as well as his taste for the divine. He chose the sea because this "reservoir of the eternal forces" symbolically represents the fulfillment and the surpassing of himself by man. A choric ode within a dramatic framework, *Amers* proclaims a magnificent solidarity with life. But it does so at the level of individual destiny and individual joy. . . .

Perse is endowed with a voice at once intensely personal, representative of modern trends, and utterly independent vis-à-vis current fashions and practices. Exploiter of etymologies, grand master of the ellipsis and the homologue, conjurer of immense and mobile images to which his prosody is the servant, Perse shuns ambiguities, ironies and the precious games of the esthete. The enormous extension and specialization of his vocabulary are often baffling; the ceremonial tone of his free verse is at times awesome. But there is no hermetic impulse here. Syntax itself plays a humble part. What matters is the substantive: the palpable reality of the world.

Compared with his highest achievements (*Anabase, Poème á l'Etrangère, Amers*), Perse's bird-poem seems to come a little short of greatness. Wavering between the poetic essay and the lyrical meditation, it occasionally even lapses into the didactic. . . .

The thematic texture is opulent; the boldness of the images and their intricate resonances remain as admirable as in some of the exemplary works. Love of the life-principle and of individual vitality are streamlined by graceful flight and by an almost spiritual luminosity. . . .

Nautical similes and metaphors have their place in most of Perse's poetry; they are exploited with singular appropriateness in *Birds*. . . . Perse is a master of technical terms. But he is also a master of grandiose and even somber images. . .

*Victor Brombert, "Perse's Avian Order," in* The Hudson Review *(copyright 1966 by The Hudson Review, Inc.; reprinted by permission), Vol. XIX, No. 3, Autumn, 1966, pp. 494-97.*

St.-John Perse is a poet who is not only highly original and modern but who is so in so original a way that those in pursuit of some avant-garde may fail to see how new and how strong a synthesis his imagination has created. One . . . example of his characteristic and inimitable beauty, precision, complexity, and contemporaneity I give in English:

"At the hypnotic point of an immense eye inhabited by the painter, like the very eye of the cyclone on its course—all things referred to their distant causes and all fires crossing —there is unity at last renewed and diversity reconciled. After such and so long a consummation of flight, behold the great round of birds painted on the zodiacal wheel and the gathering of an entire family of wings in the yellow wind, like one vast propeller hunting its blades."

This superb image is even more powerful in French; "renewed" is an imprecise translation of "renoué," which means literally reknitted, the ends as it were retied. Nor am I happy about the propeller "hunting" its blades, though at first sight it is impressive and powerful; is not "en quête de ses pales" rather "in quest of"? This would seem nearer to the suggestion of a reassembling of parts into the whole which they compose than the image of hunting, with its implicit duality of hunter and hunted.

*Kathleen Raine, "St.-John Perse's 'Birds'," in* The Southern Review, *Vol. III, No. 1, Winter, 1967, pp. 255-61.*

The pseudonym St.-John Perse was meant partly to force his work to stand on its own, and perhaps it does, but I think it stands firmer when you know the hard and willful statesman Alexis Saint-Leger is behind it, guaranteeing the reality of many of its tones and attitudes, which otherwise could seem a retarded kind of posturing. In America, for example, where anything like a feudal culture or a courtly culture is a regional ruin at best, a poet who took up an aristocratic manner and made as much of rank and ceremony, of ritual and blazonry, as Perse does, would seem only pretentious, and pretending to something silly at that. The attitudes in Perse may be exotic to us, and unsympathetic, but they are real and not to be dismissed lightly. What *panache* there is to them is a native and recurrent French thing. And of course they beautifully serve his epic manner.

His work, or the sequence of considerable works taken together—*Anabasis, Exile, Rains, Snows, Winds, Seamarks, Chronique, Birds*—is, like the Divine Comedy, not really an epic. An epic has to have a story, preferably dramatic, at least one good battle and several heroes at odds with each other. Perse's work has several properties of the epic—elevation, rapidity, a certain ferocity, and a wonderful imagination of space and movement—but his essential form is rather the dithyramb or Dionysiac hymn. . . .

Though it is not the Christian God which sustains his work (to the annoyance of Claudel), something reasonably divine does, what he calls Universal Being. It might be a dead end, but it is more essentially the source of movement, if not movement itself, manifesting itself in the movements of the elements, especially in waves, but also in the Winds, Rains, Snows, of his titles. For Perse poetry too is first of all movement, and the movement of his verse follows as closely as it can the movement of the elements, so there is a sort of ritual communion with a divine essence, even a kind of identification of the celebrant with his god, in a dance and trance, as in Dionysiac ritual. For us in America I think the high and wide movement is intoxicating, at least the most vivid pleasure his work affords, but it is also sacred and often expressed in a hieratic language, and that is rather a nuisance. . . .

The movement, the essential, one can take straight, and also the constantly varying and detailed imagery which is propelled by it and made dynamic. Almost everything in Perse travels, be it the nomadic or exiled heroes, the winds and rains, or the plants, which do more than sit there and grow—they disseminate themselves incredibly on the winds. . . . Perse's eye for telling touches of color and for curious or intricate shapes is very fine, and so is his sense of surfaces, consistencies, and materials, from feathers to castiron, from mucus to sand. The sensuality of the poems is tropical, and again quite natural, after a childhood in Guadaloupe.

It puts him in accord with our current dogma of concreteness and specificity, indeed he himself has spoken sharply against abstractions; but his work is full of abstractions both implicit and overt, some of them rather forbidding. . . .

His fondness for scientific terms, precise, rare, and exotic to the standard literary vocabulary, is as much a wish to classify as to particularize. If I were what he indiscriminately calls an Anglo-Saxon I should be happy to retort that his career as a diplomat has taken its toll, and that he sees the universe from the point of view of Administration, which has to deal in ranks, types, functions, abstractions, and Credit, as well as in funds and back files of precise Information. . . .

What is most engaging in Perse's work is not so much its elevation as its openness and expansiveness, its unrelenting sense of the frontier, geographical frontiers, but also the frontiers of human thought, or of "the human". And all of it in movement. This Whitmanesque side of him, which is large, I find congenial; the Dantesque side, with the chivalry, the scholasticism, and the "imperious" manner, I do not.

*Donald Sutherland, "Le Haut et Le Pur," in* Parnassus, *Fall/Winter, 1972, pp. 47-56.*

There is no doubt that [*Anabase*] broke new ground in the field of poetic technique. It is epic in length and subject yet lacks the clear narrative element normal in the epic. It is lyric in its attention to the details of the interrelation of sound and sense and in the personal involvement of the poet. It is dramatic in its clear characterisation and use of snatches of dialogue, a great moving fresco against a desert backcloth. Its sometimes stark juxtapositions of statements leave out what epic would indulge in the shape of extended similes, explanations and digressions. It is like a kaleidoscope in that the material does not change but the patterns and textures do, elements being related not so much by tangible material as by imaginative leaps. It is like a film in that the movement of characters, complete with dialogue and gesture, through clearly coloured archetypal spaces is always with us. It is a distillation of epic, and as such it is interesting to note that the first version was four times the length of the published one. Despite its considerable length, it is a poem of concision and ellipsis, not of expansion and dilution, and this is a principle which remains true of all Perse's subsequent poetry. What is more, it escapes from known subject-matter, traditionally drawn for the epic from Classical and Christian mythology or from history, to become a pure imaginative creation, not derivative in any direct way though not so rashly independent as to refuse echoes of past cultures. It is pagan and timeless, an archetype creating its own mythology, and as such one of the most remarkable poems of this century.

As often happens with such pioneering work, not everything is perfect, and it remains true that *Anabase* is somewhat lacking in simplicity of approach as well as of vocabulary. The notion of Perse's aloofness stems partly from this poem, and not even the deep human sympathy enlisted by *Exil* has fully dispelled the legend. (pp. 20-1)

Although the [four] separate poems [of *Exil*] may be read quite independently, they are all inter-related through the common theme of exile and through their treatment in indirect or symbolic form of Perse's renewed exploration of man's eternal solitude and of the sources of poetic inspiration. (p. 21)

It is sometimes difficult, when reading Perse's prose, to say that it is not poetry. Putting *Oiseaux* and 'Pour Dante' in separate categories . . . depends on a partly arbitrary decision. Could not the first have been subtitled 'Discours' and the second 'Méditation poétique' instead of the other way round? The style of both is similar: incantatory even if the argument is clear, dangerously near the over-rhetorical, magisterial in avoiding turgidity by sheer density of texture. (p. 65)

One cannot stress enough how completely faithful Perse is to the concrete data which form the basis of his imagery. They are never debased or denatured, and as he said . . . the more daring the poet's explorations, the more concrete must be his imagery. It is a sure guard against abstraction and in no way limits the scope or import of the work. (p. 110)

It is all the stranger therefore to find Perse charged by some critics with verbalism, with being too 'literary'. Yet the rare quotations he borrows from other writers are thoroughly assimilated. Of all modern poets, he, like Rimbaud, most invites one outside into the fresh air away from books, encourages one's powers of observation and enjoyment. His pleasure includes language—one would expect no less from a poet—but it is hardly fair to criticise a writer for knowing his craft. It seems to be the Symbolists' deprecation of 'littérature' and the subsequent babel of writers using literature to their own religious, political or other extra-literary ends that has created the confusion in readers' minds. For the poet, there is only one possible 'engagement', and that is to poetry. Literature is literary as water is wet. (pp. 110-11)

His commitment to language is seen not only in his breadth of vocabulary, textural techniques and philological interests but also in the way language takes its legitimate part in the imagery of the poems. Although poets have been known to concretise linguistic phenomena sporadically—Hugo and Baudelaire are cases in point—Perse makes them an integral and consistent part of his structures. They play an important role in fusing the various ingredients of poetic creation: the poet himself, his subject—its concrete existence and metaphysical implications—and his means of expression. Beyond the musical qualities of language lies a whole philosophy of its function as yet another barrier to be converted by the poet into a threshold. It is the fullest means of communication at man's disposal and its purity is therefore imperative if confusion is not to ensue. At the same time, it is paradoxically our most complete and subtle tool for exploring the ineffable unless the experience is to remain unshared and sterile. Those critics . . . who choose to assume that Perse plays emptily with words, that his rhetoric is verbosity and that where they do not understand a word it must be a wilful neologism could not be further from the truth. For even where, as happens on occasions in *Amers,* there are somewhat baroque volutes in the writing, they are expressive of the sea's magniloquent currents. Every word is appropriate to the theme in hand. Contrary to all appearances, Perse's poetry is spareness itself. . . . Everything in Perse is fined down to essentials, and the essential questions—those which ultimately have no answer—are posed. It is the *intensity* more than anything that holds problems for the reader. (pp. 111-12)

Beyond the contingencies of time and place, Perse seeks those values which endure. In his poems he suggests an order to which some will respond, not simply grasping at straws in the chaos of modern life, but seeking in their turn an ultimate reality which does not depend on belief in denominational orthodoxies. He offers at the same time a heartening sense of delight in things as they are—in natural phenomena and the sensual pleasure of being more alive to them. His joy is matched by an equal feeling for language: he bears an equally high sense of loyalty to the world and to the word. (pp. 113-14)

*Roger Little, in his* Saint-John Perse, *Athlone, 1973.*

* * *

## PIÑERO, Miguel 1947?-

**Piñero, a Puerto Rican, based his play "Short Eyes" on his own experience in Sing Sing prison.**

Pinero, as he himself admitted, was not a realist, but he is not a proficient artificialist either. His characters have no originality, no wit, and no comic consistency (as opposed to repetitiveness).

*Perry Pontac, in* Plays and Players, *December, 1973, p. 57.*

Pinero, for all the awkwardnesses of the script [of *Short Eyes*], hasn't come to this work out of a *theory* about theatre but out of his blood. . . . "Short Eyes" could do with subtler aesthetics, but it has a moral intelligence that makes its addicts, killers, and child rapists more than gratuitous shockers in another prison drama. Its intelligence tells us we can't simply watch.

*Arthur Sainer, in* The Village Voice *(reprinted by permission of* The Village Voice; *© 1974 by The Village Voice, Inc.), January 10, 1974, p. 55.*

According to playwright Miguel Pinero, "Short Eyes" is the term prison inmates use for a sex offender. As it's also used in his play to refer to anything sexual—pornographic novels are called "short-eyes books"—I would guess the term comes from the proverbial narrowing of a man's gaze when he focuses on a sexual object. And that, indeed, is what the play "Short Eyes" is about. When a suspected child molester is placed among a group of prisoners, their disgust for his crime makes them classify him as sexual "stuff," and the possible rapist becomes the potential rapee, a fact which summons up a goodly number of interlocking ironies about the "solidarity" of prison inmates, their sexual Puritanism, the way their classifications of each other mirror and distort the society outside, and so on.

Although Pinero ultimately pushes the irony too far, in a "surprise" epilogue whose reversal recalls "The Caine Mutiny" switcheroo, it's precisely his capacity for perceiving the ironic components of the situation that gives "Short Eyes" shape and interest, and makes me believe that we have here a playwright, and not just an earnest ex-con who's put his little bit of prison truth into a sentimental plea for compassion in the theatre. Even his mistakes, which mostly center on the alleged sex offender and his position in the play's structure, are the mistakes of someone struggling to see the world whole and put it in the shape of art, instead of whining about what a rotten time he had in stir. So I recommend "Short Eyes" as a flawed but powerful *play,* and, if you're up for a message instead, the "scorching anger" and "searing indictment," etc., that are the locus of most of the newspaper excitement over the work, can be derived very easily from the program bios of the ex-prisoner-actors, where you may read the grim details of the social contract America makes its lower classes sign. . . .

[The] message of the program notes, however, is only a starting point for the thought process behind "Short Eyes," and an ex-prisoner who can push himself that far up from the simple message on his first try is likely to have a few more plays to give us. And we may expect that on future outings he will be able to avoid the technical sandtrap into which the Epilogue of "Short Eyes" has thrown him.

That sandtrap is a real lesson in the way the structure of a play can overpower the "meaning" of the words spoken. In the first act of the play, the sex offender—a young white man who is Pinero's one awkwardly realized character—is left alone in the prison dayroom with the group's sympathetic sage, and pours out an elaborate confession about his compulsion for and sexual experiences with little girls. Later, when the others badger him about his tendencies, the confessor attempts to defend him, saying "he's a sick man, leave him alone." Still later, when the badgering has led to the molester's murder, the captain of the prison guard scourges the convicts with the news that their victim had not been identified by the child in the case and was arrested by mistake. But the confessor and the audience know better—or do they? At first I took this ending to be a final irony: the prisoners have done society a service by disposing of someone much worse than themselves, but if they admit to it their own sentences will be redoubled, because outside law takes no notice of prison law, even though its values in such cases are similar.

But the way the reversal is brought in discredits, as epilogues will, not the messenger who brings it, but his hearers. If Davis (the molester) was innocent, the prisoners have committed a crime against their own code as well as the law's. But then what is his confession—hysteria, psychopathic lying, desperation fantasy, a ploy to arouse sympathy? The flaccid, narrative-prosy writing of the confession (the weak spot in otherwise crisp and pungent dialogue), with lines like "weeks passed without a confrontation," only confuses the issue more—is it the character's fumbling prosiness, or the playwright's? The ambiguity very neatly turns the play's straightforwardness into confusion, and cuts off our empathy and understanding just where they should peak.

Still, Mr. Pinero has done well by the bulk of his play, and in a way that leads one to expect more and better work of him.

*Michael Feingold, "Wide View from Narrowed Eyes," in* The Village Voice *(reprinted by permission of* The Village Voice; *© 1974 by The Village Voice, Inc.), March 28, 1974, p. 68.*

*Short Eyes* . . . is a prison play. Its author Miguel Piñero is a 27-year-old Puerto Rican who has served time in Sing Sing. . . . This background lends *Short Eyes* positive advantages as a documentary. It is impossible to deny the circumstantial truth of the presentation. We witness the behavior of a collection of men in the day room of one of the floors in a House of Detention, gathered there during the pretrial period. . . .

The picture is one of people restricted by poverty, ignorance, disease and social corruption, through which one perceives traces of the originally healthy fiber. There are gleams of grim humor, of native imagination as well as viciousness. As information, all this is surely of moment, the matter from which we may learn much to which we ought to pay more attention than we have in the past. It is also stuff from which art may be made. But though it stirs our consciousness and thus is more than commendable, *Short Eyes* is not a "marvelous play," as one reviewer has called it. It does not sufficiently transcend its material to achieve wider human significance.

*Harold Clurman, in* The Nation, *April 6, 1974, p. 445.*

"Short Eyes" is an astonishing work, full of electrifying exuberance and instinctive theatricality. While it won't vie with Somerset Maugham or Terence Rattigan in an anthology of "well-made" plays, "Short Eyes" needs absolutely no apology—it isn't occupational therapy and it isn't a freak show; it's an authentic, powerful theatrical piece that tells you more about the anti-universe of prison life than any play outside the work of Jean Genet. . . .

"Short Eyes" portrays the tragicomedy of people festering in prison like bread being baked in a malfunctioning oven. The young convicts—heisters, muggers, druggies, whatever—act out a violent and ironic parody of straight society, complete with its racism, its conflicting codes, its moralities that are hard to tell from corruptions. For the cons the supreme sin is to be a "short eyes"—a sexual molester of children. On this one point everyone—black, white, Puerto Rican, Muslim fanatic and tough Irish Catholic—all come together, and the short eyes gets the book thrown at him, from ostracism to the indignity of being dunked in the toilet to a final act of terrible "justice."

The brilliance of the play is to show these violent young men instinctively reaching for a balance of personal expression and communal structure. It isn't easy to show the paradox of destructive impulses that want to be creative ones, but "Short Eyes" does this better than most "straight" works, especially in a number of powerful and hilarious set pieces, stunningly performed.

*Jack Kroll, "In the Oven," in* Newsweek *(copyright Newsweek, Inc., 1974; reprinted by permission), April 8, 1974, p. 81.*

There's some temptation to hate yourself at a play like *Short Eyes*. Here is a drama cut right out of some urgent social troubles of our time, performed by people (for the most part) who know firsthand what they are talking about. And yet, within the framework of an art, it's defective—even a trifle boring. Occasionally you feel a twinge of conscience for not capitulating to it. But no. At the last, no: if it was worth doing in the theater, then the theater is worth something; and theatrically *Short Eyes* is flawed. . . .

The writing of the play is schizoid. The banter, teasing, homosexual play and fights are pungent, vital. They give the impression of extemporizations that have been taped and preserved, according to a scenario, rather than of dialogue written and memorized. In clumsy contrast are such passages as Davis' long confessional narrative and the examination of the prisoners by an officer, which were written on a rusty typewriter. . . .

One critic said that attention wanders at *Short Eyes* because the audience is busy testing out the characters' emotions in themselves. Odd how infrequently that sort of wandering occurs at *Oedipus Rex*. My attention wandered because I had faced these emotions, in these renderings, so often before—on TV, in the press, on film and in other plays. The hard, admittedly cold truth is that people who get in trouble and suffer, like people who fall in love, tend to think that because it affected them so drastically, it will automatically interest others. Once the facts are familiar—and Piñero's facts are by now very familiar—only the telling can be interesting. And Piñero hasn't much skill in telling.

There *is* a strong irony in his play, but I'm not convinced that he's aware of it. These prisoners very badly need some sort of superiority. The "short eyes" gives it to them, in a surge that floods across their racial and personal differences. But the inhumanity they then practice toward their "inferior" is simply an extension of the very inhumanity, the social cruelty, that put them here in the first place. So, fundamentally, they are their own persecutors.

Because this underlying truth is left muzzy, because Piñero relies so naively on facts that have by now lost their shock value, the viewer soon conquers his impatience with himself at not being overwhelmed by the play.

*Stanley Kauffmann, in* The New Republic *(reprinted by permission of* The New Republic; *© 1974 The New Republic, Inc.), April 20, 1974, p. 20.*

* * *

## PIRSIG, Robert M. 1928-

**Pirsig, an American, wrote *Zen and the Art of Motorcycle Maintenance*.**

"Zen and the Art of Motorcycle Maintenance: An Inquiry Into Values," by Robert M. Pirsig . . ., is as willfully awkward as its title. It is densely put together. It lurches, with a deliberate shift of its grave ballast, between fiction and philosophic discourse, between a private memoir and the formulaic impersonality of an engineering or trade journal. As it stands, it is a very long book, but report has it, and fault lines indicate, that a much longer text lies behind it. . . . "Zen and the Art" is awkward both to live with and to write about. It lodges in the mind as few recent novels have, deepening its grip, compelling the landscape into unexpected planes of order and menace.

The narrative thread is deceptively trite. Father and son are on a motorcycle holiday, travelling from Minneapolis toward the Dakotas, then across the mountains, turning south to Santa Rosa and the Bay. . . .

A largesse of symbols, allusions, archetypes so spendthrift, so palpable, that only a great imaginer, shaping his material out of integral need, could afford it. A more professional contriver would have excised, he would have made his mythologies oblique, he would have felt embarrassed at the obviousness of the symbols offered. Mr. Pirsig allows himself a certain broad innocence. Everything is animate at the surface, contoured, casting exact shadows, as in the snowscape of an American primitive. Because the underlying design is covert and original to a degree.

Pirsig's work is, like so much of classic American literature, Manichaean. It is formed of dualities, binary oppositions, presences, values, codes of utterance in conflict. Father against son; the architectures of the mind against those of the machine; a modernity of speed, uniformity, and consumption (of fuel, of space, of political gimmicks) against conservancy, against the patience of true thought. But these confrontations are themselves ambiguous; they keep us off balance and straining for poise as do the swerves of the motorcycle.

Phaedrus is hunting the narrator. He is, at one level, the secret sharer, the intense questioner, the compaction of pure intellect. He has sprung directly out of the Plato dialogue that carries his name, and the device of having a living being pursued by a shadow out of Plato is by itself enough to certify Pirsig's strength, his mastery over the reader. But the chase is, to be sure, internal. . . .

The westward journey is punctuated by lengthy meditations and lay sermons that Pirsig calls "Chautauquas." They are basic to his purpose. During these addresses to the reader, Phaedrus's insinuations are registered and diagnosed. The nature of quality, in conduct as in engineering, is debated and tested against the pragmatic shoddiness of a consumer society. Much of this discursive argument, the "inquiry into values," is finely shaped. But there are pedestrian stretches, potted summaries of Kant which betray the aggressive certitudes of the self-taught man, misattributions (it was not Coleridge but Goethe who divided rational humanity into Platonists and Aristotelians), tatters out of a Great Books seminar to which the narrator once took bitter exception. The cracker-barrel voice grinds on, sententious and flat. But the book is inspired, original enough to impel us across gray patches. And as the mountains gentle toward the sea—with father and child locked in a ghostly grip—the narrative tact, the perfect economy of effect, defy criticism.

A detailed technical treatise on the tools, on the routines, on the metaphysics of a specialized skill; the legend of a great hunt after identity, after the salvation of mind and soul out of obsession, the hunter being hunted; a fiction repeatedly interrupted by, enmeshed with, a lengthy meditation on the ironic and tragic singularities of American man—the analogies with "Moby Dick" are patent. Robert Pirsig invites the prodigious comparison. It is at many points, including, even, the almost complete absence of women, suitable. What more can one say?

*George Steiner, "Uneasy Rider" (abridged with permission), in* The New Yorker, *April 15, 1974, pp. 147-50.*

From its title—which sounds freaky and pretentious, but is apt and perfectly serious—to its shattering final pages, Robert Pirsig's [*Zen and the Art of Motorcycle Maintenance: An Inquiry Into Values*] is extraordinary. It's a sort of autobiography, cast in the form of a motorcycle journey from Minneapolis across the Central Plains to the Dakotas, through the Rockies to the Pacific Coast. . . .

The shifts from exterior landscape to the slippery crevasses of the haunted narrator's interior life are usually brilliantly managed. In the later chapters, Pirsig does sometimes lapse into a Village Explainer, recapitulating Kant, Poincaré or Zen teachings with an autodidact's cumbersome fervor. One willingly endures a certain amount of tedium. The piercing clarity of feeling between father and son lifts the book to majesty.

*Walter Clemons, "Life Cycle," in* Newsweek *(copyright Newsweek, Inc., 1974; reprinted by permission), April 29, 1974, pp. 95-6.*

[In *Zen and the Art of Motorcycle Maintenance,* what Pirsig] talks about, mostly, is his lifelong compulsion to negotiate a workable intellectual contract with Ultimate Reality.

Actually, it's not the narrator's compulsion, but the compulsion of the man he used to be before all this thinking snapped his mind, and he ended up an incontinent vegetable, sitting on the floor of his Chicago apartment for three days before the court committed him to a hospital. . . .

[*Zen and the Art of Motorcycle Maintenance*] is splendidly lucid. It is even fascinating. Fascinating, at least, if you're the sort of person who got snagged by the old college conundrums such as: "If a tree falls in the woods and there's nobody there to hear it, does it make any noise?"

That sort of thinking has not been fashionable lately. Rationality has been the enemy of the great gestalt march back to Eden. THINK, we remind ourselves, was the motto of the loathed IBM. Thinking made atom bombs and factories. . . .

[This book] not only defends rationality, but insists on it. . . .

It plunges back into the mind-work our civilization is founded on. With all the ferocious energy of naive faith, it gnashes and flails and wrestles with all the anarchic epiphanies of 20th-century science, the Heisenberg-Uncertainty-Principle sort of thing, until the narrator is satisfied that he has expanded rationality to satisfy the needs of technological, quantum-physics man.

*Henry Allen, "Uneasy Rider," in* Book World—The Washington Post (© The Washington Post), *May 19, 1974, pp. 1-2.*

Dear Robert Pirsig,

I write this letter with difficulty, knowing I will not be able to disguise my confusion or my feelings, and fearing that because of this, the things I am clear about may be misunderstood too. You have written a book that in many ways I find honest and true (virtues, for me, slightly more important than artful or intelligent). But happy as I am that you are whole enough to set down the true parts of your book, I am troubled by some of your strategies of artifice—the Thoreauvian touches at the start, the quietly insistent priggishness and the parade (or is it parody?) of textbook techniques. There is also a whispered presumption of larger-than-life insight. Yet I, for one, feel reticent about imputing such presumptuousness to you, even though I find synoptic philosophy, truth-table logic and binary analysis heavily interlarded with those realities that supposedly are meant to assure a workaday existence for the airy vision—the concreteness of the bike and the down-home flavor of the Chautauqua. . . .

There is real anguish in [your book]. You reach us (me, I won't be coy) where it hurts. You're describing that feeling of being out of touch, of things slipping past, of being dead before we know it—and with a lot of regrets for having blown the scene. You explore this time and again in those real encounters between people and people, but why can't you hold the focus in just those human terms? Why the shift from human pain to a dialogue in six philosophic modes? You're making it easy on yourself and easy on your readers, especially those who will enjoy babbling about the Big Ideas in your book. Biker genuinely knows that discussing concepts is easy, but how to feel about them is hard, and how to live with them harder still. . . .

My own life is so far from tranquil that I cannot bring myself to apply the literary analyst's eye-loupe to your creation and show how it all coheres into some metaphysical, multifaceted crystal. It may well be that you are just too clever for me (no irony intended). . . .

I will remember your book indelibly for the way you checked your metric bolts and ran the threads clean with the die; I will remember it because it gave a glimpse of something that saddens me yet I know for truth—how a decent, moral and intelligent man can find more in his machine than in his own flesh and blood to solace himself. But I will forget, as quickly as I can, those abstractions presuming to edify and purporting to share great truths that are like the fine clothes of the naked emperor.

Sincerely,
Dudley Flamm

*Dudley Flamm, "The Manuals Never Tell All You Need to Know," in* New Leader, *May 27, 1974, pp. 15-17.*

Earnest, innocent, awkward, authentic—long on character and short on formal art (but that includes a blessed lack of artfulness)—[*Zen and the Art of Motorcycle Maintenance*] is an ungainly piece of do-it-yourself American Gothic. It is a novel, a travelogue, a quest, a set of lectures, and a secular confession, with some sketchy information on motorcycle maintenance thrown in for good measure. In his subtitle the author describes it as "an inquiry into values," and it's that too. But anything you call it, it's also something else. They may seem silly, but these problems of nomenclature are symptomatic; the book is exasperating and impressive in about equal measure, which is to say greatly. It's a completely heteroclite performance. . . .

As a four-square, feet-on-the-ground thinker, Pirsig leaves us bemused and quizzical; as a teller of stories, he disturbs more than he ingratiates, but the way values now stand, that's all to the good. His work mainly depends on the quality of his writing, and about this I don't think there can be two opinions. He is a stunning writer of fictional prose. With a minimum of apparatus, he can evoke a landscape or intimate a deep sense of uneasiness, allow a mood to evaporate, or touch us with compassion. Yet there's very little overwriting. . . .

Paradoxically, the novel has a sharper line as a stream of sensations than it does as an organized story. Zen and motorcycle maintenance dominate the earlier pages; but they represent the solution to a problem that is defined only in the last part of the book. That leaves them hanging out, so to speak: more like picturesque properties than working components. . . .

The real test of a prickly, rankling book like *ZAAMM* lies in its enduring power to disquiet. One can guess that even if the intense and confused metaphysics should pall (based as they seem to be on feverish interpretations of hastily read books), the wonder and fear of the novel would remain. These are loose, impressionistic words for an effect that grows, not simply out of effect making, but from quiet and deft prose on seemingly impersonal topics.

*Robert M. Adams, "Good Trip," in* The New York Review of Books *(reprinted with permission from* The New York Review of Books; *© 1974 by NYREV, Inc.), June 13, 1974, pp. 22-3.*

[*Zen and the Art of Motorcycle Maintenance*] says nothing practical about choppers, and little more about Zen. But it says plenty about cycles writ large, and implies even more about art—particularly the fiction of the American '70s. *Zen* is a novel in need of maintenance because it chops and grinds its way along, truly humming only at the end—which is part of the point. . . .

Or, perhaps I should begin with Pirsig's ending—"there is a feeling now, that was not here before, and is not just on the surface of things, but penetrates all the way through: We've won it. It's going to get better now. You can sort of tell these things." This remarkable novel is part of the evidence that there is indeed an important new victory making itself felt now, a resurgence rivaling the one that seized America in the middle of the last century. Ideas in the outdoors: we haven't seen anything like it since Melville. If Melville and his contemporaries worried about the machine in the garden, Pirsig is one of many writers now worried about slipping the garden back into the machine—art back into artifice, romantic back into classical—and it's a telling moment when Pirsig rebukes Thoreau for "talking to another situation, another time, just discovering the evils of technology rather than discovering the solution. . . . No books can guide us anymore."

Not unlike Thoreau's and Melville's books, nevertheless, Pirsig's novel is by turns exasperating and profoundly exciting. . . . [The] narrator tells us this book will be [a series of] thoughtful essays, . . . set pieces he calls Chautauquas, "intended to edify and entertain." But this novel is less about edification, besieged as it becomes, than about the relationship of edification to everything else in the world. . . .

There will be a lot of people reading this novel and it may well become an American classic.

*W. T. Lhamon, "A Fine Fiction," in* The New Republic *(reprinted by permission of* The New Republic; *© 1974 The New Republic, Inc.), June 29, 1974, pp. 24-6.*

Mr. Pirsig describes his book as a series of chautauquas. This deliberately anachronistic term evokes an image of a bygone America in the days before radio and television, or for that matter motorcycles, when people assembled in the summer outdoors for two or three days of edifying lectures, concerts, and recreation. In large part this is, to the contrary, a repellent and dispiriting work by a not very likable man. If all the speakers on the chautauqua circuit were like the author, it is no wonder the phenomenon has died out.

Perhaps it is true that some books are like thermometers which generalize for us whether the cumulative sicknesses of our society are ebbing or flowing on the fever chart. That is to say, a work that is the opposite of the platitudinizing or moral-cancer-diagnosticating the heads of church and state. *Zen and the Art of Motorcycle Maintenance* is like a thermometer protruding from the anus of America. Reading it is like taking a reading of 106° in the shade. . . .

As Eric Hoffer correctly is quoted as saying in a jacket blurb, Pirsig is a born writer. His technological instructions, whether on computers or motorcycles, are likely accurate, logical, in a way poetic. This is because he has a passion for wanting the reader to understand technology and not run away from it. If there is one valuable lesson in this book it is this: the next time your radio stops working, or your automobile breaks down, try to fix it yourself. Pirsig says the future of America is the machine and it will keep breaking down until we take the Zen approach, look upon the busted radio, in a sense, as ourselves, forbear dropping it off at the repair shop, and learn to fix it. . . .

So there are chautauquas about how to repair a motorcycle, and others again, almost lyrical, on blackbirds and grey skies in Montana, and many more on insanity, the arguments of philosophers from Phaedrus to Hegel on the meaning of quality; and so on. But if the reader is in some ways enlightened, he certainly feels little moral elevation.

What is frightful about Pirsig is his technological hatred for what he calls the Romanticist, by which he means the person who really is unable even to concentrate on reading some simple instructions on, say, how to operate an electric can-opener, or fix a tire. Pirsig has for all practical purposes metaphorized the repair of machines, trivial or complicated, as equivalent to his own rehabilitation into a "sane person." Implicit in the book is a doctrinaire Zen idea that self and thing are identical, which is nonsense.

At the end of the narrative Pirsig sketches a rather ambiguous chautauqua in which the reader is unable to determine whether the author recants, in whole or part, his technological credo or not. Patently he has been treating his son as a machine. It is the relationship of a mechanic with a troublesome set of valves, loving and hating, but above all wanting it to work *right*. . . .

Pirsig has considerable integrity. He is like a forerunner of a new kind of technological intellectual: not just the graduate out of engineering school without the least interest in the humanities; but someone who has learned a great deal about philosophy and literature only to repudiate it, or subsume it to the qualities of the machine.

Perhaps the most "romanticism" is to treat a motorcycle as the self and time as something that can be divided into equal Zen parts. Some things *are* urgent. The self is not always so important—sometimes it is the least important. When the radio falls apart one ought to try to fix it—providing one is not too busy doing something better like trying to read Tolstoy, or make Mozart live again; or, when it comes to that, writing one's own *War and Peace,* or distributing one's goods to the peasants. The invidious and paradoxical thing about Pirsig's vision of technology is that it is concerned only about "values" (the subtitle is "An Inquiry into Values"), not people. And yet the end result is to find oneself the complete egotist: everything is the self. The motorcycle and the rider are equal partners on the long journey towards eternity. The new chautauqua is the motorcycle manual. To misappropriate the words of Katherine Mansfield, if this is the future, then I'm glad I have consumption.

*John Heidenry, in* Commonweal *(reprinted by permission of Commonweal Publishing Co., Inc.), August 23, 1974, pp. 461-62.*

* * *

## PLOMER, William 1903-1973

**Plomer was born in South Africa and lived in Japan and**

**Greece before finally settling in England. Plomer wrote novels, short stories, poems, criticism, librettos, biography, and autobiography. (See also *Contemporary Authors*, Vols. 21-22.)**

William Plomer's first novel, *Turbott Wolfe,* was published in 1926, when he was a very young man. A distinguished poet and autobiographer, he has, one feels, obstinately refused to be a professional novelist. In fiction his best work has lain in the short story, and there his achievement, especially in volumes like *I Speak of Africa* and *A Child of Queen Victoria*, has been remarkable. All the same, his novels cannot be ignored and, taken with the short stories, their influence has been seminal. . . .

Plomer's . . . *Museum Pieces* appeared in 1952, eighteen years after *The Invaders*, It seems to me by far his best, and it springs out of affection, not indignation or hatred. The satirist of the early books has become a humorist.

*Walter Allen, in his* The Modern Novel: In Britain and the United States *(copyright © 1964 by Walter Allen; reprinted by permission of the publishers, E. P. Dutton & Co., Inc.), Dutton, 1964, pp. 197-99 (in the paperbound edition).*

William Plomer was the first South African writer to create a fictional hero (Ula Masondo) out of a migrant native laborer in the gold mines. His novel *Turbott Wolfe* was the first work of fiction to treat miscegenation and race relations from the point of view of political and social protest rather than as a moral shame—the quality with which earlier South African writers had invested them. (p. 208)

The theme of his novel has become an obsession with later South African writers, and *Turbott Wolfe* may be said to be the prototype of the modern liberal protest in fiction against *apartheid.* Here, Plomer deals with two examples of miscegenation: one the unfulfilled passion of Wolfe and the native girl he idealizes; the other the affair between the South African white girl and black radical. One affair ends in consummation; the other achieves nothing more solid than a sigh. It is significant that the white South African girl who marries her black lover is called "Eurafrica" and that she survives in Africa, while Wolfe feels bound to leave it. (p. 209)

Miscegenation in *Turbott Wolfe* is not only condoned—it is encouraged and demanded as a condition of health. "Eurafrica," the union of the two races, is the novel's pervasive image. Today, it is easy enough to understand why *Turbott Wolfe* stimulated much controversy on its first publication. And, because the novel calls for the abolition of the color bar in a violently sexual manner, the book has remained controversial. . . .

Plomer is a novelist of violence because he views the South African scene as an environment of tension and repressed hostility which cannot be altered by quiet good will. It is action, and not sentiment, which affects South Africa in his fiction. I have called him a novelist on the "left" because his fiction represents an attack on the existing social and moral codes of his time. (pp. 210-11)

*Martin Tucker, in his* Africa in Modern Literature: A Survey of Contemporary Writing in English, *Ungar, 1967.*

Among many trad modernists, Mr. Plomer is one of those poets who see the golden age of art and society very evidently *not* in the future. His latest book entitled *Celebrations* finds some of its best subjects in the past: the first London performance of *Cherry Orchard*, a pre-1914 afternoon with the Bloomsbury set in Bedford Square, a Victorian photographic album, an out-moded old lady in a house on a by-pass.

Mr. Plomer's verse exhibits a rare power of historical evocation, not a little of the wisdom of experience, and a bland and versatile sense of diction.

*Derek Stanford, in* Books and Bookmen, *June, 1972, p. 87.*

William Plomer seemed to be made of some absolutely clear, crystalline substance. All his qualities were windblown, sun-saturated, sparkling, and in his writing the language shines and curls like waves animated by a strong breeze on a clear day. In a self-protecting way he was mysterious, guarding the secrets of his singularity against infringement by intimacy no less than by publicity. Yet at the same time he was open, candid, friendly, and a hilarious raconteur. He kept the world of causes and salesmanship at a distance by viewing them all with the same detached irony. He was insulated (no telephone, the barest of small houses in the least inviting of suburbs) and yet to several people—some of whom did not know of the others' existence—he was a life-long friend with an amazing constancy of tolerant affection.

His last poems have all the virtues of his insight and meticulous observation. Some of them are assertions of faith, and without being subjective they are often self-revealing. . . .

Plomer had an impersonal way of stating intense personal affirmation. He can be detached and committed in the same poem, simply by ordering his impressions in a hierarchy of those about which he is more ironic, less ironic, and not ironic at all. . . .

I think that half a dozen poems in [*Celebrations*] are among the best English poems written in the present century. If I am right, it may seem odd that Plomer, while having fans and being generally respected, or patronised, has not been recognised as the maker of unique verbal objects which are peculiarly hard, clear and well-formed. It would not have seemed odd to him. He casts a very cold eye on 'the mad new Establishment/of loud disrespect'.

*Stephen Spender, "A Singular Man," in* New Statesman, *November 9, 1973, p. 690.*

It is a . . . sophisticated pleasure to read William Plomer from beginning to end, but saddening that it is now the end. The love of rhyme (and a rare talent for it), the insight into character and the offhand, sardonic tone: these are in evidence even in the early poems from South Africa and Japan, and by the time of the 'London Ballads' are habitual enough to allow him a grateful relapse into open heartlessness. I like the Hardy parody, and pieces like 'The Heart of a King', so close to comic opera. The historical poems are flexible and ingenious, and he has a fresh and alert way with landscape. But how can it be that one tolerates Plomer's bland comedy of cruelty, the Dorking Thigh and the Flying Bum?

In so many places, the rentier-intellectual's bachelor scorn of petit-bourgeois married comforts strikes an insistently false note. Christ may yet be born in a bungalow, but Plomer is very half-hearted about the notion. Better is a poem like 'Palmyra', where the feeling becomes wistful, the ghost of unfulfilled desire. One laughs at such aperçus as the female Swiss ('waxwork stuffed with cheese'), but deplores his view of female sexuality as something inevitably comic, risking nemesis. This is a precarious and misogynist poetry, with more nervous energy than Betjeman, more flair, more colour, and a fine imagination moving deftly between irritation and amusement.

*John Fuller, in* The Listener, *March 7, 1974, p. 311.*

With engaging briskness and efficiency, the air of a man doing a good job, Plomer was nevertheless misled by the ease with which verse can become "light." . . . Plomer was interested in people. Characters *are* the heart of his matter, though his quite obvious sensationalism is of the macabre sort ("The Flying Bum", "The Dorking Thigh", "Mews Flat Mona" etc.). His last two books moved away from that to a more tender characterisation, just as his earlier poems about his native South Africa must have indicated to his first readers that he might have become a lyrical and descriptive poet on fairly orthodox lines, not a poet of sensational disgruntlement. . . .

In "Tugela River", he allowed his descriptive writing free verse, pressurised by an historical forecast of revolution in South Africa. Even so, "Tugela River", powerful as it is, lacks the density and mysteriousness of a 20th-century classic. Courting clarity with such dedication, Plomer emerges as a poet like Andrew Young in his emphasis on traditional craftsmanship. . . .

[In] Plomer's intensely personal poem "The Umbrella",. . . the verse, its purposiveness, and the obligations it forces on the writer trivialise the urgency of the feeling. Outcomes and decisions are specified *too* clearly; he tells a moralised tale to himself, too consciously ordered as a story. Above all, verse can appear outmoded by the psychology of a poem. It can force categorisation on fluid states of mind, simplifying experience. Plomer's kind of verse manoeuvres back to a verse-world, a story-world, which is not unlike the secret country of [a] bucolic imagination, and certainly not unconnected to a faithfully English view of life, that queerly middle-class English outlook, "commonsensical" but not rational, crafty, with its relish of eccentricity and the grotesque, cruelly dismissive of those who are beyond the pale, despite frequent professions of a liberal humanity.

It may be a mistake to see something so programmatic in Plomer's poems, but the level of life he appears to have opted for is represented by those who inhabit "The Bungalows." The secret country has its counterpart in the secret suburb. These "semi-isolationists", the cabbage their emblem, are seen by Plomer as thankfully unambitious, thankfully contented with all that is ever likely to be granted them. Their attitudes to those who do not live in "unassuming bungalows" is not mentioned, which is characteristic of a political poem which does not realise it is a political poem. . . . Plomer . . . was able, especially in his later poems, to write in freer forms; and it is in such examples of Plomer's sort of care and attention to language that English habits can be found—contemporary and traditional at the same time—which one hopes will be perpetuated in poetry.

*Douglas Dunn, in* Encounter, *September, 1974, pp. 84-5.*

* * *

## POUND, Ezra 1885-1972

**Pound was a major American poet who lived most of his life outside the United States. He was, according to Babette Deutsh, "an alchemist of words, producing, out of the commonest substances, precious metals and life-giving elixirs." He called the *Cantos* a "history of the world" and it is because of those uneven and opaque poems, modulations of his own voice through time and space, that he is now recognized as a major force in the development of modern poetry. (See also *Contemporary Authors*, Vols. 5-8, rev. ed.; obituary, Vols. 37-40.)**

[The *Cantos*] makes greater demands on one's learning and perseverance than any other poem that has ever been written. The reader is expected, for example, to guess at the meaning of quotations and monologues in nine foreign languages: Greek, Latin, Italian, French, Old French, Provençal, Spanish, German, and Chinese (besides one name in Persian script and, in Canto 93, a group of Egyptian hieroglyphs). The reader is also expected to plow his way through many long or obscure works in order to grasp the force and appositeness of the quotations. Some of those works Pound himself found it hard to procure: for example, the letter books of the Venetian foreign office and *The Works of John Adams,* in ten volumes that provide the substance of Cantos 62-71.

In addition to undertaking such studies, the ideal reader—or "suitably sensitized apprehensor," as Mr. Kenner calls him—will make himself as familiar with the details of Pound's literary career as if they were incidents from the *Odyssey.* Even then he will understand many passages only after learning to recognize Pound's friends and minor acquaintances. . . .

[What] about the general notion of writing long poems that can be fully understood only after one has become acquainted with the poet's life, read his correspondence, published or unpublished, and studied all the books he happened to acquire? And what does Pound offer us in return for such labors?

In some ways he offers a great deal; in others, less than we have a right to expect. The *Cantos* does not present "an action of considerable magnitude," as Aristotle said that an epic must do; in fact it presents no action whatever. It does offer hundreds of incidents, all fragmentary, and thousands of separate sharp images, but usually there appears to be no connection between one incident or image and the one that follows. There are names, again by the thousands, but no true characters. Even the hero, who appears under many of the names—as Ulysses, as Hanno the Carthaginian explorer, as Sigismundo Malatesta, and as a number of early American statesmen—is only a series of faceless masks for the poet himself. Emotions are often celebrated or condemned—for example, there is a fine canto in praise of love and part of another in dispraise of pity—but they are seldom or never evoked from the reader. There are no recurrent patterns of meter or rhyme or refrain or strophe to create and satisfy one's expectations. In a poem where everything is freedom and surprise, one expects anything, and nothing at all is truly surprising. . . .

Although Pound's system of rhetoric has not proved effective in persuading any but a few scholarly critics and various members of right-wing groups, it is not something he happened upon by chance or wrongheadedness. It is truly a system, being based upon a theory of knowledge, an epistemology. In philosophical terms Pound is a nominalist, a disciple of Aristotle and Duns Scotus, as well as of Confucius, but one who carries a few of their theories to simplified extremes. He insists that the only genuine knowledge is of separate *things* (including separate actions and sensations). He distrusts all generalities except his own. . . .

Let me present an example of my own. If Pound were asked to define "vegetable," which is a generic term, and if he strictly followed his own method, he would appear with a basketful of onions, beans, lettuce, and cauliflower. Then, fearing that his statement was not sufficiently complete or qualified, he would rush back to the market and reappear with another basket, this time piled with carrots, beets, turnips, and radishes. That is essentially what he calls his "ideogrammic method," and it is the system of rhetoric he follows in the *Cantos*. There his usual means of conveying ideas is by presenting basketsful of disconnected items from the history of various countries, including Italy, China, the United States, medieval England, and the Byzantine Empire. . . .

There are obvious weaknesses in the ideogrammic method when carried to the extreme to which Pound carries it, and one of them is that it abolishes logical thinking. One cannot compare or evaluate statements that consist of vegetables by the basketful or historical items by the gross. One cannot test the statements for consistency with each other. . . .

Then too, if he puts one item after another, isn't he suggesting that the first is the cause or explanation of the second? *Post hoc, ergo propter hoc.* There are examples of this simplest logical fallacy everywhere in the later cantos, as likewise in the political prose of *Impact.* Indeed, the verse and the prose are hard to distinguish, except that the verse is more ideogrammic and harder to read. . . .

I feel no resentment against Pound for presenting this eccentric picture of history. He believes in it as in everything else: his collection of ideas, his ideogrammic method of presenting them, his bold non sequiturs, and his mission of saving the world from usury, war, and bad art. After his years of confinement let him live in peace—and in honor too, for the debt that other poets owe him. The resentment I feel is only against the critics who have been proclaiming that Pound is a genius to set beside Dante and that his endless harangue against the bankers is a poetic masterpiece to be studied in every course in modern literature. There is time in college to study only so many masterpieces. The *Cantos* would have to take the place of something else, perhaps of other modern poetry, perhaps of Wordsworth or Milton. Students might conclude, in their practical way, that poetry was damned nonsense and that critics didn't know what they were talking about.

*Malcolm Cowley, "Pound Reweighed" (originally published in a shorter version in* Reporter, *March 2, 1961), in his* A Many-Windowed-House: Collected Essays on American Writers and American Writing, *edited, with an introduction, by Henry Dan Piper (copyright © 1970 by Southern Illinois University Press; reprinted by permission of Southern Illinois University Press), Carbondale: Southern Illinois University Press, 1970, pp. 178-90.*

Ezra Pound had two very remarkable qualities: he was a poet and, despite his passion for the past, a deeply original one. He was also something rarer than a poet—a catalyst, an impresario, a person who both instinctively understood what the age was about to bring forth and who helped it to be born. We recognise this quality in Apollinaire, in Cocteau, in Diaghilev, in André Breton. . . .

1912 was an important year for Pound. He brought out his fifth book of poems, *Ripostes* (dedicated, incidentally, to William Carlos Williams), in which his authentic voice began to be heard. It is a tone of cool, relaxed dandyism, playing with the forms of the Greek and Latin epigram, yet capable of a deeper magic—as in 'Portrait d'une femme' ('Your mind and you are our Sargasso sea' or 'The Tomb at Akr Çaar', or his bleakly alliterative adaptation of the Anglo-Saxon 'The Seafarer'). . . .

Both Pound and Eliot had a very unusual combination of gifts—revolutionary élan, first-class minds, and a most fastidious and critical ear. One is always surprised by Pound's taste, he is indeed the Catullus (a *gamin* Catullus, wrote a reviewer) of Yeats's 'Scholar' poem which, I fully believe, was intended for him. . . .

The Pound of 'Lustra' is still a minor poet. With *Quia Pauper Amavi* he attains a stature which is worthy of the admiration since bestowed on him. . . . The book consists almost entirely of long poems and includes the first three Cantos and 'Homage to Sextus Propertius'. The Cantos have not yet begun to belch forth huge lumps of prose like a faulty incinerator and include the lovely Elpenor passage paraphrased from Homer, while 'Homage to Sextus Propertius', complete with howlers, grows better at each rereading, a complete identification of one fame-struck, slightly wearying dandy with his dazzling archetype. The passage of time encrusts the howlers with a hoary rightness.

*Cyril Connolly, "The Breakthrough in Modern Verse" (originally published in* The London Magazine*), in his* Previous Convictions *(© 1963), Hamish Hamilton, 1963, pp. 235-51.*

It is nothing new to say that the basis of Ezra Pound's poetics may be seen in the Imagist Movement that Pound himself brought to being in 1912 in London. Yet Imagism remains a somewhat cloudy business. . . . The repetitions about Imagist theory have obscured the fact that the earliest focus of Imagism was on a discipline involving what Pound called "living language" and "presentation," not on any theories of the Image as such. Slightly later the focus shifted to include more theoretical concerns, but the discipline remained the heart of the achievement, yielding poems that employed severe artistic control to make a few words carry a large burden of meaning. This discipline was derived to a significant degree from ideas and attitudes of Pound's good friend, the novelist Ford Madox Hueffer (later Ford Madox Ford). When talking about Hueffer's relation to them, Pound spoke of these ideas as "the prose tradition."

Pound's pre-Imagist poetry lacked this discipline, and his early poetics was a *mélange* of Aestheticism, scientistic "realism," and Browningesque "vigor" that Pound later mocked as "red-blooded." (pp. 3-4)

The "Contemporania" poems indicate that Imagism was first of all an ascetic means of dissolving impurities and of resolving the poem into "straight talk," a classic directness in the accents of contemporary speech. Next they imply a new freedom of attitude, a new unpretentiousness of subject, a new brilliance in the use of himself as *persona*—all taking rise from Pound's desire to bid good-bye to his earlier style, and the postures in which it had involved him. (p. 8)

Pound stopped trying to forge a poetics from Yeatsian ideas, and sought the "hard-edged" quality that Hueffer's doctrines seemed to promise. (p. 17)

Hueffer insisted on the unchanging nature of experience: unless he has the courage to look at and portray life, the modern poet will "never realize that Paolo and Francesca loved and suffered precisely as love and suffer the inhabitants of the flat above him" [*The Critical Attitude*]. This kind of statement did more than make Pound a modernist; it gave him the clue for a new non-derivative way to use his scholarly research into the past, and the idea of an unchanging basis of experience is certainly a key to his later poetry, especially the *Cantos*. (p. 18)

[The] fact is that Imagism was best suited to post-Victorian London, and a few other situations in which reticence is the idiomatic norm. One of these other situations can be found in classical Chinese poetry, of which Pound made good use: in his poetic development, the phase of Imagism proper was followed by a period in which his main concerns were epigrams, *haiku,* and adaptations from Chinese. (p. 31)

Pound was of course in favor of visual quality wherever it helped to achieve definite and precise "presentation," and often praised the visual imaginations of Dante and his other Italian and Provençal favorites. But he never pretended to believe that this was the only proper effect for poetry, and his own poetry even in its most Imagist phase shows no unusual reliance on visual effects or qualities; moreover, he continually warned his group against being "viewy" or "descriptive." The aim of Pound's Imagism was to produce a kind of pattern or structure of insight, to "present a complex instantaneously," and he never proposed to limit the means for such presentation to one sensuous effect. Quite often Pound talked about qualities of poetic form in a vocabulary derived from the plastic arts—"getting an outline," "hard-edgedness," and so on—but the values here were as often tactile as visual, since (as Donald Davie has pointed out [in *Ezra Pound: Poet as Sculptor*] Pound often conceived his art in sculptural terms. (p. 44)

Most critics have thought that [Ernest] Fenollosa's important gift to Pound was the "ideogrammic method," yet Pound's early outbursts of praise for Fenollosa single out not that but Fenollosa's thesis that verbs are the basis of living language [presented in his "Essay on the Chinese Written Character," 1919]. . . . In his view reality is faithfully described only by transitive verbs, for it consists entirely of actions and processes: "A true noun, an isolated thing, does not exist in nature. Things are only the terminal points, or rather the meeting points of actions, cross-sections cut through actions, snap-shots. Neither can a pure verb, an abstract motion, be possible in nature. The eye sees noun and verb as one: things in motion, motion in things, and so the Chinese conception tends to represent them." As for parts of speech, he says, "the verb must be the primary fact of nature, since motion and change are all that we can recognize in her." (pp. 58-9)

The implication in the essay is that we should in our usage try to recapture a sense of this verbal substratum in all the parts of speech. Fenollosa seems to have convinced Pound that if we will recognize the true verbal basis of language, we can write a poetry that will attain the desired closeness to nature. (pp. 59-60)

To better define the true form of predication, Fenollosa attacked the traditional definitions of the sentence-form. Rejecting the criterion of "a complete thought" because "in nature there is *no* completeness," he went on to denounce the usual "subject-predicate" definition as hopelessly subjective:

> In the second definition of the sentence, as "uniting a subject and a predicate," the grammarian falls back on pure subjectivity. *We* do it all; it is a little private juggling between our right and left hands. The subject is that about which *I* am going to talk; the predicate is that which *I* am going to say about it. The sentence according to this definition is not an attribute of nature but an accident of man as a conversational animal. If it were really so, then there could be no possible test of the truth of a sentence. Falsehood would be as specious as verity. Speech would carry no conviction.

It is amazing that this passage has received so little attention from critics; perhaps the Johnsonian use of *specious* has thrown them off. For here Fenollosa proposes nothing less than a way across the terrifying Cartesian gap between internal and external, between subjective and objective; it proceeds from the conviction that we can have a truly objective predication that will manifest the operations of reality itself. The sentence-form is not an arbitrary convention, but a structural representation of these operations: "agent—act—object." (p. 61)

Objective predication, with its aim of capturing such "moving images," is the key to Pound's idea of a "poetry of reality" and to Pound's work as a whole. For Pound is, in Charles Tomlinson's phrase, "engaged with the 'out-there'". . . . (p. 65)

It was Charles Norman, who as a biographer cannot have made such a statement lightly, who asserted that the *Cantos* form the "most autobiographical poem in the English language"; but what do we know of the private Pound or of his subjectivity when we have read the poem? The

*Cantos* give me no feeling of knowing "Pound the man" while reading; if autobiography, it is that of a reagent in history who tests what he comes into contact with. Most of the hostile criticism has complained that not enough subjective "order" is imposed. Disturbed by the idea of bits and pieces of reality predicating themselves, the critics have demanded that Pound "comment," say more as himself, develop a philosophy and elaborate it in verse. Actually Pound talks incessantly in his poem, of course, but somehow it isn't the kind of subjective "what I have to say about it" that we are used to.

The sharpness of the paradox in Pound's work is almost certainly related to a comment once made by Hueffer: "The Impressionist author is sedulous to avoid letting his personality appear in the course of his book. On the other hand, his whole book, his whole poem is merely an expression of his personality." A self-indulgent author might use that principle to pour himself all over his work under a thin disguise, but Pound would not have put it to that use. Here is his adaptation: "The artist seeks out the luminous detail and presents it. He does not comment. His work remains the permanent basis of psychology and metaphysics." This was written before he read Fenollosa, but it shows how the Imagist discipline of "presentation" [as defined by Pound in his 1913 essay "A Few Don'ts by an Imagiste"] was preparing him to become a faithful believer in the power of objective predication. (pp. 67-8)

As prose discipline signified for Pound a means toward a sweeping reform of poetry, so his apprehension of Joyce's merits seems to have been a sign of a further goal: it is almost as if Joyce showed him the way to put twentieth-century literature on a basis not only technically sound, but metaphysically solid. One theme recurs in Pound's essays on Joyce aside from praise of stylistic achievements: fascination with the way Joyce had been able to use a narrow, insular city to imply the world in general. (p. 76)

Pound believed that Joyce, and Eliot too, had attained a "poetry of reality" that not only answered the call of "presentation" for an exact proportion between detail and insight, but embodied a metaphysical world of universal meanings. The formula for such a relation between literature and reality was one that would have pleased a Schoolman of the Moderate Realist persuasion: *universalia in rebus*.

Critics of Pound ignore his statement of belief in universals to their cost. So convenient has it been to explain Pound away as a "nominalist" that many have mistaken his attack on "abstractions" as a nihilistic rejection of universals. They are therefore nonplussed when Pound says that the *Cantos* contain "magic moments or moments of metamorphosis" that lead into a "divine or permanent world" [in *Letters of Ezra Pound, 1907-1941,* 210]. . . . (p. 77)

[In] his own attempt at the re-sacralization of a profaned world, . . . [Pound] is concerned with the details of myth, seeking the moment of metamorphosis which opens into the permanent world of "gods, etc.," as he succinctly puts it [in *Letters,* 210]. Metamorphosis is a way of showing the true nature of things under the figure of swift and dramatic change; see Ovid, and Dante. Pound's assertions of the truth of myth and the reality of the gods reflect not only the hope of restoring some of the meaning dissipated by reductionist skepticism, but a sense of "striking at universals" through real particulars. (p. 83)

One aim of Pound's poetics seems to be the construction of a morphology of experience in the form of images. He renders bare, skeletal shapes of insight or feeling, creating in quick strokes the recognizable forms. Ideally the poems have no shape or form except what is produced by the applying of energy to material in the particular poem; hence the poems often seem formless to those accustomed to more traditional kinds. Yet if the poems are indeed quests for universal forms in particular images, their formal aspirations are far more ambitious than those of traditional kinds. Even to contribute to a morphology of experience is a rather high aim. If such was the ultimate goal of Imagism it helps further to explain statements like "It is better to present one Image in a lifetime than to produce voluminous works." (p. 97)

Joyce had the advantage over Pound in that he could make use of the novelistic accretion of detail, and thus his work seems more "realistic" than Pound's. But the underlying assumptions of both included a sense of potentiality in the particular, and a sense of the configurational, relational character of experience, and from these assumptions proceeded not only the use of synecdoche as the method of their symbolism, but also a generally organicist world-view —each part of the world ultimately related to every other part—that permitted the further developments of their arts. (p. 108)

[In his 1928 essay "Medievalism," Pound makes] an ingenious assertion that visionary activity leads to greater precision, not less, in perception and presentation. It is followed by a denunciation of modern thought for tolerating imprecise and formless concepts of energy: for us energy "has no borders, it is a shapeless 'mass' of force," whereas "the medieval philosopher [Guido Cavalcanti] would probably have been unable to think the electric world, and *not* think of it as a world of forms." The inseparability of force and form is a cardinal principle for Pound, and the basis of Vorticist theory. . . . A morphology of experience requires clear distinctions and separations—fittingly Pound finds his model in the Middle Ages. He did not object to what later ages scorned as pedantic fussiness about terms, or rigidities of hierarchical thinking, in medieval writers: to his mind these were all to the good, since they preserved demarcations, gradations, and values with exactness. (pp. 128-29)

Many literary comparisons have been proposed for the *Cantos*: Homer and Dante obviously, lately and suggestively *Piers Plowman,* and perhaps we should add Blake's Prophetic Books. But the best analogy of all is surely Ovid's *Metamorphoses,* a work that Pound seems unable to praise too much. Ovid, however, was not "writing" mythology, but rather constructing a living compendium of myth, gathering together metamorphic interpretations of realities. So also with Pound, who retells certain vital segments of myth, flashes of man's intercourse with the "vital universe," rendering them in his own "interpretative metaphors." Like Fenollosa he believes in language carrying alluvial deposits of these meanings, hence his interest in the layers of language, e.g., in various translations of Homer. Those layers preserve live speech. . . . (p. 136)

Ovid's great work provides yet another major analogue to the art of the *Cantos* in its organization. Pound never assumed that unity was Ovid's aim, but rather took the *Metamorphoses* to be a compendium of its varied sources and insights, multi-layered and multi-faceted. . . . Pound apparently believes that if a poet really concentrates his work, the logical result is a compendium; a long unified tale can be produced only by spreading the effort. (pp. 138-39)

If a poet proposes to himself to write not a "myth for our time" but a huge process-epic carrying the burden of a "tradition" embodied in various layers of language and racial consciousness, how could his work be anything other than a compendium? . . . But for Pound's work the root of the matter is that real concentration boils a work down to separate "gists and piths," which must seem at first fragmentary and disunified. He has never desired a unity of surface or style, nor made a secret of the "binding matter" in the *Cantos* which, while holding the poem together, has made it seem even more heterogeneous. This matter includes, for instance, annotations. . . . Insofar as Pound really hoped to write "the tale of the tribe" his work must be endless, episodic, and conglomerate, justifying itself only in the sharp etching of those bits of fact that "govern knowledge as the switchboard governs an electric circuit." The very precision demanded in the etching of those details prevents them from being subordinated to any unifying principle; tonal or thematic unity imposed by a single mind, no matter how creative, tends to diminish the sense of jagged clarity. If the texture is made smooth, the details cannot stand out sharply. . . . The *Cantos* . . . seek texture rather than major form. . . . When asked anxious questions about the form of the *Cantos,* Pound's replies usually tried to indicate that the poem was not schematic, but organic in the most literal sense—growing. . . . (pp. 140-42)

Study of Pound's writings has convinced me that even by the most hostile evaluation his mind was never so disorganized as to prevent him from imposing "form" on the *Cantos* if he had wanted to. It rather seems that his principles of composition were governed by two great values he derived from "the tradition"—medieval exact distinctions and Ovidian multiplicy. (p. 143)

Among the effects on Pound's poetics of the alliance with Eliot was a broadening of perspectives. One augmentation stands out: a new tolerance of wordplay in the form of *logopoeia.* This new interest is related to an awareness of Laforgue, whose interest for Pound went up sharply after he met Eliot. . . . Apparently Pound and Eliot decided that the age demanded sharp-edged satire, and that clipped regular form, scored in the apparently "caressable" but really disturbing "sculpture" of rhyme, would draw the ridiculous poses of the age into cramped and uncomfortable display. A technique that could mock pretentious rhetoric was required; Pound named it *logopoeia* [which he defined in his essay "How to Read"]. . . . (pp. 157-58)

In a sense, everything that is part of Pound's mature poetics was latent in the earlier conceptions of Imagism. The assured control that *logopoeia* demanded was immensely facilitated by the severities to which Pound faced up when practicing Imagism as discipline. (pp. 159-60)

Thus, while Pound owed to Eliot and Laforgue a new flexibility and a broadened sweep of perspective, he did not see that their lessons involved him in any self-contradictions. The enthusiastic practice of *logopoeia* on which he embarked implied for him no devaluation of earlier modes, only certain narrowed definitions for the sake of neatness and clarity. He triumphantly discovered *logopoeia* in Propertius, and made it part of his *Homage*; but he also discovered a "limited range" of it "in all satire," and "something like it" in Heine, who had been one of his earlier enthusiasms. (p. 161)

Though at first Pound seems much less concerned with religious ideas than his friends Yeats, Eliot, and Joyce, their place in his mind is quite central, and they are crucial not only to his beliefs about mythology but, for example, to the whole conception of Imagist discipline. Most of the ideas I have used so far [Schneidau employs several ideas and metaphors drawn from religion to clarify his analysis of Pound's thought] could roughly be characterized as Catholic ones, and the main point of the comparison is fairly simple: it can be seen in the Catholic insistence on the real and literal, not "symbolic," nature of what it deals with. Pound's belief in a "poetry of reality" starts from similar convictions. . . . Perhaps more than other modern poets Pound believes in the literal reality of what poems say; he was so irritated by the bourgeois equation of poetry with fantasy that his attack on it has been in a profound sense his life's work. (p. 174)

The fervor, urgency, and absoluteness with which he delivered his opinions testifies to his origin from a country that takes evangelism seriously, and throughout his thought, from aesthetics to economics, something that looks suspiciously like a Puritan pattern keeps revealing itself. Imagist poetics is a useful example: it was founded on the idea of discipline, an *askesis* necessary for poetic purity. The Imagists sought no elusive *poésie pure,* of course, but they did demand a poetry purified of signs of decadence like rhetoric, comment, metronomic rhythm, "emotional slither," "Tennysonianness of speech," and many other immoral practices. Most puritanically they eschewed decoration and ornament, that Victorian gingerbread that obscures truth. (pp. 177-78)

Pound himself ascribed his moral strenuousness to his belief that it is the duty of art to present reality. (p. 180)

His art continued to rest on the principle of the "universal in the particular," just as it continued to strive for objective predication, letting realities manifest themselves, rather than settling for subjective affirmation or denial. . . . He continued to render the shapes of experience, and to try to enshrine the direct knowledge that differs from our conceptual ones. All the Imagist ingredients stay in his work, in one form or another, although the poetry came to have obvious differences from the Imagist poems of the early period. (p. 188)

My concern is simply to assert that the *Cantos* have their roots in Imagist poetics. Between an Imagist poem and a Canto there is a major difference in form, of course, yet the continuity is there too, much like the one that obtains between Impressionism and contemporary art: the *Cantos* are to the short Imagist poems as today's freewheeling sculpture is to the anti-academic picture. In both Imagism and Impressionism we have a breakthrough toward dynamism; and both, by seeking truer representations, ended by breaking the stranglehold of "representationalism." The sense of the isolated "moment," of instantaneity, that inheres in a short Imagist poem had been useful to render shapes of insight or sudden illumination or realization. But Fenollosa taught Pound that the sense of activity is the sense of reality, and large-scale embodiments of it demanded a less constricted form. (p. 189)

In view of [the] merging of Imagism into reverie and phantasmagoric vision, and in view of the relationship between the precisions of Imagism and the precisions of the *Cantos,* it seems allowable to contend that the *Cantos* are not a repudiation of Imagism but a magnified projection of it. (p. 190)

Form was one of the values to which Pound was utterly committed. Not a form of objects—not "well-wrought-urn-ism"—but a form of events, of process, of lines of force as Fenollosa apprehended them: "Transferences of power." Sight alone can never come to the conception of a universe so full of vital energies that forces are being transferred constantly, but without sight we would have only a vague roaring in our ears from such apprehension. Form, for Pound, is an attempt to focus on the loci of these transferences. His is dynamic form, to be sure. . . . Reading a line from a Canto, we must have a sense that something is "going on" all the time; the words do not simply lie in limp patterns, the poem is something happening rather than something over with. But it also has a fixedness, a dance, even in its movement; Pound was a Vorticist, a man who believes that powerful force creates and maintains form. The vortex is a figure for the reconciliation of those mighty opposites, dynamic and static, in a shape whose fixedness is dependent on a certain intensity of movement. (p. 195)

If he is surely a "poet of reality," he is just as surely determined to extend the boundaries of what we call real. . . . The greatest figures in the literary tradition of the Western world have always been concerned to assert the "higher truth" of poetry, and Pound is one of their most convinced and passionate inheritors.

In the end Pound's "poetry of reality" depends on his boundless faith in language. He truly believed that words did not merely describe or point to real things, but could really body them forth. Far from wishing that poetry could be made with something other than words [as suggested by Frank Kermode in *Romantic Image*], with objects or with bodily sensations, he believed instead that words could get closer to the inner nature of reality than other apprehensions of experience. This is not to say that he believed that "words alone are certain good," or valued *verba* over *res*: on the contrary, he felt that the highest function of language could be achieved only by a severe restriction on verbalism, a discipline that would remove the "curse of mediacy" from words by making language totally efficient, making every word count. . . . What Pound saw in Egyptian statuary is what he wanted: an art of incarnation. To be sure, it is the reverse of an orthodox incarnation: it is flesh made word. . . . These conceptions depend on an idea of language in which the word has, through the centuries, in the "magic moment" received reality into it. In this moment, all analogies for language are transcended. (pp. 200-01)

*Herbert N. Schneidau, in his* Ezra Pound: The Image and the Real, *Louisiana State University Press, 1969.*

Old age closed in on the *Cantos*. Did some flaw in the scheme, as well?

Not if you say there was no scheme. But clearly there was. Already we can discern a great deal of it. I say "already" because the poem has only been *known* for some twenty years, though it has been in progress for fifty. . . .

Lacking . . . a continuous tradition of relevance, the reader of the *Cantos* must attempt an act of historical reconstruction to locate the work's point of origin, whereas the reader of *The Waste Land* need not. This points not to a defect in the *Cantos* but to a defect in the history of their reception. . . .

The volumes have always been structural units. The first unit, *A Draft of XVI Cantos,* was quite clear if there had been anyone to pay attention to it in 1925. Its span is from Homer to World War I, that watershed. . . . There is always a "now" in which the language on the page before us is being found, analogous to but no longer coincident with the "now" in which we read it, and the language normally encompasses many times simultaneously. This is perhaps Pound's most profound invention, this way of seeing the past, many pasts, without nostalgia: active now, in the words. The Malatesta documents, even, exist in two times: the fifteenth century, and today's English. . . .

In *Mauberley* Pound shed like a skin the aesthete who does not know what is going on, the author, as it were, of the first drafts of the first cantos, and replaced him with a persona who can scrutinize the times, including wars and wasted lives, and can understand the social value of perceptivity, its function as a generator of wealth.

The historical retrospection in *Mauberley* concentrates on the immediate past. In the first thirty cantos the method is similar but the scope is larger, embracing the span, from the Renaissance till now, during which the contradictions of European history had worked themselves out. Malatesta had managed to work against this current. So, for a while, had America, and the plan next called for the presentation of Jefferson as a second Malatesta. . . .

The *Rock Drill* Cantos carry us up through a vision of a syncretic heaven, which falters and vanishes when the mind can no longer sustain it. But the cosmos contains order independent of mind, the patterning vegetable energies of seed and root and flower; the governing science of *Rock Drill* is natural growth. The poem's center of gravity is moving from the human will out into nature, await with paradigms.

The governing science of the next sequence, *Thrones,* is philology: luminous words and their meanings, seeds of mental growth. The large blocks of the early cantos are reduced to a scatter of luminous particles, fulfilling the imagery of rising sparks Canto V had postulated long before. These sparks of exactness define legal systems: Byzantine, Chinese, English; the governing *subject* of *Thrones* is Law. And about the time he was conceiving *Thrones,* Pound produced one day on the lawn at St. Elizabeths a sheet of paper bearing sixteen ideograms, "for the last Canto." "That is my first Chinese quatrain." It consisted, he said, of the sixteen ideograms he found most interesting. (You cannot write a poem with the sixteen English words you find most interesting.) So the arc would close. Having brought new blood to Homer's meanings in the first Canto, he would bring new patterns of meaning to Chinese gists in the last; that was what return to Ithaca would mean. The meanings are in the characters; the poet does not impose meaning, he unlocks it in finding a new arrangement.

*Hugh Kenner, "'Drafts and Fragments' and the Structure of the 'Cantos'," in* Agenda, *Autumn-Winter, 1970, pp. 7-18.*

*Drafts and Fragments of Cantos CX-CXVII* is a very valuable little book. There is an ancient legal maxim to the effect that the deed does not establish a crime—there must also be proof of a guilty mind behind it. So it is with poetry. To produce sets of verses which in stanza form, rhyme, metre and such other characteristics as school-teachers tell their pupils are the distinguishing features of poetry is nothing. All these things may be present—and the one essential absent. Indeed, it is so in perhaps ninety-nine per cent of what is generally regarded as poetry. Almost always indeed the very presence of these things is a substitute for what alone is required. And the consequence is that such work as we have in this book is apt to be dismissed by the traditionalists as formless rubbish. It is very far from that and in fact contains more genuine poetry than is to be found in the totality of alleged volumes of poetry published annually. These scraps and trial shots are sufficient to furnish material for more good poets than have used any form of the English language for at least the past century.

*Hugh MacDiarmid, "The Esemplastic Power," in* Agenda, *Autumn-Winter, 1970, pp. 27-30.*

At the core of Pound's work is a frustrated equation. . . . This equation exists *a priori,* it is a truism, it is absolute and eternal, not subject to differences of time or cases, like all true mathematics, or even simple arithmetic. . . . In human life the obvious, God-given equations rarely work out right at all: for between the term and the term, between the desire and the act, falls the shadow. The shadow may be called Sin, the Fall, or whatever: but [it] is the way we account for the observable fact that in human life two plus two rarely equals four: some third or more factor enters to spoil the equation. . . .

The shadow for Pound is Usura, the palsied shadow that keepeth the bride from the groom (Miranda from Ferdinand), the maid from her Loom, the man from his house of good stone, the word from its true meaning, the coin from its proper value, the thing from its true price. For Pound the original sin (and he wouldn't call it that) is not sex but Usura. . . . The two worlds of nature, unfallen, and of man, fallen (not through sin but ignorance Pound would say with the Bhagavad Gita), confront each other in page after page of the Cantos, the one accusing the other, but also teaching the other, coaxing, leading back to truth, reality, the original perfection. . . . There are the images of things, realities in nature, set over against the images or whatever of non-things, the emptiness of reality created by Usury. . . . This "thinginess" of Pound's poetry in its positive mood is characteristic, and imagistic: and is not "thinginess" the meaning of "realitas"? Usury creates a world of nothingness, it creates "ex nihil", and out of nothing comes nothing—except misery. The world created by Usury is psychosis, an unreality empty of real things, a world in which no thing has a definite value, or a definite price, no money a definite correspondence to anything by which real value and price can be established. . . .

Pound's idea of the nature of the shadow that spoils our natural equations, that creates a world in which criminals are raised to power and wealth while saints are crucified and poets starved, is as much worth consideration as any other idea of it. The fact that it provokes such irrational fear and hatred would seem to suggest, indeed, that it is much more worth consideration than others all too acceptable. Where the patient winces and becomes resistant is where the trouble is: we should all probe deeper into the questions of money and Usury. And we should do it of course as writers concerned with values, not as economists or whatever concerned with pseudo-science. The kind of resistance to be looked for is plain from the treatment the greatest poet of our age has received.

*Tom Scott, "Two Plus Two Would Equal Four But For The Shadow . . .", in* Agenda, *Autumn-Winter, 1970, pp. 35-7.*

Impossible to approach the latest fragments of this impassioned poem [the *Cantos*] without bending the knee before the length and dedication of the life lived. But there is enough new seeing [in *Drafts and Fragments of Cantos CX-CXVII*] for veneration without ancestor-worship.

The sight is attained after pain, the keener for knowledge of its causes, but the tone is not sharp. It is levelled by humility, by admission of error, and by the distancing of experience through time.

Gone, years ago, concern about "how to say it"—style, verse, language, and all that. Long study and great love have brought to the work exactitudes immediate as instinct, phrases of absolute rhythm moulding the sense. The ear never errs but the tongue falters, its broken phrases sighting states of mind in motifs of nature, history and art. . . .

No-one else has so delicate an ear. The words define themselves by the movement of their sounds, more precise than the definitions of the lexicographers, but trace areas of meaning where the mind plays. Raised to another power, the technique allows lines and sequences of lines, equally precise in what they mark but do not say, to determine by their placing multiple volumes of thought and perception. The clarity of detail in multidimensional spacing makes the poetry look both simple and difficult. Historically the progression is from delineation by mots justes through dissociation of ideas to ideogram and a kind of projective geometry, but here all are used.

"Monuments" one might call them if the word did not evoke the stuffy and the overpowering. But lightness, lightness above all, with the calm and discrimination of observers of nature: *to walk with Mozart, Agassiz and Linnaeus.*

Here take thy mind's space

Just words moving, given weight by experience only, meaning the knowledge of centuries as well as the memory of an old man, words reaching out to ultimates, to live by and die with.

*Kenneth Cox, "New Things Seen," in* Agenda, *Autumn-Winter, 1970, pp. 38-9.*

Those critics who claim the *Cantos* do not cohere and who would read Pound's personal expressions of doubt as concurrence with their judgment ought to study carefully these new cantos [*Drafts and Fragments of Cantos CX-CXVII*]. The searchlight of intellect which Pound throws mercilessly upon the work does not register doubt of his accomplishment. He merely keeps to the Confucian principle of looking straight into the heart and acting on the results. He puts his work to the test, judging it by the true tones given off by the heart. Under such straight gaze, doubt that assails the human spirit at all too frequent intervals becomes affirmation. . . .

*Marcella Spann, "Beauty in Fragments," in* Agenda, *Autumn-Winter, 1970, pp. 40-3.*

*Drafts & Fragments* makes us realise that Pound probably oversimplified the world in some earlier parts of the poem. Sadness and beauty are here inextricably interwoven. These are fragments of beauty that because of their fragmentation are permeated by pain. The greatest happiness we know comes in moments which are gone before we can grasp what it is we have experienced. It is instants of this kind that these Cantos define. . . .

Cantos CX-CXVII are a cluster of things felt which spark off new relationships with themselves and with the body of the work on each rereading. They make us see, in flashes, all parts of the poem draw to a deeper unity than had once seemed possible.

*Cyril Connolly, "A Short Commentary," in* Agenda, *Autumn-Winter, 1970, pp. 44-9.*

In *The Cantos,* Pound constructs his own mythical conception of ancient and modern, eastern and western history. In so doing, he imitates the original creator as he imagines him, transforming myth into art, personal into objective experience. Pound deliberately distorts historical material; he sees historical figures as either heroes or villains, and he involves them with gods and creatures of hell. His narrator is omnipotent and his perspective messianic, for he attempts to create the great historical myth of which western society has been deprived by vulgar and unethical leaders. . . .

The laws that Pound envisions in history are not derived from the empirical evidence provided by the Italian Renaissance, China, or the American Republic, but are mythical laws of "inborn qualities of nature" which can be traced not only to ancient concepts of reality but to Pound's own messianic view of order and control. Like Zeus or Odysseus, the poet himself "pilots" all of history to conform to his own construction of an ideal past, which is more myth than history, more eccentric than universal. In *Guide to Kulchur,* Pound writes of his idea of "dynamic form," which is intrinsically related to his belief in the "dynamo" that the past must provide for the present. . . . Pound's myth of recurrence and permanence in history rises from death, for its purpose is ultimately to involve the reader in a ritual of abhorrence of the present and reversion to an idealized inner vision of the past. If his "history" contains some vital persons and events of earlier societies, these are often used to support the hatred and contempt which seem to inspire Pound's visionary pattern. History in *The Cantos* is finally Pound's own creation.

*Lillian Feder, "Ezra Pound: The Messianic Vision," in her* Ancient Myth in Modern Poetry *(copyright © 1971 by Princeton University Press; reprinted by permission of Princeton University Press), Princeton University Press, 1971, pp. 293-307.*

Despite critical pleading, the *Cantos* are an unfinished, totally flawed, almost totally destroyed poem. The recent volume (1968) of the *Cantos* is called *Drafts & Fragments of Cantos CX-CXVII*; it is not possible to distinguish these clearly labeled notes and drafts from the two earlier volumes *Thrones* and *Section: Rock Drill.* No reader can fail to note the progressive disintegration of substance and surface. The mind loses its way among the scattered bundles of torn documents and fragmentary texts translated (or not translated) from the languages of the world; the ear forgets the vigorous prosodic tune which begins Canto 1 and at the end hears little more than the mutter and buzz of free association. With the best will in the world, the most up-to-date scholarly annotation, and the sharpest exegetical tools, it is impossible to read the macaronic lines which follow and derive pleasure from their music or intellectual stimulation from their propositional sense. . . .

Nowhere do we find a basic tonality or tone-row, a consistent development or climax, a fully orchestrated page. My concern with the *Cantos,* then, centers more on intention and intended method than on intrinsic aesthetic value. The *Cantos* is not an achieved poem, "a window to existence and history," but a shattered mirror crazily reflecting historical knowledge and historical process. I take Pound at his word that he is writing "the tale of the tribe," a poem that means to be exemplary history. There is no reason why histories cannot be framed in verse or told with the grace, precision, and power which poetic form renders human experience. Pound himself discounts the *Cantos* as detached art; and *horrible dictu* and contrary to every canon of post-Symbolist literary theory, stresses their importance as naked propaganda.

Pound faces problems as old as Aristotle. If the *Cantos* is a poem "about" history, if it is a poem containing history, or if (as some critics have affirmed) it *is* history, then we stand deep in an ontological quagmire. A poem *qua* poem is not expected to tell *wie es eigentlich gewesen,* preserve chronology and sequence, or infer patterns of cause and effect. But if the *Cantos* is history told as a poem, then we should expect that it follow the canons governing the writing of humanistic history. If Pound really means to give us knowledge of the past and instruct our wills for right action, then the history of the *Cantos* must separate present and past, sift the true from the false ("the lies of history must be exposed"), and erect a structure of premises, a philosophy or a metaphysic, which shows an inner reality to events as well as their outer factuality. . . .

Pound responded to what Nietzsche so bitterly attacked: the nineteenth-century belief in History and its redemptive possibilities. History was meant to function as the major ordering structure in the *Cantos*; historical knowledge could supply a system of belief. As Dante knew his reader believed in God, Pound knew his reader believed that in History truth is revealed and salvation achieved. Far from thinking History a burden, a deterrent to action, Pound believed historical knowledge would energize men to action. . . .

The ideogrammatic or anachronistic method (they are identical) would make all of the past instantly present and hence available not only to the imagination but to the will. But the method, as Pound employs it, more nearly prevents than aids historical knowledge, more often confuses than enlightens the reader about the true nature of history. . . .

The method of ideogram and anachronism denies that history requires either verification or chronology; without the possibility of knowing truth from falsehood or what came after when, history is reduced to meaningless recurrence or regressive myth. Ideogram and anachronism deny that history reveals process or that history is available to the understanding. Thus the arrangement (I should say disarrangement) of documentary material in ideograms, in patterns of deliberate chronological disorder, produces nothing we can call historical knowledge. . . .

Pound's "study" of economics supposedly traces the deterioration of culture brought about by the abrogation of the traditional theological strictures against usury; it also traces the ways in which the corruption spread from social practice to the forms of art. However, Pound demonstrates no relationships between art and economics or between economics and politics. We must accept Pound's word that whatever is evil in the modern world is the result of usurious practices. Pound's theory is single, simple, and unequivocal; the history of western Europe and America, in all its variousness and complexity, can be understood if we recognize usury as the motivation behind human action.

Even if we find some truth in Pound's *ad hoc* definition of usury (munitions-selling *is* a despicable racket), its application is irresponsible and dangerous. . . .

To believe in a "key to History," to believe that a single historical phenomenon explains historical process means holding one of the many varieties of conspiratorial theories of history. And a conspiratorial theory of history can hardly "affirm the gold thread in the pattern. . .". . . .

Despite Pound's awareness of time passing, he reveals nothing in the *Cantos* we might call temporal process. Some critics have discovered in the *Cantos* evidence that Pound holds a cyclical concept of time or that Pound progresses *through* time: from the writhing disorder and hate of an *Inferno* to the blessed order and love of a *Paradiso*. But these integrative critics write in their criticism the poem Pound might have written but could not. . . .

The *Cantos* is not a poem sustained by circular or organic time: by myths of death and resurrection or by the return of the seasons. Quite deliberately the *Cantos* is a poem without time or sequence. . . . If the poem were sustained by an integrating myth, there would be a discoverable movement—from birth to death and resurrection; or from winter to spring. What sustains the Cantos, in those places where we can follow Pound's meanings and respond to his feelings, is tone and mood; the binding material is the pervading emotions of regret and despair. Pound's understanding of time and history is limited to his own feelings. He knows that events took place, that men and women suffered, that it all seems a terrifying waste. Time and history are thus reduced to a spectacle of undifferentiated change—a spectacle where all event is inexplicable occurrence. . . .

Pound is a learned and cultivated connoisseur of all the arts. But in both his political attachments and in the *Cantos* Pound waged a furious campaign against the bourgeois tradition, rational historiography, and anything that might be considered conventional or not sufficiently revolutionary. Always in the avant-garde, he proclaimed as his motto "Make it new!" Always the enthusiast for the latest movement, he urged the demolition of the nineteenth century—that good gray century of middle-class values. A scholar and intellectual himself, he sneered at scholars and intellectuals; in his own frivolous way, he reached for a revolver when he heard the word culture: he spelled it Kulchur. Pound was not alone in thinking that it might be fun to blow up the European cultural heritage; the Futurists and Dadaists showed a similar taste for what they felt was "creative" violence.

In all his activities Pound was neither consistent nor aware that at one and the same time he was urging the destruction of culture and thinking himself the last defender of Europe and the West. Nor was he aware that in pushing his campaign against history (for that is what the *Cantos* do), he became an enemy of the Europe he believed he was defending. At this point I am tempted to say that Pound's History, with its thousands of documents, letters, and economics of social credit; with its Greek, Latin, and Chinese words of wisdom; is, in the words of another American primitive, The Bunk. Perhaps Pound cannot be dismissed so glibly. It took tremendous effort and the work of more than fifty years to write the one hundred and seventeen Cantos; it has taken the work of a dozen critics to discover their form and unravel their obscurities. The *Cantos* is the longest modern poem in English; it offered itself as a solution to the problems of its age. Yet the *Cantos* remains an unsuccessful epic of human culture (more exactly, an epic against culture) because it is based on an idea of history and a historiographical method to which the mind, unless it abrogates its responsibility, cannot give assent.

*Harvey Gross, "The 'Cantos' of Ezra Pound," in his* The Contrived Corridor: History and Fatality in Modern Literature *(copyright © by The University of Michigan 1971), University of Michigan Press, 1971, pp. 100-23.*

For more than fifty years, the prospect of failure has haunted the *Cantos*. But during that time, Pound's ambition has proved so compelling, his effort so Promethean, that even the most severe criticisms have seemed short of the mark. Pound has, in fact, preserved for us the belief that poetry has to do with ceaseless energies, with prophecy, with the articulation of those things about which all the rest of us can be expected to fall speechless. Serving thus a rare function in a time when many poets are bled of their self-esteem, the *Cantos* persist as an artifact outreaching the judgment of failure or success.

*William M. Chace, "Talking Back to Ezra Pound," in* The Southern Review, *Vol. VIII, No. 1, Winter, 1972, p. 226.*

Ezra Pound sometimes seems less a writer than an entire literary community, one that has accidentally assembled in the body that goes by his name. Editor, poet, anthologist, critic, propagandist, cultural historian, English teacher, he has also been called patriot, traitor, sage, madman, defender of the artist, corrupter of the young. . . .

Even the reader of the *Selected Poems* is bound to be struck by Pound's extraordinary facility, his capacity to sound casually "right" in forms that range from Anglo-Saxon verse structures to the most intricate Italian, Provençal, or French ones.

What makes this facility possible is something that is less learned than innate: Pound's ability to hear and to reproduce the most subtle nuances of speech. Pound talked a great deal about the importance of the poet's sense of verse melody—the delicate weave of sound and accent that plays above the stress pattern of a line and that imposes on that pattern an author's unique voice. It is this sure ear for verse melody, I think, that makes us swear by the "rightness" of a great deal of Pound's work—whether in his own poetry (most conspicuously perhaps in the Pisan Cantos), his editorial activity (most conspicuously perhaps in his cutting of Eliot's *The Waste Land*), or his translations (most conspicuously perhaps in the translations from Li Po).

Once we have accustomed ourselves to this voice, then we are ready to discover the ways in which individual elements of Pound's work interconnect: the melodies of the Chinese, the Provençal, the Italian translations weaving into and through the historical and contemporary "events" that accent *The Cantos,* melodies that fuse in a mind like waves washing into and over each other, interpenetrations of light. . . .

*John Unterecker, "Foreword," to* Ezra Pound: An Introduction to the Poetry, *by Sister Bernetta Quinn, O.S.F. (reprinted by permission of the publisher), Columbia University Press, 1972, pp. vii-x.*

If a reader regards Pound's *The Cantos* as too formidable an introduction to his poetry, he can begin with the highly readable prose. Here the writer very often assumes the role of preceptor, a word stemming from *praecipire,* "to know beforehand," and, as applied to Pound, meaning one who promulgates working rules respecting the techniques of an art. The rationale of all that he has written is contained in his critical essays, a factor which renders them decidedly useful to one who wants to know Pound. Moreover, his ideas are so influential that they have changed the character of four decades in American letters, have truly given poems . . . new directions. (p. 37)

Pound himself in his early years considered his criticism more a form of rhetoric than a lasting genre of appraisal. . . . [But Eliot believed that, despite] the absence of any evaluation of drama, no critic of our time . . . can less be spared. He stresses the need to bear in mind the contexts in which the selections were written, none being produced in a vacuum or as ultimate; rather each is a landmark in the growth of a great sensibility. . . . Pound's prose is much more lively than that of any other poet-critic of his age, brimming over as it is with apothegm, image, wit. (p. 38)

That the poet conceived of himself as preceptor is clear from that essay of his, in Eliot's culling [*The Literary Essays of Ezra Pound*], entitled "The Teacher's Mission." He envisions this mission as a restoration of language from its corruption through journalism, in order that the "Health of the National Mind" be maintained. No one can achieve success as a teacher unless he first examine his own interior condition—a flashback to Confucius—and then turn toward the light in all openness. In the study of poetry Pound desires, as the furthest possible remove from abstraction, a comparison of masterpieces. This method rests upon disciplined concreteness such as is found in the ideogram's union of word and thing. (p. 45)

Accuracy for Pound is a goal consistently held to. . . . At least five Cantos enshrine his love for conciseness in their employment of the *ching ming* ideogram, which might well serve as emblem for the intent of all his critical prose. (pp. 45-6)

Most hostile critics accuse Pound of violating the adage "Shoemaker, stick to your last" because his essays often range far from literature. However, a man lives his life as he chooses: style includes, among other things, the subjects one elects to write about. From at least his forties on, the lion's share of Pound's energies went into economics. (p. 46)

If one is to comprehend the last fourth of the Cantos, he will be forced to learn at least the outline of a history of money, some familiarity with which is needed in order to make any sense of them at all. Realizing how such a requirement will alienate readers, Pound nevertheless thinks the issue important enough to take that risk. (p. 48)

Some of Pound's best poetry is to be found in his translations, as exemplified at the start of *The Cantos* by his putting into magnificently economical English a Renaissance Latin version of the eleventh book of Homer's *Odyssey.* His theory of "the immortal concept," traveling down the years to emerge in era after era expressed by means of different media, has direct relevance to this aspect of his genius. Though his central thrust is to capture the spirit of each original, the vision informing the unique artifact and linking it with vanished splendor, he is no blunderer among masterpieces. Pound is a far better scholar both by education and by experience than philologists in general have recognized. (p. 75)

Sometimes one is almost tempted to divide Pound's career into before and after his contact with ideograms. (p. 95)

In more than one sense, Ezra Pound was "the son of Homer." As all readers of *The Cantos* know, its substructure is Homeric, with an Odysseus-figure as the hero, part fictional, part autobiographical. . . .

[Passages] from Cantos 1, 4, 9, 13, 14, 16 . . . represent the aged poet's advice to those who wish to acquaint themselves with his major achievement but feel at a loss as to how to start. Faced by its bulk, many hesitate, thinking the challenge too great. Others spend years reading without a plan. To have *il miglior fabbro* single out the best passages for initiation [in *Selected Cantos of Ezra Pound,* 1967] is therefore an enormous help. (p. 103)

If nothing remained of the Cantos beyond those written during the days at Pisa, especially the twenty-five pages of magnificent poetry which constitute the seventy-fourth, Pound's status as a literary genius of the first rank would be secure. It is all but incredible to find a writer considered by some to be a major poet in English (Robert Graves) denying the excellence of these Cantos [Graves' contention appears in a letter to the editor of *Esquire,* December, 1957]. Their loveliness is the more remarkable in that they were composed in captivity, under most painful conditions, after a collapse from exposure and other hardships had necessitated Pound's removal from the 6′ x 6½′ "gorilla cage" of the camp wherein he was held in secrecy. These Cantos contain the basic elements introduced and developed in the first seventy, starred by certain "epiphanies" which act as preparation for the Edenic splendors ahead.

Only rarely has Pound achieved passages of like beauty since that November in 1945 when he arrived in Washington, D.C., expecting to be tried for treason. . . .

Nowhere in *The Cantos* does he reveal more of his personal history, expressing in accents of humility his union with mankind's common pain. These "minor key" passages [in *The Pisan Cantos*] strike a new note in the music of the whole. (pp. 131-32)

Pound himself selected Cantos 81 and 84 as essential to understanding his whole work. Laughlin, his publisher, adds four and a half pages of Canto 83, perhaps because of its marked autobiographical nature, perhaps because no introduction to Pound is complete without the marvelous poetry that this section contains. Its mood is tranquil, contemplative: the meditations of philosophy (Gemistus and Scotus Erigena), the talk of writers (Yeats), the aesthetic experience as before the statue of Our Lady in Paris or the mermaids of the church in Venice. (p. 139)

Toward life's end, Pound wrestles with self-doubt. He knows what every artist must finally admit: one cannot write Paradise. But the cosmos coheres, beyond any transcript. All of that which is durable in classical literature, East and West, as he has encountered it, all of his own visions and revisions have gone into *The Cantos* as palimpsest. The "erasures" are not really that: their originals still exist under new and newer beauty. The words are done in gold light on the newest surface of the palimpsest—modest, as things human must necessarily be: "A little light, like a rushlight/ to lead back to splendour." More and more personal as they proceed, the Cantos after the hundredth frequently echo a sense of failure, "a tangle of works unfinished." Pound's humility, the direct opposite of hybris, sees far less in his total achievement than is really there; or perhaps one might say that with authentic sensitivity he judges even the highest masterpiece of man to be only "a rushlight." (p. 163)

On the last page of *The Cantos* Pound writes of how he has tried "to make a paradise/ terrestre." Paradise can never be put into words. But to try is a high enterprise—for a poet, the highest. (p. 167)

*Sister Bernetta Quinn, O.S.F., in her* Ezra Pound: An Introduction to the Poetry *(reprinted by permission of the publisher), Columbia University Press, 1972.*

[Whereas] no one, for instance, would question the fact of the modernist movement, it does not necessarily follow that one has to accept Pound as a modernist because he supported James Joyce or T. S. Eliot. Moreover, if one concedes the historical importance of certain technical innovations or such loyalties, one cannot—however much one wants to do so—close the door on the historical significance of Pound's anti-Semitism and Fascism. Similarly, one cannot argue about Pound's translations of the Provençal the same way one can about his translations of the Chinese. No one . . . is willing to claim that Pound invented Provençal poetry for his time, and the critic is consequently hard pressed to minimize that which he is coevally praising. In both cases, some of the pitfalls for a critic dealing with a contemporary figure become apparent.

First, any dismissal of Pound's anti-Semitism on the grounds that when he uses "Jew" he does not mean "Jew" seems to defeat all of Pound's pronouncements against a poet's using sloppy language. Either "Jew" is not "Jew," as [Sister Bernetta] Quinn [in her book *Ezra Pound: An Introduction to the Poetry*] would insist, and one must convict the poetry of the same imprecision that Pound attacks in politicians; or "Jew" does mean "Jew," and critics like Quinn must face up to this fact and justify the greatness of the poetry despite its content. . . .

Any defense of Pound's views of translation which does not take into account the relation of sound to word meaning invites a similar questioning. Here Pound has been subject as well to the charge of having used sloppy language, and examples like [Stuart Y.] McDougal's [in his book *Ezra Pound and the Troubadour Tradition*] of times when a rejected dictionary meaning has led the poet to inventive and exact analogues do not balance the greater number of inaccuracies that scholars cite. Pound's statement in the *ABC of Reading* that "poetry begins to atrophy when it gets too far from music" is in this matter relevant. His esteem for language seems intimately linked to both its sound value (*melopoeia*) and Walter Pater's notion of all art's aspiring to the condition of music. What the translator sees as an original work is a series of sounds to be rescored into English words. Such a vision is itself transcultural and atemporal, and it suggests *ratio* in its Augustinian sense is a better explanation for precision in language than the *res-verba* relations that most critics employ. The view also allows the poet under the international language of music to revive the past and make its poets his contemporaries as well as to hold coexistent the permanent products of any civilization. Louis Zukofsky's *Catullus* is the logical extension of such a position, just as his "upwards music/downwards speech" is a concise statement of its practice.

Nevertheless, both Quinn and McDougal are correct in assuming that language is the key to whatever greatness Pound may earn as a poet. The reader is immediately struck by an unusual vocal vividness that Pound derives from Robert Browning and that John Donne in a different way possesses. Bizarre spellings and phrases, colorful diction, and fragmented syntax evoke Ben Jonson's remark about Spenser, that "in affecting the ancients, he writ no language," and it is a charge that at various times Pound has had to bear. Yet, the very archaism, as McDougal's tracing of translations from the Provençal proves, seems deliberate. It is as if by creating an artificial language Pound is defying the lockstep of his age and, like *The Faerie Queene,* the *Cantos* projects a voice that is more than the voice of a particular community. Its vision of proper behavior and earthly paradises not only suggests the biblical prophets but the style, too, seems to have gained from a study of the King James version of the Bible. When Ford Madox Ford advised Pound that poetry should be at least as well written as prose, it was to the Bible that the poet went for one model, and various cantos owe phrases and rhetorical devices to what he learned from reading the ethical and prophetic books.

Critics have tended to play down these stylistic matters for what W. D. Snodgrass once called the "flash-card" nature of the language. Reviewing *Cantos* 96-109, he complained that "life with Ezra had come more and more to be a daily mid-semester test. I must spend hours each day watching him flash (a little faster each day) note cards containing significant phrases (a little shorter each day) past my nose. For each snippet of phrase I must produce a full historical context together with the received interpretation." Most books on Pound are precisely the laying aside of the reader's vision to memorize the poet's life view that Snodgrass indicates may result from such examinations. This laying aside of vision prevents a number of these critics from seeing in the *Cantos* what Randall Jarrell termed "the Organization of Irrelevance": "If something is somewhere, one can always find Some Good Reason for its being there, but if it had not been there would one reader have missed it; if it had been put somewhere else, would one reader have guessed where it should have 'really' gone?" It also prevents them from seeing how much a work like the *Cantos* is a cultural document and how the greatness of its poetic art consists in its triumphing over an enormous prose content. . . .

[Pound] helped clear poetry of some of its false poeticisms and was *the* important publicist and mythmaker for the modernist movement. In addition, for good or bad, he took American letters out of the coterie and put it into the marketplace where it has remained. It is to Pound—though perhaps not singly—that one owes the subsequent literary campaigns and orchestrated receptions of modern writers that have democratized literature and secured so many raises and tenure for academics. He abroad and H. L. Mencken at home helped turn literary criticism into an adjunct of journalism and, while Pound complained of comparable debasements in other fields, this debasement of criticism seemed not to have bothered him. Rather, like the cultural imperialism which underlies his practice of using foreign phrases, his references, and his translations, a belief in the ultimate good judgment of the average magazine reading citizen then common to Americans supported his actions. In fact, some of his most famous attempts at reform came out of his journalistic efforts.

*Jerome Mazzaro, in* Criticism *(reprinted by permission of the Wayne State University Press; copyright 1974 by Wayne State University Press), Vol. XVL, No. 1 (Winter, 1974), p. 85-7.*

Throughout his translation [of Guido Cavalcanti] Pound does many things to irritate the scholar. . . .

Still, . . . we must admit that there is no inarguable way of looking at Cavalcanti, and Pound is fully aware of Cavalcanti's heretical, empirical, scientific bent. If Shaw sees Cavalcanti as an orthodox Christian, Nardi aligns him more convincingly with the Averroists. If the stanzas [of the *Donna mi prega*] dealing with light sound Neoplatonic, other sections are markedly Aristotelian or Averroistic. It is no wonder, then, that Pound himself seems to employ Cavalcanti in a double way: both as a scientific observer of love and as a hymner of its metaphysical power.

Cavalcanti thus displays that tension between idealism and realism that can be found in many minds, including Dante's and Pound's. Pound could admire Cavalcanti's idealism because it was not slavishly aligned to tradition. At the very same time he could admire Cavalcanti's insistence on scientific inquiry, his defense of the sensual, and his refined use of the mot juste. For these reasons Cavalcanti is a recurring voice in the *Cantos*, operating almost as an undertone to the more conservative Dante. However much scholars such as Shaw may have condemned Pound's philosophic judgments and critical acumen, the poet allows Cavalcanti to sing from the pages of the *Cantos* more clearly than he does in any of the complex and contradictory commentaries about him.

*James J. Wilhelm, "Guido Cavalcanti as a Mask for Ezra Pound," in* PMLA, 89 *(copyright © 1974 by the Modern Language Association of America; reprinted by permission of the Modern Language Association of America), March, 1974, pp. 332-40.*

* * *

## POWERS, J(ames) F(arl) 1917-

**Powers is a Catholic American novelist and short story writer. Crisp, satirical, precise, and funny, his masterful prose has won several important awards. (See also *Contemporary Authors*, Vols. 1-4, rev. ed.)**

Mr. Powers's work is all the more interesting because its prime subject is one that has been little exploited by American writers and that would seem, in fact, to hold little promise for them. His subject is the contradictions that beset Catholicism, in practice if not in theory, because of its claim to an earthly as well as a divine mission and authority. Powers is, however, a very down to earth, very American, Catholic. In his work, the contradictions are expressed, not in any of those flagrant dramas of sin and redemption which form the staples of Christian romance but in the simple spectacle of priests going about the ordinary business of their professions. From this spectacle, however, he evokes a mingling of severity and raillery that is not simple. . . . In his own way he is a thorough realist, even a regionalist. His explorations into novelistic reality are confined to a locale that is small enough and distinct enough to be knowable in terms of what he wants to know about it. Improbably, for a writer of his faith, his locale is traditionally Lutheran Minnesota. The advantage to him of this setting, however, is just that it intensifies the essential contradictions. His fictive Minnesota is a country of interminable flats, vague lakes and woodlands, and slightly hostile natives. It is very far from [the ecclesiastical pomp of] Rome (traditional Rome) and centuries away from [the spiritual sublimities of] St. John of the Cross. The distance lends a certain unreality to [the] Church Latin, black habits, medieval vows, and dogmatic assumptions [of Minnesota Catholicism. From] this unreality arises some of the severity and much of the hilarity of the whole spectacle of priestly endeavor in Powers's domain. Yet neither the [dim] unrealities nor the all too raw realities of his Minnesota keep Powers from depicting it with restrained affection: the heart has, apparently, its regions. Nor are his ecclesiastics and their lay followers submitted to the kind of doctrinaire scrutiny which might see them as all of a piece. . . .

For the purposes of fiction, [Powers] effects a divorce between faith and morals. The question is not whether faith, in the measure [that] his characters have it, makes them greatly better or greatly worse than those outside the fold. The question is whether those inside the fold can sustain the moral life at the level of *average* good will, self-respect and taste. If this approach is necessary to Powers as a moral realist, it is also congenial to him as a storyteller; and his love of narration in all shapes, sizes and degrees of seriousness is obvious. Stories within stories, ranging from rectory-table anecdotes through biblical parables to scraps of radio serials caught from the airwaves, thicken the fictional atmosphere. Each sentence tends to be an event; yet every event, like every firm but fluent sentence, is an open door into the next half-expected, half-shocking encounter. Thus does J. F. Powers coax stories out of the shabby rectories of his not altogether mythical Minnesota.

*F. W. Dupee, "In the Powers Country," in* Partisan Review *(copyright © 1963 by Partisan Review, Inc.; reprinted by permission of F. W. Dupee), Spring, 1963, pp. 113-16.*

Powers has always been a very uneven writer. In the fashion of that prototype of fiction writers, when he is good he is very very good, and when he is bad he is horrid. Powers has published two volumes of short stories, *Prince of Darkness and Other Stories* in 1947, and *The Presence of Grace* in 1956. Most of the stories deal with the Roman Catholic clergy, given an intense scrutiny, although Powers has written a few early stories, and those his worst, dealing with Negro life.

*Stanley Edgar Hyman, "The Priest With the Fishnet Hatband," in his* Standards: A Chronicle of Books for Our Time *(© 1966; reprinted by permission of the publisher, Horizon Press, New York), Horizon, 1966, pp. 93-7.*

Although Powers tellingly satirizes both the old priest and the young one [in "The Wrong Forks"], it cannot be said that what he satirizes in either is lack of spiritual depth but rather a failure to get results. If we are to say that the two priests, each in his own way, is an activist in the American tradition, with respect focused on pragmatism, so at this time is Powers himself. There is no sign yet that he attributes ineffectiveness to failure of the spirit. That insight is yet to be expressed. . . .

Powers' stories have a bleakness we have not seen since we looked at Mauriac, and, as we will see, this bleakness persists in his novel. Waugh at least presented us with an innocent victim, Paul Pennyfeather. In Powers, if innocence is present at all, it is never drawn fully enough so that we can be really sure it is there.

Powers' novel, *Morte d'Urban,* has for its hero an almost perfect specimen of the modern American activist priest. No doubt as a former seminarian Powers had more insight into Americanism in the priesthood than the average American Catholic. Certainly he understands it, and he dissects its modes of progress with a skill almost surgical in its merciless precision. . . .

Whatever Father Urban's failings, lack of pragmatic success is not among them—and this is a reversal of the situation Powers portrayed with Father Eudex and Father Burner. Powers has developed. His target this time is failure of the spirit, not lack of success. Powers has looked at the American Catholic community and seen in it the fulfillment of the worst of the fears that almost half a century earlier had led to *Testem Benevolentiae*. . . .

It seems obvious that *Morte d'Urban* does not involve any detailed one-for-one correspondence with [Malory's *Morte d'Arthur*], but that the evocations of Malory are a loosely infused mocking refrain designed to reinvoke at suitable intervals the wildly dissonant thematic unity of the serious with the insanely funny that give the work resonance. To cast the life of Father Urban, the supersalesman of the Church, as a parody of epic was a brilliant inspiration. The story of Father Urban is as serious as it is comic. If we understand the consequence of the existence of priests like Father Urban in the American Catholic community, our laughter at his blunders is mingled with bitterness and outraged concern. . . .

Father Urban's change of character after the episode with the golf ball again raises the question of free will in Powers' fiction. We cannot say that Father Urban is like Father Eudex in weighing alternatives and choosing his way. Rather his way is chosen for him by the accident. Father Urban is not shown responding to grace, he is shown being overwhelmed by the bishop's blow. To the degree that Urban is helpless before circumstances, he at the end becomes a puppet, and Powers has swung away from his earlier orientation to enter more deeply into the spirit of the American Jansenist and Irish Puritan heritage. It is hard to stir much emotional response to the puppetlike Urban at the end. Whatever our sympathy for him before, we feel a reduction in dramatic power, and the astringent comedy of the "conversion by golf ball" does not leave us as moved as we would have been if Urban had been led to change his character by some process of self-criticism or growth of insight. But this is precisely the point. Father Urban was simply not capable of that much self-criticism or growth of insight. If his conversion had not come about by golf ball, it would not have come about at all.

The bitterness in this book is darker than any that appeared in Powers' earlier work, even in such cruel stories as "The Eye." In "The Eye" human beings were responsible for the events. In *Morte d'Urban* chance determines Urban's fate. . . . Powers never turns our attention toward eternity, and his novel thus is cast further into shadow by lack of the dimension that had been important in Catholic aesthetics since Maritain and Claudel, and, if we except Powers' master, Waugh, had played a part in nearly all the European Catholic novels since Huysmans and Belloc. Powers is so astringent, indeed so flatly earthbound, that any mention of an afterlife, or even any intimation that it exists, would be dissonant—impossible to take seriously simply by the mode of his fiction. . . .

When we considered the early growth of the Catholic novel in France, we saw that the major French Catholic authors avoided the moralizing form. Writing a novel to illustrate a thesis was not the mode of creative procedure adopted by either Bernanos or Mauriac. Waugh, however, wrote to illustrate his findings about his world, and Powers does the same. The problem with this kind of writing is its reliance on the central statement. Once Powers has made his statement that America's priests are despiritualized, he seems to have used up a large part of what he has to say. When the statement has been registered, the novel's impact exhausts itself—specially if one is familiar with Powers' short stories, many of which make the same statement.

*Gene Kellogg, "J. F. Powers," in his* The Vital Tradition: The Catholic Novel in a

Period of Convergence, *Loyola University Press, 1970, pp. 167-79.*

* * *

## PROKOSCH, Frederic 1908-

**Prokosch is an American novelist, poet, and translator. He has said that his principal themes are "perpetual search, perpetual flight, multiple identities, ambiguities of destiny, and geographical symbolisms."**

[Frederic Prokosch] is thought of today as one who writes travelogues, who does a nice job of describing places and whose work should be dutifully reviewed by third-rate reviewers—perhaps that pleasant assistant professor who could use an item in his bibliography. And yet, against this impression of Prokosch's worth must be set the opinions of some of the greatest writers of the century. In addition to Yeats, three other winners of the Nobel Prize for literature [Gide, Mann, and Camus] saw important promise in Prokosch's work. (p. 34)

[His] strange, quite beautiful poems made Frederic Prokosch for a time a popular, almost a fashionable, poet. His poems were placed in anthologies, conspicuously in those of Oscar Williams. Of more importance, however, Prokosch influenced the work of one of the most remarkable poets of the century: Dylan Thomas. (p. 40)

Frederic Prokosch's production of poetry has not been large: fewer than one hundred poems have been printed. Furthermore, the poems, roughly the product of perhaps ten years time, were written for the most part between 1930 and 1940. One can probably not treat his expression, limited both in time and amount, as anything other than a potential. Prokosch's talent for poetry remains an unfinished talent. We do not know, nor does it seem likely that we shall ever know, how he might have ended had he chosen to be a poet rather than a novelist. (p. 46)

While Prokosch's poetry is flawed by a vagueness which leads to occasional dullness and by an excess of emotional words such as "terrifying" or "frightening," which should almost never be said out loud in poetry, his gift for poetry was still a generous one. (p. 47)

World War II solved some problems for Prokosch and created others. He had, prior to the conflict, always contemplated the possibility of war as if it were the approach of doomsday. When war came and then went, and man and his problems persisted, Prokosch lost some of the basis for his world outlook, for his delicious fears. Of the three novels set in the war years, only *The Conspirators* is successful. . . . But it is not, finally, a good book because it is better unified or better conceived. It is a good book because Prokosch's old view of the collapse of Europe and civilization remained valid in the immune atmosphere of neutral Portugal. One did not in the first two years of the war know what would happen to Europe. . . . Both *Age of Thunder* and *The Idols of the Cave* are seeking for a new beginning or, better, for a new approach to the destiny of man. In *The Idols of the Cave* only the most tentative notions rise as to what the new approach might be. But one spies from time to time a fear of mechanization and of conformity in the western world. These tentative notions, however, became positive focuses in later novels. (pp. 100-01)

[Prokosch's] contribution has not been, one sees now, to participate like Hemingway in the public experience of his generation; it has been to participate in the psychic experience of his generation. He has not marched on the broad plain. He has wandered in a narrow chasm, fitfully lit, haunted by phantoms and echoing with the voices of dangerous memories. One would be foolish to take his chasm as the whole truth; but it would be equally foolish to take as the whole truth the armies marching on the plain. (p. 130)

Prokosch is not alone . . . in his depiction of the flavor of internationalism in his novels and poetry, but his contribution to the genre is unique. He is not so concerned as was Henry James with the contrast of cultures brought into confrontation. Nor is he so concerned with the comparison of cultures as is Lawrence Durrell. Prokosch is not primarily interested in the exilic or expatriate viewpoint which fascinated Hemingway and many others in this century. Prokosch's interest and concern, while partaking of cultural contrast and comparison, largely reflect a vogue, almost a mystical haloing, of the idea of internationalism. This vogue represents a condemnation, really, of American isolationism prior to World War II. Prokosch's intensity of conviction could come, really, only to an American, one supposes, and only to one whose background contained elements both of provincialism and cosmopolitanism. Only one who was born early in the twentieth century and whose youth was spent in Wisconsin, Texas, and European schools would so singleheartedly desire to collate disparate cultural elements. The word here is "collate," for there is never any impression that Prokosch wants to fuse the elements. His Asians do not change his Europeans; his Europeans do not blend with his Americans. However, when his Americans or Europeans are not destroyed by their contacts with each other—or, more particularly, by their contacts with Asians or Africans—they may enrich their lives through broadening their understanding of themselves. (pp. 131-32)

One cannot avoid the impression that Prokosch's novels rather fretfully deplore the changes wrought, and about to be wrought, by the twentieth century. Again and again his earlier novels remind us that the old Europe is dying. His later novels remind us that some change, not so great as had earlier been anticipated, has already taken place and that the future is that of an antiseptic, dull civilization. Yet what is it in the old Europe, that Prokosch so reluctantly gives up? It is not the Europe of 1910 or of the nineteenth century; it is the Europe of the Age of Reason. It is a western civilization incidentally aristocratic but naturally international and one which took man rather than five-year plans as the measure of all things. In reality, Prokosch laments the passage of an era which never in a personal way existed for him and which, indeed, had been swept away by the century preceding his birth. (pp. 132-33)

If the intent of Prokosch's internationalism is to turn life toward life, so also has his faith in freedom a similar aim: to allow the soul scope to pursue its own tragedy. Prokosch uses the word "tragedy" with a romantic largeness. He associates it with "dignity." To a degree, at least, tragedy must mean to him the weaving of individual destiny that is apparent in all of his novels. Prokosch examines both life and its destiny in two different ways. He holds western, civilized men up to the cruel, frank light of Asia, Africa, Brazil. He places them in wastelands and among primitives whose incomprehension finally begets ironic comprehension. Or, he scrutinizes his Europeans and Americans in their great cities: Paris, Rome, New York. The cities function for Prokosch somewhat as do his deserts and jungles, for they extract as well as affect the spirits of his characters. At the same time, the city is clothed in its civilization, while the desert or jungle is nude. The city thus murmurs of the heights of civilization, perhaps passed, perhaps to come, but always with a gentle insistence on the virtues of decorum and intelligence. . . . Unquestionably, Prokosch longs to coordinate instinct and civilized intelligence, but he does not wish to do so through any romantic dependence on nature. (pp. 134-35)

Frederic Prokosch creates character within a severely restricted range beyond which he cannot, or will not, go. We may easily catalogue the categories: the faceless hero, the sly but engaging aborigine, the promiscuous and ambitious heroine, the "tragic" artist, the conspirator, the homosexual, the European or American whose sensibilities are whipped into hysteria by exposure to a circumstance or to a savage setting. In addition, the novels are salted with creatures, *creatures* rather than characters, who appear briefly to present a tantalizing surface of inscrutable gesture but who disappear like figures in a nightmare without any sure resolution. (p. 136)

The fact is that Prokosch writes what Hawthorne in the nineteenth century called "romance"; that is, an allegory in which the real or surface occurrences may much of the time appear illusory, so that only meaning or theme obtains a solidity. In addition to this general aim of romance, Prokosch also writes in the tradition of legend or fable. (p. 139)

Because Prokosch apparently believes faithfully that man is born with a sacred nature, his whole concept of character is that of encouraging that nature to fulfill itself or, if need be, to cast off the disguise created by the fearful self or imposed by modern life. . . . Prokosch is speaking, of course, of what Carl Jung calls the *anima* in the layers of personality. . . . The seemingly flaccid hero of Prokosch's novels derives from the fact that Prokosch chooses to reveal primarily the innocuous surface. Yet the whole truth is that, through other characters and cryptic clues, the submerged selves of his heroes are subtly suggested. (pp. 140-41)

Frederic Prokosch's luxuriant prose style is characterized at its most elementary level by a contest between large terms, vague but suggestive, and sharp, brilliant metaphors. He hangs a very great deal—too much, one says finally—on such words as "prehistory," "primitive," and "tragedy." Such abstractions suggest an attempt to shove a number of indefinite emotions into one container in the hope that the container itself will be imposing enough to scare away questions. The terms are a literary equivalent of political jargon, a kind of jingoism of the soul. (p. 142)

Wherever one turns in Prokosch's work he finds the oblique view, the irrational desire, the strange imbalance, the subtle mood, over all of which his style blows like a hectic wind in Hansel's and Gretel's forest. If one thinks Kafka took unpredictability as far as possible, he needs only to read Prokosch to know better. If one thinks T. S. Eliot's Apeneck Sweeney struck utter simplification in saying that life is "birth, copulation and death," one need only read Prokosch to find an author who strikes birth from the list. What, one asks, is the permanent worth of this novelist who stands outside the categories of the spokesmen for the mainstream, such as Thomas Mann, E. M. Forster, Ernest Hemingway, or William Faulkner? . . . It seems unlikely that more than two or three novels of Frederic Prokosch have any chance of survival. At the same time, it seems improbable that such a unique voice as his can ever be quite lost. No picture of the whole accomplishment of the twentieth century would be complete without cognizance of, say, *The Asiatics, The Seven Who Fled,* perhaps *Nine Days to Mukalla,* or *The Seven Sisters.* For these books possess the kind of delicate tensile strength, the individuality which survives longer than many a more conventional book. . . . The modern scene does not offer equivalents to Frederic Prokosch. But even though he is not very much like any other contemporary novelist, his prospects are shared by other writers who, in rejecting the common view of life, are forced to create their own views through intensities of style and situation. They are, like Prokosch, essentially poets who in a century of prose, write novels. Julien Green, Lawrence Durrell, Vladimir Nabokov come to mind, along with Truman Capote, Carson McCullers, Paul Bowles, and possibly Isak Dinesen and James Purdy. In such a company, Frederic Prokosch has no masters—and hardly a peer. (pp. 146-47)

*Radcliffe Squires, in his* Frederic Prokosch *(copyright 1964 by Twayne Publishers, Inc.; reprinted with the permission of Twayne Publishers, a Division of G. K. Hall & Co.), Twayne, 1964.*

Frederic Prokosch's *The Wreck of the Cassandra* may produce audible groans of dismay. Who on earth would have thought that a writer would resort to the *narrenschiff* device again, but here it is, the steamer *Cassandra* this time, puffing across the Pacific in 1938 with an assorted collection of international wanderers who will (right) be shipwrecked and (right again) be forced to confront their true natures. . . .

Prokosch's characters have been recruited from the same old passenger list: Lily Domingo, a rich, bored American; Baron Kleist, a demonic German; Professor Shishnik, a meditative Slav; Laura Eccles, a virginal Englishwoman; the Americans Tony and Laura Wagenseller, partners in a disintegrating marriage. Their fates also come as standard equipment. The innocent Laura Eccles will be put to death in savage fertility rites; Lily Domingo will be murdered for her jewels by a demented Malay; the gentle Shishnik will kill the mad Teuton, Baron Kleist, in self-defense; Tony and Laura will survive with new respect for one another. And since *The Wreck of the Cassandra* uses its shopworn formula with a full awareness of the modern temper, there will also be a good deal of existentialist philosophizing. . . .

Frederic Prokosch has been writing novels since the mid-1930s, and he can spin out words with the polished ease of an old professional. More's the pity that *The Wreck of the Cassandra* is so banal and unbelievable, a docile servant of the existential mood.

*A. Sidney Knowles, Jr., in* The Southern Review, *Vol. IV, No. 3, Summer, 1968, pp. 823-25.*

[*America, My Wilderness*] is an exercise in decorative faux-naïveté. . . . Reading the elaborate, high-charged style of this book is like being confronted by a bulldozer on a narrow road: It scarcely gives you time to step back and look at it because it just keeps coming at you. The narrative —full of magic, violence, and fabulous incidents—is almost engulfed by the metaphors, and *America, My Wilderness* is a static novel. The characters don't move across the land so much as the land moves under them. The naming of towns and rivers and the animation of landscape ("Then the land grew hysterical. . . . The waves of noonday light made the sand seethe and coruscate, and the earth lay in a spasm of grotesque torment") doesn't guarantee lyricism or vitality, and when everything is like something else, it's difficult to know what anything is like. . . .

*America, My Wilderness* aspires to poetry, to a mythopoeic conception of the country as something as vast and grand and inexplicable as nature itself, and as violent. All this is a great deal for a novel to take on, and I think that the desperate and often frantic style is an indication that the author is cowed by the task he has set himself. There are moments when he rises to it, but most of the time it's very heavy going.

*Alan Hislop, in* Book World (© The Washington Post), *May 21, 1972, p. 5.*

Tag ends out of classical mythology serve to give some substance to [*America, My Wilderness*], more a brilliantly executed travelogue than a novel wherein the author in episodic fashion traces the journey of his amorphous hero across the United States, back and forth, up and down, in a fruitless search for a country closer to cloudland than America. Color, sound, and beauty often juxtaposed with ugliness all help to enchant the reader and lose him in a world of unutterable strangeness despite a haunting familiarity here and there accented by the inclusion of place names readily identifiable but rejected out of hand all the same as mere intrusions designed to give verisimilitude otherwise lacking to a tale of no considerable validity.

Virginia Quarterly Review, *Vol. 48, No. 3 (Summer, 1972), p. c.*

Frederic Prokosch is, thank God, no Bill Burroughs. The symbols, the weirdnesses he offers in [*America, My Wilderness*], are reassuringly familiar. I don't know exactly what it is about puppet-masters, photograph albums, hunchbacks, umbrellas, lepidopterists, feathers, patent medicine pedlars and tiny music boxes that makes them so immediately mysterious and intriguing and irresistibly *other*. Certainly something does. So much so, in fact, that in less delicate and precise hands than those of Mr. Prokosch they are in serious danger of becoming stock items, surrealist cliché.

*America, My Wilderness* tells stories of a young man's adventures as he travels across turn-of-the-century America, finding beauty and violence, creation and destruction everywhere inseparable. Trite old stuff, no doubt: picaresque and predictable. But illuminated here by the fresh, clear imagination of the author, and told with a lack of embarrassment, a richness, a love of language that I find quite breath-taking. . . .

The blurb boldly suggests that 'to read the novel is to inhabit again for a time a kind of Eden'. I don't quite know what that means. But I'll go along with it all the way.

*D. G. Compton, in* Books and Bookmen, *January, 1973, pp. 82-3.*

* * *

## PURDY, James 1923-

**Purdy, a masterful American novelist and short story writer, writes dark fiction about narcissism and the cruelty of love. (See also *Contemporary Authors*, Vols. 33-36.)**

For an author who uses dialogue so tellingly in his novels and stories, James Purdy is strangely inept in his two plays. . . . [There] are not even flamboyant and inventive moments—as there certainly are in the fiction—to distract me from the sense that nothing is going on. *Cracks* . . ., is an amorphous play in which an old woman, through a dream or a visitation, is assured that, despite pain, life goes on; this is apparently comfort for the kind of fear the child displays in his desire to have closed the "cracks" through which "the zephyrs of death" blow. *Children Is All* is a longer play in which Edna Cartwright waits for the return of her convict son, but she can only recognize him by an act—cradling his head in her lap as he dies—while she calls him stranger. Much of Purdy's best work deals with the way men remain close strangers to one another, but his plays use that favorite theme without illuminating it; there is more dramatic invention in *Malcolm* and the short stories than there is in either of the plays.

*Gerald Weales, in his* The Jumping-Off Place: American Drama in the 1960's *(reprinted with permission of Macmillan Publishing Co., Inc.; copyright © 1969 by Gerald Weales), Macmillan, 1969, pp. 211-12.*

In the world in which [Purdy's] Malcolm finds himself, sense is continually dissolving in contradictions. There is nothing stable enough or meaningful enough around him to enable him properly speaking to 'begin'. The word recurs as Malcolm constantly thinks or hopes that this time 'life is actually *beginning*' as a new social situation opens up to him. Yet the feeling we are left with is that he never really does *begin*; it is as though the visible, audible parts of him are not really his own but borrowed for and from the occasion. He passes through changing scenes but, instead of thickening into identity and consolidating a real self, his life is really a long fading. This paradox of passing through life without, as it were, beginning to live Purdy explores at length in his most searching novel, where the problem is written into the title, *Cabot Wright Begins*. But at this stage we can make the point that if Malcolm never begins neither does his story ever really begin—another way in which Purdy seems to want to remind us that when we finished the book we only have texture without substance. . . .

*Cabot Wright Begins* . . . gathers together all the themes opened up or touched on in Purdy's earlier work and explores them with a subtlety and humour and power which makes this, to my mind, not only Purdy's most profound novel but one of the most important American novels since the war. Cabot Wright is a Yale man who gets bored with Wall Street and his wife and who, after an unusual cure from a strange doctor, becomes a relentless rapist. Put that way the novel might seem to promise the sort of glamorous pornography one associates with a best seller. Yet it contains no detailed sexual scenes at all and it transpires that Cabot Wright can only think of 'boredom' as the motive of his rapes, not lust. More to the point, over a third of the novel is spent in discussing the problems connected with writing a book, the biography of Cabot Wright. Chapter Seven of Purdy's novel is entitled 'Cabot Wright Begins', while the first six chapters are concerned with the people involved in the decision to attempt to make a book out of his life. The frame has never intruded so far into a Purdy novel before. . . .

Just as the Invisible Man conveys the relief of finally dropping out of all 'mythic contact with the social' into his unlocatable refuge in a border area, so in this novel Purdy has demonstrated the need to escape from all the supposititious 'selves' fostered by those illusory contacts. The question again arises—is there a third realm beyond the alternatives of submission to social fabrications or escape by flowing away? Can a 'non-self' have an identity? In rejecting all this non-humanity of society, in what sense does Cabot Wright achieve real humanity? One answer that Purdy clearly intends is—simply by achieving the ability to laugh. He inserts a long rhetorical paragraph on laughter as the supreme consolation; it ends: 'Meaning there is no meaning but the laughter of the moment made it almost worth while. That's all it's about. We was here, finally laughed.' Perhaps you are only human as long as you are laughing; some such desperation is implicit in the sudden unchecked feeling of this paragraph.

*Tony Tanner, "Frames Without Pictures," in his* City of Words: American Fiction 1950-1970 *(copyright © 1971 by Tony Tanner; reprinted by permission of Harper & Row, Publishers, Inc.), Harper, 1971, pp. 85-108.*

If Petronius could pull it off, and Federico Fellini could pull it off, why not James Purdy? The identification of imperial Rome and the Empire State is, after all, a commonplace of High Camp culture. So enter Elijah Thrush, mime, poet, painter—part prophet of unspeakable corruption and eternal youth, part white, fungoid, mucous taint.

In this American *Satyricon* [*I am Elijah Thrush*], scented with Kashmir saffron and running with mascara, satire must look after itself. For the fable itself floats free into an exotic, Yellow Book fantasy world, or Firbankian romp, of unscrupulous oil millionairess, Millicent de Frayne, her mahogany buck of a spy or go-between, and antique lover (Pierrot, Narcissus, The Most Beautiful Man in the World), himself in love with his mute great-grandson, the Bird of Heaven, "a young boy with flowing raven locks, haunting wild Indian eyes, and a mouth of brilliant vermilion".

Yet what seems to ring out from the pungent flavours of this mixed curry is the old, tormented cry of hurt love—the American bitch goddess in perpetual heat and her Negro Adonis. . . .

[Perhaps], after all, this *Thrush* is not only a *Satyricon,* but an American parable. Set in a fairy-tale city of New York, this dark exotic jewel, as if fathered by Cocteau on F. Scott Fitzgerald, seems like the pianist with dark circles in his moon-pale face and a geranium in his buttonhole, flashing looks of malevolent hatred at the audience "when he was not playing Cécile Chaminade or Eric Coates".

*"Golden Suction," in* The Times Literary Supplement, *November 3, 1972, p. 1305.*

[*I Am Elijah Thrush*] is a stylish novel in which the manner is very well suited to subject matter, and the comic tone is judged to a nicety. In general it is Firbankish, an exuberantly gay exercise in the bizarre, a series of elegant acrobatics and graceful gestures which have about them a certain iridescence like the shimmer of peacock feathers. Bird analogies are appropriate because the theme of this work is the predatory nature of love, and here the characters behave like ravenous birds. Albert Pegg falls for Elijah and the plot tumbles the reader through a coruscating succession of improbable turns of fortune, of kidnapping and counter-kidnapping, to a remarkable comic climax at sea.

*J. A. Cuddon, in* Books and Bookmen, *March, 1973, p. 79.*

*Malcolm,* James Purdy's first novel, was published in 1959 and has not suffered from want of acclaim. The praise has been richly deserved, for Purdy may be the most skillful black-humorist around. No one, however, has given Purdy credit for the full achievement of *Malcolm*. The novel generally is applauded for its wit, style, and deft handling of the disturbing themes of loneliness and lack of identity in the bizarre nightmare of modern existence. In addition, Purdy's gift for sharp and sweeping satire rakes such targets as marriage, art and artists, sex, status, and adolescence. The last is a tempting critical morsel, for it makes the novel classifiable as a *bildungsroman*. Without question *Malcolm* is a story of a young man confronting adulthood, for initiation is its central theme. The novel has been called "an allegory of growing up." However, Purdy has not written merely another novel of adolescence in a century already overstocked. Instead, he has offered us a sport on that type, using the genre to satirize it, with a wry approach to form as well as content. Viewed this way, the satire of an already cheerless book is deepened, and the blackness of its humor becomes more pervasive, more complete, and more grim. . . .

Malcolm himself is a parody of the typical initiate. Such youths, no matter how primitive or unsophisticated, are usually bright young men, sensitive, quick and alert. But not Malcolm. His most consistent response is to fall asleep at crucial moments, more reminiscent of Stan Laurel than Stephen Dedalus. His single diversion is to sit in his bathrobe and listen to the ocean roar in his sea shells. Billy Budd's illiteracy was all the more inspirational because it made him appealingly ingenuous. Malcolm's stupidity is so complete it arouses distrust, not love or affection. The ultimate question is whether he has any mind at all. . . .

The innocent, saintly, and Christ-like qualities of Malcolm are too hard to miss to be taken seriously. . . .

One of the novel's major themes seems embodied in the character of Madame Girard, for she shows how much more important style is than content. Style at least equips one to survive, at times to survive well, whereas someone like Malcolm who clings to substances which are often fictions seems assured of defeat. . . .

Perhaps . . . the handling of Malcolm's death makes the extent of the parody impossible to deny. . . . The reference at his death to "Malcolm's short long life" . . . tends to turn the solid meaning of Francis Macomber's short happy life inside out. Finally, a lavish funeral is held. However, the coroner and the undertaker contend that no corpse was in the casket, that nobody (no body?) was buried in the ceremony. The only proof that Malcolm died rests ultimately with Madame Girard, and "in time her story became full of evasions". . . . Thus, if nothing proves that Malcolm is dead, nothing, likewise, guarantees that Malcolm ever lived, in any sense of the word. Instead of the novel being an allegory of a young everyman, it is more an allegory of no man—the way Purdy sees modern man. "But nobody could deny that there had been a ceremony". . . . Perhaps that is the way we must look at *Malcolm*, as ceremony, a texture with the substance deliberately removed. In a way the novel is like a whopping practical joke, because we are not supposed to hunt for meaning in a practical joke. Like life in the modern world, only the humor is important.

*Charles Stetler, "Purdy's 'Malcolm': Allegory of No Man," in* Critique: Studies in Modern Fiction, *Vol. XIV, No. 3, 1973, pp. 91-9.*

A prominent feature in the microcosm of James Purdy's six novels and numerous short stories is the relationship between a young innocent and the corrupt adult world in which he must make his way. Both terms used in this description need to be taken with some latitude: the youth is always "innocent" to one degree or another in terms of his *knowledge* of the world, but he is almost never lacking in toughness, resilience, and cunning; as he learns the harsh rules, the rough grounds, and the almost pitiless odds of the game, he copes at each stage, even if early death is frequently the goal. Nor are the mentors "corrupt" in any simple sense of the term as suggested by the villain in a melodrama: they are former innocents themselves, reenacting a shadow play of their own initiation perhaps in a vain effort to communicate with their own lost innocence. And finally, one cannot construe this theme with their own lost innocence. And finally, one cannot construe this theme as the statement of an evil practice of a morally depraved minority, which might somehow have been avoided; it must be taken as the ordinary process of living in the world as we know it. . . .

All of the innocents are bewildered about ultimate meanings; they have renounced childhood religious faith and have found no viable substitute explanation of reality or standard for behavior. The innocent almost invariably keeps notes or a journal in an attempt, first of all, to record his experiences, and secondly to find a track through the wilds by means of written meditations. . . .

In [the picaresque] tradition, gross and spectacular crime is generally eschewed, but the whole range of petty crime is the stream in which the protagonists float, and "honor among thieves," or some comradely code of standards whereby one has stable ways of relating to peers, is the prevailing moral code, quite outside dominant respectable codes of the day in most cases. The whole social ambiance of pickpockets, smugglers, thieves, bawds, pimps, prostitutes, card sharps, pardoners, mountebanks, and cheats corresponds only very roughly to "the insulted and the injured" in Purdy, but the parallel is there—and this is the same subculture in which Huckleberry Finn threads his way, in a book Purdy admires strongly. . . .

Although all his novels present a rich train of variations on the theme of the picaresque corruption of innocents, it is his masterful novella, "63: Dream Palace," that gives the most balanced treatment of all the factors in short compass.

*Frank Baldanza, "James Purdy on the Corruption of Innocents," in* Contemporary Literature *(© 1974 by the Regents of the University of Wisconsin), Vol. 15, No. 3, Summer, 1974, pp. 315-30.*

# R

## RABE, David 1940-

**Rabe, an American dramatist, has won several important awards.**

Occasionally in the theater one finds a play that drives deeper into the despair of existence than can be stated in clichés. David Rabe's *Sticks and Bones* is one such, and although I cannot fully comprehend its meaning, I am aware that it is invading with freshness and honesty some of the most painful ambiguities that afflict contemporary America. . . .

It is impossible to be very explicit about some of Rabe's implications. For instance, there's a strong hint that the behavior of American soldiers in Vietnam is the logical extension of our worship of violence, and yet Rabe seems to say that there is also an honesty and a satisfaction in our recognition of our violent natures. Our violence may be, the play seems to imply, the antidote to a comfortable but vapid family life in which a non-communicative peace hides real feelings. . . .

*Sticks and Bones* is not the complaint of one American soldier, but a remarkably ambitious attempt to explore a larger and more complex American dilemma.

*Henry Hewes, "'Only Winter is White'," in* Saturday Review *(copyright © 1971 by Saturday Review/World, Inc.; reprinted with permission), November 27, 1971, pp. 70-1.*

[Rabe's] first two plays, produced in 1971 and 1972, got much praise and many awards. Now it's 1973. His latest play, *The Orphan,* was recently produced at the Anspacher, and the critical consensus was that this writer of exceptional gifts had slipped somewhat and had written a play that didn't "work" (the current most popular critical cant word). To me, the play was merely infested with the disease that had been evident in the two earlier ones.

*The Basic Training of Pavlo Hummel* was one more good-hearted sentimental undergraduate play about the horrors of war—this time Vietnam—showing a simple-minded joe being savaged by vast cruel powers, using stale expressionist fantasy and even staler rhetoric to prove its humanitarianism and high-mindedness. Then came *Sticks and Bones,* which was at least a mixed bag. A blind Vietnam veteran returns to his home and is such a moral nuisance that his family induces him to commit suicide. The family stuff, done in sharp pop-art style (the parents were called Ozzie and Harriet), had good smiling bitterness; but the soldier's purple speeches and the device of his phantom Vietnamese girlfriend were straight out of Playwriting 435 (Permission of Instructor Required). The pop elements gave me some little hope for Rabe, which the new play drastically deferred. In *The Orphan* he opted completely for the purple prose, without let-up or remorse, the kind of rhetoric that brings a tear to the eye of a third-rate playwriting instructor. The disease hasn't just recently struck Rabe, it is now simply unopposed. . . .

His one apparent avenue to effective writing led through anti-grandness; his critical reception in general led him to think—or anyway didn't discourage him from thinking—that he is equipped for the grand. Now those who myopically encouraged him can no longer blink at the bankruptcy; after the praise, now come the tsk-tsks. I don't mean that once having praised him they were obliged to go on praising him forever; I mean that *The Orphan* is not much different from or worse than the work they praised; and now they have to know it.

*Stanley Kauffmann, in* The New Republic *(reprinted by permission of* The New Republic; *© 1973 by Harrison-Blaine of New Jersey, Inc.), May 26, 1973, pp. 22, 33-4.*

"Boom Boom Room" is not a good play, not a good play at all. . . .

The trouble is that Mr. Rabe's play never gets anywhere. . . . The play is loose, flaccid, unfocussed, wandering uncertainly in and out of realism and expressionism, comedy and serious drama—not fusing these opposites, not poising them effectively against each other, just wandering.

Mr. Rabe has not really figured out what to do with this material. . . .

Still, "Boom Boom Room" is really not **so** terrible. What it does have to say about emptiness and confusion is neither unbelievable nor untrue. There is some good, funny comic writing. . . .

If only Mr. Rabe had not been so over-praised before now,

if only his play—so wrong for **this** theatre, **this** audience, **this** occasion—had not been given the dangerous honor of planting Mr. Papp's New York Shakespeare Festival flag on the virgin shores of Lincoln Center, it might be possible to acknowledge him as a promising playwright who had not yet put it all together, and leave it at that. But as things stand, it is necessary to say that "Boom Boom Room," which was meant to mark a proud new departure in the history of the Vivian Beaumont Theatre, turns out to be only the latest of the many disasters that have taken place under that stylish, jinxed roof.

*Julius Novick, "Papp Goes Boom at Beaumont," in* The Village Voice *(reprinted by permission of* The Village Voice; *© 1973 by The Village Voice, Inc.), November 15, 1973, p. 74.*

[There] is a savage poet in Rabe rather than a naturalist. His humor contains venom, an uncontained rage. He is lacerated by the sordidness, the cruel craziness of our place and time. In his early plays *Pavlo Hummel* and *Sticks and Bones,* the objects of his horror and wrath were the war in Indochina and its aftermath at home, but in *Boom Boom Room* his aim is broader. Though the milieux here are those of the cheap night joints, the lowest working class, the detritus of U.S. civilization, the comic inferno he depicts leads to a quasi-universal accusation.

The play's colors are glaring. The intensity of the author's feeling and imagination reaches beyond verisimilitude to expressionistic declaration, a kind of super realism. Yet in its own special way there is something funny and probing within the ghastliness. The whole is uneven, at times forced and crude, but its power is unmistakable.

*Harold Clurman, in* The Nation, *November 26, 1973, pp. 572-73.*

The theme [of *Boom Boom Room*], the ravaging of a female social-sexual victim, is so familiar that one *counts* on the familiarity, in a way: one assumes that the author would never have chosen it unless he was convinced he had new insights or an artistic vision of the subject that in itself would afford new insights. . . . Not so. Not Rabe. Clearly, one can say after the fourth experience of him, his notion of playwriting is to get a clever device, impressively flashy, then just fill in the rest of the play as needed. Previously he has used old German expressionist anti-militarist dream techniques; or a blind Vietnam veteran with an invisible Vietnamese girlfriend in his Midwest home; or a combination of the Oresteia myth with Mylai and Charles Manson. After these initial gimmicks, he seems to have said, who could question my gravity or power?

Some can—even after his new gimmick. He puts *Boom Boom Room* in a multiple set, with six large gilded cages hanging from the roof, rope ladders going up to each. At the start five go-go girls come out and climb to the cages. From time to time, they writhe, comment, come down and do numbers with their leader; but their real purpose is to show that Rabe is theatrically brilliant. I didn't feel I needed them around continuously to emphasize the heroine's sex-object fate; it was Rabe who needed them.

Because without that flashy device, it would have become clear quickly that an adolescent intellect was pompously restating what all of us over 14 know: that he has padded these social-characterological clichés with torturous fake-emotional ramblings, peopled his play with stereotypes (the three principal men are a shy clerk, a truckdriver and a homosexual), and has lolled in long detours of reminiscence that are like plastic Chekhov. And besides studding his dialogue with old jokes, he keeps re-using a stale naturalistic dialogue device. Someone is talking about subject A, suddenly interpolates something about B (as if in a sting of memory), then continues with A; finishes that; pauses, then wistfully returns to B. In Rabe's heavy hands, it becomes a vaudeville formula.

*Stanley Kauffmann, in* The New Republic *(reprinted by permission of* The New Republic; *© 1973 by Harrison-Blaine of New Jersey, Inc.), December 1, 1973, p. 22.*

The new play which most interested me thus far this season is . . . David Rabe's *Boom Boom Room.* Once again, and through another milieu, this young dramatist vents his hurt and anger at a world in which moral insensibility and a lack of real values breed cruelty and grief, breakdown and horror—what an early 20th-century Russian writer once called "red laughter."

But Rabe is a man of feeling, a poet whose wounds cry out to us. His savagery does not make us turn away in disgust. In this play, as in earlier ones (*Pavlo Hummel* and *Sticks and Bones*), the "little" men and women he writes about are people in whom, beneath the filth of stupid habit, grinding mechanization, tumultuous inanity, mindless verbiage and ugly frivolity, there are still remnants of natural human desire and aspiration. . . .

The play, I repeat, begins as though it were a naturalistic study—it never strays far from the individual girl—but it gradually evolves into a soul-searing schizophrenic rave. There are, in other words, both a subjective intimacy in the play's composition and a general statement which declares itself in speeches and scenes which exceed realism.

*Harold Clurman, in* The Nation, *December 3, 1973, p. 603.*

The shock of David Rabe's play ["Boom Boom Room"] is the shock of truth, the most valid dramatic use of that emotion. Rabe's intention couldn't be clearer. By the creation of a repugnant world of anti-human cruelty, ugliness, and degradation, he throws into sharp relief the plight of his heroine, Chrissy, the go-go dancer and onetime hooker who is desperately trying to escape from that world. There is something fierce about the way he throws himself into Chrissy's tortured soul, not only examining but sharing all the doubt and pain and fear, every drop of the anguished self-loathing she feels for herself. The depth of his capacity for compassionate empathy is astonishing.

But Rabe is also hellbent on wringing the same compassion from his audience. To make you share his sympathy for the vulnerable Chrissy, his whooping pride in her tentative steps toward self-respect and self-awareness, his anguish when she is defeated, it is crucial for him to draw an uncompromising vision of the social forces which created her and which are conspiring to keep her down. In other words, Rabe has set himself the task of creating a dramatic vision of a woman's personal hell. If the hell isn't hellish, and the demons aren't loathsome, Chrissy's triumphs, defeats, and ultimate despair and capitulation lose their intensity and their value.

Neither Rabe's play nor the New York Shakespeare Festival's production of it succeeds in creating this living hell, primarily because the play's surrealism is insufficiently vivid. Chrissy's world of home and nightclub, and the family, friends, and lovers who populate it, are meant to be nightmares and the demons who populate nightmares—surreal, not in the sense of unreal, but in the sense of more-than-real. If they are grotesque, it is not for the purpose of shocking you, but to jolt your sensibilities, to make their reality so vivid you cannot ignore or escape the truth of it. That's the way Chrissy sees her life, and that is the way you must see it to understand her and feel for her.

And yet, a lot of people are shocked by "Boom Boom Room," a surprisingly large number of critics among them. Morally shocked. By the language, the ugliness, the brutality, the gross sexuality of Chrissy's world. Ironically, it might be argued that the production is too modest, too conservative in conceptualizing in theatrical terms the full scale of the horror that Chrissy calls her life. As objective reality, the dramatic landscape is overdrawn; as a vision of the surreal, the stylized abstraction of Chrissy's interior subjective reality, it is insufficiently bold, inadequately audacious. The nightmare isn't fearsome enough; the demons on stage aren't as horrifying as the devils that howl down the corridors of the mind. The audience is confused; they think they are watching the merely real, and they sense that it is too strong. And so, they are shocked.

I believe that. I believe that if Rabe and his director Joseph Papp had intensified the surreal quality of the horror, making it all noisier, dirtier, uglier—not in a naturalistic style, but in the supra-reality of nightmare—the reality of Chrissy's dilemma would have taken on a purer poignancy. . . .

The remarkable quality about David Rabe is his willingness to confront the alien culture of the Boom Boom Room and the level of society it represents. Not only does he face it head on, and attempt to understand and communicate the dynamics of the people who live in it, but he also finds amidst the wretchedness and ugliness a good deal of character and dignity. Chrissy—remember—is not one of us, but one of Them. Maybe that's the real threat, the fear that if we look hard enough at Them, "the others," we might see beyond the effects of their dehumanization. We might even see the humanity of these people we would prefer to avoid in life. And if we are forced to look through the unsavory reality that "shocks" us on a superficial level, we might feel compassion for the fellow human beings who live in this alien world; we might even feel a share of responsibility in shaping their lives. We might even feel the urge to help, to change the shape of social patterns which we have always accepted and acquiesced in.

To feel responsibility is frightening. One could almost call it shocking.

*Marilyn Stasio, in* Cue *(copyright © 1973 by Cue Publications, Inc.), December 3, 1973, p. 2.*

*Boom Boom Room* is Rabe's most ambitious play to date—it runs three hours—but for me it remains much what it was when I saw it as a work-in-progress more than a year ago at Villanova: an unnecessarily long chronicle of a not very bright girl's unsuccessful search for a self, for meaning, for love. Rabe has turned away from the direct treatment of social problems that marked his celebrated anti-Vietnam plays, *The Basic Training of Pavlo Hummel* and *Sticks and Bones,* but he retains his preoccupation with American violence and with our habit of kidding ourselves about public and private disasters. These concerns are implicit, and occasionally explicit, all through *Boom Boom Room,* and I suspect that he means Chrissy, his go-go heroine, to be a representative figure like Pavlo Hummel or the TV family of *Sticks and Bones.* America is still his subject, but Chrissy is both too idiosyncratic and too stereotypical to give *Boom Boom Room* the kind of stature for which it seems to be reaching. The characters are finally too special to tell me anything very startling about myself and my society, and what they tell me about themselves is too commonplace and too predictable to give them much dramatic validity. Oddly, in *Sticks and Bones,* Rabe begins with a situation-comedy family which, under the stress of the action, outgrows its generic limits; in *Boom Boom Room* he begins with characters, who have at least the individuality of mental and physical ties, but whose edges are knocked off by dramatic and psychological clichés.

The play is interestingly conceived because its actual dramatic line is in conflict with the one that might be presumed from the heroine's central emotional concern. *Boom Boom Room* is a quest play with the quester defeated at every turn. . . .

Although much of *Boom Boom Room* is overextended and overexplained, at his best Rabe has an oblique style which is attractive because it suggests more than it defines, because it opens the audience to possibility.

*Gerald Weales, in* Commonweal *(reprinted by permission of Commonweal Publishing Co., Inc.), December 14, 1973, pp. 294-95.*

[Unlike] most of those who have written antiwar plays, Rabe refuses to grind the axe, to present pure victims and pure monsters. Although the army helps Pavlo [of *Pavlo Hummel*] to become a killer, it does so with his own eager cooperation. It does not "dehumanize" him, to use that much overused and generally meaningless word; it gives him the occasion to cultivate his basic capacity for the inhumane. At the end, Pavlo has, perhaps, achieved a partial self-identity, but the what or the why of that identity is never really clear. It is as if Rabe himself had not quite decided. Or perhaps that is the point. Perhaps the Pavlo of Act 1 and the Pavlo of Act 2 are really very much the same, neither hero nor villain, neither bad nor good guy, but a lonely, confused, and infinitely fallible man.

If the ambiguity of Pavlo is at times disturbing, there is a reverse of the coin that gives the play much of its impact and dimension. Rabe does not make anything—apart from the hell and absurdity of war—*that* black and white. He avoids both easy sentimentality and facile point-scoring and —and this, too, is a welcome relief—he realizes that horror and comedy, like tragedy and comedy, are seldom far apart. His Vietcong are no more heroic than his Americans (which by now seems almost refreshing). It is war itself that becomes the horror story, a tragicomic nightmare in which no one really can win, in which casual cruelty and indifference are as likely to be found in the black pajamas of the Vietcong as in GI battle dress. It is that and the refusal to be simplistic, together with Rabe's ability to create pungent, evocative, and believable dialogue and unstereotyped characters, that lifts *Pavlo Hummel* above such agit-prop exercises as *Viet Rock, Pinkville,* and the rest and makes it, diffused focus and all, one of the best, if not the best play to come out of America's Vietnam nightmare.

*Catharine Hughes, "'The Basic Training of Pavlo Hummel'," in her* Plays, Politics and Polemics, *Drama Book Specialists, 1973, pp. 77-82.*

* * *

## RANSOM, John Crowe 1888-1974

**Ransom was a Southern American poet and critic. His graceful and gently ironic poems were generally consonant with the principles of New Criticism, of which "school" he was a major proponent. With Donald Davidson and Allen Tate, Ransom was also active in the "Fugitive Group" of poets living and working in Nashville from about 1915 to 1928. (See also *Contemporary Authors*, Vols. 5-8, rev. ed.; obituary, Vols. 49-52.)**

For Ransom the agrarian image is of the kind of life in which leisure, grace, civility can exist in harmony with thought and action, making the individual's life a wholesome, harmonious experience. When Ransom writes of nature, it is almost never as wilderness, but as farmland. His agrarianism is of the old Southern plantation, the gentle, mannered life of leisure and refinement without the need or inclination to pioneer. The necessity for order and stability is uppermost in Ransom's world. His poems reflect his abhorrence of (and, paradoxically, his fascination with) disorder; they are full of violence, bloodshed, gore. . . . The violence is always presented with mannered gentility, a sense of chivalric decorum in language, that serves only to underscore and emphasize the terror of the action. . . .

Ransom's poetry is that of a gentleman of culture and refinement confronting the savagery and horror that lie beneath the veneer of everyday modern life. The elegance of the diction, the quaintness of the metaphor serve to intensify the desperate nature of the predicament. Everywhere about him he sees violence and terror, and he is appalled at what he sees. Ransom's agrarianism is an assertion of the value of ritual, manners, tradition, as a way of disciplining the passionate violence of the world, while helping to realize its frail loveliness.

*Louis D. Rubin, Jr., in his* Writers of the Modern South: The Faraway Country, *University of Washington Press, 1963, pp. 166-70.*

Mr. Ransom has said that he considers the dramatic monologue the *central* poetic form, and this is one of his critical dicta rather subtly related to his practice. He has not made the dramatic monologue in the usual sense his characteristic form. But the voice which speaks his poems is always crucial to their effects, and is only deviously the poet's own. Like the fictional point of view it is maneuvered, in its more contracted space, to lead us through a series of perspectives to the essential apprehension. These perspectives may suggest roles, attitudes of participants, may be only the inflections of the unsaid. Sometimes, as with the fictional device, the point of view becomes the real protagonist. . . .

Mr. Ransom has always been as sparingly descriptive as a poet can be, although he has been masterly at suggesting the visual in its repercussions.

*Leonie Adams, "Masters in the Garden Again," in the symposium "On John Crowe Ransom," in* New World Writing, *No. 22, Lippincott, 1964.*

A poet's use of literary allusions brings up the problem of obscurity, particularly in this period which has witnessed such a supreme example of the obscure use of erudition as *The Waste Land*. There are both similarities and pertinent differences in Ransom's and Eliot's allusions. Both poets include a wide range of literature and learning in their allusions, and an understanding of those allusions aids the reader's understanding of both poets. Any kind of allusion implies a necessary obscurity to those ignorant of the thing referred to. But Ransom's allusions are not so frequent or recondite as Eliot's. And perhaps more important, in Ransom's poetry ignorance of the allusions does not destroy the continuity of the logical progress of the poem. He does not place so heavy a burden upon his allusions as Eliot often does. (p. 27)

Ransom is comic in the sense that Voltaire and Rabelais, Swift and Twain are comic: the humor is real, but it is based upon a sense of far-reaching incongruity. The times are out of joint, Ransom seems to say, but we can still take an objective look at things. And a good way to keep one's balance is to look at things through a witty and ironic style. (p. 37)

The metaphor is Ransom's favorite figure of speech, and the study of his use of it provides a good deal of understanding of his poetic techniques and achievements. Ransom infrequently uses synecdoche and metonymy; he uses only a moderate number of similes; the metaphor, the "climactic figure", is overwhelmingly his characteristic figure of comparison. (p. 38)

Whether or not metaphor is a part of everyone's speech, whether intrinsic or acquired, the important thing for the critic remains the quality of the practice of metaphor. It must be agreed that some people demonstrate a superior degree of skill and achievement in the use of metaphor, as in the use of any other element of language. The psychology of creativity remains obscure even this long after Aristotle, but the objective fact of the created work is readily available for study. (p. 39)

Structure and texture are in Ransom's theory contending forces; the logical argument tries to push forward, but the texture of irrelevant details entices the reader "away into passionate excursions". Or, another way of putting it is to say that the "science" of the poem wishes to arrive at its generalized statement while the "poetry" of the poem offers isolated aesthetic pleasures along the way. And in speaking of poetry as knowledge, Ransom places his emphasis upon the kind of thing that science cannot know, texture. Poetry is valuable because it sees the world in its fullness and complexity of details. (pp. 41-2)

The individual image or figure, then, is the key element in the ontological distinction of the poem. It is the element which gives aesthetic pleasure, the thing which recalls for us the world as we have experienced it. And so Ransom's theory of the poem and his defense of poetry as opposed to science suggest why he makes frequent and varied use of metaphors. Images and figures are for aesthetic contemplation, "for exploration and delight"; and it follows that the more striking the imagery, the more delightful it is to contemplate. (p. 42)

The typical Ransom metaphor . . . cannot be reduced to a single word; it comprises a more extended utterance. . . . The fact that Ransom's figures of comparison can so seldom be reduced to a single word is significant. His figures are not mere decoration or incidental ornamentation; they are evidences of the quality of his mind. He sees in terms of objects, which makes him a distinctly lyric poet. (p. 43)

Ransom tends to use the practical, the homely image, rather than the technical or abstract one.

These metaphysical qualities in Ransom—extended metaphors or conceits, strict logical consistency, and boldness or wit—these things indicate that the quality of Ransom's poetic performance is closer to the poetry of Donne's school than to that of any later period. Indeed, the implications of the entire study of Ransom's practice of metaphor lead to the same conclusion. The poets of the eighteenth century characteristically preferred the simile to the metaphor, and in their practice they insisted upon decorum (hence Johnson's outrage at the "excesses" of metaphysical wit). Ransom prefers the metaphor, and his ironic attitude leads him to "indecorous" conversions upward and downward. Ransom sets himself apart also from the Romantics and Victorians by his studied maintenance of aesthetic distance and avoidance of the announced message. These are generalizations to which numerous exceptions could be cited, but as generalizations they seem to agree with the conventional findings of literary history. (p. 65)

[One] must turn to symbols in order to see the full significance of Ransom's view of experience in the modern world. The progression from diction to metaphor and then to symbol is a movement in a direct line. The image, the metaphor, and the symbol are indeed so closely related that a particular image may be in the form of a figure of speech and at the same time have symbolic value. And so in turning attention to Ransom's symbolism, one is not dealing with new objects in the poems so much as with the same kind of objects but on a different level. And it is on the level of symbolism that Ransom's poetic thought may be most comprehensively examined.

Among Ransom's major themes are the dissociation of sensibility and mutability, both of which are often developed symbolically. It is not necessary to perform extensive analyses of both themes, however, for several reasons. Ransom's symbols tend to be fluid rather than fixed; that is, they have a general signification which is reduced to particular applications in particular contexts. The same symbols generally are used in developing each theme, and if a symbol's general meaning is understood, then it may be easily enough comprehended in any context. . . . Secondly, the dissociation of sensibility is Ransom's major theme. (pp. 67-8)

Obscure poetry, according to Ransom, suggests a great deal of meaning but refuses to clarify, organize, or conclude what is set forth. Pure poetry, on the other hand, aims at aesthetic effect without even suggesting any meaning or moral effect; the pure poet "has performed a work of dissociation and purified his art". The kind of poetry which Ransom prefers, however, is neither modern obscure nor modern pure poetry; it is "impure" poetry, a traditional compound of "a moral effect with an aesthetic effect". "As for poetry, it seems to me a pity that its beauty should have to be cloistered and conventual, if it is 'pure,' or teasing and evasive, if it is 'obscure.' The union of beauty with goodness and truth has been common enough to be regarded as natural. It is the dissociation which is unnatural and painful." In his practice of poetry, with its fusion of technical brilliance and significant thematic content, Ransom has avoided the kinds of dissociation which characterize modern poetry. Perhaps the poetic act has been an important means in his own experience of combating the general malady of dissociation in this age. (pp. 72-3)

Ransom has an obvious joy in the fact of physical life itself and in the concrete "world's body". And then he has a high standard for the quality of man's experience in that world. He has a vision of man as a being with a highly refined sensitivity to aesthetic and spiritual values. Man is seen as a creature with natural instincts for a life of fullness and harmony. Ransom's Garden of Eden existed in prescientific ages. . . .

The symbols which Ransom establishes to project this view of man are drawn largely from nature or from natural acts. On the one hand there are the objects, colors, and activities which suggest fullness and vitality, images representing the realm of unified experience. Modern man comprehends these qualities only in transient recollections of his pre-scientific nature. He is more familiar with the antithetical qualities of depletion and isolation, suggested by images of coldness, dullness, or unsuccessful activities. (p. 108)

The analysis of Ransom's language on the levels of diction, metaphor, and symbol reveals the richness of the technical skill employed in developing his principal effects and ideas. His diction, which has fascinated many critics by its precision and significant surprises, brings together terms from many sources and levels of language. It moves from the pedantic to the commonplace, from the euphemistic to the starkly shocking, and from the archaic to the colloquial. Ransom's metaphors reveal the boldness of his poetic approach to subjects, an approach which is typically original and markedly metaphysical. The primary quality of his diction and metaphors is irony, which results from the fusing of disparate elements of diction, from applying surprising language to subjects, or from unexpected comparisons. Things subjected to Ransom's scrutiny are placed in new focuses, sometimes being elevated and sometimes apparently being "demoted" in regard to conventional attitudes. The characteristic result is a new attitude toward the subject being presented.

Ransom's symbolism consists largely of a fairly consistent pattern of repeated images, the significance of which is easily seen and analyzed once the basis of the symbols is understood. First, Ransom delights in nature, and then he desires that man lead a full life in harmony with nature. Ransom believes that man's originally coherent relationship to nature has been perverted by the abstractionism which is the concomitant of the scientific method. And thus images and figures and events which are perverted, distorted, or dulled come to symbolize the curse of modernism: the dissociation of sensibility or the fragmentation of personality, Ransom's main concern in his poetry. (p. 110)

Ransom achieves variety in sameness; that is, though he tends to deal with aspects of the same general problem, he does so through original, bold, and varied usage of different levels of language. As concrete objects of art, his works are each distinct, none quite like any other. Only the concept or idea tends to sameness. Even the symbols which recur over and over are fresh, for they occur in different contexts and in varied juxtapositions. The fact that Ransom's variety in manner saves the matter from seeming repetitive is demonstrated by the failure of many of his pre-*Fugitive* works. Ransom had pretty much the same ideas in all his poetry, but only when he couched his ideas in his mature style did his poetry become successful as art. The significant ideas became significant poetry through skillful techniques.

Ransom is traditional in that he is deeply concerned about the condition of man in the world; he is modern in that he avoids open moralization. . . . His indirection and objectivity are most clearly indicated by two of the predominant qualities in his work, irony and aesthetic distance. The latter keeps the reader detached from the poetic object, allowing him to get a rounded view unhampered by distracting sentimentalism or other imposed attitudes. Irony, itself a device contributing to aesthetic distance, provides two or more objects or choices, and a choice is generally not easy to make. The fact that Ransom establishes tensions which are not easily resolved suggests his recognition of a difficult world. Life pulls one way and then another, and man tends to take the line of least resistance, often not knowing which choice to make.

The plight of man is Ransom's main thematic concern. In the face of modernism, the loss of God, a rapidly changing order of life, or the prospect of death, man is uncertain, hesitant, confused. Ransom's people more often than not are destroyed, whether physically or spiritually. They are often passive. (p. 111)

Ransom sees human isolation as the condition of modernism rather than as a universal fact of experience. Underlying his work is a nostalgia for a time when it was not this way. In Agrarian terms, man was capable of coherent life before industrialism. In classical terms, man was a creature of integrated experience before science destroyed his ability to see individual objects. This nostalgic view of an integrated world as opposed to the modern world of dissociation is the basic irony which informs Ransom's poetry.

If Ransom depicts the destruction of man, if he presents the cause in the form of abstractionism, and if he usually presents man as a passive object acted upon by the cause, what then keeps Ransom from being a naturalist? First of all, he is essentially classical in his attitudes. He believes in a world of order and balance, a world which at times man has realized. Modern man with his dissociation is viewed in a historical context: man has departed from the way, and the departure is wholesale, but it is viewed in a lengthy perspective of better times and conditions.

And secondly, Ransom's portrait of man is essentially noble. . . . Ransom says that man is a good deal more than his generally wretched life at present would indicate. (pp. 112-13)

Although his antagonism toward science led him to excessive emphasis upon the separateness of structure and texture, nonetheless one can see in his theory the essential conflict which he projects in all of his thought and work, the conflict between a concrete world of full experience and a debilitating abstractionism. (p. 113)

Ransom himself is apparently caught in the trap of modernism. He is an intellectual specialist in an age of intellectual specialists. (p. 114)

In a positive sense Ransom does not create a myth of man. Modern man has perhaps lost the myth-making faculty. . . . Ransom does in [one] sense offer a "fragmentary myth". His human failures and defeats are typically played against a background of natural harmony and fullness. Ransom uses nature as a picture of "what might be or ought to be". In other words, his direct approach is to depict the flaws of modernism, which is a negative task; and his indirect approach is to set up as a foil the myth of harmony and coherence. This again is his central tension and the basis of his vision of man as a noble creature fallen upon ignoble times. (p. 115)

In his treatment of a few main ideas he achieves delightful variety through the rich use of multitudinous elements from the "world's body". Because of his limited production and scope, he is a minor poet. Because of his magnificent handling of language and his concern for man's widespread confusion in a difficult world, he is a good minor poet. If he survives the tests of time, it will doubtless be because posterity will remain preoccupied with the confusions of a scientific world and because virtuosity in poetic techniques will remain an admired talent. (p. 116)

*Karl F. Knight, in his* The Poetry of John Crowe Ransom: A Study of Diction, Metaphor, and Symbol *(© Mouton 1964; reprinted by permission of Mouton & Co., Publishers), Mouton, 1964.*

[Ransom's speech] is that of the Gentleman, rather than that of the Common Man. The Gentleman is of no definite society usually—from the first the poet was determined not to "lapse" into "those amiable Southern accents"—but of the Anglo-American culture. His sentences have the effect of an ease that can indulge itself in the direction of elegance, except in a few late poems, where they become more nervously elliptical, more conventionally modern. He is learned enough and assured enough to range in his words from the colloquial to the archaic or pedantic (the latter kinds in a tone frequently of self-mockery, for he is conscious of being human, all too human, and does not want his judgments to be taken as final). Or to play a Latinate vocabulary off against an Anglo-Saxon. . . . The effects of Ransom's poetry are almost exclusively effects of language, and effects that are possible almost exclusively through language. Its irony is a subtle, and gentle, irony of tone, rather than an irony of startling juxtaposition such as we have in Eliot. Imagery is of minimum importance in Ransom, and his poetry may therefore disappoint the reader who takes one of his chief delights in the image. But it is possible, perhaps, to make too much even of image in poetry. (I mean *image* here in the restricted sense of *picture*—Eliot's crab at the end of a stick—as distinct from metaphor and simile, which are also effects and means developed best through language.) If it is the image we want more than anything else, we can get it best from the graphic artist. In one sense Ransom's poetry might be said to be of the "purest" kind: in its fidelity to its medium. (pp. 6-7)

Because of Ransom's quietly toned, frequently understated discourse, the reader first may find him "cold." . . . It is an old misreading of Ransom, and not at all peculiar to the inexperienced reader. (p. 7)

Another error is due to a confusion of the genres that is endemic among modern readers. Because Ransom's poems are based often on a kind of narrative situation—that is, on the kind of situation that the prose fictionist could work with too—the reader may be led, as one generally admiring critic has been, to compare the poet to the novelists and come away complaining that his people are only types. Or he may be led to some extreme judgments, like another critic: to count "Here Lies a Lady," "Piazza Piece," "Hilda" and others as complete failures because the "characterizations" are flat, and to prefer a possibly inferior poem, like "Puncture," because it is a little more like a short story. (p. 8)

The vagueness about the narrator of which the critic complains in "Here Lies a Lady" is due really to the fact that there is no narrator at all—that is, no speaker distinct from the poet, as long as we understand that by poet we do not mean the historical John Crowe Ransom. The *I* of "Here Lies a Lady" is no different from the *I* of "The Equilibrists," or "Special Lovers," or "Good Ships"; in these poems there is no intention to make the *I* a distinct character, with a distinct relation to other distinct characters, as the term "narrator" or "speaker" might imply. (pp. 8-9)

Ransom is subtle in his irony, and the reader who has been trained by the modern critic to have sharp ears for irony, to be wary of taking almost anything at face value, may go too far and begin to imagine a whole complex of little ironies where none are intended. (p. 9)

*Robert Buffington, "Introduction" to his* The Equilibrist: A Study of John Crowe Ransom's Poems, 1916-1963, *Vanderbilt University Press, 1967.*

Most of Ransom's poetry is concerned, in various manifestations, with divided man living between polarities, between possibilities; it asserts the honesty, even in the face of inconclusiveness, of acknowledging man's dualism in which mind and body, as in the line from "Painted Head," are "so hardly one they terribly are two." Above all, in the resolution of polarities into something of worth, that value is not necessarily commensurate with ideal moral or aesthetic standards. . . . Both [Robert Penn] Warren and Ransom record the dangers in the yearning attempts to make the ruck of a fallen, circumstantial world conform to a settled, even abstract, ideal.

The pertinence here is not the originality of this shared vision (an ancient one, which Warren himself has identified as central to several diverse writers), but rather, the similarity and significance of approach, the deployment of a technique that ratifies the vision as a relevant one for twentieth-century man. Both writers create dramatic personae to articulate a view of man struggling, of man in his "precarious balancing of antinomies." As readers have sometimes pointed out, both the Ransom and the Warren personae, however varied and endowed with whatever independent life, are rarely wholly separate from their creators.

Many of Ransom's poems are structured around the figure of an observer whose serious ambivalences help to distance the nostalgia for and sentimentality toward an older time, a more seemly "place," and the informing little ceremonies—antique and perhaps inadequate—which lent a certain meaning to man's life. "Janet Waking," "The Equilibrists," "Blue Girls," "Vision by Sweetwater," "Somewhere Is Such a Kingdom" all locate the pervasive disparity between an innocent ideality and the impossibility of its survival squarely in the sensibility of a detached but sympathetic *I*. Still others—"Antique Harvesters," "Persistent Explorer," "Captain Carpenter," "Necrological"—are given shape by nothing more felt than an authorial voice also detached but sympathetic. In both kinds of poems a hard wit and a toughminded irony prevent the breaking loose of not merely incipient romanticism but also, more threatening, despair, which may stem from either residual Calvinism or rationalistic unbelief.

The qualities of the Ransom persona have been discussed by no one better than Warren himself. The larger problem of belief in *Poems about God* (1919), he states, implied a previous split in the poet himself—"a quarrel with the self, a drama of the self." In succeeding volumes throughout the 1920's the drama is more fortunately distanced, in narrative and seminarrative situations, because the recurring persona is set against a microcosmic rural world; the drama reflects the pattern of "reduction" common to the pastoral tradition, which produces "the irony of wisdom out of innocence, the clarity of the human outline when set in the light of nature, the shock of truth out of naivete." The resulting Ransom "voice" then emerges out of the "dimensions of the persona, with both the tension and the loving interplay between a man and his heritage, the drama of 'difference from' and 'identification with.'"

*James H. Justus, "A Note on John Crowe Ransom and Robert Penn Warren," in* American Literature *(reprinted by permission of the publisher; copyright 1969 by Duke University Press, Durham, North Carolina), November, 1969, pp. 425-30.*

John Crowe Ransom is the critical champion of the existent in the world and in literature. This, it would seem, would be sufficient reason for the study of him. For if we do not know and revere existence, what do we know or revere? Ransom believes that the world and the poem, which aesthetically reveals the world, should stand inviolate against the critical pragmatists of this age who "go about seeking whom they may devour" so that all things may become their image and their likeness. In short, Ransom is an objective rather than a narcissistic critic. He wishes the world and the poem to be perceived as what they are and not as someone would have them to be. . . . Ransom is a critic who wishes to be faithful to the reality of 'the world's body', who wishes the poem aesthetically to reveal that reality, and wishes criticism to show the poem as revealing or distorting it. Those whom he calls the moral and scientific pragmatists seek to abstract from the world (that includes the poem) what is useful for their purpose and then order the world to their abstractions. For Ransom these are manipulators, not critics—interested in use, not revelation.

Ransom to a great extent fathered a 'new criticism' which was bent on letting the poem be itself and not something else; not, for example, a means of moral propaganda or psychic therapy. . . . Ransom believes that in knowing this aesthetic being, the poem, we will more surely and deeply know its correlative—the world, in the fullness and realness of its 'body'. This word 'body' is used deliberately by Ransom to connote the exquisite material being which constantly presents itself to the consciousness of man. Ransom is not a transcendentalist, an essentialist, or a mystic. He is a critic and a poet who is concerned with existent, particular being and man's revelation of it through the poem. (pp. 11-12)

John Crowe Ransom's metaphysical foundation is spread the distance of history: he is so eclectic in his conviction that I do not think that a biographer or critic will find a pure vein of any philosopher in him. What may seem a Kantian mind in one context will be empirical in the next. . . . Furthermore, Ransom is not 'willfully' idealistic, either subjectively (Kantian) or objectively (Platonic). . . .

Ransom is Platonic, but in an ironic way. That is, he has been affected by Plato but he reacts against this early affection; for example, his notions of existence, art and poetry rebel against Platonic idealism. If we understand Ransom in his anti-Platonism, we will have understood a great deal of the essential Ransom. (p. 17)

To the extent that the poet becomes a 'moral tailor', Ransom disowns him. For the tailor cuts his matter exactly to fit his blueprint. He is not a discoverer, he does not realize himself more fully for knowing the world, but he has cut the world to the size of his mind. The poet must be a voyager, a seeker who realizes the world as his dynamic and spontaneous complement, and about which he is never sure. The world is the unpredictable spouse of the poet, through whom the poet comes to know the myriad recesses of his own personality and psychic potentialities. He never superimposes his private morality, his private moral universal upon nature but lets nature engage and, if he is lucky, symbolize his moral universal.

Ransom gives an example of what he means by true aesthetical balance in the process of creation when he rephrases Kant's example of the landscape gardener in his garden. Kant's gardener has a universal of what he wants the garden to look like, but despite this universal and beneath this universal there is the free, intricate play of nature —the tissues of natural irrelevancy that escape the form of the gardener's universal, and yet give it the recalcitrant spontaneity to make it art. "Nature seems to have no inclination to reject or even to resent the human Universal, for now obtains the condition of 'freedom under law', and its consequence of beauty."

The poet cannot and must not try to determine nature, for he is not the exemplar cause of nature. Nature subsists outside himself and is not really under his control; yet it will offer itself to the poet's imagination in order that he may concretize an idea, if the poet is not too procrustean in his demands. (pp. 51-2)

Though Ransom will accept a synchronized existence of the abstract and the embodied universal in the same poem, it seems that he prefers the universal to be totally embodied in words, especially in metaphor. Metaphor is the most complete, most whole and most consonant way of incarnating the universal. (p. 56)

Though Ransom believes that the most accurate and natural poetic means for the poet to embody his notion of the world by the world itself is the metaphor, he will not *theoretically* admit that the metaphor can be the whole poem or that the attitude embodied in the metaphor can be its unity. . . . On the one hand, Ransom *practically* likes the complete submergence of the poet's universal in the flesh of words; on the other hand, he theoretically holds for the poem's ideational 'core' or 'logic' as against 'tissue of meaning' or metaphor. This oscillation and confusion in Ransom's criticism cannot be resolved, but only explained. (p. 59)

[One] might say that [for Ransom] the poem is an unpragmatic attempt to embody metaphorically a universal of man's existence in the world, within a metered and logically structured tissue of words. (p. 69)

For Ransom, the process of development in a poem, or the process of creation in a poet, is a movement from simple realization in the mind to a phrase that textures the realization and stimulates the creative mind into spinning further texture and further poetic suspension, until the original realization has been textured into the web of poetic existence. Ransom would also say that the central meaning of the finished poem would not directly correspond to the original realization of the creator. Rather, the original realization would be the stimulus that generated the concentrated attention of the mind and startled the mind into spinning its verbal web. Ransom implies a great deal of subconscious activity in the creation of the poem; there is an unpredictable predictability about what is happening. The demands of language and the excrescences of the subconscious seem to influence the focus of the conscious mind in the creative act. (pp. 77-8)

What Ransom wants is an emergence from bias and the awakening of an alert sensibility that will respond to the world and the poem as they are: the world as the total fullness of particular being and the poem as an aesthetical being with an ontological reference. The texture of the poem, for Ransom, is a testimony of the poet's faithfulness to reality and to himself, as part of reality. Ransom is almost willing to let the poem go its own unpredictable way, as the world is free to go. In his dialectical fashion, he refuses to assume any degree of critical omniscience or omnipotence. He does not seek to superimpose Platonic forms upon a world that does not fit them, nor will he seek to manipulate things in the scientific exercise of power. He and the poet are subject to the world, and the world is subject to them in their wonder and in their worded creation.

Finally, in his critical procedure he is always incomplete because he is always dialectical—he has never come, he believes, and will never come to the whole truth about anything. Thus, he is irritating in his incompleteness, but there is a reason for it. He will not attempt an exhaustive definition of poetry, perhaps, because there is none. Knowledge has an open end for Ransom.

As is evidenced in *The New Criticism*, Ransom has read Eliot long and hard, and his style resembles Eliot's. For example, neither Ransom nor Eliot is particularly logical in his critical progression. They lack the order which the mind urges when reading them. They do not define, divide, and discuss very systematically. Both critics intimate a part of a definition, make somewhat arbitrary divisions, and then discuss what they are interested in, with a casual unpredictability. I hope I am not discourteous in saying that they remind me of two venerable beachcombers who search through the sands of texts, sifting them, comparing one item with another, and unexpectedly come up with a gem of an insight, an insight with a memorable formulation: 'structure' and 'texture', 'dissociation of sensibility', 'tissue of irrelevancy', 'objective correlative', and so on. . . . They have been up and down the beach many times, and when they have discovered something in the sand, one can be sure that it is the result of much labor, much knowledge, and much sensibility. They are not the type to make razor-sharp distinction after distinction. . . . Ransom's strength is in his combination of a scholarship not as broad as Eliot's, with a poetic sensibility comparable to Eliot's, in addition to an existential philosopher's interest in existing things.

Ransom has given the critical world a redirection. . . . He has made the pragmatists clear their vision again and again, and made them focus upon the poem, whose reason for existence, he thinks, is to catch up the world beautifully in the texture of its worded being. (pp. 122-23)

*James E. Magner, Jr., in his* John Crowe Ransom: Critical Principles and Preoccupations *(© Mouton 1971; reprinted by permission of Mouton & Co., Publishers), Mouton, 1971.*

In his use of wit and irony, in the tension of paradox and ambiguity characteristic of his best verse, Ransom is distinctively a modern poet. His attitudes, however, like the poetic forms he employs, reflect his continuing interest in the traditional. One part of the double vision so obvious in Ransom's poetry reminds the modern Southerner that he must accommodate himself to the harsh and unpleasant realities of life in the twentieth century; the other encourages him to cast a glance backward at the felicities of a previous age. (pp. 23-4)

Few poets of his generation have been able to represent with greater accuracy and precision the inexhaustible ambiguities, the paradoxes and tensions, the dichotomies and ironies that make up the life of modern man. His poetry reiterates a few themes: man's dual nature and the inevitable misery and disaster that always accompany the failure to recognize and accept this basic truth; mortality and the fleetingness of youthful vigor and grace, the inevitable decay of feminine beauty; the disparity between the world as man would have it and as it actually is, between what people want and need emotionally and what is available for them, between what man desires and what he can get; man's divided sensibilities and the wars constantly raging within him, the inevitable clash between body and mind, between reason and sensibility; the necessity of man's simultaneous apprehension of nature's indifference and mystery and his appreciation of her sensory beauties; the inability of modern man, in his incomplete and fragmentary state, to experience love. (p. 26)

*Thomas Daniel Young, in his* John Crowe Ransom, *Steck-Vaughn, 1971.*

Poetry for Ransom exists on two levels: the first is the "rational surface" which can be explicitly social in meaning; the other . . . should be immediately recognizable to any student of Ransom's aesthetics. The "deeper" level is "irrational," in Ransom's use of the term, the realm of sensibility where the poet embraces the particularity of the world rather than its social abstractions. It is primarily this "deeper" meaning that, in full retreat from social norms, provided the basis for the New Criticism; yet finally it must be seen as a step toward the dream world of aesthetic vision—toward the Brooksian world "as it ought to be."

Ransom is a transitional figure for us in this study much as he has been for the general history of American critical theory. He is difficult to place not because he changes or shifts his aesthetic principles (they are . . . marvelously consistent), but because he adheres to a critical doctrine that is neither here nor there in the common canons of American aesthetic thought. For him, . . . literary theory is grounded in epistemology. Ransom finds himself confronting the ancient question of poetry and knowledge, and the ultimate criterion of value is necessarily bound up with the determination of the meaning of the poem. . . .

In many ways the most crucial work in Ransom's production was a rather early one, *God Without Thunder* (1930). He is never very far from it although he repeatedly refines his terminology. Here he makes the first lengthy announcement and exposition of the essential dualism in his theory; "Life" is conceived in Arnoldian fashion as the dichotomy of science and religion; in sociological terms as the dichotomy of city and country; in something like Marxian terms, Industrial and Pastoral; and in metaphorical terms, "Penseroso" and "Allegro." Later in his career he added a psychological dimension by adopting the Freudian oppositions between "ego" and "id." All of these, including the aesthetic dualism which most interests us here, arise from Ransom's Kantian epistemology. The essential dualism which forms the core of *God Without Thunder* is that of the faculties of reason and aesthetic sensibility. Ransom claims that each gives us a particular kind of knowledge. The reason deals in abstractions and belongs to the rational world of science and general laws based on operational postulates. The aesthetic sensibility concerns itself with the particularities of existence, the objects of perception in all their minute uniqueness and infinite quantity. The former is practical and utilitarian; the latter is fundamentally hedonistic. . . .

Ransom [in *The World's Body*] assigns the poet a prodigious Bergsonian task—to "perpetuate in his poem an order of existence which in actual life is constantly crumbling beneath his touch. Reality for Ransom is a matter of "flux and blur." There is also some evidence that Santayana entered into Ransom's thinking; the significant coupling of religion and poetry in *God Without Thunder* has a decidedly

Santayanan twist in the insistence that both are fictions which seek to grasp the meaning of the world. Ransom sees, however, a dichotomy in Santayana between the "realm of essences" and the "realm of matter," and he finds too much emphasis on the former. In his own similar dualism he would seek to tilt the balance toward the latter. . . .

Poetic discourse, he tells us [in "Criticism as Pure Speculation"] "is more cool than hot, and a moral fervor is as disastrous to it as a burst of passion itself." Consequently he sees poetic activity as reflective of "the purest esthetic experience"; it eschews all interest in utility. . . . As a result poetic discourse must avoid any temptations toward social or political activism. . . .

> The true poetry has no great interest in improving or idealizing the world, which does well enough. It only wants to realize the world, to see it better. Poetry is the kind of knowledge by which we must know what we have arranged that we shall not know otherwise.

Ransom's attitude that art ought not to participate in social movements also pervades the New Criticism. . . . Ransom relegates political activism to the speculation of prose discourse, and in its pure form sees poetry as "always something magnificently chimerical, and irresponsible if it would really commit us to an action" [*Kenyon Review,* 5 (1943)]. His dualistic theory demands that in the realm of poetic discourse the artist must never assert his own personality; he must remain as "nearly anonymous" as possible. . . .

There are a host of difficulties inherent in Ransom's dualism. There is a clear sense of mimesis in his aesthetics, particularly in his insistence on the "representation" of natural objects. He would banish the sentiment of the artist specifically to preserve a strong sense of "realism." Yet total detachment and photographic representation are not what he wants. . . . In addition, the extent of "reality" is never very clear. For the most part Ransom seems to mean by "the real" only the particularities of nature, yet more than once he proclaims that the poem must contain both particularities and universals to be truly realistic. . . .

There are, to be sure, even more crucial problems arising from the dualism of poetry and prose. A great emphasis in Ransom's theorizing is on making an absolute distinction between the two forms of discourse, yet they must also be seen as working somehow harmoniously within the individual poem. . . .

The exact balance of prose and poetry within the single poem is never clearly stated. Moreover, Ransom's concept of the poem as a whole or an "entirety" results in at least one significant effort to completely dissolve the dualism in the creative act. Murray Krieger [in *New Apologists for Poetry*] quite accurately points out those passages of *The New Criticism* where Ransom, in terms very reminiscent of his friend Allen Tate, sets the oppositions of structure and texture (here called "Determinant Meaning" and "Determinant Sound") into a relation of "tension" (to borrow Tate's term) which yields a poem having its own status in being. Such an idea, of course, forms the center of Ransom's theory of ontological criticism and is perhaps the single most influential aspect of his theory on the New Criticism and Contextualism. It is, as Krieger notes, Ransom's approach to Coleridge's organic poem which must somehow fuse into a unity the disparate elements of Imagination and Fancy. But it also runs counter to Ransom's abiding concern with "realism." The poem as an organic unit having its own unique status in being would seemingly be just one more particularity in nature's infinite supply. It would not, by anything other than mere chance, give us knowledge of our environment. . . .

The primary reason for Ransom's claim that poetry gives us knowledge is found in his religious orthodoxy. The dualism he expounded in *God Without Thunder* exists also as a dichotomy of innocence and experience. The former state is characterized by man's living in nature, the second by man's attempt to gain complete mastery over it—to reduce it to logical systems whereby he might be its god. The first is truely poetic or Edenic while the second is prosaic. . . . In *God Without Thunder* Ransom argues for a return to an Old Testament orthodoxy, to the kind of myth which by preserving man's sense of irrationality and mystery would not lead to cold abstractions about existence but would rather demand that he turn again toward a state of natural innocence. Ransom's religious commitment pushes him beyond the particularity of the world's body; not only is the idea of poetry's ontic status undercut, but poetry's balance of structure and texture is justified finally by the vision of a timeless Eden that it gives us. It is the dream of a world returned to its proper proportions.

*Wesley Morris, "John Crowe Ransom: Principles for a New Historicism," in his* Towards A New Historicism *(copyright © 1972 by Princeton University Press; reprinted by permission of Princeton University Press), Princeton University Press, 1972, pp. 108-19.*

Ransom's total output of poetry is not large; his considerable reputation as a poet rests on the work he did over a period of less than eight years, but out of those years have come a disproportionate number of the poems contained in the standard anthologies of our day. (p. 6)

Ransom is a poet as the Greek scholar in him would understand the word. He is a maker. His poems are contrived, structured, not to appear as moments torn almost intact from the actual lives of actual people. There is no attempt at realism; rarely does his dialogue afford an illusion of conversation. Ransom doesn't mind that we can see the underpinnings to the art that the welding shows. This is not theater-in-the-round. The proscenium arch is elaborately there, and we imagine that his characters are obliged now and then to step to the footlights and in the manner of Restoration actors declaim a few lines to the audience.

Ransom's poems are mostly about domestic situations; this is perhaps because in the familial he finds the condensation of those questions, essentially theological, which ultimately are the only questions worth asking.

What Ransom treats in his poetry are those concerns which hold the attention of every sensible person: sex, death and religion. Sex here, of course, encompasses all of that which belongs to romantic love, marriage, home-building and childbirth as well as the frustration and satisfaction of the libido. It is the primary life-force and is responsible for the very existence of the man and the woman whose fealty it commands. Death puts an end to that force, and religion attempts to make sense out of both death and the sexuality which tries desperately to overcome death and to make sense out of existence itself, which is anchored to sex at one end and to death at the other. (pp. 6-7)

It should be noted here that Ransom's concern with death —and he has devoted a larger part of his work to this subject than most poets—is not only with death as a dark reality which has to be examined; he is concerned not so much with mortality itself as he is concerned with the proper attitude toward mortality. The noblest characters in his poems are stoic, standing with Ransom in that tradition of the Southern Calvinists which we call Christian stoicism. Ransom dislikes any flagrant emotional display, especially of grief, as such a display reveals at least a temporary dissociation of sensibility, a breakdown in that bond of mind and spirit whose integrity Ransom cherishes. (p. 7)

[His] rhetoric serves the poem in a number of ways, but probably the most important is the laying of an aesthetic and emotional distance between the poem and the reader. Any direct expression of emotion—especially the gentler feelings—is always dangerous in a poem. In the period when Ransom was writing it was especially so. This was the time of the imagists, of the publication of *The Waste Land*. The experimenters in taste and technique were moving to the hard line, the tough and violent. It was necessary to find some sort of scrim to cover the naked feelings of love, loneliness, compassion, sorrow. But this is only half of it; Ransom was not *forced* into hiding. If there had been no imagists and no Eliot, he still would have muted his feelings, would have kept us from getting too close to the subjects of his poems. Because that would be indulgence, would play dangerously with pain and pleasure. And Ransom is stoic. (p. 8)

[Although] Ransom has been a great influence as a man of letters, he has had no perceptible stylistic influence through his poems. He has written in a style too much his own for anyone to imitate without copying slavishly. So to understand Ransom, to read him well, we have to go to Ransom. When we do, we see a poet who has known as few have, even in his time, the meaning of tension in verse. We see the poet as the balancer of force; the poet as equilibrist.

Ransom is, and has been found from his earliest publication, opposed to the science-oriented mentality of this century and an enemy of rational positivism. He has been called reactionary, romantic, and decadent. He is a poet of such skill, compassion and elegance, however, as to confound such critics. (p. 10)

In the discussion of tensions and ambiguity which has taken place during the past several years, the apparent influence of the seventeenth-century metaphysical poets on Ransom's poetry has been mentioned countless times. To emphasize this influence, I think, is to misread the poetry; it is not metaphysical except in certain of its effects. It draws considerably on the force created by the yoking together of what appear to be incompatibles, but the fairly extended forces in Ransom's work are not a result of those techniques generally thought of as metaphysical. The tension of his poetry lies not very much in the mutual repulsion of two elements of a metaphor, such as Dr. Johnson found to his displeasure in the poems of John Donne, or in the bristling of a poem against a "nonpoetic" language. Ransom is more skilled than most in these techniques, but his poems are charged with another and a stronger force. In almost every one of them, the stage is set between opposing thematic positions, and we find that we are unable to make a choice between them. The poet will not, and so the characters never can either. It is beneath this tension—the polarity of statement—that the minor stresses play through the poems.

One of his best-known pieces, "The Equilibrists," gives in its title, its structure and its texture a touchstone to the sources of this force, this peculiar power which we can call —as an inclusive term—the equilibrium-stress. In this, as in most of his poems, it is Ransom who finally is the supreme equilibrist. He gives us passion in perilous balance with honor—the polarity of statement, the major force. In the texture of the poem itself, the additional sense of balanced forces in the juxtaposing of warm Teutonic and sterner Latinate words, and in the use of slant rhyme, which come to our ears like the notes of close harmony repelling and attracting each other, in the alternate use of modern and archaic terms, the pageantry and the pedantry of the language, the homeliness and nobility of tone. (pp. 19-20)

The forces . . . that give Ransom's poems their life come from the equilibrium-stress, which is primarily the polarity of statement supported and intensified by the minor stresses of the language. The pathos, the passion of the poetry is found in the losing: it lives in the inevitable passing away. This too, being as it is oxymoronic, irreconcilable, is a polarity creating tension, and so creating life, since for the poems, of course, as well as for the reader, that is what life is. (p. 28)

A sense of irony is the abiding realization that every human statement contains its own contradiction and that every human act contains the seeds of its own defeat. From this comes the realization that there are no pure truths and that there are no pure men or pure women or pure causes or pure motives. There is neither the simply holy nor the simply unholy. John Calvin and Camus alike understood that man's very lot is one of awful irony, as he finds his rational self facing a nonrational universe, his hungering and homesick soul facing an incomprehensible and indifferent God. This is the terrible wisdom which moves perceptibly through Ransom's poems.

He gives irony its most dramatic expression in the polarity of statement. In "Armageddon" it is Christ who is bloodthirsty, while Satan tells us that he is weary of war and prefers the fellowship of good talk; the "Old Man Playing with Children" finds that he and the child are "equally boy and boy"; "The Equilibrists" are beautiful in their eternally unconsummated and undenied love; the Friar in "Necrological" becomes as one with the slain soldiers. (p. 29)

[Irony] is present, spelling out still something of Camus' absurdity, in the confrontation of Ransom's people and the real world they can neither ignore nor live in. This duality is everywhere in the poems, as are the conventionally treated ironic situations, the death of the young, the inefficacy of innocence, the self-destroying essence of sexual love.

All this is structural, but its effectiveness—as in the case of equilibrium-tension—depends on the texture, on the sense of irony which is woven into it. (p. 30)

Ransom contrives (and the term here is not pejorative)—to invest his poems with an objectivity in such a way that we are able to see the contrivance function more clearly—perhaps the word is more dramatically—than we can with most writers. We can see him when he decides to step back from his subject, and we can watch him move in again; we know when, and he intends for us to see by what means, he becomes disengaged or disengages us the readers. (pp. 30-1)

When Ransom shows us one thing to speak of another, he depends not so much upon the symbol as the metaphor.

There are a few words which recur so often in Ransom's poetry that the reader sometimes takes them to be part of a system of symbols, but in the case of substantives, in particular, this is not so. Many of the words suspected of being a part of such a system are in fact not intended to carry any special symbolic import at all. (p. 39)

Now and then Ransom gives a character in his poems a name which reveals something the poet wants us to know about the character. This is not symbolism, because the character is an important figure in his own right and will not be reduced to a symbol; it is not allegory because the character does not stand for an abstract quality, but rather embodies the quality, which interests us here only in terms of *this* character. Still the name-giving harks back to the morality play or more exactly to the names which the Puritans, in wishful thinking at least, gave to their children. (p. 48)

These are major elements in his poetry, but perhaps the most vital . . . [is] unconsummated passion, the stuff of which Ransom structures most of his polarities, abstraction though it is, is itself a symbol of that abstraction which to Ransom was most terrible and almost visibly present, almost a living enemy. This is the dissociation of sensibility, that theme which pervades most of Ransom's work and informs his use of contrast and metaphor, his understanding of color. And so the names for the poles which hold our parts apart—heat and cold, bright and dull, flames and ice, chills and fevers, all standing for the intellect and passions, the head and the body—are central to much of Ransom's poetry, as passion too much thought about and so undone, sensibility split in two. This is the schizophrenia from which the majority of Ransom's people suffer. (pp. 48-9)

*Miller Williams, in his* The Poetry of John Crowe Ransom, *Rutgers University Press (New Brunswick, N.J.), 1972.*

John Crowe Ransom's literary career may be divided into four distinct periods. From 1918 to 1927 the major portion of his creative energy was expended in writing some of the most carefully controlled and sophisticated lyrics produced in this century, and during these nine years he published four books of poetry: *Poems About God* (1919), *Grace After Meat* (1924), *Chills and Fever* (1924), and *Two Gentlemen in Bonds* (1927). . . . During the next ten years he produced more than twenty essays on political, social, and economic topics . . . and published his provocative study of religion and myth *God Without Thunder* (1930). . . .

Although Ransom has written only five or six poems since 1927, he has brought out three collections of his verse. . . . [The] appearance of each new edition is the occasion for the poet to revise his poems, and in some cases earlier versions have been so completely recast that different poems are produced. . . .

[Early] in the 1920's Ransom put aside the style of *Poems About God* and adopted an entirely new style. Instead of the conventional diction, the obvious and heavy-handed irony, and the often sentimental tone of the early verse, the poet having "mastered a new style" began to present poems in what has come to be known as his mature manner. First there is the language, which is so distinctively different as to be unmistakably Ransom's; then in and through this language comes the ironic suggestion that the distance between what man wants and what he can reasonably expect is seldom bridged. One has come to expect from Ransom a poetry composed of a nice balance of powerful forces, a poetry that appears to be both true and believable because it reflects the inexhaustible ambiguities, the tensions and paradoxes of modern life. . . . If one studies carefully the revisions of . . . almost any [poem] which the poet has been rewriting in recent years, he will find that Ransom has altered the dualistic attitude that one associates with his best known poems. Above all else this poetry of the master's old age . . . reveals a strong urge to resolve some of the conflicts and ease the tensions resulting from the attempt to hold two opposing ideas in the mind at one time. For thirty years or more some of Ransom's strongest supporters have argued that one of the poet's greatest achievements is his ability to maintain in perilous balance some of the basic contrarieties of modern life: heaven and hell, fire and ice, reason and emotion, love and honor. . . .

For the past forty years or more, as we know, the major portion of Ransom's creative energy has not gone into the writing of poetry. Instead he has turned his attention to aesthetic speculation, to probing the nature of poetry, and to demonstrating the manner in which poetry must be read if it is to provide us with the full range of the knowledge that resides within it. Since the publication of *The New Criticism* more than thirty years ago, Ransom has not, until now, issued a new book of criticism, although during this time he produced with amazing regularity a series of important and influential essays. Almost all commentators . . . agree that Ransom's career as literary critic has been characterized by a remarkably consistent attitude toward art. . . . Ransom's interest in poetry and aesthetic theory was a product of his "fury against abstraction" and his discovery that neither philosophy nor classical literature can restore the concrete particularity of "The World's Body" as modern literature can. . . .

[Between] 1925 and 1927 . . ., Ransom worked out a theory of the aesthetic process from which he has never deviated. . . . [One] of Ransom's most persistent critical principles [is that] cognition and not instruction is the most important element in the poetic experience.

During the early twenties, too, Ransom published . . . a number of brief critical pieces which contain the first public statement of some of his most important ideas. In "The Future of Poetry" . . ., he argues that poetry has to perform a dual role with words. On the one hand they must be arranged in such a manner as "to conduct a logical sequence with their meaning," and on the other they must "realize an objective pattern with their sounds." This is the earliest published statement of his structure-texture formulation, a familiarity with which is essential to anyone who would assess the value of Ransom's criticism. . . . In "Thoughts on the Poetic Discontent" . . ., Ransom first presents his argument that only through the ironic mode can man reconcile himself to some of the complexities of the world in which he must live. . . .

As early as *God Without Thunder* Ransom insisted that the aesthetic attitude is both innocent and objective because with it we look upon the world without desiring to use it or control it. Although he argues for a post-scientific poetry—a literature of experience, not of innocence—and although he admits that science produces useful and necessary knowledge of the world, the scientific attitude is destructive because it encourages man to attempt to possess and control the world and therefore lose its "body and solid substance." Art, on the other hand, "wants us to enjoy life, to taste and reflect as we drink; when we are always tending as abstract appetites to gulp it down" (*The World's Body*).

A poem, then, becomes a precious object, one that the reader should attempt to know and love in all its fullness and particularity. . . .

Ransom has not altered his critical stance as much as some commentators have suggested, and . . . the essay which seems to announce a fundamental change of critical position usually represents another attempt to clarify a misunderstood statement by supplying additional details or, as is usually the case, by changing his metaphor. . . .

In the concluding essay to *The New Criticism* Ransom utters his now famous plea for the ontological critic—one who believes that the poem is an object which has within itself its reason for being, one whose critical energy is consumed in concentration upon the poem itself, and one who is not concerned with the intentions of the poet or with the possible reaction of the reader. Although he finds several critics who participate in the method of the ontological critic, no one completely fills this demanding role. . . . Ransom comes closest to fulfilling the requirements of the ontological critic, for only to him is the text of a poem a total and consuming occupation. . . .

Some of us might resent the master's tinkering with the phrases and rhythms of the poems that, in Randall Jarrell's phrase, we have long considered "nearly perfect lyrics" because we think he is disturbing the "perilous equilibrium" that makes his poetry one of the aesthetic marvels of his age. But the essays in *Beating the Bushes,* one of which was written in his eighty-third year, suggest that Ransom's critical vision is as clear as ever, that his view of the critic's function remains unchanged, and that he has few peers in performing this function. We may not have again one who can remind us with such eloquence and force that only through poetry can we reconcile the disparate and seemingly unrelated experiences of modern life.

*Thomas Daniel Young, in* The Georgia Review, *Summer, 1973, pp. 275-82.*

John Crowe Ransom's complete theory of poetry is not to be found in any one essay, or even in one book; for Ransom, despite the determinate ring to some of his terms, has not been quite a systematic theorist. However, we can be eclectic among his writings without troubling overmuch about their chronology, for he has not changed his theory of art since *God Without Thunder* (1930), or his theory of poetry since *The World's Body* (1938). His most nearly complete formulation is in *The New Criticism* of 1941. In the thirty years since, critics from time to time have been pleased to report a shift in Ransom's position—toward organicism, or toward a theory of expressive meters; toward a theory that will resolve the tension of Ransom's definition of poetry. The general opinion of Ransom as a theorist seems to be that he is charming and well-meaning, but wrong-headed, and needs to be saved from himself. But Ransom continues unregenerate. For the opening essay of *Beating the Bushes* (1972), his first collection of prose in 17 years, he goes back to the major chapter of *The New Criticism,* "Wanted: An Ontological Critic." After his "bold designations" and "heroic dispositions" there, he does grow more modest in tone in the succeeding essays, coming down to 1970—the modesty due to his realization that as a theoretical critic "he cannot support his great ambitions." That is the only change. . . .

The dissatisfaction that . . . others feel with Ransom is due really to the fact that he does not try to define the poem as an organic unity; and that failure, if it is a failure—Ransom doubts that the world will "stop turning"—that failure has its source not in Ransom's theory of composition, but much farther back, in the philosophical dualism to which he has been faithful in prose and in verse for fifty years, except in a few recent, unhappy revisions of his poems.

*Robert Buffington, "Ransom's Poetics: 'Only God, My Dear'," in* The Michigan Quarterly Review, *Fall, 1973, pp. 353-60.*

* * *

## READ, Herbert 1893-1968

**Read, an English poet and critic of literature and art, was a lifelong friend of T. S. Eliot. (See also *Contemporary Authors*, Vols. 25-28.)**

In many ways, his war-poems are Read's most amazing productions. They have an infinite compassion, pathos and horror, an utter lack of violence (one of his most marked characteristics), and above all a detachment almost unbelievable in one so physically and mentally implicated in the job of war. (Here I almost wrote 'in the job of killing', until I remembered Read's words in *Annals of Innocence and Experience*: 'During the whole war I never deliberately or consciously killed an individual man . . .')

Observe the horror and the pity of such poems as *The Execution of Cornelius Vane,* the heart-breaking compassion of *My Company*; but observe also the restraint with which the poet shows you what has moved him so deeply, as in . . . *The Refugees*. . . .

For me, the ultimate attraction of Read's work, and of his character, for the two must always be mentioned together, lies in enigma, paradox, and perfectly wedded opposites. It is nothing as simple as 'Poet or Critic?', 'Artist or Philosopher?'. It is more nearly the 'Marriage of Heaven and Hell'; it is more nearly still a complete recognition and absorption of the totality of experience, psycho-physical, emotional and intellectual. Such a recognition and absorption as must inevitably produce the theory of lability; poems, prose, criticism and political theory. Such a wholeness as must inevitably produce within one mind, and within one body of work, strength and delicacy, permanence and lyricism, tolerance and clarity, reason and romanticism, fervour and balance, maturity and enthusiasm.

Honesty at innumerable points, a form of multiple integrity, a final anarchic sanity; the philosophical code of every adult man who has let his eyes wander over the face of the world, and his mind ponder over what they have seen. And the thing that always stupefies me at this point is that Read, who is representative of more phases of human recognition than any other writer living today, can externalise those phases with complete clarity and sincerity, so that the image is never blurred, the language never misused, the high standard of selection never impaired. . . .

The poet . . . may argue that Read has invented no spectacularly original 'form', that he has lagged behind Hopkins or even Meredith, forgetting that there is a form which is greater, more organic, than any 'form', a poetic return to the . . . 'laws of nature', laws which are so wide, even so subterranean, in their operation, as to be invisible to all but the sharpest eye and the most fully informed perception. The poet might object that the poetic *surgery* has been overdone, that to cut down to the bone of a poem is an act of cruelty rather than one of artistry. . . .

The art-critic might accuse Read of a different sort of fault; that of following too many gods, that of being only too ready to fling himself into the fight for an attractive idea. But such a critic would be denying Read his very nature, his lability, his tolerance and breadth, overlooking that generous vitality which they are too selfconscious to display in public, or even to possess in private. Such a critic would miss the whole point. . . . For Read's humility is only the obverse of his honest solidity; it is the humanity of the man who can recognise, probe and still respect the multiplicity of the world in which he walks; that of the man who knows, for all his individual complexity, that he is but one fragment. . . .

*Henry Treece, "Introduction" to* Herbert Read: An Introduction to His Work by Various Hands, *edited by Henry Treece (reprinted by permission of Faber and Faber Ltd.), Faber and Faber, 1944, pp. 7-41 (in the Kennikat reprint edition, 1969).*

An ideal of beauty that finds its most appropriate expression in reflective lyrics, or even in didactic poetry, has always formed part of the English conception of art. The work of Herbert Read follows this more than any other tendency in the English tradition. Though his poetry cannot be called didactic in the proper sense of the word, ideas are the main source of his inspiration. The clue to his critical and aesthetic work lies in the fact that he believes this kind of poetry to represent art in its highest form. On the other hand his writings, mainly those after 1931, reflect a different attitude: appreciation for unreflective art, for an art that entirely abandons the realm of conscious reason. With a glance cautious but full of expectation he bends over to gaze at the mysterious and creative depth of the human soul. And in so doing Herbert Read does justice to that other side of his nature which seeks fulfilment not in the universality of thought but in the spontaneity of feeling. . . .

Read's early contacts with peasants and craftsmen have given his mind a direction that made him a literary critic of quite a special brand. His preference for what is plastic, concrete and of good craftsmanship has supplied his art theories with a certain solid robustness, which is perhaps not quite compatible with literary refinement. Read has always been more artist than art critic. This perhaps explains why he was not recognized as one of the best English critics till 1930. . . .

Even a consideration of Read's literary methods gives one an idea of an artistic nature in which feeling plays an important part. He does not write like a scholar who builds up his work methodically and with regularity. With every new book he makes a new start. Every new book, however planned it may appear in its structure, betrays the poet impatient to communicate, the poet whom a sudden leap carries away from and beyond logical concepts. His formulation is such that it does not admit of any contradiction. His inner vision draws to itself everything that can be of use to it, silencing any critical objections. Read's thought is aphoristic, and therefore particularly suited for the essay. Where he attempts to create more systematically and on a larger scale he is not so successful.

His keen and vital intellect is matched by an open-eyed unbiased judgment. His two main subjects—literary criticism and the history of art—open for him the way to all other spheres of culture. He is widely read and shows critical understanding in every field. There may be other critics of his time his superiors in scientific training or in verbal magic: there are not many that are his equals in universality of interest and richness of aesthetic feeling.

The other pole of Read's personality [is] his sense of order [and] his deep respect for the laws of nature. . . .

The true balance . . . between [his] 'appollinic' tendencies and his fundamentally romantic sensibility is found by way of the aesthetic experience, and in particular through the work of art itself. In creative imagination Read experiences a reality that is clear and ordered as well as dynamic.

*H. W. Hausermann, "The Development of Herbert Read," translated by Léonie Cohn, in* Herbert Read: An Introduction to His Work By Various Hands, *edited by Henry Treece (reprinted by permission of Faber and Faber Ltd.), Faber and Faber, 1944, pp. 52-80 (in the Kennikat reprint edition, 1969).*

[In *The Green Child*] Read's clear, economical style is more akin to that of Hemingway's sportsman's sketches than to any other twentieth-century writing. There is a striking resemblance between the description of Olivero's walk along the bank of the stream and Hemingway's wonderful evocation of a North American river in *In Our Time*. The resemblance is not distinctly to be found in the texture of the writing for Read constructs a longer sentence and eschews Hemingway's excessive use of conjunctions, but both writers are distinguished by the cool, sharp, homesick eye and the gift of progression, and both can claim stylistic descent from Defoe. But whereas Hemingway has a forthrightness and an inherently objective vision which makes him almost 'the modern Defoe' Read's relationship to Defoe is not so simply a matter of affinity; his is not by any means a return to Defoe's documentary style, but is rather an aftermath of that style's complex and passionate flowering in *Wuthering Heights,* the heat gone and its traces calcined.

*Robert Melville, "The First Sixty-Six Pages of 'The Green Child'," in* Herbert Read: An Introduction to His Work by Various Hands, *edited by Henry Treece (reprinted by permission of Faber and Faber Ltd.), Faber and Faber, 1944, pp. 81-90 (in the Kennikat reprint edition, 1969).*

In 'The Scene of War' Read . . . adhered closely to Imagist principles. These short poems are formally perfect, classically objective word-pictures of reality. The Imagists' indifference to subject-matter appears in his treatment of the horror and desolation of war. . . .

When Read describes the havoc of war in 'Villages démolis', the pitiful fate of 'The Refugees', or the derision of 'The Crucifix', he does not want to stir our feelings of pity and indignation; he on the contrary endeavours to transmute these feelings into art. . . .

For the success of Read's artistic purpose it appears necessary that he should treat some large objective theme, some 'outer horror'; for when he chooses for his subject some inner experience of war he fails. Thus, 'Liedholz' is merely a *fait divers* which sounds unnecessarily emphatic when told in verse; in fact, the prose version of the same event in *Ambush* makes much better reading. 'Fear' is little more than a 'conceit', and 'The Happy Warrior' a naturalistic study with a satirical implication.

Read must have felt that the complexity and depth of the inner experience of war could only be handled in a longer poem. 'Kneeshaw Goes to War', 'My Company', and 'The Execution of Cornelius Vane' are progressive steps towards that end. But it is only in 'The End of a War' that Read achieves the desired impersonal beauty. Here, too, the poetry is not in the pity; but pity is not banished from the poetry as it is from 'The Scene of War'. What makes 'The End of a War' one of the few very great war poems is less its poetic form (there are some weak lines in it) than the wide range of thought and emotion which it gathers up in a perfectly adequate dramatic situation. The detachment with which the poet formerly transmuted the 'outer horror' into art is here brought to bear upon the highly complex inner experience of war. None of its essential aspects is sacrificed, neither the German officer's fanatic devotion to his vision of power and glory, nor the French girl's equally single-minded love of her country. There is no trace left of the superior, or didactic, or satirical attitudes which marred the earlier longer war poems. . . .

Most of Read's satirical poems are directed against man's reluctance or inability to follow whole-heartedly his natural intuitions and healthy instincts. In 'The Brown Book of the Hitler Terror' he shows up, if I understand it rightly, the inconsistency of our romantic heroism and noble attitudes on the one hand, and our timidity and prudent discretion on the other. In the 'Short Poem for Armistice Day', which is probably the finest of his satires, the poet finds a poignant image and haunting rhythm to bring home his feeling of anticlimax at the sight of armistice celebrations, artificial poppies, crippled and disabled soldiers, of inane gestures and dead symbols, after all that has happened in the war. . . .

It appears from a study of Herbert Read's poetry as well as of his prose works that his personality combines the talent of the poet-philosopher with that of the poet-artist. He has the desire for knowledge and the capacity for abstract argument which characterise the man of science and the philosopher; but he also has the artist's quick and highly specialised sensitiveness to outward shapes. His feelings are aroused not only by the eternal themes of nature, love, death, and religion, but also by the logical implications of modern physics, of organic mechanism, and of certain psychological discoveries. On the other hand, pure sense impressions (not altered by literary or other extraneous associations) equally speak to his affections and give him intuitions of a profounder reality.

These two modes of thinking are not always reconciled in Read's poetry. . . .

Not all of Read's lyrics show the same predominantly pictorial character. There are many in which other emotions are at least as important as the joy that comes with the vision of the 'innocent eye'. Thus 'The White Isle of Leuce', 'September Fires', 'Day's Affirmation', 'Night's Negation', 'The Falcon and the Dove', 'A Northern Legion', 'Bombing Casualties in Spain', 'To a Conscript of 1940', and 'Summer Rain' are more purely lyrical in the accepted sense of the term. They, too, show the peculiar hardness and dryness of some of the typically Imagist poems, and they always have that shyness or emotional virginity which characterises Read's personal style. Those who like their lyrical verse expansive, richly orchestrated and very explicit will find little to their taste in his poetry and they had better not waste their time trying to enjoy it. It may be doubted, however, if they can enjoy Wordsworth, for the Lake poet too achieves his finest effects by transmuting passion into impersonal things.

*H. W. Hausermann, "Herbert Read's Poetry," translated by Léonie Cohn, in* Herbert Read: An Introduction to His Work by Various Hands, *edited by Henry Treece (reprinted by permission of Faber and Faber Ltd.), Faber and Faber, 1944, pp. 91-107 (in the Kennikat reprint edition, 1969).*

Read has always committed himself to searching life at a very great depth. In so doing, he has deprived himself of almost all the traditional digging tools, taking it on faith that he must submit naked and without artifice to the presence of the Truth he is seeking. To some, he may appear to be mining coal with his bare hands. Others may see him in a nearly messianic light: a man getting at the lode of composite personal experience by the admittedly uncertain medium of words, which have served as well as they can if they show the reflected light of a Truth not so much sensory, but Absolute: opaque, heavy, and full of grandeur and mystery. . . .

To use words as sparingly as Read does, shouldn't one see that each syllable pull a great deal more weight than if it occurred in a somewhat denser line? In many of [the poems in *Moon's Farm*] the employment of language is fairly near being arid, and is substantially less successful than if the poems were to be divested of their linear structure and written as Sir Herbert's excellent prose. Again, the inadequacy is not entirely technical, but is inadequacy of insight also, the heart's blood of poetry. In these cases, the moments in which Read believes with such passion and intelligence are given no true chance to reach us. We have only

Sir Herbert's word for it that they exist, or have existed. There is too much of the will, here, and not enough of the carrying flow of passion, which, in a great poet, is inevitably and deeply connected with language. Read's verse has over it, still, a strong cast of the would-be poet, the straining inarticulateness of the amateur. In only a few places does he display the exploratory and personal sense of language that identifies the major poet.

It is amazing, therefore, after noting that it lacks the skill, the insight, and the passion requisite to his subjects and approaches, to find in Read's poetry a number of qualities which are nobly memorable, and (one hopes) of permanent value. The poems I think of most persuasively as Read's ("A World Within a War," "Moon's Farm") are about land, and its relationship to those who live on it. These poems have more of the feudal (and older) sense of *belonging* to the land than any I know since Wordsworth's. He writes, "When you live all the time in the same place / Then you become aware of time." At their most memorable, Read's lines in this vein have the profound authority of statement of words spoken by the dying, or by those who are in love: one has the same horror of asking the poet to change them for "effect" that one would have if they were, indeed, out of such actual situations. It is this naked and yet somehow imaginative and right simplicity, paired with the deep feeling for and of place, that gives Herbert Read's poetry its great spiritual and human resonance; it is fitting that after forty-five years of exemplary service to civilization, Herbert Read should make his ultimate contribution as a poet as "a man speaking to men."

*James Dickey, "Herbert Read" (1957), in his* Babel to Byzantium *(reprinted with the permission of Farrar, Straus & Giroux, Inc.; copyright © 1956, 1957, 1958, 1959, 1960, 1961, 1962, 1963, 1964, 1965, 1966, 1967, 1968 by James Dickey), Farrar, Straus, 1968, pp. 63-5.*

Sir Herbert Read's active career as a poet began in the middle years of the first World War and has continued down to the present. Only Pound's creative lifetime has been longer and more representative in our time: for although Edmund Blunden . . . was publishing his pleasant Georgian poems in 1914, they have remained essentially Georgian and unrepresentative of the line of development taken by poetry in the twentieth century. From the beginning Read's poetry has been recognizably, even insistently, modern, although it has been a modernity little disposed to outrage conservative sensibilities, even in the earlier decades of his career: and it has been a modernity that has changed surprisingly little in style over half a century. One cannot read the 286 pages of Read's *Collected Poems* without a sharp awareness of the writer's informed intelligence, and especially of his simple courageous decency that seems the strongest single quality in his best poems. The persistence of these virtues across fifty years must necessarily command a strong assent from the reader. But unfortunately these virtues we assent to so happily too often seem attached to the poems only by the most tenuous of connections. Disembodied and unincarnate, they lend the shadow but rarely the substance of power to the words on the page. . . .

Read names "the poets who were my immediate mentors," and the list includes T. E. Hulme, F. S. Flint, Ezra Pound, H. D., T. S. Eliot, Marianne Moore, and William Carlos Williams. Although I see little direct influence of Miss Moore on this verse, the others are much in evidence throughout the volume. What these poets share in common, perhaps again with the exception of Marianne Moore, is a strong element of Imagism, at least in part of their work. Despite its superficiality and general invitation to mediocrity, Imagism has been a surprising source of strength in the best of twentieth-century poetry. . . . Read's first volume of verse was predominantly Imagist in inspiration, and it was doubtless the spare economy of Imagism's visual evocations that led into the considerable achievement of his early war poems; and it continues to be an operative influence in his work.

*Marius Bewley, in* The Hudson Review *(copyright © 1966 by The Hudson Review, Inc.; reprinted by permission), Vol. XIX, No. 3, Autumn, 1966, pp. 479-83.*

The blurb for [Read's novel] says: "First published in 1935, *The Green Child* is Herbert Read's only novel. But if he had written nothing else, this one inspired book would insure his fame." This is simply not true: there are fine passages in the novel, as there are in much of Read's prose, as in his war diary . . . (*The Contrary Experience: Autobiographies* . . .), and his other autobiographical and critical prose. He is to be honored, I think, for his reasonable romantic championship of the art of others.

*David D. Harvey, in* The Southern Review, *Vol. V, No. 1, Winter, 1969, p. 259.*

As a poet Herbert Read was certainly not at the mercy of the *Zeitgeist*; his own poems—which will, I believe, outlast most of his criticism—laconic, private utterances, are the creation of his own "true voice of feeling"; his concern with groups and movements a matter of principle, or the expression of another side of his character, to which, perhaps, he often sacrificed his poetic genius on behalf of talents of less value than his own. . . .

Imagism, with its accompanying form of "free verse", was the first of the several movements with which Herbert Read was to associate himself. From the regionalism which inspired his first and enduring poetic loyalty to Wordsworth he moved, in postwar London, into the American expatriate *ethos* which, from Henry James to Ezra Pound and T. S. Eliot, introduced into English letters that internationalism which changed, perhaps permanently, the course of its native current. Eliot was to become his closest literary associate and lifelong friend; perhaps against his own natural bent he was caught up into the stronger current of the Imagist movement, whose first apologist was T. E. Hulme, whose often-quoted lines

> [I] saw the ruddy moon lean over a hedge
> Like a red-faced farmer

may be poor poetry, but are perfectly good prose. Herbert Read's natural preference for the laconic, together with his adherence to Wordsworth's view that poetry should be a selection from the language of common men, may have attracted him to a poem and a theory of poetry which do not, in retrospect, seem more than an incident in the history of English poetry. . . .

Herbert Read once confessed to me the difficulty he had in memorizing verse, even his own; a defectiveness of the inward ear which may in part have accounted for his bias. . . .

In the course of his literary life Herbert Read hastened to relate his criticism to system after system, most of them now themselves perished and replaced. Under the compulsive necessity always to have a theory, he was almost naïvely uncritical of ideas so long as they were new; and throughout his works is scattered a sequence of obscure names (most of them Germanic) of Freudian psychologists, Behaviorists, and Heaven knows what, cited as infallible authorities in one book, forgotten in the next. The root of this continual theorizing was his refusal to accept the only final sanction there is for any qualitative view of the world. . . .

[Neither] Herbert Read nor anyone else infected by the excitement of the Surrealist movement stopped to ask whether those who opposed it might have motives other than ignorant prejudice, reactionary obstructivism, and so on. The intoxication of Surrealism could not, obviously, infect believers in a spiritual order, whether Christian or theosophist, for whom the "irrational" hierarchies of heaven and hell were in any case real, and more clearly conceived than by these newcomers from Behaviorism, Freud, French anti-clerical rationalism, and what-not. It seemed easy to make light of the criticisms of so popular a writer as J. B. Priestley, who had strongly attacked the movement on the self-evident grounds that the Surrealists "stand for violence and neurotic unreason", and that "you catch a glimpse behind them of the deepening twilight of barbarism that may soon blot out the sky, until at last humanity finds itself in another long night." C. S. Lewis, scholar and Christian theologian, was another opponent. Yeats, who had been studying "the irrational" ever since the 1880's, and who could have told not only Herbert Read and the Surrealists but Freud and Jung themselves a great deal about the *memoria* and the *hodos chameleontos* which is only now beginning to be understood, reached Priestley's conclusion; "after us the savage god," he wrote, after seeing in Paris the first performance of Jarry's *"Ubu Roi"*. . . .

[Read] was always careful to say that not all Surrealism was, as he would understand the word, art; all the same, there was already in the concept of Surrealism the beginning of the confusion that has since threatened to submerge any such distinction. There has never been any precedent, in the art of the past, for the notion that the function of art can ever be "destructive"; but once art and literature are conceived of as expressions of the *Zeitgeist,* with that *Zeitgeist* itself at the service of a nihilism (as Read himself knew very well), the only possible term can be the destruction of art itself. This the Surrealists themselves were the first to proclaim, at a time when few could have foreseen the triumph of the principle of destruction they deliberately introduced into art.

*Kathleen Raine, "Herbert Read as a Literary Critic," in* Sewanee Review *(© 1969 by The University of the South; reprinted by permission of the editor), Summer, 1969, pp. 405-25.*

Read's life had an underlying shape which is best evoked not by the conceptual metaphor of the dialectic, but rather by an image of archetypal nature: the mandala, the ancient symbol of the solar cycle, the shield of Achilles, the sacred circle that, apart from its uses in ritual and contemplation, unites within a single form the universe's many aspects, and parallels the karmic wheel of existence portrayed by Tibetan Buddhists. Read himself refers to the 'magic circle' of the mandala as 'the symbol of the self as a psychic unity', a symbol whose recognition in the art of infants was for him 'an apocalyptic experience'; he sees mandalas in general as 'images of wholeness and integration, inviting withdrawal from the chaotic distraction of daily perception, inducing contemplation and selfless meditation'.

Read's two most personal books, *The Green Child* and *The Contrary Experience,* can be seen as mandalas rendered in literary form, for their meanings are multiple, yet their designs are unified within circles of experience. In *The Green Child,* the fictional hero Olivero, and in *The Contrary Experience* that character's creator, Read himself, both leave the country of childhood and afterwards both return to seek regeneration. (p. 14)

In Read's poetry and criticism, in his theories of aesthetics and education and anarchism, this consciousness of the need for a return to the pristine and the natural is always present, balanced by a knowledge that the power we gain from such an Antaeus-like contact with earth is expressed nowhere more intensely than in the work of romantic art. (p. 15)

The dialectic suggests the *mode* of progression by the interplay of reason and intuition. The mandala suggests the *direction* of progression, that of a circle returning on itself, like the world-encompassing snake, Uroboros.

The mandala also suggests Read's personal view of life in so far as it accepts a pattern and deviates from the general inclinations of our age. Most modern men have plotted their lives in the form of a trajectory of progress. The momentum may decline, the arc may fall, but when it reaches ground they are at least farther forward than they were in the beginning. They live by a concept of material advancement which Puritans share with Marxists. Read's concept, though he was in no ordinary sense a religious believer and claimed no mystical experience, was that of the spiritual man and also that of the anarchist who looks, not forward to some Utopia at the end of progress, but round a curve of intention that will lead men out of corruption into simplicity. (pp. 15-16)

It was a book of criticism that Read entitled *The Sense of Glory*; if there is any quality that unites his work, in every field, it is this. The glory of the world perceived through a child's eye and later through the awakening mind of a creative artist permeates his autobiographical writings and gives a peculiar lambent quality to his poetry and his rare works of fiction. It extends into his critical writings, where he is seeking always that special fire of inspiration which liberates man from the mere imitation of the laws of nature, and it inspires his anarchism, that doctrine of man glorified by freedom. It even extends into his organizational efforts, into the centres and societies he created, into the great lecturing journeys, all intended to stir in men the aesthetic sense that would somehow preserve in them the visionary gleam which Read detected in the art of children as Wordsworth had detected it in the perceptions of childhood, the gleam Wordsworth too had associated with glory. The causes Read supported, the artists whose work he loved, his own work in all its variety, were emanations of that wonder at life of which he had been aware from the moment when he passed out of childhood, where it had been instinctive and therefore unperceived, into adolescence. (p. 32)

*The Green Child* is no ordinary novel. It has been called a parable, a romance, a fairy tale, a Utopian fantasy, an allegory, and it contains elements of all these in its intricate symbolic suggestiveness. There is a bright and visionary clarity in its writing that brings it nearer to *The Innocent Eye* than to any other of Read's writings, and it also resembles that book, written only two years before, not only in its discontinuous, mosaic pattern, but also in the importance of spatial as opposed to chronological elements. (p. 66)

It is clear that he was by temperament and talent a poet and an essayist, not a novelist, and that *The Green Child* was the kind of *jeu d'esprit* which many poets have performed once in their lives, as a change from more familiar genres. . . . [But] *The Green Child* would not have been the small and unique classic it has now become if Read had not used in writing it his poet's complex sensitivity to words and his essayist's power to control and manipulate ideas. (pp. 78-9)

Throughout his life Read was troubled by the difficulty of achieving a proper balance between visual and conceptual elements in poetry. He did so most successfully in his shorter poems, and some of the best of these belong to the volume of imagistic verses entitled *Eclogues*. (p. 89)

There is a perceptible line of development in this poetry, and the burden of it is carried in his long, rather than in his short poems. Some of the later short poems were more complex in form and perhaps more profound in thought than the *Eclogues,* but it is hard to show development in the 'clarity and elegance of . . . sensibility' which, as Robin Skelton has remarked, is most evidently displayed in Read's briefer poems. It is in the longer poems that development takes place, a development from metaphysical abstraction towards an ever greater concreteness of vision. . . . He was, in fact, always at his best in poems—long or short—where action or the strong visual rendering of physical scenes was involved, preferably brought into a detached form through an element of indirection imposed by distance in time or space.

Conflicting with this characteristic concreteness of vision was Read's obstinate ambition to write the long contemplative work which he regarded as the sign of a major poet. He was fascinated by the genre of philosophic verse, and the poets he admired most, from Donne and Traherne, through Wordsworth and Coventry Patmore, to such innovators as Hopkins and Eliot, were all in their various ways metaphysical. Read was ill equipped, at the beginning of his career, to emulate them. He was innocent of religious experience, untutored in philosophy. His mode of thought tended to be visual rather than conceptual. He later acquired a working knowledge of philosophy as it impinged upon his fields of aesthetic and political interest, but he never won acceptance among professional philosophers, who regarded his thought as nebulous and inconsistent. Yet it is often an advantage in a poet to be an imperfect logician, for this leads him to seek the expression of philosophic truths by oblique paths, and Read moved forward, as his Imagist origins taught him, by a series of attempts to reconcile the visual and the conceptual, and by the development of a style that matched his poetic personality. (pp. 95-7)

For the solution Read eventually found for the long contemplative poem he was indebted to Browning; it lay in the substitution of a personal for an impersonal voice, which immediately set the poem within 'the structure of an event'. (p. 100)

Read rejected the characteristic attitudes of the dominant trend in English poetry during the 1930's. Though he took an active part in the Surrealist movement, with its insistence on a revolutionary art, and made public before the middle of the decade his hitherto private adherence to anarchism, he did not accept the idea of art as propaganda, and consistently rejected the doctrines of social realism fashionable at the time.

In age and experience, Read really belonged to a half generation between the classic 'modern' writers—Eliot, Pound, Lewis, Joyce—and the younger poets first introduced as a group through the publication of *New Signatures* in 1932. Despite the aristocratic element that often tinged his thinking, he retreated into none of the varieties of conservatism that Eliot, Pound and Lewis each in his own way adopted, nor was he tempted to follow Joyce into an aesthetic *cul-de-sac*. He retained his pacifism, he broadened his anarchism. And the poems he wrote between 1933 and 1945 reflected as deep an awareness of the social problems of the time as anything Day Lewis or Auden wrote. As late as the 1950's when both these poets had long abandoned social revolution in any form as a theme, Read was still, in such a poem as "The Death of Kropotkin," asserting his anarchist faith.

The circumstances of the time in fact fostered a poetic activity in Read which resulted in the production, in the twenty years between 1935 and 1955, of a series of poems superior to any but a handful of very short pieces from the preceding decades. His vision deepened in intensity and clarity; his expression sharpened in intelligibility, and in the best works of these two decades it fused feeling and form into constructions so harmonious and economical, and yet so emotionally active, that one is unsure whether to regard them as perfect examples of classicist form or perfect expressions of romantic feeling. In these poems, more than in any of his other writings, Read in fact achieves that synthesis of the abstract and the organic which had always been his goal. (pp. 106-07)

If to the end of his life Read considered himself primarily a poet the description applied only to a minor proportion of his work. Most of his writing, in volume as in numbers of titles, he did as—in his own description—'a critic and philosopher of art and literature'. . . . He went beyond the contemplation of actual works of art and literature to seek the sources of artistic creativity and to establish the relationship between the work of art and the percipient mind. And these very studies led him to the point where his aesthetic philosophy took on an ethical character, and became synthesized with the political philosophy of anarchism which he had already evolved in his youth.

Yet it is no rigid structure of metaphysical architecture that faces us when we seek Read's philosophy. It is rather a kind of coral growth, a symbiosis of attitudes related by a common urge that can perhaps most accurately be described as the dynamic equilibration of freedom and order. It was not in the nature of Read's mind to marshal his thoughts into a single summational work, even of so undisciplined a structure as Coleridge's *Biographia Literaria* which was for long his critical bible. It was his method to work out the facets of a subject in separate essays and afterwards to bring them together; a collection established in this way he regarded as a more organic entity than a book constructed on a mechanically logical plan. He did not reject the systematizers; indeed, he borrowed their ideas without concealment, but he found that in the fields of thought where he was working, so near to the spontaneous urges of creation, his own approach was the more fruitful. And in the end, if there is no system, there is certainly a recognizable pattern, a philosophy of the relationships between the arts and human society, which spans the whole horizon of human creativity from poetry where Read's criticism begins in the judgement of his own art, to the politics of the unpolitical where it emerges as a criticism of all civilization. (p. 121-22)

In the end it was towards Jung that Read felt most strongly drawn, as he moved deeper into the symbolic interpretation of the visual arts, and found in the writings of the Swiss psychologist not merely the ideas that assisted him, such as the seminal theory of the collective unconscious, but also a knowledge of the varieties of symbolism, in art, in religion, in primitive magic, of a richness unparalleled in any of his rivals. (p. 130)

As a writer, Read divided his activities between the spontaneous, lyrical approach of the poet and the logical, discursive approach of the essayist. His views on poetry tended to the romantic; his practice in prose was inclined to the classical. Poetry was a private activity; prose led him into the public world, the world of lecture rooms and conferences against which his poetic self put up a ritual fight which was doomed from the beginning to defeat. (p. 176)

Read's definitions of romanticism and classicism and his attitudes towards them fluctuated constantly, and it is significant that in the introduction to *Surrealism* he chooses to speak in his role as the poet, dedicated to romanticism, rather than as the art critic, committed to impartiality. In fact, if any real alignment as an art critic appears in Read's writings as he moves out from the shadow of the academy, it is a dedication to the interpretation of the contemporary whether it can be defined as romantic or classical. (p. 180)

Of all Read's many books the most influential was undoubtedly *Education Through Art*. Its reputation spread far beyond the cognoscenti of arts and letters who were Read's special audience; it reached and influenced many of the very people he had hoped to convert—the teachers and the instructors in colleges of education. Its influence led to the foundation in Britain of the Society for Education through Art, and a few years later, in 1951, to the establishment under UNESCO auspices of an International Society for Education through Art. Yet the success of *Education Through Art* was largely one of esteem, and to that extent transitory; today one does not hear so much talk among educators as one did a decade ago of the fresh ideas and insights that Read—an outsider—had brought into the field of educational method. This fate is at least in part due to the fact that the ideas Read advanced have been absorbed into educational theory, and have invisibly and often indirectly modified teaching methods and curricula in many parts of the world, while the book itself has receded into the background stance of an educational classic. (p. 264)

Read died believing that his philosophy of life—the aesthetic philosophy—was valid, and that some day, if the world was not destroyed by technicians, mankind would come to live by it, through true education and a life in which work and art would become indistinguishable. He never denied his anarchist convictions, and though he became reconciled to thinking of the free society as a point on a distant horizon, he refused, in republishing his early libertarian writings, 'to give an air of caution to the impetuous voice of youth. Indeed, I now envy those generous feelings.' He believed in the great art of his time, and he continued to write poetry as he felt it should be written, in spite of his lack of popularity as a poet. He realized the hollowness of much of the popularity he did enjoy in his later years, and he recognized that his works most likely to survive were precisely those least noticed in his time—the poems, the autobiographies, *The Green Child.*

In a historical sense, I believe that Read will also retain a unique place as an interpreter of his time, for few writers have probed so deeply and so intelligently into the nature of our culture, and none has brought together so suggestively the insights of modern philosophers and critics, poets and artists, psychologists and social scientists, as Read did in the varied corpus of his work. (pp. 291-92)

*George Woodcock, in his* Herbert Read: The Stream and the Source *(reprinted by permission of Faber and Faber Ltd.), Faber and Faber, 1972.*

In the remarkable diversity of Sir Herbert Read's achievement, *The Green Child* remains his masterpiece, a work as extraordinary now as when first published in 1935. Seductive, complex, self-contained, it appears at once to invite and to forbid analysis. Is there a secret to be wrested from it, or is the story obscure in the sense in which Read once defined obscurity as a poetic ideal—"vision without meaning, concrete, synthetic, but held in suspense, contemplated without question"? Read held that poetic coherence is different in kind from prose coherence and has priority over it; that poetry requires from the reader an essential submission, which renders analysis always ancillary. (Without submission, he thought, analysis is monstrous.) . . . *The Green Child* is a philosophic myth, and Read's mythmaking —as he makes clear in the book—belongs in the tradition of Plato. Although an apologist for surrealism and a defender of the night-side of the mind, Read was in his own work characteristically cerebral. Even in his poetry one remarks, in conjunction with original and striking images, a hard intellectuality, with difficult and elliptical patterns of thought, more often than "vision without meaning". What seems to have happened in *The Green Child* was that he combined his ideas in such unexpected ways and embodied them in a fantasy so entrancing as to render his readers unable or unwilling to grasp the meaning of his allegory. Yet it is the matching of image with idea in this work that is, finally, most extraordinary of all.

Read's thought was dialectical, characterized by probings and testings, tensions and contradictions. His work balances thought with sensation, reason with emotion, idea with image, order with anarchy, in an equilibrium never intended to be quite stable. There was always a center, however. His thought turned on the priority of aesthetic over rational cognition, of the image over the idea, the concrete over the abstract, and in book after book he attempted to demonstrate this priority. In *The Green Child* his thought became flesh. This strangely luminous story of a quest for the source of life is itself a complex image which embodies the idea of the priority of image over idea. . . .

Read's life work can be summed up as an attempt to construct a post-idealist romanticism, in which the Idea, the absolute of nineteenth-century romantic idealist aesthetics, is transformed into the Image. Underlying discursive thought, he maintained, is aesthetic cognition, the nondiscursive, subjective-objective complex of "superreality". The work of art, he said in "Myth, Dream, and Poem", is a "living synthesis"—"that miracle which is the only objective evidence we possess of whatever superreality is cosmic and eternal".

*Worth T. Harder, "Crystal Source: Herbert Read's 'The Green Child'," in* Sewanee Review *(© 1973 by The University of the South; reprinted by the permission of the editor), Autumn, 1973, pp. 714-36.*

* * *

## READ, Piers Paul 1941-

**Read, an English novelist, is the son of the poet and critic Sir Herbert Read. (See also *Contemporary Authors*, Vols. 23-24.)**

Piers Paul Read is a young English novelist with a speciality: exposing false innocents. He writes cool little horror stories about decent, well-intentioned people who suddenly find themselves up to their lily-white necks in evil. Good but tragically unaware Germans before World War II *(The Junkers),* for instance. Or the rich English boy *(Monk Dawson)* who sets out to be a saint, rather as if he were joining a club. Almost sinisterly quiet in tone, Read is a sad, skilled connoisseur of the moral blindness that occurs when self-righteousness and self-interest try to be one.

If the late J. P. Marquand had been crossed with Graham Greene, *The Professor's Daughter* might well have been the literary result. Here Read has zeroed in on another moral elitist, American style. Henry Rutledge is a double aristocrat—a professor at Harvard and the scion of an old Yankee family. The sort of New Deal liberal who receives $3,500,000 from his parents as a little wedding gift. . . .

Read never quite makes things clear. Clouding his own novelist's dilemmas with heavy melodrama, he kills off Henry with a bullet from the movement. Henry dies as ambivalently as he lived. Read has not so much shaped a resolution as confessed that he dare not imagine one. He seems paralyzed by suppressed hope the way other authors get paralyzed by suppressed despair.

*Melvin Maddocks, "Hope Against Hope," in* Time *(reprinted by permission from* Time, The Weekly Newsmagazine; *copyright Time Inc.), October 25, 1971, pp. 92-4.*

Piers Paul Read is a young English novelist of much talent and intelligence—cool, wry, tough intelligence—whose subject thus far has been disillusionment in its various contemporary manifestations. In his fine 1969 novel, "Monk Dawson," it is the disillusionment of a priest who flees the church in search of a more "relevant" life only to return, routed, to the sanctuary of the cloister. In "The Professor's Daughter" it is double disillusionment: of the young with their elders, and their elders with themselves. . . .

What Mr. Read has made . . . is not precisely a generation-gap novel, though there is quite enough of that in it, but an inquiry into political styles; as such it is engaging and provocative, but Mr. Read in great measure defeats himself by wrapping it in thick layers of melodrama.

*Jonathan Yardley, in* The New York Times Book Review *(© 1971 by The New York Times Company; reprinted by permission), November 7, 1971, pp. 38-9.*

At the heart of *The Upstart* is a fine tension between the conservatism of its themes and settings and characters and the anarchic vigour of much of the action. The latter quality erupts suddenly and splendidly at the moment Hilary quits Cambridge—the last arena in which he has tried and failed to win the snobs' game—and plunges into a life of vice and crime and abstract art in SW6. This middle section of the book, with its outrageous coincidences and outrageous crimes, is a success, the more so because it is unexpected and because Mr Read maintains throughout his air of dispassionate objectivity. The prose remains dry, almost studious. . . . Very chilling. . . .

*The Upstart* is a welcome book, particularly after the comparative failure of *The Professor's Daughter*. It has those qualities of unpredictability and wit and artistic ambition that distinguished Piers Paul Read's earlier novels; and it makes me, as I used to, look forward again to his next.

*Peter Prince, "Humiliations," in* New Statesman, *September 7, 1973, p. 321.*

Piers Paul Read's first novels, *Game in Heaven with Tussy Marx* and *The Junkers,* were clever, perceptive, elegantly written, but they gave some appearance of being difficult exercises he had set himself, ways of getting into training, rather than the kind of book he was best equipped to write. In *Monk Dawson* he seemed to have found his subject, a man's attempt in mid-twentieth century England to live according to his conscience and religious beliefs and his final decision that to remain true to his beliefs he had no alternative but to opt out of society and join a monastic order. In *The Upstart* the subject is similar, the conflict in one man between potential saint and actual sinner. Like the earlier books it is inventive and acutely observant, but after the first straightforward, scene-setting eighty pages the plot lurches into melodrama so lurid that the narrative strength, which is considerable, fails completely to keep disbelief suspended. . . .

The melodrama is so blatant, there are so many coincidences and dei—or diaboli—ex machina, that one must presume it all to have been part of the author's purpose. Nevertheless, whatever the Grand Design may have been, it doesn't seem to me to have been achieved. It is as if a canvas had been started by Ford Madox Brown and finished by Hieronymus Bosch. After *Monk Dawson, The Upstart* is a comedown: a good read but an unsatisfactory Read.

*John Mellors, in* London Magazine, *December, 1973-January, 1974, p. 155.*

So astonishing a story [as *Alive*] would have been easy to sensationalise but Piers Paul Read tells it with beautiful judgement. Technically, he is superb, cutting his narrative vividly from scene to scene, never losing a moment of suspense or drama, nor sacrificing any of the forward impulse that grips the reader from start to finish. . . .

Morally and emotionally, Mr Read is equally sure-footed. . . .

He never pushes his moral messages, but rather lets them rise, questioningly and disturbingly, out of the reader's own reflections. He has in short, contrived a masterly piece of story-telling about a group of human beings who rose, *in extremis,* to heights beyond their own, or anyone else's expectations. . . .

*David Holden, "Blow-Out," in* The Spectator *(© 1974 by* The Spectator; *reprinted by permission of* The Spectator*), May 18, 1974, p. 611.*

*Alive* is the story of the Uruguayan rugby team who . . . survived a winter plane crash high in the Andes mountains —a chilling tale of cannibalism and human survival, and a story that in its flat and careful telling will involve the reader as thoroughly as the best adventure novel. . . .

Read is sufficiently sensitive and skillful in his narration that the cannibalism becomes only one facet of how the diverse personalities of the survivors changed during their trials. . . .

Because Read makes each character real and distinct . . . the story gains a novelistic sort of depth. The lives most of us lead give no hint as to what we may be capable of; the value of stories like *Alive* is the way they remind us of the deepest strengths of the organism. By sighting on that, Read has risen above the sensational and managed a book of real and lasting value.

*Michael Rogers, in* Rolling Stone *(© 1974 by Straight Arrow Publishers, Inc.; all rights reserved; reprinted by permission), May 23, 1974, p. 90.*

* * *

## RHYS, Jean 1894-

**Jean Rhys was born in Dominica, West Indies, and has lived in England since 1910. She is a novelist and short story writer whose work has been called "among the most original and memorable of our time." (See also *Contemporary Authors*, Vols. 25-28.)**

*After Leaving Mr. McKenzie,* originally published in 1930 (one is tempted to say before its time), depicts with cool mordancy what it is like to try to cope as a woman, irremediably past a petted prime, in a world for the comfort of men. . . .

Perhaps it is because she is a woman, a lady, that Miss Rhys eschews the strongest colors in depicting Julia Martin's "humiliation" after leaving Mr. McKenzie. . . .

The very style of writing fights back against a smug dominant masculinity. Uncle Griffiths is pictured as a "large and powerful male," with subliminal suggestions of a gorilla, and is neatly brutalized as a man in whom selfishness and neurotic fear of penury are killing sensitivity and compassion. . . . By the same token, Horsfield, a hesitant potential successor to McKenzie in Julia's life, is shown enjoying an elegant, vegetable comfort in his "world of lowered voices, and of passions, like Japanese dwarf trees, suppressed for many generations." *After Leaving Mr. McKenzie* becomes a proleptic document for women's liberation, passionate without polemics, plain without immodesty, a cameo of helpless female dignity in a world where it does not amount to much to be a man.

*Michael Cooke, in* The Yale Review *(© 1972 by Yale University; reprinted by permission of the editors), Summer, 1972, pp. 607-09.*

To my mind, [Jean Rhys] is, quite simply, the best living English novelist. Although her range is narrow, sometimes to the point of obsession, there is no one else now writing who combines such emotional penetration and formal artistry or approaches her unemphatic, unblinking truthfulness. Even the narrowness works to her advantage. She knows every detail of the shabby world she creates, knows precisely how much to leave out—surprisingly much—and precisely how to modulate the utterly personal speaking voice which controls it all, at once casual and poignant, the voice of the loser who refuses, though neither she nor God knows why, to go down. Because of this voice, the first four novels read as a single, continuing work. They have the same heroine—although she goes by different names—the same background of seedy hotels and bedsitters for transients in Montparnasse and Bloomsbury, and they recount the single, persistent, disconnected disaster of a life in which only three things can be relied on: fear, loneliness and the lack of money. . . .

[The] world Miss Rhys creates [seems] strangely unprecedented, glassy clear yet somehow distorted, as though she were looking up at things from the bottom of a deep pool. She makes you realize that almost every other novel, however apparently anarchic, is rooted finally in the respectable world. The authors come to their subjects from a position of strength and with certain intellectual presuppositions, however cunningly suppressed. She, in contrast, has a marvelous artistic intelligence—no detail is superfluous and her poise never falters as she walks her wicked emotional tightrope—yet is absolutely nonintellectual: no axe to grind, no ideas to tout. . . .

"Wide Sargasso Sea" is her only novel to be set in the past and with a heroine not immediately identifiable with the author, except in her being, like all the others, one of those who are defeated as though by natural right. . . .

It is a hallucinatory novel, as detailed, abrupt and undeniable as a dream, and with a dream's weird and irresistible logic. It is also the final triumph of Miss Rhys's stylistic control, her persistent search for a minimal senuous notation of distaste. Despite the exotic setting and the famous, abused heroine, there is no melodrama. Her prose is reticent, unemphatic, precise, and yet supple, alive with feeling, as though the whole world she so coolly describes were shimmering with foreboding, with a lifetime's knowledge of unease and pain.

The purity of Miss Rhys's style and her ability to be at once deadly serious and offhand make her books peculiarly timeless. Novels she wrote more than 40 years ago still seem contemporary, unlike those of many more popular authors. More important, her voice itself remains young. She was about 30 before she began to write—apparently having other things on her mind before that—yet the voice she created then, and still uses, is oddly youthful: light, clear, alert, casual and disabused, and uniquely concerned in simply telling the truth.

*A. Alvarez, "The Best Living English Novelist," in* The New York Book Review *(© 1974 by The New York Times Company; reprinted by permission), March 17, 1974, pp. 6-7.*

Jean Rhys is a writer of extraordinary delicacy who has been too long neglected except for a small group of cognoscenti. . . .

The thin, faded, intellectually sensitive heroines delineated by Francoise Sagan are prefigured by Rhys in more precisely wrought prose, better sustained and consistent, richer and more horrifying for the roundness. . . .

There are a number of fascinating technical and stylistic innovations in Rhys's work which I've not seen elsewhere, and always a feeling of fidelity to reality, even if that is a somewhat colder and seamier reality than one would care to know.

The Village Voice *(reprinted by permission of* The Village Voice; *© 1974 by The Village Voice, Inc.), June 6, 1974, p. 35.*

* * *

## ROBBE-GRILLET, Alain 1922-

**A French anti-novelist and critic, Robbe-Grillet writes fiction in which cinematographic representations of "things" are accumulated in pursuit of "reality," which is defined in terms of the things themselves. Vehemently opposed to the plots, psychological development, metaphors, adjectives, and pathetic fallacies that are the apparatus of the traditional novel, he pushes language away from "meaning" in an attempt to reinvent man in terms of the total reality of things. (See also *Contemporary Authors*, Vols. 9-12, rev. ed.)**

A few points in Robbe-Grillet's reflections on his art stand out. He wishes to banish the story and all anecdotes more or less pertaining to it, as had been already the dream of Flaubert and that of Joyce. . . . In *La Maison de rendez-vous* (1965), Robbe-Grillet, forsaking all pretense of being a thinker among novelists or a psychologist competing with Flaubert and Nathalie Sarraute, even condescended to facile tricks of erotic literature and evocations of local color in a luxury prostitution establishment of Hong Kong not unworthy of the once famous Claude Farrère. Robbe-Grillet, however, discards the naïve assumption of his predecessors that the adventures alluded to had actually happened to real characters, hence that we lived in a coherent universe which the novelist was able to decipher. He is no advocate of the absurd, which amounts to the most blatant form of anthropomorphism: complaining that the world does not suit man's conveniences. To him, the world is, and that is all. Man's function is in no way to force a meaning upon it.

Robbe-Grillet aims many barbs of his irony at the second idol of dramatic and fictional literature: character. He laughs at the conventional reader's demand that the actors of a novel should have a name, a pedigree, a profession, certain material possessions, and should belong to a social and human category; even more ludicrous is our insistence that there be some inner logic in their make-up and that they be 'human.' His irony at character, that mummy just good enough to be discarded, is entertaining; but even if it were true in theory that the creation of character, that sacrosanct requirement of criticism, can be dispensed with, the desire of the reader to have the novelist impart some life to his personages cannot be so easily dismissed. . . . It may be heroic to attempt to sever oneself altogether from the outdated storytelling, character-creation, chronological sequence, and three-dimensional perspective of past fiction. It takes ingenuity to substitute anti-heroes, or insignificant people like the phantom-like lover in *La Jalousie* and like the little boy, the woman, and the soldier wading in their labyrinthine snows, for the boldly outlined characters of Zola and of Proust. But the role of a pioneer is an ungrateful one for some day, like Edouard Dujardin when he experimented with the interior monologue to be picked up by James Joyce, he may be followed by more powerful talents than his own. . . . The flabby generalization that a name, a face, a social position, a profession and possessions have ceased to count in our topsy-turvy world of 1950-70, and fiction should consequently relinquish those to Madame Tussaud's wax museum, requires more gullibility in this era of triumphant bourgeois materialism than most of us are gifted with. Paradoxical aphorisms such as 'the true writer has nothing to say but he has only a manner of saying' are about as valid as those which Oscar Wilde used to flip.

Symbols and metaphors are among the ingredients of the traditional novel which the impetuous Robbe-Grillet proclaimed as doomed. Symbols, however, are not lacking in [his work]. . . .

*Le Voyeur* (1955) takes place in a setting which, in the author's fashion, is never precisely localized. . . . In it, Robbe-Grillet has shed some of the useless means of deception by which the contriver of a detective story throws his readers on the wrong track. The plot is simple and some anguished fear in the protagonist, not unworthy of Edgar Allan Poe or of Julien Green, is imparted to the reader. . . .

The novelist's mastery of his devices is perfect here. All the details, sensations, gestures, childhood memories, or vague projects of Mathias, expressions of fear in his behavior, are presented from the outside; even if they refer to the past or the future, they are given in the present indicative. The reader is made to borrow the eyes of Mathias throughout the story and there are thus two voyeurs, the reader and the rapist-murderer. But the former is afforded no insight into the dark recesses of the killer's desires or fear. His imagination is nowhere stimulated, his sensibility is not touched; the obliteration of both past and future makes the perpetual present very thin. The proliferation of exterior details drowns the attention of the reader-voyeur. Such elimination of all poetry about objects, scenery, human beings, man's sensations of nature impoverishes fiction. Reductionism in literature proves enjoyable only for a few undaunted ascetics; those who are neither saints nor snobs will not so readily consent to being deprived of all refined pleasure.

*La Jalousie* (1957) is a marvelous clockwork, which owes little or nothing to detective stories or to the suspense of an impending murder but lets psychology enter through a back-door. . . . All the novelist's skill is spent on the objective measurement of things and on repetitions multiplied in those tales of eternal recurrence. The bewilderment of the trapped reader grows as the very precise details around him no longer seem real and turn the meticulously surveyed setting into a phantasmal scene.

'Kafkaesque' is the adjective which comes to mind when we read Robbe-Grillet's novels, and the comparison naturally belittles the French novelist, whose expertly used devices never seem to unfold with the inevitability of the events in *The Castle,* or in some of Faulkner's novels. James Joyce and his theme of a wandering anti-hero pursuing his quest for a never stated goal also come to mind. But the intensity of that metaphysical pursuit of an undecipherable meaning, which oppresses us in Kafka, has given way to a series of traps into which the more playful and wily Frenchman lures us. *Dans le labyrinthe* (1959) drove even further that disturbing sense of an author playing cat and mouse with his reader. A brief warning, in the way of preface, notifies the reader that no allegorical value is to be looked for and that gestures, words, events as they are related have no more nor less significance 'than his own life or his own death.' The very title of a Labyrinth comes down to us, nevertheless, laden with mythological and symbolical associations. . . .

[In] spite of the novelist's admonitions not to read any ulterior meaning in any details, we are bound to wonder why those were selected and whether they do not connote love, time, and death. Or else, if no further meaning is anywhere implied, our involvement in the images dimly glimpsed at through the play of a magic lantern becomes nonexistent and our interest wanes altogether. . . . The novelist's purpose is to cease being, as in Balzac or Mauriac, a god aware of all that takes place inside the skulls and the hearts of his creatures, but to act only the cool observer of their exterior behavior. All links with reality are cut off in that strange realism: the novel must be erected, like an object or a pure and cold art work, outside life, in a rarefied empyrean. The novelist is a virtuoso engineer, but it is too easy to take all his clever mechanisms to pieces and then to be left with little but naïve wonderment at his skill. Man feels superfluous, *de trop,* in that artificial world and far more of a derelict than in Sartre's universe.

*Henri Peyre, in his* French Novelists of Today *(copyright © 1955, 1967 by Oxford University Press; reprinted by permission), Oxford University Press-Galaxy, 1967, pp. 369-75.*

[There] is nothing of the traditional humanist about Robbe-Grillet, who was trained as a scientist before he turned to literature, and whose only concern with humanism is to abolish it. Robbe-Grillet is a brisk operationalist, concerned purely with questions of process and technique, and to my mind an almost perfect exponent of what Marcuse calls the one-dimensional consciousness. . . . Robbe-Grillet's aim seems to be to make the novel a fit occupant of a totalitarian society, where individuals no longer matter; it is not one I find at all congenial. At the same time there is an extraordinary ambivalence in his approach: he sees that the nineteenth-century novel was the historical product of a particular society and set of assumptions about the world which have now largely vanished; yet he also wants the 'novel', as a transcendental entity, to go on existing in a form that bears very little relation to anything previously bearing the name.

*Bernard Bergonzi, in his* The Situation of the Novel *(reprinted by permission of the University of Pittsburgh Press; © 1970 by Bernard Bergonzi), University of Pittsburgh Press, 1970, pp. 37-8.*

Robbe-Grillet is against the Rilke type of empathy, against 'the idea of interiorness' which, he says. . ., 'always leads to that of transcendence'—and indeed, as we have seen, this is just what it did with Rilke and his angels. Above all, Robbe-Grillet is against the pathetic fallacy which, in our time, has slowly brought about the 'tragification of the universe', either in the form of despair at the discovery that the external world does not after all contain the human meaningfulness with which it has been invested, or in the form of a cynical acceptance that this world is meaningless and therefore absurd. . . .

There is . . . an ultimate inconsistency in Robbe-Grillet's position, since his particular technique, based on the formal analogies between things, not only achieves an effect similar to that achieved by metaphor (which he rejects), but also, in its intensity, makes his poetic novels in fact throb with the reflected emotion in the perceiving mind that sees the things. Rilke is more consistent within his own terms, but the problem remains. 'Man looks at the world, but the world does not look back at him[,'' writes Robbe-Grillet].

*Jerzy Peterkiewicz, in his* The Other Side of Silence: The Poet at the Limits of Language *(copyright © 1970 by Jerzy Peterkiewicz; reprinted by permission of Oxford University Press, Inc.), Oxford University Press, 1970, pp. 66-7.*

In French experiments with the non-fiction novel . . . the fiction that is purged from the novel is not so much a matter of invented characters and actions as a philosophical 'fiction', or fallacy, which the traditional novel encourages—namely, that the universe is susceptible of human interpretation. The purest statement of this point of view is to be found in the theoretical writings of Alain Robbe-Grillet. Essentially his argument is that traditional realism has distorted reality by imposing human meanings upon it. That is, in describing the world of things, we are not willing to admit that they are *just* things, with their own existence, indifferent to ours. We make things reassuring by attributing human meanings or 'significations' to them. In this way we create a false sense of solidarity between man and things.

*David Lodge, in his* The Novelist at the Crossroads *(© 1971 by David Lodge and used with his permission), Cornell University Press, 1971, p. 15.*

Robbe-Grillet . . . handles language as though he were himself a camera. He views over and over again from as many angles and at as many distances as he desires, the objects and images that are his subjects. It is among the relationships that he creates in this manner that the reader must seek the meanings of the novel, for they are literally woven from the movements of the [characters] in and out and back and forth among the novel's various settings. (p. 110)

The unique feature of the perspective employed by Robbe-Grillet is that it is subjective and objective at the same time. Generally, his narrators are either unidentified, as in *Jealousy,* or concealed, as in *In the Labyrinth* and *La Maison de Rendezvous.* This uncertainty regarding whose perceptions are being described has the effect of pressing the reader into an extremely close and intimate identification with the narrator. Since there is no alternative view of things to provide a comparison, a standard by which the reader may evaluate the "reality" of what he is being told, he must accept it as fact. At the same time, the manner of the descriptions—their precision, their dryness, their lack of qualifiers and of words that evoke feelings—is objective in the extreme. Like Marc Saporta, Robbe-Grillet is presenting an intensely subjective view in an intensely objective manner. The result is a fused, a double, perspective, and it is made possible by the borrowing of camera techniques. (p. 112)

One feels that, more than anything else, Robbe-Grillet wants, in writing a novel, to build something. "Clearly, he wants his books to have the solidity and independent existence of a statue or a picture, which resists any anecdotal or intellectual summary." But since words cannot be wholly freed from their relationships to observable reality, the novel as an object cannot be Robbe-Grillet's aim, as the finished painting is that of a painter. He is using the novel, much as paints, clay, or collage materials are used, to erect an impression, an illusion, that will exist in an ultimately nonverbal relationship to the reader. Instead of a record made with words, the novel becomes, in this writer's hands, the secondary means to the construction of an independent, abstract entity. If a Robbe-Grillet novel is read swiftly at one sitting, the final impression is of a structure which is itself abstract, although it may consist of minutely detailed parts. When the book is finished, this impression will remain in the reader's mind as the illusion of a form—solid, three-dimensional, architectonic. This abstract form is the ultimate emblem of the novel's central experience, action, or emotion. (pp. 182-83)

*Sharon Spencer, in her* Space, Time and Structure in the Modern Novel *(reprinted by permission of New York University Press; copyright © 1971 by New York University), New York University Press, 1971.*

Clever is the most apt, most curt and least pretentious adjective that can serve to describe Robbe-Grillet's novels. The publishers' blurb writer has attempted to make Robbe-Grillet 'relevant', asserting that 'New York's reality [in *Project For a Revolution in New York*] has caught up with his fictional prophecy'. In fact it's hard to imagine a writer who manifests a greater lack of interest in sociological or anthropological analyses—it simply doesn't occur to him to look at things through the eyes of the social scientist. So far as he is concerned the novelist's approach is just that, and not a psychologist's, communist's, liberal's, semiologist's or whatever; whether or not he admits it—and he seems loath to do so, at least in so many words—the only doctrine to which he conforms is that of art for art's sake; and that should lead no one to consider him trivial or 'unimportant'.

The title of this, his most recent novel . . . is misleading in the most disingenuous way. Protest kids will be gulled into dipping into it; imagine their disappointment at discovering therein fine writing, fine wit, total lack of 'commitment' and not a single word of advice on how to make time bombs from Times Square parking meters. . . . Of course it's not only those who are fooled by the title who will be taken in; as usual Robbe-Grillet is determined to tease, titillate, dupe and *disappoint* his readers. His conception of New York (not so different from that of Hong Kong in *The House of Assignation,* to which he alludes a few times) owes more to his (mis)reading of lurid accounts of that city's demi-monde in *France Soir, Ici Paris* and dime (sou) novels than to any 'authentic', first-hand experience of it. Virtually every cliché relating to the violence of the city and the sexual tastes of its inhabitants is set down here—muggings, rapes, sado-sexual experiments, the dangers of riding the subway, the prowlers who lurk in apartment blocks and so on. Out of such hackneyed and threadbare material Robbe-Grillet or 'the narrator' tries, using a variety of means which despite their appearance are not cinematic, to construct a coherent 'story', to find a structure in which all his chosen and 'cardboard' characters and situations are integrated. This is the subject, the main preoccupation of the novel. Eschewing all established disciplines, Robbe-Grillet sets out to form one of his own and to demonstrate that the only pattern which can be imposed on the data with which he feeds himself and which constantly alters beneath his gaze is one that is self-contradictory and convoluted to the point where it makes no 'sense' save on a near hallucinatory level. And while it's only too clear that he enjoys puzzles, trompe l'oeil (cerveau?) exercises and games it would be both insolent and ludicrous to suggest that the diligent reader might decipher the text and reach a solution, discover a 'correct' order in which the scenes might be played or presented. Still his claims to be a 'realist' are not altogether without foundation; the most evidently effective external realism is that which is constructed along the lines of some kind of factual report, the news broadcast (like Welles' Mars scare) or an obituary, a biography, a journalistic account etc. Likewise Robbe-Grillet's fictions tends to mimic the obsessional ramblings of some schizophrenics—they are documentaries of fantasies and, as such, completely realistic; they pretend to be nothing more than what they are. . . . It appears that his ideas on the relationship of objects represented to their models are a lot closer to those of these contemporary visual artists than to those of the French novelists with whom he is generally categorized in the many tiresome tracts on the 'new novel'—whatever that is. . . .

I can think of no other writer who can render the banal so fearfully fantastic. In the subtlest, slyest and most sheerly delightful way he persuades us to look anew at the commonplace and to realise that everything we see, feel and think is phenomenal, and to consider that the word 'ordinary' could well be discredited. He thus celebrates man and his ability to conquer natural laws far more thoroughly than do 'concerned' and sentimental humanist scribes.

*Jonathan Meades, "Slicker City," in* Books and Bookmen, *April, 1973, p. 106.*

One of the criticisms frequently levelled against Robbe-Grillet's film work is that it is literary rather than cinematic. It is true that he had written four novels before he began to involve himself with the cinema, that his first completed film work was the script for Alain Resnais's *Last Year at Marienbad* and that he has continued his novel writing alongside his film work. But if one looks at all closely at the actual work produced, the label 'literary' soon proves quite inadequate. He himself makes quite a clear distinction between novel writing and film making, and all his public statements stress the differences rather than the similarities. . . .

A second charge brought against Robbe-Grillet is that of deliberate obscurity. Certainly one of the delights of his style is the taste for paradox and seeming contradiction which a whole area of modern fiction (the stories of Borges, for instance) inherits from the classic detective story. Several of Robbe-Grillet's film titles are significant in this respect: *Last Year at Marienbad* and *L'Eden et Après* chosen for films which deny the conventional time scheme of past, present and future, a before and an after, or *L'Homme qui ment* for a film in which, though the hero may be lying, his words constitute the only reality and hence the truth of the film. But this does not alter the fact that Robbe-Grillet's film work is based on a thorough re-examination of the specific qualities of film as a medium which he has articulated in straight-forward and fundamental terms in the essays collected as *Towards a New Novel*. This return to the basic attributes of film as a source of new narrative structures has been a most fruitful one, as Robbe-Grillet's progress from *Last Year at Marienbad* to *L'Eden et Après* shows. From using images to show the way in which characters actually experience a situation (such as a love affair) which conventional film-making externalizes all too glibly, Robbe-Grillet has moved on to a more radical examination of how we—the audience—see fictional images. His work gives the audience an increasingly active role—in *L'Eden et Après,* for instance, he offers us a series of images and leaves each of us to make them into a sequence meaningful to ourselves: the film is completed not on the screen but in the spectator's mind and imagination. . . .

Modern film-making is for him a form of cinema which continually draws attention to itself. All his films therefore present themselves as works of fiction, nothing more nor less, in that any attempt at verisimilitude is denied. . . . Robbe-Grillet's films explore the fact that film presents fact and fiction, truth and dream, experience and imagination undifferentiated and on the same level. Such an approach, if followed through to its full implications, results in more than a novel style of editing. If past, present and future can be fused in any order into a single flow, then all our notions of character and psychological motivation are questioned. In a world where objects lose their solidity and time its chronology our usual ethical and moral standpoints are shown to be equally suspect. This is what happens in Robbe-Grillet's films, in which image and experience are restored to their full ambiguity and multivalence. . . .

Like all the major works of modernist cinema, *L'Eden et Après* is a film that questions itself, and comprises a series of images that query the very nature of the image. Thus it is a film less about people than about colour, shape and form, less a narrative than a game with objects and images abstracted from reality.

*Roy Armes, "Robbe-Grillet in Africa," in* London Magazine, *October/November, 1973, pp. 107-13.*

Robbe-Grillet uses neither the cubist principle of searching a visual unity synthesizing a variety of objects into a single perspective, nor the Surrealist trick of bringing together distant realities. . . . He comes close to the pursuit of contemporary painters. . . .

In "Le Mannequin" Robbe-Grillet reveals what can be seen in the room and even alludes to what cannot be seen. The author remains strictly within the limits of the self-imposed frame, mentioning first the centrally situated object, then what is to its right, then what is behind or above it. Information is first provided about the color and shape of the coffeepot. Yet the recurring S shapes, the spout, the handle, the roundness of the pot surmounted by the mushroom-shaped lid point already towards the growing complexity of the exploration. Robbe-Grillet, although he remains within a limited space, and looks at plain, simple objects without going beyond their surface, never reaches a coherent, overall view. Why? In conformity with the title of the volume, the author presents but a series of snapshots. Such two-dimensional, photographic renderings occur also in the novels, e.g. the outline of the gull in *Le Voyeur* and the progressions of the shadow in *La Jalousie*. Moreover, the notion of "instantanés," by restricting perception to an instant, excludes time exposure or the unfolding of a time sequence. The room is seen for an isolated moment; a slight rearrangement of the mannequin's position separates this vision completely from all previous perceptions. . . .

The verbal inventory does not attempt to unite the visible elements by any meaning; in other words, the sum total of details does not add up to anything. Careful accounting of details meets with resistance; one statement sometimes merely corrects the previous one. . . . Simple, everyday objects, or fragments of reality cannot be automatically translated into language. A language corresponding to the objective eye of the camera has to be created or rediscovered. . . .

Instantaneous contact with a scene characterizes Rimbaud's *Illuminations*; spatial exploration on a limited scale characterizes Reverdy's *Poèmes en prose* and *Etoiles peintes*. Robbe-Grillet searches for a unity quite different from the Rimbaldian flash or the Reverdian spatial order: he conveys only the image of a moment thus pointing to our divorce from reality.

*Renée Riese Hubert, in* The International Fiction Review, *January, 1974, pp. 12-13.*

With its small but nonetheless labyrinthine setting, minute descriptions, notations of spatial relationships, numerous and sudden shifts from one time period to another, incremental repetitions, transformations and mergings of events, and series of contradictory time markers, Robbe-Grillet's *Jealousy* demands to be read with nearly the same obsessive attention to detail with which the narrator studies the objects and persons within his range of vision. In this elaborately, carefully, and cleverly constructed novel, a few purposeless contradictions seem to have escaped the watchful eye of its creator. These tiny lapses probably would go unnoticed in a novel focusing less on minutiae and requiring less exact visualization.

A reader of *Jealousy* soon becomes aware that the narrator views A. . . through three bedroom windows, two facing south (toward the central portion of the veranda and the valley) and one west. These windows, however, are numbered in an inconsistent way. . . . The numbers assigned to the windows do not appear to be dictated by the narrator's different points of observation, and, in fact, could have been avoided because of other reasonably clear details. Satisfactory explanations may be offered for other changes or contradictions in the novel (say, the enlarged centipede in the climactic sequence, or the concluding comments on the African novel), but the confusing numbering system noted here seems to be an example of a non-functional modification, the result either of carelessness or of downright perversity. . . .

[An] object in the novel mysteriously changes shape. At first A. . .'s "dressing table" is said to be "provided especially with a vertical mirror.". . . Considerably later in the novel A. . . sits at her dressing table and looks at herself "in the oval mirror." . . . Also, in several instances it is difficult to understand how the narrator, positioned on the veranda, sees or hears some of the things noted in A. . .'s bedroom. . . . Finally, during one of the dining scenes when, as usual, Franck is the only visitor, surely a reference to "the guests" . . . is an error rather than a subtlety.

Even tiny inaccuracies are surprising and jarring when they appear in the work of a master of minutiae, a novelist whose "concern for precision . . . sometimes borders on the delirious."

*Daniel P. Deneau, "Non-Functional Contradictions in Robbe-Grillet's 'Jealousy'," in* The International Fiction Review, *January, 1974, pp. 62-4.*

The purest, simplest, and in many ways still the finest example of Robbe-Grillet's art is *Dans le Labyrinthe* (1959). Here, although the text presents many apparent contradictions, it very soon strikes the reader that he can make sense of them if he assumes that the central character is inventing a story, and invention, like memory and day-dreaming, does not proceed in neat, logical steps. If it is true invention—artistic creation—and not just dreaming, coherence must be imposed on the fragments produced by the freely roaming imagination, whether it be logical or imaginative coherence. And Robbe-Grillet's narrator is preoccupied, in part, with autocriticism and revision. However his first drafts are there for us to read, and in the intricate web of variants and variations, a pattern emerges which does appeal to our imagination. But Robbe-Grillet does not leave it there. Our assumption that we are sharing the narrator's experience saves us from finding the work too incoherent, but it rests on a way of reading which derives from realism. Ultimately, Robbe-Grillet wishes us to realize that the novelist is bound only by the requirements—so subtle and intangible—of the imagination, not of logic. And so he introduces into his last chapter details which throw doubt on our interpretation, and which suggest that the novelist is manipulating the narrator as freely as the fictional narrator is manipulating his own invented characters. The same reading is probably valid for the previous novel, *La Jalousie* (1957), although that is usually taken as a portrayal of the thoughts of a jealous man. But the different chapters of that book could also be a semi-invention, with only the events of the last section "real," and there again, one or two details obstinately refuse to allow any interpretation to be water-tight. . . .

For all its fascination, I have not found *La Maison de Rendez-Vous* as satisfying as the other novels, perhaps because the "game" element seems to be developed at the expense of any deeper human meaning, by which I do not wish to dissociate form from content—the game is the meaning, I recognize—but just to suggest that the . . . story does not, to me, have the same resonance as the four novels which preceded it. . . .

Readers cannot easily shed habits acquired from "realistic" fiction, and we are bound to wonder at times just what is going on. [In *Projet d'une Révolution à New York*,] Robbe-Grillet builds this understandable reaction into the novel itself, including discussions with the reader. In one of the best of these, the reader objects to the excessive insistence on erotic detail, but the novelist can easily prove that there is much in the novel besides erotica, and he accuses the reader with incomparable elegance of living in a glass house. . . .

[We] cannot fail to notice the contrast between the violence and the exceptional elegance of the style. Robbe-Grillet could say, with the author of *Lolita,* that there are no crude expressions in his book. . . . The elegance turns the savage cruelty into comedy. . . .

There seem to me to be two ways in which *Projet d'une Révolution à New York* appeals directly to the aesthetic imagination of the reader. One is by the pattern, a very intricate one. . . . If the parallels add to the cohesion of the different levels, Robbe-Grillet's habit of crossing levels leads to incoherence on one plane, although on another plane, the book is perfectly coherent. But it follows, in Eliot's phrase, the logic of the imagination, not the logic of concepts. Secondly, it appeals by its wit, which is a form of art. Robbe-Grillet's patterns are nothing if not witty. Once we understand where we should place ourselves we can appreciate this wit. . . . There are some beautifully elegant inventions: the interrogation, . . . (one of the high spots of the novel for anyone who enjoys Marx Brothers humor), the idea that police efficiency is increased by having the criminal write the report of the crime . . ., and other slightly mad details. A *fervent* will relish particularly the use he makes of his own books, particularly the previous two novels, both by vague parallels, or by direct quotation, or by allusions to a character or a name. . . .

It is indeed a novel of astounding inventiveness, and of remarkable elegance in expression. I myself find that it has a hallucinatory power, that it is more than a fantastically ingenious joke. The things he evokes, the gestures of the characters, jump off the page and lodge in the reader's mind. Even if your intellect does not always follow, there is a hypnotic spell cast. Partly this is due to the fact that we have the feeling that although the logical explanation escapes us, it is there somewhere, tantalizing and tormenting us, and so we pay particular attention to each word. Likewise, we appreciate the elegant shape and economy of each sentence. Everything combines to grip our attention.

What assessment do we make? I know the novel will not be to everyone's taste; it does ask for a certain kind of mental pleasure, if a reader is to take it seriously enough to work at it, and the raw material itself may put some people off. Personally, though I do not say that Robbe-Grillet is another Proust, I find that he has become part of my imagination, in a way which is only possible for an artist with something very original and positive to give us.

*Anthony R. Pugh, "Robbe-Grillet in New York," in* International Fiction Review, *July, 1974, pp. 120-24.*

* * *

## ROTH, Philip 1933-

**Roth, a major Jewish-American novelist and short story writer, has often been accused of expressing "unfocused hostility" in his fiction. At the same time, he is said to have produced some of the best fiction of Jewish life in America. (See also *Contemporary Authors*, Vols. 1-4, rev. ed.)**

Roth's first novel, *Letting Go* (1962), is perhaps the first genuine attempt to write a Jewish novel of manners. The intricacies of Jewish family custom and sentimentality are combined with a species of person that needs a much more careful and astute study: the academic lower-class, the Lucky Jims of the American non-tenure rank, whose lives reveal a mixture of pride and fear, and an occasional nobility. The book's value comes from its weaving in and out of a Jewish *situation comblée,* its adapting Jewish manners to a comic and pathetic plot. Though there is much confusion, much hurrying about, the novel returns repeatedly to basic human engagements, which must be respected and above all comprehended.

*Frederick J. Hoffman, in his* The Modern Novel in America, *Regnery, revised edition, 1963, pp. 243-44.*

If the central character of Mr. Roth's shocker [*Portnoy's Complaint*], an insatiable onanist, remains an unregenerate adolescent dominated in a matriarchal society by an obsessive mother and condemned always to suffer as a Jew among hated and envied gentiles, readers must similarly endure the author's insistent intrusions of scenes depicting the self-love into which the youngster is forced as a compensation for his rejection, and are thus obliged to contemplate publicly acts best practiced in private, if at all. But Mr. Roth's hero never grows up; he never abandons his boyish proclivities; he is the tragic hero abused by life as by himself, the tortured, condemned soul who must stand at the Wailing Wall in eternal lamentation, overwhelmed by racial guilt and a sense of persecution. So corrosive and coprophilic a recital cannot of itself easily qualify as literature. If one define a good novel as a re-readable book Mr. Roth's contribution must stand on tenuous ground, sensationalism and raw appeal to one side. De gustibus non est disputandum.

Virginia Quarterly Review, *Vol. 45, No. 3 (Summer, 1969), p. lxxxviii.*

When I read several of the stories in manuscript that were to appear two years later in *Goodbye, Columbus* . . . I didn't at first know how to respond. . . .

But my resistance quickly toppled like tenpins. It was like sitting down in a movie house and suddenly seeing there on the screen a film about the block on which I had grown up: the details of place, character, incident all intimately familiar and yet new, or at least never appreciated before for their color and interest. This story of Neil Klugman and Brenda Patimkin was so simple, direct, and evident that it couldn't be "art," and yet I knew that art did advance in just this way: a sudden sweeping aside of outmoded complexities for the sake of a fresh view of experience, often so natural a view and so common an experience that one wondered why writers hadn't been seeing and doing this all along. The informal tone of the prose, as relaxed as conversation, yet terse and fleet and right on the button; the homely images . . . that make the passage glow. Such writing rang bells that not even the Jewish writers had touched; it wasn't Malamud, it wasn't even Saul Bellow: the "literary" fuzz of, say, *Augie March* had been blown away, and the actualities of the life behind it came forth in their natural grain and color, heightened by the sense of discovery.

Such writing is much more familiar today than it was ten years ago: indeed, it has become one of the staples of contemporary fiction. But at the time the only other writer who seemed to be so effortlessly and accurately in touch with his material was Salinger. For a year or so after reading *Catcher in the Rye,* I hadn't been able to walk through Central Park without looking around for Holden and Phoebe Caulfield, and now here was this young semblable of mine who dragged me off for a good corned beef sandwich or who gave me a push when my car wouldn't start, and who, somehow, was doing for the much less promising poetry of Newark, New Jersey, what the famous Salinger was doing for that of Central Park West. Moreover, if Roth's fiction had something of Salinger's wit and charm, the winning mixture of youthful idealism and cynicism, the air of immediate reality, it was also made of tougher stuff, both in the kind of life it described and in the intentions it embodied. Salinger's taste for experience, like that of his characters, was a very delicate one; Roth's appetite was much heartier, his tone more aggressive, his moral sense both broader and more decisive. . . .

So I envied Roth his gifts, I envied even more his honesty, his lack of fastidiousness, his refusal to write stories that labored for a form so fine that almost any naturalness would violate it. The gross affluences and energies of the Patimkins, the crudities of Albie Pelagutti and Duke Scarpa, even the whining and wheedling of Sheldon Grossbart turned him on rather than put him off. . . .

It was evident that *Letting Go* represented a major effort to move forward from *Goodbye, Columbus.* The theme of communal coerciveness and individual rights that dominates most of the stories had been opened out to deal with the more subtle perversions of loyalty and duty and creaturely feeling that flow through the ties of family, marriage, friendship. A very Jamesian theme: *The Portrait of a Lady* figures almost immediately in *Letting Go,* as a reference point for its interest in benevolent power plays. Also, in bringing his fiction more up to date with the circumstances and issues of his life, Roth had tried for a more chastened, Jamesian tone. . . .

[As] much as I liked *When She Was Good,* it was . . . evidence that he was locked into [a] preoccupation with female power which was carrying his fiction into strange and relatively arid terrain. . . .

But soon after came "Whacking Off" in *Partisan Review*: hysterical, raw, full of what Jews call self-hatred; excessive in all respects; and so funny that I had three laughing fits before I had gone five pages. All of a sudden, from out of the blue and the past, the comedian of those Chicago sessions of nostalgia, revenge, and general purgation had landed right in the middle of his own fiction, as Alex Portnoy, the thirteen-year-old sex maniac. . . .

This was new, all right, at least in American fiction—and, like the discovery of fresh material in *Goodbye, Columbus,* right in front of everyone's eyes. Particularly, I suppose, guess, of the "Jewish" writers' with all that heavily funded Oedipal energy and curiosity to be worked off in adolescence—and beyond. And having used his comic sense to carry him past the shame that surrounds the subject of masturbation, and to enter it more fully than I can suggest here, Roth appeared to gain great dividends of emotional candor and wit in dealing with the other matters in "Whacking Off.". . .

Having discovered that Portnoy's sexual feelings and his "Jewish" feelings were just around the corner from each other and that both were so rich in loot, he pressed on like a man who has found a stream full of gold—and running right into it, another one. Moreover, the psychoanalytic setting had given him now the freedom and energy of language to sluice out the material: the natural internal monologue of comedy and pain in which the id speaks to the ego and vice versa, while the superego goes on with its kibitzing. At the same time, Portnoy could be punched out of the analytic framework like a figure enclosed in cardboard and perform in his true role and vocation, which is that of a great stand-up comic. Further, those nagging concerns with close relationships, with male guilt and female maneuvering, from his two novels could now be grasped by the roots of Portnoy's experience of them and could be presented, not as standard realistic fare, but in a mode that was right up-to-date. If the background of *Portnoy's Complaint* is a classical Freudian one, the foreground is the contemporary, winging art and humor of improvisation and release, perhaps most notably that of Lenny Bruce.

In short, lots of things had come together and they had turned Roth loose.

> *Theodore Solotaroff, "Philip Roth: A Personal View" (1969), in his* The Red Hot Vacuum and Other Pieces on the Writing of the Sixties *(copyright © 1968, 1970 by Theodore Solotaroff; reprinted by permission of Atheneum Publishers), Atheneum, 1970, pp. 306-28.*

Philip Roth, in his first novel, *Letting Go,* written after his contained and craftsmanly first longer fiction, a novella called "Goodbye, Columbus," attempts a narrative in Bellow's style. . . . *Letting Go* is looser and freer than "Goodbye, Columbus," which is a poignant look at first love in a satirized suburban setting. (Roth's true gift is for the comic and satirical. When he is being satirical he is not ambivalent . . . about the subject of his satire.) However, *Letting Go,* the history of an activist hero, Gabe Wallach, fails as an activist novel. . .; it fails to present dramatically inside the narrative action the conflict between the existential reality and the ideal possibility. Gabe Wallach . . . fails as a figure of spiritual activism since his quest bogs down in Freudian ponderings. . . . He does not come to terms with that past and its psychological implications for his present; and his habit of looking backward while supposing himself to be moving forward has a curious effect, making of Gabe a whining and ineffectual hero with whom the reader is supposed to sympathize in spite of his unattractiveness. . . .

Roth uses the openness of the activist novel without the justification of an activist hero. . . . Roth, however, is magnificently expert at describing the individual scenes and situations of the world; it is only in the creating of the tension necessary as novelistic ingredient in the activist hero's total situation that he fails. . . .

One might argue that Roth's novel in its inability to create viable alternatives to the nihilism which informs modern life is existentially faithful to the way-it-is. But in Gabe's protests we inevitably read a larger (finer) intention—the intention to show the pitting of the choosing self against the caging of his past and the determinism of his environment—which is not realized.

> *Helen Weinberg, in her* The New Novel in America: The Kafkan Mode in Contemporary Fiction *(copyright © 1970 by Cornell University; used by permission of Cornell University Press), Cornell University Press, 1970, pp. 182, 185.*

[*Our Gang* is an] abrupt departure for Roth—who wrote this malicious and necessary book in a three month leave of absence from a novel he has returned to—but a purgative diversion for his many readers. The object of his outrage is the [Nixon] Administration in Washington; the subject is the debasement of language. Although this mordant satire . . . will not and cannot reach the depths of folly and hypocrisy represented by the original cast, it may achieve literary permanence as a brilliant protest against the meaninglessness of contemporary political speech in its infinite variety and stupefying abundance. Roth is funnier than Orwell and as acerbic as Swift; whether he is as sensitive to native political attitudes as were these two obvious predecessors remains to be seen.

> The Antioch Review *(© 1971 by The Antioch Review, Inc.; reprinted by permission of the editors), Vol. XXXI, No. 3, 1971, p. 440.*

[*Our Gang*] will be judged in the long run as an entertainment rather than a major work—a summer's diversion for the nimble author, and an evening's giggle for a hip reader.

This is the result of—as you must know by now—Roth's selecting Richard Nixon and his court as the object of his satire. As such, *Our Gang* is the all-too-probable tale of Trick E. Dixon, an improbable president of the United States who holds sway through a combination of pietistic and cliché-ridden press conferences and a feeling for language that would do justice to an Al Kelly. . . .

Up to [a] point, Roth's material is fairly predictable; its episodic and topical nature will put you in mind of Art Buchwald at best, a slew of stand-up comics at worst. Fortunately, in the last three chapters Roth's higher aspirations take over and his well-contained rage breaks loose. . . .

Unfortunately, all this will be called outrageously funny because that is a phrase that comes automatically to mind when the mass thinkers write about satire. The point is that even when you're writing an Orwellian novel, it's almost impossible to be wildly inventive about an administration either so inept or so corrupt that it has been forced to substitute amateur public relations for frank discussion. (Not for nothing has Roth chosen *Our Gang* as his title. It certainly appears that the White House has more in common with Spanky McFarland, short pants, and Hal Roach than it does with the Federalists.)

As such, *Our Gang* is an Orwellian tract; one that repeats his warning that people who begin to be lazy about the language that their leaders use can be told anything. . . .

*Michael Olmert, in* Book World (© The Washington Post), *November 7, 1971, p. 12.*

[The] strength of [*Our Gang*] is in its ability to parody the flatness, tedium, and rambling quality of the jargon of the [Nixon] administration. . . .

Roth's ear is very good, and he catches perfectly that strange mixture of jaunty self-assurance and desperate uncertainty, those bold grammatical beginnings which inevitably get lost in innumerable qualifications and additions, the curious arhythmic succession of sounds and lack of any periodic structure, and those astounding assertions of logic based on the most bizarre premises. If you believe, as most of us probably do to some extent, that the style is the man, and the society as well, then Roth has found and exposed one serious symptom of what is wrong with modern American society: it talks too much and it talks badly. *Our Gang* is almost all talk and very little action. . . .

All of this is excellent parody, but it is not great satire. . . . Alexander Pope remarks, "The Muse may give thee, but the Gods must guide," which points to something very important about satire. A good style, the ability to contrive clever effects, and the flash of wit are important gifts of the satiric muse, but the real power of satire comes finally from the gods, from the awareness that institutions and persons are finally worthy of attack not because they are "morally insensitive" (who isn't?), but because they pervert and threaten something fundamental to the order of things. In other words, the satirist, as opposed to the mere parodist, must himself believe deeply and powerfully in something whose breaking makes a difference. Only out of this kind of moral conviction can he give vice and folly the dignity satire requires of its villains, create that entire and convincingly mad world of satire in which something so fundamental has been disturbed that all the crucial institutions of society—schools, homes, churches, courts, senate houses —go mad, and life seems determined to make a grotesque joke out of itself. The "moral" principle grasped by the satirist need not be very complex—Nathanael West probably believed in little more than the superiority of straight lines over crooked—but it needs to be so deeply woven into the fabric that its removal undoes the entire weave.

It is this commitment which I find lacking in *Our Gang*. Not that Roth does not have all kinds of principles of the highest order, the value of human life, moral honesty, the value of logic, the importance of common sense, etc. But these seem mere "principles," the appropriate equipment for a man of a particular political and intellectual persuasion, rather than values so deeply felt that they inform the writing completely, the way that, say, Swift's passionate commitment to good sense is everywhere in *Gulliver's Travels*. What really comes through the actual writing of *Our Gang* is the amused disdain, not passionate hatred, of a man who writes and speaks well, who has a real sense of style, for a bunch of near illiterates who use the language atrociously because they are vain, stupid, malicious, and crafty. To believe in style is still to believe in something, better than believing in nothing, but it is not enough to enable Roth to create a villain who is more than silly or a world which does anything more serious than talk incessantly and badly. For this reason most readers will, I believe, find themselves bored after a few pages of each episode. . . .

[Hostility] and wit, while they are necessary parts of satire, are not finally enough to create more than expressions of ill will and amusing parody. Satire is not only a sacred weapon but a dangerous one as well, and chief among its dangers is the possibility that the man who uses it will reveal himself to be a part of the world he is attacking. This is what happens in *Our Gang*, where the irony ultimately becomes large enough to include the ironist, without his being aware of the fact. Satire has caught better writers than Roth in this trap, but still it is sad to see him as part of the disease he set out to cure.

*Alvin B. Kernan, "The Sacred Weapon," in* The Yale Review *(© 1972 by Yale University; reprinted by permission of the editors), Spring, 1972, pp. 407-10.*

*The Breast* seems an exercise, primarily one of self-containment, the creation of a perfect and hermetically protected closed system. . . . Beyond this, one recalls Roth's statement, about the time of *Letting Go* (1962), that in terms of interest, information, surprise, shock, reach of imagination, fact has preempted fiction. So it is possible that this exercise is indeed a serious one, an attempt to reclaim for fiction the property of imagination, to stake a claim in country that fact and reason and contemporary possibility have not yet occupied. Perhaps.

But in the meantime it must be said that Kepesh's anguish is really not very affecting, nor even, in any sustained way, very intriguing. And, though it is only an hour's read, *The Breast*, like Roth's previous satires, seems too long by half. Its satisfactions are mostly outside the book, in the not unpleasurable sensation of rising hackles and in speculations on what a most intelligent and gifted writer may be up to, now and next.

*Eliot Fremont-Smith, "Life as a Gland," in* Saturday Review of the Society *(copyright © 1972 by Saturday Review/World, Inc.; reprinted with permission), September 23, 1972, pp. 80, 82-3.*

Many readers have felt . . . that *Portnoy's Complaint* is not fair to the entire American Jewish community. But it is my belief that Roth was not concerned with the question. He took up one prevalent problem among several presently older generations of Jews, a problem which always was half way between a headache and a joke to their adolescents or perpetual adolescents in private conversation and amateur mass therapy sessions; Roth wrote a caricature bordering somewhere between the joke and the headache side of the fence. One can take the book too lightly, but only Sophie Portnoy could take it too seriously.

*Julie Braun, "Portnoy as Pure Confusion," in* The Carleton Miscellany, *Spring-Summer, 1973, pp. 73-6.*

*My Life as a Man* will probably be a controversial book, because those who like it will like it immensely—as I did; and others, perhaps not aware of the *tour de force* the novel really is, will dislike it because of its time-shifts, persona-shifts, its outrageous insistence upon the utter banality of its subject matter, and its mixture of baffled idealism and cynicism so far as love and marriage and women in general are concerned. Roth is certainly critical of romantic illusions, and one would hardly wish to have participated in his hero's experimental life as a man, but readers should be aware of the fact that Roth is as hard on his hero as he is on anyone, perhaps even more harsh, because Peter Tarnopol is supposed to be so clever.

The book is marvelously energetic and inventive. It consists of three related stories, the longest of which ("My True Story") is narrated by Peter in the first-person, as he attempts to impose a coherent form on the incoherent experiences of his adulthood; preceding this personal document are two short stories, in which a fictional hero named Zuckerman appears. For once, the fashionable "avant-garde" device of authors stepping out from behind *personae* makes legitimate, psychological sense; and the elements of comic exaggeration, absurdity, and improbable coincidence are skillfully synthesized into a whole. Roth's people are always real, painfully real, though they are being run through a bizarre melodrama of the kind William Empson and Roger Sale—one presumes—would not believe to be the material of Art. . . .

Parts of the novel are reminiscent of *Portnoy's Complaint*, but what frequently remained undeveloped in that book is more deeply attacked in this one. The stories read as if they were originally written in something approaching hysteria—but then rewritten, and rewritten again. The novel is chaotic in its emotions, but nicely controlled as conscious art, and its more subtle considerations surface when it is read a second time. It has always been my belief that a good novel is read the first time for its story—for all literature, no matter how sophisticated, should be suspenseful—and the second time for its more subtle concerns.

Roth's best work, so far, has transformed intense private experience into fiction that speaks for its era, no matter how eccentric the basic metaphor of the works might be. . . .

*My Life as a Man* is irresistibly readable and, for all its frenzy, a sadly mature work.

*Joyce Carol Oates, in* The American Poetry Review, *May/June, 1974, pp. 44-5.*

No writer, not even Mailer or Lowell, has contributed more to the confessional climate than Philip Roth. Thanks to "Portnoy's Complaint" a good slice of contemporary fiction seems to come verbatim from the writer's own hours on the couch. This would be a dubious distinction had Roth's book not also boldly altered the tone of our confessional writing, most of which had been lugubrious and realistic, smothered in *angst* and high-seriousness. Reaching back instead to the raunchy, delirious autobiographical manner of Henry Miller and Céline—indeed, perpetrating an unseemly imitation of the latter's great "Death on the Installment Plan"—Roth pitched his anguish in such a low comic strain that the effect was irresistible. If there has been a funnier novel in the last 10 years, or one that exploits sex, psychoanalysis and the "family romance" more brilliantly, I don't know what it could be. . . .

Unfortunately . . . after "Portnoy" he seems radically to have mistaken his own talents and misread the real breakthrough "Portnoy" represented. Evidently he came to feel that his three earlier books, starting with "Goodbye, Columbus" in 1959, were enfeebled by an overdose of Jamesian or Hebraic moral seriousness, which had censored a native but "sub-literary" gift for farce, mimicry and Lenny Brucean black humor. Henceforth he would take his material from low rather than high culture, from sick jokes and borscht-circuit vulgarity, from half-repressed sexual fantasies and the half-remembered pop culture of the thirties and forties, from the carney-barker rather than the genteel, owl-eyed Jamesian narrator. . . .

It became obvious that Roth had no power of what critics once called invention; he was unable to inspirit a plot or characters that were the least bit outside his own experience. . . .

"My Life as a Man" . . . confirms that despite his superb gifts as a mimic, *tummler* and hyperbolist Roth is only good at fantasticating materials from his own life. As a satirist of Nixon or Bill Veeck he is clever but uninspired. (He especially lacks any political savvy.) As a satirist of middle-class Jewish life in Newark or the suburbs he is brilliant and wicked, endowed with a perfect ear and a cold eye, a bit like the early Mary McCarthy. And faced with the traumas of family life and the conflicts of the mental and moral life in "Portnoy," Roth can be not only funny but lyrical—emotion recollected in hysteria—with the poignance of one who is so miserable he can only crack jokes. . . .

At the root of the creative problem is the pervasive ungenerosity that has always marked Roth's work. (His early Jewish critics were misguided; his quarrel was not with Jews but with people.) Even a satirist must love his characters a little, especially if he also loathes them. He must be drawn to them in an animating way, must *need* to give them life. He can't use novels simply to settle old scores. Roth's genius is all for surfaces—the telling descriptive detail, the absurd mannerism, the tics and turns of real speech, the ludicrous flaw of personality—rarely for human depths. He does have an affinity for people at their most frantic, pompous and ridiculous, in part because he admires the sheer energy of human waste, but also because they confirm his own sense of superiority.

The fatal flaw of his protagonists, which Roth never sees, is their self-righteousness. . . . Roth seems to lose all perspective—no one but his surrogate exists, no other viewpoint has meaning—and the judgmental parents and the arrogant, smart-ass kid speak directly through the mouth of the thwarted, furious adult. For all his talent, the canker of arrogance and *ressentiment* have kept Roth from becoming a truly major writer: though his work has become more anguished over 15 years, it has shown very little emotional growth.

*Morris Dickstein, in* The New York Times Book Review *(© 1974 by The New York Times Company; reprinted by permission), June 2, 1974, pp. 1-2.*

Philip Roth's new novel, his eighth work of fiction, *My Life as a Man* . . . , is the self-told and thrice-told story of a successful Jewish writer and intellectual *in extremis,* his unsatisfactory affairs with several girls, his horrific marriage and its breakup, his years of psychotherapy, and finally his obsessive attempts to force the world, his emotional drives, his ethical commitments, and his craft (a variety of narrative tones and voices) into line: to become whole, to become "mature," to be "a man." The writer and narrator is Peter Tarnopol. . . .

The elusiveness of a "right" voice, essential to truth, has been a persistent theme with Roth; as much as or more than anything else, it is what his books, starting with *Portnoy's Complaint* (1969), have been about. (Starting really much earlier: in a famous 1961 essay he despaired of making "credible" in fiction the absurdities of American reality. "The actuality is continually outdoing our talents," he wrote, "and the culture tosses up figures almost daily that are the envy of any novelist." And that was back when, from our present vantage, things seemed relatively sane and stable.) Like Roth, Tarnopol is painfully aware—it's a constant of his anguish—that the serious voice, appropriate for the expression of serious, in fact, horrifying, matters, is always in danger of parodying itself, and, what's more, of deserving that fate. . . .

*My Life as a Man* is in many important ways a recapitulation and culmination of all of Roth's previous work. Tarnopol is in one way or another reminiscent of and a development from Roth's previous protagonists. . . . (Seeing Roth's work as a whole, an opportunity *My Life as a Man* provides, incidentally emphasizes the very considerable achievement of [*The*] *Breast,* and gives the lie to the myopic critical grumping that greeted that book's publication.) . . .

Roth's book is partly quicksand, too; it shifts positions as it engulfs. But then, that's its subject. The irresolutions of the story, the various voices of its telling, the slippery vagaries of truth (finally, it's not even encircled; it may be that Tarnopol is paranoid and has been lying right along), are at once the source of its terror and the spur for its low, raucous, belly-laugh humor. It is, in invention, in perception and delineation of character (they are memorable people here, men and women), in coming to grips with the wild inconsistencies of life and art, in the exposure of the most serious and agonizing matters to outright farce, a very grand work.

*Eliot Fremont-Smith, "Peppy's Complaint," in* New York Magazine *(© 1974 by NYM Corp.; reprinted by permission of* New York Magazine *and Eliot Fremont-Smith), June 3, 1974, pp. 73, 75.*

"My Life as A Man" is Philip Roth's best novel. It is also his most complex and most ambitious. The artist's controlling hand is more clearly evident here than in any of his books since his first, "Goodbye, Columbus," and this is a more probing, more interesting book than that one. Frequently Roth has seemed willing simply to pummel an entertaining idea with as many variations as occur to his uncommonly fertile imagination—"Portnoy's Complaint" is left as an extended joke, "The Breast" as a stillborn metaphor—but the design of his new novel enables Roth to develop fully themes first introduced in his earlier fiction. Shrillness and excess are here confined to the characters and their situations; we no longer need worry that the author himself has succumbed. Indicative of the control that Roth maintains is the tone of the narrator's voice—not the free-floating maunderings of Alexander Portnoy, but a writer's varied attempts to impose a form upon his life. . . .

This novel is more successful precisely because for the first time Roth's willingness to take risks is matched entirely by his skill as a craftsman. The shrieks of pain and laughter are not muffled, but controlled—by the complexity of Roth's design and the range of tone, and response he allows his narrator.

*Peter S. Prescott, "Tarnopol's Complaint," in* Newsweek *(copyright Newsweek, Inc., 1974; reprinted by permission), June 3, 1974, pp. 79-82.*

Peter Tarnopol, the protagonist-monologist of Philip Roth's [*My Life as a Man*], is a cunning sophist and casuist, a narcissist, megalomaniac and solipsist, a tireless self-justifier, a wily paranoiac. It would be futile to point out to him these minor flaws of character and personality, which he knows both better and not as well as we. Besides, they're not flaws: flaws trumpeted to all the world, closely documented in case the inattentive auditor happened to miss their least manifestation—such flaws can be regarded by their victim as heroic virtues, evidence of the most difficult, admirable kind of integrity, attained at terrible price. . . . How was it . . . that this boy, destined for all the world's marbles—prodigiously gifted, brilliant, darkly good looking—how is it that his life can so readily have turned from a bed of roses to ashes in the mouth?

Like his kin Portnoy, Tarnopol tells us and tells us. Already predisposed to moral heroism, defenselessly vulnerable to its exigencies, Tarnopol, obedient pupil that he is, absorbs whole the graduate school religio-literary culture of the '50s, the way we were taught to reflect, feel, experience, judge, value, live by such mentors as the great Russians, Flaubert, James, Conrad, Mann—to make, so to speak, of a choice between tea and coffee one of the supreme moments in the moral history of the race; to make of his life, as it were, a lyric that could withstand (more than endure: prevail against) the most rigorous exegetical criticism. Thus armed, Childe Peter meets Maureen Johnson, for whom, it turns out, all the Empsons in the world cannot suffice. . . .

[Tarnopol's marriage to Maureen and his] consuming, devastating thrashings within its thongs occupy the center of the novel; occupy his entire consciousness and its extensions into his life as he draws—compels—the world into its net. . . .

[Maureen dies, gruesomely, in a crashed car.] "Good," says his brother when he hears of the death; and his mother, when she hears of it, asks, 250 miles from the scene of the carnage: "You're all right?" Therein lies the key, or a key, to Roth's extraordinary gifts, to the sheer pleasure one takes in reading him: at the limits of one's patience one is stunned with admiration. That's exactly what his big brother and mother would have said, that and nothing else; an image, an utterance has been perfectly observed and felicitously recorded; some scene, and there are many of them, has been beautifully shaped, the comic complication measured in just the right degree and kind. Pure admiration and pleasure, of a sometimes guilty nature, such as we take in performance when they are their own end.

But the whole is less than the sum of its parts and finally impatience tilts the balance. The trouble with the comedy of extreme situations is that it can never hold still. Starting wild it must get wilder, flail itself from excess to excessiveness. Unless we can be drawn wholly into its vortex, an obsession obsesses only the obsessed; as a clinical category obsessions are narrow and limiting. Where inventiveness ends and the flailing continues in a whirlwind, desperation sets in and breeds cruelty. . . .

[Truly] to lay [Maureen's] ghost the whole awful record must be inscribed in a book, in fact this book, which is the book Tarnopol has gone to the mountain to write.

As against this reading, a quite different version is possible, of extraction, not by main force but because it has been built in most cannily—that Tarnopol is a sonofabitch and often seems at the threshhold of discovering that transparent truth just before closing the door on it, and that Roth, cannier by far than the rest of us, knows it perfectly well. And why not, in a novel composed of dialectic, each argument hedged by counterargument, each thesis by antithesis? But in this version the synthesis has been omitted, and we are left with a portrait of the golden boy as tarnished heel; of the would-be "man" mired in the phallic or perhaps the anal stage, thereby validating Spielvogel's vulgar, "reductive" case history, and *that* the novel is certainly not. Either way, an obsession is an obsession—volatile, vivid, crafty, but still an obsession.

*Saul Maloff, "The Golden Boy," in* The New Republic *(reprinted by permission of* The New Republic; *© 1974 by The New Republic, Inc.), June 8, 1974, pp. 21-2.*

Now in his 41st year, Philip Roth still seems the most promising young novelist in America. With seven books behind him since *Goodbye, Columbus* won the National Book Award 15 years ago, he continues to apply to each succeeding title the thrust of a brilliant newcomer, as if staking out his subject and defining his voice for the first time.

The Roth determination not to repeat himself is becoming, in fact, his most famous and only predictable trait. The writer who went from *Portnoy's Complaint* to political satire *(Our Gang),* and thence to Kafkaesque fantasy *(The Breast)* is now so impatient that he cannot even wait to complete this book before trying to reconstruct himself. In *My Life as a Man,* he switches persona in mid-volume. The result is superb as a performance and uneven as a book (or rather, two books). It leads, finally, to some questions. Does a kind of bravura restlessness now not only characterize Roth but constitute the heart of his talent? Has his own range of style—an actor's gift, a writer's curse—got the better of him? . . .

In a self-circling frenzy, both funny and bitter, Roth goes on and on explaining, until at last the book seems to have spun out from under him. The author's alter ego, Tarnopol, is allowed to create his own alter ego, Nathan Zuckerman, and in a *Doppelgänger* novel-within-a-novel, Zuckerman takes 95 pages to unfold a parallel plot about still another Jewish boy-novelist and his Gentile harpy-muse.

What a fixated center there is to Roth's tormented scrambling! The letters that Roth-Tarnopol-Zuckerman scribble may appear to free-associate like a Lenny Bruce monologue. The literary-psychoanalytical-theological commentaries may come on like a marvelously clever cram course in 20th Century Anxiety. (Reader, look to your guilt-edged paperbacks: Dostoevsky, Freud, Kierkegaard.) But everything comes back to the unanswerable mystery which seems to make all of life unanswerable: why does a man embrace what he hates—perversely bond himself to what destroys him? Is this, Roth appears to be asking, a paradox of life or the straight story on death? . . .

Like Tarnopol, [Roth] may be looking for his own Maureen, the one subject that might slow down his dazzling technique, sober up his double and triple ironies, humble his sheer knowingness. The one subject, in other words, that might turn him into a matured—or at least middle-aged—novelist. In the meantime, unlike Tarnopol, he still can't lose for winning. That, for the moment, is his special talent and his special doom.

*Melvin Maddocks, "Make It New," in* Time *(reprinted by permission from* Time, The Weekly Newsmagazine; *copyright Time Inc.), June 10, 1974, p. 92.*

Some years ago Philip Roth suggested that reality had become so inventive and prolific, so replete with improbable characters like Eisenhower and his political descendants, that the writer of fiction was more or less out of a job in America. . . .

When paranoia becomes reality, the whole of sanity is left to fiction. But then sanity is not at all easy to invent, and tends to prefer rather dull narrative modes. In recent years Roth has chosen to go the other way. *Portnoy's Complaint* was an attempt to outbid extravagant reality—if life often looks like a long joke, then the long virtuoso telling of a joke may well serve as a novel. In *Our Gang* he simply (and brilliantly) accepted reality's invitation to madness; and in *The Breast* he suggested something of reality's own madness in the metaphor of a man turned into a thinking mammary gland. In *that* context, ordinary life itself seems strange, diffuse, elusive. . . .

Once the ordinary becomes extraordinary then ordinariness can be seen as a form of grail, and one might expect a novelist to set off in search of a lost normality; of the spaces, as it were, between life's exaggerations. This is partly what Roth is doing in *My Life as a Man,* but only partly. His main task seems to be to speak now without parables and hyperbole, to give up the narrative modes of paranoia, and realistically portray the horrors of the private life of one married, harried man; to create something like *The Breast* without its element of fable, or *Portnoy's Complaint* without its vaudeville and histrionics, or *Our Gang* without the all too verifiable historical existence of Richard Nixon. He is writing a *novel,* that is, hoping to offer a believable imagined world in which daily demonstrations of the unbelievable can take place.

*My Life as a Man* is a very self-conscious piece of work, a bit prone to mistake apologies for repentance, and self-accusation for self-scrutiny.

*Michael Wood, "Hooked," in* The New York Review of Books *(reprinted with permission from* The New York Review of Books; *© 1974 by NYREV, Inc.), June 13, 1974, pp. 8-10.*

there are those of us who sat and grumbled about philip roth's life and work all these years; unhappy about the quality of the work we found much to bitch about in respect to the rewards, fame, and affluence that accrued to him because of that work—or certainly, this being america, unhappy about the rewards, fame, and affluence that accrued to him, we set about denigrating his work, in any event, much of this criticism seemed justified to me, since i could see serious flaws in his books and i couldn't accept a culture in which a few writers win it all, while the rest labor unpaid, and perhaps worse, unobserved.

but the system was not his fault, and the work was. "goodbye columbus" seemed to me to be consistently stretched past its strength, the title story should have been a normal-length short story, the other stories in general would have done better as vignettes or short shorts. "letting go" and "when she was good" also seemed strung out, perhaps actually novellas. and the other major complaint i had came to the fore with "portnoy's complaint." roth's celebrated humor seemed to me to always get in the way of the book, of the writing itself. here was a man who couldn't resist a joke, and who would spoil the telling and the story to get the joke in, and by the time he came to "the breast" and "our gang" and to a certain extent, "the great american novel," the jokes had taken over the writing and the story completely. and all the while the writing stayed skimming on the surface of itself. meanwhile the critics had nothing to say but good.

and so we come to roth at a point where he had to make a decision. i have to say that in this new book i think he made it, strongly, effectively, and without copping out. but now the critics are screaming. it seems fashionable in the reviews of "my life as a man" to bemoan the fact that roth is still chewing over the same material, is still working the same mine of the poor beset jewish male. my feeling is that he is for the first time digesting the material and transmuting it, for the first time is digging deep into the mine and producing work. before things were touched beautifully and brightly and funnily, but just touched. now he has taken the problem seriously, he has tried desperately to come to grips with the age-old war between men and women—and he has done it at just the wrong time in our culture, too, which is delicious, and deliberate, the sign of a writer. granted the hero of this book, zuckerman-tarnopol is not a particularly virtuous, strong, or otherwise heroic male, but the women, sharon-lydia-monica-susan-maureen, are all worse, each in [her] own [way]. in fact, they all come across as so one-sidedly abominable that one wants desperately to hear their stories from their lips or pens—and aint that what fiction is about, in part at least?

what roth has done is to go deep inside the head and soul of his male, to try and find out where we are, instead of looking at those damned maps they hand out everywhere that don't tell us anything. in the doing of it, like them or not, he has finally created real people who breathe and suffer—and, yes, make jokes, only now we can laugh with them, and him.

the book itself is broken into two parts, the first, "useful fictions," a brace of short stories by [peter] tarnopol, and the second, an autobiographical memoir by tarnopol, and this device triumphs over itself, because it is after all tarnopol that roth is investigating, so that the multiplicity of voices, and the semi-duplication of characters (which led the distinguished reviewer for the distinguished paper to pick the wrong woman as "villain"), give tarnopol a breadth and depth that might not be possible in any other way.

It seems to me that this is the first book by roth that is both truly offensive and revelatory because it *is* offensive, because like the novelist he is, he is finally looking hard and long at his people and their lives, no one is a hero in this book. tarnopol says he would have laughed had anyone suggested that struggling with a woman over a marriage would come to occupy him in the way that exploring the south pole had occupied admiral byrd, or writing "madame bovary" had occupied flaubert. and his women, who have either had him inflicted on them, or themselves inflicted on him, each lay out their own condemnation of him, mutedly, because it comes through tarnopol's voice, but there nevertheless.

"my life as a man" is a marvelous, rich piece of work, and well worth all that went before it. the man always knew how to write, we all knew that, but now he has put it all together, and used it all, to make a living breathing story.

*joel oppenheimer, in* The Village Voice *(reprinted by permission of* The Village Voice; *© 1974 by The Village Voice, Inc.), June 20, 1974, p. 33.*

[*My Life as a Man*] is an elaborate burlesque of "honest" autobiographical writing, and as such it is the sort of one-shot stunt that probably every writer of a certain rank is entitled to when he has had too much of his critics. The only problem with this hilarious, amazing book is that the earnest elements—the pleading, the melodrama, the horror—are often upended by all the fooling around.

The New Yorker, *June 24, 1974, p. 103.*

Overpraised for his slightest work *(Goodbye, Columbus; Our Gang),* generally ignored for his most ambitious *(Letting Go, When She Was Good),* Roth has been attacked by Jews as bad for their image, by Wasps for not knowing his subject (women's lib will have a field day with [*My Life as a Man*]), and has had *Portnoy's Complaint* praised as "the funniest book since *Huckleberry Finn*"—which is rather odd, since both books strike me as not only sad but ultimately terrifying. . . .

What Roth is insisting on [in *My Life as a Man*] is his right to make fictions; that is, to transform personal experience —because it is so limited and redundant—into stories. "My True Story" is beyond autobiography, but it is a gloss and commentary on Roth's own work, a meditation on the creative act itself. . . . Roth admits that, yes, he's got only one story—that central marital trauma—but when you consider his entire work, then the virtuoso variations on the theme, the revised and contradictory histories, the wealth of different characters and associations which that one dumb liaison has apparently produced seem all the more remarkable. . . .

[What] has been overlooked and/or disparaged is that, unlike most of his contemporaries, Roth is writing about a particular time and place, and attempting to come to terms with contemporary history. His subject, it seems to me, is the disintegration of American liberalism—not the Trillingian brand, obviously. Rather, it is the liberalism fostered by middleclass families after the war in those young men who were not only the first to go to college, but who also carried their businessmen fathers' values of discipline, hard work, and duty into the humanities and reform politics, only to ultimately confuse aesthetic with political strategies, and to find the talents so carefully nurtured in the Fifties to be tangential at best to the chaos of the Sixties.

All of Roth's male protagonists are victims of this upbringing, and their predicament can hardly be said to be uniquely Jewish: indeed, the literary and psychological antecedents here are the earnest young men of Henry James. This view of experience—a relatively happy childhood, parents with achieved identities, American optimism and upward mobility refined by an *education sentimentale,* Enlightenment idealism, and the romanticism of nineteenth-century fiction —meets continual defeat at the hands of a series of ladies whose unhappy lives exemplify only the banal bourgeois egotism of self-pity and self-righteous emancipation, which trivializes even their own genuine alienation. The liberal patsy confronts the blackmailing dependent, helplessly, since he never knows whether he is acting out of guilt or charity; all his reason and responsibility are unable to come to terms with everything he is not; "I wanted," Roth intones, "to be humanish: manly, a man." . . .

Tarnopol survives his women because, essentially, he is his father's son—a made self, based not on his modestly successful career, but on the knowledge that he is neither typical nor exemplary. His is the special victimization of Henry James's Lambert Strether, Daisy Miller, and Christopher Newman, an incarnation of the idea that only those who survive can be called victims.

The cost of such survival is also clear, for Tarnopol's strength is sufficient only unto itself—he can "trust" only his own writing, his personal reconstitution of the world; he cannot relate to history except by deflating it with gross satire; he cannot protect those he loves any more than he can kill his enemies. . . .

This seems to me to constitute both the poignance and importance of Roth's unremitting story—that all the therapy, meliorism, exorcism, all those clichés of "self-realization, permissiveness, spontaneous role-playing, being open about one's problems," cannot deal with the irrational forces of our time. It is no accident that the analyst who had complex functions in *Portnoy's Complaint* is reduced here to a straight man, just another foolish literary critic *manqué*. No accident that Maureen's last grasp at self-justification is group therapy, that *collective* solipsism which presumably is the answer to Tarnopol's personalized variety. The implication is clear; Roth seems to be saying, "Okay, so I'm solipsistic, but it's the real thing, not bought off the rack, an actual sickness and not just a phenomenon of the age."

Whatever reservations one might have about Roth's work —and he forces you to have reservations—we should recognize that he is dealing with extremely serious issues for the contemporary state of mind and their literary embodiments. Literature, after all, is concerned not only with making metaphors but with trashing facile ones, and it takes some courage to point out false analogies (particularly at one's own expense) and to reject that most contemporary of vices: the desperate equation of one's personal life with the disparate history of one's time.

*Charles Newman, "The Failure of the Therapeutic," in* Harper's *(copyright © 1974, by Harper's Magazine, Inc.; reprinted from the July, 1974 issue of* Harper's Magazine *by permission), July, 1974, pp. 87-9.*

*My Life as a Man* could be the textbook Jewish novel. Tarnopol, its hero, is a writer-teacher—as are six of every 15 Jewish novel heroes. Tarnopol has made a catastrophic marriage. Maureen, the *shiksa* wife, comes on like one of those all-purpose penknives: she can cut, punch, corkscrew, or rasp him into wretchedness. Tarnopol pishers away nearly ten years trying to understand why he married her. His approach is literary; he brings New Criticism to bear on his *tsuris*. More or less typical of the Jewish novel: at some level it is attuned to its predecessors in the History of Western Fiction. Human existence treated as beginning-middle-end; event as epiphany. In fact the novel is both entertainment and an inexpensive tool for psychiatric self-help. Roth goes about it cleverly. Part III is "My True Story." Parts I and II are pieces of short fiction: Tarnopol casting his disaster in literary form, with which form (and not formless real life) he has been trained to cope. I like the concept. It works. Perhaps, though, Tarnopol's short stories represent Roth's own false starts with *My Life as a Man*. It wouldn't surprise me. Novelists, Jewish or Christian, need to be thrifty. . . .

Psychoanalysis . . . has been a peculiarly Jewish exercise since Freud first created the 50-minute hour and called it good. Jewish heroes have an aptitude for the exegesis of complex moral events. Everybody in *My Life as a Man* is supporting at least one analyst. Dr. Spielvogel's couch becomes the novel's arena: Tarnopol does his best suffering there. Moreover, the Jewish hero despises violence. As a result, violent acts, whether performed or endured, have a special resonance in the Jewish novel. They surprise. They insult. The single slap, even the hard look, are wonderfully heightened: each has to be understood, analyzed. And sex, too, is a form of physical violence. The Jewish hero can't slough it off as merely procreative. But in thinking about it so much, in elevating it, he tends to idealize women. And they, in turn, tend to disappoint him. . . .

*My Life as a Man* isn't the best novel of its kind. Nonetheless, deploying just general issue Jewish equipment, Roth has constructed a funny, imaginative, moving book. It serves to prove that the Jewish novel, in good hands, is our most enduring and resource-filled subgenre.

*D. Keith Mano, "The Novel As Shrug," in* National Review *(150 East 35th St., New York, N.Y. 10016), July 19, 1974, p. 828.*

Philip Roth's taunting . . . novel, *My Life as a Man* . . ., is a brilliant documentary on the writing of fiction, with its taxing discipline and harsh principles of selection. I know of nothing as fascinating on the subject, except the notebooks and prefaces of Henry James. . . .

The main distinction between the two versions of marrying presented in *My Life as a Man* is a literary one. "Courting Disaster" is basically objective, sequential, decorous, to the extent that Roth can muster these attributes of fiction he once admired. In "My True Story" the problem of veracity is more tentatively pursued—we are invited to assess the reliability of an obsessive narrator no less strident and rancorous than Alexander Portnoy—and the plot reconnoiters back and forth in events as if it were some Indian scout cutting brush in the forest of the psyche. Yet the more the depictions differ, the more they remain the same. . . .

Roth has always had the knack of locating his fiction in common derangements. What made *Portnoy's Complaint* a best seller was not really the flamboyant vocabulary or the lurid sexual images, but the complaint itself: the encroachment of the Jewish family on the outlook and imagination of its vulnerable offspring. Now Roth is confronting us with a relatively new phenomenon in the relations between men and women, a kind of lethal emotional democracy in which reserve has completely evaporated and no demand is considered too presumptuous. Beyond that, he may be telling us that we enter marriage as much for harassment (growth through suffering, as a European philosopher more conventionally put it) as for gratification. Yet if he is indeed striking the cosmic note, one wonders why he resorts to a braying and offensive narrator, and a few sordid, nerve-jangling episodes to represent an entire marriage.

In any case, Roth's argument at this point in his career appears to be more with Literature than with modern life. He mulls over the craft of fiction as a woman might over an old lover who did her wrong—reconstructing his relationship to it, and discarding mannerly conventions and moral pretensions. For these, Roth believes, unman his heroes and ill equip their creator to contend with the present reality.

No matter how awesome the spectacle of a writer so eager to capture every facet of the truth that he subjects us forcibly to the ignoble, the unbalanced and the disgusting in ourselves, the theme of an artist's progress is after all a highly specialized one. We expect quite reasonably that the main fascination of a novel will inhere in its persons and places. But Roth is too intensely inside to care where he is outside, and ascetic enough that he passes up without a qualm the chance to describe, in two different sections of the book, the enchanting burnt-orange aspect of Rome. The few characters we can empathize with show up in words, not action. . . .

One of the displeasures of reading *My Life as a Man* is that it is overly seismographic, trying to incorporate everything that is rife in the environment—psychoanalysis, the role of women, the struggle toward orgasm (needless to report, not successful). But at least it can be said that this is not an empty novel; for all its excesses, *My Life as a Man* can boast an ironic, recondite source of harmony that inadvertently touches us: The writer is so precisely the man—compulsively literary, modern, fastidious, hooked on the seven types of ambiguity, and extraordinarily inclined to wax wroth.

*Isa Kapp, "Roth in Progress," in* The New Leader, *July 22, 1974, pp. 16-17.*

For ten years following the appearance of *Goodbye, Columbus* in 1959, Roth struggled to find a form that would contain and objectify his sternly adversary vision of American culture, and in his two massive novels of the early and middle 60's, *Letting Go* and *When She Was Good,* he experimented with greater effectiveness than is generally recognized with the traditional form of the realistic social novel. But the difficulty of this form for Roth was that it demanded a sense of thematic coherence which he did not possess as well as a social experience definable in terms of certain implicit concepts of communal order which, as he well knew, contemporary society did not possess. As a result, Roth found himself caught in a predicament which, to one degree or another, has confounded American writers ever since Melville: he had vast quantities of material, but he could not discover and possess a subject. All he could do was describe and document at infinite length the experiences of his characters, record every word of their interminable and mostly trivial conversations, and in that way produce a certain effect of life—busy, abrasive, vibrant, but finally one-dimensional and incoherent. It also became apparent in these novels that Roth suffered from two primary weaknesses that severely limited his ability to work successfully with objectively created characters in a realistically presented social milieu: he had no power to identify or sympathize with characters who were not to some degree extensions or idealizations of himself, and his natural tendency was to recoil in horror from contemporary experience and to treat it with the contempt of one who feels that he alone is worthy of salvation.

In short, on the evidence of these novels, it was clear that the form most congenial to Roth was the novel of narcissism, just as his strongest gift was for the tragi-comedy of paranoia, and it happened that in *Portnoy's Complaint* he was able to coordinate form and gift to extraordinary effect. Yet there was still a lingering urge in Roth to make the kind of direct assault on the social and political realities of our time which in his essay he had criticized some of his contemporaries for failing to make. He accordingly produced after *Portnoy's Complaint* three very different and very bad novels: *Our Gang,* a heavy-handed and adolescent satire of the Nixon administration which only verified the truth of Roth's observation that "the actuality is continually outdoing our talents," particularly when the actuality is Richard Nixon; *The Breast,* a baffling and pretentious scrap of psychological fantasy that is ghoulish in its taste-lessness; and *The Great American Novel,* an even more baffling mélange of hyperkinetic writing about the mythology of baseball. Clearly, it was impossible for Roth to deal successfully in fiction with either the public realities or the various fantasy worlds of contemporary life, and the reasons were precisely those he had recognized in 1961. The experience of our time was stupefying and infuriating to the writer not merely because it was so often more incredible than anything he could imagine, but because it seemed to have no relation to the individual self. That, in fact, was the prime feature of its incredibility.

For a writer of Roth's particular talent and temperament there is only one reliable measure of credibility—what the self feels and thinks—and only one compelling interest—what the self experiences: in Roth's case, how events and people, especially women, have assaulted his sanity, thwarted or provoked his sexuality, and outraged his sense of moral virtue. This is the story he told in *Portnoy's Complaint,* and he tells it again in rather different terms in *My Life as a Man.* But the fact which in the former was partially obscured by the absorbing joys of book-length masturbation is here once again in full evidence: although Roth is a fine stylist and may be the funniest serious writer in America, he is gravely deficient in a sense of the novel form; he has no firm understanding of what his novels are supposed to mean; and he has no subject matter except fanatical self-infatuation.

His strategy this time is to try to convert these weaknesses into literary capital by making them part of the contrived architectural and thematic design of the novel. The theory behind this presumably is that an author is permitted to do anything in a novel provided he can convince the reader that he did it deliberately, in the service of some artistic intention, however obscure. . . .

*My Life as a Man* is . . . a totally solipsistic novel, which may well make it a perfect expression of the times. It is created out of the materials of exactly the kind of alienation from the public culture which Roth described in his essay ["Writing American Fiction," 1961]. Its form is the endless ranting monologue; its content is guilt, anxiety, and acute paranoia; its appropriate setting is the psychiatrist's office where, as was literally the case in *Portnoy's Complaint,* the only sound is the sound of the narrator's voice. Nothing is real in the world except that voice, all our separate, complaining voices.

But the problem with Roth is that he cannot function as his own psychiatrist. He cannot find the meaning of his anguish or his anger: hence, we cannot. All he can do is talk, talk, talk, sometimes brilliantly, sometimes tediously, but always toward a point that is never reached because it does not exist. What he is up to really is—to use his own phrase—a form of literary onanism.

*John W. Aldridge, "Literary Onanism," (reprinted from* Commentary *by permission; copyright © 1974 by the American Jewish Committee), in* Commentary, *September, 1974, pp. 82-6.*

# S

## SALAMANCA, J(ack) R(ichard) 1924?-

**Salamanca, an American novelist, writes hauntingly lyrical prose. Although he is best known for his interpretation of the "mad" girl Lilith, and he has always been fascinated by madness, he has been mainly preoccupied in his fiction with the failure of love. (See also *Contemporary Authors*, Vols. 25-28.)**

J. R. Salamanca's second novel is striking confirmation of the talent which aroused considerable excitement when his first novel, "The Lost Country," appeared three years ago. Although narrower in scope and less resonant in style than his first novel, "Lilith" is a subtler continuation of the author's theme: gentle innocence journeying toward self-knowledge through cruelty and corruption, unguardedly embracing with flaring intensity the secret mysteries of human intimacy. . . .

"Lilith" demonstrates again Mr. Salamanca's rare sense of place, his sensuous, tender evocation of country people and country days, for it is within the setting he has known all his life, among the familiar and beloved hills and woods which nourished his boyhood, that Vincent becomes the victim of his own generosity and violates himself. It would be possible to view this book as it seems on the surface: a chilling exposure of the manipulation of the healthy by the demented (and vice versa). But "Lilith" is really something much rarer in contemporary fiction. As in "The Lost Country," this gifted young novelist has taken the myths of masculine growing-up—the hunger of the immature for involvement with the beautiful, the brilliant, and the unattainable—and woven them into a subtle canvas behind which dance the avid dreams of youth.

It is a tribute to J. R. Salamanca's great skill as a writer that both the surface of this novel—stylish in tone, precise in language, sure in evocation of place—and the unspoken knowledge which lies beneath it combine to produce a work of mature artistry.

*Harding Lemay, "The Beautiful and Demented," in* The New York Herald Tribune —Books, *July 30, 1961, p. 9.*

It is difficult to define precisely what the novelist has done [in "Lilith"], and even more difficult to determine what he intends. In the context of a mental institution, and with concepts chosen rather promiscuously from Freud and Jung, he has recast in ironic form and studied poetic prose various conflicting materials; the character of Vincent, that most gentle of Christian saints; the rabbinical legend of the night-creature Lilith, first wife of Adam, who abandoned him for demons; the theme of romantic agony, of heightened erotic sensibility, that the Marquis de Sade, Byron, Keats and others relished in their plots of the innocent corrupted by evil.

All this emerges as a witch's brew that Mr. Salamanca has tried to flavor to everyone's taste. If the reader insists that a novel have a specific meaning, no matter how subtle, he will not find one here. The equations of sense are many and contradictory; thus, at one moment insanity is equated with creativity, then with evil and next with unreality. Yet through this book there shines the light of an authentic talent, darkened though it may be in the mirror of insanity. If this is the novel the author felt he had to write after his brilliant "The Lost Country," perhaps in the next one he will return to that same lost country of his youth and dreams.

*E. Nelson Hayes, "Love and Death in a World of Delusion," in* The New York Times Book Review *(© 1961 by The New York Times Company; reprinted by permission), August 20, 1961, p. 30.*

[*Lilith*] is a beautifully, sensitively written book, a book full of touching and memorable insights, often a moving book. Only its subject matter keeps *Lilith* from being entirely successful. . . .

The first one hundred pages, in which the hero re-creates his early life in the town, his war years and his return, contain some of the loveliest prose I have come upon in a long while. And the rest of the writing is equally impressive.

However, after Vincent goes to work at the Lodge, as the asylum is called, and meets his co-workers, the novel takes on the aspect of a fairy tale which all the beautiful writing cannot dispel. . . .

Herein lies the novel's flaw: the good, simple, troubled hero is believable; but the heroine's character, however charming, is that of a madwoman and can never be relied upon for any genuine or recognizable motivation. Thus, as Vincent is excluded from her private world, so is the reader. Without this contact there is no sympathy, and combined with the difficulties that the setting itself provides, it is easy to see how shaky becomes the whole edifice.

*Doris Grumbach, "Bewitching Madness," in* America *(© America Press, 1961; all rights reserved), September 2, 1961, pp. 691-92.*

There is an entrancing dreamlike quality to the fiction of J. R. Salamanca. In *Embarkation* as in *Lilith* and *A Sea Change* the world he creates is somewhere between reality and fantasy, past and present, the palpable and the mysterious. His novels move slowly, deliberately and powerfully through time, evoking an ambiance of legend and myth. They are tapestries, woven out of deep feeling for character, a keen awareness of the physical landscape, and a fine appreciation of ambiguity.

*Embarkation,* which may well be the best of them, is a work of artistry about the subject of artistry. . . .

Salamanca tells this wise and provocative tale with grace and feeling and no small amount of humor. Joel Linthicum [the protagonist of *Embarkation*] is a charming and wholly fascinating character, whose clumsy attempts to express love are as believable as his gusto and his genius. As so many of Salamanca's characters are, he is a man of the sea, and *Embarkation* contains passages of nautical description that are truly brilliant. Throughout, it is a novel that engages the reader, as the best fiction does, in the lives it unfolds.

*Jonathan Yardley, in* Book World—The Washington Post (© The Washington Post), *December 2, 1973, p. 3.*

Goethe, who was fascinated with the image of the superior man long before Nietzsche gave him romantic and mystical trimmings and called him Zarathustra, believed that if we are strongwilled and know our goal people will step aside for us. In [*Embarkation*] Joel Linthicum, the boat-builder as artist, would pass any test for the superior man . . . and his older son Aaron compares him with the Elizabethans. Most Englishmen and Americans today would be intimidated if a Drake or a Raleigh came swaggering among them, sea salt in his beard and blood on his hands. Aaron, the narrator of *Embarkation,* admits he's intimidated and his growing up—one of the major themes of the novel—is a quiet struggle to crawl out from under the shadow of a man who belongs to a time when there were giants in the earth.

Though Salamanca gave the title character of his best-selling novel *Lilith* a rich fantasy life, he is no maker of fantasies himself. *Lilith* was based on a year's work in an asylum and its success was owing not only to its Gothic atmosphere but also to its finespun details and its author's power in identifying with the occupational therapist who served as narrator. In *Embarkation* Salamanca . . . dipped into his own experiences as well. . . . Whether he is describing London or the odds-against struggle of the Linthicums with a gale off the Maryland coast, Salamanca writes with a lyricism that persuaded a critic of his first novel, *The Lost Country,* to chide him as a Thomas Wolfe cub.

Salamanca differs from Wolfe, however, in ways important enough to indicate that he doesn't have to crawl out from under the shadow of *that* giant. Since *The Lost Country* he has been curbing a taste for verbiage and rhetoric and producing novels that have been *progressively* shorter. He is more inventive than Wolfe, never using nostalgia as an excuse for disguised and interminable autobiography. Most important, perhaps, he turns to mythology as Joyce and Faulkner and John Updike did before him but avoids the obtrusive parallels that became a wearisome trick in Updike's *The Centaur.* The Genesis story of Noah furnished Salamanca with hints for the primitive vigor and alternating scrupulousness and waywardness of Joel Linthicum. . . .

Joel Linthicum is not entirely credible—no semi-mythic hero could be—if measured by the standards of realistic fiction. . . . [He] is above all a contrast to the anti-heroes that have long dominated fiction and an answer—if one is wanted—to the despair of the '70s. His delight in living and eagerness to take risks limit him as a human being only in that they prevent him from understanding what the whimpering of the J. Alfred Prufrocks is all about.

The artist as a comic hero rather than a sensitive plant on Shelley's model is an uncommon theme and it is handled by Salamanca with romantic overtones that would jar if his lyricism weren't under delicate control. In moving from the Gothicism of *Lilith* and the overinsistent sexuality of *A Sea Change,* he has arrived at an artistic maturity that puts *Embarkation* first among his works.

*James Walt, "No Wolfe Cub," in* The New Republic *(reprinted by permission of* The New Republic; *© 1974 by Harrison-Blaine of New Jersey, Inc.), January 5 & 12, 1974, pp. 28-9.*

* * *

## SANDBURG, Carl 1878-1967

**Sandburg, an American, was a poet of real people, of folksongs and ordinary speech. His work is characterized by his sincere and abiding love for America's beauty and brawn and he was, as a result, one of this country's most revered literary men. In addition to his poems, he wrote short stories and a well-known biography of Abraham Lincoln. (See also *Contemporary Authors*, Vols. 5-8, rev. ed.; obituary, Vols. 25-28.)**

Carl Sandburg's poems, generally, are improvisations whose wording is approximate; they do not have the exactness, the guaranteeing sharpness and strangeness of a real style. Sandburg is a colorful, appealing, and very American writer, so that you long for his little vignettes or big folk editorials, with their easy sentimentality and easy idealism, to be made into finished works of art; but he sings songs more stylishly than he writes them, says his poems better than they are written—it is marvelous to hear him say "The People, Yes," but it is not marvelous to read it as a poem. Probably he is at his best in slight pieces like "Grass" or "Losers". . . .

*Randall Jarrell, "Fifty Years of American Poetry" (1962; originally published in* Prairie Schooner, *Spring, 1963), in his* The Third Book of Criticism *(reprinted with the permission of Farrar, Straus & Giroux, Inc.; copyright © 1941, 1945, 1955, 1956, 1962, 1963, 1965 by Mrs. Randall Jarrell; copyright © 1963, 1965 by Randall Jarrell), Farrar, Straus, 1969.*

Sandburg's performance has much in common with Whitman's. It shows the same interest and delight in the American scene, as in all sorts and conditions of men and women. If it does not celebrate the physical self with the gusto of "Calamus", it speaks out against a repressive respectability. Its affirmative character shows a tie with the older poet that Allen Ginsberg, in his "hungry fatigue . . . shopping for images" in a California supermarket, trying to turn his nightmare into a vision, cannot as fully claim. Much as Whitman exalted the divine average, Sandburg tends to deify "the People". But his verse denounces the betrayers of the people in plainer accents than Whitman's. The famous phrase about blood, sweat, and tears could be paralleled in Sandburg's offering of "hunger, danger, and hate" in the war against the exploitation of man by man.

*Babette Deutsch, in her* Poetry in Our Time *(copyright by Babette Deutsch), Doubleday, revised edition, 1963, p. 53.*

Even if there had never been any New Critics to denigrate it, Sandburg's early work, with the exception of several short poems, would surely have been recognized by this time for what it was, an expression of the times that came as close to being subliterary as the work of any American poet of comparable reputation ever has. It is much more difficult, today, to understand why *this* poetry was once so greatly admired than it is to think ourselves back into the situation in which Whittier's poems were read with pleasure. However much we may approve of Sandburg's humanitarian and socialist views, and his efforts to write poetry in which "democratic" and "realistic" would amount to the same thing, we are likely to find the poetry itself, when we actually *read* it, more remote than Tuckerman's. Much of it reads like the worst of Whitman, if Whitman had had only ideology to guide him. . . .

After almost half a century of devoting his energies chiefly to things other than his own poetry, Sandburg published his best volume of verse in 1963. *Honey and Salt* would be a remarkable achievement for any poet, but for a poet in his middle eighties who gained his fame with "Chicago," it is extraordinary. The poems no longer demand to be classified as tough or tender, violent or sentimental. There is in them the mellowness and wisdom of age, which we should like to feel we could expect of very aged poets, but hardly dare to; and there is much more. This volume reminds us of the development of Williams in his last decade, both in sound and in sense. The lines now are much more strongly cadenced, yet still "free." The sound of "the American idiom," as Williams called it, is in fact more evident here than in the earlier, more "realistic," verse. And the sense is as different as the sound from what the early work prepared us to expect. The old reliance on ideology has been replaced by a concern for actual people and their actual experience and actual needs, without any loss in the strength of the vision of the family of man. . . . The old tendency to fall back from ideology into pure sentimentalism is gone, too, without any loss of the genuine, controlled and meaningful, tenderness that was the chief distinction of the best early poems. In its place, we find a mature romantic imagination manifesting itself chiefly through sympathetic identification with all forms of life.

*Hyatt H. Waggoner, "Carl Sandburg," in his* American Poets From the Puritans to the Present *(copyright © 1968 by Hyatt H. Waggoner; reprinted by permission of Houghton Mifflin Company), Houghton, 1968, pp. 452-57.*

What Sandburg had for the poor, frustrated, heroic, and ordinary, was *Einfühlung* [empathy; sympathetic understanding].

What he also had was a marvelous prosody, a perfect ear for the beautiful potentials of common speech, something he learned from folk song, but mostly he learned from just listening—on a hundred jobs, at ball games, fishing for catfish, soldiering in Puerto Rico, swapping lies in the City Room or in the nearby bar, talking to militant "hunkies, kikes, and dagoes" after a Socialist speech.

*Kenneth Rexroth, in his* American Poetry in the Twentieth Century *(copyright 1971 Herder and Herder, Inc.; used by permission of the publisher, The Seabury Press, New York), Herder, 1971, p. 48.*

Sandburg is not writing *for* the Lincolns and Shakespeares of America, primarily, . . . and not primarily for the middle class, and in [his] poems he celebrates the vitality of "the mob," arguing that the real silhouettes against the sky, the real bronzes, should be of those who do the basic work of the world. "Chicago Poems" more than anything is intent on enhancing and improving the lot of such people, and thus anathema to Sandburg is the poet or performer who misuses his skill, serving the exploitative and deadening economic powers. . . .

Like Whitman, like William James, like Pound, Mencken, Anderson, Brooks . . . Sandburg hoped, as he indicated in a dedication to Stephen Vincent Benét, "that men would act because of his words." That he wished this to be and that he worked for it through a unified perspective, purpose, and structure in "Chicago Poems" should enhance our sense of Sandburg as a writer and as a participant in the literary and cultural thrust of the early decades of this century. What he talked about doing, what he urged upon his readers' attention, and, indeed, much of what he did is, as he said of Pound's biplane spirit, "worth having."

*William Alexander, "The Limited American, the Great Loneliness, and the Singing Fire: Carl Sandburg's 'Chicago Poems'," in* American Literature *(reprinted by permission of the Publisher; copyright 1973 by Duke University Press, Durham, North Carolina), March, 1973, pp. 67-83.*

* * *

## SARRAUTE, Nathalie 1902-

**A Russian-born French anti-novelist and critic, Mme. Sarraute presents in her fiction a gallimaufry of images, evocative of antecedent sensations, in place of the plot, character, and psychological development around which the conventional novel is built. "Tropisms"—responses to people and things—are the "living substance" of her work. (See also *Contemporary Authors*, Vols. 9-12, rev. ed.)**

Nathalie Sarraute, as Sartre analyzed her intentions more lucidly than she did herself, refuses to take her characters either from the inside or from the outside, 'because we are, for ourselves and for others, both wholly outside and inside at the same time.' The meeting ground is the commonplace, which 'belongs to every one in myself and is in myself the presence of every one.' Behind the banal words uttered by the characters and their gestures, a constant flight away from oneself toward daily chores, mediocre tasks, insignificant thoughts, and all forms of inauthenticity is attempted. The reader often feels that he is on the verge of some momentous happening which never does occur: the puppets lapse back into the commonplace. An elusive inauthenticity, such as Sartre was fond of denouncing, into which human cowardice, fleeing from the assumption of freedom, takes refuge: such was the new motive which lurked behind the brief, ironical sketches of *Tropismes* and behind Nathalie Sarraute's second novel [*Portrait d'un inconnu*]. . . .

[According to Sarraute, we] distrust everything; invention, plot, character. The character with a neat label affixed, warning us that he is a miser, the lover, the jealous, the upstart, used to be the meeting ground of author and reader; 'he has now become the converging point of their mutual distrust.' Along with others today, she has declared war against him. Her aim is to explore those tenuous states, similar to those of the particles of modern physics which a feeble ray distorts. She gives the name of tropisms to those microscopic movements of attraction and repulsion that lie beneath the level of consciousness and defy analysis. They can only be deftly, poetically, elusively suggested.

Like most of the practitioners of the recent or new novel in France, Nathalie Sarraute is austere. She demands much from her readers. The mere device of refusing even to ask the Shakespearean question 'What's in a name?' and of designating the agents, or passive, half-sickly observers, as 'he,' 'she,' 'they,' inherited in part from Faulkner's confusion of names given to several characters and from Kafka's half-anonymous men, erects a hurdle of dubious value between the book and the reader. Descriptions 'à la Balzac' are derided by Nathalie Sarraute, as they had already been by Gide and Virginia Woolf; and circumstances of the extremely tenuous action are omitted. All is fake and inauthentic, and must therefore be banished: order, causation, logic, self-analysis, language all are deceptive. As a starting point for a new fictional enterprise and the antechamber to some new palace of art, the therapeutic cure advocated by Nathalie Sarraute could probably prove beneficial. *Tropismes,* her earliest volume, consisting of casual talks between ladies in a tea room, of insignificant conversations between a decrepit old man and a polished little girl, is a clever series of sketches. . . . Behind the empty or seemingly harmless chitchat, tropisms faintly appear; enmity and cruelty, envy and suspicion, never thus termed and never analyzed, are discreetly suggested by the author. Those sketches, which never assume the integrated solidity of short stories, were relieved with irony and were varied and short enough not to weary the reader's patience. Her novels, however, do. Professional technicians of the art of the novel, chiefly Bernard Pinguad, have discovered profundities in them, which are only perceptible to professionals. Others, who insist upon not divorcing literature completely from emotional, intellectual, and social life, may not feel adequately rewarded by those technical feats. Proust refused any hint that his tool was the microscope and insisted that it was rather the telescope, through which other worlds were descried and explored. Nathalie Sarraute does use a symbolic microscope to discover what we may perceive at a glance but cannot, she submits, render into words: 'an entire human being with its myriads of little movements which appear through a few things said, a laugh, a gesture.'

*Portrait d'un inconnu* (1949; *Portrait of a Man Unknown,* as it was translated in . . . 1958) and *Martereau* (1953) do not lend themselves to any analysis of plot or structure: events do not count, characters are not characterized, tension hardly mounts and certainly fails to grip the reader. The storyteller alone has some inkling of the sense, if any, of the book. . . . The apathetic observer does not discover anything and does not judge. Much subtlety and much stylistic skill are expended by the novelist on thin and brittle material in which this reader, and probably many like him, refuse to be concerned. French wits, waxing impatient at so much garrulous talk around trifles, unmindful of the serious psychological purpose of the author, have disparagingly called them 'sarrauteries,' or innocuous society dances or 'sauteries,' during which mothers, keeping an eye on their daughters and the husbands whom they might lure through their well-bred simpering, embroider their 'ouvràges de dames.'

*Le Planetarium* (1959) has been the one novel by the author which has been moderately praised. There can but be calculated irony in the title, conjuring up an artificial heavenly vault which shows the motions of stars and planets. The story is certainly laid in stuffy claustration; never a touch of nature and never an intruder from the masses. Even in Proust, servants and elevator boys brought a touch of country life and appeared to be doing something with their hands. . . .

*Les Fruits d'or* (1963; *The Golden Fruits,* 1964) is even more totally devoid of plot, character, and motion. The reader has to work his misty way among dim and gloomy alleys. The only external events consist of a man holding a shawl for a lady, an umbrella being annoyingly forgotten, the asinine acclaim of a novel entitled *Les Fruits d'or,* and equally superficial and ludicrous attacks against the novel by others, or by the same persons who have espoused another snobbery. As a satire of the would-be 'ins' in literary fashions, and of their pompous and sibylline oracles, it arouses a faint smile on our lips now and then. Snobbery, however, deserves a sounder thrashing; from La Bruyère to Proust, French satirists of pretentious fakery had accustomed us to more robust fare. 'He that drives fat oxen must himself be fat,' Dr. Johnson ironically quipped. She who intends to portray insignificance and tedium should probably not banish all humor, forcefulness, and even exaggeration from her books and incur the one unforgivable charge in literature; that of unshakable dullness.

*Henri Peyre, in his* French Novelists of Today *(copyright © 1955, 1967 by Oxford University Press; reprinted by permission), Oxford University Press-Galaxy, 1967, pp. 363-68.*

Sarraute's case against realism [set forth in *The Age of Suspicion*] is a convincing one. Reality is not that unequivocal; life is not that lifelike. The immediate cozy recognition that the lifelike in most novels induces is, and should be, suspect. (Truly, as Sarraute says, the genius of the age is suspicion. Or, if not its genius, at least its besetting vice.) I wholeheartedly sympathize with what she objects to in the old-fashioned novel: *Vanity Fair* and *Buddenbrooks,* when I reread them recently, however marvellous they still seemed, also made me wince. I could not stand the omnipotent author showing me that's how life is, making me compassionate and tearful; with his obstreperous irony, his confidential air of perfectly knowing his characters and leading me, the reader, to feel I knew them too. I no longer trust novels which fully satisfy my passion to understand. Sarraute is right, too, that the novel's traditional machinery for furnishing a scene, and describing and moving about characters, does not justify itself. Who really cares about the furniture of so-and-so's room, or whether he lit a cigarette or wore a dark gray suit or uncovered the typewriter after sitting down and before inserting a sheet of paper in the typewriter? Great movies have shown that the cinema can invest pure physical action—whether fleeting and small-scale like the wig-changing in *L'Avventura,* or important like the advance through the forest in *The Big Parade*—with more immediate magic than words ever can, and more economically, too.

More complex and problematic, however, is Sarraute's insistence that psychological analysis in the novel is equally obsolete and misguided. "The word 'psychology'," Sarraute says, "is one that no present-day writer can hear spoken with regard to himself without averting his gaze and blushing." By psychology in the novel, she means Woolf, Joyce, Proust: novels which explore a substratum of hidden thoughts and feelings beneath action, the depiction of which replaces the concern with character and plot. All Joyce brought up from these depths, she remarks, was an uninterrupted flow of words. And Proust, too, failed. . . .

Actually Sarraute's novels are not so unlike Joyce's (and Woolf's) as she thinks, and her rejection of psychology is far from total. What she wants herself is precisely the psychological, but (and this is the basis of her complaint against Proust) without the possibility of any conversion back into "character" and "plot." She is against psychological *dissection,* for that assumes there is a body to dissect. She is against a provisional psychology, against psychology as a new means to the old end. The use of the psychological microscope must not be intermittent, a device merely in the furthering of the plot. This means a radical recasting of the novel. Not only must the novelist not tell a story; he must not distract the reader with gross events like a murder or a great love. The more minute, the less sensational the event the better. . . . Sarraute's characters do not really ever act. They scheme, they throb, they shudder—under the impact of the minutiae of daily life. These preliminaries and gropings toward action are the real subject of her novels. Since analysis is out—that is, the speaking, interpreting author is out—Sarraute's novels are logically written only in the first person, even when the interior musings use "she" and "he."

What Sarraute proposes is a novel written in continuous monologue, in which dialogue between characters is a functional extension of monologue, "real" speech a continuation of silent speech. This kind of dialogue she calls "sub-conversation." It is comparable to theatrical dialogue in that the author does not intervene or interpret, but unlike theatrical dialogue it is not broken up or assigned to clearly separable characters. . . . The novel must disavow the means of classical psychology—introspection—and proceed instead by immersion. It must plunge the reader "into the stream of those subterranean dramas of which Proust only had time to obtain a rapid aerial view, and concerning which he observed and reproduced nothing but the broad motionless outlines." The novel must record without comment the direct and purely sensory contact with things and persons which the "I" of the novelist experiences. Abstaining from all creating of likenesses (Sarraute hands that over to the cinema), the novel must preserve and promote "that element of indetermination, of opacity and mystery that one's own actions always have for the one who lives them."

There is something exhilarating in Sarraute's program for the novel, which insists on an unlimited respect for the complexity of human feelings and sensations. But there is, for me, a certain softness in her argument, based as it is on a diagnosis of psychology that is both excessively doctrinaire in its remedy and equivocal. . . .

It really is science, or better yet sport, that Sarraute has in mind as model for the novel. The final justification for the novelist's quest as Sarraute characterizes it—what for her frees the novel from all moral and social purposes—is that the novelist is after truth (or a fragment of it), like the scientist, and after functional exercise, like the athlete. And there is nothing, in principle, so objectionable about these models, except their meaning for her. For all the basic soundness of Sarraute's critique of the old-fashioned novel, she still has the novelist chasing after "truth" and "reality."

*Susan Sontag, "Nathalie Sarraute and the Novel" (revised version, 1965), in her* Against Interpretation and Other Essays *(reprinted with the permission of Farrar, Straus, & Giroux, Inc.; copyright © 1961,*

*1962, 1963, 1964, 1965, 1966 by Susan Sontag), Farrar, Straus, 1966, pp. 100-11.*

As one might suspect . . . the volume *Tropisms* itself has only qualified interest and illustrates the inherent limitations of a book consisting entirely of disconnected epiphany-like fragments. Mme Sarraute handles the form about as well as can be expected, but it prevents her from *doing* anything with the tropisms she only permits herself to record: she cannot use them to enhance any general effect, to build up to anything, or to climax anything. They are just there. Presumably, these considerations explain why she has not written a second book like *Tropisms*. But, as she says, "this first book contains *in nuce* all the raw material that I have continued to develop in my later works," and "tropisms are still the living substance of all my books." . . . Part of the fragmentary, unstructured effect remains too. As a result of her de-emphasis on plot, for example, only rarely are the illuminations that her novels record truly major or climactic, like the one experienced by the narrator in *Portrait of a Man Unknown* when confronted with the portrait for the first time. Rather, the dominant note is of an incessant stream of fleeting moments of awareness: of self, of others, above all of the relationships between oneself and others. In her world, life is a trauma, and few experiences are much more traumatic than other experiences: instead we have a continual sense of the excitement and terror that can be constantly aroused by the most banal trivia.

*Morris Beja, in his* Epiphany in the Modern Novel, *University of Washington Press, 1971, pp. 222-23.*

"Subtlety" or a synonym thereof is probably the one word that occurs—and recurs—in every discussion of the art of Nathalie Sarraute. Now, it is true that as a psychological novelist she seeks to reproduce modifications of feeling so subtle and so elusive that in everyday life we are never fully conscious of them. In French she calls these modifications *mouvements,* a word that . . . can very often be translated into English simply by the word "emotion" or—more subtly—by the phrase "emotional stirring" or "stirring of emotion."

In the Foreword to *Tropisms* . . ., Madame Sarraute gives the most concise statement both of the nature of these stirrings and of the method she uses to render them in her books:

> These movements, of which we are hardly cognizant, slip through us on the frontiers of consciousness in the form of undefinable, extremely rapid sensations. They hide behind our gestures, beneath the words we speak, the feelings we manifest, are aware of experiencing, and able to define. . . .

"Undefinable" and "extremely rapid" as these sensations are, it is the novelist's task to define them and to slow them down so that the reader may take cognizance of them. . . .

> And since . . . no words express them, . . . it was not possible to communicate them to the reader otherwise than by means of equivalent images that would make him experience analogous sensations. . . .

It is her choice of "equivalent images" that makes Nathalie Sarraute's work so much less subtle—at least in its immediate effect—than it is alleged to be. . . . On almost every page one will find a contrast—slight enough at times but very often [so inappropriate as to be] breathtaking—between the banal conversation or action and the imagery used to define the underlying "movements" or "sub-conversation." . . . She conceives of human relations at [the] subconscious—not necessarily unconscious—level as furtive yet prehensile, and she believes that all Dostoevsky's characters exemplify the same urge: what Katherine Mansfield called "this terrible desire to establish contact."

Only if we bear in mind that Madame Sarraute regards this urge as the "source" of all Dostoevsky's work can we accept her insistence . . . that the Russian novelist has been the greatest influence on all her writing. Otherwise, there would seem to be no possible point of comparison between his work and hers. . . . [Unlike his novels] hers are usually short and sparsely inhabited by a handful of anonymous humans who stand aloof from "birth and copulation and death," to use T. S. Eliot's phrase. The most crucial overt act performed by a Sarraute character is likely to be the buying of a house or a piece of furniture, though we are rarely allowed to observe him in the act of earning his living; he is seldom short of money, however, for—in sharp contrast to the wide range of social classes explored by Dostoevsky—he always belongs to the middle classes or to the non-bohemian part of the literary world. . . .

Madame Sarraute has implicitly defended the absence of action and the narrowness of social reference in her novels. . . . [She asserts] that a tumultuous, Dostoevskian activity does occur in her novels, at least in metaphor if not in fact, at the subconscious level. . . . In the long run, . . . her subject matter often resembles that of the most romantic storyteller—but a displacement has occurred [as she would say] from "broad daylight" to the "secret recesses."

So much for subtlety. But the sharp contrast between conversation and sub-conversation—between the highly colloquial yet conventional upper-middle-class dialogue and the submarine, eat-and-be-eaten existence that goes on underneath—is essentially comic. All discrepancies between ideal and reality or illusion and reality are potentially either comic or tragic. When we examine each of Madame Sarraute's novels in turn, we shall see that the ultimate resolution of a potentially tragic situation is benign or, at worst, ironic. Furthermore, if we resolutely swim on the surface of the dialogue, refusing to be dragged into the depths, we can hardly help noticing—especially in *The Planetarium, The Golden Fruits*, and *Between Life and Death*, her last three novels—that on this level her work can most easily be classified as comedy of manners. Her study in *The Golden Fruits* of the passage of a meretricious novel from fashionable acclaim to equally fashionable oblivion has everything in common with the study of the fads and fancies of intellectual Paris presented by Molière in *Les Précieuses ridicules* or *Les Femmes savantes*.

Why has no critic, to my knowledge at least, written an essay on the comic vision of Nathalie Sarraute? Why has she herself, in her splendid essays on the art of the novel, which often glint with irony for pages on end, never even whispered to us that it is permissible to laugh *with*, though not *at*, her writing? . . .

It took her a long time to get fully under way as a writer, but from the beginning there has been a firm logic in her development. Her works of fiction can be viewed in pairs, perhaps: *Tropisms* contains drafts of a number of passages later reworked in *Portrait of a Man Unknown*; *Martereau* and *The Planetarium* are mature examples of her fiction, satisfying many of the expectations entertained by lovers of the traditional novel; *The Golden Fruits* and *Between Life and Death* are twin tours de force, dealing with the rise and fall of a novel, first from the point of view of its readers and then from that of its author. Yet these pairs will not remain in watertight compartments: *Martereau*, like *Portrait*, is narrated in the first person by a hypersensitive young or youngish man. *The Planetarium* uses "third-person" stream-of-consciousness technique . . . like its successors, and also deals to a great extent with the literary life. . . . I incline to believe that *The Planetarium* is Madame Sarraute's masterpiece. . . .

[As a] new art form, the "Tropism," is hard to define: it falls somewhere between the prose poem and the short-short story. . . . Madame Sarraute's book [*Tropisms*], although written for the ear as well as the eye, will probably always be classified as prose fiction, if only because of its close relationship to *Portrait of a Man Unknown*.

It may be useful to compare and contrast *Tropisms* [first published in 1939] with the short prose works that James Joyce called "Epiphanies"; we must remember, however, that nobody knew what Joyce meant by that term until the publication of *Stephen Hero* in 1944. . . . Thus there is no shadow of possiblity that Madame Sarraute was imitating Joyce. . . .

Joyce seems to believe that by recording externals with the utmost scrupulosity one can implicitly reveal the spiritual poverty of others. It apparently never occurred to the very young Joyce . . . that the inner life of others might be as rich as his own, a shortsighted attitude of which Nathalie Sarraute is never guilty. While often capturing externals skillfully, she constantly probes for the feelings underneath. . . .

In her essays on the novel, Madame Sarraute hankers after the freedom enjoyed by the abstract painter, but she has never, in fact, enjoyed greater freedom than in her first book. All her sketches are plotless, all her human figures are anonymous and to a considerable extent characterless; her urban and rural landscapes are [usually] unidentifiable . . .; indications of epoch and season hardly appear. . . . Yet she does not seem to have relished this freedom sufficiently to keep from writing novels—in which plot, characters, place, and time are difficult to keep at arm's length. . . .

Sartre called *Portrait of a Man Unknown* "this difficult, excellent book," and difficult it certainly is. Even the title is ambiguous, for the *inconnu*, the unknown man, may be either the old father or the younger narrator, or neither of them. Twice in the novel the narrator tells of a painting that haunts him: a portrait of an unknown man by an unknown artist, it hangs in a Dutch museum. The whole painting, except for the eyes, has an unfinished, fragmentary look. . . .

Later this painting is invoked as the narrator's artistic ideal; reading between the lines, one suspects that it also symbolizes Madame Sarraute's ideal for this novel. . . . We begin to see that Madame Sarraute's novel, which shares its title with the painting, has or aims to have some of the same vital incompleteness, the same anxious groping. . . .

[At the end, it] seems almost as though the entire book has melted away in the acid bath of irony that is its last chapter. . . .

The year 1953 was a significant one in French literature: Samuel Beckett's *En attendant Godot* was first performed in Paris in January; *L'Innommable*, the third in his trilogy of French novels, was first published later in the year; Alain Robbe-Grillet's *Les Gommes*, inexplicably hailed by some critics as the first example of *le nouveau roman*, also appeared that year. One might say that by publishing *Martereau* Madame Sarraute was joining the movement, but it would be truer to say that the movement was joining her, since *Portrait*, her most radical break with the traditional novel, was already five years behind her. She in turn had been preceded by the even more experimental novels of Raymond Queneau—but it is doubtful whether she knew *Le Chiendent* or the early versions of *Saint Glinglin*. Even if she had known them, they could not have offered any guidance to one who was seeking to renovate the psychological novel.

Be that as it may, *Martereau* shows us a writer in full control of her innovative technique as well as of her subject matter. . . . [As for ambiguities in *Martereau*,] Madame Sarraute, I am sure, does not want us to make up our minds one way or the other. For the book to achieve its full effect, the various ambiguities should never be resolved. The experience of each one of us probably contains one or many people about whom we cannot make up our minds. So the argument from verisimilitude—that obsession of most novel-readers and novel-critics—can be used to justify ambiguity. A better argument possibly would be that ambiguity is, if not essential to art, at least congenial to it. A psychological case history pretends to certainty for pragmatic reasons; the artist is under no such pressure to rob his characters of mystery. Besides, if our uncertainty were removed, along with it would go a great deal of the book's quiet humor. . . .

*Le Planétarium* . . ., translated as *The Planetarium* in 1960, is the least difficult of Nathalie Sarraute's novels: many of the characters, for instance, possess both first and last names. . . .

*The Planetarium* [is] an extremely entertaining comedy of manners: its surface reminds me most of Jane Austen, though its depths are Proustian; we must not forget, though, that much of Proust's work is itself comedy of manners. . . .

*The Planetarium* will seem to many readers more deserving of an award than *The Golden Fruits* [which won the International Publishers Prize in 1964], but undoubtedly the latter is Madame Sarraute's most original work. It presents a logical stage in the line of development established by her previous novels. . . .

In *The Golden Fruits* Madame Sarraute at last achieves the novelistic ideal adumbrated in her critical essays: no characters, no plot. At least there are no *human* characters, but it would be possible to argue that the imaginary novel "The Golden Fruits" by Bréhier is the central "character" of

Madame Sarraute's book and that the plot—or at any rate the story—concerns the rise, triumph, and fall of Bréhier's novel. Although there are no human characters in *The Golden Fruits*, there are human beings, most of whom have either a first or a last name and sometimes both. But each of them appears only for a page or a few pages, says his say or feels his mute feelings about the imaginary novel, and drops out of sight for good. . . .

Besides the common first names that pepper the book, there are a number of uncommon last names—usually assigned to critics or novelists—that may well have been chosen with a certain malice. They seem like the names one finds in satiric works, and there are certain passages in *The Golden Fruits* which cross the boundary between stylized realism and caricature, between comedy of manners and satire. . . .

A further question naturally arises: is this book a *roman à clef*—do most of the critics and novelists mentioned have recognizable living counterparts? So far as I know, no French critic has suggested the possibility. Indeed, the accepted view of Nathalie Sarraute as an ultra-serious writer seems to preclude the mere asking of such a question. Again, I am suspicious. I have already used the word "caricature": in one passage in particular I see a lampoon either on two living critics or on two imagined exponents of recent trends in French "highbrow" criticism. Other critics and the salon amateurs in the book employ the traditional vocabulary of literary appreciation in France, but this pair engage in a dialogue that seems well rehearsed, using the vocabulary of the new "structural criticism". . . . [In] either French or English the meaning of this duet must be opaque, except possibly to convinced "structuralists." Now that existentialism has gone out of fashion, structuralism is the all-purpose password in French intellectual circles. . . .

[*Between Life and Death* exemplifies] the Sarraute doctrine of the undifferentiated unity of human nature, as expounded in the essay "The Age of Suspicion." In fact, the whole novel preaches it. Every man or woman whose environment makes it possible for him or her to become a moderately successful novelist will have the same experiences and play the same roles. The very anonymity of the protagonist in *Between Life and Death* enables us to identify with him and assures us that we would be he under the same circumstances. . . .

In following the development of Nathalie Sarraute as a novelist, we have seen her begin with an ambition to rival Dostoevsky in his exploration of the obscure depths of human motivation. Then, as she gained mastery of her craft, her feminine humor and acute observation of the surface of upper-middle-class life seemed to be taking her out of the Dostoevskian depths into that well-lit drawing room where Jane Austen presides over the comedy of manners. But in her latest book, even as her humor and irony play over the contradictions and absurdities of the literary life, we see her filling her lungs and readying herself for the plunge. Suddenly, she is down below with Dostoevsky again, searching in the murky depths for those authentic yet unidentifiable impulses toward truth that redeem, even when they cannot excuse, all the petty vanities of the creative writer.

*Vivian Mercier, "Nathalie Sarraute: From Jane Austen to Dostoevsky," in his* The New Novel: From Queneau to Pinget *(reprinted with the permission of Farrar, Straus & Giroux, Inc.; copyright © 1966, 1967, 1968, 1971 by Vivian Mercier), Farrar, Straus, 1971, pp. 104-64.*

Mme Sarraute sees human reality as consisting of myriads of tiny impulses—the famous "tropisms." Some merge together to form streams of emotion, others die out before they reach the level of consciousness, others again oscillate indecisively as "person" comes into contact with "person," either in silence, in speech, or—as is often the case in this book [*Do You Hear Them?*]—in laughter. The word "person" has to be put with inverted commas, because the relationship of the subjective consciousness to the inarticulate behind it or beneath it is just as uncertain as any interpersonal connection. I can tell myself what I am only by means of words taken from the Not-I, that linguistic element in which my mental lungs breathe, just as my physical lungs have to operate in the general atmosphere.

But whereas the oxygen in the physical atmosphere is perpetually renewed, the linguistic atmosphere on which the mind depends is constantly going dead, because given words—"mass-produced words, ready-to-wear words that are already worn to a shred"—can never correspond exactly to the complex novelty of the fresh psychological moment. This is a never-ending complaint with Mme Sarraute. On the one hand, she is constantly dissatisfied with words, because they are always inadequate; on the other hand, she has nothing but words with which to lament their inadequacy and to struggle toward a formulation. . . .

What a Sarraute novel presents us with . . . is a mass of words writhing in dubiety. The author has inevitably to be classed as a "New Novelist," because in the first place, her primary subject or hero or anti-hero is language, rather than anything else. Additional reasons are that she discards plot, linear development, social description, characterization, and definition of the verbal source. . . .

Mme Sarraute's vision of "tropisms" is . . . of an obsessiveness. The question is: does it always bring reality into sharper focus, or does it not sometimes blur things that a more traditional technique might, with advantage, particularize? . . . My difficulty in trying to appreciate Mme Sarraute's books, like some other "New Novels," is that they produce an impression of obscurity without corresponding enlightenment. What I understand them to be saying is a banality translated into linguistic or structural strangeness, rather than a new perception caught with linguistic peculiarity. Are they really an avant-garde, or an arrière-garde making avant-garde gestures?

*John Weightman, "What's Going On Upstairs?," in* The New York Review of Books *(reprinted with permission from* The New York Review of Books; *© 1973 by NYREV, Inc.), April 19, 1973, pp. 30-2.*

Nothing would appear to be more of a fabrication than the *nouveau roman*, of which Nathalie Sarraute continues to turn out her nervertheless utterly personal, crabbed, cranky, grimly literary (at any rate not cinematic!) instances. For Mme. Sarraute, motives continue to range freely between malice and paranoia; the manner is by now as assured as a funeral director's; and the familiar substance becomes thinner and thinner. *Between Life and Death* is the last volume of her trilogy (the first two: *The Planetarium* and *The Golden Fruits*) about French literary life, which she continues to represent as pure murder. . . .

Mme. Sarraute's latest novel [*Do You Hear Them?*] is all bad feeling and no acceptable product at all. . . .

*Marvin Mudrick, in* The Hudson Review *(copyright © 1973 by The Hudson Review, Inc.; reprinted by permission), Vol. XXVI, No. 3, Autumn, 1973, p. 552.*

[In *Do You Hear Them?*] Mme. Sarraute performs exquisitely in the manner she first perfected in *The Planetarium*. There is a magnificently comic disproportion between event and imagination, and the latter swells into exotic growth that dazzles with its preposterous elaboration. . . . As in all of Mme. Sarraute's novels, doubt and distrust—the gnawing suspicion that turns to a consuming obsession—generate savage metaphors and grotesque encounters. The tension between the father and the children (whose age is not clear), so vaguely located between fantasy and actuality, attracts allegorical import: age and youth, tradition and revolution, esthetic devotion and philistinism, high art and Dada mockery, literature and the structuralists. And there are literary reminiscences, if not allusions: Stepan Verkhovensky at the fête in Dostoevsky's *The Possessed*, Mr. Ramsay and his daughters in Virginia Woolf's *To the Lighthouse*, the counterfeiters of Gide's novel. But this is to dissolve Mme. Sarraute's intensity into concepts and instances. What she gives us is brilliant dramatic tension, with all its fluctuation and violent disequilibrium. . . .

Mme. Sarraute has a genius for catching fugitive states of rancor and self-pity, self-transcendence and defensiveness. As in Virginia Woolf's novels the interest lies in the transitions between such states, but in Mme. Sarraute's work the transitions are both rapid and violent; and the metaphors in which the extremes are caught are more extravagant in their heroism or their crassness. Mme. Sarraute is a more ironic novelist than Mrs. Woolf, more ready to see the maudlin and the spiteful, and freer to laugh at them. Her exactitude in recording tropisms, minute turns and shifts of feeling, rules out the direct pursuit of metaphysical depth. She remains the pathologist of belief, serenely detached and awesomely observant.

*Martin Price, in* The Yale Review *(© 1973 by Yale University; reprinted by permission of the editors), Autumn, 1973, pp. 89-91.*

More than one critic has said, of course, that the boringness of the New Novel is a feature of its authenticity. Whereas the old-fashioned novelist strove to entertain, to cut out the dull parts where nothing happens and to present even boring people as being amusing when seen from a particular angle, the best present-day writers (like some contemporary film-makers) do not cheat in this way; the boringness of their writing is meant to correspond exactly to the boringness of existence, so that if the aunt in *Le Planétarium* fusses about her door for pages on end, she is actually intended to be as excruciating as some old dear who corners you in real life. But it is difficult to accept the view that the New Novelist actively intends to bore. . . . Mme Sarraute speaks of the expression of artistic truth as being exciting. In any case, if the aim of art were simply to reproduce the boringness of life, there would be no need for it; life itself would suffice. . . . All art *is*, of course, a stylisation, absolute realism being logically impossible, since life could be totally rendered only by life itself. Mme Sarraute, like every other novelist, is offering us a stylisation. . . .

In the last resort, her books break down into "the good bits" and the traditional or inferior passages which only serve as bridges from one good bit to the next. Fortunately, the good bits are numerous enough to make one feel happy and excited, during the process of reading, at being able to borrow her strength of mind. With the New Novel, I feel that the good bits, such as the visit to the house in *Martereau*, are too few and far between; most of the time, I am being told the obvious, plainly and minutely, and what I would really like to know about the author's mind is being, almost perversely, withheld.

Something missing in all the books, except *Les Fruits d'Or*, is a shape (but even in *Les Fruits d'Or* the shape is not organic; it is engineered from without). I am not asking for an abhorred and old-fashioned "plot", because I agree that the story element is often the least interesting part of a novel. But aesthetic shape means that the artist knows which parts of the work are most important for his sensibility and intelligence. Mme Sarraute's attempt to catch the tiniest movements of the sensibility all the time seems to involve a destruction of perspective. She often appears to be needling away at the fabric of perception to no purpose. . . .

My suspicion is that Mme Sarraute has something to say but that she is not saying it fully.

After all, most of her novels can be read as a critique, monotonous in its ruthlessness, of Parisian, middle-class *mauvaise foi*—a critique, moreover, conducted mainly by means of interior monologue and, inevitably, the interior monologue, even chopped up into very short phrases, is as dated and as artificial a convention as any. There would be nothing wrong with Mme Sarraute's use of it, if she included in her books some indication of the nature of the "authenticity", in the light of which she is presumably stigmatising *la mauvaise foi*. . . . I have to sit and wait without being told what an active form of living might be. Here again, it is not a question of asking for an old-fashioned "message", but of knowing what balance the artist is striking between the various tensions of life. If "tropisms" are pure responses to stimuli, the universe Mme Sarraute is describing is deterministic, and indeed the impression of claustrophobia her novels produce in me comes, I think, from the fact that her characters, however subtle their twitchings, are entirely passive. They never initiate anything; their emotions, which are consistently repulsive or contemptible, wash this way or that without the intervention of any act of conscience, as opposed to mere consciousness.

Now the New Novelists, generally speaking, have eliminated morality as being an antiquated encumbrance. . . . Mme Sarraute has moral feelings; one has only to talk to her to see that this is so, and her books imply the most traditional French form of social, intellectual, and aesthetic contempt for the bourgeois class to which she belongs. The element lacking in the "reality" described in her books is a most important one: the positive manifestation of the conscience which is passing the unfavourable judgment.

*John Weightman, in his* The Concept of the Avant-Garde: Explorations in Modernism, *Alcove, 1973, pp. 307-11.*

In almost all of *Tropismes* characters are referred to as *il* or *elle*, indefinite singular or plural; imperceptible movements take place between these barely delineated characters. Sarraute gives an account of their inaudible speeches, their invisible gestures, their elusive tensions, their unaccountable forces of attraction and repulsion. This hidden world is recorded, without embellishments. . . . We can no more identify the persons than the action they might carry out, we can barely account for their stress or tendencies. Sarraute who refuses to be distracted by the outer, tangible signs detects constant hidden movement. Change, progression or retraction, remain fragmentary or discontinuous, never develop into a full-fledged stage or into a persistent movement. We witness recurring birth, even its embryonic manifestations, without ever attaining an *aim*, an equilibrium. . . .

Contrary to Beckett who reduces interrelations by searching for the fundamental, Nathalie Sarraute strips them of everything but habit and contingency. When Beckett's characters threaten to part they are, merely, unable to formulate tangible reasons for staying together. In Nathalie Sarraute's universe useless tensions and nagging constitute the only level. In Beckett, contradictions express a fundamental uncertainty of human beings, in Nathalie Sarraute contradictions . . . show that our relations amount to a senseless game of hide and seek. . . . The identity of who provokes and who seduces raises unanswerable questions, not only because of complicity but also because any answer would introduce the notion of origin and give the illusion of a time sequence. . . .

What is said merely expresses stagnation. Anonymous creatures feign to look for reality but grope for nothing. Yet their game never exceeds certain limits, the laws of self-preservation governing the instinctive would never let sources of vitality die out. Nathalie Sarraute suggests the sensuality of this interrelation, stripped of outer manifestations. The poetic qualities of these texts, which show the vibration of a life in which gesture and word, self and others interfere, yet remain invisible, are fairly obvious.

*Renée Riese Hubert, in* The International Fiction Review, *January, 1974, pp. 10-11.*

In . . . *Vous les entendez?*, Nathalie Sarraute draws us down, once more, into the depths of the human mind, which she has explored so intensively now for over thirty years. The continuity of her work is remarkable, yet so is its variety, for each new novel explores a fresh aspect of those ever-changing, ambiguous relationships with others, which are as much the substance of our lives as of her novels. Technically, *Vous les entendez?* moves further in the direction which has become gradually more apparent in her last three novels. The narrative thread, never very strong and always subordinate, is here reduced to a single sequence, which is repeated time after time through the novel, and its variations reveal to us the characters and the changes in their relationships. . . .

This sequence is the starting point for an exploration of the relationships between the protagonists. Each repetition of the incident brings a change of mood and a varying of attitudes, for here, as in all her novels, Nathalie Sarraute sees human relationships as a perpetual flux and reflux where characters act, react, counteract in the unending movements which she calls *tropismes* and which she plots so remorselessly, so intimately. . . .

The struggle [in *Vous les entendez?*] between father and children which centres around a certain definition of Art, marks the continuation of a theme which, always present in Nathalie Sarraute's work, has become more dominant in her latest novels. *Les Fruits d'Or* (1963) which describes reactions to a best-selling novel, and *Entre la vie et la mort* (1968) which follows the writing of a novel from genesis to publication, both explore the almost intangible qualities which make one novel a success with the public and another a failure. *Vous les entendez?* widens the field to take in other art forms and continues the debate which Nathalie Sarraute presents, not in terms of a search for esthetic absolutes, but as a perpetual to-and-fro of fashion and of an elusive thing called "good taste." . . .

The protagonists have no physical identity in the novel. They are characterized by their words and by the cult-objects with which they surround themselves, but the link between these two, traditionally constituted by appearance and personality, is totally lacking. We do not know, for example, how many children there are, nor how old they are: they are presented as one collective consciousness from which only occasionally a single element is detached, an "elle," who is a spokeswoman and a leader. This concept of character presents to the reader only basic movements of sympathy, hostility, complicity, abnegation, and always self-justification, but these remain currents of emotion which never freeze into fixed personality traits. . . .

*Vous les entendez?* touches the limits of consciousness and the boundaries of language as communication, yet, at the same time, it emphasizes the necessity for consciousness to affirm its Self and its need for communication with the Other. Father and children are locked in a bitter conflict but neither can exist without that conflict.

*Margaret Groves, in* The International Fiction Review, *January, 1974, pp. 59-61.*

* * *

## SARTON, (Eleanor) May 1912-

**Ms Sarton, born in Belgium, has lived in the United States since 1916. She is an award-winning poet, a novelist, and an autobiographer. (See also *Contemporary Authors*, Vols. 1-4, rev. ed.)**

Miss Sarton understands that we must mistrust the betrayals of technical facility fully as much as those of inarticulateness, and that we must employ whatever skills we may summon in the service of the things that move and shape us as human beings. In almost every poem [in *In Time Like Air*] she attains a delicate simplicity as quickeningly direct as it is deeply given, and does so with the courteous serenity, the clear, caring, intelligent and human calm of the queen of a small, well-ordered country. The only regret Miss Sarton raises is that she is not likely to become much of an "influence." What good effects her practice may have on others will have to take place like the working of a charm or a secret spell: they must be felt in the loving skill with which her poems are built, rather than in the quiet, true, unspectacular sound of her voice.

*James Dickey, "May Sarton" (1958), in his* Babel to Byzantium *(reprinted with the permission of Farrar, Straus & Giroux, Inc.; copyright © 1956, 1957, 1958, 1959, 1960, 1961, 1962, 1963, 1964, 1965, 1966, 1967, 1968 by James Dickey), Farrar, Straus, 1968, p. 73.*

In the only interesting portion of her new book *A Private Mythology,* May Sarton provides us with a fragmented travelogue of Japan, India, and Greece. Practically all of the twenty-six poems in this section are occasional in nature, and many of them are devoted almost exclusively to sensory impressions. She encounters Japan with a sense of wonder. "I inhabit a marvelous world/" she tells us at an inn at Kyoto, "Where every sense is taught/ New ways of perceiving." There are two difficulties with what she learns, and they may or may not be related: the process is too self-conscious, and the products are dull too much of the time. . . . The writing is quaint but accurate, and the syntax does much to convince us that she has realized at least something of the Eastern perspective on natural detail. The poems on Japan, and some of those on India and Greece, are written in a free verse that she handles more successfully than she does the traditional line. After the book returns us to the West and to her extremely clumsy iambs, the poems are consistently bad.

*James McMichael, in* The Southern Review, *Vol. III, No. 2, Spring, 1967, pp. 435-36.*

May Sarton's newest book [*A Durable Fire*], her fourth, is . . . a book I wanted to like because so much of it attests to a difficult psychic growth and harmony perilously established; and, aside from what pain there always must be in criticizing the outcome of such a struggle, one also hopes to learn something from it. . . .

But no matter my respect for the woman for having achieved this serenity, except for an occasional lovely moment she is all too right when she says "Out of the passion comes the form,/ And only passion keeps it warm."

There are many brief evocations of an actual rural world, but it is, every bit of it, so *used* and directed, that what is concrete in it melts and re-freezes as yet another impenetrable abstraction. So, while this kind of poetry appears superficially to work by equivalencies of fact with emotion, nothing in the end has its own real life to begin from: it is all props on which, we are assured, great inner consequences lean. Looking for perceptions of observed nature, all I can find is how they are, one by one, turned immediately to the grasping uses of Human Nature. . . . And none of it convinces me of anything beyond the poet's devouring will that can soften and manipulate anything in the actual world until, sounding wholly fabricated, it can be bent to her uses.

*Rosellen Brown, in* Parnassus, *Spring/ Summer, 1973, pp. 49-50.*

An honest writer, never less than serious in her intent, May Sarton has created [in *As We Are Now*] a convincing record of evil done and good intentions gone astray. The device chosen suits her purpose and strengthens her book: the unity of viewpoint, derived from the use of the journal as a vehicle, reinforces both our sense of Caroline Spencer's isolation and helplessness and our own guilt. She is speaking to us.

But "As We Are Now" has the defects of its virtues. It is almost as if Miss Sarton became careless because she had a strong theme and a viable approach. The book is peppered with clichés . . . and weak statements. . . . There is a tendency to dissipate strong effects by the use of intensive adverbs. . . .

One might argue that this is a journal, and therefore written as the character would have written it; but it is a novel and it must make its effects by art.

*Ellen Douglas, in* The New York Times Book Review *(© 1973 by The New York Times Company; reprinted by permission), November 4, 1973, p. 77.*

Often [Sarton] gives her work (and thus provides us conveniently with) unusually indicative titles: *Kinds of Love* (1970) or the poetic account of love, aging and her time in psychiatry, *A Durable Fire* (1972). *Journal of a Solitude,* in the same year, advances her conviction that it is not in relationships but in maintaining one's aloneness that a creative woman realizes herself. And *The Small Room* (1961), [was] the book that appealed especially to academic women (I was one then) because it raised (but never tried to solve) the question of how it was possible to be productive, scholarly, creative and yet lead the life women were "destined" for.

As a longtime reader of hers I want to join the celebration because I admire the *nature* of her career—serene-seeming despite "the anguish of my life . . . its rages"; her declared traumas of bisexual love, breakdown, conflict; her increasing productivity (to my mind her book published last summer, *As We Are Now* is one of her finest achievements), everything she has written entirely professional, solid yet sensitive. . . .

Love has always lived an uneasy, fitful, secret existence in May Sarton's novels. It enters surreptitiously, it was never meant to be admitted into the ordered life, it takes possession of the reluctant spirit. In *Mrs. Stevens,* it may be because love is irregular, but more I think because it is (as in Thomas Mann) a disruptive and diminishing force working against creative fulfillment and purpose, "love as the waker of the dead, love as conflict, love as the mirage . . . Not love as . . . lasting, faithful giving . . . No, that fidelity, that giving is what the art demands, the art itself, at the expense of every human being," Hilary tells her interviewer.

It makes no difference to us that for May Sarton the Muse is, has been, feminine—love of any kind is always "a costly indulgence in primary emotion." "Would it have ended differently . . . if Dorothea had been a man?" No, because the end is brought about by a vital rage in which "the Muse vanished"; she remembers an earlier lover's words that "we are lepers, we are treated like lepers." Here Sarton is speaking not of lovers alone but of the *artist*: "the creative person, the person who moves from an irrational source of power, has to face the fact that this power antagonizes." For Hilary (and Sarton) the face of the beloved is the gorgon face: "we have turned the Medusa face around and seen our *selves*. The long solitude ahead would be the richer for it." . . .

[Sarton] has examined her sex as subject, and her art as mistress, companion and hazard. She has seen, and made us see, the dangers as well as the joys of living alone. Hers has been a durable fire, despite the fact that criticism and recognition have often ignored her; her small room seems to make most male critics uncomfortable. She accepts love now, perhaps, in a small and secret way.

*Doris Grumbach, "The Long Solitude of May Sarton," in* The New Republic *(reprinted by permission of* The New Republic; *© 1974 by The New Republic, Inc.), June 8, 1974, pp. 31-2.*

F. Hilary Stevens, the 70-year-old protagonist of "Mrs. Stevens Hears the Mermaids Singing" by May Sarton, the author of "Collected Poems (1930-1973)" and of 14 novels, is the author of two novels and six books of poetry. Like her creator, Hilary Stevens has lived abroad, now leads a relatively isolated existence in the New England countryside, loves nature, and has for most of her career been denied the critical acclaim she would have liked to enjoy. Of course, Hilary is ficticious, i. e., she serves her creator's purposes; given Hilary's beliefs and behavior, I would like to think that those purposes include irony, but the evidence suggests that she is Sarton's mouthpiece and perhaps alter ego. . . .

The predominating point of view is Hilary's. So the very form of the novel establishes her as a source of knowledge and enlightenment, an answerer, authoritative if not downright oracular.

Hilary's voice is consistent with the role, employing a public, rhetorical tone and diction even in intimate moments. She tends to make generalizations and pronouncements, particularly with regard to Writing and Women; moreover she fails to distinguish between what is acquired (historical, cultural) and what is inherent, and also among herself, some others, and all others. As a result she makes some very large claims of the form *Women Are*: "Women do not thrive in cities," and "Women are afraid of their daemon, want to control it, make it sensible like themselves," and "Women have to deal with the things men in their wildness and genius have invented."

". . . [We] agree I hope that neither the novel [nor] the poem of ideas is woman's work." Thus Hilary relegates women to literary housekeeping and renders herself incapable of dealing at all with Mary McCarthy and Simone de Beauvoir: "My opinion about these writers can have no interest. I never pretended to be a critic." But that is doubly disingenous of Hilary, because she expresses quite a few critical opinions and because the greatest achievements of these writers have been in non-fiction. Since they do not conform to her theory she dismisses (in effect erases) them, a godlike maneuver. But then *control* is one of the big issues in Hilary's life. The word is used so many times, either by Hilary or about her, that it becomes a kind of verbal tic.

Hilary's sentimental attitudes toward writing and women converge in what she and her interviewers agree is "*the* question"—i. e., the Muse, that sexist fairy-tale figure who personifies Inspiration. Actual, incarnate, female, by no means merely a way of speaking, the Muse is embodied for Hilary in female love-objects. The logical conclusion is that the position of writer is not open to homosexual men and heterosexual women; refusing to say so explicitly. Hilary falls back on the concept of women's work and men's. . . .

So the final solution in a double bind: *woman writer* is a contradiction in terms: "After all, admit it, a woman is meant to create children not works of art—that's what she has been engined to do, so to speak. . . . It's the natural order of things that (a man with talent) construct objects outside himself and his family. The woman who does so is aberrant. . . . [When] the artist is a woman she fulfills (the need to create) at the expense of herself as a woman." A female person who writes must therefore define herself as freaky and/or crippled, as not-a-writer or not-a-woman. If she defines herself as other-than-woman, women must be the Other to her, and in that case she should not pretend to speak for them.

The belief in the feminine sensibility informs Sarton's poetry, too. In "My Sisters, O My Sisters" she expresses a compassionate awareness of women's potentialities and the limits imposed on them, yet she manifests her own complicity in the traditional oppressions, reinforces and perpetuates the damaging myths, by encouraging women "To be Eve . . . To be Mary . . ." and by speaking of "the masculine and violent joy of pure creation—" It is in her intense, delicate, sensuous poems about Japan that Sarton seems to me to most successfully give herself over to and present a "universe of feeling/ Where everything is seen, and nothing mine/ To plead with or possess, only partake of."

The novel, with its special pleading and implicit self-justifying, reads like a gloss on the life work of the author of "Collected Poems" by May Sarton. She deserves more and better than its restrictive attitudes allow. We all do.

*Helen Chasin, in* The Village Voice *(reprinted by permission of* The Village Voice; *© 1974 by the Village Voice, Inc.), June 13, 1974, pp. 36-8.*

May Sarton has done her best with that now expanding novel of feminine consciousness, customarily marked by disease, suffering, old age and death. *As You Are Now* gets them all in as it wheezes to a climax at an old people's home in America. Caro Spencer looks back over a life which seems to be easily divisible into a series of diary entries: her lover, her school, her relatives and her more forbidding passions. These conventional reflections were ruined for me when I realised that their source was a most unpleasant old party, being both boring and snobbish. Mrs Sarton does not seem to realise this, a fact which I can only put down to the Wicked Witch principle of the mirror showing only the fairest of all.

*Peter Ackroyd, "Private Lies," in* The Spectator *(© 1974 by* The Spectator; *reprinted by permission of* The Spectator*), July 27, 1974, pp. 118-19.*

On a first reading, May Sarton's story [*Punch's Secret*]

seems simple and touching—lonely, Punch the parrot "longs for someone small to love," and that night "a sweet wild mouse" comes into his cage and becomes his "secret friend in the dark." But as I read this simple and touching story a second and a third time, I wondered why, like one of Miss Sarton's fine poems, it yielded increasingly complex and disturbing resonances. The book's final sentence, "it is good to have a secret friend in the dark," was not comforting but a cause for anxiety, suggesting that darkness is a more fundamental condition of life than friendship. What if one doesn't have a friend in the dark? Why should having a friend be a secret? . . .

What *is* Punch's secret? And from whom is he keeping it? As much as I was moved by this book, there's something unconvincingly passive about Miss Sarton's conception of Punch, something unacceptably accepting. I think Punch is keeping his secret to himself—that he'd really like to bite those "kind" hands that cover his cage at night, that he dreams not so much of "someone small to love" but of flapping his wings and rising swiftly above the treetops, screaming against the sky.

*Ross Wetzsteon, in* The New York Times Book Review *(© 1974 by The New York Times Company; reprinted by permission), September 1, 1974, p. 8.*

* * *

## SARTRE, Jean-Paul 1905-

**Sartre, a Frenchman, has been described as an "iconoclast, idealist, muckraker, playwright, novelist, philosopher, [and] amateur politician." All of Sartre's immense literary output may be seen as implementation of his Existentialist philosophical position. A brilliant thinker and writer, Sartre is one of the most influential literary figures in the world today. (See also *Contemporary Authors*, Vols. 9-12, rev. ed.)**

A schoolteacher, professor of philosophy, [Sartre published] his first literary work as an adult in 1938. And then, nothing less than the novel *Nausea (La Nausée)*. It is followed in 1939 by the novellas in the volume *The Wall (Le Mur)*, and then suddenly a writer emerges who commands all the forms: Horror and grim irony, formal and colloquial dialogue, dream conversations and the most precise philosophical analysis. Aside from this, there are his essays about Faulkner, Dos Passos, and Giraudoux, a philosophical novel about the power of the imagination—about the imaginary—and later a metaphysical work, *Being and Nothingness (L'Être et le néant)*. Finally, the philosopher and novelist publishes his first drama, *The Flies (Les Mouches)*, which is performed in Paris with great success. It, too, is a masterpiece of craftsmanship, as is everything which has appeared up to now under the name of Sartre. One after the other, after such a long silence, the works and actions all strengthen the impression of the extraordinary, the incomparable. They are all internally connected without showing the slightest sign of popularized or trivial thinking. They are true works of literature which have an effect and disturb in those places where their true depth is unsuspected.

However, the abyss is wide open under this work. It is totally open because it is identical with existence itself. Nietzsche's hopeful nihilism appears played out in view of this relentless, disciplined objectivism of Sartre, who does not allow existence to become endowed with any meaning. Existence in and by itself is meaningless: there is neither the Christian nor the humanistic life. Life—existence as such—means contaminated, meaningless physical drives. Whoever seeks to find in these drives meaning and order, mission or foresight, selection or predestination, deceives himself and others. . . . This lesson is drawn throughout Sartre's novels in a variety of pictures and bright parables.

But, what should become of art and genius, creative life and experience, if our existence removes itself from all categories, the ethical as well as the aesthetic? Suddenly Sartre's work reveals a totally different face. Nihilism served to make a clear division of the spheres. It was far removed from all metaphysical despair. Pessimism was a necessity for thought, not an affectation. Next to the meaningless being came nonexistent meaning. Art. It recognizes necessity and meaningful form, laws and categories, beauty and greatness. But all for a price—that of being non-existent. It is necessary because all that is created intellectually apears as unreal. It escapes time, chance, meaninglessness, which have mercilessly characterized all that which exists. . . .

Life and stories about life are irreconcilable concepts: the one is without spirit, arbitrary, meaningless; the other creates the necessary, a meaning, and laws for the price of its reality. Whoever tells stories, composes melodies, or writes stories offers form, perhaps consolation. However, only because the art works are fictitious.

Sartre's final word, however, is not this aesthetic ideality or imagination. The Atreus drama *The Flies* reveals a new aspect. Sartre combines his experimentation with a new form, the dramatic, with a new chapter in his interpretation of the world. Next to aesthetics, there is ethics. Here, too, he is concerned with Electra and Orestes, with the gods and the Eumenides—as in Giraudoux's *Electra*. A drama about the twilight of the gods, about the turning point in time just as in Giraudoux, where the last word is the double meaning of the word "dawn." Orestes frees the city from the gods. Through this deed man deliberately frees himself without remorse from a world ruled by the gods. The law of the gods is turned against the gods: the law gave man the freedom which he used to take his affairs upon himself. Here, too, existence is without a plan: the belief in a divine world scheme is pure illusion. Orestes proves this by his deed. The gods have been banished; fear is removed from man; the "metaphysical age" of Auguste Comte is replaced by the positive. In spite of all this, chaos does not emerge. The Eumenides pursue Orestes. The city is free of fear, but the individual is not free in his actions. The world of appearance and art alone cannot establish meaning. The world of action must also be included. Next to fiction stands action. Both leave behind an impression, a picture of that which they encounter. Everyone is followed by pictures and reproduction of his actions. In the final analysis, he "is" only through their reflection—as through the reflection of the art that he creates. The freedom of the act transforms itself into a necessary fiction of the picture that leaves the act for the outside world. Is this still ethics? Is it still aesthetics? Certainly the work, the act alone, conveys meaning to life, which would still be meaningless by itself. . . . But isn't there a deeper, richer meaning of meaninglessness conveyed through art? Sartre gave no answer to this. . . .

Three years after the liberation of France, Sartre undertook to answer the question. What is literature? His comprehensive essay reads as though one were climbing a mountain: excursions and digressions and a mixture of sociological, psychological, and aesthetic observations allow us to recognize the author of the philosophical treatise *Being and Nothingness* and also the Sartre who wrote the *Critique of Dialectical Reason*. His essay on literature goes around in spirals to its summit. . . .

This balance of the records by Sartre concerning the principles behind his work (this is nominally what it is about) is indeed remarkable. One of the finest works by Jean-Paul Sartre. He is possibly at his best as an *essayist*. The term is understood here not in the narrow sense of a cultural or literary critic but in the broad traditional sense which he may claim to have developed out of the tradition of Montaigne. The essay sections in Sartre's philosophical treatises are always the high points and represent for some a compensation for "weaker parts." . . .

All Sartre's literary works are demonstrations of his philosophical theories. All the figures in Sartre's stories, dramas, and novels are exemplifications and hardly have a right to exist "in and by themselves." . . .

In Sartre's novels and plays, man lives in a world that is unrecognizable to him, one which appears to him to be illogical, incomprehensible, completely meaningless. There is neither a law of history nor a transformation of reality through common efforts. Each action has a significance only for the one who acts. The narrator or the dramatist is in no better position than his characters. Since he does not know more than they do, he cannot think of assuming the attitude of the director or the omniscient narrator. . . .

An artistic contradition arises here. A contradiction that seems to be insoluble, and even Sartre, an extraordinarily gifted man, could not overcome it with all the means of his talents. He demands that the theater once again become a moral institution. This conception belongs to the theme of the Enlightenment that can be constantly observed in Sartre's thought and work. Thus, nothing would be more absurd than to bring Sartre's plays together with the so-called theater of the absurd. Sartre is the opposite of a thinker and writer of absurdity. *His opposition to Camus is based on this*. He is a moralist and cannot conceive of literature without a function.

However, the moralizing of this author with his conception of mere life situations in an unrecognizable world continually falls into conflicts. A literature with a moralizing function must strive to involve the theater audience as well as the reader with the action of the figures. Either through identification or distance. There is empathy and alienation. In both cases the author determines the nonliterary effect of his work. However, moralization and functionalism are not possible when there is only a world of situations and abrupt actions that are not based on the nature of character or causal events. Either the situational concept of a freedom in the incongruous individual action that is valid for no one else but the one who is acting, since no one else goes through the same situation, or—literary moralizing. Both together are not possible. Thus, it becomes clear why Sartre's dramas, stories, and novels, though always captivating because of their intellectual intensity, can never lead to any kind of non-literary life decision by the reader and spectator the way Sartre seems to wish they could. Sartre's heroes always live in a unique situation especially prepared for them. The way in which they cope with the situation cannot be accomplished by anyone else or repeated by anyone else. No matter what Sartre might introduce, their way must remain without a function. . . .

The writer Sartre seeks a literature of "not only/but also." . . .

It becomes apparent why writing could initially be nothing less for Sartre than literature of commitment. Moreover, one senses [that] the great essayist Jean-Paul Sartre later had to dismiss the opposition between "pure" and "committed" literature as an artifical antithesis. This was because the choice of a seemingly nonmissionary literature was understood as a special form of commitment—thus Sartre's passionate interest in Baudelaire. As is known, Sartre remained true to this basic position, which called for existential options. The complete works of this philosopher, sociologist, dramatist, politician, and novelist are rooted in a strange amalgamation of Corneille and Pardaillan. ["*Translator's note:* Pardaillan was a knight who appeared as hero of a serial written by Michael Zévaco for the newspaper *Le Matin*. As a boy Sartre read this serial with great enthusiam and Pardaillan came to represent for him a champion of the people."]

However, what happens to an author who gradually catches himself at his own tricks and must recognize that the beloved Pardaillan and the somewhat less beloved Michael Strogoff, famous courier of the Czars, are slightly degenerate epic heroes in keeping with their literary genres while they play the role of substitute redeemers in an existential sphere? After such a realization a second secularization is due. In the process the belief in a religion of art is dropped as well as the belief in the possibility and necessity of literary commitment. In anticipation of later events, Sartre accomplishes this double expulsion in the last pages of *The Words*: he banishes substitute religion and commitment. Nonetheless he continues to write. He continues to commit himself. . . .

Sartre takes his philosophy absolutely seriously. Therefore, it becomes apparent once again why, in spite of all his efforts to create a synthesis out of Marxism and existentialism, he could never really come close to Marxism. His ontology and eschatology reject the basic Marxist principle of a dialectic subject-object relationship as well as the materialistic thesis of the "primacy of the external world." Aside from this, it becomes evident the *The Words* that Sartre also had to disavow Marxist dialectics in the relationship between theory and practice. Theory as ideology, as false consciousness, is understood under the negative aspect of total atheism. A theory of history can never accept this thesis of consciousness as impersonal spontaneity. Philosophy of history and *creatio ex nihilo* cancel each other out. In other words, practice without theory. Practice in and of itself. But also, practice as a substitute religion.

The freedom, which the last pages of *The Words* appear to proclaim, proves to be a new metaphysical bond. It is merely a condition, a "situation," and therefore, it can be resolved—abrupt in action, absurd in substance—by a new decision. This is because it became clear that the situation of being totally without illusions also represented a form of commitment and, along with this, institutionalization. Sartre is well aware of this.

*Hans Mayer, "Observations on the Situation of Sartre" (originally published in Ansichten zur Literatur der Zeit; © 1962 by Rowohlt Verlag GMBH), in his* Steppenwolf and Everyman, *translated by Jack D. Zipes (copyright © 1971 by Hans Mayer; reprinted with permission of Thomas Y. Crowell Co., Inc.), Crowell, 1971, pp. 213-39.*

*Saint Genet* is a cancer of a book, grotesquely verbose, its cargo of brilliant ideas borne aloft by a tone of viscous solemnity and by ghastly repetitiveness. . . . Sartre breaks every rule of decorum established for the critic; this is criticism by immersion, without guidelines. The book simply plunges into Genet; there is little discernible organization to Sartre's argument; nothing is made easy or clear. One should perhaps be grateful that Sartre stops after six hundred and twenty-five pages. The indefatigable act of literary and philosophical disembowelment which he practices on Genet could just as well have gone on for a thousand pages. Yet, Sartre's exasperating book is worth all one's effort of attention. *Saint Genet* is not one of the truly great, mad books; it is too long and too academic in vocabulary for that. But it is crammed with stunning and profound ideas.

What made the book grow and grow is that Sartre, the philosopher, could not help (however reverentially) upstaging Genet, the poet. What began as an act of critical homage and recipe for the bourgeois literary public's "good use of Genet" turned into something more ambitious. Sartre's enterprise is really to exhibit his own philosophical style—compounded of the phenomenological tradition from Descartes through Husserl and Heidegger, plus a liberal admixture of Freud and revisionist Marxism—while writing about a specific figure. In this instance, the person whose acts are made to yield the value of Sartre's philosophical vocabulary is Genet. . . .

Sartre wants to be concrete. He wants to reveal Genet, not simply to exercise his own tireless intellectual facility. But he cannot. His enterprise is fundamentally impossible. He cannot catch the real Genet; he is always slipping back into the categories of Foundling, Thief, Homosexual, Free Lucid Individual, Writer. Somewhere Sartre knows this, and it torments him. The length, and the inexorable tone, of *Saint Genet* are really the product of intellectual agony.

The agony comes from the philosopher's commitment to impose meaning upon action. Freedom, the key notion of existentialism, reveals itself in *Saint Genet*, even more clearly than in *Being and Nothingness*, as a compulsion to assign meaning, a refusal to let the world alone. According to Sartre's phenomenology of action, to act is to change the world. Man, haunted by the world, acts. He acts in order to modify the world in view of an end, an ideal. An act is therefore intentional, not accidental, and an accident is not to be counted as an act. Neither the gestures of personality nor the works of the artist are simply to be experienced. They must be understood, they must be interpreted as modifications of the world. Thus, throughout *Saint Genet*, Sartre continually moralizes. He moralizes upon the acts of Genet. . . . Although Sartre occasionally refers to things which he knows through his own friendship with Genet, it is almost entirely the man revealed by his books of whom Sartre speaks. It is a monstrous figure, real and surreal at the same time, all of whose acts are seen by Sartre as meaningful, intentional. This is what gives *Saint Genet* a quality that is clotted and ghostly. The name "Genet" repeated thousands of times throughout the book never seems to be the name of a real person. It is the name given to an infinitely complex process of philosophical transfiguration.

Given all these ulterior intellectual motives, it is surprising how well Sartre's enterprise serves Genet. This is because Genet himself, in his writings, is notably and explicitly involved in the enterprise of self-transfiguration. Crime, sexual and social degradation, above all murder, are understood by Genet as occasions for glory. It did not require much ingenuity on Sartre's part to propose that Genet's writings are an extended treatise on abjection—conceived as a spiritual method. The "sanctity" of Genet, created by an onanistic meditation upon his own degradation and the imaginative annihilation of the world, is the explicit subject of his prose works. What remained for Sartre was to draw out the implications of what is explicit in Genet. Genet may never have read Descartes, Hegel, or Husserl. But Sartre is right, entirely right, in finding a relation in Genet to the ideas of Descartes, Hegel, and Husserl. . . .

*Saint Genet* is a book about the dialectic of freedom, and is, formally at least, set in the Hegelian mold. What Sartre wants to show is how Genet, by means of action and reflection, has spent his whole life attaining the lucid free act. Cast from his birth in the role of the Other, the outcast, Genet chose himself. This original choice is asserted through three different metamorphoses—the criminal, the aesthete, the writer. Each one is necessary to fulfill freedom's demand for a push beyond the self. Each new level of freedom carries with it a new knowledge of the self. Thus the whole discussion of Genet may be read as a dark travesty on Hegel's analysis of the relations between self and other. Sartre speaks of the works of Genet as being, each one of them, small editions of *The Phenomenology of Mind.* Absurd as it sounds, Sartre is correct. But it is also true that all of Sartre's writings as well are versions, editions, commentaries, satires on Hegel's great book. This is the bizarre point of connection between Sartre and Genet; two more different human beings it would be hard to imagine.

In Genet, Sartre has found his ideal subject. To be sure, he has drowned in him. Nevertheless, *Saint Genet* is a marvellous book, full of truths about moral language and moral choice.

*Susan Sontag, "Sartre's 'Saint Genet'" (1963), in her* Against Interpretation and Other Essays *(reprinted with the permission of Farrar, Straus, & Giroux, Inc.; copyright © 1961, 1962, 1963, 1964, 1965, 1966 by Susan Sontag), Farrar, Straus, 1966, pp. 93-9.*

In his time, Sartre has gone into the ring with nearly every literary form, except poetry: novels, plays, stories, philosophy, aesthetics, politics and criticism. With immense industry, spouting ideas like some huge, hard-working Moby Dick of the intellectual life, he has effortlessly dominated the Paris scene since the war. Yet he is a curious phenomenon: a great influence, a great figure in the landscape, yet never quite a great writer. His philosophy, apparently, is not startling original and is, certainly, expressed far too obscurely to have had anything but a most sidelong influence. How many of the professed Existentialists have really read *L'Être et le Néant*? And how many of them have really understood it? It strikes me as being written as though deliberately to defy analysis. Even more certainly, he is not a great creative writer, for all the compulsive readability of his novels—like a highbrow Ian Fleming—or the tensely dramatic situations of his plays. All that brilliance gets in the way of the human thing which is, after all, what literature is about. The books are too full of good ideas to be true. Tease them out as problems and they seem all very profound and subtle; but they *feel* shallow.

Yet this combination of talents—both exceptional, neither quite overwhelming—blends into something wholly pervasive. Sartre is influential because he is a philosopher who gave his ideas flesh and set them intriguingly in action. He is also a novelist and playwright whose work gains dignity by echoing an elaborately structured world of ideas. As such, he belongs to a special sub-division of literature, the School of Brilliance: its alumni include Voltaire and George Bernard Shaw, Anatole France and Aldous Huxley. It is a school that relies, to use old-fashioned terms, more on invention than imagination. That is, the writers' fecundity with plots, situations, aphorisms and striking, unexpected ornaments is endless, but their people are two-dimensional props for ideas, voices in a crackling but bleak world of abstractions.

*A. Alvarez, "Jean-Paul Sartre" (originally published in* The Spectator, *1964), in his* Beyond All This Fiddle: Essays 1955-1967 *(copyright © 1968 by A. Alvarez; reprinted by permission of Random House, Inc.), Random House, 1969, pp. 128-32.*

One of the most maddening things about Jean-Paul Sartre is how he continually promises, and continually fails, to be a poet of the stage. Buried somewhere deep inside of him there is an inventive theatre artist capable of fertile theatrical concepts, but while he thoroughly explores the philosophical implications of these concepts, he leaves their imaginative possibilities virtually untapped. What Sartre ultimately lacks is the artist's commitment to form: of all his dramatic works, only the short play *No Exit* seems to enjoy a structure congenial to its theme. As for the others, they all look like uneasy collaborations between a deft original thinker and a clumsy derivative playwright, for despite their intellectual vitality and suggestive scenic strategies, they invariably bog down into talky scenes, old-fashioned dramaturgy, and unconvincing character motivations that lessen the impact of their ideas. . . .

His virtues stem from an adventurous mind, his faults from an inability to be equally adventurous in his use of the stage. As a thinker, Sartre has no peers among contemporary playwrights, but he has not yet learned to forge his ideas into powerful myths. He is certainly a dramatist, but one who presently looks backward, even as he is pushing forward intellectually to the limits of human thought.

*Robert Brustein, "Sartre, the Janus" (1966), in his* The Third Theater *(copyright © 1958, 1960, 1961, 1964, 1965, 1966, 1967, 1968, 1969 by Robert Brustein; reprinted by permission of Alfred A. Knopf, Inc.), Knopf, 1969, pp. 165-68.*

In Romantic literature, of which Existentialism can be seen as a logical continuation, it is other people who are wrong in their failure to recognize the solitary man of genius when he appears. For the Sartre of *Les Mots*, the writer whom Iris Murdoch described so accurately in 1953 as a "Romantic Rationalist," it becomes the others, the handsome, agile children in the Luxembourg gardens, the "fils du peuple" who totally ignore the young Sartre when he joins their class at school, who are right to judge the solitary individual according to their lights. Moreover, this tendency to set the group above the individual is not peculiar to Sartre's autobiography. It occurs in *Le Diable et le Bon Dieu* (1951), where Goetz is presented as acting correctly when he gives up his attempt to secure individual salvation and devotes himself instead to serving the collective interests of the peasants, and the idea of preferring collective to individualistic values is already suggested by the preference given to Hoederer over Hugo in *Les Mains sales*. In *Les Séquestrés d'Altona*, Franz von Gerlach is criticized for attempting to escape the judgment of his contemporaries and seek refuge in the verdict of History, and even Jean Genet, so often considered as a kind of existentialist hero, is violently attacked in *Saint Genet, comédien et martyr* for seeking to attain through sainthood a position where he would be immune to merely mortal judgments. It is almost as if, in these individual texts as well as in his more general readiness to adopt a Marxist point of view on so many social and ethical problems, Sartre were trying to compensate for his failure to be accepted by his contemporaries when he was a child. The idea that there might, in some respects, be real though long-term advantages in having had a lonely and unhappy childhood is almost totally lacking in *Les Mots*, and it is again instructive to compare Sartre, in this respect, with those lonely children who became philosophers—Jean-Jacques Rousseau, John Stuart Mill, and Bertrand Russell. Whereas Sartre regrets the isolation forced upon him, they all come, on reflection, to look upon this early solitude as containing the ultimate source for their present strength. "Thou shalt not follow a multitude to do evil" was the text held up as an ethical ideal to the young Russell by the grandmother who brought him up, and the whole of Russell's life can be seen as a laudable if sometimes misguided effort to carry out this injunction. Sartre does not, of course, suggest that we should follow a multitude to do wrong just because it is a multitude. His refusal of the Nobel Prize for Literature, like his courageous stand on a number of controversial political issues, reveals something of the Protestant ethic so dear to the Schweitzers, and there is little doubt that he would, like Russell, have

Dared to be a Daniel
Dared to stand alone
Dared to have a purpose clear
Dared to make it known.

Yet for all the encouragement to unorthodoxy that may be derived both from his early work and from his later public attitudes, Sartre's actual description of his own early life offers at the moment little support for the basic existentialist position that it is the unhappy outsider whose experience is potentially of the most value. . . .

It is an established convention that the novels and biographies inspired by our most famous politicians and business leaders, from the real Winston Churchill to the partly fictional Citizen Kane, should begin by tracing the hero's drive and ambition to the physical or emotional deprivations of his childhood, and Sartre is only being more honest than many other highly successful men when he writes that he detests his childhood and everything that it has done to form his character (*"je déteste mon enfance et tout ce qui en survit"*). What is original and paradoxical about *Les Mots* is the lie which the book gives by its very form to the ideas which it expresses. For some two hundred brilliantly written pages Sartre derides the literary calling which alone has enabled him to impose this vision of his childhood so effectively on his readers. For all the apparent rejection of his ideas on freedom and determinism of his optimism about man and society, of the important political role which he once saw the writer as capable of fulfilling, and for all the scorn he shows towards the child whose unhappiness continues to inspire everything he does, Sartre has not abandoned the fruits to which this unhappiness has given birth. He is still, in *Les Mots* itself, one of the best stylists in modern French literature, one of the keenest and wittiest observers of other human beings, one of the most perceptive of social thinkers. Even though Sartre himself may not, in retrospect, think that the game has been worth the candle, his readers undoubtedly do. Whatever else he may have rejected of the Existentialist and Romantic position, he has certainly kept, in practice at any rate, the idea of the pearl produced by an irritation in the oyster.

*Philip Thody, "Sartre's Autobiography: Existential Psychoanalysis or Self-Denial?" in* The Southern Review*, Vol. V, No. 4, Autumn, 1969, pp. 1030-44.*

*La Nausée* is a concentrated, knotted kind of book. There is nothing much in the way of a plot—no development of situations and no ripening of human relationships. But this is deliberate, for Sartre wishes to show, among other things, the banal routine of everyday life in which people conceal from themselves the basic absurdity of their existence. Nothing meaningful will ever happen to the citizens of Bouville: they will forever continue to go to work, to sit in cafés, to discuss trivialities, and to believe in the permanence of human structures. The development of the novel is in the deepening of Roquentin's nausea and his analysis of the absurdity, the sheer contingency of existence, which is its cause. The climax is reached when he decides to return to Paris to write his 'hard as steel' book. Yet we suspect that this is really an anti-climax, for it is hard to see how a book written by a superfluous individual can declare its own inherent necessity and thereby make people 'ashamed of their existence.' The solution to Roquentin's problem does not, we feel, lie here.

On the other hand, we may feel that *La Nausée* is *too* concentrated, that too much of life is omitted and that what Sartre has presented is a distortion. Probably all of us from time to time share the feeling of Roquentin that our own existence is dissolving into Nothingness, but most of us are too busy to attend for long to these private fancies. We have our work to do and our families to support and there are even moments when the banal rountines of our day-today lives seem to clarify and reveal a glimpse of meaning. . . . Certainly there is nothing in Sartre's novel to counter-balance or alleviate the sense of nausea: all meanings crash down in ruin. Learning, culture, human friendship, even the 'perfect moments' of love—all are destroyed by the rot of absurdity.

Yet as an artist Sartre is surely entitled to concentrate as he does in *La Nausée*, for art may legitimately seek to isolate and define a bit of human experience whose significance is usually lost amid the welter of life. The question we have to ask is whether Sartre succeeds in forcing us to recognize the presence of nausea in ourselves and whether he convinces us that we have paid too little heed to it. Perhaps, like the people of Bouville, we are also guilty of living an unjustified, superfluous existence whose true nature we conceal from ourselves by routine actions and habits of thought. It may be of vital importance that we recognize the implications of nausea and stop thinking of it as a temporary malaise. Salvation may depend upon knowing the worst and shedding delusion. . . .

There is a world of difference between a nihilism so terrible and inescapable that it leads to madness or suicide, and a nihilism which is merely a fashionable pose, though it may be doubted whether the latter would exist if the former did not. It is, I think, undeniable that genuine nihilism is more common in the literature of our time than in that of other periods. As Sartre says, we have reached the stage of having to *decide* to live. In an age in which *cosmic* suicide has become possible, such a decision is of literally vital importance.

If we are Christians, we shall not despise the feelings of a Roquentin, nor shall we persuade ourselves that he is merely a poseur. We may think, rather, that nausea is not so far removed from what St. Paul called 'the exceeding sinfulness of sin'—the experience of finding that the props of culture, work, social enjoyment, and even religion itself, are shoring up a building whose foundations are unsupported. We may, from our point of view, say that nausea is the discovery that our existence is unjustified because we have lost God and cannot create ourselves; that all our substitutes for God are false and useless. We may readily agree with Sartre that man cannot be understood merely in terms of a social or cultural context and that there always comes a point at which we recognize how spurious is the confidence we place in our defensive structures, how easily they crumble away and leave us 'unaccommodated'. But we may also wish to claim that God in Christ is present with us even in the depths of our self-despair.

Behind the novels of Sartre stands his Existentialist philosophy, and one wonders whether the characters he invents are more like exemplars of a theory than possible individuals. But Existentialism is not supposed to be a theory about human existence—only one of many rival interpretations—formulated ideologically; it is meant to be descriptive of what it is actually like to be a human being, and that is why it is most appropriately expressed in dramatic form. Even Sartre's major theoretical work, *Being and Nothingness*, is full of homely examples drawn from life. The difficulty is that Sartre, like all morally serious writers, is concerned not only with what men do but also with what they *ought* to do, not only with how they actually understand themselves but with how they *ought* to understand themselves. He wants to break down all the bogus structures, to strip off the layers of falsehood and self-deception, and to reveal the authentic being of man. But this implies a theory about the nature of 'authentic' being which itself stands in need of some authentication. For the most part, Sartre's writings attempt to provide this negatively, by presenting to us a pageant of individuals who are manifestly living *in*authentically and by leaving us to infer from their failure the lines along which we are to look for success. This makes his novels and plays on the whole rather depressing and even inhuman. . . .

Nietzsche and Sartre bid us rejoice and enter exultantly into our freedom, welcoming the dawn which has at last broken after the long night of human bondage. The twentieth-century sickness turns out to be convalescence after the illness of faith, and soon we shall rise from our beds and inaugurate the reign of Man, for whom all is now permitted.

In view of the heroism and adventure implied by this gospel, we may be puzzled to know why it is that the writings of Sartre are so depressing. In them, we see people being brought, with tremendous reluctance and struggle, to the starting-line of freedom, but we seldom seem to see them actually running in the promised race. The reason for this is perhaps that it is not really possible for Sartre to make predictions or offer models without denying his own existentialist doctrine. Sartre has repudiated all absolutes and all objective values; man finds himself cast upon a meaningless universe in which there are no sign-posts, no maps, no marked-out routes to follow, not even a concept of human nature from which some sort of guidance may come. Each man must create his own essence and no one else can do it for him. To offer models is to play the part of God and to bring man back into servitude. Sartre will place you at absolute zero, the starting-line of freedom, but after that you are on your own. Absolute zero is a rather depressing spot, which is why Sartre's novels are rather depressing novels.

But Sartre's intense moral seriousness requires him to insist that it is better to be depressed than deluded. To live without God and without ultimate meanings is a difficult calling, and we prefer our delusions, the lies we tell ourselves, because they persuade us that we have a grip on existence. But to be a man in the twentieth century is to see these delusions for what they really are and to be challenged to live without them. We are being summoned by a serious call to a life of responsibility and freedom, to a work of demolition on the spurious orders of belief and convention within which men have been imprisoned throughout the centuries of faith. . . .

There is, therefore, a sense in which Sartre and other contemporary writers are recalling us to the kind of life which Jesus himself placed before us—a life, that is, which is creative and open to the future because it is free from stultifying moral prescriptions. The difference is that Sartre believes that such a life can be self-generated, whereas Jesus believed it could come only if a man opened himself up to the will of God.

*David Anderson, in his* The Tragic Protest *(© SCM Press Ltd., 1969; used by permission of John Knox Press), John Knox, 1969, pp. 27-48.*

* * *

## SCHWARTZ, Delmore 1913-1966

**Schwartz, an important American poet, playwright, and short story writer, is best known for *In Dreams Begin Responsibilities*. (See also *Contemporary Authors*, Vols. 17-18; obituary, Vols. 25-28.)**

There have been other tragic generations before the one we identify with Robert Lowell, John Berryman, Randall Jarrell, and Delmore Schwartz, perhaps Sylvia Plath as well. Yeats, in *Autobiographies*, called his "The Tragic Generation," and it was the last sentence in that chapter that A. Alvarez made the title of his book, *The Savage God*, on writers and suicide.

Theirs *has been* a tragic generation, an overpublicized truth, and with the exception of Lowell, a generation where the sons died before the fathers (in this case, John Crowe Ransom and Allen Tate). It's even possible that, having listened to their voices over and over, we know too much about them, or at least more than we should. Since Lowell, Berryman, Schwartz, and Jarrell were all close friends, and since the mode in which all of them expressed themselves was intimate, involved with self-revelation (I hope that M. L. Rosenthal's unfortunate label, "Confessional poetry," is now no longer in use), we come to learn their histories through their own poems. The biographies are there to be read. Lowell addresses Berryman in the *Notebook*, Berryman addresses God, who "wrecked our generation"; somehow, though, the magnitude of what happened to these lives is lost, and if we've learned to value the poems themselves, to be aware in our own time that *Homage to Mistress Bradstreet, Life Studies*, and Jarrell's long meditative poems are American classics, still I sense that our appreciation of their work is incomplete.

What informs this suspicion above all is that Delmore Schwartz has been so neglected; nothing demonstrates this more than the fact that virtually no book of his remains in print. . . .

In [Schwartz's] seven books I discovered a voice so brilliant, ardent, and complicated that it threatened to drown out all others. It seems to me now that Schwartz's idiom was the most accomplished and unusual of that celebrated generation, and that his odd, comical, tortured sensibility was, at least when obsessed with self-examination, the most honest. . . .

The question to be asked is the same Schwartz asked about Ring Lardner, whose life ended in a similar decline: "why so successful and gifted a human being suffered so much and so helplessly."

There are some obvious sources to examine; no writer ever revealed more than Schwartz about his own psychoanalytic history, the subject which lies at the center of all he wrote. . . . So pressing was the desire to relive traumas rooted in the child's earliest development that Schwartz turned often to verse drama, simply in order to be on stage, tormented soliloquist in a play of his own devising. . . . All the motifs and properties of Schwartz's later work are in [his] play [*Shenandoah*]: the masterful, controlled blank verse passages alternating with prose commentaries; the comical, extended metaphors (birth resembles "the descent/ Of a small grand piano from a window"); jokes, in the best tradition of ironic Jewish humor (when someone expresses the hope that the child will live to be 110, Shenandoah admonishes: "He should know better what long life avails,/ The best seats at the funerals of friends"); a serious reliance on Freud; and the sad eloquent meditations on art in its relation to society. . . .

Most of his stories take place during the Depression, and in New York, so that the landscape through which the speaker moves is intensely local: the lower middle-class apartment, awkward immigrant parents, the cut-glass chandeliers above the dining room table. Shenandoah exhorts the audience to "see the Particular as Universal," and it was this quality that Schwartz possessed in such ample measure. His portrait of that era accomplishes more than a chronicle or memoir ever could because it's anchored in references which appear in their natural context: at a party, someone takes down Edmund Wilson's *Axle's Castle* from the shelf and reads a notable passage aloud; in *The World is a Wedding*, none of the loquacious characters, in their twenties, are employed; in *A Bitter Farce*, Shenandoah teaches a class on Louis Adamic's essay, "Plymouth Rock and Ellis Island," while in another story, *New Year's Eve*, he becomes "locked in what was soon to be a post-Munich sensibility; complete hopelessness of perception and feeling."

But it is more than some vague social oppression that Schwartz's protagonists feel; their hopelessness is encouraged by those around them, who jealously guard their own insecure selves against any violation. At the disastrous party chronicled in *New Year's Eve*, Shenandoah laments "the self-pity which wept in him," while "in other cages of the room, other human beings were trying without success to get along with each other." It's no accident that the corners in which these tortured, clever, ineffectual people spar more than converse are described as cages; Schwartz's view of human relationships emerges in his prose with a terrible poignance, and among the consistent features of the situations he examined are entrapment and the claustral effects of Others on his nervous personae. In *The Child is the Meaning of This Life*, where the precocious Jasper Hart grows up amidst an oppressive environment of insensitivity and failure, only later coming to realize that "he looked at the adult world as he had had to look at his mother, suspicious, rejected, ambitious to win more than most human beings desired," these Others are family; in *The World is a Wedding*, the Others are contemporaries, whose moral ineptitude and lack of grace impose themselves, omen-like, on their creator, so that "each event lies in the heavy head forever, waiting to renew itself." Nothing illustrates this dread before what is inexorable, the lapses that always disfigure our lives, more than the story *In Dreams Begin Responsibilities*. . . .

What renders his work so valuable, what elevates it to a level where it can be compared with major American writers, is Schwartz's acute historical consciousness. . . .

Schwartz was a profoundly learned writer, whose unobtrusive erudition was made to serve his art in a manner quite opposite to Pound's; he was intimate with all those he convoked to listen to the talkative, guilt-ridden self, and especially with Freud. . . .

In the introduction to *Genesis, Book One*, he noted that "Some authors are fortunate. They live in an age when their beliefs and values are embodied in great institutions and in the way of life of many human beings." It was just this condition, expressed in a consensus about what elements compose a coherent cultural inheritance, that Schwartz missed in contemporary American life; in compensation, he looked to the tradition which could provide what elsewhere was absent, and that tradition was in literature. . . .

His desire to *know*, to be certain of reality, was possessed of such urgency that it could only fail to be achieved; in "Poetry as Imitation," he had insisted that a poem "involves knowing of some sort," that "the act of writing a poem is an act of knowing," and that the work of art is capable of "making known," disclosing what would otherwise remain indistinct. So he relied on literature to explicate existence, much in the manner of a Talmudic scholar poring over some obscure text; for Schwartz, writing could provide this gloss, it could elicit those truths buried within events. . . .

Delmore Schwartz understood the world's inviolate sadness. . .; tacit in all he wrote was Kafka's parable of "Infinite Hope, but not for us."

*James Atlas, "Delmore Schwartz: The Mind of God," in* American Poetry Review, *January/February, 1974, pp. 3-5.*

* * *

## SCHWARZ-BART, André 1928-

**A French Jew of Polish heritage, Schwarz-Bart is a novelist whose most recent enterprise has been the fictional exploration of the racial implications of *négritude*.**

André Schwarz-Bart's own life story is exceptionally rich in human interest and his . . . Jewish novel [*The Last of the Just*] is probably the most ambitious French-Jewish fictional effort of all times. Schwarz-Bart is in no way the spokesman for Jewish intellectuals today, but his mood—and that of his novel—is in a way their mood. His novel telescopes the experiences of many others. . . .

Schwarz-Bart's mood is one of gentle grief over Jewish suffering, especially that part which he himself witnessed. Very rarely does this grief turn into acrimony. Only when he speaks ironically of the Jesus of impossible love does he turn bitterly against others, implicating Christianity in the history of anti-Semitism and underscoring its unreal aspirations against a record of failure. Far more important than Schwarz-Bart's indictment of the Jew-haters of all time is his reaffirmation of the Jewish "mission," what French mystics have called the mystery of Israel. By enveloping his novel in the legend of the Lamed-Wow, Schwarz-Bart has supplied Jewish folklore as its frame and the ethical tradition as its theme. Stylistic and structural weaknesses notwithstanding, *The Last of the Just* ranks without a doubt among the great Jewish novels of all time.

Schwarz-Bart regards suffering as the distinctive feature of Jewish destiny and the actions of the non-Jewish world as responsible for this suffering. . . .

Schwarz-Bart has publicly declared that there is no Jewish existence independent of Jewish religion. This factor, more than peoplehood or culture, constitutes the real common denominator for Jews everywhere. Nevertheless, *The Last of the Just* is perhaps not a full-blown religious book. It is, to be sure, rich in Jewish lore; its customs and ceremonies are presented authentically; its ideas fit into the mainstream of the Jewish tradition. Yet its major modern characters are not mainly inspired by the Torah. The last two generations depicted in the novel. . . were neither schooled in the Law nor particularly conscious of their heritage. They are peripheral Jews. . . . They are the Jews of today, not strongly aware of any positive quality to their faith, yet unconsciously living it and suffering for it.

*Lothar Kahn, in his* Mirrors of the Jewish Mind: A Gallery of Portraits of European Jewish Writers of Our Time, *A. S. Barnes, 1968, pp. 212-15.*

A stylist, slow and fastidious in his craft, André Schwarz-Bart was awarded the Prix Goncourt for his first book, *The Last of the Just*. His novels are like miniatures painted on ivory, and, perhaps because the author himself was a member of the Maquis who had been deported to an extermination camp and escaped, his stories are poignant with the cruelty which men inflict on one another.

*Edward Weeks, in* The Atlantic Monthly *(copyright © 1973 by The Atlantic Monthly Company, Boston, Mass.; reprinted with permission), March, 1973, p. 105.*

*A Woman Named Solitude* manages to be simultaneously one of the most exquisitely wrought lyric novels of recent years and an utterly convincing representation of the reality of historical suffering. The two achievements, which may sound contradictory, are in fact inseparably linked. The texture of Schwarz-Bart's prose, beautifully rendered in Ralph Manheim's translation, is "poetic" throughout but never merely decorative, which is to say that it performs one of the primary functions of poetry, to make the strange familiar, to enable us to feel the imponderable experience of another on our own impulses. *A Woman Named Solitude* might be described as the study of a violated but heroically persistent perspective, that of black Africans torn from the organic wholeness of their traditional world by the white enslaver; and the novel's vivid metaphorical language, constantly rearranging the elements of experience in unexpected patterns, makes this perspective ours as we read. . . .

The paradox of lyric beauty in an imaginative confrontation with slavery makes particular sense because Schwarz-Bart has chosen to represent the moral outrage of enslavement as a drama of consciousness. The artistic tact of this choice is admirable. I suspect that over the last few years our collective sensibilities have simply been numbed by the deluge in film and fiction of what Stanley Kauffmann once called "the pornography of violence." In *A Woman Named Solitude*, the chains and whips, the sundry instruments of maiming and torture, the sexual despoliations, are merely alluded to quickly in passing, in a matter-of-fact tone that is far more shocking than the conventional wallowing in gore of other contemporary writers. In any case, what one feels more poignantly than the references to physical torture is the continuous presence in the novel of a consciousness pitifully deformed by slavery yet doggedly persisting in its effort to be itself, something other than a shadow in the white man's dream. . . .

In a 1967 interview, Schwarz-Bart said that after the war he had felt that the Holocaust radically isolated the Jews from the rest of mankind in an experience of suffering so profound that it could not be communicated to others. Only after his encounter with West Indians, he went on, did he realize that there might be bridges over the abyss to other islands of suffering, that with all differences recognized, there might still be a universal community of history's victims. The reader of *A Woman Named Solitude* marvels, and wonders, at Schwarz-Bart's unfaltering ability to project himself into another race, another sex, another age. It is only in the last words of the Epilogue that the author of *The Last of the Just* calls attention to his identity. The imaginative visitor, we are told, to the site of the slave rebellion's last stand might almost see human figures arise from the long-moldering ruins—just as other phantoms are said to rise before other travelers at the ruins of the Warsaw Ghetto. This last gesture is, I think, a psychologically necessary one for the novelist, and with a little shock it throws a whole added perspective on the story that has been told. Schwarz-Bart in this book has brilliantly solved the problem of writing a novel after the great novel of the Holocaust by using Jewish suffering as a window of perception to the suffering of others. . . . It is hard to think of many living novelists who are able to use the novel so convincingly to bear witness for humanity in its harshest historical trails.

*Robert Alter, "History's Victims" (reprinted from* Commentary *by permission; copyright © 1973 by The American Jewish Committee), in* Commentary, *May, 1973, pp. 94-6.*

[For Schwarz-Bart], as for Herodotus, true history is that which gives us the past as it applies to our own present condition. . . .

Having successfully synthesized the accounts of history and fable, ledger and legend [in *A Woman Named Solitude*], he has added a unique volume to that slim shelf of books whose words "hold up the house." Moreover, he has given a name to the millions who died as mere entries in a slaver's register, and a voice to those who freed themselves from bondage by swallowing their tongue.

*Alan Cheuse, "Legacy of the Middle Passage," in* The Nation, *October 29, 1973, pp. 440-41.*

* * *

## SELBY, Hubert, Jr. 1928-

**Selby is a controversial American novelist. (See also *Contemporary Authors*, Vols. 15-16.)**

Criticism of Hubert Selby's *Last Exit to Brooklyn* has been generally hostile. The book is usually mentioned in passing as an example of corruption and/or decay in modern literature and/or society. *Time* magazine even went so far as to assert, in its review, that anyone who gave the book a good notice would obviously be in the employ of Grove Press. I liked *Last Exit to Brooklyn*, but since I cannot produce any notarized affidavits certifying my independence of the publisher's payroll, the reader will have to be content merely with my most emphatic denial of any such relationship. . . .

In all the furor over Selby's book as a perhaps appropriate victim of censorship, little progress has been made in evaluating it in terms of literary criteria. Could it be that Selby seems so dangerous precisely because he is an effective and persuasive writer of prose fiction?

Before answering this question in detail we should determine for ourselves exactly what the intention of the book is. The title provides us with a clue. The stories are not about Brooklyn but about the *last exit* to Brooklyn. Selby is making no claim to encyclopedic sociological thoroughness in laying before us the hoodlums, queers, and whores of city-planned slums. He presents us with an exit, a point of departure, a specific view which can be tested only in terms of its inner viability, its effectiveness in dominating the imagination with its own standards of reality. . . .

The only appropriate question is, does Selby's Brooklyn work?

It does not work in all the details, a fact which separates Selby as a good writer from the first-raters. His ear for language is often quite inept ("did yadig" for "didya dig"), and his insistence upon including gratuitous sexual episodes to liven up quiet movements (as in "Strike") indicates a lack of confidence. Perhaps he is making capital out of the well-known fact that a censored book is an automatic best-seller in this country. In any case, his control over the world of his stories is not uniformly sound; given his subject-matter, the slip from the pathetic to the bathetic is all too easy.

In general, however, Selby presents us with a compelling vision. It is difficult to choose any one story to illustrate this, because the whole collection is interdependent. The first story, for example, may frighten many readers away because it is an apparently senseless presentation of violence and brutality. This story contains, however, the most radical expression of all the principles which inform the rest of the book. It is told from the point of view of a group, an uneasy grammatical construction in our singular-oriented language. This group functions under a set of rules which will be alien to most readers. The cohesive principle is *kicks*, that vague word which elbows its way into our consciousness usually by way of the tabloids. The word is not vague when Selby is through. *Kicks* is anything that counteracts the forces that bring the members of the group into individual self-consciousness: boredom, lack of money, lack of purpose. . . .

Critics are wrong to dismiss Selby on the grounds that this picture is "tasteless" or "obscene." But they are right if they recognize that Selby has presented only part of the picture, a modern Inferno, if you will. Comparisons with Dante are likely to be fruitless, but we have a right to hope, if not expect, that Selby will see fit to exercise his talents in the more difficult direction of writing about those people in Brooklyn he loves, not pities.

*W. J. T. Mitchell, in* Studies in Short Fiction, *Fall, 1965, pp. 77-8.*

What Selby is saying [in "The Room"] is that in the lives of the powerless nothing occurs. Or rather everything occurs but to no effect. Their debasement and triumph are all fiction. Day-dreaming. Nothing is changed by their lives. Whether they live or die, suffer or not, are good or evil means nothing. For, being impotent, they are outside history. They are casualties numbered on a list and forgotten. . . .

[The novel] is a nightmare and pain. It is an exquisite, meticulous examination of the curious piteous lust between oppressor and oppressed. It documents the sexual basis of power and criminality. As a work of the imagination, I think it assures Hubert Selby's place in the first rank of American novelists. . . . In "The Room" and "Last Exit to Brooklyn" Selby has created characters with a concreteness, force and individuality seldom found in American fiction. And yet they are eminently American characters. They could exist nowhere else. That is why to understand Selby's work is to understand the anguish of America. . . .

Selby's genius is that he compels us to feel. And that is a marvelous thing. Think of it: a writer has come along and created a novel which sensitizes us to the pain of others, a novel profoundly concerned, perhaps too deeply, with America and yet a novel that refuses to sentimentalize the American experience. "The Room" is a great, moral book.

*Dotson Rader, in* The New York Times Book Review *(© 1971 by The New York Times Company; reprinted by permission), December 12, 1971, pp. 5, 28-9.*

"This book is dedicated,/with love,/to the thousands/who remain nameless/and know." The dedication page of Hubert Selby's new novel [*The Room*] suggests that—as in the fated and, later, fêted *Last Exit to Brooklyn*—the author's primary role is that of social critic. The criminals, in *Last Exit*, were not the mindless sadists it so often depicted so much as those who ran the society which gave rise to such people: it was not the savage sex that was nauseating, but the social conditions that fostered it. That, in any case, would seem to have been the thesis; and if Mr. Selby was out to turn the average stomach with *Last Exit*, then he probably succeeded, though whether he managed at the same time to stir the average conscience is quite another matter.

In *The Room*, the range is narrowed a little. The malign influence depicted here is still, by implication, society at large, but it is personified by the most obvious example of its repressive influence: the police.

*"Pig Sticking," in* The Times Literary Supplement *(reproduced by permission), February 25, 1972, p. 209.*

[Selby's novel] *The Room* [is] his portrait of a festering mind. . . . From human dregs, from the unremittingly tormented, Selby extracts the very odor of rage, the essence of that free-floating anger that lies like a pall over all of us. . . .

His preoccupations are the relentless pursuit of machismo through all the ways of cruelty, the fear of failure and worthlessness that drives men into deeper and deeper vileness. Selby is a clinician of male violence, dissecting straight to the center of sexual chaos and cruelty. . . .

Where *Last Exit to Brooklyn* focused on the social scene of violence, from brawls to sexual infighting, *The Room* is the story of one mind riveted on fury. Sadism is the only means of survival for Selby's nameless hero, who festers in prison as he awaits trial for an unnamed crime. . . .

This is Selby's vision of a culture's bedrock psyche, a portrait of an American mind gone the limit in its acceptance of cruelty as life's only fixed principle. Selby perceives pain, whether inflicted or felt, as the basic bond between people. If he does not gloat over the cruelty he describes, Selby nevertheless sees nothing else, nothing but the terror of those dismal, festering characters who spring from his imagination so fully formed in their vileness. He does write of them with love, with an energy and purity of style that is absolute in its insistence on your glimmer of recognition and assent: is their life yours? Whether it is or not, reading Selby is like being mugged.

*Josephine Hendin, "Angries: S-M as a Literary Style," in* Harper's *(copyright © 1974, by Harper's Magazine, Inc.; reprinted from the February, 1974 issue of* Harper's Magazine *by permission), February, 1974, pp. 87-93.*

* * *

## SEXTON, Anne 1928-1974

**Ms Sexton, an American poet, wrote frank and forceful "confessional" poems. Her principal themes were motherhood and love, life, death, and madness. (See also *Contemporary Authors*, Vols. 1-4, rev. ed.)**

Anne Sexton is a very talented poet whose honesty may be her undoing. Normally, candor is a virtue in art: the poet is not afraid to look at things as they are and is not afraid to speak out, even at the risk of displeasing his audience. But confession, while good for the soul, may become tiresome for the reader if not accompanied by the suggestion that something is being held back, that there is an interior life, too costly and rare to be hawked in the market-place. In [*Live or Die*] Miss Sexton's toughness approaches affectation. Like a drunk at a party who corners us with the story of his life, or an exhibitionist who undresses in Times Square, the performance is less interesting the third time, despite the poet's high level of technical competence. The flyleaf of "Live or Die" speaks of "total frankness," and indeed Miss Sexton gives us an almost day-by-day account of her intimate life: one poem dated November 7, 1963, is called "Menstruation at Forty." One thinks of all that Emily Dickinson *didn't* tell and recalls Heraclitus' aphorism: "The lord whose oracle is at Delphi neither speaks nor conceals, but gives signs."

Virginia Quarterly Review, *Vol. 43, No. 1 (Winter, 1967), p. xvii.*

Anne Sexton's *Love Poems* are like choppy-surfaced puddles and she has no qualms about offering them exactly as they are. Sometimes the wind blowing on them has considerable force, which makes this volume more readable than her last, *Live or Die*, but most of the poems seem to have been written far too quickly, as if she were rather nervous of overcooking the emotional raw material. Some of them are like slightly abbreviated transcripts of a patient's free associations during a session with an analyst. . . .

In her first two volumes, *To Bedlam and Half Way Back* and *All My Pretty Ones*, Anne Sexton worked a "confessional" mode to considerable effect. The *Love Poems* are no less honest—often they seem too honest—and the emotional pressure behind them may be no less urgent, but the tension is no longer captured in the verse itself, which is thin-textured and rhythmically flaccid. Nothing is left of the breakneck movement from one tight cluster of images and ideas to the next. We get more clarity, but at the cost of a pedestrian pace.

*Ronald Hayman, in* Encounter, *December, 1970, p. 77.*

*Transformations* are retellings, in jokey, prosaic language, of seventeen tales by the Brothers Grimm. I have tried but I cannot take any interest in them, any more than I'd want to drive a Chrysler 'Imperial' or live in Weston, Massachusetts. I fear Miss Sexton and I would not be entertaining to each other. I am so deaf and blind to her possible virtues that I surely cannot give them to you. (And, to say it just one more time, that is one of the dangers of one poet writing about another poet.) Anyway, I have vague memories of Uncle Milty doing cute revisions of fairy tales on tv that seemed better than these.

*Jonathan Williams, in* Parnassus, *Fall/Winter, 1972, p. 101.*

Although Anne Sexton has been intensely aware of herself as a woman and a woman poet, there is a new militancy here [in *The Book of Folly*] that I have never detected in her previous work. At best, it is part of a larger impulse in the book which would challenge not just what are male and female worlds, but what constitutes sane and insane, prosaic and poetic, sacred and secular domain.

A concern with breakthrough, as much as breakdown, continues to distinguish Anne Sexton's work in this book; and, since literary influences are quirky, tricky matters, I kept having to remind myself that if I found some bad, unfortunate debts to Robert Lowell and Sylvia Plath in these pieces, that it was Anne Sexton who was also important in influencing Plath and possibly even Lowell. What I am more worried over, however, is how this new book raises the same problems that have marked her books—an unevenness that often derives from the inclusion of unmistakably bad poems and even entire, unsuccessful sequences; an overuse of apostrophe and appositives to conceal some terrible failures of language and imagination, feeling and thought; recurrent metaphor and simile that are either too banal or not outrageous enough to work. These may seem like harsh criticisms, but I say them because I also find here important poems by an important poet, and a poet whose best poems ought not to run the risk of being dwarfed by lesser things. At its best, *The Book of Folly* has poems and prose poems—"The Ambition Bird," "The Doctor of the Heart," "Oh," "The Wifebeater," "The One-Legged Man," "The Red Shoes," "The Death of the Fathers," "Three Stories"—that can stand up to the stronger pieces in what for me are her best books, *To Bedlam and Part Way Back, All My Pretty Ones*, and *Love Poems*, this last book a book that never received the kind of attention it deserved. . . .

What moves me most in this book is a relentless vision and weird abundance which marked the best of Anne Sexton's earlier work, a hard-earned knowing that need is not quite belief.

*Arthur Oberg, in* Shenandoah *(copyright by* Shenandoah; *reprinted from* Shenandoah: *The Washington and Lee University Review with the permission of the Editor), Fall, 1973, pp. 87-8.*

When Hawthorne rewrote Greek myths for children, he removed the gore, the deaths, the tragedies and the sex, rendering that gritty material into an insubstantial stew of false bliss considered suitable for the children of the time. Anne Sexton certainly couldn't be accused of siding too much with the angels in her versions [*Transformations*], not at first glance anyway. Whom she sides with, finally, are the live ones, the survivors who stay intact, partaking of a vitality neither moral nor immoral. In the process, she ruthlessly attacks the fairy tales which have sprung from the original Grimm tales and simultaneously attacks the aspects of our culture which have used those fairy tales "to banquet / at behest of usura." . . .

Anne Sexton . . . [keeps] her eye on the movement of each tale, although one could hardly fail to notice the spice she dashes into it. Above all, the tales do entertain. There are moments when they strain a bit to entertain ("her secret was as safe / as a fly in an outhouse"), but these moments are overwhelmed by the main force of a dark and often direly sympathetic laughter. The voice, primarily witty and knowing, frequently is possessed by a lyricism that is stunning.

*William Pitt Root, in* Poetry *(© 1973 by The Modern Poetry Association; reprinted by permission of the Editor of* Poetry*), October, 1973, p. 50.*

Whenever Anne Sexton's poems are mentioned, the term "confessional poetry" is not far behind. It has always seemed a silly and unilluminating term to me; one of those pigeonholing categories critics invent so as not to talk about poetry as poetry. I think it's an especially unfortunate term because it implies that the raw sexy truth is finally being told—as in *True Confessions*. It also implies that poetry (or any other literary form) can be utterly revealing of autobiographical truth. In fact, this is impossible. . . .

If any term is needed, I think it would be fairer to call Anne Sexton a psychological poet. She has always dared to explore areas of the human psyche which lesser poets shrank back from. . . .

She is an important poet not only because of her courage in dealing with previously forbidden subjects, but because she can make the language sing. . . .

This newest collection, *The Death Notebooks*, contains all that is best about Anne Sexton and all that is worst. Best: her honesty, her vulnerability, her splendid ear for language, her psychological insight. Worst: her repetitiveness, her excess.

*The Death Notebooks* contains (according to the publisher's press release) poems that Anne Sexton had originally planned to save for posthumous publication, and one of the main themes of the book is the curious fate of the poet: to make a living out of her death. This is a rich and fascinating paradox. The writer's death provides her with both her *raison d'être* and her livelihood. . . .

[In] Anne Sexton's case, poetry is the reincarnation, the regurgitation, the living she is making out of the jaws of death.

*Erica Jong, "Giving Birth to Death," in* Ms., *March, 1974, pp. 36-7.*

[Anne Sexton] is already an established "confessional" poet. . . . *The Death Notebooks* continues in the confessional mode and speaks through her characteristically exhibitionist, iconoclastic "I." The major change in *Notebooks* is its underlying religious metaphor. Consequently, the predicament of Woman, with her awful knowledge of "water breaking," blood and creation, now leads her to the temple. With prosodic roar, Sexton finds her deity [for example] in the mysteries of the toilet. . . .

After sharing in Sexton's epiphanies, one cannot help feeling that perhaps the lady doth protest too much. All the irreverence begins to resemble old-fashioned Puritan repression. The further paradox lies in the coy and very unliberated way Sexton pursues God, her ultimate seduction!

*Norma Procopiow, "The Ladies Do Protest Too Much," in* Book World—The Washington Post (© The Washington Post), *May 26, 1974, p. 3.*

When Wordsworth went looking for God, he walked into the woods of his childhood and there He was. In [the poems in *The Death Notebooks*] Anne Sexton looks in many strange places for God (oddly, she doesn't try the woods); she apparently finds him in the lavatory. This excremental view of religion and life (buttocks, backsides, enemas, crappers abound in the poems) is a central strand of *The Death Notebooks*. . . .

However it's not necessary to compare her to Wordsworth to feel that she writes from a narrow and insecure base, making a virtue (and a subject) of her weakness. I was surprised that many of my best female students were infuriated at her seeming dependence (in *Love Poems*, 1969) on male love and sex, as if without them she was worthless, a nothing (by "she," of course, I mean the persona of her poems, not Sexton herself). In *The Death Notebooks* this insecurity, this feeling of abandonment, is transferred from men to God. . . . I'm not looking for happy poetry, but for poetry with balance, a center of gravity. The fear of death, of growing old, very strong here, is universal, but there are many ways to face it. One sometimes—not always—gets the feeling that Sexton is asking too heavily for our sympathy: the poet as loser.

For a major poet with a strong voice of her own, she often lapses into definite echoes of other poets, particularly Sylvia Plath or . . . Berryman . . . or Ginsberg. . . . But . . . Sexton's weaknesses are general and vague, her strengths specific and clear: a lean energetic line, a technical and formal virtuosity, a sharp visual talent applied to psychological states and human situations that we all can recognize.

*Peter Meinke, "Poet as Loser," in* The New Republic *(reprinted by permission of* The New Republic; *© 1974 by The New Republic, Inc.), June 22, 1974, pp. 27-8.*

In Anne Sexton's *The Death Notebooks* there is a good deal of the same chic diction and glib irony that to my mind vitiated the energy of many of her earlier poems. Indeed I have always thought it a great pity that she could not break through this self-consciousness more often, because her energy was clearly there to be tapped, along with intelligence and humane concern, though at the same time her self-consciousness was understandable—and more!—to those of us who have shared her topic: the experience of emotional illness. The important point is that in all her books at least a few poems have made it; they have broken through. Sometimes she has succeeded by converting self-consciousness of style to a genuine formal attribute, at other times by smashing artifice in the heat of feeling. Her new book is no exception, and is well worth having for its few real poems.

*Hayden Carruth, in* The Hudson Review *(copyright © 1974 by The Hudson Review, Inc.; reprinted by permission), Vol. XXVII, No. 2, Summer, 1974, p. 315.*

No matter what else you think about Anne Sexton's poetry, you have to concede its extraordinary and persistent vitality. Like that awful child with the curl, when she's good Anne Sexton is very, very good, and when she's bad she sometimes really is rather horrid—but, nonetheless, vital. Always energetic, brimful of her own pains and passions, as if *she*, whoever and whatever she is (and that's an issue which continually concerns her) is about to leap out of her own skin in her ironic/demonic quest for Love, Life, Art, Intensity.

All of which may seem, at first, particularly odd in view of the brooding, apparently "neurotic" preoccupation with death which her poetry has displayed from *To Bedlam and Part Way Back* onwards, and which now comes fully to the surface in *The Death Notebooks*. Yet even in her earliest books, Sexton's thoughts of death were expressed with a breathless and often comic vitality that lightened what might otherwise have been unmitigated gloom. . . .

Vital as her early volumes were, however, *The Death Notebooks* goes far beyond them in making luminous art out of the night thoughts that have haunted this poet for so long. The book's epigraph is a line from Hemingway's *A Moveable Feast*—"Look, you con man, make a living out of your death"—which succinctly summarizes the poet's goal, a goal both shrewdly ironic (at least she can write, and thus make a living out of her obsession) and ambitiously metaphysical (what is there to make a *living* from except death?). But if irony and shrewdness have always characterized Anne Sexton's work, the largeness of her metaphysical ambition is what is newly notable about *The Death Notebooks*.

*Sandra M. Gilbert, "Jubilate Anne," in* The Nation, *September 14, 1974, pp. 214-15.*

* * *

## SHAPIRO, Karl 1913-

**Shapiro, an American poet, critic, and editor, won the Pulitzer Prize for Poetry in 1945. One of Shapiro's more remarkable accomplishments has been the successful handling of prose poems built around prose paragraphs. (See also *Contemporary Authors*, Vols. 1-4, rev. ed.)**

Shapiro . . . has never seemed to me . . . a passionate poet; his own work is striking for its concrete but detached insights; it is witty and exact in the way it catches the poet's subtle and guarded impressions, and it is a poetry full of clever and unexpected verbal conceits. It is a very professional poetry—supple, adaptable, by no means Dionysian. Like much contemporary lyric poetry, it seems to me imprisoned in "sensibility," muscle-bound except in relation to the poet's specific rendering of a place, a time, a mood. Shapiro's essays [*In Defense of Ignorance*] are full of the same excellent and detached insights. He is often brilliant in his judgment of particular texts, as luminous and witty then as he is unnaturally programmatic and self-defeating and even a bit hysterical on Eliot as the evil genius of modern literature. . . .

Yet when Shapiro lives up to his own prescription that the critic should do nothing but judge works of art, when as a fellow poet he takes up those pieces of Eliot's which in university classes are often read only as a puzzle to decipher or as necessary condemnations of contemporary society, he is exhilarating.

*Alfred Kazin, "The Poet Against the English Department" (copyright © 1960 by Alfred Kazin; reprinted by permission of Little, Brown and Co. in association with The Atlantic Monthly Press), in his* Contemporaries, *Little, Brown, 1962, pp. 489-93.*

The 'Jewish' aspect of [Karl] Shapiro is worth consideration. Like [Delmore] Schwartz and [Stanley] Kunitz, he brings his Jewish background into his poetry. More than either of them, however, he has called special attention to it, even publishing a collection of his pieces called *Poems of a Jew*. In this volume, he seems to define Jewishness as a psychological state very much like the one that dominates his poetry: 'The Jew represents the primitive ego of the human race. . . . The free modern Jew, celebrated so perfectly in the character of Leopold Bloom, is neither hero nor victim.' As self-evident truths, these and like formulations by Shapiro are wanting. However, the choice of Leopold Bloom, who certainly suffers from 'the wound of consciousness,' and who is so much an outsider and insider at once in the little world Joyce put him in, is apt for Shapiro. In his view, the awareness of pain life thrusts upon the helpless, the human predicament which is Jarrell's great theme, is the essence of Jewishness.

*M. L. Rosenthal, in his* The Modern Poets: A Critical Introduction *(copyright © 1960 by M. L. Rosenthal; reprinted by permission of Oxford University Press, Inc.), Oxford University Press, 1960, p. 249.*

Karl Shapiro's poems are fresh and young and rash and live; their hard clear outlines, their flat bold colors create a world like that of a knowing and skillful neoprimitive painting, without any of the confusion or profundity of atmosphere, of aerial perspective, but with notable visual and satiric force. The poet early perfected a style, derived from Auden but decidedly individual, which he has not developed in later life but has temporarily replaced with the clear Rilke-like rhetoric of his Adam and Eve poems, the frankly Whitmanesque convolutions of his latest work. . . .

Both in verse and in prose Shapiro loves, partly out of indignation and partly out of sheer mischievousness, to tell the naked truths or half-truths or quarter-truths that will make anybody's hair stand on end; he is always crying: "But he hasn't any clothes on!" about an emperor who is half the time surprisingly well dressed.

*Randall Jarrell, "Fifty Years of American Poetry" (1962; originally published in* Prairie Schooner, *Spring, 1963), in his* The Third Book of Criticism *(reprinted with the permission of Farrar, Straus & Giroux, Inc.; copyright © 1941, 1945, 1955, 1956, 1962, 1963, 1965 by Mrs. Randall Jarrell; copyright © 1963, 1965 by Randall Jarrell), Farrar, Straus, 1969, pp. 330-31.*

Karl Shapiro is [a] "social poet" who found impetus and subject matter in the public crises of the 1940's, when his private predicament as a soldier in the war against Germany and Japan merged with the predicament of American society as a whole, fighting for its survival. But, although a slow, subdued anger is the permanent emotional climate of an army, Shapiro's tone is rarely angry, even in the poems in which he points out the shortcomings of society—the racial, religious, and economic injustices that he sees about him. . . . He is bitter and ironic, but possesses enough spiritual equilibrium to be "at rest in the blast," as Marianne Moore would say. He achieves the sort of cosmic consciousness that makes possible an objectification and dramatization of inner tensions and polarities. All of his best work was done during the years 1940-1948. . . .

Of all contemporary poets, he is the least interested in projecting "the anarchy of experience." His poems always have a point of view, often so strongly stated that it amounts to an "ideology." . . .

[All his] poems of the 1940's have their social meaning. Ideologically, they seem to be liberal, and the formulations of political and social attitude, the abstractions of an intellect at work in categories, owe a great deal to W. H. Auden, who, ironically enough, had already abandoned his liberalism by 1941. Shapiro owes a great deal to Auden in matters of technique also, in his handling of stanza and line, for, like Auden, he works in traditional measures, knowing that a relatively prosaic content requires meter. . . .

A study of the poems in *The Bourgeois Poet* (1964) shows that Shapiro is now writing a very prosaic free verse but that his subject matter is unchanged: he still writes social commentaries, as the very title of his book indicates. His poems have, in the past, been saved from prose by an underpinning of meter; now he has the problem of creating a strong substitute rhythm that can organize his essentially prosaic subject matter.

*Stephen Stepanchev, "Karl Shapiro," in his* American Poetry Since 1945: A Critical Survey *(copyright © 1965 by Stephen Stepanchev; reprinted by permission of Harper & Row, Publishers, Inc.), Harper, 1965, pp. 53-68.*

A turning point in Shapiro's search for his identity occurred between [1953 and 1960] when he discovered Whitman. How much like a conversion the discovery was for Shapiro was not immediately apparent, for no volume of wholly new poems appeared between 1947 and 1964, the two volumes of verse that appeared in the 1950's being largely or entirely made up of reprintings of earlier poems. But when *The Bourgeois Poet* appeared in 1964, it was clear that Shapiro had turned a sharp corner in his career. Only certain similarities of attitude and certain personal mannerisms might suggest that the poems in *Person, Place and Thing*, his first mature book, and the "antipoems" in *The Bourgeois Poet* were written by the same man. . . .

A comment in one of the jottings that make up a section of *The Bourgeois Poet* suggests the reason why Whitman became, in the middle and later 1950's, so very important to Shapiro. "Now all things are the measure of man, it's hard to find a decent god or muse." That Whitman had gained another disciple who valued him chiefly for the help he had given in the two-pronged search is everywhere apparent. . . . Whitman . . . is the friend, the good one, in a world of unnamed enemies who are determined to exterminate what is good. . . .

In *Trial of a Poet* Shapiro continued to explore the possibilities of the style ["Modernist"] he had already, theoretically, and in his heart, renounced. . . . But the title poem of the volume, which I must confess I find extremely dull, was something else again. Here was a rehearsal, in a poetic drama with the speakers listed as "Poet, Public Officer, Doctor, Priest, and Chorus of Poets," of the cloudy and too-excited rhetoric of *Beyond Criticism*, which appeared six years later. Echoing Pound and Eliot in phrase and image, the poem ends by recommending poetry as "an independent faith," yet having the Poet speak in prose, as being less dishonest than verse!

After *Trial of a Poet*, Shapiro, not surprisingly, wrote very few poems for the next fifteen years. Trying to reconstruct the reasons for his imaginative exhaustion, I can only suppose that his vein of implicit social criticism, after the manner of "Drug Store," has run out; and that in such religious explorations as he had recorded in "The Convert," he had come to a dead end. For a poet sensitive to the meaning of religious questions, Freud and Marx, to whom, obviously, he was listening in the 1930's, were not helpful. Nor was his tendency (under the influence of Eliot, primarily) to equate "religion" with High Church orthodoxy. In poem after poem of this period, the "age of faith" is equated with rigidly intellectualistic formulations of dogma and with ceremonial that lacks all inwardness. No wonder he later described Whitman, quite contrary to Whitman's stated intentions, as having "contempt" for religion. "Religion" for Shapiro was defined by Eliot's position. Whitman appealed to him because he attacked "priestcraft" in "Song of Myself," yet affirmed his almost doctrineless faith in the triumph of persons over time and fate. . . .

*The Bourgeois Poet*, whatever we may decide about its doing away with *verse* as the distinguishing element in "poetry," has the great merit of appearing to be—for the very first time in Shapiro's poetic career—wholly representative of the voice we hear in it speaking to us. We are, after all, the poet has at last discovered, beyond both the "age of faith," as he understands the term, and the age of rational doubt. We are in the age of the scientific datum considered as a "construct," of the work of art constructed out of "found objects," and of the "nonfiction novel." . . .

*The Bourgeois Poet* seems to me to be a work of greater poetic integrity than any of Shapiro's earlier volumes. Whitman and Hart Crane, Blake and Jesus are openly his heroes now. His capacity for self-deception is recognized and explored. . . .

*The Bourgeois Poet* exhibits Shapiro in his chosen role as the primeval American poet, the "man who begins at the beginning—all over again," the "first white aboriginal." The role demands immense renunciations, which only future development of the poet can justify.

*Hyatt H. Waggoner, "Karl Shapiro," in his* American Poets From the Puritans to the Present *(copyright © 1968 by Hyatt H. Waggoner; reprinted by permission of Houghton Mifflin Company), Houghton, 1968, pp. 585-96.*

In "The Bourgeois Poet," Karl Shapiro dared to write prose-poems that were really prosy. It is sad to see that strong experiment go by the boards. "White-Haired Lover," a cycle of twenty-nine love poems from life (and mostly sonnets at that!), is neither as interesting nor as carefully wrought. Shapiro is too self-conscious here. He poses and exposes himself. Still, he can do interesting things with the sonnet, and there's no doubt that this subject requires the form. Without it, these poems would be impossibly out of control. Even with it, there are numerous fuzzy spots, where, for example, a colloquial rhyme is forced in: "The laughter of the goddess cool as hell/Pinged like a Cellini shell"; or, in another couplet, where the tone becomes Ogden Nashian: "And if I've lost you who is there to blame?/(Faulty communications are my middle name)." As Shapiro says over and over again, he's too old for this kind of thing. He has the technique, but his emotions seem to be too shook up. Only a few times in the whole book can this fine poet bring it off—for example, in these stately lines: "You are going into your beauty/And it is I who am opening all the doors as you pass/From room to room of your life till you walk to my grave."

Virginia Quarterly Review, *Vol. 45, No. 1, Winter, 1969, pp. xvi, xviii.*

Shapiro has been enacting the role of the not terribly bright village reformer ever since 1945, when, in *Essay on Rime*, he called for "a plainer art." What he wants is a turning from received and thus discredited English and European techniques of focus in favor of honest encounters with the stuff of local experience, which I'm afraid he takes to be uncomplicated. His masters in this enterprise have been Whitman and W. C. Williams, but he has served neither very well, lacking the sensitivity to idiom of the one and the talent for a rude and consistent honesty of the other. . . .

Seeing nothing defective in either the rhetoric he practices or the simpleminded critical dialectic he has embraced, Shapiro cannot be expected to write interesting poems, and those in *White-Haired Lover*—an implausible but I suppose comforting oxymoron—will disappoint critics and lovers alike. . . .

Despite all his pleas for the "non-moral society," Shapiro has not been able to rid himself of a lurking concern with making a good—here, a respectable—impression, and despite his strenuous antipathy to traditional poetic forms, here he clutches the sonnet as his *cache-sexe*, a device which will provide him with the fig leaves and pasties for which, as an essentially decent person, he feels a need. These poems pretend to send up the sonnet ("stab it" is Shapiro's awkward way of putting it), but actually they naïvely capitulate to its norms. Sonnet VIII ("How Do I Love You?") is an example. The force of the rigid rhyming system of the sestet invites Shapiro, devoid as he is of language resources, to juxtapose warring idioms, and we end with a mixture, destructive rather than explosive, of Mrs. Browning, Pope, Edna Millay, the Beatles and Auden. . . .

But one exposes the sleaziness of Shapiro's achievement at the same time that one doesn't really dislike the familiar character he has undertaken to play. It is the character of the bumbling, well-intentioned Good American, too good to be wasted in the aluminum-siding business, but not of course good enough to compete with sensibilities of real literary delicacy and accuracy. Shapiro has carefully made himself into a Sherwood Anderson or Sinclair Lewis character, the kind of American who thinks opera silly but who is willing, if pressed, to contribute handsomely to his local "Cultural Center." Shapiro thinks *Herzog* a "brilliant novel"; Henry Miller seems to him a great writer; he considers M. B. Tolson a distinguished poet who has not made it only because "critics" can't stand poets who are black. In folk judgments like these, Shapiro comes to resemble a sort of Yvor Winters reversed. In both, the program has quite corrupted the perceptions, and perhaps it is a similar kind of American parochialism, with all its invitations to crankhood, that has actuated both.

*Paul Fussell, Jr., "The Bourgeois Poet," in* Partisan Review *(copyright © 1969 by Par-*

*tisan Review, Inc.), Winter, 1969, pp. 141-45.*

Karl Shapiro [is] a poet of very considerable power and unusual attractiveness, and a critic whose increasing disaffection with criticism and affirmation of neo-Romanticism makes an interesting and perhaps representative story.

Shapiro made his reputation as poet during World War II, under the aegis of the New Criticism. . . . He repudiated the New Criticism in the essays collected as *Beyond Criticism* (1953; reprinted in paperback as *A Primer for Poets*, 1965), and by *In Defense of Ignorance* (1960) he had made an explicit commitment to the visionary and occult tradition and had become increasingly vindictive toward his former allegiances. The thesis of this last volume is stated in the preface: "The dictatorship of intellectual 'modernism,' the sanctimonious ministry of 'the Tradition,' the ugly programmatic quality of twentieth-century criticism have maimed our poetry and turned it into a monstrosity of literature." The motto is "everything we are taught is false," and Shapiro apologizes for not being more rigorously anti-intellectual.

*Monroe K. Spears, in his* Dionysus and the City *(copyright © 1970 by Monroe K. Spears; reprinted by permission of Oxford University Press, Inc.), Oxford University Press, 1970, p. 216.*

Give a poet enough breathing space and time, sooner or later he'll do that novel he's had on his mind. And, since Shapiro's mind is flinty, vibrantly imaginative, tender, and (it turns out) extremely funny, his *Edsel* is a welcomed occasion, despite its stigmatic status as yet another college novel. . . . Shapiro's faintly disguised portrait of Allen Ginsberg as the goofy Harry Peltz is in itself enough to make this whole trip worth taking.

The Antioch Review *(© 1971 by The Antioch Review, Inc.; reprinted by permission of the editors), Vol. XXXI, No. 3, 1971, p. 439.*

The anti-intellectual distrust so often (and so often hysterically) evident in Karl Shapiro appears . . . in [*White-Haired Lover*] as a fear of the very art which has always best celebrated love. Shapiro's problem is how to show in art one's great luck in an emotional commitment that is at bottom a welling-up of spontaneity, of sincerity. And how to show sincerity in that most hoary artifice, the love poem? To be a maker exposes one's most bravely sincere declarations of love as vulnerable to such technical concerns as beat, rhyme, alliteration, and such intellectual matters as wit and wisdom.

Shapiro's solution is at times to be the "natural" poet who will have no truck with a fancyman's bag of tricks but who will lay out, in terms as simple as the artifice of language will allow, the bare feeling, the sheer joy of surprise that love is still possible. Hence those poems (or most often parts of poems) which rely heavily on patterns most conventionalized by the "natural" poet: I love you too much for thought or image or wit. And the fear of that artifice lurks everywhere, as if someone of his own persuasion might accuse him of Eliotic tendencies. The best poems are those in which he frankly admits to being maker as well as lover, asserting the uncomfortable paradox that the lover must sacrifice love long enough to write a love poem. . . .

Like most love poets, Shapiro would like it both ways: to love sincerely and to write good poems out of that love. . . .

For all the poems addressed to *you*, the title is *White-Haired Lover*. However he cherishes his private love, Shapiro is never far from recognizing that what counts is commodity, *himself* as subject, and that the public must be served as well as the mistress. We are serviced rather than served. Art can, I suppose, betray love, but Shapiro's statements on the dilemma are bogus, unpersuasive tacks to divert our attention from the patchy and predictable art itself. He might well ask, "Where are the poems that got lost in the shuffling spring?"

*James H. Justus, "Some Middle Generation Poetry," in* The Southern Review, *Vol. IX, No. 1, Winter, 1973, pp. 264-65.*

* * *

## SHEED, Wilfrid 1930-

**Sheed is an Anglo-American novelist, short story writer, critic, and essayist. His fiction, crisp and satirical, is concerned with social and intellectual encounters and is characterized by an immensely attractive style.**

As it happens, Wilfrid Sheed is indeed one of the nation's most gifted writers. . . . Sheed has been gathering points for years with such novels as *A Middle Class Education, The Hack, Square's Progress* and the [other] works. . . .

Curiously, Max Jamison has been greeted by most book reviewers as a fair approximation of a critic but a foul caricature of a human being. Apparently, nothing is too bad for a critic, nor too good for a human being. My reaction to Jamison is quite the opposite in that I find him believable as a human being and unbelievable as a critic. I simply can't buy the utter joylessness and egregiousness of the scene he covers. But then, . . . I have always thought of Sheed as more of a novelist than a critic even when he was writing criticism. Movies and plays do not exist as autonomous entities in his prose, thereby lumpily distending it and blocking its marvelous flow. No, even old Anton Chekhov must be ground down into a joke, a vaudeville routine, or, at most, a controlling metaphor in the ever-ripening process of a sensibility already too refined for most workaday critical functions. Max Jamison is therefore something of a fraud when he sets himself up as the definitive critic striving to be a human being. . . .

What Sheed has isolated in Max Jamison's persona is merely the somewhat comical paradox that as much as the intellect wishes to treat existence as a gloomily speculative Samuel Beckett play, the emotions persist in reducing family life to a mushy Walt Disney movie. Sheed is especially good with children. . . . Sheed's creative feat in *Max Jamison* is to make us aware of the dangerous tightrope between art and life, career and family, mind and heart we must all walk in order to fulfill our duties and possibilities on this earth. . . .

The ability to confront the invidious implications of one's own rhetoric at the peak of its persuasiveness is the mark of a fair-minded writer. That too many of his targets are propped-up straw men and sitting ducks attests not so much to Sheed's lack of fairness as to his lack of interest in the logic and nuance of cultural heresies. But that isn't the real problem with *Max Jamison* as far as certain portions of the literary establishment are concerned. Sheed's real offense against decorum is his minute examination of all the disagreeable details of being a middle-class intellectual in a society where only inherited money is truly admired. How gloriously grubby are Sheed and Jamison on the lecture circuit, in academe, in the corridors of the castrating news magazines, in the cluttered dungeons of avant-garde pretense, and, above all, at dinner with the breadwinning wife who must be kept in her place so that her husband is not as emasculated psychically as he will always be economically. What grubby book reviewer can forgive Sheed for exposing the grubbiness we all share as we lurch onward and upward with the arts?

*Andrew Sarris, "Brawling Brotherhood of Critics," in* The Village Voice *(reprinted by permission of* The Village Voice; *copyrighted by The Village Voice, Inc., 1971), August 26, 1971, pp. 23, 52.*

At first glance the irony in Sheed's new novel ["People Will Always Be Kind"] seems to flow outward toward its author's life and toward recent public events. In the first part of the novel we read how Brian Casey—athletic, just past puberty—is stricken with polio. Thereafter, "Brian's legs were a wasteland where no life would stir again." In the second part we read an account by Sam Perkins, speech writer, Ivy-league smartie and civil-rights activist, of Senator Brian Casey's campaign for the Democratic party's Presidential nomination.

Sheed has already written how in his own athletic adolescence he was stricken with polio. And he has also written how he traveled with Eugene McCarthy making speeches during the Senator's campaign for the Democratic nomination. But Casey, Sheed and McCarthy are not alike, except in their Irishness, their "Commonweal-Catholicism," and their compulsive wittiness. . . .

The detail-work in Sheed's account of the process by which Casey's contrary wills and many minds are formed is only one of this novel's pleasures. The inside dope on the dealing of politicians and on the sordid highs of campaigning gives the reader another pleasure—the kind that has always addicted readers to the novels of major as well as minor old-fashioned craftsmen. The prose, the pace, the humor are pleasures neither old-fashioned nor new-fangled, but simply unique to Sheed's writing. So is a certain quality of moral intelligence, one graced by an unflappable and chastened sanity, a charity precise and unsentimental.

Robert Graves, who has been called a minor poet for over 50 years now, once pointed out that the distinction between major and minor writers tells us less than the distinction between good and bad ones. "People Will Always Be Kind" is a very good novel by a very good novelist.

*George Stade, in* The New York Times Book Review *(© 1973 by The New York Times Company; reprinted by permission), April 8, 1973, pp. 1-2.*

[*People Will Always Be Kind*] is the most substantial novel yet from Wilfrid Sheed, and that is saying something. Aside from being one of the finest essayists and critics we have, Sheed is a novelist of depth, complexity and compassion. Though his early work, notably *Office Politics*, gained him a reputation as a wit, his fiction has grown steadily darker over the years—more interesting, more thoughtful.

*People Will Always Be Kind* continues that trend. It is a very funny book, but its wit is essentially a decoration; Sheed is concerned here with a considerable range of subjects, and he has woven them into a sympathetic, convincing study of political man—one of the best political novels we have. . . .

*People Will Always Be Kind* is, in its refusal to see Casey or any of its other characters in simplistic terms, admirably appreciative of human complexity. The first section seems more deeply felt on Sheed's part than the second, and it touches the reader more directly, but the novel is consistently persuasive throughout. Sheed gets better with each new novel, and there are few writers of whom that can be said.

*Jonathan Yardley, "Wheeling and Dealing," in* Book World—The Washington Post *(©* The Washington Post*), April 29, 1973, p. 3.*

*People Will Always Be Kind* seems a before-and-after book with a hole in its middle, just where readers would want to look for the connection. . . .

Probably one should forget Part One while reading Part Two, which may suggest something less than the economy of means one hopes for in a novel. It may be that Sheed's experience—as a polio victim and a campaigner for Eugene McCarthy in 1968—has led him to write two stories. The first, a compassionate but unsentimental picture of a young mind bewildered by the sudden, inexplicable loss of its anticipated future, strikes me as imperfectly suited to Sheed's talent as a writer, though not to his intelligent, self-mocking Catholicism. His account of how it feels to gain self-consciousness through a suffering that estranges you from family, friends, community, God, all the modes of love and security most people are permitted to give up or redefine more gradually, is rather too reminiscent of Joyce, who after all did it without giving Stephen Dedalus a crippling disease on top of everything else. Like Stephen's, the young Brian Casey's experience has no ending compatible with fictional convention; but where *Ulysses* proceeds from *A Portrait* (without in any simple way being predicted by it), the story of the mature Casey seems disjointed.

But Casey II comes off very nicely on his own. Sheed's treatment of the tantalizing gap between the behavior of public men and our understanding of them capitalizes upon the recent intense interest in practical politics without descending to the melodramatic banalities of popular "political" novels. . . . Sheed makes no appeals to vulgar paranoia. There are no lurid conspiracies, no shocking scandals, no patriotic sermons to tie it all together. The hectic, duplicitous, improvisational hubbub of real political business is theater enough for a novelist like Sheed, part *farceur* and part theologian—like Brian Casey himself. . . .

*People Will Always Be Kind* [is] what is rare these days, a convincing political novel.

*Thomas R. Edwards, "Surprise, Surprise," in* The New York Review of Books *(reprinted with permission from* The New York Review of Books; *© 1973 by NYREV, Inc.), May 17, 1973, pp. 35-7.*

[*People Will Always Be Kind*] is an unusual and provocative novel. It is often compelling, intuitive and funny, yet, in the outcome, one is uncertain as to its purpose and development. It is difficult, in short, to decide whether it is a book about politics or one about the effects of illness. Perhaps it is both. . . .

In drawing out the essence of the politician, in its humor, satire, and ultimate anguish, Mr. Sheed's book is brilliantly contrived, a *tour de force*. It makes one wonder whether, in terms of the individuals who operate the system, pluralist, liberal politics are any less nightmarish than the patterns of totalitarianism with which we have been presented since the thirties in the writing of Koestler, Orwell and others whose communist idealism turned into disillusionment and dismay. In this sense, *People Will Always Be Kind* is indeed a political novel for our times. . . .

Is it, in fact, a political novel exploring the psychological make-up of *this* politician in *this* political context? Does it, in other words, seek to give us a particular explanation of a generally interesting question, namely, what psychological characteristics and experiences account for the development of the politician, given the morally debilitating pressures which are placed upon such an individual? If this is the case, then the long exploration of Casey's adolescence and coming of age shows us how such characteristics might develop, and his illness is a spectacular (and symbolic?) catalyst. Or, is it an exploration of the traumatic effects of an illness which, in this case, leads the victim into politics, and ends with the imposition of his trauma on the political scene? In either case, the linkage of the parts of the book is uncertain unless, of course, in his cleverness Mr. Sheed intended it to be so.

*David Cox, in* The International Fiction Review, *January, 1974, pp. 66-7.*

If being a New York Jew, born preferably in the Bronx, is worth a cliché's headstart to any aspirant American novelist, then at first sight Wilfrid Sheed is tied to a handicap somewhere below the horizon. Not only an Englishman but a certain sort of Englishman, an expatriate Oxford-educated Catholic, Mr Sheed lives in New York and now writes ostensibly American novels about Americans. As such he is competing on strange terrain against the best the East Coast has to offer, and that best is very good indeed. Mr Sheed, let it be said, positively flourishes on the comparison. . . .

The danger for an English novelist writing about a cast of high-powered Americans is that, culturally speaking, he's likely to sound either patronising or over-impressed, where he wouldn't be with a comparable group of Englishmen.

One negative measure of Mr Sheed's achievement is the critical distance he has put between himself and the run of novels with an American setting. He writes with the authority and insight of a native American but there is a precision and traditionalism about the structure of his novels that is very English. However, environment has its effect. . . . He [Casey, the protagonist of *People Will Always Be Kind,*] is Mr Sheed's finest creation so far, the creation of a novelist of great power at the top of his form.

*Timothy Mo, "Sick Fantasy," in* New Statesmen, *January 18, 1974, p. 86.*

* * *

## SHEPARD, Sam 1943-

**An American dramatist and screenwriter, Shepard has forged a "theatre of the mythic West" from hillbilly language, late-night TV westerns, country and western music, and legend. Shepard's plays, according to one critic, are "words and sounds, and the lost American idioms."**

*Operation Sidewinder* would be a great deal easier to talk about if I could dismiss it, as some reviewers did, as the self-indulgence of a precocious child or if I could celebrate it as a shattering statement about contemporary America. I can do neither. Sam Shepard has fascinated me ever since I first picked up a copy of *Five Plays*. He has a bizarre theatrical imagination, an ability to create workable dramatic turns which preclude any desire to dismiss him. Yet his plays seem designed to forestall any cumulative effect. His early one-acters—including the admirable *Red Cross*—are uneasy combinations of images—verbal and visual—but even after plot invaded his work, in *Melodrama Play* (1966), his plays remained saltatory, effective bits popping in for quick bows without the traditional justifications of story, character or theme. At *Operation Sidewinder*, predictably, I was amused, intrigued, interested, occasionally bored, infrequently annoyed, but never shattered. . . .

[The] virtues [of *Operation Sidewinder*] are all theatrical. There are too many moments when the conscious corn becomes self-defeating, bores in its cuteness, but for the most part it is at the service of a genuine stage imagination. The attenuation of the full-length play and the collector's quaintness in the pop gathering make the Shepard of *Operation Sidewinder* less interesting than the young man who wrote *Red Cross*. The new play can be seen with pleasure, perhaps even with self-recognition, as long as the audience understands that it is an artifact not a critique. Reduced to an ideational line it would be as sentimental as it is silly. It deserves better than that.

*Gerald Weales, "The Little Shepard," in* Commonweal *(reprinted by permission of Commonweal Publishing Co., Inc.), May 8, 1970, pp. 193-94.*

Sam Shepard works with an extraordinary freshness and humour and lightness of touch. He is one of the few living playwrights who seem to think directly in theatrical terms: most of them seem to have ideas which they then translate into drama.

Shepard's ideas are at once interesting, funny, moving and capable of organic development which is inseparable from that of the action.

*Randall Craig, in* Drama, *Autumn, 1973, p. 39.*

Laden with symbolism—both obvious and subtle—Sam Shepard's *Back Bog Beast Bait* creates a situation that can be understood on many levels. And it is only the author's own self-indulgence in continuing on long after his point has been made, that keeps the play from measuring up to its promise. . . .

Much to Mr. Shepard's credit, although these people remain archetypal, they are still individuals, acting and reacting consistently within an established reality. . . .

*Back Bog Beast Bait* is so near to being a significant work that it would be well worth Mr. Shepard's efforts to polish up some of the overwriting and tone down the overstatements.

*Debbi Wasserman, in* Show Business, *January 31, 1974, p. 7.*

Best known for his script work on Antonioni's *Zabriskie Point*, Sam Shepard has written a curious and disturbing first book in *Hawk Moon: A Book of Short Stories, Poems and Monologues*—full of perverse, often gratuitous bloodlust, moodiness, retribution fantasies, Indians, run-on sentences, pop mysticism, and intensely imagined fragments.

There is a sense in which, one might argue, the obsessive, extreme, arbitrary violence and necrophilia of *Hawk Moon* dramatizes life in our culture and is therefore somehow "right" for us. . . .

One does not have a sense, [though,] that he is expressing any special or sophisticated aesthetic theory or attitude toward character or characterization as he works, rather that he is freaked out on media tempos and disunities and/or figures he is writing for media freaks. So, he parcels out the intense close-up, the quick cut, the precise sense of rhythm and timing (which he is very good at, by the way), the corny mysticism, or the cheap thrill of blood on the carpet. . . .

If his intent is to take potshots at the culture, he usually fails to strike home, it seems to me, because too frequently his understanding of the culture seems simplistic, or the targets of his animosity seem so stiffly stereotyped, nothing but straw men to mow down. . . . We have all become "connoisseurs of anti-Americanism"; we have such a lot of it to choose from. Why rig a fictional America that is *nothing but* a justification for violent destruction?

If the bad guys in *Hawk Moon* are straw men, the good guys are monsters. . . . At times, the Shepard of *Hawk Moon* seems to have embraced the ghoulishness and sadism of media-distorted aspects of the culture he wishes to attack and rationalized it as Indian lore and the wisdom of savagery, a bizarre interpolation. If Charles Manson could write fiction, *Hawk Moon* is what it might look like—there is so much hate and incredible mixed up voodoo in this book.

*Joe David Bellamy, in* Partisan Review *(copyright © 1974 by Partisan Review, Inc.), Vol. XLI, No. 2 (Spring, 1974), pp. 314-16.*

Sam Shepard . . . is in the opinion of many, including myself, the most original and artistically disciplined of the Off-Off Broadway playwrights.

In his early plays like *Chicago* and *Red Cross* Shepard attracted attention by the startling way in which he juxtaposed powerful visual and verbal images producing an immediate and often disconcerting impact on the spectator's mind. He has in his more recent plays developed and refined this technique of dramatic collage and has employed it increasingly to create complex and unexpected combinations of cultural elements. In *Operation Sidewinder* Shepard shows a world of mad scientists and military men that recalls the film *Dr. Strangelove*, uses (in the first version of the play) excerpts from a speech by Stokely Carmichael, and recreates a Hopi snake ceremony. In *The Unseen Hand* he presents a cowboy gang styled on Western movies, confronts them with a science fiction character from another planet, and ends by introducing a "typical" all-American boy cheerleader. Finally, in . . . *The Tooth of Crime*, which describes how one rock singer and life style is replaced by another, he forges a new language by drawing on the dissimilar vocabularies and speech patterns of joke books, sportscasters, disk jockeys, rock musicians, hunters, and gangsters.

*Mad Dog Blues*, produced in 1971, is Shepard's third full length play, written after *La Turista* and *Operation Sidewinder* and before *The Tooth of Crime*. In it he again demonstrates his mastery of dramatic collage and treats many of the same themes found in his other plays—the search for innocence, the loss of identity, the tensions and fragility of human relations, and the obsessive presence of death. *Mad Dog Blues* differs from Shepard's other works in that the cultural elements he utilizes to develop these themes are more directly the center of interest. The play is in fact an intricate dramatization of the value and limits of popular culture, our attitudes toward it, and its effects on us. . . .

*Mad Dog Blues* is clearly an American play, and only an imagination that has grown on American movies, radio shows, pulp magazines, and music could have conceived it. Shepard's presentation emphasizes this fact, for each character in his costume, language, gestures, and songs appears as the pure expression of his own image, and each, like saints in a cathedral of American popular culture, carries his identifying attributes. . . .

Shepard's collage includes more than just the characters and costumes. . . . Even the sound effects are drawn from our cultural memories. . . . Shepard like Kerouac, a writer he admires, describes the rootlessness of American life, an existence of scattered friends, short-term affairs, and separations. Kosmo and Yahoodi [Shephard's protagonists] support each other's "inability to function," a condition which is true of most of the couples in Shepard's plays. . . .

For the spectator the presence of all these cultural figures, images, and allusions produces a definite, if limited, comic effect—an effect that is not, however, based on anything that could accurately be called parody, satire, or camp. Compared to the plays of many of his contemporaries, and especially to the wild dramatic exercises of Tavel or Charles Ludlam, Shepard's presentation is remarkably straight. The spectator of *Mad Dog Blues* laughs or smiles for the simple reason that the figures he sees on stage, by their very recurrence in yet another work, reaffirm their existence as clichés. He also takes obvious delight in an imagination that is able to draw on such a variety of sources. This delight comes easily because none of the cultural allusions, despite their relative complexity, are hidden or in any way obscure. On the contrary, they are immediately recognizable, if not blatant. The problem Shepard is posing for Kosmo and for the spectator is not that of identifying images and figures already known to everyone, but of finding a way to live and to deal with them. Shepard's own technique of dealing with popular culture is the key to the play's significance. While *Mad Dog Blues* does have a dazzling and often slick surface that directly strikes the senses, it also forces the spectator to view the surface, so to speak, from behind, from within the imagination that conceived it. In other words, the play is at once a pop-like display and a psychodrama. Also, the surface itself is not uniform, but is broken repeatedly by the characters who momentarily step out of the plot or adventure in order to comment on it and on their own lives. In this way Shepard's collage is not just a combination of different cultural elements but also of different dramatic tones and points of view. . . .

In his plays Shepard is in fact showing to what extent the mind, and particularly the modern American mind, can become and has become entrapped by its own verbal and imaginative creations. . . . The impression produced by the play is that the mind is so saturated by popular culture that almost any idea introduced into it acts as a catalyst around which an endless series of other ideas and images immediately crystallize. . . .

Shepard has a real love for the popular myths of our culture and a genuine nostalgia for some lost age of innocence when life was simpler in America. He also knows that this world may never have existed, that even at the time things were not the way the media represented them, and that our memory and imagination may well be based on lies. . . . Indeed, *Mad Dog Blues* suggests that all America is a society of ghosts, and that modern American civilization in general has taken on the attributes of its popular culture, has become a country where nothing lasts, where people pursue visions that lead nowhere, and where all relationships are transitory. America, too, carries the taint of mortality. . . .

It is not Shepard's purpose . . . to arrive at any kind of pat conclusion. . . . The value of *Mad Dog Blues* is in its ambiguity, or rather in the multiplicity of points of view it offers. . . . The quality of [Shepard's] performance can be judged by his ability to give a voice to the cultural confusion without succumbing to it as a playwright. There is nothing self-indulgent or contrived about his art in *Mad Dog Blues*. On the contrary, the play reveals his total commitment to the problems he is treating, as if he himself were attempting to discover his own identity in the cultural material inherited from the past.

Like many of his fellow playwrights Shepard knows that the old frontier myths of America's youth are no longer a valid expression of our modern anxieties, even though they continue to influence our thoughts. . . . [It] is clear that Shepard is searching for a new mythology that will encompass all the diverse figures of our cultural history together with the psychological and social conditions they represent. . . . Shepard's greatest contribution to a new American mythology may well be his elaboration of a new myth of the modern artist. Whatever judgment is finally made on his work, it is certain that in a society drifting rapidly into the escapism of a permanent, and often instant, nostalgia, Shepard's plays are a sign of artistic health and awareness, and are, therefore, worthy of our attention.

*George Stambolian, "Shepard's 'Mad Dog Blues': A Trip Through Popular Culture," in* Journal of Popular Culture, *Spring, 1974, pp. 776-86.*

[Shepard's] plays are not *about* America. In fact, it's hard to say what his plays are about. Sam himself says, 'I never know what to say when somebody says what are the plays about. They're about the moment of writing.' No, instead of trying to say what the plays are about, I'll simply call them American graffiti—images of America with a language pounding with the pulse beat of America. Take a play like *The Tooth of Crime*. Ostensibly set in the future. Yet it contains more of the *feel* of the modern American nightmare than any other American play written in the past few years. . . .

Sam is Indians, cowboys, rockers and greyhounds. He is also Wakan, cars, Cody, Wyoming and the Coasters with a fullblown vet underneath. But Sam is not just these things alone. He's far too unique to be ever captured in print. . . .

Sam is very aware of the problems involved in an art in which his vision must be transmuted and made three-dimensional through the agency of others. Like Genet, the uniqueness of this vision and the very way it is expressed confounds you. No two directors can agree on which is the best way of communicating Sam's vision, of making his words flesh. This vision has been seen, heard and felt so clearly by Sam, but its physical expression on the stage remains elusive.

*Walter Donahue, in* Plays and Players, *April, 1974, pp. 14-18.*

America is the only society that defines itself by a dream. Its stage legends and literature are cluttered with desperate dreamwalkers—men staggering through life in a state of perpetual anticipation or dazed acceptance. . . .

Usually, these dreamwalkers don't understand their condition; and that's where Sam Shepard's newest hero, Cody, in *The Geography Of A Horsedreamer* . . . differs from his theatrical ancestors. Cody has a genius for tipping the horses, a gift which puts him, and the two thugs that guard him, for the syndicate in fat city. But then his dreaming goes stale. When the curtain comes up, Cody is manacled to a hotel bed. He's predicting old winners. Cody tries to explain the problem to his bodyguards who wait, terrified, for Cody's dreaming to pay-off. 'It's very delicate work, dreaming a winner. . . . It takes certain special conditions. A certain internal environment.'

Cody is talking creativity. The thugs are talking cash. They refer to him as 'Mr Sensitive', 'Mr Artistic Cowboy', 'Beethoven'. Like any voracious audience living off somebody else's energy and insight, the thugs only want the result not the process. They need Cody's winners, not his non-starters. Uncreative themselves, their impatience is magnified by their impotence. The thugs won't let Cody out of his hotel room. He doesn't know where he is or what time of day it is. He's caged and adrift. Cody has the expatriate shivers which Shepard, now living in London, knows all too well. . . .

No Sam Shepard play is ever naturalistic. Every freak or cowboy who takes centre stage in his fantasy life has a sharp line of hip metaphysical chat. Since Shepard's plays are meditations, his characters are often plagued by inconcreteness, leaving the actors to struggle with ideas to play rather than character. But *The Geography Of A Horsedreamer*, which suffers from this disease, doesn't succumb to it. . . .

Shepard has subtitled *The Geography Of A Horsedreamer* a 'mystery play'. Certainly, it's a work whose characters and debate emerge out of the continual reassessment about America that goes on in the unconscious when you leave the States. As Cody is led away and back to his homeland, he speaks about dreaming and coming to terms with being a perpetual exile from the world. Dreaming is no longer an escape from an oppressive world but a creative source for survival. 'In a sacred way. This day. Sacred. I was walking in my dreams. A great circle. I was walking and I stopped. Even after the smoke cleared I couldn't see my home. Not even a familiar rock. You could tell me it was anywhere and I'd believe ya. You could tell me it was any old where . . .'.

Shepard, who has put himself outside the killing commercial climate of American life and theatre for the last few years, seems to be saying in this beautiful speech that the only real geography is internal. The world of keepers and the kept, the debased dreamers and the prophets, remains in every society. But once you've conquered the inner landscape, knowing how to use the visionary power and protect it, then it doesn't matter where you do your dreaming.

*John Lahr, in* Plays and Players, *April, 1974, pp. 46-7.*

* * *

## SILONE, Ignazio (pseudonym of Secundo Tranquilli) 1900-

**Silone, an Italian novelist of great power, is best known for *Bread and Wine*, his compelling fictional indictment of Italian Fascism. (See also *Contemporary Authors*, Vols. 25-28.)**

With his very first novels, *Fontamara* and *Bread and Wine*, Ignazio Silone won a following of readers who soon came to feel they were his secret friends. Silone could go almost anywhere in the world and find men who, having like himself experienced the failure of socialism, would immediately know how to register and value the muted slyness and sadness of his books, quite as old companions can speak to one another through a shrug or a smile.

For such readers, but surely for others, too, Silone's every word seems to bear a special quality, a stamp of fraternal but undeluded humaneness. It is really something of a mystery, which literary criticism with all its solemnities seems unable to penetrate: how a man who writes so simply and unpretentiously can nevertheless make everything he publishes uniquely his own. For almost four decades—the most terrible of our century, perhaps the most terrible in Western history—Silone has been a transforming presence: the least bitter of ex-Communists, the most reflective of radical democrats.

His work is wry, sometimes saturnine; sardonic, sometimes disillusioned. Brought up in the Abruzzi, he knows and loves the Italian peasants, but knows and loves too well for even a trace of sentimentalism. Educated in Italy, a nation cursed with the gift of rhetoric, he seems immune to all the enticements of verbal display. He can make small things (a casual gesture by a character, a quiet phrase of his own, a minor anecdote) into tokens of all the redemptive possibilities in this century of betrayal. He brings together in his writing the grit of the peasant and the fever of the intellectual, so that to read him is to encounter the oldness, the weariness of Europe: all those wise and tormented priests who keep moving through his stories, all those hunted and doubting revolutionists broken on the wheel of memory. . . .

What moves us, I think, is the sense we gain that while no wiser or politically "more correct" than the rest of us, Silone is, both as writer and person, profoundly contemptative, with every problem, every doubt, every failure of this age of failed revolutions having become part of his inner being.

And there is something else: the miracle—for it *is* a miracle—of his relationship to the people about whom he writes, the peasants of Italy. Silone is entirely free of the false identifications and grandiloquent delusions of Populism; for while he comes from the people, he is no longer of them. . . . Yet in all his books he is utterly free of those sins of aristocratism which stain the work of so many twentieth-century European writers. The miracle of Silone's relation to the peasants lies neither in distance nor in immersion, but in a readiness to leave and return, to experience estrangement yet maintain affection, to know in himself both the relief of deracination and the steadiness of rootedness. In this balance of response there is at least as much desperation as affection. Silone cares neither to deceive himself nor others: he does not romanticize the peasant figures who, together with the heretical priests and dissident revolutionists, embody his notion of character as moral example. He knows these peasants too well. . . . Yet he believes in the peasants, at least in those potentialities of which they themselves are seldom aware. For Silone has learned how to wait, even for that which may never come. (pp. 280-82)

*Fontamara* is the one important work of modern fiction that fully absorbs the Marxist outlook on the level of myth or legend; one of the few works of modern fiction in which the Marxist categories seem organic and "natural," not in the sense that they are part of the peasant heritage or arise spontaneously in the peasant imagination, but in the sense that the whole weight of the peasant experience, at least as it takes form in this book, requires an acceptance of these categories. What makes *Fontamara* so poignant as a political legend . . . is that he is a *patient* writer, one who has the most acute sense of the difference between what is and what he wishes. The peasants are shown in their nonpolitical actuality and the political actuality is shown as it moves in upon them, threatening to starve and destroy them; Silone does not assume the desired relationship between the two, though he shows the possibilities for a movement into that relationship; the book is both concrete—wonderfully concrete—in its steady view of peasant life and abstract—a brilliant paradigm—in its placing of peasant life in the larger social scheme. The political theories behind the book resemble the lines signifying longitude and latitude on a map; . . . they are indispensable for locating oneself among the mountains and plains and oceans; they are what gives the geography of society meaning and perspective. (p. 284)

[It] is precisely from . . . scrupulous examinations of conscience and commitment that so much of the impact of *Bread and Wine* derives; no other twentieth-century novelist has so fully conveyed the pathos behind the failure of socialism. *Bread and Wine* is a book of misery and doubt; it moves slowly, painfully, in a weary spiral that traces the spiritual anguish of its hero. The characteristic turning of the political novelist to some apolitical temptation is, in Silone's case, a wistful search for the lost conditions of simple life where one may find the moral resources which politics can no longer yield. This pastoral theme, winding quietly through the book and reaching full development only in its sequel, *The Seed Beneath the Snow*, is not an easy one for the modern reader to take at face value: we are quick, and rightly so, to suspect programs for simplicity. But in Silone's work it acquires a unique validity: he knows peasant life intimately and, perhaps because he does not himself pretend to be a peasant, seldom stoops to pseudo-folk romanticizing. (p. 287)

*Bread and Wine* is a work of humility, unmarred by the adventurism or occasional obsession with violence which disfigures the political novels of André Malraux and Arthur Koestler. Whatever the ideological hesitations of Silone's novels, they remain faithful to the essential experience of modern Europe; and to the harsh milieu of political struggle they bring a cleansing freshness, a warmth of fraternity. (p. 288)

After some years of silence . . . Silone managed a notable recovery. In the late fifties and early sixties he published two short novels, *The Secret of Luca* and *The Fox and the Camellias*, which seem to me . . . works that are both pleasing and fresh. Though never a literary modernist (Verga, not Joyce, is his master), Silone has always been an original writer, most notably in his use of anecdote as a major element in narration and in his readiness to employ the novel as a medium of conversation with the reader. These two novels show that in his quietly restless way he succeeded in breaking past the crisis of the middle years, not because he had solved his problems of belief but because he now wrote with the ease of a man who knows these problems will stay with him until the day of his death. (p. 289)

The form Silone developed in these books is peculiarly adapted to his intellectual condition. He now favors a brief, compact, and unadorned narrative, with very little of his earlier richness of anecdote or contemplation. The validating detail we associate with the novel as a genre is almost entirely absent. Silone drives his events forward with such a singleness of purpose that one soon realizes he has some commanding idea in sight; yet these tales—for they are more tales than novels—do not succumb to the abstractness or didacticism of allegory. They demand to be read, at all but one crucial point, as accounts of ordinary human experience. I would be inclined to call them realistic fables: realistic in that they are clearly meant as imitations of "real" life, and fables in that they are strictly pruned to the needs of Silone's theme, composing themselves in the reader's mind as a kind of quizzical *exemplum*. (p. 290)

Silone's novels contain a profound vision of what heroism can be in the modern world. Like Malraux, he appreciates the value of action, but he also realizes that in the age of totalitarianism it is possible for a heroic action to consist of nothing but stillness, that for . . . [many] there may never be the possibility of an outward or public gesture. For Ernest Hemingway heroism is always a visible trial, a test limited in time and symbolized in dramatic confrontations. For Silone heroism is a condition of readiness, a talent for waiting, a gift for stubbornness; the heroism of tiredness. Silone's heroic virtues pertain to people who live, as Bertolt Brecht put it, in "the dark ages" of twentieth-century Europe. (p. 293)

*Irving Howe, "Silone: A Luminous Example" (originally published in a different version in his* Politics and the Novel*; © 1957; reprinted by permission of the publisher, Horizon Press, New York), in his* Decline of the New, *Harcourt, 1970.*

A new book by Ignazio Silone is both a literary and a political event. A novelist and essayist, he was one of the outstanding figures in Italy's early Communist movement. During the 1920s he was actually in charge of its underground activities against the Fascist régime.

In 1927 a visit to Moscow and participation in a session of the Executive Committee of the Communist International marked the beginning of his estrangement from the movement, which he finally left in 1930. The incident that led to his eventual "renegacy"—as his disenchantment and withdrawal was termed by his erstwhile comrades—is vividly described in the main chapter of *Emergency Exit,* and supplies the title of the volume.

[He is a] pure-in-heart idealist and not a politician, whether "regular" or revolutionary. . . .

Hatred of Fascist and Communist tyranny and duplicity did not blind Silone to the shortcomings of the masses, all his compassion for their plight not withstanding. . . .

Silone is just as disappointed in the bulk of the radical intelligentsia which in some countries, and particularly in France, went along with the Kremlin rulers. He has bitter words for Jean-Paul Sartre, who in the name of "progress" justified the Soviet massacres in Hungary in 1956. In a remarkable passage Silone says: "In [Sartre's] view, a writer who is really alive cannot be for anything but progress; on the other hand, progress, in the modern era, is identified with the working class, which, in turn, is 'identified' with the Communist Party: the Communist Party, as everyone knows, 'is identified' with Soviet Russia and the People's Republics, which of course are to be 'identified' with History." . . .

*Max Nomad, "Cutoff from Hammer and Sickle," in* Saturday Review *(copyright © 1968 by Saturday Review/World, Inc.; reprinted with permission), November 9, 1968, pp. 40-1.*

The genius of Ignazio Silone lies in his faculty of [dealing] with the world not through an intercessor—some political, social, or psychological theory—but directly, and on the simplest terms. In this scholastic age, when every activity has a theory to explain and obscure it, so ideal a Protestantism on the part of a cultivated man is bound to appear perverse or disingenuous. The human preoccupations of Silone's books scandalize our sophisticated humanism; they are as unseemly as an outburst of religion within the church. Just such an untimely intrusion of the spirit is the theme of *The Story of a Humble Christian.*

The author is well aware that he is in a false position among the schoolmen of the scientific era. In the introduction to this powerful work, entitled "What Remains," Silone says: "Now it's clear that I'm interested in the fate of a certain type of man, how a certain type of Christian fits into the machinery of the world, and I wouldn't know how to write about anything else." The Christian he has in mind is the man often miscalled saint, prophet, or mystic—the man who sees what is real and declares it. Direct and simple, how can he help but antagonize orthodoxies and institutions? Silone has himself passed through two great orthodoxies, official Christianity and official Marxism, and that experience has led him to certain conclusions about the nature of our business as men. . . .

Silone's plain and vigorous style is infinitely more difficult to reproduce in a translation than a more elegant, more bookish prose would be. . . .

The spirit that animates the six acts of *The Story of a Humble Christian* is the spirit of religion—in despite of dogma and institutions. It should not be necessary to suggest that that spirit is at the origin of any reasonable philosophy, any reasonable view of our own nature and needs. But the idea of religion, like the idea of politics, has been so traduced by the actions of its official servants that to decent men it almost necessarily means obscurantism, as politics means fraud. Silone has never made either of those errors. He has always suggested that religion is properly the sum of our values, and politics the conduct that promotes those values. In his earlier books the polity that might incarnate our values had come more and more to appear incompatible with government. In this play, his conclusion is more explicitly anarchist: men cannot find God or the good while their institutions separate them from their fellows. It is our privilege that so sound a moralist is also a great artist.

*Emile Capouya, in* Saturday Review *(copyright © 1971 by Saturday Review/World, Inc.; reprinted with permission), April 24, 1971, pp. 31, 41.*

What can a writer do—I mean the kind of writer who yields himself to the political struggles of his time yet wishes to remain faithful to his calling and his craft? He can bear witness and tell the truth. He can assault the cant of brutal men in power and of hard-spirited ideologues lusting for power. He can tell us stories and fables that recall the imagination to humaneness. And if he is brave, stubborn and unafraid of loneliness, he can even help redeem the age in which he lives.

I think of Solzhenitsyn, Grass, Orwell, Camus and Silone, all sneered at these days by our campus guerrillas and pop revolutionists, yet the writers who ought to be seen as the true heroes of our culture. Immune to the virus of authoritarianism, these writers insist upon linking the hope for social change with the values of political liberty. They move in and out of popularity, going their own way, independent and authentic.

Foremost among them stands Ignazio Silone . . ., author of "Fontamara," a fable of peasant revolt in Fascist Italy, and "Bread and Wine," a profound novel about the disillusionment of a sincere Italian Communist. Silone is a writer whose every word yields a radiance of good faith, a pleasure of spirit that is indifferent to power and hostile to ideology. He is a churchless Christian and a partyless Socialist who keeps returning to a central problem of modern life: the problem of power, its tendency to corrupt those who hold it, to leave impotent those who refuse it, and to torment those who wish to shorten the distance between the ends for which they suppose themselves to live and the means by which they do live.

So generalized, the problem may be beyond solution. Yet in a number of his works Silone deliberately creates extreme situations in which a good man finds himself torn between the demands of action and the constraints of morality. He offers no solution, and knows that the actuality of experience is more shaded than this counterposition of absolutes might suggest. What interests him is a fictional test case, the experience of the man who submits himself to this terrible problem—"the fate of a certain type of man, how a certain type of Christian fits into the machinery of the world."

It is the mystery of the good man, his appearance and persistence, that absorbs Silone, just as, in a different context, it absorbs Solzhenitsyn.

*Irving Howe, in* The New York Times Book Review *(© 1971 by The New York Times Company; reprinted by permission), May 2, 1971, pp. 4, 5, 42.*

* * *

## SIMON, Claude 1913-

**Simon, a French novelist, is considered one of the most brilliant of the New Novelists.**

Along with other experimenters among recent novelists, Claude Simon attempts to bypass literature in communicating an experience directly and with an immediacy such as painting could have; but few styles are more consciously literary than his. The overall impression is that he possesses the greatest gifts of any prose writer among the modern French since Huysmans and Giono, but hardly those of a writer of fiction, if fiction must engage and maintain a reader's interest. Poets, since Mallarmé and George, have eventually created a limited audience of fervent lovers of their poetry and influenced philosophers, fiction writers, painters, and musicians. It is more doubtful whether novelists can likewise relinquish the spacious realm which once was theirs, cultivate an impossible purity, and survive. The history of the artistically written novel, from Chateaubriand to Walter Pater and George Moore, is strewn with mishaps.

*Henri Peyre, in his* French Novelists of Today *(copyright © 1955, 1967 by Oxford University Press; reprinted by permission), Oxford University Press-Galaxy, 1967, pp. 375-79.*

Claude Simon learned much from both Albert Camus and William Faulkner. His first novel, *Le Tricheur* (1945; *The Trickster*), is very much in the vein of Camus's *The Stranger*. By the time he had reached his fifth novel, *Le Vent* (1957; *The Wind*), Simon was using Faulkner-like thousand-word sentences and elongated parentheses. But, like Faulkner, Simon by means of such methods often achieves impressive effects; the wind of his story, for example, is supremely orchestrated, the wind blowing across the vineyards over which Simon's central character, the saintly simple Antoine Montès, wanders. *L'Herbe* (1958; *The Grass*) is even more poetic, and the story plays a more important part in the book this time, as a group of characters look back on their lives, which once covered the earth like the blowing grass. . . .

In *La Route des Flandres* (1960; *The Flanders Road*), Simon seems more the follower of Conrad and Proust than of Faulkner, though by this time he has developed a vision distinctly his own.

*Harry T. Moore, in his* Twentieth-Century French Literature Since World War II *(copyright © 1966 by Southern Illinois University Press; reprinted by permission of Southern Illinois University Press), Carbondale: Southern Illinois University Press, 1966, pp. 143-44.*

Claude Simon began his literary career after the Liberation with a traditional novel, *Le Tricheur,* whose hero is very close to Meursault in [Camus's] *L'Etranger.* But there is no question of direct influence. Simon expresses through his hero not so much the impossibility of taking an absurd world seriously as a difficulty in living at all. After some years of self-searching and silence, he wrote *Gulliver* and *Le Sacre du Printemps,* in which obsessive material breaks through the traditional narrative style that is imposed upon it. The rhythm is a syncopated one. A number of separate stories interweave and overlap. One feels that the author has read Faulkner and that he has learnt something from his reading. He appears in his own guise in *Le Vent* . . . and *L'Herbe*. . . .

[History, in] all Claude Simon's novels, is fatalistic. . . . The characters of *L'Herbe* . . . have, in fact, no history, or at least one so banal as not to be worth mentioning. What interests the author is the material that can be extracted from the events of a life; and again, it is this matter that he makes so fascinating. His unimportant, scarcely distinguishable characters take on a relief that no analysis could have given them. The whole construction of the novel forms a block in which we are made prisoners.

[In] *La Route des Flandres* . . . each individual carries about him a boundless world which intersects with other worlds. It is enough for him simply to live, and it is this life, merging with others, taken up by the vast movement of the world, tossed about at the mercy of events, sinking into memory or spreading out over the surface of things, that Claude Simon has striven to express in words, in a language dense and obscure. . . .

[In *Le Palace*] Claude Simon makes brilliant use of his heavily-weighted, meandering, serpentine sentence. Imperceptibly it has become for him an instrument of discovery and creation. It passes over reality like a sponge, sucking it dry.

*Maurice Nadeau, in his* The French Novel Since the War, *translated by A. M. Sheridan-Smith (reprinted by permission of Grove Press, Inc.; copyright © 1967 by Methuen and Co., Ltd.), Methuen, 1967, pp. 137-38 (in the Grove-Evergreen paperbound edition, 1969).*

[Claude Simon] started his career as a painter and he envisaged the problem of writing fiction as not dissimilar from that of the painter: to convey, not a succession in time and a sense of duration, but simultaneousness; to transpose one dimension into another and organize images which coexist in memory. Hence his inordinately long sentences, meandering over several pages, and his dismissal of all punctuation. His demands upon the reader's attention are cruelly exacting and not a few critics have refused to accede to them. . . . As to the public, Claude Simon, who nowhere attempts to outwit his readers with detective story trickery, firmly asserts that it can be disregarded by the novelist, as it was by Van Gogh and Picasso: the primary duties of a creator are to himself. . . .

What distinguishes "Histoire" from so many dreary and boring *nouveau roman* attempts at capturing the truths of reality is that Claude Simon structures his remembrances around crucial centripetal happenings that manage to sustain the reader's interest in the novelist's frenzied and puzzling involvement with past events and impressions. The clever counterpointing of banal incidents with lyrically intense realities rescues the novel from deteriorating into the painfully labored and pretentious exercise on human complexity that has marred so many of the new French novelists' excursions into the fictional world. "Histoire" is a novel worthy of a second reading and careful examination.

Virginia Quarterly Review, *Vol. 44, No. 4 (Autumn, 1968), p. cxlviii.*

Like his predecessors, the narrator of *Histoire* seeks to discover in the past the meaning of his present existence and finds only reasons for discarding what remains of his ideals. Because he achieves no epiphany, however, he falls short of the heroic possibilities suggested by Montès [in *The Wind*] and Georges [in *The Grass*]. These two figures best represent Simon and best express his view of the dignity of the man who maintains his ideals and aspirations despite his disillusionment. In the tradition of Leopold Bloom, they are the heroes of the contemporary novel; theirs is a humanity which the essentially intellectual heroes of Robbe-Grillet and Butor can never achieve.

Because of them Simon must be distinguished from the New Novelists, even though his narrative method seems so closely to parallel theirs. We find in his works the same balance of strict objectivity and intense subjectivity; the same use of myth and symbol as a form of analogue—functioning, in effect, as a parallel point of view; the same combination of logic and uncertainty as in Robbe-Grillet, and the same interaction of various levels of time as in Butor. If this technique differs from theirs, it is only in the frequent occurrence of the word "reconstruction" and the Proustian process which it entails. But the possibilities which Simon has developed in this process are wonderfully enriching.

By affording his narrators the power to recreate events of which they have little direct knowledge, Simon provides them with much of the freedom of authorial omniscience at the same time that he offers insight into the characters themselves. In their need to recreate the past, in their effort to understand their present lives as a product of their past, in their need to make of their lives—past and present—a formal and consistent pattern like that of Proust's Marcel, Simon's characters are most enlightening. This compulsion makes them susceptible to disillusionment and makes them figures with whom the reader can identify, providing for character and reader alike the possibility of epiphany and catharsis. The peculiar contemporaneity of their narrative method arises because their apparent omniscience provides not greater certainty—as in the traditional novel—but greater possibilities of uncertainty, reasons for abandoning their ideals at the same time that they retain them. It is this ambiguity which makes their situations so moving.

*Morton P. Levitt, "Disillusionment and Epiphany: The Novels of Claude Simon," in* Critique: Studies in Modern Fiction, *Vol. XII, No. 1, 1970, pp. 43-70.*

Of the French novelists who have come into prominence in the last twenty years, only two have emerged from the blurred crowd of new names as genuine artists, as writers of genuine wisdom and stature: Alain Robbe-Grillet and Claude Simon. Both are difficult writers, for they are testing the very fiber and form of the novel with each book they write. Robbe-Grillet is better known because of his association with films, but Simon is as brilliant and exciting a writer and deserves a wider audience in this country than he has. "The Battle of Pharsalus" is his sixth novel, and it is a rich exemplification of the power of the imagination to create value in the flux of experience, to make the real from a confusion of sensations, of percepts and concepts. Like Robbe-Grillet's "In the Labyrinth" or Nabokov's "The Gift" and "Pale Fire" the novel becomes itself the tangible fact of the imagination of its central character. In it, O. the man without certain identity unravels his personal past and the larger past of Caesar's battle at Pharsalus, but he does not arrive at a static moment of truth but rather at an open door into the living future. By being able through an imaginative act to be both his wife in an adulterous sexual act and himself outside the door discovering her, he frees himself to be all men, to become not what the past made him, but whatever he chooses to be. Just as no memory or landmarks of the battle of Pharsalus exist in the present Greek town called the Battle of Pharsala, the past does not exist in O.'s present unless he chooses it, unless he transmutes it into words on the page as Caesar did in his war commentaries. One may believe Caesar or present fact. O. may believe in his present or allow himself to be locked in the past. He chooses the present in the form of the novel, "The Battle of Pharsalus." And by making that choice he creates the values of his own future and influences those of us, the readers of the novel, as well. The novel is a brilliant book.

Virginia Quarterly Review, *Vol. 47, No. 3 (Summer, 1971), p. civ.*

Claude Simon is plainly the most "impure" artist among [the New Novelists], in the sense that he excludes no aspect of life from his purview: "birth and copulation and death," politics, economics, science, the arts. In his crowded, turbulent books we find scenes of war, crime, revolution, and imprisonment; details of farming and the care of horses; the lure of alcohol, fast cars, and gambling; the technicalities of sport, dress, and interior decoration. . . .

If we are tempted to regard Simon as an impure artist because of his great concern with the minutiae of life, we run the risk of classifying him as impure in another, related, way by attributing to him an insufficient concern with form. Such a judgment would be a gross error, whether it referred to Simon's intention or to his achievement. Far from being unconcerned with form, Simon consciously strives for it, as his apprenticeship to painting presumably trained him to do. His less successful novels—notably *The Palace*—suffer from too great rigidity of structure rather than too little. As epigraph to *The Wind* he quotes a dictum of Paul Valéry: "The world is incessantly threatened by two dangers: order and disorder." Simon himself, as a novelist, is threatened by these twin dangers, but in his best work to date, *The Flanders Road,* he triumphantly passes between Scylla and Charybdis, creating a precarious balance between order and disorder. Paradoxically, though life is meaningless to Simon as a man, to Simon as an artist it is never entirely formless. This concern with form, even more than his skepticism about the possibility of knowing anything for certain about the stream of phenomena, classifies him indisputably as a New Novelist.

Two other characteristics of many of the New Novelists have become increasingly important in Simon's work. One is the passion for minute description which has led some critics to name the New Novelists *l'école du regard* ("the school of the gaze"). . . . As a result, "things *are there*" in Simon's novels, often endowed with an intrinsic importance unrelated to their symbolic value for the human mind that perceives them. The other characteristic, ultimately of more importance, is the attempt to convert the novel from an art of time to an art of space, so that when we have read a book through—probably not for the first time, however—we can get the impression of "seeing it all at once," just as we do a painting or a map. . . .

Simon has been deeply influenced by Proust, and all his later novels are "remembrance of things past." . . . Note that the final word of *The Flanders Road*, as of Proust's *Remembrance of Things Past*, is *temps*, "time.". . .

[If] the pattern of . . . lives [in *The Flanders Road*] is shattered, the pattern of Simon's book remains, raising its triune symbol of order triumphantly above the fragmentary disorder of history and time. And hand in hand with order, as always, goes beauty, not merely the sort of beauty one can find in Goya's terrifying series of etchings, *The Disasters of War*, but also a more familiar kind that gains poignancy from Simon's oppressive awareness of its transience: the beauty of young women, of jockey's silks and thoroughbred horses, of a cavalry squadron before battle, of the French landscape not yet defaced and eroded by the tide of war, of the archaic ideals upheld by a dying aristocracy. Life may be meaningless for Simon, but he cannot persuade either us or himself that it is not good. Thus a book like *The Flanders Road* is not merely a work of art, it is a means to knowledge—of ourselves and of the world.

*Vivian Mercier, "Claude Simon: Order and Disorder, Memory and Desire," in his* The New Novel: From Queneau to Pinget *(reprinted with the permission of Farrar, Straus & Giroux, Inc.; copyright © 1966,*

*1967, 1968, 1971 by Vivian Mercier), Farrar, Straus, 1971, pp. 266-75.*

After somewhat difficult beginnings, Claude Simon is today prominent, prolific, and probably the most solid writer on the French literary scene. His tenth novel [*Les corps conducteurs*] shows a significant evolution in his art. In previous novels there still was, if not a story, at least a visible anecdotal level which has disappeared altogether here. . . .

[This] novel is made up of a series of descriptions seemingly disconnected, for it is impossible to place them in any sort of logical time sequence. The impression given by the book is that of a giant collage or patchwork, reminiscent of contemporary art works and especially of the famous "combines" of Rauschenberg whom Claude Simon admires very much. . . .

This particular conception of the novel can best be appreciated through a rapprochement with painting because it attempts to escape time in order to achieve a spatial representation of the mind. As in painting, it requires a great artist to select the material, arrange, blend, and link the varied components so masterfully. Visual, auditive, emotional associations or pure word assonances are used in a fade-dissolve technique to transport us from one theme to the other, and back and forth. Another point of comparison with the plastic arts is that, just as an amateur in art is free to imagine a story while looking at a work, say, by Rauschenberg, a reader can do the same with Claude Simon. Of course, in an "abstract" novel, a myriad of possible "stories" exists.

*Claude DuVerlie, in* Books Abroad, *Vol. 46, No. 2, Spring, 1972, pp. 262-63.*

I have nothing but admiration for M Simon's intrepid integrity in the solution of technical problems of style and form in the novel. His novels are properly experimental and this one [*The Battle of Pharsalus*] shows great ingenuity and considerable powers of imagination. He has more than once been compared with William Faulkner, and it is clear from his method and style that he has been indebted to writers like Beckett and Joyce. But I am beginning to wonder now whether the 'stream of consciousness' technique, which has been exploited on and off for at least 50 years, can be much furthered.

*J. A. Cuddon, in* Books and Bookmen, *August, 1972, pp. 69-70.*

Claude Simon's latest book *Triptyque* is another product of the art of "scription," as understood by some new novelists. . . . As in some of his former fiction, particularly *Histoire . . ., Bataille de Pharsale . . .* and *Les corps conducteurs . . .,* Simon explores language. Opposed to the concept of the omniscient writer who tells a story, Simon . . . claims that he is "the product of his work." Words generate the text in constant transformation. Combining fictional fragments and placing them into new contexts, the scriptor creates a closely-knit network of textual relationships as the fiction develops.

*Triptyque*, composed of three major fictional fragments, is an example of how close Simon's art of writing is to the painter's form. (In painting, a triptyque consists of three different segments, placed side by side, which share theme, form, and/or colors.) His outline, unfortunately not included in the book, shows that he divided his pages into three sections: A deals with a wedding that ends in sorrow; B gives episodes from the lives of two boys in the country and the drowning of a little girl; and C refers to an evening on the Mediterranean (and contains references to a former book). There is a great deal of intertextuality, particularly with references to movie and circus posters on a billboard, marked by lines and arrows that overlap the three divisions.

In the book itself the fragments occasionally offer a substantial portion of thematically connected prose. At other times, there is also overlapping. For example there is the same blond actor in two of the film posters, as well as in two fictional fragments. . . .

Although it is tempting to analyze *Triptyque* in terms of structural components, it is better to step back, as when viewing an impressionistic painting, to enjoy the impact of the whole work. At the end, we may, like one of the characters, destroy the jigsaw puzzle, or step out into the street with the audience that has just seen the film. All is over, all can begin again.

*Anna Otten, in* Books Abroad, *Vol. 48, No. 1, Winter, 1974, pp. 86-7.*

* * *

## SIMPSON, Louis 1923-

**Simpson is a Jamaican-born American poet, critic, and editor. He won the Pulitzer Prize for poetry in 1964. (See also *Contemporary Authors*, Vols. 1-4, rev. ed.)**

[Simpson] demonstrates that the best service an American poet can do his country is to see it all: not just the promise, not just the loss and the "betrayal of the American ideal," the Whitmanian ideal—although nobody sees this last more penetratingly than Simpson does—but the whole "complex fate," the difficult and agonizing *meaning* of being an American, of living as an American at the time in which one chances to live. If it comes out sad, as it does with Simpson despite all his wit and compassion, it is a whole and not a deliberately partial sadness, and this gives the pervasive desperate sadness of [*Selected Poems*] a terrific weight of honesty and truth. . . .

Through the used-car lots, through the suburbs, through the wars that are only the intensification and temporary catharsis of the life we lead now, Simpson moves in this book, and moves memorably and skillfully. Principally there is the feeling of the great occasions of a man's life being veiled, being kept from him by the soft insulations of his civilization, he being all his life comfortable and miserable, taken care of and baffled. Since there is no primitive singleness of response anywhere, since one cannot hope for spontaneity, one takes it out in wit. Simpson's tone is often much like Randall Jarrell's, although more nervous, irritable, and biting. Jarrell's poems deal with the slow wonder of loss; Simpson's less resigned ones are more bewilderedly angry. If I had any objections to Simpson's work they would tend to group around a knowledgeable glibness, an easy literary propensity to knock off certain obvious sitting ducks, But [*Selected Poems*] is a very good book, a good spread of Simpson's work, and the intensity of his intelligent despair throughout it is harrowing.

*James Dickey, "Louis Simpson" (1965), in his* Babel to Byzantium *(reprinted with the permission of Farrar, Straus & Giroux, Inc.; copyright © 1956, 1957, 1958, 1959, 1960, 1961, 1962, 1963, 1964, 1965, 1966, 1967, 1968 by James Dickey), Farrar, Straus, 1968, pp. 195-97.*

A poet of liberal persuasion, [Simpson] is interested in public issues, in social and philosophical questions relating to the destiny of Europe and America. . . . In . . . *At the End of the Open Road,* [he] asks us to forget the Adamic innocence of the American past and recognize the seriousness of life in the present; we must cultivate our gardens in full awareness of the imminence of death.

Although he wrote some free verse as a young man, Simpson was deeply committed to traditional technique until 1959; he counted his accented and unaccented syllables carefully and built structures of pleasing but conventional sound, nailed with rhyme. After 1959, largely under the influence of the subjective-image poets, he changed his style drastically. The prosaism of his early work—which required metrics and rhyme in order to give it character as verse—now gave way to rich, fresh, haunting imagery. His philosophical and political speculations achieved a distinction and brilliance that they had lacked before.

*Stephen Stepanchev, "Louis Simpson," in his* American Poetry Since 1945: A Critical Survey *(copyright © 1965 by Stephen Stepanchev; reprinted by permission of Harper & Row, Publishers, Inc.), Harper, 1965, pp. 198-200.*

Simpson, especially since his Pulitzer Prize volume, *At the End of the Open Road*, 1963, has come to rely largely upon the emotive imagination.

Thematically, Louis Simpson is a powerfully guilt ridden poet and the most recent poems [in *Selected Poems*] intensify this strain. There are several explicit motivations for this: disillusionment with the enthusiasm of his own generation's war torn hopes to build a better society ("The Silent Generation") or a grudging resignation to middle class inertia in "In the Suburbs". . . . Simpson's disgust with postwar America occasionally lapses into acrimony and outrage which thwarts his native lyric tongue; it is a tendency I hope that he will be able to overcome. The theme of guilt emotively explored, particularly the tension between his self-conscious middle class respectability and the variously impoverished figures who confront him, is the basic idiom of his poetry now. Stripped of its excesses, it can provide a firm foundation for his growth.

*George Lensing, in* The Southern Review, *Vol. III, No. 1, Winter, 1967, pp. 205-06.*

Mr. Simpson's first three volumes are better [than the new work in *Selected Poems*]. They convey the same themes more excitingly, more satisfyingly, and no little part of the earlier successes is an adherence to tight and demanding forms, which Mr. Simpson handles with great skill. The new freedoms he has allowed himself have not made it possible to do the old things better. I know at last that the Pulitzer award was not for past works as well as present. It was bestowed for the more open and direct acknowledgment of the poet's master Whitman, which had always been there, but which in the earlier poems had been filtered through Hart Crane. . . .

One hopes that Mr. Simpson will return to a more formal utterance; one hopes that verse in English will recover strength, order, grace—its former sanity.

*Harry Morris, in* Sewanee Review *(© 1969 by The University of the South; reprinted by permission of the editor), Spring, 1969, p. 325.*

Mr Simpson seems embarrassed by his blessings. In a world full of naked pain and cruelty, he is almost ashamed to be sane, competent, free. He is also embarrassed by his fellow-countrymen, saddened by the false finale of the American idyll. Implicit in his irony and humour are many of the judgments passed by [Robert] Duncan. But his understatements linger in one's ear; his elegies for an over-ripe civilization lure and surprise one with their delicate changes of tone, their witty plaintiveness. Surely Mr Simpson's road would be a good one for more poets to travel.

*"Dubious Seer," in* The Times Literary Supplement *(reproduced by permission), July 23, 1971, p. 855.*

Louis Simpson's work is unbuttoned, genial, the kind of particularly American poetry that approaches a reader with an easy confidence in a shared language and an ironic civilization of attitude. . . . Simpson's achievement is to keep a total casualness of manner while paring and heightening the language so that it conveys a great deal poetically.

*Julian Symons, "Unbuttoned," in* London Magazine, *December, 1971/January, 1972, p. 128.*

[Simpson's] war poems are not witty, clever, gay, or humorous, but they are indeed moving and ironic. The other qualities, including irony, abound in the love poems, which, like the war poems, constitute about a third of the lyrics in *The Arrivistes*. In these love poems, Simpson resorts at times to inversions and to other archaic conventions in order to achieve rhyme. He often sounds, in fact, like an Elizabethan song-maker or like a Cavalier poet. Several of the love poems succeed better than others in infusing modern situations with the standard techniques of some time ago. (p. 41)

From the war poems included in *The Arrivistes* and in *Good News of Death and Other Poems*, certain consistent attitudes emerge. . . . Men in war, particularly those who serve in the infantry, are led to combat like children in a schoolyard to play a game with which they are unfamiliar. The men are, for the most part, unable to understand for what or why they are fighting. War is a dehumanizing force. . . . Yet men in war strive to maintain their basic dignity as human beings, and for this attempt they deserve sympathy. There is neither glory nor glamor in modern war, yet there are heroes and heroic acts. After war, the heroes, or their memories, are mistreated by a society that does not know what to do with them and that wants to forget anything to do with war as quickly and as conveniently as possible. (pp. 55-6)

Forty-one of the seventy-five pages of *A Dream of Governors* are devoted to the subject of war, thirty-one of which make up "The Runner," Louis Simpson's longest poem. This subject . . . is such a consistent one that there is little doubt, as we have observed before, that Simpson is the major American poet of World War II. In fact, he is probably the major American war poet, a position won not because he has written considerably on the subject, but because of the qualities that distinguish his war poems. (p. 76)

Although "The Runner" contains instances of fine descriptive and dramatic writing, it is nevertheless quite a conventional narrative. Thus it is not surprising that most reviewers of *A Dream of Governors* and the *Selected Poems* in which the long poem appeared find it unsatisfactory, by and large. . . .

I must disagree with the critical consensus; "The Runner" satisfies the basic requirements of the long narrative poem. The plot moves well to its exciting climax. As the protagonist, Dodd is well defined; we are led to feel with his emotional turmoil over man's archetypal need to be strong, brave, and accepted. And we can understand the forces working outside of and within him that bring about his alleged act of cowardice. Dodd is no hero, and herein lies a major point: there are no heroes, and there is no glory in war. War is inimical to the human condition; and it is especially alien to a man like Dodd who is sensitive and who *thinks*. "The Runner" succeeds in what it sets out to do, and what it sets out to do is significant. (p. 84)

Simpson, along with William Stafford, James Wright, and Robert Bly, best represents the Emotive Imagination, though there are of course, other American poets whose work fits into this category. (p. 94)

Although my intent is not to label Simpson or to put him squarely within the definitive boundaries of a movement, I believe that an awareness that other poets share similitudes of techniques, subject matter, and attitudes helps to place his poetry within a meaningful context that is all the more significant because Simpson is pioneering these efforts. Of course, he is an individual poet, especially in his vision of America; but his poems since 1959 do resemble those of others, and this resemblance is important to notice.

The poems of the Emotive Imagination are, for the most part, not directed by concerns for rhyme, meter, or specific stanza divisions. The diction and rhythms are colloquial; images juxtaposed to create fresh and invigorating perceptions abound in poems of this movement. Since most of the poems of the Emotive Imagination are short, exact timing in the placing of these images is an important consideration. The images in these generally nonviolent (but not always) poems create a muted shock effect insofar as the reader's expectations are concerned. For example, some of Simpson's shortest poems begin with seemingly dull and uninspired lines; then, as the poems progress, the imaginative leaps through images take place; and, in the closing lines, the reader is confronted with images that seem irrationally arrived at but that contain the emotional messages of the poems. The reader is led to understanding, therefore, through feeling rather than through a logically charted progression of symbols. Assuredly, intellect is involved in the progression and images in the poem of the Emotive Imagination, but understanding depends frequently on what appears to be an irrationally oriented imagination. Coleridge's "willing suspension of disbelief" is asked of the reader, who, if he is willing to comply, is rewarded.

The imaginative leaps the reader is asked to accept are founded on metaphors, and Simpson believes that metaphor in poetry makes us "experience thought as sense-perception, and so understand it." Often the metaphoric qualities in the images that characterize poems of the Emotive Imagination work through personifications. Stafford, Wright, and Bly employ the personification method with more consistency than Simpson, but his use of it is extremely effective. (pp. 95-6)

[Although the] other poets of the Emotive Imagination work within the context of defining America, Simpson alone has come directly to terms with America's failure to fulfill promises it seemed once to hold. Although this thematic consideration is apparent to an extent in his earlier poems, [*At the End of the Open Road*] contains the substance of his vision. (p. 96)

The influence, rather the force, of Whitman on Simpson lies primarily in the subject choice and attitude—and, more exactly, in providing Simpson with a way of looking at America, its spirit, character, philosophy, and direction. Nonetheless, the attitudes are entirely Simpson's; they are not extensions or refinements of those Whitman seems to hold. Since, more than any other American poet, Whitman tries to embrace and embody all of America, it is only reasonable that he provides a point of departure for Simpson, a set of attitudes about the country from which Simpson departs; for, assuredly, Simpson is not the optimistic celebrator of America that Whitman is; moreover, the poetry of Simpson is original in thought and in execution. (p. 109)

The last four lines of "Walt Whitman at Bear Mountain," . . . have frequently been cited by Simpson's critics and reviewers as a brilliantly imagistic ending to an outstanding poem. But no one has yet offered an explanation for the rational sense of these lines. The fact that they are striking and, at the same time, seemingly inexplicable is strong testimony to the efficacy of the Emotive Imagination. (p. 114)

[Regarding "Walt Whitman at Bear Mountain,"] I can think of no other recent poem about America which so incisively and artistically probes at the core of the American spirit. Even in a literary sense, Simpson has provided a valuable service by placing Whitman's so-called prophecies in a sensible and meaningful perspective. In addition and more importantly, Simpson has questioned the validity of "American dreams." Our headlong plunge into self-aggrandizement is the primary object of his indictment. His prescription is offered in the perhaps too confusing closing lines of the poem. (p. 115)

The first three volumes of Simpson's poetry abound in poems shining with ironic humor. The irony remains in the fourth volume, *At the End of the Open Road,* and in the poems following to date; but the humor, largely a matter of dry, understated wit, is not as apparent. Like the early poetry, *Riverside Drive* can be humorous. . . .

*Riverside Drive* is a good novel. To serious students of Louis Simpson, it is an important novel. . . . The novel confirms, among other things, the thematic judgments his poems on war make; and its style is superior. (p. 171)

*Ronald Moran, in his* Louis Simpson *(copyright 1972 by Twayne Publishers, Inc,; reprinted with permission of Twayne Publishers, a Division of G. K. Hall & Co.), Twayne, 1972.*

[*Adventures of the Letter I*] is the first full-length collection of new poems by Louis Simpson since "At the End of the Open Road," which startled readers with its radical departures from Simpson's earlier, more traditional manner. Simpson's shift in style was something like James Wright's: from rhyme, meter, and traditional subject matter to free-verse explorations of the subjective image and of what must be called, loosely, politics. He continues in his new vein in this book, but with what a difference! He has abandoned the owlishness that characterized "At the End of the Open Road"; the sense of serious play so important to his earlier work has given his new poetry a strength and serenity that it had lacked. The book begins with a series of poems which try to recapture an imagined land, the Russia in which the poet's mother grew up. From there he moves to explorations of politics as a human reality, in poems concerned with Indians, Walt Whitman, and Kafkaesque visions of contemporary bureaucracy, always with control and even with love. This is perhaps Simpson's best book so far.

Virginia Quarterly Review, *Vol. 49, No. 1 (Winter, 1973), pp. xii-xiii.*

A poet has written ["North of Jamaica"]. No praise is higher than that—that is, if the poet has succeeded in mastering the words for it, the "handful of words" it takes to write the poem one intended or the book one had in mind. "North of Jamaica," a story of Louis Simpson's life, is told in prose with the clarity, precision, condensation of poetry. Through its six parts, he speaks in many voices, yet amazingly each voice is his own: quiet, dispassionate, amusing, disturbing—separate voices. By listening to the tone, one hears them all.

*Helen Bevington, in* The New York Times Book Review *(© 1973 by the New York Times Company; reprinted by permission), April 8, 1973, p. 3.*

* * *

## SNOW, C(harles) P(ercy) 1905-

**Snow is a British novelist and physicist best known for his "Strangers and Brothers" series of eleven novels. In his novels, Snow deals with problems of power and morality in English society. (See also *Contemporary Authors*, Vols. 5-8, rev. ed.)**

[Critical] consideration of Mr. Snow comes back to his style, that style which in its alkaline flatness blandly ignores half a century of experimental writing. The style is not the man. Mr. Snow is not imperceptive of the revolution in the novel's technique connected with the names of James Joyce, Wyndham Lewis, Joyce Cary and many others: he ignores them deliberately in pursuit of an aesthetic which has never been openly formulated, but is perhaps his own version of realism—a realism that looks back to Trollope rather than to the symbolic naturalism of Zola or the photographic technique of such an American novelist as James T. Farrell. The style is that of a lucid and uncommonly honest recorder, rather than of an artist. When the whole ten or eleven volumes of Lewis Eliot's saga ["Strangers and Brothers"] are ranged on the shelf Mr. Snow may well be regarded as the most faithful recorder of the figure to whom his work is really devoted, the corporate individual, the harassed and virtuous administrator, the bureaucratic man.

*Julian Symons, "Of Bureaucratic Man" (1954), in his* Critical Occasions, *Hamish Hamilton, 1966, pp. 68-73.*

Snow . . . is quite satisfied to take over, entirely unaltered, the machinery devised by Trollope. Sir Charles's interests are those of a practical man; he is concerned primarily with how the world works and how things get done. Since this kind of preoccupation has not altered very much in the last century, there is no reason why Sir Charles should trouble himself to adapt the Trollopian form; it will do as it stands; Galsworthy in *The Forsyte Saga* found that form perfectly suited to the task of describing the Edwardian social scene and Sir Charles finds it equally suited, for his own special purposes, to the mid-twentieth century. And indeed it may be that this kind of copious realistic novel, generously inventive as to episode and detail but entirely uninventive in regard to everything that concerns the art of the novel, can usefully be written in each generation. But there seems to be no possibility of any give and take between Snow and any other contemporary English novelist. . . .

*John Wain, "The Conflict of Forms in Contemporary English Literature," in his* Essays on Literature and Ideas *(reprinted by permission of Macmillan, London and Basingstoke), St. Martin's, 1963, p. 40.*

The remarkable thing about all of [Snow's] novels, written over a period of thirty years, is how little stylistic change or development there is from one novel to the next. By 1934, in *The Search*, Snow's style had become set to such an extent as to show almost no important change thirty years later in *Corridors of Power*.

Snow's prose style is level, unadorned, realistic in the manner of many Victorian novelists. Considering his use of chapter titles and his interest in politics, he is most like Trollope. He scrupulously avoids any sort of poetic effects in his prose, and he particularly excludes experimental effects from his novels; as he has often said in his literary criticism, he is totally opposed to the James Joyce-Virginia Woolf experimental techniques.

In effect this means that Snow has eschewed all devices such as allusion, symbolism, the stream of consciousness, complex uses of time (there are rarely even any flashbacks in his books); little attention is given to the sounds of words or the rhythms of sentences; rarely are there any vivid passages or striking metaphors; and there is no conscious use of allegory or myth. Instead the prose is straightforward and never difficult to understand—"readable," as Snow puts it. In this respect Snow's style is similar to that of many popular writers—H. G. Wells or J. G. Cozzens, for instance—who tried never to baffle their readers.

The prose in Snow's novels is often ponderous; when he wishes to emphasize a point he repeats it. . . .

In opposing the experimental writers, Snow has frequently come out against "poetic" fiction and verbal innovation; his own fiction shows, perhaps, too little concern with individual words and concentrates more on the plot. Despite the fact that the use of a strong plot line had never fallen into disuse among popular writers of fiction, Snow was one of the first postexperimental writers to reassert the value of the plot, make his verbal texture subservient to the plot, and justify this shift of emphasis by actively opposing (rather than merely ignoring) those experimental writers who had deemphasized the value of the plot in their works. . . .

His novels represent a new phenomenon in that they deal with modern technical innovations, such as the development of the atomic bomb; but the language and style he uses in describing these phenomena are derived from the Victorian and Edwardian novelists. . . .

The greatest impact of modern science on the experimental novelists came in an area which Snow ignores entirely: psychology. . . . Modern psychology may still be in its infancy, but it is the best knowledge we have in this area. Snow, however, prefers to use a more intuitive, pre-Freudian psychological approach. . . . What Snow has done, actually, is to reject the idea of the psychological unconscious. His fictional use of psychological motivation is similar to the method of the Victorian novelists; that is, a particular character will pursue only goals which he consciously recognizes as goals. . . .

In Snow's fiction, the men at the top are seldom evil; they may have odd prejudices, like Lord Boscastle, or curious habits, like Thomas Bevill; but in general they are decent men. No one who is really villainous, in Snow's novels, holds a place of power very long. In this way Snow subtly equates the idea of goodness with success. This type of evaluation is generally common today, as much in the capitalistic Horatio Alger view of man as in the socialist-realist view of the Marxist. . . .

Snow's moral system is society-oriented in this way. He praises those values in men which are most useful socially, and even his social criticism is of the socially acceptable variety: he makes few suggestions for social change which would offend the people in power. Such a moral system must forgo abstract concepts of justice and appeal instead to ambiguous phrases like "fairness" and "decency"; these terms do not so much refer to any moral code as simply mean actions which society would approve of. . . .

Snow's hero is the bureaucratic man, and by romanticizing the roles of people in essentially mundane occupations Snow has endeared himself to readers in the countries with the largest bureaucracies, regardless of their political point of view. His heroes engage in no heroic quests; they seek good incomes, but not fortunes; instead of fame they are happy with a bit of official recognition; if they have any really great ambition, it is to be able to control their fellow men. People like to read about themselves: the professional, middle-class people Snow writes about are also his greatest readers.

*Rubin Rabinovitz, "C. P. Snow as Novelist," in his* The Reaction Against Experiment in The English Novel, 1950-1960 *(reprinted by permission of the publisher), Columbia University Press, 1967, pp. 128-65.*

[Snow's] *Strangers and Brothers* has many admirers and it does investigate whole areas of contemporary experience that other novelists are either disinclined or unequipped to deal with. Snow is uniquely concerned with the public life, with power struggles and politics, whether in a small, enclosed society, or in the state itself, and part of the interest of his sequence is in watching his narrator, Lewis Eliot, move, with immense deftness, onwards and upwards through one area of society after another. We start with Eliot as a young man in a provincial town in the twenties, then follow him to the Inns of Court in London, to the senior common-room of a Cambridge college, and into an ever-widening circle of acquaintances, taking in aristocratic life in a country house, big business and the intimate friendship of a wealthy Anglo-Jewish family. During the Second World War Eliot joins the civil service, and we see through his eyes the inner workings of an atomic research establishment. In recent years Eliot has been awarded a knighthood and has become the friend and confidant of cabinet ministers; now he seems to have given up public life and is devoting his time to writing. Snow himself has been involved in more kinds of occupation than most writers; first as a scientist, then as an administrator in the civil service and in business; and briefly as a junior minister in the Wilson government. Nor has he denied his own identification with Lewis Eliot. . . .

In practice, whatever his overt beliefs, Snow is the most deeply backward-looking and nostalgic of living English novelists, forcing his civil servants and businessmen and scientists into a Trollopian mode that is maintained without the faintest hint of conscious pastiche. . . .

[*Strangers and Brothers*] proceeds by a method of simultaneous rather than successive progression. That is to say, two or three novels may cover the same period of time, and in each of them Eliot will be concerned with a different set of events. Thus, by cross-referring between *The Light and the Dark, The New Men* and *Homecomings,* one can work out that in the autumn of 1941 Eliot was falling in love with Margaret Davidson, involved in his official capacity with the atomic project at Barford, and deeply concerned about the marriage of his friend Roy Calvert. Were Eliot really presented to us as a whole man, then these separate strands of experience would be co-existing in his consciousness and sensibility, modifying each other and converging to form new patterns. Instead of which they are presented in separate watertight compartments. Although Snow may have been prompted in his fictional project by the laudable intention of showing the unreality of our customary rigid separation between the personal and the social, in practice he has only made the distinction seem more absolute. . . .

In his stress on pragmatic worldly wisdom, and his fascination with a world of manipulation and operation, Snow has come close to providing a fictional embodiment of what Marcuse calls 'one-dimensional man', where the very terms of reference preclude the possibility of transcendence. These strictures apply with much less force to the most recent volume in the sequence, *The Sleep of Reason,* where some new elements seem, very late in the day, to have entered into Lewis Eliot's understanding. Much of the book is taken up, it is true, with familiar and mechanically efficient committee-room stuff; Eliot serves on the court of a new university, and mounting pressure is put on the vice-chancellor to resign. But, more interestingly, Eliot is made to encounter death in a fuller way than at any point previously in the sequence. . . . Here, for the first time in Snow's fiction, we find not tragedy, but some faint realisation of the meaning of tragedy. The insufficiencies of a world of sensible men and practical solutions are exposed. . . . What is good in *The Sleep of Reason* is not enough to redeem the whole novel, which is more than usually shapeless, and Snow's linguistic resources are still inadequate to meet his emotional demands. Yet the new sense of self-knowledge, and indeed, self-doubt, that Eliot acquires in this book represents a significant development in the sequence, and one which is likely to make us see the preceding volumes in a different, though scarcely more flattering, light.

*Bernard Bergonzi, in his* The Situation of the Novel *(reprinted by permission of the University of Pittsburgh Press; © 1970 by Bernard Bergonzi), University of Pittsburgh Press, 1970, pp. 134-48.*

Snow has little sense of tonality in dialogue, because the central obsession with decision means that the dialogue should be in short, clipped sentences; at a moment of decision, and at the really hard moments (a mother dies, a wife leaves us, we are sacked from our job) we all talk in clichés. The apparent aridity of Snow's dialogue may be an aesthetic decision: He may have chosen to represent and record only the properly dramatic moments, the moments of choice.

But this concentration on moments of choice does mean that, compared to the two novelists who offer us a rather similar range of observation of social change in England over the last thirty or forty years, Angus Wilson and Anthony Powell, Snow lacks certain dimensions. There is a certain sick and angry feeling about contemporary England, a feeling of humbug, which Wilson conveys admirably by means of Dickensian exaggeration. Socially, Wilson is a radical, and the English class system, growingly nonfunctional, growingly taking refuge in fantasies, makes him sick. At moments, he seems to see the modern English as a nation of compulsive role-players, infantile and regressive. If Wilson is a little like Dickens, Powell is a little like William Thackeray: The sheer rumness and oddity of the English establishment, the loose London network in which everybody "knows" everybody else and in which bumbling and determined ineptitude like that of Widmerpool gets to the top, fascinates him, but a sense of comedy gets the better of any sense of furious indignation. He feels, and rightly feels, how full of irreducible individuality, how lacking in faceless men, the English scene still is. It is the fine failures, like Thackeray's Dobbin or Esmond or his own Stringham, the rogues and oddities who are not such bad rogues after all, the Rawdon Crawley or Captain Costigan types, the battered, worldly women with good hearts, like his Lady Molly, who interest him. Some of Powell's characters in *The Music of Time* could have met some of Snow's in *Strangers and Brothers*—the areas partly interact—but I do not know what they would have talked about.

I think Powell and Wilson together give a richer picture than Snow of what England has been like since 1935, say, but it is a picture of what England means to an intelligent man with a firm artist's bias, a wish to see life in a certain way, because that way suits his gifts. A much flatter writer than either of them, eschewing the delights of accumulation of resonance, Snow, like Stendhal (see Stendhal's letter to Honoré de Balzac about Balzac's flattering review of *La Chartreuse de Parme*), wishes to sacrifice "style," atmosphere, "fine writing," for the sake of "small facts." . . .

Snow has not the great gift, which very great novelists as different as Tolstoy, Dickens, Thackeray, and Proust and also some minor writers of talent like Arthur Conan Doyle or Edith Oenone Somerville and Ross Martin have, of creating a character whom we feel we would recognize—his appearance, costume, tone of voice, idiom, bearing—if he came into the room. Nor has he that related but different gift, the peculiarly individual tone of voice that makes us go on listening to Thackeray, Henry James, James Joyce, or Virginia Woolf when they are being self-indulgent; doodling, freewheeling, over-elaborating, filling up blanks with arabesques. More broadly than this, one could say that Snow (who seems to me, as a man, like Sydney Smith in Thomas Carlyle's description of him, to have a great and generous sense of fun but little sense of humor, little natural relish for the oddities and anfractuosities of human character as something intrinsically valuable, to be appreciated for their own sakes) avoids exaggerative humor, like Angus Wilson's, and even the slow-motion comedy of exaggerated precision, like Anthony Powell's, for the sake of the seriousness to him of his subject matter. His is a sort of puritan prose; he does not convey the oddly self-enjoying quality of human life half as much in his novels as he does in some of his prose memoirs. He writes, I think, good puritan, or perhaps good early Royal Society, prose: a naked, plain, and natural style. One wouldn't guess from reading him that, as a person, he is an exuberant, boisterous character, eager and clumsy: a touch of Falstaff, a touch of Dr. Johnson (he snorts and heaves himself about), a touch of Peter Bezhukhov. . . .

In novels like *The Masters, The New Men, The Affair,* and *Corridors of Power* Snow is dealing with centrally important questions of "pure" politics, in the sense that I have defined that: the relationships between knowledge and power (or knowledge and charisma), between expedience and justice, between one's affection for a certain person, say, and one's perception that another person, for whom one has little affection, is the better man for a certain job. These interests may possibly be "impoverished" in Leavis's connotational sense; Leavis feels that Snow's university characters seem to be indifferent to their subjects, as far as their conversation shows, but terribly keen about who shall be master, president, or whatever it may be. Professor Helen Gardner, on the other hand, seems to find the picture accurate enough; and if Snow's characters tend often to seem predictable and dim, so, to be sure, in my own experience, do many of one's university colleagues. . . .

I sometimes wish that Snow had been a historian. But his novels are at least unique in modern fiction in giving us a dry but accurate notion of how we are ruled and some quite deep insights into the consciences of our rulers. They are the novels, also, of a good man who sees how very easily the human race could, through its representative institutions, destroy itself and who is anxious to improve these institutions and prevent that from happening.

*G.S. Fraser, "C. P. Snow (1905- )," in* The Politics of Twentieth-Century Novelists, *edited by George Panichas (reprinted by permission of Hawthorn Books, Inc.; copyright © 1971 by The University of Maryland; all rights reserved), Hawthorn, 1971, pp. 124-33.*

What is familiar about "The Malcontents" is Snow's habitual tone, characterization and obsessions. The tone is flat and explicatory, laying down sentences like railroad ties, without graces but also without many foibles; the occasional rare word ("lanthanide," "aphesis," "nepenthe") flashes across the scene like an exotic bird. The characterization is matchingly stolid: people are seen initially through a ready-made set of physical descriptions, and later through conscientious but inert summings-up of their gestures and manners. . . . As for the obsessions, as usual they are power and the motives for power; classic stuff for the novelist, certainly. Snow seems to suppose that the urge for power is our basic human drive. . . .

Snow is not a seductive or ingratiating writer. When his novels work, they do so through sudden old-fashioned turns of speed . . . and through an involvement of a detective-story kind ("who did it, and why?"—just as in "The Masters" the question is "who will get it, and through whom?").

*Anthony Thwaite, "In the Comfortably Ruminative Snow Manner," in* The New York Times Book Review *(© 1972 by The New York Times Company; reprinted by permission), May 7, 1972, p. 5.*

*The Malcontents* explores radical political thought and action during a state of adversity, when the activist—often for the first time—is compelled agonizingly to scrutinize self and purpose. . . .

*The Malcontents*—not a part of Snow's massive "Strangers and Brothers" series—provides fascinatingly successful evidence that contemporary science can be incorporated into literature with enriching results. The subtlety that predominates is remarkable. Snow has wisely abandoned the reflective, discursive first-person narrator of his earlier fiction and reduced exposition and summary to a minimum. The result is a tautly structured skein of conflict and anxiety so dramatically projected that stage adaptation seems destined. . . .

The "Two Cultures" controversy in which Snow, F. R. Leavis, and others were embroiled more than a decade ago has passed into history; yet it should not be forgotten. Then, Snow—trained as a physicist, but a novelist and social critic by choice—insisted that the general culture must begin knowledgeably to absorb the arcane specifics of its scientific subculture. He placed extraordinary responsibility for the erasure of a dangerous, internal cultural lag upon the artistic subculture, of which he was a part. At the time Snow evoked incomprehension and negation when he insisted that up-to-date understanding of the Second Law of Thermodynamics was as humanistically essential and vitalizing as a reading of Shakespeare. *The Malcontents* is an exciting novel, displaying not only the continued ripening of Snow's literary art but also a model for those still doubtful that science and art can be harmoniously combined.

*Brom Weber, in* Saturday Review of the Arts *(copyright © 1972 by Saturday Review/World, Inc.; reprinted with permission), June 17, 1972, pp. 76-7.*

Since the middle 1930s, C. P. Snow has been known as a writer of somewhat plodding novels, curiously old fashioned and solid in an age in which we have come to expect important things to be said in experimental forms. His novels have typically been saved by his sympathetic understanding of his subject—the stresses of men whose decisions influence large masses of people. Nothing has changed. *The Malcontents* are too young to be so influential, but someday they probably will be. Each of the malcontents is dissatisfied with the status quo—some because they have never been deprived and have an abstract longing for justice, others because they have been deprived. Their plans for a demonstration involving the exposure of a slum landlord who is a powerful political figure are exposed at the start of the novel; the remainder deals with the effects of the exposure on the group. Although Snow never gets inside his characters, he has a remarkable ability to present them and their conflicting social attitudes with fairness, warmth, and, above all, understanding.

*Lee T. Lemon, in* Prairie Schooner *(© 1972 by University of Nebraska Press; reprinted by permission from* Prairie Schooner*), Fall, 1972, pp. 267-68.*

The world of C. P. Snow is clearly circumscribed, it has evident limits. Inside, there is a large population of usually very busy people. They, too, are conscious of limits. Sometimes these are imposed on them by their families, their jobs, the society in which they live, even the country they serve. Sometimes they are self-created, barriers thrown up by the temperament and moral character of the individual who strives to overcome them. Also, in spite of the large public issues raised in it, the world of C. P. Snow has rigorous physical limits. For the most part it is contained in a triangle drawn between the three points of an anonymous midland town (Leicester), Cambridge and London. Excursions from any of these three points into unknown territory are rare. When they do occur, the place at which we arrive is never in any important respect different from the places we left behind. Its inhabitants are still scientists, academics, Civil servants and government officials, with one or two other professional people (especially lawyers) and their appendages (clerks, landladies, messengers, wives) thrown in for good measure. They live in large detached houses and professional flats (one of them prefers a modest four-roomed flat in a Victorian high rise, but he is being uncharacteristically eccentric); they work in government offices, colleges, laboratories and law courts; and they spend their leisure time going to parties and watching cricket. . . .

[Snow] displays quite remarkable powers of narrative. . . . It is a conventional narrative skill—the ability to control the pace of events, the tact with which information is disclosed at the right time, the handling of suspense—indeed, all those attributes which . . . are mid-nineteenth century ones. . . . [His] narrative power [sometimes] falters, and usually it is not co-existent with the form of the novel to which it belongs. With the exception of *The Masters*, individual novels in the *Strangers and Brothers* sequence are loosely constructed—tautly organized episodes alternating haphazardly with perfunctory incidental matter. Nevertheless the dominant plot is usually strong, oddly so, since it exists independently of most other kinds of control. . . .

Snow is at his best where the circumstances of the action he is describing almost automatically produce a plot . . . Snow excels at touching up plots which are almost 'given' to him by the procedures inherent in the situations he has chosen to describe. When there is no pre-existent plot, he usually fails. And this is pre-eminently the case where the lives of the individuals at the centre of his novels conspicuously lack plot. . . . A tragic action, as Aristotle spent most of the *Poetics* explaining, requires a plot. But the plots C. P. Snow is able to work with are just those plots, those 'given' plots, that tragedy must do without. Although Snow has a marked sense of symmetry . . . he has an equally marked inability to construct his own artificial plots; and this is precisely what is required to bring out the truth of suffering through the quite unrealistic patterns of action such plots produce. The plots of *Oedipus Rex*, or *Hamlet*, or *Phèdre*, or even *The Wild Duck* are not 'realistic'. A tragic action seems to require this evident and unrealistic patterning of events. But Snow's commitment to a realistic picture of people in society prevents him from exercizing the imagination that would free his tragic picture of personal life from the constraints of his, in the *best* sense, pedestrian respect for facts. . . .

None of this would matter if Snow had stuck to the [social] representation of life that occupies most space in the novels he has written. . . . However, the fact is that Snow does evince particular interest in [the] unsocial self, this mysterious repository of energy and suffering, of creative power and tragic depression. But it refuses to disclose itself in the plots that suit the other, social self so well. . . .

On the one hand his meliorist—not merely scientific, but also humane and humanist—attitude to life has encouraged him to write a long novel of almost epic proportions (if not epic events) which for much of the time functions satisfactorily as a critique of English society. He has tried to produce the effect of lifelikeness by incorporating devices that I should judge he discovered in the Russian and the Victorian/Edwardian novel. But his clumsiness in using these devices, combined with the resistance that is set up against them by the highly plotted texture of his fiction, has left him with a patchy success at best. On the other hand he has often felt constrained to do something quite different. A powerful apprehension of the essential loneliness of life, of its absurd precariousness and its inevitable end, has forced him to explore levels of personality which fail to connect continuously, in terms of cause and effect, or plot, with that 'epic' life of the surface. . . . He cannot avoid, therefore, being pulled in two directions. . . .

The tragic vision remains muddled and blurred. . . . No wonder the novels seem, with all their intelligence and humanity, a little remote from the lives most of us know, and that most of us live.

*Patrick Swinden, "The World of C. P. Snow," in* Critical Quarterly, *Winter, 1973, pp. 297-313.*

Snow's refusal to analyze and experiment, representing faith in the validity of the experience we live by, "infuriates Snow's harriers." However, when Snow's critics deplore his realism as the manifestation of an invalid form, they misstate the terms of argument. Snow's realism is less a matter of faithfulness to life than one of adherence to the conventions of genre. Snow's critics are objecting to the storyteller's necessary honesty, and ironically this honesty is an innate feature of storytelling form. The realism of the "Strangers and Brothers" sequence possesses an inherently valid form, a form we may first seek in another surface medium—the film. The avant-garde film-making concept of *cinéma vérité* incorporates in its union of cinematic surface and documentary realism a useful analogy. Considering "Strangers and Brothers" as C. P. Snow's *cinéma vérité* summons parallels that are the necessary parameters of subsequent discussion.

Snow is a linear writer. Unlike dramatists who attempt to reveal what is customarily hidden inside characters, he lets the weakness and blindness that defeat his characters appear right on the surface. His Chekhovian surface is therefore one that a camera might easily record, and "Strangers and Brothers" is cinematic in this sense of the word, not in the popular connotation of lyrical. The two-dimensional universe of the film is equivalent to the two-dimensional reality of Snow's fiction. That fiction also shares a second linear aspect with film. Both the film and "Strangers and Brothers" are sequential in construction; time is their third dimension. As still photographs are animated to make a movie, so Snow animates tales to construct a sequential novel. Snow's sequential art of the surface is cinema; seeking the inherent relationship between realism and the form of Snow's fiction means discovering that his cinema is *cinéma vérité*. . . .

C. P. Snow's *cinéma vérité* refers to a synthesis of surface and verity, giving rise to an important recovered modern form. . . .

An examination of Snow's verity suggests that his realism is never more than what Lewis Eliot describes in *The Light and the Dark* as "a sort of libellous verisimilitude" (p. 163). His cinema is a sequential art of the surface, that resists analysis to participate in the storyteller's circle. *Cinéma vérité* is actually no more than what we refer to colloquially as "the movie of the book," only in Snow's case the book is a movie of a play—as real as a television commercial. Another way to conceive of this is to think of Snow composing an analytical novel, then enclosing it in a narrative, and finally repressing the inner work. We are left with the surface alone, and Snow becomes the storyteller free from the burden of explanation. If the details of the story are only exigencies of plot, we arrive at stereotype reality. If, however, three dimensions have been reduced to two in an art of the surface, the surface will be experientially valid. Finally by animating that surface in a temporal dimension, we create a record of event; not a history but a *chronicle*, a chronicle entitled "Strangers and Brothers." . . .

"Strangers and Brothers" is a chronicle of conscience. . . . [The] modern novelist turned to the chronicle, discovering a form that expresses the underlying morality of realism in art. The chronicle recovers the ethical basis of realism. In "Strangers and Brothers," Snow stands against apocalypse. He recognizes the solipsism underlying contemporary nihilism; modern literature is irresponsible when it willfully solicits chaos. . . .

The eleven volumes of "Strangers and Brothers" do not tell the same story, but all are about fraud public and private. The interrelationship stretches Snow's surface. Omission and ironic detail frequently indict acquiescent pragmatism in the early novels; later, gaps are filled to measure progress. Lewis Eliot does not simply or immediately discover himself or recover a previously hidden reality. Conscience is instead counseled into consciousness of hospitality in its classical sense—a welcome to a community of being. The governance of this community is shared and is a function of individual governance in its archaic sense of self-control, manner of life, good conduct. We are welcomed by the brightly illuminated window in "Strangers and Brothers"; when it shines in the dark, man is at home in a structural and humanistic sense. The storyteller and his companions, arriving home, are greeted with revelation. There is no apocalypse; instead the oldest character in "Strangers and Brothers" the singularly positive M. H. L. Gay, falls asleep in his chair at home—and the entire sequence ends with the announcement of the birth of his great-grandson. . . .

The storyteller is the artisan of literature, and the governance expressed in "Strangers and Brothers" is rooted in Snow's disciplined prose style, in prose subservient to use. There is little lyricism or ornament in Snow's straightforward exposition and dialogue of plain (but learned) speech. His sentences are built by handicraft and functional skill. . . . Forgetting the craftsmen and remembering dada, we often believe use and permanence antithetical to unique aesthetics. But the governed prose of "Strangers and Brothers" evolves symmetry from the craftsman's demands, achieving economical style, perhaps Shaker beauty. . . . The storyteller counsels us with community, and the unfolding of a sequential novel is a chronicle of conscience. When all is unfolded, consciousness comes into being, a moral consciousness—predicated on the ethics of realism. From governed form comes governed content. Returning to our earlier analogy with *cinéma vérité*, we may think of each frame of film as a disciplined unit, a moral emblem in a connected chronicle; when the film is animated and played to completion, the emblem becomes an identity whose consciousness we have created from validated experience.

*Thomas L. Ashton, "Realism and the Chronicle: C. P. Snow's 'Cinéma Vérité'," in* South Atlantic Quarterly *(reprinted by permission of the Publisher; copyright 1973 by Duke University Press, Durham, North Carolina), Autumn, 1973, pp. 516-27.*

Snow's open-ended world was a hopeful world, demanding from the man of hope and science in the early novels and the man of affairs in the later ones a ceaseless attention and moral energy. In the aesthetic rightness of all this we had acquiesced. In ending the sequence, that sense of rightness has to be rescinded, and one of the strange merits of *Last Things* is that it does achieve that striking change of direction, if by somewhat odd means. In the course of *Last Things*, Lewis Eliot makes a struggling renunciation of political office, of 'the world'; he has made them before in earlier books, and it has been part of a certain moral banality in him that he has never made them properly, as if we knew that the world's plot needs an Eliot to untie it with reconciling efficiency. But this time a sort of finality, an obituary sentiment, suffuses the entire novel. For here we have a world that does *not* seem to need an Eliot, a world in which a generation comes to an end and with it an entire set of possibilities and affections; the end of it all is, appropriately enough, a roll-call of the dead.

Finality, the closing of the open doors, in fact dominates *Last Things*, and it is in this larger mood rather than in local detail that one senses Snow's novelistic authority. The big world of the earlier novels is seen shrivelling. Whether we took it *as* the world or not, we had to recognize it; it contained a large movement tracked through twentieth-century history and society, the movement of a meritocratic class towards power and responsibility, the movement of a certain kind of decent, optimistic, rational, mediating mind towards pre-eminence in the affairs of men. The mediation had its authority and its proper compulsions, but it constituted an odd version of modern heroism when one measured it against the literary witness, though not the witness of one's own social and political world. . . .

Like Fitzgerald, who took the world of the rich as the place where, for better or worse, men act on the front edge of history, Snow took the world of power and gave it meaning as a line of force and morals running through the society. In his novels, social mobility, the emergence of the bright young man, is a metaphor for the mobility of the human race; he is a fairly exact heir of Wells and the evolutionary writers of the turn of the century who could make plots out of the belief that the emergence of a new class was a manifestation both of the life-force and a redeeming kind of knowledge, the special knowledge in question being that socially emergent and hence radical doctrine, science, a doctrine of responsibility and problem-solving redemption. Lewis Eliot carries this temper, and it is because of this that his emergence from lower-class provincialism into the world of universities, law, and government could be taken, of itself, as a working of history, a generalized manifestation of man. But Snow's universe has always been one in which the general moral and biological movement which he catches, first in *The Search* and then in the eleven-volume sequence, has also been at odds with the position of the individual, for whatever his part in the general human affair he has always been left to seek his personal validity, his emotional poise, his human assuagement, in tragic isolation. And his arrogant, powerful women, his self-seeking men, his politicians and dons and scientists, his fervent radicals, are the embodiments of a life force often dangerously untempered by reason, the power to be fair, or compromise. They perform frenziedly and fall back into lonely *angst*. In the New Men there is always the Old Adam, and it is a world of strange hauntings and disorders lying outside the firelight rooms of reason where Lewis so often sits. . . .

Snow's sense of family and place, of the momentousness of these things, and of their continuing energy even after one has left them behind, as Eliot was always about to do, is powerful and remarkable, a striking effort of literary colonization—which is one reason why he so interested a number of novelists in the 1950's. What in fact seems to lie behind Snow's fascination with these things is not simply the function of memory, nor only the desire for cultural distillation; he finds in this dense contingency forces of reason and growth at work, and in some of the later novels about the good family at the top he saw a rational social development, man using those decencies, those gifts of morally filling out his place, to make a reasonable society which was a fair embodiment of experience. History would move and times would change; generation would grow in new form out of generation; but this was the natural evolution of life, like sons leaving mothers and striking out into the feel of their own world. It was humane evolution, and it simply needed the right kind of administration. Snow's model for that becomes something like that of the good committee, where man adjusts to the new business thrown up by the evolutionary cycle, and above all the momentous changes of science itself. The college meeting or the parliamentary committee is a characteristic focus of his literary action, and whatever the separate passions at work in it, it is morally decisive. Of course between the thesis and the antithesis falls the Eliot, who comes out of the novels as an odd and morally disconcerting mixture of the good committee man and the struggling moral agent. There is the family of man moving densely through history, then; but there is another motion in the world, which belongs to the self. For, outside the meeting, man is left prey to Tolstoyan fears about his own place in that history.

*Malcolm Bradbury, "C. P. Snow's Bleak Landscape," in his* Possibilities: Essays on the State of the Novel *(© 1973 by Malcolm Bradbury; reprinted by permission of Oxford University Press, Inc.), Oxford University Press, 1973, pp. 201-10.*

* * *

## SOLZHENITSYN, Aleksandr I(sayevich) 1918-

**Solzhenitsyn is a Nobel Prize-winning Russian novelist and playwright of awesome erudition. His themes are in the great Russian literary tradition rooted in nineteenth-century naturalism and his novels, taken together, form a loving and deeply concerned examination of troubled Russia. (See also *Contemporary Authors*, Vols. 25-28.)**

When advance reviews of [*The First Circle*] compared Solzhenitsyn's talent with that of Tolstoy, people who had nothing but "One Day in the Life of Ivan Denisovich" to go on raised their eyebrows more than a little. The eyebrows will still be up after the skeptics read [*The First Circle*], but they will be raised in admiration and wonder. This is very clearly a great book, perhaps the finest novel to come out of Europe and America since the 1930's. Solzhenitsyn may not yet be Tolstoy's equal, but in one sense Tolstoy was not Solzhenitsyn's: Tolstoy did not spend eleven years in a Stalinist prison camp. Aleksandr Solzhenitsyn came out of the camp with his health ruined, but his genius was unimpaired; prison indeed sharpened his talents, as it frequently has for the great Russian writers (one thinks immediately of Dostoevsky, who learned to write in Siberian exile). All of Solzhenitsyn's books . . . deal with prison and prisoners. Is he then a writer of limited range? The point of his novels is that twentieth-century existence involves only jailer and prisoner.

Virginia Quarterly Review, *Vol. 45, No. 1 (Winter, 1969), p. xv.*

[*The First Circle*] is, I think, a very great book, which itself verifies the truth which it tries to convey, in the same way that the greatest novels of the past, of Stendhal, or Dickens, of Balzac, or Tolstoy or Dostoevsky, are the evidence of their own truth, and perhaps for this reason in reading Solzhenitsyn it is to such models that one's mind instinctively recurs.

Why is it then that it is the book which comes out of the land of tyranny which conveys a message, not of despair, but hope, and not of hatred, but love, more vividly, I think, than anything I have read recently in the literature of the West? And how is it that one man, with one book, seems to be able to tell us more about his own society, from which he is an outcast, than any number of probes can tell us about our own society, which we are so much better equipped to understand, so much so indeed that it seems more vivid and real to us than our own? Even more, why is it that such a book and such a writer, the products of such terrible circumstances, should convey to us the sense of human freedom, of the infinite capacities and potentialities of human beings, more vividly than any Western writer has been able to do in recent years?

I do not know the answer to these questions, and indeed there is a kind of paradox in them which I myself do not wholly understand. It would be easy to say that it is the quality of genius to produce such effects, but I do not think it is a sufficient answer, nor would it explain why it is precisely Russia which has produced this particular kind of genius. Again, it would be easy to argue that it is precisely the immensity of Russia's experience of suffering, and Solzhenitsyn's own share in it, which has made him into the writer he is; and no doubt this would partly be true, but again it does not explain why it is the sense, not so much of suffering in itself, but of the power to comprehend and transcend it, which suffuses *The First Circle*, so that in some extraordinary way it is possible, in spite of its almost unrelieved picture of oppression, hypocrisy and brutality, to speak of it as an optimistic book, in a sense which it would be impossible to apply to any writer of comparable literary stature to Solzhenitsyn's in the West today.

Indeed, one could say with every confidence that it would be quite impossible for any Western novelist to write such a book today; not so much because of the particular experiences and environment which it embodies, but because of the intellectual and spiritual standards by which they are judged. For despite all his imagination, his capacity for sympathy and understanding, Solzhenitsyn retains the faculty of judgment and that is not a quality which we any longer look to literature for in the West today. Moreover, though he writes of experiences which to us are infinitely unfamiliar except by hearsay, we instinctively trust his judgment because it is based on standards which are universally acceptable and intelligible, and are such indeed as any ordinary man might understand. He writes indeed as a human being might write if he also possessed the highest degree of literary talent, and this also is something which for many years now we have been unaccustomed to meet in the West. One reason for this, I think, is the obsessive attention which Western writers have devoted to those aspects of human life which find their most complete expression in PAD ["Pill, Abortion, Drugs," made into an acronym by the columnist, R, as "a useful abbreviation for the Society as a whole"]. They form, for the West, that First Circle of Hell which is the subject of Solzhenitsyn's book; but it is an even narrower and more constricting circle and I think it could be shown that by definition the Western version excludes the kind of qualities which make Solzhenitsyn so remarkable a writer.

*R, in* Encounter, *May, 1970, p. 48.*

The sober, documentary tone of the style employed in *One Day in the Life of Ivan Denisovich*, the swift brushstrokes of characterization, shrewd but not—with the exception of Ivan Denisovich himself—in depth, the fleeting descriptions and functional dialogue are all part of an endeavor to maintain a quiet voice in the book. There is a deliberate refusal of sensationalism, of the desire to shock: Solzhenitsyn never stoops to melodrama; he never exaggerates; he never pushes the horrors of the camps to their bitter end. In fact, he deliberately chooses a relatively good day in Ivan Denisovich's life in the camp: "A day without a dark cloud. Almost a happy day." Precisely in that refusal to go beyond the daily mundane facts is the novel's great power; by carefully sticking to those facts, by his macabre humor, by his irony and understated sense of horror, Solzhenitsyn gives an even greater reality to the cruelty of the camps, to the systematic criminality of the Soviet penal system, than a shriller voice and an emphasis on the killing, the suicides, the self-mutilation, the torture would have given.

But just as there is power in so defining and confining his indignation, so too there is limitation. In restricting himself to a documentary tone, in limiting himself to a first-person account through the eyes of a kolkhoz peasant of great guile but of limited knowledge and sophistication, Solzhenitsyn deliberately narrows the scope of the novel. In limiting himself to Ivan Denisovich's sensibility, the novelist willingly sacrificed a more profound point of view for the symbolic creation of an innocent Ivan. Shukhov is perhaps the Russian peasant at his best, the epitome of the simple and decent countryman, hardworking and skillful with his hands, shrewd, with common sense, ignorant though cunning when necessary, but neither vicious nor violent, a man responsible and compassionate, who automatically detests the Soviet method of "one man works, one man watches," and who would, as he remarks of Alyosha and the Baptists, help another man if that man asked him for help. If there is in Solzhenitsyn's portrait of Shukhov some of the old Populist hope for the peasant as the regenerating factor in Russian life, there is nothing of sentimentality about the peasant: he knows peasants too well, and Denisovich is therefore neither an ideal hero nor what orthodox Soviet critics like to call a "positive hero." There is in Shukhov the peasant deference, the peasant superstition, the peasant ignorance, the peasant's passive resistance. For Ivan, as perhaps for most of Russia's citizens, the problem is how to get through a single day, each day, one day—and hence the aptness of the title. . . . For more intelligent and complex personalities such as Tsezar or Buinovsky or Prisoner X 123, it is not enough merely to survive the day, or even to seize it; they must make sense of their experiences, understand the relationships between ends and means, cause and effect, they must integrate the one day with the many, with the years and the "current of history," see some pattern or meaning in what is happening to them, to their country, and to the world. Out of all these things they must seek to answer the most important of the "accursed questions" that have plagued Russian writers: how is one to live and how is life to be organized.

In confining himself to Ivan Denisovich's skull, in the careful hewing to fact in dealing with the holocaust of Stalinist terror, purge, and concentration camp, Solzhenitsyn opposes the tendency to falsify, inflate, and distort reality either by "lacquering" or by the overblown rhetoric so endemic in officially approved Soviet writing. In speaking of the unspeakable, Solzhenitsyn is saying, one must show an ascetic restraint in choosing one's words. Yet both these strengths are also limitations, for they prevent the book from rising, from transcending the boundaries of the specifically Soviet experience to a general experience; in brief, the camp is a metaphor for Russian life but not quite for most of human life elsewhere.

*Abraham Rothberg, "One Day—Four Decades: Solzhenitsyn's Hold on Reality," in* Southwest Review, *Spring, 1971, pp. 109-24.*

Not since the days of Tolstoy has Russian letters produced a novelist of the stature of Alexander Solzhenitsyn. The early promise of his "One Day in the Life of Ivan Denisovich" has been more than fulfilled in his "Cancer Ward" and "The First Circle. . . ." [*Stories and Prose Poems*], a collection of six short stories and what the editors term "prose poems," should continue to enhance the reputation for literary excellence which Solzhenitsyn enjoys in the West. Contrary to the assertions of the Soviet government and the Soviet Writers' Union, there is little in many of these stories that could be called "political" or even "anti-Soviet." They are, rather, rich in the kind of characterization and plot for which the Russian literary masters of the nineteenth century were famous: The short stories, "Matryona's House" and "Sakhar-the-Pouch" are particularly memorable from this standpoint and from the standpoint of an evocative prose style not often achieved in Soviet literature. In fact, they are comparable to the stories of Tolstoy at his prime in the depth and complexity of character, plot and theme development.

Equally striking is Solzhenitsyn's remarkable similarity to Tolstoy in his naturalistic religion and love of peasant value. . . .

Less complex, less well plotted and less well written overall are the stories with obvious political overtones. Not even a writer of Solzhenitsyn's stature can help but stumble over basically awkward themes. Into this category, unfortunately, must fall "For the Good of the Cause"—the longest of the stories in this collection and the only one which has been published by itself in another format—and "The Right Hand" where the author's commentaries on the corruption, selfishness, and pettiness of the bureaucracy of a hospital get the best of his native ability and degenerate into something of a polemic at the end.

Finally, the prose poems present in clear detail the true depth of Solzhenitsyn's genius. Without claiming for him the invention of an entirely new genre, suffice it to say that, by their brevity (running to an average of 35 to 40 lines), Solzhenitsyn is able to bring to bear in a concentrated form the full power of his evocative prose on a variety of subjects while setting an example that few Western writers could emulate.

*George E. Snow, in* Best Sellers, *October 1, 1971, p. 305.*

While following in his own incomparable way the naturalistic traditions in the description of the way of life in the concentration camp in *One Day in the Life of Ivan Denisovich*, Solzhenitsyn also knows how to compel us to see that the soul of his unsophisticated hero lives not by bread alone. Apart from the tremendously vital stamina of Ivan Denisovich and his good-natured, peasant cunning, we feel in him a man of goodwill whose spirit is not filled with bitterness, despite the crying injustice of his punishment and despite, too, the inhuman conditions of life in the so-called corrective labor camp. On the contrary, his soul is radiated by his belief in humanity, by the ease with which he establishes human contacts. . . .

Solzhenitsyn's best works really do convey the impression of being literary miracles, achieved through a rare combination of naturalness, deep insights, and incomparability of artistic talent—talent denied in a tone of aggressive hypocrisy by those in power in the Soviet Union. Indeed, the phenomenon of Solzhenitsyn is not only a literary miracle but also a spiritual miracle.

The ethical element appears in an especially dramatic way in two main novels by Solzhenitsyn, *Cancer Ward* and *The First Circle*. The ethical aspect of these novels can be considered under three headings: Solzhenitsyn's exposition of the negative ethical essence of some of his heroes, his skill in detecting the sparks of goodness even in the souls of his negative (though not hopelessly so) heroes, and his ethical views, expressed when the author speaks through his positive heroes or in the form of author's remarks. . . .

[Without] a single word of the external condemnation of a tyrant, Solzhenitsyn makes us feel the inner nemesis of the mania of total power. This nemesis is the absolute solitude, aggravated by the inner foreboding of a close, inevitable end. Men who commit evil deeds but whose conscience is still alive usually feel remorse. No trace of this is to be found in Stalin, however, as presented through the magic prism of Solzhenitsyn's art. There is not a trace of the prick of conscience, because leaders like Hitler and Stalin are full of the evil will with which they identify themselves. They strangle their own conscience. Indeed, how could they feel any pricks of an already dead conscience?

It is claimed that the essence of *The First Circle* lies in the unmasking of the evils of Stalinism. This claim is, of course, true, but to see this as the central meaning of the novel would mean a gross politicizing of Solzhenitsyn's creativity. The very idea of *The First Circle* does indeed have an intrinsically political aspect, but Solzhenitsyn is primarily concerned with denouncing the spiritual evil of Stalinism: the lives mutilated by a regime of terror, the bleeding wounds of human souls—in short, the external triumph of evil. . . .

On the basis of . . . the overall impression of Solzhenitsyn's creativity, there can be no doubt about the presence of a deep ethical pathos in the writer and that his moral intuition borders on ethical clairvoyance. In our time it is often the fashion to discredit moral values, and the very word "morality" is often placed in quotation marks. Against this negative background, it is to Solzhenitsyn's great merit that, by his literary works, in which he so boldly denounces an externally triumphant immorality, he has contributed greatly to the rehabilitation of ethics. There is a deep and urgent need for this rehabilitation today. Solzhenitsyn reminds his readers of that which makes men human: of their ethical essence, of the Eternal in man.

*Sergei Levitzky, in* The Politics of Twentieth-Century Novelists, *edited by George Panichas (reprinted by permission of Hawthorn Books, Inc.; copyright © 1971 by The University of Maryland; all rights reserved), Hawthorn, 1971, pp. 207-14.*

The text of Alexander Solzhenitsyn's Nobel Lecture, released recently in Stockholm, may eventually prove to be as much a key to understanding this controversial writer as a knowledge of *My Confession* and the essay "What is the basis of my faith?" is essential to appreciate Tolstoy's moral stance. Solzhenitsyn's lecture, constructed around his unerringly ruthless logic, states explicitly what has been becoming increasingly clear to those who have been following the course of his career. He is a man with a crusading sense of mission and he is not shy of confronting his own government or the whole world in the pursuance of his ideals.

Solzhenitsyn has been termed "a nineteenth-century man", with some justice. To Western eyes there is, indeed, an ingenuousness about Solzhenitsyn's didactic, patriarchal announcements which may cloud the basic truth underpinning them. The West has come to distrust the twentieth-century crusader, whether he is a Joseph McCarthy or a Che Guevara, a Jean-Paul Sartre or a Norman Mailer. . . .

[Solzhenitsyn's] conviction that art is the supreme achievement of mankind and the vehicle of truth places him firmly in the mould of the old pre-Revolutionary intelligentsia. It also demonstrates yet again his affinity with another Russian writer-scientist, Yevgeny Zamyatin, whose view of socio-political entropy Solzhenitsyn appears to share. "Genuine literature can only be created by madmen, hermits, heretics, dreamers, troublemakers and sceptics", wrote Zamyatin in 1921.

*"Russia's Conscience," in* The Times Literary Supplement *(reproduced by permission), September 22, 1972, p. 1086.*

Alexander Solzhenitsyn's "August 1914" is the first part of a major work of historical reconstruction and judgment that, according to Solzhenitsyn, may take twenty years to complete. This fact makes it difficult to pass definitive judgments on the author's position regarding many of the issues raised, at least implicitly, by the book. This difficulty is increased by Solzhenitsyn's attempt to combine fictional and historical modes of presentation. However, the core of "August 1914" consists of a heavily detailed semi-fictional analysis of the modes and causes of Russian defeat and German victory in the East Prussian campaign of August, 1914, which centers around the rousing, suspense-filled story of the remarkable exploits at the front of a Colonel Vorotyntsev, a General Staff officer. Vorotyntsev clearly belongs to the category termed by the late Edmund Wilson that of "Solzhenitsyn-figure"; his rôle corresponds to that of Kostoglotov in "The Cancer Ward" and Nerzhin in "The First Circle." Vorotyntsev, on a mission dreamed up by himself, but sanctioned by the Commander-in-Chief of the Russian armed forces, Grand Duke Nicholas, finds himself witnessing and in some instances participating in, all of the major episodes involved in the encirclement and virtual annihilation of the Russian Second Army, commanded by General Samsonov, whose well-intentioned ineptitude, ill-treatment at the hands of his superiors, especially the fatuous General Zhilinsky, and suicide in the depths of the Grünfliess forest, seem to symbolize, to Solzhenitsyn, the doom awaiting the military forces of a backward Tsarist Russia in their combat against a modernized, skillfully led German military machine. . . .

By its very nature as a reconstruction of events that, to the Western reader at least, are well known or easily accessible, "August 1914" lacks the elements of surprise and revelation to be found in "The Cancer Ward" and "The First Circle." It is, nevertheless, an interesting, illuminating, and provocative work. This story, told in an often didactic and polemical fashion, and in a tone of high moral indignation, but also with considerable objectivity and fairness, will force many readers to reflect on the complexity and contradictoriness of history. . . .

Ironically, in view of the continued, even intensified persecution and vilification to which Solzhenitsyn has been subjected by the Soviet authorities, since the appearance in the West of "August 1914," the novel contains much that helps us to understand why the Bolsheviks were determined to make Soviet Russia so strong, economically and militarily, that it would never again suffer the defeats listed by Stalin in his famous speech to industrial executives in 1931, and why in his 1946 "pre-election" speech Stalin demanded a program of preparedness for "all eventualities." In view of this, one is inclined to some puzzlement that the Soviet press and high Soviet spokesmen have so scathingly criticized "August 1914."

However, despite some overlap between Solzhenitsyn's attitude toward the tsarist régime and that of the Soviet leadership, it is not very surprising that "August 1914" is criticized and its author vilified. As far as the régime is concerned, it is intolerably presumptuous of Solzhenitsyn to boldly and independently express an individual, personal point of view. The leadership's quarrel with Solzhenitsyn and a few other bold spirits has always revolved around this issue of private conscience *versus* official formulas. To be more specific, the régime finds objectionable Solzhenitsyn's failure to engage in standard propaganda denunciations of German—and British and French—"imperialism," to record in detail the vogue for American, British, and German gadgets and wares prevalent in 1914 Russia, and of course it is irked by his unsympathetic, even slightly contemptuous treatment of revolutionaries. . . .

Still, we can rejoice that Alexander Solzhenitsyn, working under incredibly difficult conditions, has produced an instructive work of historical imagination from which open-minded readers everywhere can derive much wisdom and understanding.

*Frederick C. Barghoorn, "An Instructive Work of Historical Imagination," in* Virginia Quarterly Review, *Vol. 49, No. 2 (Spring, 1973), pp. 316-20.*

Despite the stir in the intellectual community over [*August 1914*], it is not a good place for a newcomer to Solzhenitsyn to start. It is the first of his novels not to be based on his personal experiences. Instead, it is a monumental effort to reconstruct a specific moment in Russian history, a subject unfamiliar to most Americans. A great effort at historical research went into the making of this book, and Solzhenitsyn has complained that he was forbidden access to vital archival materials. . . .

Nevertheless, *August 1914* displays a continuity with the rest of the Solzhenitsyn corpus. Its slow beginning and heavy pace are not dissimilar to those of *The First Circle* and *Cancer Ward*. It also shares with them a large cast of characters and a compact time span. At least as measured by our usual expectations, plotting has never been a strong point with Solzhenitsyn. Rather, he offers something like a painting, the depiction of a social panorama. His humanist themes of individualism and freedom are consistent throughout his work, a testimony to the coherence of his world view. If his career is ever divided into periods by the literary historians, it will not be on the basis of major shifts in his thinking about life. . . .

Several major themes thread their ways through the novel. Of these, the primary one is Solzhenitsyn's concern for truth. The novel concludes with the epigram, *"Untruth did not begin with us; nor will it end with us."* The truth which he is after in particular in this novel is the truth of history and its meaning. But one cannot speculate on the meaning without first having the facts at his disposal; thus the importance of the details of his historical reconstruction, even if at the expense of boring some of his readers. . . .

Another theme of the novel, which is congruent with the author's other writings, is the nobility of the individual. This theme is enunciated by one of his minor figures, Varsonofiev—and Solzhenitsyn includes a series of minor figures to speak his mind and to place his interpretation upon events. . . .

Another major theme of *August 1914* is one's responsibility toward his fellows. The great example of this is Colonel Vorotyntsev, one of the two sympathetic major characters and the closest thing to an authorial *alter ego* in this novel. . . . If there is one watershed issue, one separator of sheep from goats, in this novel, it is just this. Who will help his brothers? Those who do not are the villains. Those who do are the heroes.

It is precisely at this point that Solzhenitsyn chiefly takes issue with Tolstoy (who appears briefly as a character in the book). Running throughout the novel is a love-hate relationship with the author of *War and Peace*, and in important ways *August 1914* can be seen as his version of the subject and even his rebuttal of his master. On this crucial issue Tolstoy avers that men do not control their own destinies, do not make history, but rather that impersonal forces of history rule the fates of men. For all his love of Tolstoy the writer, Solzhenitsyn feels compelled to draw a sharp line of distinction from him here, and Vorotyntsev is his answer.

The final theme which we will consider is the one embodied in Solzhenitsyn's other hero, General Samsonov: the theme of tragedy. And here we come to a theme which transcends anything which has appeared in the earlier fiction of Solzhenitsyn. In the novels rooted in his autobiography, he presented a vivid picture of suffering, but it was always undeserved suffering inflicted upon innocents by totalitarian oppressors. The books were protests against that oppression. Now we come to something different and more elemental. In Samsonov we have a character who approximates the tragic heroes of the Western literary tradition, a man who suffers and dies and whose tragic end grows in large measure out of his own failures, yet a man who retains his dignity and integrity to the end. The meaning of the tragic events escapes him, but he dies affirming the will of God. . . .

What we have, then, in this novel is the expression of a man who is profoundly anti-collectivist, anti-determinist, anti-utopian, anti-revolutionary, and even anti-liberal, but who is equally adamantly pro-individual, pro-patriotism, pro-nationalism, pro-history, pro-tradition, pro-religion. So far Solzhenitsyn, as a dissenter against totalitarianism, has received an almost uniformly good press from American liberals. Yet with each passing work and pronouncement of his, it becomes increasingly clear that he is at odds with them. So it should not come as a surprise, the virus of ideology being as strong as it is today, that eventually some liberals would begin to express some hesitancy about and even reaction against him.

*Edward E. Ericson, Jr., "Solzhenitsyn and the Truth of History," in* Intercollegiate Review, *Spring, 1973, pp. 177-82.*

Most reviewers of *August 1914* have stressed the fact that it is but the 'initial presentation' of a much longer work which Solzhenitsyn thinks may well take him twenty years, so that therefore judgment must be deferred. Yet in all fairness, it is hard to imagine how the multitude of pages to come can redeem large swatches of the book to hand. At least I do not know any other novel which strings out its endless list of characters to quite this extent, introducing new ones after three or four hundred pages have already elapsed. Somehow, we trust, all this will eventually come clear; yet the strain on even the willing reader is finally intolerable—one simply groans when, for example, Chapter 43 begins, "Terenty Chernega hardly remembered his father; he was brought up by his stepmother . . ." etc. Much of the time we barely remember a character whom we may have met ten chapters previously—or did we?

For Solzhenitsyn is a monotonous writer with little variation in the tone used to treat all subjects. Compared to *War and Peace*, and I am not sure the comparison deserves to be made in spite of Solzhenitsyn's overt concern with Tolstoy, there is a flatness and sameness about the experience of *August 1914*. Much of the military action in Tolstoy's book takes place either after we thoroughly know some of the characters involved, or is meditated on through the comforting presence of Kutuzov. With Solzhentisyn the word is gravity, gravity, more gravity, no matter whose character's experience is supposed to be at the center of things. . . .

On the credit side there are good portraits of the heroic General Samsonov who nobly pays the full price for his and others' mistakes; of Colonel Vorotyntsev who lives through the battle and comes back to try and make truth known; of the Ferapontych family who come on early in the book, then disappear, no doubt to be seen again later; and of the student Sanya whom the opening chapters introduce, whose hero is Tolstoy, and who is later shown (in a finely-rendered scene) with a fellow student taking leave of Moscow in preparation for their army life. On the debit side, a number of "camera eye" and newspaper headline inserts . . . provide a kind of warmed-over Dos Passos atmosphere. Yet it must be said that Solzhenitsyn admits in his foreword to the difficulty of "retelling history" and asks with future volumes in mind for the "cooperation of readers who still remember the period." Perhaps then in view of this admirable man's enormous labors, it does not greatly matter that my own activity as a reader of fiction is severely limited.

*William H. Pritchard, in* The Hudson Review *(copyright © 1973 by The Hudson Review, Inc.; reprinted by permission), Vol. XXVI, No. 1, Spring, 1973, pp. 225-27.*

I daresay as an expression of one man's indomitable spirit in a tyrannous society we must honor [Solzhenitsyn]. Fortunately the Nobel Prize is designed for just such a purpose. Certainly it is seldom bestowed for literary merit. . . .

Solzhenitsyn is rooted most ambitiously in literature as well as in films. Tolstoy appears on page three [of *August 1914*] and Tolstoy hangs over the work like a mushroom cloud. In a sense the novel is to be taken as a dialogue between the creator of *War and Peace* and Solzhenitsyn, with the engineer opposing Tolstoy's view of history as a series of great tides in which the actions of individuals matter not at all. I'm on Solzhenitsyn's side in this debate but cannot get much worked up over his long and wearisome account of Russian military bungling at the beginning of the First World War. The characters are impossible to keep straight, though perhaps future volumes will clarify things. . . .

At the book's core there is nothing beyond the author's crypto-Christianity, which is obviously not going to please his masters; they will also dislike his astonishing discovery that "the best social order is not susceptible to being arbitrarily constructed, or even to being scientifically constructed." To give the noble engineer his due he is good at describing how things work, and it is plain that nature destined him to write manuals of artillery or instructions on how to take apart a threshing machine. Many people who do not ordinarily read books have bought this book and mention rather proudly that they are reading it, but so far I have yet to meet anyone who has finished it. I fear that the best one can say of Solzhenitsyn is *goré vidal* (a Russian phrase meaning "he has seen grief").

*Gore Vidal, in* The New York Review of Books *(reprinted with permission from* The New York Review of Books; *© 1973 by NYREV, Inc.), May 31, 1973, pp. 15-16.*

With the publication of "Candle in the Wind," almost the full body of Aleksandr Solzhenitsyn's major work is now available in English translation. . . .

The importance of "Candle in the Wind" in Solzhenitsyn's *oeuvre* is that it is one of two plays he is known to have completed—and it is his only work that, ostensibly, does not possess Russia as its locale. . . .

"Candle in the Wind" is a minor work by one of the major writers of our time. It is significant for its variations on the issues he deals with in both "The First Circle" and "Cancer Ward." It includes one important statement of principle which Solzhenitsyn places in the mouth of a scientist who swims against the stream of state control:

> "Apart from the obvious aims which are visible to everyone, science has concealed aims as well. Like art. Science is needed not only

> by our intellect, but also by our soul. Perhaps it's just as necessary for us to understand the world and to understand mankind as it is to . . . have a conscience! Yes, that's my hypothesis. We need science also as a conscience." . . .

The literalness of the [translation] is in keeping with Solzhenitsyn's preference for a precise version, even at the cost of smoothness and readability.

*Harrison E. Salisbury, in* The New York Times Book Review *(© 1973 by The New York Times Company; reprinted by permission), September 9, 1973, p. 43.*

It was well before the twentieth anniversary of Stalin's death that Aleksandr Solzhenitsyn emerged. First as the author of *A Day in the Life of Ivan Denisovich*, which appeared in print during the brief Soviet experiment with what was then thought of as a cultural thaw and is now recognized as a brief historical sally by an experimental anti-Stalinist faction. Soon after *Ivan* was published, it was proscribed; and, with the persecution of Pasternak, Soviet cultural life returned to normal.

But Solzhenitsyn persisted, and a very great novel surfaced —*The First Circle*. It is a work of genius—and in it is a portrait of Josef Stalin that clings to the mind and soul. It is comparable to the greatest portraits in literature. This *was* Stalin; and the fictional liberties taken by the portraitist—whatever they were—advance the truth, rather than obscure it. . . .

It is neither exaggeration nor melodrama to say that, on the twentieth anniversary of Stalin's death, the great struggle is: between Solzhenitsyn and Stalin, whose indelible portrait, as done by his most eloquent enemy, will survive in literature, poetry, and history, irrespective of who wins that great struggle between the spirit of the free man and the spirit of his oppressor.

*William F. Buckley, Jr., "Solzhenitsyn's Stalin," in* National Review *(150 East 35th St., New York, N.Y. 10016), October 12, 1973, pp. 1104-06.*

[In the] Khrushchev-Brezhnev era, . . . what happened to *Ivan Denisovich* and its author was what happened to the "thaw," to destalinization and liberalization. Issues were raised and not only not pursued, but rejected. The problem of eliminating the monstrous caprice and arbitrariness of Stalin's rule, while at the same time sustaining the absolute authority of the party that Stalin had used as the administrative instrument of that caprice, was confronted by the leadership and then withdrawn. The waters pressing against the gates were too dark, too full, too threatening. In that withdrawal Solzhenitsyn kept calling attention to the darkness, kept insisting that the mission of literature was truth, that without the truth of memory there could be no literature and no life worth living. At first his message seemed to reinforce what the party leaders themselves had begun to say. But then he wouldn't stop talking—about the camps, about the past, about Czechoslovakia, about the KGB, about the Writers' Union subservience to a politics that was death to literature. He refused to recognize the "legitimacy" of KGB harassments; he refused to recognize the authority of unlettered party officials over literature, or any authority other than open discussion and informed criticism. To allow him to go on would mean for the party "to give up literature."

Protected in part by his enormous reputation, Solzhenitsyn has nevertheless been hounded, isolated and muted. There is a kind of cossack, Old Believer stubbornness in his resistance. At the same time he has responded deeply to the representative nature of his role and he has been one of the very few Soviet dissidents able to bridge, however precariously, the great gaps among dissenters themselves—between the revolutionary and the national conscience, religion and socialism, the intelligentsia and the mass. He has spoken out not only for the freedom of his own work, but also for all the oppressed.

Spokesmanship and artistic integrity do not go well together. Yet Solzhenitsyn has managed to sustain them both. He has resisted the temptation that must have confronted him for his martyrdom itself, to usurp the truth being witnessed, that "right thing for the wrong reason," as T. S. Eliot called it. His range and depth as a novelist have constantly increased. At no point has he become a "message" novelist: those who have read his play *Candle in the Wind* know that the critics who attributed a "technocratic" message to his *August 1914* wrote nonsense. Technocracy was a theme and not a message. Nor is his ongoing argument with Tolstoy either Tolstoyism or anti-Tolstoyism; it is rather a dialogue with one of the powerful presences—Dostoevsky is another—that preside over his work. He has recently begun a historical novel of immense scope and great complexity. No doubt the conflict between his "spokesmanship" and his art is a tearing one, and on that fire he burns, yet it has enhanced and not diminished his gifts as an artist. It is extraordinary, and this chronicle of persecution and resistance shows only indirectly what has to be seen directly in the works themselves—Solzhenitsyn keeps growing.

*Sidney Monas, "That Fire Burns," in* The New Republic *(reprinted by permission of* The New Republic*; © 1973 by Harrison-Blaine of New Jersey, Inc.), December 22, 1973, pp. 26-7.*

Moments of revelation, of sudden and often oppressive and demoralising freedom, are not uncommon in the great Russian novels. In the same East Prussia in which Solzhenitsyn was arrested, Nikolai Rostov, in *War and Peace*, undergoes a similar experience when his Colonel gets into trouble with the authorities, and all sorts of frightening and dangerous thoughts about power and injustice, about the adored Emperor and the peace he has just made with Napoleon, begin to crowd into Rostov's mind. They do not remain there of course: he can burrow back into the enormous friendly bosom of the Russian family, the home and haven of the novel, though in its final chapter such ideas are beginning to raise their heads again. But the comparison serves to underline Solzhenitsyn's point: tyranny, even Russian tryanny, was as nothing in the past, compared to the present; its present monumental scale and scope dwarf the majestic proportions of Tolstoy's novel to a kind of child-like innocence. If Solzhenitsyn still thinks of Russia as a family, it is clearly as one in which, to adapt Orwell's phrase, the wrong members are in charge. . . .

[*The Gulag Archipelago*] is certainly written with immense nervous force and feeling, idiomatic, allusive, and filled with exclamation and parenthesis which in Russian give an impression of total unselfconsciousness, but which would be exceedingly difficult to translate in such a way that their almost Voltairian tone came across. There is a great contrast with the calm and craftsmanship of the novels; and much of the edgy, explosive reminiscence exhibits that curious lack of verisimilitude which shows the author to be a novelist who needs to distance and regroup his material before it takes on the three-dimensional truth of fiction.

*John Bayley, "'The Gulag Archipelago'," in* The Listener, *February 14, 1974, pp. 193-96.*

Britain's leading specialist in Soviet literature, Max Hayward, points out that "Solzhenitsyn is already a fully formed, great writer who has completed many major works in Russia. Exile is hardly likely to affect him now as a writer." Leonard Schapiro of the London School of Economics adds that "even if he is cut off from the living speech of Russia, he is now engaged in writing historical works, and there is no doubt that he has a tremendous gift of bringing history alive that is denied to us mere historians."

Before his exile, Solzhenitsyn spoke of his "relief and calmness" in the accomplishment of his mission. This he perceives as a memorial to the dead of the archipelago. But his books are also Solzhenitsyn's gift to the living. Mindful of George Orwell's dictum that he "who controls the past controls the future," he has already wrested Soviet history from those bent on obliterating it and restored it to his people. In the future, he may also succeed in quickening the conscience of both the oppressed and the oppressors in his unhappy country. For, as he wrote in his Nobel Prize lecture, "The persuasiveness of a true work of art is completely irrefutable; it prevails even over a resisting heart."

Time *(reprinted by permission from* Time, The Weekly Newsmagazine; *© 1974 by Time Inc.), February 25, 1974, p. 40.*

Almost all reviews of "1914" have been deliberately neutral, predictable tributes to the author's "courage" and "independence" and "moral greatness," qualities seemingly too lofty to be questioned or elucidated. But Solzhenitsyn is not a Tolstoy, he is not a Dostoevsky, he is not the soul of Holy Russia, and it is unfortunate that his critics have made his reputation in the perspective of these categories.

His previous major works, in fact, concerned themselves with extreme experiences highlighted against a condensed time and space: a day in the life of a Denisovich or a clash of fates in the purgatory of a labor camp. Here, for the first time, Solzhenitsyn extends himself into the outside world—the battlefield of Western Europe—on a grand scale. But at no time does he aspire to the exhilarating neutrality of a Tolstoy; indeed, the outstanding tension in the work is that between Solzhenitsyn the writer, with his unique obsessions and perceptions, and the public history he is endeavoring to scrutinize.

In his earlier works, the concentration of time and space imposed a ready-made form on the material he was struggling with; here Solzhenitsyn has no such luck, and his habitual method of stringing together loosely or not at all related episodes suffers somewhat—one is a little puzzled as to where Solzhenitsyn will finally locate an organizing center for this roman fleuve (this historical novel seems to proclaim both implicitly and through the speeches of the author's mouthpiece the irrationality, the ultimate elusiveness of history from rational grasp).

However, one must not forget that this is only the first of who knows how many volumes, and at this point Solzhenitsyn's self-imposed task is slightly reminiscent of Musil, who also at the midpoint of his life discovered the work that would occupy him for the rest of his days. These 600-odd pages are not self-contained, and it would be whimsical and presumptuous for me to render a judgment or an evaluation with insufficient evidence. What is more important is to try to see Solzhenitsyn through the distorting murk of mass media reputation, international good will, and cliched notions of Russian literature.

In the deepest sense, "August 1914" is a local affair. By this I do not mean that Solzhenitsyn's values and sentiments are essentially Russian, nor do I mean that the novel, perverted through a barbaric English translation, can only be read and appreciated by one who reads Russian and understands its internal references. The fact is that Solzhenitsyn is trying to rewrite Russian history in the very prosaic sense that one rewrites a textbook: to correct a biased or one-sided version of historical events. This kind of enterprise assumes an intimacy with Russian propaganda and legend that we are not privy to. We can catch the overtones, but much of the essential melody is lost.

"August 1914" is open-ended not only formally but in the sense of carrying the burden and tension of dialogue *to the reader*. Solzhenitsyn, in all his isolation, in all his apartness, in all his estrangement from the social life around him, is literally reaching out to his fellow Soviet citizens through his work. Psychologically there is, I would guess, little difference for Solzhenitsyn in the feeling of isolation that he carries with him now, living in Western Europe rather than in the labor camps and hospitals where he passed a good deal of his adult life. If there ever was an internal outcast, Solzhenitsyn is it. Ideas and convictions in "1914" exist for the most part in the give and take of animated conversation. But unlike the long dithyrambic exchanges that occur in "Cancer Ward" or "War and Peace" or "Doctor Zhivago," the time for debate must be snatched up from the demands of duty and public life. And the dialogue that does take place is too often a desperate gallows kind of conversation—it has to bear more meaning than it can. . . . Human contact is sought out as an end in itself—Solzhenitsyn even accepts war for the human contact it delivers. Not once in "1914" is the traumatic aspect of battle revealed: its experience is too closely analogous to that of the camp or the cancer ward to be viewed as particularly horrifying or existentially negative. Man or men will *survive* it. The contemplative life does not exist: just as one must memorize the anecdotes and impressions in the labor camp to record them later on bits of scrap paper, so does Solzhenitsyn evince an almost conspiratorial sympathy for the officers who write their accounts quickly, against time, between battles.

It should be clear by now what I meant when I suggested that Solzhenitsyn was an "extreme" writer. He writes not only out of the bowels of extreme deprivation—in the labor camp or prison or cancer ward—but from a *sense* of whose substance, the suffering or bad luck or fate of his life, is transmuted into a sentiment of what must be called messianism. . . .

I'm afraid that Solzhenitsyn is akin to Kostoglotov in "Cancer Ward," whose only wish is to leave the ward—but when released his first satisfactory contacts with freedom degenerate into a helpless disorientation and aimlessness. Kostoglotov is possessed by his former life, and once free of the terror that both usurped his being and fortified it, he is at a loss. Solzhenitsyn, qua writer, is the same, and it explains why he has opted for this long novel of historical upheaval and also for the lack of vigor in the scenes that do not occur on the battlefield or under the stress of its impact. Solzhenitsyn is, unlike Pasternak, an artist of war, not peace; the pleasures and complacencies of domesticity and physical love are beyond him and his renderings of them are feeble indeed.

Robert Jay Lifton recently suggested that one major current of post-World War II literature could be identified as the literature of survival. Solzhenitsyn's work would certainly fall into this category. . . . Solzhenitsyn himself is one of the innocents who barely survived, and while he, like Camus, is basically an ethical writer, or even if you will a moralist, he finds his equivalent of sun and sea in a mystical caring embrace of dying and death. United by their ethical preoccupations, one remains loyal to the Mediterranean sense of life as energy and the other to his Slavic mysticism or vitalism. But for both the noblest survivor is the doctor, the giver and sustainer of life. Dr. Rieux, in "The Plague," is certainly the only unambiguously noble person in Camus's novels, while Donsova, in "Cancer Ward," is the model of intellectual and moral self-awareness whose professional duty to healing evolves, under the threat of death from cancer, into that moral duty of *living* with humanity which Solzhenitsyn's example signifies.

I am skeptical of reducing literature to categories or movements, but in this case a "literature of survival" serves to bring together literary responses to contemporary experience that are at once universally shared and half-articulated. If Solzhenitsyn's version of all this seems to the Western reader a bit blunt and heavy-handed, it only illustrates the importance of Solzhenitsyn for Soviet letters, which, after all, has to catch up with its West European neighbors, and the indomitability of Solzhenitsyn's will, his will to work, his will to survive, his willingness to go on. . . .

Despite the lengths of "Cancer Ward" and "The First Circle," they were, along with "One Day in the Life of Ivan Denisovich," essentially set pieces, static allegories where men played out their destinies against an unchanging background. Solzhenitsyn the creator has never before had to move through time, and here he will have to deal with the historical and psychological transitions that are prefigured in "August 1914": the movement from civilian to military, from youth to maturity, from speculation and dream to praxis, and the breakdown of old but formidable class structures.

Solzhenitsyn is returning to pre-revolutionary times to dig out from under the rubble a post-revolutionary ethic. He sees this as his mission and I see no reason not to accept his understanding of what he is doing. Thus, if one is going to "place" Solzhenitsyn, it seems to me that, for the moment, he belongs not with a Tolstoy or a Dostoevsky but with a contemporary, Miklos Jancso. Solzhenitsyn's anthropology, like Jancso's, is locked into the fate of his society as he tries to comprehend it, to sing its glories, to entrap and exorcise its errors . . ., and finally to re-structure it, sharing with Jancso the positive and negative of this search—a concern with the promise of a new socialist man and a revision to a kind of mystical populism. . . .

Solzhenitsyn's previous novels take place against static backdrops which allow individual lives to unfold under a universal eye—no private world here, no sanctuaries or homes; everything is visible, hyper-visible, taking on a sort eerie magnificence. But in "1914" Solzhenitsyn parts by necessity with this spatial and temporal uniformity and for the first time struggles with new [forms] and the demands of organizing diverse and disconnected events. And in this regard one must—caution—say that Solzhenitsyn shows signs of failing to find the container for his ideas and characters. His . . . documentary insertions (random newspaper clippings from the year 1914, military summaries . . ., and descriptions of battle action in scenario form) [do] not work to objectify the narrative, or connect loosely linked sketches separate in time and space, or distance the reader from his intense involvement. . . .

Solzhenitsyn is such a richly endowed writer and significant cultural figure that I have barely traced the most salient features of "August 1914." More seriously perhaps, I have failed to discuss his unusual metaphysical attitude toward women, who symbolize for him, as for Jancso, a full life at the far end of history and the struggle for survival, and who serve for him as the constant reminder of the meaning of estrangement from the community. But Solzhenitsyn is estranged largely through choice and through the whims of history. The twists and turns and clots of 20th century Russian history seem to have effected a split right down the middle of life, separating the public from the private.

Pasternak in a sense re-invents Christianity and romantic love, but artistically he finds himself at a loss with the social or historical side of contemporary reality; Solzhenitsyn is the master of everything military, of the response of man to the threat of danger and death and humiliation, but the entire middle ground of the civilian and the quotidian and the contemplative is beyond his grasp.

It may be that this apparent limitation of Solzhenitsyn's creative range—the poverty of his imagining of the inner life—is the one situation from which he cannot escape. Or it may be that he will grow with the characters of "August 1914," with Vorotyntsev and Lenortovich, and that this ongoing work will be another of his great novels on a richer and more comprehensive scale.

*Randall Green, "Alexander Solzhenitsyn and the Literature of Survival," in* The Village Voice *(reprinted by permission of* The Village Voice; *© 1974 by the Village Voice, Inc.), April 4, 1974, pp. 34, 36, 44.*

Even if [*Gulag Archipelago*] had registered no more than we know already, it is written by a man whose courage, whose integrity, and whose experience will give it overwhelming authority throughout the world. It is a truly exceptional work: For in it literature transcends history, without distorting it.

It is indeed an important aspect of Solzhenitsyn's book, though by no means the only one, that he confirms and further details many horrors that have been reported. (Medvedev, an ideological opponent of Solzhenitsyn, has, incidentally, gone on record as saying that all the factual material in *Gulag Archipelago* is true.) . . .

[A] major aspect of Solzhenitsyn's book is that it breaks totally with the myth that has corrupted and deluded so many commentators on the Russian Revolution and the Soviet regime: the myth of a constructive and humane Lenin.

*Robert Conquest, "Evolution of an Exile," in* Saturday Review/World *(copyright © 1974 by Saturday Review/World, Inc.; reprinted with permission), April 20, 1974, pp. 22-4, 30.*

Tolstoy's literary influence is evident in all of Solzhenitsyn's work, reaching extreme proportions in *August 1914*, in which whole episodes are modeled on scenes from *War and Peace* and many characters are no more than latter-day simplifications of the Rostovs and the Bolkonskys. Tolstoy dominates the content of the book, too: his pictures adorn the walls of bourgeois homes, his views are followed and debated, and, in a hopelessly stereotyped scene, Tolstoy himself appears, sententiously preaching about "good" and "love."

As a novelist, however, Solzhenitsyn is no Tolstoy. In later life Tolstoy renounced his earliest (and greatest) novels, alleging that they contradicted his teachings. As his writing became increasingly didactic, it was saved from utter tediousness only by his monumental talent as an artist. It may, in fact, be said that what accounts for the incredible vitality of Tolstoy's work is the conflict between his intuitive sensibilities and his conscious goals. This conflict does not exist for Solzhenitsyn. His work, for the most part, is didactic, as he intends it to be, and it is often dull and ponderous.

Soviet readers, however, brought up on the aridities of socialist realism, have been electrified by Solzhenitsyn's concern with what he calls "eternal values" and his dealing with such forbidden themes as Stalinist terror. . . .

The situation is different in the West, where Solzhenitsyn is probably one of the least read of best-selling novelists. Despite the inflated praise he has received from Western reviewers, whose admiration for Solzhenitsyn's courage is often mistakenly expressed as esteem for his works, many Western readers appear to find his novels heavy-handed, humorless, and monotonous. Solzhenitsyn's characters lack dimension: his heroes are all passive, prisoners not so much of themselves as of immutable circumstance. The political and philosophical theories for which the novels serve as vehicles are oversimplified and irritatingly presented with a repetitious, self-indulgent verbosity. His works often seem like morality plays, with each character representing a specific abstract idea. This is why *One Day in the Life of Ivan Denisovich*, the least ambitious of Solzhenitsyn's writings, is in some ways the most successful: it *is* a morality play.

There are admittedly a number of fine moments in Solzhenitsyn. Even *August 1914*, the most cumbersome of his novels, contains a few scenes—bourgeois life at the Tomchaks, Samsonov's suicide—that recall the best of Russian 19th-century realism. But Solzhenitsyn seems to tire quickly of such moments, no doubt feeling driven to go on to "weightier" problems. Like his life, Solzhenitsyn's novels have become increasingly didactic over the years. Again in a manner reminiscent of Tolstoy, he may well decide one day to abandon fiction altogether in favor of polemics; if so, *Gulag Archipelago* will have been the harbinger.

*Jeri Laber, "The Real Solzhenitsyn" (reprinted from* Commentary *by permission; copyright © 1974 by The American Jewish Committee), in* Commentary, *May, 1974, pp. 33-4.*

[For] all its faults (which, Solzhenitsyn notes in his introduction, he is ready to correct if confronted with "cogent and constructive criticism"), [*Letter to the Soviet Leaders*] may ultimately be regarded as one of the most important documents to come from the pen of a contemporary Russian writer. . . .

Solzhenitsyn . . . is not a political thinker, but a chronicler; not a political analyst, but a critic — if you will, a poet. These deficiencies and qualities, as well as their inherent contradictions, emerge most forcefully in the passages where the author gives vent to his nostalgia for the past, his idealization of simple *Russian* virtues, and his spirited rejection of Western values—especially the belief in industrial and technological progress. Understandably, many Western observers have taken him to task for advocating such "retrogressive" notions. . . .

Solzhenitsyn's hostility to the West derives as much from a reaction to the rampant cynicism and hypocrisy that he perceives in contemporary Western societies as from the traditional Slavophile abhorrence of Western civilization. Essentially a moralist, he is equally revolted by the systematic violence of the Soviet regime and by the acquiescence to it on the part of individuals and governments in the West. His credo, affirmed in his Nobel Lecture, is disarmingly simple: "All internal affairs have ceased to exist on our crowded Earth. The salvation of mankind lies only in making everything the concern of all. People in the East should without exception be concerned about what people are thinking in the West; people in the West should without exception care about what is happening in the East." . . .

In sum, Solzhenitsyn's *Letter* is not of the same order as most of his fictional writings or the remarkable *Gulag Archipelago*. It is a profoundly *Russian* work—extreme, passionate, at times mystical, and frequently at odds with itself. It belongs in the mainstream of Slavophile writings, in that it seeks to find Russia's salvation in the country's unique historical and religious traditions. It sets Solzhenitsyn apart from many other Soviet dissenters, particularly Sakharov, who strongly advocates Western concepts of political freedom and democracy. . . .

In assessing the importance of the *Letter to the Soviet Leaders*, one must take into account not only the author's lack of realism but his humanity and uncompromising dedication to moral values. Above all, one must view the *Letter* against the background of Solzhenitsyn's long, courageous and often lonely struggle for decency and truth in a country that for more than half a century has known little of either.

*Abraham Brumberg, "Understanding Sol-*

*zhenitsyn," in* New Leader, *May 27, 1974, pp. 10-13.*

[Unlike] any living American writer you can think of, Solzhenitsyn is destined to remain a political symbol and may very well have a lot of political influence—whether he wants it or not. Solzhenitsyn seems to be the one writer produced by Soviet society itself who is determined to expose Leninism, root and branch—to destroy the fiction that the tyranny of the bureaucracy represents anything but the perpetuation of its own power and of the old Czarist belief that the only function of the masses is to obey. . . .

Writers in America cannot easily understand that the function of literature in the Soviet Union—even of the most arcane poetry—has for a long time now been to expose propaganda, those unbelievable, generally unbelieved but enforced fictions on which the system rests. American society is full of profound class and race violence, is marked by terrible deprivations, is plainly unjust to many people. But we have no lack of documentation, of truth-telling exposés, of resources for demolishing the myth, if myth there remains, of America as an "ideal" society. *Our* literature suffers not from telling lies but from having no great truths. It suffers from triviality, the absurdity of purely sexual or material goals, from the exhaustion of pursuing success and of generally achieving it. Above all, it suffers from the fact, as is true everywhere in Western society, that our quest for individuality does not have the requisite sources in personality. . . .

Now Solzhenitsyn is not a "great" writer, at least not a writer on the grand scale, as "August 1914" showed. It may be that writers on the grand scale, as we can see in the case of that deluded super-rationalist Sartre, are not what we particularly need just now. But Solzhenitsyn is something better than that chimera of the "great" writer, the universal genius, left over to us from the 19th century: he is a documentarian, a truth-teller, in the deepest sense of the word a *fact* man. Thanks to his voluminous intelligence, the kind of absolute pitch that writers do bring to their memories (especially about prison), and his scientific training (from Pushkin to Nabokov the mark of the really "enlightened" writer in Russia), he has planted in his mind everything he has ever learned and read about the Russian penal system. And the particular thing that makes him so exhilarating to Russians in and out of Russia, despite the painful nature of his material in "One Day in the Life of Ivan Denisovich," "Cancer Ward," and especially "The First Circle," that prime document of the absolute hell that Soviet Communism has been for millions of innocent people, is his exposé of the absolute unreality on which Leninism rests. . . .

Solzhenitsyn has been more feared by the régime than any other Soviet writer, and more hated by the toadies in the Writers' Union, because he has completely and systematically removed himself from Leninism. As the six members of the Writers' Union in Ryazan complained when they expelled the seventh, Solzhenitsyn, he is a "talented enemy of Socialism"—by which they mean Leninism.

*Alfred Kazin, "Tired of Solzhenitsyn?," in* The Village Voice *(reprinted by permission of* The Village Voice; *© 1974 by The Village Voice, Inc.), May 30, 1974, pp. 18-19.*

Unpalatable though it may be, the fact is that many a coward and scoundrel has written far, far better than Solzhenitsyn at his worst. He is, in fact, an artist of very uneven attainment, who seems to call for reassessment with the publication of every new item.

Solzhenitsyn's finest work is surely *One Day in the Life of Ivan Denisovich*, which also happened to be the first to appear. A short sketch written in peasant language, it surveyed the routine of Stalinist concentration camp life through the eyes of a simple uneducated man. It was immediately compared—and by no means undeservedly—with such masterpieces of Russian penological literature as Dostoyevsky's *House of the Dead*, Tolstoy's *Resurrection* and Chekhov's *Sakhalin Island*. *One Day* seemed to put the reader behind the barbed wire and make his bones ache with the cold. It is taut, terse, economical; it has a precise, exactly calculated verbal texture.

That this masterpiece of a few dozen pages would be followed, as it has been, by a succession of cumbrous blockbusters of ten times its length—works in which the virtues of terseness and economy are ostentatiously neglected—few would have predicted. From these succeeding writings a quite different Solzhenitsyn seemed to emerge. A think-tank for convict-scientists, a Central Asian hospital, the Battle of Tannenberg . . . these subjects were explored one after the other—exhaustively, not economically—in the superbly atmospheric *First Circle*, the mediocre *Cancer Ward* and the disappointing *August 1914*. These three works all take the form of fictionalised documentaries and all confirm the author as a formidable documentarist whose writing suffers to the extent to which it admits fictional elements. Within this documentary world his best writing always seems to emerge when he treats the concentration camp theme which he has made so peculiarly his own.

These auguries all bode well for *Gulag Archipelago*, which is exclusively documentary and which contains no traceable or avowed fictional element whatever, but sticks relentlessly to its forbidding penological theme. The exposition is systematic, dealing with the history of the institution, with techniques of arrest and interrogation, with the transport of prisoners, with conditions in prisons, in transit camps and in concentration camps proper. . . .

By cumulative effect, by battering away relentessly, Solzhenitsyn here gives the reader, once again, the feeling of having been 'inside': a compliment which one cannot pay to many items in Soviet penological literature. The work also gains depth from the author's concern for Russian history and literature. . . .

Yet was Solzhenitsyn wise to indulge in so much rhetoric, so much overt denunciation of the conditions which he describes? Could not their appalling nature have been allowed to speak for itself? Dostoyevsky and Chekhov, in their penological works, Solzhenitsyn himself in his *One Day*—all had been content to describe without parading any personal indignation, whereas here the reader has the author jogging his elbow all the time and seeming to tell him what to think. . . .

This is, in short, an important book which cannot be ignored as a work of art—for all its numerous defects and its failure to rise to the level of its author's own best work. As for its political message, that of course will be ignored by the world at large, as it always has been. That the dead Hitler maintained atrocious concentration camps we all know and are being continually reminded. That Soviet concentration camps have a record every bit as evil in [a] very different way—and one which is by no means dead—is a fact too inconvenient to be accepted even with the eloquence of a Solzhenitsyn to present it.

*Ronald Hingley, "The Trouble With Solzhenitsyn," in* The Spectator *(© 1974 by* The Spectator; *reprinted by permission of* The Spectator*), June 29, 1974, pp. 801-02.*

Whether Solzhenitsyn ultimately occupies a place in literary history comparable to his current prominence in the headlines may depend on how future critics judge *The Gulag Archipelago*. In scope and density it is worthy of its subject, which is nothing less than the most massive and systematic repression of a people by its leaders that the world has ever known. . . .

Solzhenitsyn scrutinized the fate of the victims and the role of the authorities, from the anonymous to the notorious. He concluded that both Stalin's predecessor, Lenin, and his successors (including some still in power) must share the blame for the crimes of the Stalin era, and that the enormity of the Stalinist evil mitigated the actions of Soviet soldiers and civilians who collaborated with the Germans during World War II. These verdicts infuriated the present Russian rulers more than anything else Solzhenitsyn has written.

*Gulag* is subtitled "An Experiment in Literary Investigation." The phrase suggests that the author's methodology was scholarly and the contents of the book are factual but that the form is novelistic; the style is—in Solzhenitsyn's highly idiosyncratic way—literary, and the judgments are as bold and absolute as those of an Old Testament prophet.

*Strobe Talbott, "Solzhenitsyn's Excruciating Exposé," in* Harper's *(copyright © 1974, by* Harper's Magazine, *reprinted from the July, 1974 issue of* Harper's Magazine *by permission), July, 1974, pp. 37-8.*

Much of the best Russian writing is obsessive, resembling a literary epileptic seizure in which the author lays hands upon his subject and then becomes its prisoner, unable to shake it loose until he has wrestled with it in the dirt, called it by all its names, and then come back to stamp along its spine once more. This kind of performance informs this huge volume [*The Gulag Archipelago: 1918-1956*], the first of three (the second has just been published in Russian in Paris) in which Aleksandr Solzhenitsyn combines personal narrative, research and his recollections of what others have told him to create a national epic of life in that peculiarly Russian underworld, the network of political prisons.

The result is mind-boggling: we are in turn appalled, excited, numbed and bored. For Solzhenitsyn in this book, and in others he has written, the only visible, tangible universe is captivity: the world is honeycombed with walls whose doors will open at any moment to snatch us in. He is writing for his fellow Russians, of course, but Russians are not allowed to read him; this book, apparently written in 1968, fell into the hands of State Security and was the cause of Solzhenitsyn's expulsion to the West. . . .

[His] book is an indictment of Russians for not caring enough for their own freedom, and an apology on the ground that they never knew what the real situation was. Solzhenitsyn has dug up every record of prisons he could find, and listened to stories told by hundreds who were processed through what he calls the archipelago of prison camps; he is determined to be a memorialist of the unknown and almost-forgotten, recording everything, every name and experience, until his facts, stories, statistics acquire a hypnotic rhythm, like a strobe light flashing in the dark. . . .

[His] tone is sarcastic, indignant, and his prose, which has always been rough, seems here to be hurried. He reaches for abstractions and generalizations; he seems to accept without question whatever he is told; indeed, his manner might provoke skepticism had not the principal lines of his story been sketched before by such disparate historians as Robert Conquest, Adam Ulam and Roy Medvedev.

*Peter S. Prescott, "The Prison State," in* Newsweek *(copyright Newsweek, Inc., 1974; reprinted by permission), July 1, 1974, p. 65.*

The going literary view . . . is that Solzhenitsyn's fame depends on politics more than art, that he is a great man, but not a great writer. That is probably a shortsighted judgment. In America it will be necessary to wait for first-rate translations of his books, since each succeeding volume (*Gulag* will be no exception) stirs more than the usual storm about inaccuracies and betrayal of spirit that mars most translations. More important, one will have to see completed the already vast and elaborate mixture of fact and fiction through which he is attempting to restore to his countrymen the history of Russia since 1914. Solzhenitsyn is also clearly working on the creation of a rich, interlocking literary world that will revive a 19th century conception of man, shorn of his fond hopes for progress, but still a creature endowed with conscience and a soul who has need for piety, loyalty, continuity and simplicity in order to survive.

*Timothy Foote, "Towering Witness to Salvation," in* Time *(reprinted by pe-rmission from* Time, The Weekly Newsmagazine; *© 1974 by Time Inc.), July 15, 1974, pp. 90, K15, 92.*

Even where it moves and instructs us most, "The Gulag Archipelago" is a work violently at odds with the Western style of feeling and argument. It is filled with Slavophile, liturgical rhetoric. . . .

The prose is often crude, demotic, overblown (features that Thomas P. Whitney has, as far as I can surmise, rendered admirably in his translation). But the crudity lies not only in the prose. Western authors, "peering through a microscope at the living cells of everyday life, shaking a test tube in the beam of a strong light," would no doubt require "another ten volumes" to deal with the problem of how to urinate in a cell filled to twenty times its capacity and with no latrine bucket. "Our Russian pens write only in large letters." To make this point, Solzhenitsyn refers to "Remembrance of Things Past." As it happens, Proust's sounding of human evil and suffering is as unsparing as Solzhenitsyn's and the moral intelligence he brings to the enterprise more comprehensive. Though it is universal in its appeal, "The Gulag Archipelago" is also a thoroughly Russian, culturally specific work. Only an "insider" can judge Solzhenitsyn's history of the Soviet apparatus and the formula he puts forward of a future symbiosis of émigré and motherland.

*George Steiner, in* The New Yorker *(abridged with permission), August 5, 1974, pp. 78-87.*

* * *

## STAFFORD, Jean 1915-

**Ms Stafford is an American novelist and short story writer praised for her sensitive depictions of adolescence and childhood. (See also *Contemporary Authors*, Vols. 1-4, rev. ed.)**

In some respects, the symbolism of *The Mountain Lion* is too profuse and mechanical, but in the case of this contrapuntal death motif [Molly's death-wish has its counterpart in Ralph's ever-increasing desire to be rid of her], Miss Stafford has made symbol synonymous with theme. Read as an account of two differing reactions to initiation, the novel makes perfectly good sense. But it is equally meaningful viewed as an extended metaphor depicting the initiation of a single adolescent. Psychology generally accepts that one level of maturity is achieved when the adolescent abandons bisexuality and asserts the dominant sexual quality, simultaneously repressing its opposite. Now, sexual knowledge and physical development are the elements specifically denoted as the determinants of Ralph's estrangement from Molly, together with Ralph's resentment of Molly's pre-empting his dreams. Most of the novel, one notes, is presented from Ralph's point of view. Finally and significantly, the lion which Ralph desires to destroy is feminine, and he shoots Molly while ostensibly aiming at it. Ralph, by destroying that part of himself which has resisted initiation, prepares himself for entry into the "good" world of the merchants.

Ralph's successful initiation can be achieved only at the expense of Molly's total alienation. Significantly, Molly never accepts Ralph's definition of the world's being divided into "Kenyon men" and "Bonney merchants." Ralph's definition is objective, based upon a recognition of the social and moral complexity of the adult world. Molly subjectively evaluates people according to the sole criterion of whether or not they are forgivable. . . .

Just as the details of Ralph's and Molly's diverging physical attributes function to dramatize their respective movements toward integration and alienation, so do their differing attitudes toward the central symbol of the novel. To Ralph, the mountain lion represents in part a trophy, the acquisition of which would qualify him for entry into manhood. To Molly, Goldilocks is a vision of loneliness and loveliness—a creature envied for her beauty and independence, hated for that quality of wildness which has united Ralph and Claude in the common bond of pursuit, and yet somehow loved for her pristine and ferocious virginity. Both children's destinies are clearly bound to the fate of the mountain lion, but a shared quality of isolation links Molly [more] closely and directly with Goldilocks. Although the causes obviously differ, both are the prey of a hostile society. Molly's subconscious recognition of their common dilemma prompts her anxiety for Goldilocks's safety. But with deliberately arrested innocence, she has never progressed beyond childish ritual: "She lit the incense in the gilt incense Buddha burner which she had brought from Covina and very briefly prayed that the mountain lion would . . . clear out of the hills. . . . She hoped neither Ralph nor Uncle Claude would get her" (215). . . .

In its final form, then, *The Mountain Lion* is not only a novel of adolescent initiation but a saga of a changing America. The violence of the concluding scene represents, symbolically, the cataclysmic disruption of American society. On this panoramic scale, Ralph's violent initiation dramatizes the plight of a whole generation growing up to discover an America tragically unlike that which their forebears had taught them to expect. Through a contrapuntal structure, Miss Stafford has depicted the disastrous fate awaiting the uncompromising innocent in his encounter with modern society, while pointing out that a loss of innocence and a compromise of ideals go hand in hand. Molly, the uncompromising innocent, adherent to the ideals of a vanished nineteenth-century society, fails to achieve self-realization; Ralph succeeds, but only by abandoning most of his ideals. Since Miss Stafford obviously prefers the values inherent in the earlier society, both plots are tragic, but the real tragedy implicit in *The Mountain Lion* is that, in order to achieve self-realization in a changing society, the individual must compromise or deny those very qualities which constitute the self.

*Stuart L. Burns, "Counterpoint in Jean Stafford's 'The Mountain Lion'," in* Critique: Studies in Modern Fiction, *Vol. IX, No. 2, 1967, pp. 20-32.*

If one opens Jean Stafford's *Collected Stories* to, say, "The Lippia Lawn", which begins, "Although its roots are clever, the trailing arbutus at Deer Lick had been wrenched out by the hogs," he is promised the work of a kind of poet and this promise the other stories generally keep. It's the "clever", employed for all its worth, including *its* root sense that does it *almost* all; and this as it should be, if, as I suppose with a few other theorists, the short story is most like the lyric and its agent is neither plot nor character but diction. When the diction is felicitous and decorous, the tone and feeling will cradle characterization, enhance idea, and imply action which the novel must always dramatize—or fail. But this is not to say that the short story *is* a poem and here, too, is where some writers (and not a few critics) have gone wrong.

The short story is not quite a poem any more than it is [not] quite a short novel boiled conveniently down to bite size. So it cannot, therefore, be done with sounds, sights, and symbols alone. . . .

This "collection" (some of Miss Stafford's stories are not here), thirty strong, is grouped geographically under these headings: "The Innocents Abroad"; "The Bostonians" and "Other Manifestations of the American Scene"; "Cowboys and Indians" and "Magic Mountains"; and "Manhattan Island". This arrangement is, Miss Stafford in her prefatory note acknowledges, "arbitrary". In any case it is merely descriptive, and since she is not presuming to be critic of her own work, it is legitimate enough. As a practitioner here of evaluative criticism I would elect to see them as falling naturally into two rather than four groupings: real stories with sufficient verbal magic to compensate nicely for the absence of explicit causal-temporal logic essential only to the longer fictional forms; and alleged stories which no amount of verbal magic can rescue from a poverty of implied plot and other formal features. I found few of the latter in this book and even those got out of this pedant a grudging approval.

"The Captain's Gift" isn't, I think, a story, and neither, I suspect, is "Between the Porch and the Altar". Both seem to me programmatic tales calculated to make a fictional statement without ample fictional means. . . .

> *M. M. Liberman, in* Sewanee Review *(reprinted by permission of the editor; © 1969 by The University of the South), Summer, 1969, pp. 516-21.*

Jean Stafford's "A Country Love Story" begins in this way:

> An antique sleigh stood in the yard, snow after snow banked up against its eroded runners. . . .

[The] beginning of Jean Stafford's story, in comparison with the more recent fictions [of, for example, Donald Barthelme, Richard Brautigan, and Robert Coover], reads like something from the other side of the moon. The most immediately striking differences lie in what Jean Stafford does, and the more recent writers do not do, with time and with physical objects.

"An antique sleigh," "snow after snow," "eroded runners," phrases like these from the first sentence begin to present a durational mode that is little short of obsessive, projecting us immediately into a world of waiting, expecting, contemplating, appreciating, hoping, wondering, all of those experiences in which the mind and the sensibility are deployed around the central object of their contemplation, slow change. Both objects and people bear with them the marks of their own past; everything decays and disintegrates; both nature and people present the appearance of cyclic or ritualistically recurring behavior. In addition, time, in such fiction, always carries with it an implicit valuation. . . . [We] are unsure, in that first paragraph, whether the sleigh is worn out, and should be discarded, or is an authentic antique, and should be preserved. . . .

There is a perverse kind of time sense at work in new fiction, centering especially around a fascination with the junk of our culture, both linguistic and material. But it is in no way comparable to the durational quality of Jean Stafford's story. If we recall the enormous amount of critical attention given to the philosophy of Bergson and the temporal techniques of Proust, Virginia Woolf, and Joyce, and if we then regard the use of time in Jean Stafford's story as a stylized domestication of one of the chief modernist preoccupations, then the atemporality of such fiction as Barthelme's, the indifference to slow change and the lack of interest in the value-conferring process I have described all become highly significant. . . .

Secondly, to return to Jean Stafford's [story], a set of relationships is evoked between two different modes of existence, in this case the man-made object and the forces of the natural world, and these relationships are played upon in a symbolistic way. The function of a sleigh is to ride on the snow, not be covered by it. And we know, even from the first sentence, that the presence of the sleigh, immobile and nonfunctional, will be made into a metaphor, charged with a flexible, ironic, noncommittal value, a metaphor for the presence of man in the world. As in the case of time, such a man-nature dichotomy, as a center for a symbolistic charge of meaning, is a convention, present in a large amount of modernist fiction, extended and refined in the kind of sensibility fiction which Jean Stafford represents. But here again it is a convention of no use to new fiction, in which the made and the born, the authentic and the schlock, the natural and the manufactured are all taken as the given data of a difficult world which simply cannot be divided into two halves.

Thirdly, there is, in Jean Stafford's story, the presence of the thing itself, an object pulled out of the background and conspicuously placed before our attention, . . . a marvelously versatile structural device, which compresses and gathers together a number of attitudes axial to the story that follows. But there is not much doubt that the image of the sleigh is more than a trope or a structural device to Jean Stafford and her readers; it is a thing, with intricacy of contour, complexity of texture, solidity, and the marks of its own past. Whatever its usefulness in the story, it is an image that issues from the imagination of a writer fascinated with the material objects of daily, sensory existence.

Such "solidity of specification," in James's phrase, is central to the purpose of the classic realistic novel. . . . [Allowing] an affectionate interest in things to stand at the very center of one's fiction is in the Anglo-American tradition. . . . Take the phenomenal settings, for a further example [of] the ways in which the character's conscious experience is controlled by the spaces in which the [author chooses] to present it. . . . In due course certain exterior events will take place [in Stafford's story], but the characters' most intense emotional scenes are lived out within rooms. It is not merely a convenience of staging to place the characters within those spaces in which they most conveniently interact. And it is not merely the realistic result of the fact that the characters, being upper middle class, do spend most of their time in rooms. There is an obsessive, house-bound quality in such fiction, reminiscent of Samuel Richardson, in which doors and windows, corridors and stairs, beds, tables, and chairs all figure heavily. Once again, it occurs to me that there was a time when it seemed to all of us that that was simply the way very much fiction was written, with characters condemned to work out their fates in studies, kitchens, and living rooms. . . . If the action in new fiction does take place in houses, it is never for purposes of defining the "usualness" of a cast of domestic characters or for rendering the room-bound effect so useful to Jean Stafford. . . .

In some seemingly indefinable way, Jean Stafford's opening paragraph sounds not only characteristic of her work as a whole. It also sounds like countless other stories of about the same period. . . .

In Jean Stafford's story, the events consist of tensions made only partly overt, harsh words, misunderstandings. Any sharply exterior events clearly exist to figure forth the moral and psychological dynamics of the characters. Ultimately the story ends with a kind of plateau of understanding toward which the rest of the fiction has worked.

Epiphany is too facile and imprecise a word for what happens at the end of the story. It is a moment both of resignation and of awesome frustration in the face of the future, and any word, such as epiphany, which implies sudden insight is misleading. Still, the structure of the story is in the tradition of epiphany fiction, which is to say that it values the private and the domestic over the public and the external, that it demonstrates a belief in the possibility that an intuitive self-knowledge can cut through accumulations of social ritual and self-deception, a belief so firm that it permits the intuitive act to serve as dramatic end point and structural principle, indeed as the very moral justification for the fiction. . . .

[The] most conventionalized, imitated, standardized feature of modernist fiction, especially shorter fiction, of the last generation [is] the epiphanic illumination, or, as in Jean Stafford, the self-generated plateau of understanding which transcends the plane of social conventionality and habitual self-deception which has made the self-understanding both possible and necessary. . . .

We have a conventional desire when we are led to expect events, devices, and tonal manipulations typical of the genre. Jean Stafford's story is full of such conventional desires and fulfillments, the sophisticated mastery of the characters alternating with their humiliation and ineffectuality, the compassion of the author alternating with her ironic distance, the diminuendo into generalized pathos at the end, all of these being typical of the genre.

*Philip Stevick, "Scheharazade runs out of plots, goes on talking; the king, puzzled, listens: an essay on new fiction," in* Tri-Quarterly 26 *(© 1973 by Northwestern University Press), Winter, 1973, pp. 332-62.*

* * *

## STAFFORD, William 1914-

**Stafford is a prize-winning American poet and critic. (See also *Contemporary Authors*, Vols. 5-8, rev. ed.)**

[William Stafford] has been called America's most prolific poet, and I have no doubt that he is. He turns out so much verse not because he is glib and empty, but because he is a real poet, a born poet, and communicating in lines and images is not only the best way for him to get things said; it is the easiest. His natural mode of speech is a gentle, mystical, half-mocking and highly personal daydreaming about the landscape of the western United States. Everything in this world is available to Mr. Stafford's way of writing, and I for one am very glad it is. The things he chooses to write about—I almost said "talk"—seem in the beginning more or less arbitrary, but in the end never so. They are caught up so genuinely and intimately in his characteristic way of looking, feeling, and expressing that they emerge as fresh, glowing creations; they *all* do, and that is the surprising and lovely fact about them. . . .

*James Dickey, "William Stafford" (1961), in his* Babel to Byzantium *(reprinted with the permission of Farrar, Straus & Giroux, Inc.; copyright © 1956, 1957, 1958, 1959, 1960, 1961, 1962, 1963, 1964, 1965, 1966, 1967, 1968 by James Dickey), Farrar, Straus, 1968, pp. 139-40.*

Stafford familiarizes his reality, makes it often subject to a "we," generalizing in that way the personal insight. The primary tones of his work are those of nostalgia, of a wry wit, often, which can make peace with the complexities of times and places. He says "that some kind of organization/ is the right way to live." The danger is simply that things will become cozy ("The earth says have a place . . ."), and that each thing will be humanized to an impression of it merely. When the irony can outwit this tendency, then an active intelligence comes clear.

*Robert Creeley, "'Think what got away . . .'," in* Poetry *(© 1963 by The Modern Poetry Association; reprinted by permission of the Editor of* Poetry*), April, 1963.*

William Stafford . . . is a poet of Existential loneliness and Western space. He seems to write out of an autobiographical impulse, a need to describe and understand his personal experience of the mountains and forests of the Far West. He was born in Kansas, was educated in Iowa, and teaches in Oregon. His memories range widely over these territories and fill his books with images of tornadoes, prairie towns, deserts, mountain-climbing, etc. The technique is not dazzling—there are no verbal fireworks—but Stafford describes the objects of his world carefully and exactly: he has the power to see, the patience to wait for his insights, and the ability to construct strong structures of sound and meaning. He is a sort of Western Robert Frost, forever amazed by the spaces of America, inner and outer. . . .

Sometimes he sees ironic reversals in the old struggle between man and nature and makes wry comment. . . .

Out of such awareness comes not defeatism but a sharp appraisal of one's surroundings and a self-reliance in tune with nature—reminiscent of Emerson. . . .

*Stephen Stepanchev, "William Stafford," in his* American Poetry Since 1945: A Critical Survey *(copyright © 1965 by Stephen Stepanchev; reprinted by permission of Harper & Row, Publishers, Inc.), Harper, 1965, pp. 201-02.*

Plain in diction, plaintive in spirit, the poems in ["The Rescued Year"] are unspectacular but splendid. Kansas born, now a resident of Oregon, Stafford writes with a touching humanity of the spatial and temporal dimensions of his world, a large world centering in and symbolized by the American West. Jack London, Daniel Boone, and Ishi, the Last Wild Indian, are among the figures from the vanishing frontier who remind us in Stafford's poems that we must be regardful of "a world that offers human beings / a lavish, a deepening abode. . . ." The frontier experience and his own childhood experiences enrich most of the poems in "The Rescued Year" but they do not in any sense define the limits of Stafford's vision. Like Dag Hammarskjöld, whose "Markings" are the inspiration for a sequence of seven moving poems in the collection, William Stafford is blessed with the gift of seeing and showing the universal in the local.

Virginia Quarterly Review, *Vol. 43, No. 1 (Winter, 1967), p. xvi.*

William Stafford's . . . collection, *The Rescued Year*, is a deceptive book. On first glance it may appear somewhat colorless. It is simple and direct. It lacks clutter. Mr. Stafford has no need of frothy garnish, hysterical adjectives, or gimmicks. The poems communicate. . . . Value judgments are carefully weighed, and for the most part, calmly asserted. The poems reestablish the valid relationship between the speaker and his surroundings. As such, what could be ground into sentimentality in the hands of a lesser poet, assumes, in Mr. Stafford's hands, a force that goes beyond the poem. . . .

For those interested in obscure puzzles, indirect communication, this is not their book. But for those who know simplicity and individual perception are the hardest and most elusive qualities a poet can attempt, this book will be read and re-read. Its language is exact and beautiful, inviting the reader to an involvement with words and silence. Here is poetry, written with a knowledge that goes beyond mere craftsmanship. I come away richer having read *The Rescued Year.*

*Adrianne Marcus, in* Shenandoah *(copyright by* Shenandoah; *reprinted from* Shenandoah: *The Washington and Lee University Review with the permission of the Editor), Spring, 1967, pp. 82-4.*

William Stafford's grip is always loose, his touch light—almost feathery. Often, a very good poem slips through his fingers, slides away from him, in the closing lines; and this is the risk he takes by his unwillingness to tighten his hold to protect his interests. If the reader feels let down, disappointed, he also senses the poet is content to have lost the poem to save the quiet tenderness of the human voice weaving through it. If we read on, we learn that a few poems end with a magic and bewitching mysticism that is a perfect arrival, a blossoming and fulfillment of the poet's voice. . . . His best lines don't necessarily have the ring of inevitability: rather, they are on exactly the right wavelength, in the right tone of voice. They could as easily have been other lines, we feel, but we know they have been intimately listened—not worried!—into being. . . .

The scale chosen may disturb the reader, since it automatically restricts itself to the limitations of a softly whispered one-man's viewing, but we are never led to doubt that Stafford has perfectly secured his most telling angle of vision. The style of seeing is usually the mover behind the poem's subject, not the reverse; and the poem becomes a way of creating a sensibility, not just discovering one already inherent in himself: a way of shaping a manner of feeling, wording inner responses and fitting them to the world. . . .

In his characteristic mode, Stafford, making a powerful effort to resist the usual habits of his senses, slowly discovers the remarkable hidden beauty in ordinary low-keyed experience. The world is somehow to be learned by arduously and freshly observing average, middle experience—not extreme or fantastic experience. In this sense, he has been developing in a direction opposite to James Dickey, though both writers have been richening a personal and mystical vision.

*Laurence Lieberman, in* The Yale Review *(copyright © 1968 by Yale University; reprinted by permission of the editors), Winter, 1968, pp. 262-64.*

Stafford is three very hard things to find in America: an adult, a poet, and an adult poet—and he does a very hard thing in *Allegiances*. He drops out. He can afford to; in his case it's being a good citizen. *Traveling through the Dark* and *The Rescued Year* are what we have come to think of as archetypal Stafford—wise, witty observations in plain, rich verse at once sustaining and confection, like a *kuchen*. While I wouldn't like to say that these two are a necessary preface to *Allegiances*, the [latter] book will strike many as more like edible lichen. When I leafed through it in a shop it seemed thin. In fact the poems are very dense, I think the most deliberate I ever read. Reading them slowly is almost frightening because you see how thoroughly they are *meant*. It isn't "sincerity," which is meaning what one says (and has nothing to do with art), but a trick he's developed of signaling that the act of saying is meant too.

Though Stafford's poems show up in prominent journals of opinion, *Allegiances* is beneath that level of dogfighting. Like Frost, he's more interested in griefs than grievances. . . . American buildings look temporary. Our architecture makes it look as if we don't really think we'll always be here; a white wood church is as transient as a tepee. What Stafford has done since "Lake Chelan" is dig in—sit quiet and feel out what relation is possible between us and the frightening land buried under all that asphalt, and how such a peculiar people as ourselves can live together with something like dignity. To do this you have to get away from the movers ("Deerslayer's Campfire Talk"):

> Wherever I go they quote people
> who talk too much, the ones who
> do not care, just so they take the center
> and call the plans. . . .

In terms of content, *Allegiances* is the most dangerous American book since *Walden*. In terms of art, particularly as a work to hearten other artists who wonder whether fribble and propaganda exhaust the choices, it is of inestimable value. I should say that *at least* from a writer's point of view Stafford has given us a country to write in and write about, which is to say he is for us a kind of Hesiod. To *review* an achievement that important would be an impertinence, to reward it honorable.

*Gerald Burns, "A Book to Build On," in* Southwest Review*, Summer, 1970, pp. 309-10.*

Stafford is a poet who allows the world's language to move in on him, nuances and suggestions, intimations; a poet who wants to keep himself ready for "those nudges of experience," as he calls them. And: "it's like fishing—the person who keeps his line wet catches a fish." But as the world does move in on him, he gathers it together, for his poem's sake, line by line, whole poem by whole poem. Notice the internal rhymes, the natural break at one sound and the locking-in of that sound at line's end, road's end. The art of successful repetition. Sort of a refrain. Lovely, really, the echoes in the lines, and the pacing (for there are in the end only two sounds, silence and non-silence), the pauses and then the poem going on. Resonance. The poem coming off the page, toward our bodies. . . .

And I would think that Stafford, more than nine out of ten American poets, would *sound* like a poet to someone who couldn't understand English. The full rhymes are infrequent, pyrotechnics are at a minimum, but the lines are held together by a sort of unstudied point-counterpoint. It is apparent that they were said in a lot of different ways before just the right combination of sounds and silences declared themselves inseparable forever.

Well, anyway, I am an admirer of William Stafford's poetry. First, for the craft that does not call attention to itself—Stafford admits that he almost flaunts nonsophistication in his work—but which is always there, being necessary and important just by being there; second, though this is never distinct from the craft, for the downright power of what he has to say.

*William Heyen, "William Stafford's Allegiances," in* Modern Poetry Studies, *Vol. I, No. 6, 1970, pp. 310-11.*

[*Allegiances* contains] attractive pieces, full of gentle memories and quiet affection. The daily world of nonurban America lives in its simple fact. And yet, somehow, the manner too frequently moves into the oversimplifications of the sentimental:

> Like a little stone, feel the shadow of the great earth;
> let distance pierce you till you cling to trees.
> That the world may be all the same,
> close your eyes till everything is,
>    and the farthest sand can vote.

There are too many passages in the volume of this kind, too many poems that lack the tautness and the vigorous imagery of one of the better poems in the book, "Montana Eclogue":

> We glimpse that last storm when the wolves
> get the mountains back, when our homes will flicker
> bright, then dull, then old; and the trees
> will advance, knuckling their roots or lying in
> windrows to match the years. We glimpse
> a crack that begins to run down the wall,
> and like a blanket over the window at night
> that world is with us and those wolves are here.

This is a hard style to handle, with its colloquial informality and easy directness. Stafford can't afford to rest on his many laurels: he needs to keep his wit sharp and his mode terse.

*Louis L. Martz, in* The Yale Review *(© 1971 by Yale University; reprinted by permission of the editors), Spring, 1971, p. 412.*

[Stafford's is poetry] with a sustained force and directness of its own, a steadily maintained vision and a resonant music, and a legitimate claim on the reader's attention. . . .

In Stafford's poems a simple vocabulary serves every purpose—"the language we all use every day and forgive each other for." Simple scenes—small-town streets, camping in woods, walking on a beach, closing down a high mountain ranch for the winter—are described, usually elliptically, often with wild juxtaposition of highly disparate images. These descriptions set the reader's mind reverberating, and the horizons of his spirit move back a little bit farther than ever before. . . .

This poetry is pervaded by a love of the land and its life, a love for people as they move through experiences by which, under the poet's calm close scrutiny, they become exemplars of the way human beings live among other human beings.

*Tom P. Miller, "'In Dear Detail, by Ideal Light': The Poetry of William Stafford," in* Southwest Review, *Autumn, 1971, pp. 341-45.*

There was an earlier Stafford who was more engaged in discovering the size of the universe in which he wandered, sometimes scarily free. In this fifth book of poetry ["Someday, Maybe"], he has settled down in a known place.

"Someday, Maybe" expresses a humanized relation with the world of big spaces. Above him and on every side, Stafford looks into the enormous dimensions of desert, prairie, mountains or sky, and he gives a center of lived human experience to the wide expanse. For him the wonder is that amidst such vast contexts to our individuality, nothing ever drops away into insignificance or forgetting. He feels comfortable in the density of his relations, sure that, while he lives, his single life includes the earth and other people. Domestic and rusticated, he has the viewpoint of a private but not alienated citizen.

He responds to the world in quiet, penetrating short lines that sharply focus each poem on a single objective. . . .

Stafford is in tune with his surrounding and his poems are like celebratory songs and prayers. But there is some danger that his mellowness in the world can become too anti-individual like the gross wisdom of folk-ideals. . . .

Stafford's complacencies have turned him away from any experience that is potentially not his own. He does not reach to the edge of his composed life and touch the alien beyond it, but he opens his attention fully to the center of his charmed circle.

*David Cavitch, in* The New York Times Book Review *(© 1973 by The New York Times Company; reprinted by permission), December 9, 1973, p. 45.*

One of the rich unexpected rewards of Stafford's maturity was the discovery that the many years of cultivating a bare plain idiom capable of the widest range of expressiveness in the lowest registers of the quiet tones of language—the low-pitched key of our human voice (consider the narrow range of the bass viol, but the unearthly over-tones sung by the instrument in the hands of a virtuoso performer!)—have produced a medium in which his own great calm would be a fit conductor for violent hidden movements of the earth, quaking in concert with deep temblors of the human spirit. Stafford celebrates the common bonds—the mediating site—between the earth and the single frail human vessel, astonished to find that any one of us in depths of "our stillness" can *contain* such magnitude of subterranean currents. . . . Stafford is inundated with the ecstasy of beautiful surging communion with the land, and he is so stubbornly committed to thinking himself an average simple person, his experience ordinary and shared by everyone, by anyone else—any reader, certainly—why, he petitions, isn't each one of us this very moment out running on the hills of night, of day, to become swept up into this love affair with our great benefactor, this marriage to our most faithful patron. . . .

Stafford's voice is so quiet, so low-keyed, his taciturnity may be mistaken for frailness, timidity; his humble cries for self-diminishment, or self-depreciation. Yet he makes the highest possible claims for his humanity and his art. . . .

William Stafford has continued, unwaveringly, . . . to develop and refine one of the most delicate supersensitive recording instruments in our poetry. He has been training himself to hear and feel his way back in touch with distant places, ages, epochs. . . .

He would re-endow our poetry with a Frostian vernacular, a level directness of delivery of sufficient plainness to win back to the reading of verse a wide readership of unsophisticated caring humans. He is a civic manager legislating urban renewals of the heart. Stafford is our poetry's ambassador to the provinces.

*Laurence Lieberman, in* The Yale Review *(copyright © 1974 by Yale University; reprinted by permission of the editors), Spring, 1974, pp. 454-55, 458, 462.*

* * *

## STERN, Richard G(ustave) 1928-

**Stern is an American novelist, short story writer, and poet. (See also *Contemporary Authors*, Vols. 1-4, rev. ed.)**

All along the scale from "Moby Dick" to the Bugs Bunny factory, American imaginations have worked for more than a century at the Republic's craft, the arraying of particulars. "No ideas but in things," said William Carlos Williams, sensing that, like the view through a scanning electron microscope, our very sense of reality was growing ever more particulate. The corresponding art-form is the purposeful miscellany, like the list of names Fitzgerald put into "The Great Gatsby," allegedly copied from notes on an old timetable. . . .

Richard Stern, . . . collecting old pieces, finds imperturbability alien to his nature. He takes for his title "The Books in Fred Hampton's Apartment" and evidently is most himself in his eager pursuit of diversities he can itemize. Fred Hampton was one of the young Black Panthers slain in a Chicago shootout. . . .

You can see Mr. Stern's eye seizing on components, sorting effects and impressions into the elements that produced them. Hemingway thought young writers should learn to write down "what the actual things were which produced the emotion that you experienced." The emotion, though, was Hemingway's starting-point, and there seemed not to be many shades of emotion. Mr. Stern is sufficiently post-Hemingway to welcome multiplicities and let emotion form as it will. . . .

Always, knitting and linking variety, he's concerned with ways such actuality might expand a fictionist's domain. Judiciousness might recoil from "the new democracy of art, in which camera-owners think they are doing Leonardo's work, hi-fi possessors that they are fusions of Beethoven and Edison, 'candid-camera' characters that they are brilliant performers, the subjects of interviewers that they are dispensers of wisdom (and this while they step from the shattered store window, television sets in arm)," but none of this folk bravado depresses the miscellanist. Remembering how "the Cubists found new eyes in African sculpture and children's art," he glimpses new energies for the narrative artist. Which is how Mr. Stern differs from a Gay Talese or a Tom Wolfe, from a spray-can practitioner of fluorescent new journalism. His multiplicity of surface perceptions bespeaks the novelist's dedication to a deft economy, like Calder elaborating *assemblages* with an eye toward keeping them in moving balance, no detail simply for kicks. Devoted to the imagination's autonomies, he lets us sense what the boundary between fiction and journalism feels like. For it's false to suppose that fiction is being crushed these days by reportage, as false as it would have been in 1850 to predict that Mr. Melville's imagination was about to perish of cetacean statistics.

*Hugh Kenner, in* The New York Times Book Review *(© 1973 by The New York Times Company; reprinted by permission), March 25, 1973, p. 6.*

Despite Henry James's unshrill insistence that we must grant the artist his subject, his *donnée*, that we must not take the fearful responsibility of prescribing starting-points, it's difficult to imagine any sensitive reader not finding himself absolutely compelled to caution Richard Stern against the destructive folly of publishing a novel about a post-40-year-old Harvard physiologist abandoning his wife and four children for a carnal (and surely doomed) liaison with a 20-year-old summer session student from Swarthmore ["Other Men's Daughters"]. . . .

Of course, this same overwary reader would have warned Tolstoy away from "Anna Karenina" and the Master himself from "The Golden Bowl," probably because it's still not easy to believe that execution is all: "The advantage, the luxury, as well as the torment and responsibility of the novelist, is that there is no limit to what he may attempt as executant—no limit to his possible experiments, efforts, discoveries, successes." Yes. And Richard Stern does execute wonders with his apparently hopelessly melodramatic subject.

Almost flawless technique and nearly impeccable taste—easy terms but entirely applicable to "Other Men's Daughters" (a most unfortunate, forgettable and misleading title). . . .

One of the miracles of this novel is how such comprehensiveness is achieved with so much economy, so many ellipses.

Occasionally [Stern's] insistence on compression and minimal detail threatens to [oversimplify], to reduce characterization to caricature. . . .

Though not really experimental in structure, "Other Men's Daughters" makes use of some unusual time-patterns, with convolutions and overlays, flashbacks and flash-forwards. The end result is not obscurantism but enrichment.

*James R. Frakes, in* The New York Times Book Review *(© 1973 by The New York Times Company; reprinted by permission), November 18, 1973, pp. 4-5.*

Celebrations are due many a good writer languishing under an excess of obscurity, but few deserve them as much as Richard (G.) Stern. The author of five novels, two volumes of short stories—one of them, *1968*, incorporating the dazzling novella *Veni, Vidi . . . Wendt*, which should be immediately hunted out and read by everyone who thinks he has learnt by heart the complete list of contemporary prose masters—and a revealing collection of journalistic pieces, Stern has been publishing for 14 years, getting stronger and more audacious with each new novel, inventing a distinctive and mature narrative style, and always following his own elegant hard-won line. The generosity and sophistication of his mind, those characteristics which emerge first in depth of style, evident in his first novel, *Golk* (1960), were fully present a year later in his second, *Europe; or, Up and Down with Baggish and Schreiber*, giving deep tones to that book's comedy—the bank he's been drawing on ever since. (Except, I should say, in his short stories: most of them seem to me honorable flops.) . . .

Stern, a novelist who began by writing poetry, was always concerned with, and fiercely delighted by, the possibilities within language and narrative technique, and shares with the best American prose its self-awareness and daring. All of Stern's work boils along on a high verbal head of steam, full of energy and finesse, with constant inversions and surprises of diction. . . . Writing like Stern's derives from a root sense that to give expression is to give life, that the world cannot be taken as given, that verbal awareness, artifice, accuracy and strategy are the incarnations of insight and feeling. Stern was clearly influenced by Bellow, encouraged by both his style and his regal example, and learned from him that fiction might seek large rich freedoms discouraged by the American academic ideas of discreet literary perfection; influence is a loaded issue, but Bellow's work, beginning with *The Adventures of Augie March*, taught many writers in America and England how to escape the strictures of the too modestly 'well-made' novel. If the word 'mandarin' can be stripped of its more precious connotations and allowed to represent the sort of sensibility in which morality and aesthetics make a dense, lively unity, it fits Richard Stern. The novel of his which shows this best is probably *In Any Case*. Every chapter is packed with know-how and knowingness, a hundred different kinds of sentence, stunning usages, metaphorically apt information, brilliant speculation and question.

*Peter Straub, in* New Statesman, *May 10, 1974, pp. 668-69.*

The plot of *Other Men's Daughters* may be the old, old story, but it is Stern's telling that counts. His writing achieves at times the compressed strength of a Tacitus, and you read a sentence twice not because it is obscure but because you want to make sure you are extracting every nuance. The comment (e.g. on MacBundy- and Kissinger-style whizz-kids at Harvard) is caustic. The dialogue glitters but remains credible conversation. The lovers' shared humour, and their inevitable misunderstandings, make their relationship convincing. . . . All the minor characters—Merriwether's Harvard colleagues, his children's friends—are three-dimensional. Also, Stern takes infinite trouble with his hero's work background: Dr Merriwether really does come over as a learned, but not quite top-flight, physiologist. . . .

[This] is a book to restore one's faith in academic if not political America, in its tolerance of nonconformism and its recognition that knowledge, intelligence and intellectual honesty and tenacity are virtues to be cultivated and defended. Henry James would have approved of Stern's Bostonians.

*John Mellors, in* The Listener, *May 16, 1974, p. 641.*

Ten years ago, on the strength of his first two novels, *Golk* and *Europe; or, Up and Down with Baggish and Schreiber,* [Richard Stern] looked like a savage and resourceful joker, unafraid of meddling with the world or of being in bad taste. His new book [*Other Men's Daughters*] is tame, well-groomed, and strenuously inoffensive. It comes worryingly close to being the thinking man's *Love Story*; a routinely ironic account of a Harvard professor's affair with a peachy Southern blonde who comes up for summer school and stays to change his life—a little. There's not a page on which Stern does not display his considerable technical accomplishments: his ear for lightly-pointed, studiedly self-aware academic dialogue; his eye for small exactitudes of place and person; his sprightly control of interior monologue which enables him to shift, most convincingly, from character to character at the turn of a paragraph. But by the end of the book I didn't feel that he had established a single particularly good reason for putting these enviable attainments to use.

The trouble is that he is so thoroughly of a piece with his characters that we are expected to take them all at their own valuations of themselves. So cultivated, so unruffled, so anxious to understand each other's motives, they move through Cambridge, as they move through the novels, like painted figurines, made out of some finer clay than flesh. With such paragons for characters, it's hard to precipitate any action more violent than conversation. . . . They are simply too urbane for fiction. . . .

As a nightmare prophecy about a new breed of perfectible humans now being distilled in some laboratory off Harvard Square (Merriwether does teach physiology), *Other Men's Daughters* is rich in dark possibilities. After all, Swift's feelings about the Houyhnhnms were none too clear, either, and Stern's irony has an uncertain, conceivably dangerous, depth. But the novel seems softly approving, easily shockable, oddly unwilling to follow its own insights through beyond a certain cautious point. It exudes a simple faith in the mildest of all forms of irony—the value of being able to smile wryly at your own actions, as if that alone put them beyond censure.

*Jonathan Raban, in* Encounter, *July, 1974, pp. 75-6.*

Richard Stern is a good American novelist, not quite of the first rank, less obsessed and stylistically less bold than his best-selling contemporaries—Bellow, Mailer and Malamud—whose influence on his own writing is evident. But *Golk* (1960) and *Stitch* (1965) have excellent things in them, the writing is always intelligent and strongly shaped . . . and his dedication to the craft an honourable one. Intelligence and stylistic energy is also observable throughout this miscellany [*The Books in Fred Hampton's Apartment*], though its overall effect is less than overwhelming. Stern has seemingly tracked down every bit of nonfictional utterance he's committed in the last twenty years or so. . . .

Pretty miscellaneous stuff it is, but this . . . collection will justify itself if it shakes us into taking another look at Stern's novels which will still be around when ninety-five percent of post-1965 absurdist fiction is judged to be in fact absurd.

*William Pritchard, in* London Magazine, *August/September, 1974, pp. 147-49.*

* * *

## STOPPARD, Tom 1937-

**Stoppard, an English dramatist, screenwriter, novelist, and short story writer, is a brilliant and witty stylist.**

It would be tempting to label Tom Stoppard as the intellectual among our young playwrights, if 'intellectual' did not always tend, in the British theatre anyway, to have the ring of a dirty word. Also, he does deny very firmly that it's true: however precisely calculated his plays look, he insists that when he starts writing them he has no clearer idea of exactly where they are going, or exactly how they will get there, than the most innocent, uninformed member of a first-night audience. Nevertheless, the most striking, and most strikingly individual, effect Stoppard's plays make comes from their evident concern with structure, with overall pattern. Where other dramatists produce big, untidy effects, spilling out their materials generously, and often too generously, with little apparent concern for economy, concentration and scrupulous adaptation of means to ends, Stoppard works by neatness, precision, a meticulous tying-in of loose ends. He professes to mistrust most of all the arbitrary in art, the play which works as linear experience from moment to moment; he likes and works towards the feeling of completeness as one piece after another falls into place, and finds it very important for him that the structure of his plays should lock finally into a clear pattern with a 'clunk' at the end. . . .

[*Rosencrantz and Guildenstern are Dead*] is a long play in which virtually nothing happens: as soon as we meet the principals for the first time, playing some interminable game of coin-tossing, which defies all the rules of chance by coming up heads eighty-five times in a row, we know (primed with Beckett and all that crush) that Godot will never come, nothing will ever change, the two will remain perforce waiting in the wings for the rest of their lives, never quite grasping what is happening centre-stage of life. They can perhaps make a choice of some kind, decide to act instead of merely being acted upon; but if they do, they will be denying their essential nature, and will be able to assert their own existence only by independently choosing to extinguish it.

Which is fair enough: a pattern of Stoppard's imposed upon, or neatly dovetailed with, the pre-existing pattern of Shakespeare's play. . . . But what are their private lives like? Do they have any? Stoppard thinks not. They live, suspended in existential doubt, on the fringes of life. They never know what's happening, who is who and what is what. . . . They recognize, in spite of themselves, that life, like laughter, is always in the next room. In the end they go so far as to make a choice, or at least acquiesce in the choice of another, but it is only death that they choose, a death which will at last define and give shape to their pointless, shapeless lives.

The conception is cool, cunning, and intellectual: not for Stoppard the romantic inventions of those who choose to speculate on the nature of King Lear's wife, the number of children Lady Macbeth had, or what happens next to Katharina and Petruchio—the whole point of his play is to reinforce the strict classical viewpoint that dramatic characters do not have any independent, continuing existence beyond the confines of what their inventor chooses to tell us about them. This, it seems to me, Stoppard's play does with great skill and virtuosity; but, it is very evidently the working out of an intellectual, almost one might say a scholarly, conceit, with I would have thought little to capture the interest of a non-specialist audience once the pattern has become patent. It is not, to put it mildly, a play mad with too much heart.

And yet I am obviously wrong in this assessment; the play has not only had great success on its home ground, but has gone on to almost universal success abroad. This proves, if anything does, that audiences are not by any means so impervious to the appeal of writing which sets out to work on them primarily by way of their intelligence as we always, much too loftily, tend to assume. . . .

All Stoppard's works since have been relatively slight, at least in terms of physical scale. . . .

[We] may accept fairly happily Stoppard's insistence that intellect is not the prime motive-force in his work, just as we recognize that there are passages in it, notably in the monologues of Gladys in *If You're Glad I'll be Frank* and Albert in *Albert's Bridge,* which are beyond the reach of intellectual calculation. Perhaps the doubts I feel to some extent about all Stoppard's work boil down, rather surprisingly, to a feeling that he lacks a sort of fundamental seriousness as a playwright, that his ideas remain, in the Coleridgean definition, on the level of fancy rather than imagination. But all the same, it is pleasing to note that there is at least one young dramatist who, whatever the starting-point of his dramatic work, feels that intelligence and conscious art in the shaping of his material are necessary, are indeed a positive source of inspiration, rather than some dangerous outsider, to be tangled with very much at his peril.

*John Russell Taylor, "Tom Stoppard," in his* The Second Wave: British Drama for the Seventies *(reprinted by permission of Hill and Wang, a division of Farrar, Straus & Giroux, Inc.; copyright © 1971 by John Russell Taylor), Hill & Wang, 1971, pp. 94-107.*

The Stoppard comedies do not pretend to be much more than clever exercises. *The Real Inspector Hound* sets out to combine a parody of a mouldy British whodunit with a witty fantasy in which a third-string drama critic nefariously manages to become number one. . . .

Stoppard [accepts] the difficult challenge of making his . . . spoofs merge into something that both adroitly completes the exercise and also reflects a certain degree of surreal truth. . . .

*After Magritte* is an interesting and remarkably successful attempt by the playwright to create a theater piece that has the quality of the Belgian surrealist painter René Magritte, or, that is, the quality Magritte would have had if he had been dealing with aspects of British middle-class society.

*Henry Hewes, in* Saturday Review of the Society *(copyright © 1972 by Saturday Review/World, Inc.; reprinted with permission), August 26, 1972, p. 66.*

On Broadway, "Rosencrantz and Guildenstern" was verbally so dazzling—the English language seems a treasure chest just opened for Stoppard—and the acting was so polished that one tended to think of it as the most exciting, witty intellectual treat imaginable. It is that, of course, but much more. In the midst of all the word games and punning, even in the first scene, as the two young heroes toss that coin in the air and it comes down heads time after time after time, feeling seeps in—bewilderment, gathering melancholy, and, finally, tragedy—so subtly that the line, near the end, "There must have been a moment, at the beginning, where we could have said no" comes as a shattering and sobering surprise. "Rosencrantz" is, among other things, about having no control over events, over what happens next. Why didn't I realize the first time that these two were waiting for Godot?

*Edith Oliver, in* The New Yorker, *March 4, 1974, p. 70.*

Seven years ago, in *Rosencrantz and Guildenstern Are Dead,* British Playwright Tom Stoppard turned *Hamlet* inside out and seemed to prove that even for bit players, great tragedy has no silver lining. When critics inquired about the play's message, Stoppard averred that this is no age for message in the theater. "One writes about human beings under stress," he said, "whether it is about losing one's trousers or being nailed to a cross." To risk a play whose primary level was philosophical, he added, "would be fatal." In *Jumpers,* that is just the gamble he has taken —in London with triumphant results. . . .

[The] goings-on may be taken as the kind of crazy crime and panachement that Stoppard displayed so well in *The Real Inspector Hound.* But the playwright also offers a long, rambling monologue by Dotty's rumpled husband, George Moore. . . .

By itself, George's discourse is exquisite parody. By themselves, the goings-on in Dotty's room are surrealist—eventually futurist—farce, which reflect the cumulative personal and political effects on the modern world of not believing in absolute values. Together, they make up an extraordinary statement: if God does not exist, it will shortly be necessary to re-invent him.

*Timothy Foote, "Crime and Panachement," in* Time *(reprinted by permission from* Time, The Weekly Newsmagazine; *copyright Time Inc.), March 11, 1974, p. 103.*

Stoppard's problem [in *Jumpers*] is, first of all, that he is himself the archetypal jumper, always in mid-*salto mortale* between metaphysical puns and absurdist metaphors: swinging brilliantly from an epigram, but fatally neglecting the safety network of solid character, plot, and structure to protect his neck. George and Dotty interest us, but Stoppard tells us far too little about them, seldom even letting them inhabit the same side of the stage. Problematic, too, is the piquant stage image of philosophers as jumpers, which stumbles over the difficulty of finding actors and acrobats in the same skin. The roles, regrettably, remain divided into jumping and non-jumping ones, and the play's basic concept fails to coalesce.

Subjects proliferate profligately; philosophy, religion, politics, love, the survival of mankind, psychiatry, linguistics, the music hall (i.e., Pop art) and its influence on culture—even the acting out of the paradoxes of Zeno. The stage cannot cope with all this: it is a muscle-bound Achilles vainly lumbering after Stoppard's tortuous tortoise. And there is even something arrogant about trying to convert the history of Western culture into a series of blackout sketches, which is very nearly what *Jumpers* is up to. But, undeniably, there are funny bits jumping all over the stage like performing fleas; hilarious as they bounce about, but capable also of drawing a little blood.

*John Simon, in* New York Magazine *(© 1974 by NYM Corp.; reprinted by permission of* New York Magazine *and John Simon), March 11, 1974, p. 84.*

There is no doubt that *Jumpers* was conceived by a bright mind, for (our knowledge of his previous writing aside) author Tom Stoppard makes several intelligent points as he manipulates words and concepts into parodies of themselves. But what might look good on paper, or sound humorous during late-night discussions, does not necessarily make good theatre.

Caught up in its own cleverness, the play is over-run with Mr. Stoppard's witticisms. Consequently, his characters all sound alike and the absurdity of the basic situation . . . is lost in verbosity. . . .

[In] spoofing cliche philosophy and boring philosophers, [the play] becomes cliche and boring itself.

*Debbi Wasserman, in* Show Business, *April 25, 1974, p. 13.*

In his waggishly donnish way, Mr. Stoppard is tremendously clever. George's lecture is a very witty parody of inane philosophical discourse: no professional philosopher will want to miss ["Jumpers"], and it might do some of them a lot of good. . . .

[In] spite of all its merits, the first act of "Jumpers" left me unsatisfied. Mr. Stoppard's basic joke is the old one about the absent-minded professor; George's preposterous lecture is really a set of variations on this joke, and as George bombinates on and on, the joke begins to wear thin. (This parody-lecture, by the way, owes a good deal to a Jonathan Miller sketch from "Beyond the Fringe," in which the Cambridge philosopher G. E. Moore figured very prominently. Mr. Stoppard's George, of course, is also a G. Moore. And while we're at it, Inspector Bones of the Yard bears a distinct resemblance to Inspector Truscott in Joe Orton's play "Loot.") The bickerings between George and Dorothy verge at times on the tiresome. Worse, the play seems to be about nothing in particular at all; it appears to be a self-indulgent, wayward excuse for Mr. Stoppard to be too clever by at least three-quarters. . . .

[The] second act, for me, tips the balance in the play's favor. Just in time, it becomes clear that Mr. Stoppard's cleverness is not just cleverness in a vacuum. My point is not that pathos is more satisfying than comedy, but that coherence is more satisfying than sprawl; coherence is what "Jumpers" attains, just in time.

*Julius Novick, "Saved by the Second Act," in* The Village Voice *(reprinted by permission of* The Village Voice; *© 1974 by The Village Voice, Inc.), May 2, 1974, pp. 83-4.*

What Mr. Stoppard and the Reverend Mr. Dodgson have in common is an interest in symbolic logic, in puzzles that embody that logic, and in animals that embody the puzzles (a hare, a tortoise, and a goldfish play significant roles in "Jumpers"); they are also interested—if I may animadvert upon so delicate a topic without disturbing Dodgson's diffident ghost—in naked girls. Dodgson as a photographer and Stoppard as a playwright use nakedness as a metaphor for purity of apprehension; in Dodgson this would imply innocence, in Stoppard experience. . . .

Because Stoppard is such a fiendishly clever fellow, anything I say about ["Jumpers"] after but a single viewing of it is bound to be provisional, save this—that I find it as amusing as it is mysterious, and that a few more viewings of it will no doubt diminish its mystery without diminishing my amusement.

*Brendan Gill, "Tumbling onto the Truth," in* The New Yorker, *May 6, 1974, p. 75.*

British Playwright Tom Stoppard chain-smokes ideas like cigarettes and emits the smoke with puffs of mirth. The latest display of his intellectual curiosity, verbal agility and quirky sense of humor is *Jumpers* . . ., a philosophical roller coaster careering dizzyingly along the parallel tracks of wit and logic over such subjects as the existence or non-existence of God, the nature of good and evil, and the interdependence of ethics and metaphysics. . . .

Though Stoppard ravels and unravels the destinies of these characters, that is not his prime concern. Utilizing the Socratic method of perpetual questioning, he is assessing the destinies of 20th century man in a Shavian play of jousting ideas. In dramatic kinship, *Jumpers* is a child of Shaw's *Heartbreak House*. In that play, written shortly before World War I, Shaw dramatized the sundering of the social fabric of Western civilization. Stoppard is concerned with the moral fabric, the abyss of non-belief. He sees man, devoid of metaphysical absolutes, as rending his fellow man and reducing the planet to a desolate, lifeless cipher rather like the moon, which is a key symbol in *Jumpers*.

*T. E. Kalem, "Ping Pong Philosopher," in* Time *(reprinted by permission from* Time, The Weekly Newsmagazine; *copyright Time Inc.), May 6, 1974, p. 85.*

When *Jumpers* opened at the Kennedy Center, the production was pronounced unready; to me, it seemed that the playwright was unripe. And the short time between Washington and New York was hardly enough for Tom Stoppard to ripen. A well-known English critic insists that Stoppard is nothing but a clever sophomore, which strikes me as oversimplified and unjust. An author who has read as much as Stoppard has, who has a facile but sophisticated way with mathematics, philosophy, and linguistics, is no bright, snotty kid; at the very least, he is the prince of sciolists. Moreover, Stoppard at his wittiest is very funny indeed—take the scene in which Archie tries to bribe or brainwash Inspector Bones, where almost every line is a swift, masterly cut to the quick of comedy. And the attempt to cut political satire, murder mystery, metaphysical speculation, and bedroom farce into one multifaceted, highly polished diamond is no sophomore's prank. If Ludwig Wittgenstein, who is evoked in the play, and whose spirit to some extent informs it, could speculate about theology as grammar, why not philosophy as farce?

Yet for all that, Stoppard's is more of a ready wit than a ripe good humor. Time was when I wondered how Shakespeare could stoop to plagiarizing himself by writing in *Hamlet,* "the readiness is all," and then, in a similar context, "ripeness is all" in *King Lear*. Now I know better: this is no reiteration but an emendation, the maturer phrasing of the same great truth. Translated into comedic terms, it means that you must have more than a tart epigram for every occasion: a sense of underlying character from which the comic retort or aphorism springs. Stoppard's George Moore, the uxorious metaphysician, is somewhat schematic but believable, with the manically heightened credibility of a Beckett or Ionesco character; but Dotty, the moral philosopher's wife, is no character at all. She shuttles between a brainless sexpot and a bitterly disillusioned intellectual, and even if some of her gaping contradictions could perhaps be yoked together into a theatrical zeugma, Stoppard hasn't begun to try. . . .

I admire Stoppard's intelligence and wit (wistfully I think of the times when "wit" meant intelligence), but I await the day when he puts them to their best uses. Even his admirable love of words does not yet protect Stoppard from solecisms, notably so ugly a lapse as that of the opening stage direction: "a screen, hopefully forming a backdrop. . . ." No person with any pretension to culture can permit himself that ghastly Teutonicism, the impersonal use of "hopefully." Let me hope, then, that the still very young Stoppard will ripen in every way into a more humane and considered playwright. . . .

*John Simon, "Ripe, or Merely Ready?," in* New York Magazine *(© 1974 by NYM Corp.; reprinted by permission of* New York Magazine *and John Simon), May 13, 1974, p. 98.*

*Jumpers* is superior by virtue of felicitous wit and its cleverness in making bright stage fare of its ideological content. But it fails to turn its material into true drama; its point or "thesis" is not revealed through action: it is only *stated.* There is no basic confrontation, conflict or delineation of real characters. What keeps the show going, apart from the amusing "mask" of the author's spokesman and his brilliant verbiage, is mere window dressing: acrobatics, pastiche mystery melodrama and dollops of nudity.

The intellectual substance of the play hardly ever challenges one's mind, nor is it made emotionally penetrating.

What, in sum, does the play tell us? As against the so-called "radical-liberals" of Stoppard's invention we are told that God exists. *"Cogito, ergo Deus est,"* Stoppard's professor says. I am pleased that he takes this positive position at a time when most drama and literature are hell-bent on negation. But to assert rather than to make manifest God's existence is to go no further than does any sensible humanist, not specifically a "believer." There is more of God in the tragicomedies of Chekhov, in the murk of Gorky's *Lower Depths,* even in Beckett's bleak despair or in Shaw's cheerfulness than in all Stoppard's literary exercises.

*Harold Clurman, in* The Nation, *May 18, 1974, pp. 637-38.*

Tom Stoppard, the Englishman who wrote [*Jumpers*], is the author of *Rosencrantz and Guildenstern Are Dead,* which was hailed for its novelty and its existential explorations. The latter seemed to me even more tenuous than its novelty: W. S. Gilbert wrote a *Rosencrantz and Guildenstern* in 1891. Stoppard's *R&G* was only a bright undergraduate's one-act prank waffled out to three acts. Then we got a bill of his one-act plays *The Real Inspector Hound* and *After Magritte,* which showed the undergraduate being less bright, merely facetious. In 1972 we read about Stoppard's new play, *Jumpers,* produced at the (British) National Theater and hailed as a work of philosophical richness and wit.

Sorry. *Jumpers,* in proof, is a work of copious philosophical *allusion,* written in that rhetorically ornate style brandished by the dramatist who has more wish than need to write and who takes the offensive stylistically in order to cow us. (Latter-day Albee is another example.) But Stoppard slides even further. He tries to fob off one more example of a stage-worn shallow genre: the play in which the author shows he has cosmic itches and tries to scratch them with a mixture of facile intellectual rotundities and self-conscious theater mystique. Examples: Philip Barry's *Here Come the Clowns,* Thornton Wilder's *The Skin of Our Teeth,* Max Frisch's *The Chinese Wall.*

Stoppard attempts a triple counterpoint between his vaudeville, a murder-mystery farce, and an intellectual comedy. . . . This braiding of vaudeville-farce-cogitations is supposed to stun us into perception of the relation of one to the other: the acrobats as visual equivalent of moral flip-flop, the murder-farce and sexual innuendo as gloss on the professor's moral speculations and vice versa. Not one shadow of a hair of such relation or supportive resonance is established. The elements are merely juxtaposed, that is all; and the mere juxtaposition is itself supposed to create weight—more, to bully us into fear of doubting that weight. Some physical connections (the corpse's tumbler costume, the stripper-secretary) are made; but there is no thematic resonance whatsoever between the scurrying antics in the boudoir and the intellectual meanderings in the study. And those meanderings end with the usual bland cop-out in this kind of purportedly probing work. It turns its back on query after the appropriate two-and-a-half hours, and accepts the universe so that we can all go home. . . .

The play is fake, structurally and thematically. . . . [Stoppard] is just one more half-baked egoist anxious for a cosmic grab, who thinks that the size of his ambition will certify his seriousness, particularly if he is comic, most particularly if he is reflexively theatrical.

*Stanley Kauffmann, in* The New Republic *(reprinted by permission of* The New Republic; *© The New Republic, Inc.), May 18, 1974, pp. 18, 33.*

Since *Rosencrantz and Guildenstern,* a play I admired but found a little too coy and dramatically forced in its darker moments, Stoppard has come closer and closer to a successful wedding of theatrical artistry and intelligence. He is already the best playwright around today, the only writer I feel who is capable of making the theater a truly formidable and civilized experience again. In George Moore [protagonist in *Jumpers*] he has created, with humor and familiar authority, a moving and comical attitude toward a modern intellectual dilemma, and I wish only that in place of "attitude" I might have said "character."

*Jack Richardson, in* Commentary *(reprinted from* Commentary *by permission; © 1974 by the American Jewish Committee), June, 1974, p. 80.*

It is a long time since my hands smarted so from applause for a flawed play as they did when the curtain fell on *Travesties.* There had been moments during the second half of the play when I feared that the whole thing might fall disastrously to pieces, mostly during a scene in which Tom Stoppard seemed not quite to have involved Lenin as persuasively as James Joyce and the Dadaist, Tristan Tzara, in the pattern of Oscar Wilde's *The Importance of Being Earnest,* but this was a passing anxiety. . . .

The idea of having such disparate characters as Joyce, Lenin and Tzara—comparable only in that each, in his way, was a revolutionary innovator—in the same play has doubtless struck you already as unlikely; to see them, respectively, as analogous to Lady Bracknell, Miss Prism and John Worthing is plainly so bizarre as to verge upon the impossible, and Stoppard's notion is always a little inebriated by its own temerity; but the overall effectiveness of his theatrical legerdemain is incontrovertible. The skill and wit and irony displayed in the trick are impudently dazzling. . . .

The form of the play reminded me vaguely of Anouilh's *The Rehearsal,* in which the characters, rehearsing a comedy by Marivaux, were themselves involved in a situation that paralleled the events in their play. Anouilh wrote his piece in the style of Marivaux, and Stoppard—finding echoes of *The Importance of Being Earnest* in his own invention—writes his very largely in the style of Wilde, often pitched so little above or below the key of the original that anyone hearing samples of both might be legitimately confused. . . . [The] Wildean trick of inverting a cliché to coin an epigram is not neglected: "If Lenin did not exist it would be unnecessary to invent him." This is, of course, parody of a high and rare order. Stoppard supplements it by applying an equally astute and effective comic invention to Joyce . . . and to Tzara, who is dealt with mainly in puns ("My art belongs to Dada"), a literary form shrewdly calculated to be precisely right for burlesquing this particular subject. The Stoppard irreverence sprays in all directions . . ., and with such lavish flippancy that there will almost certainly be those who will fail to appreciate the essentially serious nature of the play's discussion of the place of art and revolution in society; but this is the inevitable lot of writers who inform criticism with a genial sense of humour and a texture of wit. Stoppard clearly knows all about the importance of being earnest, and happily ignores it.

*Kenneth Hurren, "Wilde about Stoppard," in* The Spectator *(© 1974 by* The Spectator; *reprinted by permission of* The Spectator), *June 22, 1974, p. 776.*

* * *

## STOREY, David 1933-

**Storey is a British playwright and novelist whose work explores problems of alienation in contemporary society.**

[A] talented young English novelist, David Storey, followed two sharply perceptive novels about class and love in northern England with a fantastic parable in *Radcliffe* (1963). *Radcliffe* has two heroes who alternately attract and repel each other in a series of violently improbable actions. On one level, the heroes represent the two social classes in a northern town, and their attractions and repulsions are given a social dimension. But the upper-class character is also made the "soul" and the lower-class the "body," their friendship representing an uneasy, frequently violent, and finally destructive alliance. Storey has claimed that all his novels fit a pattern that the first, the novel of the professional rugby player, *This Sporting Life* (1960) was the novel of "body," that the second, *Flight into Camden* (1960) was the novel of "soul," and that the third, *Radcliffe*, is the impossible combination of the two. Yet, despite Storey's intention, the first two novels did not depend on their symbolic function; they conveyed a kind of complex verisimilitude that overwhelmed and enlivened the symbols. Only in *Radcliffe* is the symbolic machinery obtrusive, solemnly necessary to provide both coherence and relevance.

*James Gindin, in his* Harvest of a Quiet Eye: The Novel of Compassion, *Indiana University Press, 1971, pp. 339-40.*

[In] many respects Storey's plays seem rather anachronistically balanced, direct and realistic, beautifully shaped and with a meticulous notation of everyday speech. So much so that critics have started bandying the name of Chekhov about in their vicinity, and commenting on how well-made and—what was until very recently the last word in polite damnation—'well-written' they are. . . .

It is precisely this quality—the teasing and elusive feeling that the plays have a sort of weight and density which one cannot logically justify—which makes David Storey's plays (and for that matter his novels) so distinctive in the contemporary British scene. One would guess, I think, that though the plays have an extraordinary and unerring instinct for what works in the theatre, they were written by someone with no passionate interest in the theatre or close involvement in the latest movements, the approved positions for a modern playwright. A lot of their material is clearly autobiographical—not so much, presumably, in the details of plot, character and situation, but in the backgrounds and ways of life evoked. . . . The experiences give immediacy and body to his works; but finally any documentary interest is strictly coincidental. They are so compelling because of the intensity with which they summon up one man's private vision of the world. . . .

[*Home*] is built of great gaping silences, and words which are hardly better, or hardly different—Pinter's second silence, when speech is speaking of a language locked beneath it. Thus *Home* is completely non-literary in its effect; it makes sense only in the theatrical situation of people on a stage, speaking and moving, and people in an audience, watching and listening, and understanding more through their instincts than through their intelligences.

This is rather a remarkable development in Storey, though his plays have been becoming progressively less literary, less dependent on the words of dialogue, for the principal effect. His strength as a dramatist up to now has been his isolation from fashion, his ability to follow his own vision unswervingly in the theatre and find to his hand precisely the right means of doing so. One could label his earlier three plays produced 'conservative' in technique if one wanted to, but the question does not arise because one never feels that there was any real choice of technique: the idea determined its form of expression, and that was that. In *Home* this remains so, even if the ideas have changed and the form of expression has changed with them. The slight flurry of discussion when the play opened about whether Storey had undergone an influence from Pinter seemed, more than usual, grotesquely irrelevant.

*John Russell Taylor, "David Storey," in his* The Second Wave: British Drama for the Seventies *(reprinted by permission of Hill and Wang, a division of Farrar, Straus & Giroux, Inc.; copyright © 1971 by John Russell Taylor), Hill & Wang, 1971, pp. 141-54.*

*The Changing Room*, by David Storey, is documentary theatre with social implications and symbolic overtones. It takes place in the locker room (changing room) of a North-of-England Rugby League team, a bunch of semi-professionals ranging from miners and mill workers to a few teachers and such. The play covers the period from just before to just after a game and includes among its characters the team owner, a successful, knighted businessman, the club secretary, the players, coaches, trainers, referee, masseur and, at the bottom of the hierarchic scale, the cleaner, a crazy old man muttering about the cold weather being part of a sinister Russian plot to Communize the world. This spectrum, extending from bluffly jovial but shrewdly calculating owner, through various intermediary stages, down to semidemented drudge, gives the play its slice-of-life, societal-cross-section aspect. There is some suggestion of the slackening and reshuffling of the caste system, but also a clear sense of its persisting all the same.

Principally, though, the play is an almost *cinéma-vérité* rendering of the shedding of civilian identities to become players and teammates; of the effort and dirtying, the injuries and pain that make up the game; of the elation and rowdy horseplay after the victory; and of the changing back into civilians, with the locker room becoming once again a soiled, disheveled disaster area for the cleaner to confront with his grudging, cantankerous ministrations. But here the title itself becomes significant: *The Changing Room*, the space in which a change comes to pass. The owner has moved up the social scale, some of the players have improved their status by becoming star athletes; others, cuckolded by their very buddies, have been pushed down the ladder. Yet, in a deeper sense, nothing changes in this changing room. . . .

David Storey is a minimalist, as we know from such other plays of his as *Home* and *The Contractor*. Within his narrow range, he works with sure and suggestive brushstrokes. But such is the duration of a play [here, *The Changing Room*] that it requires more brushstrokes to fill it out than are consistent with minimalism. The minutiae have a way of becoming too numerous for stark simplicity, and still remaining too minute.

*John Simon, in* The Hudson Review *(copyright 1973 by The Hudson Review, Inc.; reprinted by permission), Vol. XXVI, No. 2, Summer, 1973, pp. 340-41.*

*A Temporary Life* . . . is not the tragedy of the elderly, but the tragedy of the younger and the more disaffected ciphers of our society. It is a novel of provincial life. Specifically, the provincial life of one Colin Freestone, an art-teacher and (so that we know he's not one of these art-teacher 'types') an ex-boxer. . . . He is not a hero in anything but the technical sense, but I got the impression that his laconic and often brutal manner was designed to be interesting. I found it as aimless and as incomprehensible as all of the other lives in the novel, and that may well be the point. And I am not one to scoff at *angst*.

As befits the fall . . . of an ex-boxer, the style of Mr Storey's novel is hard and abrupt. He uses the present indicative in what is a perpetually interrupted stream of northern consciousness. Conversations and movement are of the mechanical variety, as though the distance between author and character is the length of a puppet's string. . . .

[Like] the beat of the tom-tom in the jungle, there may be passions lurking beneath the staccato. But in fact it turns out that there are none, and when these brief conversations are decoded they add up to nothing more than fashionable *angst* and alienation. Complete with the romantic landscape of chimneys and bed-sits, moors and tenements. But Mr Storey protests too much. Now there is a genuine and human sadness about the novel. . . . But futility and incoherence become the status quo of the narrative, and Storey becomes the victim of his mood.

Adultery, violence and boredom are the universal constituents of human life (said Samuel Johnson as he kicked *himself*), and I don't know why Mr Storey takes them so seriously. When they become central to the narrative, they also become portentous and trite—to go back to my original point, they are low matters treated in a high style. They are better as the vehicle for comedy or farce, and it is when Mr Storey is being funny that he is at his best.

*Peter Ackroyd, in* The Spectator (© *1973 by* The Spectator; *reprinted by permission of* The Spectator), *September 22, 1973, p. 377.*

One shouldn't confuse ambition with effect, but in Storey's case his talent only seems completely itself when stretched in contention with the greatest, wrestling with the memories of Hardy, the Brontës and Lawrence. It wasn't just the fact that his earlier plays seemed easy that I objected to. It was that their facility made them seem more trivial than he is.

*Ronald Bryden, in* Plays and Players, *October, 1973, p. 49.*

The parlour of David Storey's fine new play, *The Farm* . . . , is stuffed with easy furniture and the collected bric-a-brac of a lifetime. You might remove your muddy boots if you went in, but you wouldn't need to dress up. As in so many [Storey plays] you feel yourself, in a very rare way, almost able to project your own physical presence into the world they so mesmerically create. It's a world that stays in your head for days after, and it's not a particularly comfortable parasite.

The twentieth century has not allowed this Yorkshire farm —isolated as it might seem if seen from road, rail or plane— to by-pass its buffetings. Although, as at Haworth Parsonage, the windows give out on to the moors, the three sisters are as unlikely to write tortured classics as they are to die of consumption; their brother may share with Branwell the spirit of a failed poet, but the spit and anger have gone out of him. On the great white road of worldly progress they, like most of us, are feeling somewhat rootless.

As in *Home,* where the home was no home at all, so the farm, which should be the symbol of growth and fertility, nurtures only dashed hopes; behind the smell of a good old-fashioned breakfast, there's an odour of waste. The household is not just a clutch of characters but emblems in an entirely natural form. . . .

Storey writes about women in *The Farm* with far more clarity than I remember in his earlier plays. The three sisters are carefully individualised, each caught at a precise moment of their development. . . .

After Storey's last foray, *Cromwell, The Farm* may seem like a return to less adventurous ground, to the home territory of *In Celebration* and *The Contractor,* but . . . I see no reason to complain. After all, Cézanne painted plenty of apples.

*Helen Dawson, in* Plays and Players, *November, 1973, pp. 42-3.*

There is not much in the way of illumination [in *Pasmore*], apart from Mr. Storey's general observations about our precarious grasp on sanity in a loony, hostile world or his suggestion that British meaninglessness is just like everyone else's, except rather more laconic. The real difficulty is that Mr. Storey doesn't find his character sufficiently interesting to make him articulate. The result is an utterly barren and unrewarding book.

*Paul Theroux, in* The New York Times Book Review *(© 1974 by The New York Times Company; reprinted by permission), March 17, 1974, p. 40.*

Mr. Storey is an absorbing writer, and he captures in a completely believable way the terrible bleakness of Pasmore's family's coal-mining town and the bewilderment and anguish of a family falling apart. But the wife, the children, and all of Pasmore's friends enter and exit so rapidly (if dramatically) that we never really get to know who any of them are, and the expression that the characters utter so frequently—"Ah, well"—is more or less what comes to mind when Pasmore returns home, feeling all around him "an intensity, like a presentiment of love, or violence: he found it hard to tell."

The New Yorker, *March 25, 1974, pp. 141-42.*

Families are a funny breed. They draw, spill, suck and drink the blood they share. They seem to survive everything with dumb granitic tenacity. What they give to each other is measureless, like divine grace; what they take is inexorable, like mortal fate.

David Storey's *In Celebration* . . . is in the tradition of the finest family plays. Its relatives leap to mind: *Long Day's Journey Into Night, Death of a Salesman, The Glass Menagerie, The Homecoming.* Like them, it is incessantly poised between laughter, tears and the unfathomable mystery of existence. Like them, it is a loving, sorrowing armistice with the past.

Written years before *Home, The Changing Room* and *The Contractor, In Celebration* is Storey's most personal play. The first three are exactly observed, but in them Storey distances author and subject with fastidious detachment. *In Celebration* seems to have been axed out of the playwright's heart. While writing this work, Storey must sometimes have seen blood red.

*T. E. Kalem, "Family Communion," in* Time *(reprinted by permission from* Time, The Weekly Newsmagazine; *copyright Time Inc.), June 10, 1974, p. 106.*

David Storey's *Life Class* . . . may perhaps turn out to be one of his less substantial works; even if it does, it is full of resonant overtones informing a basically simple structure. . . .

We are . . . plunged into the interaction and isolation of students and teachers in a north-country art school during one day's session . . . where the students reluctantly set about learning to look at, and draw, an actual object—in this case a naked female model—under the weary supervision of a failed artist who has become, in the words of one of his colleagues, a 'purveyor of the invisible event'. . . .

[At] the end of the first half . . . we have been given an amusing, if saddening, . . . picture of aimless young people and dotty or depressed mentors. What next? Quite a bit, as it happens, for instead of post-prandial torpor pressures rise, and vague theoretical questions need urgent practical answers. Shall art, or life, conform to disciplines, rules of conduct; shall art, or life, remain faithful to the outside world reported by the senses? A discipline of drawing, a discipline of decency? That they should is urged most strongly by the head of the school . . ., convinced that 'If life itself is degenerate, then art should set ideals'. But Allott, the man actually taking the life class (the irony of the title becomes keener as the play goes on) is too far gone for that. Perhaps he was a good artist himself, once; now, when not actually peering despondently at his students' feeble efforts, or drawling sarcastically at them, he takes refuge in the idea of the artist as a disinterested person, himself confining his creativity to the writing of comic doggerel. Even his private life has disintegrated, and disintegrates further in the course of the play.

*J. W. Lambert, in* Drama, *Summer, 1974, pp. 39, 41.*

Storey, [in his novel *Pasmore*] as in his plays, creates a world that is full of intimations but without fixities. Events are not traced to causes; motives are not such as we can easily specify. We are suspended in a situation that seems at once lucid in its universality and yet as arbitrary and impenetrable as the least predictable accident. The novel never departs from the circumstantial detail that we expect of realism, but it never quite gives us the kind or amount of detail we seek. The result is a series of events that are obsessive and almost hallucinatory. . . .

Storey's language never tries for the fluidity of dream in its own idiom; instead we are given a crisp, often epigrammatic, sense of factuality. The matter-of-factness only confirms the power of the obsession, which will not offer itself as less than reality.

*Martin Price, in* The Yale Review *(© 1974 by Yale University; reprinted by permission of the editors), Summer, 1974, p. 557.*

"A Temporary Life" represents a beautiful homogenization of English fictional themes—past, present and future. From David Storey's earlier orientation comes a touch of class turmoil. From even farther back come wildly idiosyncratic characters that might be at home in "Crome Yellow." From the dawn of the novel comes our hero, Colin Freestone, a natural man who faces experience with the uninhibited flexibility of Tom Jones. Plus, the novel exudes a post-modern Zeitgeist that might be described as nihilistic. . . .

Storey's hero gives enough of a damn to be a man worth watching. He reacts to immediate stimuli. Rudeness he repays with a punch in the nose. He responds to the misfortune of others with enlightened concern. But in the long run, well, there is no long run. A temporary life consists of disconnected encounters that call for individual strategies. . . .

The novel is bitter, funny, enriching.

*Martin Levin, in* The New York Times Book Review *(© 1974 by The New York Times Company; reprinted by permission), September 22, 1974, p. 40.*

* * *

## SUKENICK, Ronald 1932-

**Sukenick is an American experimental novelist and short story writer. (See also *Contemporary Authors*, Vols. 25-28.)**

Since 1968, when John Barth declared that literature was "exhausted" and Leslie Fiedler, Susan Sontag, Norman Mailer, and other critics cheered along that the novel at least was dead, Ronald Sukenick has been proving that there is a great deal of life to be rediscovered in the form. His first novel, *Up* . . ., followed Barth with a generous indulgence in aesthetic allegory, but instead of painting itself into a corner or disappearing up its own fundament, *Up* pointed a way out. . . .

Ronald Sukenick would revalidate our imaginations so that

we can look at our environment in a real way. For [Carlos Castaneda's] Don Juan, it's a question of two distinct manners of perceiving. "'Looking' referred to the ordinary way in which we are accustomed to perceive the world, while 'seeing' entailed a very complex process by virtue of which a man of knowledge allegedly perceives the 'essence' of the things of the world." For fiction, it is the ability to transcend a mere describing of life (always a danger in this most mimetic of forms) to a revelation of the truth of experience, which may be at odds with the popular consensus. To stop the world—to call a halt to having one's personal, provisional view of things as absolute—may be a key to the cultural turnabout so apparent around us, reflected in Sukenick's new style of fiction, Castaneda's great popularity, and the appeal environmentalist Aldo Leopold has for such a broad intellectual audience. . . .

To arrive at "seeing," Castaneda learned in *Ixtlan,* one must stop the world. "'Stopping the world' was indeed an appropriate rendition of certain states of awareness in which the reality of everyday life is altered because the flow of interpretation, which ordinarily runs uninterruptedly, has been stopped by a set of circumstances alien to that flow." Don Juan's task, as exercised in *A Separate Reality,* "was to disarrange a particular certainty which I shared with everyone else, the certainty that our 'common-sense' views of the world are final." The imagination, Sukenick has said, makes reality seem more real—and Don Juan's methods are a paradigm for liberating oneself from the obstructed, unimaginative view. "'The little smoke removes the body and one is free, like the wind'" and the metaphor of bodily flight becomes "the sorcerer's capacity to move through nonordinary reality and then to return at will to ordinary reality." The fullest possibilities of vision—not just the documentary records of what historically occurred—are what Sukenick wants for his fiction, and Don Juan is the master who can show how "'There are worlds upon worlds, right here in front of us'." . . .

Fiction plays its tricks, but in his own *Village Voice* essay on Castaneda's work Sukenick insists that "All art deconditions us so that we may respond more fully to experience." The wealth of that response has been his aim since *Up,* through the efforts to capture the truth of experience in *The Death of the Novel and Other Stories* . . . and most recently *Out.* While others would let fiction die, Sukenick argues that its great advantage "over history, journalism, or any other supposedly 'factual' kind of writing is that it is an expressive medium. It transmits feeling, energy, excitement. Television can give us the news, fiction can best express our response to the news. . . . No other medium, in other words, can so well keep track of the reality of our experience." Technically, his novel *Out* proves that a novel can be a concrete as well as an imaginative structure, and offers art for the eye and the page-turning hand as well as for the mind. But ultimately Sukenick's genius rests with his discovery that the reality we know is only a description, and that "The power of a sorcerer is the power of the feeling he can invest in his description so it is felt as a persuasive account of the world." This same persuasiveness is the measure of good fiction, which Ronald Sukenick brings to life, proving what an unexhausted novelist can do.

*Jerome Klinkowitz, "A Persuasive Account: Working It Out With Ronald Sukenick," in* North American Review, *Summer, 1973, pp. 48-52.*

Sukenick makes a point of (no, makes a novel of) art that does not conceal art. The scaffolding remains on the completed building. . . .

The medievalists understood this kind of writing. See Augustine especially. Solve the conundrum whose center is divine truth. Art proposes revelation as its end. The pleasure comes through teasing the mind until it sees clearly the kernel within the husk. Whether the several apologists (Sontag, Pynchon etc.) for Sukenick's kind of writing like it or not, works such as "Out" demand an interpretation, an exegesis if you like. Despite the surface glitter we look for more because language asks us to. . . . Contemporary innovators reject an older tradition's view of plenitude and significance for emptiness, the void. I don't question their moral posture, but I would say that they are on a very well-worn track: the one leading through and beneath phenomena to a static truth. Old wine, new bottles.

*Tim O'Hara, in* Best Sellers, *July 15, 1973, pp. 157-58.*

Sukenick is not only an uncommonly talented writer, but a sensitive and purposeful one. "Out" is precisely what it says it is, a novel that walks right out of itself, whose central character himself rejects all possible human pathways save that of total disappearance. . . .

[Not] only has Sukenick taken the devices of the literature of the id and turned them on their heads to produce a humanistic—and hence, intellectual—document, he has followed the whole trend to its logical conclusion. There he has discovered a brick wall, a blank page. There is no future in the id, only instinct, madness and ultimate death. The id cannot create, it can only destroy; monkeys do not build cities. Such resources as it possesses may be all very well when it comes to describing present states and moral revulsion, as Sukenick amply demonstrates, but a whole literary movement that ends screaming in a blind alley is going to do very little to increase the measure of man. And that, in the last analysis, is the only thing that art is all about.

*L. J. Davis, in* The New York Times Book Review *(© 1973 by The New York Times Company; reprinted by permission), October 21, 1973, p. 49.*

Ronald Sukenick's *Out* reads like a bizarre fantasy of sexual brutality, violence on the streets, and fear in the guts. Here is a world where names change at the drop of an introduction, where those who are part of the plot or part of the counterplot keep talking, keep moving, although they can rarely find, identify, or understand each other. . . .

The point of this complex onslaught is to induce the character, the writer, and the reader to abandon linear perception for the more inclusive second sight of the artist or the mystic. . . .

Throughout the book, major incidents are portrayed at least twice—each time a combination of the real and the fantastic. They resemble the constant word plays, anagrams, and puns of the novel's language, which delight the reader. . . . But the incidents that follow this pattern do not delight, because while we can accept and enjoy play on words, play on experience quickly becomes threatening and frightening. The reader is threatened because traditional perceptual tools are useless when characters change names and traits irrationally, when he can only choose between equally dissatisfying combinations of reality and fantasy. The character, sharing this frustration, must be purged of the inclination to stuff all experience into the insufficient frameworks of words and incidents and "meaningful question." . . .

The reason for the free-form language and the peculiar physical shape of the book grows clearer as the work progresses. The traditional structure of the novel—words, sentences, paragraphs, chapters of nearly equal length—constructs experience into artificial forms from which the novel must find a way out if it is to be capable of imitating contemporary experience. Words, like characters, like incidents, have affinity groups, move sideways as well as straight ahead, and in so connecting and moving reach equally "real" ends. As the main stream of character learns that it is not necessary to keep talking, the size of Sukenick's chapters diminishes, but not in the traditional sense. The chapter numbers, running from 9 to 0, indicate the number of lines in each of the three sections clearly separated on each page. The constantly diminishing number of words on each page pulls the reader along at an ever increasing rate until, finally, only three lines per page force the eye and the mind to rush through the words and out to the blank expanse of the last chapter. The reader is thus still literally experiencing the novel after it runs out of words. Language is itself a symbol, a form into which experience is put. Experience is not less full when fewer words delineate it, nor does it cease when words stop describing it.

This not particularly new line of thought has obvious limitations: how could we have any fiction that does not codify experience, that does not substitute characters for human consciousness, words for sight and sound and movement, or a plot for real action. It does, however, allow Sukenick to give the impression of direct, amorphous experience, and in this is the book's force. This book moves the reader, producing vivid sensations of fear, lust, confusion, frustration, and, at the end, produces a flooding sensation of relief in the rapid whoosh out. Form, content, and technique are welded into a fluid whole that engages the reader in growth similar to that of the character, and gives him a glimpse of a broader mode of perception. Sukenick's elaborate code tempts the reader into critical abstraction even though Sukenick (the character) attests its futility. But the abstracted code leads away from the book, limiting perception. The reader—and the reviewer—caught, must flow with the book, or lose it. . . .

Acceptance of the mix of life, of the asymmetry of incidents, of the unclearness of reality, of the formlessness of perception, is demanded by the dissolving and reforming skywriting that indicated the way out at the end of the novel. This does not negate meaning so much as grope toward a deeper, more inclusive, more ecstatic understanding.

And to some extent the reader can share this experience with character, responding to before quite understanding the changes he is undergoing. For Sukenick seduces the reader into a mode of perception in which characters, situations, and even words are stretched to their limits in exploitation of their latent possibilities. *Out* is rich with the fantasies and foibles of contemporary America—from city doors covered with locks to campers in the mountains teeming with the junk of civilization. The verbal style is rich, the erratic sentence structure congealing puns and word play from the simple to the gross. Characteristically, Sukenick twists the familiar into strangeness or absurdity. For all its richness, the novel is uneven; although he usually carries it off, Sukenick cannot always escape triteness, sometimes even foolishness. And the physical structure of the book imparts a strangeness that, although justified, threatens to obscure rather than to enrich. His ideas are not new, his incidents almost irritatingly familiar, his clichés not always renovated. But the novel overcomes these flaws, sometimes brilliantly, with overall force and wit.

*Linda S. Bergmann, "Out. A Novel by Ronald Sukenick" (reprinted by permission of* Chicago Review; *copyright © 1974 by* Chicago Review*), in* Chicago Review, *Vol. 25, No. 3, 1974, pp. 9-12.*

* * *

## SWENSON, May 1919-

**Ms Swenson is an award-winning American poet and critic. (See also *Contemporary Authors*, Vols. 5-8, rev. ed.)**

[May Swenson's] distinction is that she is able to make poems of ordinary public realities, offering precise images of urban life with an amazed reporter's skill—a reporter with pity—making her reader see clearly what he has merely looked at before. The public squares, parks, subways, museums, and zoos of New York City provide the scenes and incidents for her scrutiny, though there are easy references to Rome, Venice, Paris, and Arles as well, for Miss Swenson has been traveling. She is at her strongest in poems about people riding a subway to work or driving along a highway or feeding pigeons or sitting in a park—lonely people in a world without anchor in the cosmic sea. . . .

Miss Swenson works in a free verse that is supple but rather prosaic, despite her picturemaking efforts. She lacks formal subtlety and profundity of insight. And some of her poems are badly in need of pruning. But at her best she succeeds in giving the reader a sense of what it feels like to be alive in a large American city in the middle of the twentieth century.

*Stephen Stepanchev, "May Swenson", in his* American Poetry Since 1945: A Critical Survey *(copyright © 1965 by Stephen Stepanchev; reprinted by permission of Harper & Row, Publishers, Inc.), Harper, 1965, pp. 202-04.*

May Swenson begins and ends in mannerism. She is forever tinkering, taking apart a cat, a watch, a poem. . . . She is endlessly feeling things and relentlessly fashionable about what there is to grab: "On Handling Some Small Shells From the Windward Islands"—the pretentious-unpretentious title tells the story, as does the chic disposition of words on the page, . . . in old-fashioned pentameter. . . . For May Swenson things exist so that poems can be written about them, and if most things have been discovered there's always "A Basin of Eggs". . . . May Swenson has nothing to say, and her many ways of saying it drove me to exasperation.

*William H. Pritchard, in* The Hudson Review *(copyright © 1967 by The Hudson Review, Inc.; reprinted by permission), Vol. XX, No. 2, Summer, 1967, pp. 307-08.*

Existence, its mystery, and therefore, its reality [is the tantalizing subject of May Swenson's poetry]. Whatever is, is not and therefore is *more* when the poet apprehends it through the ever living word. This is her subject. She is forever in this world (her last collection is called *To Mix with Time*), and therefore apprehends the isness that is beyond, which is within—this world. She says this over and over again in her poetry as she moves from a city garden, the ocean, kites, a watch, an astronaut in his capsule, cats, shells, trees, a dentist's needle, lightning, Provincetown, the moon. It doesn't matter the whatness. Through her language she probes existence, takes what is apart (and not in a surrealistic way, but in a scientific way that becomes through accuracy seemingly metaphysical), puts it together again because she has set it down in words, and it then exists. There, look at it. It is behovely. It disappears. It begets other worlds. And is. Existence. . . .

Apprehension is the magic, apprehension through the excitement of language. Ezra Pound found that a successful poetic presentation or rendering gave "that sense of sudden liberation; that sense of freedom from time limits and space limits; that sense of sudden growth, which we experience in the presence of the greatest works of art.". . . [The] tremendous sense of liberation in the poems of May Swenson, in her rhymes, her depiction of objects, her expert use of typography and line . . . is not a liberation away from time but into time, not esoteric in intention but descriptive, even analytic. The liberation, that metaphysical accompaniment, is that quivering equation that is reached when object and word are aptly mated.

*Harriet Zinnes, "In This World," in* Prairie Schooner *(© 1968 by University of Nebraska Press; reprinted by permission from* Prairie Schooner*), Spring, 1968, pp. 86-9.*

It is as an observer that May Swenson has become best known. Such a comment as Robert Lowell's "Miss Swenson's quick-eyed poems should be hung with permanent fresh paint signs," represents a common reaction. Miss Swenson achieves this freshness by a good eye enlivened by imagination. But however imaginative, her poetry is continually tied to accuracy of sight, to truth to the literal and concrete. This is so even when the truth is conveyed by metaphor or in a spirit of aesthetic play. . . .

Though she revels in the world of objects and is concerned with surfaces, Miss Swenson is also aware of depths and changes. Her poems have many possibilities for interpretation on levels beyond the literal. In the introduction to *Another Animal,* John Hall Wheelock gave an elaborate summary of the levels in "The Greater Whiteness," and many of her other poems contain materials for such analysis. Some, like "The Primitive," are clearly symbolic, while remaining true to the literal. Starting with the line "I walk a path that a mountain crosses," the poem seems to present a primitive point of view, but the reader immediately wonders "who is the primitive?" All the comments of the poem apply to walking up any mountain, but they have to do also with the special mountain which this is. Is it the mountain on the other side of which is death? The primitive does not know. The poem ends with a series of questions and speculations, some contradictory, all of them subjects of a separate inquiry in relation to its symbolic structure. But the symbolism in this and other poems, like May Swenson's magic, grows most often out of a tangible phenomenon, like the path and the mountain, where the poet has an observably solid base.

Miss Swenson's involvement with the perceptibly solid is further seen in her placement of the poem on the page. Lines and spaces are carefully arranged in patterns appropriate to the subject. Some words are given typographical emphasis by being set off and repeated. Even punctuation and capitalization—or the lack of them—are arranged for visual effect.

There are several variants of the shaped poem. The shape may be that of the object involved as in "Out of the Sea, Early" where the poem is round to represent the rising sun. Or there may be an uneven margin which undulates or steps back and forth to give the poem a shape of a black figure against a white background as in "Fountain Piece." The margin may be placed at the right side of the page instead of the left. Or two columns of narrow stanzas may be placed on the page, their center margins straight.

Other poems use alphabetical devices or whole words which occur in a repeated pattern in a line, emphasized by the spacing of the line. . . .

This linking of the parts of the poem, the care in its visual physical arrangement, is not related to form alone. It reflects the careful observation, the respect for the whole range of the senses, that goes into the language and concepts that Miss Swenson presents. Her poems are not limited to linear time; they are patterns in space as well. The shaped poem represents the poet's response to the aesthetic need for structure, a need met in other poets by the formal stanza or the syllabic or metric line. The enclosing of the poem within spatial boundaries rather than auditory-rhythmic limits is especially appropriate to the perceptual qualities of Miss Swenson's art.

*Ann Stanford, "May Swenson: The Art of Perceiving," in* The Southern Review, *Vol. V, No. 1, Winter, 1969, pp. 58-75.*

With all its virtues, *Half Sun Half Sleep* is not a completely successful book of poems. Miss Swenson abjures thematic or stylistic organization and, by printing the poems in alphabetical order, defers to the contingency she sees around her. While this is a perfectly valid theory of arrangement, the fact remains that some of the poems need the support of a definite context to make them work, or to make them less obtrusively second-rate; for this volume is uneven, varying greatly in quality not only from one poem to another, but also within individual pieces. . . . Miss Swenson's right to experiment with typography and repetition of elements must be respected; but it is only fair to say that the results are not always impressive. And elsewhere, otherwise successful poems are seriously damaged by ready-made imagery: "Farms are fitted pieces of a floor,/tan and green tiles" ("Flying House"); "buttermilk skies" ("On Handling Some Small Shells . . ."). Still other poems do not succeed because of less obvious faults; they simply lack the special sharpness of wit necessary to prevent the close detailing of experience from becoming mechanical. Nonetheless, when successful, as she often is, May Swenson is among the best of those poets who can effectively show us what all of reality is like by examining closely a small fragment.

*Karl Malkoff, in* The Southern Review, *Vol. IV, No. 2, Spring, 1970, pp. 574-75.*

The variety in [*Iconographs*] is wide and rare, and because I am not used to a strong vein of overt passion in May Swenson's poems, I was particularly taken with a series of love poems: *Feel Me, A Trellis for R., Wednesday at the Waldorf,* and *The Year of the Double Spring.* The subjects of these poems are persons rather than the bird, the flower, or stunning artifact so often used as levers in her poems. . . . There are [many] very fine poems in this collection; no clinkers, no duds. These poems combine ecstasy with exactness, and speak the truth in truthful language. May Swenson is an established, rather than an establishment, poet.

*Nancy Sullivan, "Iconodule and Iconoclast," in* Poetry *(© 1971 by The Modern Poetry Association; reprinted by permission of the Editor of* Poetry*), November, 1971, pp. 107-08.*

May Swenson since her first collection, *Another Animal* (1954), obviously, even nervously has been devoted to craft. Formal sloppiness would be impossible for her. . . . Out of close observation of urban and rural landscapes, of faraway places and tourist spots, of birds, horses, waves or the sun, she has built her poems upon the page. It is the way May Swenson has built her poems that needs comment. . . . [The] poet *typed* the poems ([*Iconographs*] is a photo-offset publication). In effect, the photographed typescript creates an enclosed, graphic object upon the page. The whole is seen as a significant spatial object even before the eye relents and begins to read. The poem evolves into something almost plastic, a form of conceptual art. The words that are the poem do not lose their integrity within the poem, and the mold, the shape, is a possible new dimension. . . .

May Swenson's solution is interesting because she seeks the form *after* the poem, the text, has been written. In other words, her mold does not determine the verbal structure. First the words are on the page, and then like a draftsman she draws her icon with her text as pencil and pen. The advantage of this method is that there is no distortion of the original language, and thus of perception. The poetic text has not been violated in any way. But what May Swenson is saying, in effect, is that language is not enough today, that poetry has suffered a diminution. She feels the need to "make an existence in space, as well as in time, for the poem." . . .

I would add, however, that this complex contains language, and the poetry of May Swenson reveals a brilliant use of language: definitions of visible and evocative worlds. . . . In May Swenson's shaped verse there is never a failure of form in the sense that William H. Gass meant when he recently commented that "an unfeelable form is a failure." But even May Swenson's shaped verse is at the least a distraction. . . .

[*Iconographs*] is a triumph of poetry. I go backward as I read. I read the text *before* the shape has been imposed, and then I see that her singular devotion to her craft has led to a new dimension in her art. Through assonance and internal rhyme, she delicately maneuvers new feelings. . . .

In this volume May Swenson's metaphysical wit has become less Dickinsonian and more like Beckett. Primarily interested in concrete experience ("No to and from/There is only here," as she writes in an earlier volume), she sees the *here* more firmly rooted in the *now,* without embellishment. . . .

This new volume attests that May Swenson is one of the most distinguished poets writing. With an uncanny ear, a sense of line directed by an inner energy and a way with language that is ever a discovery, she stands almost alone as a poet who has triumphed over the continuing skepticism among her colleagues toward their own craft.

*Harriet Zinnes, "No Matter What the Icons Say," in* The Nation, *February 28, 1972, pp. 282-83.*

# T

## TATE, (John Orley) Allen 1899-

**Tate, an American poet, critic, and man of letters—one of America's foremost writers—was an influential member of the "Fugitive Group" of poets writing about the agrarian South. His poetry, according to David J. Parkes, "has the intellectual discipline of Eliot, the turn of conceit of the metaphysicals and the macabre imagery of Poe." (See also *Contemporary Authors*, Vols. 5-8, rev. ed.)**

Allen Tate's mind is exceptional in its harmony. . . . His personality is as whole and undivided, and it is as steady, as it is vivid. Allen would readily have found his role in the Golden Age of Hellenism, or in classical Rome, or the Elizabethan Renaissance. All the powers of the mind engaged at once in the great figures of those ages. And if he had been of middle age in Virginia during the Civil War, he would have been a statesman, or a warrior, and he would have retired like General Lee afterwards to the university, but in the role of poet in residence. Yes, and if it had been fated—and even in this age it may be fated, in view of the religious establishment which survives so resolutely from "the age of faith"—Allen would have been a theologian and a poet in those Middle Ages when there was a sort of closure of the whole mind under the religious prescription. There was not in theory any division within that mind. It was not necessarily contemplated that the right hand would have to be jealous of the freedom of the left hand. And here I take the right hand as standing for religion, and the left hand as standing for poetry and literature.

*John Crowe Ransom, "In Amictia," in* Sewanee Review *(© 1959 by The University of the South), Autumn, 1959, pp. 528-39.*

Every serious writer has one subject, I believe, which he spends his life exploring and delivering as fully as he may. Tate's subject is simply what is left of Christendom, that western knowledge of ourselves which is our identity. He may be classed as a religious writer, and that from the very beginning. The literary historian is likely to see his work as the best expression of the crucial drama of our time. "We've cracked the hemispheres with careless hand!" Does language more poetically describe the plight of western civilization? He has many voices: verse, biography, criticism, essay, even fiction—but one language and one subject. In rereading him I was surprised to find that, even as a young man, especially a young man in the 'twenties, he saw the religious doubt, the failure of belief, as crucial. In the same way he accepted the South's defeat not as a private or local affair but as the last great defense in a going society of those values, particularly human, we know as Christian. Even in the earlier verse such as "Causerie" and "Last Days of Alice" the ironic complaint derives from and hangs upon this ambiguity of belief. In *I'll Take My Stand* it was his essay which argued the religious position. The diversity and range, certainly in the verse, can be seen in the manner he divides his collected poems into sections. Early pieces are put by the latest, but the book opens with the larger treatments of his position, the historical and cultural past, not as background but as vision immediately related to the poet and all others now living. The first section opens with "The Mediterranean" and closes with the "Ode to the Confederate Dead." The final irony of the sound of nature's soughing of the leaves serves for a transition to the other parts of the book.

Behind Allen Tate lies a body of work anyone would be proud to call a life's work.

*Andrew Lytle, "Allen Tate: Upon the Occasion of His Sixtieth Birthday," in* Sewanee Review *(reprinted by permission of the editor; © 1959 by The University of the South), Autumn, 1959, pp. 542-44.*

[Tate's] poems, all of them, even the slightest, are terribly personal. Out of splutter and shambling comes a killing eloquence. Perhaps this is the resonance of desperation, or rather the formal resonance of desperation. I say "formal" because no one has so given us the impression that poetry must be burly, must be courteous, must be tinkered with and recast until one's eyes pop out of one's head. How often something smashes through the tortured joy of composition to strike the impossible bull's-eye! The pre-Armageddon twenties and thirties with all their peculiar fears and enthusiasms throb in Tate's poetry; imitated ad infinitum, it has never been reproduced by another hand.

*Robert Lowell, "Visiting the Tates," in* Sewanee Review *(© 1959 by The University of the South), Autumn, 1959, pp. 557-59.*

One has only to recall those Arnoldian "touchstones"

which Allen Tate gave in his essay on "Tension in Poetry" to see the romanticism openly confessed—not one of these touchstones could conceivably be given as an example of classical precision or elegance. The whole concept of "tension," central to much of Allen Tate's thought, is a romantic concept. The classicist ideal is not tension, but serene security. . . .

I am not instructed in the hierarchies of American criticism, but I have never seen Allen Tate in the battle-dress of one of its factions, and I imagine that he cannot easily be classified. That, to me, is the mark of a sound critic, forever dwelling in uncertainties, forever qualifying categorical logic with intuitive *finesse*. I think it is a characteristic to his credit that although he has voluntarily accepted the rigors of a dogmatic faith, he has never sought to subordinate his criticism to morality. Perhaps he has never confused morality with religion, or faith with belief. He knows that Satan, if put to it, could write his own *Paradise Lost*. . . .

Allen Tate knows that poetry survives and has meaning for survival only to the extent that it is and remains a symbolic language. In an Introductory Note to his translation of the *Pervigilium Veneris* (one of the few translations that exist in their own poetic virtue) he suggested that this great poem of antiquity is trying to tell us (with contemporary philistines in mind) that the loss of symbolic language may mean the extinction of our humanity. This is perhaps the most urgent note in Allen Tate's poetry, and the purpose of his criticism. He has had many forces working against him, in American civilization (which is merely the perfection of the frustrations we all suffer) and in American academies (which are advanced posts of our desolate rationalism), but the protest cannot be ignored.

*Herbert Read, "Our Cousin, Mr. Tate," in* Sewanee Review *(© 1959 by The University of the South), Autumn, 1959, pp. 572-75.*

There is such a thing as being so truly sophisticated, if one must use the word, as to enjoy immunity to all so-called sophistication, the fads, foibles and novelties of the moment, that actually are anything but new. Yet a thorough grounding in what has been done in the past would not, of itself, have been enough without an imaginative perception of what is relevant to the present. Mr. Tate's poetry represents, to my mind, an achievement that could only have come about through the happy and inspired coincidence of these two uncommon qualifications. In that poetry, contemporary sensibility finds embodiment in forms that are timeless.

This balance of perception, of judgment, of taste is exerted by a true poet throughout the entire structure of a poem, from the grand scheme down to the smallest detail.

*John Hall Wheelock, "Allen Tate," in* Sewanee Review *(© 1959 by The University of the South), Autumn, 1959, pp. 577-78.*

[The] singular virtue of Tate [is] that both in his verse and his criticism his mind operates upon insight and observation as if all necessary theory had been received into his bones and blood before birth. That is why what is controversial in him is so often a matter either of temperament or temper, and there is a strength to his language superior to any ideas that may be detached from it. From this one virtue stem his two talents as a critic: one, to see through or around or beyond the methods of other critics into an image or insight (for an insight is seen like an image, that it gives light) of what those methods left out; two, when he is practising direct criticism, his extraordinary skill, surpassed only by Eliot, at illuminating quotation, especially those made for the purpose of exemplifying what he calls the tension between the different elements in a poem. Anybody who writes poetry will understand what he is up to, even if disagreeing; anybody who does not write poetry will feel as if he did. Tate is the man who is concerned with poetry as it always was. His taste is deep; hence the love at the bottom of his contentiousness.

*R. P. Blackmur, "San Giovanni in Venere: Allen Tate as Man of Letters," in* Sewanee Review *(© 1959 by The University of the South), Autumn, 1959, pp. 614-31.*

[For] me Allen Tate was, and has remained, one of the indispensable writers. I would say, moreover, that insofar as I understand the development of modern literature in this country, Tate has played a role which has been central, and in some ways unique. . . .

"The Cross," with its extraordinary realization of conceptual and emotional experience in primarily visual imagery, is probably the best example I know of what most critics have usually thought they were describing when they spoke of *metaphysical* poetry, and that it is one of relatively few twentieth-century poems which will bear genuine comparison to the methods of the poems of John Donne. By "comparison" I do not mean to suggest a facile identifying of the work of a seventeenth-century poet and a twentieth-century poet; we have, surely, learned better than that, and like any modern poem "The Cross" can be compared only analogously with the poetry of the past. For if it is anything, "The Cross" is a twentieth-century poem. It exists in an area which is very close to the heart of some of the most, shall I say, *crucial* dilemmas which we have faced in this time. . . .

Though the poem is short, its controlling idea is as large and vital as any in our experience; the handling of it is very fine. It is apparent, I believe, that although the poem is in a sense explicitly religious, its meaning expands until it includes the large historical and cultural concerns which inform all Tate's work.

*R. K. Meiners, in his* The Last Alternatives: A Study of the Works of Allen Tate *(© 1963 by R. K. Meiners; reprinted with permission of The Swallow Press, Inc.), Swallow, 1963, pp. 145-52.*

Tate's . . . criticism has always been exact, authoritative and subtle, unencumbered with the self-consciousness so often found in the modern Freudian approach. For a brief time his reputation as an outstanding critical authority tended to overshadow his poetry. But poetry is Tate's chief concern. . . .

A basic element that has nourished Tate's poetic response is his relationship to his land and his view of its history—the Southern civilization both in its flowering and its decadence. He is the only modern American poet so deeply involved. One thinks of John Crowe Ransom and Robert

Penn Warren, but Tate is less romantic, less tolerant, and, though less limited in his approach, is more passionate. His "angry love" of the South, as an English critic has said, has made him criticize but never abandon the image of what that life once was. In his memory, land and people together express the beauty, intelligence, and wit of a classic age. His memory of actual events has supported his poetic vision. The tragedy of defeat adds to its heroism.

His agrarian theories, which he shares with other Southern writers . . .—once centered in the Fugitive group at Vanderbilt University—sprang from a belief in the essential relationship between the land and the living. Tate would keep the values of the South, with its noble past, though now a poor section of the earth, against the sterile and anonymous environment of vast urban conditioning. He does not think of agrarianism alone as restoring the old South—something new must be created in the moral and religious outlook of Western man. That the Southern way of living inevitably took for granted the existence of a class society has not troubled Tate, though it has disturbed some of his liberal admirers. . . .

His sense of tragedy springs from the frustration that comes from the ever unresolved conflict between the ideal and the actual.

Tate expresses this frustration in a poetry that cannot be read or understood "inadvisedly or lightly." His meaning is not often on the surface. His style is elliptical and powerful. There are qualities like the poetry of the 17th Century, particularly Donne, in the baroque wit, the play on words, the metaphysical slant, and the religious circle of emotion.

The intellectual vision is so emphatic in Tate that emotion is seldom loosened or set free at once. Rather it is embedded in the image and must be forced out to reach the reader. Violence is never the primary motivation of a poem; the pulse, the feeling comes first and the explosive expressions, far from being elaborately induced for effect, are held back in a tight leash. What has been called the violence of his style is found in the startling union of opposites: "the bleak sunshine shrieks its chipped music," or "the idiot greens the meadows with his eyes." And these opposites can also create a sensuous melodic tempo. . . . Sometimes there is a lack of tenderness or warmth in his poems, a shining bleakness; more often a deeper sense of horror than any sense of hope. One does not expect to find consolation, and there is little spontaneous joy. But there is stimulation of honesty and challenge of courage in what one might call his "stance" to meet calamity head on; he summons defenses in which irony is a weapon, not an escape, though it may act as a shield. The wound can still bleed behind the shield, but the spear is lifted and the voice speaks: There is a moment of respite in the midst of an encounter with life at a dark hour. The courage of irony is Tate's unique contribution, and the originality and power of his language are poetry of "a mind imperishable if time is." . . .

The style of vers libre has never tempted Tate. His form, so essentially a part of his thought—"the language of the poem is the poem"—fits into two general modes, a meditative blend of rhymed verse which introduces a theme and then discusses it; or in what he calls "the immaculate conception of its essence in itself." To me Tate's most successful poems are his condensed lyrical perceptions. Tate is not a man of action, he is a man of thought, of books, of language. But his scholarship is never dry.

*Katherine Garrison Chapin, "The Courage of Irony: The Poetry of Allen Tate," in* The New Republic *(reprinted by permission of* The New Republic; *© 1965 by Harrison-Blaine of New Jersey, Inc.), July 24, 1965, pp. 4-5, 22-4.*

For the most part Mr. Tate has (by his own account) been able to limit his criticism to subjects which are of genuine interest to him, and usually he has written on poets whom he could use, at the same time justifying, however consciously or unconsciously, his own poetic procedures. This is also true in similar ways with the other subjects he has wrestled with. Tate has accordingly been able to bring a special concentration to bear upon the work at hand, a special urgency and authority. Moreover, he has the enormous advantage of a classical education, a far-ranging mind, and an incisive wit. (I often get the uncomfortable feeling when reading Tate that he sprang into the world, like Athena from the head of Zeus, with a fully-formed intelligence and style. Skeptics should read "Emily Dickinson" which he wrote in part at the old age of twenty-nine.) Tate also "enjoys the power of received philosophy," as R. P. Blackmur puts it; and he is possessed of an imagination which is both literal and historical. . . .

There are three myths which Tate has used metaphorically to define the South. The first is the obvious one—that the Old South was a medieval society patterned after the feudal autocracies of the Middle Ages; the second pattern of likeness he remarked (some thirty years after writing "Religion and the Old South") in "A Southern Mode of Imagination" is the parallel with Sparta—and, more clearly, Republican Rome; the third, mentioned casually in the obituary on Faulkner in 1962, is still farther back in history—the Greco-Trojan myth. This last parallel takes us a good deal further than the first two, at least to the extent that we have often encountered the others. Tate develops the analogy in "Sanctuary and the Southern Myth," a major statement about Faulkner and Southern letters, even though it repeats things the author has said elsewhere. Tate sees Faulkner's principal subject—and that of his contemporaries—as the Greco-Trojan myth. "The 'older' culture of Troy-South was wiped out by the 'upstart' culture of Greece-North. *Sunt lacrimae rerum*; and the Yankees were therefore to blame for everything—until, as I have pointed out, the time of the first World War. This myth, inadequate as it may appear to the non-Southern reader, has permitted a generation of Southern novelists to understand and to dramatize (that is, depict in action) much of the Southern historical reality." Needless to say *The Fathers* is, among other things, one of the most powerful fictive embodiments of this myth so transformed.

This view of the South provides the foundation for Tate's many trenchant observations on its literature. . . . Tate has said that "myth should be in conviction immediate, direct, overwhelming" and that it is "a dramatic projection of heroic action . . . upon the reality of the common life of a society." The society which embodies such a mythology is regional and religious, traditional and unified, primitive or highly refined, "extroverted" and unselfconscious. The last traditional society in this country was largely extinguished by the Civil War, and in entering the modern world and becoming a part of the United States after the First World War, it became aware of its peculiarly historical predicament in a way that had escaped it previously; and the agency of self-consciousness was accomplished through the determined work of many brilliant writers, of whom Allen Tate is of course one.

In seeking to define the strange brilliance of the Southern renascence Tate is at once probing his own artistic conscience with the intense historical, aesthetic, and moral judgment which is typical of him. Since the Old South provides Tate with the concrete model for a traditional Christian society, it is only natural that he fully understands the fictive works which have sprung from the consciousness of writers who like himself have painfully recognized that society's passing. Tate is perfectly aware of the failings of the Old South, yet it remains his chief model for his whole life—and one much closer in time and more palpable than, say, Yeats's Byzantium, which is largely a historical and mythopoeic reconstruction by one man. Hence Tate's connections with the South—by inheritance, kinship, custom, and manner—have furnished him with what Blackmur has deemed a central allegiance. Out of the tension between Tate's personal allegiance and his awareness of what he has called "a deep illness of the modern mind" has come the enkindling subject of his work as a whole. . . .

Again and again one encounters this historic and mythic perspective in Tate's criticism. As Blackmur noted in 1934, Tate writes as though we are not living in a largely post-Christian age. . . . [He] has steered towards literature as a form of expression more complete than that offered by any other discipline or mode of discourse. In arguing this position he has, however, too often involved himself in elaborate operations against the enemies of art—positivism, social science, semantics, and the other myopias which have slowly eroded classical education and have at once caused, or been caused by, education of the modern dispensation. He has smitten these enemies of culture and civilization, much as Arnold and Eliot did in their separate ways. But he has not been so involved in these preoccupations as his friend Eliot who once complained that Arnold couldn't find time for literature because he was too busy cleaning up the country.

*George Core, "A Metaphysical Athlete: Allen Tate as Critic," in* The Southern Literary Journal, *Autumn, 1969, pp. 138-47.*

I shall not patronize Allen Tate by pretending to be impartial: it is precisely because he is more than a man of parts, because he is a whole, that I am partial to him; I shall take him, merely, at his word, the only place to take a poet, even in his prose. And in his prose Tate's word is the same as in his poems—why, forty years ago he admonished us: "all the books of a poet should ultimately be regarded as one book—it was to this end he worked." And the word I take him at is that *he has never been able to concentrate on what could not be useful to him*. . . .

And the effect, when the books of this poet *are* ultimately regarded as one book, is of life pressing round a dedicated victim decked with all the gauds of immolation—dedicated, that victim, to the grand-mannerist acknowledgment of the Natural Order, which is the Repudiation of Eschatology. His criticism is a part, . . . the contralto part, a middle voice taken and sustained within what Blackmur has called Allen Tate's *virtuosity of presence*: one utterance among many voices—verse, fiction, biography, essay, history, gossip, invective—though the voices speak but one language to articulate but one subject. . . .

Nothing ends without having to be broken off, for everything—the poet tells us, in his poems—everything is endless. That is why the South, in these essays, is regarded as a *style of life* representative of the continuities of blood, and so of ritual and tradition. . . . Again and again, the critic rehearses what the poet calls "the deep coherence of hell," reiterates "a commitment to the order of nature, without which the higher knowledge is not possible to man." He wants one thing to lead to another, wants it so hard that his thirst becomes aphoristic. . . .

We must judge the past and keep it alive by being alive ourselves. Thus he rejects Basic English (the secularization of the mind) as he rejects the Protestant, scientific North (the secularization of the body politic) because it leads to communication without prior or following communion. "Poe," he says in one of his great dismissals, "Poe circumvented the natural world. Since he refused to see nature he was doomed to see nothing. He overleaped and cheated the condition of man." Essentially Catholic, then, Tate's imagination (and he would say, all imagination) rejects an heretical Apocalypse, rejects that compulsion to cast out nature, to uproot whatever seems external to redemption, whatever might intervene between the self and God. "The task of the civilized intelligence," Tate insists, "is one of perpetual salvage." His is the tact, as he says of Dante somewhere, "the tact of mediation between universals and particulars in the complex of metaphor."

Patience, then, in the full sense of the word, the sense that shares, with passion, *suffering*—patience, salvage, and death ("the general symbol of nature is Death") are this poet's articles of faith, and they work to his concentration in the criticism. "The singular passion/abides its object" one poem says, and that is the attainment of his prose.

*Richard Howard, "A Note on Allen Tate's Essays," in* Poetry *(© 1970 by The Modern Poetry Association; reprinted by permission of the Editor of* Poetry*), April, 1970, pp. 43-5.*

Emerging from the exuberant literary climate of the first postwar period, Allen Tate's poetry has had to face the dizzy changes of perspective that took place in the last three decades. These changes mirror the modern writer's endeavor to throw light on his spiritual predicament in a world beset by the demonic dynamism of the atomic age. An unquestionable vitality marks Tate's poetry when we set it beside so much of the derivative elegiac production that sprouted from Eliot's *Waste Land* only to wither shortly after at the first change of weather. Tate's poetry endured—thanks to its incisive language, its structural rigor, and its seminal authenticity. . . .

Only today, after such a crowded time, the value of his poetical work shows fully, and his contribution to twentieth-century poetry is understood in its cognitive and ethical implications. For his writing hovers in an interstellar emptiness, between a very remote world of aristocratic culture where the individual had fulfilled the supreme ambition of making himself the spiritual legislator of reality, and a closer yet equally (for the artist) unattainable world where the machine is king and levels out of existence whatever proves irreducible to the standards of industrial use in a Babelic civilization.

Tate's authentic note rings out from the permanent structures of his ironic vision. His knife-sharp paradox cuts into our consciousness. He has filled the emptiness with a real anguish, with a tension of suffering which bespeaks a dramatic perception of life. Intellectual bewilderment at a dehumanized world wore very thin, and actually evaporated, in the cosmic poetry of the "Wastelanders," whose prophetic attitude degenerated into a mannered posture of "metaphysical" cast and wailing tone. In Allen Tate's poetry the bitter awareness of a hopeless split between past and present finds such graphic expressions as this line (from "The Mediterranean"): "We've cracked the hemispheres with careless hand!" It always implies the concrete experience of a place, of a time, of a history. Like William Faulkner's fiction, Allen Tate's vision is linked to the myth and reality of the South. It is the South that looms behind both writers' work: a motherland harboring darkness and splendor, haunted by images of heroism and human misery, obsessed by the tragedy of slavery and by the yearning for a lost tradition of spiritual freedom. . . .

A child of his time, Allen Tate had to claim the resources of metaphysical poetry, the only kind to offer him a model of total application of the mind to poetry, both to react against the tired *fin de siècle* Decadentism so widespread in the early twentieth century and to shape the tools for exploring a world seemingly inaccessible to any other "strategy." . . . Actually by subsuming sensuous imagery and musical verse to an intense realization of intellectual values, Tate places himself on the opposite side of Symbolism and pure poetry. These are just a portion of the experiences absorbed by his poetry, which in the last resort, as Herbert Read has seen, flaunts a paradoxical union of romantic with classical elements, the former implied by the very concept of "tension," the latter by the necessity of a formal rigor. As a matter of fact, even while sharing the thrill of discovering metaphysical poetry, Tate was never completely imprisoned by a poetics which mirrored a time-worn mechanism of sensibility. In his eyes, Metaphysical conception represents one extreme, with the other extreme supplied by a Romantic or Symbolist conception: one tends toward the other, in the urge to occupy all the possible intervening space in this range of tensions. His poetics, thanks to the awareness of a last alternative, marks a step beyond a strictly metaphysical conception. It aims at an ultimate fusion of "extensive" and "intensive" values of experience and language, in the median point, so hard to reach nowadays, which our poet illustrates with a few lines of Dante's, the model he has chosen in his recent work characterized by terza rima. This median point would be where the harmony of verse in the individual poem becomes one with the recaptured harmony of a vaster order.

*Alfredo Rizzardi, "An Introduction to the Poetry of Allen Tate," translated by Glauco Cambon, in* Ode ai Caduti Confederati e Altre Poesie, *translated by Alfredo Rizzardi (© 1970 by Arnoldo Mondadori, Editore, Milano), Arnoldo Mondadori, 1970.*

Certain critics have called the verse of Allen Tate Augustan, pointing out in particular his affinity to Pope; others have labeled it metaphysical, after the poetry of Donne's age; still others, in the tradition of the Greco-Roman classics. Yet his basic concern, especially as revealed in *Poems: 1922-1947,* is medieval. In the Middle Ages there was one drama which took precedence over all other conflict: the struggle of Everyman to win beatitude and to escape eternal reprobation. Tate recognizes the issue as a subject most significant for literature. With the old veteran of "To the Lacedemonians" he announces: "Gentlemen, my secret is / Damnation." One way to penetrate the meanings of his work, the difficulty of which is largely due to the complexity of his ideas rather than to verbal experimentation, is to trace the implications of this secret throughout his lyrics.

*Sister Mary Bernetta, O.S.F., "Allen Tate's Inferno," in* Renascence, *Spring, 1971, pp. 113-19.*

The poetry of Allen Tate is remarkably consistent in mode and in theme. Many of his poems, including some of the most moving of them, have to do with the impact of modern science, the consequent withering away of man's sense of the supernatural, and his radically altered conception of nature. Thus, in his "Last Days of Alice," Tate uses as a symbol for modern man Lewis Carroll's child heroine of *Alice in Wonderland* and *Alice Through the Looking Glass*. . . .

Alice, looking into the mirror, suddenly found that she had stepped through its polished surface into a world which was like that of the room in which she had been sitting but with everything reversed, a world of marvels in which chess pieces talk; white rabbits consult their watches; and a grinning cat fades away until nothing is left save—a miracle of abstraction!—the grin itself. Twentieth-century man also finds himself in a world of wonders, beautifully logical, quite self-consistent, conforming relentlessly to its own special laws, but a world in which man is lost and baffled. In Lewis Carroll's books, Alice is rescued from her nightmare world by waking up. Unfortunately, modern man cannot wake up and find himself back once more in the world which he has known throughout history and in which he has achieved his humanity. . . .

Many of Tate's poems deal with a related blight, that which has fallen over history, which has become impersonal process and as such, drained of meaning. Tate's most celebrated poem, his "Ode to the Confederate Dead," has to do with this theme and only incidentally with the Confederacy. This is by no means the only poem in which Tate has used his native region as a special vantage point, from which to comment upon Everyman, specifically the modern Everyman, who, deprived and emptied, rootless and uncommitted, is attempting to live in a world which, in the process of making a gigantic extension of its technology, has lost its grip on values. . . .

Like William Butler Yeats, Tate finds in history, not only the ground for his discourse, but the central excitement of his poetry. With the possible exception of Yeats, no poet of our time has possessed a more penetrating discernment of the predicament of modern man with reference to nature and history. In the old Christian synthesis, nature and history were related in a special way. With the break-up of that synthesis, man finds himself caught between a meaningless cycle on the one hand, and on the other, the more extravagant notions of progress—between a nature that is oblivious of man and a man-made "unnatural" Utopia.

In Tate's poetry nature comes in for a great deal of attention—"The Seasons of the Soul" is a typical instance —but Tate rarely exhibits nature for its own sake and never as a kind of innocently pastoral backdrop for man's activities. Since man, who had once thought his journey had a destination, the return to the meaningless round of the seasons is not comforting but terrifying. . . .

Tate sometimes impresses one as an almost desperate poet who, in order to convey to his reader the profound irony of modern man's plight, is willing to startle and shock him and is quite prepared to take the risk of putting him off the poem altogether. So also with Tate's rhythms. He sometimes seems trying deliberately to deform the metrical structure to achieve a richer and more subtle effect. All of this is to say that Tate puts a great burden upon his reader. He insists that the reader himself, by an effort of his own imagination, cooperate with the poet to bring the violent metaphors and jarring rhythms into unity.

For the casual and careless reader, the poem may seem to explode in his face. The recalcitrant elements that Tate insists on binding into one pattern will not stay bound, but fly apart. Yet, the reader who is willing to wrestle with a bold and adventurous poetry and is not insistent on easy harmonies will find Tate's poetry remarkably exciting and rewarding. Robert Lowell has made the point in his own way: "Out of splutter and shambling comes a killing eloquence."

*Cleanth Brooks, "On the Poetry of Allen Tate," in* Michigan Quarterly Review, *Fall, 1971, pp. 225-28.*

[We must] take cognizance of the astounding diversity of Allen Tate's achievement. But in a last analysis the divisions are an Aristotelian nicety, an arbitrary convenience. His work is really all of a piece. It has all derived from the same energy, the same insights. It has all had a single aim. When I try to explain that aim I am drawn toward a quaint analogy or a metaphor whose coordinates are very distant from each other. There used to exist in elementary courses in physics an apparatus intended to instruct students in principles of pressure. Consisting of a sealed jar nearly filled with liquid, it had some provision for pumping air into the space at the top. As the air pressure was increased, from the bottom of the jar would rise a little imago—an ivory-colored homunculus, one thought at first. Then, as it rose higher one saw that it was a representation of a medieval Satan. The synergy of Allen Tate's poetry, fiction, and essays has had the aim of applying pressure—think of his embossed, bitterly stressed lines, his textured metaphors—until it brings up before our eyes a blanched parody of the human figure, which is our evil, the world's evil, so that we begin to long for God. That has seemed to him a worthwhile task to perform for modern man threatened by such fatal narcissism, such autotelic pride that he is in danger of disappearing into a glassy fantasy of his own concoction. We shall need his help for a long time to come.

*Radcliffe Squires, in his "Introduction" to* Allen Tate and His Work: Critical Evaluations *(© 1972, University of Minnesota), University of Minnesota Press, Minneapolis, 1972, p. 8.*

Like Ezra Pound, Allen Tate is one of those twentieth-century writers whose works have until recently been available only to a small company of readers, fortunate in their apprenticeship or else heroic in their lonely perserverance. Indeed the two have been victims of the great ideological wars of the modern world, and against both the philistines have mounted the same two-pronged attack: charging on the one hand political heresy and on the other, literary obscurantism. In fact, because of the notorious Bollingen Prize controversy, Tate is often linked with Pound and Eliot as members of the same reactionary and elitist cabal.

But Allen Tate's work is perhaps best understood in contrast with Pound's (and to some extent Eliot's), though the three were literary "modernists" preoccupied with the preservation of an endangered cultural heritage. Pound was a temperamental exile and latter-day gnostic who seemed to feel at times that he could save the world with economic pleading and translations of lyric poetry. Eliot, like Pound, strayed far from home, but ultimately sank his roots deep into English tradition and bloomed like a hothouse plant. Tate, on the other hand, can only be fully understood as a Southerner; for, though he too lived in Paris during the 'twenties, he never really left his native soil. . . .

[In] Tate's use of manners one sees the epitome of the order he was attempting to define and preserve in his poetry, fiction, and criticism. What are manners, after all, but the form whose "content" is the very nature of humanity itself? Manners, it should be evident, control and order our purely natural impulses; they are one means of defining man's transcendent being, to distinguish him from those creatures whose drive to survive and reproduce is all-consuming. Manners are also essential to a hierarchical society, where communion between unequals is facilitated through such mutually agreeable rituals. It is such a civilized society that Tate has always advocated in his art and in his discursive prose, a society with a transcendent view of man. His working model, more often than not, has been that of the South, which by 1930 he came to understand as somehow deriving its structure from Western European civilization in a way that, say, New England did not.

Thus Mr. Tate's manners can be viewed as something more than the quaint vestiges of a Southern childhood. On the conscious level they are the weaponry of active combat against hostility and chaos, the walls of the city against which the barbarians throw their hoards. Unconsciously they are the expression of man's highest concept of being. . . .

Because Tate's latter-day work is so singularly infused with a commitment to Christianity, it is surprising to be reminded by Monroe Spears' 1949 essay ("The Criticism of Allen Tate") that Tate was a skeptic until the 1950's, devoted to the *idea* of religious faith as the most important element informing a traditional society, yet unable to accept that faith as anything more than a useful, indeed necessary, myth. . . .

In the medieval world, which he publicly admired as much as did his friend Eliot, he found the archetypal model for his own vision of the dying South; and he also found in

Dante the poet who had invented the aesthetic which linked the classical world with Christendom and thus provided Western civilization with a necessary continuity which defined the Middle Ages not as a descent into theological darkness but as a fulfillment of the promise of order and ultimate truth found in Homer and Vergil. Dante, after all, was something of a modern in that he was preoccupied with the internal world and thus was the hero of his own epic struggle for salvation. . . .

His impeccable manners, his generosity, his fierce loyalty to his Southern heritage, his preoccupation with the formal elements in poetry, his innate classicism—all of these qualities crystallize in his later essays and in such a poem as "The Buried Lake," a hymn to St. Lucy which is one of the most moving religious statements of the twentieth century.

Indeed, in rereading the body of Tate's work one is struck by its remarkable unity of vision and also by its extraordinary timeless quality. Though one of the "moderns"—a term still used to designate a poetry outmoded by the late 1950's—few of his poems have become period pieces like "Prufrock" or *The Waste Land,* which for all their technical virtuosity contain a heavy-handed irony which sounds "cheap" to the contemporary ear. Though Tate is perhaps not as historically important a poet as Eliot, he may well be a more durable (that is to say, a *better*) one.

For one thing, there is a little more of what has been called "the native strain" in Tate's poetry, a directness of diction, despite its textural difficulties. These difficulties usually can be traced to the subtlety of his mind rather than to a flamboyant use of modernist technique, with its formal fragmentation and its arcane allusions. (Tate's poetry is occasionally arcane, but he never leans so heavily on a tissue of allusion that it requires extensive footnoting.)

Then, too, at a time when poetry is highly personal—at its worst confessional—a poem like "The Swimmers" has a distinctly contemporary flavor. . . .

Eliot's conservative Anglicanism has provided trouble enough for the literary establishment, which accorded him his laurels before he made his later commitment to high Toryism. Tate's Southern conservation was militant almost from the beginning of his career.

For this reason, I suspect, those troublesome though essential allies, the explicators, have steered clear of the difficult challenge that Tate's work has always posed. The Squires volume [*Allen Tate and His Work: Critical Evaluations*], therefore, is something of a godsend, since it gathers together some of the most important criticism necessary to make Tate available to a wider audience of younger readers. In an age of bad manners and literary barbarism it is perhaps too much to hope that a host of critics will immediately follow suit.

*Thomas Landess, "Allen Tate: Southern Man of Letters," in* Intercollegiate Review, *Winter, 1973-74, pp. 54-7.*

* * *

## TAYLOR, Elizabeth 1912-

**An English novelist and short story writer, Ms Taylor is a quietly elegant stylist whose principal themes are loneliness and isolation. (See also *Contemporary Authors*, Vols. 13-14.)**

Elizabeth Taylor is a pastel stylist, a celebrant of delicately-drawn losers. . . .

In Miss Taylor's epiphanies, pitiful frauds are exposed, and old wounds laid bare. Yet the tone of her fiction is urbane rather than morbid. Her characters have enough vitality to be interesting, but not enough to be tragic.

*Martin Levin, in* The New York Times Book Review *(© 1972 by The New York Times Company; reprinted by permission), April 23, 1972, p. 41.*

Elizabeth Taylor must surely now be among the four or five most distinguished living practitioners of the art of the short story in the English-speaking world. Some have reservations—this reviewer among them—about her range as a novelist; there is an assumption of English middle-class habits, preoccupations, and woes which, however accurately and indeed sometimes waspishly documented, excludes perhaps too much of modern experience to give her broader canvases the significance she herself might intend. And harking back to Jane Austen is not, in the media-influenced society we now have, a relevant rejoinder.

But when it comes to the isolation—in the symbolic as well as technical sense—of a particular relationship, a particular incident in which the apparently ordinary, stock individual is momentarily exposed, then there is no writer so skilled at imprinting forever on the reader's mind *how* significant that moment can be. . . .

[The] gentle reminder, implied even in Mrs Taylor's most sardonic descriptive details [in *The Devastating Boys and Other Stories*] that we are all as ludicrously self-seeking, as blind and petty, as . . . faded snapshot figures. . . . Perhaps it is the humble wisdom of experience that all story-tellers need to focus the moment against the insignificant wastes of time that lie around.

*"Escape Into Irony," in* The Times Literary Supplement *(reproduced by permission), June 9, 1972, p. 649.*

Elizabeth Taylor's fifteenth book [*The Devastating Boys and Other Stories*] contains eleven elegant stories that decisively demonstrate her mastery of the techniques of traditional fiction. And yet, the reader wonders, so what?

Miss Taylor evokes middle-class Englishmen and Englishwomen at home and abroad. . . . All the characters function in realistic settings and obey the laws of psychological verisimilitude. They press flowers, have black children to the country, or risk a middle-life sex affair while on Mediterranean holidays. The stories have tension, suggestion, mood, irony, insight, humor, compassion, and complete believability. The book is flawless—and totally unmemorable. . . .

The techniques she employs here were developed to reflect the realities and sensibilities of another era; they do not reflect our own. In 1972 one does not write fiction under the banner of Guy de Maupassant. These stories about and for the upper middle class do little more than provide minor insights and provoke minor questions. The accepted language and form correspond to the accepted society they describe, and, like it, resist acknowledgment of change or even the need for change.

*William Beauchamp, in* Saturday Review of Science *(copyright © 1972 by Saturday Review/World, Inc.; reprinted with permission), June 10, 1972, p. 69.*

* * *

## TAYLOR, Peter 1919-

**Taylor is an American short story writer, novelist, and playwright. Considered a master of the short story, Taylor is usually associated with the so-called Southern Renaissance. (See also *Contemporary Authors*, Vols. 15-16.)**

Over the years Taylor piled up a stodgily respectable list of honors, including Fulbright, Guggenheim, and Ford Foundation mementos. His stories turned up unobtrusively in prize anthologies and college textbooks, and he himself regularly manned lecterns at an assortment of universities, including Harvard and Oxford. The proper literary surveys gave him dutiful nods, and his unanimously delighted critics compared him not unflatteringly to Trollope, James, Katherine Anne Porter, Turgenev, Tolstoi, and Chekhov.

Yet, for all this, Peter Taylor is not much better known to the general American reading public now at the time of his retrospective *Collected Stories* than he was thirty years ago. *New Yorker* readers know him, and *aficionados* of Southern fiction, but who else? The sad fact is that in an age of exploitation, when pressagentry often means more than art, Peter Taylor remains a perfectly unpromotable writer, landing just as close to one end of the exploitation spectrum as Jacqueline Susann does to the other.

Take Taylor's typical subject matter, for instance. His protagonists are small town doctors and state senators and scholars on sabbatical, cotton brokers and colored cooks and country club brides—all remote in a thousand ways from the "relevant" obsessions of the sixties. Though Taylor deals with communication breakdowns between races and classes and generations, the resultant conflicts are personal, internalized, revealed in muted symbolic gestures rather than in shrieks and sorties. . . .

There is no sensationalism, either, in Taylor's treatment of the South—no wild Faulknerian rhetoric, no violent melodrama, no Gothic grotesqueries. Taylor's Southerners are not the usual decadent aristocrats or earthy primitives; they are mostly unpicturesque well-to-do upper-middle-class urbanized professional people who have moved up from and out of small country towns to big Southern cities like Memphis or Nashville or even outside the South to foreign climes like St. Louis and Detroit and Chicago. Their lives have crises . . ., but they are more like the crises of Silas Lapham or Emma Woodhouse than those of Thomas Sutpen or Peyton Loftis. . . .

[His] reputation at this point must rest almost entirely on his short fiction—some forty-odd stories spread out over three decades. These stories, moreover, are unapologetically old-fashioned: devoid of dazzling stunts or pyrotechnics, lucid in style, genteel in language, detached or gently ironic in tone, eschewing both the esoteric and the scatological, tantalizing neither the academic explicators on the one hand or the media markets on the other. The basic form Peter Taylor uses most frequently, in fact, is the memoir story—leisurely, digressive, reflective, casual but complex, sifting past experience through the time-wrought wisdom of a civilized intelligence.

*Albert J. Griffith, in* Commonweal *(reprinted by permission of Commonweal Publishing Co., Inc.), February 6, 1970, pp. 516-18.*

Taylor, in his later work, is able to create his effects with far less carpentry work and sheer words than he required when he began. [His] stories center on character and for this reason Taylor has been called the "American Chekhov." Actually, Taylor is, if anything, even more delicate in the way he proceeds by indirection and by irony to reveal the most heartrending apprehensions about humanity. His razor is so keen that the deepest cuts may go unnoticed; one can imagine a grandmother gently smiling over a story which would terrify her granddaughter. And here is the greatness of [his] stories. They offer something to every reader without descending to a mediocre level of technique or interest.

Virginia Quarterly Review, *Vol. 47, No. 1 (Winter, 1971), pp. xii, xiv.*

While there is in these plays [*Presences*] a movement and tone in the dialogue I normally associate with poetry, there is something about the settings that is remarkable in quite another way. They have a pervasive "elegance"—sometimes fading, sometimes flourishing—that is unusual in modern American theater. The plays nearly always take place in houses that are very grand. Through the glass of fashion darkly, here are the gentry with a vengeance, in their parlors and bedrooms, all fiercely respectable, conscious of origins and with a sense of their own past. It strikes me that this socially ambitious concern for appearances—all that elegance and old-family vapor of prosperity—might be the very thing that inspires ghosts: a fear of failure calling up images of the dead. The banal formality of the lives—but that elegance is not every American's—somehow makes the specters more possible. It would be interesting to know if Taylor is aware of how select a crowd his haunted people are.

The publication of these seven plays will certainly establish Peter Taylor as a playwright of the first rank, excelling in both the technical and imaginative aspects of drama. It is not just that he has given the ghost a chance to make a comeback; he has added a dimension to dramatic experience by giving voice and shape to what is most private in our mental lives.

*Paul Theroux, "Old-Family Vapors," in* Book World—The Washington Post (© The Washington Post), *February 25, 1973, p. 33.*

Like his stories, Taylor's plays [*Presences: Seven Dramatic Pieces*] are heavily concerned with *family* and *place* —and with people's uneasy experiences being in or out of these. At emotional quarters thus close, such "presences" are easily acceptable. Less acceptable are Taylor's awkward dependence on contemporaneous themes (drugs, abortion, homosexuality), and the absence of what gives his best stories their density—the restrained suggestion of turbulent drama, painstakingly rendered through social detail.

But he has found a fresh way of dramatizing the small agonies that boil insistently at the edges of our lives, yet seldom erupt into open confrontations. It is also a new way of presenting multiple viewpoints in conflict. This collection is a quiet, unpretentious contribution to the rhetoric of fiction, but it may prove a lasting one.

The Antioch Review *(© 1973 by The Antioch Review, Inc.; reprinted by permission of the editors), Vol. XXXII, No. 4, 1973, pp. 700-01.*

Taylor's fiction takes up directly the subtle moral disarrangements and dislocations within a seemingly immobile middle class. Taylor is all fiction writer and does not seem to want to be anything more. The "little inch of ivory" on which everything is worked out gives his stories an effect of necessity and realization. The shifts are entirely within the stories, do not take us through those harshly contrasting changes of time, scene, history which in many big-writing Southern novelists embody violence to the person even when the novelist seems to be doing all the moving around. . . .

[The] surface of Taylor's stories, entirely domestic, often suburban, conceals the intense Brownian movement of emotions under the surface. Yet these dislocations or rearrangements of authority are more than usually quiet; the manner of a Taylor story is entirely part of the manners it describes, and seems to follow from them; Taylor has just left the party to think it over, but will rejoin it presently. . . .

There is far less violence in Peter Taylor than there is in Carson McCullers and Flannery O'Connor; but this seemingly intact world in which drama follows only from slight, soundless changes of consciousness has as its center a woman's sensibility precisely because of the contrast between the position she upholds and the slow, inner sapping of her life. The absence of "scenes," friction, strong movement of any kind, is the mark of a good breeding that seems to have worn the material smooth. The craftsmanship, like good manners, makes its points quietly; we are kept in a world in which nothing very much seems to happen only because Taylor is more chivalrous in writing about Southern ladies than they are in writing about themselves.

*Alfred Kazin, in his* Bright Book of Life: American Novelists & Storytellers from Hemingway to Mailer *(copyright © 1971, 1973 by Alfred Kazin; reprinted by permission of Little, Brown and Co. in association with the Atlantic Monthly Press), Atlantic-Little, Brown, 1973, pp. 46-9.*

In *Presences: Seven Dramatic Pieces,* Peter Taylor explains that he has resorted to plays rather than fiction to present the experience of ghosts and fantasies because fiction requires too much artifice to present them convincingly, "whereas in a play, the ghost simply walks upon the stage. We do not question his presence." But there are as many kinds of stage ghosts as there are ways of being present. There is Hamlet's father and Mrs. Alving's husband and Maeterlinck's bluebird. Only one of Taylor's pieces, *Maisie,* deals with ghosts who are supernatural spirits rather than psychological projections; the other plays dramatize "conceits" about self-deceptions and illusions in the domestic conflicts of the upper-middle classes. The condensed form of the drama works against the delicacy of relationships that Taylor handles so well in his short stories. Ironically, then, the weakness of these dramatic playlets is that they show too much artifice, are too schematic and too neatly paradoxical, so that the effect is more often that of O. Henry than of Hamlet.

*B. H. Fussell, in* The Hudson Review *(copyright © 1974 by The Hudson Review, Inc.; reprinted by permission), Vol. XXVI, No. 4, Winter, 1973-74, p. 755.*

* * *

## TOMLINSON, (Alfred) Charles 1927-

**Tomlinson is a British poet whose work is characterized, according to William Cookson, by "an intelligence of eye and ear," and whose poems "fix moments of heightened perception." (See also *Contemporary Authors*, Vols. 5-8, rev. ed.)**

Aside from two volumes of translations, [*American Scenes, and Other Poems*] is Charles Tomlinson's fifth collection of poems. It was in his second collection, *The Necklace* (1955), under the influence of Wallace Stevens, that he first found a style to suit his particular poetic temper and preoccupations. Taking other American poets as his models—Marianne Moore and Williams—he has since progressively extended his technical range to give fuller expression to his personal voice and vision. In the construction of the moral and mental framework that supports his poetic insights the strongest single influence seems to have been D. H. Lawrence—for example, Lawrence on self-consciousness and mental idealism. But in their intellectual rigour and a 'metaphysical' quality his poems have also something in common, though it is less easily illustrated, with Laura Riding's work.

What most impresses a reader of Tomlinson's successive collections is the deeply pondered character—and the consistency—of his reading of experience. He began life as a painter and in his poems he feels through what he sees; and it is prior training in a visual medium that probably accounts for his bias away from the romantic, subjective interpretation of reality: trust in the act of perception has led him, in considering the relation between subject and object, the person and what is external to him, to lay the emphasis on the object and the external. His poems have the air of laying bare the essentials for an objective, impartial view of the world. The perceptual ideal is an image for a moral ideal: Tomlinson celebrates the eye that sees coolly and precisely, that sees objects and events in all their relations, and that orders what it sees; which is to celebrate not only right seeing but right thinking and right feeling. The ideal is classical but includes also a modern scepticism: the objective world cannot be fully possessed by the mind, and so to apprehend it we approach it by comparison—'naked nature/Clothed by comparison alone' and thus *'related'* ('Glass Grain', *Seeing is Believing*). Relating things to their likes is a strategy designed to represent them in their totality. If reality has a central meaning, then it is inaccessible to the mind, but the clue to it is that it embraces *contraries,* and to register in one's art these contraries is the objective procedure, one also adopted by Tomlinson, that brings one to the point of entry. And this, too, is a way of seeing life whole. *Relations and Contraries* (1951) was the title of his first volume; they have ever since remained central to his investigation of reality.

The development his poems have shown is in the direction of greater humanity. Whereas, for instance, the poems of *The Necklace* were still lifes—objects and moments whose 'facets of copiousness' were presented separately to the eye of the reader, analyzed in a taut, vibrant verse, those of *Seeing is Believing* (1960) were organized in the sentences of careful conversation, words and rhythms pinpointing every nuance of meaning and inflection of voice. The poems of *A Peopled Landscape* (1963) were human in a different sense: previously, as Tomlinson has pointed out, the things he wrote about—houses, cities, walls, landscapes—were already saturated in human presence and traditions, and this was his point in writing about them, but now people themselves move to the centre. *A Peopled Landscape* showed yet another development in style, several of the poems having the look of Williams's and Marianne Moore's poems. In 1961, . . . Tomlinson referred to this technique as the 'experiments of Cummings and Williams of letting the look of the poem on the page prompt and regulate through the eye the precise tone of the voice'. Its usefulness for Tomlinson, then, was that it reflected even more faithfully the cadences of the speaking voice (humanizing his verse in yet another way), at once increasing the possibilities of precision and enabling the poet to unbend from a posture of steely formality.

The verse of *American Scenes* continues in the direction laid down in *A Peopled Landscape*: movement and line-division function primarily as pointers to voice inflection; the verse reflects exactly speech stress and the patterns that emerge, picked out also by assonances and internal rhymes, are the patterns of the argument, the symmetries and emphases that belong to careful, ordered thought. The values and the conception of reality that informed the previous three volumes are affirmed with the same assurance in these poems. The attitude of tough resilience exemplified in all his poems and the theme of many of them finds expression in now familiar terms and imagery:

again you bend
joint and tendon to encounter
the wind's force and leave behind
the nameless stones, the snow-shrouds
of a waste season. . . .

The experiments of Williams strongly influenced the form of poems in *A Peopled Landscape*; it is from the experiments of Williams's successors that his American and Mexican poems have benefitted. The results are a decrease in the pedantries of meticulous analysis and a greater reliance on the simplicities of the (apparently) casual statement and the unsymbolic anecdote. The subtlety of the poem's thought is there in the satisfyingly exact notation of voice-movement and in the juxtaposition of facts the connections between which are unstated but 'add up' to a flavour that cannot be defined because it is the flavour of life in all its fortuitousness.

*Michael Kirkham, "Negotiations," in* Essays in Criticism, *July, 1967, pp. 367-74.*

Just as an actor gets type-cast, a poet in our literary climate is all too liable to go on being discussed in the same terms that are applied to him in his first set of reviews. "Painterly," "visual," "microscopic"—the words were relevant to Tomlinson's 1955 collection *The Necklace,* but while he is no less precise an observer than he was, he has developed so much since then that to go on thudding out the same adjectives is to tell a small part of the truth.

The position he took in *The Necklace* is defined in its first two lines:

*Reality is to be sought, not in concrete,*
*But in space made articulate*

In the poems which follow and in his second book *Seeing is Believing,* the basic assumption is that clarity of vision is the prerequisite for an adequate grasp on reality. *"When the truth is not good enough/We exaggerate."* The poems record and advocate the discovery and practice of a discipline by which distortion can be avoided. The poems observe not only the surfaces of things, but the play of light and shade in the spaces between them. . . .

This is poetry for all the senses, but its concern is to wake them up, not to put them to sleep with facile gratification. . . .

Instead of asserting himself subjectively, Tomlinson uses himself as a medium through which he realises natural life more vividly than any poet since Hopkins. No one writing today is more sensitive than Tomlinson to the turn of the seasons and though he most often opts for a winter setting, his attitude of reverent gratitude in face of the natural landscape which surrounds us and his keen awareness of the processes of self-renewal which are constantly and copiously at work in it put him emotionally at the antipodes of Beckett and the writers whose preoccupations are one-sidedly with decay, the gradual failing of the individual body's faculties. . . .

But it is only in *The Way of a World* that the assertion of the human will comes into the foreground of the serious poems. "Assassin" is by far the most dramatic poem Tomlinson has yet written. . . .

In "Prometheus" Tomlinson not only sets up a more complex interrelationship between the visual, aural, and tactual references than before, but he develops a new rhythm, no less subtle but less reticent, more committed than in the earlier poems. Altogether this is a less private voice, a controlled rhetoric which claims and commands a wider space, ranges over a more impressive variety of tones than ever before.

*Ronald Hayman, in* Encounter, *December, 1970, pp. 72-3.*

"Civic and close-packed" is how Charles Tomlinson describes a town in one of his new poems [in *Written on Water*], and like many a Tomlinson phrase it covertly characterizes the poem itself as much as its subject. Flexing, modulating, compacting, interchanging—these stately abstractions refer at once to qualities of natural process and to the poetic structure which elicits them, so that the poems enact an epistemological harmony of mind and matter, becoming the structure of what they see. They are well-bred, elaborate mental artifices but also pared, laconic statements, cavalier in their civilized formality but puritan in their relentless sobriety. Resolute objectivizing creates, paradoxically, an impression of dense, subtle interiority, so that the poetry seems saturated with speculation even in its least apparently reflective, most rigorously descriptive moments. . . .

One wonders if Mr. Tomlinson's world isn't a bit *too* harmonic. Certain conflicts, potential contradictions even, do seem implicit in his epistemology—that the mind hunts for forms in an evanescent world, for instance—but they tend not to be developed. Instead, motion and stasis, natural flux and aesthetic structure, "presentness" and melting time seem everywhere to form agreeable marriages, in a world of almost-suspended animation. On the other hand, the fine concluding poem "Movements" does betray—more candidly and explicitly than in most of Mr. Tomlinson's previous work—something of the moral tentativeness which underlies the dry self-composure. Here, in what may be an important new departure, problems of believing as well as seeing are tackled in a more open, richly meditative way than before.

*"From Waterways to Soupy Streams," in* The Times Literary Supplement *(reproduced by permission), October 20, 1972, p. 1249.*

Charles Tomlinson is the most considerable English poet to have made his way since the Second World War. There is more to see along that way, more to meditate, more solidity of achievement, more distinction of phrase, more success as, deftly turning, hand and mind execute the difficult knot that makes the poem complete, than in the work of any of Tomlinson's contemporaries. It is true that the way is strait; but Tomlinson would have it so. For his is a holding action: he is out to save the world for the curious and caring mind. And if he is narrow, he is only so narrow as a searching human eye and a mind that feeds and reflects on vision—an eye that to everything textured, spatial, neighbouring, encompassing, humanly customary, and endlessly and beautifully modulated by light, dusk, weather, the slow chemistry of years, comes like a cleansing rain—as also like a preserving amber. The quality everywhere present in Tomlinson's poetry is a peculiarly astringent, almost dry, but deeply meditated love; this is true whether his subject is human beings, houses, lamplight, chestnuts, lakes, or glass. Tomlinson is a poet of exteriority and its human correlatives: the traditional, the universal, the unchangeable, the transparencies of reflection. And he is thus the opposite of a lyric or "confessional" poet. Yet what a mistake it would be to confuse this outwardness with superficiality. To read Tomlinson is continually to *sound*: to meet with what lies outside the self in a simultaneous grace of vision and love. Tomlinson's chief theme is, in his own phrase, "the fineness of relationships". And though his poetry is in great measure restricted to this theme, the theme itself is an opening and a wideness.

Tomlinson's theme, or his strict relation to it, is one with his originality; and this originality is most salient in his poems on the world's appearances. We have been asked to admire so many poets of "nature" that we can but sigh, or look blank, to hear it announced that still another one has come along; and we will greet with scepticism any claims to originality. But Tomlinson is unmistakably an original poet. There is in him, it is true, a measure of Wordsworth: the at-homeness in *being* as against *doing,* the wise passivity, the love of customariness, and what Pater spoke of as Wordsworth's "very fine apprehension of the limits within which alone philosophical imaginings have any place in true poetry". Both poets awaken, moreover, in Shelley's phrase, "a sort of thought in sense". But how different in each is the relation of sense to thought. In Wordsworth, sense fails into thought. Nature strikes Wordsworth like a bolt; it is the charred trunk that he reflects upon. His thought looks back to sense and its elation, hungering. In Tomlinson, by contrast, the mind hovers over what the eye observes; the two are coterminus. Together, they surprise a sufficiency in the present; and if passion informs them, it is a passion for objectivity. For the most part, Wordsworth discovers himself in nature—it is this, of course, that makes him a Romantic poet. Tomlinson, on the other hand, discovers the nature of nature: a classical artist, he is all taut, responsive detachment.

The sufficiency (or something very near it) of the spatial world to Tomlinson's eye, mind, and heart, the gratefulness of appearances to a sensibility so unusual as his, at once radically receptive and restrained, separates him from such poets as D. H. Lawrence and Wallace Stevens—though the latter, indeed, exerted a strong early influence. This marked spiritual contentment—which makes up the message and quiet power and healing effluence of Tomlinson's work—[is] conveniently illustrated by one of his shorter poems, "The Gossamers." . . .

An ascetic of the eye, Tomlinson pushes poetry closer to natural philosophy than it has ever been before—and at the same time proselytises for fine relationships with space, writes and persuades in earnestness, if not in zeal. Into an area crowded with hedonists, mystics, rapturous aesthetes, he comes equipped with a chaste eye and a mind intent upon exactitude. Nature may indeed be a book; but not until now, say the chaste eye, the intent mind, has the book been more than scanned. The fine print, the difficult clauses, the subtle transitions, the unfamiliar words—Tomlinson will pore over them all. And his language will be as learned and meticulous, his dedication as passionate, his ego as subdued, as that of the true scholar—though mercifully he will also exercise, what few scholars possess, a deft and graceful feeling for form.

The clue to Tomlinson's originality lies in the apparent incongruity between his chosen subject and his temperament. In part, the subject is all the opulence of the visual world—jewelled glass, golden gossamers, fiery clouds. The temperament, by contrast, is strict and chaste, not far from sternness. . . .

Tomlinson looks outward, and what he sees becomes, not himself exactly, but his content. Seeing discovers his limits—but they are the limits of a vase or a window, not of a prison. Indeed, to Tomlinson it is a happy circumstance that the world is "other"; were it identical with the self, there would be no refuge from solitude, nothing to touch as one reaches out. . . . Observer and observed stand apart, then, as the necessary poles of a substantiated being. The eye is the first of philosophers; seeing turns up the soil of ontology. Beholding thus applies to the spirit a metaphysical balm. The "central calm" of appearances, their very thereness, gives a floor to the world. So Tomlinson walks and looks, and he finds it enough. Philosophically, he begins in nakedness—in nakedness, not in disinheritance; for the scrutinising eye detects no twilight of past dreams of transcendence, only a present wealth of finite particulars, an ever shifting but sharply focused spectacle. In Tomlinson, the spirit, as if ignorant of what once sustained it—Platonic forms, Jehovah, the Life Force, the whole pantheon of the metaphysical mind—finds bliss in trees and stones that are merely trees and stones. And doubtless this implies an especially fine, not a particularly crude, capacity for wonder. Tomlinson is one of the purest instances in literature of the contemplative, as distinct from the speculative, mind. No poet has ever before regarded the intricate tapestry of Space with such patient and musing pleasure, with so little dread or anxiety to retreat through a human doorway or under the vaulted roof of a church. On the other hand, neither has any poet been less inclined to eat of the apples in his Eden. Tomlinson holds up to the tapestry a magnifying glass: he is all absorption, but, courteously, he keeps his place. . . .

Like the hills and seas of his poems, Tomlinson is conservative through and through. If he could, one feels, he would bring all the world to a halt: to the "luminous stasis" of contemplation. The dread he conveys is not of nature, nor even of human nature, but of the "rational" future and its present busy machines—of what is happening to the earth, our host, and to the distinctively human source of our contentment, the filaments of custom that hold us lovingly to place. . . .

Tomlinson's poems have something of the severity of a religious cell. Whitewashed of the self, chill, close-packed as stone walls, they are rooms for intense and selfless meditation. Austerity marks both their language and their movement. The diction has the dryness of exposure to mental weather—though the dryness of living bark, not of stones. Learned and exact, it joins the concrete with academic abstraction. . . .

[His] rhythm . . . is neither extroverted nor introverted, but emotionally suspended, stilled and poised in meditation. . . . Reading Tomlinson, one comes instinctively to look for [a] sort of rough yet reliable recurrence. Like the next bead in a rosary, the accentual repetition provides a necessary sense of stability. On the other hand, shifting and uncertain as it is, it discourages complicities of the pulse. It leaves the mind strung, alert, and waiting. . . .

What makes Tomlinson an important poet is partly his originality; but of course it is not his originality that makes him a poet. If his poetry contained observation alone, it would be of no more interest—though of no less interest, either—than a camera set rolling in a snowy field or by the sea. Tomlinson is a poet, in part, because of a consistent, masculine elegance of language, and also in part because of his feeling for rhythm. But mostly he is a poet because he uses, and excites, imagination, and because this imagination is not of a light or gratuitous kind, but steeped in feeling, organic, pregnant with a response to life. Deeply and richly conceived, Tomlinson's poems are neither the mere notations of a stenographic eye, nor cold slabs of reflection; they begin, they vault, and they conclude in feeling. . . .

Tomlinson's imagination *attends* to observable reality with almost the patience that characterises and gives distinction to his eye. Like a fine atmosphere, it can be gentle to the point of invisibility, so that objects and places, and not the poet himself, seem to be communicants of feeling. And when it does grow dense, it thickens as light thickens, making its objects as well as itself more vivid. Impossible to imagine a closer co-operation between the conceiving mind and the receiving eye. Tomlinson's imagination takes its cues, its colours, its composure, from the Persian carpet of the visual world itself. . . .

If Tomlinson's poems are imaginative, it is almost in their own despite. They are imaginative, so to speak, only because they must be in order to qualify as poetry. Granted their way, so it seems, they would be, instead, only a wondering silence. . . .

Listen to the poems and you will conclude that Tomlinson is but the servant or the guest of appearances. Experience the poems, on the other hand, and you will know that he is something more, and more difficult—namely, their abettor, their harvest, their fulfilment. And this is to say that there is a notable discrepancy, widening at times into a contradiction, between what the poems declare and what they are and do. They speak, as it were, in ignorance of themselves. Thus, though they recommend passivity, it is through their own activity. Though they would teach us to conserve, they themselves are creative and therefore innovative. As they urge us to silence before the multiple voices of space, they impress us with a distinctively human voice. And as they praise nature as our replenishment, they replenish us. So it is that what the right hand gives, the left hand takes away. . . .

The essential confession of Tomlinson's art is, I believe, the essential confession of all art: that man is forced to be, and also needs to be, his own replenishment, perpetually renewed out of himself. So it is that, merely by existing, Tomlinson's poetry completes the real but limited truth—namely, the gratefulness of the world to the senses—whose thousand faces the poems seek out and draw. . . .

It was in his third volume, *Seeing is Believing* (1960), that Tomlinson first became both the distinct and the distinguished poet that he is today. His first volume, *Relations and Contraries* (1951), is haunted by Yeats and Blake, and though brilliant in patches, is not of much consequence. Tomlinson next moved a good deal nearer to himself in *The Necklace* (1955), which ranks, at the least, as a prologue to his real achievement. It zeroes in on the great Tomlinson theme, but vitiates it by a kind of enamelled elegance; it has Stevens's epicurean quality, but not his saving gusto and bravura. Precious in both senses of the word, *The Necklace* is a book to be valued, but—too beautiful, too exquisite—not to feel at home in: you must park your muddy shoes at the door. The very title of the third volume, *Seeing is Believing,* suggests a homely improvement over *The Necklace.* Here the earth takes on some of the earthiness that, after all, becomes it; and the manner is more gritty, rubs more familiarly with the world. In the subsequent two volumes, *A Peopled Landscape* (1962) and *American Scenes* (1966), the same manner—at once meticulous, prosaic, and refined (for Tomlinson's early elegance is roughened rather than lost)—is extended, as the titles indicate, to new subjects if not exactly to new themes. It is largely to the Tomlinson of these three volumes and of a fourth, *The Way of a World,* that I have addressed my remarks, and it is this Tomlinson who, as I began by declaring, has produced the most considerable body of poetry, to date, of any postwar English poet. . . .

Because of both an increased dynamic clarity and a more definite music, Tomlinson's latest poems are probably his most readily accessible; they still, however, constitute a language to be learned, a flavour to be found, and to care about Tomlinson is to approve of this difficulty.

*Calvin Bedient, "On Charles Tomlinson,"*

*in* British Poetry Since 1960: A Critical Survey, *edited by Michael Schmidt and Grevel Lindop (reprinted by permission of Dufour Editions, Inc.), Carcanet, 1972, pp. 172-89.*

Contemplation of the visible world is the gradual filling up of a closed container. The fullness is wonderful: the finitude chafes. Yet Charles Tomlinson, England's truest contemplative since the Hopkins of the notebooks, blessed with a classical self-possession, on "I" as modest as a pane of glass, inhabits the day-long sphere of contemplation so variously and peaceably that he reconciles one to it, makes looking seem as large as vision. The only way to live in time without restlessness, he seems to say, is to learn to see it as a wealth of unresting changes: "Time present beyond all bargain," as he says in a poem on Midas, "liquid gifts."

For Tomlinson wisdom is acquiescence, acquiescence an allowing of the inward and the outward to meet and be, each stilled in the other, and fulfilled there. For this is what contemplation is, this mutual calming. We find this repose on duration difficult; after all, the depths of duration are death. . . .

But the consolation of contemplation—its metaphysical deliverance—is the healing touch of reality. . . . No poet has ever seemed at once so intelligent and immune to anxiety as Tomlinson. His mind is superbly serene, inhumanly human. He descends upon appearances like a calm of love.

An instinctive poet, Tomlinson has invented, as William Carlos Williams said, a "new measure" that "gives a refreshing rustle" to the language. His lines break ascetically, his pace has a mellowed deliberation. . . .

As a poet, he is complete, a convincing voice, at once a strict musician and a relentless philosopher of seeing. Since 1958, with the publication of "Seeing Is Believing," he has been the most consistently admirable poet writing in England. The English themselves have been tardy in taking to him, for somehow they get a wild smell of Williams off his work and, besides, have complained that he seldom writes about people. This last is true, but he is himself so powerfully civilized a presence in his poems (in this regard, so *English*) that the criticism amounts to a quibble.

The high point of Tomlinson's career to date is the first long section of poems in "The Way of a World" (1969)—poems dense with his loving intellection, his stringent sensuousness, his difficult grace, his strong dry beauty. Unfortunately, the comparably ambitious meditative poems in "Written on Water" hamper as much as they restrain the sensuous. The brilliance of the world is hidden behind the smoked glass of reflection; the *display* of contemplation is more apparent than its joy. . . .

Still, almost all the new poems [in "Written on Water"] are in some part fine (it is hard for this poet to fail), and as many as a dozen give that rare happiness of knowing that someone alive in your own day is a master. . . .

*Calvin Bedient, in* The New York Times Book Review *(© 1973 by The New York Times Company; reprinted by permission), April 29, 1973, p. 7.*

For Charles Tomlinson, the formative energies of poetry are predicated upon certain normative conditions, analogous to the continual flux, the movement and motion, of music, memory, and the water on and about which he writes. These conditions are sustained in his poems by a modulating diction which repeatedly "halts (the) progress (of thought), / A clear momentary silhouette, before it / Dips and disappears into wordlessness." For Tomlinson is a connoisseur of incessant transmutations and disappearances, of that "coherent chaos . . . that refuses to declare itself," yet contains a poetic declaration, since "to say / Is to see again by the light of speech / Speechless." . . .

The "solid vacancies" of Tomlinson's poetry are the particular accomplishment of his supple language, and by employing this language—"the unspoken/ Familiar dialect of habitation—speech/ Behind speech, language that teaches itself/ Under the touch and sight"—to explore "the crossings and the interlacings" of his shifting and mutable, though highly contrived, perceptions, Tomlinson provides us with a compelling "liturgy of changes." . . .

*J. E. Chamberlin, in* The Hudson Review *(copyright © 1973 by The Hudson Review, Inc.; reprinted by permission), Vol. XXVI, No. 2, Summer, 1973, pp. 395-96.*

[Tomlinson's] great strength as a translator [is that while] he has not (exactly) used other poets to develop the resources of English poetry, nor . . . aimed centrally at new types of translation, . . . his renderings, delicately faithful, where I can judge, to the essential feel, do stand as consummately executed new works. He is, indeed, one of the rare translators to read even when one has no need of a translation. 'His' *Renga* is decidedly a poem in its own right. . . .

Tomlinson has always been concerned . . . with transcending personality. His contribution to *Renga* is remarkable for the tightly organized intent with which he uses the encounter of the poets and the collaborative nature of their poem as a means to enlarge his theme. His painting involves a similar disciplining of the self. . . .

Tomlinson's poetry belongs to the literature of *pietas*. . . . *Pietas* is an ample tradition, Latin and subsequently European, founded largely in Virgil and Horace and fertile over here in divers ways—in Pope, say, and also in Wordsworth, and in those, like George Eliot, whom Wordsworth influenced. It stirs in Tomlinson's care for rightness and richness of relationship, with others, with nature, with the past and—if not exactly with the gods—with death, the dead and all that encompasses and bounds us. His *pietas* sizes the self and opens it to the otherness of the real. It is often pastoral, though it engenders no idyll: his verse sings the multiple interweavings of a man with the earth and its seasons, with space and time, but balances them, as one knows, against fundamental threats; and it records the passing of those communal meshings, with worked land and the practice of generations, which depend on a rural order now menaced by 'the soft oppression of prosperity'.

The source of his most sustained quickening of the tradition is his sense of place. Among his most potent words are 'where', 'here', 'there'. In the earlier books he celebrates buildings, in their just craftsmanship and their penetration by age and neighbourhood. Everywhere, he devises moments of spatial awareness, when a person is called out and made more vividly present by an illuminated perception of surroundings. . . . Deeply, his poetry is a search for 'Eden', a cherished word, and a lament for every loss of the piety of place. . . .

It is likewise a Latin decorum, a neoclassical propriety, which motivates his deriding of literary exhibition and of extremity in life-styles and art-styles, in, among others, 'Ars Poetica'. And which stresses movingly sober poems about death, like 'Remembering Williams', . . . from *Written on Water,* that in its charged restraint is both casual and, in the end, dramatic, reticent and raw.

Tomlinson's concerns here generate what seems to me a poetry of obvious human, moral, imaginative richness. Though his outspokenness does expose limitations. One may feel that he asks too much of a seasoned attentiveness to the world outside as a solution to our problems, and one can regret that the self within is dismissed at once so easily and so curtly. It is also true that for anyone who believes nature to have a meaning that Tomlinson would disallow as mythic, his sense of reality, which is so beautifully and so copiously revealing of fact, nevertheless prevents itself ultimately from achieving fact's 'proper plenitude'.

While writing out of a tradition and interpreting a nexus of common themes, Tomlinson also admits into his verse some of that tradition's poets. If I have understood him, he is not only declaring his descent: he is essentially assembling and manifesting the tradition, and giving it tongue. . . .

In all [his] poems taken together, Tomlinson has managed an original method of assimilating other poets. The tradition that he gathers, though diverse, is a whole, with the result that a clarified and particular communal voice is found to be speaking. It also includes many near-contemporaries, so that when Tomlinson writes, modern poetry is involved. Furthermore, the consequent impersonality is new, or at least newly established. . . .

Tomlinson's diverse engaging with tradition and impersonality poses problems, both evaluative and theoretical. It clearly needs to be examined at greater length than here. Yet his poetry can be seen already, I believe, through this approach, to be a stimulating, ample enterprise. It maintains contact with the past. It defines a present. It opens up large technical possibilities for the future.

*Michael Edwards, "Charles Tomlinson: Notes on Tradition and Impersonality," in* Critical Quarterly, *Summer, 1973, pp. 133-44.*

Charles Tomlinson's new book [*Written on Water*] is virtually free from violence. He continues in the same mode in which he has developed his exacting and admired craftsmanship. Though he is occasionally grouped with Creeley and other Black Mountain poets, I think the link is tenuous. The American poet he most resembles is Marianne Moore, who wrote: "Ecstasy provides the occasion, but expediency determines the form." Tomlinson's precision derives from just such an emotional expediency. Both have mastered the tone of urgent conversation, and their poems are wrought with great pressure and energy. This volume is finer than his earlier *American Scenes,* and longer poems in a British locale, like "Mackinnon's Boat," give us the rare pleasure of things that are both beautiful and instructive. . . . Neither knobby to the ear nor abandonedly primitive, Tomlinson's lines work with trustworthy but surprising inventiveness.

*Charles Molesworth, in* The Nation, *March 16, 1974, p. 347.*

Tomlinson . . . practices and advocates an anti-romantic viewpoint. He urges us to curb our egocentric imaginations in the interest of acquiring accurate information about external nature, and his own poems exemplify his advice. From his experience as both painter and poet, however, he is intensely aware of the difficulties confronting those who wish to apprehend in undistorted fashion the "plenitude" of fact in the natural world. Particularly his earlier poems deal with various problems of perspective. He recognizes, for example, that the position which we adopt for purposes of observation necessarily constitutes a restricted and arbitrary focus upon unbounded and undifferentiated phenomena. We cannot embrace everything at a glance; we must be satisfied with what our vision encompasses. Nor will our attending carefully to an event necessarily permit us to distinguish all of its features. As disinterested observers we may admire the power and grace of the hawk's deadly stoop, but the hawk itself is conscious only of its hunger, nor is its descent beautiful in the eyes of its prey huddled in "the shrivelled circle / Of magnetic fear." A comparable relativity hedges round such universal physical features as space and light. It is important to realize as the Impressionists did that an object will assume different features depending upon the degree of light to which it is exposed. . . .

Problems involving relativity of perspective are inseparable from omnipresent mutability, which interpenetrates all natural phenomena and complicates our efforts to understand ourselves as well as our surroundings. We yearn for a static and predictable realm in which we may order events and assign meaning to them. . . . [But] Tomlinson finds that the natural world has not been ordained specifically for human happiness, domination, and moral edification. He . . . recognizes that its immense power is dreadful, threatening, and unchallengeable, but he shares with his fellow poets the conclusion that by intelligently recognizing and deferring to natural forces, we can achieve a measure of dignity and peace.

*Julian Gitzen, "British Nature Poetry Now," in* The Midwest Quarterly, *Summer, 1974, pp. 232-37.*

* * *

## TOOMER, Jean 1894-1967

**Toomer was a Black American novelist, short story writer, and poet.**

Toomer turned to mystical religion and denounced poetry and renounced race—he was certainly the best American Negro poet until the upsurge of creativity amongst Blacks after 1960. He refused to allow his poetry to be reprinted or anthologized, and as he was dying turned over his literary estate to his friend Arna Bontemps, and his one book of poems and stories, *Cane,* was republished with great success. (pp. 96-7)

Toomer is the first poet to unite folk culture and the elite culture of the white avant-garde, and he accomplishes this difficult task with considerable success. He is without doubt the most important Black poet, although he was practically white and easily passed, until recent years. (p. 153)

> *Kenneth Rexroth, in his* American Poetry in the Twentieth Century *(copyright © 1971 Herder and Herder, Inc.; used by permission of the publisher, The Seabury Press, New York), Herder, 1971.*

"Cane" also means "Cain," and it is not by accident that Toomer wanted to depict the black experience in mythic terms. [Toomer accidentally wrote *Cain* for *Cane* when referring to his novel. Later he corrected his typing "error" in his own handwriting, as may be seen in the Toomer papers at Fisk University Library, Box 32, Folder 7.] Hart Crane, Van Wyck Brooks, Waldo Frank, and others had been urging American artists to exploit the mythic possibilities of America's past. Here specifically was one myth ready-made for black people and already a part of American folklore; the color of the black man's skin was the mark of Cain. . . .

Toomer uses Cain as a symbol of the African in a hostile land, tilling the soil of the earth, a slave, without enjoying her fruits. Yet strangely enough, this Cain receives another kind of nourishment from the soil, spiritual nourishment, which the owners of it are denied.

Also, the Bible states that Cain's nomadic existence leads him to found a city in the land of Nod, "east of Eden" (Genesis 4:16-17). An apocryphal legend develops from this event, for he and his descendants become known as the first city-dwellers. Toomer treats this side of the myth as part of the curse. As the blacks move into northern cities "east of Eden," they are cut off from their spiritual roots in the agrarian South; their lives grow pale like the "white-washed wood of Washington" to which Toomer refers in "Seventh Street." But there is a fate worse than moving to the desolate northern cities; it is moving to those desolate cities inside your mind, as Kabnis does when he accepts the myth of the black Cain as a curse and not a badge of divine protection. . . .

The second approach to a fuller understanding of *Cane* comes from Toomer's letter to Waldo Frank upon completion of the novel. Critics may be skeptical about finding any structure in the work, and certainly *Cane* may be appreciated without one, but Toomer himself apparently had a plan. "My brother!" he says to Frank on December 12, 1922:

> Cane is on its way to you! For two weeks I have worked steadily at it. The book is done. From three angles, Cane's design is a circle. Aesthetically, from simple forms to complex ones, and back to simple forms. Regionally, from the South up into the North, and back into the South again. Or from the North down into the South and then a return North. From the point of view of the spiritual entity behind the work, the curve really starts with Bona and Paul (awakening), plunges into Kabnis, emerges in Karintha etc. swings upward into Theatre and Box Seat, and ends (pauses) in Harvest Song. . . . Between each of the three sections, a curve. These, to vaguely indicate the design. [Toomer papers, Fisk University Library, Box 3, Folder 6.]

Toomer's outline both puzzles and informs. It puzzles because, although the novel moves from South to North to South, it does not parallel the spiritual pattern he employs. The published work begins with the Karintha section and ends with "Kabnis." The curves drawn on separate pages between the sections hint at a circular design, but the reader tends to associate them only with the South-North-South structural scheme.

The key, I think, lies in the word "pauses" (". . . and ends (pauses) in Harvest Song"). Toomer is describing *Cane* in organic terms, and therefore it never really ends. It is simply a matter of beginning all over again with "Bona and Paul," the story that follows "Harvest Song.". . .

Paul has had a vision of wholeness in the Gardens, but in his excitement to explain it, to understand it, he loses it. Paul's epiphany then is ironic; the purple of the Gardens at dusk suggests a fusion of the white and black worlds, specifically of Bona and Paul, but it is a fusion whose nature, like that of dusk, is only temporary. The color purple also suggests passion; Paul's passion thins out before he has a chance to experience its fullness.

Nevertheless, Paul's dream haunts Toomer. The conflict between the world of the Crimson Gardens and the world outside, like that of art and life, is a preface to the Kabnis-Cain who believes that the real Kabnis "is a dream" and that "dreams are faces with large eyes and weak chins and broad brows that get smashed by the fists of square faces. The body of the world is bull-necked. A dream is a soft face that fits uncertainly upon it. . ." (p. 158).

The myth of Cain is most relevant as the lowest point on the circle. It is crucial to the understanding of Kabnis's emotional anguish. Based upon Toomer's own experience, the story documents his spiritual conflict, for Kabnis is Toomer, or one side of Toomer, a Toomer who has yet to reach the artistic and spiritual wholeness of the singer of "Harvest Song." . . .

The mark of Cain upon Kabnis represents, as Toomer suggests in his letter to [Waldo] Frank, the spiritual nadir of the book. It stands thematically in direct opposition to "Harvest Song," the lyric which completes the "spiritual entity" of the novel by providing an answer to Kabnis's dilemma. Also, since "Kabnis" concludes the novel, it forces a comparison with the lyrical opening ("emerging") story, "Karintha." For instance, Kabnis's spiritual alienation underscores Karintha's spiritual health. . . .

The spiritual quest which gains momentum in the agrarian South "swings upward" in the electric beehive of Washington. The "cane-fluted" world does not die in the North. It continues to haunt the dreams and lives of those who have strayed far from their roots to dwell in the cities. Avey, for instance, is a Fern come North where the only outlet for her natural, instinctual life is that of prostitution. The story as it progresses shifts its focus to the narrator, a wandering Cain who cannot cope with Avey for the same reason that Kabnis cannot cope with Georgia: she is too immediate. He tries to romanticize her: "I talked, beautifully I thought, about an art that would be born, an art that would open the way for women the likes of her" (p. 87). But her unresponsiveness convinces him that she is lazy, a "cow." Only at the end of the story does he understand her in a light which links their common humanity. . . .

"Harvest Song" completes the cycle. The poem answers Kabnis's spiritual despair, and in its lyric simplicity it restates the thematic conclusion of "Box Seat," the peace that passes understanding. In the poem, the reaper sings of his suffering. Like Cain, he tills the soil but the bread he earns by the sweat of his brow is not enough to sustain him. . . .

The theme of Cain suggests even broader possibilities. Americans have tended to mythologize their experience, and they found most suitable the myth of Adam. Scholars like R. W. B. Lewis *(The American Adam)* have persuaded us that this identification was by no means accidental; it grew out of man's contact with the New World, a garden in which the vices of Europe were unknown and in which man could return to his primal innocence. For some (Thoreau, Emerson, Whitman), the world lay before this New Adam and nothing seemed impossible; for others (Hawthorne and Melville), the world constricted around his heart to remind him that evil existed even in Eden. Thus, if the dominant culture can make sense out of its experience through the myth of Adam, I would suggest that Negroes have used the myth of Cain to explain their own uprootedness, an experience antithetical to the outer culture.

*Charles W. Scruggs, "The Mark of Cain and the Redemption of Art: A Study in Theme and Structure of Jean Toomer's 'Cane'," in* American Literature *(reprinted by permission of the Publisher; copyright 1972 by Duke University Press, Durham, North Carolina), May, 1972, pp. 276-91.*

At the time he was writing *Cane,* the book that is said to have launched the Harlem Renaissance, Jean Toomer was on the road to becoming an "essentialist.". . . Basically, this means two things. First, it means that Toomer believed in the reality of the soul and attainment of spiritual truth through intuition. . . .

In other words, Toomer the poetic realist was well on the way to becoming Toomer the poet/priest.

*Cane* is an intricately structured, incantational book. Divided into three major parts, it progresses from a highly poetic to a heavily dramatic form. . . . Because of its hybrid nature, *Cane* defies categorical classification as any single distinctive form.

*Cane's* structure, for example, also reflects Toomer's reading in psychoanalysis, philosophy and aesthetics. The three major divisions of *Cane* can be compared to the Freudian theory of personality, a Hegelian construct, or the Gurdjieffian triad [Bell is referring to George I. Gurdjieff, a Greek spiritualist]. In fact, a good case can be made that all three constitute the unifying force of the book. Part One, with its focus on the Southern past and the libido, presents the rural thesis, while Part Two, with its emphasis on the modern world and the superego, offers the urban antithesis. Part Three, then, functions as a synthesis of the earlier sections, with Kabnis representing the Black writer whose difficulty in reconciling himself to the dilemma of being an Afro-American prevents him from tapping the creative reservoir of his soul. Unlike the appeal to logic of a Hegelian construct, Toomer attempts to overwhelm the reader with the truth of his mystical theory of life through images and symbols whose appeal is more to our power of intuition and perception than to our cognition.

For these reasons, I believe *Cane* can be meaningfully approached as a poetic novel. By poetic novel, I mean that the book's theme grows out of its rhetorical structure. Neither its characters nor its plot is developed sufficiently to sustain the reader's interest. The strong appeal of *Cane,* its haunting, illusive beauty, lies in Toomer's fascinating way with words. The meaning of the book is implicit in the arabesque pattern of imagery, the subtle movement of symbolic actions and objects, the shifting rhythm of syntax and diction, and the infrastructure of a cosmic consciousness. When analyzed as a poetic novel, the disparate elements and illusive meanings of the book coalesce into an integral whole and provide a poignant insight into the dilemma of the modern Black artist.

On the surface, *Cane* is a pastoral work, contrasting the values of uninhibited, unlettered Black rustics with those of the educated, class-conscious Black bourgeoisie. On this level, Toomer draws on the Afro-American tradition of music as a major structural device. The melancholic fragments of spirituals and work songs that appear throughout the sketches create a flowing rhythm and intricate pattern of Gothic images that unify the dissimilar Christian and non-Christian elements of the book. While in Georgia, Toomer was deeply moved by the beauty of the folk songs he heard and saddened by the belief that the industrialization of the South would soon make them relics of the past. Adapting the conventions of the pastoral to his subject, he therefore employs folk songs as symbols of the folk spirit of Black Americans and, by extension, of the external soul of man.

Equally important as a symbol of the rural life is sugar cane itself. Purple in color, pungently sweet in odor, mysteriously musical in sound, and deep-rooted in growth, cane represents the beauty and pain of living close to nature. It also represents the Gothic qualities of the Black American's African and southern past, especially his ambivalent attitude toward this heritage. . . .

Although following the publication of *Cane* he turned his primary attention to people rather than books, Toomer did continue to write voluminously. But the bulk of these writings, which reveal the repudiation of racial classifications and the celebration of a Gurdjieffian vision of life, remains unpublished. *Cane,* thus, marked the death of an Afro-American poet-realist and the birth of a Gurdjieffian high priest of soul.

*Bernard W. Bell, "Jean Toomer's 'Cane'," in* Black World *(copyright © 1974, by Bernard W. Bell; reprinted by permission of* Black World *and Bernard W. Bell), September, 1974, pp. 4-6, 97.*

# V

## VASSILIKOS, Vassilis 1933-

**Vassilikos is a Greek novelist, playwright, and screenwriter best known for the novel *Z*.**

Most Left-of-center novelists, following in the Marxist tradition, get tangled in their message, producing caricatures and losing sight of artistic goals. Vassilikos almost always remembers that he is first of all a novelist. He accepts experimental techniques as compatible with his didactic purpose and as by no means an intrusion of form into content. Obviously [he is] well-read in the European new novel. . . .

*Robert J. Clements, "Prefiguring the Coup," in* Saturday Review/World *(copyright © 1968 by Saturday Review/World, Inc.; reprinted with permission), November 16, 1968, p. 51.*

In [*Z*,] his only book available here since "The Plant, The Well, The Angel," . . . Vassilis Vassilikos . . . demonstrates new and considerable storytelling and lyric powers. Designing a pattern as gracefully complex as an oriental carpet, he weaves fact with poetic fantasy, produces a texture peopled with dozens of characters, and knots them tightly one to the next. . . .

Transcending the grisly tale is its poetry. Images ripple, cascade, flood through every page. Other-worldly spirits, voices from the dead, great birds with human souls, all harking back to Olympian deities of old, hover in the murky air, wail for persecuted man, now and again swoop down to caress him. At times, these lyric flights rampage into a deluge of verbiage. (Shades of Thomas Wolfe in a Hellenic idiom!) But Vassilikos's gifts are dazzling, and these excesses of the imagination are also his book's chief beauty.

*Albert J. Zuckerman, in* The New York Times Book Review *(© 1968 by The New York Times Company; reprinted by permission), November 17, 1968, p. 81.*

In his . . . novel, *The Photographs,* Vassilikos has chosen the title for its symbolic resonance: literally 'writing with light'. The author means, presumably, that he is trying to cast light into dark corners of his native country. The city in the novel, Necropolis, the same as in *Z* is, of course, the city of the dead. The deadness is due to the passive conformity of its people. . . .

*The Photographs* . . . is a kind of surrealist dream or, at times, nightmare that makes reality more acceptable than if the author had used a more traditional 'naturalistic' method. In this way, too, he conveys more effectively the poetic nature of his hero. Naturally, for a Greek expatriate writer, politics can never be far away. . . .

Vassilikos wants to make the point surely that man chooses his own destiny; he is not at the mercy of outside forces, the sport of the gods or a Hardyesque President of the Immortals. The death-wish is inside each one of us—Freud turned to the Greek in naming it 'Thanatos'—but a man can choose not to yield to it and opt instead for life and freedom. By saying that 'nothing can happen in Necropolis' Vassilikos is insisting that no creativity is possible where men are not free to express themselves as they wish. There is an insistence, too, on the necessity to choose the freedom and pain of exile rather than be stifled as an artist. No doubt he has felt the need to justify his own position.

*The Photographs* is a novel that works on various levels and is therefore open to various interpretations. Its terms of reference are both public and private. Yet it cannot be dismissed as merely another propagandist effort since the 'message' is so subtle and so ably woven into the total structure.

*Robert Greacen, in* Books and Bookmen, *December, 1971, pp. 64, 66.*

*The Photographs* is a novel in which the main emphases are verbal, structural and thematic. Vassilis Vassilikos is too competent a novelist to let the lavish application of "technique" completely suffocate the human lack which is expressed by his story. . . .

This potentially interesting theme is vitiated by the iambic prose reverie which the translation offers us at so many points. It may sound like poetry in Greek; in English the banality of the prose rhythm merely emphasizes the whimsicality of so many of Mr. Vassilikos's inventions, and distorts the seriousness of the book's subject, the perennially interesting relations between life and art, illusion and reality, man and woman.

*"Fidgeting," in* The Times Literary Supplement *(reproduced by permission), December 17, 1971, p. 1568.*

Since 1967 in Paris as an exile from his native land, Vassilikos has published seven books and has been considered a promising modern Greek writer who gracefully balances the imagery of film and light as seen internally and externally and the inner landscape of the mind with the scenery of Greece.

*John E. Rexine, in* Books Abroad, *Autumn, 1972, Vol. 46, No. 4, pp. 721-22.*

Vassilis Vassilikos' earlier novel "Z" was based on the murder of the Greek Socialist deputy Lambrakis in Salonika before the advent of the regime of the colonels in 1967. Its strength was based on a shrewd understanding of the dynamics of cold-blooded behind-the-scenes political manipulation. At the end of that book, the fates of those involved in the affair are told: evil was handsomely rewarded and ordinary decency carried a heavy price.

One price can be exile, a Greek solution to political questions since the time of Cleisthenes. Vassilikos himself, since "Z" was banned by the present Government, has lived in exile from his own country, and exile is the subject of "The Harpoon Gun."

It consists of two novels and 13 stories. After a section of bafflingly little interest, which woodenly recounts the kidnapping of an American officer by anti-Government Greeks bent on obtaining the release of political prisoners through an exchange, Vassilikos presents us with a gallery of exiles—sketches of their lives abroad. . . .

Granted the unifying theme, these sections have little else to do with each other in the ordinary sense; one has to strain the symbolic imagination to make connections of a sort. This might be all right if that unifying theme were systematically developed. But it scarcely gains in velocity as the book proceeds; the constant jumping from one anecdotal situation to another begins to suggest that Vassilikos may be a rather fickle lover of his characters. . . .

[Along] with satire . . . , Vassilikos sometimes achieves a simple and convincing poignancy. In "Sarandapikhou Street," an exile has traveled from Belgium to Paris for one evening; in his homesickness he has gone to such lengths just to see a program of Greek documentary films made by young directors before the time of the colonels. Suddenly "the camera came to rest on what used to be his own balcony with its pots of basil and jasmine. He could see his own initials on the sheet hung out to air."

*Peter Sourian, in* The New York Times Book Review *(© 1973 by The New York Times Company; reprinted by permission), May 6, 1973, p. 39.*

The nineteen selections [in *Le fusil-harpon et autres nouvelles*, "The Harpoon Gun and Other Stories"] are not "short stories" strictly speaking, but open-ended "pieces," with elements akin to new journalism, tape transcriptions, cinéma-vérité, and the like. Two major pieces frame a group of seventeen others, much shorter and sometimes loosely connected by the presence of a book salesman who, like an ambulatory recorder, travels in Western European circles of Greek exiles, émigrés and workers. Vassilikos focuses on the Resistance at home and especially abroad, through individuals shown in a painfully realistic, very objective (warts and all) fashion: they are nostalgic, helpless, powerless, pathetic, tragic, flawed, sincere, opportunistic, ineffectual, yet not crushed. . . .

[The] tone in *Le fusil-harpon* is low-key, with no grand gestures, speeches or acts. Anger is present of course, but controlled, contained and suffused by . . . sadness. . . .

[Anxiety], the self-torture of memories and psychological violence are the focal points, not explicit physical violence. . . . The book is not entertainment or a stylistic exercise—in fact it sags occasionally when the author indulges in "literature." It is essentially a treatise on sociopolitical conditions, but of such a specifically Greek nature that allusions, references and "personnages à clé" will be fully appreciated only by those readers who are familiar with the particulars and who are able to become involved in the protracted dialectics of the Resistance.

*Edwin Jahiel, in* Books Abroad, *Spring, 1974, Vol. 48, No. 2, p. 409.*

* * *

## VIDAL, Gore 1925-

**Vidal is an American novelist, playwright, critic, essayist, and *raconteur*. He is considered a brilliant essayist and his principal themes for both fiction and nonfiction are social and political. He has also written detective stories under the pseudonym Edgar Box. (See also *Contemporary Authors*, Vols. 5-8, rev. ed.)**

[While] outwardly flattering to the political opinions of the spectator, *The Best Man* is secretly destructive of all intelligent politics: complex ideas harden into ideology, and liberalism itself is tainted with the demagoguery it professes to abhor. It is worth observing that while we are encouraged to sympathize with the upright Russell . . . in his uncompromising concern with issues rather than personalities, there is not a single political issue of any consequence discussed in the play. And at the same time that we are hooting Joe Cantwell's low-road penchant for malicious scandal, we are giggling at gossipy wisecracks about the sex life, drinking habits, and personal idiosyncrasies of prominent political figures and their wives. That these politicians are presented in composite serves not to disguise them so much as to multiply the scandals in their public and private lives. . . .

In short, *The Best Man* demonstrates that expediency can be operative in playwriting as well as in politics, and that there is not such a wide gulf between our commercial drama and our national life as one might imagine. Since one can hear an author's true voice speaking in only one of his lines, it is difficult to say how committed Mr. Vidal is to the flaccid attitudes he grinds out in his play. "As a playwright," he once wrote in an article, "I am a sport, whose only serious interest is the subversion of a society which bores and appalls me." Whether wittingly or not, he is certainly realizing his objective with this cynical and mechanical work.

*Robert Brustein, "Politics and the Higher*

*Gossip" (1960), in his* Seasons of Discontent: Dramatic Opinions 1959-1965 *(© 1959, 1960, 1961, 1962, 1963, 1964, 1965 by Robert Brustein; reprinted by permission of Simon and Schuster, Inc.), Simon & Schuster, 1965, pp. 108-10.*

The Broadway theatre has this much in common with American society: It is rapidly becoming an operation of hipsters for the bilking of squares. The hipster—if you are still unfamiliar with the term—is a sophisticated careerist who adapts himself to meretricious surroundings for the sake of advancement, concealing his derisive contempt for his customers while prospering on their gullibility, pretentiousness, and bad taste. He is identified, therefore, by the schizoid split that separates his public from his private personality: he wears a mask of charm and sincerity over a face of scorn. . . .

The smoothest of these legitimized con men is the cultural hipster. . . .

Let me cite, as evidence of the hipster's flourishing influence, the recent adaptation of Duerrenmatt's *Romulus der Grosse*—or GORE VIDAL'S ROMULUS, as the program more shrewdly identifies it. . . . [Vidal's] dramatic writings, while superficially sophisticated, are carefully designed for squares. Confirming in spades his press agent's boast that "Vidal has done it again," he has even managed to make *Romulus* indistinguishable from his other two Broadway opiates, transforming Duerrenmatt's tough parable into an effeminate charade enacted by the theatrical smart set.

What Duerrenmatt wrote was a bitter comedy about the last Roman Emperor. . . . Vidal has preserved the shell of the original while hollowing out the center, adding a confectionery filling sprinkled with witless political jokes, irrelevant anachronisms, and open thefts from Wilde and Shaw. . . .

[In] our theatre, no artist is safe from the cultural hipster—or, for that matter, from the square spectator, because despite their contrasted natures, both are the natural antagonists of genuine art.

*Robert Brustein, "Hipster Dramatists, Square Spectators" (1962), in his* Seasons of Discontent: Dramatic Opinions 1959-1965 *(© 1959, 1960, 1961, 1962, 1963, 1964, 1965 by Robert Brustein; reprinted by permission of Simon and Schuster, Inc.), Simon & Schuster, 1965, pp. 130-33.*

To work one's way through Mr. Vidal's collected essays [*Homage to Daniel Shays: Collected Essays 1952-1972*] is to feel with a peculiar immediacy the tone of years long over and done with. Most collections of this sort are timepieces, to be sure. But Mr. Vidal has a gift for catching the tremors of the moment as they occur, and he does so with an alertness usually reserved for the beneficiaries of hindsight. . . . Mr. Vidal is scarcely ever only cruel, or even only adept. One of the pleasant things about him is a modulating tone, which varies, from time to time, with temper, but which is drawn, one thinks, from reliable reserves and from a certain warmth of mind. This was called personality once, and there is no doubt that its pleasant abundance in Mr. Vidal makes him agreeable, even when he offends. He is seldom strident, except when he is carrying on about sexual freedom for all, or when he is tenting under the skirts of the women's movement, puffing away about the oppression of the second sex, and of Kate Millet in particular. . . . He has other preoccupations as well. Mr. Vidal's broadsides at the middle class are delivered with a classy hauteur, but their origins are the dank and weary nether regions to which the clichés of the leftish mind retire when they go to breed. His self-confident throwaways about "the moral nullity at the center of American life" have a similar birthplace. . . .

These things said, there is a good deal of intellectual, as well as plain, old-fashioned literary, pleasure to be had in nearly all else Mr. Vidal has written here. He is a moralist, of course, and a man of considerable humor, and those two qualities have usually gone well together in the history of letters. The last essay in the book is on Eleanor Roosevelt, and it is quite the most moving piece on that subject in one's memory. Like any real moralist, the author of this collection has an abundance of feeling, which factor works quite as well for the affections as it does for the spleen.

*Dorothy Rabinowitz, in* World *(copyright © 1972 by Saturday Review/World, Inc.; reprinted with permission), December 19, 1972, p. 73.*

Despite its more or less foreclosed partisanship in favor of Burr, this latest and, with *Julian* and *Myra Breckinridge,* best of Vidal's 13 novels is not designed merely to change the mind of anyone who has been brought up to venerate Jefferson and Hamilton at the expense of Burr. Because while [*Burr*] is prejudiced against Jefferson, disdainful of Washington, and somewhat demonological about Hamilton, it nonetheless exhibits Vidal's characteristically 18th-century detachment about human follies, and this extends to the reader's presuppositions about the beginnings of our nation.

If this detachment were merely imposed *de haut en bas,* as in some of Vidal's writing, then the results would be merely charming, evocative, exciting—and superficial. Instead, Vidal's detachment here is a form of meditative skepticism about our beginnings. . . .

If the novel is about treason, it is also about a much larger problem: to what does anything or anyone truly belong? The success and power of *Burr* derives from the ingenuity with which this question is probed, even to the point of making it a question about the legitimacy of writing such a book. In the afterword, Vidal asks "Why a historical novel and not a history? To me, the attraction of the historical novel is that one can be as meticulous (or as careless!) as the historian and yet reserve the right not only to rearrange events but, most important, to attribute motive—something the conscientious historian or biographer ought never do." The oddity of this statement is in the lack of ambition it betrays not about history but about the novel itself. It proposes for the writer of fiction absolutely nothing which is not also, though Vidal refuses to grant this, the privilege of the biographer and historian. These latter are of course forever rearranging events and attributing motives; it is hard to imagine what else importantly they ought to do. Vidal's 18th-century inclination extends here to a faith in the decorum of genres, and his concern is of a piece with the whole anxiety in the book about what properly does belong with what and to whom: not only to the Constitution or to the branches of government, not only to the nation or to the family, but also to novelists and/or historians. It is an exciting and most promising dilemma for a novel, and Vidal has worked out a great many variations on it. But in *Burr,* as in its afterword, he is sometimes prevented by his decorousness from pushing ahead as a novelist, imaginatively and stylistically, into precisely the strange territories he has mapped out for himself and for us. . . .

My primary criticism of *Burr* is not that it seems sometimes to violate the historical record, especially with respect to Jefferson's attitude toward slavery. . . . Rather, the main trouble with *Burr* is that it does not dare quite enough and that Vidal remains just a bit too loyal not so much to "the record" as to a world of essential rationality. This in spite of the fact that his entire structural apparatus, his very principle of organization would seem to commit him to stylistic evocations of the mysterious, the murky, the grotesque in an effort to comprehend those submerged forces that began and set the course for our nation. There are a few attempts to open the book up to the kinds of inquiry that seem to be called for . . . [but they do not] come off, partly because nothing in the book has habituated us to the treatment of resemblances at any such level of intensity and partly because, as a result, Vidal's natural energies are not fired up by such possibilities.

Nonetheless, *Burr,* when taken with *Julian, Myra Breckenridge* and *Two Sisters,* suggests that Vidal is moving into fictional terrains more hazardous and more rewarding than ever before. He is working out ways by which characters from the past find versions of themselves in characters of later times and are then projected by Vidal as the manipulator of the material, in such a way as to make it all seem immediately contemporaneous and autobiographical. It doesn't matter if this effort isn't always wholly successful. What does matter is that Vidal, who now might lean on or merely transplant his laurels, is instead taking big and exciting chances. In *Burr* the chances have begun to pay off rather handsomely.

*Richard Poirier, "The Heart Has Its Treasons," in* Book World—The Washington Post (© The Washington Post), *October 28, 1973, p. 3.*

Gore Vidal . . . is to American letters what, in Burr's time, Thomas Rowlandson was to English painting: a cartoonist, an excellent draftsman, a satirist fond of the bawdy and perverse. Vidal understands that the best way to revise history without accepting responsibility for one's conclusions is to write a novel. The novelist, certain that few readers object to seeing the mighty look incompetent, may simply attribute every motive and action of the great to ambition, stupidity and malice. These days, cynicism, sharpened by style and research, seems a reasonable approach to political reality. . . .

Vidal is not above reaching for easy effects, but "Burr" is an extraordinarily intelligent and entertaining novel. He has done his homework. He has re-created the smells and noises of the time. Vidal's principal triumph, however, is that he has made of Burr more than a political cartoon. . . .

*Peter S. Prescott, "Great American Monster," in* Newsweek *(copyright Newsweek, Inc., 1973; reprinted by permission), November 5, 1973, p. 98.*

Vidal has a wonderful talent both for mimicry and evocation. . . . Vidal has also the love of learning which is so often best guarded by its distance from American university education. He has never let himself be distracted by inferior models or merely satisfied with the greatest ones. Gibbon pointed—but only pointed—him toward Julian the Apostate; and *Julian* has the particular charm of making us imagine that we have come not upon one of Gibbon's pupils but upon one of his sources. . . .

Vidal himself has observed that his is one of those spirits that are keenest when they are quickened partly out of a sense of mischief and partly out of a sense of justice. *Burr* has, therefore, some elements of the prank, but it is more a serious attack on the notion of an original American innocence.

*Murray Kempton, "Discovering America," in* The New York Review of Books *(reprinted with permission from* The New York Review of Books; *© 1973 by NYREV, Inc.), November 15, 1973, pp. 6-8.*

Vidal . . . is something very few American novelists have been: a wit. Humorists we have had aplenty, but novelists who could actually write sparkling repartee have been rarer among us than saints, and rather more sorely missed. If you look at today's crop of novelists, except for Vidal, only Wilfrid Sheed can be considered a reputable wit, and even he is English-born. If for nothing else but their rarity, therefore, wits are precious hereabouts.

*John Simon, "Clinging to A. Burr," in* The New Leader, *December 10, 1973, pp. 10-12.*

[Vidal] is something like the last gentleman of American letters, a stylish politician of the mother tongue, and our most ingratiating snob—a snob of conscience, contemptuous of all that is not Quality. More completely than any other conspicuous novelist of his generation (those who began writing in the immediate postwar period), Vidal sees himself as a man of letters in an old-fashioned sense, which only two or three middle-to-low-circulation magazines and, bewilderingly, Carson and Cavett have allowed to survive into the second half of the century. And among his peers, Vidal assumes the role most successfully. Norman Mailer is too obsessive and self-referring to belong in the great tradition I have in mind. To draw the usual untenable distinction: The man of letters writes not about himself but about the world; he is fundamentally a critic. At his best, Mailer is a far more exciting writer than Vidal, but the excitement is bought at the price of a frequently maundering self-examination that Vidal would never allow on the page. It is boring. If you are able to turn the nifty trick of looking at either the self or the world steadily, the world turns out to be steadily interesting and the self—albeit intermittently consuming—simply not. . . .

The ghostly man of letters I see Vidal fleshing out for us was born in the eighteenth century—think of Voltaire's thin, sneering smile—and he has survived numberless corruptions and transformations on his way to the "David Susskind Show." But he is always political; he is, in fact, usually a politician *manqué*. . . .

And so Vidal became an unconventional politician in the republic of letters: novelist, playwright, scenarist, television playwright, essayist, and talk-show pundit supreme. He also became—to modify Edmund Wilson's crowning touch on W. H. Auden—"one of the great American men of the world." Worldliness. Is there any American anywhere more worldly than Gore Vidal?. . . Though not always the most attractive of characteristics, worldliness is—short of being possessed by a great idea—perhaps the best possible perspective for the critical mind ("I was born to be a critic"), and Vidal is one of the most superbly deflationary and entertaining (if not completely persuasive) critics I know.

The man of letters I'm thinking of sees himself as the Ideal Citizen, speaking out of his imagined place in the dead center of society ("I still see America as my turf and a country continually in need of my ministrations"). He addresses neither himself nor the angels of transcendence, but the plain old, faintly simple-minded body politic. The prime virtue for such a man is not passion but articulation. "Writing, for me," says Vidal, "is almost entirely a matter of making sense." He seems to have no interest at all in blowing the mind anywhere. . . . Vidal talks straight. For all his reputation for glacial, unapproachable archness, his are the simple virtues. Be clear. Think carefully. Talk about something important. Do not be a bore. . . .

In both his essays and novels, Vidal functions best as an acid and urbane witness. His eye alternates between being a very cold eye and a very evil eye—God knows he can turn a phrase like a knife in the heart—but it is never a dazzled eye (bedazzlement is not quite worldly enough), and consequently what he says is almost never dazzling. . . . The pleasures [I experience with Vidal's fiction are] . . . the joys of style, the engrossment of argument, the fascination of evil, and, at its best, the pleasure of being hit square between the eyes. Bull's-eye.

These are the joys of connoisseurship, rather than of intellectual—well—adventure. In his criticism, advancing his various causes (repeal of the sex laws, legalization of drugs and making addiction a strictly medical matter, political attacks and exposés, the concern for the environment and overpopulation), Vidal's ideas are—like those of even the best politicians—never original or, for that matter, even all that unusual. (One peculiar result, for me, is that his works turn out almost always to be more interesting than they promise to be at first blush.) But not even Camus was original: The fact is that the role of the man of letters is simply not big enough to accommodate a really powerful new idea. The role consists in lucidly defending intelligence and quality, drawing distinctions, and scourging the bogus and corrupt—at which Vidal has no peer: Contempt could be his middle name. This is usually done in the name of values that—like the rest of the writing—are very clear, finally simple.

But a worldly connoisseurship also tends to suggest decadence: And, indeed, there is a Vidal the good and a Vidal the bad. In Vidal the bad, the Ideal Citizen gives way to the author of *Julian,* prestidigitator of depravity. He becomes the author of *Myra Breckenridge,* that comedy of sexual degradation that suggests nothing so much as a buffo unconscious recapitulation of *Les Liaisons dangereuses,* possibly the most evil masterpiece of all literature.

Then Vidal the good turns around—well, he is never very, *very* good—and startles the sophisticates with something like this:

> To read of Eleanor and Franklin is to weep for what we have lost. Gone is the ancient American sense that whatever is wrong with human society can be put right with human action. . . . Whether or not one thought of Eleanor Roosevelt as a world ombudsman or as a chronic explainer or as a scourge of the selfish, she was like no one else in her usefulness. As the box containing her went past me, I thought, well, that's that. We're really on our own now.

Somewhere in Vidal's mind there is an ever more improbable convocation of superior people—highly intelligent, incorruptible, at once serious and wordly, philosophical and practical—whose duty it is to make egalitarian democracy the social condition of this land, to fulfill the eighteenth-century promise of a republic of the just, a promise that really was a great experiment, which has in turn become a great tradition, which in turn the little foxes have systematically and all but completely destroyed.

*Stephen Koch, "Gore Vidal: Urbane Witness to History," in* Saturday Review/World *(copyright © 1973 by Saturday Review/World, Inc.; reprinted with permission), December 18, 1973, pp. 24-9.*

Wit and intelligence can disinfect almost anything. It is such a relief . . . to come across a book which deals with decadent material in a sparkling, ironical way. If it is true that an important part of American culture has gone straight from provincial primitivism to metropolitan decadence, then [*Myra Breckenridge*] stands in more or less the same relation to the decadence as Laclos's *Les Liaisons Dangereuses* to the gameyness of late 18th-century French society. It is both part of the phenomenon it describes and a marvellously spirited comment on it. . . .

Most pornographic or erotic works are depressingly simple; but one of the charms of this book is the difficulty of deciding whether it is a pure spoof, written for the fun and the money, or a spoof with a core of genuineness.

*John Weightman, "Myth of the Butch Bitch," in his* The Concept of the Avant-Garde: Explorations in Modernism, *Alcove, 1973, pp. 281-84.*

Given the circumstances of the nation's inception it is not surprising, Vidal suggests, that American mythology has chosen to sanctify a social-climbing, power-hungry bastard from the West Indies like Alexander Hamilton, and a slave-owning, megalomaniacal satrap like Thomas Jefferson, while writing off a man of genuine greatness like Aaron Burr as an adventurer and a scoundrel. For Burr was a man of moral imagination and intelligence far too refined and subtle for the American herd, which has always been inhospitable to greatness of every sort, and tended to idolize all that is small and vulgar. He was, in short, much the kind of man that Gore Vidal takes himself to be, one of the "host of choice spirits" forced to live among coarse, materialistic, and hypocritical people who remain callously indifferent to the moral instruction he offers them.

While many individual episodes in *Burr* are entertaining in themselves, the plotting tends to sluggishness; the book's separate story lines and sections never achieve the structural coherence necessary to sustain a work as large as this. As the narrative moves forward, we are always conscious of the very thing good novels make us forget, that the whole business is a contrivance. The book, moreover, is written in a curious "period" language that is probably supposed to promote historical verisimilitude, but a great deal of both the dialogue and the narration is simply stiff or grandiloquent. The transitions between Burr's sections and Schuyler's eventually come to seem wooden and obviously schematic; the momentum built up in any single segment stops abruptly at its close; and the effect is that while the novel is technically well-organized, its spirit is static and crude.

The flaws in *Burr*'s architecture are serious, but its fatal shortcoming is the attempt to fob off its simplistic and polemical obsessions about America as "themes," and its carefully positioned strawmen as "characters." This is a book written in the interest of debunking some myths about the nature of the American experiment and its primary energy derives from the ironic juxtaposition of "reality," as represented in Burr's supposed truthtelling, and the "ideal," or all those casually accepted conventional notions of American history that the reader theoretically brings with him. The strategy works for a while, but it soon becomes apparent that all the events, all the observations, all the interactions among the characters make, essentially, variations on the same small point. What at first passes for naughty iconoclasm eventually becomes predictable and tedious; there is only so much shock value to be derived from learning that George Washington had carbuncles, or that Thomas Jefferson repeated himself tiresomely in conversation.

*Jane Larkin Crain, "Above the Herd" (reprinted from* Commentary *by permission; © 1974 by the American Jewish Committee), in* Commentary, *March, 1974, pp. 76-8.*

I suppose that to write an historical novel is the kind of temptation it was, once, to compose an oratorio. It is a solid task to apply yourself to; it lends respectability; and it gives a chance to preach, which is a natural desire. Of course, Gore Vidal has often preached already in his essays —preached a sort of patriotic gloom, not so much unlike Edmund Wilson's. . . . [In] the same spirit, he has written a novel about Aaron Burr, who (as, according to Vidal, every American schoolboy does *not* know) tied with Jefferson for the Presidency in 1800, killed Alexander Hamilton in a duel and was eventually tried for plotting to dismember the Union. . . .

However, though Gore Vidal preaches, he also wants to entertain, and here trouble arises. For, if his homily is to have its full effect, we must expect honest republican integrity in him as an artist, and we do not always get it. To put it bluntly, he cheats—as most historical novelists do, blithely or shamefacedly, consciously or unconsciously. (It is what makes it a bothersome genre.) His way of cheating is to make Burr a 20th-century-style novelist, closely resembling Gore Vidal. . . .

Aaron Burr could never have spoken or written in [the style Vidal attributes to him], not having had the advantage of studying Conrad or Graham Greene. This, for good or evil, is the prose of 20th-century fiction. . . . Vidal is at some pains to give Burr, and his [fictional] biographer, 'period' speech-habits, providing Burr with a terse, sub-Voltairean wit. And elsewhere again, he provides prose which contains no anachronism in the choice of words but is a total anachronism in the way they are put together. . . .

The truth is, Vidal is not interested in making and observing rules for himself, in this matter of 'period' style. His only rule is convenience. If his 'Regency' standard-lamp actually suggests the Regency to his client, so much the better, but the main thing is that it should work. To have written about the Washington of the Kennedys seems to him a good motive for now writing about Washington's Washington—as in a way it is—and he will cut as many corners as need be to bring his special expertise to bear. With some success, I think. At moments, Washington and Hamilton and Van Buren are brought up close to our faces as if at a party or on a television screen, in a way that is outside the scope of history-books. In this novel, for the first time, Washington in particular became real to me, with his unready speech and cold serpent-like eye.

All the same, probity and Jamesian scruple in artistic method are not lightly neglected. What is lost by neglecting them may be not some pedantic accuracy but life itself; and I do think that Vidal, in manipulating Burr so much to his own convenience, loses some of the life of his hero. Burr, when in exile, kept a private journal for his daughter, and the contrast with *Burr* is striking. Here, indisputably, is a living man; and, by contrast, Vidal's Burr seems all in an attitude, a machine for manufacturing epigrams and Voltairean ironies. Indeed, they seem rather different persons.

*P. N. Furbank, "Gore Vidal's Voltairean Gentleman," in* The Listener, *March 21, 1974, p. 372.*

*Williwaw* . . . by Gore Vidal was *not* the Great American World War II Novel. But it *was* something else. It was an almost classically *perfect* first novel. Perfect, at least, for a young man embarking upon a career in what is called (around the bar at Elaine's in New York anyway), "Serious Lit." It was short. It was modest. It was tidy. It was impeccably written in a naturalistic style well suited to the times. But it had something else too.

Reading it, you got the sense that (a little portentous musical underscoring, please) *the author knew exactly what he was doing!* Not for *him* the passionate . . . tell it *all!* tell it *all!* . . . first-novel-outpouring that can frequently catapult the writer to instant Fame and Fortune and afterwards, when the passion is spent, and his greying hair spills across the pillow in the moonlight, to a lifetime of trying to figure out how he did it that one time so long ago but can't seem to be able to do it no more baby blues.

Wisely, Mr. Vidal did not, and had no intention of, shooting his bolt the first time out. . . .

Mr. Vidal is too serious a man ever to permit himself to be caught being "serious." It is his pleasant custom to conceal his seriousness beneath a gift-wrapping of savage wit. Some years ago (much impressed by his *photograph* and his *name*) I produced a play of his in which a visitor from outer space in a polite, if somewhat patronising attempt to make small talk with his primitive hosts cheerfully remarked, "Isn't hydrogen fun?"! Mr. Vidal comes to *us* from an intelligence operating in another system. Mr. Aaron Burr came to the simple folk of the nineteenth century in much the same way.

It is Mr. Vidal's pleasure to use Burr as a rear view mirror into history. Mr. Vidal's sort of history. In it, George Washington appears as an inarticulate Eisenhower. Jefferson, who is said by many to be the author of the Constitution of the United States, is shown to be, through Burr's eyes, but vaguely literate.

And then Mr. Vidal comes up with a master stroke of the novelists' art. Cumbersome though it may seem, he employs the use of a fictitious first person narrator who is ostensibly engaged in assisting the ageing Burr in the preparation of his memoirs. Crafty Mr. Vidal! He gets to say any damned thing he wants about American history, not once but *twice* removed.

The central event of Burr's life was, very probably, the duel with Hamilton. There is no way that Mr. Vidal, as Mr. Vidal, could have made this well-known footnote to American history either new or dramatically workable. Even Burr, recounting *his* version in first person narrative, could not have been as effective as the *tour de force* which Gore brings off by (and I know this sounds ridiculous) having Burr *re-enact* the shooting for the benefit of the *narrator,* playing both parts himself.

*Burr* has been, for endless weeks, at the top of the American best seller list. There are excellent reasons for this. It is allegedly about 'American history', and therefore a *safe* book. It makes an excellent gift.

*George Axelrod, "George Axelrod on Gore, a Novelette Without Parts," in* The Spectator (© *1974 by* The Spectator; *reprinted by permission of* The Spectator), *March 23, 1974, pp. 362-63.*

After hearing Gore Vidal rationalise a career in which literary success has only been achieved at the expense of political ambition, the whimsical thought occurred to me that his parents must have made the same mistake as the Sleeping Beauty's: they left one old fairy off the guest list at his birth, and, true to form, she revenged herself in a peculiarly spiteful way. Having seen her colleagues bestow upon the baby boy every gift that a future politician could desire, including the most highly prized of all in our post-Gutenburg age, a natural aptitude for Television, the vindictive sprite trumped them by decreeing that he should also possess the one quality that is incompatible with political office of any sort: a writer's concern for the truth. So the very real chance Mr Vidal might have had of becoming President—'the unfinished business of my life' he calls it—was scuppered from the start, although it was not until he began to write *The City and the Pillar,* twenty-one years later, that the penny finally dropped.

Still, America's loss has been the English-speaking peoples' gain. Had Gore Vidal contrived the hold he sought upon the slippery pole, we should be the poorer for a huge body of work that includes at least a half a dozen fine novels and three entertaining and informative plays. More importantly, perhaps, for Anglo-American letters, the sadly-neglected art of the essay would lack one of its few modern champions, a cool, witty stylist whose prose is informed by Shavian verdicts like this one, on President Nixon's choice as Ambassador to the Court of St. James's: 'Had he not been born with money he might have found a happy niche for himself as a sales manager in some small firm where his crudeness and lack of civilisation would have been a virtue.' Clearly, Mr Vidal has a rather different set of values from the man who at present orders his country's affairs; values consistent with a background which, by any standards, was cultivated, worldly and very well connected.

*Michael Barber, "Crusader Against Cant," in* Books and Bookmen, *May, 1974, pp. 65-9.*

For nearly thirty years Gore Vidal has been publicly struggling with the two-headed monster of Lust. One of its heads is Power, the other is Sex. Vidal's Herculean struggle is not raw and sweaty, like Norman Mailer's. The wily Vidal, greased with urbane ambiguities, slips more smoothly from the monster's strangling grasp. Unfortunately (though perhaps fortunately for literature), the grease works both ways and the monster slips from the hero's grasp, too. Thus the struggle goes on and on, through the several million words of Vidal's thirteen novels and scores of plays, stories, essays and TV appearances.

Vidal's first novel, *Williwaw* (1946), is the least typical; the last, *Burr,* is the most mellow. By now the struggle seems more a game, a parody, a treacherously amusing pastime. . . .

The ambivalences of a writer are the most exquisite, for words are both substitutes for, and prods to (or even forms of) action. In the paradoxical power of words—those vicars of the gods, those angel javelins which have only as much power as there is belief—lies both redemption and corruption. While Vidal as an avowed atheist can hardly qualify as vicar of the Judeo-Christian Lord, he takes vicarious pleasure as restorer of the pagan gods, prophesying doom and castigating Christians (often for not being better ones!). Ostensibly down on Christianity and Puritanism—despite his Episcopalian upbringing—he is up on the Greek gods and Roman conquerors whose myths and fables fed his youth. But even at his most Dionysian, there is an evangelical fervor to his scathing pronouncements on the Galileans (as the Christians are called) of *Julian,* and on the "romantic-puritans" of our time who turn book reviewing into "pulpiteering.". . .

One can sympathize with Vidal's impatient attitude to the sloppy and transient sentiment that is often characterized as love; but without its aspects of empathy, the lusting after sex and power throughout his novels renders his characters ignoble, trivial, destructive, tragic, or (most outrageously in *Myra Breckinridge*) ludicrous. That they are all these as well as "stupid" is, apparently, what he has to say about their lustings, those commitments without compassion. But it is when empathy—implied mostly by its absence—is sought more explicitly that the earlier promises of a seriously engaged writer, a "great novelist," seem on the point of being realized, and fail. While Vidal's politics as expressed in both essays and novels is Socialist-humanist, it is accompanied by a bloodlessness, a defensive aloofness, lacking in the empathy of love. The fusion of sexes heralded in *Myra Breckenridge,* the bisexuality and androgyny to which Vidal has long given lip service, may also be taken as a metaphor for that mysterious mixture of lust and love, of assertion and compassion, which Vidal has not yet grasped or portrayed. Self-sufficient as the androgynous state may appear, and impossible as it is to achieve, its pursuit also suggests, at its fullest, an engagement of feeling that Vidal has so far not seemed willing to make. It is this elusiveness that makes his grappling with the two-headed monster, while entertaining, not entirely serious.

*Ann Morrissett Davidon, "Gore Vidal and the Two-Headed Monster," in* The Nation, *May 25, 1974, pp. 661-62.*

Telling the reading public that homosexuality is a recurrent theme in Vidal's fiction is almost like explaining to musicologists that the leitmotif is Richard Wagner's trademark. (p. 21)

Except for a few poetic passages in *The City and the Pillar,* Vidal has never approached homosexuality with either Genêt's lyrical rapture or Gide's silken diabolism. It is calculated barter where the language of exchange does not even require a translator's ear for idiom. Only to adolescents, thrown into each other's arms from fear of estrangement, is Vidal sympathetic; it is assumed that consenting adults are beyond pathos. (p. 27)

Now it is difficult to think of *The City and the Pillar* in terms of degeneration of any sort. . . . *The City and the Pillar* with its once-subtle distinctions between shrill transvestites and manly lovers, sentimental queens and introspective dreamers, is no longer the Baedeker for anyone journeying through the circles of the gay inferno. Vidal simply charted the terrain which others have apportioned. (p. 30)

If *The City and the Pillar* were merely the father of contemporary homosexual fiction, one should only accord it the homage patriarchs usually receive—a quick nod or a hasty genuflection. But within the Vidal canon it occupies a more significant position: *The City and the Pillar* reworks material from *Williwaw* and *In a Yellow Wood* into the myth of natural man as the original homoerotic. In homosexuality, Vidal discovered a crucible that could melt down his first two novels to their components—sexual rivalry and the lost boyhood dream. . . . A homosexual sensibility was completely absent from both novels; yet their themes—a rivalry between males that reduces the contestants to epicene tormenters, a friendship that ends when paths no longer converge—could easily form the basis of a homosexual novel if they were united as cause and effect.

But if, as Leslie Fiedler argued in *Love and Death in the American Novel* (1960), there is constant ritual warfare between the female as the dark intruder and the male as the fair defender of a sacred boyhood, then there is an even closer connection between a brawl over a bedmate and the termination of a friendship. In *The City and the Pillar,* Vidal restored these motifs to their original form, where they were part of a homoerotic paradise myth—an all-male Eden that ripens with purity and rots with experience.

In his depiction of this paradise before and after the fall, Vidal uses—and explodes—Mark Twain's symbols of the Mississippi boyhood: the cabin, the enchanted woods, the brown river, the barefoot boys defying mortality, and civilization as the meddling female. It is almost as if Vidal set out to write an anti-*Huckleberry Finn* merely to prove what Judge Brack said at the end of *Hedda Gabler:* "People don't do things like that!" (pp. 31-2)

In the essay, Fiedler alluded to "a recent book" of Vidal's where "an incipient homosexual, not yet aware of the implications of his feelings, indulges in the apt reverie of running off to sea with his dearest friend". . . .

Melville, Cooper, and Twain projected the popular concept of male friendship in its purest form; but it was a dream that could only exist in a Neverland that was pastoral enough to unsex the youths who romped through it. Admit a woman to the sylvan paradise and the cool form of boyhood begins to glower; remove the Arcadian illusion and the form becomes flesh.

In *The City and the Pillar,* . . . Jim and Bob are the Good Bad Boys demythologized who cannot endure the limits of the classic American friendship. (pp. 32-3)

[Today] *The City and the Pillar* is important as a mythic novel, not a homosexual one. (p. 38)

*The City and the Pillar* did prove that anyone who could crack the surface of *Huck Finn* and *The Last of the Mohicans* would eventually discover original sin. Vidal concluded it came into being when a pair of rebellious lads secularized the sacred rites of boyhood by enacting the forbidden parts of the rubrics. Read in the light of *Love and Death in the American Novel, The City and the Pillar* contains many of the recurrent themes Fiedler detected in Melville, Cooper, and Twain—the boyhood idyll, the intrusive woman, the miraculous sea, Cooper's redskin brother-surrogate for the white male in the guise of the red-haired Bob Ford, the lost frontier friendship. *The City and the Pillar* is the American wilderness novel demythologized; or rather it exposes the awesome truth the myth concealed. (p. 39)

In the opening pages of *Myra* [*Breckenridge,*] Vidal has made clear to those who have read Sartre and Robbe-Grillet (that blessed minority) exactly what he is doing. The novel is a joke, a literary and even an academic one. The recording of banality has become the apotheosis of banality, a characteristic of both the New Novel and the films of the forties. . . .

*Myra* is also a parody of literature, showing the nadir to which art can plunge when it abandons its canons. (pp. 152-53)

To anyone who respects symmetrical prose and subtle argumentation, Vidal's essays are nonpareil. Yet the essays exist in collections; while they are excerptable and eminently teachable as models of an all-but-abandoned-art, they do not add up to a full-scale work of nonfiction. (p. 192)

When it comes to fiction, Vidal is a classicist; his novels

are as plot-centered as Aristotle would want them to be—traditional, often intricate, but rarely innovative. It is his classicism, not his expatriation or even his charmed life, that sets him apart from his contemporaries. . . .

While his colleagues were innovating, bleeding over Vietnam, discovering entropy, and going with the flow, Vidal went about his business writing fiction with the proverbial beginning-middle-end, preferring to address himself to current affairs in his essays and quadrennial plays. Vidal the essayist faces the present, but Vidal the novelist looks to the past. The fact that *Why Are We in Vietnam?* (1967) appeared in the same year as *Washington, D.C.* not only crystallizes the difference between these two literary rivals but also explains why Mailer has become the voice of his generation while Vidal has become its mocking persona. Even *Myra,* which supposedly reflected the sexual freedom of the sixties, had more in common with the Age of Petronius than it did with the Age of Aquarius. (pp. 193-94)

Vidal has not published enough verse or short stories to qualify either as a poet or as a short story writer. But he has perfected his own brand of fiction—the literary novel with echoes from Crane, Melville, Twain, Cooper, the eighteenth-century *Bildungsroman,* futuristic fiction, the *Satyricon, Nausea,* the New Novel, and even the films of the forties now studied on the campus as "documents of the age." Despite his dislike for the theatre, *Visit to a Small Planet* (which has been anthologized in college readers) and *The Best Man* are extremely well-crafted. Technically, they are melodramas in Lillian Hellman's careful definition of the term—tautly constructed plays relying on conventions (sudden disclosures, chance occurrences) which naturalistic drama avoids but which can be valid if the tricks never become ends in themselves. (pp. 195-96)

*Bernard F. Dick, in his* The Apostate Angel: A Critical Study of Gore Vidal *(copyright © 1974 by Bernard F. Dick; reprinted by permission of Random House, Inc.), Random House, 1974.*

* * *

## VIERECK, Peter 1916-

**Viereck is a Pulitzer Prize-winning American poet, novelist, critic, and essayist. His poetry is conservative in form, witty, intelligent, and analytical. (See also *Contemporary Authors*, Vols. 1-4, rev. ed.)**

Mr. Viereck is a humanist who believes that poetry must communicate and that it must celebrate the emotional life, the life of meaning rather than gesture. He writes for the intelligent common reader, in the traditional forms he is intent on preserving. He writes with wit, spirit, conviction and a great understanding of history and modern Western culture—a culture whose increasing dehumanization and vulgarization he finds pernicious. His poetry ranges widely but is basically one of ideas, ideas often fleshed in fresh and surprising ways. Nevertheless, there are poems in [*New and Selected Poems: 1932-1967*] which, for me, never get off the ground. I believe the trouble lies partly in the use of metaphors that are turgid and come thick and fast, and partly in the versification, which employs severely regular meters and end-stopped lines in conjunction with very close, frequent rhyme and alliteration. Not that any of these devices are unintentional . . . [but] deliberate or not, it sometimes works against him, especially in intellectually complex poems, which seem to need a larger, more flexible, basic unit than the single line. Since then, however, Mr. Viereck has written some poems of far greater suppleness, including some in blank verse, a form he handles admirably. ("Frutta" and "A Walk on Moss" . . . .) Here the images flow as naturally as waves, and the poems move by stanza rather than line. And then there is the last, previously uncollected, sequence, "Five Walks on the Edge," which seems to me the best thing Mr. Viereck has done. Technically, it is a brilliant and varied tour de force, but it is really the fluent lyricism which makes it the wonderful work it is.

*Lisel Mueller, in* Shenandoah *(copyright by* Shenandoah; *reprinted from* Shenandoah: *The Washington and Lee University Review with the permission of the Editor), Spring, 1968, pp. 66-7.*

It isn't easy . . . to mistake a poem by Peter Viereck. Impulse in the saddle, with unbounded energy raring to take on any subject, is the outstanding impression one gets from his work. Playing the role of Poet as Broncobuster (of Pegasus, of course), he frequently takes his reader for a wild ride from which he alone, the poet, returns. And when the reader does manage to hang on, he is apt to find himself soaring from the plain of reasonable discourse into a realm of Higher Jugglery, somewhat like Marc Chagall's world of identified flying objects.

There is fortunately, however, another Viereck, the memorable one, who can and does rein his mount in tightly after the wilder rides. This happens often enough to make the present collection [*New and Selected Poems*], old and new poems spanning a thirty-year period, worth the time of anyone concerned with the question: who are our memorable poets?

*Ernest Kroll, in* Michigan Quarterly Review, *Summer, 1969, p. 204.*

On a first reading, Peter Viereck's poetry seems to have great variety. This apparent diversity, however, is not characteristic. For, as he once said, to him "A key word is 'obsessive'"; and in his first book of verse this word and its derivatives appear at least five times. The phrase "obsessive crystals" from "A Walk on Snow" in *Terror and Decorum* describes his consistency in theme, idea, technique, and subject matter. An important obsessive crystal is "Manhattan classicism," a term Viereck coined to name the type of poetry which he thought he and other poets of his generation were writing. . . .

[Four] requirements [of "Manhattan classicism"] in form and content—"traditional forms and metrics," clarity, ethical responsibility, and lyrical passion—Viereck summed up in 1966 in the phrase "strict wildness": it means "spontaneous absent-mindedness accompanied by the strictest, most conscious discipline of craftsmanship." . . .

In Viereck's poetry "form" means, first of all, conventional stanzas, rhyme, and meter. "Free verse I write not at all," he said in 1949, "on principle". . . . (pp. 33-4)

Viereck frequently writes long poems—perhaps because they more easily convey ideas. In 1950 he thought that, in his "*typical* poem," "lyrical emotions and philosophical ideas are equally present and are fused into unity by expressing the ideas in sensuous metaphors." "Mine," he continued, "is a poetry of ideas." . . . His first volume of verse won praise for its fertility of idea; but much of its content was an intellectual "classicism" from which he has moved away. In much of his work since then his best poetry is romantically sensuous; in spirit, style, and idea his poetry is like that of Yeats and also like that of the modern American romantic poet Hart Crane. (p. 35)

For Viereck "Manhattan classicism," or the "baroque synthesis," was a term under which he subsumed the characteristics of his revolt against revolt. It meant coming to terms with contemporary life, using urban materials—the heart, spirit, and mind of urban man as well as (early) actual urban landmarks and machines. It meant also "clarity," explicit and meaningful statements about "intellectual and moral values implied by the content." And, finally, it meant "exacting forms," "traditional metrics," and, within these, "romantic wildness of music and lyrical passion . . ." . . . . In Viereck's verse this "romantic classicism" means themes such as the supreme importance of man and love, beauty, and poetry in the face of the "mystery of mortality." (p. 37)

Viereck retains a touch of [his] early comic manner—one transmuted with a delight in the indecorous—in his mature, serious poetry. . . .

Restoring "fun" and "human-ness" to poetry is to Viereck one of his central poetic functions, and in his best poems the tone is often still jocose but with a serious intention. (p. 40)

Like many twentieth-century men who fiercely refuse the panacea of any "friend in the sky" and who also share what has been called the modern world's "amazement at the silence of God," Viereck remains bound to earth and humanity. But . . . Viereck does not negate; he affirms vigorously, sadly, and joyously "that life cannot be altered for the better either by retreat from humanity or by superimposing on man the authority of any institution, stately or godly." (p. 41)

With his fondness for a variety of forms, his wealth of ideas, and his ability to cull quotations from other writers, Viereck would be better at putting together a commonplace book than trying to write one around a single theme. For in prose the problem of form is one that he has not solved. Both *Metapolitics* and *Conservatism Revisited* lacked it to some extent; *Shame and Glory* lacks it completely. . . . [All] attempts to evaluate the book involve Viereck's prose style. Hortatory, exclamatory, imperative, subjunctival, rhetorical, bombastic, pun- and fun-loving, it is characteristically crammed with coinages, paradoxical linkings, and other devices. (pp. 93-4)

As a poet Viereck is justly praised for his "audio-imagination," but he has little ear for sound in prose. It is heavy, Germanic, reminiscent of Carlyle or Nietzsche. (p. 103)

In estimating Viereck's . . . prose works, one must, first, concede that he is important to American intellectual life, even though he is not an original thinker or a writer of organized books. Students of political science, writers of intellectual history, historians of contemporary times, and journalists cite his works, object to his opinions, honor his concepts, and acknowledge him as a leading new conservative. Writing easily and seldom rewriting, Viereck has, of course, no faultless book. *Conservatism: From John Adams to Churchill,* the text of which he worked over carefully, shows his possible prose economy. But it is his poetry, not his prose, which he constantly revises and rearranges. He writes prose out of a sense of duty, an impulse to "do good." No more than a breeze can Peter Viereck "sit" and choose not to act. In his prose books many turbulent ideas are poured out with energy and exuberance. On occasion he makes careful discriminations, expositions, and definitions. (p. 124)

As a stimulant to thought and intellectual self-examination, Viereck has been read and reread for his humane and wise overview of life.

Viereck's place in American literature, however, is established by his poetry, not his prose. The forms, attitudes, subjects, and themes . . . result in many excellent poems that stand in today's literature along with the best work of his contemporaries: Richard Wilbur, Robert Lowell, and Theodore Roethke. Speaking trees and tree-girls are uniquely Viereck. He is also notable for metaphor, phrase and line arrangements, as well as for unexpected juxtapositions. (p. 126)

His diction is varied but not precious; his syntax is straightforward and conversational; he seldom reverts to inversion. The simplicity of the diction and syntax in some of his recent verse is, indeed, its success. . . .

This punctiliousness of diction, careful line arrangement, and exact images are what one remembers about his poems. . . . Most importantly, Viereck's development in poetry has been away from a stress on ideas, simile, metaphor, and content for their own sake toward a pure rhythmical lyricism. In 1959 he said that he often had "the rhythm earlier than the words. . . ." Nonetheless, his early verse tended to be, though versatile, conventional in rhythm. Since the mid-1950's, rhythmical patterns have increasingly conveyed the meaning in his best work. (p. 127)

*Marie Henault, in her* Peter Viereck *(copyright 1969 by Twayne Publishers, Inc.; reprinted by permission of Twayne Publishers, a Division of G. K. Hall & Co.), Twayne, 1969.*

* * *

## VONNEGUT, Kurt, Jr. 1922-

**Vonnegut, an American novelist, fantasy writer, short story writer, and playwright, is one of America's best-known and most influential writers of fiction. His great achievement has been the combination of black humor and science fiction to form a powerful commentary on contemporary culture and its destiny. (See also *Contemporary Authors*, Vols. 1-4, rev. ed.)**

For years the literary establishment viewed Kurt Vonnegut, Jr., as a writer of science fiction, certainly nobody to be taken seriously. In 1969 when *Slaughterhouse-Five* was published, critics seemed confused. The novel did contain flying saucers and robots, but its protagonist, Billy Pilgrim, seemed more concerned with problems of morality and religious faith. What was a science fiction writer doing writing a modern sequel to *Pilgrim's Progress?* A reading of Vonnegut's earlier novels reveals that rather than a science fiction writer, he has always been a social critic whose marked use of ambivalence and complex personas serves as an objective correlative with which to present his view of man and man's proper role in the universe.

One point that must be stressed is that Vonnegut is a novelist and not a theologian. If his readers keep this in mind, they will find it easier to grapple with the implications of Vonnegut's intermingling of Old Testament and New Testament characters in his novels, especially the intriguing relationship between an Old Testament Jonah figure and a New Testament Messiah or Jesus figure. Vonnegut's protagonists in at least four of his novels assume the role of a Jonah figure when urged to follow . . . a course of action by a Messiah figure. . . . Apparently for Vonnegut Jonah's most significant characteristic is his marked passivity, especially when contrasted with the Messiah figure. While Vonnegut indicates that the Jonah and Messiah figures are polar in intentions while achieving the same end and carrying the same message, he does not clarify the precise nature of this relationship or how it varies from novel to novel. The many parallels in Vonnegut's fiction to various other aspects of the biblical Jonah tale, particularly the conception of human and divine love, offer possible answers to these questions. . . .

[There] is a definite progression from a situation in which a Jonah figure faces a hostile world with only an ineffectual, indifferent, or even hostile Messiah figure to help him, to a situation in *God Bless You, Mr. Rosewater* in which the Jonah figure has the full support and encouragement of Kilgore Trout. . . . Yet, even though this self-confessed Jesus figure expresses his full support for Eliot [Rosewater], he does not follow the young altruist's example. . . . The difference between the two now becomes clear. While Eliot lives by Trout's precepts and becomes an altruist, Trout . . . accepts a job within the corrupt society and receives something in return for the gifts he dispenses. . . . Vonnegut is ambiguous, but at this point it appears that Trout is speaking for the author and that his words are more important than his actions.

Vonnegut appears to believe that whether or not man lives in a godless universe is really inconsequential. What man must do is to seek to create a better world in which human love and compassion are paramount.

*Stanley Schatt, "The Whale and the Cross: Vonnegut's Jonah and Christ Figures," in* Southwest Review, *Winter, 1971, pp. 29-42.*

The life of [*Cat's Cradle*] is in its movement, the turns of plot, of character, and of phrase which give it vitality. Vonnegut's prose has the same virtues as his characterization and plotting. It is deceptively simple, suggestive of the ordinary, but capable of startling and illuminating twists and turns. He uses the rhetorical potential of the short sentence and short paragraph better than anyone now writing, often getting a rich comic or dramatic effect by isolating a single sentence in a separate paragraph or excerpting a phrase from context for a bizarre chapter-heading. The apparent simplicity and ordinariness of his writing masks its efficient power, so that we are often startled when Vonnegut pounces on a tired platitude or cliché like a benevolent mongoose and shakes new life into it. . . .

Despite his mastery of the prose medium and a sense of the ridiculous which is always on duty, Vonnegut never abandons himself to relentless verbal cleverness. . . . Sometimes we may wrongly suspect him of this kind of self-indulgence, as in the opening sentence of *Cat's Cradle*—"Call me Jonah"—which seems like a gratuitous though delightful parody of the opening of Moby Dick, until we realize that by invoking Jonah and his whale, along with the biblical leviathan, Vonnegut is preparing us for a story on the Job theme. . . .

Vonnegut's prose always serves his vision and helps to make narrative structures of that vision. This process is illustrated nicely by a longish passage from the introduction he wrote in 1966 for the new edition of *Mother Night*. In it he speaks of his actual experience as a prisoner of war in Dresden, in prose which has the lucidity of the best journalism enriched with poetic resources of a born story-teller. (One falls naturally into the word "speaks" in discussing this prose, which gives a strong sense of a voice behind the words.) . . .

In Vonnegut, as in his contemporaries, we do not find the rhetoric of moral certainty, which has generally been a distinguishing characteristic of the satirical tradition. The writers of modern dark comedy do not seek the superior position of the traditional moralists. Nor do they point to other times and customs as repositories of moral values, or to any traditional system as The Law. Even in essaying to abstract a moral from his own book, Vonnegut makes no special claim for its virtues, or his. The book itself must be the test. Our experience of it must be satisfying and healthy. If this is so, then it may nourish our consciences without requiring reduction to a formula. My feeling is that, far from manifesting sickness (as some critics seem to feel it does), Black Humor is a sign of life and health.

*Robert Scholes, "'Mithridates, he died old': Black Humor and Kurt Vonnegut, Jr.," in* The Sounder Few: Essays from the "Hollins Critic," *edited by R. H. W. Dillard, George Garrett, and John Rees Moore, University of Georgia Press, 1971, pp. 173-85.*

The universe of Kurt Vonnegut's novels is a hostile and ridiculous one, in which a sense of humor and an eye for the absurd are necessary. The humanist in Vonnegut is often defeated by the pessimist in a continuous teleological tug-of-war. The tussle is to decide whether or not there is any meaning in Stonehenge beyond its ironic and essentially useless message to the Tralfamadorian messenger, whether the destruction of the earth by fire or ice would subtract from a universal total, or merely exchange some frozen popsicles or charred hunks of steak for a figure that already adds up to zero. (p. 1)

Except for the brilliant *Sirens of Titan* and its implication of nothingness, each of Vonnegut's novels indicates a belief in a meaningful universe, and each of his heroes (again with the exception of *Sirens*)—Proteus, Howard W. Campbell, Jr., Jonah, Rosewater, and Billy—is a modern pilgrim engaged in an uncertain quest along an unmapped route. Although the pilgrim often must go it alone, Vonnegut provides an unusually large number of messiahs, real and phony, major and minor, to aid in the quest. [Not] surprisingly, the first one, Winston Niles Rumfoord, is as deluded as those he seeks to lead, yet his messianic intentions, if a bit cynical, are nonetheless sincere. He is out to prove to the inhabitants of Earth that their old religions are useless and myopic, while his at least has the benefit of being headed by someone who can see into the future. (pp. 1-2)

The next major messiah to appear is, of course, Lionel Boyd Johnson, alias Bokonon. His contributions seem more substantial, because they are based on love and compassion for others, but they are basically as cynical and turn out to be as illusory as Rumfoord's. (p. 3)

Vonnegut's aims in this respect seem clear. He is attempting to show, in *Sirens* and *Cat's Cradle,* the futility of, first, metaphysics, and then organized religion, while conceding the comforting qualities of each. And each time he is employing the satirist's weapon of dystopian divorcement to remove his targets from the battleground of uncomfortable reality. The character and role of Kilgore Trout, the next messiah, seems somewhat less clear. When he first appears in *Rosewater* it seems apparent that if he is not actually the reincarnation of Jesus Christ, representing the ineffectuality of the Christian ethic today, he is at least a Christ figure. . . . If one interprets Eliot's recovery from his nervous breakdown and subsequent acknowledgement of all the bastards of Rosewater County, Indiana, as a triumph, then Trout must be given at least part of the credit for it, which would make him the most effective messiah in the novels. This is the impression one gets from *Rosewater.* However, in the next novel, Vonnegut goes to some length to vitiate this impression by showing his "cracked messiah" at Billy Pilgrim's eighteenth wedding anniversary party, "gobbling canapes, . . . talking with a mouthful of Philadelphia cream cheese and salmon roe to an optometrist's wife," and in general playing the litterateur among the peasantry. . . . In the basically absurd world of Vonnegut's writing, it would be asking too much of any person to make perfect sense. (pp. 4-5)

With the exception of *Player Piano,* which contains a political messiah, Paul Proteus, each of Vonnegut's novels has at least one figure who is concerned with the theological well-being of the race, even if, like Rumfoord, he is a Machiavel, or like Bokonon, a fraud, or, as Billy Pilgrim says of Trout in a moment of candor, "his prose [is] frightful."

One hesitates to draw more implications from this extensive use of the messiah other than the obvious one that Vonnegut, like Hesse, is a writer who is interested in theological problems and thus by including characters who represent various forms of the Promised One is able to comment on His illusory nature, yet indicate a yearning for Him nonetheless. . . .

There is indeed a definite tendency away from nihilism and toward some sort of tentative affirmation in the . . . novels. . . . Placing the first book [*Player Piano*] in the category of "preparation," it is possible to make the following analysis of the thematic progress of his work:

*The Sirens of Titan*—Early disillusionment
*Mother Night*—Preoccupation with guilt
*Cat's Cradle*—Folly of collective answers such as religion
*God Bless You, Mr. Rosewater*—Possibility of individual answers
*Slaughterhouse-Five*—Mature acceptance of man's condition (p. 5)

It is difficult to understand why Vonnegut was dismissed for so long with the disreputable title of science-fiction writer, since from the very beginning he has been dealing with metaphysical, ethical, and epistemological questions in his work. One must conclude that his imagination and talent for eccentric detail actually worked against him with the critics, who rarely looked beneath the surface gloss to the rugged terrain underneath. On first reading, the intricate plot and fascinating detail of *The Sirens of Titan* can indeed obscure the serious intent and probing, if not traditionally scholarly examination of the cosmological question. Vonnegut, after all, is a novelist, not an academician or a philosopher, and he deals with theme in the manner of a creative writer—with all the stylistic devices at his command. Certainly he is fond of space ships, time travel, and other gimmickry, but these phenomena, after all, represent the latter half of the twentieth century far better than would the riverboat journeys of Twain, the small town life of Sherwood Anderson, or the physical encounters with death of Ernest Hemingway. At any rate, neither Vonnegut's motives nor techniques need be defended in a discussion of his themes, which are without doubt as respectable a collection as could be found anywhere in the modern American novel. (pp. 6-7)

*David H. Goldsmith, in his* Kurt Vonnegut: Fantasist of Fire and Ice, *Bowling Green University Popular Press, 1972.*

In spite of the numerous articles appearing on the work of Kurt Vonnegut, Jr., certain aspects of his fiction consistently seem to be ignored or misinterpreted. One such element is what David H. Goldsmith [in *Kurt Vonnegut: Fantasist of Fire and Ice*] calls a "teleological tug-of-war," in his discussion of the "messiahs" that he finds prevalent in Vonnegut's work. To refer to such characters as Bokonon, Malachi Constant, Eliot Rosewater, and Kilgore Trout as "messianic" seems at least an irresponsible use of the term. . . . Goldsmith's assumption that the Vonnegut characters are theologically concerned is open to strong disagreement. . . .

Perhaps Goldsmith and others have tended to ignore the obvious in Vonnegut, seeking instead to raise certain of his characters to more resonant, mythic dimensions, such as the messianic. But the most recurring Biblical reference in Vonnegut's works is to Jonah. It is tempting to consider Jonah one of the earliest representatives of the absurd antihero in Western literature. As a man protesting his fate, seeing no meaning in it, finding that all his attempts to escape his destiny merely contribute to its fulfillment, Jonah's story concludes with his still not understanding the bizarre events in his life. It would seem that anyone familiar with Vonnegut's writing could not overlook this parallel. . . .

Vonnegut's main characters, from Paul Proteus and Ed Finnerty in his first novel *Player Piano,* to Billy Pilgrim in *Slaughterhouse-Five,* are caught, "like bugs in amber." But there does seem to be a greater degree of rebellion expressed against the Jonah-role in his earlier works. Confusion, dismay, active rebellion and final frustration are more applicable to the characters in *Player Piano, Sirens of Titan, Mother Night,* and even *Cat's Cradle* than to Eliot Rosewater and Billy Pilgrim in Vonnegut's last two novels. But this does not necessarily lead to Mr. Goldsmith's conclusion that there is "a definite tendency away from nihilism and toward some sort of tentative affirmation" in the progression of novels. Neither *God Bless You, Mr. Rosewater* nor *Slaughterhouse-Five* bears this out. . . .

Because Trout is portrayed as a misunderstood, overlooked science-fiction writer, one could easily assume that he speaks for Vonnegut. But to view Trout as either messiah/prophet or Vonnegut-mouthpiece is, seemingly, to deny Vonnegut's depiction of writers throughout all his works, as well as the special circumstances surrounding Trout in *God Bless You, Mr. Rosewater.*

I think it can be adequately argued that Vonnegut has never portrayed a writer in simplistic or totally favorable terms. . . .

He consistently portrays the masses, the "little people" like the Diana Moon Glampers, as grotesque or despicable, or just stupid, unthinking sheep. But he also creates main characters who, for all their wit or intelligence or superior powers, are just as caught, "like bugs in amber," as their followers. In fact, to further the Jonah theme, when the main characters act as leaders, they merely serve to act as catalysts for the inevitable doom, neither proving nor improving anything. . . .

In contrast to Goldsmith, I would suggest that Vonnegut's most affirmative passage, if not most affirmative work, is in his second novel, *The Sirens of Titan.*

*Joyce Nelson, "Vonnegut and 'Bugs in Amber'," in* Journal of Popular Culture, *Winter, 1973, pp. 551-57.*

For better or for worse, Vonnegut's science-fiction stories [published in popular magazines during the 1950's] read at times like television situation comedies. The hallmark of these stories is that although technology changes, sociology remains the same. Familiar people encountering a new life have nevertheless familiar problems. . . .

By far the greater majority of Vonnegut's stories feature no science or technology at all, and are simple, sometimes sentimental tales of middle-class America. . . . Most are written from a very stable point of view, that of an average citizen, often "a salesman of storm windows and doors, and here and there a bathtub enclosure.". . .

Vonnegut wrote these stories, dozens of them, from a consistently middle-class point of view. This point of view is often their best asset, offering Vonnegut some of his strongest plots, clearest themes, and funniest lines. The middle-class slant is not simply a requirement of the form; if we look at Vonnegut's nonfictional work, we will see that it is an integral part of his expression. . . . Daily life as a measure of judgment pervades Vonnegut's work. High school, big and small business, are frequent standards: so is family life. . . .

When Vonnegut criticizes middle-class American life, he does not do it from a position of superiority. In *God Bless You, Mr. Rosewater* Eliot's sophisticated wife is herself criticized because "She had never seen Rosewater County, had no idea what a night-crawler was, did not know that land anywhere could be so deathly flat, that people anywhere could be so deathly dull." Vonnegut knows it well, and, like Asa Leventhal in Bellow's *The Victim,* is frequently mindful of that part of humanity which "did not get away with it," in this case those who have not escaped the Middle West. . . .

The most conclusive proofs for Vonnegut as a spokesman of the middle class are that he does not view himself as an intellectual writer, and that in fact much of his material is grossly anti-intellectual. In *Player Piano* he expressed the same aversion to rule by "experts" that Richard Hofstadter [in *Anti-Intellectualism in American Life*] says anchors anti-intellectualism in middle-class American life. . . .

Vonnegut's major novels speak against man's position as romantic center of the universe, a posture which makes him responsible for all evil and hence hopelessly alienated from himself. When Vonnegut applies the same distinctions to youth he is clearly repeating statements characteristic of his writing for middle-class magazines. He is a pacifist; he distrusts the unbridled intellect; he argues for simple, humane values. All are elements of a fundamental American decency, dating to his childhood in the 1930's and sustained in his writing of the 1950's, which perhaps in the last decade has been submerged under new forces and ideas against which youth rightly protests. When Vonnegut so accurately reflects that protest, it should be no surprise that he is forty-eight years old, has kids, a car, and pays his bills on time. He is simply speaking for its ultimate origins.

*Jerome Klinkowitz, "Why They Read Vonnegut," in* The Vonnegut Statement, *edited by Jerome Klinkowitz and John Somer (copyright © 1973 by Jerome Klinkowitz and John Somer; used with permission of Delacorte Press/Seymour Lawrence), Dell-Delta, 1973, pp. 18-30.*

The great psychic migration of American youth since World War II can be charted by the novels they read and the novelists whose reputations they created: Jack Kerouac and the Beats for getting out of plastic suburbia and On the Road. Beginning a search for authenticity and soul, for poetry not spindled on the printed page and dissected by Footnote Kings but hurled from a lectern by a reeling Dylan Thomas, chanted at jazz and poetry concerts, wailed out of jukeboxes by Hank Williams, Lightnin' Hopkins, Creedence Clearwater, and Bob Dylan. Kerouac and the Beats represent the psychic revolt of the 1950's; J. D. Salinger represents the inner flight from McCarthyism, from the Corporation, from the Other-Directed self: the lacerating self-consciousness of Holden Caulfield and the Glass family.

Then Golding and *Lord of the Flies* for the early 1960's, with a vision of human limitation and capacity for evil that matched the 1950's generation's sense of helplessness before the rapidly escalating cold war and certain bomb at the end of it all. We also dug Golding because of the classy symbolism, so neat and easy to figure out: see, we can be New Critics too.

Then somewhere in the late 1960's Kurt Vonnegut, Ken Kesey, and Joseph Heller took a generation's consciousness on a sharp left turn down the crooked road to the absurd. Yet it was a recognition of the absurd that was not a surrender to meaninglessness but a wholehearted, raucous Bronx cheer for the false pieties and Aesopean language of rampant technology and the cold war. . . .

The structural discontinuities (which are really a new continuity) and radical juxtapositions of space fantasy and homely everyday existence in Vonnegut's novels catch the imagination of a generation born and bred to the TV montage reality of contemporary life. Moving from his early formula short stories through his novels, Vonnegut has perfected his version of what I call social surrealism, a fictional technique utilizing the radical juxtapositions, nonspatial time sense (i.e., the world of dreams), and radical irony for purposes of social satire. The social surrealist sensibility flickers like heat lightning in the films of Godard and Fellini; the novels of Thomas Pynchon, Jakov Lind, Friedrich Dürrenmatt, Günter Grass, and Joseph Heller; in the music of Country Joe MacDonald, Bob Dylan, and Frank Zappa; in the incredible put-on *Esquire* reportage and novels of Terry Southern and Dan Wakefield. . . .

Vonnegut's fictional method of radical juxtaposition is a product of his richly comic sense of the absurd. . . . To Vonnegut and his audience, the noble, isolated grandeur of classic tragedy is no longer possible in an age of concentration camps and mass death by bombing. Tragicomedy is the style of the age, a style that establishes the juxtapositions of *God Bless You, Mr. Rosewater, Slaughterhouse-Five, Dr. Strangelove, Bonnie and Clyde, Little Big Man,* Lenny Bruce's Masked Man, and Country Joe and the Fish's "Fixin' to Die Rag.". . .

Basically, a comic recognition of the absurd is a counter-strategy, giving the absurd meaning. Vonnegut's ordinary-language echoes of this recognition *place* the absurd, fit it into the everyday affairs of his characters. From *Mother Night* to *Slaughterhouse-Five,* the absurd is ordered around by "Hi Ho," "So be it," "Busy, busy, busy," "So it goes." Vonnegut's uneasy canonization by the Yippies, for example, makes perfect sense; both Abbie Hoffman and Vonnegut use the put-on, radical irony, as an analytical tool for stripping away the masks of the absurd. Paul Krassner, founder of the archetypal underground magazine *The Realist,* seems to be writing most newspaper headlines. . . .

[Students] talk about Vonnegut's world, his *mythos.* They react to him as a myth-maker and fabulist rather than as a dramatic and narrative novelist. Vonnegut hangs ideas on his fables, making them easily accessible to young readers. In this sense, he is no science-fiction writer; science fiction as such is part of his store of fables. Vonnegut uses Kilgore Trout, his invented science-fiction writer, as one of many *voices,* voices speaking multidimensional fables. . . .

The literature of aesthetic alienation and escape-into-art doesn't go down very well with a generation struggling for physical and ecological survival. Vonnegut's fables get a leg up on present dizzying reality, and that's what this generation of readers wants. . . .

And yet I get disquieting evidence that many of Vonnegut's younger readers appreciate him for not quite the right reasons. While his techniques may be hip, his morality is strictly sober middle class. In this respect, he greatly resembles George Orwell, the Orwell who returned to a solid assertion of basic middle-class values in *Keep the Aspidistra Flying.* Certainly Vonnegut's recurring fictional themes hit at the central concerns of his readers—runaway technology, the enormity of evil, a detestation of the rich and their indifference to human need and want. . . .

Above all, however, Vonnegut's readers appreciate his act of bringing fiction out into the streets, making it easily available in cheap paperbacks full of inventive, teasing fables and metaphysical tomfoolery. He's not afraid of sentimentality, salting it down, though, with acerbic absurdist humor—a tonality of irony that matches perfectly the watchful, wary irony of a generation choking in corporate solemnity.

*Jess Ritter, "Teaching Kurt Vonnegut on the Firing Line," in* The Vonnegut Statement, *edited by Jerome Klinkowitz and John Somer (copyright © 1973 by Jerome Klinkowitz and John Somer; used with permission of Delacorte Press/Seymour Lawrence), Dell-Delta, 1973, pp. 31-42.*

While it is true, to a great extent, that the times have finally caught up with Vonnegut, part of his emergence as a major figure, as should now be clear, must be credited simply to his growth and improvement as a writer. Though heresy to admit, it is nonetheless accurate, I think, to observe that the benign neglect of Vonnegut's first decade as a writer was partially justified. Here was a marvelously original but erratic writer. He was a "skilled seducer" in the making, but a long way from fulfilling his potential, tempering steadily in the hard-nosed slick and exploding mass-circulation-paperback trade, a uniquely modern professional initiation. . . .

[The] maturing of Vonnegut's comic-satiric vision, his feeling for, or just plain synchrony with, the Zeitgeist, and his improving technical finesse must be considered as dominant factors in the upswing of his fortunes. At a time when critics such as Susan Sontag and Richard Poirier were learning to appreciate the Beatles and the Supremes *as well as* Bach, and comic strips as well as Shakespeare—without shame—and were providing sophisticated justifications for such tastes, Vonnegut could begin to assume something of a position merely as a "pop" writer. The age of "pop" was at hand. But Vonnegut was more than just a pop writer; he was the thinking man's pop writer. He was an American writer who was actually writing about ideas and incorporating contemporary experiences in his work; and his basic assumptions, his attitudes and prejudices, were, as Benjamin DeMott has pointed out [in "Vonnegut's Otherworldly Laughter," *Saturday Review,* May 1, 1971], "perfectly tuned to the mind of the emergent generation. To the surging youth culture, the proper conduct of life, man's inhumanity to man, and the possibility of the end of the world, were and are viable issues. And Vonnegut as fatalistic moralist, cynical pacifist, holy atheist, anti-intellectual philosopher, apocalyptic futurist, and grim humorist complexly encompassed all the right paradoxes.

And not only that: but, more important, I think, than anyone has yet to emphasize, Vonnegut had latched on to a truly original contemporary idiom, as American as TV or napalm or napalm-abhorrers, as fragmented and discontinuous as contemporary experience. A consideration of Vonnegut's idiom, I would say, should take into account everything from his great ear, his sense of the way Americans talk, his sense of timing (as active and keen as Paul McCartney's—a compliment one does not bestow lightly), to his formal idiosyncrasies, beginning with *Mother Night* in 1961: the short chapter form; the sharp image; the short, quick scene; the fragmented time sequence; the speed of narration generated by these formal characteristics. If one were to play Marshall McLuhan here, one might point out that Vonnegut's fiction is a clever formal approximation of, or at least shares many elements of the experience of, watching television. This might offer another explanation for Vonnegut's appeal to the TV generation, those who have *always* had television, not to mention those of us, more or less aged, who, according to McLuhan, have also had our sense ratios hopelessly rearranged by it.

*Joe David Bellamy, "Kurt Vonnegut for President: The Making of an Academic Reputation," in* The Vonnegut Statement, *edited by Jerome Klinkowitz and John Somer (copyright © 1973 by Jerome Klinkowitz and John Somer; used with permission of Delacorte Press/Seymour Lawrence), Dell-Delta, 1973, pp. 71-89.*

Vonnegut's first novel, *Player Piano,* is one of the best science-fiction novels ever written, and it rests uneasily in the science-fiction genre precisely because it is such a good novel—a novel, that is, in the Jamesian sense, a detailed examination of human experience. The devotee of science fiction comes away from *Player Piano* with the uneasy feeling that somehow this isn't science fiction at all, that there is something wrong here. What is wrong here is that someone finally wrote a science-fiction novel that puts the emphasis on characters—upon human experience and actions. . . . What Vonnegut has done in *Player Piano* is to turn conventional science fiction inside out. Science fiction traditionally, as literature of idea, works from the premise that in the beginning was the idea. . . . At its normal best, the characters still manage somehow either to get in the way of the ideas being developed or to get all but ignored in the rush to develop those ideas. Vonnegut's inversion is simply to have realized that people are the most important things in both the real and the fictional universe. He begins, not with the idea, but with Paul Proteus, possibly the most solidly realized character in all of science fiction. . . .

Throughout the novel the emphasis remains on the frailties, the failings, the small heroisms, the tiny joys and gigantic sorrows which make up the experience of all the characters of the book, from Dr. Paul Proteus and his wife, Anita, right down to the small boy who sails paper boats when the fire hydrants are flushed down in Homestead. Science provides the conflict, but Vonnegut resolves his novel with people being basically the same, with universal elements being put up against the test—in this case a very contemporary one. . . .

It is . . . through [his] very "noticing" of technology that Vonnegut manages to get across much of what he has to say. The *idea* paramount in *Player Piano* is simply what Vonnegut has stated it to be—that machines frequently get the best of it. . . . Conventional writers may choose to ignore the technological infringement upon our lives and grope faint-heartedly for the cause of the dismay in the lives of their characters. Vonnegut knows the cause, and for him the communication of the idea of *Player Piano,* and of nearly all his works, has been to admit that science exists and has become vastly important to our lives. The communication of such an idea would not be easy to accomplish without the techniques of science fiction. Therefore Vonnegut both philosophizes and characterizes, and when a statement is made, it draws as much importance from who says it, and how, as from the idea itself. Context is as important as content. . . .

The absurd, alienated nature of the universe is dealt with in each novel, always with some new depth of perception, some new slant; characters from the short stories and the earlier novels find their way into the later works. The same city, Ilium, in upstate New York, remains a central symbol of the twisted future of mankind. . . .

The concretizing of abstract ideas has always been a major goal of art; perhaps the most abstract and important idea of all has been the question of the ultimate destiny of the human race. This has been a constantly reiterated theme of artists through the ages. In dealing with this motif, Vonnegut has most clearly illustrated his ability to integrate science fiction into the mainstream of literature. There is in his work a constant effort to project something of today as it must become if the human race continues into its insane self-created future.

*Karen and Charles Wood, "The Vonnegut Effect: Science Fiction and Beyond," in* The Vonnegut Statement, *edited by Jerome Klinkowitz and John Somer (copyright © 1973 by Jerome Klinkowitz and John Somer; used with permission of Delacorte Press/Seymour Lawrence), Dell-Delta, 1973, pp. 133-57.*

[In such displays as the catalog of "twinkling treasures" littering the streets of Ilium, in *Player Piano,* pp. 290-91,] Vonnegut begins to suggest that his real literary interests lie in the *nonliterary,* in the inarticulate, the subliterary. He begins to suggest, indeed, that his real mode will be more polyphonic than the conventional novel, more expansive in its range of human expression, more interested in the puns, alliteration, and aphorisms of vernacular speech, less concerned with sequential plot, developed and motivated character, coherent explanations. In short, the mode for which Vonnegut is searching through the wreckage of *Player Piano*'s Ilium is the old popular oral mode of the storyteller expanded by the varied artifacts of print and electronic communications. . . .

There is no way to assess the value, then, of the artifacts of expression Vonnegut gives us. Like rocks brought back from the moon, these artifacts could help us understand untold histories if we could only reconstruct the experience represented in each—every word, phrase, sentence, however common. . . .

By accepting . . . expressive artifacts—all those sermons, prayers, speeches, letters, advertisements, chants, poems, doggerels, mnemonics, stories, tales, legends, scholarly extracts, photographs, paintings, statues, architecture, decorations—*The Sirens of Titan* invades the uniform, lineal, and merely visual universe of McLuhan's Gutenberg Galaxy. By investing all such artifacts with value, Vonnegut consecrates the verbal and physical objects, the furniture, of human existence. As a writer he becomes an "interior decorator," that most useful of artists as Vonnegut once called them in a speech. By such resacralizing he brings man back into the center of his existence, like the tribal man who exists in an acoustical enclosed space, unlike the punctual, civilized, literate man who exists in a vast linear universe that stretches perspectivistically and infinitely beyond him. . . .

Robert Scholes has said that Vonnegut, as a black humorist, cannot employ the "rhetoric of moral certainty" found in the tradition of satire to which Vonnegut has also been allied. But if Vonnegut is a black humorist, he certainly does not suffer from the ethical unease Scholes attributes to that mode. As a popular writer in a naïve mode, Vonnegut employs not the rhetoric but the *sententiae* of moral certainty. At its highest the naïve mode Vonnegut has regenerated achieves what somewhere Northrop Frye has called the "aphoristic pinnacle of *sententiae*," though Vonnegut's aphorisms are appropriately hip to the new indeterminate world we have made. . . .

From *Player Piano* to *The Sirens of Titan,* Vonnegut moves from a traditional mode, associated with a visual model of the world, to a new mode that begins to re-create an acoustic model. He also moves from an almost reflexive analysis of what McLuhan calls the major themes of mass culture, mechanics and sex, to a much more conscious, albeit fantastic, effort to create a world in which counter values can be revealed.

*James M. Mellard, "The Modes of Vonnegut's Fiction: Or, 'Player Piano' Ousts 'Mechanical Bride' and 'The Sirens of Titan' Invade 'The Gutenberg Galaxy'," in* The Vonnegut Statement, *edited by Jerome Klinkowitz and John Somer (copyright © 1973 by Jerome Klinkowitz and John Somer; used with permission of Delacorte Press/Seymour Lawrence), Dell-Delta, 1973, pp. 178-203.*

There are two ways of portraying the end of things in Vonnegut's work that are especially important and worth singling out. Taken together they show how the kind of fiction Vonnegut writes is related to the kind of religious "message" that is felt in his work. These are first of all the death of the novel, and secondly, linked with it, the passing of a sense of history and tradition. . . .

Vonnegut rejects both Western religion, with its insistence on God's acts in history, and the novel, the Western art form which more than any other finds meaning in history. The linkage of the two in *Cat's Cradle* can be seen in the book's plot, which is both a conversion story (from Christianity to Bokononism) and a parody of the *Bildungsroman.* It can also be seen in Bokononism itself, which is a parody both of the *Bildungsroman* and of religion: Bokononism provides a set of terms for a new religion, but they work equally well as terms of literary criticism for the novel. . . .

A regret for the loss of tradition, and with it a sense of historical purpose, has been common in Western literature at least since *The Waste Land,* and there is some of this regret in Vonnegut. . . . [But for] the most part his work accepts the loss of tradition rather gladly as a fact, and even demands that it become a fact. Vonnegut's work as a whole gives us a satiric version of the sense of tradition and of God's movement in history; it shows the kind of faith which is built on that sense to be at best foolish and at worst demonic. . . .

Finally for Vonnegut there is no meaning or purpose in history. God is not interested. *Deo volente* becomes, in *Slaughterhouse-Five,* "if the accident will." There is no such thing as Progress, or Providence, or Manifest Destiny. . . .

Vonnegut's vision of life and history has several features in common with the world view that Martin Buber [in *Two Types of Faith*] has called Paulinism. . . . One feature of Paulinism is its vision of the enslavement of the cosmos by powers which are hostile to or indifferent to man. Vonnegut's vision of history, in *The Sirens of Titan,* as arranged by Tralfamadorians in order to communicate something about a missing part for a spaceship, is simply a more dramatic rendering of the view taken in *Cat's Cradle* and *Slaughterhouse,* where history is an accident or a joke. A second feature of Paulinism is the problematic nature of the law: in Paul, the moral law revealed to man by God is recognized as opposed to the law which God established in creation. Similarly in *Slaughterhouse-Five* Vonnegut tells us that the Tralfamadorians, though they can foresee evils, particularly wars, are powerless to stop them; and that past, present, and future are "among the things" which Billy Pilgrim can do nothing about. Throughout *Slaughterhouse-Five* Vonnegut's language emphasizes this vision of the world by using Newtonian terms for humans (they "flow" like liquid, or "expel fluid" like machines) and organic terms for the nonhuman (light "seeks to escape," and bubbles of air seek to climb out of a glass). Those who try to follow the moral law are either pathetic or futile, like Edgar Derby "becoming a character," or evil themselves, like all those who commit massacres for what they feel are righteous causes. A third common feature is man's response to his condition of enslavement. In Paul it is conversion; and conversion is effected by belief in a mediator and his action in history. In Vonnegut there is no mediator (unless he be the bringer of the message, Billy or Bokonon), and there is no action upon history, whose facts remain the same. But there is a conversion, a "belief," which is a new perspective, a new way of seeing things called Bokononism or Tralfamadorianism. Billy's job as spiritual optometrist is to provide the spectacles for a new, converted vision. Conversion to Bokononism and Tralfamadorianism brings results similar to Paul's conversion to Christianity: Bokononism gives a sense of purpose, Tralfamadorianism gives belief "that we will all live forever, no matter how dead we may sometimes seem to be."

*Glenn Meeter, "Vonnegut's Formal and Moral Otherworldliness: 'Cat's Cradle' and 'Slaughterhouse-Five'," in* The Vonnegut Statement, *edited by Jerome Klinkowitz and John Somer (copyright © 1973 by Jerome Klinkowitz and John Somer; used with permission of Delacorte Press/Seymour Lawrence), Dell-Delta, 1973, pp. 204-20.*

Because Vonnegut's existential problems find their way into his art, his struggles to return from his annihilation [the Dresden fire-bombing], to survive the return, and to communicate what he had learned are clearly mirrored in his novels, specifically in his attempt to create a hero who could survive with dignity in an insane world. In *Player Piano,* Vonnegut created his first "hero," Paul Proteus, who is perhaps no better than a protagonist. . . .

Malachi Constant, the hero of *The Sirens of Titan,* is Vonnegut's next attempt at creating a hero capable of facing the terrors of Dresden. . . .

In this, his second novel, Vonnegut discovered an answer to Dresden, but he did not yet know how to apply it. Winston Niles Rumfoord's discovery that "everything that ever has been always will be, and everything that ever will be always has been" (p. 26) lies inert in the novel, separate from its aesthetic resolution. In order to exorcise Dresden with his new vision, Vonnegut had to rid himself of his youthful notions of romanticism and liberalism, to acquire a context for Rumfoord's theory of time, and to isolate and to define the aesthetic problem raised by Dresden.

In *Mother Night* Vonnegut dismisses romanticism, with its anthropocentric notion of guilt, as a valid response to Dresden. . . . While Campbell learns much about the world, he fails to establish a rapport with it. He cannot stand the prospect of being free to return to an insane world, to an insanity that he also shares. . . .

In *Cat's Cradle* Vonnegut dismisses liberalism, with its anthropocentric notion of duty, and dramatizes the principle of Dynamic Tension, a state of careful and proportioned alignment of stresses that creates a geodesic dome of balanced forces, forces so arranged that they contain one another's energies. Jonah, the narrator and protagonist, fares better than Campbell. Again this is a story written after the fact, but this time the narrator has acquired some understanding of himself as well as the rest of mankind. He is a Bokononist and knows that no one can assume the responsibility for the end of the world. . . .

In *God Bless You, Mr. Rosewater* Vonnegut finally confronted Dresden. When his hero, Eliot Rosewater, sees the imaginary fire storm devouring Indianapolis, he goes insane and sees the "inner core of white" in the flames. Upon his recovery, he discards his liberal sense of duty, his romantic guilt, and lives. . . . He has not only been trying to enlighten his heroes to their role in a universe devoid of spiritual values, but he has been trying to define the void in contemporary man's life and trying to create a symbol, a literary device that could manifest an answer to this problem. With Eliot he almost succeeded. He created a hero who understands that the universe touches man in accidental ways, a hero who responds affirmatively to the insanity epitomized by the Dresden fire-bombing, and a hero who survives his return to the everyday world. Vonnegut needed one thing more, however—a literary device capable of manifesting the process that his hero must experience if he is to achieve a vision of reality that could encompass the implications of Dresden without surrendering to utter despair. It took him four more years to unite Rumfoord's theory of time and Bokonon's theory of dynamic tension into a structural principle for his Dresden book. It took him four years to dramatize the gap in Rosewater's life, the gap that defined the problem of contemporary man and its answer, four years to conceive his schizophrenic manner of writing, an aesthetic that could re-create and nurture a hero destroyed by Dresden. . . .

*Slaughterhouse-Five* is composed of equal parts of autobiography and fiction, of Vonnegut and Billy, of body and soul, of consciousness and unconsciousness, of intellect and intuition, of punctual time and schizophrenic time, and of spatial and temporal narrative devices. Thus, Vonnegut has technically acknowledged the indelible cleft in Western man's psyche. The challenge he has accepted in *Slaughterhouse-Five* is not to destroy or suppress one part of the mind or the other, nor is he naïve enough to assume that he can fuse them into an organic whole. His technical problem is to synchronize the two parts of the book, bring their conflicting times, rhythms, together so both plots may reach a simultaneous climax and create a structural dynamic tension, a book that can fall on a geodesic path through its readers' minds. . . .

Thus, in his schizophrenic manner, Kurt Vonnegut discovers a means of re-inventing himself and his universe. The principle of dynamic tension informs not only the fabric and structure of the novel, but it also informs the existential relationship between Vonnegut and his transcendent hero, Billy Pilgrim. This relationship dramatizes Vonnegut's rite of initiation. We have [elsewhere in this essay] defined the rite of initiation as the absorption of the ego by a concept of reality that the ego itself has created, and we have observed the frightening aspects of the Einsteinian world that frustrate such a traditional process. As a result of man's inherent fear of the fourth dimension, Vonnegut's rite of initiation is not founded on the notion of annihilation by absorption but on the notion of creation by synchronization. Just as Vonnegut, in his twenty-second year, picked his way through the rubble of Dresden, Billy Pilgrim, toward the end of *Slaughterhouse-Five,* picks his way through the squalid ruins of a pornographic shop and finds there the inarticulate wisdom of Kilgore Trout, one of Vonnegut's masks, finds his "impossible hospitable world." Just as Vonnegut, twenty years later, is struggling to leave his autobiography and to enter his own fictive world to seek Billy out, Billy is pursuing Vonnegut in the guise of Trout with the same relentless tenacity. Both the intellect and the intuition are struggling to march to the same beat, striving to arrive simultaneously at the same image. At the end of *Slaughterhouse-Five* both Vonnegut and Billy, caught in different time dimensions, are synchronized by space, Dresden, and . . . rebirth. . . .

Because his moral confrontation with Dresden was steady and persistent throughout his career, the affirmation of life, vibrating in this climactic novel is based not on self-deception but upon the greatness of the human spirit confronted by great adversity. More important, though, the integrity of this affirmation signals the aesthetic strength and freedom of Vonnegut's vision, a vision that captures the essential spiritual dilemma of contemporary man and represents an enduring contribution to his literary heritage and to man's quest for "wonderful *new* lies."

*John Somer, "Geodesic Vonnegut; or, If Buckminster Fuller Wrote Novels," in* The Vonnegut Statement, *edited by Jerome Klinkowitz and John Somer (copyright © 1973 by Jerome Klinkowitz and John Somer; used with permission of Delacorte Press/Seymour Lawrence), Dell-Delta, 1973, pp. 221-54.*

In Kurt Vonnegut's *Slaughterhouse Five* the Time Machine, as in countless more mundane sf sagas, is . . . a spaceship, a flying saucer from the planet of Tralfamadore. What the transported Billy Pilgrim learns from the Tralfamadorians is, in effect, not just a quietistic philosophy but also the dispensability of the aeroplane-spaceship for the novelist: "All moments, past, present and future, always have existed, always will exist. The Tralfamadorians can look at all the different moments just the way we can look at a stretch of the Rocky Mountains. . . ." Vonnegut treats the story of Billy Pilgrim like that, switching in time at will, with or without a flying saucer. Other worlds can be all about us at any moment, beneath our feet or in the nearest hillside, as the makers of Greek myths and mediaeval romances knew only too well. The signals from Tralfamadore are a metaphor for the reclaimed narrative freedom of the novelist, a freedom staked out most clearly by the Time Traveller in Trieste, James Joyce.

*Clive Jordan, in* Encounter, *February, 1974, p. 62.*

[Those] who think [Vonnegut's] fiction thin, unformed and full of cheap tickles will find these essays [*Wampeters, Foma, & Granfalloons*] just that.

Vonnegut seems an honest man, which is admirable enough these days. Yet honesty leaves him confessing many sad things. . . .

Vonnegut is a sneaky moralist. He admires the simplicity and untextured responses of the young, just as they admire his reductiveness and his untextured precepts. He speaks to an audience which has not been compromised by the corruptions and conventions of getting on. And he hankers for an age that has not suffered the same fate. His analogies, therefore, are to the 19th century. Since the 19th century will not return, his plots are into the vague future. And so on.

The phrases *and so on* and *so it goes* are so essential to Vonnegut that even though his critics have complained that such expressions are irking, he's not about to excise them. He can't. The world is full of binary and-so-ons for him: people whose lives are compromised and those whose lives are not; bad officers and nice enlisted men; innocent scientists who cause harm, and cynical scientists who hate the destruction to which they inevitably contribute; smart people and dumb people; happy people and lonely people; and so it goes. People who are caught in this world, and those with the liberated perspective of having lived in space, and so on. People who are substantial and those who are not: the somebodies and the nothings; those who are the "merest wisp of an implication" and those who slip back into Nothing, and so it goes. He's not trying to be vague. Rather he's emphasizing how eternally the world is a simple place which we overcome or in which we are overcome. And so on.

The world is not that sort of place: not so clean nor well-lighted. It is messy, in fact, and most of us keep on going during and after being overcome by the dirt and the dark. Vonnegut knows that, and his life shows it if his writing does not.

*W. T. Lhamon, "Family Man," in* The New Republic *(reprinted by permission of* The New Republic; *© 1974 by The New Republic, Inc.), June 1, 1974, pp. 27-8.*

The most distinctive voice in recent American fiction is that of Kurt Vonnegut Jr., the author of seven likable but sometimes hopelessly tacky novels and a couple of unsuccessful plays. In this collection of commencement speeches, book reviews and other shavings from under a busy writer's workbench [*Wampeters, Foma & Granfalloons*], his tone has the usual rarefied diffusion of tiredness and rue. It may be time to ask why this tone is so attractive.

Tiredness is part of the answer. When Vonnegut writes, it is as if a favorite uncle had just driven 1,200 miles nonstop from Indianapolis, slugged down two stiff drinks, and collapsed on the sofa, body becalmed but mind still blasting along at 80 m.p.h., voice spinning on and on, talking of horrors with rumpled brilliance. In this strange mood of elation and exhaustion, there is no time or energy for calculation, artifice, rewriting (as it seems), or anything except the wild sputter of ideas and the sigh "So it goes."

Niceness is part of the answer. In this collection, Vonnegut quotes a critic friend, who told him in exasperation that what Vonnegut does is put bitter coatings on sugar pills. This is perfectly true, and the sugar pill is Vonnegut's own character. He is (or makes himself seem) a kindly, decent fellow. When the young hear from him that the world is decaying, this message is to some extent reassuringly contradicted by his wry and understanding smile.

The way to enjoy Vonnegut is to pick out the raisins. The idea of writers' conferences is absurd, he says, because writers cannot confer; "it's all they can do to drag themselves past one another like great, wounded bears." That is a raisin. He reports without undue enthusiasm that his wife and daughter have become followers of the Maharishi. "Nothing pisses them off anymore," says Vonnegut. "They glow like bass drums with lights inside." Another raisin.

. . . There is a lot of solid, sad talk, and it makes the reader feel sorry that this gentle, tired uncle is so gloomy. "I have always thought of myself as a paranoid," he writes, "as an overreactor, and a person who makes a questionable living with his mental diseases." The arts, he believes, are benign frauds: "Films and books and plays show us people talking much more entertainingly than people really talk. . . . Singers and musicians show us human beings making sounds far more lovely than human beings really make. Architects give us temples in which something marvelous is obviously going on. Actually, practically nothing is going on inside. And on and on." If Vonnegut really were an uncle, the reader would take him to see *The Sting,* maybe, and buy him a couple of beers afterward to cheer him up. Or lose patience and tell him to pull up his socks. People really do feel this way about Vonnegut. A twelve-year-old boy wrote a letter after reading *Breakfast of Champions,* the author reports, saying. "Dear Mr. Vonnegut, Please don't commit suicide." Vonnegut says he is fine.

Nevertheless the idea of taking care of the author as a relative is surprisingly attractive. It is, in fact, a rather Vonnegutian idea. . . .

"Wampeters," by the way, are objects (like the Holy Grail) around which the lives of otherwise unrelated people revolve. "Foma" are "harmless untruths, intended to comfort simple souls,"—such as "prosperity is just around the corner." A "granfalloon" is a "proud and meaningless association of human beings." As members of the Vonnegut granfalloon know, the words first appeared in one of Uncle Kurt's early novels, *Cat's Cradle.*

*John Skow, "Raisin d'Etre," in* Time *(reprinted by permission from* Time, The Weekly Newsmagazine; *copyright Time Inc.), June 3, 1974, p. 77.*

Kurt Vonnegut, Jr., gave the latest fatherly advice when he told a group of graduates Shakespeare was wrong to say, "The smallest worm will turn, being trodden on": "I have to tell you that a worm can be stepped on in such a way that it can't possibly turn after you remove your foot." Vonnegut's authority derives from exactly this sense of total vulnerability. His fiction is really one voice from under the cosmic heel. He is the writer who takes charge of wormhood, who speaks for the ground-down man.

Vonnegut is the hero of the American male under seige. How else to explain the coexistence in his work of the uneventful dreariness of the average man and the wildest flights through space and time? Vonnegut is a double-threat hero who provides an accurate statement of both the trivial surface of American life and the charged innards of male fantasy. He uses science fiction as the vehicle for emotional truth, for the large frustrations contained in the small cliché, the pain canned in the aluminum-sided house.

Vonnegut is the one writer who is an instinctive pop artist. What people require is not more social criticism, but reassurance, truth in a better wrapper than reality. In irresistible tales, he packages the downs of the average man. With brilliant tenderness he reproduces the talk of car dealers, salesmen, beauticians, optometrists, whose astonishing verbal flatness is their strength. Through such simplicity Vonnegut builds characters who are American Everymen, whose sheer banality is what saves them. Vonnegut makes out of their trivia a necessary burden, an anchor that keeps them from flipping out from the force of their unhappiness. He is our hero because he has made a monument out of insecurity and turned the crushed, ground-down man into an unmistakable model of masculinity. . . .

In *Wampeters, Foma, and Granfalloons,* Vonnegut is nothing less than the voice of the many who are one with their limitations. In this collection of fascinating odds and ends—reviews, speeches, fiction, interviews—he is totally open and marvelously crafty at giving everything that happens to him or the world the force of a good one-liner. His peremptory style, his folksy cracks are geared to silence. That style permits no development after the laugh, the snort of recognition, the encapsulating cliché. Vonnegut can administer his truths in doses that stop thought. He is a master of the instant defense, the immediate retreat, the phrase that simultaneously expresses his point and blocks your disagreement. He is the new man considering what he can count on. . . .

Ordinariness, sameness, the sheer mindlessness of heroes who are poor slobs like the rest of us, is one pole of Vonnegut's fiction. Fragmentation in space, the easy collapse of body and mind into a universal molecular flow or the mud of Earth is the other. Both meet in Vonnegut's belief in the step beyond personality, the disappearance into stereotype or chemical process. Vonnegut gives up on people getting together, on synchronizing the different cravings of even one mind. He sees wholeness and satisfaction as inconceivable in purely human terms. But as the walking mud people are in *Cat's Cradle,* or the fragments they become in *Sirens of Titan* or *Slaughterhouse-Five,* they can connect through their common chemistry, their shared anonymity, the mutual restackability of their minds and bodies, their reducibility to movable objects.

A culture creates its heroes even as its heroes create novels. Vonnegut's ideas of fusion reflect a male flight from frustration, the greatest possible withdrawal from taking charge. They reflect a widespread will to get beyond the confines of individual responsibility and out of the single, beleaguered self. Vonnegut's ability to be that ravaged figure has made him one of the most beloved writers in America. His novels arouse not only our admiration but our protectiveness. His least works are praised along with his best. He offers an unthreatening, instantly recognizable portrait of man ground under the heel of American expectations. What Vonnegut pleads for in his weird, alien images is the end of damaging hope, the end of those hierarchies of moral and aesthetic worth, of status, money, and intelligence that divide men from each other and make them adversaries. Physical and psychic coalescence means the end of differences. In the recognition of shared hardship dies the self-assertive urge, the adversary-seeking competitive life. You are your enemy and he is you. You're both walking mud. . . .

Vonnegut's antidote is dullness. His true hero is the man slightly cracked by his own frustrations but holding himself together with his triviality—his aluminum siding, his humdrum marriage, his empty job, the boredom that keeps him from thinking or feeling. Vonnegut is the champion of the average American who spaces out of his heart and mind so as not to have to hurt.

*Josephine Hendin, "The Writer as Culture Hero, the Father as Son," in* Harper's *(copyright © 1974, by Harper's Magazine, Inc.; reprinted from the July, 1974 issue of* Harper's Magazine *by permission), July, 1974, pp. 82-6.*

A young poet recently described his daily journal as an asterisk-ridden affair. He used an asterisk, it seems, to indicate a passage that was not necessarily his absolute or final statement on a particular subject. Another volume, just published, would benefit from a similar method of notation. It's called *Wampeters, Foma & Granfalloons* and its author, ostensibly a novelist, is really the world-famous public relations man, Kurt Vonnegut Jr.

It may be 20 years since Mr. Vonnegut officially held that title (he was employed in that capacity by General Electric of Schenectady), but the spirit of pr lives on in his fiction and in this collection of previously published articles, speeches, and interviews. Taken individually, each of the pieces is a delightful unit of casual and well focused prose designed both to inform and to sedate the reader. But by bringing these pieces together, publisher Seymour Lawrence has locked in, between hard covers, a composite picture that accurately reveals the extent of Vonnegut's essentially schizophrenic world view.

You will notice as you read this book that the author contradicts himself from essay to essay, speech to speech. Contradiction is a pr device, and its use here calls for asterisks or some other system to alert the reader to Vonnegut's Jekyll-Hyde approach. . . .

In spite of the contradictions, though, maybe even because of them, Vonnegut accomplishes what few other writers would dare to attempt: he makes Americans see themselves. By contradiction, he reveals the contradictions in our lifestyle. There are times when Vonnegut needs to have his hands slapped for the errors in his doctrine, but more often he raises valid points and describes the world in a way that reveals much about Americans.

His favorite scheme is the cosmic overview. He uses it in his novel *Breakfast of Champions,* when he writes about "two lonesome, skinny, fairly old white men on a planet which was dying fast." He uses it again, with great effectiveness, in his *Harper's* article on the 1972 Republican convention. It is in his speeches, though, that Vonnegut comes on strongest, with statements on the political influence of writers, on the Vietnam war, on science, and on the art of being humane.

*Steven Kosek, "Through Ambiguities, Lightly," in* National Review *(150 East 35th St., New York, N.Y. 10016), July 5, 1974, p. 771.*

# W

## WAKOSKI, Diane 1937-

**Ms Wakoski is an imaginative American poet whose work, often "confessional," is characterized by dark and violent imagery. (See also *Contemporary Authors*, Vols. 15-16.)**

Diane Wakoski is another young poet(ess) of *turned-on* imagination. This is what the young seem to be doing these days. And, really, isn't it much more demanding than the fashion of an older generation, when everybody was struggling to turn the corpses of run-over squirrels into lugubrious meditations on the nature of original sin? Except in spots, [*Inside the Blood Factory*] lacks high seriousness—but so did Chaucer. The poems tend to be long, long-lined, surrealistic monologues, and "Filling the Boxes of Joseph Cornell" is certainly one of the best. It is an entertaining book—strange thing to say about a book of poems.

Virginia Quarterly Review, *Vol. 45, No. 3 (Summer, 1969), pp. xciii-xciv.*

When "Inside the Blood Factory" was published in 1968, it was clear that in the poetry of Diane Wakoski a new sort of energy had been tapped. A fierce impulse toward confession and autobiography moved through her poems, but it took unexpected detours into an imagery of elusive beasts, colors and bizarre precious stones. The "me" she confessed to was not contained by situations; it was not an object of complaint. Although her poems were stirred by angers and fears, they did not include gestures toward suicide, the madhouse or the pill bottle. Instead, she confessed to the hippogriff in her soul, which carried her like an exulting spirit among the men who loved her, or betrayed her. The blend of exotic shapes and swift spoken language was often startling. . . .

Diane Wakoski wrote poems of loss. The loss of childhood; the loss of lovers and family; the perpetual loss a woman lives with when she thinks she is not beautiful. These losses created a scorched earth of isolation around her, which she described harshly and precisely. . . .

But "Inside the Blood Factory" was also an erratic book. Many of the longer poems rambled inconclusively. Miss Wakoski's very exuberance tended to play tricks on her by allowing the intensely personal core of the poems to become stifled in a mesh of images that moved far away from any recognizable center. In a sense, the failures of the book were very much in the image of its power; the best and the worst belonged to each other, for both resulted from the poet's defiant commitment to her freedom. It might have been better if we'd been spared the bad poems, but their rambling may have formed the only ground from which Diane Wakoski's imposing inwardness could spring. There is, after all, a bravery that artists may need more than most people: a willingness to risk being ridiculous, in order to expose the reluctant figures in their lives. . . .

"The Motorcycle Betrayal Poems" are more open than much of Miss Wakoski's earlier work. . . .

The directness of [her] lines describing the combat that art enables the poet to wage against the bitterness of her life is one of the very best qualities in the book. In much of it, Miss Wakoski achieves an intensity of simple speech that is rare in contemporary poetry. . . .

These poems are not declarations of feminine independence. Their rage is not ideological, as in many Women's Liberation tracts. Miss Wakoski's tactic is different. She digs her teeth into the slaveries of woman, she cries them aloud with such fulminating energy that the chains begin to melt of themselves. The rage is that of a prisoner whose bitterness is her bondage but also her freedom.

In many poems, however, the anger becomes thin, repetitious, and this is perhaps the book's most serious weakness. All too often, the stridency does not turn into poetry; the words are flattened almost into helplessness by the very anger they express. . . .

But this is far from general in the book. Many poems survive, and they are like nothing I know in contemporary poetry. Often enough, the vindictive rage is rounded into whimsy and self-knowledge, or into asides of sheer fantasy that charm the reader while they are chilling him with insight. . . .

Yes, there are failures in "The Motorcycle Betrayal Poems." But they are the sort of failures that lesser poets could have avoided without improving themselves. At her best—and the best is frequent enough—Diane Wakoski is an important and moving poet.

*Paul Zweig, in* The New York Times Book Review *(© 1971 by The New York Times Company; reprinted by permission), December 12, 1971, pp. 5, 18, 20.*

Miss Wakoski's poetry [here, *Greed, Parts 5-7*], if intense, is immediate. Still, one cannot help being much impressed with the singular precision and scope of her work. Thus, what seems "sheer confession" at first, never degenerates into clever self-analysis. Her poetry is never self-centered or purely self-directed: "I wonder," she asks, "if it is a story everyone knows?"

Virginia Quarterly Review, *Vol. 48, No. 1 (Winter, 1972), p. xxiii.*

Diane Wakoski is expansive—her poems need space to conquer, and she is certainly out to conquer. These are part of an endless autobiography to establish character in a largely male-dominated world, instanced as the bike scene —not so much speed as engineering made into the central male fascination. . . .

Her work has a baroque effect; it is not a book to be read too much at a time, since there is little variety of voice or theme ("Conversations with Jan" contains more invention, especially the sixth). Her poems are letters never sent: "this letter writer, / this passionate piece of paper / you will all / someday / read." The threatening tone here and in the murderous epigraph continues throughout, and fools no one, let alone Diane Wakoski; but the desperation is substantial. She operates in a world of women as adjuncts to men and the erotics of bikes; the poems are survival gestures. . . . They are dense with information used as defensive attack: a passionately alert sense of the uselessness of self-regard. . . . Diane Wakoski's love poems care for facts rather than psychological convention and those orgasmic obsessions brandished by the mob who discovered Reich last month. . . . She takes over the trite masculine imagery of guns, bullets, bikes, the Angels, mustaches, and male Beethoven-playing maestros, for her own usage and dumps them for the man who relaxes as a man with his own kind of body and life, exercising his ability to live as the necessary other coupling of sexual love. The rest is, broadly, perversion and its main image, games and women as adjuncts to sport. . . .

Diane Wakoski has a radically metaphorical imagination, rare in contemporary American poetry, and nearly old-fashioned. Her conception of female vulnerability in the male-dominated world, with all its nagging obsessiveness, maps its region conclusively. What is missing is family and babies, and the endless sense of vulnerability felt in the working classes. . . . [It] is essentially poetry for the leisured and intellectually trained, who wish to follow their own processes in representative forms.

*Eric Mottram, in* Parnassus, *Fall/Winter, 1972, pp. 160-62.*

All that is real or invention about the several surfaces of [the] poems [in "Smudging"] seem but incredible facets of this woman's imagination and a child's urge towards warmth and a mythic life. There is throughout a sure note in the poet's voice of one who knows oneself and moves out into multiple relationships, that these too will reflect the self. There is, however, continually the problem that the other somehow is not a smooth nor a clear reflecting surface. The imagination can create its own relationship with another, as in "The George Washington Poems," but the image projected is not as finely etched as that of the poet in "Smudging."

Virginia Quarterly Review, *Vol. 49, No. 1 (Winter, 1973), p. xiii.*

Diane Wakoski knows how to make words into poems. Her precise and straightforward style organizes not-quite-reality, and pushes it into the right contact. At all times in these two books [*The Motorcycle Betrayal Poems* and *Smudging*] Wakoski is in control, she is the craftsman. Although her poems are not traditional structures, she builds them solidly with words which feel chosen, with repetition of images throughout a poem (as in the carefully woven *Motorcycle Betrayal* poem, "The Catalogue of Charms"), and with exact observation, as in "To A Friend Who Cannot Accept My Judgment Of Him": "his former/ black worm self,/ fringed with delicate green spires,/ crawling along branch,/ angling and curving under leaves," from *Smudging*.

When I first read *The Motorcycle Betrayal Poems,* I thought, help, here is a neurotic woman whose mind can't get untracked from the loss of her man. Who wants to read all this? And then I read "Thanking My Mother For Piano Lessons." In this poem Wakoski tells us of "the relief/ of putting your fingers on the keyboard,/ played my way/ on the old upright piano/ obtained for $10,/ played my way through fear." The other poems in the book are now seen as variations on a theme, as in music. Because the one continuous theme beats beneath all the poems, we see beauty in the variations of language, images, and approach. A single subject, the man-woman relationship, serves as the light source for a flowering of imagination. . . .

Her latest book, *Smudging,* is equally well-crafted and the subject matter encompasses a wider range. Among other things, she examines poetry, her parents, pain, and "That Abomination In The By-Now 20th Century Aesthetic Tradition: Meditation On A Wet Snowy Afternoon." The book's title poem refers to the process of putting smoke pots in orchards to protect the fruit from frost, and hints that poetry can be a protective structure, too. . . . These two books are remarkable because Diane Wakoski has successfully balanced the life of emotion against the life of intelligent reflection, through the medium of poetry. The poems sound true in your heart, true in your mind, and true in your ear.

*Debra Hulbert, "True Poems," in* Prairie Schooner *(© 1973 by University of Nebraska Press; reprinted by permission from* Prairie Schooner), *Spring, 1973, pp. 81-3.*

[Diane Wakoski's] poems create a persona who is not heroic but who is demanding nonetheless; the apotheosis of all our own plainness to a level where its other, presumably more basic, virtues *must* begin, mercifully, to be searched for. . . . Wakoski has had the good sense to make her whole style out of this ordinariness, which she expresses in plain talk, no shit, an unadorned, "straight," anti-poetic voice—in skillful alternation with its opposite. For all her unfeigned simplicity and the accommodation to reality her lack of conventional, hence easy, beauty demands (as metaphor for all the other good reasons for being open and honest), it is hard to think of a poet who writes more lyrically: invoking jewels and flowing hair, exotic animals, landscapes as stylized and exaggerated as fairy tales—in these she is Diana of the moon. So, she has hit her readers, especially the young ones on the college circuits, twice: first precisely where they live and then where they go to dream. In this her poetry is more like Brautigan's prose than even his own poetry: cool, syntactically innocent, damn hard sometimes, fresh with the insights given only to the undeceived—while underneath beats a heart as sentimental as old gold. . . .

With Wakoski's long wordy books, one can reach in anywhere for an illustration of flaccid writing. . . . Granted she achieves her effects by building somewhat crudely with big blocky statements. If one were to see Wakoski's poems as whole languages, they would be synthetic, rather than analytic—structures that heap up and join words rather than build long and complex and precise single words which enclose meaning. . . . [Although] Wakoski . . . chats and ambles and declaims in full voice, unashamed, raunchy, idealizing, . . . I find myself, ungratefully, looking at this her twelfth book [*Smudging*] and wondering, if there were less, would more of it be strong and shapely? She is a marvelously abundant woman who sounds, in her non-goddess moments (which predominate), like some friend of yours who's flung herself down in your kitchen to tell you something urgent and makes you laugh and respect her good old-fashioned guts at the same time ("So then I told him. . ."). Would that flow itself be curtailed if less of it were to see the light of print?

She can write poems with extreme and immaculate care. See the disciplined tone, no less "realistic" and conversational than in the lesser poems, of "Steely Silence," of "Sour Milk." See the tour de force "Screw, A Technical Love Poem," which manages in spite of its ostensible subject, to be a poem about love, with all the other implications of its title held quite miraculously at bay. See "The Joyful Black Demon of Sister Clara Flies Through the Midnight Woods on Her Snowmobile," whose title is a joyous catalog of the remarkable contents of Wakoski's mind when it is really engaged; whose lines are a richly orchestrated music which feels like a vastly extended sestina because of the tolling recurrence of words and images.

*Smudging* contains so much that is good that I resent being worn into satiety and inattention by its length, and by all that is easy and disheveled and nagging in it. What she is trying to do is well-served by her two kinds of voices, the broad and profane and the more precise and intellectualizing, and she deserves a lot of latitude in return for that versatility. ("Building up/ in any way/ a structure that will permit you to say/ no,/ a structure that will permit you to say/ yes.") There is little this poet says that is uninteresting per se; but she can and should be more than interesting. . . . But if, by design or default, she can't become a more consistent poet, then let her have a harsher editor. A fine poet three-quarters disciplined does not have to apologize.

*Rosellen Brown, in* Parnassus, *Spring/ Summer, 1973, pp. 52-9.*

The speaker of [*Greed: Parts 8, 9, 11*] is a bully to people who are not her kind. Awesomely disingenuous while giving advice, she slaps with one hand and fondles with another, so that the victim of her lecture (one supposes), convinced of his worthlessness, will go away placidly accepting her wisdom. Her language, tepid here, lumpy with sugar there, is loud with self-justification. Yet this poem, the confessional, is not weepy and often opens out in an admirable way. The trouble is that the vanity of the speaker, who is pragmatic and sophomoric by turns, sucks the air out of the room.

Virginia Quarterly Review, *Vol. 49, No. 4 (Autumn, 1973), p. cxl.*

There is a plague. "Ever since we began to see death as an absolute end, *everybody writes*" (E. M. Cioran). If anything on earth could, this might justify the presence on the printed page of Diane Wakoski, a type that never flourished before the New World invented the spoiled child. Her sticky fingers are into everything, tearing pistils and stamens out of the calyx, prying open every oyster, unscrewing the back of every clock, fumbling at the tripes of the poor, carrying torches for negroes and dead women, permanently in a lather about *men*—which *she* spells with four letters. Her manifesto, introducing her so-called Part 9 [in *Greed, Parts 8, 9, 11*] might have been distinguished as *unbelievable* if anything else she had said were believable; an example—"to make the male chauvinists of the world [*of the world,* no less!] stop comparing me with Sylvia Plath —as if all women of the world who write well must be similar." *(They're not?)* At random, I pluck a line from her writing-well, on the subject of Sylvia Plath's husband: "I know how his gravity pulled on you like a diesel truck attached to yr lip. . ." (the *ou* is silent as in *your*). In every "slim volume" she becomes more fatuous, more immodest, more importunate, as if she could repair the absence of talent by screaming it into life. There is not an educated thought in this pamphlet. Yet it's not entirely devoid of uneasy recognitions. "For a woman/ there is only one thing which makes sense:/ a man who loves her faithfully and keeps her warm at night. . . ." I thought she'd never say it.

*Vernon Young, in* The Hudson Review *(copyright © 1974 by The Hudson Review, Inc.; reprinted by permission), Vol. XXVI, No. 4, Winter, 1973-74, pp. 724-25.*

Diane Wakoski's poems *come close* to being terrible; some are almost soap operas, others the grotesque fantasies of some overly imaginative and under-experienced little girl. They're self-indulgent almost to the point of obsession, over-blown almost to the point of being naive and foolish. At times she is as prosey as garden manuals and as inviolate as sophomore philosophy exams. She can be indiscreet and voluble, excessively symbolic and annoyingly hung-up on being a poet. Constantly she is the essayist discoursing on relationships. She is probably the first candidate to be hung on her own theorem that a poet's poetry is only as interesting as his life, judging by what she lets on about herself in these poems [in *Smudging*]. I happen to disagree with her theorem. To me, a poet is only valuable or interesting to the extent he has developed his power of penetration, his vision, substance.

Many of her poems sound as if they're constantly in trouble, falling into triteness, clumsiness, or indirection. She is constantly jumping into deep water to save a drowning stanza or into a burning building to recover disintegrating meaning, always managing to pull these rescues off, sometimes with what appears to be a superhuman determination, drawing gasps from witnesses who never lose that initial impression of diaster. Perhaps she too much loves to write.

It is hardly a fault, yet it is possibly what is responsible for poems that haven't found their natural skins, positioned before a mirror trying on Macy's complete offering in ladies' fashions, flirting with marshmallow fictions. I am sure that writing can also be painful for her, but when she launches a poem so sweeping in implication, sparked by that love for the process of writing and can't fulfill its potential because she really wasn't ready, I'm not at all sure that this is the sort of pain conducive to the solid vision of genius.

This is the price paid when a poet throws his entire self into his poetry, when the poem becomes a veritable extension of his inch-by-inch living and thinking throughout a day. The poem suffers because it is too much the poet—almost the persona of the poet; or, at least, an oxydized image of his personality. But "suffers" isn't the correct term because the poem is actually divinized by having the poet in it, only with all the human drawbacks added it appears heterogeneous, askew, vulnerable. One has to revel in human contact and possess a love, not mere tolerance, for fallibility to benefit from such poems. Then too, the poet must be good, damned good, dynamic, unrelenting, and blessed with a gut-intuitive wisdom.

Wakoski has these attributes. She is saved. Her poems are saved. This inordinate degree of intelligence, both in what she says and how she handles her poems, not only saves but is the guiding force that makes her best poems more total, more liveable, more penetrable, with more results than those written by so very many of our more dichotomized poets. Her poems are always *working*. They are constantly going in the right direction for all of us.

If she isn't explaining herself, describing what she does, recapturing clipped instances from her past, then she is focusing upon her relationships with whatever enters her life. In fact, she spends most of her psychic energy examining how she relates to objects, events, feelings, people; always seeking the gold that is their essence, always sending herself into their plasma to steal it for her poems. . . .

Wakoski's imaginative excursions and side-journeys (she can get strung-out in just about any poem over a page long) are well-founded in her life—they're not just facile language cyclone-spinning itself to naught. They are doors into her psyche. Veritable adventures-in-image to the Land of True Sight and Knowledge. Virtually everything in her poems is a clue to what she is. Jung wrote an autobiography of the evolution of his mind as a consequence of his life experiences, while Diane Wakoski writes the autobiography of her imagination as a consequence of *her* life experiences. She doesn't evade, fortunately, I believe, because her unconscious mind is the driveshaft that propels her imagination, with a conspicuously rational and perceptive mind doing the steering. This is a first rate combination and supplies her poems with the substance necessary to qualify them notches above the works of creative "geniuses", "stylists", and "cultural avatars" who have little to say.

*Douglas Blazek, in* Poetry *(© 1974 by The Modern Poetry Association; reprinted by the permission of the Editor of* Poetry*), June, 1974, pp. 170-72.*

Diane Wakoski has seemed to me one of the most interesting poets of the past decade. Her language usually leaves me cold—perhaps because I have never heard her read her poems aloud. . . . Her new book, *Dancing on the Grave of a Son of a Bitch*—and what a title! magnificent, though the book is by no means as triumphant as this might suggest—is a somewhat random collection, perhaps not up to the level of previous work, but it contains good poems. Wakoski has a way of beginning her poems with the most unpromising materials imaginable, then carrying them on, often on and on and on, talkily, until at the end they come into surprising focus, unified works. With her it is a question of thematic and imagistic control, I think; her poems are deeply, rather than verbally, structured.

*Hayden Carruth, in* The Hudson Review *(copyright © 1974 by The Hudson Review, Inc.; reprinted by permission), Vol. XXVII, No. 2, Summer, 1974, pp. 311-12.*

* * *

## WALCOTT, Derek 1930-

**Walcott is a West Indian playwright and poet. The relationships between men and God and men and society have been the principal themes of his intelligent and sophisticated poems and plays.**

Derek Walcott's . . . plays range through myth and folklore, against backgrounds as much allegorical as they are Caribbean. The laments of superstitious fishermen, charcoal-burners and prisoners are quirkily counter-pointed by talking crickets, frogs and birds. Demons are raised, dreams take actual shape, supernatural voices mingle with the natural lilting elliptical speech rhythms of downtrodden natives. Mr Walcott . . . is a social commentator who conceals his messages in elaborate poetic wrappers not always easy to unfold, but he is a powerful visionary as well as a compassionate observer of misfits lost in a world they never made.

*Romilly Cavan, in* Books and Bookmen, *April, 1972, pp. 59-61.*

Publication of the seminal West Indian works of literature in English is a fairly recent development in the United States. Derek Walcott is one of the few whose names may be familiar. His plays, "Ti-Jean and His Brothers" and "Dream on Monkey Mountain," have already earned him a certain distinction in the New York theater. "Another Life" is his fourth book of verse, a single poem which extends over some 4,000 lines of self-inquiry and cultural assessment in the context of a Caribbean life. It is the history of an imagination. . . .

[The] increasing pressures of race and politics in Caribbean society always threaten to put such a writer on trial. Walcott is not popular among a later generation of cultural nationalists who, in his view, have sought to turn white mythology on its head by discovering in blackness a new aristocracy of skin. This is an argument which increases in intensity. If the Caribbean House is to be designated black and African, what human or national status is to be given (and by whom) to the numerous descendants of those grandfathers who crossed the water from other continents? Moreover, the cultural inheritance does not allow for any precision of ancestral bond. The society's sinews reach out to Africa and Asia. It announces its wishes through a European alphabet. How truly to name what it really sees is the intricate task of the creative artists. This is the burden of Walcott's turbulent meditation on the dilemma of his time. The result is a formidable achievement.

*George Lamming, in* The New York Times Book Review *(© 1973 by The New York Times Company; reprinted by permission), May 6, 1973, pp. 36-7.*

Because this autobiographical poem [*Another Life*] suffers from a metaphor glut, it will hold the attention in a way a leaner work will not. Every four lines or so a fresh assault is made on the sensibilities, setting up a queer anticipation in the reader. One might wince after several baroque passages of Corelli or gape in amazement at the gingerbread excesses of certain German cathedrals, yet the mind adjusts, uneasily, to this aesthetic of irritation. In Derek Walcott's case I adjusted, but did not enjoy it. I was fascinated by his ingenuity but somewhat put off by the dazzling images and diction. The attention is violated in poetry like this rather than held as it should be.

Granted that one must write as one is able to write, yet in "Another Life" the plan of the poem and its artistic philosophy probably account for its density as much as the tumors in Mr. Walcott's style. As an epigraph to the poem's first section, he uses this statement by Malraux: "What makes the artist is the circumstance that in his youth he was more deeply moved by the sight of works of art than by that of the things which they portray." Fair enough. This explains the continued invocation of VanGogh, Cezanne, Verocchio, Vermeer, Gauguin and other paraphernalia of the "bookish." The past, and eventually the present, is valued as artifact. The creative source becomes the invention, the fabrication, instead of the natural and the temporal. Now this choice has often been made; when it produces a rich scaffolding of language with little substance behind it and too little air and space then, understandably, we feel cheated. When it extends over 150 pages or so we feel worn out. . . .

[Because] Mr. Walcott is a gifted poet he quite often constructs memorable set pieces. . . . These are damaged in the long run by their engraftment to a tenuous narrative line that includes tendrils and undergrowth and a rhetoric too ponderous for storytelling. Poetry of this sort is best read in separate chunks and perhaps should have been published, after judicious editing, as a collection of independent lyrics in one volume. I don't doubt for a moment Mr. Walcott's abilities, but "Another Life" doesn't work as a long poem.

*T. O'Hara, in* Best Sellers, *June 15, 1973, p. 134.*

Derek Walcott is a poet of enormous talent laboring under an enormous burden of obligation. *Another Life* is his third volume of poetry, and is the testament of a West Indian "AfroSaxon". It tells the truths Mr. Walcott has sworn an oath to tell, the truth of the West Indies: its landscape; its people and their aspirations, defeats, and victories; their religion and history; their harbors and towns; all of it down to "every neglected, self-pitying inlet." Interwoven is a personal testament of Mr. Walcott's crucial relationships: with Harry, a painter who commits suicide; with Anna, the lover with whom the poet shares an aching, deep, doomed passion; with art, especially poetry and painting; with the West Indies. *Another Life* is a big book, over 150 pages, over four thousand lines. It is a restless mixture of lyric and narrative, of the local and the European, of the evocative and the didactic; ultimately, its elements don't cohere or reconcile, and most readers will probably seek, according to preference, their own favored poetry-within-the-poem. . . .

The quality of the lyric moments of *Another Life* seems to me far superior to the narrative and didactic two-thirds. There are many exceptions, of course, for Mr. Walcott's immense talent never really quits, and the descriptions of the landscape and—especially—of the people are often wonderful. . . . But, overall, it is the intense lyric moments which hold the reader in awe and substantially deepen his understanding of the world. . . .

There is in this book, too, a stunning though sometimes obstructive erudition. Often an apt allusion seems to arrive in a packing crate, from a source far from the poem's center —the allusions are gracefully made, but the unwieldy crates remain. As we know that deep obligations to country and race are being fulfilled here, we sense also that Mr. Walcott feels the need to establish himself as a citizen of a world larger than the West Indies. He displays impeccable intellectual credentials, stamped in many countries, many centuries; but the poetry is so often so remarkable that all this seems a gross waste of paper, paper on which he could and should write lyrics with the power to change his readers' lives.

I urge everyone who cares for the wonders of fresh metaphor in the service of deep thought and feeling to sift *Another Life* for its triumphs.

*Paul Smyth, "Less Tit Than Tat," in* Poetry *(© 1973 by The Modern Poetry Association; reprinted by permission of the Editor of* Poetry*), December, 1973, pp. 171-72.*

*Another Life* should make it clear, if it was ever in doubt, that Derek Walcott's superlative descriptions are far more than description, that they are the only feasible expression of his situation. They have rather the function that Ian Hamilton defined for the visual images in Lowell's *For The Union Dead*: they are 'felt to be profoundly ingrained elements of the poet's morality, and untranslatable; they press upon him as in some way an important aspect and perhaps the source of his present desolation but they will not surrender to the explicating intelligence'—except that, as Walcott hasn't the history of Boston and the Lowell family to draw on, only a history snapped at the root, the sense of his puzzlement before these images is considerably greater. He sometimes seems stunned, almost inhibited by them.

Here, again, *Another Life* may have an essential role to play: it is a work of making sense, of bringing the puzzlement into shape. Not one image in this long poem is casual in its role. That images should enter so casually and recur so naturally is merely a tribute to the fluency with which this impressive work conceals its organization: as each of the motifs recurs, its meaning is altered or accentuated to reflect the poet's changing experience of the island, the constant features of which, cumulatively, they define. This is autobiography in the best sense, not a memoir but an exploration into the past, a work of rediscovery and reconciliation; as such, it may well mark a new phase in the development of this lucid but essentially complex poet.

*Roger Garfitt, "Poetry: The Domestic Age," in* London Magazine, *December, 1973-January, 1974, pp. 123-29.*

Reading the West Indian poet's long autobiographical poem [*Another Life*] with its North American counterparts inevitably in mind, one is struck, first, by the lavishness of metaphor and figurative language; second, by the lack of obsession with structure. The straightforward, and yet rambling, narration allows a great deal of the life around the poet to crowd into the picture. The poem is uneven; the accumulation of metaphors can be artificial and confusing as well as breath-taking. Some parts of the plot are treated hastily and obscurely; others at too great length, the set-pieces of the Artist's Progress—though Walcott's concern with the contradictions of the colonial imagination gives them a special, tragic tinge. In sum, "Another Life" is a large-spirited book with passages of extraordinary beauty; everyone interested in poetry should read it.

Virginia Quarterly Review, *Vol. 50, No. 1 (Winter, 1974), p. xiv.*

There is a lot in [Derek Walcott's long poem *Another Life*] that I do not like and much that I do not understand. It seems to me too long, too choked with people, places, and things, and there is too much foreign talk and far too much British style. Even as the poet repudiates the intrusion of European "culture" into Black West Indian life, he proves at the same time that he can write a poem in which very little that is recognizably Black West Indian survives.

Perhaps this is unfair. Perhaps there is no such thing as a Black West Indian sensibility, that quality of *difference* that, in the United States, informs the work of even the most academic black poets. I do not know. What I do know is that Walcott writes an English line that can at times rise to perfection, and that his mastery of language and expression—though occasionally rendered with a 19th century twist—is complete and beautiful to see. He is a fine, mature, often brilliant and moving poet, which makes it harder than ever to determine exactly what it is that is missing. What it is, I think for me, is a view of Mr. Walcott's West Indies that escapes the camouflage of an essentially European interpretation. Eager to know Mr. Walcott's West Indies, *his* island, *his* people, *his* greenness, *his* sea, I am disappointed that what he chooses to tell me comes hidden behind names from Greek myths I only half remember, or written in Latin I never studied, or so sprinkled with the "glories" of English empire days that I, finally, can recognize nothing without a debilitating struggle; but must pick my way laboriously from page to page, choosing bits and pieces that speak to me and leaving the rest for the dons of Oxford.

*Alice Walker, in* The Village Voice *(reprinted by permission of* The Village Voice; *© 1974 by The Village Voice, Inc.), April 11, 1974, p. 26.*

[Walcott's long autobiographical poem, *Another Life,*] is a poetry that doesn't conceal its influences (here mostly Pound, I should think). Walcott is a cultivated cosmopolitan poet who is black, and as such he risks irrelevant praise as well as blame, whites finding it clever of him to be able to sound so much like other sophisticated poets, blacks feeling that he's sold his soul by practicing white arts. Whatever hardships this situation may create for Walcott, its difficulty is at least poetically profitable. . . .

The sense of having to live and work, however masterfully, within a culture never quite to be felt as one's own is a predicament that any provincial writer or artist has to cope with, one (for example) from which white American writers haven't yet escaped, and it does lend a fine authentic nervousness to provincial art at its best, Walcott's included. . . .

[This] is a finished poem of deep and complex self-awareness, one that preserves the distinction between the elegiac and the merely sentimental . . . firmly. . . . Derek Walcott tells me about as much about being both black and human as I feel I have any reasonable right to know.

*Thomas R. Edwards, in* The New York Review of Books *(reprinted with permission from* The New York Review of Books; *© 1974 by NYREV, Inc.), June 13, 1974, p. 39.*

* * *

## WARREN, Robert Penn 1905-

**Warren is a celebrated American poet, novelist, short story writer, literary critic, essayist, and editor. Warren was an original member of the influential "Fugitive Group" of poets and is often associated with New Criticism in literature. The moral and intellectual welfare of men in complex contemporary society, an abiding aspect of his agrarian sensibility, has been a prevailing theme in his work. (See also *Contemporary Authors*, Vols. 13-14.)**

[Robert Penn Warren is] a writer of great talent, great sophistication, and great intellect. The most notable characteristic of Warren's work is his serious concern with religious and philosophical ideas. He attempts to write the novel of ideas in which the essentially southern view of man is dramatized through melodramatic actions involving southern characters.

For Warren the problems of man are the twin problems of finding identity and expiating guilt. In finding identity man moves, he believes, from nontime to time, from innocence to guilt; for guilt is an inevitable property of identity. Warren repeatedly tells the story of that guilt and that search in poetry, short stories, and novels, frequently laid in the historical past or involving legendary folk characters.

Warren's novels are uniformly technical tours de force, in which the normal demands of their apparent type of fiction are set aside in order to achieve meaning through the manipulation of action and the special use of witty, knowing, and metaphysical language which can express meaning in its complexity and ambiguity.

*C. Hugh Holman, "The Novel in the South," in* A Time of Harvest, *edited by Robert E. Spiller (reprinted by permission of Hill and Wang, a division of Farrar, Straus & Giroux, Inc.; copyright © 1962 by Robert E. Spiller), Hill & Wang, 1962, pp. 83-94.*

In discussing the ideas in Mr. Warren's novels one pays, inevitably, insufficient attention to the effect of his luxurious, and in its way undoubtedly magnificent, romantic style upon his material. This style is seen at its full reach in *World Enough and Time,* a book in which the invented quotations from early nineteenth-century histories, autobiographies, newspapers and pamphlets are done with such skill and at such leisurely length that they have an air of absolute fidelity. In spite of all its rhetorical glitter the style is used here positively to enhance the force with which Mr. Warren puts forward his ideas about man's place in history.

*Julian Symons, "Fables for our Time" (1962), in his* Critical Occasions, *Hamish Hamilton, 1966, pp. 119-25.*

Robert Penn Warren's lyric poetry . . . depicts the condition of modern man suffering from unbelief. . . . Warren's modern man . . . is entirely isolated within the society, and suffers only his own private agonies. . . . There are only solitary individuals discovering their own predicament, for the most part devoid of the responsibility for any historical or social representation. His people are locked in with their loneliness; it is not a mode of thought with them,. . . but a literal fact, a condition of being. . . .

For Warren . . . the agrarian image is an assertion of the supremacy of dumb nature, the massive reality of the natural world as contrasted with the doubt, the ignorance of thinking men with their pathetic searching for values beyond those of nature. In this respect Warren seems almost Emersonian, but without the earlier poet's easy optimism about cosmic unity and Transcendental purpose. . . .

His agrarians are not virtuous husbandmen; there is little of the pastoral corrective in them. . . . Warren's men in nature are anguished mortals caught in time, for whom the stony fields of winter are withering reminders of human transience, and the forest a place where the crimes of culpable humanity may be re-enacted.

*Louis D. Rubin, Jr., in his* Writers of the Modern South: The Faraway Country, *University of Washington Press, 1963, pp. 176-82.*

If Warren is a first-rank novelist, it is not because he is "wise"; he simply brings the most energy and knowledge to bear imaginatively on [the] point of collision. No other novelist so committed to modernism—with its devotion to truth of the inner life, its alliance with a presumably superior past, its confidence in its vision of something better than commercial industrial society—so powerfully conveys the surprise at being given world enough and time to try translating arrogance into actuality. In all of his best novels, this pent-up anger finds itself freer than it had dreamed possible to press upon living flesh. Where in Faulkner violence counterattacks against unbearable stasis, violence in Warren acts calculatingly in the name of concretely envisaged freedom. Warren is a true shock novelist—not in his plots or his embarrassed sexuality, but in his focus on the tender, murderous imagination of the twentieth century suddenly authorized to practice control upon events. He shows more forcefully than any of his rivals what enthusiasm for control is and where it hurts most. He writes the emerging novel of forces with a more violent drive than Snow or Greene or Sartre or Camus. . . .

[The] limits of Warren's explanations appear more starkly now than they did fifteen or twenty years ago. Essentially, he depends upon a commonwealth of guilt grounded in the family romance. Though fewer people now question this chart, more recognize its crudity. Such sophistication can make the wish behind the cross-referencing drama seem too tensely held. Straightening everything into a tight pattern may be impossible and undesirable—may be, as Herzog's psychiatrist says, a dangerous inability to tolerate ambiguous situations. . . .

In *Night Rider* the fundamental drive is for definiteness. Kenneth Burke first recognized the importance of its division into day and night worlds, and one point should be added. The day world is radically indefinite. It consists of claustrophobia in the train, the miscellaneous crowd, release and exhilaration in Munn's speech followed by letdown and question, victory in Trevelyan's trial succeeded by doubts as to justice. But the night world makes definiteness seem a possibility. In the dark the great fantasies can be acted out. Munn can lead a search of the negro cabin and terrorize its inhabitants; can retry Trevelyan and exact punishment in the lynching; can recreate Confederate myth in the Morgan raid and ambush at the ford; can try Senator Tolliver, the avatar of the day world, in his own mind and set out to destroy him. This militant search for definitions grand enough to encompass all complexities is basic to Warren's best work. And he represents the resistance thoroughly, ranges all over for every complication that might thwart definition. . . .

If Warren is to remain among the major novelists, though, *All the King's Men* must stand as more than a monument to some minor Muse like the American Political Novel. Warren makes this rereading hard to do. Unlike most contemporaries, he does not automatically enlist the reader's collaboration. His drive for definiteness leads him to finish sentences that his fellow novelists like to leave dangling. Above everything else, he is an anxious writer. At the end of *All the King's Men,* his fear of the ferocity within leads him to tie up loose ends in a frenzy of reconciliations—with Jack's mother, Judge Irwin, the Scholarly Attorney, Anne, and Cass Mastern. He has to protect the new life at every point from the threat of emotional kickback. So he returns to that fountain of modern renewal, youthful hopes, and tries to carry them intact across the barrier of adult years.

But up to that point he had been doing better than most novelists. He writes powerful dramatic scenes. He brings together militant energy and a theatrical imagination at a time when theatricality carried man's hope; and he fixes these upon a double locale admirably suited to testing their range. . . . Warren's theatricality sets up a conflict between subtler ambivalent feelings—a love-fear for the integrity of anger, a love-hatred for slyness, and an impossible yearning for personal force. . . .

The critical conflict in *All the King's Men* occurs not between ends and means, but between spontaneity and technique. More than anything else, Jack Burden expresses distrust for the use of mind divorced from the integrity of anger. Loss of an exciting, unifying vision determines the opening attitude toward Willie. The means he uses in the drug store speech at Mason City are not immoral in the sense that his coercing Judge Irwin is. They are not even seriously false. They amount to little more than what courses in public speaking inculcate daily in respectable universities—adapting the material to the audience. . . .

The traditional case for Warren rests on his "wise" perception of conflicts between means and ends plus his understanding the self in relation to them. But his great claim to endurance rests on his "immoral" impulse, his secret sharing with the enemy. No other contemporary touches Warren's powerful identification with energetic intelligence —his enthusiasm for the efficient producer. In dramatizing the drive that Snow only suggests, he expresses better than anyone else the spirit of the forties. Politics in Warren appeals through its ruthlessness, its ethic of the imposed will, its by-passing the claims of decency and the civilian rules for muffling conflict. It allies with war and hero worship rather than democratic referral to committee. Only because Warren feels this drive in his bones can he raise the serious moral issue for an organizing society—the question of *degrees* of flexibility.

*James Hall, "The Poet Turned First-Degree Murderer: Robert Penn Warren," in his* The Lunatic Giant in the Drawing Room: The British and American Novel Since 1930, *Indiana University Press, 1968, pp. 81-110.*

Both speculative philosopher and intuitive explorer, Robert Penn Warren keeps pushing ever further toward a resolved truth that will satisfy a mind that longs for easy answers but will have none of them and a body acutely open to sense impressions, inescapably vivid however they are interpreted. His latest report on the world [*Incarnations*] finds it charged with the grandeur of God and plagued with the obscenity of man's grief. As the ripe fig incarnates the glowing light of the sun that brought it to maturity, so all the radiance of sentient things is proof of the soul in them and the divinity at their source. And yet the world goes its way careless of meaning, and the restless mind inquires at its own peril. The man facing electrocution for murder in a Southern jail begs for morphine to ease his intolerable dread of death, and the Warden of a place in which such horrors can occur has no reason to think that *he* is above the Law. Nothingness can be a powerful presence of things that deny the logic of their own being, or a dazzling sea of ineffable light. All flesh is one flesh, and though the *logos* may appear hideous—a hunchback Aphrodite—it guarantees an everlasting (?) reincarnation. These poems are sometimes gnarled, even gnomic, in their essays at dark wisdom and sometimes funny in their sharp anecdotal observations. Warren has not lost his gift for narrative nor his fondness for finding sermons in stones and other things. But the reality behind the slippery appearances of mortal experience demands expression with a new urgency. Where if not here will the heart discover its own meaning? There is no other place. However difficult and uncertain the enterprise may be, "We must try / To love so well the world that we may believe, in the end, in God."

Virginia Quarterly Review, *Vol. 45, No. 1, Winter, 1969, pp. xv-xvi.*

The influence [on Warren] of [John Crowe] Ransom is of course pervasive, but it is also to be seen in particular and tangible ways. The similar vision of man that dominates Warren's major themes is one; the manipulation of those themes is another. From his earliest protagonists (in *Night Rider,* 1939, and *At Heaven's Gate,* 1943) to his later ones (in *Wilderness,* 1961, and *Flood,* 1964) Warren has systematically explored the possibilities of a persona projected out of his own obsessive concerns. The persona emerges out of the self-delusions of idealism, innocence, and narcissism into the shattering knowledge that he participates in evil, that he shares, even exacerbates, the already imperfect human condition, and that to recognize this complicity is to take the first step toward healing his divided self.

One critic has happily applied to Warren the term *Homo Viator,* man on the road, the poet seeking for all the clues he can find—in external nature and in his own experience—that will justify an Emersonian faith in the glory of man's selfhood in the very face of theological and rationalistic assertions that deny that possibility. Jack Burden, Jeremiah Beaumont, Amantha Starr, Adam Rosenzweig are themselves protagonists on the road, all groping toward that integration which will confirm the worth in their particular lump of clay, a worth that must nevertheless be tested again and again. But if these familiar protagonists are one version of the dramatically achieved (and sometimes beautifully rendered) persona, there is another kind, more transparent, more personal: the authorial voice which interrupts the story of Billie Potts ("The Ballad of Billie Potts") and closes the agony of Beaumont's search (*World Enough and Time*), the barely disguised "R.P.W." (*Brother to Dragons*) and the outright *I* of the later poetry (notably in *Promises, You, Emperors, and Others,* and *Incarnations*).

It may be argued that Warren all too often extends the deft ironies of Ransom's domestic vignettes into full-scale obvious ones most commonly associated with melodrama, and that his antinomies, though they may begin as precariously balanced, always threaten to topple awkwardly into first one extreme, then another. This characteristic is perhaps Warren's most obvious divergence from Ransom. Certainly some of those qualities which Warren found in Ransom both as friend and poet—gaiety, an easy gallantry, a spirit of play—never saw full expression in his own career. . . . Behind the heavyhanded probing of ideas that we read in fits and starts in *World Enough and Time* or in *You, Emperors, and Others* lurks the tough grace of Ransom. But the edged wit, the settled assurances, the confident vision of unconfident man, and even the serious exercise of one's craft compete more vitally, more frenetically, more obsessively, than they ever do in Ransom's best work. "Man must make his life somehow in the dialectical process," Warren observes in a typical statement, "and in so far as he is to achieve redemption he must do so through an awareness of his condition that identifies him with the general human communion, not in abstraction, not in mere doctrine, but immediately. The victory is never won, the redemption must be continually re-earned." That comment on the great theme of "the philosophical novelist" must finally define Warren as his own man rather than as anybody's student.

*James H. Justus, "A Note on John Crowe Ransom and Robert Penn Warren," in* American Literature *(reprinted by permission of the publisher; copyright 1969 by Duke University Press, Durham, North Carolina), November, 1969, pp. 425-30.*

It's always a little hard to place Penn Warren's work, perhaps because so much of his poetry at first seems unresolved, built from a conflict of tensions: the strong narrative and historical sense he has of the frontier landscapes of the nineteenth century, in which hard characters play out their lives in violent actions, as opposed to an intense lyrical perception of an absorption in pristine nature, its animals and plants seen as if for the first time by a sensitive and reflective mind. That mind belongs to a philosophical poet whose method, like Faulkner's is to embody his thoughts in persons who, like most of the few naturally aristocratic, genuinely superior and simple Americans we have had, seem to live situated amidst a savagery both very nearly unthinkable yet obviously so common that it's taken for granted. Perhaps the poetry appears unresolved because our lives cannot be otherwise in America, and it is this recurrent fact that has always obsessed Penn Warren. As Faulkner did, he has evoked the wilderness sweetness and brutality and the obscure, doom-haunted destinies of American men and women: he has made poems out of them that seem like dreams of beauty and horror frozen in amber and preserved for our contemplation, a terrible contemplation of what it means to live, to have lived always, in a world without rules, a world where rules are irrelevant—the American world, in fact.

*Jascha Kessler, in* Saturday Review *(copyright © 1970 by Saturday Review/World, Inc.; reprinted with permission), May 2, 1970, pp. 35-6.*

Warren has been the most open in texture and personal in tone of the Fugitive poets; when he began writing poetry again in 1954, after a ten-year interval during which he wrote none except for the long "play for verse and voices," *Brother to Dragons* (1953), these tendencies were much accentuated. Partly in response, no doubt, to the same pressures that caused a number of other poets to write "open poetry" or "confessional poetry" at about the same time, and partly as a result of private and internal developments, Warren's poems have grown steadily more open, more unabashedly personal, more overtly psychological and religious, and more interdependent. (There is, in most cases, no attempt to make each poem self-sufficient; the poems come in sequences of some length, and knowledge not only of the rest of the sequence, but often of the whole context of Warren's recent poetry, is required in order to apprehend the full meaning of any single poem.) The themes are similar to those . . . in the novels; and there is, in the latest poetry, the same new sense of blessedness, joy, redemption as really possible.

*Monroe K. Spears, in his* Dionysus and the City: Modernism in Twentieth-Century Poetry *(copyright © 1970 by Monroe K. Spears; reprinted by permission of Oxford University Press, Inc.), Oxford University Press, 1970, p. 186.*

Robert Penn Warren. The name is like a bell calling me back to those halcyon days when I was a student at Ohio State and Prof. Eliseo Vivas was having us ponder the profound resolutions of moral perplexities in Penn Warren's "Night Rider," his first novel. Now, nearly a quarter century later, I find myself on the same ground. In "Meet Me in the Green Glen" there is the same craftsmanship in narrative, the same attention to nature as a reflection of man's primitive self, the same fondness for Elizabethan blood-and-guts melodrama, the same morality play dimensions of good versus evil, the same inexplicable punishment of good while evil prospers. Above all, there is the same ability to rivet the reader's attention until the climax and the sustaining of a profound sadness in knowing the story has to end.

*John J. Murray, in* Best Sellers, *October 15, 1971, p. 318.*

The question of the relation between subject and object, feeling and episode, seems to me one of the grand questions, and in Mr. Warren's fiction the crucial matter. "Blackberry Winter" exemplifies a natural law, true to Coleridge's sense of imagination and reality, interdependent. The reality proffered by the story gives an impression of being single, that is to say, single-minded, and I take this to be a proof of its validity. But often in Mr. Warren's longer fictions and especially in his big novels I find the relation between episode and feeling insecure, and generally the feeling is exorbitant. Feeling and interpretation flow in, but their abundance is often gross, if we think of what occasioned them. . . .

Like Mr. Warren's *World Enough and Time,* [*Meet Me in the Green Glen*] is a story of sin and expiation, and it is concerned more with the motive than the deed. . . . The theme is what Jeremiah called it in *World Enough and Time,* "the crime of self, the crime of life." Making subject and object interdependent once and for all, Jeremiah says, "The crime is I." . . .

Mr. Warren's . . . characters [in *Meet Me in the Green Glen*] have no freedom, and only as much vitality as is consistent with imprisonment, a life sentence in their nature. They are so empty that he must himself produce the fullness of the world and give it to the narrator, the narrative voice.

Mr. Warren has to do that as well as everything else. He must do what these wretched characters cannot do for themselves: imagine, understand, perceive. Their slightest gestures must be eked out, glossed, driven to mean something. The narrative voice never rests. . . .

The narrator is equally generous to all his characters: each of them . . . is amplified, protected, filled from resources not his own. After a while, and no wonder, they all sound the same. . . . Mr. Warren should have told his narrator to shut up. Like Murray Guilford, the narrator "could sure swing the English language," but the swinging wrecks what might have been a good novel.

*Denis Donoghue, "Life Sentence," in* The New York Review of Books *(reprinted with permission from* The New York Review of Books; *© 1971 by NYREV, Inc.), December 2, 1971, p. 28.*

In light of [Warren's] whole corpus, any single work within it is seen as at once more complex and more lucid. One should begin with *Billie Potts* and the *Eleven Poems,* for they state most clearly the first of his two compulsive themes: Original Sin.

In a score of fables, Warren has tried to re-create our sense of awakening into a web of guilt and responsibility we never made, and our dawning consciousness that we, knowing or unknowing, in every act extend and involve that web for lives of which we may never be aware. . . .

To the moralist like Warren, the act can never be judged pragmatically by its fruits, but only by its motives, the state of the will that puts it in motion. And are such motives really knowable?

The ineluctable ambiguity of justice is the second central theme of Warren's work. To his very first published fiction, Warren prefixed the tag from Horace that mocks Spenser's Romantic dream of a Golden Age when Truth was simple and apparent. "Nor is nature able to distinguish between iniquity and justice, as it separates the good from the bad, and what is to be sought from what is to be avoided." The illusion of a primal innocence makes living possible for those who cannot face up to the fact that experience is ambiguous, truth elusive, the only certainty that we are born to sin and death. . . .

[Insofar] as Romanticism is pledged to the mirage of a natural Innocence, Warren is anti-Romantic. If [*World Enough and Time*] is called a "Romantic Novel" to the confusion of some critics, it is as an irony, a truth to be understood on the second convolution. His whole work is a critique of Romanticism, whether it be an explicit defense of John Donne and a deflation of Shelley, or "just a story." In the "impure" art of Warren, the Garden into which his lovers enter is the Garden of Shakespeare and not of Tennyson. What Romeo and Juliet momentarily forget within the wall, Mercutio remembers outside, and the Nurse mutters in the bedroom: the toad is as real as the rose, the chancre as true as the moon.

What makes the anti-sentimental, ironic Robert Penn Warren palatable to the mass audience, which instinctively prefers the easiest romanticisms, the lushest sentimentalities; and asserts that they detest "ideas" in fiction? Warren's appeal depends primarily upon his deep flair for narrative, an instinct not merely for "telling a good yarn," which is within the scope of the weariest hack, but of touching archetypal plot material that embodies, quite apart from any explicit statement, ultimate mythic meanings. The author who can exploit plot significance, concrete meaning beside abstract, has a *chance* at least of reaching the great public whose responses and perceptions, where they have not been already vulgarized, are still more *mythos* than *logos*. Such great modern fictionists as Mann and Joyce, even Proust, have surrendered the direct use of the fable—and can move relatively few, though those deeply. To the naturalist, the pragmatist, the nominalist, plot can only be a "machine" and must in honesty be abandoned; but to the believer in the reality of guilt and grace, the "fable" with its immemorial reversals and recognitions is the formal vestige of a way of believing and a celebration of belief. The hunger for plot among the people is a hunger for ritual satisfaction, and the writer who can feed their hunger without condescension may satisfy them and his own alienated self at the same time. Besides Warren, only Graham Greene and perhaps Faulkner among contemporaries have this talent.

In the world of Shakespeare or the Greek dramatists, playwrights were happily *required* to draw on a body of archetypal material; in our world, it is only with great daring that they can attempt to kidnap for high art such popular, mythic forms as the "thriller" or the "historical romance." Warren has moved uncertainly, fumblingly in this direction. In *Night Rider* he touches his authentic material, but apparently without knowing it; in *At Heaven's Gate,* the most incoherent of his books, he loses it almost completely; in *All the King's Men,* he exploits a modern instance of the myth of the tragic hero, vaguely adumbrated in the life of Huey Long (had not three or four popular novelists already compulsively approached it?). But before his current novel [*World Enough and Time*], he seems to have clearly realized his proper subject matter and approach only in *The Ballad of Billie Potts,* a poetic version of a story, told in a score of literatures as "true," and for all one can tell erupting again and again from the fable into "real life," the account of the son of murdering innkeepers, who returns home rich and unrecognizable and is murdered for his money by his mother and father before he confesses his identity. . . .

If *World Enough and Time* has any major flaw, it is the insistence on remaining still a novel—the expected, popular form; for it constantly aspires to become a narrative poem, an epic. One feels that the finally successful work toward which Warren has been groping will finally accept what is for narrative in our time, alas, the *burden* of verse. Certainly, Warren's imagery and command of texture, his concern with music and pattern, his sensitivity to language, all demand the freer scope and tighter discipline of poetic form. Perhaps his talent and skill, which have redeemed the metaphysical novel for the mass audience, may accomplish as much for the serious verse narrative. . . .

To one who has followed Warren from nightmare to nightmare, [*Brother to Dragons*] is a reminder that there is only a single bad dream from which he has always striven to awake to art, a suggestion that perhaps for all of us there is a single archetypal experience of terror, unsayable and, therefore, forever to be said. This is not quite the point that the critics continue to make about Warren's works, observing that he returns to the same themes of Justice and Guilt, to the same reflections on the ambiguity of History, to the same exploitation of the dissonance between the intent of an act in time and its infinitely echoing meaning, to the same symbolisms of West and East, Wilderness and City, to the same Faulkner-ridden milieu.

These are the excrescences of something deeper, and by themselves suggest only an accidental entrapment, an obsession harmful to art. The reader of Warren who sees just so far is tempted to suggest that it might be well for him to find other concerns, to move on. . . . But his major theme seems to me to be precisely the paucity of possible themes, the terrible singleness of the truth under the multiplicity of our lies, the ineffable oneness of Nightmare, or, as he preferred to call it in an early poem, Original Sin. . . .

This is a bombastic poem in the technical sense of the word: bombast as in Seneca or the Jacobean dramatists, a straining of language and tone toward a scream which can no longer be heard, the absolute cry of bafflement and pain. Such a tone becomes in Warren, as in Seneca or Torneur or Thomas Lovell Beddoes, ridiculous on occasion, ridiculous whenever we lapse from total conviction. . . .

It is a Senecan tragedy that Warren has composed, a play

that cannot be played, a poem that must be imagined as acted in the high, ranting style, complete with ghosts and prophecies and dire forebodings, shakings of the earth and raw skulls, suicides and obscene murders and crimes too horrible to define. . . .

Here, for the first time, his form has allowed Warren to use all the trappings proper to the shrillness of his need. *All the King's Men* suffered not only because its hysterical rhetoric had to be disguised as the tough-guy patter of Jack Burden, but because its historicity prevented the appearance on stage of gibbering ghosts and portents out of nature. Even the considerably superior *World Enough and Time* permitted itself only a literary, metaphorical dragon; and the excuse of its Romantic milieu did not quite justify the more than Byronic bombast. . . .

[Warren] represents a line of development which begins with Faulkner's vision of the South as the landscape proper to the terror of us all; but he is not what we ordinarily mean these days by a "Southern Writer," not one of those feminizing Faulknerians, who via Katherine Anne Porter and Eudora Welty have burgeoned into the full-blown epicene school.

Warren, however, manages to preserve the shrillness of Faulknerian tone, the provinciality of his diction and the sense of a rhetoric more controlled by passion than design. He is, indeed, the only serious contemporary writer I know able to achieve the typical Faulknerian corkscrew motion of action, that inward and downward circling toward a climax of horror, which makes of plot an outward symbol of our inward flight from and attraction toward the revelation of guilt. But the author who clings to plotting remains by that token closer to the semiliterate reader than any exponent of sensibility; and this is by no means the only "popular" aspect of Warren's art. He is different from Faulkner in this respect, but no less sympathetic to those lovers of a "good story" so often baffled by current literature; for he has relinquished the hunting yarn, the comic folk tale of sharp dealing and the detective story only to substitute for them the Historical Romance, the debased and apparently unredeemable Bosom Book. We should be aware, however, that Warren's turning to the Historical Romance is an accommodation neither mercenary nor naïve, he exploits it for sophisticated and strategic ends. . . .

I have been convinced for a long time that Warren was feeling his way toward a form which would be neither prose nor poetry, but I have never been able to find a metaphor to define it. Since reading *Band of Angels,* I have become aware that what he has been approaching for so long is something not very different from nineteenth-century Italian opera: a genre full of conventional absurdities, lapses of good taste, strained and hectic plots—all aimed at becoming myth and melody. Though I feel deeply the *necessity* of such a contrivance and respect the courage of Warren's attempt, I am not quite sure that either the novel or the long poem intended to be read as a novel can stand such a metamorphosis.

Given the vast distances of the opera house as it has evolved, the glare of lights and the stir of the audience, one can accept the bellowing, the gilt trimmings, even the vulgarities as finally satisfactory, part of a gross but coherent whole. In the intimate situation of reading a novel, however, there is not enough public rumor, not enough basic space to save the illusion. I see the grease paint; I am aware of the contrived effects; I cannot believe in the pasteboard sets. Or rather, by fits and starts I am carried away; and then my doubt returns. There is, at last, no sufficient poetry, perhaps no way of attaining it, to make an equivalent for the music into which all the oafishiness and coarseness of effect of the opera flow and are redeemed.

*Leslie Fiedler, "Three Notes on Robert Penn Warren," in* The Collected Essays of Leslie Fiedler, Volume I *(copyright © 1971 by Leslie A. Fiedler; reprinted with permission of Stein and Day/Publishers), Stein and Day, 1971, pp. 33-53.*

With the best will in the world a reader will still find this new American Gothic [*Meet Me in the Green Glen*] a chilling, disappointing experience, in which Warren's considerable talents are only rarely matched by material that continually seems frozen, motionless, as if refrigerated too long in too-familiar Faulknerian rhetoric and stereotypes.

The Antioch Review *(© 1972 by The Antioch Review, Inc.; reprinted by permission of the editors), Vol. XXXI, No. 4, 1971-72, p. 589.*

*Meet Me in the Green Glen* is stylistically Warren's most satisfying work. In dealing with the elemental human truths of pain and loneliness and identity and aging and pleasure it is not surprising that the author allows himself occasionally to lapse into a Faulknerian syntax—which from anyone but Faulkner is annoying. Now and then there are reminiscences of Stein. But most of the time the prose moves with a subtle indirection which portrays with great precision the torturous movement of introspection. . . . Warren's characters are real, their world is real, the slow evolution of their story to a sudden crisis is all too real. The poetry of the novel lies in its distillation of humanity, in its artistic combination of all elements—which we call vision.

*Kenneth John Atchity, in* Mediterranean Review, *Spring, 1972, pp. 64-5.*

[One] would dare speculate that Robert Penn Warren's *Meet Me in the Green Glen,* with its elements of romance, stream-of-consciousness, melodrama, and sex, with its ostensible *familiarity,* will work to crystallize a new category in fiction, the neohexameral or comtemplative novel, when what is contemplated is one's own coming into conscious sustained being, rather than going through more or less conscious (perceptible) local experience. . . .

The novel proceeds . . . by adumbrations, intersections, and gentle epiphanies emerging out of mechanical, almost obsessive, dutifulness and habit. . . . Warren does not undermine the simplicity of his characters, but he articulates their consciousness, gives them an unpretentious language that nevertheless has profound reverberations. . . .

The sense that Warren, while keeping up a *nearly* flawless simplicity of surface, is doing something metaphysically and esthetically adventurous gets ample reinforcement from the evidence that other novelists are trying to do what he has done, represent the creation of the delight and dignity of being human out of our modern "chaos" in a plausible idiom, on a workable ground of action, and with plausible characters who are not philosophical taws.

*Michael Cooke, in* The Yale Review *(© 1972 by Yale University; reprinted by permission of the editors), Summer, 1972, pp. 600-03.*

Since his first and best novel, *Night Rider* (1939), each of Warren's novels has been less interesting than its predecessor. In his early novels one is still aware of Warren the voice, the teacher, the exponent of a traditionalist view of the world that is essentially a philosophy of literature. Warren knows what makes certain literary works great; no critic in our generation has persuaded more people of just what there is to "understand" in poetry and fiction. He tends to *apply* understanding to his own imaginative creations—the understanding is in his voice, his will, his fluent skill. Warren is always in command of the narrative rather than the other way around, expounding the contradictions in human nature and breathing on its symbols. The omnipresent Warren voice, struggling with History, the contradictions of Human Nature and Original Sin as ideas for stories, makes him a sayer of contraries.

*Alfred Kazin, in his* Bright Book of Life: American Novelists & Storytellers from Hemingway to Mailer *(copyright © 1971, 1973 by Alfred Kazin; reprinted by permission of Little, Brown and Co. in association with the Atlantic Monthly Press), Little, Brown, 1973, pp. 45-6.*

There is all the bad writing anyone could hope for in Robert Penn Warren's *All the King's Men.* Could this really have been the runaway best seller of 1946 and could Mr. Penn Warren really be a distinguished American poet? The style is a messy mixture of Faulkner and pulp 'tec writing, the sort of tough-guy talk used by the narrating heroes of 1940s murder-mystery movies. . . . [If] the hero is a sensitive, serious student of history why does he write like somebody talking out of the side of his mouth?

*Stanley Reynolds, "Jungle Dust," in* New Statesman, *January 11, 1974, p. 55.*

George Orwell once remarked that 'in all novels about the East the scenery is the real subject matter'. By a similar generalization one might say that in all novels about the American Deep South violence, or the threat of violence, is the real subject matter. Racial tension, political and social feuding, ignorance, poverty, corruption, the ugliest possible face of capitalism presented by the big, greedy corporations, *machismo* and the Sanctity of Southern Womanhood —all these factors so charge the atmosphere that a spark can cause an explosion. Any drama, however tame, performed against this backcloth acquires elements of passion and excitement which compensate for limitations of plot, character or dialogue. Witness the flaccid sub-Freudian posturings of Tennessee Williams, which are infused with intense melodramatic vigour by the lurid situation in which they are set. A genuine tragedy, in such circumstances, attains epic proportions.

Robert Penn Warren's Pulitzer Prize-winning novel is not quite of that stature. . . . [*All the King's Men*] is a finer novel than other American blockbusters by such competitors as James Gould Cozzens, William Styron or Harper Lee. But it is not a great novel (it is jejune when placed beside the densely textured works of Faulkner, for example) and, indeed, it is difficult to sort out how far it relies, as a work of art, on its considerable intrinsic merit and how far on the volcanic background of the Deep South in the depression years. . . .

It is convincingly constructed, the characters are subtly portrayed, great depths of moral and imaginative insight are plumbed and there are large dollops of folk humour expressed in hammer-hard nail-on-the-head vernacular. What is more, Warren's novel relies as much on these virtues for its effect as on its setting, the submerged Southern jungle of which Huey Long was, so briefly, Kingfish.

*Piers Brendon, in* Books and Bookmen, *March, 1974, p. 87.*

Robert Penn Warren's first two novels have often seemed better as the trying-out of *All the King's Men* than as novels in their own right. Certainly, as studies of the nature and uses of political power, *Night Rider* and *At Heaven's Gate* are anticipatory. Both touch on big bossism in its corporate and individual forms, and both dramatize the dangers to the morally insensitive individual posed by abstract embodiments of power. . . . And compared to the firm assurances of the third novel, both seem tentative: they lack a particularized, sensuously immediate politician whose motives and acts are examined in a context of rich circumstantiality, as well as an engaging figure who is articulate enough to justify his credibility as a man both morally aware and expediently knowledgeable. . . .

There are flaws aplenty in *At Heaven's Gate,* not the least of which are the undisguised threads stitching the various segments together like a patchwork quilt. There are occasional spurts of fancy writing, and its more self-conscious effects are obviously derivative and uncertainly controlled. (The derivation is mostly from Faulkner: there are detectable echoes from *The Sound and the Fury, The Wild Palms,* and perhaps *Sanctuary.*) . . .

Despite [the] flaws *At Heaven's Gate* is finally more interesting than *Night Rider.* Its stylistic modulations, its scattergun point of view, and its deployment of multiple narratives can be seen as both untidy and typically Warrenesque. For the first time we see the rich profusion of favorite words and phrases—"the blind, unqualified retch and spasm of the flesh, the twist, the sudden push, the twitch, the pinch of ejection and refusal"—and the lengthy segments of second-person idiom, faintly ironic and precisely detailed, straight out of the tough-guy and private-eye tradition of the 1920s and 1930s. And, in its more discursive moments, *At Heaven's Gate* achieves a kind of lyric naturalism that becomes a hallmark of Warren's prose: periods of closely observed details strung out in an evocative rhetoric which invites nostalgia for a specific time and place or which invokes awe for a mythic history that seems to explain national and even human urges.

Someone once noted that *At Heaven's Gate* is Warren's only city novel. In a technical sense this is true. But it is also the closest Warren ever came to writing an agrarian novel. The values associated with southern Agrarianism—

integration of personality, mutual responsibility, and a general harmony of man and nature—are conspicuously missing in the lives of the major characters, but their very absence is a measure of their importance. . . .

*At Heaven's Gate* is Warren's only work in which the combined effects of technology, finance capitalism, and political power are examined so explicitly, even obviously. . . .

The novel is a brilliant example of Warren's insight into the manipulative uses of technique. The roles his characters play are desperate, and the techniques of their playing serve to mask, distract, or deceive. The major psychological patterns of the novel involve rejection and repudiation, often in violent ways. In most cases what the characters react against is the continuing relationship of the individual with the home, the past, and tradition. In Warren's own Unreal City the uses of technique are necessarily efforts to remake the self after new images, to fill the gaps left by the repudiation, to heal what Jack Burden of *All the King's Men* calls the terrible division of the age. What usually results in these efforts to create the self anew is to widen the division and make it all the more terrible. . . .

Warren's emphatic and iterated references to calculated effects, artifice, rhetorical patterns, deployment of manners and gestures, tricks of phrasing and bons mots, and cultivation of personal images for public consumption: all point up the plight of the fragmented self who is not at home even in the world it tries to make. In an urban milieu liberated from the demands of family, past, or tradition, values that celebrate man's responsibility for man are few and fragile. Techniques can only oil the machinery of an impersonal, dehumanized, and abstract society. . . .

As in most of his novels with strong political strains *At Heaven's Gate* is not about Warren's views of politics—even Agrarian politics—or politicians. It is a study of individuals who in the "blur of the world" strive to find a focus in their own shape and weight, apart from such piecemeal definitions as economic man or aesthetic man.

*James H. Justus, "On the Politics of the Self-Created: 'At Heaven's Gate'," in* Sewanee Review *(reprinted by permission of the editor; © 1974 by The University of the South), Spring, 1974, pp. 284-99.*

* * *

## WHITE, Patrick 1912-

**White, an Anglo-Australian novelist, short story writer, and playwright, won the Nobel Prize for Literature in 1973. His cyclopean novels, according to Hal Porter, are created by "putting together razor-bright sentences, glassy clauses, vitreous jigsaw slices of paradox and poetry, [and] the fastidious gluing on of sharp-edged fragments." His fiction is mythic, evoking the whole of Australian culture.**

[White's] sumptuous fiction shows one of the most considerable novelists writing today, at the pitch of his powers and form. *The Vivisector* joins the imaginative resources of the writer's *Riders in the Chariot* with the firmer, more abstinent manner developed in *The Solid Mandala.* What might have been in Patrick White's earlier work no more than a gratuitous flourish or creative frolic, is in this book, where there is an almost papal certainty about means, blended into the text and the texture. Descriptive wit enlivens the blandest things. . . .

Patrick White's talent is sad, furious, powerful. His method is the poet's, who struggles to compose, or rather to compel glimpses of significance and shades of meaning into a solid structure of being. To help him he has his vision, at certain moments his dazzling vision, of man, since he is a writer whose work is the application of his vision, not one who manipulates a plot or cultivates a sensibility or chronicles a period; and he has, as well, a gluttonous eye for details and the gift to render them palpably and exactly. His art, dense and image-ridden, stained with anxiety and sometimes with loathing, is, this novel confirms, a substantial and a genuine thing.

*William Walsh, "'The Vivisector'," in* Encounter, *May, 1971, pp. 81-2.*

White . . . deals with the integration of dualities within the individual.

One of White's techniques . . . is his utilization of the structural unit of the inward spiritual quest of the protagonist. [One can place] his work within the context of "the Judao-Christian cultural heritage from which it flowers.". . .

White is an heir to Henry James's objective narrative. . . .

*The Aunt's Story* (1948) marks the emergence of White's maturity as a writer. An interlacing framework of allegory, myth, and archetype provides a rich, seemingly evergreen form around which White constructs this and his remaining novels. However, . . . this could be deemed a fault in White's work, that all of his later works apparently spring from the same concerns and that the similarities of form and theme among the novels are too visible. . . .

*Riders in the Chariot* (1961), in my opinion, is perhaps of all of White's novels the one most blatantly patterned on the Christian myth. In contrast to *Voss,* the meaning of this novel frequently seems "arbitrarily imposed." Nevertheless, it works because of the enormity of the work and the fine delineation of character, but subtlety and allusiveness are lacking here. . . .

Any admirer of White must admit that some of his characters hover on the edge of stereotype—and that a didacticism now and then breaks through the lyricism of White's narrative. White occasionally cannot resist the urge to spell out the ideas to which he alludes. Another weakness I see in White is his failure to experiment with new forms and themes, or at least to lessen his reliance on allegory and archetype to inform his work. . . .

White's novels are novels, not mystical essays. What makes his writing, regardless of its excesses, so multilayered and exquisite is his use of the many literary traditions available to the probing, gifted writer.

*Nancy Winegardner Whichard, in* The Georgia Review, *Winter, 1973, pp. 619-21.*

Because White is obsessed by the implication of soul, of transcendent vision in bone and bowel, he harks back relentlessly to the process of aging. Incontinence, the worn skin, the sour odors of senility, the toothless appetites and spasms of the old, are worse than farcical. They lay bare the ignoble, perhaps accidental fact that the spirit is so meanly housed. White, like the Jacobean dramatists, like the tomb-sculptors of the baroque, pries at the skull beneath the skin and the thought beneath the skull—hammering for exit. If the rose flaunts its earthbound flesh, it is "in an honourably failed attempt to convey the ultimate." With old age this attempt grows desperate and ludicrous. Hence the studies of senescence in earlier novels by White —in "Riders in the Chariot," in "The Solid Mandala," probably his best. Hence, too, the brutal appositeness of Australia: a land, according to White, of strident muscularity, young, raw as new meat, hating the transcendent. To be old in Australia is to die twice. . . .

The reciprocities of minute material detail and vast time sweeps, the thread of hysteria underneath the dreary crust, the play of European densities against the gross vacancy of the Australian setting, are the constant motifs of White's fiction. . . .

[Exemplary] as it is of White's distinctive powers, "The Eye of the Storm" remains a disappointing book. The formula is inherently lopsided. In plot, in carpentry, it is intensely Jamesian. More than one touch in the miserable matrimonial chronicle of the Princesse derives from "The American" and from James's repeated novellas of overseas innocence or social climbing entrapped in the sheer malignity of French aristocratic usage. . . . Patrick White shares the Master's feel for the constricting vitality of family structures, for the feverish opportunism bred of idle wealth. He has the selfsame trick of spinning a kind of verbal terror and complexity out of terms that are psychological and abstract. But at the very same time White is, like James Purdy, one of the current virtuosos of the grotesque, of the carnal. The result is strain. White forces his style. . . .

There is in almost every one of White's novels and tales an eruption of savagery, an incident in which the volatile mixture of soul and flesh explodes. In "The Solid Mandala" it is the fratricide, the body being eaten by starved dogs, which ends the twinned lives of Arthur and Waldo Brown (one of the great studies of love in modern literature). It is the apocalyptic fire in "Riders in the Chariot," mirroring the fires in the Nazi ovens. But, however Gothic, these occurrences stem from the logic of the narrative. The incest of Dotty and Basil Hunter strikes one as merely histrionic, a stroke of terror and uncleanliness staged only for effect.

There is, in fact, not a touch of redeeming elegance, of disinterested humanity in "The Eye of the Storm." Everything tilts to ugliness or lumbering ferocity. God knows the world is in a tawdry season, and no serious novelist need feel optimistic. But unrelieved blackness rings false. It celebrates itself.

*George Steiner, "Carnal Knowledge" (abridged with permission), in* The New Yorker, *March 4, 1974, pp. 109-13.*

Is it possible, one wonders, to advance the name of a modern British novelist who might conceivably be a candidate for the Nobel Prize? There are indeed a number of distinguished novelists in Britain, but I would find it hard to suggest one with the quality and largeness of creative achievement which one must suppose to be the requirement. If we look for energy, creative energy, in the novel, it seems to me that we have at present to go outside Britain. It is indeed energy which characterizes so much work in a number of Commonwealth countries, whether in the creative insouciance and sumptuous imagination of Patrick White, the endless multiplying incident of R. K. Narayan's Malgudi, or the passionate lucidity of V. S. Naipaul. The sense of a more uninhibited life, which the reader finds in these writings, comes, I suppose, from a more substantial, if not necessarily better-grounded, confidence in the future, which is itself related to a more aspiring and perhaps less uncertainly complex national purpose than we know in Britain. As serious writers each of these novelists cannot but be involved in accumulating the spiritual experience of the race. He is concerned to draw the exact curve of the specific sensibility of his own time and nation. He is the analyst and the critic of his society. And he is doing these things with the powerful pressure of English literature removed some way from him. He is, to some degree, free from the suffocating conviction that it has all been done before and so much better.

Certainly the qualities of largeness, uninhibited confidence, potent creative energy are present in *The Eye of the Storm. The Eye of the Storm* appeared just three years after *The Vivisector* and at the end of a fifteen-year cycle which included *Voss, Riders in the Chariot,* and *The Solid Mandala.* In quality and authority it suggests a strong and continuing creative power. It is a work saturated with death. The novelist's grim infatuation is animated by an incessant, probing curiosity. . . . Creative inquisitiveness is joined in White's novels with the hunger to illustrate. Each is more than satisfied in a story of domination, possession and jealousy which is romantically unflagging in energy and also classically concentrated, a handful of Elizabeth Hunter's connections constituting the dramatis personae and their relationships the plot.

White's power to refine from the grossness of a bodily condition the subtlety of a mental state has the fullest scope in this re-creation of decrepitude and decease. Mrs. Hunter pours as much vitality into her dying as agitates the whole lives of most people. Her character and situation are designed to figure White's vision of death as an intense specification, almost as the point, of life. . . .

White, who has shown himself elsewhere (in *Riders in the Chariot* and *The Solid Mandala* in particular) as horrified by the cruelty of communities and their blind fervor in favor of the average, is appalled in this novel by the savagery of individuals. . . . [The] book's strongest and most vibrant value, against which I suppose we are to measure the distortions of life, is not virtue in the conventional sense in which it exists in the husband and the nurse but rather the absolute intensity of life represented by Mrs. Hunter herself and instanced supremely in her dying.

What makes Patrick White so rare in the contemporary novel in English is his power to discover and present in the grubbiness of life, in the wretchedness of senility in this novel, the depths and distances which Wordsworth found in the life of childhood. That capacity showed itself first in *The Aunt's Story* in 1948. . . .

*The Aunt's Story,* of course, is neither a passive history nor clinical description but the rendering in terms of art of the process of mental collapse, and one is conscious from the first, in the tone, in the nuance of word and image, of some disturbing irregularity in the material of Theodora's experience. But the story of mental decay, the fiction which constitutes the material of the novel, is itself a means in the development of a profound and powerful theme, which is an ordering and clarifying force in the novel and the current managing the drift of event and detail. It has to do with the nature of the self and more particularly with the release from the self and even indeed with the obliteration of the self. It is this complication, this further resonance, which turns what might have been a medically exact account of mental disintegration into a richer and more humanly significant composition.

There is a certain toughness and palpability in the idiom of *The Tree of Man* (1955) which is very different from the attenuated and neurotic fineness of *The Aunt's Story* but which is in keeping with the centrality of the common human experience it deals with. It comes out in the feeling for the land which sustains every event and each character in the tale. It is a double sense of the creative force in the earth and the homely forms and shapes that man can make it assume. . . .

Just as *The Aunt's Story* shows how neurosis can be the means to an apprehension fuller than the conventionally "normal" one, so *The Tree of Man* shows the capacity of decent ordinariness to be transformed into a higher order of existence altogether. It requires a kind of genius, the genius for staying, in Henry James's phrase, the subject's "truth of resistance."

*The Tree of Man* and *Voss* (1957) represent Patrick White's different reactions to what he once called his panic at the exaltation of the average. *The Tree of Man* burrows into the commonplace; *Voss* reconstructs the extreme. The wilderness which was to be domesticated in *The Tree of Man* in *Voss* is to school the hero. If we use a biblical analogy, which seems distinctly appropriate to the character of Patrick White's work, we can say that *The Tree of Man* is his version of Genesis and Redemption, and *Voss* his John the Baptist. (But leading to what Christ, the reader may wonder. The answer, if there is an answer, suggested by the novel, seems to be some intrinsic or buried Christ in Voss himself.) . . .

The upheaval of the substantial world is the great shaping activity working through *Riders in the Chariot*. The novel follows the favored White pattern—a strong central conception, development by means of a biographical method, and an endless multiplication of palpable detail. . . .

Patrick White belongs to a line of novelists whose art embodies a concentrated and dazzling vision of man. Such writers are not manipulators of plot or cultivators of a sensibility or critics of manners or chroniclers of a period. Their art is initiated by their vision, and its form is determined more by a force from within than by any extrinsic scaffolding. It is somewhere between imaginative power and authenticity and crispness of detail that Patrick White's work is imperfect, in the area where architectural capacity and taste are required. The failure is not in the generating concept nor in the worked-out detail—in neither the idea nor the vocabulary, that is—but somewhere between, in what one might call the syntactical structure. *Voss* and *Riders in the Chariot* certainly answer this account, I believe: impressive in the constructive idea, superb in their palpable concreteness, but apt on occasion to offer an imposed and gratuitous symbolism in place of organic design.

One novel exempt from this weakness is *The Solid Mandala* (1966), the story of the Brown twins—shambling, simple-minded Arthur and brittle, "gifted" Waldo. The movement between idea and material in the novel is unbroken, and the complex theme intimately informs the dense material. The tension between cerebrally abstract and intuitively concrete understanding, which Patrick White is so conscious of, is sustained throughout. . . .

[In] *The Solid Mandala* . . . [there] is an unbroken circular movement connecting the old men. . . . Indeed the structure of the novel is composed of a series of similar movements or concentric circles. . . .

*The Vivisector* (1970) shows White at the top of his power and form. . . . The subtlety and scope, the intuitive rightness . . . put [*The Vivisector*] on a level with *Voss* and *Riders in the Chariot*. The business of the artist, the novel implies, is both to register his perception of reality with the most rigorous precision, and by a painful discipline of self-sacrifice to compose these into a more inclusive and healing truth. But Hurtle Duffield, the artist, the vivisector, uses the damaging razor more than the healing scalpel. It is art as cruelty which is most stressed in *The Vivisector,* art as the torturer of accepted realities; there is a near-Swiftian force behind the negative knife. The hints of art's other and positive functions are more dispersed.

It is characteristic of White's sensibility that this perception about art should so naturally find expression in metaphor. His work abounds in these initiating creative metaphors, just as his mode of presentation and narrative is conducted through choking thickets of imagery. Other central metaphors of this kind are those of the explorer and life at the extremes in *Voss*; of the heavenly chariot which is the intuitive, immediate poetic and religious consciousness in *Riders in the Chariot*; of the glass marble whose enigmatic lights mirror the cloudy depths of personality in *The Solid Mandala*. Art as the knife and the artist as the tormented but disciplined surgeon; life as an unexplored desert, and the extremes of suffering and simplicity as the conditions of man's deepest experience; neurosis as a figure of the effort towards a purer vision; twins as the image of the divided self; the disruption of the common world of substance by the single and singular soul: it is in this play of metaphorical life that one comes to see the lesson of White's art—the lesson, that is, in Henry James's sense, that "deeply lurks in any vision prompted by life."

The comparable figure in *The Eye of the Storm* . . . is the metaphor in the title. Mrs. Hunter's life had been transfigured by a certain entranced experience of pure existence she had undergone in a typhoon on an island off the Queensland coast, where she had entered the very eye of the storm. This constitutes for her a model or shape of perfection that she had struggled to make her life and then the act of dying itself conform to, in spite of the intervention of treachery, greed, guilt, or even love. This is the profound and powerful theme which is the ordering and clarifying influence in the novel, which turns what might have been a clinically exact account of disintegration into a more complex, more humanly significant composition. It is this which makes *The Eye of the Storm* a fit member of an impressive family of novels. It shows us insistently the ravaged harshness of Patrick White's reading of human reality. . . . At the same time we are aware, though more obliquely, less positively, in *The Eye of the Storm* than in *The Tree of Man, Riders in the Chariot,* or *The Solid Mandala,* of the flow of love, of the possibility of illumination, of the conditions under which something rich and healing could be constructed. It takes a talent of a rare order to keep the two themes in place and in proportion.

*William Walsh, "Fiction as Metaphor: The Novels of Patrick White," in* Sewanee Review *(reprinted by permission of the editor; © 1974 by The University of the South), Spring, 1974, pp. 197-211.*

The plot of Patrick White's new novel, *The Eye of the Storm,* . . . patently has its affinities with an Angus Wilson short story. And that is part of the trouble, or at any rate part of the question. Is Patrick White—Nobelist novelist—a giant or a gigantist? Does he have the amplitude of mind, the variety of solicitude, the range of scrutiny, that demand more than 600 pages for their true telling?

The works of literature that do have such amplitude are continually invoked throughout *The Eye of the Storm*: *King Lear* and *La Chartreuse de Parme. King Lear* is mentioned or alluded to dozens of times. . . .

Yet, although the reader is aware that it is as much the unlikenesses between the modern happenings and the masterpiece of ancientness as the likenesses that Mr. White is insisting upon, the effect of the re-reiterated parallel is at once muffled and strident, partly because insisting upon it is indeed what Mr. White does. I should go further, and say that there are very few respects in which either the likenesses or the unlikenesses amount to anything at once penetrating and truly substantial. But even those who go less far may still feel that there is something perfunctorily obsessional about the novel's always having *King Lear* so handily to hand. . . .

[What] matters to Mr. White is oddly at odds with itself. He wishes that profound possibilities should judge and rebuke the shallow hurtfulness of modern life, and yet almost all his own gift is for punishing shallow hurtfulness. When Basil describes vermouth as "only an excuse for gin," he winces at himself: "His knowingness appalled him." Yet the knowingness is that of his creator too, knowingly putting down the knowing, and Mr. White is trapped within the very terms that he deplores. The sharp eye which Mr. White undoubtedly has is for people flashing a sharp eye; yet the vistas do not open out, they shrivel in. "Whichever way she looked she could see no end to her dishonesty: a vista of mirrors inside a mirror."

This has been a strain within Mr. White's work from early days. His second novel, *The Living and the Dead,* published thirty-three years ago, was out to unite "those who have the capacity for living," and "oppose them to the destroyers, to the dealers in words, to the diseased, to the most fatally diseased—the indifferent." Yet Mr. White, even then, wrote as a dealer in words, his style mannered, acute, self-congratulatory. His style is now richer and more various, and it truly has more to congratulate itself upon—and yet it is still at its best when it is bent upon its most questionable activity, morally and artistically: despising the despisers. To keep describing a character at a party as "the detergent knight" (and to cap this with "The detergent knight at one stage was unable to contain a fart")—this is to use language no more responsibly than do the detergent people. This is to observe, not with the eye—and ear—of the storm, but with the eye and ear of a snooping private detective. Mr. White dwindles into being merely the private eye of the storm. . . .

[The] presiding genius of *The Eye of the Storm* is not, as it hopes, Stendhal (a writer never predictable and often profoundly magnanimous) but a very different Frenchman. It is characteristic of the way in which this novel is trapped within its deplored knowingness that it cannot bring itself to utter his name—but he figures as the author of *The Master of Santiago,* and Basil recalls the author, "a cantankerous, hostile Frenchman arriving unannounced to catch you out." The phrase does wonderfully catch Henry de Montherlant out (a writer whom I was once given the opportunity to deplore in *NYR,* June 5, 1969), Montherlant being a writer whose whole aim was to catch the human race out. But Mr. White catches himself out too. For the great critical statement on Stendhal is this, by T. S. Eliot:

> Stendhal's scenes, some of them, and some of his phrases, read like cutting one's throat; they are a terrible humiliation to read, in the understanding of human feelings and human illusions of feeling that they force upon the reader.

The trouble with Mr. White, as with Montherlant, is, first, that his scenes and his phrases read like cutting someone else's throat, not one's own at all; and second, that his self-gratifying obsession with human illusions of feeling has become eerily independent of any understanding of human feelings. . . .

What was once the glory of the novel—its specificity, its knowledgeability, its being in possession of and putting you in possession of so much of the evidence (all of it?) on which you could judge for yourself—is at present the stunting impoverishment of the novel, since it is a permanent and well-nigh irresistible invitation to irresponsibility, to cheating, to the crucial immorality of the artist which Lawrence stigmatized as putting the thumb on the scale.

The novelist who deplores the egregious and corrosive knowingness of our times finds that he cannot resist the temptations of the falsely specific, the synthetic authenticity of the selectively invented. Poetry, just because it can traditionally establish its authenticity other than through the easy substantiation of invented detail, is able to escape this dilemma.

*Christopher Ricks, "Gigantist," in* The New York Review of Books *(reprinted with permission from* The New York Review of Books; *© 1974 by NYREV, Inc.), April 4, 1974, pp. 19-20.*

White's thesis in [*The Eye of the Storm*] is simply this: We are all alone in a chaotic world, and only we ourselves can help ourselves during our brief tenure. Others are predators who hinder rather than help. "Families can eat you," one of White's characters says, and his novel proceeds to demonstrate just that. . . .

Central to the novel is Elizabeth Hunter, the heroine

(though none of White's characters are "heroic"—she is destined to remain forever a mere "hunter" after truth). . . .

[White] is not . . . an instinctive, non-analytical writer, an objective realist or a subjective romanticist. Every scene seems an ordered, deliberate counterpoint to another, all of which are parts of a single artistic whole rather than a reflection of life's chaos. Further, White is a bit of a symbolist. When a rare platypus, or pink sapphire, or basin of mould, [makes] an appearance, he intends [it] to carry secondary significance; when a character is badly named Flora Manhood, we can also assume he means the name to bear symbolic freight. And the repeated references to *King Lear* and to *The Charterhouse of Parma* bear scrutiny for their relation to White's own book. (The son Basil and the daughter Dorothy are more than a bit like Shakespeare's Goneril and Regan, concerned only with the division of the kingdom rather than the verities of the heart, and Mrs. Hunter herself could be compared with Stendhal's Contessa, a composite vision of the *bellezza folgorante* [the beauty that blinds like lightning] of all the women of Stendhal's and White's dreams.)

Unlike Stendhal, for whom the surface of life had no appeal, White seems near-preoccupied with surfaces. He documents every drop of dew on the rose, every mote of dust in the air. His descriptions give the novel a rich texture: Sentence for sentence he writes the most beautiful novelistic prose since Elizabeth Bowen. Occasionally the texture is too rich, a bit like over-indulgence in chocolate *mousse*. . . .

Yet White's attention to minutiae has its rewards. When Sir Basil continues drowsily smiling, "till a hair bent in one of his nostrils, making him sneeze," we recognize a writer who perceives the little annoyances of man. He is particularly good at recording our most embarrassing moments. . . . White shows us stumble as well as sail, and he is particularly good describing the awkwardness of sex.

A further attribute of White's technique is the sheer epigrammatic quality of his prose. Phrase after phrase cries out to be underlined, memorized. . . .

Finally there are White's essays into stream-of-consciousness. For the most part, these are brief and seem pre-Joycean. White pricks at the surface, but never succeeds in stripping away whole layers. Despite his excellences—and there are many—what White says of Elizabeth Hunter must finally apply to his own work, at least as evidenced in this novel: "Elizabeth Hunter was never womanly enough, her flaws too perfectly disguised under appearance, enormous, gaping, at times agonizing flaws." After all the fascinating descriptions and adroit aphorisms, White's characters while not quite types, are exceedingly thin of blood. The blood they lack is White's own, and if they are less than human, it is because he seems less than humane. With perhaps the exception of Frau Lippman, the author shows no compassion for any of these people. He is a demiurge, looking down, pulling strings, unsmilingly.

*Robert Phillips, in* Commonweal *(reprinted by permission of Commonweal Publishing Co., Inc.), May 17, 1974, pp. 269-70.*

[There] are few contemporary novelists who have the fastidious eye and ear of Patrick White. His prose is instantly recognizable; it has a South American sonority and plumpness. You could poke it and it would yield. *The Cockatoos* is a collection of his short and shorter stories, but, like a natural exhibitionist, Mr. White returns throughout to the same knots of life; the brunt of his prose in these stories is directed against his old enemies, the hysterical women of the title, scheming, winning small victories, the matrons of a dying breed.

These are the stuff of which conventional fiction is made, but Mr. White has gone to exhausted soil and brought forth hot water. And at the centre, of course, is White's breeding ground—vast Australia, tottering from the mist with a few colonials clinging to its rubbery slopes. . . . [The] short story, even the novella, cramps Mr. White somewhat. The narrative is occasionally too cluttered, with protagonists knocking against each other like real people, or alternatively too abstract when it loses the fine specificity of White's social observation. His vision is too intense for a small compass.

*Peter Ackroyd, in* The Spectator *(© 1974 by* The Spectator; *reprinted by permission of* The Spectator*), June 22, 1974, pp. 771-72.*

[A] novel must live in characters and action, not by claims of profundity or an intricate surface of language. *The Eye of the Storm* does not live. . . . *The Eye of the Storm* overpowers the reader with hurricanes and lesbians and horrible parties, all rich in symbolic significance. Its characters, from the grand old lady, her face grotesquely painted for company, dying while sitting on her commode, to her refugee housekeeper (her family dead in concentration camps, she enjoys dressing in male costume to do music hall dances), display the author's invention rather than his knowledge of human nature.

*Patricia Meyer Spacks, in* The Hudson Review *(copyright © 1974 by The Hudson Review, Inc.; reprinted by permission), Vol. XXVII, No. 2, Summer, 1974, p. 287.*

Patrick White's *The Cockatoos* inspects with a fine amplitude the constrictings and minimisings of ageing time, and possesses, with the confidence his fictions have worked hard for years at earning, a varied set of people whose problem is, above all, the sapping away of former confidence. There's certainly little—apart from the novelist's superb command of the medium—to alleviate the bleakness. Bodies become unlovely and scarcely lovable—flabby and wrinkled with the slackness of age or skinny with its emaciation; loved ones die; ambitions come to naught; savings and possessions dwindle; people are greedy, or proud, or snobbish, or just humdrum. And love and sex that should bind us defensively in couples and families scarcely manage to be more than negative factors.

*Valentine Cunningham, in* New Statesman, *July 5, 1974, p. 23.*

* * *

## WHITTEMORE, (Edward) Reed 1919-

**Whittemore, a gifted American poet and essayist, is concerned with middle-class values and aspirations and topical issues. (See also *Contemporary Authors*, Vols. 9-12, rev. ed.)**

[Whittemore] is as wittily cultural as they come, he has read more than any young man anybody knows, has been all kinds of places, yet shuffles along in an old pair of tennis shoes and khaki pants, with his hands in his pockets, saying to every head-down, hustling graduate student he meets, "Shucks, fellow, don't take all this so seriously. Learn, as I was born to know, that all literature, all life, is secretly funny." . . .

Whittemore has plenty of whatever it takes to get you to "reassess the world around you," and is not much interested in the other thing, that makes you *like*, or hate in any significant way, anything you know, or think you know. The Subjects of the world stand around you, during your reading of Whittemore's poems, revealed in their inconsequentially ridiculous, very recognizable, and humorously contemptible attitudes, and never in their most deeply characteristic and unknown gestures, in unmanageable love. I suppose this is to say that Whittemore is essentially a satirist—yet even as I write I am not sure of that "essentially." But it *is* true that almost all the poems [in *An American Takes a Walk*] are full of very telling satiric invention and observation, Americanized Auden, and "wonderful fun" (as in "Paul Revere's Ride," which is just that). For Whittemore is himself the perfect *Furioso* poet. Certainly I never saw anything published in that genuinely lamented magazine half so good of its kind as the best of these poems. Yet . . . what *is* it, exactly, in terms of the immovable values of real poetry, to be or to have been "the perfect *Furioso* poet"? To have been wittily uncommitted to anything save a few vague humanistic principles that have no issue except to mock, condescendingly and as from a great distance, inhumanly cool with the scintillant remove of knowledgeable superiority, a few of the things we are all against: War, the City, the Army, Science Divorced from Man?. . . Strength of feeling, it is true, uncritical and breathless with unsanction, comes in a few times, but, save in one or two wonderful exceptions, the effect is that of a jar, and we tend to look up guiltily, saying, "What is *wrong* with Whittemore here, anyway?" Yet we are saying this of the poet who wrote, "And the laced-in hazards of the covert hills," and, for anybody's terror and helpless acquiescence, "Caught in an offshore breeze / A butterfly will turn / Too late to fight the air . . .". Truly hearing the way that "fight" works, no one could argue the effectiveness of this passage. Yet it is more than *effective*. If the theory of the "objective correlative" takes any value from examples, it ought to stand deep in the theorist's mind through this one, bearing with it all the latent terror of the natural world. The image realized here is part of that world, and finally that of man, gained, in an unforeseen and indispensable way, through Whittemore's words. Of the two (or more) poets in Whittemore, I should like most to see the one who wrote those lines emerge.

*James Dickey, "Reed Whittemore" (1956), in his* Babel to Byzantium *(reprinted with the permission of Farrar, Straus & Giroux, Inc.; copyright © 1956, 1957, 1958, 1959, 1960, 1961, 1962, 1963, 1964, 1965, 1966, 1967, 1968 by James Dickey), Farrar, Straus, 1968, pp. 49-52.*

In so many of Reed Whittemore's poems, the ear is flawless. His voice is perfectly pitched, immaculate, suave, urbane. There are no slips, no mistakes—if he trips, it is always accidentally-on-purpose, he comes up smiling, and we smile with him, not at him. He is one of our dwindling few tasteful and intelligent satirists, and we don't dare risk putting him off on some other track; but we do wish he would surprise us a bit more.

When the good poem starts to unwind, to uncoil, it serpentines cunningly, and as the poem rises to a perfect little loop at the finish, and sticks its little forked tongue out at me, I am genuinely tickled and stung. But there is always a moment just before the finish when I want to slash through the poem's sleek hide and expose the rough second skin, and this devilishness of mine lingers with me as an aftertaste when I finish reading the poem. . . . Whittemore's style, tone, manner, and range of targets had become too predictable. He has stuck to the same mode for so long, I had begun to associate only one type of poetry with him—the low guttural chuckle of a highbrow Ogden Nash. Perhaps the comparison is unfair; his sensibility is sophisticated, closer to Jules Pfeiffer's cartoons.

*Laurence Lieberman, in* The Yale Review *(© 1968 by Yale University; reprinted by permission of the editors), Winter, 1968, pp. 267-68.*

[In *Poems, New & Selected*,] Mr. Whittemore carries on his quarrel with himself and the world in a tone that is casual, witty, civilized, detached; he likes to deflect anger into irony; he is cool. . . . Mr. Whittemore *has* caught the note of sadness by now. It shows through more and more in the new poems, especially those which most deeply involve his feelings, poems about himself as a man and a poet in an environment not geared to either humanity or poetry. "The Seven Days," a long sequence, falls, I suppose, under the "public summation" category, and it is a beautiful and highly inventive combination of tongue-in-cheek brightness and the sadness that comes with understanding. Among the old poems there are many occasional ones: frankly funny ones, and those that are straight and serious, but remain lightweight, either because the specific subject doesn't really involve Mr. Whittemore, or because a more deeply affecting treatment would have meant greater lyrical intensity, something which is not, or at least was not, Mr. Whittemore's *forte*. His most remarkable characteristic surely is his mental and verbal nimbleness. In the new poems, however, he is both sharper and deeper. He is willing to drop the insistent tone of self-mockery; he does not mind being exasperated, unhappy, and just plain angry.

*Lisel Mueller, in* Shenandoah *(copyright by* Shenandoah; *reprinted from* Shenandoah: *The Washington and Lee University Review with the permission of the Editor), Spring, 1968, pp. 67-8.*

When not simply low-pitched light verse, Reed Whittemore's . . . poems [in *Fifty Poems Fifty*] are dry, wry, and wrinkled. One of them is called *A Song of Wrinkles*: a far more accurate and appropriate title for his book than *Fifty Poems Fifty*. The poem has all the outstanding Whittemore characteristics. It starts as though it were going to be a facetious bit of self-irony or a satirical squib against advertising. The kind of rhymes and half-rhymes it begins with support the impression, yet there is just enough serious edge to allow a quite forceful ending to develop. It is as though the voice began with a wobble, then discovered its true spin just in time to hit a Popean note of wit, put to a serious purpose, at the very end. Whittemore's desire to keep to an idiom that is absolutely natural and only minimally emotional and "poetic" is a bit self-defeating. Still, once one accepts the book as a collection of dry pods rattling in the wind, a certain wind-harp music starts up from it after all, as in some of the poems of Kenneth Burke or William Empson. No doubt a staunchly deliberate rejection of the whole romantic complex is implied in Whittemore's poetic reductionism.

*M. L. Rosenthal, "Plastic Possibilities," in* Poetry *(© 1971 by The Modern Poetry Association; reprinted by permission of the Editor of* Poetry*), November, 1971, pp. 102-03.*

* * *

## WINTERS, Yvor 1900-1968

**Winters was an American poet and critic. His literary criticism was among the most influential in modern letters. (See also *Contemporary Authors*, Vols. 9-12, rev. ed.; obituary, Vols. 25-28.)**

Winters is a serious man, and in some respects quite a useful one, and it is regrettable that to a generation of writers younger than himself he has become largely a comic figure, the man who thinks that Elizabeth Daryush is our foremost living poet and that Edith Wharton is a better writer than Henry James. Winters has made these statements, and others more extreme, but he is our foremost and perhaps sole representative of a vanishing art, Johnsonian criticism, and he is well worth careful study. . . .

Implicit in [his] view of the moral nature of art and criticism is the obligation on the critic to "correct" traditional opinion in so far as he believes it to be wrong. Without question, this wearying ethical burden is in part responsible for some of Winters's wilder evaluations. . . . [There is] a possibility that after disposing of American literature he looks forward to rearranging the history of English literature or even of world literature.

Into this giant project in the correction of opinion only now beginning to emerge, all of Winters's critical writing is designed to fit. . . .

It is obvious that Yvor Winters is . . . a throwback to the violent oracular tradition of an earlier century, [for he] bases his evaluations in classicism and traditionalism, and . . . enlists his evaluations in the cause of political reaction. . . .

The vocabulary and examples of Winters's criticism are contemporary, but his heart and mind seem firmly back in the London of 1700. . . .

Winters has contributed a number of things of value to contemporary criticism: some good metrical analyses; some brilliant close reading and studies of poetic structure; . . . salutary insistence on "the intellectual and moral significance of literary forms," and the relationship between beliefs and forms (although most of the specific relationships and significances he points out are foolish). Most important, he has, almost single-handedly, kept an important critical function, evaluation, alive for us. His evaluations tend to be made in terms that are semantically meaningless, contradictory, purely subjective, and never defined. . . . He gives only his conclusions, almost never with any evidence approaching adequacy, and in a form in which it is impossible to argue with him or even understand what he is trying to say. Nevertheless, he does evaluate, does compare, contrast, grade, rate, and rank, at a time when most serious criticism only analyzes and interprets. . . . What criticism can adopt from Winters is his vigor and boldness of evaluation, while making sounder evaluations than his, making them on a basis of more significance to literature than his concepts of "rationality" and "morality," and with them giving the reader the whole structure of analysis, to serve as a basis for the reader's checking the evaluation or making his own on the evidence. Winters's own five-stage process culminating in evaluation [elaborated elsewhere in Hyman's essay] is a fairly good basis for such a process. Winters himself has seldom taken advantage of it. Testing it first by turning it on him, as this essay has attempted to do, it works out pretty well. We find Yvor Winters, in a "unique act of judgment" dogmatic and impolite enough to flatter his methods, an excessively irritating and bad critic of some importance.

*Stanley Edgar Hyman, "Yvor Winters and Evaluation in Criticism," in his* The Armed Vision: A Study in the Methods of Modern Literary Criticism *(copyright © 1947, 1948, 1955 by Alfred A. Knopf, Inc.; reprinted by permission of the publisher), Knopf-Vintage, 1955, pp. 23-53.*

[Professional critics] are those who are vowed to the job by a kind of act of faith. They make their living out of literature in the true sense, which is not a question of cash but of moral habit. In short, they use literature to build up for themselves a world of values. Inevitably, they don't like much, for in all viable moralities the elect are, of necessity, few. So their work is devoted to keeping up the standards, always with an intellectual passion, sometimes with a certain savagery. Like old-fashioned doctors, they believe that blood must at times be let to preserve the health of the system. In England, the foremost professional critic is in this sense F. R. Leavis; in America, he is Yvor Winters.

*In Defense of Reason* has taken a long time to reach us. . . . It is a pity that the book has been so long on the way, for original ideas spread their light before them; a number of Winters's suggestions have become fashions and he has not been given credit for them. He was, for instance, the first man to debunk Eliot's claims to classicism by showing how his theories descend straight from the late Romantics; he attacked the vagaries of neo-Symbolism and the craze for Laforguian irony (which he blandly equated with 'careless writing'); he praised Melville, James and, with reservations, Stevens, Crane and Hawthorne, long before any of them had become cult-figures. All this he had writ large in the thirties and early forties. We are just catching up with him.

But Winters would wish to base his ultimate reputation less on his originality or on the profundity of his insights than on his ability to produce a system that works. He has a rage for order and is fierce in proportion to an author's lack of it. He calls himself an absolutist, which means he demands nothing less than everything. . . .

[There] is no arguing with Winters. But principles, particularly when they concern the enormous complexity of artistic and moral judgement, are better left brief or implicit than explained. The critic creates his audience and his context more by his intellectual tone than by spelling things out. Leavis, when challenged to define one of his terms, would, I imagine, prefer to point to a work of art than to launch into abstractions. Winters, on the other hand, is determined to have everything down in black and white. The results are often less flexible and profound than his practice. . . . The business of the poet is to know himself: by his art he makes clearings of sanity in the encroaching jungle of experience; and because of his skill, these clearings are more lucid, more precise, more generally meaningful than those of other people. His method, for Winters as for Wordsworth, is that of 'emotion recollected in tranquillity'. . . .

Winters makes it sound as though the *rational* understanding always came before the poem rather than during the process of writing, or even after it; as though each poem were accreted round a separate pearl of wisdom. He also implies that there are rules for the degree of emotion proper to each subject. It sounds more like a Renaissance than a modern theory. What he is describing, I suggest, is less the act of poetry than the act of criticism.

It is easy to see why. Like Winters, I too dislike obscurantism and the cant of blind inspiration. I am all for poets knowing what they mean. But knowing is not a clear-cut business. In the twentieth century, to be intelligent does not mean simply to be rational. It means the ability to make one's reason supple and subtle enough to include the irrational without being overwhelmed by it. The physicists have long worked with this element of irrationality, which they call entropy, the measure of chance or probability. In other terms, the whole of Freud's work was devoted to showing how irrational desires and fears run deep and compulsively below the most rational motives. The irrational, in short, is a vital element in modern reason.

When Winters, however, calls his book *In Defense of Reason* he really means it. He is not only Johnsonian in style; like the Doctor, he believes absolutely in the power of rational common sense. Because he is a peculiarly fine critic, his logic is always instinct with feeling, but he seeks to reduce everything to its terms. It doesn't always work. Eliot's importance, for example, has nothing to do with his Symbolist tricks and obscurity: instead it is in the way he worked out for our time a language in which great formal intelligence combines with great psychological depth, in which the rational and irrational meet and illuminate each other. But Winters will have none of him. He opts instead for the totally rational. And that means Robert Bridges, Adelaide Crapsey and Elizabeth Daryush, 'the finest British poet since T. Sturge Moore'—'that sheep', Yeats called him, 'in sheep's clothing'.

It is perhaps the least distinguished 'great tradition' any important critic has produced. Yet although Winters has deliberately set his face against American modernism, his choice is not dictated by mere perversity. Like Zeno with his arrow, he is in a logical quandary: Winters admires above all sureness and clarity of moral choice; therefore he is against the experimental because it attempts to cope more or less directly with 'the confused and therefore frightening emotion' of unregulated experience; therefore he makes a virtue out of the traditional which 'endeavours to utilize the greatest possible amount of the knowledge and wisdom, both technical and moral . . . to be found in precedent poetry. It assumes the ideal existence of a normal quality of feeling'; therefore he chooses Bridges & Co. The flying arrow does not move; the great poets are the consolidators, not the transformers of art. For all his originality, Winters is, by force of logic, profoundly reactionary.

Yet this taste for clear logic and moral certainty is also the strength of his criticism. His method is to combine literary insight with the history of ideas. Lucidly, stringently, he builds up the world of ideas and beliefs in which his authors wrote. He then goes through their works showing how the ideas were transformed and coloured by the writers' sensibilities. It is a kind of paraphrase done from the inside, so that at the moment of defining what a work of art says, Winters is defining how it feels. . . . It takes a major critic to combine that degree of aesthetic understanding with so firm and pervasive a judgement.

So in the end, his tight, restrictive moral system seems not only justified but necessary. He is a man of acute moral instincts with no strong moral system to which he can instinctively adhere. Although he deeply understands the New England tradition, he is not part of it. He belongs, apparently, to no organized church. So he is left with his belief in literature, his logic and his considerable ability as a writer (he is also a distinguished poet). From these he has erected, by Johnsonian reasonableness, a moral and literary tradition of his own. One may not agree with it, but it is impossible not to admire his skill, his courage and the superb criticism it has enabled him to write.

*A. Alvarez, "Yvor Winters" (originally published in* The New Statesman, *1960), in his* Beyond All This Fiddle: Essays 1955-1967 *(copyright © 1968 by A. Alvarez; reprinted by permission of Random House, Inc.), Random House, 1968, pp. 255-59.*

[The] early poems which Winters has seen fit to supersede are very much influenced by those of William Carlos Williams, but they seem to me better than any poems Williams has ever written. They not only show great spontaneity and imagination—an imagination really working with and in and *through* its subjects—but also a high degree of intuitive linguistic perceptiveness; above all, they are wonderfully free of the will, that Medusa-face that turns hearts and poems to stone. They are very much the poems of a man who, though not quite sure of what he is doing, is yet seeing and experiencing newly, freshly, in each poem as if for the first time, his world and the words by which it may be explored and lived. I believe this Winters entirely when he says, "Adventurer in / living fact, the poet / mounts into the spring, / upon his tongue the taste of / air becoming body." Among certain reviewers in the past it has been a commonplace to denigrate Winters's later poems by praising his earlier ones, but these first poems exist, and there are always going to be people like myself who prefer them. Their most surprising characteristic is their wonderful feeling for motion—one somehow thinks of Winters as inert—their feeling for color and light, set down with young uncertainty and eagerness. . . .

[The later style makes its appearance] in a poem called

"The Moralists." It begins, "You would extend the mind beyond the act, / Furious, bending, suffering in thin / And unpoetic dicta; you have been / Forced by hypothesis to fiercer fact." Here in full force is the kind of writing by which Winters wishes to be remembered: the strict metrics, the hard, obvious rhymes, the hard-jawed assurance, the familiar humorless badgering tone, the tendency to logic-chop and moralize *about* instead of presenting, the iron-willed determination to come up with conclusions, to "understand" and pass definitive judgments no matter what. As one reads, it gets more and more difficult to believe that a man's *life* is supposed to be contained in these pages, with the warmth, joy and sorrow, the disappointments and revelations that must surely have been parts of it. One can't help being struck by the poverty of Winters's emotional makeup; there are only a few things which seem to have made much of an impression on him. The principal one of these is what he conceives to be the function of the university intellectual, the teacher, whose role it is to instill "precision" in the students' minds. . . .

The tightness and concision of his writing are bought at altogether too high a price: that of deliberately stifling the *élan* and going-beyond that first-rate poets count on blindly and rightly. This results in calcified and unlikely poems, academic and "correct" according to the set of rules one has arrived at, and doubtless from this standpoint capable of being defended logically and/or eloquently, but only in arguments which are, in view of what they come to in the poems themselves, simply beside the point. It is evident that this kind of poem is principally an exercise of the logical faculties, a display of what one has come to deem proper as to method and statement. Even this might be all right if the qualities Winters has chosen were not so drastically limiting, or if his means of embodying them were other than they are. The kind of thinking and writing that Winters fosters is good enough for small poets, and doubtless enables them to concentrate and consolidate their modest gifts in a way which is as good as any they may hope for. But for a big talent, which must go its own way, it is and probably has been ruinous, and I am haunted by the vision of a Yeats or Dylan Thomas or W. S. Graham laboring diligently to get into the same Stanford Parnassus with J. V. Cunningham, Donald Drummond, Howard Baker, and Clayton Stafford. The trouble with verse of this sort is, quite simply, that is is all but dead, not only to the power of giving something of the mystery and fortuitous meaningfulness and immediacy of life to the reader, but dead also, and from conception, to the possibilities of receiving these upon itself.

This is not quite, however, the whole story on Winters's later verse. From poems like "To the Holy Spirit" and "Moonlight Alert," one comes to see that Winters's most enduring and characteristic theme is not really the teacher's part, but Nothingness, and the perhaps illusory stand of the mind against it. The pessimism and stoicism and honesty of his poems about himself, not as laying down the law in the William Dinsmore Briggs Room, but as a solitary night-watching man, are utterly convincing. Though they are not free of the moralizing tendency that ruins so many of the later poems, the occasions for this and his other familiar qualities seem more nearly right, and for that reason, and because of Winters's awesome unflinchingness in the face of approaching old age, they are good poems, and compare favorably with the best of the early ones.

*James Dickey, "Yvor Winters" (1962), in his* Babel to Byzantium *(reprinted with the permission of Farrar, Straus & Giroux, Inc.; copyright © 1956, 1957, 1958, 1959, 1960, 1961, 1962, 1963, 1964, 1965, 1966, 1967, 1968 by James Dickey), Farrar, Straus, 1968, pp. 182-86.*

[Winters] was *the* poet-critic of our time who combined an understanding of general philosophical ideas with a sensibility almost hypersensitive in its awareness of the most minute particulars of poetic style. For him, criticism was nothing unless it was evaluative. He constantly applied his general principles to individual poets—and not only to individual poets, but to specific poems, lines, and phrases. His unorthodox judgments were the delight of his graduate students and the irritated despair of his colleagues, particularly those who specialized in the romantic and Victorian periods.

His early poems from which, shortly before his death, he published a selection with an illuminating introduction, were in the free verse forms of the imagists. His mature work, all of it in conventional meter—is not imitative of but has affinities with certain poems of Gascoigne, Greville, Jonson, Hardy, and Bridges. In a lecture given at the Johns Hopkins Poetry Festival he spoke of a post symbolist poetry which would combine the rational content and structure of medieval and Elizabethan lyrics with that peculiarly modern awareness of the sensory world so beautifully found in the verse of Valéry and Wallace Stevens. This synthesis is, I believe, what he himself was striving to achieve in some of his finest poems: "Sir Gawaine and the Green Knight," "To the Holy Spirit," and "At the San Francisco Airport." . . .

[No] other critic was so capable of fully entering into the spirit of a poem, of perceiving its virtues and its weaknesses, of discovering ways of revising in keeping with the intentions of the author. His greatness as a teacher of young poets lay in his enthusiasm for the job, the seriousness with which he took their efforts, and his uncanny ability to discern potential talent in a welter of bad adolescent writing. His influence on American poetry of the last thirty-five years has been far greater than is generally recognized.

*Donald E. Stanford, "Yvor Winters, 1900-1968," in* The Southern Review, *Vol. IV, No. 3, Summer, 1968, pp. 861-63.*

[Winters] was our most cantankerous literary critic, willing to take on any of his colleagues in a no-holds-barred free-for-all the like of which is seldom seen in this age of polite tolerance for any opinion about anything. In *Forms of Discovery* he writes off the poetry between George Herbert and Thomas Hardy as decadent in thought and language, with rare and curious exceptions; he writes off the work of other scholars and critics as foolish for foisting off on their readers and students literature he considers second rate; and, unlike most contemporary critics, he prefers the right-handed insult to the left-handed compliment. When he does compliment a living poet or scholar, his reader is likely to learn that the fortunate person had been a student of Winters. . . .

Yvor Winters was arrogant, and arrogance always looks a bit foolish; he called himself an absolutist, and if one's own absolute or one's own skepticism runs counter to that of Winters, Winters will appear thoroughly ridiculous. If Winters found very few poems worthy his praise and few scholars and critics whom he did not attack, it was because of his extremely high standards for literature and for literary study. As a theorist, Winters asked for poetry that appeals to the senses, to the emotions, and to the mind; a poem that fails to work on all three levels is, for Winters, distinctly minor—it is not bad, it just has not come up to the highest standards, and those are the standards by which Winters believed that poetry must be judged. As a polemicist, Winters was a savage opponent because he took literature seriously and because he trusted his own judgment infallibly; as a professional critic, he felt it his responsibility to challenge his colleagues whenever, in his opinion, they erred. To leave professional stupidity unchallenged would have been, for Winters, a sin of the gravest kind; literature for Winters was something very special, and those who professed to understand it were under obligation to prove their competence. . . .

One could make a long list of Winters' eccentricities of judgment and an almost equally long list of absurd categorical statements. But despite the faults, there are advantages to reading Winters. He is a critic who states his position so clearly and so forcefully that readers are shocked into thought; and his theoretical position is so strong that, in disagreeing honestly with Winters, one is forced to think about literature widely and deeply.

*Lee T. Lemon, "Winters as Critic," in* Prairie Schooner *(© 1968 by University of Nebraska Press; reprinted by permission from* Prairie Schooner*), Fall, 1968, pp. 277-78.*

I am far from intimating that the earlier books have been rendered obsolete by *Forms of Discovery*. On the contrary, Winters was working on major problems and recording major discoveries in them, and one can now use those discoveries much better than before. . . .

I suggest that if occasionally the theoretical assertions in *Forms of Discovery* should appear a trifle blunt, they are capable of being sharpened, unlike, say, almost any of the more ambitious generalizations of Northrop Frye. They point to real phenomena, like gunsights which might benefit from a little adjustment but with the aid of which a marksman can still hit the target. . . .

Winters has helped to bring more distinguished poems into the light than any other American critic, both directly and through the activities of people intelligent enough to learn from him. . . .

Despite the protestations of catholicity one hears, there is indeed an official map of poetry, and the quickest way to find out what it is is to go through a few historically organized anthologies for undergraduates, bearing in mind that such anthologies probably do more to shape the history of poetry for their readers than anything that normally comes their way later. . . .

[Part] of Winters' greatness is that he does not operate in terms of systems or "worlds" or of minds considered as wholes, and neither permits his readers to relax illegitimately nor seeks to force them into a position of *de jure* subservience to poems as things to be gratefully "understood." He is looking all the time at this or that specific piece of discourse without any preconceptions as to how it relates to other pieces from the same hand, and without any presumption that either goodness or badness travels osmotically. His condemnations of particular poems, and sometimes of almost the whole body of poems, by writers to some of whose poems he gives high praise are frequently as vigorous as anyone could wish; it is not Bridges and Moore *as wholes* that he is elevating, for example. Similarly the greatness that he discerns in, say, part of Bridges' "The Affliction of Richard" is not presumed to make the rest of it great, any more than he sees the faults of Wordsworth's Mutability sonnet as militating against the undoubted greatness of the last two-and-a-half lines of it. In this connection his essay elsewhere on "The Audible Reading of Poetry" is indeed, as he says, of the utmost importance, with its emphasis on poems as discourse and not as maps—discourse that may in some places falter and fumble and in others rise to greatness, just as happens in prose. And his insistence that "if poets have any value, it is because of their superior intelligence . . ." is salutary in the extreme. I believe that when he demonstrates that the assertions made in this or that poem are foolish or naïve or patently unsound by any reasonable standards, and that the line of argument in a "serious" argumentative poem is self-contradictory or in some other way confused, and that specific metaphors and similes are grossly untrue to the hard physical realities that they purport to remind us of, he has made unanswerable objections, he has pointed to *faults*. . . .

I think that Winters has called a number of major bluffs. And I believe that his doing so is of especial importance today, when the emphasis on romantically freer and "truer" ways of seeing and modes of expression seems to be, if anything, intensifying. . . . The notion of the unarmored simpleton or inspired madman traveling by very different roads from most of us and getting much further has its charms, I suppose. And it is true that there have been a few men of genius, such as the Douanier Rousseau, whose work has sometimes been characterized by an almost magical freshness and innocence of vision, and that there have been others, such as Céline and Van Gogh, whose lives have been characterized by the most appalling intensities and anguishes. But the two I have just mentioned, during the periods in which they were doing their greatest work at least, were highly intelligent and articulate men with a formidable mastery of the technical resources of their art, and when their control in fact deteriorated, so did their art. . . .

[Where] I think Winters most right and most important is in his challenge to our continuing, if unconscious, professional contemplation of poetry through the distorting medium of the Romantics. (I am, of course, taking a tip from his brilliant paragraph about the effects of reading Keats when young.) That bias manifests itself in a variety of ways, of course, among them an excessive esteem for the Romantics themselves, a naïvely organicist notion of what poems are, an uneasy mixture of expressive and mimetic theories of art, a preference for magniloquence to truth, and a superstitious awe of poets and poetry in general. The continuing excessive appeal of Romanticism for academics derives substantially, I suspect, from the fact that judged by their own standards the Romantics were failures and that it is by the same standards that many academics secretly judge themselves. . . . Hence it is natural enough to want to see the Romantic pattern as the norm—I mean, to see muddle and weakness and decline of one sort or another as being inevitable and somehow rather noble. Some such hypothesis, at any rate, seems called for to explain our collective over-indulgence towards such things in poetry, given that we are in a profession that pays a good deal of lip-service to the idea of a steady and self-disciplined advance in knowledge, skill, and wisdom during one's professional lifetime, and a passing on of such virtures to the young, especially the young who desire to enter our guild.

*John Fraser, "Winter's Summa," in* The Southern Review, *Vol. V, No. 1, Winter, 1969, pp. 184-202.*

Though his admirers are far-flung, Winters is still largely a coterie poet. It is not that he wrote only for the delectation of a select group, but most critics and readers have never discerned his intentions and recognized his accomplishments. . . . Most of his best poems are written according to a method or style which he called post-Symbolist. This is, briefly, a way of charging sensory details with abstract meaning: a particular variety of metaphoric language. The post-Symbolist method repairs deficiencies in each of the two other principal methods Winters used at various times to relate the concrete and the abstract: the style of his free verse and his later abstract style.

In the twenties Winters was writing experimental free verse which was rapid in movement, spare, and frequently violent. He was influenced by Williams, by the Imagist movement and its offshoots, by translations of American Indian poetry. His early poetry aimed at intensity of individual images and lines; rational content was not a primary concern. He described his early poems later as "material cohering by virture of feeling and rhythmic structure, and very little by virture of intelligible theme." Some of the poems confine themselves to description, or description for the sake of mood, and make no attempt to deal with ideas. . . .

In some of the early poems Winters deals with intellectual themes, but never straightforwardly. For a brief time in the twenties he favored the term "anti-image" to describe an idea in a poem. An idea was only poetic if it fused with sensory images and sound patterns, or other, apparently unrelated, ideas, to become an anti-image. The single idea, directly expressed, had no place in his system. "Even perspicuous generalities do not constitute poetry." Intellectual statements sometimes appear in the early poetry, but they never have an easily definable relation to each other, and to the other elements of the poem. If the ideas were obscure, Winters believed, this might facilitate the real work of the poem. . . .

When Winters switched abruptly from free verse to regular meters in 1928, he began to make increasing use of undisguised abstraction in his poetry. He was no longer opposed to perspicuous generalities. Most of his poems still depended primarily on sensory detail, but by the time of *Before Disaster* (1934) he had developed an almost purely abstract style, and he wrote in this style intermittently throughout the rest of his career. . . . The influence of the plain-style poets of the Renaissance, especially Ben Jonson, is perceptible in some of these poems. One frequently expressed view of his poetry as a whole is that it slavishly imitates Renaissance models; Winters is a warmed-over George Gascoigne. This is true to a degree of those poems in the abstract style, though there are other influences, and though some of the poems are vigorous and memorable whatever their affinities; but his abstract style is only a minor part of his mature poetic work. . . .

Winters' post-Symbolist poems are the most characteristic and important of his mature work. They belie the common view of Winters as primarily a poet of abstractions; and if he is didactic and moralistic, these qualities inhere in poems displaying a surface texture of intense sensuousness. In discussing these poems I have concentrated on their abstract significance, in order to show something of the way his method works. This sort of analysis is one-sided, and it makes the poems sound mechanical. The poems I have discussed are extraordinarily perceptive in respect to the external world they describe and in respect to language; the precise yet evocative language is, in his own phrase, a form of discovery. The lines are living lines.

Winters is, I think, a major poet, a poet of no less stature than Williams, Pound, Eliot, Crane, or Frost. If this is true, then the low state of his reputation may seem to require some explanation. One problem is that to many readers his poems have seemed old-fashioned, having nothing to say to them, not "modern." His restrained tone, his emphasis on rationality and control of the emotions, his sometimes explicit moralism, are partly the basis of this feeling, along with the regularity of his metrical and stanzaic forms. Even poets like Frost or the early Robert Lowell, who use regular meters, are rougher in their rhythms, closer to speech. Neither Winters' ideas, his tone, nor his forms provide for many readers anything they can identify as modern, and it seems reasonable to them to conclude that he is irrelevant to the course of poetry in this century. . . .

Winters' matter is modern in that it builds upon the romantic and Symbolist traditions in opposing them. As a "counter-romantic," he was on the same track as Yeats and Crane, though he was going the other way. J. V. Cunningham, who called him a "congenital romantic" despite Winters' notorious repudiation of romanticism, recognized that Winters' concern with self-control arises out of a specifically romantic context. The temptations which the poet of "The Slow Pacific Swell" must resist are the temptations which Wordsworth and Crane invited. "A Spring Serpent" and "Midas" are replies to Mallarmé, rather than abstract speculations about poetic pitfalls. . . .

The majority of reviewers have taken his poems in the abstract style as typical of his later verse; they have not been aware of how the post-Symbolist poems work, or what they are about. There is also a tendency to regard his poems as versified footnotes to his criticism, which has attacked virtually every well-known literary figure since the eighteenth century and earned Winters the reputation of a crank. Winters' best post-Symbolist poems, though their paraphrasable content is consistent with his critical essays, are less assertive and dogmatic. His ideas, in the adventure with form that produces poetry, are complicated and qualified; but critics have used his more immediately accessible poems in the abstract style to attack his "banality and over-simplification." The effect of Winters' criticism is to imply a position of exclusiveness: if you admire Robert Bridges, you cannot admire T. S. Eliot. His detractors have taken him at his word, and admiring the poets he denigrates, they have brushed aside his own poetry. Scornful of his claims for Elizabeth Daryush or T. Sturge Moore, they have assumed that Winters' poems must be more of the same.

Winters' poetry commends patience, fortitude, thoughtfulness, and self-control. He does not commend passion, perhaps the cardinal virtue to the modern mind, and this has led many readers to suppose that his poems must be passionless. For them, the self-discipline which restrains the forces of the irrational is the only visible element in the poems. It is as if a party of the gods were to yawn at the tableau in Venus' boudoir; were, unconscious of the activity caught beneath the remorseless fibers, to find the workmanship of Vulcan's net empty formalism. . . .

When young, Winters was obsessed with what he called "the metaphysical horror of modern thought," and this was an immediate fear, almost a physical fear. The state of mind in the poems verges on madness, and the poet, the voice speaking, knows this. After 1928, the horror, the violence, the madness are restrained, but their effect on the poetry is as important as before; they are the impetus behind his adamant faith in reason. Irrationality, spontaneous impulse, "spiritual extroversion" seemed to him the first step to madness; and the annihilation of the mind was associated with physical dissolution. "Ruin has touched familiar air," he wrote of a garden, and ruin was always imminent. This is the central theme of his mature poetry; it is the theme even of so apparently "literary" a poem as "Midas." . . .

To see Winters' later poetry as cold and emotionless is to miss half the point.

There is a hardness, a "cold certitude," an immobility in Winters' poems, but this is the result of the spiritual discipline which formed the man and the poems, not the result of congenital stolidity. He achieved the stasis of his poetry only at great cost, and the cost is evident in the poetry.

*Howard Kaye, "The Post-Symbolist Poetry of Yvor Winters," in* The Southern Review, *Vol. VII, No. 1, Winter, 1971, pp. 176-97.*

Yvor Winters is a very considerable poet indeed, with a most curious career. . . . When most of his friends and most of his literary generation went to Paris and met the great, Winters discovered he had fairly advanced tuberculosis and was forced to live the rest of his life in a dry climate. He taught school for a while in an ugly mining town, Raton, New Mexico, and then college in Moscow, Idaho, and finally in the late Twenties he came to Stanford, where he remained for the rest of his life. He was the true exile, the true *aliené*. Years must have gone by where nobody knew what he was talking about except his wife, or his echoing students. He became cranky and cantankerous and is responsible for some of the most wrong-headed and eccentric criticism ever written.

He changed the style of his verse to a stark neo-classicism of his own invention, which he always insisted owed much to, of all people, the late Tudor writer of doggerel, Barnaby Googe. . . . Winters stood Dadaism on its head, as Marx did Hegel, and his critical ideas cannot be appreciated unless this is understood.

*Kenneth Rexroth, in his* American Poetry in the Twentieth Century *(copyright © 1971 Herder and Herder, Inc.; used by permission of the publisher, The Seabury Press, New York), Herder, 1971, pp. 92-3.*

* * *

## WRIGHT, Richard 1908-1960

**Wright, a Black American novelist and short story writer, was one of this country's most highly respected spokesmen for Black problems and attitudes.**

Wright's short fiction of the 1930s is essentially an imaginative re-creation of the atmosphere and milieu of his childhood experiences. The fears, frustrations, and pent-up angers of the Southern Negro are posed against the sadism of the white Southerner. Until, in two of the stories, Marxism enters the lives of some of his Negroes and whites, there are no influences outside of Southern culture to alter an environment generally hostile to the black man. Each story represents a Negro reaction to the white world during a moment of crisis and, usually, of violence. Furthermore, the stories collected in *Uncle Tom's Children* are so arranged that each marks a progressive increase in resistance to their lot on the part of Negro characters or groups. "Uncle Tom's Children" look less and less like "Uncle Tom." In many respects, the stories could be classified as biased sociological studies, with Negroes created as the human beings and whites as the generalized evil figures. The tone of the stories reflects Wright's attitude of protest, prefiguring his outlook in his celebrated novel of protest set in a Northern metropolis, *Native Son*.

The stories, too, are filled with the kind of literary naturalism so often linked by commentators to *Native Son*. Deterministic and materialistic forces are shown as components in an environment of external forces obstructing human freedom. Also stressed are genetic and subconscious limitations on human rationality. . . . In his terse, dialogue-filled novellas of protestation set in what is basically the rural South, Wright seems to have combined his knowledge of the fictional forms he had met in his reading and his personal impressions of a ghastly South that was antagonistic toward the Negro. In his later writings his adoption of literary naturalism is as consistent, and a posture of protest continues to inform the narratives. Thus, Wright's short fiction of the 1930s provides a valuable introduction to the themes and techniques of his later works. (pp. 20-1)

As a work of art, *Lawd Today* is beset by numerous shortcomings. The amount of sheer dialogue is overburdening; the meager, often-monosyllabic vocabulary is shallow and poorly descriptive; and the unrelenting stress upon the smallest of details, even to the extent of picturing the card distributions in bridge games, is tedious. The fact that Wright did not offer the novel to the public—his wife had it published after his death—may be an indication of how Wright himself felt about the quality of the work. Nevertheless, *Lawd Today* is an interesting prelude to *Native Son*. Because of it, we can imagine Wright's groping to translate his Chicago experiences into an artistic genre. The novel has two significant features: one is Wright's placing of a single Negro character at the center, while at the same time examining all of the events and objects in his environment immediately touching upon his life; the other is an absence of specific white characters who could represent threats to the central figure's being. Wright's emphasis is upon Negro people and Negro life amid the cold forces of Northern urban surroundings. (pp. 22-3)

*Native Son* differs . . . from the autobiography and from most of the earlier writings in an important respect: a conscious attempt is made by Wright to picture certain whites as human beings sympathetic to and communicating with Negroes. (p. 37)

Thematically, *The Long Dream* characterizes a relationship between the whites and the blacks of the South distinguished again by a curtain drawn by the ruling whites. Threats and dangers to Negro property, life, and personality are unrelentingly present. However, the novel differs from Wright's other fiction in two ways: it depicts a middle-class, entrepreneur Negro existence, and it portrays the psychological and emotional growth of a central figure over a period of time. Aritistically noteworthy are the ironies in dialogue and action and the inclusion of mirrored episodes. (p. 43)

*The Long Dream* is a protest novel. As such, it makes little distinction between the Negro-white relations Wright grew to comprehend during the days of his youth described in *Black Boy* and the relations he could only read about and sense during his final years in Paris. *The Long Dream* reiterates a consistent Wright theme that in America a curtain hangs between the black and white races. This curtain is not only an outgrowth of white prejudice, but also a barrier against the elimination of that prejudice through communication between the races. Furthermore, it creates an impediment to the full development and expression of all American Negroes. (pp. 47-8)

Wright's proletarian poetry . . . generally reflects a movement from propaganda-making to poetry-making. It tends to move from blatant Marxist and Party words to a utilization of words for their beauty and subtle suggestive powers. There is an obvious advance in Wright's skills and techniques, but poetic forms apparently were not large enough to satisfy his desire to encompass the emotion-packed details of his Southern and Northern experiences. They were abandoned for a concentration on the short-story and novel forms. (p. 59)

In *Uncle Tom's Children*, both the first and the expanded editions, Wright generally relocates his arenas of conflict, racial and class, from the poverty-stricken farms to the small towns of the South. An exception is the setting for "Long Black Song"; however, the town is only a few hills away, and the white men whose respect Silas craves are townspeople, not farmers. This shift parallels a geographical movement in Wright's own life, which offered the live experiences from which the stories could be conceived. In addition, an urban setting provides a convenient basis for a broader Marxist application, even though, because of the geography of Wright's Southern experience, the masses of industrial workers are not incorporated into the plots. The collection of stories is most easily understood on the obvious level of racial conflict. However, as one tale leads into the next, the Marxist undertones develop progressively into functioning materials of the stories until, at last, personal fulfillment and social salvation is identified with action and hope in the Communist Party. Therefore, since the militancy of action increases with successive episodes, *Uncle Tom's Children* creates the impression of having a novel-like development. (pp. 60-1)

In a sense, *12 Million Black Voices* is the symbolic rendering of a political-philosophical dilemma so evidently protruding from the pages of *Lawd Today* and *Native Son*, Wright's two novels written during his Communist Party period. In both works, the Negro artist primarily shouts his protest against racial injustice and prejudice. Secondarily, he attempts to superimpose upon his plots and major themes the tenets of a seemingly useful and "rational" motivation for his protest; that is to say, Wright's head seems to have been vying with his heart. In *12 Million Black Voices*—an emotional piece really—his heart wins, at the expense of a rigid and "rational" Marxist dialectic. That Wright's position in the Party was shaky is not surprising. (pp. 70-1)

*Lawd Today* does not openly advocate the Marxist revolution as the solution, but Marxism and the Communist Party survive the novel as unexplored possibilities for hope and salvation, even though they have been battered and beleaguered by the clichés of Jake and his friends. Unlike the later *Native Son, Lawd Today* assumes on the part of its reading audience a knowledge of both Marxism and the expressed aims of the American Communist Party. Although scenes and speeches in the novel that are literally anti-Marxist are balanced with none that are literally pro-Marxist, the anti-Marxist materials are planted in such a way as to appeal to the reader's ironic sense and to evoke from him a sympathy for a Marxist solution to racial problems. Nevertheless, the reader is never able to forget that the subject of the novel is black men in a white world, not workers in a capitalistic world. There is no assurance that even if the Marxist revolution were to fire and transform America, racial conflict would subside and then swoon in a predictable death. (p. 71)

*Lawd Today* is artistically unappealing for many reasons, but Wright's method of inserting the Marxist motif shows an admirable skill. The unobtrusiveness, subtlety, and irony with which these particular socio-politico-economic materials are handled are, in fact, especially commendable in the light of how Wright later uses Marxism in the last section of his larger and generally finer novel *Native Son*. (pp. 76-7)

Wright's treatment of the Marxist materials in the first two sections of *Native Son* is much the same as in the whole of *Lawd Today*, although the inclusion of Jan in *Native Son* accentuates the Marxist motif more strongly. In both novels the concept of salvation through a Marxist revolution is held above the plots as an uninvestigated alternative to a social and economic system that exploits Negro labor and personality. In both, too, the main Negro figures and their cronies are depicted as the uninformed but innocent foes of their possible salvation. Wright does establish early in both novels that the Negro characters are searching in their own half-hearted, unguided manner for some type of plan or leadership to capture the unconscious emotions of all black people and direct them to a willed, dignified, and better fate. (p. 80)

The didacticism of the final section in *Native Son* seems then to have been intended to be just that, and presumably it was meant to contribute to the artistic unity of the novel. However, intention and effect do not always correspond, and it is precisely the divergence of the two that detracts from the sense of unequivocal achievement for *Native Son*.

It is not Marxism as such that detracts from the themes of the novel; in fact, a Marxist interpretation does provide a useful tool for partially explaining the sociological and economic backgrounds for American Negro-white relations. Instead, Wright's emphasis on socio-politico-economic explanations of Bigger's predicament causes an undesirable shift in focus from the fascinating personal story of Bigger's psychological life. (p. 82)

After 1953, the publication date for *The Outsider*, Wright apparently felt a need to retrace the steps of his own philosophical development, including his odyssey from political ignorance, to Marxist belief, to an anti-Marxist position. In his nonfiction of the last half decade of his life—the European, African, and Asian political journey books to be examined in the next chapter—we learn that though Wright experienced urgent impulses to discuss Marxism as a real force in the larger world of continents of many races and ideas, he remained staunchly anti-Communist. Although in his nonfiction of the 1950s he could not avoid treating, and even dwelling upon, Marxist themes and materials, he shunned all such references in his later novels, *Savage Holiday* (1954) and *The Long Dream* (1958), both written in France but narrowed to American settings. In effect, Wright may have been confirming that Marxism and America, let alone Marxism and the American-Negro artist, have not mixed well historically. (pp. 85-6)

Wright's years of self-imposed exile in Paris and on his Normandy farm, from 1947 until his death in 1960, were not years of withdrawal and isolation. He continued to write fiction and, near the end of his life, to compose hokku and "haiku" poetry. Furthermore, he became friendly with French writers and philosophers, especially the existentialists, and notably Jean-Paul Sartre. Through Sartre and the other existentialists he probably clarified his own quasi-existential thinking and discovered the ideas and terms that form a basis for *The Outsider*. His contacts with French intellectuals and thought also helped Wright to extend his sentiments about race and social structures, including Marxism, beyond the boundaries of his American experiences. However, his years away from America provided him with even greater opportunities to enlarge his thinking and to add new subject matter to his writing. As significant in the development of his own ideas and the direction of his prose were his travels to other countries, scattered on different continents. These trips expanded Wright's vision to a world of many races and cultures so that he felt impelled to comment in his nonfiction on what he saw and sensed in such places as Spain, Indonesia, and the African Gold Coast (now Ghana). (pp. 87-8)

In *Pagan Spain* as in his other nonfictional works resulting from his travels during the 1950s, there is that consistent framework of thought which had helped to influence his embracement in the 1930s of the seemingly rational, pseudo-scientific, secular tenets of Marxism. Perhaps, too, from a related conviction that man's rational mind could and should be the source for the resolution of Negro-white problems, Wright sounds his protest, trusting that his voice will be heard and heeded by other rational men. Although such works as *Black Power, The Color Curtain, White Man, Listen!* and *Pagan Spain* indicate new and wider concerns on the part of Wright, the messages found in each identify and establish a basis from which these concerns stemmed—Wright's desire for an orderly and rational universe, created by man out of the concept of his own rational and humane image. (pp. 118-19)

For the sake of Wright's literary reputation, *Savage Holiday* would best be left untouched between its sensational paperback covers. However, for a fuller picture of the influences on Wright's thinking, especially during his residence in France, the novel is valuable, even if painfully so. Although it focuses on the irrational aspects of man's mind and the irrational mode of his behavior, it also suggests that the irrational has a rational explanation. Possibly too, in the case of Fowler, his violent and destructive actions would never have occurred had his mother given him the love he craved and needed and, correlatively, had she not tramped off with many men in her sexual abandonment. There is a temptation, of course, to extrapolate further and to call Wright a moral Puritan; however, the bulk of his writings would not substantiate such a theory. *Savage Holiday* is, then, a poorly constructed, too-seriously articulated, overstated work, purposely employing Freudian devices and a few ideas from Nietzsche. It neatly fits the pattern of Wright's attitudes toward Christianity, and it may be linked to the rationalist impulses behind the type of humanism he seems to have been formulating sometime after he had left the United States. (pp. 142-43)

*Native Son* is a perplexing novel. Because of Wright's obtrusive pro-Marxism and because of the predominant theme of protest against a particular social injustice, it defies an easy categorization into purely existential literature. The protest in *Native Son* asks that social changes occur. It also implies that man can bring them about. To the degree that existentialism views man as set free from the claims of a God, Wright also perceives man's position as such. When Bigger meets his death not in despair but with a belief that he has at last been able to acquire a new freedom by shaping his own destiny—though through violence and killing—he symbolizes an authorial tenet that man's freedom is within his grasp, here on earth, if he is willing to accept the responsibility and consequences for it. The message is an existential one; but it does mirror the same social, not metaphysical, concerns and protests that powerfully emerge from *Black Boy*. (pp. 147-48)

*The Outsider* is proof not of Wright's existentialism but of his rejection of existentialism. In his portrayal of the destruction left in the path of a man who had walked outside history and society, Wright was really asking man to be responsible for others as well as for himself. Although in his nonfiction after *The Outsider* he found certain existential tenets useful, especially for exposing the myths he thought man often irrationally lived by, and although he may not have fully realized what he was doing philosophically in *The Outsider*, the direction of his thinking in the 1950s had shifted away from the grim and dark side of existentialism seen in "The Man Who Lived Underground." (p. 163)

[Though] Wright's later novel, *The Long Dream*, has been attacked for protesting an American racial situation that by 1958 bore no resemblance to contemporary fact, the inspiration for Wright's protest was consistent with that for such diverse works as *Native Son* and *The Outsider*—that man's reason could discover a way out of a history of injustices and irrationalities. Finally, *Savage Holiday*, by exploring a chain of absurdities built upon the unwillingness of the main character to view rationally his motivations and his existence, underscores how reason should be the key to reality. In many ways it mirrors the approach taken by Wright more than twenty years before in his early short story, "Superstition."

Marxism at one time apparently provided for Wright the pseudo-scientific foundation for the construction of a rational and peaceful world. His later disillusionment with the Communist Party could possibly have influenced his writing of the pessimistic "The Man Who Lived Underground." However, *The Outsider* is a return to older concepts once held by Wright—feelings and ideas that really grew out of *Black Boy*. (p. 164)

Nothing in Wright's late works dissolves the thesis that his efforts were those of a black man who, even in his anger, fear, outrage, and frustration, was generally sounding his pleas for change to the ears and minds of rational men, especially white men. If anything, the last short pieces suggest that Wright, the man, was mellowing and that he now could occasionally smile. (p. 171)

*Russell Carl Brignano, in his* Richard Wright: An Introduction to The Man and His Works, *University of Pittsburgh Press, 1970.*

* * *

## WURLITZER, Rudolph 1938?-

**Wurlitzer is an American novelist.**

In grisly detail [Wurlitzer] describes [in *Nog*] an interlude in the lives of a few young acid heads freaking out in various habitats ranging from California and Panama to New York, where the yarn abruptly terminates. Prose fiction outside the novel form is momentarily fashionable, and here for all to regard is an example of the genre composed with no little skill and confidence.

Virginia Quarterly Review, *Vol. 45, No. 2 (Spring, 1969), p. xlix.*

No one waits for Godot in [the] somber pages [of *Flats*], yet the Beckett influence is manifest as in the course of the narrative private fantasy reveals a central figure wandering aimlessly in the blackness of night over the swampy flats of a garbage and refuse dump, while a blue light flashes to no purpose and an engine drones overhead. Symbolism is here for the choosing in sufficient supply to please the most exacting of readers accompanied by an opacity both puzzling and superfluous. Mr. Wurlitzer's brief book can be only designated a novel by courtesy, for all commonly accepted criteria are conspicuously absent. His work has every affectation of profundity.

Virginia Quarterly Review, *Vol. 47, No. 1 (Winter, 1971), p ix.*

Samuel Beckett sometimes writes like this: "It was midnight. It was raining. It was not midnight. It was not raining." Such particularity has been described as a dogged persistence in getting at the bare truth. Rudolph Wurlitzer is similarly persistent: "I don't want to manage the repetitions. I know about that. I don't know about that. I don't want to create a conclusion. That has already happened." The similarity of style is plain enough: so too are theme and setting. Beckett should be flattered: Mr Wurlitzer gives the impression of having read no one else. . . .

The characters [in *Flats*] inhabit a waste land. It might be a dump at the edge of town, or a public park in the post-pollution age, and the characters no more than tramps enacting the absurdities the fiction of terminus so easily invites. Or they are the derelict survivors of apocalypse. . . .

What can be commended in *Flats* is the success with which Mr Wurlitzer teases (in a grim sort of way) rather than informs. The sustained, grey image of desolation is powerfully cumulative, and the motives and preoccupations of the characters appropriately trivial or pointless. Grovelling among the rubbish of the twentieth century, treasuring bars of soap and paper cups, Mr Wurlitzer's garbage-people experience the American Nightmare. But people have lived in dustbins before.

*"Dead End Game," in* The Times Literary Supplement *(reproduced by permission), November 26, 1971, p. 1469.*

Rudolph Wurlitzer in *Nog*, his brilliant first novel, makes the most serious effort since Pynchon to create a style that renders similar states of being in which separate identities can barely be located and, when they are, seem merely accidental. Identities fuse and separate without intention and without feeling, as if persons had the consistency of air, with no one able to find himself in himself, in anyone else or, with any certainty, even in space. For Wurlitzer to have achieved a stylistic approximation of these conditions is an accomplishment of some historic consequence, showing that our language can manage to reach into those areas of contemporary life where, among its young inhabitants, there is mostly silence.

*Richard Poirier, in his* The Performing Self *(copyright © 1971 by Oxford University Press, Inc.; reprinted by permission), Oxford University Press, 1971, p. 26.*

Wurlitzer . . . has had outside help, notably from Thomas Pynchon and Donald Barthelme, the former of whom proclaimed on publication of Wurlitzer's novel, *Nog*, that "The novel of Bullshit is dead" while the sly wag Barthelme praised it as "an excellent book, full of unhealthy mental excitement." Since *Nog* Wurlitzer has given us *Flats*, the only novel ever written where American cities do what they've always wanted to: "Houston sat up and peered at the field"; "Duluth slowly took off his remaining shoe and sock." Now with *Quake* ("a testament to man's ability to struggle for life with humor and courage") he has successfully achieved Lawrence's accurate prediction of the "phantasmal boredom" and "final atrophy of the feelings," above all of the "inertia, inertia, inertia" that's built into the texture of every sentence. . . .

Contradicting Pynchon, we can admit that on the evidence of this new book the novel of Bullshit is not dead at all but humorlessly alive as ever, Wurlitzer's work being an egregious instance of it.

*William H. Pritchard, in* The Hudson Review *(copyright © 1973 by The Hudson Review, Inc.; reprinted by permission), Vol. XXVI, No. 1, Spring, 1973, p. 230.*

Rudolph Wurlitzer's *Nog* (1969) and *Flats* (1970) offer convincing evidence of the continuing vitality of prose fiction. Both novels take us to the heart of the American malaise and do so by reaching deeply into the best traditions of our literature. Both novels force us to re-examine the American dream in the light of present realities; and both stand in the rich tradition of the American parable: Ishmael, Huck, Nick Adams, and Nick Carraway, for example, are the formidable predecessors of the anonymous, profoundly fragmented narrators of *Nog* and *Flats*. Wurlitzer's spokesmen bring the solipsism and negation of Melville's Bartleby up to date. In the disintegrative and maddened present the only thinned-out authenticity left is found in the "freedom" of the naked "I"—the uncompromised nay-sayer. . . .

*Nog* and *Flats* are worthy experiments and possess the form and finesse that will win them increasing acceptance. . . . The best experimental fiction of recent years has revealed few limitations beyond which genuinely creative writers cannot take us. Wurlitzer shares with many of them an interest in probing beneath the layers of cultural conditioning and compromise to expose the truth of man's solitary being.

*Douglass Bolling, "Rudolph Wurlitzer's 'Nog' and 'Flats'," in* Critique: Studies in Modern Fiction, *Vol. XIV, No. 3, 1973, pp. 5-15.*

Rudolph Wurlitzer's new novel, *Quake*, his third in three years, assumes the American apocalypse as [fact], brute surface fact, violence served up without comment in all its dehumanizing reality. Despite its blunt naturalistic technique, the novel is complete fable, an act of imagination which locates the specific collapse of American civilization in Los Angeles, fittingly enough, and which refuses any statement but the most symbolic. Its narrative consciousness comes from a young, nameless wanderer whose basic life style (an actual absence of life style) makes him the perfect medium for transmitting all the ugly details, chalking up another literary debt to Ernest Hemingway. . . .

As sociological fable, *Quake* is clever and chillingly apt, but it weakens its own firm, if far too narrow, *raison d'être* through its adolescent obsession with sexual quirks. True, the sexual fantasies of masculine America are one with its more violent urges, but the sex here is too often arbitrary, external, the result of the author's personal hang-up rather than a legitimate causal or thematic factor. Sensationalism clouds much of what is valuable in the book, and I suspect that Mr. Wurlitzer is himself too enmeshed in his hero's lost identity to offer us a reliable mirror for the fragmented profile of our cultural heritage.

*Edward Butscher, in* Carleton Miscellany, *Fall/Winter, 1973-74, pp. 133-34.*

# Z

## ZUKOFSKY, Louis 1904-

**Zukofsky, an American, is a brilliant and idiosyncratic poet and novelist. (See also *Contemporary Authors*, Vols. 9-12, rev. ed.)**

Louis Zukofsky's poetry is compounded of great love, equal care, and a singular perception of the nature of words in all their manifold senses. There is no one who writes with greater intelligence of what our common world is, nor of the tradition of the family in it, nor of the mind itself asked to see reason in the flux of war and economic confinement. His long poem, *"A"* . . ., is itself a singular history of a man's will to relate, in all senses, the circumstances in which he lives.

*Robert Creeley, "Louis Zukofsky: 'A' 1-12 & 'Barely and Widely'," in* Sparrow #18, *November, 1962.*

Louis Zukofksy has defined his poetics as a function, having as lower limit, speech, and upper limit, song. It is characteristic of him to say that a poet's ". . . major aim is not to show himself but that order that of itself can speak to all men. . . ." It is his belief that a poet writes one poem all his life, a continuing *song*, so that no division of its own existence can be thought of as being more or less than its sum. This is to say, it *all* is. . . .

I can think of no man more useful to learn from than Zukofsky, in that he will not 'say' anything but that which the particulars of such a possibility require, and follows the *fact* of that occasion with unequalled sensitivity.

*Robert Creeley, "'paradise/ our/ speech . . .'," in* Poetry *(© 1965 by The Modern Poetry Association; reprinted by permission of the Editor of* Poetry*), October, 1965.*

"Love is to reason as eyes are to the mind." Louis Zukofsky has written a book of 470 large pages on that eloquent bit of philosophical algebra, his occasion being the whole corpus of Shakespeare. To which his wife, Celia Thaew Zukofsky, has appended her opera *Pericles*, as a second volume. This radiant set of books is one of the great *tractati* on poetry. Its title, *Bottom: On Shakespeare*, is as eccentric as all the poet's titles *(A, It Was, Prepositions, Barely and Widely, All)*. In time it will probably transmute into "Zukofsky on Shakespeare," and eventually into "Zukofsky's Poetics." All of Zukofsky's writing seems to have happened outside time; the demon *Zeitgeist* has had no more luck with him than with John Clare or Christopher Smart. *Bottom* belongs spiritually to the seventeenth century; it is contemporary, in Spengler's sense, with the mind of Spinoza, as Wittgenstein is a contemporary of Heracleitus and R. Buckminster Fuller of Pythagoras.

Zukofsky's poetry is out of time in another sense. For all its kinship to the harmonies of Dowland and the perpetual motion of Bach, its native enterprise is to *play*, if we can grasp all the punning senses of that dangerous word. The immediate sense must be that of *ludens*—the play of thought over a subject. This sense must not be detached from that of *playing* music. Neither discursive, incantatory, nor molendinary, Zukofsky's poetry is a playing of the intellect over a choice inventory of observations and predilections.

The long poem *A* is a procession of poems of various lengths. Like the *Cantos* of Pound and the *Paterson* of William Carlos Williams, it grows out of the inventions of the Imagists and Vorticists, and reflects many of their strategies. Spiritually, however, it is that most American of poetic forms, a large structure built up over a lifetime, copious enough to contain all that the poet wants to put into it, but strict enough of form to grow organically. It may be one of the eloquent reactions of the century that America, which makes everything quickly and moreover makes everything shoddily, should have in its best poets men who are in no hurry to dash off their work, and who build slowly and painstakingly.

The patient and laborious construction of *A* is something of a paradox, for the poem is as spare and weightless as a bicycle wheel in its wit, terseness, and agility. Zukofsky's deft playfulness is so singular among modern poets that we must adjust our expectations or be flipped backwards like Don Quijote from the windmill. The very title discloses simply the letter A, the author being Z: the extremes of the poet's wherewithal, the alphabet. In A-7 the letter A becomes a sawhorse in a cycle of Shakespearean sonnets, a cone in A-9, and so on throughout the poem—playfulness is always liberal and always obeys rules of its own making. A-9, for instance, is not only a verbal pattern in which certain letters of the alphabet define conic sections; it is a translation of Cavalcanti's great canzone on love, and its phrases are taken, all of them, from the Everyman edition of Marx's *Kapital*.

So serious is the matter of Zukofsky's playing with words that we must recognize it as a major source of his poetics. . . .

One lesson is a matter which has to be learned over and over; that poetry is artifice. Dance rhythms and end-rhymes were once giddily revolutionary; so were polyphony and flying buttresses and perspective and zero as a number. Whether the poet's new game is going to lead other poets into its labyrinth remains to be seen. But a more immediate lesson must be pondered first. And that is the poet's English. He has allowed no neologisms in the rules of his game, and has therefore had to resort not to the well zoned diction which poets have always considered it meet and proper to cleave to, but to all the Englishes, as it were, all the jargons, dialects, and ages of the language. We note that an early work of the poet is *Le Style Apollinaire*, a study of the French poet who, taking the next revolutionary steps after Rimbaud, Laforgue, and Corbière, threw the diction of French poetry wide open, cancelling the rules by which poetry was restricted to these words only, and never those. . . .

Zukofsky has needed, and has used, all the Englishes, showing that it can be done, and even that there is a glittering abstractness in the result. The words in the Zukofsky *Catullus* clash against each other like so many wild monads; for an analogy we must turn to the dancing facets of a cubist painting, which, like Zukofsky's whole-dictionary range of words, draw a picture of the world, though the drawing is not like anything we've seen before. You can best read the Catullus, I think, by forgetting the Latin. Zukofsky's "Catullus" is not the native of Sirmione; he is a New Yorker whose second language is English, and who but for historical accident might have figured among the Petrograd Futurists, a figure comparable to Khlebnikov, and would have probably been on the same friendly terms with Mayakovsky as, in the way things turned out, with William Carlos Williams. The poetry of Catullus was simply a bright object over which the poetic inventiveness of Zukofsky might play.

What Zukofsky is about in his poetry is always reasonably obvious, often so obvious that we reject what we can see and look for matters which we suppose to be wonderfully hidden. . . .

We might note that Zukofsky is anti-Joycean. The poet speaks for himself and his family; he is the counter-vision of the inarticulate Bloom and the nightmare of industrial city man in *Finnegans Wake*. Ultimately, at great distance, the portable piece of knowledge about Zukofsky, the tag to be inserted in handbooks and encyclopedias, will be that he was the poet who saw how to be wise about love in a time of madness and hate. And yet his significance at the moment would seem to be his uniqueness as an artist. Neither school nor movement contains him; he is without precedent or heirs. He is a deeply intelligent, witty, passionate Roman poet placed by some playful Fate in our time and world. Or he is a Chinese poet of subtlest sensibility plucked from his mountains and pines and put into a time of subways and rockets to the moon.

*Guy Davenport, "Louis Zukofsky," in* Agenda, *Autumn-Winter, 1970, pp. 130-37.*

# Cumulative Index to Critics

# Cumulative Index to Authors